Understanding Turbo Pascal: Programming and Problem Solving

Understanding Turbo Pascal: Programming and Problem Solving

Douglas W. Nance
CENTRAL MICHIGAN UNIVERSITY

WEST PUBLISHING COMPANY
MINNEAPOLIS/ST. PAUL NEW YORK LOS ANGELES SAN FRANCISCO

To Estefania and Tye with love. Welcome to our family.

Copyediting: Mary George
Indexing: Schroeder Indexing Services
Interior design: Paula Schlosser, Lucy Lesiak, and John Rokusek; enhanced and reinterpreted by Roslyn Stendahl, Dapper Design
Illustrations: Miyake Illustration and Design; DBA Design and Illustration
Cover image: Gregory MacNicol
Composition: Carlisle Communications

WEST'S COMMITMENT TO THE ENVIRONMENT

In 1906, West Publishing Company began recycling materials left over from the production of books. This began a tradition of efficient and responsible use of resources. Today, up to 95 percent of our legal books and 70% of our college and school texts are printed on recycled, acid-free stock. West also recycles nearly 22 million pounds of scrap paper annually—the equivalent of 181,717 trees. Since the 1960s, West has devised ways to capture and recycle waste inks, solvents, oils, and vapors created in the printing process. We also recycle plastics of all kinds, wood, glass, corrugated cardboard, and batteries, and have eliminated the use of styrofoam book packaging. We at West are proud of the longevity and the scope of our commitment to our environment.

Production, Prepress, Printing and Binding by West Publishing Company.

 PRINTED ON 10% POST CONSUMER RECYCLED PAPER 

Printed in the United States of America
01 00 99 98 97 96 8 7 6 5 4 3 2

Library of Congress Cataloging-in-Publication Data

Nance, Douglas W.
Understanding Turbo Pascal : programming and problem solving / Douglas W. Nance.
p. cm.
Includes index.
ISBN 0-314-02812-9 (hardcover)
1. Pascal (Computer program language) 2. Turbo Pascal (Computer file) I. Title.
QA76.73.P2N355 1993
005.13'3--dc20 93-28875
CIP

Contents

CHAPTER **1** ■ Computer Science: Architecture, Languages, Problem Solving, and Programs 1

Preface

This text was originally intended to be a Turbo Pascal version of *Pascal: Understanding Programming and Problem Solving,* Second Alternate Edition. I naively thought a few changes could be made, programs rewritten in Turbo Pascal, and a new text would result. Instead, extensive changes resulted in a two-year project. Virtually every page in the previous text has been changed (these changes are detailed later). Before examining elements of this text, I would like to state my philosophy regarding its preparation.

Those who teach entry-level courses in computer science are familiar with the problems that beginning students encounter. Initially, students can get so involved in learning a language that they may fail to grasp the significance of using the language to solve problems. Conversely, it is possible to emphasize problem solving to the extent that using a particular language to solve problems becomes almost incidental. The intent of this text is to provide a happy medium between these two extremes. Besides providing a complete, one-semester course in Turbo Pascal, the broader goals are for students to understand language concepts and subsequently be able to use them to solve problems.

Turbo Pascal is an excellent vehicle to be used for the purpose of accomplishing these goals. Turbo Pascal's popularity is due primarily to the availability of an affordable compiler and its ease of use with personal computers. In many respects, Borland's Turbo Pascal has become a second standard.

In addition to the affordability and portability of Turbo Pascal, some other advantages of using this version of Pascal as a programming language are:

a. The Integrated Development Environment using a mouse and pull-down menus is user-friendly.
b. An improved debugger makes debugging programs easier.
c. The ability to construct units is consistent with the emphasis on data abstraction and abstract data types.
d. The support for object-oriented programming allows this exciting concept to be presented to students relatively early in their programs.

Overview and Organization

The material in Chapters 1 and 2 includes the basics of most programming languages: input, output, data types, arithmetic, and standard functions. Even if students are well versed in these mechanics from another programming language, they should not skip these two chapters. The fundamental issues of computer science as a science and program development by top-down design are contained in this material. I feel it is very important for students to have a broad perspective of the discipline of computer science and to use a problem-solving approach when designing solutions to solve problems. Chapters 1 and 2 set the stage for this kind of development.

Section 1.4 contains a detailed development of the Turbo Pascal Integrated Development Environment. Upon completion of this section, students should be able to activate Turbo Pascal, write, edit, and run a program, save the file, and exit Turbo Pascal.

Throughout the text, I have attempted to explain and develop concepts carefully. These are illustrated by frequent examples and diagrams. New concepts are then used in complete programs to show how they aid in solving problems. An early and consistent emphasis has been placed on good writing habits and on producing neat, attractive output. I firmly believe program documentation and readability are important. Thus, I frequently discuss them in the text, and I offer style tips where appropriate.

There are at least three general scenarios for which this text would be appropriate.

1. A deliberately paced, thorough presentation of concepts would allow you to get through records and/or files in a one-semester course.
2. An accelerated pace with students who have previous computing experience would allow you to get through Chapter 12 in a one-semester course.
3. A deliberate pace with a thorough presentation would allow you to present the material in Chapters 1–12 and at least one chapter of Chapters 13–15 in a two-quarter sequence.

Subprograms are presented fairly early in this text. Procedures and user-defined functions are presented in their entirety in Chapter 3 before either selection statements (Chapter 4) or repetition statements (Chapter 5). This facilitates good problem solving habits in that a completely modular approach can be emphasized early in the course.

A completely interactive environment is assumed for the first five chapters. The first part of Chapter 6 introduces text files. From that point on, examples and programming problems use a combination of interactive and noninteractive environments. If you prefer, it would be possible to present the material on text files (Section 6.1) earlier in the course.

Chapters 7 and 8 develop arrays. Due to the significance of this concept, these chapters contain numerous examples, illustrations, and applications. Both the selection sort and bubble sort are presented in Chapter 7. Insertion sort and quick sort are discussed in Chapter 11. The insertion sort could be brought forward, but the quick sort requires the material on stacks to be covered before the sorting algorithm is presented. Records and files are discussed in Chapters 9 and 10, respectively. Their placement there is traditional. These chapters, combined with Chapters 7 and 8, present a detailed treatment of static data structures.

Chapter 11 is an optional chapter that discusses recursion and sorting. Recursion has been placed in this chapter so that an expanded presentation would be more appropriate. This also allows the quick sort to be developed. For advanced classes, material in this chapter could be used to motivate additional work with data structures.

Chapter 12, Sets, could be presented any time after Chapter 6. Although a full chapter has been devoted to this topic, a working knowledge could be given to students in one or two days. Chapter 13 is a complete development of graphics in Turbo Pascal. Conceptually, this material could be presented anytime after selection and repetition have been studied. However, reviewers overwhelmingly favored a late placement, so it is placed after the chapter on Sets. It has been written in such a way that it can be utilized at different times during the course depending on the instructor's preference.

Chapter 14 is a chapter on object-oriented programming. This introductory material will enable students to understand the basic concepts of OOP and to be able to write short programs using objects. Object-oriented programming is a rapidly growing field in computer science. It is my belief that students should have a relatively early introduction to using objects. Since Turbo Pascal supports OOP, it is appropriate to include this material here. Dynamic variables and data structures are introduced in Chapter 15. A reasonable discussion and development of pointers, linked lists, and binary trees is included. However, a full development of these concepts would have to come from a second course with a different text.

S Pascal statements in this text conform to Turbo Pascal. Standard Pascal references are included in the margins (see left margin) to indicate where Turbo Pascal differs from standard Pascal. These references refer to Appendix 7.

Features

This text has a number of noteworthy pedagogical features.

- Communication and Style Tips—suggestions for programming style, intended to enhance readability. A conscious attempt to emphasize the need for solid communication skills is developed in this text.
- Exercises—short-answer end-of-section questions.
- Programming Problems and Projects—suggestions for complete programs and projects given at ends of chapters.
- Module specifications for program modules.
- Structure charts to reflect modular development. These include use of data flow arrows to emphasize transmission of data to and/or from each module. This sets the stage for understanding use of value and variable parameters when procedures are introduced.
- Notes of Interest—brief essays intended to create awareness of and interest in various aspects of computer science.
- Suggestions for test programs—ideas included in exercises that encourage the student to use the computer to determine answers to questions and to see how to implement concepts in short programs.
- Focus on Program Design—when appropriate, a complete program at the end of the chapter that illustrates utilization of concepts developed within the chapter.
- Running and debugging hints preceding each summary and programming problems at the ends of chapters.
- New terms are italicized when first introduced.
- Communication in Practice—Suggestions and assignments which emphasize oral and written communication are included at the end of every chapter.

In the back of the book there is a complete glossary, as well as appendixes on reserved words, standard identifiers, syntax diagrams, character sets, compiler error messages, standard Pascal references, compiler directives, utilities programs, debugging features, and the **GOTO** statement. The final section of back matter provides answers to selected exercises.

Changes for this Version

The standard editions of earlier texts carefully presented and illustrated new concepts. It was assumed students had some previous computing experience; hence, introductory material was brief and subprograms were introduced very early (Chapter 3).

This version continues these assumptions. Furthermore, as the discipline of computer science evolves, there are two issues that its textbook authors must address. First, students in introductory courses have increasing experience and sophistication with computers. Second, the nature of an entry-level course should reflect current trends and meet current needs.

All development and programs in this edition assume a Turbo Pascal environment. Using the Integrated Development Environment (IDE) is covered early in Chapter 1. Complete chapters on graphics and object-oriented programming have been included. Turbo Pascal Version 6.0 was used for development reference throughout the text. All examples of code in the text will also run in Turbo Pascal Version 7.0. An appendix that details the differences between versions 6.0 and 7.0 is provided. Whenever we discuss an aspect of Pascal for which Turbo 7.0 offers additional features, a Turbo 7.0 logo (shown at the left) is used to furnish a convenient reference to this appednix. Such references are not widespread since most differences between Turbo 6.0 and 7.0 are of such an advanced nature to be of importance only to professional programmers. Consequently, students using this book will not be affected by the version of Turbo being used.

7.0

This text maintains the philosophy that computer science is a dynamic discipline. Although Pascal is still the language most used in entry-level courses, many concepts are presented in a language-independent manner. Thus, learning a language for the sake of learning the language is frequently deemphasized in favor of emphasizing concepts and problem-solving skills.

Consistent with the philosophy that Pascal is evolving as an introductory course in computer science, this version features the following:

- Continuing emphasis on the design of solutions to problems.
- Graphic documentation to illustrate how sections of code work.
- Two sections on using assertions.
- A section on software engineering and subsections throughout the text indicating how new concepts relate to software engineering.
- A section on the software system life cycle.
- Material on abstraction, including subsections on procedural abstraction, data abstraction, and abstract data types.
- A high level of rigor in the development and use of current terminology associated with subprograms, including discussions of cohesion, encapsulation, and interface.
- Material emphasizing communication in computer science. This includes periodic Communication and Style Tips as well as text references and exercises in every chapter designed to allow students to interview people, write reports, give oral reports, and write program specifications without writing code.

- Graphic documentation of some algorithms has been included to enable students to more easily understand code by using visual illustrations.
- Occasional use of photographs to clarify and enhance presentations.
- A significant number of mathematical examples and programming problems.
- Emphasis on programming problems. Beginning with Chapter 1, problems are provided to enhance the student's skills in problem solving and communication.
- A complete chapter on graphics in Turbo Pascal.
- A complete chapter on object-oriented programming.

All of these changes have been made with two thoughts prevalent in my mind. It is essential that this edition reflect current trends and future directions of computer science. It is also essential that concepts continue to be presented in such a manner that beginning students understand a concept and see how it can be used to design a solution to solving some problem. In this regard, every attempt has been made to retain the pedagogical features that have proven to be the trademark of other editions. These include frequent use of examples, clear exposition of new concepts, use of test programs, and varied end-of-section exercises.

Ancillaries

It is our belief that a broad-based teaching support package is essential for an introductory course in Pascal. Thus, the following ancillary materials are available from West Publishing Company:

1. Laboratory Manuals—In keeping with our intent to provide a modern approach and to meet the growing need for laboratory experience as put forth by the new ACM Curriculum Guidelines, there is a laboratory manual tied closely to the text's pedagogy. Authored by Carol Wilson, (Western Kentucky University) and class-tested with students at two universities, it provides excellent sets of lab exercises to promote students' understanding.
2. Instructor's Manual—This manual, by Jim Cowles of the Ohio University–Lancaster, contains the following for each chapter:
   - **a.** outline
   - **b.** teaching suggestions
   - **c.** answers to all end-of-section exercises
   - **d.** sample test questions
   - **e.** answers to test questions
3. Transparency Masters—More than 85 transparency masters are available to adopters of the text. The set of masters includes figures, tables, and selected other material from the text.
4. Software with Machine-readable Programming Problems—This software contains at least four complete programming problem solutions for each chapter and the complete Focus on Program Design problem. This software will run on IBM-PCs and compatibles, Apple Macintoshes, and DEC Vaxes.

Each program and program segment in the text and all ancillaries have been compiled and run. Every effort has been made to produce an error-free text, although this is virtually impossible. I assume full responsibility for all errors and omissions. If you detect any, please be tolerant and notify me or West Publishing Company so they can be corrected in subsequent printings and editions.

Acknowledgments

I would like to take this opportunity to thank those who in some way contributed to the completion of this text. Several reviewers contributed significant constructive comments during various phases of manuscript development. They include:

Deborah Byrum
Texas A & M University

Darrell Holland
Okaloosa-Walton Community College

Martin Holoien
University of California–Santa Barbara

Dennis Lynch
Elgin Community College

Leon Levine
University of California–Los Angeles

William R. Nico
California State–Hayward

Marilyn Jussel
University of Nebraska-Kearney

C.J. Knickerbrocker
St. Lawrence University

Jack Olson
Merritt College

Anne-Louise Radimsky
California State University–Sacramento

Parley P. Robinson
Brigham Young University

Melanie Wolf-Greenburg
California State–Fullerton

Dean DeChambeau, Developmental Editor, coordinated production of all ancillaries. Jim Cowles, Ohio University in Lancaster, has done yeoman's work in preparing many of the ancillaries. Carol Wilson, Western Kentucky University, contributed two Notes of Interest and prepared a Laboratory Manual, which can be used with this text. Tom Naps, Lawrence University in Wisconsin, contributed many helpful suggestions and recommendations.

Three other people deserve special mention because, without their expertise, this book would not exist. They are:

Mary George, copyeditor. She has amazing attention to detail. If you find the text readable, it is in large part due to her suggestions, changes, and rewordings.

Deb Meyer, Assistant Production Editor. This is my first book with Deb. She is efficient and well organized. She is very adept at coordinating all aspects of producing a textbook on schedule. She has a pleasant demeanor while maintaining a no-nonsense attitude about getting the project finished on time.

Jerry Westby, Manager, College Editorial. This is our twelfth book together, and my respect for Jerry keeps increasing. He has an excellent sense for what makes a book useful. Most of the special features of this text are the result of Jerry's suggestions. He has offered constant support and invaluable suggestions.

My family and friends deserve special mention for their support and patience. Most of my spare time and energy during the last decade have been devoted to writing textbooks. This would not have been possible without their encouragement and understanding.

Finally, there is one person without whose help this project would not have been possible. Helen, who was a student in my first Pascal class, has been of tremendous assistance since the inception of this effort. She served as an "in-house" copyeditor and made many helpful suggestions regarding presentation of the material. She keyed in all programs in the text. She read all the material during the copyedit, galleys, and pages stages of production.

This is the eighth text for which she has done all of the above. Her unfailing patience and support were remarkable. Fortunately for me, she has been my wife and best friend for thirty-five years.

Douglas W. Nance

Computer Science: Architecture, Languages, Problem Solving, and Programs

CHAPTER OUTLINE

This chapter provides a quick introduction to computer science, computer languages, and computer programs. Section 1.1 provides a preview of the study of computer science. Section 1.2 begins to explore the relationship between computers, computer languages, and computer programs. Section 1.3 lays the foundation for what many consider to be the most important aspect of entry-level courses in computer science: program development. The problem-solving theme started in this section is continued throughout the text. The remainder of Chapter 1 is intended to enable you to write complete programs as early as possible. You will thus be able to use the computer and to be an active participant from the initial stages of your study of computer science.

As you read this chapter, do not be overly concerned about the introduction and early use of terminology. All terms will be subsequently developed. A good approach to an introductory chapter like this is to reread it periodically. This will help you maintain a good perspective as to how new concepts and techniques fit in the broader picture of using computers. Finally, remember that learning a language that will make a computer work can be exciting; being able to control such a machine can lead to quite a sense of power.

■ 1.1 Computer Science: A Preview

Computer science is a very young discipline. Electronic computers were initially developed in the 1940s. Those who worked with computers in the 1940s and 1950s often did so by teaching themselves about computers; most schools did not then offer any instruction in computer science. However, as these early pioneers in computers learned more about the machines they were using, a collection of principles began to evolve into the discipline we now call computer science. Because it emerged from the efforts of people who used computers in a variety of disciplines, the influence of these disciplines can often be seen in computer science. With that in mind, the next sections briefly define what computer science is (and what it is not).

Computer Science Is Not Computer Literacy

Computer literate people know how to use a variety of computer software to make their professional lives and home lives more productive and easier. This software includes, for instance, word processors for writing and data management systems for storing every conceivable form of information from address lists to recipes.

However, knowing how to use specific pieces of computer software is not the same as acquiring an understanding of computer science, just as being able to drive a car does not qualify you to be an expert mechanic. The user of computer software must merely be able to follow instructions about how to use the software. On the other hand, the modern computer scientist must, more than anything else, be a skillful problem solver. The collection of problems that computer science encompasses and the techniques used to solve those problems are the real substance of this rapidly expanding discipline.

Computer Science Is Mathematics and Logic

The problem-solving emphasis of computer science borrows heavily from the areas of mathematics and logic. Faced with a problem, computer scientists must first formulate a solution. This method of solution, or *algorithm*, as it is often called in computer science, must be thoroughly understood before the computer scientist makes any attempt to implement the solution on the computer. Thus, at the early stages of problem solution, computer scientists work solely with their minds and do not rely upon the machine in any way.

Once the solution is understood, computer scientists must then state the solution to this problem in a formal language called a *programming language*. This parallels the fashion in which mathematicians or logicians must develop a proof or argument in the formal language of mathematics. This formal solution as stated in a programming language must then be evaluated in terms of its correctness, style, and efficiency. Part of this evaluation process involves entering the formally stated algorithm as a programmed series of steps for the computer to follow.

Another part of the evaluation process is distinctly separate from a consideration of whether or not the computer produces the "right answer" when the program is executed. Indeed, one of the main areas of emphasis throughout this text is in developing well-designed solutions to problems and in recognizing the difference between such solutions and ones that work, but inelegantly. True computer scientists seek not just solutions to problems but the best possible solutions.

Computer Science Is Science

Perhaps nothing is as intrinsic to the scientific method as the formulation of hypotheses to explain phenomena and the careful testing of these hypotheses to prove them right or wrong. This same process plays an integral role in the way computer scientists work.

Upon observing a problem, such as a long list of names that should be arranged in alphabetical order, computer scientists formulate a hypothesis in the form of an algorithm that they believe will effectively solve the problem. Using mathematical techniques, they can make predictions about how such a proposed algorithm will solve the problem. But because the problems facing computer scientists arise from the world of real applications, predictive techniques relying solely upon mathematical theory are not sufficient to prove an algorithm correct. Ultimately, computer scientists must implement their solutions on computers and test them in the complex situations that originally gave rise to the problems. Only after such thorough testing can the hypothetical solutions be declared right or wrong.

Moreover, just as many scientific principles are not 100 percent right or wrong, the hypothetical solutions posed by computer scientists are often subject to limitations. An understanding of those limitations—of when the method is appropriate and when it is not—is a crucial part of the knowledge that computer scientists must have. This is analogous to the way in which any scientist must be aware of the particular limitations of a scientific theory in explaining a given set of phenomena.

Do not forget the experimental nature of computer science as you study this book. You must participate in computer science to truly learn it. Although a good book can help, *you* must solve the problems, implement those solutions on the computer, and then test the results. View each of the problems you are assigned as an experiment for which you are to propose a solution, and then verify the correctness of your solution by testing it on the computer. If the solution does not work exactly as you hypothesized, do not become discouraged. Instead, ask yourself why it did not work; by doing so, you will acquire a deeper understanding of the problem and your solution. In this sense, the computer represents the experimental tool of the computer scientist. Do not be afraid to use it for exploration.

Computer Science Is Engineering

Whatever the area of specialization, an engineer must neatly combine a firm grasp of scientific principles with implementation techniques. Without knowledge of the principles, the engineer's ability to creatively design models for a problem's solution is severely limited. Such model building is crucial to the engineering design process. The ultimate design of a bridge, for instance, is the result of the engineer considering many possible models of the bridge and then selecting the best one. The transformation of abstract ideas into models of a problem's solution is thus central to the engineering design process. The ability to generate a variety of models that can be explored is the hallmark of creative engineering.

Similarly, the computer scientist is a model builder. Faced with a problem, the computer scientist must construct models for its solution. Such models take the form of an information structure to hold the data pertinent to the problem and the algorithmic method to manipulate that information structure to actually solve the problem. Just as an engineer must have an in-depth understanding of scientific principles to build a model, so must a computer scientist. With these principles, the computer scientist may conceive models that are elegant, efficient, and appropriate to the problem at hand.

An understanding of principles alone is not sufficient for either the engineer or the computer scientist. Experience in the actual implementation of hypothetical models is also necessary. Without such experience, you can have only very limited intuition about what is feasible and how a large-scale project should be organized to reach a successful conclusion. Ultimately, computers are used to solve problems in the real world. There, you will need to design programs that come in on time, that are within (if not under) the budget, and that solve all aspects of the original problem. The experience you acquire in designing problem solutions and then implementing them is vital to being a complete computer scientist. Hence, remember that you cannot actually study computer science without actively doing it. To merely read about computer science techniques will leave you with an unrealistic perspective of what is possible.

Computer Science Is Communication

As the discipline of computer science continues to evolve, communication is assuming a more significant role in the undergraduate curriculum. The Association for Computing Machinery, Inc., Curriculum Guidelines for 1991 state, "... undergraduate programs should prepare students to ... define a problem clearly; ... document that solution; ... and to communicate that solution to colleagues, professionals in other fields, and the general public." [page 7]

It is no longer sufficient to be content with a program that runs correctly. Extra attention should be devoted to the communication aspects associated with such a program. For instance, you might be asked to submit a written proposal prior to designing a solution, to carefully and completely document a program as it is being designed, and/or to write a follow-up report after a program has been completed.

These are some ways in which communication can be emphasized as an integral part of computer science. Several opportunities are provided in the exercises and problems of this text which focus on the communication aspects associated with computer science.

Computer Science Is Interdisciplinary

The problems solved by computer scientists come from a variety of disciplines—mathematics, physics, chemistry, biology, geology, economics, business, engineering, linguistics, and psychology, to name a few. As a computer scientist working on a problem in one of these areas, you must be a quasi-expert in that discipline as well as in computer science. For instance, you cannot write a program to manage the checking account system of a bank unless you thoroughly understand how banks work and how that bank runs its checking accounts. At minimum, you must be literate enough in other disciplines to converse with the people for whom you are writing programs and to learn precisely what it is they want the computer to do for them. Since such people are often very naive about the computer and its capabilities, you will have to possess considerable communication skills as well as knowledge of those other disciplines.

Are you beginning to think that a computer scientist must be knowledgeable about much more than just the computer? If so, you are correct. Too often, computer scientists are viewed as technicians tucked away in their own little

A NOTE OF INTEREST

Ethics and Computer Science

Ethical issues in computer science are rapidly gaining public attention. As evidence, consider the following article from the *Washington Post.*

Should law-enforcement agencies be allowed to use computers to help them determine whether a person ought to be jailed or allowed out on bond? Should the military let computers decide when and on whom nuclear weapons should be used?

While theft and computer viruses have not gone away as industry problems, a group of 30 computer engineers and ethicists who gathered in Washington recently agreed that questions about the proper use of computers is taking center stage. At issue is to what degree computers should be allowed to make significant decisions that human beings normally make.

Already, judges are consulting computers, which have been programmed to predict how certain personality types will behave. Judges are basing their decisions more on what the computer tells them than on their own analysis of the arrested person's history. Computers are helping doctors decide treatments for patients. They played a major role in the July 1988 shooting of the Iranian jetliner by the USS Vincennes, and they are the backbone of this country's Strategic Defense Initiative ("Star Wars").

Representatives from universities, IBM Corp., the Brookings Institution, and several Washington theological seminaries [recently discussed] what they could do to build a conscience in the computer field.

The computer industry has been marked by "creativity and drive for improvement and advancement," not by ethical concerns, said Robert Melford, chairman of the computing-ethics subcommittee of the Institute of Electrical and Electronics Engineers.

Computer professionals, Melford said, often spend much of their time in solitude, separated from the people affected by their programs who could provide valuable feedback.

Unlike hospitals, computer companies and most organized computer users have no staff ethicists or ethics committees to ponder the consequences of what they do. Few businesses have written policies about the proper way to govern computers. But there is evidence that technical schools, at least, are beginning to work an ethical component into their curricula. [For example, in recent years,] all computer engineering majors at Polytechnic University in Brooklyn [have been required to take a course in ethics.] The Massachusetts Institute of Technology is considering mandating five years of study, instead of the current four, to include work in ethics.

Affirmation that such questions should be addressed by computer scientists is contained in the 1991 curriculum guidelines of the Association for Computing Machinery, Inc. These guidelines state that "Undergraduates should also develop an understanding of the historical, social, and ethical context of the discipline and the profession."

You will see further Notes of Interest on this area of critical concern later in this book.

worlds, not thinking or caring about anything other than computers. Nothing could be further from the truth. The successful computer scientist must be able to communicate, to learn new ideas quickly, and to adapt to ever-changing conditions. Computer science is emerging from its early dark ages into a mature process, one that I hope you will find rewarding and exciting. In studying computer science, you will be developing many talents; this text can get you started on the road to that development process.

■ 1.2 Computer Architecture and Language

This section is intended to provide you with a brief overview of what computers are and how they are used. Although there are various sizes, makes, and models of computers, you will see that they all operate in basically the same straightforward manner. Whether you work on a personal computer that costs a few hundred dollars or on a mainframe that costs in the millions, the principles of making the machine work are essentially the same.

In this section, we will look at components of a computer and the idea of language for a computer. Also, we will continue to emphasize the notion of problem solving, which is independent of any particular language.

Modern Computers

The search for aids to perform calculations is almost as old as number systems. Early devices include the abacus, Napier's bones, the slide rule, and mechanical adding machines. More recently, calculators have changed the nature of personal computing as a result of their availability, low cost, and high speed. The development of computers over time is highlighted in Figure 1.1. For more complete information, see John F. Vinsonhaler, Christian C. Wagner, and Castelle G. Gentry, *People and Computers, Partners in Problem Solving* (Eagan, MN: West Publishing Company, 1989).

The last few decades have seen the most significant change in computing machines in the world's history as a result of improvements that have led to modern computers. As recently as the 1960s, a computer required several rooms because of its size. However, the advent of silicon chips has reduced the size and increased the availability of computers, so that parents are able to purchase personal computers as presents for their children. These computers are more powerful than the early behemoths.

What is a computer? According to *Webster's New World Dictionary of the American Language* (2nd College Edition), a computer is "an electronic machine which, by means of stored instructions and information, performs rapid, often complex calculations or compiles, correlates, and selects data." These stored instructions can also be altered by the user. Basically, a computer can be thought of as a machine that manipulates information in the form of numbers and characters. This information is referred to as *data*. What makes computers remarkable is the extreme speed and precision with which they can store, retrieve, and manipulate data.

Several types of computers currently are available. An oversimplification is to categorize computers as mainframe, minicomputer, or microcomputer. In this grouping, *mainframe computers* are the large machines used by major companies, government agencies, and universities. They have the capability of being

FIGURE 1.1
Development of computers

Era	Early Computing Devices		Mechanical Computers	Electro-mechanical Computers
Year	1000 B.C.	A.D. 1614	1650	1900 — 1945
Development	Abacus	Napier's bones	Adding machine Slide rule Difference engine Analytic engine	Cogged wheels Instruction register Operation code Address Plug board Harvard Mark I Tabulating machine

used by as many as 100 or more people at the same time and can cost millions of dollars. *Minicomputers,* in a sense, are smaller versions of large computers. They can be used by several people at once but have less storage capacity and cost far less. *Microcomputers* are frequently referred to as personal computers. They have limited storage capacity (in a relative sense), are generally used by one person at a time, and can be purchased for as little as a few hundred dollars.

As you begin your work with computers, you will hear people talking about hardware and software. *Hardware* refers to the actual machine and its support devices. *Software* refers to programs that make the machine do something. Many software packages exist for today's computers. They include word processing, database programs, spreadsheets, games, operating systems, and compilers. You can (and will!) learn to create your own software. In fact, that is what this book is all about.

A *program* can be thought of as a set of instructions that tells the machine what to do. When you have written a program, the computer will behave exactly as you have instructed it. It will do no more or no less than what is contained in your specific instructions. For example, consider the following complete program:

```
PROGRAM ComputeAverage;
USES
  Crt;

VAR
  Score1, Score2, Score3 : integer;
  Average : real;

BEGIN
  ClrScr;
  writeln ('Enter three scores and press <Enter>.');
  readln (Score1, Score2, Score3);
  Average := (Score1 + Score2 + Score3) / 3;
  writeln (Average:20:3);
  readln
END.
```

FIGURE 1.1
(continued)

Noncommercial Electronic Computers	Batch Processing	Time-Sharing Systems	Personal Computers
1945 – 1950	1950 – 1965	1965 – 1975	1975 – Present
First-generation computers	Second-generation computers	Third-generation computers	Fourth-generation computers
Vacuum tubes	Transistors	Integrated circuit technology	Fifth-generation computers (supercomputers)
Machine language programming	Magnetic core memory	Operating system software	Microprocessors
ENIAC	Assemblers	Teleprocessing	Workstations
	Compilers		
	UNIVAC I		
	IBM 704		

This Turbo Pascal program allows three scores to be entered from a keyboard, computes their average, and then displays the result. Do not be concerned about specific parts of this program. It is intended only to illustrate the idea of a set of instructions. Very soon, you will be able to write significantly more sophisticated programs.

Learning to write programs requires two skills.

1. You need to be able to use specific terminology and punctuation that can be understood by the machine: you need to learn a programming language.
2. You need to be able to develop a plan for solving a particular problem. This plan—or algorithm—is a sequence of steps that, when followed, will lead to a solution of the problem.

Initially, you may think that learning a language is the more difficult task because your problems will have relatively easy solutions. Nothing could be further from the truth! **The single most important thing you can do as a student of computer science is to develop the skill to solve problems.** Once you have this skill, you can learn to write programs in several different languages.

Computer Hardware

Let's take another look at the question, What is a computer? Our previous answer indicated it is a machine. Although there are several forms, names, and brands of computers, each consists of a *main unit* that is subsequently connected to peripheral devices. The main unit of a computer consists of a *central processing unit (CPU)* and *main (primary) memory.* The CPU is the "brain" of the computer. It contains an *arithmetic/logic unit (ALU),* which is capable of performing arithmetic operations and evaluating expressions to see if they are true or false, and the *control unit,* which controls the action of the remaining components so that your program can be followed step-by-step, or *executed.*

Main memory can be thought of as mailboxes in a post office. It is a sequence of locations where information representing instructions, numbers, characters, and so on can be stored. Main memory is usable while the computer is turned on. It is where the program being executed is stored along with the data it is manipulating.

As you develop a greater appreciation of how the computer works, you might wonder, How are data stored in memory? Each memory location has an address and is capable of holding a sequence of *binary digits,* (0 or 1) which are commonly referred to as *bits.* Instructions, symbols, letters, numbers, and so on are translated into an appropriate pattern of binary digits and then stored in various memory locations. These are retrieved, used, and changed according to instructions in your program. In fact, the program itself is similarly translated and stored in part of main memory. Main memory can be envisioned as shown in Figure 1.2, and the main unit can be envisioned as shown in Figure 1.3.

Peripherals can be divided into three categories: input devices, output devices, and secondary (auxiliary) memory devices. *Input devices* are necessary to give information to a computer. Programs are entered through an input device, and then program statements are translated and stored as previously indicated. One input device (a typical keyboard) is shown in Figure 1.4.

Output devices are necessary to show the results of a program. These devices are normally in the form of a screen, line printer, impact printer, or laser printer (see Figure 1.5). Input and output devices are frequently referred to as *I/O devices.*

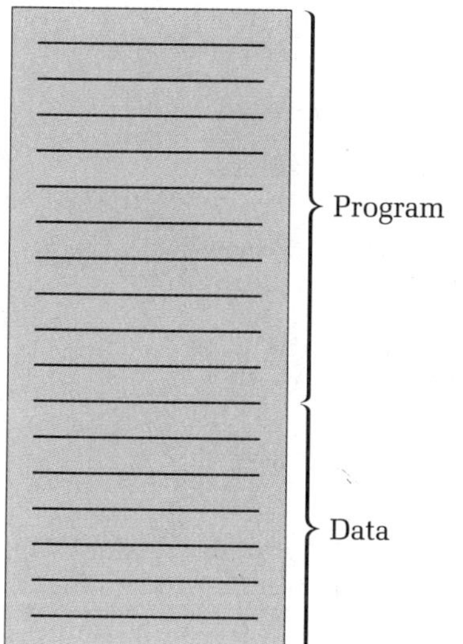

FIGURE 1.2
Main memory

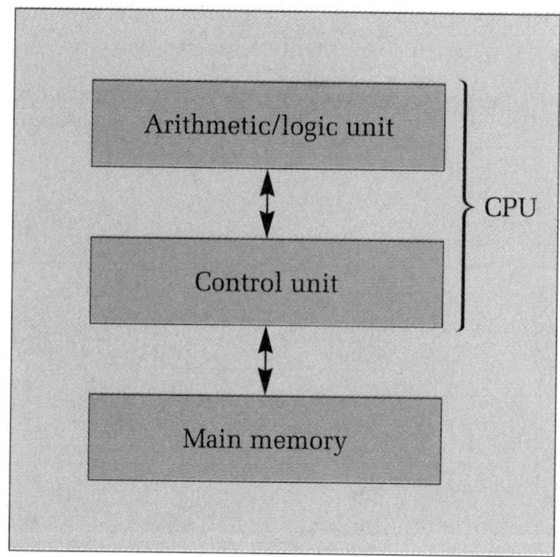

FIGURE 1.3
Main unit

FIGURE 1.4
Keyboard

Secondary (auxiliary) memory devices are used if additional memory is needed. On small computers, these secondary memory devices could be floppy disks or hard disks (Figure 1.6), magnetic tapes, or magnetic bubbles. Programs and data waiting to be executed are kept "waiting in the wings" in secondary memory.

Communication between components of a computer is frequently organized around a group of wires called a *bus*. The relationship between a bus and various computer components can be envisioned as shown in Figure 1.7.

A photograph of a bus is shown in Figure 1.8. What appear to be lines between the slots are actually wires imprinted upon the underlying board. Boards with wires connected to peripheral devices may be inserted into the slots.

Computer Software

As previously stated, software refers to programs that make the machine do something. Software consists of two kinds of programs: system software and applications software.

FIGURE 1.5
(a) Screen, (b) line printer (mainframe), (c) impact printer (microcomputer), and (d) laser printer

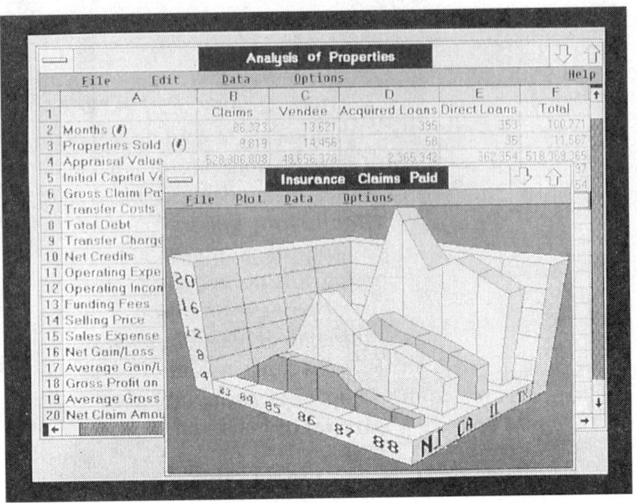

(a)

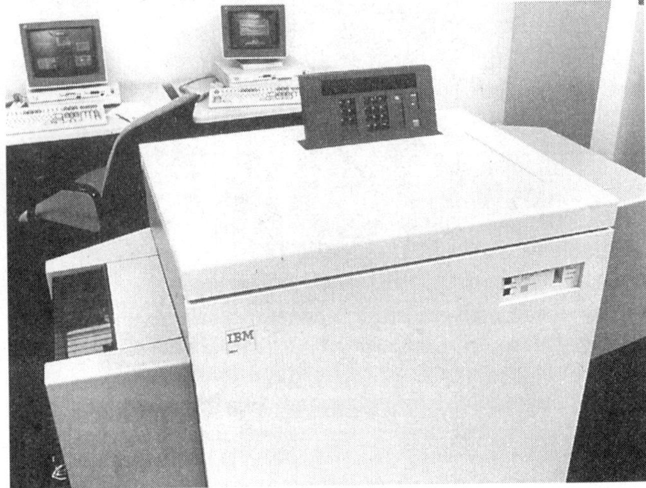

(b)

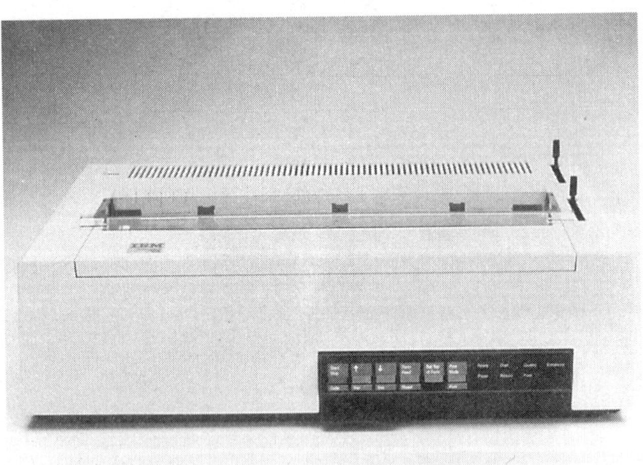

(c)

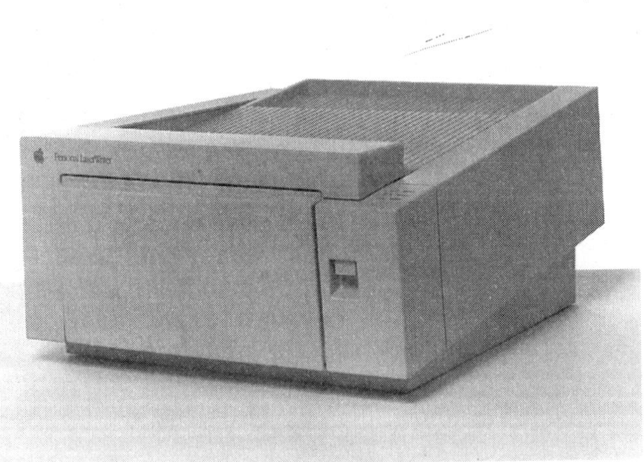

(d)

System software includes what is often called the *operating system.* (You may have heard reference to DOS, which is an acronym for Disk Operating System.) The operating system for a computer is a large program and is usually supplied with a computer. This program allows the user to communicate with the hardware. More specifically, an operating system might control computer access (via passwords), allocate peripheral resources (perhaps with a printer queue), schedule shared resources (for CPU use), or control execution of other programs.

Applications software consists of programs designed for a specific use. Examples of applications software include programs for word processing, text editing, simulating spreadsheets, playing games, designing machinery, and figuring payrolls. Most computer users work with applications software and have little need for learning a computer language; the programs they require have already been written to accomplish their tasks.

FIGURE 1.6
(a) Disk drive, and (b) microcomputer with internal hard disk

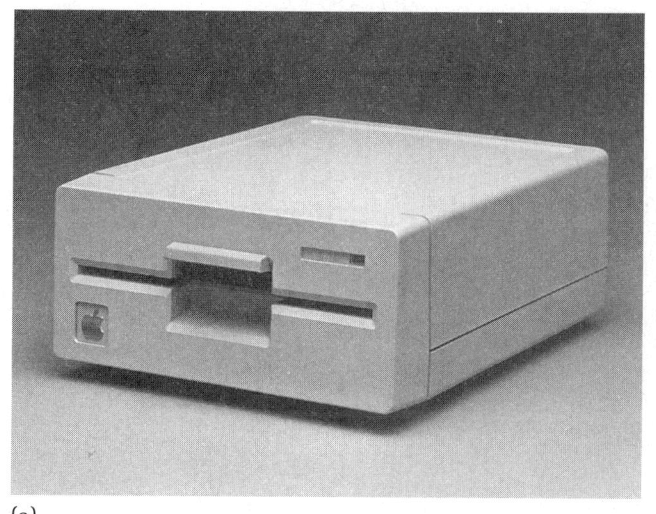
(a)

(b)

FIGURE 1.7
Illustration of a bus

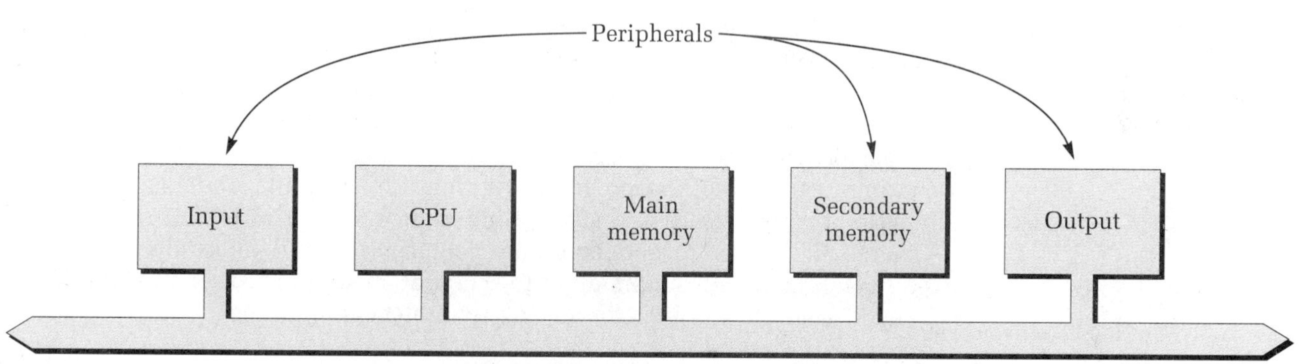

FIGURE 1.8
Bus

A NOTE OF INTEREST

Data Loss on Floppy Disks

Why is it important to keep the dust covers on your diskettes? Look at the figure shown here. It illustrates how some very small particles look huge in comparison to the distance between the surface of a diskette and the read/write head. If these particles become lodged between the head and the surface of the diskette, the surface may be scratched, resulting in data loss. So consider yourself warned; handle your disks carefully, and keep copies of important programs on more than one diskette.

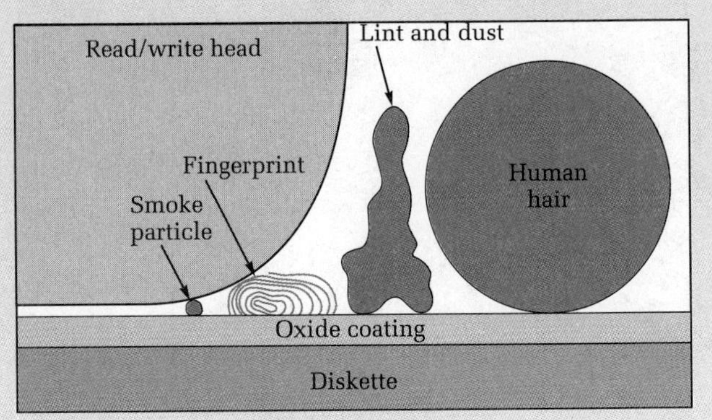

Computer Languages

What is a computer language? All data transmission, manipulation, storage, and retrieval is actually done by the machine using electrical pulses generated by sequences of binary digits. If eight-digit binary codes were used, there would be 256 numbered instructions from 00000000 to 11111111. Instructions for adding two numbers would consist of a sequence of these eight-digit codes.

Instructions written in this form are referred to as *machine language.* It is possible to write an entire program in machine language. However, this process is very time consuming, the program is difficult to read and understand, and the language is hard to learn and susceptible to programmer errors.

Therefore, the next level of computer language allows words and symbols to be used in an unsophisticated manner to accomplish simple tasks. For example, the sequence of machine codes for adding two integers might be

```
010000110011101000111101010000010010101101000010
```

This is replaced by

```
LOAD A
ADD B
STORE C
```

This causes the number in A to be added to the number in B and the result to be stored for later use in C. This computer language is an *assembly language,* which is generally referred to as a *low-level language.* What actually happens is that words and symbols are translated into appropriate binary digits and the machine uses the translated form.

Although assembly language is an improvement on machine language in terms of readability and program development, it is still a bit cumbersome. Consequently, many *high-level languages* have been developed; these include Pascal, PL/I, FORTRAN, BASIC, COBOL, C, Ada, Modula-2, Logo, and others. These languages simplify even further the terminology and symbolism needed to direct the machine to perform various manipulations of data. For example, in these languages, the task of adding two integers would be written as

C := A + B;	(Pascal)	C = A + B;	(C)
C = A + B;	(PL/I)	C := A + B;	(Ada)
C = A + B	(FORTRAN)	C := A + B;	(Modula-2)
C = A + B	(BASIC)	MAKE "C :A + :B	(Logo)
ADD A,B GIVING C	(COBOL)		

A high-level language makes it easier to read, write, and understand a program. This book develops the concepts, symbolism, and terminology needed to use Pascal as a programming language for solving problems. After you have become proficient in using Pascal, you should find it relatively easy to learn the nuances of other high-level languages.

For a moment, let's consider how an instruction such as

```
C := A + B;
```

gets translated into machine code. The actual bit pattern for this code varies according to the machine and software version, but it could be as previously indicated. In order for the translation to happen, a special program called a *compiler* "reads" the high-level instructions and translates them into machine code. This compiled version is then run using some appropriate data. The results are then presented through some form of output device. The special programs that activate the compiler, run the machine-code version, and cause output to be printed are examples of system programs (software). The written program is a *source program,* and the machine-code version generated by the compiler is an *object program* (also referred to as *object code*).

As you will soon see, the compiler does more than just translate instructions into machine code. It also detects certain errors in your source program and prints appropriate messages. For example, if you write the instruction

```
C := (A + B;
```

where the parentheses are not matched, when the compiler attempts to translate this line into machine code, it will detect that ")" is needed to close the parenthetical expression. It will then give you an error message, such as

```
'')'' EXPECTED
```

You will then need to correct the error (and any others) and recompile your source program before running it with the data.

Before leaving this introductory section, let's consider the question, Why study Pascal? Various languages have differing strengths and weaknesses. Pascal's strong features include the following:

1. It incorporates program structure in a reasonable approximation of English. For example, if a certain process is to be repeated until some condition is met, this could be written in the program as

```
REPEAT
   } (Process here)
UNTIL (Condition here)
```

2. It allows the use of descriptive words for variables and data types. Thus, programs for computing payrolls could use words like Hours-Worked, StateTax, FICA, TotalDeductions, and GrossPay.
3. It facilitates good problem-solving habits; in fact, many people consider this to be Pascal's main strength. As previously noted, the skill to solve a problem using a computer program is the most important trait to develop as a beginning programmer. Pascal is structured in such a manner that it encourages—indeed, almost requires—good problem-solving skills.

You are now ready to begin a detailed study of Pascal. You will undoubtedly spend much time and encounter some frustration during the course of your work. I hope your efforts result in an exciting and rewarding learning experience. Good luck.

■ 1.3 Program Development: Top-Down Design

We are now ready to examine problems that computers can solve. First, we need to know how to solve a problem, and then we need to learn how to use a programming language to implement our solution on the computer.

Before looking at problem solving and writing programs for the computer, we should consider some psychological aspects of working in computer science. Studying computer science can cause a significant amount of frustration because

1. Planning is a critical issue. First, you must plan to develop instructions to solve your problem, and then you should plan to translate these instructions into code before you sit down at the keyboard. You should not attempt to type in code "off the top of your head."
2. Time is a major problem. Writing programs is not like completing other assignments. You cannot expect to complete a programming assignment by staying up late the night before it is due. You must begin early and expect to make several revisions before your final version will be ready.
3. Successful problem solving and programming require extreme precision. Generally, concepts in computer science are not difficult; however, implementation of these concepts allows no room for error. For example, one misplaced semicolon in a 1000-line program could prevent the program from working.

In other words, you must be prepared to plan well, start early, be patient, handle frustration, and work hard to succeed in computer science. If you cannot do this, you will probably neither enjoy computer science nor be successful at it.

The key to writing a successful program is planning. Good programs do not just happen; they are the result of careful design and patience. Just as an artist commissioned to paint a portrait would not start out by shading in the lips and eyes, a good computer programmer would not attack a problem by immediately trying to write code for a program to solve the problem. Writing a program is like writing an essay: an overall theme is envisioned, an outline of major ideas is developed, each major idea is subdivided into several parts, and each part is developed using individual sentences.

Six Steps to Good Programming Habits

In developing a program to solve a problem, six steps should be followed: analyze the problem, develop an algorithm, write code for the program, run the program, test the results and document the program. These steps will help you develop good problem-solving habits and, in turn, solve programming problems correctly. A brief discussion of each of these steps follows:

A NOTE OF INTEREST

Why Learn Pascal?

From the point of view of many potential users, Pascal's major drawback is that it is a compiled rather than an interpreted language. This means that developing and testing a small Pascal program can take a lot longer and involve many more steps than it would with an interpreted language like BASIC. The effect of this drawback has been lessened recently with the development of interpreter programs for Pascal. [For example, some current versions of Pascal, such as Turbo Pascal, have quick compilation, and are as easy to use as most interpreted languages.] Even so, most programs written by users of personal computers are small ones designed for quick solutions to particular problems, and the use of Pascal for such programs may be a form of overkill.

Ironically, the characteristics of Pascal that make it relatively unsuited for small programs are a direct consequence of its strengths as a programming language. The discipline imposed by the language makes it easier to understand large programs, but it may be more than a small program demands. For serious development of large programs or for the creation of tools that will be used over and over again (and require modifications from time to time), Pascal is clearly superior.

Experts generally consider Pascal an important language for people who are planning to study computer science or to learn programming. Indeed, the College Entrance Examination Board has designated Pascal as the required language for advanced-placement courses in computer science for high school students. While it is true that an experienced programmer can write clearly structured programs in any language, learning the principles of structured programming is much easier in Pascal.

Is Pascal difficult to learn? We don't think so, but the question is relative and may depend on which language you learn first. Programmers become accustomed to the first language they learn, making it the standard by which all others are judged. Even the poor features of the familiar language come to be seen as necessities, and a new language seems inferior. Don't let such subjective evaluations bar your way to learning Pascal, a powerful and elegant programming language.

Step 1. Analyze the Problem. This is not a trivial task. Before you can do anything, you must know exactly what it is you are to do. You must be able to formulate a clear and precise statement of what is to be done. You should understand completely what data are available and what may be assumed. You should also know exactly what output is desired and the form it should take.

Step 2. Develop an Algorithm. An algorithm is a finite sequence of effective statements that, when applied to the problem, will solve it. An *effective statement* is a clear, unambiguous instruction that can be carried out. Each algorithm you develop should (1) have a specific beginning; (2) at the completion of one step, have the next step uniquely determined; and (3) have an ending that is reached in a reasonable amount of time.

Step 3. Write Code for the Program. When the algorithm correctly solves the problem, you can think about translating your algorithm into a high-level language. An effective algorithm will significantly reduce the time you need to complete this step.

Step 4. Run the Program. After writing the code, you are ready to run the program. This means that, using an editor, you type the program code into the computer, compile the program, and run the program. At this point, you may discover errors that can be as simple as typing errors or that may require a reevaluation of all or parts of your algorithm. The probability of having to make some corrections or changes is quite high.

Step 5. Test the Results. After your program has run, you need to be sure that the results are correct, that they are in a form you like, and that your program produces the correct solution in all cases. To be sure the results are correct, you must look at them and compare them with what you expect. In the case of using a program with arithmetic operations, this means checking some results with pencil and paper. With complex programs, you will need to thoroughly test the program by running it many times using data that you have carefully selected. Often you will need to make revisions and return to a previous step.

Step 6. Document the Program. It is very important to completely document a working program. The writer knows how the program works; if others are to modify it, they must know the logic used. As you develop the ability to write programs to solve more complex problems, you will find it helpful to include documentation in Step 3 as you write the code.

Developing Algorithms

Algorithms for solving a problem can be developed by stating the problem and then subdividing the problem into major subtasks. Each subtask can then be subdivided into smaller tasks. This process is repeated until each remaining task is one that is easily solved. This process is known as *top-down design,* and each successive subdivision is referred to as a *stepwise refinement.* Tasks identified at each stage of this process are called *modules.* The relationship between modules can be shown graphically in a *structure chart* (see Figure 1.9).

FIGURE 1.9
Structure chart illustrating top-down design

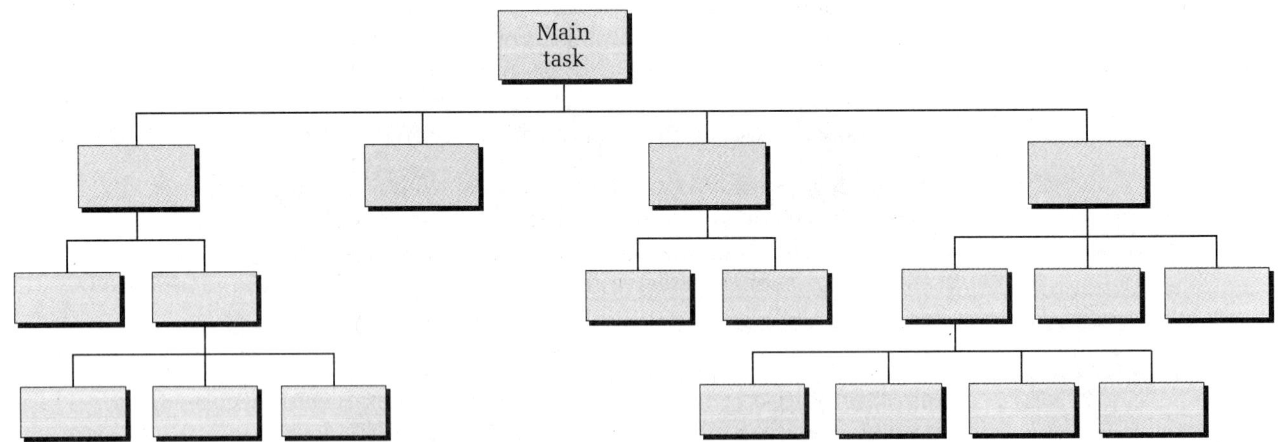

To illustrate developing an algorithm, we will use the problem of updating a checkbook after a transaction has been made. A first-level refinement is shown in Figure 1.10. An arrow pointing into a module means information is needed before the task can be performed. An arrow pointing out of a module means the module task has been completed and information required for subsequent work is available. Each of these modules could be further refined as shown in Figure 1.11. Finally, one of the last modules could be refined as shown in Figure 1.12. The complete top-down design could then be envisioned as illustrated in Figure 1.13. Notice that each remaining task can be accomplished in a very direct manner.

FIGURE 1.10
First-level refinement

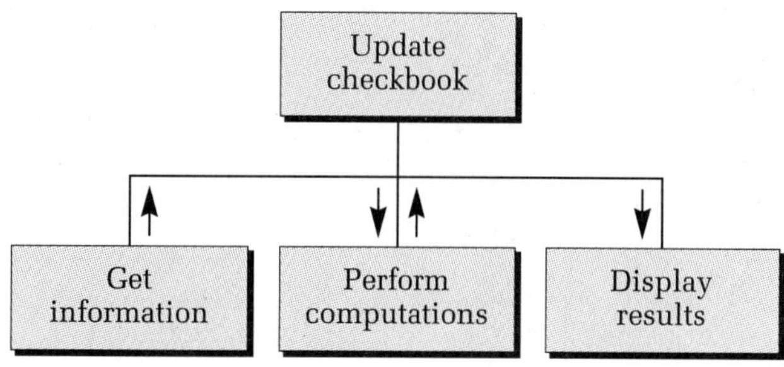

FIGURE 1.11
Second-level refinement

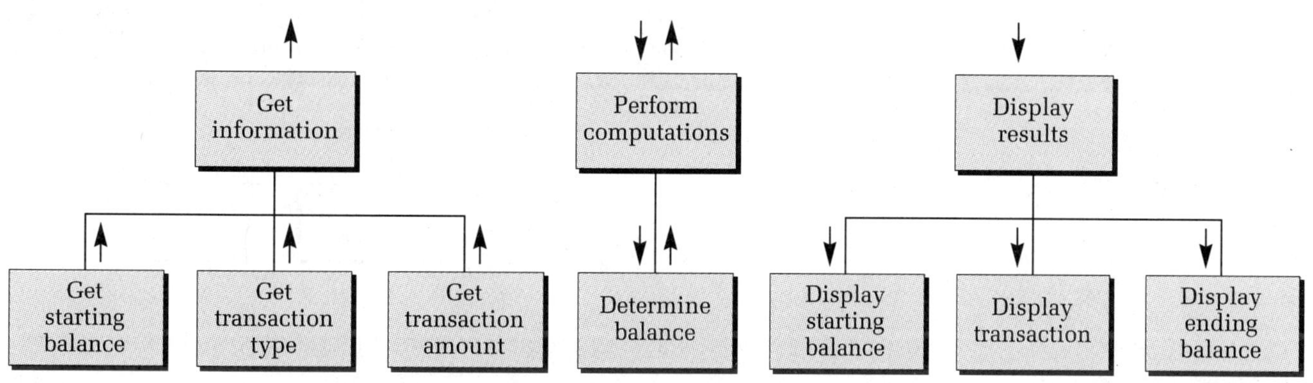

FIGURE 1.12
Third-level refinement

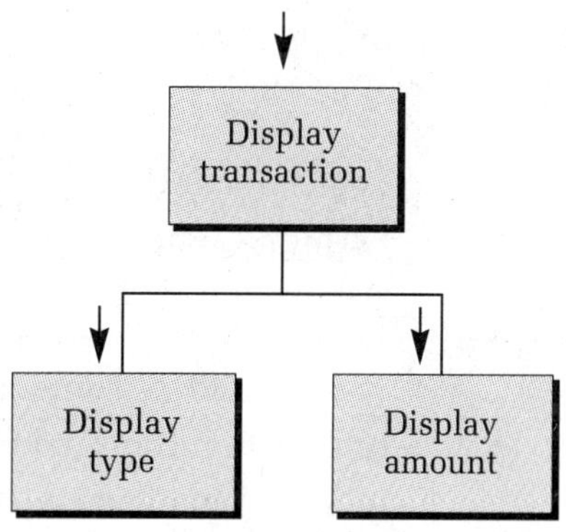

As a further aid to understanding how data are transmitted, we will list *module specifications* for each main (first-level) module. Each module specification includes a description of data received, information returned, and logic used in the module. Module specifications for the Get Information module are

<u>Get Information Module</u>

Data received: None

Information returned: Starting balance
Transaction type
Transaction amount

Logic: Have the user enter information from the keyboard.

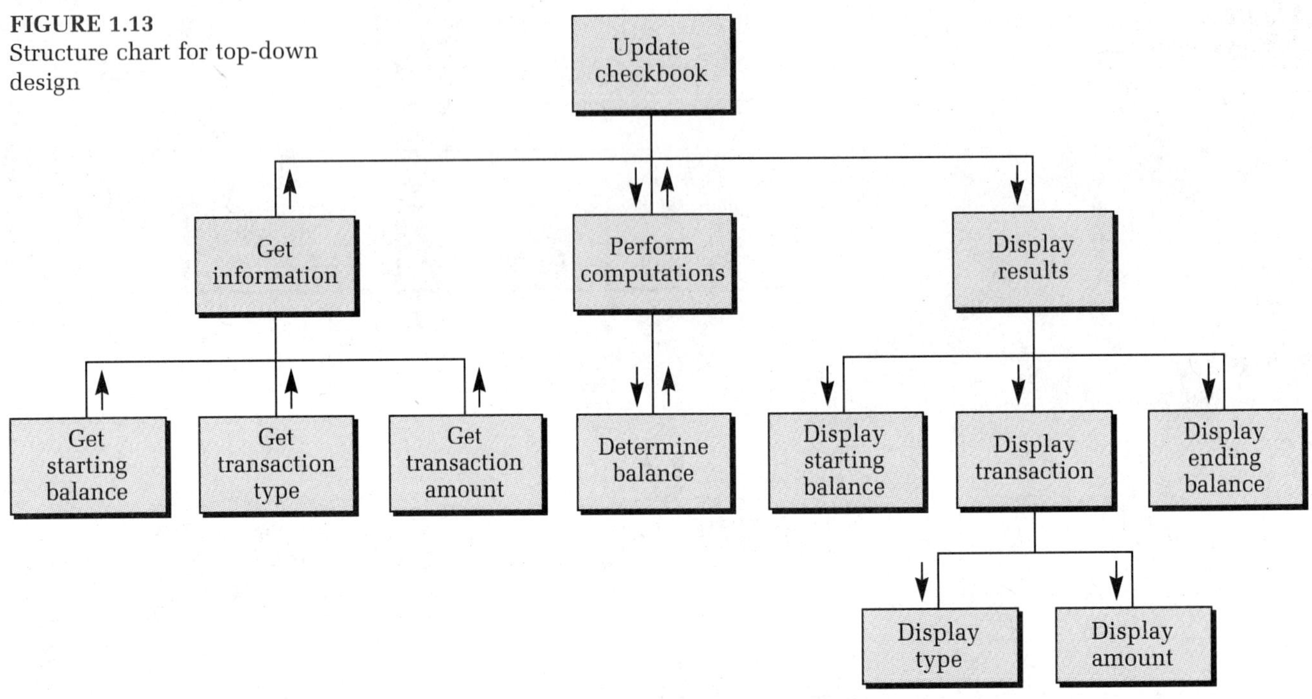

FIGURE 1.13
Structure chart for top-down design

For the checkbook-balancing problem, complete module specifications are

1. Get Information Module

   Data received: None

   Information returned: Starting balance
   Transaction type
   Transaction amount

   Logic: Have the user enter information from the keyboard.

2. Perform Computations Module

   Data received: Starting balance
   Transaction type
   Transaction amount

   Information returned: Ending balance

   Logic: If transaction is a deposit, add it to the starting balance; otherwise, subtract it from the starting balance.

3. Display Results Module

   Data received: Starting balance
   Transaction type
   Transaction amount
   Ending balance

   Information returned: None

   Logic: Display results in a readable form.

At least two comments should be made about top-down design. First, different people can (and probably will) have different designs for the solution of a problem. However, each good design will have well-defined modules with functional subtasks. Second, the graphic method just used helps to formulate

A NOTE OF INTEREST

Software Verification

Sitting 70 kilometers East of Toronto on the shore of Lake Ontario, the Darlington Nuclear Generating Station looks much like any other large nuclear power plant of the Canadian variety. But behind its ordinary exteriors lies an unusual design feature.

Darlington is the first Canadian nuclear station to use computers to operate the two emergency shutdown systems that safeguard each of its four reactors. In both shutdown systems, a computer program replaces an array of electrically operated mechanical devices—switches and relays—designed to respond to sensors monitoring conditions critical to a reactor's safe operation, such as water levels in boilers.

When completed in 1992, Darlington's four reactors will supply enough electricity to serve a city of 2 million people. Its Toronto-based builder, Ontario Hydro, opted for sophisticated software rather than old-fashioned hardware in the belief that a computer-operated shutdown system would be more economical, flexible, reliable, and safe than one under mechanical control.

But that approach carried unanticipated costs. To satisfy regulators that the shutdown software would function as advertised, Ontario Hydro engineers had to go through a frustrating but essential checking process that required nearly three years of extra effort.

"There are lots of examples where software has gone wrong with serious consequences," says engineer Glenn H. Archinoff of Ontario Hydro. "If you want a shutdown system to work when you need it, you have to have a high level of assurance."

The Darlington experience demonstrates the tremendous effort involved in establishing the correctness of even relatively short and straightforward computer programs. The 10,000 "lines" of instructions, or code, required for each shutdown system pale in comparison with the 100,000 lines that constitute a typical word-processing program or the millions of lines needed to operate a long-distance telephone network or a space shuttle.

general logic for solving a problem but is somewhat awkward for translating to code. Thus, we will use a stylized, half-English, half-code method called *pseudocode* to illustrate stepwise refinement in such a design. This will be written in English, but the sentence structure and indentations will suggest Pascal code. Major tasks will be numbered with whole numbers; subtasks, with decimal numbers. First-level pseudocode for the checkbook-balancing problem is

1. Get information
2. Perform computations
3. Display results

A second-level pseudocode development produces

```
1. Get information
   1.1 get starting balance
   1.2 get transaction type
   1.3 get transaction amount
2. Perform computations
   2.1 IF deposit THEN
           add to balance
       ELSE
           subtract from balance
```

3. Display results
   3.1 display starting balance
   3.2 display transaction
   3.3 display ending balance

Finally, Step 3.2 of the pseudocode is subdivided as previously indicated into

   3.2 display transaction
      3.2.1 display transaction type
      3.2.2 display transaction amount

Two final comments are in order. First, each module developed should be tested with data for that module. Once you are sure each module does what you want it to, the whole program should work when the modules are used together. Second, the process of dividing a task into subtasks is especially suitable for writing programs in Pascal. As you will see, the language supports development of subprograms for specific subtasks.

A Turbo Pascal program for this problem follows:

```
PROGRAM Checkbook;

USES
  Crt;

VAR
  StartingBalance,
  EndingBalance,
  TransAmount : real;
  TransType : char;

BEGIN  {  Program  }

  {  Module for getting the data  }

  ClrScr;
  writeln ('Enter the starting balance and press <Enter>.');
  readln (StartingBalance);
  writeln ('Enter the transaction type (D) deposit or (W) withdrawal');     1*
  writeln ('and press <Enter>.');
  readln (TransType);
  writeln ('Enter the transaction amount and press <Enter>.');
  readln (TransAmount);

  {  Module for performing computations  }

  IF TransType = 'D' THEN
    EndingBalance := StartingBalance + TransAmount                          2
  ELSE
    EndingBalance := StartingBalance - TransAmount;

  {  Module for displaying results  }

  writeln;
  writeln ('Starting Balance        $', StartingBalance:8:2);
  writeln ('Transaction             $', TransAmount:8:2, TransType:2);
  writeln ('---------':33);
  writeln ('Ending Balance          $', EndingBalance:8:2);                 3
  readln
END.  {  of program  }
```

*These numbers refer to the modules previously developed with module specifications.

Notice how sections of the program correspond to module specifications. Sample runs of the program produce the output below. Input from the keyboard is shown in color.

```
Enter the starting balance and press <Enter>.
235.16
Enter the transaction type (D) deposit or (W) withdrawal
and press <Enter>.
D
Enter the transaction amount and press <Enter>.
75.00

Starting Balance         $  235.16
Transaction              $   75.00 D
                         ---------
Ending Balance           $  310.16

Enter the starting balance and press <Enter>.
310.16
Enter the transaction type (D) deposit or (W) withdrawal
and press <Enter>.
W
Enter the transaction amount and press <Enter>.
65.75

Starting Balance         $  310.16
Transaction              $   65.75 W
                         ---------
Ending Balance           $  244.41
```

You probably would not use the power of a computer for something as simple as this program. You could just press a few calculator keys instead. However, as you will see, the language supports development of subprograms for specific subtasks. You will, for example, soon be able to enhance this program to check for overdrafts, save the new balance for later use, and repeat the process for several transactions. Learning to think in terms of modular development now will aid you not only in creating algorithms to solve problems, but also in writing programs to solve problems.

Software Engineering

The phrase *software engineering* is used to refer to the process of developing and maintaining very large software systems. Before becoming engrossed in the specifics of solving problems and writing relatively small programs, it is instructive to consider the broader picture faced by those who develop software for "real world" use.

It is not unusual for software systems to be programs that, if written in this size type, would require between 100 and 150 pages of text. These systems must be reliable, economical, and subject to use by a diverse audience. Because of these requirements, software developers must be aware of and practice certain techniques.

As you might imagine, such large programs are not the work of a single individual but are developed by teams of programmers. Issues such as communication, writing style, and technique become as important as developing algorithms to solve particular parts of the problem. Management, coordination, and design are major considerations that need resolution very early in the process. Although you will not face these larger organizational issues in this

COMMUNICATION AND STYLE TIPS

Effective communication is an important part of learning computer science. In recognition of this factor, this text contains two threads that consistently emphasize communication. First, several "Communication and Style Tips" contain notes about communication and suggestions for improving communication as it relates to developing programs.

The second thread is contained in the Programming Problems and Projects section, which appears at the end of each chapter. Beginning with this chapter, each chapter contains some "Communication in Practice" problems, which emphasize communication rather than program development. This is consistent with the Association for Computing Machinery, Inc., Curriculum Guidelines for 1991, which state, "Students should be encouraged to develop strong communication skills, both oral and written."

You are encouraged to discuss these ideas with your instructor and to incorporate them as part of your program development when appropriate.

course, you will see how some of what you learn has implications for larger design issues.

Software engineering has been so titled because techniques and principles from the more established engineering disciplines are used to guide the large-scale development required in major software. To illustrate, consider the problems faced by an engineer who is to design and supervise construction of a bridge. This analysis was presented by Alfred Spector and David Gifford in an article entitled "A Computer Science Perspective on Bridge Design" published in *Communications of the ACM* (April 1986).

> *Engineers designing a bridge view it first as a hierarchy of substructures. This decomposition process continues on the substructures themselves until a level of very fundamental objects (such as beams and plates) ultimately is reached. This decomposition technique is similar to the stepwise refinement technique used by software designers, who break a complex problem down into a hierarchy of subproblems, each of which ultimately can be solved by a relatively simple algorithm.*
>
> *Engineers build conceptual models before actually constructing a bridge. This model-building allows them to evaluate various design alternatives in a way which eventually leads to the best possible design for the application being considered. This process is analogous to the way in which a skilled software designer builds models of a software system using structure charts and first-level pseudocode descriptions of modules. The designer then studies these conceptual models and eventually chooses the most elegant and efficient model for the application.*
>
> *By the fashion in which engineers initially break down the bridge design, they insure that different aspects of the design can be addressed by different subordinate groups of design engineers working in a relatively independent fashion. This is similar to the goal of a software designer who oversees a program development team. The design of the software system must insure that individual components may be developed simultaneously by separate groups whose work will not have harmful side effects when the components are finally pulled together.*

This overview is presented to give you a better perspective on how developments in this text are part of a greater whole. As you progress through your study of Pascal, you will see specific illustrations of how concepts and techniques can be viewed as part of the software engineering process.

Software System Life Cycle

Software engineering is the process by which large software systems are produced. As you might imagine, these systems need to be maintained and modified; ultimately, they are replaced with other systems. This entire process parallels that of an organism: there is a development, maintenance, and subsequent demise. Thus, this process is referred to as the *software system life cycle*. Specifically, a system life cycle can be viewed in the following phases:

1. Analysis
2. Design
3. Coding
4. Testing/verification
5. Maintenance
6. Obsolescence

It probably comes as a surprise that computer scientists view this process as having a phase that precedes the design phase. However, it is extremely critical that a problem be completely understood before any attempt is made to design a solution. The analysis phase is complicated by the fact that potential users may not supply enough information when describing their intended use of a system. Analysis requires careful attention to such items as exact form of input, exact form of output, how data entry errors (there will be some) should be handled, how large the data bases will become, how much training in using the system will be provided, and what possible modifications might be required as the intended audience increases/decreases. Clearly, the analysis phase requires an experienced communicator.

The design phase is what much of this text is about. This is where the solution is developed using a modular approach. Attention must be paid to techniques that include communication, algorithm development, writing style, and teamwork.

Coding closely follows design. Unfortunately, many beginning students want to write code too quickly. This can be a painful lesson if you have to scrap several days of work because your original design was not sufficient. You are encouraged to make sure your designs are complete before writing any code. In the real world, teams of designers work long hours before programmers ever get a chance to start writing code.

The testing phase of a large system is a significant undertaking. Early testing is done on individual modules to get them running properly. Larger data sets must then be run on the entire program to make sure the modules interact properly with the main program. When the system appears ready to the designers, it is usually field tested by selected users. Each of these testing levels is likely to require changes in the design and coding of the system.

Finally, the system is released to the public and the maintenance phase begins. This phase lasts throughout the remainder of the program's useful life. During this phase, we are concerned with repairing problems that arise with the system after it has been put into use. These problems are not necessarily bugs introduced during the coding phases. More often they are the result of user needs that change over time. For instance, annual changes in the tax laws necessitate changes in even the best payroll programs. Or problems may be due to misinterpretation of user needs during the early analysis phase. Whatever the reason, a program should be expected to undergo numerous changes during its lifetime. During the maintenance phase, the time spent documenting the original program will be repaid many times over. One of the worst tasks imaginable in software development is to be asked to maintain an undocumented program. Undocumented code can quickly become virtually unintelligible, even to the program's original author. Indeed, one measure of a good program is how well it stands up to the maintenance phase.

Of course, no matter how good a program may be, it will eventually become obsolete. At that time, the system life cycle starts all over again with the development of a new system to replace the obsolete one. Hence, the software system life cycle is never-ending, being itself part of a larger repetitive pattern that continues to evolve with changing user needs and more powerful technology.

Exercises 1.3

1. Which of the following can be considered effective statements—that is, clear, unambiguous instructions that can be carried out? Explain why each statement is effective or why it is not.
   a. Pay the cashier $9.15.
   b. Water the plants a day before they die.
   c. Determine all positive prime numbers less than 1,000,000.
   d. Choose X to be the smallest positive fraction.
   e. Invest your money in a stock that will increase in value.
2. What additional information must be obtained in order to understand each of the following problems?
   a. Find the largest number of a set of numbers.
   b. Alphabetize a list of names.
   c. Compute charges for a telephone bill.
3. Outline the main tasks for solving each of the following problems.
   a. Write a good term paper.
   b. Take a vacation.
   c. Choose a college.
   d. Get a summer job.
   e. Compute the semester average for a student in a computer science course, and print all pertinent data.
4. Refine the main tasks in each part of Exercise 3 into a sufficient number of levels so that the problem can be solved in a well-defined manner.
5. Use pseudocode to write a solution for each of the following problems. Indicate each stage of your development.
   a. Compute the wages for two employees of a company. The input information will consist of the hourly wage and the number of hours worked in one week. The output should contain a list of all deductions, gross pay, and net pay. For this problem, assume deductions are made for federal withholding taxes, state withholding taxes, social security, and union dues.
   b. Compute the average test score for five students in a class. Input for this problem will consist of five scores. Output should include each score and the average of these scores.
6. Develop an algorithm for finding the total, average, and largest number in a given list of 25 numbers.
7. Develop an algorithm for finding the greatest common divisor (GCD) of two positive integers.
8. Develop an algorithm for solving the system of equations

$$ax + by = c$$
$$dx + ey = f$$

9. Draw a structure chart and write module specifications for
   a. Exercise 5a. b. Exercise 5b. c. Exercise 6.
10. Discuss how the top-down design principles of software engineering are similar to the design problems faced by a construction engineer for a building. Be sure to include anticipated work with all subcontractors.
11. Using the construction analogy of Exercise 10, give an example of some specific communication required between electricians and the masons who finish the interior walls. Discuss why this information flow should be coordinated by a construction engineer.
12. State the phases of the software system life cycle.
13. Contact some company or major user of a software system to see what kinds of modifications might be required in a system after it has been released to the public. (Your own computer center might be sufficient.)

■ 1.4 Operating Systems and Turbo Pascal

This section is designed for you to learn how to write and run your own programs on a personal computer. If you are using a networking system, it is assumed a comparable "Getting Started" handout for that system is available.

Before developing this section, a discussion of terminology is appropriate. Turbo Pascal 6.0 and 7.0 are the versions used in preparing material for this text. It is possible you may be using some other version. Since we will not be analyzing the differences between the various versions of Turbo Pascal, the phrase Turbo Pascal will be used consistently. When differences exist between versions 6.0 and 7.0, a logo (as shown at left) will be used to indicate a reference in Appendix 7, which contains explanations of the differences.

7.0

Turbo Pascal varies from standard Pascal in many ways. It is important that students using Turbo Pascal know these differences. This text highlights the differences by placing an "S" logo in the margin, as shown here. These logos refer to Appendix 8, which contains explanations of how Turbo Pascal differs from standard Pascal. Each logo is matched by a specific page reference in Appendix 8.

S

Our intent here is to get you started; to accomplish this, some essential aspects of using a computer and Turbo Pascal are presented. You should be aware that Turbo Pascal contains many more features than the ones discussed here. However, since our goal is to teach Pascal using Turbo Pascal, this presentation is consistent with that intent.

Disk Operating System

Each computer needs some kind of an operating system to manage the various tasks of finding programs on a disk, saving files, copying files, erasing files, transferring information to and from the computer's memory, and so on. This text has been prepared assuming you are using MS-DOS, which stands for Microsoft Disk Operating System. This is the most popular system for IBM and IBM-compatible PCs. Turbo Pascal has been developed to work with this system.

MS-DOS components include a command processor, a file manager, and utilities programs. The command processor allows you to request DOS services. For example, if you wish to know the current time or date, you can type

```
Time
```

or

```
Date
```

and press the <Enter> key. The requested information will be displayed with an option for you to make a change if you wish.

The file manager handles information for the system. MS-DOS is configured in such a manner that all information is stored in files. A directory of these files is maintained by MS-DOS. You may see what files are available by typing either

```
DIR
```

or

```
DIR/w
```

and pressing <Enter>. A list of the files contained on the disk in the active drive will then be displayed on the screen. If you wish to see the files available on the disk in another drive, you may change drives by typing the desired drive followed by a colon and pressing <Enter>; for example

```
A: <Enter>
```

causes drive A to be active. You then display the directory as before. You may also see a directory from any drive by typing the desired drive after DIR. Thus, from drive C, the sequence

```
DIR A: <Enter>
```

causes the directory for the disk in drive A to be displayed while keeping the current drive active.

MS-DOS contains several utilities programs that allow you to perform a wide variety of tasks. For example, you need to be able to format disks, copy files from one disk to another, erase files from a disk, display the contents of a file to the screen, and so on. To illustrate one of these, display the directory as shown above and note that

```
CONFIG  SYS
```

is included in the list of files. If you want to see what this file contains, type

```
TYPE CONFIG.SYS
```

and press <Enter>. The contents of this file will be displayed on the screen. Explanations of the use of several other utilities programs appear in Appendix 9.

Entering Turbo Pascal

It is assumed you are using a personal computer and Turbo Pascal has been installed according to the installation directions that came with the disks. If Turbo Pascal has not yet been installed, do it now. Furthermore, it is assumed your personal computer uses an MS-DOS operating system and has at least two disk drives, one of which may be a hard disk.

Using a Hard Disk

When you turn on the computer and respond to the start-up messages, you eventually get a display indicating which drive is active. If you have a hard disk, the display is

```
C>
```

or perhaps

```
C:\>
```

which indicates the operating system is contained on the hard disk (drive C). You then change the directory to the TP directory that contains Turbo by entering

```
CD\TP
```

which produces

7.0
```
C>CD\TP
```

Now press <Enter> and you get a screen display such as

```
C:\TP>
```

or

```
CTP>
```

This indicates you are now in the subdirectory that contains Turbo Pascal. You then activate Turbo by typing

```
Turbo
```

to produce

```
C:\TP>Turbo
```

or

```
CTP>Turbo
```

Press <Enter> one more time and you will activate the Turbo Pascal Integrated Development Environment (IDE), commonly referred to as "entering Turbo."

Without a Hard Disk

If your system does not have a hard disk, insert the operating system disk into drive A and turn on the computer. This produces a display of

```
A>
```

Now put your Turbo Pascal disk into drive B and change directories by typing B: to produce

```
A>B:
```

Press <Enter> to get

```
B>
```

Type Turbo to produce

```
B>Turbo
```

and press <Enter>. At this point, Turbo should be activated.

Main Menu

7.0 The first screen display you see when you enter Turbo Pascal is shown in Figure 1.14. There are three aspects of this display with which you should become familiar. The shaded bar running across the top of the screen is the *menu bar.* Each symbol or word represents a menu of choices. You may open any of these menus by placing the mouse on the desired title and then clicking. If you do not have a mouse, press function key <F10> to activate the menu bar and then use the arrow keys at the lower right portion of your keyboard to move the highlight bar to the desired location. Explanations in this section assume a mouse is not available.

Once you have highlighted the desired title, you open the menu for that title by pressing the <Enter> key. To illustrate, suppose you want to open the **File** menu. The sequence of keystrokes

<F10>
<→>
<Enter>

should produce the **File** menu, as shown in Figure 1.15.

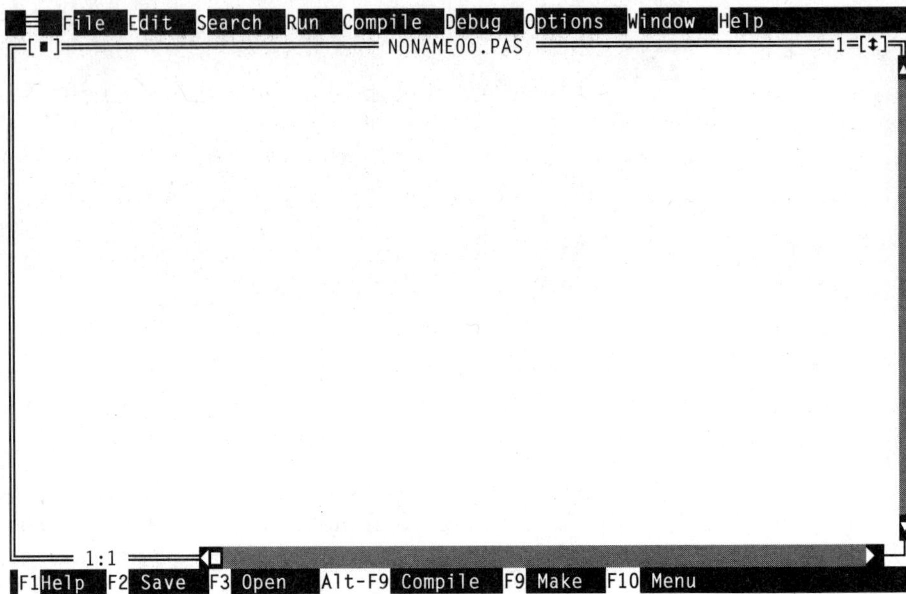

FIGURE 1.14
Turbo Pascal 6.0 Main Menu

FIGURE 1.15
The **File** Menu

You use the up and down arrow keys to move the highlight bar up and down the menu. You select an option by first highlighting it and then pressing <Enter>. Thus, if you want to save a file, you move the highlight bar down by pressing <↓> twice and then pressing <Enter>. You may close a menu by pressing function key <F10>. This puts the highlight bar back in the main menu bar.

Now let's take another look at the **File** menu shown in Figure 1.15. In particular, note the lines

```
Open...   F3
Save      F2
```

This means that pressing function key <F3> causes the same action as selecting this menu choice and then pressing <Enter>. In a similar manner, pressing <F2> is a quick way to save the file on which you are currently working. These are examples of *hot keys,* or *quick keys.* Turbo Pascal provides several such shortcuts through the use of the function keys, and you will become more familiar with them as you continue working in Turbo Pascal. A summary of the hot keys is given in Table 1.2 at the end of this section.

There is yet another way to select a menu. Instead of pressing the <F10> function key and the arrows, you may just press

<Alt><F> (Hold down the <Alt> key, and type F.)

to open the **File** menu. This method works for any of the nine menu choices that have titles. You always press the first letter of the title of the desired menu while holding down the <Alt> key. You may also use the function key <F5> to exit from the menu bar.

The second aspect of the screen display in Figure 1.14 is the **Help** menu at the bottom of the screen. This contains reminders about which function keys can be used for which operations. In particular, pressing the <F1> key causes a **Help** menu to be displayed. When reading a **Help** menu, you can scroll up and down by using the arrow keys. You can change pages by using the <PgUp> and <PgDn> keys, and you can exit the **Help** menu by pressing the <Esc> key. In general, different windows have different **Help** menus.

The third aspect of the screen display in Figure 1.14 that requires special mention is the part of the screen that is neither the menu bar nor the **Help** menu. The main portion of the screen is shown in Figure 1.16. This is an *edit window.*

FIGURE 1.16
An edit window

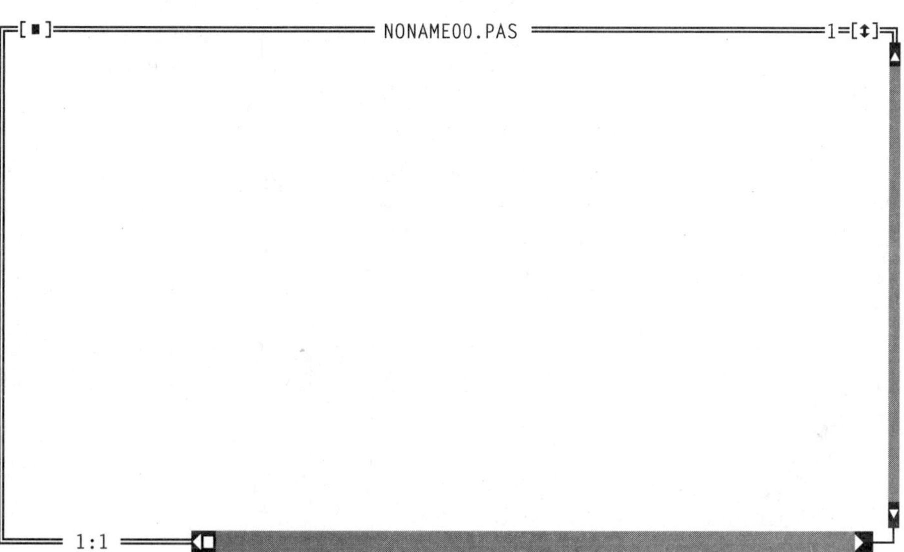

An edit window is where you type in and edit the programs you wish to run on the computer. The edit window which first appears is called NONAME00.PAS. We will soon see how to open other edit windows and how to change the default name.

Writing a Program

Now let's write our first program. Place the cursor in the edit window NONAME00.PAS using <F5> from the menu bar or the <Esc> key from the **Help** menu. Type in the following code

```
PROGRAM Rookie;
BEGIN
  writeln ('This is my first one.');
  writeln ('It is short, but it works!')
END.
```

Press <Enter> at the end of each line. If you make a mistake, use the backspace key to erase and retype.

Congratulations! You have written your first program. Although it isn't very elaborate, note the following. All programs are written in an edit window. For long programs, the lines scroll up. All corrections (editing) are made while you are in an edit window. Several editing features will be discussed soon.

Saving a File

You will want to save many of the programs you write. This can be done from the edit window by simply pressing the function key <F2>, as stated in the **Help** menu at the bottom of the edit window. You may also save a file by opening the **File** menu, selecting the **Save** option, and pressing <Enter>.

When you save a file, it is stored on a disk for subsequent retrieval and use. It is very important that you develop the habit of frequently saving your work. Many tears have been shed and much anguish experienced because beginning students did not save their work and a power failure or computer lock-up caused several hours of work to be lost. When this happens, there is no alternative except to recreate what was lost—a truly frustrating experience! It is also a good idea to periodically save a hard copy of your program or a copy on another disk.

To continue our example, after you type in the sample program Rookie, you wish to save it. When you press <F2>, you get the screen display shown in Figure 1.17.

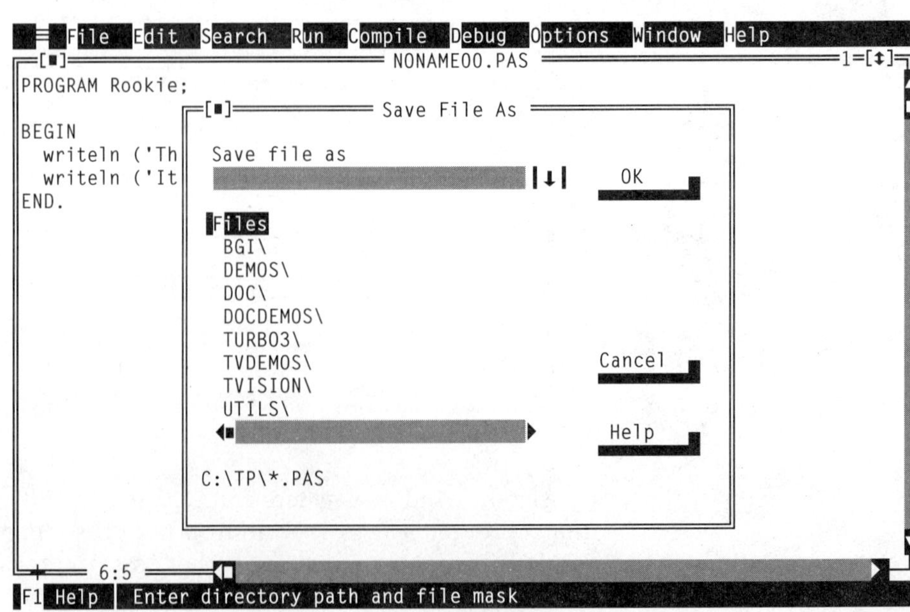

FIGURE 1.17
Saving a file

You are now asked to give your file a name so you can find it in the list of all the files you have created. This is not a trivial task! Always use descriptive names to name your files. You can only use eight characters, so think carefully about what you want to call your files. For this example, type in FirstOne and press <Enter>.

You have now created a file which appears in the directory as FIRSTONE.PAS. (Note that the default extension .PAS has been added.) Turbo automatically returns you to the edit window, which is now named FIRSTONE.PAS. Any subsequent saves will merely update FIRSTONE.PAS without interrupting the edit window. To illustrate, press <F2> again and note what happens.

Using a Work Disk

The previous description of saving a file assumes you have the luxury of saving a file on a hard disk where Turbo Pascal is installed. In reality, you may be asked not to do this. It is more likely you will be required to save your files on a floppy disk. In order to do this, you must first create a work disk by formatting a blank disk (see Appendix 9). Insert the work disk into a disk drive. (For purposes of this discussion, we assume this to be drive A.)

You now have a work disk in a drive different from the drive where Turbo Pascal has been loaded. In order to save files onto your work disk, you proceed as before but, when you are asked to name your file, you must specify the drive containing your work disk before typing in the file name. Thus, you type

```
A:\FirstOne
```

instead of just

```
FirstOne
```

When you press <Enter>, your file is then stored on the disk in drive A as FIRSTONE.PAS.

Choosing the Correct Extension

The previous process of saving a file resulted in having a file be designated as FIRSTONE.PAS. The three letters following the period, PAS, are referred to as the extension. The default extension is PAS. If you are saving a program that will subsequently be compiled and/or run, the default PAS extension is suitable. However, you will eventually want to save files for a different purpose. In particular, you will need to create and save data files. When this happens, you may specify the extension by typing it in when you first enter the file name. To illustrate, if you want to save a data file on drive A, you can type

```
A:\PROB3DAT.DAT
```

in the "Save file as" window and then press <Enter>. If you then look at the directory for drive A, you will see

```
PROB3DAT   DAT
```

in the listing.

Compiling a Program

Now that you have a program written in the edit window, it must be compiled before it can be run. You may compile your program by selecting the **Compile** menu, highlighting the

Compile   Alt-F9

option, and pressing <Enter> (or pressing the <Alt> key along with <F9> initially). If you do everything correctly, you get the message shown in Figure 1.18. Note that the phrase "Press any key" is flashing. When you press a key, you are returned to the edit window.

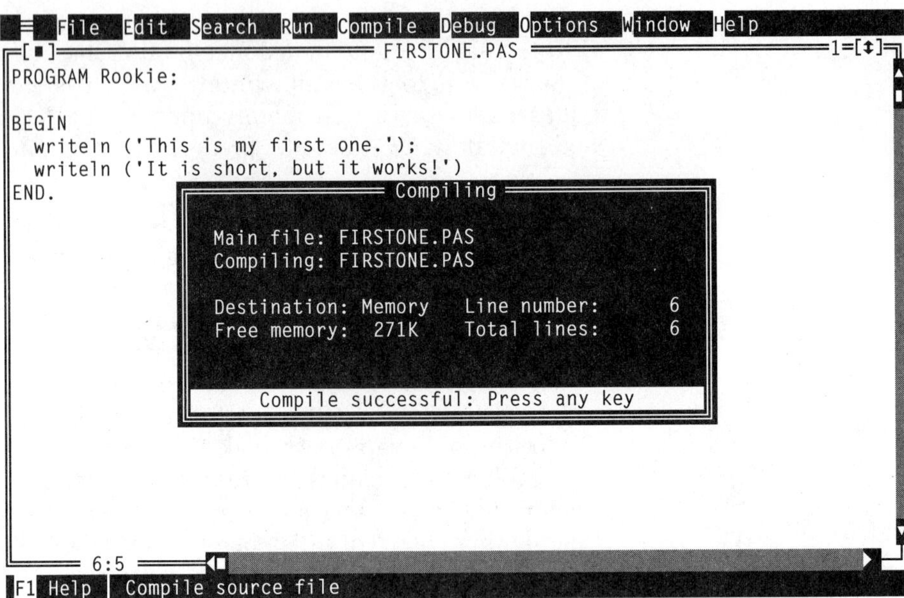

FIGURE 1.18
Successful compilation message

A successful compilation means the compiler did not detect any syntax errors in the typing of the program. If there are any syntax errors, a different screen message will appear. We will soon see how to handle compilation errors; for now, however, we assume the program is correct, so we are ready to run the first program.

Running a Program

After a successful compilation, you may run your program by selecting the **Run** menu, highlighting the

Run Ctrl-F9

option, and pressing <Enter> (or pressing <Ctrl> <F9> initially). At this point, it may appear that nothing happens. However, your program has been executed, and the output is on the output screen, which can be seen by pressing <Alt> <F5>. You can get back to the edit window by pressing <Enter>.

It is somewhat inconvenient not to have the program output readily visible to the user. Also, the screen contains some messages that are not intended to be part of the output. Both of these problems are solved when we look at how to edit a program in the following section.

At this point, it should be noted that it is possible to select a **Run** option without first selecting a **Compile** option. When this is done, program compilation automatically occurs before the program is run.

Editing a Program

Often you will want to make changes and/or corrections in your programs. This is done in the edit window. A complete description of editing features is beyond the scope of this text, but they are available in your reference manual. We will now discuss some of the more frequently used features.

The most direct method for changing a program is to position the cursor at the character position where you wish to make a change. The arrow keys can be used for this purpose. You may also use the keys as illustrated in Table 1.1.

TABLE 1.1
Keys for cursor movement

Key	Cursor Movement
Home	Moves to beginning of current line
End	Moves to end of current line
PgUp	Moves up one screen
PgDn	Moves down one screen
Ctrl Home	Moves to top of the edit window
Ctrl End	Moves to bottom of the edit window
Ctrl PgUp	Moves to first character in the program
Ctrl PgDn	Moves to last character in the program

As previously mentioned, you erase characters to the left of the cursor using the backspace key. You insert a new character at the cursor position by typing the character. If other text is on the line, it is moved to the right.

Now let's practice these features by modifying the program Rookie. First, place the cursor at the end of line 1 and press <Enter> to get a blank line. Now type the two lines

```
USES
  Crt;  {  Allows us to use screen commands  }
```

to produce

```
PROGRAM Rookie;
USES
  Crt;  {  Allows us to use screen commands  }
BEGIN
  writeln ('This is my first one.');
  writeln ('It is short, but it works!')
END.
```

Second, place the cursor after **BEGIN** and press <Enter> to produce

```
PROGRAM Rookie;
USES
  Crt;  {  Allows us to use screen commands  }
BEGIN

  writeln ('This is my first one.');
  writeln ('It is short, but it works!')
END.
```

You are now ready to add another new line by typing

```
ClrScr;  {  Screen command to clear the screen  }
```

indented two spaces in the blank line to produce

```
PROGRAM Rookie;
USES
  Crt;  {  Allows us to use screen commands  }
BEGIN
  ClrScr;  {  Screen command to clear the screen  }
  writeln ('This is my first one.');
  writeln ('It is short, but it works!')
END.
```

Now, move the cursor down two lines and then to the end of the line and type a semicolon. Press <Enter>, and then type

```
readln  {  Hold the display screen  }
```

indented two spaces. This produces

```
PROGRAM Rookie;
USES
  Crt;  {  Allows us to use screen commands  }
BEGIN
  ClrScr;  {  Screen command to clear the screen  }
  writeln ('This is my first one.');
  writeln ('It is short, but it works!');
  readln  {  Hold the display screen  }
END.
```

Now let's save this version by pressing <F2> and then run it by pressing <Ctrl> <F9> (or compile it first and then run it). If you made no errors, the screen display is

```
This is my first one.
It is short, but it works!
```

Note that there are no unwanted messages on the screen due to the **ClrScr** command added to the program. Now press <Enter> to return to the edit window. (This is necessary because **readln** holds the display screen.)

Another way to view the output window is to run the program without the **readln.** After running the program, pull down the **Window** menu (<F10> and arrow movement), select **User** screen, and press <Enter> (or just use the sequence <Alt> <F5>). After viewing the **User** screen, press <Enter> to return to the edit window.

There is a third way to view the screen output from a program. Run the program as before without a **readln.** Again, pull down the **Window** menu, but select **Output** from the menu. Press <Enter>, and you get the screen display shown in Figure 1.19.

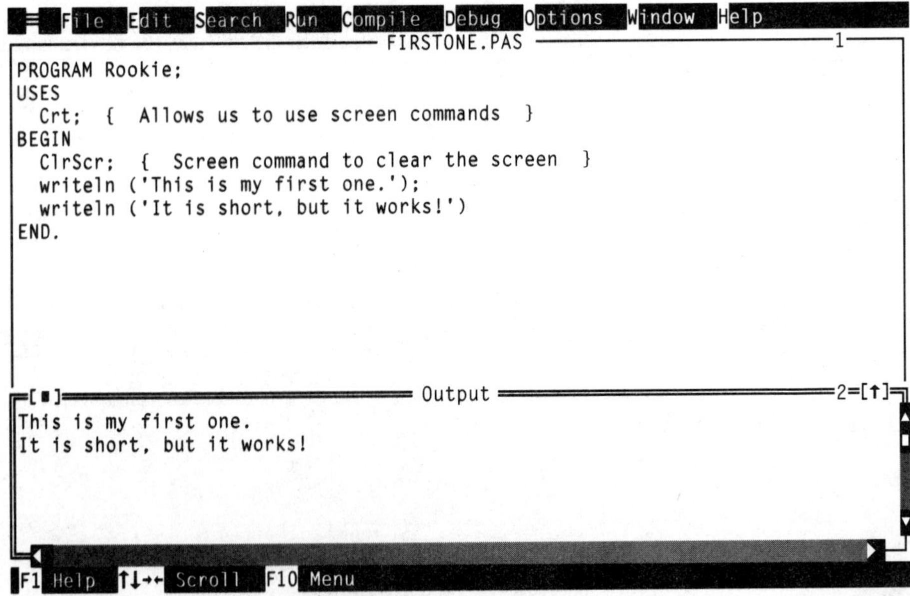

FIGURE 1.19
Split screen with Output window

Note that the screen is now divided into two windows. The lower window is the Output window and is currently the active window, as shown by the double lines across the top of the window. When you have finished viewing the Output window, press <Alt> <F3>. This closes the Output window and makes the edit window the active window.

Debugging a Program

It is frequently the case that you will make some mistake when typing a program. The process of identifying these mistakes is referred to as *debugging* a program. Turbo Pascal handles this during the compilation stage. If an error is detected, compilation halts, an error message is printed, and you are returned to the edit window with the cursor at the position where the compiler detected an error. The error is either at the point of the cursor or in the line above the cursor. You must then identify the error, correct it, and recompile. The process continues until you get an error-free compilation. To illustrate, let's change our sample program by dropping an ending quote in line 6 and omitting the semicolon at the end of line 7 to produce

```
PROGRAM Rookie;
USES
  Crt;  {  Allows us to use screen commands  }
BEGIN
  ClrScr;  {  Screen command to clear the screen  }
  writeln ('This is my first one.);
  writeln ('It is short, but it works!')
  readln  {  Hold the display screen  }
END.
```

Now, when you compile this program, you get the error message

```
Error 8: String constant exceeds line.
```

at the top of the edit window and the cursor is at the end of the line

```
writeln ('This is my first one.);
```

Insert a single quotation mark before the closing parenthesis, recompile, and you get

```
Error 85: '';'' expected.
```

at the top of the edit window with the cursor beneath the "r" of **readln.** Insert a semicolon at the end of the previous line by first moving the cursor up one line and then pressing the key <End>. At this stage, you should have an error-free compilation.

In summary, the following general sequence should be followed when you are writing a program:

1. Write the program in an edit window.
2. Save the program (<F2>).
3. Compile the program (<Alt> <F9>).
4. Correct and recompile the program as necessary.
5. Run the program (<Ctrl> <F9>).

A more elaborate discussion of several of Turbo Pascal's debugging features is contained in Appendix 10.

Closing a Window

At some point, you are going to want to close an active window. This can be accomplished by the keystroke sequence

<Alt> <F3>

or by using the **Window** menu. If you want to use the **Window** menu, select it by using the <F10> and arrow keys or by pressing the

<Alt> <W>

keys. Once the **Window** menu has been selected, use the arrow keys to select the

Close Alt-F3

line and then press <Enter>.

Although it is a good habit to close one edit window before opening another, you are not required to do so. It is possible to open another window without closing the currently active window. If you select

Open... F3

from the **File** menu, the screen display will contain an Open a File window, as shown in Figure 1.20.

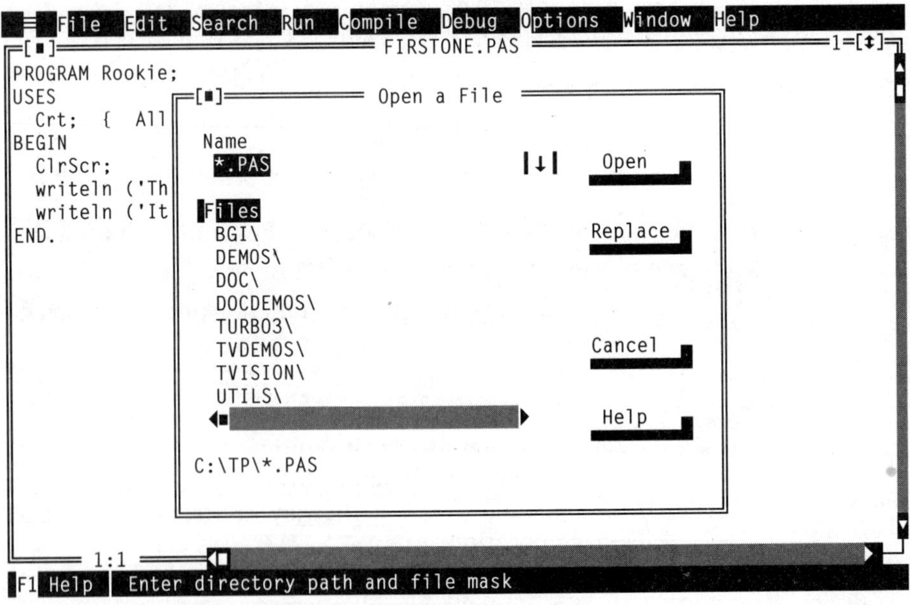

FIGURE 1.20
Open a File window

You may then select any existing file by first pressing <Enter> and then using the <↑> and <↓> keys to highlight the desired file. Press <Enter> after the desired file has been selected, and it will be opened and become the active edit window. You may also type the name of the desired file to be opened in the space just below Name as

Name

*.PAS

If you choose this method, press <Enter> after typing the name and an appropriately titled edit window will be opened.

Retrieving a File

Eventually, you will have several files that contain programs. You may examine and retrieve files by using the **File** menu. To illustrate, use <F10> and the arrow keys to select the **File** menu. Highlight the

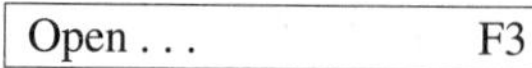

bar, and press <Enter>. (This can all be accomplished by pressing the <F3> key.) This produces a display in the edit window that contains a list of your existing files (the ones you have saved). Part of this display is

Name
☐ *.PAS [ ] ↓
↑
cursor

with a list of available files a few lines down in another window. You may select the desired file either by typing the file name where the cursor is below the asterisk or by pressing <Enter> and using the arrow keys to highlight the file you want. In either case, press <Enter> when you are finished and the file will be opened and placed in an edit window. (*Note:* If you accidentally open too many windows or the wrong edit windows, they can be closed using the **Window** menu or <Alt> <F3>.)

If the file you wish to retrieve is stored on your work disk in some other drive (say, drive A), you may retrieve it by typing A: before the file name. For example, if you want to retrieve FirstOne from your work disk, you type

```
A:FirstOne
```

or

```
A:\FirstOne
```

and then press <Enter>.

Leaving Turbo Pascal

When you are ready to leave the Turbo Integrated Development Environment (you did save your most recent work, didn't you?), go to the menu bar (<F10>) and highlight the left-hand column designated by

Press <Enter> to display the menu, and use the arrow keys to highlight

Clear desktop

Now press <Enter> (last chance to save your modifications!), and you will be returned to the main menu. You can then safely exit Turbo Pascal by pressing <Alt> X.

Function Keys or Hot Keys

As previously indicated, Turbo Pascal makes use of the function keys to allow you to use a variety of shortcuts. Function keys used in this manner are often

TABLE 1.2
Turbo Pascal 6.0 hot keys

Key	Menu item	Description
F1	Help	Displays a help screen
F2	File | Save	Saves the file in the active edit window
F3	File | Open	Brings up a dialog box for opening a file
F4	Run | Go to Cursor	Runs a program to the line where the cursor is positioned
F5	Window | Zoom	Zooms the active window
F6	Window | Next	Cycles through all open windows
F7	Run | Trace into	Runs the program in debug mode, tracing into procedures
F8	Run | Step Over	Runs the program in debug mode, stepping over procedure calls
F9	Compile | Make	Compiles the program in the active edit window
F10	(none)	Takes you to the edit window
Alt-F3	Window | Close	Closes the active window
Alt-F5	Window | User Screen	Displays user screen
Ctrl-F2	Run | Program Reset	Resets running program
Ctrl-F9	Run | Run	Runs program

referred to as hot keys (or quick keys). Table 1.2 contains a list of some of these hot keys, together with a brief description of the purpose of each one. A complete listing of all hot keys appears in the Turbo Pascal User's Guide.

Exercises 1.4

1. Discuss why the designers of Turbo Pascal provide more than one method for accomplishing tasks. For example, files may be opened by simply pressing <F3> or by a sequence of selecting the file menu, highlighting the "open" bar, and pressing <Enter>. List several advantages and disadvantages of each method.
2. Get into the main menu, and select the <F1> help key. Read all of this menu. How can you exit from a **Help** menu?
3. After you get into the **Help** menu as directed in Exercise 2, examine the new **Help** menu at the bottom of the screen. Try all of the options listed in this menu.
4. Write, run, and save **PROGRAM** Rookie as first presented in this section; then exit Turbo Pascal.
5. After completing Exercise 4, reenter Turbo Pascal, retrieve the file, modify the program to the final version, and then save it under a different name.

1.5 Writing Programs

Words in Turbo Pascal

Consider the following complete Turbo Pascal program.

```
PROGRAM Example;

USES
  Crt;

CONST
  Skip = ' ' ;
  LoopLimit = 10;
```

S

```
VAR
  J, Number, Sum : integer;
  Average : real;

BEGIN
  ClrScr;
  Sum := 0;
  FOR J := 1 TO LoopLimit DO
    BEGIN
      writeln ('Enter a number and press <Enter>.');
      readln (Number);
      Sum := Sum + Number
    END;
  Average := Sum / LoopLimit;
  writeln;
  writeln (Skip:10, 'The average is', Average:8:2);
  writeln;
  writeln (Skip:10, 'The number of scores is', LoopLimit:3);
  readln
END.
```

This program—and most programming languages—requires the use of words when writing code. In Pascal, words having a predefined meaning that cannot be changed are called *reserved words.* Some other predefined words (called *standard identifiers*) can have their meanings changed if the programmer has strong reasons for doing so. Other words (programmer-supplied *identifiers)* must be created according to a well-defined set of rules but can have any meaning subject to those rules.

In the body of this text, reserved words are capitalized and in bold type; standard identifiers are lowercase and in bold type. Reserved words used in the text's sample programs are capitalized and standard identifiers are lowercase. These conventions are not required by the language.

Reserved Words

In Turbo Pascal, reserved words are predefined and cannot be used in a program for anything other than the purpose for which they are reserved. Some examples are **AND, OR, NOT, BEGIN, END, IF,** and **FOR.** As you continue in Turbo Pascal, you will learn where and how these words are used. At this time, however, you need only become familiar with the reserved words in Table 1.3; which are also listed in Appendix 1.

TABLE 1.3
Reserved words

AND	**END**	**MOD**	**THEN**
ARRAY	**FILE**	**NIL**	**TO**
BEGIN	**FOR**	**NOT**	**TYPE**
CASE	**FORWARD**	**OBJECT**	**UNTIL**
CONST	**FUNCTION**	**OF**	**USES**
CONSTRUCTOR	**GOTO**	**OR**	**VAR**
DESTRUCTOR	**IF**	**PRIVATE**	**VIRTUAL**
DIV	**IMPLEMENTATION**	**PROCEDURE**	**WHILE**
DO	**IN**	**PROGRAM**	**WITH**
DOWNTO	**INTERFACE**	**RECORD**	**XOR**
ELSE	**LABEL**	**REPEAT**	
		SET	

Standard Identifiers

A second set of predefined words, standard identifiers, can have their meanings changed by the programmer. For example, if you could develop a better algorithm for the trigonometric function **sin,** you could then substitute it in the program. However, these words should not be used for anything other than their intended use. Some standard identifiers are listed in Table 1.4 and in Appendix 2. The term *keywords* is used to refer to both reserved words and standard identifiers in subsequent discussions.

TABLE 1.4
Standard identifiers

S

Data Types	Constants	Functions	Procedures	Files
boolean	false	abs	dispose	input
byte	maxint	arctan	get	output
char	true	chr	new	lst
comp		cos	pack	
double		eof	page	
extended		eoln	put	
integer		exp	read	
longint		ln	readln	
real		odd	reset	
shortint		ord	rewrite	
single		pred	unpack	
string		round	write	
text		sin	writeln	
word		sqr		
		sqrt		
		succ		
		trunc		

Syntax and Syntax Diagrams

Syntax refers to the rules governing the construction of valid statements. Syntax includes the order in which statements occur, together with appropriate punctuation. *Syntax diagramming* is a method that formally describes the legal syntax of language structures. Syntax diagrams show the permissible alternatives for each part of each kind of sentence and where the parts may appear. The symbolism we use is shown in Figure 1.21. A combined listing of syntax diagrams is contained in Appendix 3.

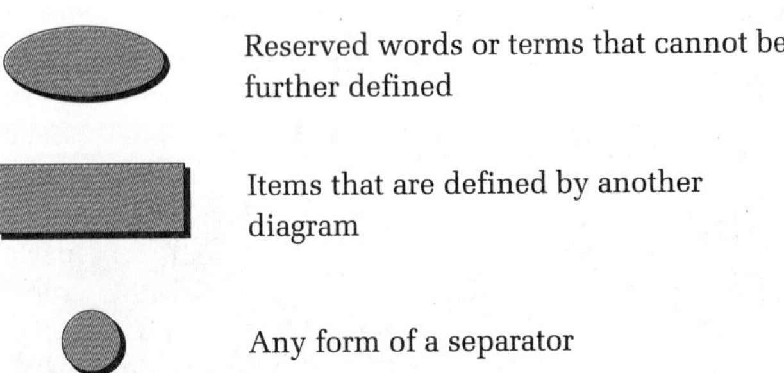

FIGURE 1.21
Symbols used in syntax diagrams

Arrows are used to indicate possible alternatives. To illustrate, a syntax diagram for forming simple words in the English language is

If the word must start with a vowel, the diagram is

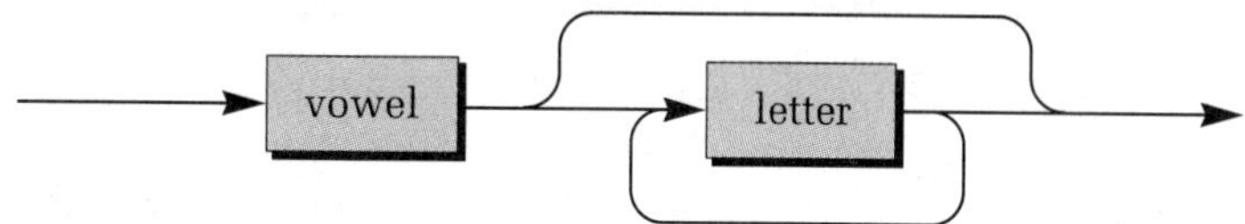

where vowel and letter are defined in a manner consistent with the English alphabet. Syntax diagrams are used throughout the text to illustrate formal constructs. You are encouraged to become familiar with them.

Identifiers

Reserved words and standard identifiers are restricted in their use. Most Turbo Pascal programs require other programmer-supplied identifiers; the more complicated the program, the more identifiers are needed. **A valid identifier must start with a letter of the alphabet and must consist of only letters and digits.** Turbo Pascal also allows the underscore character to be used in place of a letter. A syntax diagram for forming identifiers is

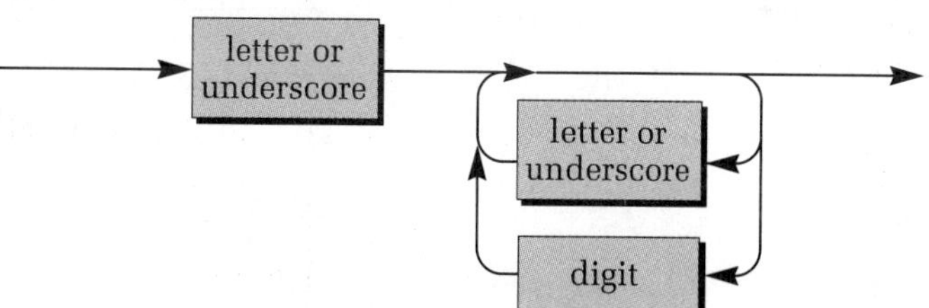

Table 1.5 gives some valid and invalid identifiers along with the reasons for those that are invalid. A valid identifier can be of any length. However, some versions of Turbo Pascal recognize only the first part of a long identifier (for example, the first eight or the first ten characters). Therefore, identifiers such as MathTestScore1 and MathTestScore2 might be the same identifier to a computer and could not be used as different identifiers in a program. Thus, you should learn what restrictions are imposed by your compiler.

TABLE 1.5
Valid and invalid identifiers

Identifier	Valid	If Invalid, Reason
Sum	Yes	
X+Y	No	"+" not allowed
Average	Yes	
Text1	Yes	
1stNum	No	Must start with a letter or underscore
X	Yes	
K mart	No	Spaces not allowed
ThisIsaLongOne	Yes	
Exam_1	Yes	

The most common use of identifiers is to name the variables to be used in a program. Other uses for identifiers include the program name, symbolic constants, new data types, and subprogram names, all of which are discussed later. Always use descriptive names for identifiers, even though single-letter identifiers are permitted; as you'll see, descriptive names are easier to follow in a program.

Basic Program Components

A program in Turbo Pascal consists of three components: a program heading, an optional declaration section, and an executable section. These three components are illustrated in the program shown in Figure 1.22. The syntax diagram for a program is

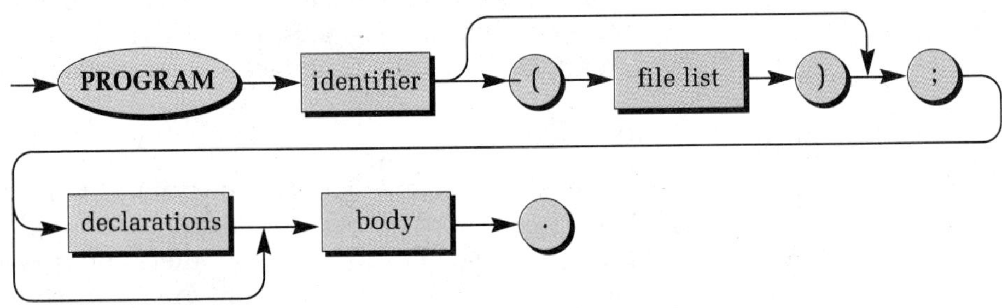

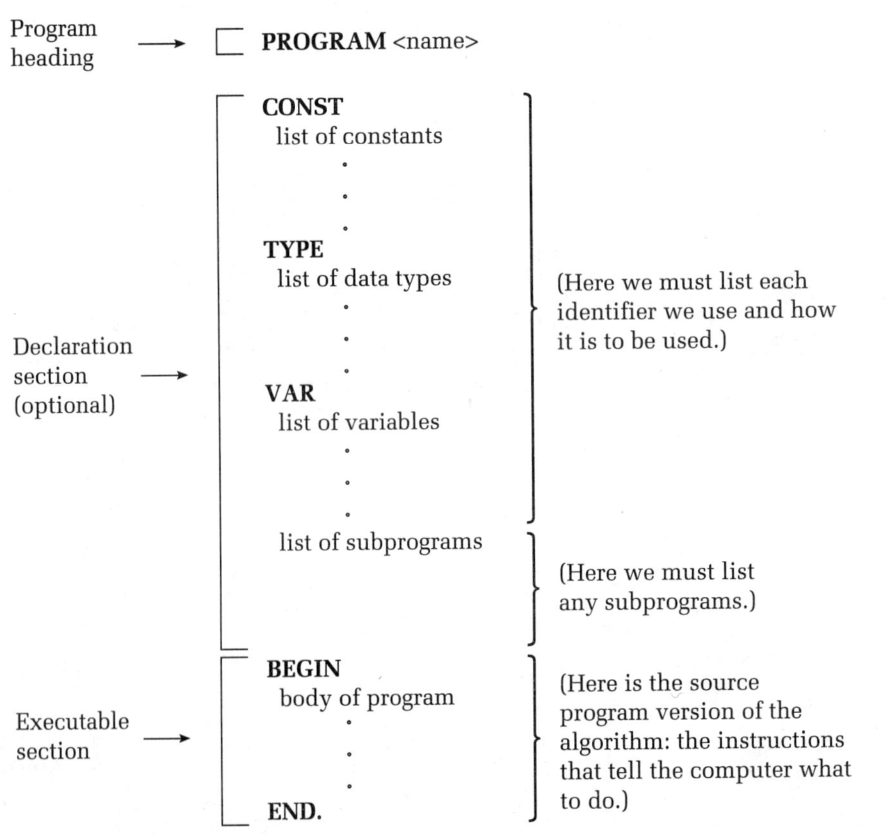

FIGURE 1.22
Components of a program

Figure 1.23 illustrates the program components of the sample program (**PROGRAM** Example) that started this section; appropriate program parts are indicated.

FIGURE 1.23
Components of **PROGRAM** Example

Program heading →

```
PROGRAM Example;
```

Declaration section →

```
USES
  Crt;

CONST
  Skip = ' ';
  LoopLimit = 10;

VAR
  J, Number, Sum : integer;
  Average : real;
```

Executable section →

```
BEGIN
  ClrScr;
  Sum := 0;
  FOR J := 1 TO LoopLimit DO
    BEGIN
      writeln ('Enter a number and press <Enter>.');
      readln (Number);
      Sum := Sum + Number
    END;
  Average := Sum / LoopLimit;
  writeln;
  writeln (Skip:10, 'The average is', Average:8:2);
  writeln;
  writeln (Skip:10, 'The number of scores is', LoopLimit:3);
  readln
END.
```

The *program heading* is the first statement of any Turbo Pascal program. It is usually one line and must contain the reserved word **PROGRAM;** the program name, which must be a valid identifier; and a semicolon at the end. It can also contain an optional file list. The respective parts of a program heading are

PROGRAM <name>;

The template or fill-in-the-blanks form just presented is used throughout this book. Reserved words and standard identifiers are shown. You must use identifiers to replace the words in lowercase letters and enclosed in arrowheads "< >". Thus

PROGRAM <name>;

could become

```
PROGRAM Rookie;
```

A syntax diagram for a program heading follows:

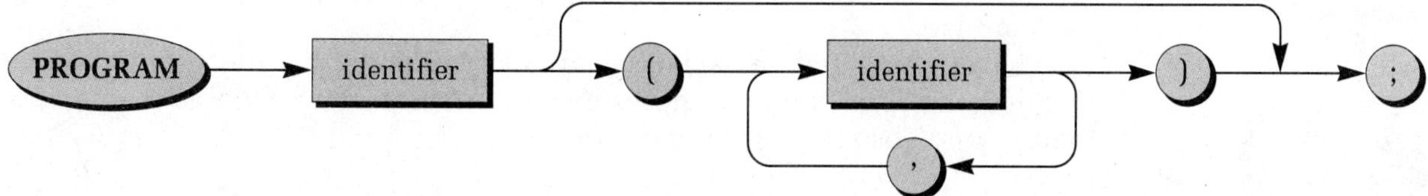

The remainder of the program is sometimes referred to as the main block; major divisions are the declaration section and the executable section. The *declaration section* is used to declare (name) all symbolic constants, data types, variables, and subprograms that are necessary to the program. All constants named in the declaration section are normally referred to as being defined. Thus, we generally say variables are declared and constants are defined.

When constants are defined, they appear in the *constant definition* portion of the declaration section after the reserved word **CONST.** The form for defining a constant is

```
CONST
  <identifier1> = <value 1>;
  <identifier2> = <value 2>;
      .
      .
      .
  <identifiern> = <value n>;
```

The syntax diagram for this part is

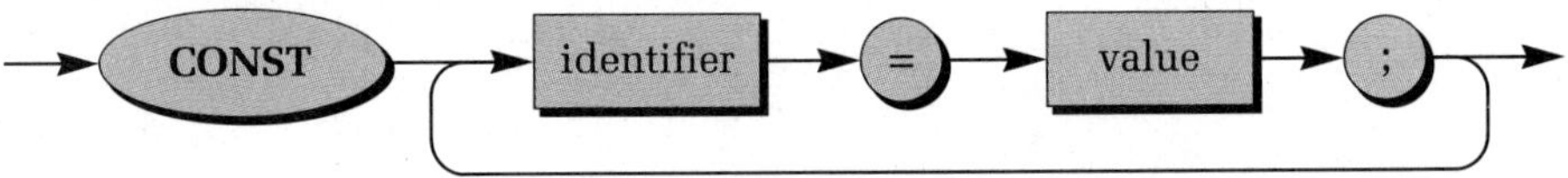

Values of constant identifiers cannot be changed during program execution.

If a value is one character or a string of characters, it must be enclosed in single quotation marks (apostrophes). For example

```
CONST
  Date ='July 4, 1776';
```

Any number of constants may be defined in this section. A typical constant definition portion of the declaration section could be

```
CONST
  Skip = ' ';
  Date = 'July 4, 1776';
  ClassSize = 35;
  SpeedLimit = 65;
  CmToInches = 0.3937;
  Found = true;
```

The **TYPE** portion of the declaration section will be explained in Section 6.2. For now, we assume data used in a Turbo Pascal program is one of the four *standard simple types*: **integer, real, char,** or **boolean.** Discussion of additional integer and real types and type **char** is in Section 1.6; discussion of **boolean** is in Section 4.1.

The *variable declaration* portion of the declaration section must be listed after the **TYPE** portion, if present, and must begin with the reserved word **VAR.** This section must contain all identifiers for variables to be used in the program; if a variable is used that has not been declared, an error will occur when the program is compiled.

The form required for declaring variables is somewhat different from that used for defining constants: it requires a colon instead of an equal sign and specific data types. The simplest correct form is

```
VAR
   <identifier1> : <data type 1>;
         .
         .
         .
   <identifiern> : <data type n>;
```

The syntax diagram is

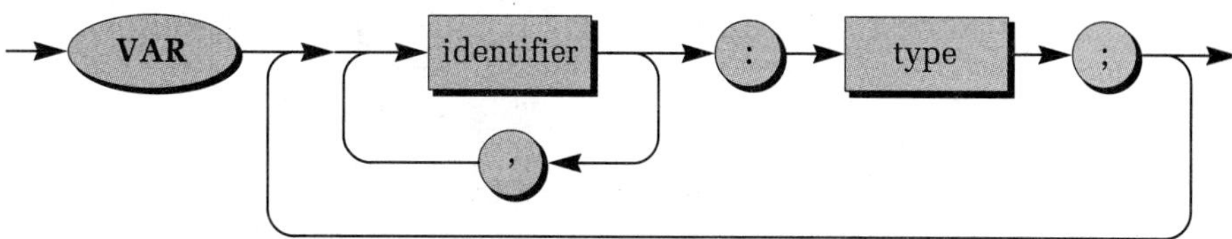

The reserved word **VAR** may appear only once in a program. (Exceptions will be noted when subprograms are developed.) If no variables are to be used, a variable declaration section is not needed; however, this seldom happens. A typical variable declaration section could look like this:

```
VAR
  Sum : integer;
  Average : real;
  I, J, K : integer;
  Ch : char;
```

The third basic program component is the *executable section.* This section contains the statements that cause the computer to do something. It must start with the reserved word **BEGIN** and conclude with the reserved word **END.** Also, a period must follow the last **END** in the executable section. The syntax diagram is

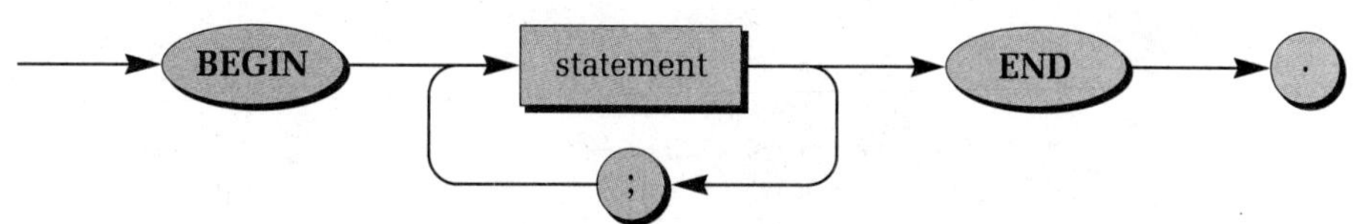

Writing Code in Turbo Pascal

We are now ready to examine the use of the executable section of a program. In Turbo Pascal, the basic unit of grammar is an *executable statement,* which consists of valid identifiers, standard identifiers, reserved words, numbers, and/or characters together with appropriate punctuation.

One of the main rules for writing code in Turbo Pascal is that a semicolon is used to separate executable statements. For example, if the statement

```
writeln ('The results are':20, Sum:8, 'and', Aver:6:2)
```

were to be used in a program, it would (almost always) require a semicolon between it and the next executable statement. Thus, it should be

```
writeln ('The results are':20, Sum:8, 'and', Aver:6:2);
```

In one instance, an executable statement does not need a following semicolon. When a statement is followed by the reserved word **END,** a semicolon is not required. This is because **END** is not a statement by itself but part of a **BEGIN . . . END** pair. However, if a semicolon is included, it will not affect the program. You can visualize the executable section as shown in Figure 1.24.

FIGURE 1.24
Executable section

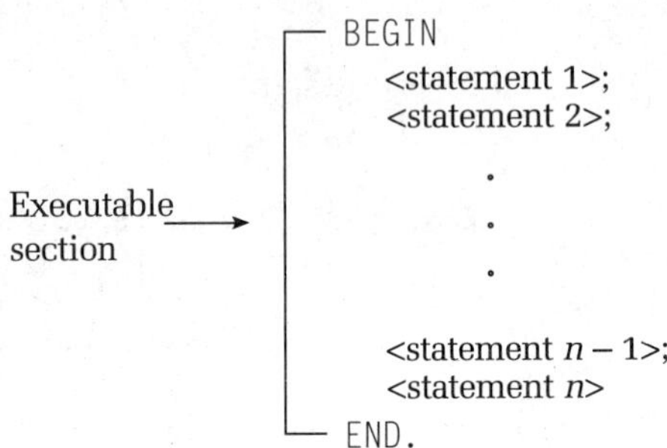

Turbo Pascal does not require that each statement be on a separate line. Actually, you could write a program as one long line (which may wrap around to fit the screen) if you wish; however, it would be difficult to read. Compare, for example, the readability of the following two programs.

```
PROGRAM ReadCheck; USES Crt; CONST Name = 'George'; Age =
26; VAR J, Sum : integer; BEGIN ClrScr; Sum := 0; FOR
J := 1 TO 10 DO Sum := Sum + J; writeln ('My name is ':
28, Name); writeln ('My age is ' :27, Age); writeln;
writeln ('The sum is ' :28, Sum); readln END.
```

```
PROGRAM ReadCheck;

USES
  Crt;

CONST
  Name = 'George' ;
  Age = 26;

VAR
  J, Sum : integer;

BEGIN
  ClrScr;
  Sum := 0;
  FOR J := 1 TO 10 DO
    Sum := Sum + J;
  writeln ('My name is ':28, Name);
  writeln ('My age is ':27, Age);
  writeln;
  writeln ('The sum is ':28, Sum);
  readln
END.
```

You are not expected to know what the statements mean at this point, but it should be obvious that the second program is much more readable than the first. In addition, it is easier to change if corrections are necessary. However, these programs are executed identically because Turbo Pascal ignores extra spaces and line boundaries.

A NOTE OF INTEREST

Blaise Pascal

Blaise Pascal (1623–1662) began a spectacular, if short, mathematical career at a very early age. He was a brilliant child. As a youngster of 14, he attended meetings of senior French mathematicians. At age 16, he had so impressed the famous mathematician Descartes with his writings that Descartes refused to believe the author could be so young.

Two years later, Pascal invented a calculating machine, the Pascaline (shown at right), that stands as the very remote predecessor of the modern computer. The Pascaline could add and subtract; it functioned by a series of eight rotating gears, similar to an automobile's odometer. Pascal's machine was opposed by tax clerks of the era, who viewed it as a threat to their jobs. Pascal presented his machine to Queen Christina of Sweden in 1650; it is not known what she did with it.

In spite of his obvious talent for mathematics, Pascal devoted most of his adult life to questions of theology; his work in this area is still regularly studied. A man who often perceived omens in events around him, Pascal concluded that God's plan for him did not include mathematics and dropped the subject entirely. However, while experiencing a particularly nagging toothache when he was 35, Pascal let his thoughts wander to mathematics and the pain disappeared.

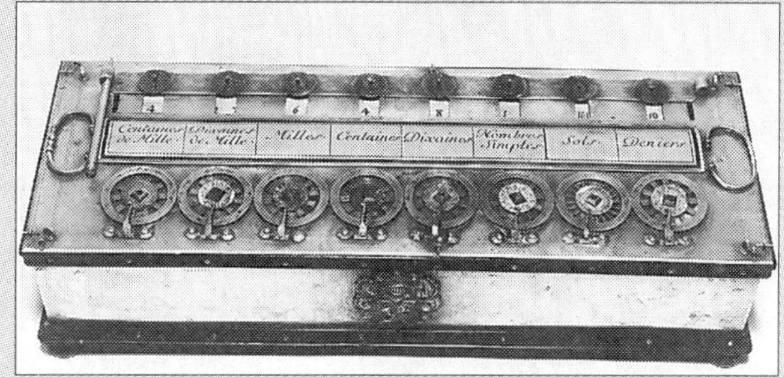

He took this as a heavenly sign and made a quick but intensive return to mathematical research. In barely a week, he managed to discover the fundamental properties of the cycloid curve. With that, Pascal again abandoned mathematics, and in 1662, at the age of 39, he died.

Program Comments

Programming languages typically include some provision for putting *comments* in a program. These comments are nonexecutable and are used to document and explain various parts of the program. In Turbo Pascal, the form for including comments in a program is either

```
{ ... comment ... }

or

(* ... comment ... *)
```

COMMUNICATION AND STYLE TIPS

This text contains several suggestions for using program comments to make your programs more readable. One suggestion is to create an information section for inclusion in every program to be given to your instructor. The style and content of this section may vary according to your instructor's wishes. A sample for consideration is

```
{  Course Number         CPS-150  }
{  Assignment                One  }
{  Due Date         September  20  }
{  Author              Mary Smith  }
{  Instructor           Dr. Jones  }
```

Typically, such a section would be placed at the beginning of the program.

Exercise 1.5

1. List the rules for forming valid identifiers.
2. Which of the following are valid identifiers? Give an explanation for those that are invalid.

   a. `7Up`
   b. `Payroll`
   c. `Room222`
   d. `Name List`
   e. `Name_List`
   f. `A1`
   g. `1A`
   h. `Time&Place`
   i. `CONST`
   j. `X*Y`
   k. `ListOfEmployees`
   l. `Lima,Ohio`

3. Which of the following are valid program headings? Give an explanation for those that are invalid.

   a. `PROGRAM Rookie`
   b. `PROGRAM Pro;`
   c. `TestProgram;`
   d. `PROGRAM;`
   e. `PROGRAM GettingBetter;`
   f. `PROGRAM Have Fun;`
   g. `PROGRAM Have_Fun;`
   h. `PROGRAM 2ndOne;`

4. Name the three main sections of a Turbo Pascal program.
5. Write constant definition statements for the following:

   a. Your name
   b. Your age
   c. Your birth date
   d. Your birthplace

6. Find all errors in the following definitions and declarations:

   a.
   ```
   CONST
     Company : 'General Motors';
   VAR
     Salary : real;
   ```
   b.
   ```
   VAR
     Age = 25;
   ```
   c.
   ```
   VAR
     Days : integer;
     Ch : char;
   CONST
     Name = 'John Smith';
   ```
   d.
   ```
   CONST
     Car : 'Cadillac';
   ```
   e.
   ```
   CONST
     Score : integer;
   ```
   f.
   ```
   VAR
     X, Y, Z : real;
     Score,
     Num : integer;
   ```

7. Discuss the significance of a semicolon in writing Turbo Pascal statements. Include an explanation of when semicolons are not required in a program.

1.6 Data Types and Output

Integer Data Types

Turbo Pascal requires that all data used in a program be given a *data type.* Numeric data can be classified in two general categories: integers or reals. Turbo Pascal provides five varieties of integers. The standard simple integer type is **integer,** which includes integers that are positive, negative, or zero.

Some rules that must be observed when using integers are

1. Plus "+" signs do not have to be written before a positive integer.
2. Minus "−" signs must be written when using a negative number.
3. Leading zeros are ignored.
4. Decimal points cannot be used when writing integers. Although 14 and 14.0 have the same value, 14.0 is not of type **integer.**
5. Commas cannot be used when writing integers: 271,362 is not allowed; it must be written as 271362.

The syntax diagram for an integer is

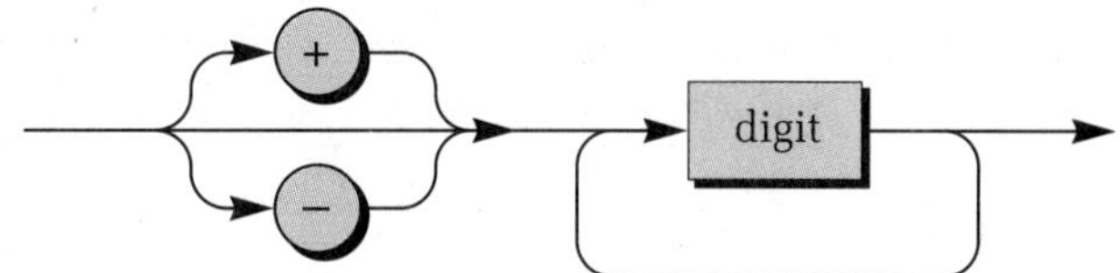

There is a limit on the largest and the smallest integer constant. The largest such constant is **maxint,** and the smallest is usually −**maxint** or (−**maxint**−1). The constants **maxint** and −**maxint** are recognized by every version of Pascal. In Turbo, **maxint** is 32767. The other kinds of integer types available in Turbo Pascal are **shortint, longint, byte,** and **word.** Table 1.6 shows the range of values

S

TABLE 1.6
Turbo integer data types

Data Type	Range	Bytes of Storage
integer	−32768 ... 32767	2
shortint	−128 ... 127	1
longint	−2147483648 ... 2147483647	4
byte	0 ... 255	1
word	0 ... 65535	2

for each of these data types and the amount of storage required for a value of that type. The variety of data types for integers allows programmers some flexibility. For the most efficient speed and use of memory allocation, you should select the data type with the smallest range sufficient for the values needed. Since this is not a matter of major concern in this text, most examples are written using the **integer** data type.

Operations with integers will be examined in the next section, and integer variables will be discussed in Section 2.2.

Real Data Types

The second general category for numeric data is that of real numbers. The standard simple data type for these values is **real.** When using decimal notation, numbers of type **real** must be written with a decimal point with at least one digit on each side of the decimal. Thus, .2 is not a valid **real,** but 0.2 is.

Plus "+" and minus "−" signs for data of type **real** are treated exactly as they are for data of type **integer.** When working with reals, however, both leading and trailing zeros are ignored. Thus, +23.45, 23.45, 023.45, 23.450, and 0023.45000 have the same value.

All reals seen thus far have been in *fixed-point form.* The computer will also accept reals in *floating-point,* or exponential, *form.* Floating-point form is an equivalent method for writing numbers in scientific notation to accommodate numbers that may have very large or very small values. The difference is, instead of writing the base decimal times some power of 10, the base decimal is followed by E and the appropriate power of 10. For example, 231.6 in scientific notation would be 2.316×10^2 and in floating-point form would be 2.316E2. Table 1.7 sets forth several fixed-point decimal numbers with the equivalent scientific notation and floating-point form.

Floating-point form for real numbers does not require exactly one digit on the left of the decimal point. In fact, it can be used with no decimal points written. To

TABLE 1.7
Forms for equivalent numbers

Fixed-point Form	Scientific Notation	Floating-point Form
46.345	4.6345×10	4.6345E1
59214.3	5.92143×10^4	5.92143E4
0.00042	4.2×10^{-4}	4.2E–4
36000000000.0	3.6×10^{10}	3.6E10
0.000000005	5.0×10^{-9}	5.0E–9
–341000.0	-3.41×10^5	–3.41E5

illustrate, 4.16E1, 41.6, 416.0E–1, and 416E–1 have the same value and all are permissible. However, it is not a good habit to use floating-point form for decimal numbers unless exactly one digit appears on the left of the decimal. In most other cases, fixed-point form is preferable.

The syntax diagram for a floating-point number is

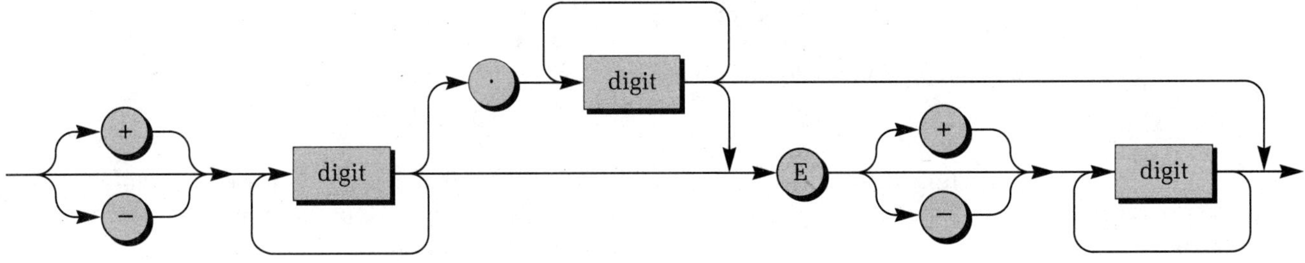

When using reals in a program, you may use either fixed-point or floating-point form. But the computer prints out reals in floating-point form unless you specify otherwise. Formatting of output is discussed later in this section.

Enhanced Real Data Types

S There are four enhanced real data types available in Turbo Pascal: **single, double, extended,** and **comp.** Table 1.8 shows the range of values for each of these data types, the number of significant digits for each type, and the amount of memory required to store a value of that type.

TABLE 1.8
Turbo Pascal real data types

Data Type	Range	Significant Digits	Bytes of Storage
real	2.9×10^{-39} ... 1.7×10^{38}	11–12	6
single	1.5×10^{-45} ... 3.4×10^{38}	7–8	4
double	5.0×10^{-324} ... 1.7×10^{308}	15–16	8
extended	1.9×10^{-4951} ... 1.1×10^{4932}	19–20	10
comp*	-2^{64} ... 2^{62}	19–20	8

***comp** holds only integer values

The use of any of the enhanced real data types requires special processing for additional precision. This processing is provided in one of two ways. Your computer may contain an 8087 numeric coprocessor. This is a special computer chip installed for the purpose of achieving greater precision when working with enhanced real data types. If your computer has an 8087 coprocessor, you activate it by using the compiler directive

```
{$N+}
```

This is typically done at the beginning of a program, just after the program heading. Thus, you may have

```
PROGRAM ComputePrac;

{$N+}
      } (Rest of program here)
```

Once the coprocessor has been activated, you may use any of the enhanced real types. Furthermore, any arithmetic involving real type values is performed with the range and precision of the **extended** data type. To illustrate the effect of using an 8087 coprocessor

```
writeln (Pi);
```

when used with a coprocessor, causes the output

```
3.14159265358979E+0000
```

Without a coprocessor, the output is

```
3.1415926536E+00
```

If your computer does not have the 8087 coprocessor installed, Turbo Pascal (after version 4.0) provides routines that emulate the arithmetic processor of a coprocessor. You may activitate these emulator routines by using the compiler directive

```
{$E+}
```

Since you may not know whether or not a coprocessor is available, the combined compiler directive

```
{$N+, E+}
```

causes the computer to use the coprocessor if it is available and the emulating routines if it is not available.

The data type **comp** works only with integral values. However, the extended precision required for computing uses the same coprocessor (or emulation) required for enhanced real types. Thus, **comp** is typically listed as one of the enhanced real data types.

Data Type **char**

Another data type available in Pascal is **char,** which is used to represent character data. Data of type **char** can be only a single character (which could be a blank space). These characters come from an available character set that differs somewhat from computer to computer but always includes the letters of the alphabet (uppercase and lowercase); the digits 0, 1, 2, 3, 4, 5, 6, 7, 8, and 9; and special symbols such as #, &, !, +, –, *, /. ASCII, the character set used in Turbo Pascal, is given in Appendix 4.

Character constants of type **char** must be enclosed in single quotation marks when used in a program. Otherwise, they are treated as variables and subsequent use causes a compilation error. Thus, to use the letter A as a constant, you would type 'A'. The use of digits and standard operation symbols as characters is also permitted; for example, '7' is considered a character, but 7 is an integer.

If a word of one or more characters is used as a constant in a program, it is referred to as a *string constant.* String constants, generally called *strings,* may be defined in the **CONST** portion of the declaration section. The entire string must be enclosed in single quotation marks.

When a single quotation mark is needed within a string, it is represented by two single quotation marks. For example, if the name desired is O'Malley, it would be represented by

```
'O''Malley'
```

When a single quotation mark is needed as a single character, it can be represented by placing two single quotation marks within single quotation marks. When typed, this appears as ''''. Note that these are all single quotation marks; use of the double quotation mark character here will not produce the desired result.

Data Type **string**

Standard Pascal does not provide for a **string** data type; however, Turbo Pascal does. Having the data type **string** available allows a programmer to design programs that are capable of using strings of characters as well as numeric data. This is particularly useful when using names of people and companies, for example. Later we will see how such strings can be incorporated into a program; for now, it is sufficient that you be aware that Turbo Pascal provides a **string** data type. (Also see the discussion on reading strings at the end of Section 2.3.)

Output

The goal of most programs is to print something. What gets printed (either on paper or on a screen) is referred to as *output.* The two program statements that produce output are **write** and **writeln** (pronounced "write line"). They are usually followed by character strings, numbers, numerical expressions, or variable names enclosed in parentheses. The general form is

write (<expression 1>, <expression 2>, . . . , <expression *n*>)

or

writeln (<expression 1>, <expression 2>, . . . , <expression *n*>)

A simplified syntax diagram for **write** (applicable also for **writeln**) is

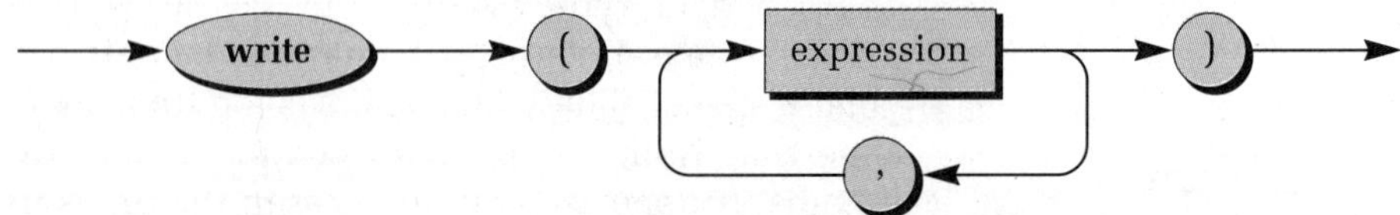

For more information on syntax diagrams for **write** and **writeln**, see Appendix 3.

A **writeln** can also be used as a complete statement, for example:

```
writeln;
```

causes a blank line to be displayed. This technique is frequently used to produce more readable output.

The **write** statement causes subsequent output to be on the same line; **writeln** causes the next output to be on the next line. This is because **writeln** is actually a **write** statement followed by a line feed. When output is to a monitor, **writeln** causes the cursor to move to the next line for the next I/O operation. To illustrate

```
write ('This is a test.');
writeln ('How many lines are printed?');
```

causes the output

```
This is a test.How many lines are printed?
```

whereas

```
writeln ('This is a test.');
writeln ('How many lines are printed?');
```

causes the output

```
This is a test.
How many lines are printed?
```

Some implementations require **writeln** to be the last output statement. Otherwise, output gathered in a buffer does not get printed.

Character strings can be printed by enclosing the string in single quotation marks within the parentheses. Numerical data can be printed by including the desired number or numbers within the parentheses. Thus

```
writeln (100)
```

produces

```
100
```

S Default output appears on the monitor. Output can be directed to the printer by using **lst** (short for list) within a **write** or **writeln** statement. Thus

```
writeln ('Hello');
```

directs the output to the screen, and

```
writeln (lst, 'Hello');
```

directs the output to the printer.

In Turbo Pascal, the use of **lst** to send output to the printer is only available by linking a library procedure to your program. This is accomplished by including

```
USES
  Printer;
```

following the program heading.

EXAMPLE 1.1 Let's write a complete Turbo Pascal program to print the address

1403 South Drive
Apartment 3B
Pittsburgh, PA   15238

A complete program to print this is

```
PROGRAM Address;

BEGIN
  writeln ('1403 South Drive');
  writeln ('Apartment 3B');
  writeln ('Pittsburgh, Pa      ', 15238)
END.
```

When this program is run on a computer, you get

```
1403 South Drive
Apartment 3B
Pittsburgh, PA     15238
```

Formatting Integers

Output of integers can be controlled by *formatting.* Within a **write** or **writeln** statement, an integer, identifier, or integer expression can be followed by a colon and another integer to specify the field width. The value will then be printed on the right side of the specified field. Thus

```
writeln (100, 50:10, 25:10);
```

produces

```
100--------50--------25
```

where each "–" indicates a blank.

The general form for formating integers is

> **write** (<integer> : <*n*>);
> or
> **writeln** (<integer> : <*n*>);

Some illustrations for formatting integer output are

Program Statement	Output
`writeln (123:6);`	`---123`
`writeln (15, 10:5);`	`15---10`
`writeln (−263:7, 21:3);`	`---−263-21`
`writeln (+5062:6);`	`--5062`
`writeln (65221:3);`	`65221`

Note that in line five, an attempt is made to specify a field width that is smaller than the number of digits contained in the integer. Most versions of Pascal will automatically print the entire integer; however, some versions will print only in the specified width.

Formatting Reals

Output of reals can also be controlled by formatting. The general form is

> **write** (<real> : <*n*1> : <*n*2>);
> or
> **writeln** (<real> : <*n*1> : <*n*2>);

where *n*1 specifies the total field width (including the decimal point) and *n*2 specifies the number of positions to the right of the decimal. Thus

```
writeln (736.23:8:2);
```

produces

```
--736.23
```

COMMUNICATION AND STYLE TIPS

Using **writeln** at the beginning and end of the executable section will separate desired output from other messages or directions. Thus in Example 1.1, the program for printing an address could have been

```
PROGRAM Address;
BEGIN
  writeln;
  writeln ('1403 South Drive');
  writeln ('Apartment 3B');
  writeln ('Pittsburgh, PA      ', 15238);
  writeln
END.
```

Formatting reals causes the following to happen:

1. The decimal uses one position in the specified field width.
2. Leading zeros are not printed.
3. Trailing zeros are printed to the specified number of positions to the right of the decimal.
4. Leading plus "+" signs are omitted.
5. Leading minus "–" signs are printed; each uses one position of the specified field.
6. Digits appearing to the right of the decimal have been rounded rather than truncated.

As with integers, if a field width is specified that is too small, Turbo Pascal will default to the minimum width required to present all digits to the left of the decimal as well as the specified digits to the right of the decimal. Reals in floating-point form can also be used in a formatted **writeln** statement. The following table illustrates how output using data of type **real** can be formatted.

Program Statement	Output
`writeln (765.432:10:3)`	`   765.432`
`writeln (023.14:10:2)`	`     23.14`
`writeln (65.50:10:2)`	`     65.50`
`writeln (+341.2:10:2)`	`    341.20`
`writeln (-341.2:10:2)`	`   -341.20`
`writeln (16.458:10:2)`	`     16.46`
`writeln (0.00456:10:4)`	`    0.0046`
`writeln (136.51:4:2)`	`136.51`

Formatting Strings

Strings and string constants can be formatted using a colon followed by a positive integer "*n*" to specify field width. The general form for formatting strings is

write ('<string>': <*n*>);
or
writeln ('<string>' : <*n*>);

The string will be right-justified in the field. Unlike reals, strings are truncated when necessary. Thus

```
writeln, ('field', 'width':10, 'check':15);
```

would produce

```
field-----width----------check
     \____:10__/\____:15___/
```

Test Programs

Programmers should develop the habit of using *test programs* to improve their knowledge and programming skills. The test program should be relatively short and written to provide an answer to a specific question. For example, in our earlier discussion of **maxint** in this section, it was mentioned that the value of **maxint** is 32767. You could use a test program to verify that this is what your computer uses for **maxint.** A complete program that accomplishes this is

```
PROGRAM TestMax;

BEGIN
  writeln ('Maxint is ', maxint);
  readln
END.
```

Notice that the brief message 'Maxint is ' is included to explain the output. Such a message or output label is almost always desirable.

Test programs allow you to play with the computer. You can answer "What if . . . " questions by adopting a "try it and see" attitude. This is an excellent way to become comfortable with your computer and the programming language you are using. For example, you might change the previous test program to

```
PROGRAM TestMax;

BEGIN
  writeln ('Maxint is ', maxint);
  writeln ('TooMuch is ', maxint + 1);
  readln
END.
```

Exercises 1.6

1. Which of the following are valid integers? Explain why the others are invalid.

a. 521	**c.** 5,621	**e.** +65	**g.** −0
b. −32.0	**d.** +00784	**f.** 6521492183	**h.** 6E3

2. Which of the following are valid reals? Explain why the others are invalid.

a. 26.3	**d.** 492.	**g.** −0.2E−3	**i.** −176.52E+1
b. +181.0	**e.** +017.400	**h.** 43,162.3E5	**j.** 1.43000E+2
c. −.14	**f.** 43E2		

3. Change the following fixed-point decimals to floating-point decimals with exactly one nonzero digit to the left of the decimal.

a. 173.0	**c.** −0.000000023	**e.** −5.2
b. 743927000000.0	**d.** +014.768	

4. Change the following floating-point decimals to fixed-point decimals.

   a. −1.0046E+3 c. 9.020E10 e. −8.02E−3
   b. 4.2E−8 d. −4.615230E3

5. Indicate the data type for each of the following:

   a. −720 c. 150E3 e. '150' g. 23.4E−2
   b. −720.0 d. 150 f. '23.4E2'

6. Write and run a test program for each of the following:

   a. Examine the output for a decimal number without field width specified; for example

   ```
   writeln (2.31)
   ```

   b. Try to print a message without using quotation marks for a character string; for example

   ```
   writeln (Hello);
   ```

7. For each of the following, write a program that would produce the indicated output.

   a.

   ```
   Score
   -----
     86
     82
     79
   ```

   where "S" is in column 10.

   b.

   ```
    Price
    -----
   $ 19.94
   $100.00
   $ 58.95
   ```

   where "P" is in column 50.

8. Assume the hourly wages of five students are

   3.65 4.10 2.89 5.00 4.50

   Write a program that produces this output, where the "E" in "Employee" is in column 20.

   ```
   ------------------------
   Employee       Hourly Wage
   ------------------------
      1             $ 3.65
      2             $ 4.10
      3             $ 2.89
      4             $ 5.00
      5             $ 4.50
   ------------------------
   ```

9. What is the output from the following segment of code on your printer or terminal?

   ```
   writeln ('My test average is', 87.5);
   writeln ('My test average is':20, 87.5:10);
   writeln ('My test average is':25, 87.5:10:2);
   writeln ('My test average is':25, 87.5:6:2);
   ```

10. Write a program that produces the following output. Start Student in column 20 and Test in column 40.

   ```
   Student Name         Test Score

   Adams, Mike               73
   Conley, Theresa           86
   Samson, Ron               92
   O'Malley, Colleen         81
   ```

11. The Great Lakes Shipping Company is going to use a computer program to generate billing statements for their customers. The heading of each bill is to be

```
             GREAT LAKES SHIPPING COMPANY
              SAULT STE. MARIE, MICHIGAN
-----------------------------------------------
  Thank you for doing business with our company.
  The information listed below was used to
  determine your total cargo fee. We hope you
  were satisfied with our service.
-----------------------------------------------
CARGO      TONNAGE        RATE/TON       TOTAL DUE
```

Write a complete Turbo Pascal program that produces this heading.

12. What output is produced by each of the following statements or sequence of statements when executed by the computer?

a. `writeln (1234, 1234:8, 1234:6);`

b. `writeln (12:4, -21:4, 120:4);`

c.
```
writeln ('FIGURE  AREA  PERIMETER');
writeln ('-----------------------');
writeln;
writeln ('SQUARE', 16:5, 16:12);
writeln;
writeln ('RECT ', 24:5, 20:12);
```

13. Write a complete program that produces the following table:

```
WIDTH    LENGTH    AREA
  4         2        8
 21         5      105
```

14. What output is produced when each of the following is executed?

a. `writeln (2.134:15:2);`

b. `writeln (423.73:5:2);`

c. `writeln (-42.1:8:3);`

d. `writeln (-4.21E3:6:2);`

e. `writeln (10.25);`

f. `writeln (1.25, 1.25:6:2, 1.25:6:1);`

15. Write a complete program that produces the following output:

```
Hourly Wage    Hours Worked      Total

    5.0            20.0          100.00
    7.50           15.25         114.375
```

16. What type of data would be used to print each of the following?

a. Your age

b. Your grade point average

c. Your name

d. A test score

e. The average test score

f. Your grade

■ Summary

Key Terms

algorithm
applications software
arithmetic/logic unit (ALU)
assembly language
binary digits
bits
bus
central processing unit (CPU)
comment
compiler

constant definition
control unit
data
data type
debugging
declaration section
edit window
effective statement
executable section
executable statement
executed
fixed-point form
floating-point form
formatting
hardware
high-level language
hot (quick) keys
identifier
input device
I/O devices
keyword
low-level language
machine language
main (primary) memory
main unit
mainframe computer
menu bar
microcomputer
minicomputer
module
module specifications
object code
object program
operating system
output
output device
program
program heading
programming language
pseudocode
reserved word
secondary (auxiliary) memory devices
software
software engineering
software system life cycle
source program
standard identifier
standard simple type
stepwise refinement
string
string constant
structure chart
syntax
syntax diagram
system software
test program
top-down design
variable declaration

Keywords

BEGIN
byte
char
ClrScr
comp
CONST
Crt
double
END
extended
integer
longint
maxint
Printer
PROGRAM
real
shortint
single
string
USES
VAR
word
write
writeln

Turbo Pascal Menus and Options

Compile menu
File menu
Help menu
Output option
Run menu
Save option
User option
Window menu

Key Concepts

- Six steps in problem solving include: analyze the problem, develop an algorithm, write code for the program, run the program, test the results against answers manually computed with paper and pencil, and document the program.
- Top-down design is a process of dividing tasks into subtasks until each subtask can be readily accomplished.
- Stepwise refinement refers to refinements of tasks into subtasks.
- A structure chart is a graphic representation of the relationship between modules.
- Software engineering is the process of developing and maintaining large software systems.
- The software system life cycle consists of the following phases: analysis, design, coding, testing/verification, maintenance, and obsolescence.
- Valid identifiers must begin with a letter or underscore and can contain only letters, digits, and underscore.
- The three components of a Turbo Pascal program are the program heading, declaration section, and executable section.
- Semicolons are used to separate executable statements.
- Extra spaces and blank lines are ignored in Turbo Pascal.
- Output is generated by using the **write** or **writeln** statement.
- Strings are formatted using a single colon followed by a positive integer that specifies the total field width; for example

```
writeln ('This is a string.':30);
```

- The following table summarizes the use of the data types **integer, real, char,** and **string.**

Data Type	Permissible Data	Formatting
integer	numeric	one colon; for example `writeln (25:6);`
real	numeric	two colons; for example `writeln (1234.5:8:2);`
char	character	one colon; for example `writeln ('A':6);`
string	string of characters	one colon; for example `writeln ('Hello':10);`

■ Programming Problems and Projects

Write and run a short program for each of the following:

1. A program to print your initials in block letters. Your output could look like

```
  JJJJJ             A              CC
     J             A A           C    C
     J            A   A         C
     J            AAAAA         C
 J   J            A   A          C    C
  JJ              A   A            CC
```

2. Design a simple picture; then print it out using **writeln** statements. If you plan the picture using a sheet of graph paper, it will be easier to keep track of spacing.
3. A program to print out your mailing address.
4. Our Lady of Mercy Hospital prints billing statements for patients when they are ready to leave the hospital. Write a program that prints a heading for each statement as follows:

```
/////////////////////////////////////////
/                                       /
/        Our Lady of Mercy Hospital     /
/        --------------------------     /
/                                       /
/            1306 Central City          /
/          Phone (416) 333-5555         /
/                                       /
/////////////////////////////////////////
```

5. Your computer science instructor wants course and program information included as part of every assignment. Write a program that can be used to print this information. Sample output is

```
***************************************
*      Author:          Mary Smith    *
*      Course:          CPS-150       *
*      Assignment:      Program #3    *
*      Due Date:        September 18  *
*      Instructor:      Mr. Samson    *
***************************************
```

6. As part of a programming project that will compute and print grades for each student in your class, you have been asked to write a program that produces a heading for each student report. The columns in which the various headings should be are as follows:

   - The border for the class name starts in column 30.
   - Student Name starts in column 22.
   - Test Average starts in column 42.
   - Grade starts in column 57.

   Write a program to print the heading as follows:

```
                             *************************
                             *                       *
                             *    CPS-150    Pascal  *
                             *                       *
                             *************************
                     Student Name       Test Average   Grade
                     ------------       ------------   -----
```

Communication in Practice

1. Exchange complete programs with a classmate, and critique the use of comments for program documentation. Offer positive suggestions as to where and what kind of comments would be helpful for others who wish to read and understand the program.
2. Contact a programmer, and discuss the use of documentation from a programmer's perspective. Get answers to such questions as, "What percent of your time is spent in writing documentation?," "Where and when do you include documentation in your programs?," and so forth. Give an oral report of this discussion to your class.
3. Contact an individual whose responsibility is to maintain and modify existing software. Discuss the significance of documentation from his or her perspective. Compare these responses to the responses you obtained when talking to a programmer (Exercise 2). Prepare a written report for class that lists the similarities and differences of both sets of responses.
4. Secure an early version of Turbo Pascal that does not have an Integrated Development Environment (IDE). Write, compile, run, edit, and save a program using the early version. Write a short paper discussing the differences between the earlier environment and the IDE. Indicate which environment you prefer and why.
5. To mouse or not to mouse, that is the question! Ask instructors, typists, professional programmers, computer users, and/or upper-level computer science students, to outline the advantages and disadvantages of using a mouse. Prepare a report of your findings, and present it to your class.

Arithmetic, Variables, Input, Constants, and Standard Functions

■ CHAPTER OUTLINE ■

In this chapter, we will discuss arithmetic operations, using data in a program, obtaining input, and using constants and variables. We will also discuss the use of functions to perform standard operations, such as finding the square root or absolute value of a number.

■ 2.1 Arithmetic in Turbo Pascal

Basic Operations for Integer Types

Integer arithmetic in Pascal allows the operations of addition, subtraction, and multiplication to be performed. The notation for these operations is

Symbol	Operation	Example	Value
+	Addition	`3 + 5`	8
-	Subtraction	`43 - 25`	18
*	Multiplication	`4 * 7`	28

Noticeably absent from this list is a division operation. This is because *integer arithmetic operations* are expected to produce integer answers. Since division problems might not produce integers, Pascal provides the two operations **MOD** and **DIV** to produce integer answers.

In a standard division problem, there is a quotient and a remainder. In Pascal, **DIV** produces the quotient and **MOD** produces the remainder when the first operand is positive. For example, in the problem 17 divided by 3, 17 **DIV** 3 produces 5, and 17 **MOD** 3 produces 2. Avoid using **DIV** 0 (zero) and **MOD** 0 (zero). A precise description of how **MOD** works in standard Pascal is given in the *Second Draft ANSI Standard for Pascal* as "A term of the form *i* mod *j* shall be an error if *j* is zero or negative; otherwise, the value of *i* mod *j* shall be that value of $(i - (k * j))$ for integral *k* such that $0 <= i \bmod j < j$."

In Turbo Pascal, the **MOD** operator returns the remainder obtained by dividing its two operands; that is

I **MOD** J = I – (I **DIV** J) * J

The sign of the result of **MOD** is the same as the sign of I. An error occurs if J is zero. To illustrate the difference between this Turbo definition and the ANSI standard, in Turbo

(–17) **MOD** 3 = –2

whereas the result in standard Pascal is

(–17) **MOD** 3 = 1

TABLE 2.1
Values of integer expressions

Expression	Value
`-3 + 2`	–1
`2 - 3`	–1
`-3 * 2`	–6
`3 * (-2)`	–6
`-3 * (-2)`	6
`17 DIV 3`	5
`17 MOD 3`	2
`17 DIV (-3)`	–5
`(-17) DIV 3`	–5
`(-17) MOD 3`	–2
`(-17) DIV (-3)`	5

Several integer expressions and their values in Turbo Pascal are shown in Table 2.1. Notice that when 3 is multiplied by –2, the expression is written as 3 * (–2) rather than 3 * –2. This is because consecutive operators cannot appear in an arithmetic expression. However, this expression could be written –2 * 3.

Order of Operations for Integers

Expressions involving more than one operation are frequently used when writing programs. When this happens, it is important to know the order in which these operations are performed. The priorities for these operations are:

1. All expressions within a set of parentheses are evaluated first. If there are parentheses within parentheses (the parentheses are nested), the innermost expressions are evaluated first.
2. The operations *, **MOD**, and **DIV** are evaluated next in order from left to right.
3. The operations + and – are evaluated last, from left to right.

These are similar to algebraic operations; they are summarized in Table 2.2.

TABLE 2.2
Integer arithmetic priority

Expression or Operation	Priority
( )	1. Evaluate from inside out.
*, **MOD, DIV**	2. Evaluate from left to right.
+, –	3. Evaluate from left to right.

To illustrate how expressions are evaluated, consider the values of the expressions listed in Table 2.3. As expressions get more elaborate, it can be helpful to list partial evaluations in a manner similar to the order in which the computer performs the evaluations. For example, suppose the expression

```
(3 - 4) + 18 DIV 5 + 2
```

TABLE 2.3
Priority of operations

Expression	Value
`3 - 4 * 5`	−17
`3 - (4 * 5)`	−17
`(3 - 4) * 5`	−5
`3 * 4 - 5`	7
`3 * (4 - 5)`	−3
`17 - 10 - 3`	4
`17 - (10 - 3)`	10
`(17 - 10) - 3`	4
`-42 + 50 MOD 17`	−26

is to be evaluated. If we consider the order in which subexpressions are evaluated, we get

```
(3 - 4) + 18 DIV 5 + 2
   ↓
  -1    + 18 DIV 5 + 2
               ↓
  -1    +      3   + 2
           ↓
           2       + 2
               ↓
               4
```

Using MOD and DIV

MOD and **DIV** can be used when it is necessary to perform conversions within arithmetic operations. For example, consider the problem of adding two weights given in units of pounds and ounces. This problem can be solved by converting both weights to ounces, adding the ounces, and then converting the total ounces to pounds and ounces. The conversion from ounces to pounds can be accomplished by using **MOD** and **DIV**. If the total number of ounces is 243, then

243 **DIV** 16

yields the number of pounds (15), and

243 **MOD** 16

yields the number of ounces (3).

Basic Operations for Real Types

The operations of addition, subtraction, and multiplication are the same for data of real types as they are for data of integer types. Additionally, division is now permitted. Since **MOD** and **DIV** are restricted to data of integer types, the symbol for division of data of real types is "/". The *real arithmetic operations* are

Symbol	Operation	Example	Value
+	Addition	`4.2 + 19.36`	23.56
−	Subtraction	`19.36 - 4.2`	15.16
*	Multiplication	`3.1 * 2.0`	6.2
/	Division	`54.6 / 2.0`	27.3

Division is given the same priority as multiplication when arithmetic expressions are evaluated by the computer. The rules for order of operation are the same as those for evaluating integer arithmetic expressions. A summary of these operations is shown in Table 2.4.

TABLE 2.4
Real arithmetic priority

Expression or Operation	Priority
( )	1. Evaluate from inside out.
*, /	2. Evaluate from left to right.
+, −	3. Evaluate from left to right.

Some example calculations using data of type **real** are

Expression	Value
`-1.0 + 3.5 + 2.0`	4.5
`-1.0 + 3.5 * 2.0`	6.0
`2.0 * (1.2 - 4.3)`	–6.2
`2.0 * 1.2 - 4.3`	–1.9
`-12.6 / 3.0 + 3.0`	–1.2
`-12.6 / (3.0 + 3.0)`	–2.1

As with integers, consecutive operation signs are not allowed. Thus, if you want to multiply 4.3 by –2.0, you can use –2.0 * 4.3 or 4.3 * (–2.0), but you cannot use 4.3 * –2.0. As expressions get a bit more complicated, it is again helpful to write out the expression and evaluate it step by step. For example

```
18.2 + (-4.3) * (10.1 + (72.3 / 3.0 - 4.5))
                         ↓
18.2 + (-4.3) * (10.1 +    (24.1     - 4.5))
                                ↓
18.2 + (-4.3) * (10.1 +           19.6)
                    ↓
18.2 + (-4.3) *           29.7
             ↓
18.2 +        (-127.71)
       ↓
    -109.51
```

Note that exponentiation has not been listed as an available operation for either integers or reals. Turbo Pascal does not have an exponentiation operator. A method for overcoming this problem is presented in Section 3.4.

Overflow and Underflow

Arithmetic operations with computers have some limitations. One of these is the problem of *overflow.* For example, integer overflow occurs when a variable of type **integer** is assigned a value that exceeds **maxint.** This does not cause a run-time error in Turbo Pascal. Instead, a meaningless value is assigned, and the program continues. In Section 4.3, we discuss how to protect a program against this problem.

Real overflow occurs when the absolute value of a real type is too large to fit into a memory location. In Turbo Pascal, program execution is halted and an overflow message appears on the screen.

A second problem occurs when working with reals. If a real number is too small to be represented, it is replaced by zero. This is called *underflow.* Thus, your computations may produce a real of the magnitude $1.0 * 10^{-100}$, but your system could replace this with a zero.

In general, underflow is less of a problem than overflow; however, it cannot be completely ignored. Some mathematical approximations require use of numbers as they approach zero. Some financial calculations (such as computing interest) also require the use of very small numbers. If your computations do not require use of small numbers, you can ignore underflow. However, if you do use such numbers, you must know the system limitations before writing programs that need them. Consult your system manual to find the limitations of your system. Figure 2.1 illustrates the overflow and underflow possibilities.

FIGURE 2.1
Overflow and underflow

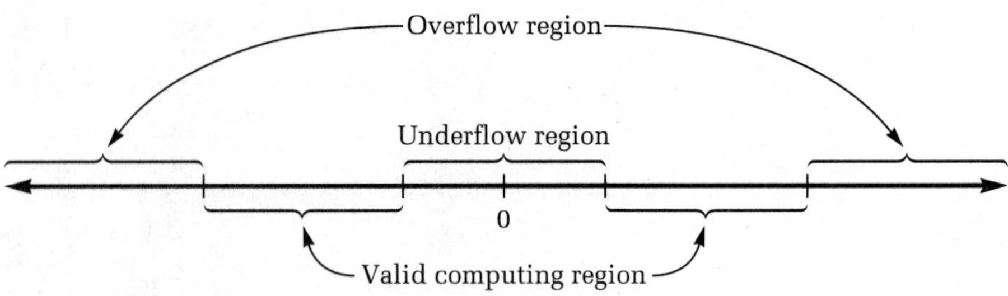

Which Numbers to Use

As previously mentioned, if you need to work with an integer type of number, you should select the type with the smallest range that will suit your purpose. Working with real types poses other problems.

If you do not use a math coprocessor ({$N+}) or an emulator ({$E+}) (recall Section 1.6), you are restricted to using only the data type **real.** However, if you do use a math coprocessor or an emulator, any of the types **single, double, extended,** or **comp** are available to you. Furthermore, using data of type **real** causes the coprocessor to be avoided by special software, resulting in a loss of efficiency in processing. Consequently, any time you activate a coprocessor or an emulator, avoid using a **real** data type.

Mixed Expressions

Arithmetic expressions using data of two or more types are called *mixed-mode expressions.* When a mixed-mode expression involving both **integer** and **real** data types is evaluated, the result will be of type **real.** A real also results if division (/) is used with integers. When formatting output of mixed expressions, always format for reals. (*Note:* Avoid using **MOD** and **DIV** with mixed-mode expressions.)

Exercises 2.1

1. Find the value of each of the following expressions:
   - **a.** `17 - 3 * 2`
   - **b.** `-15 * 3 + 4`
   - **c.** `123 MOD 5`
   - **d.** `123 DIV 5`
   - **e.** `5 * 123 DIV 5 + 123 MOD 5`
   - **f.** `-21 * 3 * (-1)`
   - **g.** `14 * (3 + 18 DIV 4) - 50`
   - **h.** `100 - (4 * (3 + 2)) * (-2)`
   - **i.** `-56 MOD 3`
   - **j.** `14 * 8 MOD 5 - 23 DIV (-4)`
2. Find the value of each of the following expressions:
   - **a.** `3.21 + 5.02 - 6.1`
   - **b.** `6.0 / 2.0 * 3.0`
   - **c.** `6.0 / (2.0 + 3.0)`
   - **d.** `-20.5 * (2.1 + 2.0)`
   - **e.** `-2.0 * ((56.8 / 4.0 + 0.8) + 5.0)`
   - **f.** `1.04E2 * 0.02E3`
   - **g.** `800.0E-2 / 4.0 + 15.3`
3. Which of the following are valid expressions? For those that are, indicate whether they are of type **integer** or **real.**
   - **a.** `18 - (5 * 2)`
   - **b.** `(18 - 5) * 2`
   - **c.** `18 - 5 * 2.0`
   - **d.** `25 * (14 MOD 7.0)`
   - **e.** `1.4E3 * 5`
   - **f.** `28 / 7`
   - **g.** `28.0 / 4`
   - **h.** `10.5 + 14 DIV 3`
   - **i.** `24 DIV 6 / 3`
   - **j.** `24 DIV (6 / 3)`

4. Evaluate each valid expression in Exercise 3.
5. What output is produced by the following program?

```
PROGRAM MixedMode;
BEGIN
  writeln;
  writeln ('    Expression    Value');
  writeln ('    ----------    -----');
  writeln;
  writeln ('    10 / 5' , 10/5:12:3);
  writeln ('    2.0+7*(-1)', 2.0 + 7 * (-1));
  writeln
END.
```

6. Find all errors in the following Turbo Pascal statements:
   a. `writeln (-20 DIV 4.0:8:3);`
   b. `writeln (-20 DIV 4:8:3);`
   c. `writeln (-20 DIV 4:8);`
   d. `writeln (8 - 3.0 * 5:6);`
   e. `writeln (7 * 6 DIV 3 / 2:6:2);`
   f. `writeln (-17.1 + 5 * 20.0:8:3);`
7. Write a test program to see what overflow message appears when real overflow occurs.

■ 2.2 Using Variables

Memory Locations

It is frequently necessary to store values for later use. This is done by putting each value into a *memory location* by using a symbolic name to refer to this location. If the contents of the location are to be changed during a program, the symbolic name is referred to as a *variable;* if the contents are not to be changed, it is referred to as a *constant.*

A graphic way to think about memory locations is to envision them as boxes; each box is named, and a value is stored inside. For example, suppose a program is written to add a sequence of numbers. If we name the memory location to be used Sum, initially we have

Sum

S which depicts a memory location that has been reserved and can be accessed by a reference to Sum. In Turbo Pascal, the value 0 is assigned at the time the variable is declared. If we then add the integers 10, 20, and 30 and store them in Sum, we have

60
Sum

It is important to distinguish between the name of a memory location (Sum) and the value or contents of a memory location (60). The name does not change during a program, but the contents can be changed as often as necessary. (Note that contents of memory locations that are referred to by constants cannot be changed.) If 30 were added to the contents in the previous example, the new value stored in Sum could be depicted as

90
Sum

A NOTE OF INTEREST

Herman Hollerith

Herman Hollerith (1860–1929) was hired by the United States Census Bureau in 1879 at the age of 19. Since the 1880 census was predicted to take a long time to complete (it actually took until 1887), Hollerith was assigned the task of developing a mechanical method of tabulating census data. He introduced his census machine in 1887. It consisted of four parts:

1. a punched paper card that represented data using a special code (Hollerith code),
2. a card punch apparatus,
3. a tabulator that read the punched cards, and
4. a sorting machine with 24 compartments.

The punched cards used by Hollerith were the same size as cards still in use today.

Using Hollerith's techniques and equipment, the 1890 census tabulation was completed in one-third the time required for the previous census tabulation. This included working with data for 12 million additional people.

Hollerith proceeded to form the Tabulating Machine Company (1896), which supplied equipment to census bureaus in the United States, Canada, and western Europe. After a disagreement with the census director, Hollerith began marketing his equipment in other commercial areas. Hollerith sold his company in 1911. It was later combined with 12 others to form the Computing-Tabulating-Recording Company, a direct ancestor of International Business Machines Corp.

In the meantime, Hollerith's successor at the census bureau, James Powers, redesigned the census machine. He then formed his own company, which subsequently became Remington Rand and Sperry Univac.

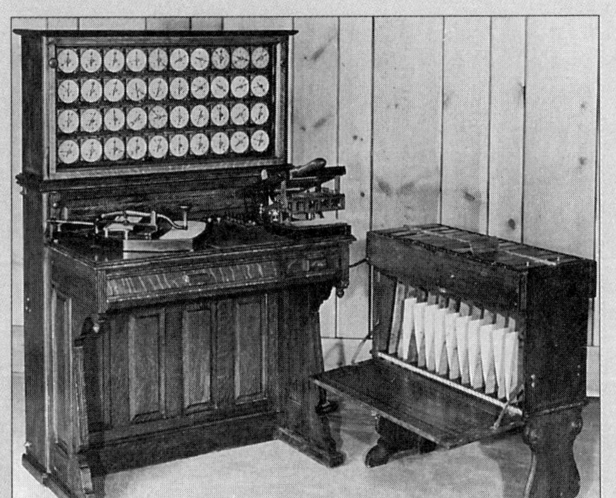

Symbolic names that represent memory locations containing values that will be changing must be declared in the **VAR** section of the program (as indicated in Section 1.5). For example

```
VAR
  Sum : integer;
```

Symbolic names that represent memory locations containing values that will not be changing must be declared in the **CONST** section.

Assignment Statements

Now let's examine how the contents of variables are manipulated. A value may be put into a memory location with an *assignment statement* in the form of

<variable name> := <value>;
or
<variable name> := <expression>;

where "variable name" is the name of the memory location. For example, if Sum was initially zero, then

```
Sum := 30;
```

changes

0	to	30
Sum		Sum

The syntax diagram for this is

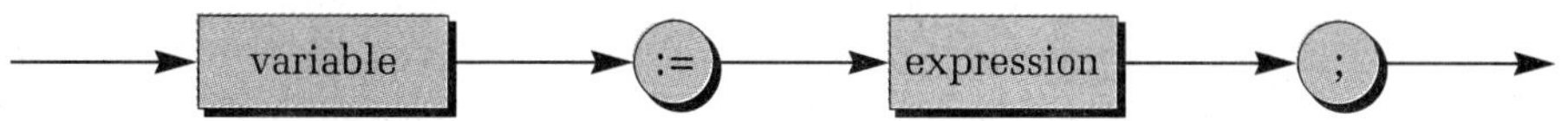

Some important rules concerning assignment statements are:

1. The assignment is always made from right to left (←).
2. The syntax for assigning requires a colon followed immediately by an equal sign (:=).
3. Only one variable can be on the left side of the assignment symbol.
4. Constants cannot be on the left side of the assignment symbol.
5. The expression may be a constant, a constant expression, a variable that has previously been assigned a value, or a combination of variables and constants.
6. Values on the right side of the assignment symbol are not changed by the assignment.
7. The variable and expression must match in data type, except that an integer expression may be assigned to a real variable, in which case the result of the expression evaluation gets converted to a real value.

Two common errors made by beginners are trying to assign from left to right and forgetting the colon when using an assignment statement.

Repeated assignments can be made. For example, if Sum is an integer variable, the statements

```
Sum := 50;
Sum := 70;
Sum := 100;
```

produce first 50, then 70, and finally 100 as shown.

~~50~~ ~~70~~ 100
Sum

In this sense, memory is destructive in that it retains only the last value assigned.

Turbo Pascal variables are symbolic addresses that can hold values. When a variable is declared, the type of values it will store must be specified (declared). Storing a value of the wrong type in a variable leads to a program error. This means that data types must match when using assignment statements: reals must be assigned to one of the real type variables; integers to one of the integer type variables; and characters to **char** or **string** variables. The only exception is that an integer type can be assigned to a real type variable. However, the integer is then converted to a real. If, for example, Average is a **real** variable and the assignment statement

```
Average := 21;
```

is made, the value is stored as the real 21.0.

The assignment of a constant to a character variable requires that the constant be enclosed in single quotation marks. For example, if Letter is of type **char** and you want to store the letter C in Letter, use the assignment statement

```
Letter := 'C';
```

This could be pictured as

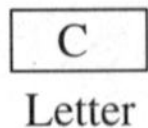

Letter

Furthermore, only one character can be assigned or stored in a character variable.

To illustrate working with assignment statements, assume that the variable declaration portion of the program is

```
VAR
  Sum : integer;
  Average : real;
  Letter : char;
  Message : string;
```

Examples of valid and invalid assignment statements using the variables just declared are shown in Table 2.5.

TABLE 2.5 Assignment statements

Statement	Valid	If Invalid, Reason
`Sum := 50;`	Yes	
`Sum := 10.5;`	No	Data types do not match.
`Average := 15.6;`	Yes	
`Average := 33;`	Yes	
`Letter := 'A';`	Yes	
`Letter := 'HI';`	No	Not a single character
`Letter := 20;`	No	Data types do not match.
`Letter := 'Z';`	Yes	
`Letter := A;`	?	Valid if A is a variable or constant of type **char**.
`Sum := 7;`	Yes	
`Letter := '7';`	Yes	
`Letter := 7;`	No	Data types do not match.
`Sum := '7';`	No	Data types do not match.
`Message := 'Hello';`	Yes	

Expressions

Actual use of variables in a program is usually more elaborate than what we have just seen. Variables may be used in any manner that does not violate their type declarations, including both arithmetic operations and assignment statements. For example, if Score1, Score2, Score3, and Average are **real** variables, then

```
Score1 := 72.3;
Score2 := 89.4;
Score3 := 95.6;
Average := (Score1 + Score2 + Score3) / 3.0;
```

is a valid fragment of code.

Now let's consider the problem of accumulating a total. Assuming NewScore and Total are integer variables, the following code is valid:

```
Total := 0;
NewScore := 5;
Total := Total + NewScore;
NewScore := 7;
Total := Total + NewScore;
```

As this code is executed, the values of memory locations for Total and NewScore could be depicted as

	Total	NewScore
`Total := 0;`	0	
`NewScore := 5;`	0	5
`Total := Total + NewScore;`	5	5
`NewScore := 7;`	5	7
`Total := Total + NewScore;`	12	7

Output

Variables and variable expressions can be used when creating output. When used in a **writeln** statement, they perform the same function as constants do. For example, if the assignment statement

```
Age := 5;
```

has been made, the two statements

```
writeln (5);
writeln (Age);
```

produce the same output. If Age1, Age2, Age3, and Sum are integer variables and the assignments

```
Age1 := 21;
Age2 := 30;
Age3 := 12;
Sum := Age1 + Age2 + Age3;
```

are made, the three statements

```
writeln ('The sum is ', 21 + 30 + 12);
writeln ('The sum is ', Age1 + Age2 + Age3);
writeln ('The sum is ', Sum);
```

all produce the same output.

Formatting variables and variable expressions in **writeln** statements follows the same rules as those presented in Chapter 1 for formatting constants. The statements needed to write the sum of the previous example in a field width of four are

```
writeln ('The sum is ', (21 + 30 + 12):4);
writeln ('The sum is ', (Age1 + Age2 + Age3):4);
writeln ('The sum is ', Sum:4);
```

The next two examples illustrate the use of variables, assignment statements, and formatting.

■ **EXAMPLE 2.1**

Suppose you want a program to print data about the cost of three textbooks and the average price of the books. The variable declaration section could include

```
VAR
  MathText, BioText,
  CompSciText,
  Total, Average : real;
```

A portion of the program could be

```
  MathText := 23.95;
  BioText := 27.50;
  CompSciText := 19.95;
  Total := MathText + BioText + CompSciText;
  Average := Total / 3;
```

The output could be created by

```
  writeln ('Text             Price');
  writeln ('----             -----');
  writeln;
  writeln ('Math', MathText:18:2);
  writeln ('Biology', BioText:15:2);
  writeln ('CompSci', CompSciText:15:2);
  writeln;
  writeln ('Total', Total:17:2);
  writeln;
  writeln ('The average price is', Average:7:2);
```

The output would then be

```
Text              Price
----              -----

Math              23.95
Biology           27.50
CompSci           19.95

Total             71.40

The average price is  23.80
```

■ **EXAMPLE 2.2**

Now let's see how we can use a variable of type **integer** to examine the problem of integer overflow. Recall the value of **maxint** is 32767. If we try to store an integer larger than **maxint** in a variable of type **integer,** we cause integer overflow. A test program to see what occurs is

```
PROGRAM IntOverFlow;
VAR
  Num : integer;
BEGIN
  Num := 32767 + 1;
  writeln (Num);
  readln
END.
```

When this program is typed exactly as it appears here and then compiled, the following error message will be given:

```
Error 76: Constant out of range.
```

Software Engineering Implications

The communication aspect of software engineering can be simplified by the judicious choice of meaningful identifiers. Systems programmers must be aware that others will need to read and analyze the code over time. Some extra time spent thinking about and using descriptive identifiers provides great time savings during the testing and maintenance phases. Code that is written using descriptive identifiers is referred to as *self-documenting code.*

COMMUNICATION AND STYLE TIPS

A relatively standard use of program comments is to establish a *variable dictionary.* In short programs, the need for this is not obvious; however, it is essential for longer programs.

Several styles can be used to describe variables. One method is to place comments on the same line as the variables in the variable declaration section. For example, in Example 2.1, we might use

```
VAR
  MathText, BioText,  {  Costs of textbooks in Math,     }
  CompSciText,        {  Biology, and Computer Science   }
  Total,              {  Total cost of textbooks         }
  Average : real;     {  Average cost of each textbook   }
```

A second method is to create a separate comment section preceding the variable declaration section, such as

```
{            Variable Dictionary                       }
{                                                      }
{  MathText      Cost of math textbook                 }
{  BioText       Cost of biology textbook              }
{  CompSciText   Cost of computer science textbook     }
{  Total         Total cost of textbooks               }
{  Average       Average cost of each textbook         }
```

You are encouraged to try both styles of describing variables, as well as any variation you might like.

Exercises 2.2

1. Assume the variable declaration section of a program is

```
VAR
  Age, IQ : integer;
  Income : real;
```

Indicate which of the following are valid assignment statements. Give the reason why each of the remaining statements is invalid.

a. `Age := 21;`
b. `IQ := Age + 100;`
c. `IQ := 120.5;`
d. `Age + IQ := 150;`
e. `Income := 22000;`
f. `Income := 100 * (Age + IQ);`
g. `Age := IQ / 3;`
h. `IQ := 3 * Age;`

2. Write and run a test program to illustrate what happens when values of one data type are assigned to variables of another type.

3. Suppose A, B, and Temp have been declared as integer variables. Indicate the contents of A and B at the end of each sequence of statements.

a.
```
A := 5;
B := -2;
A := A + B;
B := B - A;
```

b.
```
A := 31;
B := 26;
Temp := A;
A := B;
B := Temp;
```

c.
```
A := 0;
B := 7;
A := A + B MOD 2 * (-3);
B := B + 4 * A;
```

d.
```
A := -8;
B := 3;
Temp := A + B;
A := 3 * B;
B := A;
Temp := Temp + A + B;
```

4. Suppose X and Y are real variables and the assignments

```
X := 121.3;
Y := 98.6;
```

have been made. What **writeln** statements would cause the following output?

a.
```
The value of X is  121.3
```

b.
```
The sum of X and Y is  219.9
```

c.
```
X =      121.3
Y =       98.6
         -----
Total =  219.9
```

5. Assume the variable declaration section of a program is

```
VAR
  Age, Height : integer;
  Weight : real;
  Gender : char;
```

What output is created by the following program fragment?

```
Age := 23;
Height := 73;
Weight := 186.5;
Gender := 'M';
writeln ('Gender', Gender:10);
writeln ('Age', Age:14);
writeln ('Height', Height:11, ' inches');
writeln ('Weight', Weight:14:1, ' lbs');
```

6. Write a complete program that allows you to add five integers and then print

a. the integers. b. their sum. c. their average.

7. Assume Ch and Age have been appropriately declared. What output is produced by the following?

```
Ch := 'M';
Age := 21;
writeln ('******************************':40);
writeln ('*':11, '*' : 29);
write ('*':11, 'Name': 7, 'Age' :9);
writeln ('Gender' :9, '*': 4);
writeln ('*': 11, '----':7, '---': 9, '------':9, '*':4);
writeln;
write ('*':11, 'Jones':8, 'Age':8, Ch: 6, '*':7);
writeln;
writeln ('*': 11, '*': 29);
writeln ('******************************':40);
```

8. Assume the variable declaration section of a program is

```
VAR
  Weight1, Weight2 : integer;
  AverageWeight : real;
```

and the following assignment statements have been made:

```
Weight1 := 165;
Weight2 := 174;
AverageWeight := (Weight1 + Weight2) / 2;
```

   a. What output is produced by the following section of code?

```
writeln ('Weight');
writeln ('------');
writeln;
writeln (Weight1);
writeln (Weight2);
writeln;
writeln ('The average weight is', (Weight1 + Weight2) / 2);
```

   b. Write a segment of code to produce the following output (use Average-Weight).

```
            Weight
            ------

              165
              174
              ---
  Total       339

  The average weight is 169.5 pounds.
```

9. Assume the variable declaration section of a program is

```
VAR
  Letter : char;
```

and the following assignment has been made:

```
Letter := 'A';
```

What output is produced by the following segment of code?

```
writeln ('This reviews string formatting,':40);
writeln ('When a letter', Letter, 'is used,');
writeln ('Oops!':14, 'I forgot to format.':20);
writeln ('When a letter':22, Letter:2, 'is used,':9);
writeln ('it is a string of length one.':38);
```

10. Modify Example 2.2 to be

```
PROGRAM IntOverFlow;
VAR
  Num : integer;
BEGIN
  Num := maxint;
  writeln (Num);
  writeln (Num + 1);
  readln
END.
```

Run this program, and discuss the results.

11. Write a test program that allows you to examine the output for variables declared as different extended types. For example, if you have the declarations

```
VAR
  Num1 : single;
  Num2 : double;
```

and the assignments

```
Num1 := 10 / 7;
Num2 := 10 / 7;
```

what values are assigned to Num1 and Num2?

■ 2.3 Input

Earlier, "running a program" was subdivided into the three general categories of getting the data, manipulating it appropriately, and printing the results. Our work thus far has centered on creating output and manipulating data. We are now going to focus on how to get data for a program.

Input Statements

Data for a program are usually obtained from an input device, which can be a keyboard, terminal, card reader, disk, or tape. Your program heading will (probably) have the form

PROGRAM <program name>;

With this heading, input is expected from the keyboard by default. Later, we will see how input from a disk allows a file listing to become part of the program heading. When that happens, the form for a program heading is

PROGRAM <program name> (<file list>);

S The file list is optional. However, its use is recommended for documentation purposes.

The Turbo Pascal statements used to get data are **read** and **readln.** These statements are analogous to **write** and **writeln** for output. General forms for these *input statements* are

read (<variable name>);
read (<variable 1>, <variable 2>, . . . , <variable *n*>);
readln (<variable name>);
readln (<variable 1>, <variable 2>, . . . , <variable *n*>);
readln;

A simplified syntax diagram for **read** and **readln** statements is

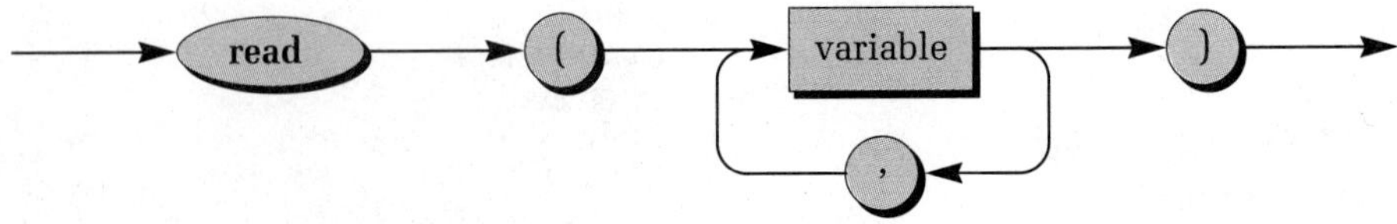

See Appendix 3 for a more detailed diagram.

When **read** or **readln** is used to get data, the value of the data item is stored in the indicated memory location. Data read into a program must match the type of variable in the variable list. To illustrate, if a variable declaration section includes

```
VAR
  Age : integer;
  Wage : real;
```

and the data items are

```
21        5.25
```

then

```
readln (Age, Wage);
```

results in

21	5.25
Age	Wage

Interactive Input

Interactive input refers to entering values from the keyboard while the program is running. Programs that get data from the keyboard are *interactive programs.* All interactive programs should use **readln** instead of **read** to get data. The **readln** statement causes the program to halt and wait for data items to be typed. A *prompt* will appear on the screen. For example, if you want to enter threescores at some point in a program, you can use

```
readln (Score1, Score2, Score3);
```

as a program statement. At this point, you must enter at least three integers and press <Enter> (or some sequence of integers and <Enter> until at least three numbers, with a space between each pair of integers, are read as data items). The remaining part of the program is then executed. To illustrate, the following program reads in three integers and prints the integers and their average as output.

```
PROGRAM ComputeAverage;

USES
  Crt;

CONST
  Skip = ' ';

VAR
  Score1, Score2, Score3 : integer;
  Average : real;

BEGIN
  ClrScr;
  readln (Score1, Score2, Score3);
  Average := (Score1 + Score2 + Score3) / 3;
  writeln;
  writeln (Skip:10, 'The numbers are', Score1:4, Score2:4, Score3:4);
  writeln;
  writeln (Skip:10, 'Their average is', Average:8:2);
  readln
END.
```

When the program runs, if you type in

```
89 90 91
```

and press <Enter>, the output is

```
The numbers are  89  90  91
Their average is   90.00
```

Interactive programs should have a prompting message to the user so the user knows what to do when a prompt appears. For example, the problem in the previous example can be modified by the lines

```
writeln ('Please enter 3 scores separated by spaces');
writeln ('and then press <Enter>.');
```

before the line

```
readln (Score1, Score2, Score3);
```

The screen will display the message

```
Please enter 3 scores separated by spaces
and then press <Enter>.
```

when the program is run.

Clearly stated screen messages to the person running a program are what make a program *user-friendly.* For long messages or several lines of output, you might wish to use **readln** as a complete statement to halt execution. When you press <Enter>, the program will continue. When **readln** is used for input, <Enter> must be pressed before program execution will continue.

The next example is a complete interactive program that illustrates the use of screen messages.

EXAMPLE 2.3

Pythagorean triples are sets of three integers that satisfy the Pythagorean theorem: that is, integers a, b, and c such that $a^2 + b^2 = c^2$. The set of integers 3, 4, 5 is such a triple because $3^2 + 4^2 = 5^2$. Formulas for generating Pythagorean triples are $a = m^2 - n^2$, $b = 2mn$, and $c = m^2 + n^2$, where m and n are positive integers such that $m > n$. The following program allows the user to enter values for m and n and then have the Pythagorean triple printed.

```
PROGRAM PythagoreanTriple;

USES
  Crt;

VAR
  M, N, A, B, C : integer;

BEGIN
  ClrScr;
  writeln ('Enter a positive integer and press <Enter>.');
  readln (N);
  write ('Enter a positive integer greater than ', N);
  writeln (' and press <Enter>.');
  readln (M);
  A := (M * M) - (N * N);
  B := 2 * M * N;
  C := (M * M) + (N * N);
  writeln;
  writeln ('For M = ', M, ' and N = ', N);
  writeln ('the Pythagorean triple is ', A:5, B:5, C:5);
  readln
END.
```

Sample runs of this program (using data 1,2 and 2,5) produce

```
Enter a positive integer and press <Enter>.
1
Enter a positive integer greater than 1 and press <Enter>.
2

For M = 2 and N = 1
the Pythagorean triple is     3    4    5

Enter a positive integer and press <Enter>.
2
Enter a positive integer greater than 2 and press <Enter>.
5

For M = 5 and N = 2
the Pythagorean triple is    21   20   29
```

COMMUNICATION AND STYLE TIPS

A variable or expression may be used as a field width specifier for formatting. When running interactive programs, this idea can be used to control desired accuracy as follows:

```
writeln ('How many places of accuracy?');
readln (Places);
    .
    .
    .
writeln ('Result is ', Result:Places+2:Places);
```

Reading Numeric Data

Reading numeric data into a program is reasonably straightforward. At least one blank must be used to separate numbers. The <Enter> character is read as a blank, so any sequence of numbers and spaces or <Enter> can be used to enter the required data.

Since the type of data items entered must match the data types for variables in an input statement, we must exercise caution when using both reals and integers as input. To illustrate, if a variable declaration section is

```
VAR
  A : integer;
  X : real;
```

and we wish to enter the data items 97.5 and 86, respectively, **readln** (X,A) achieves the desired result. However, **readln** (A,X) results in an error. Since A is of type **integer,** only the 97 is read into A. The next character is a period, and when an attempt is made to read this period into the memory location for X, a type mismatch error occurs. One exception is that an integer type can be read into a real type variable. However, it is stored as a real and must be used accordingly.

Character Sets

Before we look at reading character data, we need to examine the way in which character data are stored. In the **char** data type, each character in the set of allowable characters is associated with an integer. Thus, the sequence of characters is associated with a sequence of integers. The particular sequence used by a machine for this purpose is referred to as the *collating sequence* for that *character set.* The sequence used by Turbo Pascal is the American Standard Code for Information Interchange (ASCII). This collating sequence contains an ordering of the characters in a character set and is listed in Appendix 4. Fifty-two of these characters are letters, 10 are digits, and the rest are special characters, as shown in Table 2.6.

TABLE 2.6
ASCII code

b̸ ! " # $ % & ' ( ) * + , – . / 0 1 2 3 4 5 6 7 8 9 : ; < = > ? @

A B C D E F G H I J K L M N O P Q R S T U V W X Y Z [\ ] ^ — '

a b c d e f g h i j k l m n o p q r s t u v w x y z { | } ~

Note: Of the special characters, b̸ is the symbol to denote a blank.

Reading Character Data

Reading characters is much different from reading numeric data. The following features apply to reading data of type **char.**

1. Only one character can be read at a time.
2. Each blank is a separate character.
3. The <Enter> character is read as a blank.
4. Each digit of a number is read as a separate character.

If you want to read in a student's initials followed by three test scores

```
readln (FirstInitial, MiddleInitial, LastInitial);
readln (Score1, Score2, Score3);
```

accomplishes this. When program execution is halted, you type in something like

```
JDK
```

and press <Enter>; then type in three integers, such as

```
89 90 91
```

and press <Enter> again.

Some errors are caused by not being careful with character data. For example, suppose you want to enter three test scores followed by a student's initials. You might try the program statement

```
readln (Score1, Score2, Score3, FirstInitial, MiddleInitial, LastInitial);
```

When program execution halts for expected input, suppose you enter

```
89 90 91 JDK
```

When you try to print these values using

```
writeln (Score1, Score2:5, Score3:5);
writeln (FirstInitial, MiddleInitial, LastInitial);
```

the output is

```
89   90   91
 JD
```

because the blank following 91 is read as a character when an attempt is made to read FirstInitial. Note that the first three characters following 91 are a blank followed by 'J' and 'D'. This problem can (and should) be avoided by entering the scores on one line and the initials on a separate line. In general, you should use separate input lines for separate data. This topic of reading character data is expanded when text files are introduced in Chapter 6.

A NOTE OF INTEREST

Communication Skills Needed

Emphasis on communication has been increasing in almost every area of higher education. Evidence of this is the current trend toward "writing across the curriculum" programs implemented in many colleges and universities in the 1980s. Indications that this emphasis is shared among computer scientists was given by Paul M. Jackowitz, Richard M. Plishka, and James R. Sidbury, University of Scranton, when they stated, "Make it possible to write programs in English, and you will discover that programmers cannot write in English."

All computer science educators are painfully aware of the truth of this old joke. We want our students to be literate. We want them to have well-developed writing skills and the capacity to read technical journals in our area. But too often we produce skilled programmers whose communication skills are poor and who have almost no research skills. We must alleviate this problem. Since the organizational techniques used to write software are the same ones that should be used to write papers, computer science students should have excellent writing skills. We should exploit this similarity in skills to develop better writers.

Further, Janet Hartman of Illinois State University and Curt M. White of Indiana-Purdue University at Fort Wayne noted: "Students need to practice written and oral communication skills, both in communications classes and computer classes. Students should write system specifications, project specifications, memos, users' guides or anything else that requires them to communicate on both a nontechnical and technical level. They should do presentations in class and learn to augment their presentations with audiovisual aids."

On a more general note, the need for effective communication skills in computer science has been acknowledged in the 1991 curriculum guidelines of the Association for Computing Machinery, Inc. These guidelines state that "undergraduate programs should prepare students to apply their knowledge to specific, constrained problems and produce solutions. This includes the ability to . . . communicate [those] solution[s] to colleagues, professionals in other fields, and the general public."

Reading Strings

S Turbo Pascal permits reading textual data in strings as well as one character at a time. Strings may be declared by either

```
VAR
  Name : string;
```

or

```
VAR
  Name : string [<length>];
```

where <length> denotes the maximum number of characters in a string. If you know the longest string that you will be using will contain at most 30 characters, you can declare

```
VAR
  Name : string [30];
```

When a variable is declared to be of type **string,** 256 bytes of memory are allocated to this variable: one for the string length, and 255 bytes for up to 255 characters. For reasons of memory efficiency, it is usually better to declare a string length rather than to accept the default of 256 bytes. Thus, in

```
VAR
  Name : string [20];
```

21 bytes of memory are allocated: one for the string length, and 20 for the number of characters in a string.

With either declaration, string names can be entered by

```
writeln ('Enter your name and press <Enter>.');
readln (Name);
```

A note of caution is in order. If you wish to enter a string and a numeric value, you must make sure that the number is not part of the string. For example, using the declaration for Name having type **string** [20],

```
writeln ('Enter your name and age.    ');
readln (Name, Age);
```

could result in the user entering

```
Joan Smith 23
```

and then pressing <Enter>. Since the 23 is entered before column 20, it is considered part of the string of length 20. To avoid this problem, ask the user a separate question for each piece of information desired.

Exercises 2.3

1. Write a test program to see what happens when you try to store or print values that exceed their type ranges. For example, if Num is of type **word,** what happens if you use a value greater than 65535 or less than 0?

2. Assume a variable declaration section is

```
VAR
  Num1, Num2 : integer;
  Num3 : real;
  Ch : char;
```

and you wish to enter the data

```
15 65.3 -20
```

Explain what results from each of the following statements. Also indicate what values are assigned to appropriate variables.

a. `readln (Num1, Num3, Num2);`
b. `readln (Num1, Num2, Num3);`
c. `readln (Num1, Num2, Ch, Num3);`
d. `readln (Num2, Num3, Ch, Num2);`
e. `readln (Num2, Num3, Ch, Ch, Num2);`
f. `readln (Num3, Num2);`
g. `readln (Num1, Num3);`
h. `readln (Num1, Ch, Num3);`

3. Write a program statement to be used to print a message to the screen directing the user to enter data in the form used for Exercise 2.

4. Write an appropriate program statement (or statements) to produce a screen message, and write an appropriate input statement for each of the following.
   a. Desired input is the number of hours worked and hourly pay rate.
   b. Desired input is three positive integers followed by −999.
   c. Desired input is the price of an automobile and the state sales tax rate.
   d. Desired input is the game statistics for one basketball player. (Check with a coach to see what must be entered.)
   e. Desired input is a student's initials, age, height, weight, and gender.
   f. Desired input is a person's name and age.

5. Assume variables are declared as in Exercise 2. If an input statement is

```
readln (Num1, Num2, Ch, Num3);
```

indicate which lines of data do not result in an error message, then indicate the values of the variables. For those that produce an error, explain the error.

a. 83 95 100	d. 83 -72 93.5	g. 91 92 93 94
b. 83 95.0 100	e. 83.5	h. -76 -81 -16.5
c. 83 -72 93.5	f. 70 73 -80.5	

6. Why is it a good idea to print out values of variables that have been read into a program?
7. Write a test program that allows the user to enter her or his name, age, and social security number. Have these values printed by the program.
8. Write a complete program that will read your name and five test scores. Your program should then compute your test average and print out all information in a reasonable form with suitable messages.
9. Explain why it is a good idea to declare string variables to be of a maximum length (for example, **string**[30]) rather than to have the variables be of type **string**.
10. Write a short program to show how interaction with the user can be personalized by displaying messages containing the user's name.

■ 2.4 Using Constants

The word "constant" has several interpretations. In this section, it will refer to values defined in the **CONST** definition subsection of a program. Recall that a Turbo Pascal program consists of a program heading, a declaration section, and an executable section. The declaration section contains a variable declaration subsection (discussed in Section 1.5) and possibly a constant definition subsection. When both are used, the **CONST** subsection must precede the **VAR** subsection. We will now examine uses for constants defined in the **CONST** subsection.

Rationale for Uses

There are many reasons to use constants in a program. If a number is to be used frequently, the programmer may wish to give it a descriptive name in the **CONST** definition subsection and then use the descriptive name in the executable section, thus making the program easier to read. For example, if a program includes a segment that computes a person's state income tax and the state tax rate is 6.25 percent of taxable income, the **CONST** section might include

```
CONST
  StateTaxRate = 0.0625;
```

This defines both the value and type for StateTaxRate. In the executable portion of the program, the statement

```
StateTax := Income * StateTaxRate;
```

computes the state tax owed.

Perhaps the most important use of constants is for values that are currently fixed but subject to change for subsequent runs of the program. If such a value is defined in the **CONST** section, it can be used throughout the program. If the value changes later, only one change has to be made to keep the program current. This prevents the need to locate all uses of a constant in a program. Some examples might be

```
CONST
  MinimumWage = 4.25;
  SpeedLimit = 65;
  Price = 0.75;
  StateTaxRate = 0.0625;
```

Constants can also be used to name character strings that occur frequently in program output. Suppose a program needs to print two different company names. Instead of typing the names each time they are needed, the following definition could be used:

```
CONST
  Company1 = 'First National Bank of America';
  Company2 = 'Metropolitan Bank of New York';
```

Company1 and Company2 could then be used in **writeln** statements.

Constants may also be defined for later repeated use in making output more attractive. Included could be constants for underlining and for separating sections of output. Some definitions could be

```
CONST
  Underline = '----------------------------------';
  Splats = '***********************************';
```

To separate the output with asterisks, the statement

```
writeln (Splats, Splats);
```

could be used. In a similar fashion

```
writeln (Underline);
```

could be used for underlining.

Software Engineering Implications

The appropriate use of constants is consistent with principles of software engineering. Communication among teams of programmers is enhanced when program constants have been agreed upon. Each team should have a list of these constants for use as members work on their part of the system.

The maintenance phase of the software system life cycle is also aided by use of defined constants. Clearly, a large payroll system is dependent upon being able to perform computations that include deductions for federal tax, state tax, FICA, Medicare, health insurance, retirement options, and so on. If appropriate constants are defined for these deductions, system changes are easily made as necessary. For example, the current salary limit for deducting FICA taxes is $57,600. Since this amount changes regularly, one could define

```
CONST
  FICALimit = 57600.00
```

Program maintenance is then simplified by changing the value of this constant as the law changes.

Formatting Constants

Formatting numerical constants is identical to formatting reals and integers, as discussed in Section 1.6. Real constants are formatted as reals; integer constants,

A NOTE OF INTEREST

Defined Constants and Space Shuttle Computing

An excellent illustration of the utilization of defined constants in a program was given by J. F. ("Jack") Clemons, former manager of avionics flight software development and verification for the space shuttle on-board computers. In an interview with David Gifford, editor for *Communications of the ACM*, Clemons was asked, "Have you tried to restructure the software so that it can be changed easily?"

His response was, "By changing certain data constants, we can change relatively large portions of the software on a mission-to-mission basis. For example, we've designed the software so that characteristics like atmospheric conditions on launch day or different lift-off weights can be loaded as initial constants into the code. This is important when there are postponements or last-minute payload changes that invalidate the original inputs."

as integers. When a character string is defined as a constant, a single positive integer can be used for formatting. This integer establishes the field width for the character string and right justifies the character string in the output field. The following example illustrates formatting numerical constants in output.

EXAMPLE 2.4 This example shows how numerical constants can be formatted as part of the output of a program.

```
PROGRAM ConstantPrac;

USES
  Crt;

CONST
  CurrentYear = 1993;
  MinimumWage = 4.25;

BEGIN
  ClrScr;
  writeln ('The minimum wage in', CurrentYear:6, '  is',
           MinimumWage:6:2);
  readln
END.
```

When this program is run, the output is

```
The minimum wage in  1993 is  4.25
```

Exercises 2.4

1. One use of constants is for values that are used throughout a program but are subject to change over time (minimum wage, speed limit, and so on). List at least five items in this category that were not mentioned in this section.
2. Assume the **CONST** definition section of a program is

```
CONST
  CourseName = 'CPS 150';
  TotalPts = 100;
  Underline = '--------------------------------------';
```

You want to obtain the following output:

```
COURSE:             CPS 150       TEST #1
-----------------------------------------

TOTAL POINTS      100
```

Fill in the appropriate formatting positions in the following **writeln** statements to produce the indicated output.

```
writeln ('COURSE:':7, CourseName:    , 'TEST #1':13);
writeln (Underline:    );
writeln;
writeln ('TOTAL POINTS':12, TotalPts:   );
```

3. Using the **CONST** definition section in Exercise 2, what output is produced by the following segment of code?

```
writeln;
writeln (CourseName:10, 'TEST #2':20);
writeln (Underline);
writeln;
writeln ('Total points':15, TotalPts:15);
writeln ('My score':11, 93:19);
writeln ('Class average':16, 82.3:14:1);
```

4. Use the constant definition section to define appropriate constants for the following:

   a. Your name.
   b. Today's date.
   c. Your social security number.
   d. Your age.
   e. The name of your school.
   f. The number of students in your class.
   g. The average age of students in your class.
   h. The average hourly wage of steelworkers.
   i. The price of a new car.

■ 2.5 Standard Functions

Some standard operations required by programmers are squaring numbers, finding square roots of numbers, rounding numbers, and truncating numbers. Because these operations are so basic, all versions of Pascal provide *standard (built-in) functions* for them. Various versions of Pascal and other programming languages have different standard functions available, so you should always check on which functions can be used with a particular version. Appendix 2 lists the standard functions available in most versions.

A function can be used in a program if it appears in the form

<function name>(<argument>)

where *argument* is a value or variable with an assigned value. When a function is listed in this manner, it is said to be *invoked,* or *called.* A function is invoked by using it in a program statement. If, for example, you want to square the integer 5

```
sqr(5)
```

produces the desired result.

The syntax diagram for this is

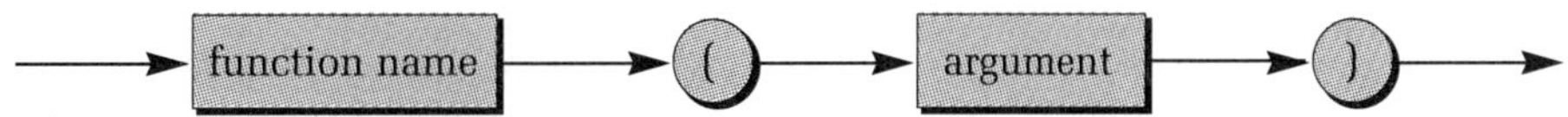

Many functions operate on numbers, starting with a given number and returning some associated value. Table 2.7 shows five standard functions, each with its argument type, data type of return, and an explanation of the value returned.

TABLE 2.7
Numeric function calls and return types

Function Call	Argument Type	Type of Return	Function Value
sqr(argument)	**real** or **integer**	Same as argument	Returns the square of the argument
7.0 **sqrt**(argument)	**real** or **integer** (nonnegative)	**real**	Returns the square root of the argument
abs(argument)	**real** or **integer**	Same as argument	Returns the absolute value of the argument
round(argument)	**real**	**integer**	Returns the value rounded to the nearest integer
trunc(argument)	**real**	**integer**	Returns the value truncated to an integer

Several examples of specific function expressions together with the value returned by each expression are depicted in Table 2.8.

TABLE 2.8
Values of function expressions

Expression	Value
`sqr(2)`	4
`sqr(2.0)`	4.0
`sqr(-3)`	9
`sqrt(25.0)`	5.0
`sqrt(25)`	5.0
`sqrt(0.0)`	0.0
`sqrt(-2.0)`	Not permissible
`abs(5.2)`	5.2
`abs(-3.4)`	3.4
`abs(-5)`	5
`round(3.78)`	4
`round(8.50)`	9
`round(-4.2)`	−4
`round(-4.7)`	−5
`trunc(3.78)`	3
`trunc(8.5)`	8
`trunc(-4.2)`	−4
`trunc(-4.7)`	−4

Using Functions

When a function is invoked, it produces a value in much the same way that 3 + 3 produces 6. Thus, use of a function should be treated similarly to use of a constant or value of an expression. Since function calls are not complete Turbo Pascal statements, they must be used within some statement. Typical uses are in assignment statements

```
X := sqrt(16.0);
```

in output statements

```
writeln (abs(-8):20);
```

or in arithmetic expressions

```
X := round(3.78) + trunc(-4.1);
```

Arguments of functions can be expressions, variables, or constants. However, be sure the argument is always appropriate. For example

```
A := 3.2;
X := sqrt(trunc(A));
```

is appropriate, but

```
A := -3.2;
X := sqrt(trunc(A));
```

produces an error since **trunc**(−3.2) has the value −3 and **sqrt**(−3) is not a valid expression.

The following example illustrates how functions can be used in expressions.

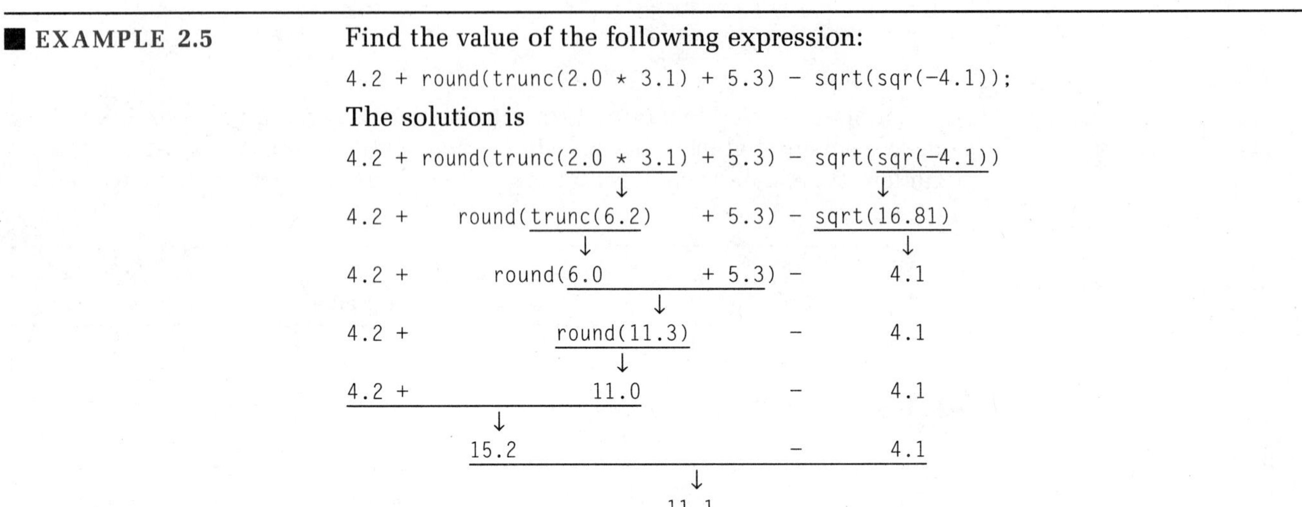

■ **EXAMPLE 2.5**

Find the value of the following expression:

```
4.2 + round(trunc(2.0 * 3.1) + 5.3) - sqrt(sqr(-4.1));
```

The solution is

```
4.2 + round(trunc(2.0 * 3.1) + 5.3) - sqrt(sqr(-4.1))
                    ↓                        ↓
4.2 +    round(trunc(6.2)     + 5.3) - sqrt(16.81)
                  ↓                          ↓
4.2 +       round(6.0         + 5.3) -      4.1
                        ↓
4.2 +            round(11.3)         -      4.1
                    ↓
4.2 +               11.0             -      4.1
          ↓
         15.2                        -      4.1
                           ↓
                          11.1
```

Character Functions

Ordering a character set requires associating an integer with each character. Data types ordered in some association with the integers are known as *ordinal data types.* Each integer is the ordinal of its associated character. Integers are therefore considered to be an ordinal data type. Character sets are also considered to be an ordinal data type, as shown in Table 2.9. In each case, the ordinal of the character appears to the left of the character.

TABLE 2.9
ASCII ordering of a character set

Ordinal	Character	Ordinal	Character	Ordinal	Character
32	b̸	64	@	96	‘
33	!	65	A	97	a
34	”	66	B	98	b
35	#	67	C	99	c
36	$	68	D	100	d
37	%	69	E	101	e
38	&	70	F	102	f
39	’	71	G	103	g
40	(	72	H	104	h
41	)	73	I	105	i
42	*	74	J	106	j
43	+	75	K	107	k
44	,	76	L	108	l
45	–	77	M	109	m
46	.	78	N	110	n
47	/	79	O	111	o
48	0	80	P	112	p
49	1	81	Q	113	q
50	2	82	R	114	r
51	3	83	S	115	s
52	4	84	T	116	t
53	5	85	U	117	u

TABLE 2.9
(continued)

Ordinal	Character	Ordinal	Character	Ordinal	Character
54	6	86	V	118	v
55	7	87	W	119	w
56	8	88	X	120	x
57	9	89	Y	121	y
58	:	90	Z	122	z
59	;	91	[	123	{
60	<	92	\	124	|
61	=	93	]	125	}
62	>	94	^	126	~
63	?	95	—		

Note: Codes 00–31 and 127 are nonprintable control characters.

Using ASCII, as shown in Table 2.9, the ordinal of a capital a ('A') is 65, the ordinal of the character representing the arabic number one ('1') is 49, the ordinal of a blank ('b̸') is 32, and the ordinal of a lowercase a ('a') is 97.

Turbo Pascal provides several standard functions that have arguments of ordinal type. They are listed in Table 2.10 together with a related function **chr** that returns a character when called.

TABLE 2.10
Function calls with ordinal arguments or character values

Function Call	Argument Type	Type of Result	Function Value
ord(argument)	Any ordinal type	**integer**	Ordinal corresponding to argument
pred(argument)	Any ordinal type	Same as argument	Predecessor of the argument
succ(argument)	Any ordinal type	Same as argument	Successor of the argument
chr(argument)	**integer**	**char**	Character associated with the ordinal of the argument

TABLE 2.11
Values of character functions

Expression	Value
`ord('E')`	69
`ord('9')`	57
`ord(9)`	9
`ord('>')`	62
`pred('N')`	M
`pred('A')`	@
`succ('(')`	)
`succ('!')`	"
`chr(74)`	J
`chr(32)`	b̸
`chr(59)`	;
`chr(114)`	r

Again using the ASCII collating sequence shown in Table 2.9, we can determine the value of these functions, as shown in Table 2.11.

Variables and variable expressions can be used as arguments for functions. For example, if Ch is a **char** variable and the assignment statement

```
Ch := 'D';
```

is made, then **ord**(Ch) has the value 68.

Now let's consider a short program that allows the use of the standard functions **ord, pred, succ,** and **chr.**

```
PROGRAM FunctionTest;

USES
  Crt;

VAR
  Num : integer;
  Ch : char;
```

```
BEGIN
  ClrScr;
  Ch := 'C';
  writeln ('Ord of C is', ord(Ch):5);
  writeln ('Succ of C is', succ(Ch):4);
  writeln ('Pred of C is', pred(Ch):4);
  writeln ('Chr of 67 is', chr(67):4);
  Num := 0;
  writeln ('The ordinal of Num is ', ord(Num));
  readln
END.
```

When this program is run, the output is

```
Ord of C is   67
Succ of C is   D
Pred of C is   B
Chr of 67 is   C
The ordinal of Num is 0
```

Note that **chr**(n) is nonprintable for $n < 32$ or $n > 126$.

One of the uses for functions **chr** and **ord** is to convert between uppercase and lowercase letters. Closely related is the conversion of a digit (entered as a **char** value) to its integer value. In the next example, we show how to convert an uppercase letter to lowercase. Other conversions are deferred to the exercises.

■ EXAMPLE 2.6

To show how functions **chr** and **ord** can be used to convert an uppercase letter to lowercase, let's assume that our task is to convert the letter 'H' to the letter 'h'. Using the ASCII chart shown in Table 2.9, we first note that the ordinal of 'H' is 72. We subtract the ordinal of 'A' from this to obtain

```
ord('') - ord('A')
```

which is

```
72 - 65 = 7
```

We now add the ordinal of 'a' to get

```
ord('H') - ord('A') + ord('a')
```

which yields

```
72 - 65 + 97 = 104
```

This is the ordinal of 'h'. It can be converted to the letter by using **chr**. Thus

```
chr(ord('H') - ord('A') + ord('a'))
```

produces the letter 'h'.

In general, the following is sufficient for converting from uppercase to lowercase:

```
Lowercase := chr(ord(Uppercase) - ord('A') + ord('a'));
```

Note that if you always use the same ASCII ordering

```
- ord('A') + ord('a')
```

could be replaced by the constant 32. If you choose to do this, it should be done in the **CONST** section. A typical definition is

```
CONST
  UpperToLowerShift = 32;
```

You would then write the lowercase conversion as

```
Lowercase := chr(ord(Uppercase) + UpperToLowerShift);
```

A NOTE OF INTEREST

Debugging or Sleuthing?

Investigating why programs don't work as expected requires ingenuity. The reason can be quite bizarre. To illustrate, consider two situations reported by Jon Bentley in *Communications of the ACM.*

1. "When a programmer used his new computer terminal, all was fine when he was sitting down, but he couldn't log in to the system when he was standing up. That behavior was 100 percent repeatable: he could always log in when sitting and never when standing."
2. "A banking system had worked for quite some time, but halted the first time it was used on international data. Programmers spent days scouring the code, but they couldn't find any stray command that would return control to the operating system."

What do you think are possible solutions? The answers can be found in Programming Problems and Projects for this chapter.

String Functions

S Turbo Pascal provides several functions for working with strings. Recall, **string** (or **string** [<n>]) is a data type. Variables of this type may be assigned a sequence of characters. A string containing only one blank is an *empty string.* To see how a string can be declared and used, let's consider the following program:

```
PROGRAM StringPrac;

USES
  Crt;

VAR
  Name : string [20];

BEGIN
  ClrScr;
  writeln ('Enter your name and press <Enter>.');
  readln (Name);
  writeln (Name);
  readln
END.
```

A sample run of this program yields

```
Enter your name and press <Enter>.
Mary Jones
Mary Jones
```

The first string function we examine is **length.** The correct form for using **length** is

length(<argument>);

where argument is a string constant or a variable of type **string.** When this function is called, it returns the number of characters contained in the argument. Thus

```
length('This is a test.');
```

would return the value 15. To see how **length** works with a variable, modify the previous program by adding the code

```
write ('The length of string ', Name, ' is ');
writeln (length(Name));
```

after the line

```
writeln (Name);
```

When appropriately inserted in the program, a sample run is

```
Enter your name and press <Enter>.
Mary Jones
The length of string Mary Jones is 10
```

The second string function we examine is **concat.** This is short for *concatenation,* which means joining strings one after another. The form for using **concat** is

concat(<string 1>, <string 2>, . . . , <string n>);

When this function is called, it returns a single string that starts with the first letter of string 1 and ends with the last letter of string n. The following example illustrates a use of this function.

■ **EXAMPLE 2.7**

This program has the user enter a first name and a last name and then prints the full name in two different ways: first name first, and last name first.

```
PROGRAM ConcatPrac;

USES
  Crt;

VAR
  FirstName, LastName, FullName : string;

BEGIN
  ClrScr;
  writeln ('Enter your first name and press <Enter>.');
  readln (FirstName);
  writeln ('Enter your last name and press <Enter>.');
  readln (LastName);
  FullName := concat(FirstName, ' ', LastName);
  writeln (FullName);
  FullName := concat(LastName, ', ', FirstName);
  writeln (FullName);
  readln
END.
```

A sample run of this program yields

```
Enter your first name and press <Enter>.
Mary
Enter your last name and press <Enter>.
Jones
Mary Jones
Jones, Mary
```

Note how the strings ' ' and ', ' are used in **concat** to make the concatenated strings have the correct form.

Several more string functions are available in Turbo Pascal and will be developed in Section 8.3. Until then, we restrict work with string functions to **length** and **concat.**

Exercises 2.5

1. Find the value of each of the following expressions.
   - **a.** `abs(-11.2) + sqrt(round(15.51))`
   - **b.** `trunc(abs(-14.2))`
   - **c.** `4 * 11 MOD (trunc(trunc(8.9) / sqrt(16)))`
   - **d.** `sqr(17 DIV 5 * 2)`
   - **e.** `-5.0 + sqrt(5 * 5 - 4 * 6) / 2.0`
   - **f.** `3.1 * 0.2 - abs(-4.2 * 9.0 / 3.0)`
2. Write a test program that illustrates what happens when an inappropriate argument is used with a function. Be sure to include something like **ord**(15.3).
3. Two standard algebraic problems come from the Pythagorean theorem and the quadratic formula. Assume variables *a*, *b*, and *c* have been declared in a program. Write Turbo Pascal expressions that allow you to evaluate
   - **a.** the length of the hypotenuse of a right triangle

     $(\sqrt{a^2 + b^2})$
   - **b.** both solutions to the quadratic formula

     $$\frac{-b \pm \sqrt{b^2 - 4ac}}{2a}$$
4. Indicate whether the following are valid or invalid expressions. Find the value of each valid expression; explain why the others are invalid.
   - **a.** `-6 MOD (sqrt(16))`
   - **b.** `8 DIV (trunc(sqrt(65)))`
   - **c.** `sqrt(63 MOD (2))`
   - **d.** `abs(-sqrt(sqr(3) + 7))`
   - **e.** `sqrt(16 DIV (-3))`
   - **f.** `sqrt(sqr(-4))`
   - **g.** `round(14.38 * 10) / 10`
   - **h.** `length(Is this a string?);`
   - **i.** `concat('Kyler', 'Jesse');`
5. The standard function **round** permits you to round to the nearest integer. Write an expression that permits you to round the real number X to the nearest tenth.
6. Using ASCII, find the values of each of the following expressions.
   - **a.** `ord(13 + 4 MOD 3)`
   - **b.** `pred(succ('E'))`
   - **c.** `succ(pred('E'))`
   - **d.** `ord(5)`
   - **e.** `ord('5')`
   - **f.** `chr(ord('+'))`
   - **g.** `ord(chr(40))`
7. Assume the variable declaration section of a program is

   ```
   VAR
     X : real;
     A : integer;
     Ch : char;
   ```

   What output is produced by each of the following program fragments?
   - **a.**
     ```
     X := -4.3;
     writeln (X:6:2, abs(X):6:2, trunc(X):6, round(X):6);
     ```

b.
```
X := -4.3;
A := abs(round(X));
writeln (ord(A));
writeln (ord('A'));
```

c.
```
Ch := chr(76);
writeln (Ch:5, pred(Ch):5, succ(Ch):5);
```

8. Write a complete program to print each uppercase letter of the alphabet and its ordinal in the collating sequence used by your machine's version of Turbo Pascal.

9. Using ASCII, show how each of the following conversions can be made.
   a. A lowercase letter converted to its uppercase equivalent.
   b. A digit entered as a **char** value converted to its indicated numeric value.

10. Write a test program to determine whether or not the string function **length** counts blanks at the beginning or at the end of a string entered from the keyboard. Discuss your results.

The following Communication and Style Tips provides a quick reference to writing styles and suggestions. These tips are intended to stimulate rather than to terminate your imagination.

COMMUNICATION AND STYLE TIPS

1. Use descriptive identifiers. Words (Sum, Score, Average) are easier to understand than letters (A, B, C or X, Y, Z.)
2. Constants can be used to create neat, attractive output. For example

```
CONST
  Splats = '*****************************';
  Underline = '------------------------';
  Border = '*                           *';
```

3. Use the constant definition section to define an appropriately named blank, and use it to control line spacing for output. Thus, you could have

```
CONST
  Skip = ' ';
  Indent = ' ';
```

and then output statements could be

```
writeln (Skip:20, <message>, Skip:10, <message>);
```

or

```
writeln (Indent:20, <message>, Skip:10, <message>);
```

4. Output of a column of numeric values of any real data type should have decimal points in a line.

```
 14.32
181.50
 93.63
```

5. Output can be made more attractive by using columns, left and right margins, underlining, and blank lines.
6. Extra **writelns** at the beginning and end of the executable section will separate desired output from other messages:

```
BEGIN
  writeln;
          .
          . (program body here)
          .
  writeln
END.
```

FOCUS ON PROGRAM DESIGN

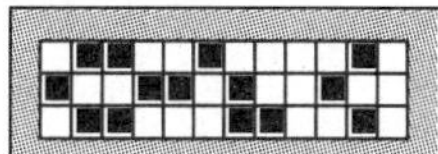

Complete programs are used to illustrate concepts developed throughout the text. In each case, a typical problem is stated. A solution is developed in pseudocode and illustrated with a structure chart. Module specifications are written for appropriate modules. Now, on to the problem for this chapter.

Let's write a complete program to find the unit price for a pizza. Input for the program consists of the price and size of the pizza. Size is the diameter of the pizza ordered. Output consists of the price per square inch. A first-level development is

1. Get the data
2. Perform the computations
3. Print the results

A structure chart for this problem is given in Figure 2.2.

FIGURE 2.2
Structure chart for the pizza problem

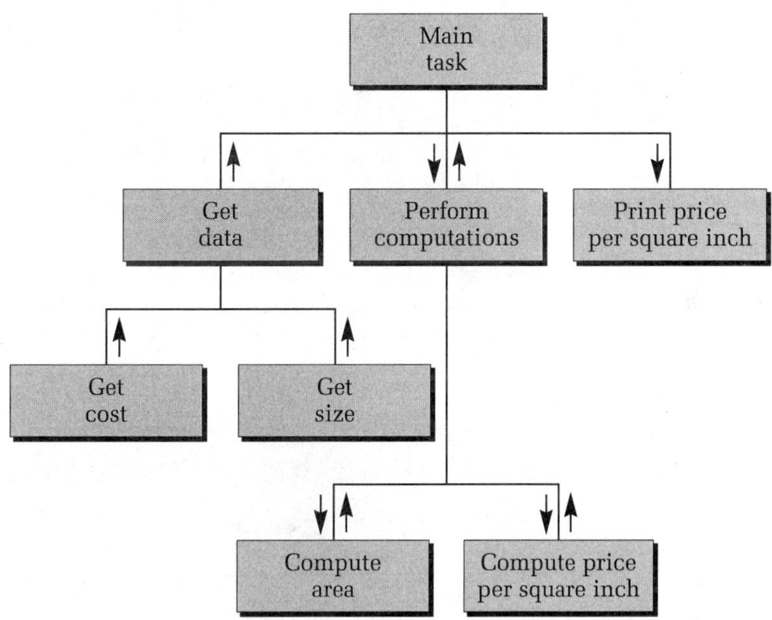

Module specifications for the main modules are

1. Get Data Module
Data received: None
Information returned: Cost
Size
Logic: Have the user enter cost and size.

2. Perform Computations Module
Data received: Cost
Size
Information returned: Price per square inch
Logic: Given the diameter, find the radius.
Compute the area using Area = Pi * Radius * Radius.
Price per square inch is found by dividing Cost by Area.

3. Print Results Module
   Data received: PricePerSquareInch
   Information required: None
   Logic: Print the price per square inch.

Further refinement of the pseudocode produces

1. Get the data
   1.1 get cost
   1.2 get size
2. Perform the computations
   2.1 compute area
   2.2 compute unit price

Step 3 of the pseudocode ("Print the results") only requires printing the price per square inch, so no further development is required.

A complete program for this is

```
PROGRAM PizzaCost;

USES
  Crt;

VAR
  Size, Radius, Cost, Area,
  PricePerSquareInch : real;

BEGIN
  ClrScr;

  {  This module gets the data.  }
  writeln ('Enter the pizza price and press <Enter>.');
  readln (Cost);
  writeln ('Enter the pizza size and press <Enter>.');
  readln (Size);

  {  This module computes the unit price.  }
  Radius := Size / 2;
  Area := Pi * sqr(Radius);
  PricePerSquareInch := Cost / Area;

  {  This module prints the results.  }
  writeln ('The price per square inch is $',
            PricePerSquareInch:4:2);
  readln
END.
```

A sample run of this program yields

```
Enter the pizza price and press <Enter>.
10.50
Enter the pizza size and press <Enter>.
16
The price per square inch is $0.05
```

■ Summary

Key Terms

argument
assignment statement
character set
collating sequence: ASCII
concatenation
constant
empty string
input statement

integer arithmetic operations: +, −, *, **MOD, DIV**
interactive input
interactive program
invoke (call)
memory location
mixed-mode expression
ordinal data type
overflow
prompt
real arithmetic operations: +, −, *, /
self-documenting code
standard (built-in) function
underflow
user-friendly
variable
variable dictionary

Keywords

abs	**length**	**read**	**sqrt**
chr	**MOD**	**readln**	**succ**
concat	**ord**	**round**	**trunc**
DIV	**pred**	**sqr**	

Key Concepts

- Operations and priorities for data of type **integer** and **real** are summarized as follows:

Data Type	Operations	Priority
integer	*, **MOD, DIV**	1. Evaluate in order from left to right.
	+, −	2. Evaluate in order from left to right.
real	*, /	1. Evaluate in order from left to right.
	+, −	2. Evaluate in order from left to right.

- Mixed-mode expressions return values of type **real.**
- Priority for order of operations on mixed-mode expressions is
  1. *, /, **MOD, DIV** in order from left to right
  2. +, − in order from left to right
- Overflow is caused by a value too large for computing on a particular machine.
- Underflow is caused by a value too small (close to zero) for computing. These numbers are automatically replaced by zero.
- A memory location can have a name that can be used to refer to the contents of the location.
- The name of a memory location is different from the contents of the memory location.
- Self-documenting code is code that is written using descriptive identifiers.
- Assignment statements are used to assign values to memory locations; for example

```
Sum := 30 + 60;
```

- Variables and variable expressions can be used in output statements.
- The **readln** statement is used to get data. Correct form is
  readln (<variable name>);
  readln (<variable 1>, <variable 2>, . . . , <variable *n*>);
- The statement **readln** (<variable name>) causes a value to be transferred to the variable location.
- Interactive input expects data items to be entered from the keyboard at appropriate times during execution of the program.
- Data types for variables in a **readln** statement should match data items read as input.
- Appropriate uses for constants in the **CONST** definition section include frequently used numbers; current values subject to change over time (for example, Minimum Wage = 4.25); and character strings for output.
- Character strings are formatted using a single colon.
- Five standard numeric functions available in Turbo Pascal are **sqr, sqrt, abs, round,** and **trunc.**
- Functions can be used in assignment statements

```
X := sqrt(16.0);
```

in output statements

```
writeln (abs(-8):20);
```

and in arithmetic expressions

```
X := round(3.78) + trunc(-4.1);
```

- Four standard character functions available in Turbo Pascal are **ord, pred, succ,** and **chr.**
- Two string-handling functions are **length** and **concat.**

■ Programming Problems and Projects

Write a complete Turbo Pascal program for each of the following problems. Each program should use one or more **readln** statements to obtain necessary values. Each **readln** should be preceded by an appropriate prompting message.

1. Susan purchases a computer for $985. The sales tax on the purchase is 5.5 percent. Compute and print the total purchase price.
2. Find and print the area and perimeter of a rectangle that is 4.5 feet long and 2.3 feet wide. Print both rounded to the nearest tenth of a foot.
3. Compute and print the number of minutes in a year.
4. Light travels at $3*10^8$ meters per second. Compute and print the distance that a light beam travels in one year. (This is called a light year.)
5. The 1927 New York Yankees won 110 games and lost 44. Compute the team's winning percentage, and print it rounded to three decimal places.
6. A 10-kilogram object is traveling at 12 meters per second. Compute and print its momentum. (Momentum is mass times velocity.)
7. Convert 98.0 degrees Fahrenheit to degrees Celsius.
8. Given a positive number, print its square and square root.
9. The Golden Sales Company pays its salespeople $0.27 for each item they sell. Given the number of items sold by a salesperson, print the amount of pay due.
10. Given the length and width of a rectangle, print its area and perimeter.
11. The kinetic energy of a moving object is given by

    $KE = (\frac{1}{2})mv^2$

    Given the mass m and the speed v of an object, find its kinetic energy.
12. Miss Lovelace wants you to write a program to enable her to balance her checkbook. She wishes to enter a beginning balance, five letters for an abbreviation for the recipient of the check, and the amount of the check. Given this information, write a program that will find the new balance in her checkbook.
13. A supermarket wants to install a computerized weighing system in its produce department. Input to this system will consist of a three-letter identifier for the type of produce, the weight of the produce purchase (in pounds), and the cost per pound of the produce. A typical input screen is

```
Enter each of the following:

Description <Enter>
ABC
Weight <Enter>
2.0
Cost/lb. <Enter>
1.98
```

A NOTE OF INTEREST

Debugging or Sleuthing? (Answers)

1. "The problem was in the terminal's keyboard: the tops of two keys were switched. When the programmer was seated, he was a touch-typist and the problem went unnoticed, but when he stood, he was led astray by hunting and pecking."

2. "When [the programmers] observed the behavior more closely, they found that the problem occurred as they entered data for the country of Ecuador: when the user typed the name of the capital city (Quito), the program interpreted that as a request to quit the run!"

Print a label showing the input information along with the total cost of the purchase. The label should appear as follows:

```
%%%%%%%%%%%%%%%%%%%%%%%%%%%%%%%%%%%%%%%%%%%

         Penny Spender Supermarket
             Produce Department

  ITEM      WEIGHT       COST/lb      COST
   ABC      2.0 lb        $1.98      $3.96

                 Thank you!

%%%%%%%%%%%%%%%%%%%%%%%%%%%%%%%%%%%%%%%%%%%
```

14. The New Wave Computer Company sells its product, the NW-PC, for $675. In addition, it sells memory-expansion cards for $69.95, disk drives for $198.50, and software packages for $34.98 each. Given the number of memory cards, disk drives, and software packages desired by a customer purchasing an NW-PC, print out a bill of sale that appears as follows:

```
***************************
    New Wave Computers

  ITEM                COST
1  NW-PC           $ 675.00
2  Memory card       139.90
1  Disk Drive        198.50
4  Software          139.92
                    -------

       TOTAL       $1153.32
```

15. Write a test program that allows you to see the characters contained within the character set of your computer. Given a positive integer, you can use the **chr** function to determine the corresponding character. On most computers, only integers less than 255 are valid for this. Also, remember that most character sets contain some unprintable characters, such as ASCII values less than 32. Print your output in the form

```
Character number nnn is x.
```

16. Mr. Vigneault, a coach at Shepherd High School, is working on a program that can be used to assist cross-country runners in analyzing their times. As part of the program, a coach enters elapsed times for each runner, given in units of minutes, seconds, and hundredths. In a 5000 meter (5K) race, elapsed times are entered at the one-mile and two-mile marks. These elapsed

times are then used to compute "splits" for each part of the race—that is, how long it takes a runner to run each of the three race segments.

Write a complete program that will accept three times, given in units of minutes, seconds, and hundredths, as input and then produce output that includes the split for each race segment. Typical input is

```
Runner number          234
Mile times:       1    5:34.22
                  2    11:21.67
Finish time:           17:46.85
```

Typical output is

```
Runner number          234
Split one              5:34.22
Split two              5:47.45
Split three            6:25.18
Finish time            17:46.85
```

■ Communication in Practice

1. Modify one of the programs you have written for this chapter by changing all constant and variable identifiers to single-letter identifiers. Exchange your modified program with another student who has done the same thing. After reading the exchanged program, discuss the use of meaningful identifiers with the other student. Suggest identifiers for the program you are reading.
2. Remove all documentation from a program you have written for this chapter. Exchange this version with another student who has done the same thing. Write documentation for the exchanged program. Compare your documentation with that originally written for the program. Discuss the differences and similarities with the other student.
3. Find one of the early programs in your Turbo Pascal User's Guide (Program MyThird, pages 26–27, if you are using version 6.0). Write complete documentation for this program. Compare your results with the results of another student who performed the same task.
4. Many (but not all) instructors in beginning computer science courses encourage their students to use meaningful identifiers when writing code. It is natural to wonder to what extent this practice is followed outside the educational world. Investigate this issue by contacting several programmers who work for nearby companies. Prepare a complete written report of your conversations for distribution to class members. Include charts that summarize your findings.

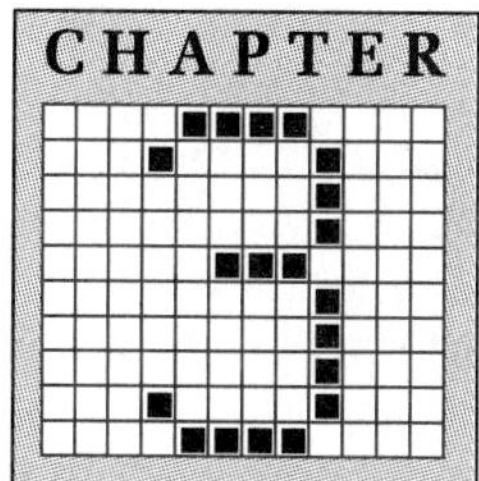

Subprograms: Procedures and Functions for Problem Solving

CHAPTER OUTLINE

Recall from Section 1.3 the process of solving a problem by stepwise refinement of tasks into subtasks. This top-down design method is especially suitable for writing Pascal programs to solve problems using subprograms.

This concept is not difficult to understand. A *subprogram* is a program within a program and is provided by most programming languages. Each subprogram should complete some task, the nature of which can range from simple to complex. You could have a subprogram that prints only a line of data, or you could rewrite an entire program as a subprogram. The main idea is to use a subprogram to perform some specific task.

3.1 Program Design

Modularity

We have previously discussed and illustrated the process of solving a problem by top-down design. Using this method, we divide the main task into major subtasks and then continue to divide the subtasks (stepwise refinement) into smaller subtasks until all subtasks can be easily performed. Once an algorithm for solving a problem has been developed using top-down design, the programmer then writes code to translate the general solution into a Pascal program.

As you have seen, code written to perform one well-defined subtask is referred to as a module. One should be able to design, code, and test each module in a program independently from the rest of the program. In this sense, a module is a subprogram containing all definitions and declarations needed to perform the indicated subtask. Everything required for the subtask (but not needed in other parts of the program) can be created in the subprogram. Consequently, the definitions and declarations have meaning only when the module is being used.

A program that has been created using modules to perform various tasks is said to possess *modularity.* In general, modular programs are easier to test, debug, and correct than programs that are not modular because each independent module can be tested by running it from a test driver. Then, once the modules are running correctly, they can become part of a longer program. This independent testing of modules is referred to as *bottom-up testing.*

Structured Programming

Structured programming is the process of developing a program where emphasis is placed on the communication between independent modules. Connections between these modules are specified in parameter lists and are usually controlled by the main program. Structured programming is especially suitable for large programs being worked on by teams. By carefully designing the modules and specifying what information is to be received by and returned from each module, a team of programmers can independently develop their module and then have it connect to the complete program.

The remainder of this chapter is devoted to seeing how subprograms can be written to accomplish specific tasks. There are two types of subprograms in Pascal: procedures and functions. We will first examine the writing and use of procedures. We will then learn how to write user-defined functions. (We discussed built-in functions in Section 2.5.)

A NOTE OF INTEREST

Structured Programming

From 1950 to the early 1970s, programs were designed and written on a linear basis. A program written and designed on such a basis can be called an unstructured program. Structured programming, on the other hand, organizes a program around separate semi-independent modules that are linked together by a single sequence of simple commands.

In 1964, mathematicians Corrado Bohm and Guiseppe Jacopini proved that any program logic, regardless of complexity, can be expressed by using sequence, selection, and iteration. This result is termed the structure theorem. This result, combined with the efforts of Edger W. Dijkstra, led to a significant move toward structured programming and away from the use of **GOTO** statements.

In fact, in a letter to the editor of *Communications of the ACM* (Volume 11, March 1968), Dijkstra stated that the **GOTO** statement "should be abolished from all 'higher level' programming languages . . . . [The **GOTO** statement] is just too primitive; it is too much an invitation to make a mess of one's program."

The first time structured programming concepts were applied to a large-scale data processing application was the IBM Corporation's "New York Times Project" from 1969 to 1971. Using these techniques, programmers posted productivity figures from four to six times higher than those of the average programmer. In addition, the error rate was a phenomenally low 0.0004 per line of coding.

■ 3.2 Procedures as Subprograms

Procedures can be used as subprograms for a number of purposes. Two significant uses are to facilitate the top-down design philosophy of problem solving and to avoid having to write repeated segments of code.

Procedures facilitate problem solving. Recall the Focus on Program Design problem in Chapter 2. In that problem, you were asked to compute the unit cost for a pizza. The main modules were

1. Get the data
2. Perform the computations
3. Print the results

A procedure can be written for each of these tasks, and the program can then call each procedure as needed. Thus, the main portion of the program would have the form

```
BEGIN {  Main program  }
  GetData (<parameter list>);
  PerformComputations (<parameter list>);
  PrintResults (<parameter list>)
END.  {  of main program  }
```

This makes it easy to see and understand the main tasks of the program.

Before learning how to write procedures and the significance of the "parameter list" in the previous program segment, a few comments are in order. First, once you develop the ability to write and use subprograms, you will usually write programs by writing the main program first. Your main program should be written so it can be easily read by a nonprogrammer but still contains enough structure to enable a programmer to know what to do if asked to write code for the tasks. In this sense, it is not necessary for a person reading the main program to understand *how* a subprogram accomplishes its task; it need only be apparent *what* the subprogram does.

Second, we should briefly consider the problem of data flow. The most difficult aspect of learning to use subprograms is handling transmission of data. Recall from the structure charts used earlier that arrows indicate if data are received by and/or sent from a module. Also, each module specification indicates if data are received by that module and if information is sent from it. Since a subprogram will be written to accomplish the task of each module, we must be able to transmit data as indicated. Once you have developed this ability, using procedures and functions becomes routine.

Form and Syntax

Procedures are placed in the declaration section of the main program. The form for a procedure is

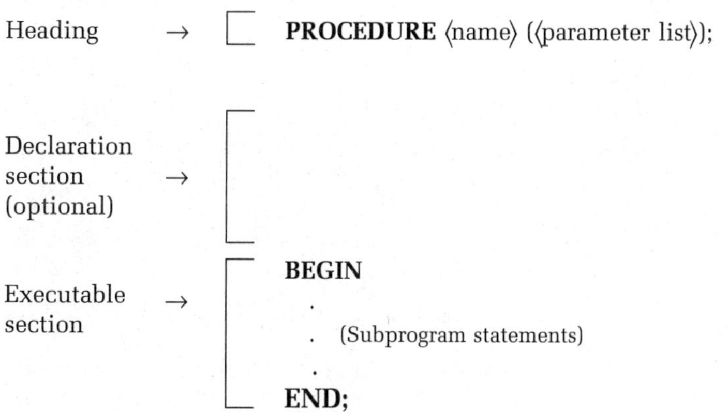
Heading →
PROCEDURE ⟨name⟩ (⟨parameter list⟩);
Declaration section (optional) →
Executable section →
BEGIN
(Subprogram statements)
END;

The syntax diagram is

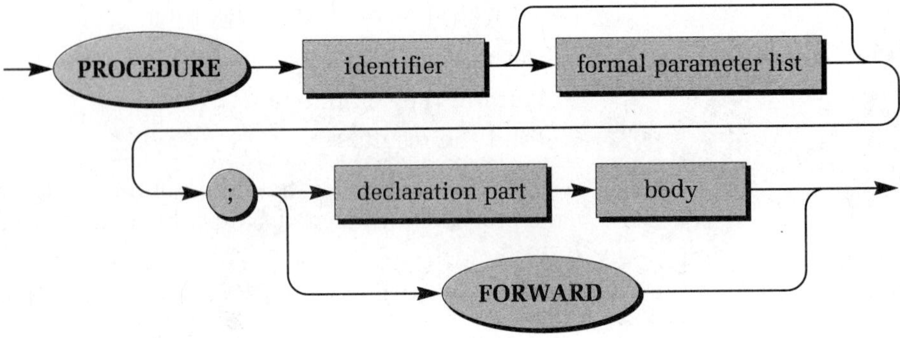

Procedures without Parameters

Some procedures are written without parameters because they require no data transmission to or from the main program or any other subprogram. Typically, these procedures print headings or closing messages for output. For example, suppose you are writing a program for Our Lady of Mercy Hospital and you wish the billing statement for each patient to have the heading

```
/////////////////////////////////////////
/                                       /
/       Our Lady of Mercy Hospital      /
/       --------------------------      /
/                                       /
/           1306 Central City           /
/          Phone (416) 333-5555         /
/                                       /
/////////////////////////////////////////
```

A procedure DisplayHeading can be written to print this message, and you can then call it from the main program when needed by

```
DisplayHeading;
```

The procedure to perform this task is

```
PROCEDURE DisplayHeading;

  CONST
    Marks = '/////////////////////////////////////////';
    Edge = '/                                       /';
    Skip = ' ';

  BEGIN
    writeln;
    writeln (Skip:10, Marks);
    writeln (Skip:10, Edge);
    writeln (Skip:10, '/', Skip:7,
             'Our Lady of Mercy Hospital', Skip:6, '/');
    writeln (Skip:10, '/', Skip:7,
             '--------------------------', Skip:6, '/');
    writeln (Skip:10, Edge);
    writeln (Skip:10, '/', Skip:11, '1306 Central City',
             Skip:11, '/');
    writeln (Skip:10, '/', Skip:10, 'Phone (416) 333-5555',
             Skip:9, '/');
    writeln (Skip:10, Edge);
```

```
    writeln (Skip:10, Marks);
    writeln
  END;
```

Later we will see how to draw a box of any size using any character for the border.

Parameters

Parameters are used so that values of variables may be transmitted, or passed, from the main program to the procedure and from the procedure to the main
7.0 program. If values are to be passed only from the main program to the procedure, the parameters are called *value parameters.* If values are to be changed in the main program, the parameters are called *variable parameters.*

When using parameters with procedures, the following should be noted:

1. The number and order of parameters in the parameter list must match the number and order of variables or values used when calling the procedure from the main program.
2. The type of parameters must match the corresponding type of variables or values used when calling the procedure from the main program.
3. The parameter types are declared in the procedure heading.

Parameters contained in the procedure are *formal parameters.* Formal parameters can be thought of as blanks in the heading of the procedure waiting to receive values from actual parameters in a calling program. Parameters contained in the procedure call from the main program are *actual parameters.* Actual parameters are also referred to as arguments.

To illustrate formal and actual parameters used with procedures, consider the following complete program.

```
PROGRAM ProcDemo;

USES
  Crt;

VAR
  Num1, Num2 : integer;
  Num3 : real;

{*******************************************}

PROCEDURE PrintNum (N1, N2 : integer;
                    N3 : real);
  BEGIN
    writeln;
    writeln ('Number 1 = ', N1:3);
    writeln ('Number 2 = ', N2:3);
    writeln ('Number 3 = ', N3:6:2)
  END;  {  of PROCEDURE PrintNum  }

{*******************************************}

BEGIN  {  Main program  }
  ClrScr;
  Num1 := 5;
  Num2 := 8;
  Num3 := Num2 / Num1;
  PrintNum (Num1, Num2, Num3);
  readln
END.  {  of main program  }
```

When this program is run, the output is

```
Number 1 =    5

Number 2 =    8

Number 3 =    1.60
```

In this program, N1, N2, and N3 are formal parameters and Num1, Num2, and Num3 are actual parameters. Now let's examine the relationship between the parameter list in the procedure

```
PROCEDURE PrintNum (N1, N2 : integer; N3 : real);
```

and the procedure call in the main program

```
PrintNum (Num1, Num2, Num3);
```

In this case, Num1 corresponds to N1, Num2 corresponds to N2, and Num3 corresponds to N3. Notice that both the number and type of variables in the parameter list correspond with the number and type of variables listed in the procedure call.

Value Parameters

The preceding procedure demonstrates the use of value parameters or of one-way transmission of values. Different memory areas have been set aside for the variables Num1, Num2, and Num3 and for N1, N2, and N3. Thus, initially we have

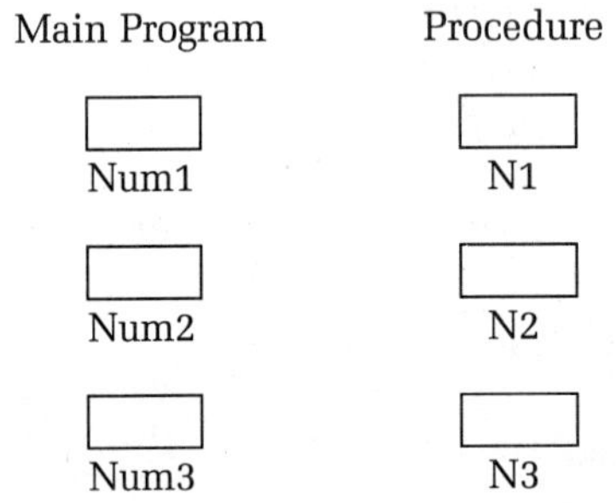

Main Program	Procedure
[ ] Num1	[ ] N1
[ ] Num2	[ ] N2
[ ] Num3	[ ] N3

The assignment statements

```
Num1 := 5;
Num2 := 8;
Num3 := Num2 / Num1;
```

produce

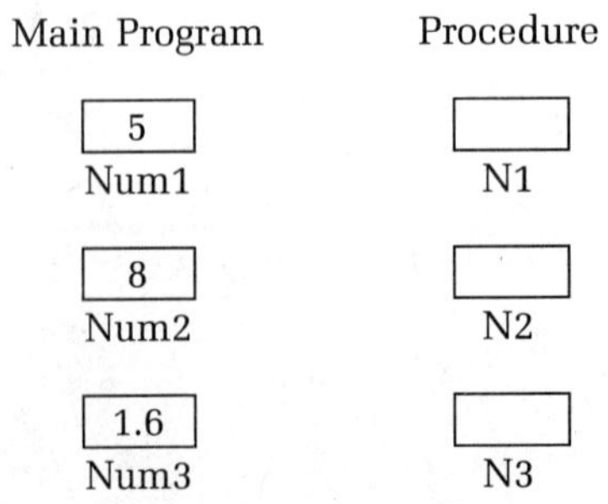

Main Program	Procedure
[5] Num1	[ ] N1
[8] Num2	[ ] N2
[1.6] Num3	[ ] N3

When the procedure PrintNum is called from the main program by

```
PrintNum (Num1, Num2, Num3);
```

the values are transmitted to N1, N2, and N3, respectively, as follows:

Main Program	Procedure
5	5
Num1	N1
8	8
Num2	N2
1.6	1.6
Num3	N3

At this stage, the procedure PrintNum can use N1, N2, and N3 in any appropriate manner.

These are value parameters because values are passed from the main program to the procedure only. If the procedure changes the value of N1, N2, or N3, the corresponding value of Num1, Num2, or Num3 will not be changed. For example, suppose the procedure is changed to

```
PROCEDURE PrintNum (N1, N2 : integer; N3 : real);
  BEGIN
    writeln;
    writeln (N1:10, N2:10, N3:10:2);
    N1 := 2 * N1;
    N2 := 2 * N2;
    N3 := 2 * N3;
    writeln (N1:10, N2:10, N3:10:2);
    writeln
  END;  {  of PROCEDURE PrintNum  }
```

Furthermore, suppose the main program is changed to

```
BEGIN  {  Main program  }
  ClrScr;
  Num1 := 5;
  Num2 := 8;
  Num3 := Num2 / Num1;
  writeln;
  writeln (Num1:10, Num2:10, Num3:10:2);
  PrintNum (Num1, Num2, Num3);
  writeln (Num1:10, Num2:10, Num3:10:2);
  readln
END.  {  of main program  }
```

When this program is run, the output is

```
         5         8      1.60      (from main program)
         5         8      1.60      (from procedure)
        10        16      3.20      (from procedure)
         5         8      1.60      (from main program)
```

The first line of this output is produced by the first

```
writeln (Num1:10, Num2:10, Num3:10:2);
```

of the main program. The next two lines of output come from the procedure. The last line of output is produced by the second

```
writeln (Num1:10, Num2:10, Num3:10:2);
```

of the main program. You should carefully note that although the procedure changes the values of N1, N2, and N3, the values of Num1, Num2, and Num3 have not been changed. Thus, we have

Main Program		Procedure	
5	Num1	10	N1
8	Num2	16	N2
1.6	Num3	3.2	N3

Variable Parameters

You will frequently want a procedure to change values in the main program. This can be accomplished by using variable parameters in the parameter list. Variable parameters are declared by using the reserved word **VAR** to precede appropriate formal parameters in the procedure heading. This causes all of the formal parameters listed between **VAR** and the subsequent data type to be variable parameters. If value parameters of the same type are needed, they must be listed elsewhere. A separate **VAR** declaration is needed for each data type used when listing variable parameters. The use of **VAR** in a parameter list is slightly different from its use in the declaration of variables, yet it is the same reserved word.

When variable parameters are declared, transmission of values appears to be two-way rather than one-way: that is, values are sent from the main program to the procedure and from the procedure to the main program. Actually, when variable parameters are used, values are not transmitted at all. Variable parameters in the procedure heading are merely aliases for actual variables used in the main program. Thus, variables are said to be *passed by reference* rather than by value. When variable parameters are used, any change of values in the procedure produces a corresponding change of values in the main program.

To illustrate the declaration of variable parameters, consider the procedure heading

```
PROCEDURE PrintNum (VAR N1, N2 : integer; N3 : real);
```

In this case, N1 and N2 are variable parameters corresponding to integer variables in the main program; N3 is a value parameter corresponding to a real variable. This procedure can be called from the main program by

```
PrintNum (Num1, Num2, Num3);
```

To illustrate the passing of values, assume the procedure is

```
PROCEDURE PrintNum (VAR N1, N2 : integer; N3 : real);
  BEGIN
    writeln (N1:5, N2:5, N3:10:2);
    N1 := 2 * N1;
    N2 := 2 * N2;
    N3 := 2 * N3;
    writeln (N1, N2, N3:10:2)
  END;  { of PROCEDURE PrintNum }
```

If the corresponding variables in the main program are Num1, Num2, and Num3, respectively, initially we have

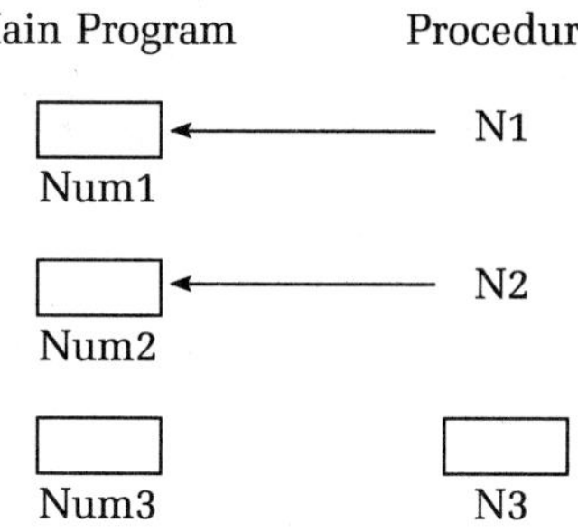

Technically, N1 and N2 do not exist as variables. They contain pointers to the same memory locations as Num1 and Num2, respectively. Thus, a statement in the procedure such as

```
N1 := 5;
```

causes the memory location reserved for Num1 to receive the value 5; that is, it causes the net action

```
Num1 := 5;
```

Thus, constants cannot be used when calling a procedure with variable parameters. For example

```
PrintNum (3, 4, 5);
```

produces an error because 3 and 4 correspond to variable parameters.

If the main program makes the assignment statements

```
Num1 := 5;
Num2 := 8;
Num3 := Num2 / Num1;
```

we have

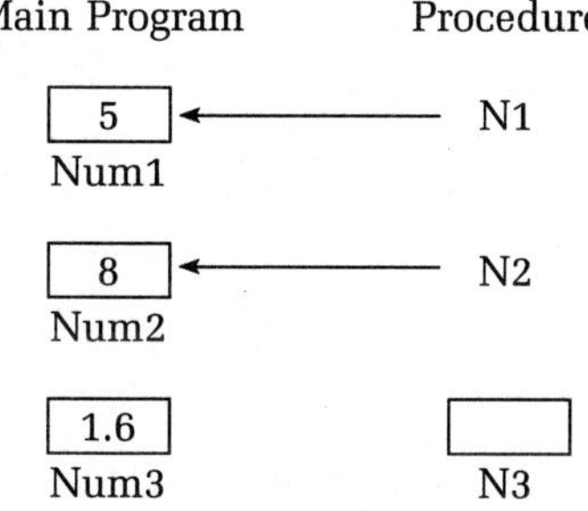

When the procedure is called by

```
PrintNum (Num1, Num2, Num3);
```

we have

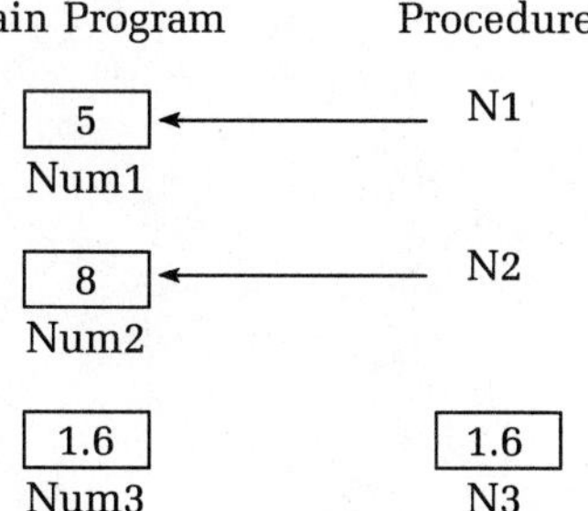

When the statements from the procedure

```
N1 := 2 * N1;
N2 := 2 * N2;
N3 := 2 * N3;
```

are executed, we have

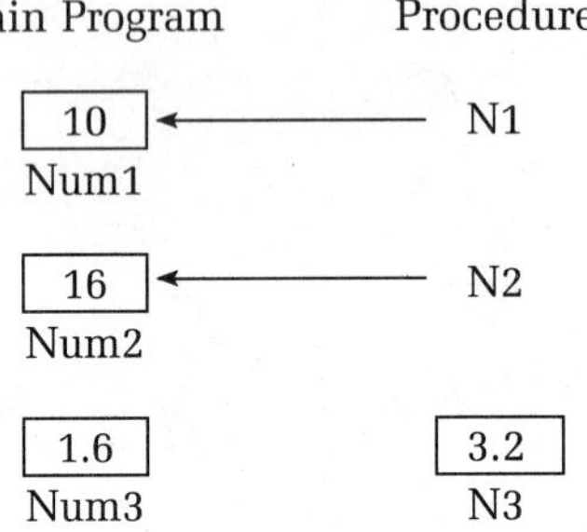

Notice that the variable parameters N1 and N2 produce changes in the corresponding variables in the main program but that the value parameter N3 does not.

Now let's consider a short, complete program that illustrates the difference between variable and value parameters. In this program (and throughout the text), the graphic documentation that accompanies the program highlights the ways in which parameters are passed between the main program and the procedure.

```
PROGRAM ProcDemo2;

USES
  Crt;

VAR
  X, Y : real;
  Ch : char;

{*******************************************}

PROCEDURE DemonstrateVAR (VAR X1 : real;
                          Y1 : real;
                          VAR Ch1 : char);
  BEGIN
    writeln (X1:10:2, Y1:10:2, Ch1:5);
    X1 := 2 * X1;
    Y1 := 2 * Y1;
    Ch1 := '*';
    writeln (X1:10:2, Y1:10:2, Ch1:5)
  END;  {  of PROCEDURE DemonstrateVAR  }

{*******************************************}

BEGIN  {  Main Program  }
  ClrScr;
  X := 3.6;
  Y := 5.2;
  Ch := 'A';
  writeln (X:10:2, Y:10:2, Ch:5);
  DemonstrateVAR (X, Y, Ch);
  writeln (X:10:2, Y:10:2, CH:5);
  readln
END.  {  of main program  }
```

Main Program | Procedure

3.6 (X) ← X1

5.2 (Y) | 5.2 (Y1)

'A' (Ch) ← Ch1

The output from the program is

```
3.60      5.20    A     (from main program)
3.60      5.20    A     (from procedure)
7.20     10.40    *     (from procedure)
7.20      5.20    *     (from main program)
```

The variables can be depicted as

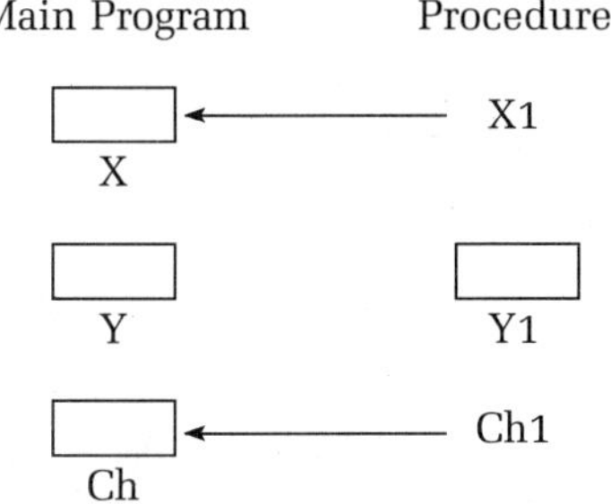

The assignment statements

```
X := 3.6;
Y := 5.2;
Ch := 'A';
```

produce

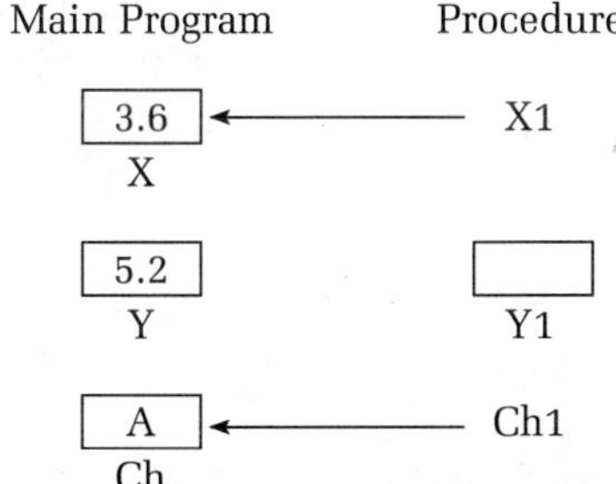

When the procedure is called by

```
DemonstrateVAR (X, Y, Ch);
```

the contents can be envisioned as

Main Program Procedure

3.6 ← X1
X

5.2 5.2
Y Y1

A ← Ch1
Ch

When the procedure assignment statements

```
X1 := 2 * X1;
Y1 := 2 * Y1;
Ch1 := '*';
```

are executed, the variables become

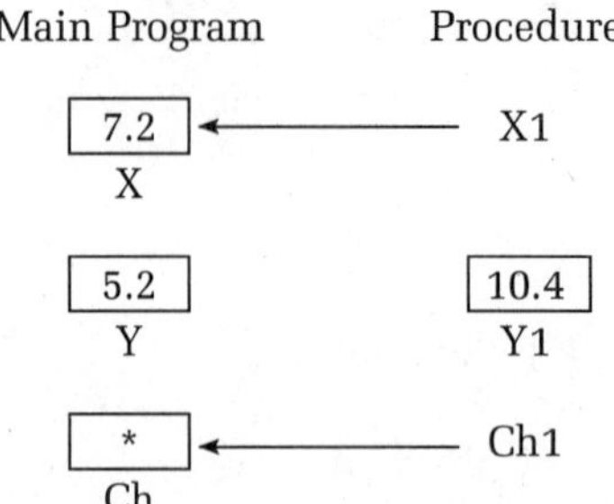

Notice that changes in the variable parameters X1 and Ch1 produce correspond-
7.0 ing changes in X and Ch but that a change in the value parameter Y1 does not
produce a change in Y.

Side Effects

A *side effect* is an unintentional change in a variable that is the result of some action taken in a program. Side effects are frequently caused by the misuse of variable parameters. Since any change in a variable parameter causes a change in the corresponding actual parameter in the calling program or procedure, you should use variable parameters only when your intent is to produce such changes. In all other cases, use value parameters.

To illustrate how a side effect can occur, suppose you are working with a program that computes the midterm and final grades for students in a class. For the midterm grade, Quiz 1 and Quiz 2 are doubled and then added to Test 1. Using variable parameters in a procedure for this yields

```
PROCEDURE ComputeMidTerm (VAR Q1, Q2, Test1 : integer);
  BEGIN
    Q1 := 2 * Q1;
    Q2 := 2 * Q2;
        .
        .      (rest of procedure)
        .
```

When this is called from the main program by

```
ComputeMidTerm (Quiz1, Quiz2, Test1);
```

the values in Quiz1 and Quiz2 will be changed. This was probably not the intent when ComputeMidTerm was called. This unwanted side effect can be avoided by having Q1 and Q2 be value parameters. Thus, the procedure heading becomes

```
PROCEDURE ComputeMidTerm (Q1, Q2, Test1 : integer);
```

Cohesive Subprograms

The cohesion of a subprogram is the degree to which the subprogram performs a single task. A subprogram that is developed in such a way is called a *cohesive subprogram.* As you use subprograms to implement a design based on modular development, you should always try to write cohesive subprograms.

The property of cohesion is not well defined. Subtask complexity varies in the minds of different programmers. In general, if the task is unclear, the corresponding subprogram will not be cohesive. When this happens, you should subdivide the task until a subsequent development allows cohesive subprograms.

To briefly illustrate the concept of cohesion, consider the first-level design of a problem to compute grades for a class. Step 3 of this design could be

3. Process grades for each student

Clearly, this is not a well-defined task. Thus, if you were to write a subprogram for this task, the subprogram would not be cohesive. When we look at the subsequent development

3. Process grades for each student
   WHILE NOT eof DO
   3.1 get a line of data
   3.2 compute average
   3.3 compute letter grade
   3.4 print data
   3.5 compute totals

we see that procedures to accomplish subtasks 3.1, 3.2, 3.3, and 3.4 will be cohesive because each subtask consists of a single task. The final subtask, compute totals, may or may not result in a cohesive subprogram. More information is needed before you can decide what is to be done at this step.

Procedural Abstraction

The purpose of using procedures is to simplify reasoning. During the design stage, as a problem is subdivided into tasks, the problem solver (you) should have to consider only what a procedure is to do and not be concerned about details of the procedure. Instead, the procedure name and comments at the beginning of the procedure should be sufficient to inform the user as to what the procedure does. Developing procedures in this manner is referred to as *procedural abstraction.*

Procedural abstraction is the first step in designing and writing a procedure. The list of parameters and comments about the action of the procedure should precede writing the procedure body. This forces clarity of thought and aids design. Using this method might cause you to discover that your design is not sufficient to solve the task and that redesign is necessary. Therefore, you could reduce design errors and save time when writing code.

Procedural abstraction becomes especially important when teams work on a project. Each member of the writing team should be able to understand the purpose and use of procedures written by other team members without having to analyze the body of each procedure. This is analogous to the situation in which you use a predefined function without really understanding how the function works.

Procedural abstraction is perhaps best formalized in terms of preconditions and postconditions. A *precondition* is a comment that states precisely what is true before a certain action is taken. A *postcondition* states what is true after the action has been taken. Carefully written preconditions and postconditions used with procedures enhance the concept of procedural abstraction. (Additional uses of preconditions and postconditions are discussed in Sections 4.6 and 5.5.)

In summary, procedural abstraction means that, when writing or using procedures, you should think of them as single, clearly understood units that each accomplishes a specific task.

Encapsulation

Encapsulation can be thought of as the process of hiding the implementation details of a subprogram. This is just what we do when we use a top-down design to solve a problem. We decide which tasks and subtasks are necessary to solve a problem without worrying about how the specific subtasks will be accomplished.

A NOTE OF INTEREST

Computer Ethics: Hacking and Other Intrusions

A famous sequence of computer intrusions was originally detailed by Clifford Stoll. The prime intruder came to Stoll's attention in August 1986, when he attempted to penetrate a computer at Lawrence Berkeley Laboratory (LBL). Instead of denying the intruder access, management at LBL went along with Stoll's recommendation that they attempt to unmask the intruder, even though the risk was substantial because the intruder had gained system-manager privileges.

Markus H., a member of a small group of West Germans, was an unusually persistent intruder, but no computer wizard. He made use of known deficiencies in the half-dozen or so operating systems, including UNIX, VMS, VM-TSO, and EMBOS, with which he was familiar, but he did not invent any new modes of entry. He penetrated 30 of the 450 computers then on the network system at LBL.

After Markus H. was successfully traced, efforts were instituted to make LBL's computers less vulnerable. To insure high security, it would have been necessary to change all passwords overnight and recertify each user. This and other demanding measures were deemed impractical. Instead, deletion of all expired passwords was instituted; shared accounts were eliminated; monitoring of incoming traffic was extended, with alarms set in key places; and education of users was attempted.

The episode was summed up by Stoll as a powerful learning experience for those involved in the detection process and for all those concerned about computer security. That the intruder was caught at all is a testimony to the ability of a large number of concerned professionals to keep the tracing effort secret.

In a later incident, an intruder left the following embarrassing message in the computer file assigned to Clifford Stoll: "The cuckoo has egg on his face." The reference is to Stoll's book, *The Cuckoo's Egg*, which tracks the intrusions of the West German hacker just described. The embarrassment was heightened by the fact that the computer—owned by Harvard University, with which astronomer Stoll is now associated—is on the Internet network. The intruder, or intruders, who goes by the name of Dave, also attempted to break into dozens of other computers on the same network—and succeeded.

The "nom de guerre," Dave, was used by one or more of three Australians recently arrested by the federal police down under. The three, who at the time of their arrest were, respectively, 18, 20, and 21 years of age, successfully penetrated computers in both Australia and the United States.

The three Australians went beyond browsing to damage data in computers in their own nation and the United States. At the time they began their intrusions in 1988 (when the youngest was only 16), there was no law in Australia under which they could be prosecuted. It was not until legislation making such intrusions prosecutable was passed that the police began to take action.

In the sense of software engineering, encapsulation is what allows teams to work on a large system. It is only necessary to know what another team is doing, not how they are doing it.

Interface and Documentation

Independent subprograms (whether procedures or functions) need to communicate with the main program and other subprograms. A formal statement of how such communication occurs is called the *interface* of the subprogram. An interface usually consists of comments at the beginning of a subprogram and includes all the documentation the reader will need to use the subprogram. This information typically consists of

1. What is received by the subprogram when called
2. What task the subprogram performs
3. What is returned after the subprogram performs its task
4. How the subprogram is called

This information aids in debugging programs. In this text, our interface consists of the three-part documentation section

```
{  Given:  <Statement of information sent from the program>       }
{  Task:   <Statement of task(s) to be performed>                  }
{  Return: <Statement of value(s) returned to the program>         }
```

The headings of subprograms in complete programs are given in this manner. When subprograms are separately developed and illustrated, this documentation is not included; instead, text development immediately preceding the subprogram serves the same purpose. How a subprogram is called is usually apparent from the identifiers listed in the subprogram heading.

Software Engineering Implications

Perhaps the greatest difference between beginning students in computer science and "real world" programmers is how the need for documentation is perceived. Typically, beginning students want to make a program run; they view anything that delays this process as an impediment. Thus, some students consider using descriptive identifiers, writing variable dictionaries, describing a problem as part of program documentation, and using appropriate comments throughout a program to be a nuisance. In contrast, system designers and programmers who write code for a living often spend up to 50 percent of their time and effort on documentation.

There are at least three reasons for this difference in perspective. First, real programmers work on large, complex systems with highly developed logical paths. Without proper documentation, even the person who develops an algorithm will have difficulty following the logic six months later. Second, communication between and among teams is required as systems are developed. Complete, clear statements about what the problems are and how they are being solved is essential. And third, programmers know they can develop algorithms and write subsequent code. They are trained so that problems of searching, sorting, and file manipulation are routine. Knowing that they can solve a problem allows them to devote more time and energy to documenting how to achieve the solution.

We close this section with a revision of the program from Chapter 2 that found the unit cost for a pizza. The structure chart is shown in Figure 3.1.

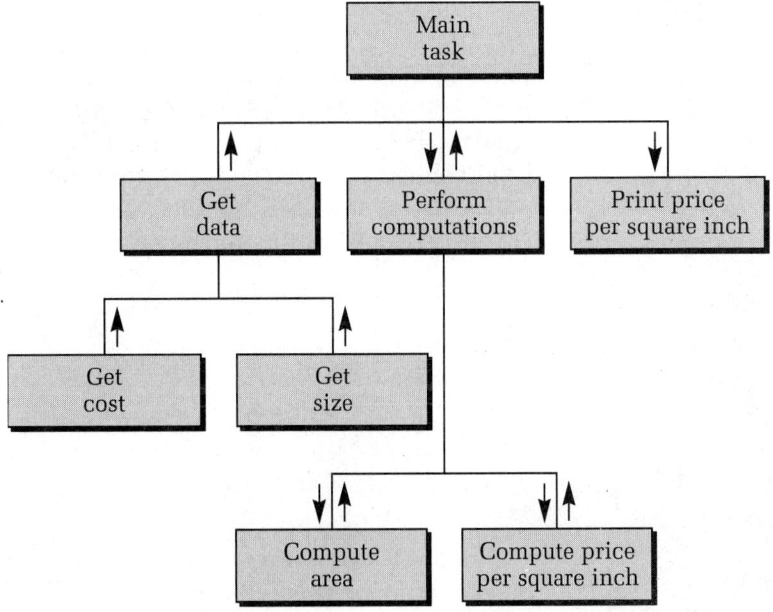

FIGURE 3.1
Structure chart for the pizza problem

The module specifications are

1. GetData Module
   Date received: None
   Information returned: Cost
                                         Size
   Logic: Have the user enter cost and size.
2. PerformComputations Module
   Data received: Cost
                           Size
   Information returned: Price per square inch
   Logic: Given the diameter, find the radius.
             Compute the area using Area = Pi * sqr(Radius).
             Price per square inch is found by dividing Cost by Area.
3. PrintResults Module
   Data received: PricePerSquareInch
   Information returned: None
   Logic: Print the price per square inch.

A procedure for getting the data requires two variable parameters—one for the size, and one for the cost—since these values will be returned to the main program. This procedure is

```
PROCEDURE GetData (VAR PizzaCost : real;
                   VAR PizzaSize : integer);
  BEGIN
    writeln ('Enter the pizza price and press <Enter>.');
    readln (PizzaCost);
    writeln ('Enter the pizza size and press <Enter>.');
    readln (PizzaSize)
  END;  {  of PROCEDURE GetData  }
```

Now let's write a procedure for performing the desired computations. (Later we will learn how this task would be done with a function instead of a procedure.) This procedure receives the Cost and Size and then returns the PricePerSquareInch. Thus, Cost and Size are value parameters and PricePerSquare-Inch is a variable parameter. This procedure also requires variables Radius and Area to be declared in the declaration section of the procedure. Assuming Pi has been defined as a constant, the procedure is

```
PROCEDURE PerformComputations (PizzaCost : real;
                               PizzaSize : integer;
                               VAR PricePerSqInch : real);
  VAR
    Radius, Area : real;
  BEGIN
    Radius := PizzaSize / 2;
    Area := Pi * sqr(Radius);
    PricePerSqInch := PizzaCost / Area
  END;  { of PROCEDURE PerformComputations }
```

Finally, a procedure to print the results receives the unit cost. Thus, a value parameter is declared and the procedure is

```
PROCEDURE PrintResults (PricePerSqInch : real);
  BEGIN
    ClrScr;
    write ('The price per square inch is $');
    writeln (PricePerSqInch:6:2);
   readln
  END;  {  of PROCEDURE PrintResults  }
```

With these procedures written, the main program becomes

```
BEGIN  {  Main program  }
  GetData (Cost, Size);
  PerformComputations (Cost, Size, PricePerSquareInch);
  PrintResults (PricePerSquareInch)
END.  {  of main program  }
```

The complete program for this problem is as follows:

```
PROGRAM Pizza;

USES
  Crt;

VAR
  Cost, PricePerSquareInch : real;
  Size : integer;

{*******************************************************}

PROCEDURE GetData (VAR PizzaCost : real;
                   VAR PizzaSize : integer);
  BEGIN
    writeln;
    writeln ('Enter the pizza price and press <Enter>.');      1
    readln (PizzaCost);
    writeln ('Enter the pizza size and press <Enter>.');
    readln (PizzaSize)
  END;  {  of PROCEDURE GetData  }

{*******************************************************}

PROCEDURE PerformComputations (PizzaCost : real;
                               PizzaSize : integer;
                               VAR PricePerSqInch : real);
  VAR
    Radius, Area : real;
  BEGIN                                                          2
    Radius := PizzaSize / 2;
    Area := Pi * sqr(Radius);
    PricePerSqInch := PizzaCost / Area
  END;  {  of PROCEDURE PerformComputations  }

{*******************************************************}

PROCEDURE PrintResults (PricePerSqInch : real);
  BEGIN
    ClrScr;
    write ('The price per square inch is $');                   3
    writeln (PricePerSqInch:6:2);
    readln
  END;  {  of PROCEDURE PrintResults  }

{*******************************************************}
```

```
BEGIN  {  Main program  }
  GetData (Cost, Size);
```

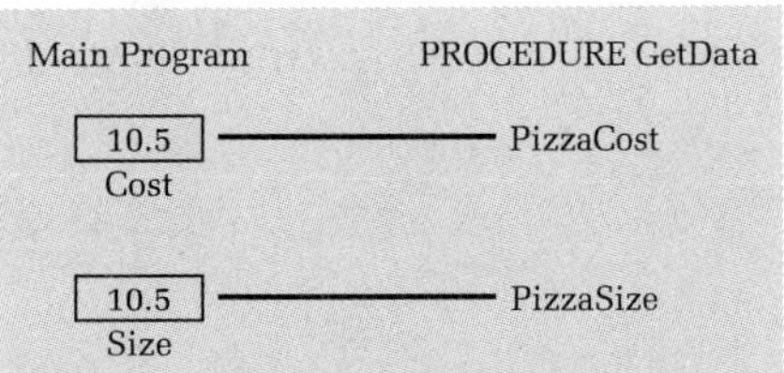


```
  PerformComputations (Cost, Size, PricePerSquareInch);
```

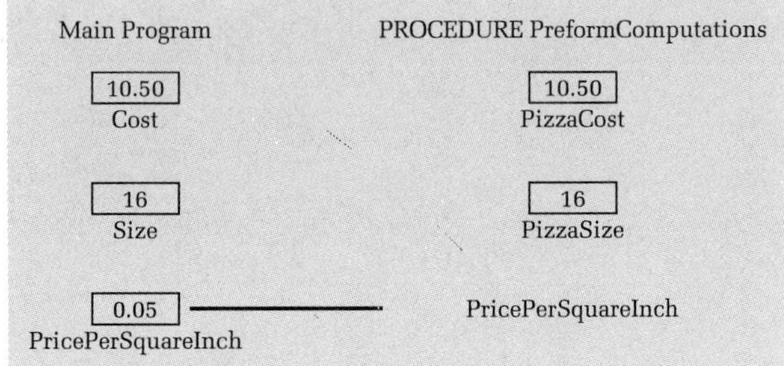


```
  PrintResults (PricePerSquareInch)
END.  {  of main program  }
```

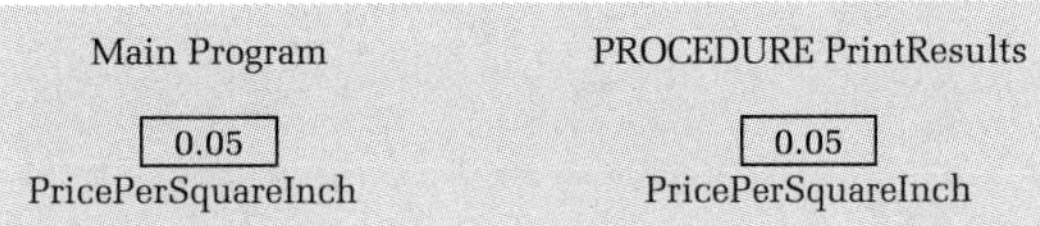

Sample runs of this program produce

```
Enter the pizza price and press <Enter>.
10.50
Enter the pizza size and press <Enter>.
16

The price per square inch is $  0.05

Enter the pizza price and press <Enter>.
8.75
Enter the pizza size and press <Enter>.
14

The price per square inch is $  0.06
```

Exercises 3.2

1. Explain the difference between value parameters and variable parameters. Between formal and actual parameters.
2. Write a test program to find what happens if the parameter lists do not match when a procedure is called from the main program. Investigate each of the following:
   a. Correct number of parameters, wrong order
   b. Incorrect number of parameters
3. Indicate which of the following parameters are variable parameters and which are value parameters.
   a.
   ```
   PROCEDURE Demo1 (VAR A, B : integer;
                        X : real);
   ```

b.
```
PROCEDURE Demo2 (VAR A : integer;
                 B : integer;
                 VAR X : real;
                 Ch : char);
```
c.
```
PROCEDURE Demo3 (A, B : integer;
                 VAR X, Y, Z : real;
                 Ch : char);
```

4. Indicate which of the following are appropriate procedure headings. Explain what is wrong with those that are inappropriate.

a. `PROCEDURE Prac1 (A : integer : Y : real);`

b. `PROCEDURE Error? (Ch1, Ch2 : char);`

c. `PROCEDURE Prac2 (A, VAR B : integer);`

d.
```
PROCEDURE Prac3 (A, B, C : integer
                 VAR X, Y : real
                 Ch : char);
```
e.
```
PROCEDURE Prac4 (VAR A : integer,
                 X : real);
```

5. Indicate how each of the following procedures would be called from the main program.

a.
```
PROCEDURE Prob5 (A, B : integer;
                 Ch : char);
```
b. `PROCEDURE PrintHeader;`

c.
```
PROCEDURE FindMax (N1, N2 : integer;
                   VAR NewMax : integer);
```
d. `PROCEDURE Switch (VAR X, Y : real);`

6. Suppose a program contains the following procedure:

```
PROCEDURE Switch (VAR A, B : integer);
  VAR
    Temp : integer;
  BEGIN
    Temp := A;
    A := B;
    B := Temp
  END;  {  of PROCEDURE Switch  }
```

Indicate the output from each of the following fragments of code in the main program.

a.
```
Num1 := 5;
Num2 := 10;
writeln (Num1, Num2);
Switch (Num1, Num2);
writeln (Num1, Num2);
Switch (Num1, Num2);
writeln (Num1, Num2);
```
b.
```
N := 3;
M := 20;
Switch (M, N);
writeln (M, N);
Switch (N, M);
writeln (N, M);
```

7. Write a procedure for each of the following, and indicate how it would be called from the main program.

a. Print the heading for the output.

```
Acme National Electronics
  Board of Directors
    Annual Meeting
```

b. Find the maximum and average of three reals. Both values are to be returned to the main program.

c. Convert Fahrenheit temperature to Celsius.

8. Assume a program contains the variable declaration section

```
VAR
  Num1, Num2 : integer;
  X, Y : real;
  Ch1, Ch2 : char;
```

Furthermore, suppose the same program contains the procedure heading

```
PROCEDURE Demo (VAR N1, N2 : integer;
                X1 : real;
                Ch : char);
```

Indicate which of the following are appropriate calls to the procedure Demo. Explain why the others are inappropriate.

a. `Demo (Num1, Num2);`

b. `Demo (Num1, Num2, X);`

c. `Demo (Num1, Num2, X, Ch1);`

d. `Demo (X, Y, Num1, Ch2);`

e. `Demo (Num2, X, Y, Ch1);`

f. `Demo (Num1, Num2, Ch2);`

g. `Demo;`

h. `Demo (Num2, Num1, Y, Ch1);`

■ 3.3 Scope of Identifiers

Global and Local Identifiers

Identifiers used to declare variables in the declaration section of a program can be used throughout the entire program. For purposes of this section, we will think of the program as a *block* and each subprogram as a *subblock* or block for the subprogram. Each block may contain a parameter list, a local declaration section, and the body of the block. A program block for **PROGRAM** ShowScope may be envisioned as shown in Figure 3.2. Furthermore, if X1 is a variable in Show-Scope, we will indicate this as shown in Figure 3.3, where an area in memory has

FIGURE 3.2
Program heading and main block

PROGRAM ShowScope

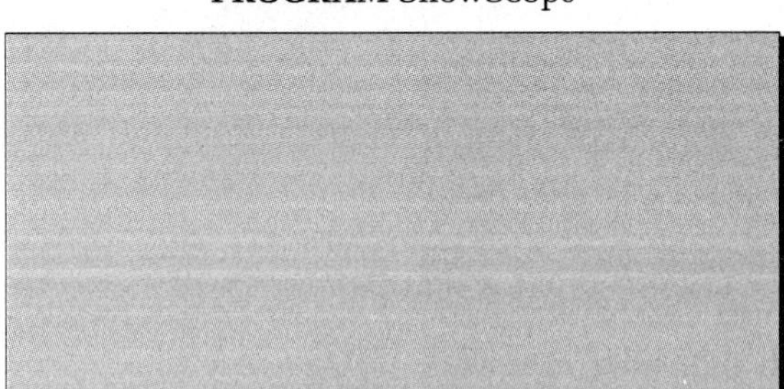

FIGURE 3.3
Variable location within main block

PROGRAM ShowScope

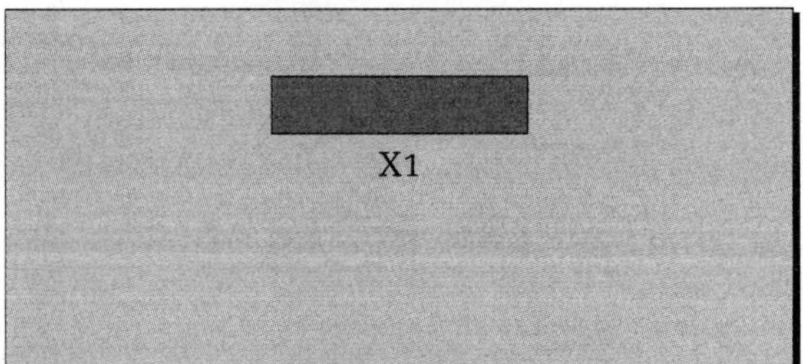

been set aside for X1. When a program contains a subprogram, a separate memory area within the memory area for the program is set aside for the subprogram to use while it executes. Thus, if ShowScope contains a procedure named Subprog1, we can envision this as shown in Figure 3.4. If Subprog1 contains the variable X2, we have the program shown in Figure 3.5. This could be indicated in the program by

```
PROGRAM ShowScope;

VAR
  X1 : real;

PROCEDURE Subprog1 (X2 : real);
```

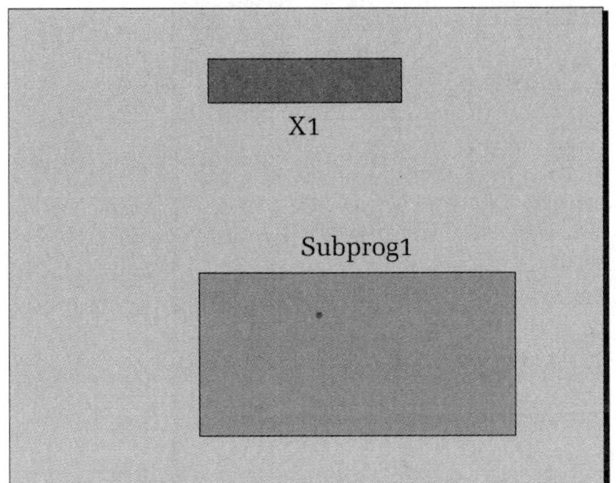

FIGURE 3.4
Illustration of a subblock

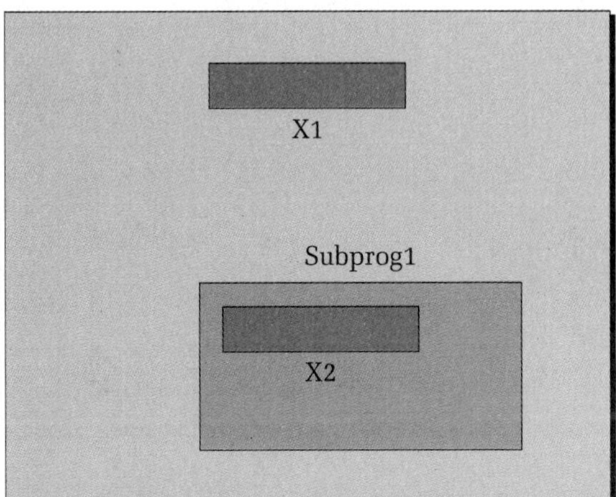

FIGURE 3.5
Variable location within a subblock

The *scope of an identifier* refers to the block in which it is declared or defined. When subprograms are used, each identifier is available only to the block in which the identifier is declared; this includes all subprograms contained within the subprogram's block. Identifiers are not available outside their blocks.

Identifiers that are declared in the main block are called *global identifiers* (or *global variables*); identifiers that are restricted to use within a subblock are called *local identifiers* (or *local variables*).Variable X1 in Figure 3.5 can be used in the main program and in the procedure Subprog1; therefore, it is a global identifier. On the other hand, variable X2 can only be used within the procedure where it is declared; it is a local identifier. Any attempt to reference X2 outside the procedure will result in an error. Identifiers used in a block in which they are not declared are said to be *nonlocal* to that block.

Figure 3.6 illustrates the scope of identifiers. In this figure, the scope of X3 is **PROCEDURE** Inner, the scope of X2 is **PROCEDURE** Outer, and the scope of X1 is **PROGRAM** ShowScope. When procedures are nested like this, the scope of an identifier is the largest block in which it is declared.

Now let's examine an illustration of local and global identifiers. Consider the program and procedure declaration

```
PROGRAM ScopePrac;

VAR
  A, B : integer;

PROCEDURE Subprog (A1 : integer);
  VAR
    X : real;
```

Blocks for this program can be envisioned as shown in Figure 3.7.

Since A and B are global identifiers, the statement

```
writeln (A:5, B:5, A1:5, X:10:2);
```

could be used in **PROCEDURE** Subprog although A and B have not been specifically declared there. However, this statement could not be used in the main program because A1 and X are local to **PROCEDURE** Subprog.

FIGURE 3.6
Scope of identifiers

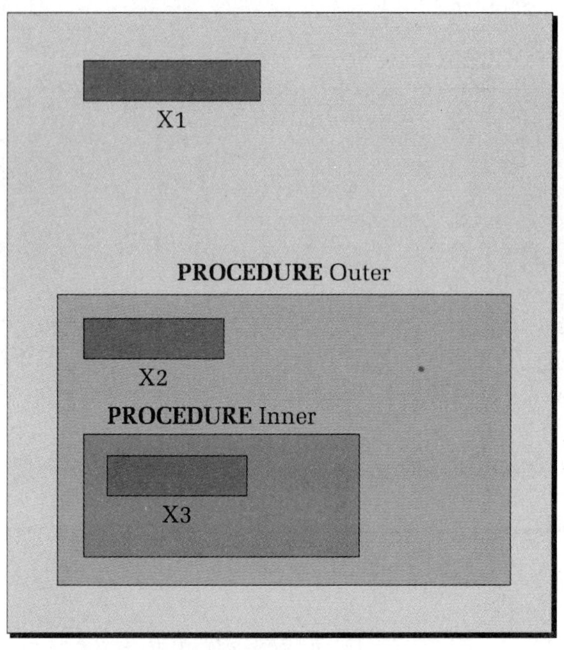

FIGURE 3.7
Relation of identifiers for **PROGRAM** ScopePrac

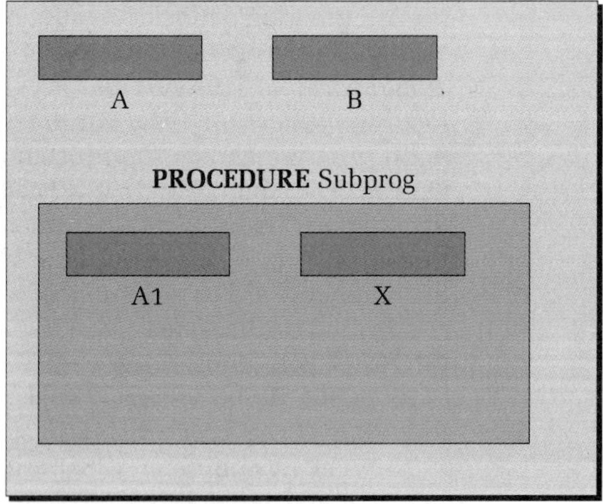

Using Global Variables and Constants

In general, it is not good practice to refer to global variables within procedures. Using locally defined variables helps to avoid unexpected side effects and protects your programs. In addition, locally defined variables facilitate debugging and top-down design and enhance the portability of procedures. This is especially important if a team is developing a program by having different people work on different procedures.

Using global constants is different. Since constant values cannot be changed by a procedure, it is preferable that constants be defined in the **CONST** section of the main program and then be used whenever needed by any subprogram. This is especially important if the constant is subject to change over time (for example, StateTaxRate). When a change is necessary, one change in the main program is all that is needed to make all subprograms current. If a constant is used in only one procedure (or function), some programmers prefer to have it defined near the point of use. Thus, they would define it in the subprogram in which it is used.

Name of Identifiers

Because separate areas in memory are set aside when subprograms are used, it is possible to have identifiers with the same name in both the main program and a subprogram. Thus

```
PROGRAM Demo;

VAR
  Age : integer;

PROCEDURE Subprog (Age : integer);
```

can be envisioned as shown in Figure 3.8.

FIGURE 3.8 Using identifiers in subprograms

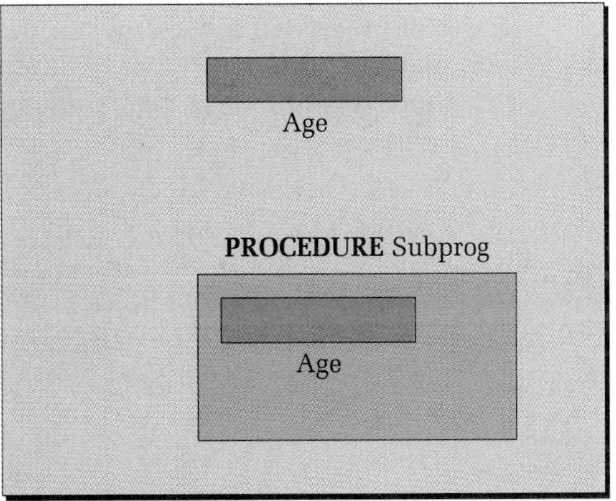

When the same name is used in this manner, any reference to this name results in action being taken as locally as possible. Thus, the assignment statement

```
Age := 20;
```

made in **PROCEDURE** Subprog assigns 20 to Age in the procedure but not in the main program (see Figure 3.9).

FIGURE 3.9 Assigning values in subprograms

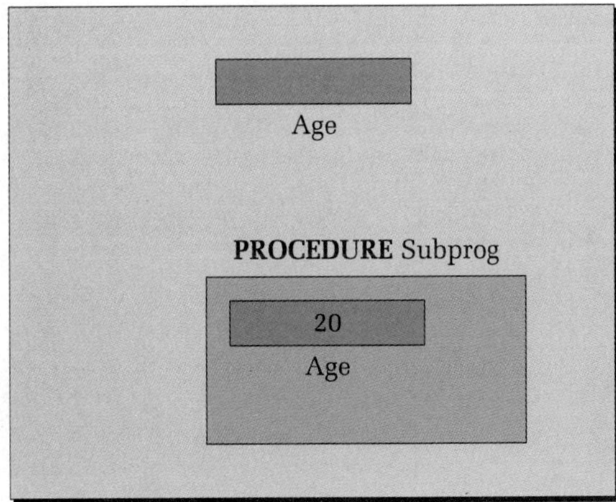

Now that you know you can use the same name for an identifier in a subprogram and in the main program, the question is, "Should you?" There are two schools of thought regarding this issue. If you use the same name in the procedures as you do in the main program, it facilitates matching parameter lists and independent development of procedures. However, this practice can be confusing when you first start working with subprograms. Thus, some instructors prefer using different, but related, identifiers. For example

```
GetData (Score1, Score2);
```

in the main program could have a procedure heading of

```
PROCEDURE GetData (VAR Sc1, Sc2 : integer);
```

In this case, the use of Sc1 and Sc2 is obvious. Although this may facilitate better understanding in early work with subprograms, it is less conducive to portability and independent development of procedures. Both styles are used in this text.

Multiple Procedures

More than one procedure can be used in a program. When this occurs, all the previous uses and restrictions of identifiers apply to each procedure. Blocks for multiple procedures can be depicted as shown in Figure 3.10. Identifiers in the

FIGURE 3.10
Blocks for multiple subprograms

PROCEDURE A

PROCEDURE B

PROCEDURE C

FIGURE 3.11
Identifiers in multiple subprograms

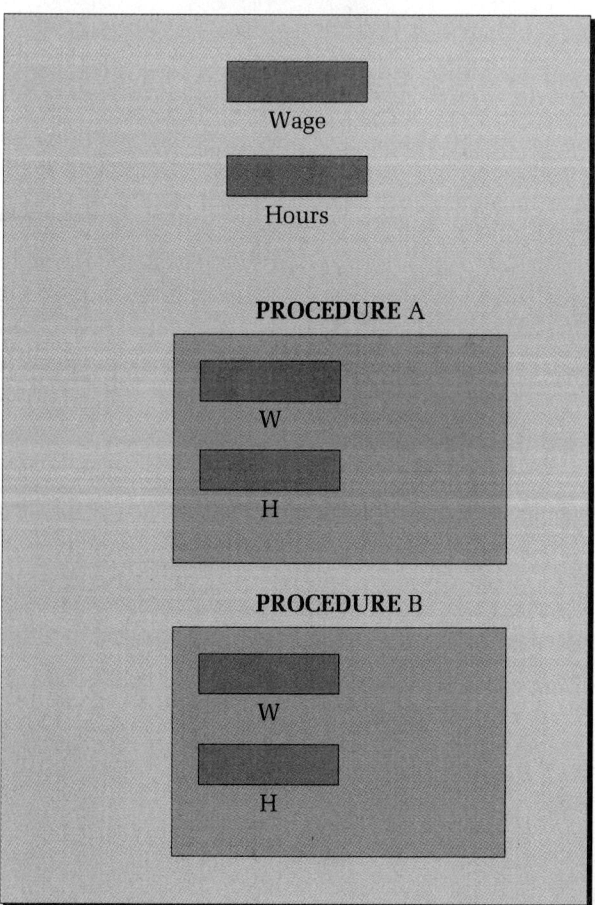

main program can be accessed by each procedure. However, local identifiers in the procedures cannot be accessed outside their blocks.

When a program contains several procedures, they can be called from the main part of the program in any order. Procedures may be called from the main program only if they are not nested in another procedure. If one procedure contains a call to another procedure (or function), the subprogram being called must appear before the procedure from which it is called. (An exception is available if the **FORWARD** statement is used; see Appendices 1 and 3.)

The same names for identifiers can be used in different procedures. Thus, if the main program uses variables Wage and Hours, and both of these are used as arguments in calls to different procedures, you have the situation shown in Figure 3.11. Using the same names for identifiers in different procedures makes it easier to keep track of the relationships among variables in the main program and their associated parameters in each subprogram.

Exercises 3.3

1. Explain the difference between local and global identifiers.
2. State the advantages of using local identifiers.
3. Discuss some appropriate uses for global identifiers. List several constants that would be appropriate global definitions.
4. What is meant by the scope of an identifier?
5. Write a test program that will enable you to see
   a. What happens when an attempt is made to access an identifier outside of its scope.
   b. How the values change as a result of assignments in the subprogram and the main program when the same identifier is used in the main program and a procedure.
6. Review the following program.

```
PROGRAM Practice;

VAR
  A, B : integer;
  X : real;
  Ch : char;

PROCEDURE Sub1 (A1 : integer);
  VAR
    B1 : integer;
  BEGIN
    .
    .
    .
  END;  {  of PROCEDURE Sub1  }

PROCEDURE Sub2 (A1 : integer;
                VAR B1 : integer);
  VAR
    X1 : real;
    Ch1 : char;
  BEGIN
    .
    .
    .
  END;  {  of PROCEDURE Sub2  }
```

a. List all global variables.
b. List all local variables.
c. Indicate the scope of each identifier.

7. Provide a schematic representation of the program and all subprograms and variables in Exercise 6.

8. Using the program with variables and subprograms as depicted in Figure 3.12, state the scope of each identifier.

FIGURE 3.12

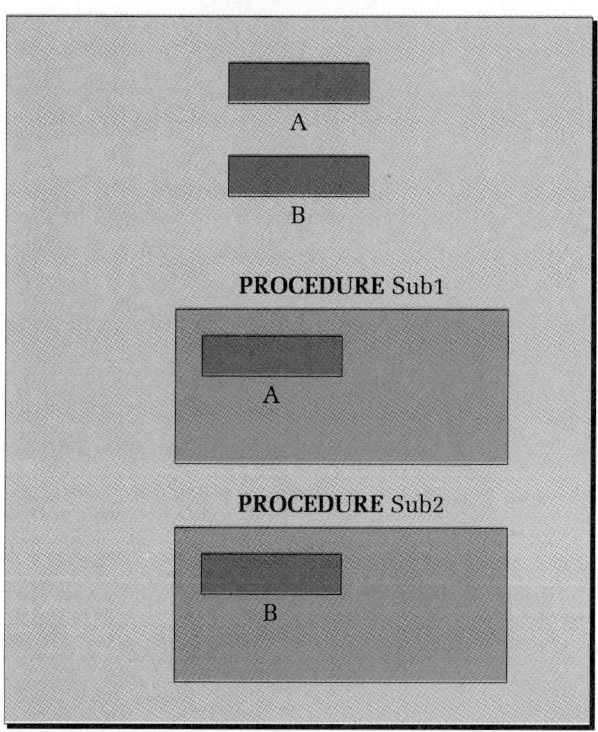

9. What is the output from the following program?

```
PROGRAM Exercise9;

VAR
  A : integer;

PROCEDURE Sub1 (A : integer);
  BEGIN
    A := 20;
    writeln (A)
  END;  {  of PROCEDURE Sub1  }

PROCEDURE Sub2 (VAR A : integer);
  BEGIN
    A := 30;
    writeln (A)
  END;  {  of PROCEDURE Sub2  }

BEGIN  {  Main program  }
  A := 10;
  writeln (A);
```

```
  Sub1 (A);
  writeln (A);
  Sub2 (A);
  writeln (A)
END.  {  of main program  }
```

10. Review the following program.

```
PROGRAM ExerciseTen;

VAR
  Num1, Num2, : integer;

PROCEDURE Change (X : integer;
                  VAR Y : integer);
  VAR
    Num2 : integer;
  BEGIN
    Num2 := X;
    Y := Y + Num2;
    X := Y
  END;

BEGIN
  Num1 := 10;
  Num2 := 7;
  Change (Num1, Num2);
  writeln (Num1:5, Num2:5)
END.
```

a. What is the output of the program as written?

Determine the output of the program if the following procedure headings are substituted.

b. `PROCEDURE Change (VAR X : integer; Y : integer);`

c. `PROCEDURE Change (X, Y : integer);`

d. `PROCEDURE Change (VAR X, Y : integer);`

11. Assume the variable declaration section of a program is

```
VAR
  Age, Hours : integer;
  Average : real;
  Initial : char;
```

Furthermore, assume procedure headings and declaration sections for procedures in this program are as follows. Find all errors in each.

a.
```
PROCEDURE Average (Age1, Hrs : integer;
                   VAR Aver : real);
```

b.
```
PROCEDURE Sub1 (Hours : integer;
                VAR Average : real);
  VAR
    Age : integer;
    Init : char;
```

c.
```
PROCEDURE Compute (Hrs : integer;
                   VAR Aver : real);
  VAR
    Age : real;
```

12. Write appropriate headings and declaration sections for the program and subprograms illustrated in Figure 3.13 on the following page.

FIGURE 3.13

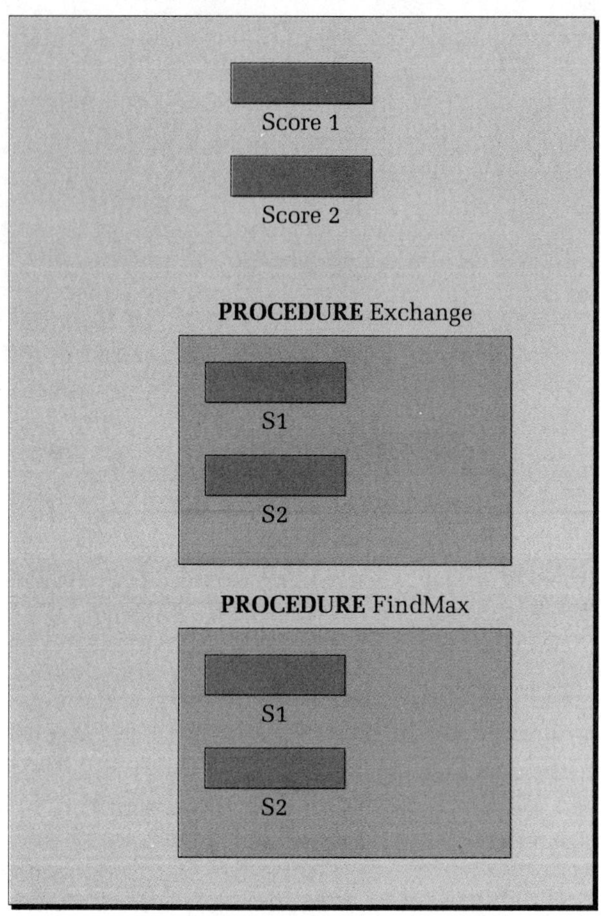

13. Find all errors in the following program.

```
PROGRAM Exercise13;

VAR
  X, Y : real;

PROCEDURE Sub1 (VAR X1 : real);
  BEGIN
    writeln (X1:20:2);
    writeln (X:20:2);
    writeln (Y:20:2)
  END;  {  of PROCEDURE Sub1  }

BEGIN  {  Main program  }
  X := 10.0;
  Y := 2 * X;
  writeln (X:20:2, Y:20:2);
  Sub1 (X);
  writeln (X1:20:2);
  writeln (X:20:2);
  writeln (Y:20:2)
END.  {  of main program  }
```

14. Discuss the advantages and disadvantages of using the same names for identifiers in a subprogram and in the main program.

■ 3.4 User-Defined Functions

The standard functions **sqr, sqrt, abs, round,** and **trunc** were introduced in Section 2.5. To briefly review, some concepts to note when using these functions are

1. An argument is required for each; thus, **sqrt**(Y) and **abs**(−21) are appropriate.
2. Standard functions can be used in expressions; for example

```
X := sqrt(Y) - sqrt(Z);
```

3. Standard functions can be used in output statements; for example

```
writeln (sqr(3):8);
```

Need for User-Defined Functions

It is relatively easy to envision the need for functions that are not on the list of standard functions available in Turbo Pascal. For example, if you must frequently cube numbers, it would be convenient to have a function Cube so you could make an assignment such as

```
X := Cube(Y);
```

Other examples from mathematics include an exponential function (x^Y), computing a factorial ($n!$), computing a discriminant ($b^2 - 4ac$), and finding roots of a quadratic equation

$$\left(\frac{-b \pm \sqrt{b^2 - 4ac}}{2a}\right)$$

In business, a motel might need to have a function available to determine a customer's bill given the number in the party, the length of stay, and any telephone charges. Similarly, a hospital might need a function to compute the room charge for a patient given the type of room (private, ward, and so on) and various other options, including telephone (yes or no) and television (yes or no). Functions such as these are not standard functions. However, in Turbo Pascal, we can create *user-defined functions* to perform these tasks.

Form for User-Defined Functions

A user-defined function is a subprogram and, as such, is part of the declaration section of the main (or calling) program. It has the components

Heading →

Declaration section →

Executable section →

The general form for a function heading is

FUNCTION ⟨function name⟩(⟨parameter list⟩): ⟨return type⟩;

A syntax diagram for this is

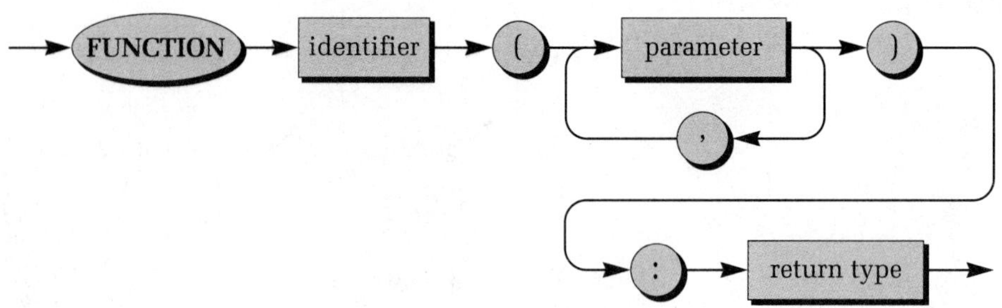

As with procedures, the formal parameter list (variables in the function heading) must match the number and corresponding types of actual parameters (variables in the function call) used when the function is called from the main program. Thus, if you are writing a function to compute the area of a rectangle and you want to call the function from the main program by

```
RectArea := Area(Width, Length);
```

the function Area might have

```
FUNCTION Area (W, L : integer) : integer;
```

as a heading. The two formal parameters W and L correspond to the actual parameters Width and Length, assuming Width and Length are of type **integer**. In general, you should make sure the formal parameter list and actual parameter list match up as indicated:

```
(W, L : integer)
(Width, Length)
```

An exception to this is that an actual parameter of type **integer** may be associated with a formal parameter of type **real.**

A function to compute the cube of an integer could have the following heading:

```
FUNCTION Cube (X : integer) : integer;
```

Several additional comments on the general form for a function heading are now in order.

1. **FUNCTION** is a reserved word and must be used only as indicated.
2. The term "function name" is any valid identifier.
   a. The function name should be descriptive.
   b. Some value must be assigned to the function name in the executable section of the function. The last assigned value is the value returned to the main program; for example, in the function Cube, we have

      ```
      Cube := X * X * X;
      ```

   c. The function name can be used only on the left side of an assignment statement within the function. For example

      ```
      Cube := Cube + 1;
      ```

      produces an error. (An exception to this rule involves recursion and is discussed in Section 11.1.)
3. The term "return type" declares the data type for the function name. This indicates what type of value will be returned to the main program.

4. A function can return values of any of the simple types: **real, char, boolean,** or **integer.** In Turbo Pascal, a function can also return a value of type **string,** which is not allowed in standard Pascal.

As in the main program, there does not have to be a declaration section for a function. When there is one, only variables needed in the function are declared. Further, the section is usually not very elaborate because the purpose of a function is normally a small, single task.

Finally, the executable section for a function must perform the desired task, assign a value to the function name, terminate with a semicolon rather than a period, and have the general form

```
BEGIN
  .
  . (work of function here)
  .
END;
```

We will now illustrate user-defined functions with several examples.

EXAMPLE 3.1

Write a function to compute the cube of an integer. Since the actual parameter from the main program will be of type **integer,** we have

```
FUNCTION Cube (X : integer) : integer;
  BEGIN
   Cube := X * X * X
  END;
```

A typical call to this function from the main program is

```
A := Cube(5);
```

EXAMPLE 3.2

Let's write a function to perform the task of computing unit cost for pizza. (We did this using a procedure in Section 3.2.) Data sent to the function are cost and size. The function returns the unit cost. Formal parameters are Cost and Size. Using the function name PricePerSquareInch, we have

```
FUNCTION PricePerSquareInch (Cost, Size : real) : real;
  VAR
    Radius, Area : real;
  BEGIN
    Radius := Size / 2;
    Area := Pi * sqr(Radius);
    PricePerSquareInch := Cost / Area
  END;  {  of FUNCTION PricePerSquareInch  }
```

This can be called from the main program by

```
UnitCost := PricePerSquareInch(Cost, Size);
```

EXAMPLE 3.3

Turbo Pascal does not provide a power function. However, now that you know how to write a function, you can use the built-in functions **ln** and **exp** to write a power function. Before writing this, however, let's consider how these functions can be used to produce the desired result.

First, **exp** and **ln** are inverse functions in the sense that

$$\mathbf{exp}(\mathbf{ln}(X)) = X$$

for all positive X. Thus, we have

$$3^{2.5} = \mathbf{exp}(\mathbf{ln}(3^{2.5}))$$

Using properties of logarithms,

$$\mathbf{ln}(a^b) = b * \mathbf{ln}(a)$$

Hence

$$\exp(\mathbf{ln}(3^{2.5})) = \mathbf{exp}(2.5 * \mathbf{ln}(3))$$

Since each of these operations can be performed in Turbo Pascal, we can compute $3^{2.5}$ by

$$3^{2.5} = \mathbf{exp}(2.5 * \mathbf{ln}(3))$$

or more generally

$$A^X = \mathbf{exp}(X * \mathbf{ln}(A))$$

If we let Base denote the base A and Exponent denote the exponent X, we can now write a function Power as

```
FUNCTION Power (Base, Exponent : real) : real;
  BEGIN
    Power := exp(Exponent * ln(Base))
  END;  {  of FUNCTION Power  }
```

This can be called from the main program by

```
Base := 3;
Exponent := 2.5;
Num := Power(Base, Exponent);
```

Use in a Program

Now that you have seen several examples of user-defined functions, let's consider their use in a program. Once they are written, they can be used in the same manner as standard functions, usually in one of the following forms:

1. Assignment statements

```
A := 5;
B := Cube(A);
```

2. Arithmetic expressions

```
A := 5;
B := 3 * Cube(A) + 2;
```

3. Output statements

```
A := 5;
writeln (Cube(A):17);
   .
   .
   .
```

Multiple Functions

Programs can contain more than one function. When several user-defined functions are needed in a program, each one should be developed and positioned in the program as previously indicated.

When a program calls several functions, they can generally be positioned above the main program body in any order. However, if one function contains a call to another function, the function being called must appear before the function from which it is called.

Exercises 3.4

1. Discuss the difference between a procedure and a function.
2. Write a test program to see what happens when the function name is used on the right side of an assignment statement. For example

```
FUNCTION Total (OldSum, NewNum : integer) : integer;
  BEGIN
    Total := OldSum;
    Total := Total + NewNum
  END;
```

3. Indicate which of the following are valid function headings. Explain what is wrong with those that are invalid.
   a. `FUNCTION RoundTenth (X : real);`
   b. `FUNCTION MakeChange (X, Y) : real;`
   c. `FUNCTION Max (M1, M2, M3 : integer) : integer;`
   d. `FUNCTION Sign (Num : real) : char;`
   e. `FUNCTION Truth (Ch : char, Num : real) : boolean;`
4. Find all errors in each of the following functions.
   a.
```
FUNCTION AvOf2 (N1, N2 : integer) : integer;
  BEGIN
    AvOf2 := (N1 + N2) / 2
  END;
```
   b.
```
FUNCTION Total (L1, L2 : integer) : integer;
  VAR
    Sum : integer;
  BEGIN
    Total := 0;
    Sum := L1 + L2
  END;
```
5. Write a function for each of the following.
   a. Round a real to the nearest tenth.
   b. Round a real to the nearest hundredth.
   c. Convert degrees Fahrenheit to degrees Celsius.
   d. Compute the charge for cars at a parking lot; the rate is $0.75 per hour or a fraction thereof.
6. Write a program that uses the function you wrote for Exercise 5(d) to print a ticket for a customer who parks in the parking lot. Assume the input is in minutes.
7. The factorial of a positive integer n is defined as
   $n! = n * (n - 1) * \cdots * 2 * 1$ for $n > 1$

   Write a function (Factorial) that will compute and return $n!$.
8. Write a complete program using Cube and Factorial that will produce a table of the integers 1 to 10 together with their squares, cubes, and factorials.
9. Use the functions **sqr** and Cube to write a program to print a chart of the integers 1 to 5 together with their squares and cubes. Output from this program should be

```
Number     Number Squared     Number Cubed
------     --------------     ------------
  1              1                  1
  2              4                  8
  3              9                 27
  4             16                 64
  5             25                125
```

10. Write a program that allows the user to enter a Base (a) and Exponent (x) and then have the program print the value of a^x.

11. Write a function (Arithmetic) that will receive a sign (+ or *) and two integers (N1, N2) and then compute and return either N1 + N2 or N1 * N2, depending on the sign received.

12. Algebra teachers often have students play "guess the rule." This consists of having the first person write down a rule (function), such as $y = x^2 + 1$. A second person then gives a value for x. The first person indicates the function value associated with the input. Thus, for $x = 3$, y would be 10 if $y = x^2 + 1$. The game continues until the second person guesses the rule.

    Write a program that allows you to play this game with another student. Write it in such a way that it can be easily modified to use different functions.

■ 3.5 Using Subprograms

Use of subprograms facilitates writing programs for problems with solutions that have been developed using top-down design. A procedure or function can be written for each main task. Each subprogram can contain its own subprograms if needed.

7.0

How complex should a procedure or function be? In general, functions should be relatively short and perform a specific task. Procedures can be longer but probably should not be more than one page of printout. Some programmers prefer to limit procedures to no more than one full screen. If a procedure is longer than a page or screen, you might consider subdividing the task into smaller procedures or functions.

Functions versus Procedures

When should you use a function instead of a procedure in a program? A general rule is to think of a function as a construct that returns only one value. Thus, a function would be used when a single value is required in the main program. Variable parameters can be used with functions, but this is discouraged in good programming practices.

What Kind of Parameters Should Be Used?

Use variable parameters when information is going to be returned to the main program; otherwise, use value parameters. The choices will be apparent if you use data flow arrows or module specifications when designing the solution to the problem.

Using Stubs

As programs get longer and incorporate more subprograms, a technique frequently used to get the program running is *stub programming.* A stub program is a no-frills, simple version of what will be a final program. It does

A NOTE OF INTEREST

Niklaus Wirth

Niklaus Wirth began his work in the computing field by taking a course in numerical analysis at Laval University in Quebec, Canada. However, the computer (Alvac III E) was frequently out of order and the hexadecimal code programming exercises went untested. He received his doctorate from the University of California, Berkeley, in 1963.

After other early experiences in programming, it became apparent to Wirth that computers of the future had to be more effectively programmable. Consequently, he joined a research group that worked on developing a compiler for an IBM 704. This language was NELIAC, a dialect of ALGOL 58. In rapid succession, he developed or contributed to the development of Euler, ALGOL W, and PL360. In 1967, he returned to Switzerland and established a team of three assistants with whom he developed and implemented the language Pascal.

Pascal was the first major programming language to implement the ideas and methodology of structured programming and was initially developed to teach programming concepts. It is particularly successful as a teaching language because it allows the teacher to focus on structures and concepts rather than features and peculiarities. However, it has rapidly expanded beyond its initial purpose and has found increasing acceptance in business and scientific applications.

not contain details of output and full algorithm development. It does contain a rough version of each subprogram and all parameter lists. When the stub version runs, you know your logic is correct and values are appropriately being passed to and from subprograms. Then you can fill in necessary details to get a complete program.

Using Drivers

The main program is sometimes referred to as the *main driver*. When subprograms are used in a program, this driver can be modified to check subprograms in a sequential fashion. For example, suppose a main driver is

```
BEGIN  {  Main driver  }
  Initialize (Sum, Count);
  GetData (Sum, Count);
  PerformComputations (Sum, Count);
  PrintResults (Sum, Count)
END.  {  of main driver  }
```

Procedures can be checked by putting comment indicators around the remainder of the program and temporarily adding a statement to print values of variables. Thus, you could run the following version:

```
BEGIN  {  Main driver  }
  Initialize (Sum, Count);
  GetData (Sum, Count);
  writeln ('Sum is ', Sum, 'Count is ', Count);
{ PerformComputations (Sum, Count);
  PrintResults (Sum, Count)  }
END.  {  of main driver  }
```

Once you are sure a subprogram is running, you can remove the comment indicators and continue through the main driver to check successive subprograms.

COMMUNICATION AND STYLE TIPS

Each subprogram should contain documentation sufficient to allow the reader to understand what information is given to the subprogram, what task is to be performed, and what information is to be returned to the calling program. This information aids in debugging programs. In this text, the headings of subprograms in complete programs will be followed by documentation in the form

```
{  Given:    <Statement of information sent to the subprogram>  }
{  Task:     <State of task(s) to be performed>                 }
{  Return:   <Statement of value(s) to be returned>             }
```

When subprograms are separately developed and illustrated, this documentation will not be included. Instead, text development immediately preceding the subprogram will serve the same purpose.

FOCUS ON PROGRAM DESIGN

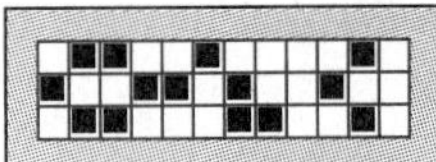

In order to encourage people to shop downtown, the Downtown Businesses Association partially subsidizes parking. They have established the E-Z Parking parking lot, where customers are charged $0.75 for each full hour of parking. There is no charge for part of an hour. Thus, if someone uses the lot for less than an hour, there is no charge.

The E-Z Parking parking lot is open from 9:00 A.M. until 11:00 P.M. When a vehicle enters, the driver is given a ticket with the entry time printed in military style. Thus, if a car enters the lot at 9:30 A.M., the ticket will read 0930. If a vehicle enters at 1:20 P.M., the ticket will read 1320. When the vehicle leaves, the driver presents the ticket to the attendant and the amount due is computed.

Now let's develop a solution and write a program to assist the attendant. Input consists of a starting and ending time. Output should be a statement to the customer indicating the input information, the total amount due, a heading, and a closing message. Sample output for the data 1050 (10:50 A.M.) and 1500 (3:00 P.M.) is

```
Please enter the time in and press <Enter>.  1050
Please enter the time out and press <Enter>.  1500


           E - Z Parking
           -------------

      Time in:    1050
      Time out:   1500

      Amount due       $  3.00

   Thank you for using E - Z Parking

             BUCKLE UP
                and
           DRIVE SAFELY
```

A first-level development for this problem is

1. Get the data
2. Compute the amount
3. Print the results

A structure chart for this problem is given in Figure 3.14. (Recall that an arrow pointing into a module indicates data are being received and that an arrow pointing out indicates data are being sent from the module.)

FIGURE 3.14
Structure chart for the parking lot program

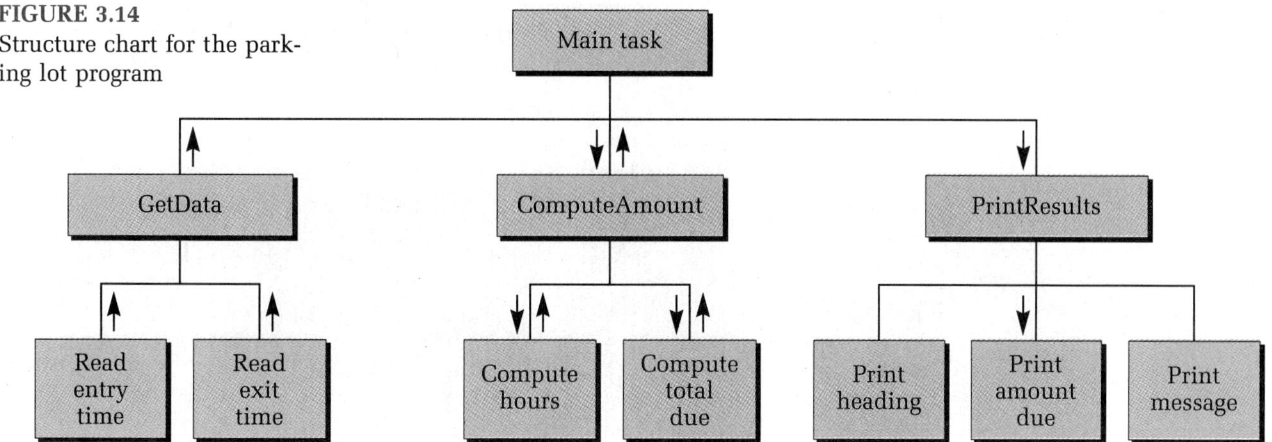

Module specifications for the three main modules are

1. GetData Module
   Data received: None
   Information returned: Entry time
   Exit time
   Logic: Have the user enter information from the keyboard.
2. ComputeAmount Module
   Data received: Entry time
   Exit time
   Information returned: Amount due
   Logic: Subtract the entry time from the exit time and use **DIV** 100 to get the number of full hours.
3. PrintResults Module
   Data received: Entry time
   Exit time
   Amount due
   Information returned: None
   Logic: Print the heading, entry time, exit time, amount due, and closing message.

By examining the module specifications, we see that two variable parameters are needed for GetData. ComputeAmount needs two value parameters and one variable parameter, and PrintResults needs three value parameters.

A second-level pseudocode development is

1. Get the data
   1.1 read time entered
   1.2 read time exited
2. Compute the amount
   2.1 compute number of hours
   2.2 compute amount due
3. Print the results
   3.1 print a heading
   3.2 print amount due
   3.3 print a closing message

The main driver is

```
BEGIN  {  Main program  }
  GetData (Entrytime, ExitTime);
  AmountDue := ComputeAmount(EntryTime, ExitTime);
  PrintResults (EntryTime, ExitTime, AmountDue)
END.  {  of main program  }
```

A complete program for this is

```
PROGRAM Parking;

{  This program prints statements for customers of the E-Z    }
{  Parking parking lot.  Interactive input consists of entry  }
{  time and exit time from the lot.  Output consists of a     }
{  customer statement.  Emphasis is placed on using           }
{  procedures and a function to develop the program.          }

USES
  Crt;

CONST
  HourlyRate = 0.75;
  Indent = ' ';

VAR
  EntryTime,               {  Time of entry into parking lot  }
  ExitTime : integer;      {  Time of exit from parking lot   }
  AmountDue : real;        {  Cost of parking in lot          }

{*************************************************************}

PROCEDURE GetData (VAR EntryTime, ExitTime : integer);

  {  Given:   Nothing                                         }
  {  Task:    Enter EntryTime and ExitTime from the keyboard  }
  {  Return:  EntryTime, ExitTime                             }

  BEGIN                                                              1
    writeln ('Please enter the time in and press <Enter>.');
    readln (EntryTime);
    writeln ('Please enter the time out and press <Enter>.');
    readln (ExitTime)
  END;  {  of PROCEDURE GetData  }

{*************************************************************}

FUNCTION ComputeAmount (EntryTime, ExitTime : integer) : real;

  {  Given:   EntryTime and ExitTime                        }
  {  Task:    Find full hours and multiply by HourlyRate    }
  {  Return:  AmountDue                                     }

  VAR                                                                2
    NumberOfHours : integer;
  BEGIN
    NumberOfHours := (ExitTime - EntryTime) DIV 100;
    ComputeAmount := NumberOfHours * HourlyRate
  END;  {  of FUNCTION ComputeAmount  }

{*************************************************************}
```

```
PROCEDURE PrintHeading;

  {  Given:   Nothing                                       }
  {  Task:    Print a suitable heading for the ticket       }
  {  Return:  Nothing                                       }

  BEGIN
    writeln;
    writeln (Indent:11, 'E - Z Parking');
    writeln (Indent:11, '-------------');
    writeln
  END;  {  of PROCEDURE PrintHeading  }

{*************************************************************}

PROCEDURE PrintMessage;

  {  Given:   Nothing                                       }
  {  Task:    Print a closing message for the ticket        }
  {  Return:  Nothing                                       }

  BEGIN
    writeln;
    writeln (Indent:1, 'Thank you for using E - Z Parking');
    writeln;
    writeln (Indent:13, 'BUCKLE UP');
    writeln (Indent:16, 'and');                                    3
    writeln (Indent:11, 'DRIVE SAFELY');
    writeln
  END;  {  of PROCEDURE PrintMessage  }

{*************************************************************}

PROCEDURE PrintResults (EntryTime, ExitTime : integer;
                        AmountDue : real);

  {  Given:   EntryTime, ExitTime, AmountDue                }
  {  Task:    Print a customer receipt;  calls both         }
  {                PrintHeading and PrintMessage            }
  {  Return:  Nothing                                       }

  BEGIN
    ClrScr;
    PrintHeading;
    writeln (Indent:4, 'Time in: ', EntryTime:6);
    writeln (Indent:4, 'Time out:', ExitTime:6);
    writeln;
    writeln (Indent:4, 'Amount due     $', AmountDue:6:2);
    PrintMessage;
    readln
  END;  {  of PROCEDURE PrintResults  }

{*************************************************************}

BEGIN  {  Main program  }
  GetData (EntryTime, ExitTime);
  AmountDue := ComputeAmount(EntryTime, ExitTime);
  PrintResults (EntryTime, ExitTime, AmountDue)
END.  {  of main program  }
```

A sample run using the data 0930 as entry time and 1320 as exit time produces

```
Please enter the time in and press <Enter>.
0930
Please enter the time out and press <Enter>.
1320

            E - Z Parking
            -------------

    Time in:    0930
    Time out:   1320

    Amount due       $  2.25

 Thank you for using E - Z Parking

              BUCKLE UP
                 and
            DRIVE SAFELY
```

RUNNING AND DEBUGGING HINTS

1. Each subprogram can be tested separately to see if it is producing the desired result. This is accomplished by a main program that calls and tests only the subprogram in question.
2. You can use related or identical variable names in the parameter lists. For example

   ```
   PROCEDURE Compute (N1, N2 : integer;
                      VAR Av : real);
   ```

   or

   ```
   PROCEDURE Compute (Number1, Number2 : integer;
                      VAR Average : real);
   ```

   could be called by

   ```
   Compute (Number1, Number2, Average);
   ```

3. Be sure the type and order of actual parameters and formal parameters agree. You can do this by listing them one below the other. For example

   ```
   PROCEDURE GetData (VAR Init1, Init2 : char; Sc : integer);
   ```

   could be called by

   ```
         GetData (Initial1, Initial2, Score);
   ```

4. Carefully distinguish between value parameters and variable parameters. If a value is to be returned to the main program, it must be passed by reference using a variable parameter. This means it must be declared with **VAR** in the procedure heading.

Summary

Key Terms

actual parameter
block
bottom-up testing
cohesive subprogram
encapsulation
formal parameter
global identifier (variable)
interface
local identifier (variable)
main driver
modularity
nonlocal
passed by reference
postcondition
precondition
procedural abstraction
procedure

scope of an identifier
side effect
structured programming
stub programming
subblock
subprogram
user-defined function
value parameter
variable parameter

Keywords

FUNCTION **PROCEDURE** **ln** **exp**

Key Concepts

- A subprogram is a program within a program; procedures and functions are subprograms.
- Subprograms can be utilized to perform specific tasks in a program. Procedures are often used to initialize variables (variable parameters), get data (variable parameters), print headings (no variables needed), perform computations (value and/or variable parameters), and print data (value parameters).
- The general form for a procedure heading is
  PROCEDURE ⟨name⟩ (⟨parameter list⟩);
- Value parameters are used when values are passed only from the main program to the procedure; a typical parameter list is

```
PROCEDURE PrintData (N1, N2 : integer;
                     X, Y : real);
```

- Variable parameters are used when values are to be returned to the main program; a typical parameter list is

```
PROCEDURE GetData (VAR Init1, Init2 : char;
                   VAR N1 : integer);
```

- A formal parameter is one listed in the subprogram heading; it is like a blank waiting to receive a value from the calling program.

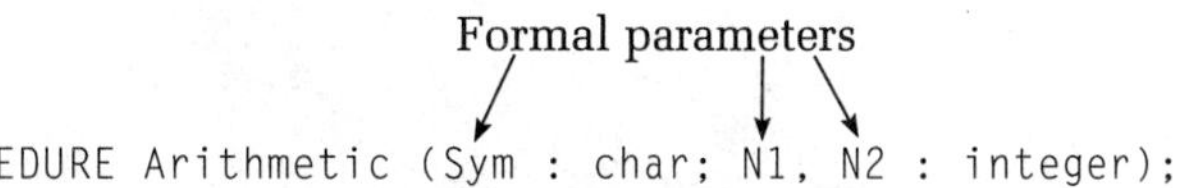
Formal parameters
PROCEDURE Arithmetic (Sym : char; N1, N2 : integer);

- An actual parameter is a variable listed in the subprogram call in the calling program.

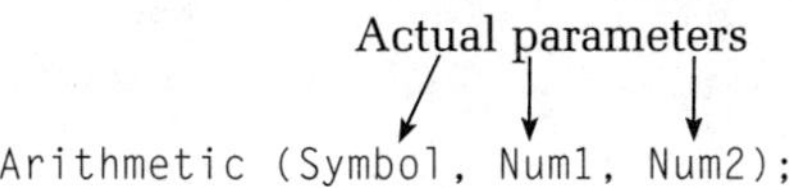
Actual parameters
Arithmetic (Symbol, Num1, Num2);

- The formal parameter list in the subprogram heading must match the number and types of actual parameters used in the main program when the subprogram is called.

```
PROCEDURE Arithmetic (Sym : char; N1, N2 : integer);
Arithmetic (Symbol, Num1, Num2);
```

- Global identifiers can be used by the main program and all subprograms.
- Local identifiers are available only to the subprogram in which they are declared.
- Each identifier is available to the block in which it is declared; this includes all subprograms contained within the block.
- Identifiers are not available outside their blocks.
- The scope of an identifier refers to the blocks in which the identifier is available.
- Understanding the scope of identifiers is aided by graphic illustration of blocks in a program; thus

```
PROGRAM Practice;
VAR
  X, Y, Z : real;
PROCEDURE Sub1 (X1 : real);
  VAR
    X2 : real;
```

```
  BEGIN
    .
    .
    .
  END;  {  of PROCEDURE Sub1  }
PROCEDURE Sub2 (X1 : real);
  VAR
    Z2 : real;
```

can be visualized as shown in Figure 3.15.

FIGURE 3.15
Scope of identifiers

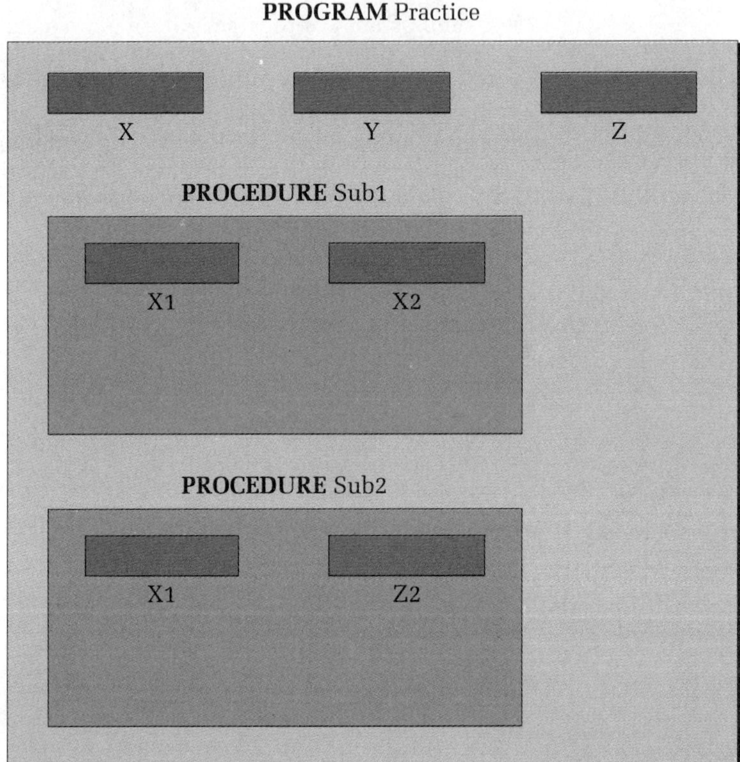

- A user-defined function is a subprogram that performs a specific task.
- The form for a user-defined function is

```
FUNCTION ⟨function name⟩ (⟨parameter list⟩) : ⟨return type⟩;
VAR
BEGIN
  .
  .  (work of function here)
  .
END;
```

- An assignment must be made to the function name in the body of the function.
- Within a function, the function name can be used only on the left side of an assignment statement.

■ Programming Problems and Projects

The following programming problems will be run on a very limited set of data. In later chapters, as you build your programming skills, you will run these problems with larger data bases and subprograms for various parts. Problems marked with a box to the left of the number are referred to and used repeatedly; carefully choose the ones on which to work, and then develop them completely.

1. Write a program to get the coefficients of a quadratic equation

   $ax^2 + bx + c = 0$

   from the keyboard and then print the value of the discriminant

   $b^2 - 4ac$

   A sample display for getting input is

```
Enter coefficients a, b, and c for the quadratic equation
  ax^2 + bx + c = 0

a = 1
b = 2
c = 3
```

   Run this program at least three times, using test data that result in $b^2 - 4ac = 0$, $b^2 - 4ac > 0$, and $b^2 - 4ac < 0$.

2. Write a program to compute the cost for carpeting a room. Input should consist of the room length, room width, and carpet price per square yard. Use constants for the pad charge and installation charge. Include a heading as part of the output.

   A typical input screen would be

```
What is the room length in feet? <Enter>
What is the room width in feet?  <Enter>
What is the carpet price/square yard? <Enter>
```

   Output for a sample run of this program (without a heading) could be

```
    Dimensions of the room (in feet) are 17 × 22.
    The area to be carpeted is 41.6 square yards.
    The carpet price is $11.95 per square yard.

        Room dimensions                17 × 22
        Carpet required                41.6 square yards
        Carpet price/square yard        $11.95
        Pad price/square yard           $ 2.95
        Installation cost/square yard   $  .95
                                        ------
        Total cost/square yard          $15.85
        Total cost                               $659.36
```

3. Williamson's Paint and Papering store wants a computer program to help them determine how much paint is needed to paint a room. Assuming a room is to have four walls and the ceiling painted, input for the program should be the length, width, and height of the room. Use a constant for the wall height (usually eight feet). One gallon of paint should cover 250 square feet. Cost of paint for the walls and ceiling should be entered by the user. Output should be the amount and cost of each kind of paint and the total cost.

4. The Fairfield College faculty recently signed a three-year contract that included salary increments of 7 percent, 6 percent, and 5 percent, respectively, for the next three years. Write a program that allows a user to enter the current salary and then prints out the compounded salary for each of the next three years.

5. Several instructors use various weights (percentages of the final grade) for test scores. Write a program that allows the user to enter three test scores

and the weight for each score. Output should consist of the input data, the weighted score for each test, and the total score (sum of the weighted scores).

6. The Roll-Em Lanes bowling team would like to have a computer program to print the team results for one series of games. The team consists of four members whose names are Weber, Fazio, Martin, and Patterson. Each person on the team bowls three games during the series; thus, the input will contain three lines, each with four integer scores. Your output should include all input data, individual series totals, game average for each member, team series, and team average.

   Sample output is

```
NAME          GAME 1    GAME 2    GAME 3    TOTAL    AVERAGE

Weber           212       220       190      622      207.3
Fazio           195       235       210      640      213.3
Martin          178       190       206      574      191.3
Patterson       195       215       210      620      206.7

     Team Total:  2456

     Team Average:  818.7
```

■ 7. The Natural Pine Furniture Company has recently hired you to help them convert their antiquated payroll system to a computer-based model. They know you are still learning, so all they want right now is a program that will print a one-week pay report for three employees. You should use the constant definition section for the following:

   a. Federal withholding tax rate   18%
   b. State withholding tax rate   4.5%
   c. Hospitalization $25.65
   d. Union dues $ 7.85

   Each line of input will contain the employee's initials, the number of hours worked, and the employee's hourly rate. Your output should include a report for each employee and a summary report for the company files. A sample employee form follows:

```
Employee:        JIM
Hours Worked:  40.00
Hourly Rate:    9.75

     Total Wages:                            $390.00

     Deductions:
          Federal Withholding     70.20
          State Withholding       17.55
          Hospitalization         26.65
          Union Dues               7.85
                                 ------
               Total Deductions  122.25

     Net Pay                                 $267.75
```

   Output for a summary report could be

```
          Natural Pine Furniture Company
                  Weekly Summary

          Gross Wages:
```

```
Deductions:
     Federal Withholding
     State Withholding
     Hospitalization
     Union Dues
          Total Deductions

Net Wages
```

■ 8. The Child-Growth Encyclopedia Company wants a computer program that will print a monthly sales chart. Products produced by the company, prices, and sales commissions for each are

a. Basic encyclopedia	$325.00	22%
b. Child educational supplement	$127.50	15%
c. Annual update book	$ 18.95	20%

Monthly sales data for one region consist of a two-letter region identifier (such as MI) and three integers representing the number of units sold for each product listed above. A typical input screen would be

```
What is your sales region?
MI
How many Basic Encyclopedia were sold?
150
How many Child Supplements were sold?
120
How many Annual Updates were sold?
105
```

Write a program that will get the monthly sales data for two sales regions and produce the desired company chart. The prices may vary from month to month and should be defined in the constant definition section. The commissions are not subject to change. Typical output could be

```
                          MONTHLY SALES CHART

                            Basic           Child          Annual
       Region            Encyclopedia     Supplement       Update

Units sold   MI              150             120             105
(by region)  TX              225             200             150
                            -----           -----           -----
Total units sold:            375             320             255

  Price/unit               $325.00         $127.50          $18.95

Gross Sales:             $121,875.00      $40,800.00       $4,832.25

  Commission rate            22%             15%             20%

Commissions paid:        $26,812.50       $6,120.00        $966.45
```

9. The Village Variety Store is having its annual Christmas sale. The store manager would like you to write a program to produce a daily report for the store. Each item sold is identified by a code consisting of one letter followed by one digit. Your report should include data for three items. Each of the three lines of data will include item code, number of items sold, original item price, and reduction percentage. Your report should include a chart with the input data, sale price per item, and total amount of sales per item. You should also print a daily summary. Sample input is

```
A1 13 5.95 15
A2 24 7.95 20
A3 80 3.95 50
```

Typical output form could be

```
Item Code  # Sold  Original Price  Reductions  Sale Price  Income
---------  ------  --------------  ----------  ----------  ------
   A1        13        $5.95           15%         $5.06    $65.78

Daily Summary
-------------
   Gross Income:
```

10. The Holiday-Out Motel Company, Inc., wants a program that will print a statement for each overnight customer. Each line of input will contain room number (integer), room rate (real), number of nights (integer), telephone charges (real), and restaurant charges (real). You should use the constant definition section for the date and current tax rate. Each customer statement should include all input data, the date, tax rate and amount, total due, appropriate heading, and appropriate closing message. Test your program by running it for two customers. The tax rate applies only to the room cost. A typical input screen is

```
Room number?
135
Room rate?
39.95
Number of nights?
3
Telephone charges?
3.75
Meals?
57.50
```

A customer statement form is

```
     Holiday-Out Motel Company, Inc.
     ------- --- ----- -------- ---
Date: XX-XX-XX
Room #                         135
Room Rate:                  $39.95
Number of Nights:                3

Room Cost:                 $119.85
Tax:  XXX%                    4.79
     Subtotal:                        $124.64

Telephone:                               3.75
Meals:                                  57.50

     TOTAL DUE                        $185.89

    Thank you for staying at Holiday-Out
                Drive safely
              Please come again
```

■ **11.** As a part-time job this semester, you are working for the Family Budget Assistance Center. Your boss has asked you to write and execute a program that will analyze data for a family. Input for each family will consist of

Family ID number	**(integer)**
Number in family	**(integer)**

Annual income (**real**)
Total debts (**real**)

Your program should output the following:

a. An appropriate header
b. The family's identification number, number in family, income, and total debts
c. Predicted family living expenses ($3000 multiplied by the size of the family)
d. The monthly payment necessary to pay off the debt in one year
e. The amount the family should save [family size multiplied by 2 percent of the income – debt, or family size * 0.02 * (income – debt)]
f. Your service fee (0.5 percent of the income)

Run your program for the following two families:

Identification Number	Size	Income	Debt
51	4	$18000.00	$2000.00
72	7	26000.00	4800.00

Output for the first family could be

```
        Family Budget Assistance Center
                  March 1993
            Telephone: (800)555-1234

Identification number                  51
Family size                             4
Annual income                  $ 18000.00
Total debts                    $  2000.00
Expected living expenses       $ 12000.00
Monthly payment                $   166.67
Savings                        $  1280.00
Service fee                    $    90.00
```

■ **12.** The Caswell Catering and Convention Service has asked you to write a computer program to produce customers' bills. The program should read in the following data.

a. The number of adults to be served
b. The number of children to be served
c. The cost per adult meal
d. The cost per child meal (60 percent of the cost of the adult's meal)
e. The cost for dessert (same for adults and children)
f. The room fee (no room fee if catered at the person's home)
g. A percentage for tip and tax (not applied to the room fee)
h. A deduction from the bill of any prior deposit.

Write a program and test it using data sets 2, 3, and 4 from the table shown.

Data Set	Adult Count	Child Count	Adult Cost	Dessert Cost	Room Rate	Tip/Tax	Deposit
1	23	7	$12.75	$1.00	$45.00	18%	$50.00
2	54	3	13.50	1.25	65.00	19%	40.00
3	24	15	12.00	0.00	45.00	18%	75.00
4	71	2	11.15	1.50	0.00	6%	0.00

Note that data set 1 was used to produce the following sample output.

```
   Caswell Catering and Convention Service
                 Final Bill

            Number of adults:        23
          Number of children:         7
Cost per adult without dessert:  $   12.75
Cost per child without dessert:  $    7.65
             Cost per dessert:   $    1.00
                     Room fee:   $   45.00
            Tip and tax rate:          0.18

    Total cost for adult meals:  $  293.25
    Total cost for child meals:  $   53.55
        Total cost for dessert:  $   30.00
               Total food cost:  $  376.80
              Plus tip and tax:  $   67.82
                 Plus room fee:  $   45.00
                  Less deposit:  $   50.00

                   Balance due:  $  439.62
```

13. The Maripot Carpet Store has asked you to write a computer program to calculate the amount a customer should be charged. The president of the company has given you the following information to help in writing the program.
    a. The carpet charge is equal to the number of square yards purchased multiplied by the carpet cost per square yard.
    b. The labor cost is equal to the number of square yards purchased multiplied by the labor cost per square yard. A fixed fee for floor preparation is added to some customers' bills.
    c. Large-volume customers are given a percentage discount, but the discount applies only to the carpet charge, not to the labor costs.
    d. All customers are charged 4 percent sales tax on the carpet: there is no sales tax on the labor cost.

Write the program and test it for customers 2, 3, and 4.

Customer	Sq. yds.	Cost per sq. yd.	Labor per sq. yd.	Prep. Cost	Discount
1	17	$18.50	$3.50	$38.50	0.02
2	40	24.95	2.95	0.00	0.14
3	23	16.80	3.25	57.95	0.00
4	26	21.25	0.00	80.00	0.00

Note that the data for customer 1 were used to produce the following sample output.

```
Square yards purchased:        17
  Cost per square yard:   $   18.50
 Labor per square yard:   $    3.50
Floor preparation cost:   $   38.50
       Cost for carpet:   $  314.50
        Cost for labor:   $   98.00
    Discount on carpet:   $    6.29
         Tax on carpet:   $   12.33
    Charge to customer:   $  418.54
```

14. The manager of the Croswell Carpet Store has asked you to write a program to print customers' bill. The manager has given you the following information.

- The store expresses the length and width of a room in terms of feet and tenths of a foot. For example, the length might be reported as 16.7 feet.
- The amount of carpet purchased is expressed as square yards. It is found by dividing the area of the room (in square feet) by 9.
- The store does not sell a fraction of a square yard. Thus, square yards must always be rounded up.
- The carpet charge is equal to the number of square yards purchased multiplied by the carpet cost per square yard. Sales tax equal to 4 percent of the carpet cost must be added to the bill.
- All customers are sold a carpet pad at $2.25 per square yard. Sales tax equal to 4 percent of the pad cost must be added to the bill.
- The labor cost is equal to the number of square yards purchased multiplied by $2.40, which is the labor cost per square yard. No tax is charged on labor.
- Large-volume customers may be given a discount. The discount may apply only to the carpet cost (before sales tax is added), only to the pad cost (before sales tax is added), only to the labor cost, or to any combination of the three charges.
- Each customer is identified by a five-digit number, and that number should appear on the bill. The sample output follows.

```
     Croswell Carpet Store
        Invoice

Customer number:          26817

       Carpet :          $574.20
          Pad :          $ 81.00
        Labor :          $ 86.40

     Subtotal :          $741.60
Less discount :          $ 65.52

     Subtotal :          $676.08
     Plus tax :          $ 23.59
        Total :          $699.67
```

Write the program, and test it for the following three customers.

a. Mr. Wilson (customer 81429) ordered carpet for his family room, which measures 25 feet long and 18 feet wide. The carpet sells for $12.95 per square yard, and the manager agreed to give him a discount of 8 percent on the carpet and 6 percent on the labor.

b. Mr. and Mrs. Adams (customer 04246) ordered carpet for their bedroom, which measures 16.5 feet by 15.4 feet. The carpet sells for $18.90 per square yard, and the manager granted a discount of 12 percent on everything.

c. Ms. Logan (customer 39050) ordered carpet that cost $8.95 per square yard for her daughter's bedroom. The room measures 13.1 by 12.5 feet. No discounts were given.

15. Each week Abduhl's Flying Carpets pays its salespeople a base salary plus a bonus for each carpet they sell. In addition, the company pays a commission of 10 percent of the total sales by each salesperson.

Write a program to compute a salesperson's salary for the month by inputting Base, Bonus, Quantity, and Sales and making the necessary calculations. Use the following test data.

Salesperson	Base	Bonus	Quantity	Commission	Sales
1	$250.00	$15.00	20	10%	$1543.69
2	280.00	19.50	36	10%	2375.90

The commission figure is 10 percent. Be sure you can change this easily if necessary. Sample output follows.

```
     Salesperson :     1
            Base : $ 250.00
           Bonus : $  15.00
        Quantity :    20
     Total Bonus : $ 300.00
      Commission :    10%
           Sales : $1543.69
Total Commission : $ 154.37
             Pay : $ 704.37
```

■ Communication in Practice

1. Modify one of your programs from this section by saving *only* the documentation, constant definitions, variable declaration section, subprogram headings, and main driver. Exchange your modified version with a student who has prepared a similar version. Using the modified version, reconstruct the tasks of the program. Discuss your results with the student who wrote the program.
2. Modify one of your programs from this section by deleting all documentation. Exchange your modified version with a student who has prepared a similar version. Using the modified version, write documentation for the program. Compare your results with the other student's original version.
3. "Think Metric" is the preferred way of having members of a nonmetric society become familiar with the metric system. Unfortunately, during the transition, many people are forced to rely on converting from their present system to the metric system. Develop a solution and write a program to help people convert their height and weight from inches and pounds to centimeters and kilograms. The program should get input of a person's height (in feet and inches) and weight (rounded to the nearest pound) from a keyboard. Output should consist of the height and weight in metric units.
4. Discuss the issue of documenting subprograms with instructors of computer science, upper-level students majoring in computer science, and some of your classmates. Prepare a report for the class on this issue. Your report should contain information about different forms of documentation, the perceived need for documentation by various groups, the significance of documenting data transmission, and so forth. If possible, use specific examples to illustrate good versus poor documentation of subprograms.
5. Reread the material in Section 3.2 concerning procedural abstraction. Then, from Problems 5, 7, 8, and 11, select one that you have not yet worked. Develop a structure chart and write module specifications for each module required for the problem you have chosen. Also, write a main driver for your program and write complete documentation for each subprogram, including comments about all parameters.

Selection Statements

■ CHAPTER OUTLINE ■

The previous chapters set the stage for using computers to solve problems. You have seen how programs in Turbo Pascal can be used to get data, perform computations, and print results. You should be able to write complete, short programs, so it is now time to examine other aspects of programming.

A major feature of a computer is its ability to make decisions. For example, a condition is examined and a decision is made as to which program statement is next executed. Statements that permit a computer to make decisions are called *selection statements.* Selection statements are examples of *control structures* because they allow the programmer to control the flow of execution of program statements.

■ 4.1 Boolean Expressions

Before looking at decision making, we need to examine the logical constructs in Turbo Pascal, which include a new data type called **boolean.** This data type allows you to represent something as true or false. Although this sounds relatively simple (and it is), this is a very significant feature of computers.

The **boolean** Data Type

Thus far, we have used data types for integers, reals, characters, and strings; another data type is **boolean.** A typical declaration of a Boolean variable is

```
VAR
  Flag : boolean;
```

In general, Boolean variables are declared by

```
VAR
  ⟨variable 1⟩,
  ⟨variable 2⟩,
      .
      .
      .
  ⟨variable n⟩ : boolean;
```

There are only two values for variables of the **boolean** data type: **true** and **false.** These are both constant standard identifiers and can only be used as Boolean values. When these assignments are made, the contents of the designated memory locations will be the assigned values. For example, if the declaration

```
VAR
  Flag1, Flag2 : boolean;
```

is made

```
Flag1 := true;
Flag2 := false;
```

produces

true	**false**
Flag1	Flag2

As with other data types, if two variables are of type **boolean,** the value of one variable can be assigned to another variable as

```
Flag1 := true;
Flag2 := Flag1;
```

and can be envisioned as

Note that quotation marks are not used when assigning the values **true** or **false** because these are Boolean constants, not strings.

The **boolean** data type is an ordinal type. Thus, there is an order relationship between **true** and **false**: **false** < **true**. Furthermore, the **ord** function can be applied to the **boolean** values: **ord(false)** = 0 and **ord(true)** = 1.

Output of boolean

S Boolean variables can be used as arguments for **write** and **writeln.** Thus

```
Flag := true;
writeln (Flag);
```

produces

```
TRUE
```

The field width for Boolean output can be controlled by formatting with a colon followed by a positive integer to designate the field width. The Boolean value will appear right justified in the field.

Although Boolean variables and constants can be assigned and used in output statements, they cannot be used in input statements in Turbo Pascal. Thus, if Flag is a Boolean variable, a statement such as

```
readln (Flag);
```

produces an error. Instead, the user typically reads some value and then uses this value to assign an appropriate Boolean value to a Boolean variable. This technique will be illustrated later.

Relational Operators and Simple Boolean Expressions

In arithmetic, integers and reals can be compared using equalities (=) and inequalities (<, >, ≠, and so on). Turbo Pascal also provides for the comparison of numbers or values of variables. The operators used for comparison are called *relational operators,* and there are six of them. Their arithmetic notation, Turbo Pascal notation, and meaning are given in Table 4.1.

TABLE 4.1
Relational operators

Arithmetic Operation	Relational Operator	Meaning
=	=	Is equal to
<	<	Is less than
>	>	Is greater than
≤	<=	Is less than or equal to
≥	>=	Is greater than or equal to
≠	<>	Is not equal to

When two numbers or variable values are compared using a single relational operator, the expression is referred to as a *simple Boolean expression.* Each simple Boolean expression has the Boolean value **true** or **false,** according to the arithmetic validity of the expression. In general, only data of the same type can be compared; thus, integers must be compared to integers, reals must be compared to reals, and characters must be compared to characters. The usual exception can be applied here: reals can be compared to integers. When comparing reals, however, the computer representation of a real number might not be the exact real number intended. Therefore, the equality (=) comparison should be avoided. Instead, the absolute value of the difference should be checked to see if it is smaller than a given value.

Table 4.2 sets forth several Boolean expressions and their respective Boolean values, assuming the assignment statements A := 3 and B := 4 have been made.

TABLE 4.2
Values of simple Boolean expressions

Simple Boolean Expression	Boolean Value
`7 = 7`	**true**
`-3.0 = 0.0`	**false**
`4.2 > 3.7`	**true**
`-18 < -15`	**true**
`13 < 100`	**true**
`13 <= 100`	**true**
`13 <= 13`	**true**
`0.012 > 0.013`	**false**
`-17.32 <> -17.32`	**false**
`A <= B`	**true**
`B > A`	**true**

Arithmetic expressions can also be used in simple Boolean expressions. Thus

```
4 < (3 + 2)
```

has the value **true.** When the computer evaluates this expression, the parentheses dictate that (3 + 2) be evaluated first and the relational operator be evaluated second. Sequentially, this becomes

```
4 < (3 + 2)
4 <     5
TRUE
```

What if the parentheses are not used? Can the expression be evaluated? This type of expression requires that priority levels be set for the relational operators and the arithmetic operators. A summary of the priorities of these operations is

Expression	Priority
( )	1
*, /, **MOD, DIV**	2
+, -	3
=, <, >, <=, >=, <>	4

Thus, we see that the relational operators are evaluated last. As with arithmetic operators, these are evaluated in order from left to right. Thus, the expression

```
4 < 3 + 2
```

can be evaluated without parentheses and will have the same Boolean value.

The following example illustrates the evaluation of a somewhat more complex Boolean expression.

■ **EXAMPLE 4.1**

Indicate the successive steps in the evaluation of the Boolean expression

```
10 MOD 4 * 3 - 8 <= 18 + 30 DIV 4 - 20
```

The steps in this evaluation are

```
10 MOD 4 * 3 - 8 <= 18 + 30 DIV 4 - 20
   ↓
   2     * 3 - 8 <= 18 + 30 DIV 4 - 20     first pass
           ↓
           6 - 8 <= 18 + 30 DIV 4 - 20
                              ↓
           6 - 8 <= 18 +      7    - 20
             ↓        ↓                    second pass
              - 2 <=    25         - 20
                                     ↓
              - 2 <=                 5     third pass
                      ↓
                     true
```

As shown in Example 4.1, parentheses are not required when using arithmetic expressions with relational operators. However, it is usually a good idea to include them to enhance the readability of the expression and to avoid using an incorrect expression.

Logical Operators and Compound Boolean Expressions

Boolean values may also be generated by using *logical operators* with simple Boolean expressions. The logical operators used by Turbo Pascal are **AND, OR,**

XOR, and **NOT**. **AND**, **OR**, and **XOR** are used to connect two Boolean expressions. The operator **NOT** is used to negate the Boolean value of an expression; hence, it is sometimes referred to as *negation.* When these connectives or negation are used to generate Boolean values, the complete expression is referred to as a *compound Boolean expression.*

If **AND** is used to join two simple Boolean expressions, the resulting compound expression is **true** only when both simple expressions are **true.** If **OR** is used, the result is **true** if either or both of the expressions are **true.** If **XOR** is used, the result is **true** when exactly one of the expressions is **true.** These rules can be summarized as follows:

Expression 1 (E1)	Expression 2 (E2)	E1 AND E2	E1 OR E2	E1 XOR E2
true	**true**	**true**	**true**	**false**
true	**false**	**false**	**true**	**true**
false	**true**	**false**	**true**	**true**
false	**false**	**false**	**false**	**false**

Expression (E)	NOT E
true	**false**
false	**true**

As previously indicated, **NOT** merely produces the logical complement of an expression. (See table in margin).

When using these operators with relational expressions, parentheses are required because logical operators are evaluated before relational operators. Illustrations of the Boolean values generated using logical operators are given in Table 4.3.

TABLE 4.3
Values of compound Boolean expressions

Compound Boolean Expression	Boolean Value
(4.2 >= 5.0) **AND** (8 = (3 + 5))	**false**
(4.2 >= 5.0) **OR** (8 = (3 + 5))	**true**
(−2 < 0) **AND** (18 >= 10)	**true**
(−2 < 0) **XOR** (18 >= 10)	**false**
(−2 < 0) **OR** (18 >= 10)	**true**
(3 > 5) **AND** (14.1 = 0.0)	**false**
(3 > 5) **OR** (14.1 = 0.0)	**false**
NOT (18 = 10 + 8)	**false**
NOT (− 4 > 0)	**true**

Operator	Priority
NOT	1
AND	2
OR, XOR	3

Complex Boolean expressions can be generated by using several logical operators in an expression. The priority for evaluating these operators is shown in the marginal table.

When complex expressions are being evaluated, the logical operators, arithmetic expressions, and relational operators are evaluated during successive passes through the expression. The priority list is now as follows:

Expression or Operation	Priority
( )	1. Evaluate from inside out.
NOT	2. Evaluate from left to right.
*, /, **MOD, DIV, AND**	3. Evaluate from left to right.
+, −, **OR, XOR**	4. Evaluate from left to right.
<, <=, >, >=, =, <>	5. Evaluate from left to right.

A NOTE OF INTEREST

George Boole

George Boole was born in 1815 in Lincoln, England. Boole was the son of a small shopkeeper, and his family belonged to the lowest social class. In an attempt to rise above his station, Boole spent his early years teaching himself Latin and Greek. During this period, he also received elementary instruction in mathematics from his father.

At the age of 16, Boole worked as a teacher in an elementary school. He used most of his wages to help support his parents. At the age of 20 (after a brief, unsuccessful attempt to study for the clergy), he opened his own school. As part of his preparation for running his school, he had to learn more mathematics. This activity led to the development of some of the most significant mathematics of the nineteenth century.

Boole's major contributions were in the field of logic. An indication of his genius is given by the fact that his early work included the discovery of invariants [properties that do not change, such as shape, length, area, and so on]. The mathematical significance of this is perhaps best explained by noting that the theory of relativity developed by Albert Einstein would not have been possible without the previous work on invariants.

Boole's first published contribution was *The Mathematical Analysis of Logic*, which appeared in 1848 while he was still working as an elementary teacher and the sole support for his parents. In 1849, he was appointed Professor of Mathematics at Queen's College in Cork, Ireland. The relative freedom from financial worry and time constraints the college appointment provided allowed him to pursue his work in mathematics. His masterpiece, *An Investigation of the Laws of Thought, on which Are Founded the Mathematical Theories of Logic and Probabilities*, was published in 1854. Boole was then 39, relatively old for such original work. According to Bertrand Russell, pure mathematics was discovered by Boole in this work.

The brilliance of Boole's work laid the foundation for what is currently studied as formal logic. The data type, Boolean, is named in honor of Boole because of his contribution to the development of logic as part of mathematics. Boole died in 1864. His early death resulted from pneumonia contracted by keeping a lecture engagement when he was soaked to the skin.

Thus, an expression like

```
0 < X AND X < 2
```

produces an error. This expression must be written as

```
(0 < X) AND (X < 2)
```

The following examples illustrate the evaluation of some complex Boolean expressions.

EXAMPLE 4.2

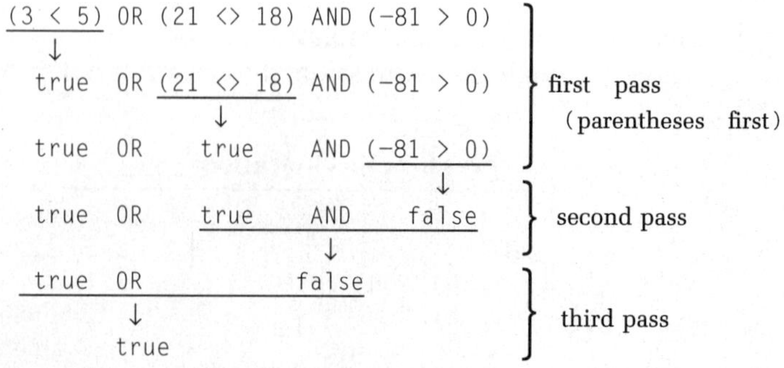

■ **EXAMPLE 4.3**

```
NOT ((-5.0 >= -6.2)  OR  ((7 <> 3)  AND  (6 = (3 + 3))))
          ↓                   ↓                  ↓
NOT (    true        OR  (  true     AND  (6 =    6    )))
                                             ↓
NOT (    true        OR  (  true     AND  (true        ))
                                   ↓
NOT (    true        OR            true                )
                      ↓
NOT                  true
          ↓
        false
```

Short-Circuit Boolean Evaluations

Turbo Pascal provides a compiler directive that may speed up the process of evaluating Boolean expressions. The compiler directive {$B–} causes the compiler to use short-circuit evaluation. More specifically, the compiler generates code to terminate evaluation of a Boolean expression as soon as possible. To illustrate, consider the Boolean expression

```
(2 > 3) AND ((Num > 0) OR (7 = 3 + 4))
```

Using complete Boolean evaluations, every expression would be evaluated in a manner similar to that shown in Example 4.2. However, if the compiler is using short-circuit evaluation, as soon as it is determined that (2 > 3) is **false** and the rest of the expression is connected by **AND**, evaluation of the remainder of the expression is terminated.

The default setting is {$B–}. If you want full Boolean expression evaluation, use the {$B+} compiler directive or choose the Complete Boolean Eval option from the **Options | Compiler** menu.

Exercises 4.1

1. Assume the variable declaration section of a program is

```
VAR
  Flag1, Flag2 : boolean;
```

What output is produced by the following segment of code?

```
Flag1 := true;
Flag2 := false;
writeln (Flag1, true:6, Flag2:8);
Flag1 := Flag2;
writeln (Flag2:20);
```

2. Write a test program that illustrates what happens when Boolean expressions are not enclosed in parentheses. For example

```
3 < 5 AND 8.0 <> 4 * 3
```

3. Assume the variable declaration section of a program is

```
VAR
  Ch : char;
  Flag : boolean;
```

Indicate if the following assignment statements are valid or invalid.

a. `Flag := 'true';`
b. `Flag := T;`
c. `Flag := true;`
d. `Ch := Flag;`
e. `Ch := true;`
f. `Ch := 'T';`

4. Evaluate each of the following expressions.

   a. `(3 > 7) AND (2 < 0) OR (6 = 3 + 3)`

   b. `((3 > 7) AND (2 < 0)) OR (6 = 3 + 3)`

   c. `(3 > 7) AND ((2 < 0) OR (6 = 3 + 3))`

   d. `NOT ((-4.2 <> 3.0) AND (10 < 20))`

   e. `(NOT (-4.2 <> 3.0)) OR (NOT (10 < 20))`

5. Indicate whether each of the following simple Boolean expressions is **true,** **false,** or invalid.

   a. `-3.01 <= -3.001`

   b. `-3.0 = -3`

   c. `25 - 10 <> 3 * 5`

   d. `42 MOD 5 < 42 DIV 5`

   e. `-5 * (3 + 2) > 2 * (-10)`

   f. `10 / 5 < 1 + 1`

   g. `3 + 8 MOD 5 >= 6 - 12 MOD 2`

6. Indicate whether each of the following expressions is valid or invalid. Evaluate those that are valid.

   a. `3 < 4 OR 5 <> 6`

   b. `NOT 3.0 = 6 / 2`

   c. `NOT (true OR false)`

   d. `NOT true OR false`

   e. `NOT true OR NOT false`

   f. `NOT (18 < 25) AND OR (-3 < 0)`

   g. `8 * 3 < 20 + 10`

7. Assume the variable declaration section of a program is

```
VAR
  Int1, Int2 : integer;
  Rl1, Rl2 : real;
  Flag1, Flag2 : boolean;
```

   and the values of the variables are

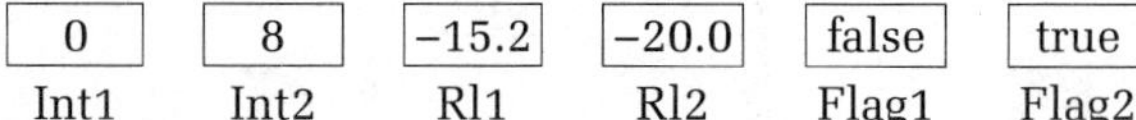

Int1 Int2 Rl1 Rl2 Flag1 Flag2

   Evaluate each of the following expressions.

   a. `(Int1 <= Int2) OR NOT (Rl2 = Rl1)`

   b. `NOT (Flag1) OR NOT (Flag2)`

   c. `NOT (Flag1 AND Flag2)`

   d. `((Rl1 - Rl2) < 100 / Int2) AND ((Int1 < 1) AND NOT (Flag2))`

   e. `NOT ((Int2 - 16 DIV 2) = Int1) AND Flag1`

8. DeMorgan's Laws state the following:

   a. **NOT** (A **OR** B) is equivalent to (**NOT** A) **AND** (**NOT** B)

   b. **NOT** (A **AND** B) is equivalent to (**NOT** A) **OR** (**NOT** B)

   Write a test program that demonstrates the validity of each of these equivalent statements.

■ 4.2 IF . . . THEN Statements

The first decision-making statement we will examine is the **IF . . . THEN** statement. **IF . . . THEN** is used to make a program do something only when certain conditions are met. The form and syntax of an **IF . . . THEN** statement are

IF ⟨Boolean expression⟩ **THEN** ⟨statement⟩;

where ⟨statement⟩ represents any Turbo Pascal statement.

The Boolean expression can be any valid expression that is either **true** or **false** at the time of evaluation. If the expression is **true,** the statement following the reserved word **THEN** is executed. If it is **false,** control is transferred to the first program statement following the complete **IF . . . THEN** statement. In general, code has the form

⟨statement 1⟩; **IF** ⟨Boolean expression⟩ **THEN** ⟨statement 2⟩; ⟨statement 3⟩;

as illustrated in Figure 4.1.

FIGURE 4.1
IF . . . THEN flow diagram

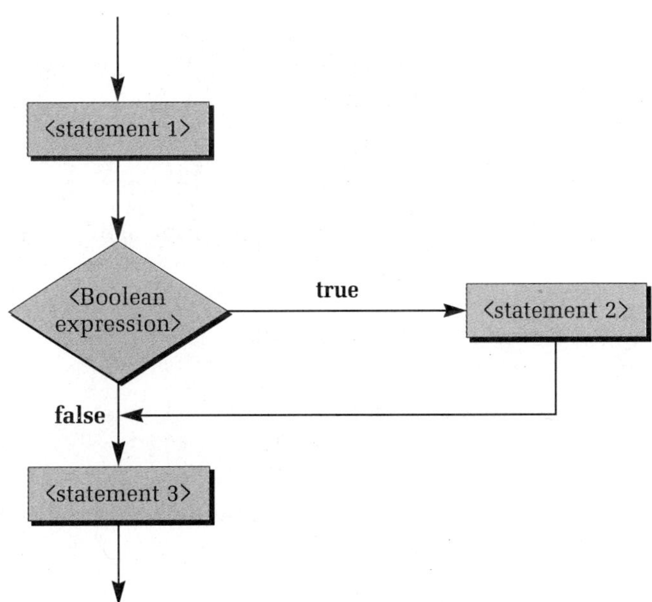

As a further illustration of how an **IF . . . THEN** statement works, consider the program fragment

```
Sum := 0.0;
readln (Num);
IF Num > 0.0 THEN
  Sum := Sum + Num;
writeln (Sum:10:2);
```

If the value read is 75.85, then prior to execution of the **IF . . . THEN** statement, the contents of Num and Sum are

75.85	0.0
Num	Sum

The Boolean expression Num > 0.0 is now evaluated; since it is **true,** the statement

```
Sum := Sum + Num;
```

is executed and we have

75.85	75.85
Num	Sum

The next program statement is executed and produces the output

```
    75.85
```

However, if the value read is −25.5, then the variable values are

−25.5	0.0
Num	Sum

The Boolean expression Num > 0.0 is **false,** and control is transferred to the line

```
writeln (Sum:10:2);
```

Thus, the output is

```
    0.00
```

Now let's suppose you want one objective of a program to be to count the number of zeros in the input. Assuming suitable initialization and declaration, a program fragment for this task could be

```
readln (Num);
IF Num = 0 THEN
  ZeroCount := ZeroCount + 1;
```

One writing style for using an **IF . . . THEN** statement calls for indenting the program statement to be executed if the Boolean expression is **true.** This, of course, is not required.

```
IF Num = 0 THEN
  ZeroCount := ZeroCount + 1;
```

could be written

```
IF Num = 0 THEN ZeroCount := ZeroCount + 1;
```

However, the indenting style for simple **IF . . . THEN** statements is consistent with the style used with more elaborate conditional statements.

Compound Statements

The last concept we need to consider before looking further at selection in Turbo Pascal is the *compound statement.* Simple statements conform to the syntax diagram for statements shown in Appendix 3. In a Turbo Pascal program, simple statements are separated by semicolons. Thus

```
readln (A, B);
A := 3 * B;
writeln (A);
```

are three simple statements.

In some instances, it is necessary to perform several simple statements when some condition is true. For example, you may want the program to do certain things if a condition is true. In this situation, several simple statements that can be written as a single compound statement would be helpful. In general, several Turbo Pascal constructs require compound statements. A compound statement is created by using the reserved words **BEGIN** and **END** at the beginning and end of a sequence of simple statements. Correct syntax for a compound statement is

```
BEGIN
  ⟨statement 1⟩;
  ⟨statement 2⟩;
      .
      .
      .
  ⟨statement n⟩
END;
```

Statements within a compound statement are separated by semicolons. The last statement before **END** does not require a semicolon; however, if a semicolon is used here, it will not affect the program.

When a compound statement is executed within a program, the entire segment of code between **BEGIN** and **END** is treated as a single action. This is referred to as a ***BEGIN . . . END*** *block.* It is important that you develop a consistent, acceptable writing style for writing compound statements. What you use will vary according to your instructor's wishes and your personal preferences. In examples in this text each simple statement within a compound statement will indent two spaces. Thus

```
BEGIN
  readln (A, B);
  A := 3 * B;
  writeln (A)
END;
```

is a compound statement in a program; what it does is easily identified.

Using Compound Statements

As you might expect, compound statements can be (and frequently are) used as part of an **IF . . . THEN** statement. The form and syntax for this are

```
IF ⟨Boolean expression⟩ THEN
  BEGIN
    ⟨statement 1⟩;
    ⟨statement 2⟩;
        .
        .
        .
    ⟨statement n⟩
  END;
```

Program control is exactly as before, depending upon the value of the Boolean expression. For example, suppose you are writing a procedure to keep track of and compute fees for vehicles in a parking lot where separate records are kept for senior citizens. A segment of code in the procedure could be

```
IF Customer = 'S' THEN
  BEGIN
    SeniorCount := SeniorCount + 1;
    AmountDue := SeniorCitizenRate
  END;
```

IF . . . THEN Statements with Procedures

The following example designs a program to solve a problem using an **IF . . . THEN** statement with procedures.

EXAMPLE 4.4

Let's write a program that reads two integers and prints them in the following order: larger first, smaller second. The first-level pseudocode solution is

1. Read numbers
2. Determine larger
3. Print results

A structure chart for this is given in Figure 4.2.

FIGURE 4.2
Structure chart for integer problem

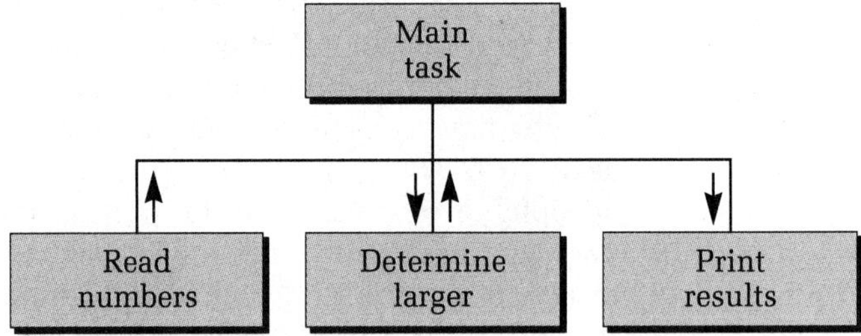

The procedures for ReadNumbers and PrintResults are similar to those used previously, so let's consider the module DetermineLarger. Data sent to this procedure will be two integers. Information returned will be the same two integers in the following order: larger, smaller. Code for this is

```
IF Num1 < Num2 THEN
  Switch (Num1, Num2);
```

where Switch is a procedure as follows:

```
PROCEDURE Switch (VAR Num1, Num2 : integer);
  VAR
    Temp : integer;
  BEGIN
    Temp := Num1;
    Num1 := Num2;
    Num2 := Temp
  END;  { of PROCEDURE Switch  }
```

Note that an additional variable Temp is needed to temporarily hold the value of Num1. This type of exchange is used frequently throughout the text.

The main program for this is

```
BEGIN {  Main program  }
  ReadNumbers (Num1, Num2);
  IF Num1 < Num2 THEN
    Switch (Num1, Num2);
  PrintResults (Num1, Num2)
END.  {  of main program  }
```

A complete program for this is

```
PROGRAM UseIFTHEN;

{  This short program illustrates using an IF...THEN       }
{  statement; two numbers are read, then printed in        }
{  order, larger first.                                     }
```

```
USES
  Crt;

CONST
  Skip = ' ';

VAR
  Num1, Num2 : integer;      {  Two numbers to be arranged  }

{*************************************************************}

PROCEDURE ReadNumbers (VAR Num1, Num2 : integer);

  {  Given:   Nothing                                          }
  {  Task:    Read two numbers entered from the keyboard       }
  {  Return:  Two integers                                     }
                                                                  1
  BEGIN
    ClrScr;
    writeln ('Enter two integers and press <Enter>.');
    readln (Num1, Num2)
  END;  {  of PROCEDURE ReadNumbers  }

{*************************************************************}

PROCEDURE Switch (VAR Num1, Num2 : integer);

  {  Given:   Two integers, Num1 and Num2                      }
  {  Task:    Use variable parameters to switch values         }
  {  Return:  Two integers, Num1 and Num2, with values         }
  {                switched, if in wrong order                 }

  VAR                                                             2
    Temp : integer;
  BEGIN
    Temp := Num1;
    Num1 := Num2;
    Num2 := Temp
  END;  {  of PROCEDURE Switch  }

{*************************************************************}

PROCEDURE PrintResults (Num1, Num2 : integer);

  {  Given:   Two integers                                     }
  {  Task:    Print the integers with a suitable heading       }
  {  Return:  Nothing                                          }

  BEGIN
    writeln;                                                      3
    writeln (Skip:19, 'Larger number',
             Skip:10, 'Smaller number');
    writeln (Skip:19, '-------------',
             Skip:10, '--------------');
    writeln;
    writeln (Num1:26, Num2:23);
    readln
  END;  {  of PROCEDURE PrintResults  }

{*************************************************************}
```

```
BEGIN  { Main program }
  ReadNumbers (Num1, Num2);
  IF Num1 < Num2 THEN
    Switch (Num1, Num2);
  PrintResults (Num1, Num2)
END.  { of main program }
```

Sample runs of this program produce

```
Enter two integers and press <Enter>.
35 115

                   Larger number          Smaller number
                   -------------          --------------

                       115                      35

Enter two integers and press <Enter>.
85 26

                   Larger number          Smaller number
                   -------------          --------------

                        85                      26
```

Note that two runs of this program are required to test the logic of the **IF . . . THEN** statement.

Exercises 4.2

1. What is the output from each of the following program fragments? Assume the following assignment statements precede each fragment:

```
A := 10;
B := 5;
```

a.
```
IF A <= B THEN
  B := A;
writeln (A:5, B:5);
```

b.
```
IF A <= B THEN
  BEGIN
    B := A;
    writeln (A:5, B:5)
  END;
```

c.
```
IF A < B THEN
  Temp := A;
A := B;
B := Temp;
writeln (A:5, B:5);
```

d.
```
IF A < B THEN
  BEGIN
    Temp := A;
    A := B;
    B := Temp
  END;
writeln (A:5, B:5);
```

e.
```
IF (A < B) OR (B - A < 0) THEN
  BEGIN
    A := A + B;
    B := B - 1;
    writeln (A:5, B:5)
  END;
writeln (A:5, B:5);
```

f.
```
IF (A < B) AND (B - A < 0) THEN
  BEGIN
    A := A + B;
    B := B - 1;
    writeln (A:5, B:5)
  END;
writeln (A:5, B:5);
```

2. Write a test program to illustrate what happens when a semicolon is inadvertently inserted after **THEN** in an **IF . . . THEN** statement. For example

```
IF A > 0 THEN;
  Sum := Sum + A;
```

3. Find and explain the errors in each of the following program fragments. You may assume all variables have been suitably declared.

a.
```
IF A := 10 THEN
  writeln (A);
```

b.
```
X := 7;
IF 3 < X < 10 THEN
  BEGIN
    X := X + 1;
    writeln (X)
  END;
```

c.
```
Count := 0;
Sum := 0;
A := 50;
IF A > 0 THEN
  Count := Count + 1;
  Sum := Sum + A;
```

d.
```
readln (Ch);
IF Ch = 'A' OR 'B' THEN
  writeln (Ch:10);
```

4. What is the output from each of the following program fragments? Assume variables have been suitably declared.

a.
```
J := 18;
IF J MOD 5 = 0 THEN
  writeln (J);
```

b.
```
A := 5;
B := 90;
B := B DIV A - 5;
IF B > A THEN
  B := A * 30;
writeln (A:5, B:5);
```

5. Can a simple statement be written using a **BEGIN . . . END** block? Write a short program that allows you to verify your answer.

6. Discuss the differences in the following programs. Predict the output for each program using sample values for Num.

a.
```
PROGRAM Exercise6a;

USES
  Crt;

VAR
  Num : integer;

BEGIN
  ClrScr;
  writeln ('Enter an integer and press <Enter>.');
  readln (Num);
  IF Num > 0 THEN
    writeln;
    writeln ('The number is':22, Num:6);
    writeln;
    writeln ('The number squared is':30, Num * Num:6);
    writeln ('The number cubed is':28, Num * Num * Num:6);
    readln
END.
```

b.
```
PROGRAM Exercise6b;

USES
  Crt;

VAR
  Num : integer;

BEGIN
  ClrScr;
  writeln ('Enter an integer and press <Enter>.');
  readln (Num);
```

```
    IF Num > 0 THEN
      BEGIN  {  Start output  }
        writeln;
        writeln ('The number is':22, Num:6);
        writeln;
        writeln ('The number squared is':30, Num * Num:6);
        writeln ('The number cubed is':28, Num * Num * Num:6);
        readln
      END  {  output for one number  }
  END.
```

7. Discuss the writing style and readability of compound statements.

8. Find all errors in the following compound statements.

   a.
   ```
   BEGIN
     readln (A)
     writeln (A)
   END;
   ```
   b.
   ```
   BEGIN
     Sum := Sum + Num
   END;
   ```
   c.
   ```
   BEGIN
     readln (Size1, Size2);
     writeln (Size1:8, Size2:8)
   END.
   ```
   d.
   ```
   BEGIN
     readln (Age, Weight);
     TotalAge := TotalAge + Age;
     TotalWeight := TotalWeight + Weight;
     writeln (Age:8, Weight:8)
   ```

9. Write a single compound statement that will:
   a. Read three integers from the keyboard.
   b. Add them to a previous total.
   c. Print the numbers on one line.
   d. Skip a line (output).
   e. Print the new total.

10. Write a program fragment that reads three reals, counts the number of positive reals, and accumulates the sum of positive reals.

11. Write a program fragment that reads three characters and then prints them only if they have been read in alphabetical order (for example, print "boy" but do not print "dog").

12. Given two integers, A and B, A is a divisor of B if B **MOD** A = 0. Write a complete program that reads two positive integers A and B, and then if A is a divisor of B
    a. Print A.
    b. Print B.
    c. Print the result of B divided by A.

    For example, the output could be

    ```
    A is 14
    B is 42
    B divided by A is 3
    ```

■ 4.3 IF . . . THEN . . . ELSE Statements

Form and Syntax

In Section 4.2, we discussed the one-way selection statement **IF . . . THEN.** The second selection statement we will examine is the two-way selection statement **IF . . . THEN . . . ELSE.** Correct form and syntax for **IF . . . THEN . . . ELSE** are

```
IF 〈Boolean expression〉 THEN
  〈statement〉
ELSE
  〈statement〉;
```

Flow of control when using an **IF . . . THEN . . . ELSE** statement is as follows:

1. The Boolean expression is evaluated.
2. If the Boolean expression is **true,** the statement following **THEN** is executed and control is transferred to the first program statement following the complete **IF . . . THEN . . . ELSE** statement.
3. If the Boolean expression is **false,** the statement following **ELSE** is executed and control is transferred to the first program statement following the **IF . . . THEN . . . ELSE** statement.

A flow diagram is given in Figure 4.3.

FIGURE 4.3
IF . . . THEN . . . ELSE flow diagram

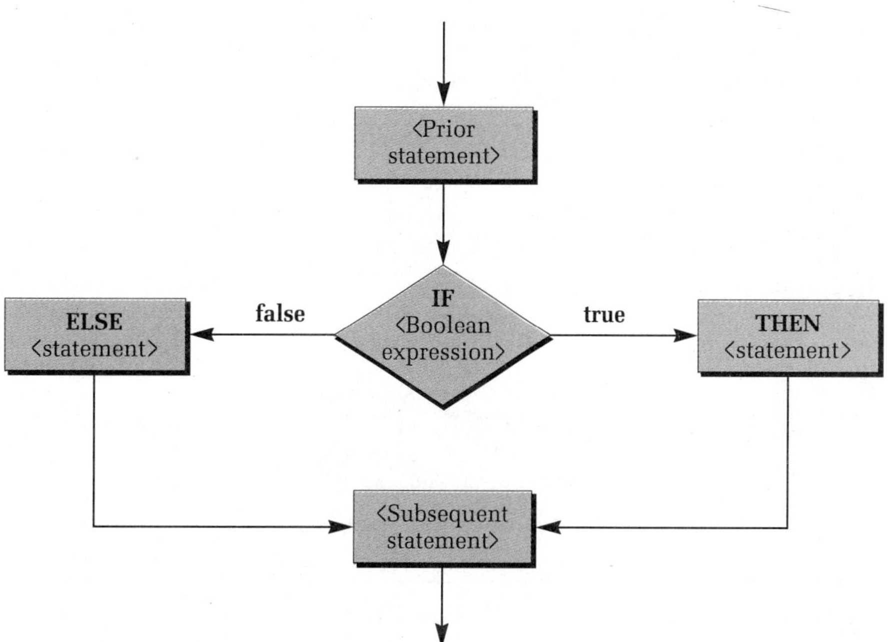

A few points to remember concerning **IF . . . THEN . . . ELSE** statements are:

1. The Boolean expression can be any valid expression having a value of **true** or **false** at the time it is evaluated.
2. The complete **IF . . . THEN . . . ELSE** statement is one program statement and is separated from other complete statements by a semicolon whenever appropriate.
3. There is no semicolon preceding the reserved word **ELSE.** A semicolon preceding the reserved word **ELSE** causes the compiler to treat the **IF . . . THEN** portion as a complete program statement and the **ELSE** portion as a separate statement. This produces an error message indicating that **ELSE** is being used without an **IF . . . THEN.**
4. Writing style should include indenting in the **ELSE** option in a manner consistent with indenting in the **IF . . . THEN** option.

■ **EXAMPLE 4.5**

Let's write a program fragment to keep separate counts of the negative and nonnegative numbers entered as data. Assuming all variables have been suitably declared and initialized, an **IF . . . THEN . . . ELSE** statement could be used as follows:

```
writeln ('Please enter a number and press <Enter>.');
readln (Num);
IF Num < 0 THEN
  NegCount := NegCount + 1
ELSE
  NonNegCount := NonNegCount + 1;
```

Using Compound Statements

Program statements in both the **IF . . . THEN** option and the **ELSE** option can be compound statements. When using compound statements in these options, you should use a consistent, readable indenting style. Remember to use **BEGIN . . . END** for each compound statement, and do not put a semicolon before **ELSE.** We next consider examples that require the use of compound statements within **IF . . . THEN . . . ELSE** statements.

■ **EXAMPLE 4.6**

Suppose you want a program to read a number, count it as negative or nonnegative, and print it in either a column of nonnegative numbers or a column of negative numbers. Assuming all variables have been suitably declared and initialized, the fragment might be

```
writeln ('Please enter a number and press <Enter>.');
readln (Num);
IF Num < 0 THEN
  BEGIN
    NegCount := NegCount + 1;
    writeln (Num:15)
  END  { of IF...THEN option  }
ELSE
  BEGIN
    NonNegCount := NonNegCount + 1;
    writeln (Num:30)
  END;  { of ELSE option  }
```

■ **EXAMPLE 4.7**

Let's write a function that computes gross wages for an employee of the Florida OJ Canning Company. Input includes hours worked and the hourly rate. Overtime (more than 40 hours) pay is computed at "time-and-a-half." A function would be

```
FUNCTION ComputeWages (Hours, PayRate : real) : real;
  VAR
    Overtime : real;
  BEGIN
    IF Hours <= 40.0 THEN
      ComputeWages := Hours * PayRate
    ELSE
      BEGIN
        Overtime := 1.5 * (Hours - 40.0) * PayRate;
        ComputeWages := 40 * PayRate + Overtime
      END
  END;  { of FUNCTION ComputeWages  }
```

Robust Programs

If a program is completely protected against all possible crashes from bad data and unexpected values, it is said to be *robust.* The preceding examples have all assumed that desired data is accurately entered from the keyboard. In actual practice, this is seldom the case. **IF . . . THEN . . . ELSE** statements can be used to guard against bad data entries. For example, if a program is designed to use positive numbers, you could guard against negatives and zero by

```
writeln ('Enter a positive number and press <Enter>.');
readln (Number);
IF Number <= 0 THEN
  writeln ('You entered a nonpositive number.');
ELSE
  .
  .  (code for expected action here)
  .
```

This program protection can be used anywhere in a program. For example, if you are finding square roots of numbers, you can avoid a program crash by

```
IF Num < 0 THEN
  writeln ('The number ', Num, ' is negative.')
ELSE
  .
  .  (rest of action here)
  .
```

In actual practice, students need to balance robustness against amount of code and efficiency. An overemphasis on making a program robust can detract from time spent learning new programming concepts. You should discuss this with your instructor and determine the best course of action for you to follow. Generally, there should be an agreement between the programmer and the customer regarding the level of robustness required. For most programs and examples in this text, it is assumed that valid data are entered when requested.

Guarding against Overflow

As we discussed in Chapter 2, integer overflow occurs when the absolute value of an integer exceeds **maxint** and real overflow occurs when a value is obtained that is too large to be stored in a memory location. The maximum value of an integer is stored in **maxint**. Unfortunately, there is no convenient analogue for reals.

One method used to guard against integer overflow is based on the principle of checking a number against some function of **maxint**. Thus, if you want to multiply a number by 10, you first compare it to **maxint DIV** 10. A typical segment of code could be

```
IF Num > maxint DIV 10 THEN
  .
  .  (overflow message here)
  .
ELSE
  BEGIN
    Num := Num * 10;
     .
     .  (rest of action here)
     .
  END;
```

We can now use this same idea with a **boolean** valued function. For example, consider the function

A NOTE OF INTEREST

New Legal Research Uses English, Not Boolean

In October, 1992, West Publishing, Inc. introduced WESTLAW Is Natural (WIN), a new method to allow legal researchers to access most computer data bases for necessary information. Before WIN, researchers had to phrase their questions in Boolean language format, using connectors and providing synonyms for important words. For example, suppose a person was injured by exposure to radiation during his or her service in the armed forces, and wanted to sue the government. The attorney would need to determine if the government was obligated to inform the person of the dangers from such exposure. Previously, the question entered in WESTLAW would have had to take the following format:

```
(government or military) w/50 warn*** w/50
(soldier or sailor or service member or
service-man or serviceman) w/50 radiation
```

WIN allows the user to enter the query in plain English; for example,

```
What is the government's obligation to warn
military personnel of the dangers of past expo-
sure to radiation?
```

WIN works by making its big computer recognize concepts within a question and then compare the concepts with documents in its files. By statistically and linguistically weighting the documents that match the request, the cases and rulings are offered to the researcher in what the computer determines is probably the most useful order and amount.

```
FUNCTION NearOverflow (Num : integer) : boolean;
  BEGIN
    NearOverflow := (Num > maxint DIV 10)
  END;
```

This could be used in the following manner:

```
IF NearOverflow (Num) THEN
  .
  .  (overflow message here)
  .
ELSE
  BEGIN
    Num := Num * 10;
      .
      .  (rest of action here)
      .
  END;
```

Exercises 4.3

1. What output is produced from each of the following program fragments? Assume all variables have been suitably declared.

a.
```
A := -14;
B := 0;
IF A < B THEN
  writeln (A:5, abs(A):5)
ELSE
  writeln (A * B);
```

b.
```
A := 50;
B := 25;
Count := 0;
Sum := 0;
IF A = B THEN
  writeln (A:5, B:5)
ELSE
  BEGIN
    Count := Count + 1;
    Sum := Sum + A + B;
    writeln (A:5, B:5)
  END;
writeln (Count:5, Sum:5);
```

c.
```
Temp := 0;
A := 10;
B := 5;
IF A > B THEN
  writeln (A:5, B:5)
ELSE
  Temp := A;
  A := B;
  B := Temp;
writeln (A:5, B:5);
```

2. Write a test program that illustrates what error message occurs when a semicolon precedes **ELSE** in an **IF . . . THEN . . . ELSE** statement. For example

```
PROGRAM SyntaxError;

VAR
  A, B : integer;

BEGIN
  A := 10;
  B := 5;
  IF A < B THEN
    writeln (A);
  ELSE
    writeln (B)
END.
```

3. Find all errors in the following program fragments.

a.
```
IF Ch <> '.' THEN
  CharCount := CharCount + 1;
  writeln (Ch)
ELSE
  PeriodCount := PeriodCount + 1;
```

b.
```
IF Age < 20 THEN
  BEGIN
    YoungCount := YoungCount + 1;
    YoungAge := YoungAge + Age
  END;
ELSE
  BEGIN
    OldCount := OldCount + 1;
    OldAge := OldAge + Age
  END;
```

c.
```
IF Age < 20 THEN
  BEGIN
    YoungCount := YoungCount + 1;
    YoungAge := YoungAge + Age
  END
ELSE
  OldCount := OldCount + 1;
  OldAge := OldAge + Age;
```

4. Write a program to balance your checkbook. Your program should get an entry from the keyboard, keep track of the number of deposits and checks, and keep a running balance. The data consist of a character, D (deposit) or C (check), followed by an amount.

■ 4.4 Nested and Extended IF Statements

Multiway Selection

In Sections 4.2 and 4.3, we examined one-way (**IF . . . THEN**) selection and two-way (**IF . . . THEN . . . ELSE**) selection. Since each of these is a single Turbo Pascal statement, either one can be used as part of a selection statement to achieve multiple selection. In this case, the multiple selection statement is referred to as a *nested* **IF** *statement.* Nested statements can be any combination of **IF . . . THEN** or **IF . . . THEN . . . ELSE** statements.

To illustrate, let's write a program fragment to issue interim progress reports for students in a class. If a student's score is below 50, the student is failing. If the score is between 50 and 69 inclusive, the progress is unsatisfactory. If the score is 70 or above, the progress is satisfactory. The first decision to be made is based upon whether the score is below 50 or not; the design is

```
IF Score >= 50 THEN
  .
  .  (progress report here)
  .
ELSE
  writeln ('You are currently failing.':34);
```

We now use a nested **IF . . . THEN . . . ELSE** statement for the progress report for students who are not failing. The complete fragment is

```
IF Score >= 50 THEN
  IF Score > 69 THEN
    writeln ('Your progress is satisfactory.':38)
  ELSE
    writeln ('Your progress is unsatisfactory.':40)
ELSE
  writeln ('You are currently failing.':34);
```

One particular instance of nesting selection statements requires special development. When additional **IF . . . THEN . . . ELSE** statements are used in the **ELSE** option, we call this an *extended* **IF** *statement* and use the following form:

```
IF ⟨condition 1⟩ THEN
    .
    .        (action 1 here)
    .
ELSE IF ⟨condition 2⟩ THEN
    .
    .        (action 2 here)
    .
ELSE IF ⟨condition 3⟩ THEN
    .
    .        (action 3 here)
    .
ELSE
    .
    .        (action 4 here)
    .
```

Using this form, we can redesign the previous fragment that printed progress reports as follows:

```
IF Score > 69 THEN
  writeln ('Your progress is satisfactory.':38)
ELSE IF Score > 50 THEN
  writeln ('Your progress is unsatisfactory.':40)
ELSE
  writeln ('You are currently failing.':34);
```

If you trace through both fragments with scores of 40, 60, and 80, you will find they produce identical output.

Another method of writing the nested fragment is to use sequential selection statements as follows:

```
IF Score > 69 THEN
  writeln ('Your progress is satisfactory.':38);
IF (Score <= 69) AND (Score >= 50) THEN
  writeln ('Your progress is unsatisfactory.':40);
IF Score < 50 THEN
  writeln ('You are currently failing.':34);
```

However, this method is less efficient because each **IF . . . THEN** statement is executed each time through the program. You should generally avoid using sequential **IF . . . THEN** statements if a nested statement can be used; this reduces execution time for a program.

Tracing the flow of logic through nested or extended **IF** statements can be tedious. However, it is essential that you develop this ability. For practice, let's trace through the following example.

EXAMPLE 4.8

Consider the nested statement

```
IF A > 0 THEN
  IF A MOD 2 = 0 THEN
    Sum1 := Sum1 + A
  ELSE
    Sum2 := Sum2 + A
ELSE IF A = 0 THEN
  writeln ('A is zero':18)
ELSE
  NegSum := NegSum + A;
writeln ('All done':17);
```

We will trace through this statement and discover what action is taken when A is assigned 20, 15, 0, and −30, respectively. For A := 20, the statement A > 0 is **true;** hence

```
A MOD 2 = 0
```

is evaluated. This is **true,** so

```
Sum1 := Sum1 + A
```

is executed and control is transferred out of the nested statement to

```
writeln ('All done':17);
```

For A := 15, A > 0 is **true** and

```
A MOD 2 = 0
```

is evaluated. This is **false,** so

```
Sum2 := Sum2 + A
```

is executed and control is again transferred out of the nested statement to

```
writeln ('All done':17);
```

For A := 0, A > 0 is **false;** thus

```
A = 0
```

is evaluated. Since this is **true,** the statement

```
writeln ('A is zero':18)
```

is executed and control is transferred to

```
writeln ('All done':17);
```

Finally, for A := −30, A > 0 is **false;** thus

```
A = 0
```

is evaluated. This is **false,** so

```
NegSum := NegSum + A;
```

is executed and control is transferred to

```
writeln ('All done':17);
```

Note that this example traces through all possibilities involved in the nested statement. It is essential to do this to guarantee that your statement is properly constructed.

Designing solutions to problems that require multiway selection can be difficult. A few guidelines can help. If a decision has two courses of action and if one is complex and the other is fairly simple, nest the complex part in the **IF . . . THEN** option and the simple part in the **ELSE** option. This method is frequently used to check for bad data. An example of the program design for this is

```
    .
    .  (get the data)
    .
IF DataOK THEN
    .
    .  (complex action here)
    .
ELSE
  (message about bad data here)
```

This method can also be used to guard against dividing by zero in computation. For instance, we can have

```
Divisor := <value>;
IF Divisor <> 0 THEN
  .
  .  (proceed with action)
  .
ELSE
  writeln ('Division by zero');
```

When there are several courses of action that can be considered sequentially, an extended **IF . . . THEN . . . ELSE** statement should be used. To illustrate, consider the program fragment in the following example.

EXAMPLE 4.9

Let's write a program fragment that allows you to assign letter grades based on students' semester averages. Grades are to be assigned according to the scale

$100 \geq X \geq 90$	A	$70 > X \geq 55$	D
$90 > X \geq 80$	B	$55 > X$	E
$80 > X \geq 70$	C		

Extended **IF**s can be used to accomplish this as follows:

```
IF Average >= 90 THEN
  Grade := 'A'
ELSE IF Average >= 80 THEN
  Grade := 'B'
ELSE IF Average >= 70 THEN
  Grade := 'C'
ELSE IF Average >= 55 THEN
  Grade := 'D'
ELSE
  Grade := 'E';
```

Since any Average over 100 or less than zero would be a sign of some data or program error, this example could be protected with the following statement:

```
IF (Average <= 100) AND (Average >= 0) THEN
  .
  . (compute letter grade)
  .
ELSE
  writeln ('There is an error. Average is':38, Average:8:2);
```

Protecting parts of a program in this manner will help you avoid unexpected results or program crashes. It also allows you to identify the source of an error.

Form and Syntax

The rule for matching **ELSE** statements in nested selection statements is

> *When an* **ELSE** *statement is encountered, it is matched with the most recent* **THEN** *statement that has not yet been matched.*

Matching **IF . . . THEN** statements with **ELSE** statements is a common source of errors. When designing programs, you should be very careful to match them correctly.

A situation that can lead to an error is an **IF . . . THEN . . . ELSE** statement such as

```
IF ⟨condition 1⟩ THEN
    .
    .  (action 1 here)
    .
ELSE
    .
    .  (action 2 here)
    .
```

where action 1 consists of an **IF . . . THEN** statement. Specifically, suppose you want a fragment of code to read a list of positive integers and print those that are perfect squares. A method of protecting against negative integers and zero could be

```
readln (Num);
IF Num > 0 THEN
  .
  . (action 1 here)
  .
ELSE
  writeln (Num, ' is not positive.');
```

If we now develop action 1 so that it prints only those positive integers that are perfect squares, it is

```
IF abs(sqrt(Num) - trunc(sqrt(Num))) < 0.0001 THEN
  writeln (Num)
```

Nesting this selection statement in our design, we have

```
readln (Num);
IF Num > 0 THEN
  IF abs(sqrt(Num) - trunc(sqrt(Num))) < 0.0001 THEN
    writeln (Num)
ELSE
  writeln (Num, ' is not positive.');
```

If you now use this segment with input of 20 for Num, the output is

```
  20 is not positive.
```

Thus, this fragment is not correct to solve the problem. The indenting is consistent with our intent, but the actual execution of the fragment treated the code as

```
readln (Num);
IF Num > 0 THEN
  IF abs(sqrt(Num) - trunc(sqrt(Num))) < 0.0001 THEN
    writeln (Num)
  ELSE
    writeln (Num, ' is not positive.');
```

COMMUNICATION AND STYLE TIPS

It is very important to use a consistent, readable writing style when using nested or extended **IF** statements. The style used here for nested **IF** statements is to indent each nested statement two spaces. Also, each **ELSE** in an **IF . . . THEN . . . ELSE** statement is in the same column as the **IF** of that statement. This allows you to see at a glance where the **ELSE**s match with the **IF . . . THEN**s. For example

```
IF . . . THEN
  IF . . . THEN
  ELSE
ELSE
```

An extended **IF** statement has all the **ELSE**s on the same indenting level as the first **IF**. This reinforces the concept of extended **IF**. For example

```
IF . . . THEN
ELSE IF . . . THEN
ELSE IF . . . THEN
ELSE
```

because the **ELSE** is matched with the most recent **THEN**. This problem can be resolved in several ways. You could use an **ELSE** option with an *empty (null) statement*. Thus, you would have

```
readln (Num);
IF Num > 0 THEN
  IF abs(sqrt(Num) - trunc(sqrt(Num))) < 0.0001 THEN
    writeln (Num)
  ELSE  {  Do nothing  }
ELSE
  writeln (Num, ' is not positive.');
```

You could isolate the second **IF . . . THEN** statement by enclosing it in a **BEGIN . . . END** block. Thus, you would have

```
readln (Num);
IF NUM > 0 THEN
  BEGIN
    IF abs(sqrt(Num) - trunc(sqrt(Num))) < 0.0001 THEN
      writeln (Num)
  END
ELSE
  writeln (Num, ' is not positive.');
```

Or you could redesign the fragment as follows:

```
readln (Num);
IF Num <= 0 THEN
  writeln (Num,' is not positive.');
ELSE IF abs(sqrt(Num) - trunc(sqrt(Num))) < 0.0001 THEN
  writeln (Num);
```

We conclude this section with an example that uses nested **IF** statements.

■ EXAMPLE 4.10

Write a program that computes the gross pay for an employee of the Clean Products Corporation of America. The corporation produces three products: A, B, and C. Supervisors earn a commission of 7 percent of sales, and representatives earn 5 percent. Bonuses of $100 are paid to supervisors whose commissions exceed $300 and to representatives whose commissions exceed $200. Input is in the form

S 18 15 10

where the first position contains an 'S' or 'R' for supervisor or representative, respectively. The next three integers include the number of units of each of the products sold. Since product prices may vary over time, the constant definition section will be used to indicate the current prices. The section for this problem will be

```
CONST
  SuperRate = 0.07;
  RepRate = 0.05;
  APrice = 13.95;
  BPrice = 17.95;
  CPrice = 29.95;
```

A first-level pseudocode development for this problem is

1. Get the data
2. Compute commissions and bonus
3. Print heading
4. Print results

The structure chart for this problem is given in Figure 4.4.

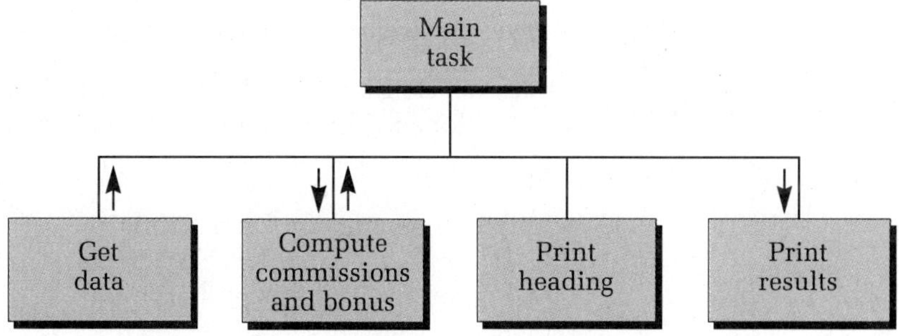

FIGURE 4.4
Structure chart for the Clean Products Corporation of America problem

Module specifications for each of the main modules are

1. GetData Module

   Data received: None

   Information returned: Employee classification
   Sales of products A, B, and C

   Logic: Read input data from the keyboard.

2. ComputeCommAndBonus Module

   Data received: Classification
   ASales
   BSales
   CSales

   Information returned: ACommission
   BCommission
   CCommission
   TotalCommission
   Bonus

Logic: **IF** a supervisor **THEN**
compute total commission
compute bonus
ELSE
compute total commission
compute bonus

3. PrintHeading Module

   Data received: None

   Information returned: None

   Logic: Use **writeln** statements to print a heading for the report.

4. PrintResults Module

   Data received: Classification
   ASales
   BSales
   CSales
   ACommission
   BCommission
   CCommission
   TotalCommission
   Bonus

   Information returned: None

   Logic: Use **writeln** statements to print the employee's report.

Modules for GetData, PrintHeading, and PrintResults are similar to those previously developed. The module ComputeCommAndBonus requires some development. Step 2 of the pseudocode, "Compute commissions and bonus" becomes

2. Compute commissions and bonus
   2.1 **IF** employee is supervisor **THEN**
   compute supervisor's earnings
   ELSE
   compute representative's earnings

where "compute supervisor's earnings" is refined to

2.1.1 compute commission from sales of A
2.1.2 compute commission from sales of B
2.1.3 compute commission from sales of C
2.1.4 compute total commission
2.1.5 compute supervisor's bonus
2.1.5.1 **IF** total commission > 300 **THEN**
bonus is 100.00
ELSE
bonus is 0.00

A similar development follows for computing a representative's earnings (commission and bonus). Step 3 will be an appropriate procedure to print a heading. Step 4 will contain whatever you feel is appropriate for output. It should include at least the number of sales, amount of sales, commissions, bonuses, and total compensation.

The main program for this problem is

```
BEGIN  {  Main program  }
  GetData (Classification, ASales, BSales, CSales);
  ComputeCommAndBonus (Classification, ASales, BSales, CSales,
                       AComm, BComm, CComm, TotalCommission, Bonus);
  PrintHeading;
  PrintResults (Classification, ASales, BSales, CSales,
                AComm, BComm, CComm, TotalCommission, Bonus)
END.  {  of main program  }
```

A complete program for this is

```
PROGRAM ComputeEarnings;

{  This program computes gross pay for an employee.  Note the    }
{  use of constants and selection.                               }

USES
  Crt;

CONST
  CompanyName = 'Clean Products Corporation of America';
  Line = '-------------------------------------';
  SuperRate = 0.07;
  RepRate = 0.05;
  APrice = 13.95;
  BPrice = 17.95;
  CPrice = 29.95;
  Month = 'June';
  Skip = ' ';

VAR
  ASales, BSales,
  CSales : integer;         {  Sales of products A, B, C         }
  AComm, BComm, CComm,      {  Commission on sales of A, B, C    }
  Bonus,                    {  Bonus, if earned                  }
  TotalCommission : real;   {  Commission on all products        }
  Classification : char;    {  S-Supervisor or R-Representative  }


{***************************************************************}


PROCEDURE GetData (VAR Classification : char;
                   VAR ASales, BSales, CSales : integer);

  {  Given:   Nothing                                          }
  {  Task:    Have classification and sales amounts entered    }
  {               from the keyboard                            }
  {  Return:  Classification, ASales, BSales, CSales           }
                                                                  1
  BEGIN
    ClrScr;
    writeln ('Enter S or R for classification.');
    readln (Classification);
    writeln ('Enter ASales, BSales, CSales');
    readln (ASales, BSales, CSales)
  END;  {  of PROCEDURE GetData  }

{***************************************************************}
```

```
PROCEDURE ComputeCommAndBonus (Classification : char;
                               ASales, BSales, CSales : integer;
                               VAR AComm, BComm, CComm,
                               TotalCommission, Bonus : real);

  {  Given:   Employee classification and sales for products    }
  {               A, B, and C                                   }
  {  Task:    Compute commission and bonus                      }
  {  Return:  Commission for each of products A, B, and C;      }
  {               TotalCommission; and Bonus                    }

  BEGIN
    IF Classification = 'S' THEN          {  Supervisor  }
      BEGIN
        AComm := ASales * APrice * SuperRate;
        BComm := BSales * BPrice * SuperRate;
        CComm := CSales * CPrice * SuperRate;
        TotalCommission := AComm + BComm + CComm;                   2
        IF TotalCommission > 300.0 THEN
          Bonus := 100.0
        ELSE
          Bonus := 0.0
      END
    ELSE
      BEGIN
        AComm := ASales * APrice * RepRate;
        BComm := BSales * BPrice * RepRate;
        CComm := CSales * CPrice * RepRate;
        TotalCommission := AComm + BComm + CComm;
        IF TotalCommission > 200.0 THEN
          Bonus := 100.0
        ELSE
          Bonus := 0.0
      END  {  of ELSE option  }
  END;  {  of PROCEDURE ComputeCommAndBonus  }

{*****************************************************************}

PROCEDURE PrintHeading;

  {  Given:   Nothing                                           }
  {  Task:    Print a heading for the output                    }
  {  Return:  Nothing                                           }

  BEGIN
    writeln;
    writeln (Skip:10, CompanyName);
    writeln (Skip:10, Line);
    writeln;
    writeln (Skip:10, 'Sales Report for:', Skip:3, Month);          3
    writeln;
    write (Skip:10, 'Classification:');
    IF Classification = 'S' THEN
      writeln (Skip:5, 'Supervisor')
    ELSE
      writeln (Skip:5, 'Representative');
    writeln;
    writeln (Skip:12, 'Product     Sales     Commission');
    writeln (Skip:12, '-------     -----     ----------');
    writeln
  END;  {  of PROCEDURE PrintHeading  }

{*****************************************************************}
```

```
PROCEDURE PrintResults (Classification : char;
                        ASales, BSales, CSales : integer;
                        AComm, BComm, CComm,
                        TotalCommission, Bonus : real);

  {  Given:   Employee classification;  sales of products A,    }
  {               B, and C; commissions for products A, B,      }
  {               and C; total commission; and bonus            }
  {  Task:    Print the results in a readable form              }
  {  Return:  Nothing                                           }

  BEGIN                                                              4
    writeln (Skip:15, 'A', ASales:13, AComm:14:2);
    writeln (Skip:15, 'B', BSales:13, BComm:14:2);
    writeln (Skip:15, 'C', CSales:13, CComm:14:2);
    writeln;
    writeln ('Subtotal':31, '$':3, TotalCommission:9:2);
    writeln;
    writeln ('Your bonus is:':31, '$':3, Bonus:9:2);
    writeln ('-------':43);
    writeln ('Total Due':31, '$':3, (TotalCommission + Bonus):9:2);
    readln
  END;  {  of PROCEDURE PrintResults  }

{***************************************************************}

BEGIN  {  Main program  }
  GetData (Classification, ASales, BSales, CSales);
  ComputeCommAndBonus (Classification, ASales, BSales, CSales,
                       AComm, BComm, CComm, TotalCommission, Bonus);
  PrintHeading;
  PrintResults (Classification, ASales, BSales, CSales, AComm,
                BComm, CComm, TotalCommission, Bonus)
END.  {  of main program  }
```

A sample run produces

```
Enter S or R for classification.
S
Enter ASales, BSales, CSales
1100 990 510

          Clean Products Corporation of America
          -------------------------------------

          Sales Report for:   June

          Classification:     Supervisor

            Product      Sales      Commission
            -------      -----      ----------

              A          1100          1074.15
              B           990          1243.93
              C           510          1069.21

                      Subtotal  $   3387.30

                 Your bonus is:  $    100.00
                                     -------

                      Total Due  $   3487.30
```

Program Testing

In actual practice, a great deal of time is spent testing programs in an attempt to make them run properly when they are installed for some specific purpose. Formal program verification is discussed in Section 4.6 and is developed more fully in subsequent course work. However, examining the issue of which data are minimally necessary for program testing is appropriate when working with selection statements.

As you might expect, test data should include information that tests every logical branch in a program. Whenever a program contains an **IF . . . THEN . . . ELSE** statement of the form

```
IF ⟨condition⟩ THEN
  .
  .  (action 1 here)
  .
ELSE
  .
  .  (action 2 here)
  .
```

the test data should guarantee that both the **IF . . . THEN** and the **ELSE** option are executed.

A bit more care is required when selecting test data for nested and extended **IF** statements. In general, a single **IF . . . THEN . . . ELSE** statement requires at least two data items for testing. If an **IF . . . THEN . . . ELSE** statement is nested within the **IF . . . THEN** option, at least two more data items are required to test the nested selection statement.

For purposes of illustration, let's reexamine **PROCEDURE** ComputeComm-AndBonus from Example 4.10. This procedure contains the logic

```
IF Classification = 'S' THEN
  .
  .
  .
  IF TotalCommission > 300.00 THEN
    .
    .
    .
  ELSE
    .
    .
    .
ELSE
  .
  .
  .
  IF TotalCommission > 200.00 THEN
    .
    .
    .
  ELSE
    .
    .
    .
```

Classi-fication	Total Commission
'S'	400.00
'S'	250.00
'R'	250.00
'R'	150.00

To see what data should minimally be used to test this procedure, consider the marginal table. It is a good idea to also include boundary conditions in the test data. Thus, the table could also have listed 300.00 as the total commission for 'S' and 200.00 as the total commission for 'R'.

In summary, you should always make sure every logical branch is executed when running the program with test data.

Exercises 4.4

1. Consider the program fragment

```
IF X >= 0.0 THEN
  IF X < 1000.00 THEN
    BEGIN
      Y := 2 * X;
      IF X <= 500 THEN
        X := X / 10
    END
  ELSE
    Y := 3 * X
ELSE
  Y := abs(X);
```

   Indicate the values of X and Y after this fragment is executed for each of the following initial values of X.

   a. `X := 381.5;`
   b. `X := -21.0;`
   c. `X := 600.0;`
   d. `X := 3000.0;`

2. Write and run a test program that illustrates the checking of all branches of nested **IF . . . THEN . . . ELSE** statements.

3. Rewrite each of the following fragments using nested or extended **IF**s without compound conditions.

   a.
```
IF (Ch = 'M') AND (Sum > 1000) THEN
  X := X + 1;
IF (Ch = 'M') AND (Sum <= 1000) THEN
  X := X + 2;
IF (Ch = 'F') AND (Sum > 1000) THEN
  X := X + 3;
IF (Ch = 'F') AND (Sum <= 1000) THEN
  X := X + 4;
```

   b.
```
readln (Num);
IF (Num > 0) AND (Num <= 10000) THEN
  BEGIN
    Count := Count + 1;
    Sum := Sum + Num
  END
ELSE
  writeln ('Value out of range':27);
```

   c.
```
IF (A > 0) AND (B > 0) THEN
  writeln ('Both positive':22)
ELSE
  writeln ('Some negative':22);
```

   d.
```
IF ((A > 0) AND (B > 0)) OR (C > 0) THEN
  writeln ('Option one':19)
ELSE
  writeln ('Option two':19);
```

4. Consider each of the following program fragments.

   a.
```
IF A < 0 THEN
  IF B < 0 THEN
    A := B
ELSE
  A := B + 10;
writeln (A:5, B:5);
```

b.
```
IF A < 0 THEN
  BEGIN
    IF B < 0 THEN
      A := B
  END
ELSE
  A := B + 10;
writeln (A:5, B:5);
```

c.
```
IF A >= 0 THEN
  A := B + 10
ELSE IF B < 0 THEN
  A := B;
writeln (A:5, B:5);
```

d.
```
IF A >= 0 THEN
  A := B + 10;
IF B < 0 THEN
  A := B;
writeln (A:5, B:5);
```

Indicate the output of each fragment for each of the following assignment statements.

i. `A := -5;` `B := 5;` **ii.** `A := -5;` `B := -3;` **iii.** `A := 10;` `B := 8;` **iv.** `A := 10;` `B := -4;`

5. Look back to Example 4.9, in which we assigned grades to students, and rewrite the grade assignment fragment using a different nesting. Could you rewrite it without using any nesting? Should you?

6. Many nationally based tests report scores and indicate in which quartile the score lies. Assuming the following quartile designation

Score	Quartile
100–75	1
74–50	2
49–25	3
24–0	4

write a program to read a score from the keyboard and report in which quartile the score lies.

7. What are the values of A, B, and C after the following program fragment is executed?

```
A := -8;
B := 21;
C := A + B;
IF A > B THEN
  BEGIN
    A := B;
    C := A * B
  END
ELSE IF A < 0 THEN
  BEGIN
    A := abs(A);
    B := B - A;
    C := A * B
  END
ELSE
  C := 0;
```

8. Create minimal sets of test data for each part of Exercise 4 and for Exercise 7. Explain why each data item has been included.

9. Discuss a technique that could be used as a debugging aid to guarantee that all possible logical paths of a program have been used.

■ 4.5 CASE Statements

Thus far, this chapter has examined one-way selection, two-way selection, and multiway selection. Section 4.4 illustrated how multiple selection can be achieved using nested and extended **IF** statements. Since multiple selection can sometimes be difficult to follow, Turbo Pascal provides an alternative method of handling this concept, the **CASE** statement.

Form and Syntax

CASE statements can often be used when there are several options that depend upon the value of a single variable or expression. The general structure for a **CASE** statement is

```
CASE ⟨selector⟩ OF
  ⟨label list 1⟩ : ⟨statement 1⟩;
  ⟨label list 2⟩ : ⟨statement 2⟩;
        .               .
        .               .
        .               .
  ⟨label list n⟩ : ⟨statement n⟩
END;
```

which is shown graphically in Figure 4.5.

FIGURE 4.5
CASE flow diagram

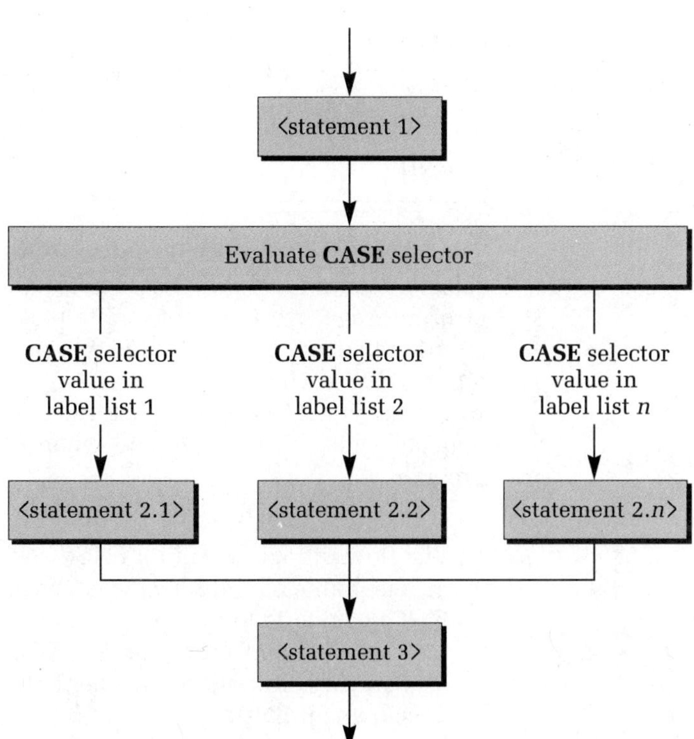

The selector must be of a byte-sized or word-sized ordinal type. Thus, **string** types and the integer type **longint** are invalid selector types. Values of the selector constitute the label list. Thus, if Age is an integer variable with values restricted to 18, 19, and 20, we could have

```
CASE Age OF
  18 : <statement 1>;
  19 : <statement 2>;
  20 : <statement 3>
END;
```

When this program statement is executed, the value of Age will determine to which statement control is transferred. More specifically, the program fragment

```
Age := 19;
CASE Age OF
  18 : writeln ('I just became a legal voter.');
  19 : writeln ('This is my second year to vote.');
  20 : writeln ('I am almost twenty-one.')
END;
```

produces the output

```
This is my second year to vote.
```

S Turbo Pascal provides an optional **ELSE** that can be used with a **CASE** statement. The form for using this is

CASE ⟨selector⟩ **OF**
    ⟨label list 1⟩ : ⟨statement 1⟩;
    ⟨label list 2⟩ : ⟨statement 2⟩;
    .   .
    .   .
    .   .
    ⟨label list *n*⟩ : ⟨statement *n*⟩
ELSE
    . (action to be taken when none
    . of the above are selected)
    .
END

The purpose of this **ELSE** option is to guard against the possibility that the selector contains a value that is not in the list of labels for action. Typically, some error message or other appropriate message is included in the **ELSE** option. You are not required to include this option, but it is recommended to avoid mysterious results. If you do not include an **ELSE** option and the selector contains a value that is not in the label list, the entire **CASE** statement will be skipped. This is usually not what you intend when you choose to use a **CASE** statement in a program.

Before considering more examples, several comments are in order.

1. The flow of logic within a **CASE** statement is as follows:
   a. The value of the selector is determined.
   b. The value is found in the label list.
   c. The statement following the value in the list is executed.
   d. Control is transferred to the first program statement following the **CASE** statement **END**.

2. The selector must be of a byte-sized or word-sized ordinal type. Thus, **string** types and the integer type **longint** are invalid selector types.
3. Several values, separated by commas, may appear on one line. For example, if Age can have any integer value from 15 to 25 inclusive, the **CASE** statement can appear as

```
CASE Age OF
  15, 16, 17     : <statement 1>;
  18, 19, 20, 21 : <statement 2>;
  22, 23, 24     : <statement 3>;
  25             : <statement 4>
END;
```

4. All possible values of the **CASE** selector do not have to be listed. However, if you wish to list them even when certain values require no action, you may list them on the same option with a null statement; for example

```
CASE Age OF
  18 : <statement 1>;
  19 : ; {  Do nothing  }
  20 : <statement 2>
END;
```

5. Values for the selector can appear only once in the list. Thus

```
CASE Age OF
  18      : <statement 1>;
  18, 19  : <statement 2>;   (error)
  20      : <statement 3>
END;
```

   produces an error since it is not clear which statement should be executed when the value of Age is 18.
6. Proper syntax for using **CASE** statements includes:
   a. A colon separates each label from its respective statement.
   b. A semicolon follows each statement option except the statement preceding **END.**
   c. Commas are placed between labels on the same option.
7. For the first time, **END** is used without a **BEGIN.** An appropriate program comment should indicate the end of a **CASE** statement. Therefore, our examples will include

```
END;  {  of CASE  }
```

8. Statements for each option can be compound. If they are, they must be in a **BEGIN . . . END** block.
9. The **ELSE** option should be used to guard against selector values not contained in the label list.

At this stage, let's consider two examples that illustrate different uses of **CASE** statements. Since these examples are for the purpose of illustration, they will be somewhat contrived. Later examples will serve to illustrate how these statements are used in solving problems.

■ EXAMPLE 4.11

The selector can have a value of type **char,** and the ordinal of the character determines the option. Thus, the label list must contain the appropriate characters in single quotation marks. If Grade has values 'A', 'B', 'C', 'D', or 'E', a **CASE** statement can be

```
CASE Grade OF
  'A' : Points := 4.0;
  'B' : Points := 3.0;
  'C' : Points := 2.0;
  'D' : Points := 1.0;
  'E' : Points := 0.0
ELSE
  writeln ('Value of Grade out of range.')
END;  {  of CASE Grade  }
```

EXAMPLE 4.12

Compound statements can be used with any or all of the options in the following form:

```
CASE Age OF
  18 : BEGIN
         .
         .
         .
       END;
  19 : BEGIN
         .
         .
         .
       END;
  20 : BEGIN
         .
         .
         .
       END
ELSE
  writeln ('Value of Age out of range.')
END;  {  of CASE Age  }
```

COMMUNICATION AND STYLE TIPS

Writing style for a **CASE** statement should be consistent with your previously developed style. The lines containing options should be indented, the colons should be lined up, and **END** should start in the same column as **CASE.** Thus, a typical **CASE** statement is

```
CASE Score OF
  10, 9, 8        : writeln ('Excellent');
  7, 6, 5         : writeln ('Fair');
  4, 3, 2, 1, 0 : writeln ('Failing')
END;  {  of CASE Score  }
```

Equivalent of Extended IFs

As previously indicated, **CASE** statements can sometimes (with ordinal data types) be used instead of extended **IFs** when multiple selection is required to solve a problem. The following example illustrates this use.

EXAMPLE 4.13

Let us rewrite the following program fragment using a **CASE** statement.

```
IF (Score = 10) OR (Score = 9) THEN
  Grade := 'A'
```

```
ELSE IF (Score = 8) OR (Score = 7) THEN
  Grade := 'B'
ELSE IF (Score = 6) OR (Score = 5) THEN
  Grade := 'C'
ELSE
  Grade := 'E';
```

If we assume Score is an integer variable with values 0, 1, 2, . . . , 10, we can use a **CASE** statement as follows:

```
CASE Score OF
  10, 9         : Grade := 'A';
  8, 7          : Grade := 'B';
  6, 5          : Grade := 'C';
  4, 3, 2, 1, 0 : Grade := 'E'
ELSE
  writeln ('Value of Score out of range.')
END;  {  of CASE Score  }
```

Use in Problems

CASE statements should not be used for relational tests that involve large ranges of values. For example, if we want to examine a range from 0 to 100 to determine test scores, it is better to use nested selection than a **CASE** statement. We close this section with some examples that illustrate how **CASE** statements can be used in solving problems.

EXAMPLE 4.14

Suppose you are writing a program for a gasoline station owner who sells four grades of gasoline: regular, premium, unleaded, and super unleaded. Your program reads a character (R, P, U, S) that designates which kind of gasoline was purchased and then takes subsequent action. The outline for this fragment is

```
readln (GasType);
CASE GasType OF
  'R' : <action for regular>;
  'U' : <action for unleaded>;
  'P' : <action for unleaded plus>;
  'S' : <action for super unleaded>
ELSE
  writeln ('Value of GasType out of range.')
END;  {  of CASE GasType  }
```

EXAMPLE 4.15

An alternative method of assigning letter grades based on integer scores between 0 and 100 inclusive is to divide the scores by 10 and assign grades according to some scale. This idea could be used in conjunction with a **CASE** statement as follows:

```
NewScore := Score DIV 10;
CASE NewScore OF
  10, 9         : Grade := 'A';
  8             : Grade := 'B';
  7             : Grade := 'C';
  6, 5          : Grade := 'D';
  4, 3, 2, 1, 0 : Grade := 'E'
ELSE
  writeln ('Value of NewScore out of range.')
END;  {  of CASE NewScore  }
```

A NOTE OF INTEREST

A Software Glitch

The software glitch that disrupted AT&T's long-distance telephone service for nine hours in January 1990, dramatically demonstrates what can go wrong even in the most reliable and scrupulously tested systems. Of the roughly 100 million telephone calls placed with AT&T during that period, only about half got through. The breakdown cost the company more than $60 million in lost revenues and caused considerable inconvenience and irritation for telephone-dependent customers.

The trouble began at a "switch"—one of 114 interconnected, computer-operated electronic switching systems scattered across the United States. These sophisticated systems, each a maze of electronic equipment housed in a large room, form the backbone of the AT&T long-distance telephone network.

When a local exchange delivers a telephone call to the network, it arrives at one of these switching centers, which can handle up to 700,000 calls an hour. The switch immediately springs into action. It scans a list of 14 different routes it can use to complete the call, and at the same time hands off the telephone number to a parallel, signaling network, invisible to any caller. This private data network allows computers to scout the possible routes and to determine whether the switch at the other end can deliver the call to the local company it serves.

If the answer is no, the call is stopped at the original switch to keep it from tying up a line, and the caller gets a busy signal. If the answer is yes, a signaling-network computer makes a reservation at the destination switch and orders the original switch to pass along the waiting call—after that switch makes a final check to insure that the chosen line is functioning properly. The whole process of passing a call down the network takes 4 to 6 seconds. Because the switches must keep in constant touch with the signaling network and its computers, each switch has a computer program that handles all the necessary communications between the switch and the signaling network.

AT&T's first indication that something might be amiss appeared on a giant video display at the company's network control center in Bedminster, N.J. At 2:25 P.M. on Monday, January 15, 1990, network managers saw an alarming increase in the number of red warning signals appearing on many of the 75 video screens showing the status of various parts of AT&T's worldwide network. The warnings signaled a serious collapse in the network's ability to complete calls within the United States.

To bring the network back up to speed, AT&T engineers first tried a number of standard procedures that had worked in the past. This time, the methods failed. The engineers realized they had a problem never seen before. Nonetheless, within a few hours, they managed to stabilize the network by temporarily cutting back on the number of messages moving through the signaling network. They cleared the last defective link at 11:30 that night.

Meanwhile, a team of more than 100 telephone technicians tried frantically to track down the fault. Because the problem involved the signaling network and seemed to bounce from one switch to another, they zeroed in on the software that permitted each switch to communicate with the signaling-network computers.

The day after the slowdown, AT&T personnel removed the apparently faulty software from each switch, temporarily replacing it with an earlier version of the communications program. A close examination of the flawed software turned up a single error in one line of the program. Just one month earlier, network technicians had changed the software to speed the processing of certain messages, and the change had inadvertently introduced a flaw into the system.

From that finding, AT&T could reconstruct what had happened.

Exercises 4.5

1. Discuss the need for program protection when using a **CASE** statement.
2. Write a test program to see how the **ELSE** option works on your system.
3. Show how the following **CASE** statement could be protected against unexpected values.

```
CASE Age DIV 10 OF
  10, 9, 8, 7 : writeln ('These are retirement years':40);
      6, 5, 4 : writeln ('These are middle age years':40);
         3, 2 : writeln ('These are mobile years':40);
            1 : writeln ('These are school years':40)
END;  { of CASE Age  }
```

4. Find all errors in the following statements.

a.
```
CASE A OF
  1        :  ;
  2        : A := 2 * A
  3        ; A := 3 * A;
  4; 5; 6 : A := 4 * A
END;  {  of CASE A  }
```

b.
```
CASE Num OF
  5           : Num := Num + 5;
  6, 7        ; Num := Num + 6;
  7, 8, 9, 10 : Num := Num + 10
END;  {  of CASE Num  }
```

c.
```
CASE Age OF
  15, 16, 17 : YCount := YCount + 1;
               writeln (Age, YCount);
  18, 19, 20 : MCount := MCount + 1;
  21         : writeln (Age)
END;  {  of CASE Age  }
```

d.
```
CASE Ch OF
  A : Points := 4.0;
  B : Points := 3.0;
  C : Points := 2.0;
  D : Points := 1.0;
  E : Points := 0.0
END;  {  of CASE Ch  }
```

e.
```
CASE Score OF
  5       : Grade := 'A';
  4       : Grade := 'B';
  3       : Grade := 'C';
  2, 1, 0 : Grade := 'E';
```

f.
```
CASE Num / 10 OF
  1 : Num := Num + 1;
  2 : Num := Num + 2;
  3 : Num := Num + 3
END;  {  of CASE Num  }
```

5. What is the output from each of the following program fragments?

a.
```
A := 5;
Power := 3;
CASE Power OF
  0 : B := 1;
  1 : B := A;
  2 : B := A * A;
  3 : B := A * A * A
END;  {  of CASE Power  }
writeln (A:5, Power:5, B:5);
```

b.
```
GasType := 'S';
write ('You have purchased ');
CASE GasType OF
  'R' : write ('Regular');
  'P' : write ('Premium');
  'U' : write ('Unleaded');
  'S' : write ('Super Unleaded')
END;  {  of CASE GasType  }
writeln (' gasoline');
```

c.
```
A := 6;
B := -3;
CASE A OF
  10, 9, 8 : CASE B OF
               -3, -4, -5 : A := A * B;
                0, -1, -2 : A := A + B
             END;
   7, 6, 5 : CASE B OF
               -5, -4 : A := A * B;
               -3, -2 : A := A + B;
               -1,  0 : A := A - B
             END
END;  {  of CASE A  }
writeln (A:5, B:5);
```

d.
```
Symbol := '-';
A := 5;
B := 10;
CASE Symbol OF
  '+' : Num := A + B;
  '-' : Num := A - B;
  '*' : Num := A * B
END;  {  of CASE Symbol  }
writeln (A:5, B:5, Num:5);
```

6. Rewrite each of the following program fragments using a **CASE** statement.

   a.
```
IF Power = 1 THEN
  Num := A;
IF Power = 2 THEN
  Num := A * A;
IF Power = 3 THEN
  Num := A * A * A;
```

   b. Assume Score is an integer between 0 and 10.
```
IF Score > 9 THEN
  Grade := 'A'
ELSE IF Score > 8 THEN
  Grade := 'B'
ELSE IF Score > 7 THEN
  Grade := 'C'
ELSE IF Score > 5 THEN
  Grade := 'D'
ELSE
  Grade := 'E';
```

   c. Assume Measurement is either M or N.
```
IF Measurement = 'M' THEN
  BEGIN
    writeln ('This is a metric measurement.':37);
    writeln ('It will be converted to nonmetric.':42);
    Length := Num * CMToInches
  END
ELSE
  BEGIN
    writeln ('This is a nonmetric measurement.':40);
    writeln ('It will be converted to metric.':39);
    Length := Num * InchesToCM
  END;
```

7. Show how a **CASE** statement could be used in a program to compute college tuition fees. Assume there are different fee rates for undergraduates (U), graduates (G), foreign students (F), and special students (S).

8. Use nested **CASE** statements to design a program fragment to compute postage for domestic (nonforeign) mail. The design should provide for four weight categories for both letters and packages. Each can be sent first, second, third, or fourth class.

■ 4.6 Assertions (Optional)

An *assertion* is a program comment in the form of a statement about what we expect to be true at the point in the program where the assertion is placed. For example, if you wish to compute a test average by dividing SumOfScores by NumberOfStudents, you could use an assertion in the following manner:

```
{ Assertion: NumberOfStudents <> 0 }
ClassAverage := SumOfScores / NumberOfStudents;
```

Assertions are usually Boolean-valued expressions and typically concern program action. Assertions frequently come in pairs: one preceding the program action, and one following the action. In this format, the first assertion is a precondition and the second is a postcondition.

To illustrate preconditions and postconditions, consider the following segment of code:

```
IF Num1 < Num2 THEN
  BEGIN
    Temp := Num1;
```

```
    Num1 := Num2;
    Num2 := Temp
  END;
```

The intent of this code is to have Num1 be greater than or equal to Num2. If we intend for both Num1 and Num2 to be positive, we can write

```
{  Assertion: Num1 >= 0 AND Num2 >= 0  }  ←—  precondition

IF NUM1 < Num2 THEN
  BEGIN
    Temp := Num1;
    Num1 := Num2;
    Num2 := Temp
  END;

{  Assertion: Num1 >= Num2 >= 0  }       ←——  postcondition
```

In practice, you may choose to label preconditions and postconditions, as the following comments illustrate.

```
{  Precondition: Num1 >= 0 and Num2 >= 0  }

IF Num1 < Num2 THEN
  BEGIN
    Temp := Num1;
    Num1 := Num2;
    Num2 := Temp
  END;

{  Postcondition: Num1 >= Num2 >= 0  }
```

As a second example, consider a **CASE** statement used to assign grades based on quiz scores.

```
CASE Score OF
  10          : Grade := 'A';
  9, 8        : Grade := 'B';
  7, 6        : Grade := 'C';
  5, 4        : Grade := 'D';
  3, 2, 1, 0  : Grade := 'E'
ELSE
  writeln ('Value of Score out of range.')
END;  {  of CASE Score  }
```

Assertions can be used as preconditions and postconditions in the following manner.

```
{  Precondition:  Score is an integer between 0 and 10 inclusive  }

CASE Score OF
  10       : Grade := 'A';
  9,8      : Grade := 'B';
  7,6      : Grade := 'C';
  5,4      : Grade := 'D';
  3,2,1,0  : Grade := 'E'
ELSE
 writeln ('Value of Score out of range.')
END;  {  of CASE Score  }

{  Postcondition:  Grade has been assigned a letter grade
                   according to the scale
              10           ——→ A
              8, 9         ——→ B
              6, 7         ——→ C
              4, 5         ——→ D
              0, 1, 2, 3   ——→ E  }
```

Assertions can be used in *program proofs*. Simply put, a program proof is an analysis of a program that attempts to verify the correctness of program results. A detailed study of program proofs is beyond the scope of this text. If, however, you use assertions as preconditions and postconditions now, you will better understand them in subsequent courses. If you do choose to use assertions in this manner, be aware that the postcondition of one action is the precondition of the next action.

FOCUS ON PROGRAM DESIGN

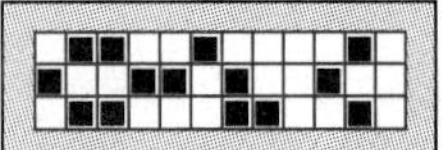

The Gas-N-Clean Service Station sells gasoline and has a car wash. Fees for the car wash are $1.25 with a gasoline purchase of $10.00 or more and $3.00 otherwise. Three kinds of gasoline are available: regular at $1.149, unleaded at $1.199, and super unleaded at $1.289 per gallon. Write a program that prints a statement for a customer. Input consists of number of gallons purchased, kind of gasoline purchased (R, U, S, or, for no purchase, N), and car wash desired (Y or N). Use the constant definition section for gasoline prices. Your output should include appropriate messages. Sample output for this data is

```
Enter number of gallons and press <Enter>.
9.7
Enter gas type (R, U, S, or N) and press <Enter>.
R
Enter Y or N for car wash and press <Enter>.
Y


               ****************************************
               *                                      *
               *     Gas-N-Clean Service Station      *
               *                                      *
               *            July 25, 1993             *
               *                                      *
               ****************************************


            Amount of gasoline purchased      9.700 Gallons
            Price per gallon               $  1.149
            Total gasoline cost                    $ 11.15
            Car wash cost                          $  1.25
                                                   --------
                           Total due               $ 12.40

                       Thank you for stopping

                         Please come again

               Remember to buckle up and drive safely
```

A first-level pseudocode development is

1. Get data
2. Compute charges
3. Print results

A structure chart for this problem is given in Figure 4.6.

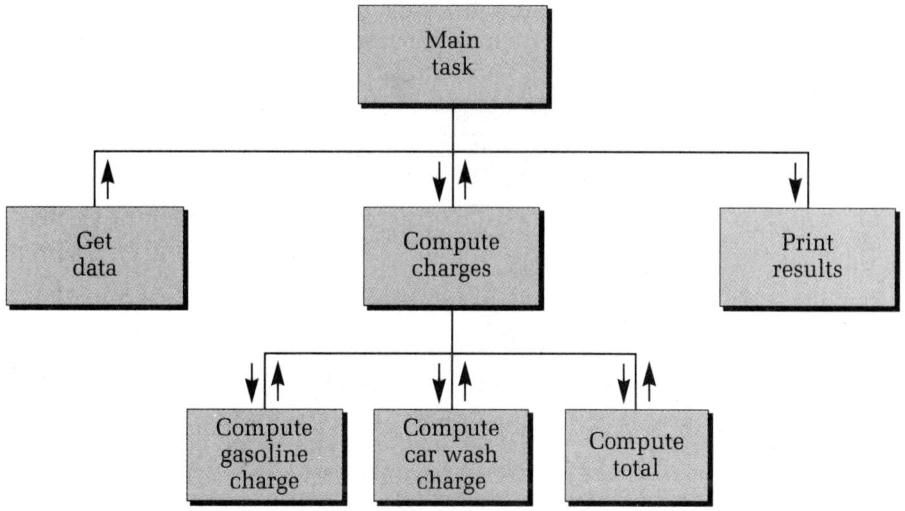

FIGURE 4.6
Structure chart for the Gas-N-Clean Service Station problem

Module specifications for the main modules are

1. GetData Module
   Data received: None
   Information returned: Number of gallons purchased
   Type of gasoline
   Whether or not a car wash is desired
   Logic: Get information interactively from the keyboard.
2. ComputeCharges Module
   Data received: NumGallons
   GasType
   WashOption
   Information returned: GasCost
   WashCost
   TotalCost
   Logic: Use a **CASE** statement to compute the GasCost.
   Use nested selection to determine the WashCost.
   Sum GasCost and WashCost to get TotalCost.
3. PrintResults Module
   Data received: NumGallons
   GasType
   WashOption
   GasCost
   WashCost
   TotalCost
   Information returned: None
   Logic: Use a procedure for the heading.
   Use several **writeln** statements.

Further refinement of the pseudocode produces

1. Get data
   1.1 read number of gallons
   1.2 read type of gas purchased
   1.3 read car wash option

2. Compute charges
   2.1 compute gasoline charge
   2.2 compute car wash charge
   2.3 compute total
3. Print results
   3.1 print heading
   3.2 print information in transaction
   3.3 print closing message

Module 2 consists of three subtasks. A refined pseudocode development of this step is

2. Compute charges
   2.1 compute gasoline charge
      2.1.1 **CASE** GasType **OF**
         'R'
         'U'
         'S'
         'N'
   2.2 compute car wash charge
      2.2.1 **IF** WashOption is yes **THEN**
            compute charge
         ELSE
            charge is 0.0
   2.3 compute total
      2.3.1 Total is GasCost plus WashCost

A Turbo Pascal program for this problem follows.

```
PROGRAM GasNClean;

{  This program is used to compute the amount due from a         }
{  customer of the Gas-N-Clean Service Station.  Constants are   }
{  used for gasoline prices.  Note the use of nested selection   }
{  to compute cost of the car wash.                               }

USES
  Crt;

CONST
  Skip = ' ';
  Date = 'July 25, 1993';
  RegularPrice = 1.149;
  UnleadedPrice = 1.199;
  SuperUnleadedPrice = 1.289;

VAR
  GasType,              {  Type of gasoline purchased (R,U,S,N)  }
  WashOption : char;    {  Character designating option (Y, N)   }
  NumGallons,           {  Number of gallons purchased            }
  GasCost,              {  Computed cost for gasoline             }
  WashCost,             {  Car wash cost                          }
  TotalCost : real;     {  Total amount due                       }

{*************************************************************}
```

```
PROCEDURE GetData (VAR NumGallons : real;
                   VAR GasType, WashOption : char);
  {  Given:   Nothing                                          }
  {  Task:    Have NumGallons, GasType, and WashOption entered }
  {               from the keyboard                            }
  {  Return:  NumGallons, GasType, and WashOption              }

  BEGIN
    ClrScr;
    writeln ('Enter number of gallons and press <Enter>.');      1
    readln (NumGallons);
    writeln ('Enter gas type (R, U, S, or N) and press <Enter>.');
    readln (GasType);
    writeln ('Enter Y or N for car wash and press <Enter>.');
    readln (WashOption)
  END;  {  of PROCEDURE GetData  }

{*****************************************************************}

PROCEDURE ComputeCharges (VAR GasCost, WashCost, TotalCost : real;
                          NumGallons : real;
                          GasType, WashOption : char);

  {  Given:   NumGallons, GasType, and WashOption              }
  {  Task:    Compute GasCost, WashCost, and TotalCost         }
  {  Return:  GasCost, WashCost, and TotalCost                 }

  BEGIN

  {  Compute gas cost  }
    CASE GasType OF
      'R' : GasCost := NumGallons * RegularPrice;
      'U' : GasCost := NumGallons * UnleadedPrice;
      'S' : GasCost := NumGallons * SuperUnleadedPrice;          2
      'N' : GasCost := 0.0
    ELSE
      writeln ('Value of GasType is out of range.')
    END;  {  of CASE GasType  }

  {  Compute car wash cost  }
    IF WashOption = 'Y' THEN
      IF GasCost >= 10.0 THEN
        WashCost := 1.25
      ELSE
        WashCost := 3.0
    ELSE
      WashCost := 0.0;
    TotalCost := GasCost + WashCost
  END;  {  of PROCEDURE ComputeCharges  }

{*****************************************************************}

PROCEDURE PrintHeading;

  {  Given:   Nothing                                          }
  {  Task:    Print a heading for the output                   }
  {  Return:  Nothing                                          }
```

```
  BEGIN
    ClrScr;
    writeln (Skip:13, '****************************************');
    writeln (Skip:13, '*                                      *');
    writeln (Skip:13, '*     Gas-N-Clean Service Station      *');
    writeln (Skip:13, '*                                      *');
    writeln (Skip:13, '*', Skip:12, Date, Skip:13, '*');
    writeln (Skip:13, '*                                      *');
    writeln (Skip:13, '****************************************');
    writeln
  END;  {  of PROCEDURE PrintHeading  }

{****************************************************************}

PROCEDURE PrintMessage;

  {  Given:    Nothing                                          }
  {  Task:     Print an appropriate closing message             }
  {  Return:   Nothing                                          }

  BEGIN
    writeln;
    writeln (Skip:21, 'Thank you for stopping');
    writeln (Skip:23, 'Please come again');
    writeln;
    writeln (Skip:13, 'Remember to buckle up and drive safely');
    writeln;
    readln
  END;  {  of PROCEDURE PrintMessage  }

{****************************************************************}

PROCEDURE PrintResults (NumGallons : real;
                        GasType, WashOption : char;
                        GasCost, WashCost, TotalCost : real);

  {  Given:    NumGallons, GasType, WashOption, computed costs   }
  {                for GasCost, WashCost, and TotalCost         }
  {  Task:     Print customer statement                         }
  {  Return:   Nothing                                          }

  BEGIN
    PrintHeading;

    writeln (Skip:10, 'Amount of gasoline purchased:', Skip:3,
             NumGallons:6:3, 'gallons');
    write (Skip:10, 'Price per gallon:', Skip:13, '$');          3

    CASE GasType OF
      'R' : writeln (RegularPrice:7:3);
      'U' : writeln (UnleadedPrice:7:3);
      'S' : writeln (SuperUnleadedPrice:7:3);
      'N' : writeln (0.0:7:3)
    ELSE
      writeln ('Value of GasType is out of range.')
    END;  {  of CASE GasType  }
```

```
    writeln;
    writeln (Skip:10, 'Total gasoline cost', Skip:19, '$',
             GasCost:6:2);
    IF WashCost > 0 THEN
      writeln (Skip:10, 'Car wash cost', Skip:25, '$',
               WashCost:6:2);
    writeln (Skip:48, '-------');
    writeln (Skip:25, 'Total due', Skip:14, '$', TotalCost:6:2);

    PrintMessage
  END;  {  of PROCEDURE PrintResults  }

{***************************************************************}

BEGIN  {  Main program  }
  GetData (NumGallons, GasType, WashOption);
  ComputeCharges (GasCost, WashCost, TotalCost, NumGallons,
                  GasType, WashOption);
  PrintResults (NumGallons, GasType, WashOption, GasCost,
                WashCost, TotalCost)
END.  {  of main program  }
```

A sample run of this program produces

```
Enter number of gallons and press <Enter>.
11.3
Enter gas type (R, U, S, or N) and press <Enter>.
S
Enter Y or N for car wash and press <Enter>.
N
            ***************************************
            *                                     *
            *     Gas-N-Clean Service Station     *
            *                                     *
            *            July 25, 1993            *
            *                                     *
            ***************************************

          Amount of gasoline purchased:   11.300 Gallons
          Price per gallon:             $  1.289

          Total gasoline cost                    $ 14.57
                                                 -------
                         Total due               $ 14.57

                     Thank you for stopping
                       Please come again

            Remember to buckle up and drive safely
```

■ RUNNING AND DEBUGGING HINTS

1. **IF . . . THEN . . . ELSE** is a single statement in Turbo Pascal. Thus, a semicolon before the **ELSE** creates an **IF . . . THEN** statement and **ELSE** appears incorrectly as a reserved word.
2. A misplaced semicolon used with an **IF . . . THEN** statement can also be a problem. For example

Incorrect	*Correct*
`IF A > 0 THEN;` `  writeln (A);`	`IF A > 0 THEN` `  writeln (A);`

3. Be careful about using compound statements as options in an **IF . . . THEN . . . ELSE** statement. They must be in a **BEGIN . . . END** block.

Incorrect

```
IF A >= 0 THEN
  writeln (A);
  A := A + 10
ELSE
  writeln ('A is negative');
```

Correct

```
IF A >= 0 THEN
  BEGIN
    writeln (A);
    A := A + 10
  END
ELSE
  writeln ('A is negative');
```

4. Your test data should include values that will check both options of an **IF . . . THEN . . . ELSE** statement.

5. **IF. . . THEN . . . ELSE** can be used to check for other program errors. In particular:

   a. Check for bad data by

   readln (⟨data⟩);
   IF ⟨good data⟩ **THEN**
   .
   . (proceed with program)
   .
   ELSE
   .
   . (error message here)
   .

   b. Check for reasonable computed values by

   IF ⟨reasonable value⟩ **THEN**
   .
   . (proceed with program)
   .
   ELSE
   .
   . (error message here)
   .

   For example, if you were computing a student's test average, you could have

   IF (TestAverage <= 100) **AND** (TestAverage >= 0) **THEN**
   .
   . (proceed with program)
   .
   ELSE
   .
   . (error message here)
   .

6. Be careful with Boolean expressions. You should always keep expressions reasonably simple, use parentheses, and minimize use of **NOT.**

7. Be careful to properly match **ELSE**s with **IF**s in nested **IF . . . THEN . . . ELSE** statements. Indenting levels for writing code are very helpful.

```
IF ⟨condition 1⟩ THEN
  IF ⟨condition 2⟩ THEN
      .
      .  (action here)
      .
  ELSE
      .
      .  (action here)
      .
ELSE
      .
      .  (action here)
      .
```

8. The form for using extended **IF** statements is

```
IF ⟨condition 1⟩ THEN
    .
    .  (action 1 here)
    .
ELSE IF ⟨condition 2⟩ THEN
    .
    .  (action 2 here)
    .
ELSE
    .
    .  (final option here)
    .
```

9. Be sure to include the **END** of a **CASE** Statement.

■ Summary

Key Terms

BEGIN . . . END block
compound Boolean expression
compound statement
control structure
empty (null) statement
extended **IF** statement
logical operators: **AND, OR, XOR, NOT**
negation
nested **IF** statement
relational operator
robust
selection statement
simple Boolean expression

Key Terms (optional)

assertion
program proof

Keywords

AND	**ELSE**	**NOT**	**THEN**
boolean	**false**	**OF**	**true**
CASE	**IF**	**OR**	**XOR**

Key Concepts

- Relational operators are =, >, <, >=, <=, <>.
- Priority for evaluating relational operators is last.
- Logical operators **AND, OR, XOR,** and **NOT** are used as operators on Boolean expressions.
- Variables of type **boolean** may only have values **true** or **false.**
- A complete priority listing of arithmetic operators, relational operators, and logical operators is

Expression or Operation	Priority
( )	1. Evaluate from inside out.
NOT	2. Evaluate from left to right.
*, /, **MOD, DIV, AND**	3. Evaluate from left to right.
+, −, **OR, XOR**	4. Evaluate from left to right.
<, <=, >, >=, =, <>	5. Evaluate from left to right.

- A selection statement is a program statement that transfers control to various branches of the program.
- A compound statement is sometimes referred to as a **BEGIN . . . END** block; when it is executed, the entire segment of code between the **BEGIN** and **END** is treated like a single statement.
- **IF . . . THEN . . . ELSE** is a two-way selection statement.
- A semicolon should not precede the **ELSE** portion of an **IF . . . THEN . . . ELSE** statement.
- If the Boolean expression in an **IF . . . THEN . . . ELSE** statement is **true,** the command following **THEN** is executed; if the expression is **false,** the command following **ELSE** is executed.
- Multiple selections can be achieved by using decision statements within decision statements; this is termed multiway selection.
- An extended **IF** statement is a statement of the form

```
IF ⟨condition 1⟩ THEN
        .
        .  (action 1 here)
        .
ELSE IF ⟨condition 2⟩ THEN
        .
        .  (action 2 here)
        .
ELSE IF ⟨condition 3⟩ THEN
        .
        .  (action 3 here)
        .
ELSE
        .
        .  (action 4 here)
        .
```

- Program protection can be achieved by using selection statements to guard against unexpected results.
- **CASE** statements sometimes can be used as alternatives to multiple selection.
- **CASE** statements use an **END** without any **BEGIN.**
- **CASE** statements may contain an **ELSE** option that can be used to control action when an unexpected selector value is encountered.

■ Programming Problems and Projects

The first 13 problems listed here are relatively short, but to complete them you must use concepts presented in this chapter. Again, some of the remaining programming problems are used as the basis for writing programs for subsequent chapters as well as for this chapter.

1. A three-minute telephone call to Scio, N.Y., costs $1.15. Each additional minute costs $0.26. Given the total length of a call in minutes, print the cost.
2. When you first learned to divide, you expressed answers using a quotient and a remainder rather than a fraction or decimal quotient. For example, if you divided 7 by 2, your answer was given as 3 r. 1. Given two integers, divide the larger by the smaller and print the answer in this form. Do not assume that the numbers are entered in any order.
3. Revise Problem 2 so that if there is no remainder, you print only the quotient without a remainder or the letter r.
4. Given the coordinates of two points on a graph, find and print the slope of a line passing through them. Remember that the slope of a line can be undefined.
5. ■ Dr. Lae Z. Programmer wishes to computerize his grading system. He gives five tests and then averages only the four highest scores. An average of 90 or better earns a grade of A; 80–89, a grade of B; and so on. Write a program that accepts five test scores and prints the average and grade according to this method.
6. Given the lengths of three sides of a triangle, print whether the triangle is scalene, isosceles, or equilateral.
7. Given the lengths of three sides of a triangle, determine whether or not the triangle is a right triangle using the Pythagorean theorem. Do not assume that the sides are entered in any order.
8. Given three integers, print only the largest.
9. The island nation of Babbage charges its citizens an income tax each year. The tax rate is based upon the following table:

Income	Tax Rate
$0–5000	0
5001–10,000	3%
10,001–20,000	5.5%
20,001–40,000	10.8%
over $40,000	23.7%

   Write a program that when given a person's income, prints the tax owed rounded to the nearest dollar.
10. Many states base the cost of car registration on the weight of the vehicle. Suppose the fees are as follows:

Weight	Cost
0–1500 pounds	$23.75
1501–2500 pounds	27.95
2501–3000 pounds	30.25
over 3000 pounds	37.00

   Given the weight of a car, find and print the cost of registration.
11. The Mapes Railroad Corporation pays an annual bonus as a part of its profit-sharing plan. This year, all employees who have been with the

company for 10 years or more receive a bonus of 12 percent of their annual salary, and those who have worked at Mapes between five and nine years receive a bonus of 5.75 percent. Those who have been with the company less than five years receive no bonus.

Given the initials of an employee, the employee's annual salary, and the number of years employed with the company, find and print the bonus. All bonuses are rounded to the nearest dollar. Output should be in the following form:

```
          MAPES RAILROAD CORP.

Employee xxx    Years of service nn
    Bonus earned: $ yyyy
```

12. A substance floats in water if its density (mass/volume) is less than 1 g/cc (1 gram per cubic centimeter) and sinks if its density is 1 g/cc or more. Given the mass and volume of an object, print whether it will sink or float.
13. Mr. Arthur Einstein, your high school physics teacher, wants you to develop a program for English-to-metric conversions. You are given a letter indicating whether the measurement is in pounds (P), feet (F), or miles (M). Such measures are to be converted to newtons, meters, and kilometers, respectively. (There are 4.9 newtons in a pound, 3.28 feet in a meter, and 1.61 kilometers in a mile.) Given an appropriate identifying letter and the size of the measurement, convert it to metric units. Print the answer in the following form:

```
3.0 miles = 4.83 kilometers.
```

■ 14. The Caswell Catering and Convention Service (Chapter 3, Problem 12) has decided to revise its billing practices and is in need of a new program to prepare bills. The changes Caswell wishes to make follow.
   a. For adults, the deluxe meals will cost $15.80 per person and the standard meals will cost $11.75 per person, dessert included. Children's meals will cost 60 percent of adult meals. Everyone within a given party must be served the same meal type.
   b. There are five banquet halls. Room A rents for $55.00, room B rents for $75.00, room C rents for $85.00, room D rents for $100.00, and room E rents for $130.00. The Caswells are considering increasing the room fees in about six months, and this should be taken into account.
   c. A surcharge (currently 7 percent) is added to the total bill if the catering is to be done on the weekend (Friday, Saturday, or Sunday).
   d. All customers will be charged the same rate for tip and tax (currently 18 percent). It is applied only to the cost of food.
   e. To induce customers to pay promptly, a discount is offered if payment is made within 10 days. This discount depends upon the amount of the total bill. If the bill is less than $100.00, the discount is 0.5 percent; if the bill is at least $100.00 but less than $200.00, the discount is 1.5 percent; if the bill is at least $200.00 but less than $400.00, the discount is 3 percent; if the bill is at least $400.00 but less than $800.00, the discount is 4 percent; and if the bill is at least $800.00, the discount is 5 percent.

   Test your program on each of the following three customers.

   Customer A: This customer is using room C on Tuesday night. The party includes 80 adults and 6 children. The standard meal is being served. The customer paid a $60.00 deposit.

Customer B: This customer is using room A on Saturday night. Deluxe meals are being served to 15 adults. A deposit of $50.00 was paid.

Customer C: This customer is using room D on Sunday afternoon. The party includes 30 children and 2 adults, all of whom are served the standard meal.

Output should be in the same form as that for Problem 12 in Chapter 3.

■ **15.** State University charges $90.00 for each semester hour of credit, $200.00 per semester for a regular room, $250.00 per semester for an air-conditioned room, and $400.00 per semester for food. All students are charged a $30.00 matriculation fee. Graduating students must also pay a $35.00 diploma fee. Write a program to compute the fees that must be paid by a student. Your program should include an appropriate warning message if a student is taking more than 21 credit hours or fewer than 12 credit hours. A typical line of data for one student should include room type (R or A), student number (in four digits), credit hours, and graduating (T or F).

16. Write a program to determine the day of the week a person was born, given his or her birth date. You should use the following steps to find the day of the week corresponding to any date in this century.

a. Divide the last two digits of the birth year by 4. Put the quotient (ignoring the remainder) in Total. For example, if the person was born in 1983, divide 83 by 4 and store 20 in Total.

b. Add the last two digits of the birth year to Total.

c. Add the last two digits of the date of birth to Total.

d. Using the following table, find the "month number" and add it to Total:

January = 1	May = 2	September = 6
February = 4	June = 5	October = 1
March = 4	July = 0	November = 4
April = 0	August = 3	December = 6

e. If the year is a leap year and if the month you are working with is either January or February, then subtract 1 from Total.

f. Find the remainder when Total is divided by 7. Look up the remainder in the following table to determine the day of the week the person was born. Note that you should not use this procedure if the person's year of birth is earlier than 1900.

1 = Sunday	4 = Wednesday	6 = Friday
2 = Monday	5 = Thursday	0 = Saturday
3 = Tuesday		

Typical input is

```
5 - 15 78
```

where the first entry (5 – 15) represents the date of birth (May 15) and the second entry (78) represents the birth year. An appropriate error message should be printed if a person's year of birth is before 1900.

■ **17.** Community Hospital needs a program to compute and print a statement for each patient. Charges for each day are as follows:

a. room charges

i. private room: $125.00

ii. semiprivate room: $95.00

iii. ward: $75.00

b. telephone charge: $1.75
c. television charge: $3.50

Write a program to get a line of data from the keyboard, compute the patient's bill, and print an appropriate statement. Typical input is

5PNY

where 5 indicates the number of days spent in the hospital, P represents the room type (P, S, or W), N represents the telephone option (Y or N), and Y represents the television option (Y or N). A statement for the data given follows.

```
         Community Hospital

      Patient Billing Statement

Number of days in hospital:      5
Type of room:                Private

Room charge              $625.00
Telephone charge         $  0.00
Television charge        $ 17.50
                         -------

     TOTAL DUE           $642.50
```

18. Write a program that converts degrees Fahrenheit to degrees Celsius and degrees Celsius to degrees Fahrenheit. In the input, the temperature is followed by a designator (F or C) indicating whether the given temperature is Fahrenheit or Celsius.

■ **19.** The city of Mt. Pleasant bills its residents for sewage, water, and sanitation every three months. The sewer and water charge is figured according to how much water is used by the resident. The scale is

Amount (gallons)	Rate (per gallon)
Less than 1000	$0.03
1000 to 2000	$30 + $0.02 for each gallon over 1000
Greater than 2000	$50 + $0.015 for each gallon over 2000

The sanitation charge is $7.50 per month.

Write a program to read the number of months for which a resident is being billed (1, 2, or 3) and how much water was used; then print out a statement with appropriate charges and messages. Use the constant definition section for all rates, and include an error check for incorrect number of months. Typical input is

3 2175

■ **20.** Al Derrick, owner of the Lucky Wildcat Well Corporation, wants you to develop a program to help him decide whether or not a well is making money. Data for a well will consist of one or two lines. The first line contains a single character (D for a dry well, O for oil found, and G for gas found) followed by a real number for the cost of the well. If an O or a G is detected, the cost will be followed by an integer indicating the volume of oil or gas found. In this case, there will also be a second line containing an N or S indicating whether or not sulfur is present. If there is sulfur, the S will be followed by the percentage of sulfur present in the oil or gas.

Unit prices are $5.50 for oil and $2.20 for gas. These prices should be defined as constants. Your program should compute the total revenue for a well (reduce output for sulfur present) and print out all pertinent information with an appropriate message to Mr. Derrick. A gusher is defined as a well with profit in excess of $50,000. Typical input is

```
G 8000.00 20000
S 0.15
```

21. The Mathematical Association of America hosts an annual summer meeting. Each state sends one official delegate to the section officer's meeting at this summer session. The national organization reimburses the official state delegates according to the following scale:

Round-trip Mileage	Rate
Up to 500 miles	15 cents per mile
501 to 1000 miles	$75.00 plus $0.12 for each mile over 500
1001 to 1500 miles	$135.00 plus $0.10 for each mile over 1000
1501 to 2000 miles	$185.00 plus $0.08 for each mile over 1500
2001 to 3000 miles	$225.00 plus $0.06 for each mile over 2000
Over 3,000 miles	$285.00 plus $0.05 for each mile over 3000

Write a program that will accept as input the number of round-trip miles for a delegate and compute the amount of reimbursement.

■ **22.** Dr. Lae Z. Programmer (Problem 5) wants you to write a program to compute and print out the grade for a student in his class. The grade is based on three examinations (worth a possible 100 points each), five quizzes (10 points each), and a 200-point final examination. Your output should include all scores, the percentage grade, and the letter grade. The grading scale is

$90 \leq$ average ≤ 100 A
$80 \leq$ average < 90 B
$70 \leq$ average < 80 C
$60 \leq$ average < 70 D
$0 \leq$ average < 60 E

Typical input is

80 93 85 (examination scores)
9 10 8 7 10 (quiz scores)
175 (final examination)

■ **23.** Dr. Lae Z. Programmer now wants you to modify Problem 22 by adding a check for bad data. Any time an unexpected score occurs, you are to print an appropriate error message and terminate the program.

24. A quadratic equation has the form

$$ax^2 + bx + c = 0$$

where $a \neq 0$. Solutions to this equation are given by

$$x = \frac{-b \pm \sqrt{b^2 - 4ac}}{2a}$$

where the quantity $(b^2 - 4ac)$ is referred to as the discriminant of the equation. Write a program to read three integers as the respective coefficients

(a, b, and c), compute the discriminant, and print out the solutions. Use the following rules:

a. discriminant = 0 → single root
b. discriminant < 0 → no real number solution
c. discriminant > 0 → two distinct real solutions

25. Write a program that receives as input the lengths of three sides of a triangle. Output should first identify the triangle as scalene, isosceles, or equilateral. The program should use the Pythagorean theorem to determine whether or not scalene or isoceles triangles are right triangles. An appropriate message should be part of the output.

■ 26. The sign on the attendant's booth at the Pentagon parking lot is

PENTAGON VISITOR PARKING

Cars:	
First 2 hours	No charge
Next 3 hours	$0.50/hour
Next 10 hours	$0.25/hour
Trucks:	
First 1 hour	No charge
Next 2 hours	$1.00/hour
Next 12 hours	$0.75/hour
Senior Citizens:	No charge

Write a program that will accept as input a one-character designator (C, T, or S) followed by the number of minutes a vehicle has been in the lot. The program should then compute the appropriate charge and print a ticket for the customer. Any part of an hour is to be counted as a full hour.

27. Milt Walker, the chief of advertising for the Isabella Potato Industry, wants you to write a program to compute an itemized bill and total cost of his "This Spud's for You!" ad campaign. The standard black and white full-page ads have base prices as follows:

Drillers' News (code N)	$ 400
Playperson (code P)	2000
Outdoors (code O)	900
Independent News (code I)	1200

Each ad is allowed 15 lines of print with a rate of $20.00 for each line in excess of 15 lines. Each ad is either black and white (code B) and subject to the base prices or is in color (code C) and subject to the following rates:

Three color (code T)	40 percent increase over base
Full color (code F)	60 percent increase over base

Write a program to input Milt's choice of magazine (N, P, O, or I), the number of lines of print (integer), and either black and white (B) or color (C) with a choice of three colors (T) or full color (F). Output should include an appropriate title, all the information and costs used to compute the price of an ad, the total price of the ad, and finally the total price of all ads.

28. Write a program that will add, subtract, multiply, and divide fractions. Input will consist of a single line representing a fraction arithmetic problem as follows:

integer / integer operation integer / integer

For example, a line of input might be

2/3 + 1/2

Your program should:

a. Check for division by zero.
b. Check for proper operation symbols.
c. Print the problem in its original form.
d. Print the answer.
e. Print all fractions in horizontal form.

Your answer need not be in lowest terms. For the sample input

```
2/3 + 1/2
```

sample output is

```
2   1   7
- + - = -
3   2   6
```

29. Write an interactive program that permits the user to print various recipes. Write a procedure for each recipe. After the user enters a one-letter identifier for the desired recipe, a **CASE** statement should be used to call the appropriate procedure. Part of the code could be

```
readln (Selection);
CASE Selection OF
 'J'  :  Jambalaya;
 'S'  :  Spaghetti;
 'T'  :  Tacos
END;  {  of CASE Selection  }
```

30. The force of gravity is different for each of the nine planets in our solar system. For example, on Mercury it is only 0.38 times as strong as it is on Earth. Thus, if you weigh 100 pounds (on Earth), you would weigh only 38 pounds on Mercury. Write an interactive program that allows you to enter your (Earth) weight and your choice of planet to which you would like your weight converted. Output should be your weight on the desired planet together with the planet name. The screen message for input should include a menu for planet choice. Use a **CASE** statement in the program for computation and output. The relative forces of gravity are

Earth	1.00	Mercury	0.38	Saturn	1.17
Jupiter	2.65	Neptune	1.23	Uranus	1.05
Mars	0.39	Pluto	0.05	Venus	0.78

■ 31. Cramer's Rule is a method for solving a system of linear equations. If you have two equations with variables x and y written as

$$ax + by = c$$
$$dx + ey = f$$

the solution for x and y can be given as

$$x = \frac{\begin{vmatrix} c & b \\ f & e \end{vmatrix}}{\begin{vmatrix} a & b \\ d & e \end{vmatrix}} \qquad y = \frac{\begin{vmatrix} a & c \\ d & f \end{vmatrix}}{\begin{vmatrix} a & b \\ d & e \end{vmatrix}}$$

Using this notation

$$\begin{vmatrix} a & b \\ d & e \end{vmatrix}$$

is the determinant of the matrix

$$\begin{bmatrix} a & b \\ d & e \end{bmatrix}$$

and is equal to $ae - bd$.

Write a complete program that will solve a system of two equations using Cramer's Rule. Input will be all coefficients and constants in the system. Output will be the solution to the system. Typical output is

```
For the system of equations

     x  +  2y  =  5
    2x  -   y  =  0

we have the solution

     x  =  1
     y  =  2
```

Use an **IF . . . THEN . . . ELSE** statement to guard against division by zero.

■ Communication in Practice

1. Using a completed program from this chapter, remove all documentation pertaining to selection statements. Exchange this version with another student who has prepared a similar version. Write documentation for all selection statements in the other student's program. Compare your results with the program author's original version. Discuss the differences and similarities with your class.
2. Using the **File** menu, select the file path DEMOS\ and then open the file CRTDEMO.PAS. Identify all selection statements in this program. Write documentation for the selection statements. Compare your results with those of another student who has the same assignment.
3. Contact a programmer and discuss the concept of robustness in a program. Prepare a report of your conversation for class. Your report should include a list of specific instances illustrating how programmers make programs robust.
4. Conduct an unscientific survey of at least two people from each of the following groups: students in upper-level computer science courses, instructors of computer science, and programmers working in industry. Your survey should attempt to ascertain the importance and use of robustness at each level. Discuss the similarities and differences in your findings with those of other class members.
5. Selecting appropriate test data for a program that uses nested selection is a nontrivial task. Create diagrams that allow you to trace the flow of logic when nested selection is used. Use your diagrams to draw conclusions about minimal test data required to test all branches of a program that uses nested selection to various levels.

Repetition Statements

CHAPTER OUTLINE

The previous chapter on selection introduced you to a programming concept that takes advantage of a computer's ability to select. A second major concept utilizing the speed of a computer is repetition. Many problems require a process to be repeated. When this is the case, some form of controlled repetition is needed.

This chapter examines the different methods Turbo Pascal permits for performing a process repeatedly. For example, we still cannot conveniently write a program that solves the simple problem of adding the integers from 1 to 100 or processing the grades of 30 students in a class. By the end of this chapter, you will be able to solve these problems in three different ways. The three forms of repetition (loops) are

1. **FOR . . . TO . . . DO**
2. **WHILE . . . DO**
3. **REPEAT . . . UNTIL**

Each of these three loops contains the basic constructs necessary for repetition: a variable is assigned some value, the variable value changes at some point in the loop, and repetition continues until the value reaches some predetermined value. When the predetermined value (or Boolean condition) is reached, repetition is terminated and program control moves to the next executable statement.

■ 5.1 Classifying Loops

Pretest and Posttest Loops

A loop that uses a condition to control whether or not the body of the loop is executed before going through the loop is a *pretest* or *entrance controlled loop.* The testing condition is the *pretest condition.* If the condition is **true**, the body of the loop is executed. If the condition is **false,** the program skips to the first line of code following the loop. The **FOR** loops and the **WHILE . . . DO** loop are pretest loops.

A loop that examines a Boolean expression after the loop body is executed is a *posttest* or *exit controlled loop.* This is the **REPEAT . . . UNTIL** loop.

Fixed Repetition versus Variable Condition Loops

Fixed repetition (iterated) loops are used when it can be determined in advance how many times a segment of code needs to be repeated. For instance, you might have a predetermined number of repetitions of a segment of code for (1) a program to add the integers from 1 to 100, or (2) programs using a fixed number of data lines (say, game statistics for a team of 12 basketball players). The number of repetitions need not be constant. For example, a user might enter information during execution of a program that would determine how many times a segment is to be repeated. **FOR** loops are fixed repetition loops.

Variable condition loops are needed to solve problems where conditions change within the body of the loop. These conditions involve sentinel values, Boolean flags, arithmetic expressions, or end-of-line and end-of-file markers (see Chapter 6). A variable condition loop uses a control feature that provides more power than is available in many old languages, such as BASIC and FORTRAN. **WHILE . . . DO** and **REPEAT . . . UNTIL** are variable condition loops.

■ 5.2 FOR Loops

There are two kinds of **FOR** loops: the **FOR . . . TO . . . DO** loop and the **FOR . . . DOWNTO . . . DO** loop. These loops are pretest and fixed repetition loops.

FOR . . . TO . . . DO Loops

The form necessary for using a **FOR . . . TO . . . DO** loop is

```
    FOR ⟨index⟩ := ⟨initial value⟩ TO ⟨final value⟩ DO
      ⟨statement⟩;
or
    FOR ⟨index⟩ := ⟨initial value⟩ TO ⟨final value⟩ DO
      BEGIN
        ⟨statement 1⟩;
        ⟨statement 2⟩;
              .
              .
              .
        ⟨statement n⟩
      END;
```

A **FOR . . . TO . . . DO** loop is considered to be a single executable statement. The actions performed in the loop are referred to as the body of the loop. The *index* is an identifier that is assigned values for each repetition of the loop. The internal logic of a **FOR . . . TO . . . DO** loop is

1. The index is assigned the initial value.
2. The index value is compared to the final value.
3. If the index value is less than or equal to the final value:
   a. The body of the loop is executed.
   7.0 b. The index value is incremented by 1.
   c. Another check with the final value is made.
4. If the index value exceeds the final value, control of the program is transferred to the first statement following the loop.

A flow diagram of the loop is given in Figure 5.1.

FIGURE 5.1
FOR . . . TO . . . DO
flow diagram

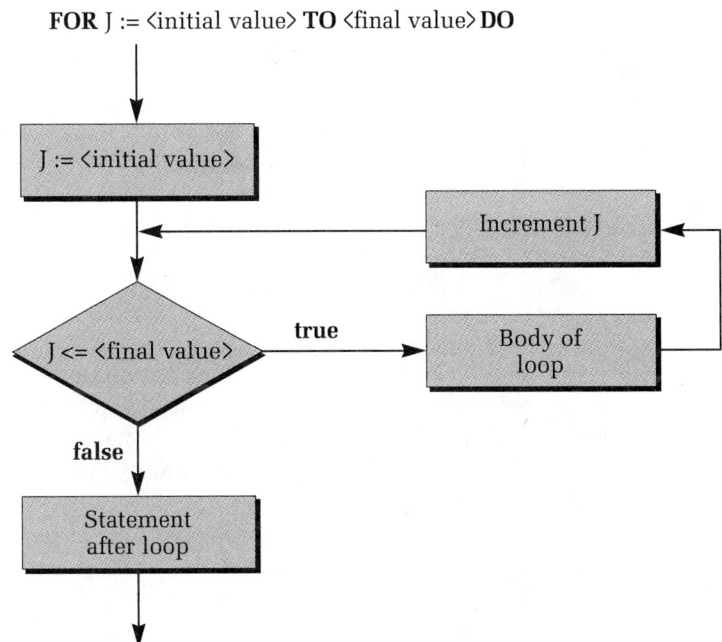

Accumulators

The problem of adding the integers from 1 to 100 requires only one statement in the body of the loop. This problem can be solved by code that constructs an *accumulator* which merely sums values of some variable. In the following code, the index variable LCV (loop control variable) successively assumes the values 1, 2, 3, . . . , 100.

```
Sum:= 0;
FOR LCV := 1 TO 100 DO
  Sum := Sum + LCV;
```

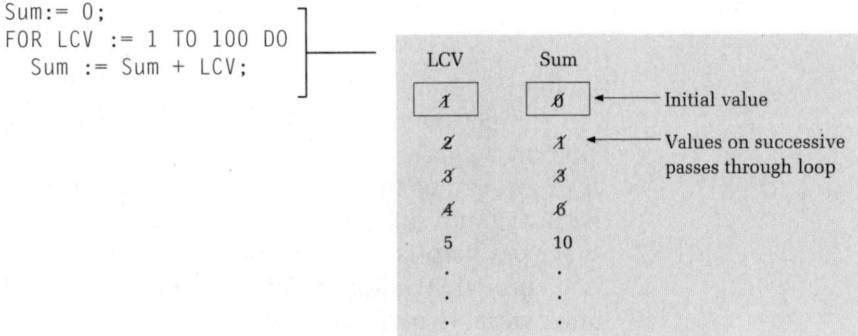

This program segment contains another example of graphic documentation. Throughout the text, these insets will be used to help illustrate what the code is actually doing. The insets are not part of the program; they merely show what some specific code is trying to accomplish.

To see how Sum accumulates these values, let's trace through the code for several values of LCV. Initially, Sum is set to zero by

```
Sum := 0;
```

When LCV is assigned the value 1

```
Sum := Sum + LCV;
```

produces

1	~~0~~ 1
LCV	Sum

For LCV = 2, we get

2	~~1~~ 3
LCV	Sum

LCV = 3 yields

3	~~3~~ 6
LCV	Sum

Note that Sum has been assigned a value equal to 1 + 2 + 3. The final value for LCV is 100. Once this value has been assigned to Sum, the value of Sum will be 5050, which is the sum 1 + 2 + 3 + · · · + 100.

Accumulators are frequently used in loops. The general form for this use is

```
Accumulator := 0;  {  Before loop  }
FOR LCV := <initial value> TO <final value> DO
  BEGIN
      .
      .  (loop body here)
      .
    Accumulator := Accumulator + <new value>
  END;  {  of FOR loop  }
```

Some comments concerning the syntax and form of **FOR . . . TO . . . DO** loops are now necessary.

1. The words **FOR, TO,** and **DO** are reserved and must be used only in the order **FOR . . . TO . . . DO.**
2. The index must be declared as a variable. Although it can be any ordinal data type, we will use mostly integer examples.
3. The index variable can be any valid identifier.
4. The index can be used within the loop just as any other variable. The value of the index variable should never be changed by the statements in the body of the loop.
5. The initial and final values may be constants or variable expressions with appropriate values.
6. The loop will be repeated for each value of the index in the range indicated by the initial and final values.
7. When the loop is finished, the index retains the value it had during the last time through the loop. For some versions of Pascal other than Turbo, the index variable may revert to a state of having no assigned value.

At this point you might try writing some test programs to see what happens if you don't follow these rules. Then consider the following examples, which illustrate the features of **FOR . . . TO . . . DO** loops.

EXAMPLE 5.1

Write a segment of code to list the integers from 1 to 10 together with their squares and cubes. This can be done by

```
FOR J := 1 TO 10 DO
  writeln (J:10, J * J:10, J * J * J:10);
```

This segment produces

```
         1         1         1
         2         4         8
         3         9        27
         4        16        64
         5        25       125
         6        36       216
         7        49       343
         8        64       512
         9        81       729
        10       100      1000
```

EXAMPLE 5.2

Write a **FOR . . . TO . . . DO** loop to produce the following design.

Assuming the first asterisk is in column 20, the following loop will produce the desired result. Note carefully how the output is formatted.

```
FOR J := 1 TO 5 DO
  writeln ('*':21-J, '*':2*J-1);
```

EXAMPLE 5.3

When computing compound interest, it is necessary to evaluate the quantity $(1 + R)^N$, where R is the interest rate for one time period and N is the number of time periods. A **FOR . . . TO . . . DO** loop can be used to perform this computation. If we declare a variable Base, the solution can be found by

```
{  Initialize Base  }
Base := 1;
FOR J := 1 TO N DO
  Base := Base * (1 + R);
```

Base

1 ← Initial value

$(1 + R)^1$ ← Values on successive passes through loop

$(1 + R)^2$

$(1 + R)^3$

.

.

.

$(1 + R)^N$

FOR . . . DOWNTO . . . DO Loops

A second pretest, fixed repetition loop is the **FOR . . . DOWNTO . . . DO** loop. This loop does exactly what you expect; it is identical to a **FOR . . . TO . . . DO** loop except the index variable is decreased by 1 instead of increased by 1 each time it passes through the loop. This is referred to as a *decrement*. The test is index value ≥ final value. The loop terminates when index value < final value. Proper form and syntax for a loop of this type are

```
FOR ⟨index⟩ := ⟨initial value⟩ DOWNTO ⟨final value⟩ DO
  ⟨statement⟩;
or
FOR ⟨index⟩ := ⟨initial value⟩ DOWNTO ⟨final value⟩ DO
  BEGIN
    ⟨statement 1⟩;
    ⟨statement 2⟩;
        .
        .
        .
    ⟨statement n⟩
  END;
```

The conditions for **FOR . . . DOWNTO . . . DO** loops are the same as those for **FOR . . . TO . . . DO** loops. We now consider an example of a **FOR . . . DOWNTO . . . DO** loop.

EXAMPLE 5.4

Illustrate the index values of a **FOR . . . DOWNTO . . . DO** loop by writing the index value during each pass through the loop. The segment of code for this could be

```
FOR K := 20 DOWNTO 15 DO
  writeln ('K =', K:4);
```

and the output is

```
  K =  20
  K =  19
  K =  18
  K =  17
  K =  16
  K =  15
```

From this point on, both **FOR . . . TO . . . DO** and **FOR . . . DOWNTO . . . DO** loops will be referred to as **FOR** loops. The form intended should be clear from the context.

Writing Style for Loops

As you can see, writing style is an important consideration when writing code using loops. There are three features to consider. First, the body of the loop should be indented. Compare the following:

```
FOR J := 1 TO 10 DO
  BEGIN
    readln (Num, Amt);
    Total1 := Total1 + Amt;
    Total2 := Total2 + Num;
    writeln ('The number is', Num:6)
  END;
```

```
writeln ('The total amount is', Total1:8:2);
Average := Total2 / 10;
```

```
FOR J := 1 TO 10 DO
BEGIN
readln (Num, Amt);
Total1 := Total1 + Amt;
Total2 := Total2 + Num;
writeln ('The number is', Num:6)
END;
writeln ('The total amount is', Total1:8:2);
Average := Total2 / 10;
```

The indenting in the first segment makes it easier to determine what is contained in the body of the loop. In the second segment, without any indenting, the beginning and end of the body of the loop are not as well defined.

Second, blank lines can be used before and after a loop for better readability. Compare the following:

```
readln (X, Y);
writeln (X:6:2, Y:6:2);
writeln;

FOR J := -3 TO 5 DO
  writeln (J:3, '*':5);

Sum := Sum + X;
writeln (Sum:10:2);
```

```
readln (X, Y);
writeln (X:6:2, Y:6:2);
writeln;
FOR J := -3 TO 5 DO
  writeln (J:3, '*':5);
Sum := Sum + X;
writeln (Sum:10:2);
```

Again, the first segment is a bit clearer because it emphasizes that the entire loop is a single executable statement and makes it easy to locate the loop.

Third, appropriate comments make loops more readable. Comments should always be given prior to entering a loop. They should state the purpose of the loop and the condition for entering the loop. A comment should always accompany the **END** of a compound statement that is the body of a loop. The general form for this is

```
{ Get a test score.  There are 50 scores. }
FOR J := 1 TO 50 DO
  BEGIN
    .
    . (body of loop)
    .
  END; { of FOR loop }
```

Example 5.5 uses a **FOR** loop to solve a problem. Example 5.6, which closes this section shows how **FOR** loops can be used in a procedure to accomplish a task.

COMMUNICATION AND STYLE TIPS

There are three features you may wish to incorporate as you work with **FOR** loops. First, loop limits can be defined as constants or declared as variables and then assigned values. Thus, you could have

```
CONST
  LoopLimit = 50;
```

Second, the loop control variable can be declared as

```
VAR
  LCV : integer;
```

The loop could then be written as

```
FOR LCV := 1 TO LoopLimit DO
      .
      . (body of loop here)
      .
```

Third, a loop limit can be declared as a variable and the user can then enter a value during execution:

```
VAR
  LoopLimit : integer;
    .
    .
    .
  writeln ('How many entries?');
  readln (LoopLimit);
  FOR LCV := 1 TO LoopLimit DO
    .
    .
    .
```

EXAMPLE 5.5

Suppose you have been asked to write a segment of code to compute the test average for each of 30 students in a class and the overall class average. Data for each student consist of the student's initials and four test scores.

A first-level pseudocode development is

1. Print a heading
2. Initialize Total
3. Process data for each of 30 students
4. Compute class average
5. Print a summary

A **FOR** loop can be used to implement step 3. The step could first be refined to

3. Process data for each of 30 students
   3.1 get data for a student
   3.2 compute average
   3.3 add to Total
   3.4 print student data

The code for this step is

```
FOR LCV := 1 TO ClassSize DO
  BEGIN
    writeln ('Enter three initials and press <Enter>.');
    readln (Init1, Init2, Init3);
    writeln ('Enter four test scores and press <Enter>.');
    readln (Score1, Score2, Score3, Score4);
```

A NOTE OF INTEREST

Charles Babbage

The first person to propose the concept of the modern computer was Charles Babbage (1791–1871), a man truly ahead of his time. Babbage was a professor of mathematics at Cambridge University, as well as an inventor. As a mathematician, he realized the time-consuming and boring nature of constructing mathematical tables (squares, logarithms, sines, cosines, and so on). Since the calculators developed by Pascal and [Gottfried Wilhelm] Leibniz [1646–1716] could not provide the calculations required for these more complex tables, Babbage proposed the idea of building a machine that could compute the various properties of numbers, accurate to 20 digits.

With a grant from the British government, he designed and partially built a simple model of the difference engine. However, the lack of technology in the 1800s prevented him from making a working model. Discouraged by his inability to materialize his ideas, Babbage imagined a better version, which would be a general-purpose, problem-solving machine—the analytical engine.

The similarities between the analytical engine and the modern computer are amazing. Babbage's analytical engine, which was intended to be a steam-powered device, had four components:

1. A "mill" that manipulated and computed the data
2. A "store" that held the data
3. An "operator" of the system that carried out instructions
4. A separate device that entered data and received processed information via punched cards

After spending many years sketching variations and improvements for this new model, Babbage received some assistance in 1842 from Ada Augusta Byron (see the next Note of Interest).

```
    Average := (Score1 + Score2 + Score3 + Score4) / 4;
    Total := Total + Average;
    writeln;
    write (Init1:4; Init2, Init3);
    write (Score1:6, Score2:6, Score3:6, Score4:6);
    writeln (Average:10:2)
  END;
```

EXAMPLE 5.6 One of the tools used by professional programmers is a box of any size, which can be created by using any available character from the keyboard. This task can be accomplished by implementing a procedure with value parameters for the width, length, edge character, and starting position of the upper-left corner.

A procedure for this is

```
PROCEDURE DrawBox (Width, Length : integer;
                   EdgeCharacter : char;
                   ColumnStart, RowStart : integer);
  VAR
    Row, Position, LineNumber : integer;
  BEGIN
    ClrScr;

    {  Start in desired row  }
    FOR Row := 1 TO RowStart-1 DO
      writeln;

    {  Start in desired column  }
    write (' ':ColumnStart-1);

    {  Draw the top border  }
    FOR Position := 1 TO Length DO
      write (EdgeCharacter);
    writeln;                  {  Advance to next line  }

    {  Draw the side edges  }
    FOR LineNumber := 2 TO Width-1 DO
      writeln (EdgeCharacter:ColumnStart,
               EdgeCharacter:Length-1);

    {  Draw the bottom border  }
    write (' ':ColumnStart-1);
    FOR Position := 1 TO Length DO
      write (EdgeCharacter);
    writeln                   {  Advance to next line  }
  END;  {  of PROCEDURE DrawBox  }
```

This procedure can be called from the main program by

```
DrawBox (Width, Length, EdgeCh, ColumnStart, RowStart);
```

where all variables have been suitably declared and initialized.

Exercises 5.2

1. What is the output from each of the following segments of code?
   a.
   ```
   FOR K := 3 TO 8 DO
     writeln ('*':K);
   ```
   b.
   ```
   FOR J := 1 TO 10 DO
     writeln (J:4, ' :', (10 - J):5);
   ```
   c.
   ```
   A := 2;
   FOR J := (3 * 2 - 4) TO 10 * A DO
     writeln ('**', J:4);
   ```
   d.
   ```
   FOR J := 50 DOWNTO 30 DO
     writeln (51 - J:5);
   ```
2. Write a test program for each of the following.
   a. Illustrate what happens when the loop control variable is assigned a value inside the loop.
   b. Demonstrate how an accumulator works. For this test program, sum the integers from 1 to 10. Your output should show each partial sum as it is assigned to the accumulator.

3. Write segments of code using **FOR . . . TO . . . DO** or **FOR . . . DOWNTO . . . DO** loops to produce the following designs. Start each design in column 2.

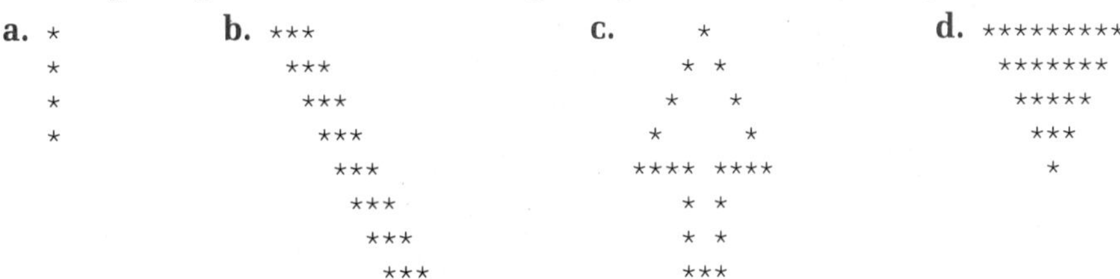

4. Which of the following segments of code do you think accomplish their intended task? For those that do not, what changes would you suggest?

a.
```
FOR K := 1 TO 5 DO;
  writeln (K);
```

b.
```
Sum := 0;
FOR J := 1 TO 10 DO
  readln (A);
  Sum := Sum + A;
writeln (Sum:15);
```

c.
```
Sum := 0;
FOR J = -3 TO 3 DO
  Sum := Sum + J;
```

d.
```
A := 0;
FOR K := 1 TO 10 DO
  BEGIN
    A := A + K;
    writeln (K:5, A:5, A + K:5)
  END;
writeln (K:5, A:5, A + K:5);
```

5. Produce each of the following outputs using both a **FOR . . . TO . . . DO** loop and a **FOR . . . DOWNTO . . . DO** loop.

a.
```
1  2  3  4  5
```

b.
```
*
 *
  *
   *
    *
```

6. Rewrite the following segment of code using a **FOR . . . DOWNTO . . . DO** loop to produce the same result.

```
Sum := 0;
FOR K := 1 TO 4 DO
  BEGIN
    writeln ('*':21+K);
    Sum := Sum + K
  END;
```

7. Rewrite the following segment of code using a **FOR . . . TO . . . DO** loop to produce the same result.

```
FOR J := 10 DOWNTO 2 DO
  writeln (J:J);
```

8. Write a complete program that produces a table showing temperature equivalents in degrees Fahrenheit and degrees Celsius. Let the user enter the starting and ending values. Use the formula

CelsTemp = 5/9 * (FarenTemp − 32)

9. Write a complete program to produce a chart consisting of the multiples of 5 from −50 to 50 together with the squares and cubes of these numbers. Use a procedure to print a suitable heading and user-defined functions for square and cube.

10. The formula $A = P(1 + R)^N$ can be used to compute the amount due A when a principal P has been borrowed at a monthly rate R for a period of N months. Write a complete program that will read in the principal, annual interest rate (divide by 12 for monthly rate), and number of months and then produce a chart that shows how much will be due at the end of each month.

11. Consider Example 5.6 where a procedure is used to draw a box of any size using any available character.
    a. Write a complete interactive program that allows the user to specify the box size and character to be used for the border.
    b. Make the program in (a) more robust by insuring that the user specifies both a width and a length so the box will fit on the screen.

■ 5.3 WHILE . . . DO Loops

FOR loops—loops in which the body of the loop is repeated a fixed number of times—were presented in Section 5.2. This loop is inappropriate for some problems, however, since a segment of code may need to be repeated an unknown number of times. The condition controlling the loop must be variable rather than constant. Recall that Turbo Pascal provides two repetition statements with variable control conditions: one with a pretest condition, and one with a posttest condition.

The pretest loop with variable conditions in Turbo Pascal is the **WHILE . . . DO** loop. The condition controlling the loop is a Boolean expression written between the reserved words **WHILE** and **DO.** Correct form and syntax for such a loop are

```
    WHILE ⟨Boolean expression⟩ DO
        ⟨statement⟩;
or
    WHILE ⟨Boolean expression⟩ DO
        BEGIN
            ⟨statement 1⟩;
            ⟨statement 2⟩;
                .
                .
                .
            ⟨statement n⟩
        END;
```

The flow diagram for a **WHILE . . . DO** loop is given in Figure 5.2.

Program control when using a **WHILE . . . DO** loop is in the following order:

1. The loop condition is examined.
2. 7.0 If the loop condition is **true,** the entire body of the loop is executed before another check is made.
3. If the loop condition is **false,** control is transferred to the first line following the loop. For example

```
A := 1;
WHILE A < 0 DO
  BEGIN
    Num := 5;
    writeln (Num);
    A := A + 10
  END;
writeln (A);
```

FIGURE 5.2
WHILE . . . DO flow diagram

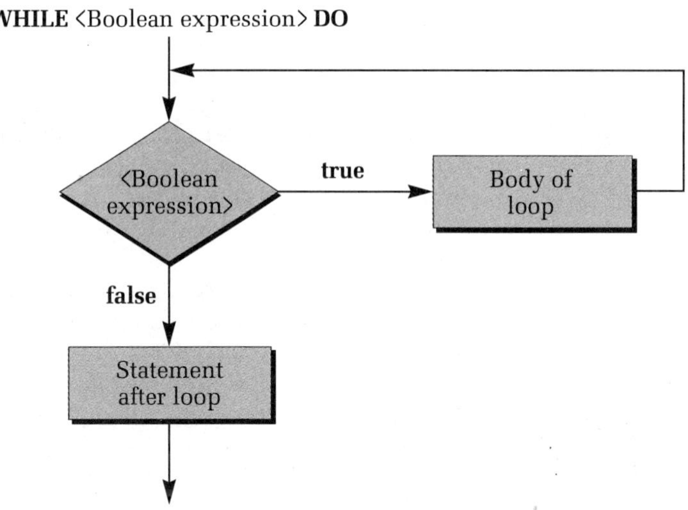

produces the single line of output

```
1
```

Before analyzing the components of the **WHILE . . . DO** statement, let's consider a short example.

EXAMPLE 5.7 This example prints some powers of 2.

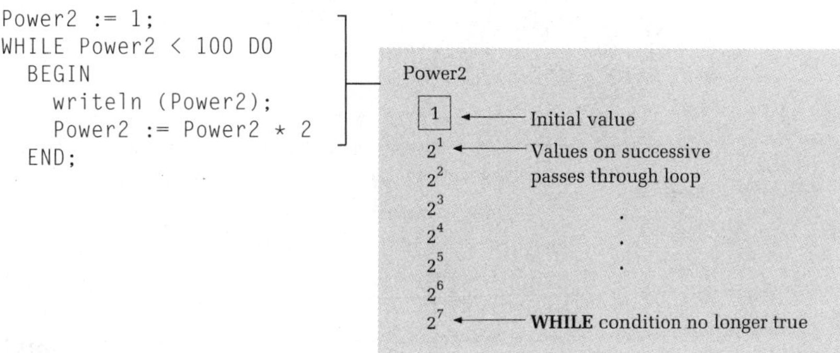
```
Power2 := 1;
WHILE Power2 < 100 DO
  BEGIN
    writeln (Power2);
    Power2 := Power2 * 2
  END;
```


The output from this segment of code is

```
1
2
4
8
16
32
64
```

Keeping this example in mind, let's examine the general form for using a **WHILE . . . DO** loop.

1. The Boolean expression can be any expression that has Boolean values. Standard examples include relational operators and Boolean variables; thus, each of the following would be appropriate:

```
WHILE J < 10 DO
WHILE A <> B DO
WHILE Flag = true DO
WHILE Flag DO
```

2. The Boolean expression must have a value prior to entering the loop.
3. The body of the loop can be a single statement or a compound statement.
4. Provision must be made for appropriately changing the loop control condition in the body of the loop. If no such change is made, the following could happen.
   a. If the loop condition is **true** and no changes are made, a condition called an *infinite loop* is caused. For example

   ```
   A := 1;
   WHILE A > 0 DO
     BEGIN
       Num := 5;
       writeln (Num)
     END;
   writeln (A);
   ```

   The condition A > 0 is **true,** the body is executed, and the condition is retested. However, since the condition is not changed within the loop body, it will always be **true** and will cause an infinite loop. It will not produce a compilation error, but when you run the program, the output will be a list of 5s.
   b. If the loop condition is **true** and changes are made but the condition never becomes **false,** you again have an infinite loop. An example of this is

   ```
   Power3 := 1;
   WHILE Power3 <> 100 DO
     BEGIN
       writeln (Power3);
       Power3 := Power3 * 3
     END;
   ```

   Since the variable Power3 never is assigned the value 100, the condition Power3 <> 100 is always **true** and you never get out of the loop.

   The best way to avoid an infinite loop is to make sure the loop control variable eventually reaches the terminating condition, which causes loop execution to cease. An alternate, less efficient method is to put a counter inside the loop and add a Boolean condition to the loop control statement. Thus, if you want the loop to terminate after at most 100 repetitions, the general form could be

   ```
   Counter := 0;
   WHILE <condition> AND (Counter < 100) DO
     BEGIN
       .
       .
       .
       Counter := Counter + 1  {Guard against infinite loop  }
     END;
   ```

Sentinel Values

The Boolean expression of a variable control loop is frequently controlled by a *sentinel value.* For example, a program may require the user to enter numeric data. When there are no more data, the user will be instructed to enter a special (sentinel) value, which signifies the end of the process. The following illustrates the use of such a sentinel.

EXAMPLE 5.8 Let's write a segment of code that allows the user to enter a set of test scores and then print the average score:

```
NumScores := 0;
Sum := 0;
writeln ('Enter a score and press <Enter>, -999 to quit.');
readln (Score);
WHILE Score <> -999 DO
  BEGIN
    NumScores := NumScores + 1;
    Sum := Sum + Score;
    writeln ('Enter a score and press <Enter>, -999 to quit.');
    readln (Score)
  END;
IF NumScores > 0 THEN
  Average := Sum / NumScores;
  writeln;
  writeln ('The average of ', NumScores:4, ' scores is ',
           Average:6:2);
```

Writing Style

The writing style for **WHILE . . . DO** loops should be similar to that adopted for **FOR** loops. Indenting, skipping lines, and comments should all be used to enhance readability.

Using Counters

Since **WHILE . . . DO** loops may be repeated a variable number of times, it is a common practice to count the number of times the loop body is executed. This is accomplished by declaring an appropriately named integer variable, initializing it to zero before the loop, and then incrementing it by 1 each time through the loop. For example, if you use Count for your variable name, Example 5.7 (in which we printed some powers of 2) could be modified to

```
Count := 0;
Power2 := 1;

{  Display powers less than 100  }
WHILE Power2 < 100 DO
  BEGIN
    writeln (Power2);
    Power2 := Power2 * 2;
    Count := Count + 1
  END;  {  of WHILE...DO  }

writeln ('There are', Count:4,
         ' powers of 2 less than 100.');
```

The output from this segment of code is

```
1
2
4
8
16
32
64
There are   7 powers of 2 less than 100.
```

Although the process is tedious, it is instructive to trace the values of variables through a loop where a *counter* is used. Therefore, let us consider the segment of code we have just seen. Before the loop is entered, we have

0	1
Count	Power2

The loop control is Power2 < 100 (1 < 100). Since this is **true,** the loop body is executed and the new values become

1	2
Count	Power2

Prior to each successive time through the loop, the condition Power2 < 100 is checked. Thus, the loop produces the sequence of values shown in the marginal table. Although Power2 is 128, the remainder of the loop is executed before checking the loop condition. Once a loop is entered, it is executed completely before the loop control condition is reexamined. Since 128 < 100 is **false,** control is transferred to the statement following the loop.

Count	Power2
1	2
2	4
3	8
4	16
5	32
6	64
7	128

Compound Conditions

All previous examples and illustrations of **WHILE . . . DO** loops have used simple Boolean expressions. However, since any Boolean expression can be used as a loop control condition, compound Boolean expressions can also be used. For example

```
readln (A, B);
WHILE (A > 0) AND (B > 0) DO
  BEGIN
    writeln (A:2, B:8);
    A := A - 5;
    B := B - 3
  END;
```

A NOTE OF INTEREST

Ada Augusta Byron

Ada Augusta Byron, Countess of Lovelace (1815–1852), became interested in Charles Babbage's efforts when she was translating a paper on the analytical engine from French to English. Upon meeting Babbage, she began the task of writing an original paper. Through the process, she documented Babbage's ideas and made it possible to understand Babbage's original intentions. Over time, she became a full collaborator on the project, correcting some errors and suggesting the use of the binary system of storage rather than the decimal.

Lady Lovelace's most important contribution was her concept of a loop. She observed that a repetition of a sequence of instructions often was necessary to perform a single calculation. Thus, she discovered that by using a single set of cards and a conditional jump facility, the calculation could be performed with a fraction of the effort. This idea has earned her the distinction of being the first programmer.

In honor of her role as the first computer programmer, the United States Department of Defense named its newly designed programming language Ada.

will go through the body of the loop only when the Boolean expression (A > 0) **AND** (B > 0) is **true.** Thus, if the values of A and B obtained from the keyboard are

17 8

the output from this segment of code is

```
17        8
12        5
 7        2
```

Compound Boolean expressions can be as complex as you wish to make them. However, if several conditions are involved, the program can become difficult to read and debug. Therefore, you may wish to redesign your solution to avoid this problem.

Exercises 5.3

1. Compare and contrast **FOR** loops with **WHILE . . . DO** loops.
2. Write a test program that illustrates what happens when you have an infinite loop.
3. What is the output from each of the following segments of code?

   a.
   ```
   K := 1;
   WHILE K <= 10 DO
     BEGIN
       writeln (K);
       K := K + 1
     END;
   ```
   b.
   ```
   A := 1;
   WHILE 17 MOD A <> 5 DO
     BEGIN
       writeln (A:5, 17 MOD A:5);
       A := A + 1
     END;
   ```
   c.
   ```
   A := 2;
   B := 50;
   WHILE A < B DO
     A := A * 3;
   writeln (A:5, B:5);
   ```
   d.
   ```
   Count := 0;
   Sum := 0;
   WHILE Count < 5 DO
     BEGIN
       Count := Count + 1;
       Sum := Sum + Count;
       writeln ('The partial sum is', Sum:4)
     END;
   writeln ('The count is', Count:4);
   ```
   e.
   ```
   X := 3.0;
   Y := 2.0;
   WHILE X * Y < 100 DO
     X := X * Y;
   writeln (X:10:2, Y:10:2);
   ```

4. Indicate which of the following are infinite loops, and explain why they are infinite.

   a.
   ```
   J := 1;
   WHILE J < 10 DO
     writeln (J);
     J := J + 1;
   ```
   b.
   ```
   A := 2;
   WHILE A < 20 DO
     BEGIN
       writeln (A);
       A := A * 2
     END;
   ```
   c.
   ```
   A := 2;
   WHILE A <> 20 DO
     BEGIN
       writeln (A);
       A := A * 2
     END;
   ```
   d.
   ```
   B := 15;
   WHILE B DIV 3 = 5 DO
     BEGIN
       writeln (B:5, B DIV 5:5);
       B := B - 1
     END;
   ```

5. Write a **WHILE . . . DO** loop for each of the following tasks.

   a. Print a positive real number (Num), and then print successive values where each value is 0.5 less than the previous value. The list should continue as long as values to be printed are positive.

b. Print a list of squares of positive integers as long as the difference between consecutive squares is < 50.

6. Write a segment of code that reads a positive integer and prints a list of powers of the integer that are $< 10{,}000$.

■ 5.4 REPEAT . . . UNTIL Loops

In the previous two sections, we discussed two kinds of repetition. We looked at fixed repetition using **FOR** loops and variable repetition using **WHILE . . . DO** loops. Turbo Pascal provides a second form of variable repetition, a **REPEAT . . . UNTIL** loop, which is a posttest or exit controlled loop.

The basic form and syntax for a **REPEAT . . . UNTIL** loop is

```
REPEAT
   ⟨statement 1⟩;
   ⟨statement 2⟩;
        .
        .
        .
   ⟨statement n⟩
UNTIL ⟨Boolean expression⟩;
```

A flow diagram for a **REPEAT . . . UNTIL** loop is given in Figure 5.3.

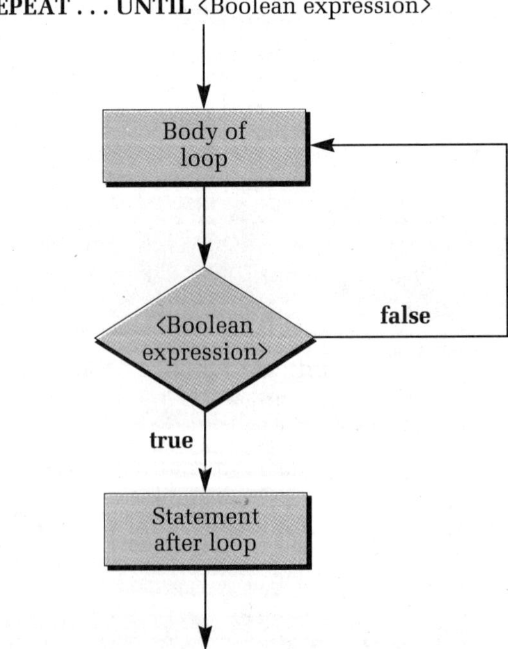

FIGURE 5.3 **REPEAT . . . UNTIL** flow diagram

Prior to examining this form, let us consider the fragment of code

```
Count := 0;
REPEAT
  Count := Count + 1;
  writeln (Count:8)
UNTIL Count = 5;
writeln ('All done');
```

The output for this fragment is

```
         1
         2
         3
         4
         5
All done
```

Keeping this example in mind, the following comments concerning the use of a **REPEAT . . . UNTIL** loop are in order.

1. The program statements between **REPEAT** and **UNTIL** are executed in order as they appear. Thus, a **BEGIN . . . END** block is not necessary.
2. A semicolon is not required between the last statement in the body of the loop and the reserved word **UNTIL.**
3. The Boolean expression must have a value before it is used at the end of the loop.
4. The loop must be entered at least once because the Boolean expression is not evaluated until after the loop body has been executed.
5. When the Boolean expression is evaluated, if it is **false,** control is transferred back to the top of the loop; if it is **true,** control is transferred to the next program statement.
6. Provision must be made for changing values inside the loop so that the Boolean expression used to control the loop will eventually be **true.** If this is not done, you will have an infinite loop, as in the following code:

```
J := 0;
REPEAT
  J := J + 2;
  writeln (J)
UNTIL J = 5;
```

7. Your writing style for using **REPEAT . . . UNTIL** loops should be consistent with your style for using other loop structures.

There are two important differences between **WHILE . . . DO** and **REPEAT . . . UNTIL** loops. First, a **REPEAT . . . UNTIL** loop must be executed at least once, but a **WHILE . . . DO** loop will be skipped if the initial value of the Boolean expression is **false.** For this reason, **REPEAT . . . UNTIL** loops are generally used less frequently than **WHILE . . . DO** loops.

The second difference is that a **REPEAT . . . UNTIL** loop is repeated until the Boolean expression becomes **true.** In a **WHILE . . . DO** loop, repetition continues until the Boolean expression becomes **false.**

■ EXAMPLE 5.9

An early method of approximating square roots, the Newton–Raphson method, consisted of starting with an approximation and then getting successively better approximations until the desired degree of accuracy was achieved.

Writing code for this method, each NewGuess is defined to be

```
NewGuess := 1/2 * (OldGuess + Number / OldGuess)
```

Thus, if the number entered is 34 and the first approximation is 5, the second approximation will be

```
1/2 * (5 + 34 / 5)          (5.9)
```

and the third approximation will be

```
1/2 * (5.9 + 34 / 5.9)      (5.83135593)
```

Let's see how a **REPEAT . . . UNTIL** loop can be used to obtain successively better approximations until a desired degree of accuracy is reached.

Assume we wish to approximate the square root of the value contained in Number, OldGuess contains a first approximation, and DesiredAccuracy is a defined constant. A loop used in the solution of this problem is

```
writeln (NewGuess:12:8);
{  Compute and list approximations  }
REPEAT
  OldGuess := NewGuess;
  NewGuess := 1/2 * (OldGuess + Number / OldGuess);
  writeln (NewGuess:10:8)
UNTIL abs(NewGuess - OldGuess) < DesiredAccuracy;
```

If DesiredAccuracy is 0.0001, Number is 34, and NewGuess is originally 5, the output from this segment is

```
5.00000000
5.90000000
5.83135593
5.83095191
5.83095189
```

■ EXAMPLE 5.10

Interactive programming frequently requires the use of a menu to give the user a choice of options. For example, suppose you want a menu to be

```
Which of the following recipes do you wish to see?

  (T)acos
  (J)ambalaya
  (G)umbo
  (Q)uit

Enter the first letter and press <Enter>.
```

This screen message could then be written as the procedure Menu and the main program could use a **REPEAT . . . UNTIL** loop as follows:

```
REPEAT
  Menu;
  readln (Selection);
  CASE Selection OF
    'T' : Tacos;
    'J' : Jambalaya;
    'G' : Gumbo;
    'Q' : GoodbyeMessage
  END  {  of CASE Selection  }
UNTIL Selection = 'Q';
```

where Tacos, Jambalaya, Gumbo, and GoodbyeMessage are each separate procedures with appropriate messages.

Compound Conditions

The Boolean expression used with a **REPEAT . . . UNTIL** loop can be as complex as you choose to make it. However, as with **WHILE . . . DO** loops, if the expression gets too complicated, you might enhance program readability and design by redesigning the algorithm to use simpler expressions.

Choosing the Correct Loop

"Which loop should I use?" is a question often faced by programmers. A partial answer is easy. If a loop is to be repeated a predetermined number of times during execution, a **FOR** loop is preferable. If the number of repetitions is not known, one of the variable control loops should be used.

The more difficult part of the answer is deciding which variable control loop is appropriate. Simply stated, if a control check is needed before the loop is executed, use a **WHILE . . . DO** loop. If a control check is needed at the end of the loop, use a **REPEAT . . . UNTIL** loop. Remember, however, a **REPEAT . . . UNTIL** loop must always be executed at least once. Therefore, if there is a possibility that the loop will never be executed, a **WHILE . . . DO** loop must be used. For example, when reading data (especially from files, see Chapter 10), if there is a possibility of no data, a **WHILE . . . DO** loop must be used with a prompting read or other control check prior to the loop. Thus, you could have

```
writeln ('Enter a score, -999 to quit.');
readln (Score);
MoreData := (Score <> -999);
WHILE MoreData DO
  BEGIN
    .
    .  (process data)
    .
    writeln ('Enter a score, -999 to quit.');
    readln (Score);
    MoreData := (Score <> -999)
  END;  {  of WHILE loop  }
```

If the three lines of code required to get a score were written as a procedure, this would appear as

```
GetData (Score, MoreData);
WHILE MoreData DO
  BEGIN
    .
    .  (process data)
    .
    GetData (Score, MoreData)
  END;  {  of WHILE loop  }
```

In the event either variable control loop can be used, the problem itself may help with the decision. Does the process need to be repeated until something happens, or does the process continue as long as (while) some condition is true? If either of these is apparent, use the code that most accurately reflects the solution to the problem.

Data Validation

Variable condition loops can be used to make programs more robust. In particular, suppose you are writing an interactive program that expects positive integers to be entered from the keyboard, with a sentinel value of −999 to be entered when you wish to quit. You can guard against bad data by using the following:

```
REPEAT
  writeln ('Enter a positive integer; <-999> to quit.');
  readln (Num)
UNTIL (Num > 0) OR (Num = -999);
```

This process of examining data prior to its use in a program is referred to as *data validation*, and loops are useful for such validation. A second example of using a loop for this purpose follows.

EXAMPLE 5.11

One problem associated with interactive programs is guarding against typing errors. This example illustrates how a **REPEAT . . . UNTIL** loop can be used to prevent the user from entering something other than the anticipated responses. Specifically, suppose users of an interactive program are asked to indicate whether or not they wish to continue by entering either a Y or N. The screen message could be

```
Do you wish to continue? <Y or N>
```

You wish to allow any of Y, y, N, or n to be used as an appropriate response. Any other entry is considered an error. This can be accomplished by the following:

```
{  Read one of Y, y, N, or n  }
REPEAT
  writeln ('Do you wish to continue? <Y or N>');
  readln (Response);
  GoodResponse := (Response = 'Y') OR (Response = 'y') OR
                  (Response = 'N') OR (Response = 'n')
UNTIL GoodResponse;
{  A valid response has been read  }
```

Any response other than those permitted as good data (Y, y, N, n) results in GoodResponse being **false** and the loop being executed again.

Exercises 5.4

1. Explain the difference between a pretest loop and a posttest loop.
2. Write a test program that illustrates what happens when the initial condition for a **REPEAT . . . UNTIL** loop is **false.** Compare this result with a similar condition for a **WHILE . . . DO** loop.
3. Indicate what the output will be from each of the following.

a.
```
A := 0;
B := 10;
REPEAT
  A := A + 1;
  B := B - 1;
  writeln (A:5, B:5)
UNTIL A > B;
```

b.
```
Power := 1;
REPEAT
  Power := Power * 2;
  writeln (Power)
UNTIL Power > 100;
```

c.
```
J := 1;
REPEAT
  writeln (J);
  J := J + 1
UNTIL J > 10;
```

d.
```
A := 1;
REPEAT
  writeln (A:5, 17 MOD A:5);
  A := A + 1
UNTIL 17 MOD A = 5;
```

4. Indicate which of the following are infinite loops, and explain why.

a.
```
J := 1;
REPEAT
  writeln (J)
UNTIL J > 10;
J := J + 1;
```

b.
```
A := 2;
REPEAT
  writeln (A);
  A := A * 2
UNTIL A > 20;
```

c.
```
A := 2;
REPEAT
  writeln (A);
  A := A * 2
UNTIL A = 20;
```

d.
```
B := 15;
REPEAT
  writeln (B:5, B DIV 5:5);
  B := B - 1
UNTIL B DIV 3 <> 5;
```

5. Write a **REPEAT . . . UNTIL** loop for each of the following tasks.
   a. Print a positive real number (Num), and then print successive values where each value is 0.5 less than the previous value. The list should continue as long as values to be printed are positive.
   b. Print a list of squares of positive integers as long as the difference between consecutive squares is less than 50.
6. Discuss whether or not a priming read (a read before the loop is entered) is needed before a **REPEAT . . . UNTIL** loop that is used to get data.
7. Give an example of a situation that would require a predetermined number of repetitions.
8. In mathematics and science, many applications require that a certain level or degree of accuracy be obtained by successive approximations. Explain how the process of reaching the desired level of accuracy would relate to loops in Turbo Pascal.
9. Write a program that utilizes the algorithm for approximating a square root as shown in Example 5.9. Let the defined accuracy be 0.0001. Input should consist of the number for which the square root is desired. Your program should guard against bad data entries (negatives and zero). Output should include a list of approximations and a check of your final approximation.
10. Compare and contrast the three repetition structures discussed in this chapter.

■ 5.5 Loop Verification (Optional)

Loop verification is the process of guaranteeing that a loop performs its intended task. Such verification is part of program testing and correctness, which we discussed in Section 4.4.

Some work has been done on constructing formal proofs that loops are "correct." We now examine a modified version of loop verification; a complete treatment of the issue will be the topic of subsequent course work.

Preconditions and Postconditions with Loops

Preconditions and postconditions can be used with loops. Loop preconditions are referred to as *input assertions*. They are comments that indicate what can be expected to be true before the loop is entered. Loop postconditions are referred to as *output assertions*. They are comments that indicate what can be expected to be true when the loop is exited.

Integer	Proper Divisors	Sum
6	1, 2, 3	6
9	1, 3	4
12	1, 2, 3, 4, 6	16

To illustrate input and output assertions, let's consider the mathematical problem of summing the proper divisors of a positive integer (see table in margin).

Consider a program with a positive integer as input and the following as output: a determination of whether the integer is perfect (Sum = integer), abundant (Sum > integer), or deficient (Sum < integer). As part of the program, it is necessary to sum the divisors. A loop to perform this task is

```
DivisorSum := 0;
FOR TrialDivisor := 1 TO Num DIV 2 DO
  IF Num MOD TrialDivisor = 0 THEN
    DivisorSum := DivisorSum + TrialDivisor;
```

An input assertion for this loop is

```
{  Precondition: 1. Num is a positive integer.          }
{                2. DivisorSum = 0.                     }
```

An output assertion is

```
{  Postcondition: DivisorSum is the sum of all proper  }
{                 divisors of Num.                     }
```

When these are placed with the previous code, we have

```
DivisorSum := 0;

{  Precondition: 1. Num is a positive integer.         }
{                2. DivisorSum = 0.                    }

FOR TrialDivisor := 1 TO Num DIV 2 DO
  IF Num MOD TrialDivisor = 0 THEN
    DivisorSum := DivisorSum + TrialDivisor;

{  Postcondition: DivisorSum is the sum of all proper  }
{                 divisors of Num.                     }
```

Invariant and Variant Assertions

A *loop invariant* is an assertion that expresses a relationship between variables that remains constant throughout all iterations of the loop. In other words, it is a statement that is true both before the loop is entered and after each pass through the loop. An invariant assertion for the preceding code segment could be

```
{  DivisorSum is the sum of proper divisors of Num that  }
{  are less than or equal to TrialDivisor.               }
```

A *loop variant* is an assertion that changes in terms of its truth between the first and final execution of the loop. The loop variant expression should be stated in such a way that it guarantees the loop is exited. Thus, it should contain some statement about the loop variable being incremented (or decremented) during execution of the loop. In the preceding code, we could have

```
{  TrialDivisor is incremented by 1 each time through the  }
{  loop. It eventually exceeds the value Num DIV 2, at     }
{  which point the loop is exited.                         }
```

Variant and invariant assertions usually occur in pairs.

We now use four kinds of assertions—input, output, variant, and invariant—to produce the formally verified loop that follows.

```
DivisorSum := 0;

{  Precondition: 1. Num is a positive integer.   }  (input
{                2. DivisorSum = 0.              }   assertion)

FOR TrialDivisor := 1 TO Num DIV 2 DO

{  TrialDivisor is incremented by 1 each time    }  (variant
{  through the loop. It eventually exceeds the   }   assertion)
{  value Num DIV 2, at which point the loop is   }
{  exited.                                       }

  IF Num MOD TrialDivisor = 0 THEN
    DivisorSum := DivisorSum + TrialDivisor;

{  DivisorSum is the sum of proper divisors of   }  (invariant
{  Num that are less than or equal to            }   assertion)
{  TrialDivisor.                                 }

{  Postcondition: DivisorSum is the sum of       }  (output
{  all proper divisors of Num.                   }   assertion)
```

In general, code that is presented in this text does not include formal verification of the loops. This issue is similar to that of robustness. In an introductory course, a decision must be made as to the trade-off between learning new concepts and writing robust programs with formal verification of loops. We encourage the practice, but space and time considerations make it inconvenient to include such documentation at this level. We close this discussion with another example illustrating loop verification.

EXAMPLE 5.12 Consider the problem of finding the greatest common divisor (GCD) of two positive integers. To illustrate, we have

Num1	Num2	GCD (Num 1, Num2)
8	12	4
20	10	10
15	32	1
70	40	10

A segment of code to produce the GCD of two positive integers after they have been ordered as Small, Large is

```
TrialGCD := Small;
GCDFound := false;
WHILE NOT GCDFound DO
  IF (Large MOD TrialGCD = 0) AND
     (Small MOD TrialGCD = 0) THEN
    BEGIN
      GCD := TrialGCD;
      GCDFound := true
    END
  ELSE
    TrialGCD := TrialGCD - 1;
```

Using assertions as previously indicated, this code would appear as

```
TrialGCD := Small;
GCDFound := false;

{  Precondition: 1. Small <= Large                    }
{                2. TrialGCD (Small) is the first     }
{                   candidate for GCD                 }
{                3. GCDFound is false                 }

WHILE NOT GCDFound DO

{  TrialGCD assumes integer values ranging from Small  }
{  to 1. It is decremented by 1 each time through the  }
{  loop. When TrialGCD divides both Small and Large,   }
{  the loop is exited. Exit is guaranteed since 1      }
{  divides both Small and Large.                       }

  IF (Large MOD TrialGCD = 0) AND
     (Small MOD TrialGCD = 0) THEN
    BEGIN

    {  When TrialGCD divides both Large and Small,     }
    {  then GCD is assigned that value.                }
```

```
      GCD := TrialGCD;
      GCDFound := true
    END
  ELSE
    TrialGCD := TrialGCD - 1;

{   Postcondition: GCD is the greatest common divisor  }
{                  of Small and Large.                 }
```

Exercises 5.5 (Optional)

1. Write appropriate input assertions and output assertions for each of the following loops.

   a.
   ```
   readln (Score);
   WHILE Score <> -999 DO
     BEGIN
       NumScores := NumScores + 1;
       Sum := Sum + Score;
       writeln ('Enter a score; -999 to quit.');
       readln (Score)
     END;
   ```
   b.
   ```
   Count := 0;
   Power2 := 1;
   WHILE Power2 < 100 DO
     BEGIN
       writeln (Power2);
       Power2 := Power2 * 2;
       Count := Count + 1
     END;
   ```
   c. (From Example 5.9)
   ```
   REPEAT
     OldGuess := NewGuess;
     NewGuess := 1/2 * (OldGuess + Number / OldGuess);
     writeln (NewGuess:12:8)
   UNTIL abs(NewGuess - OldGuess) < DesiredAccuracy;
   ```
2. Write appropriate loop invariant and loop variant assertions for each of the loops in Exercise 1.
3. The following loop comes from a program called HiLo. The user enters a number (Guess), and the computer then displays a message indicating whether the guess is correct, too high, or too low. Add appropriate input assertions, output assertions, loop invariant assertions, and loop variant assertions to the following code.

   ```
   Correct := false;
   Count := 0;
   WHILE (Count < MaxTries) AND (NOT Correct) DO
     BEGIN
       Count := Count + 1;
       writeln ('Enter choice number ', Count);
       readln (Guess);
       IF Guess = Choice THEN
         BEGIN
           Correct := true;
           writeln ('Congratulations!')
         END
       ELSE IF Guess < Choice THEN
   ```

```
      writeln ('Your guess is too low')
    ELSE
      writeln ('Your guess is too high')
  END;
```

■ 5.6 Nested Loops

In this chapter, we have examined three loop structures. Each of them has been discussed with respect to syntax, semantics, form, writing style, and use in programs. But remember that each loop is treated as a single statement in Turbo Pascal. In this sense, it is possible to have a loop as one of the statements in the body of another loop. When this happens, the loops are said to be *nested loops.*

Loops can be nested to any depth; that is; a loop can be within a loop within a loop, and so on. Also, any of the three types of loops can be nested within any type of loop. However, a programmer should be careful not to design a program with nesting that is too complex. If program logic becomes too difficult to follow, it is better to redesign the program. For example, the inner logic could be split off into a separate subprogram.

Flow of Control

As a first example of using a loop within a loop, consider

```
FOR K := 1 TO 5 DO
  FOR J := 1 TO 3 DO
    writeln (K + J);
```

When this fragment is executed, the following happens.

1. K is assigned a value.
2. For each value of K, the following loop is executed:

```
FOR J := 1 TO 3 DO
  writeln (K + J);
```

Thus, for K := 1, the "inside" or nested loop produces the output

```
2
3
4
```

At this point, K := 2, and the next portion of the output produced by the nested loop is

```
3
4
5
```

The complete output from these nested loops is

```
2 }
3 } from K := 1
4 }
3 }
4 } from K := 2
5 }
4 }
5 } from K := 3
6 }
5 }
6 } from K := 4
7 }
6 }
7 } from K := 5
8 }
```

As you can see, for each value assigned to the index of the outside loop, the inside loop is executed completely. Suppose you want the output to be printed in the form of a chart as follows:

```
2  3  4
3  4  5
4  5  6
5  6  7
6  7  8
```

The pseudocode to produce this output is

1. **FOR** K := 1 **TO** 5 **DO**
   produce a line

A refinement of this is

1. **FOR** K:= 1 **TO** 5 **DO**
   1.1 print on one line
   1.2 advance the printer

The code for this development becomes

```
FOR K := 1 TO 5 DO
  BEGIN
    FOR J := 1 TO 3 DO
      write ((K + J):4);
    writeln
  END;
```

Our next example shows how nested loops can be used to produce a design.

EXAMPLE 5.13

Use nested **FOR** loops to produce the output

```
*
**
***
****
*****
```

where the left asterisks are in column 10.

The first-level pseudocode to solve this problem could be

1. **FOR** K := 1 **TO** 5 **DO**
   produce a line

A refinement of this could be

1. **FOR** K := 1 **TO** 5 **DO**
   1.1 print on one line
   1.2 advance the printer

Step 1.1 is not yet sufficiently refined, so the next level could be

1. **FOR** K := 1 **TO** 5 **DO**
   1.1 print on one line
      1.1.1 put a blank in column 9
      1.1.2 print K asterisks
   1.2 advance the printer

We can now write a program fragment to produce the desired output as follows:

```
FOR K := 1 TO 5 DO
  BEGIN
    write (' ':9);
    FOR J := 1 TO K DO
      write ('*');
    writeln
  END;  {  of outer loop  }
```

A significant feature has been added to this program fragment. Note that the loop control for the inner loop is the index of the outer loop.

Example 5.13 is a bit contrived, and tracing the flow of control is somewhat tedious. However, it is important for you to be able to follow the logic involved in using nested loops.

Thus far, nested loops have been used only with **FOR** loops, but any of the loop structures may be used in nesting. The following example illustrates a **REPEAT . . . UNTIL** loop nested within a **WHILE . . . DO** loop.

■ EXAMPLE 5.14

Trace the flow of control and indicate the output for the following program fragment.

```
A := 10;
B := 0;
WHILE A > B DO
  BEGIN
    writeln (A:5);
    REPEAT
      writeln (A:5, B:5, (A + B):5);
      A := A - 2
    UNTIL A <= 6;
    B := B + 2
  END;  {  of WHILE...DO  }
writeln;
writeln ('All done':20);
```

The assignment statements produce

10	0
A	B

and A > B is **true;** thus, the **WHILE . . . DO** loop is entered. The first time through this loop, the **REPEAT . . . UNTIL** loop is used. Output for the first pass is

```
   10
   10    0   10
```

and the values for A and B are

8	0
A	B

The Boolean expression A <= 6 is **false.** The **REPEAT . . . UNTIL** loop is executed again to produce the next line of output

```
    8    0    8
```

and the values for A and B become

6	0
A	B

At this point, A <= 6 is **true** and control transfers to the line of code

```
B := B + 2;
```

Thus, the variable values are

6	2
A	B

and the Boolean expression A > B is **true.** This means the **WHILE . . . DO** loop will be repeated. The output for the second time through this loop is

```
6
6   2   8
```

and the values for the variables are

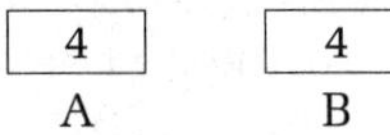

Now A > B is **false** and control is transferred to the line following the **WHILE . . . DO** loop. Output for the complete fragment is

```
10
10    0   10
 8    0    8
 6
 6    2    8

          All done
```

Writing Style

As usual, you should be aware of the significance of using a consistent, readable style of writing when using nested loops. There are at least three features you should consider.

1. **Indenting.** Each loop should have its own level of indenting. This makes it easier to identify the body of the loop. If the loop body consists of a compound statement, **BEGIN** and **END** should start in the same column. Using our previous indenting style, a typical nesting might be

```
FOR K := 1 TO 10 DO
  BEGIN
    WHILE A > 0 DO        {  Start WHILE loop  }
      BEGIN
        REPEAT            {  Start REPEAT loop  }
          .
          .
          .
        UNTIL ⟨condition⟩;  {  end of REPEAT loop  }
          ⟨statement⟩
      END;  {  of WHILE...DO loop  }
    ⟨statement⟩
  END;  {  of FOR loop  }
```

   If the body of a loop becomes very long, it is sometimes difficult to match the **BEGIN**s with the proper **END**s. In this case, you should either redesign the program (for example, write a separate subprogram) or be especially careful.

2. **Using comments.** Comments can precede a loop and explain what the loop will do, or they can be used with statements inside the loop to explain what

COMMUNICATION AND STYLE TIPS

When working with nested loops, use line comments to indicate the effect of each loop control variable. For example

```
FOR K := 1 TO 5 DO        {  Each value produces a line  }
  BEGIN
    write (' ':9);
    FOR J := 1 TO K DO   {  This moves across one line  }
      write ('*');
    writeln
  END;  {  of outer loop  }
```

the statement does. They should be used to indicate the end of a loop where the loop body is a compound statement.

3. **Skipping lines.** This is an effective way of isolating loops within a program and making nested loops easier to identify.

A note of caution is in order with respect to writing style. Program documentation is important; however, excessive use of comments and skipped lines can detract from readability. You should develop a happy medium.

Statement Execution in Nested Loops

Using nested loops can significantly increase the number of times statements get executed in a program. Suppose a program contains a **REPEAT . . . UNTIL** loop that gets executed six times before it is exited. This is illustrated by

```
          ┌─ REPEAT
          │     .
6 times ──┤     .          (action here)
          │     .
          └─ UNTIL  ⟨condition 1⟩;
```

If one of the statements inside this loop is another loop, the inner loop will be executed six times. Suppose this inner loop is repeated five times whenever it is entered. This means each statement within the inner loop will be executed 6 × 5 = 30 times when the program is run. This is illustrated by

```
          ┌─ REPEAT
          │     .
          │     .              (action here)
          │     .
          │     WHILE  ⟨condition 2⟩ DO        ┐
          │        BEGIN                       │
6 times ──┤          ⟨statement⟩ ┐──── 30 times├──── 5 times
          │        END;  {  of WHILE . . . DO  } ┘
          │        .
          │        .
          │        .
          └─ UNTIL ⟨condition 1⟩;
```

When a third level of nesting is used, the number of times a statement is executed can be determined by the product of three factors, $n_1 * n_2 * n_3$, where n_1 represents the number of repetitions of the outside loop, n_2 represents the number of repetitions for the first level of nesting, and n_3 represents the number of repetitions for the innermost loop.

We close this section with an example of a program that uses nested loops to print a multiplication table.

■ **EXAMPLE 5.15** This example presents a complete program that outputs the multiplication table from 1 × 1 to 10 × 10. A suitable heading is part of the output.

```
PROGRAM MultTable;

USES
  Crt;

CONST
  Indent = ' ';

{***********************************************************************}

PROCEDURE PrintHeading;

  {  Given:   Nothing                                                    }
  {  Task:    Print a heading for the multiplication table               }
  {  Return:  Nothing                                                    }

  BEGIN
    writeln;
    writeln (Indent:22, 'Multiplication Table');
    writeln (Indent:22, '--------------------');
    writeln (Indent:15, '( Generated by nested FOR loops )');
    writeln
  END;  {  of PROCEDURE PrintHeading  }

{***********************************************************************}

PROCEDURE PrintTable;

  {  Given:   Nothing                                                    }
  {  Task:    Use nested loops to print a multiplication table           }
  {  Return:  Nothing                                                    }

  VAR
    Row, Column : integer;
  BEGIN

    {  Print the column heads  }
    writeln (Indent:11, '    1   2   3   4   5   6   7   8   9  10');
    writeln (Indent:8, '---!----------------------------------------');

    {  Now start the loop for printing rows  }
    FOR Row := 1 TO 10 DO
      BEGIN  {  Print one row  }
        write (Row:10, ' !');
        FOR Column := 1 TO 10 DO
          write (Row * Column:4);
        writeln;
        writeln (Indent:11, '!')
      END;  {  of each row  }
    readln
  END;  {  of PROCEDURE PrintTable  }

{***********************************************************************}

BEGIN  {  Main program  }
  PrintHeading;
  PrintTable
END.  {  of main program  }
```

The output from this program is

```
                 Multiplication Table
                 --------------------
         ( Generated by nested FOR loops )

         1   2   3   4   5   6   7   8   9  10
---!-----------------------------------------------
 1 !     1   2   3   4   5   6   7   8   9  10
   !
 2 !     2   4   6   8  10  12  14  16  18  20
   !
 3 !     3   6   9  12  15  18  21  24  27  30
   !
 4 !     4   8  12  16  20  24  28  32  36  40
   !
 5 !     5  10  15  20  25  30  35  40  45  50
   !
 6 !     6  12  18  24  30  36  42  48  54  60
   !
 7 !     7  14  21  28  35  42  49  56  63  70
   !
 8 !     8  16  24  32  40  48  56  64  72  80
   !
 9 !     9  18  27  36  45  54  63  72  81  90
   !
10 !    10  20  30  40  50  60  70  80  90 100
   !
```

Exercises 5.6

1. Write a program fragment that uses nested loops to produce each of the following designs.

a.
```
*****
 ****
  ***
   **
    *
```

b.
```
   *
  ***
 *****
*******
 *****
  ***
   *
```

c.
```
***
***
***
***
******
******
******
```

2. What is the output from each of the following fragments?

a.
```
FOR K := 2 TO 6 DO
  BEGIN
    FOR J := 5 TO 10 DO
      write (K + J:5);
    writeln
  END;
```

b.
```
FOR K := 2 TO 6 DO
  BEGIN
    FOR J := 5 TO 10 DO
      write (K * J:5);
    writeln
  END;
```

c.
```
Sum := 0;
A := 7;
WHILE A < 10 DO
  BEGIN
    FOR K := A TO 10 DO
      Sum := Sum + K;
    A := A + 1
  END;
writeln (Sum);
```

d.
```
Sum := 0;
FOR K := 1 TO 10 DO
  FOR J := (10 * K - 9) TO (10 * K) DO
    Sum := Sum + J;
writeln (Sum);
```

3. What output is produced from the following segment of code?

```
A := 4;
B := 7;
REPEAT
  Num := A;
  WHILE Num <= B DO
    BEGIN
      FOR K := A TO B DO
        write (Num:4);
      writeln;
      Num := Num + 1
    END;  { of WHILE...DO }
  writeln;
  A := A + 1
UNTIL A = B;  { end of REPEAT...UNTIL loop }
```

4. Write a program fragment that uses nested loops to produce the output

```
2    4    6    8   10
3    6    9   12   15
4    8   12   16   20
5   10   15   20   25
```

■ 5.7 Repetition and Selection

Selection within Repetition (Loops)

In Chapter 4, we discussed the use of selection statements. In this chapter, we have discussed the use of three different types of loops. It is now time to see how they are used together. We will first examine selection statements contained within the body of a loop.

■ **EXAMPLE 5.16**

Write a program fragment that computes gross wages for employees of the Florida OJ Canning Company. The data consist of three initials, the total hours worked, and the hourly rate; for example

JHA 44.5 12.75

Overtime (more than 40 hours) is computed as time-and-a-half. The output should include all input data and a column of gross wages.

A first-level pseudocode development for this program is

1. **WHILE** MoreEmployees **DO**
   1.1 process one employee
   1.2 print results

This can be refined to

1. **WHILE** MoreEmployees **DO**
   1.1 process one employee
      1.1.1 get data
      1.1.2 compute wage
   1.2 print results

Step 1.1.2 can be refined to

```
        1.1.2 compute wage
              1.1.2.1 IF Hours <= 40.0 THEN
                            compute regular time
                      ELSE
                           compute time-and-a-half
```

and the final algorithm for the fragment is

```
1. WHILE MoreEmployees DO
   1.1 process one employee
        1.1.1 get data
        1.1.2 compute wage
              1.1.2.1 IF Hours <= 40.0 THEN
                            compute regular time
                      ELSE
                           compute time-and-a-half
   1.2 print results
```

The code for this fragment is

```
writeln ('Any employees?  <Y> or <N>');
readln (Choice);
MoreEmployees := (Choice = 'Y') OR (Choice = 'y');
WHILE MoreEmployees DO
  BEGIN
    writeln;
    writeln ('Enter three initials and press <Enter>.');
    readln (Init1, Init2, Init3);
    writeln ('Enter hours worked and press <Enter>.');
    readln (Hours);
    writeln ('Enter payrate and press <Enter>.');
    readln (PayRate);
    IF Hours <= 40.0 THEN
      TotalWage := Hours * PayRate
    ELSE
      BEGIN
        Overtime := 1.5 * (Hours - 40.0) * PayRate;
        TotalWage := 40 * PayRate + Overtime
      END;  {  of ELSE option  }
    writeln;
    write (Init1:5, Init2, Init3);
    write (Hours:10:2, PayRate:10:2);
    writeln ('$':10, TotalWage:7:2);
    writeln;
    writeln ('Any more employees?  <Y> or <N>');
    readln (Choice);
    MoreEmployees := (Choice = 'Y') OR (Choice = 'y')
  END;  {  of WHILE...DO  }
```

Repetition (Loops) within Selection

The next example illustrates the use of a loop within an **IF . . . THEN** statement.

EXAMPLE 5.17

Write a program fragment that allows you to read an integer from the keyboard. If the integer is between 0 and 50, you are to print a chart containing all positive integers less than the integer and their squares and cubes. Thus, if 4 is read, the chart is

```
1        1        1
2        4        8
3        9       27
```

A first-level pseudocode development for this problem is

1. **readln** Num
2. **IF** (Num > 0) **AND** (Num < 50) **THEN**
   2.1 print the chart

Step 2.1 can be refined to

   2.1 print the chart
      2.1.1 **FOR** K := 1 **TO** Num − 1 **DO**
         2.1.1.1 print each line

We can now write the code for this fragment as follows:

```
readln (Num);
IF (Num > 0) AND (Num < 50) THEN
  FOR K := 1 TO Num - 1 DO
    writeln (K, K * K:10, K * K * K:10);
```

Exercises 5.7

1. Find and explain the errors in each of the following program fragments. You may assume all variables have been suitably declared.

a.
```
A := 25;
Flag := true;
WHILE Flag = true DO
  IF A >= 100 THEN
    BEGIN
      writeln (A);
      Flag := false
    END;
```

b.
```
FOR K := 1 TO 10 DO
  writeln (K:5, K * K:5);
  IF K MOD 3 = 0 THEN
    BEGIN
      write (K);
      writeln (' is a multiple of three')
    END;
```

2. What is the output from each of the following program fragments? Assume variables have been suitably declared.

a.
```
FOR K := 1 TO 100 DO
  IF K MOD 5 = 0 THEN
    writeln (K);
```

b.
```
J := 20;
IF J MOD 5 = 0 THEN
  FOR K := 1 TO 100 DO
    writeln (K);
```

c.
```
A := 5;
B := 90;
REPEAT
  B := B DIV A - 5;
  IF B > A THEN
    B := A + 30
UNTIL B < 0;
writeln (A:5, B:5);
```

d.
```
A := 5;
B := 2;
IF A < B THEN
  FOR K := A TO B DO
    writeln (K)
ELSE
  FOR K := A DOWNTO B DO
    writeln (K);
```

e.
```
Count := 0;
FOR K := -5 TO 5 DO
  IF K MOD 3 = 0 THEN
    BEGIN
      write ('K = ' , K:4, '  output  ');
      WHILE Count < 10 DO
        BEGIN
          Count := Count + 1;
          writeln (Count:4)
        END;
      Count := 0;
      writeln
    END;
```

f.
```
FOR K := -5 TO 5 DO
  BEGIN
    write ('K =  ', K:4, '  output  ');
    A := K;
    IF K < 0 THEN          { K = -5, -4, -3, -2, -1 }
      REPEAT
        writeln (-2 * A:5);
        A := A + 1
      UNTIL A > 0
    ELSE                   {   K = 0, 1, 2, 3, 4, 5 }
      WHILE (A MOD 2 = 0) DO
        BEGIN
          writeln (A);
          A := A + 1
        END;  {  of IF...THEN...ELSE  }
    writeln
  END;  {  of FOR loop  }
```

3. Write a program fragment that reads reals from the keyboard, counts the number of positive reals, and accumulates their sum.
4. Given two integers *A* and *B*, *A* is a divisor of *B* if *B* **MOD** *A* = 0. Write a complete program that reads a positive integer *B* and then prints all the positive divisors of *B*.

FOCUS ON PROGRAM DESIGN

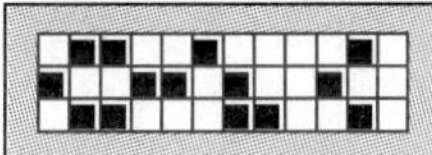

This program illustrates the combined use of repetition and selection statements. The problem statement is

> Write a program that allows positive integers to be entered from the keyboard. For each such entry, list all primes less than or equal to the number. The program should include a check for bad data and use of a sentinel value to terminate the process.

Typical output for the integer 17 is

```
Enter a positive integer; <-999> to quit.
17
          --------------------------------------------------
                    The number is 17.  The prime numbers
                    less than or equal to 17 are:

                                 2
                                 3
                                 5
                                 7
                                11
                                13
                                17

Enter a positive integer; <-999> to quit.
-999
```

For purposes of this program, note the mathematical property that a number K is prime if it has no divisors (other than 1) less than its square root. For example, since 37 is not divisible by 2, 3, or 5, it is prime. Thus, when we check for divisors, it is only necessary to check up to **sqrt** (K). Also note that 1 is not prime by definition.

A first-level pseudocode development for this problem is

1. Get a number
   WHILE MoreData **DO**
   2. Examine the number
   3. Get a number

A structure chart for this problem is shown in Figure 5.4.

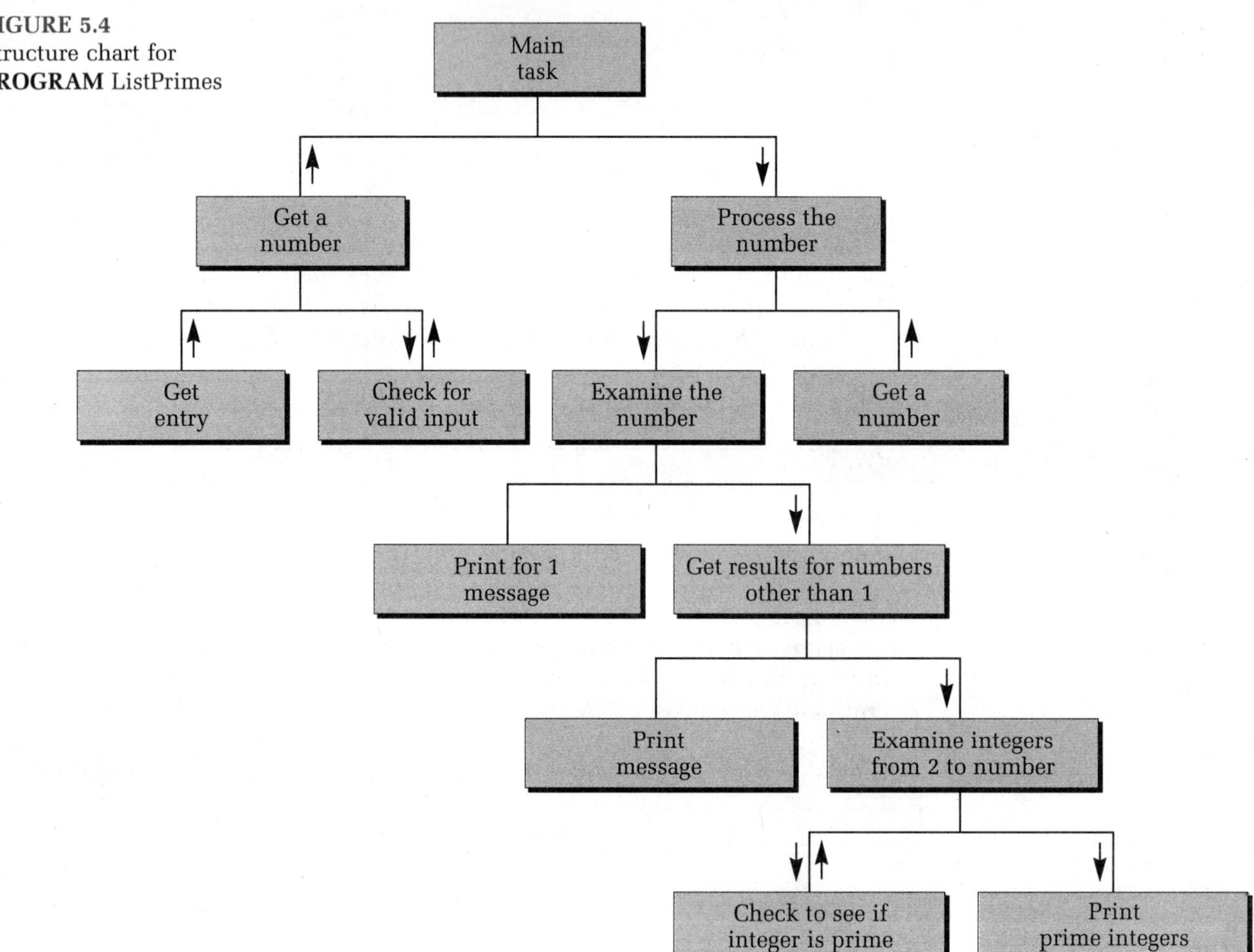

FIGURE 5.4
Structure chart for **PROGRAM** ListPrimes

The module specifications for the main modules are

1. <u>GetANumber Module</u>
   Data received: None
   Information returned: Number
   Boolean flag MoreData
   Logic: Get an entry from the keyboard.
   Make sure it is a valid entry or the sentinel value for terminating the process.
   If it is the sentinel value, set the Boolean variable MoreData to **false**.

```
2. Examine The Number Module
   Data received: The integer read
   Information returned: None
   Logic: IF the number is 1 THEN print a message
            ELSE
              Print a heading.
              FOR K := 2 TO Number DO
                Check K for a prime number.
                IF K is prime THEN print it.
```

A second-level development is

```
1. Get a number
   1.1 Get entry from the keyboard
   1.2 Check for valid entry
WHILE MoreData DO
2. Examine the number
   IF Number is 1 THEN
   2.1 print a message for 1
   ELSE list the primes
   2.2 print a message
   2.3 check for primes less than or equal to Number
3. Get a number
   3.1 Get entry from the keyboard
   3.2 Check for valid entry
```

Step 2.3 can be refined to

```
   2.3 check for primes less than or equal to Number
       FOR K := 2 TO Number DO
       2.3.1 check to see if K is prime
       2.3.2 IF K is prime THEN
                print K in list of primes
```

Thus, the complete pseudocode development is

```
1. Get a number
   1.1 Get entry from the keyboard
   1.2 Check for valid entry
   WHILE MoreData DO
2. Examine the number
   IF Number is 1 THEN
   2.1 print a message for 1
   ELSE list the primes
   2.2 print a message
   2.3 check for primes less than or equal to Number
       FOR K := 2 TO Number DO
       2.3.1 check to see if K is prime
       2.3.2 IF K is prime THEN
               print K in a list of primes
3. Get a number
   3.1 Get entry from the keyboard
   3.2 Check for valid entry
```

With this pseudocode development, the main program would be

```
BEGIN  {  Main program  }
  ClrScr;
  GetANumber (Number, MoreData);
  WHILE MoreData DO
    BEGIN
      ExamineTheNumber (Number);
      GetANumber (Number, MoreData)
    END  {  of WHILE loop  }
END.  {  of main program  }
```

A complete program for this problem is

```
PROGRAM ListPrimes;

USES
  Crt;

CONST
  Skip = ' ';
  Dashes = '--------------------------------------------------';

VAR
  Number : integer;
  MoreData : boolean;

{******************************************************************}

PROCEDURE GetANumber (VAR Number : integer;
                      VAR MoreData : boolean);

  {  Given:   Nothing                                               }
  {  Task:    Read an integer entered from the keyboard             }
  {  Return:  The integer read                                      }

  BEGIN
                                                                       1
    {  Get valid input from the keyboard  }
    REPEAT
      writeln;
      writeln ('Enter a positive integer; <-999> to quit.');
      readln (Number);
      MoreData := Number <> -999
    UNTIL (Number > 0) OR (Number = -999)  {  Assumes valid data  }
  END;  {  of PROCEDURE GetANumber  }

{******************************************************************}

PROCEDURE PrintOneMessage;

  {  Given:   Nothing                                               }
  {  Task:    Print a message for 1                                 }
  {  Return:  Nothing                                               }

  BEGIN
    writeln;
    writeln (Skip:10, Dashes);
    writeln;
    writeln (Skip:20, '1 is not prime by definition.')
  END;  {  of PROCEDURE PrintOneMessage  }

{******************************************************************}
```

```
PROCEDURE PrintMessage (Number : integer);

  {  Given:   The integer read                                        }
  {  Task:    Print a heading for the output                          }
  {  Return:  Nothing                                                 }

  BEGIN
    writeln;
    writeln (Skip:10, Dashes);
    writeln;
    writeln (Skip:20, 'The number is ', Number,
             '.  The prime numbers');
    writeln (Skip:20, 'less than or equal to ', Number, ' are:');
    writeln
  END;  {  of PROCEDURE PrintMessage  }

{*****************************************************************}

PROCEDURE ListAllPrimes (Number : integer);

  {  Given:   The integer read                                        }
  {  Task:    List all primes less than or equal to the integer       }
  {             read                                                  }
  {  Return:  Nothing                                                 }

  VAR
    Prime:  boolean;
    Candidate, Divisor : integer;
    LimitForCheck : real;
  BEGIN

    {  Check all integers from 2 to Number  }
    FOR Candidate := 2 TO Number DO
      BEGIN
        Prime := true;
        Divisor := 2;
        LimitForCheck := sqrt(Candidate);

        {  See if Candidate is prime  }
        WHILE (Divisor <= LimitForCheck) AND Prime DO
          IF Candidate MOD Divisor = 0 THEN
            Prime := false              {  Candidate has a divisor  }
          ELSE
            Divisor := Divisor + 1;
        IF Prime THEN                   {  Print in list of primes  }
          writeln (Candidate:35)
      END  {  of FOR loop  }
  END;  {  of PROCEDURE ListAllPrimes  }

{*****************************************************************}

PROCEDURE ExamineTheNumber (Number : integer);

  {  Given:   The integer read                                        }
  {  Task:    Print primes less than or equal to Number               }
  {  Return:  Nothing                                                 }

  BEGIN
    IF Number = 1 THEN
      PrintOneMessage
    ELSE
      BEGIN
        PrintMessage (Number);
```

2

```
      ListAllPrimes (Number)
    END  {  of ELSE option  }
  END;  {  of PROCEDURE ExamineTheNumber  }

{**************************************************************}

BEGIN  {  Main program  }
  ClrScr;
  GetANumber (Number, MoreData);
  WHILE MoreData DO
    BEGIN
      ExamineTheNumber (Number);
      GetANumber (Number, MoreData)
    END  {  of WHILE loop  }
END.  {  of main program  }
```

Sample runs of this program produce the output

```
Enter a positive integer; <-999> to quit.
10
          ------------------------------------------------

                    The number is 10.  The prime numbers
                    less than or equal to 10 are:

                                  2
                                  3
                                  5
                                  7

Enter a positive integer; <-999> to quit.
17
          ------------------------------------------------

                    The number is 17.  The prime numbers
                    less than or equal to 17 are:

                                  2
                                  3
                                  5
                                  7
                                 11
                                 13
                                 17

Enter a positive integer; <-999> to quit.
1
          ------------------------------------------------

                    1 is not prime by definition.

Enter a positive integer; <-999> to quit.
25
          ------------------------------------------------

                    The number is 25.  The prime numbers
                    less than or equal to 25 are:

                                  2
                                  3
                                  5
                                  7
                                 11
                                 13
```

```
                                17
                                19
                                23

Enter a positive integer; <-999> to quit.
-3
Enter a positive integer; <-999> to quit.
2
          ------------------------------------------------

                   The number is 2.  The prime numbers
                   less than or equal to 2 are:

                                2

Enter a positive integer; <-999> to quit.
-999
```

More efficient algorithms than the one we used here do exist. However, the purpose of this program is to see how loops can be used to solve a problem.

RUNNING AND DEBUGGING HINTS

1. Most errors involving loops are not compilation errors. Thus, you will not be able to detect most errors until you try to run the program.
2. A syntax error that will not be detected by the compiler is a semicolon after a **WHILE . . . DO**. The fragment

```
WHILE MoreData DO;
  BEGIN
    readln (A);
    writeln (A)
  END;
```

   is incorrect and will not get past

```
WHILE MoreData DO;
```

   Note that this is an infinite loop.
3. Carefully check entry conditions for each loop.
4. Carefully check exit conditions for each loop. Make sure the loop is exited (not infinite) and that you have the correct number of repetitions.
5. Loop entry, execution, and exit can be checked by:
   a. Pencil and paper check on initial and final values
   b. Count of the number of repetitions
   c. Use of debugging **writeln**s
      i. Boolean condition prior to loop
      ii. Variables inside loop
      iii. Values of the counter in loop
      iv. Boolean values inside loop
      v. Values after loop is exited

Summary

Key Terms

accumulator
counter
data validation
decrement
fixed repetition (iterated) loop
index
infinite loop
nested loop
posttest (exit controlled) loop
pretest condition
pretest (entrance controlled) loop
sentinel value
variable condition loop

Key Terms (optional)

input assertion, loop invariant, loop variant, loop verification, output assertion

Keywords

DO, **DOWNTO**, **FOR**, **TO**, **REPEAT**, **UNTIL**, **WHILE**

Key Concepts

- The following table provides a comparison summary of the three repetition structures discussed in this chapter.

Traits of Loops	**FOR . . . TO . . . DO Loop**	**WHILE . . . DO Loop**	**REPEAT . . . UNTIL Loop**
Pretest loop	Yes	Yes	No
Posttest loop	No	No	Yes
BEGIN . . . END for compound statements	Required	Required	Not required
Repetition	Fixed	Variable	Variable
Loop index	Yes	No	No
Index automatically incremented	Yes	No	No
Boolean expression used	No	Yes	Yes

- A fixed repetition loop (**FOR . . . TO . . . DO**) is to be used when you know exactly how many times something is going to be repeated. The basic form for a **FOR . . . TO . . . DO** loop is

  FOR ⟨index⟩ := ⟨initial value⟩ **TO** ⟨final value⟩ **DO**
  ⟨statement⟩;

  or

  FOR ⟨index⟩ := ⟨initial value⟩ **TO** ⟨final value⟩ **DO**
  BEGIN
  ⟨statement 1⟩;
  ⟨statement 2⟩;
  .
  .
  .
  ⟨statement *n*⟩
  END;

  After the loop is finished, program control is transferred to the first executable statement following the loop.
- A **WHILE . . . DO** loop is a pretest loop that can have a variable loop control. A typical loop is

```
Score := 0;
Sum := 0;
MoreData := true;
WHILE MoreData DO
  BEGIN
    Sum := Sum + Score;
    writeln ('Enter a score; -999 to quit.');
    readln (Score);
    MoreData := (Score <> -999)
  END;
```

- A counter is a variable that indicates how often the body of a loop is executed.

- An accumulator is a variable that sums values.
- An infinite **WHILE . . . DO** loop is caused by having a **true** loop control condition that is never changed to **false.**
- A posttest loop checks a Boolean condition after the loop body has been completed.
- A **REPEAT . . . UNTIL** loop is a posttest loop; a typical loop is

```
REPEAT
  writeln ('Enter a positive integer; <-999> to quit.');
  readln (Num)
UNTIL (Num < 0) OR (Num = -999);
```

- **REPEAT . . . UNTIL** and **WHILE . . . DO** are variable control loops; **FOR** is a fixed control loop.
- **WHILE . . . DO** and **FOR** are pretest loops; **REPEAT . . . UNTIL** is a posttest loop.
- Any one of these loops can be nested within any other type of loop.
- Indenting each loop is important for program readability.
- Several levels of nesting make the logic of a program difficult to follow.
- Loops and conditionals are frequently used together. Careful program design will facilitate writing code in which these concepts are integrated; typical forms are

```
WHILE ⟨condition1⟩ DO
   BEGIN
     .
     .
     .
     IF ⟨condition2⟩ THEN
        .
        .
        .
      ELSE
        .
        .
        .
     .
     .
     .
   END;  { of WHILE . . . DO }
```

and

```
IF ⟨condition⟩ THEN
  BEGIN
     .
     .
     .
    FOR ⟨index⟩ := ⟨initial value⟩ TO ⟨final value⟩ DO
      BEGIN
        .
        .
        .
      END;  { of FOR loop }
     .
     .
     .
  END  { of IF . . . THEN }
ELSE
   .
   .
   .
```

■ Programming Problems and Projects

■ 1. The Caswell Catering and Convention Service (Problem 12, Chapter 3; Problem 14, Chapter 4) wants you to upgrade their program so it can be used for all customers.

2. Modify your program for a service-station owner (Focus on Program Design, Chapter 4) so it can be used for an unknown number of customers. Your output should include the number of customers and all other pertinent items in a daily summary.

3. Modify the Community Hospital program (Problem 17, Chapter 4) so it can be run for all patients leaving the hospital in one day. Include appropriate bad data checks and daily summary items.

4. The greatest common divisor (GCD) of two integers a and b is a positive integer c such that c divides a, c divides b, and for any other common divisor d of a and b, $d \leqslant c$. (For example, the GCD of 18 and 45 is 9.)

   One method of finding the GCD of two positive integers (a, b) is to begin with the smaller (a) and see if it is a divisor of the larger (b). If it is, then the smaller is the GCD. If it is not, find the next largest divisor of a and see if it is a divisor of b. Continue this process until you find a divisor of both a and b. This is the GCD of a and b.

   Write an interactive program that will accept two positive integers as input and then print out their GCD. Enchance your output by printing all divisors of a that do not divide b. A sample run could produce

```
Enter two positive integers.
42 72

The divisors of 42 that do not divide 72 are:

     42
     21
     14
      7

The GCD of 42 and 72 is 6.
```

5. The least common multiple (LCM) of two positive integers a and b is a positive integer c such that c is a multiple of both a and b and for any other multiple m of a and b, c is a divisor of m. (For example, the LCM of 12 and 8 is 24.)

   Write a program that allows the user to enter two positive integers and then print the LCM. The program should guard against bad data and should allow the user the option of "trying another pair" or quitting.

6. A perfect number is a positive integer such that the sum of the proper divisors equals the number. Thus, 28 = 1 + 2 + 4 + 7 + 14 is a perfect number. If the sum of the divisors is less than the number, it is deficient. If the sum exceeds the number, it is abundant.
   a. Write a program that allows the user to enter a positive integer and then displays the result indicating whether the number entered is perfect, deficient, or abundant.
   b. Write another program that allows the user to enter a positive integer N and then displays all perfect numbers less than or equal to N.

   Your programs should guard against bad data and should allow the user the option of entering another integer or quitting.

7. In these days of increased awareness of automobile mileage, more motorists are computing their miles per gallon (mpg) than ever before. Write a program that will perform these computations for a traveler. Data for the program will be entered as indicated in the marginal table.

Odometer Reading	Gallons of Fuel Purchased
18828 (start)	
19240	9.7
19616	10.2
19944	8.8
20329	10.1
20769 (finish)	10.3

The program should compute the mpg for each tank and the cumulative mpg each time the tank is filled up. Your output should produce a chart with the following headings:

```
Odometer    Odometer  Fuel     Miles   Fuel    Miles   mpg     mpg
(begin)     (end)    (tank)   (tank)  (trip)  (trip)  (tank)  (trip)
```

8. Parkside's Other Triangle is generated from two positive integers: one for the size, and one for the seed. For example:

```
Size 6, Seed 1          Size 5, Seed 3
1 2 4 7 2 7               3 4 6 9 4
  3 5 8 3 8                 5 7 1 5
    6 9 4 9                   8 2 6
      1 5 1                     3 7
        6 2                       8
          3
```

Size gives the number of columns. Seed specifies the starting value for column 1. Column *n* contains *n* values. The successive values are obtained by adding 1 to the previous value. When 9 is reached, the next value becomes 1.

Write a program that reads pairs of positive integers and produces Parkside's Other Triangle for each pair. The check for bad data should include checking for seeds between 1 and 9, inclusive.

9. Modify the sewage, water, and sanitation problem (Problem 19, Chapter 4) so it can be used with data containing appropriate information for all residents of the community.
■ 10. Modify the program for the Lucky Wildcat Well Corporation (Problem 20, Chapter 4) so it can be run with data containing information about all of Al Derrick's wells.
11. Modify the program concerning the Mathematical Association of America (Problem 21, Chapter 4). There will be 50 official state delegates attending the next summer national meeting. The new data file will contain the two-letter state abbreviation for each delegate. Output should include one column with the state abbreviation and another with the amount reimbursed.
12. In Fibonacci's sequence

0 , 1, 1, 2, 3, 5, 8, 13, . . .

the first two terms are 0 and 1 and each successive term is formed by adding the previous two terms. Write a program that will read positive integers and then print the number of terms indicated by each integer read. Be sure to test your program with data that include the integers 1 and 2.
■ 13. Dr. Lae Z. Programmer is at it again. Now that you have written a program to compute the grade for one student in his class (Problems 5, 22, and 23, Chapter 4), he wants you to modify this program so it can be used for the entire class. He will help you by making the first entry a positive integer representing the number of students in the class. Your new version should compute an overall class average and the number of students receiving each letter grade.
■ 14. Modify the Pentagon Parking Lot problem (Problem 26, Chapter 4) so it can be used for all customers in one day. In the new program, time should be entered in military style as a four-digit integer. The lot opens at 0600 (6:00 A.M.) and closes at 2200 (10:00 P.M.). Your program should include appropriate summary information.

15. The Natural Pine Furniture Company (Problem 7, Chapter 3) now wants you to refine your program so it will print a one-week pay report for each employee. You do not know how many employees there are, but you do know that all information for each employee is on a separate line. Each line of input will contain the employee's initials, the number of hours worked, and the hourly rate. You are to use the constant definition section for the following:

federal withholding tax rate	18%
state withholding tax rate	4.5%
hospitalization	$25.65
union dues	$ 7.85

Your output should include a report for each employee and a summary report for the company files.

16. Orlando Tree Service, Incorporated, offers the following services and rates to its customers:

a. tree removal	$500 per tree
b. tree trimming	$80 per hour
c. stump grinding	$25 plus $2 per inch for each stump with a diameter exceeding 10 inches. The $2 charge is only for the diameter inches in excess of 10.

Write a complete program to allow the manager, Mr. Sorwind, to provide an estimate when he bids on a job. Your output should include a listing of each separate charge and a total. A 10-percent discount is given for any job with a total that exceeds $1000. Typical data for one customer are

```
R 7
T 6.5
G 8
8 10 12 14 15 15 20 25
```

where R, T, and G are codes for removal, trimming, and grinding, respectively. The integer following G represents the number of stumps to be ground. The next line of integers represents the diameters of the stumps to be ground.

17. A standard science experiment is to drop a ball and see how high it bounces. Once the "bounciness" of the ball has been determined, the ratio gives a bounciness index. For example, if a ball dropped from a height of 10 feet bounces 6 feet high, the index is 0.6 and the total distance traveled by the ball is 16 feet after one bounce. If the ball continues to bounce, the distance after 2 bounces will be 10 ft + 6 ft + 6 ft + 3.6 ft = 25.6 ft. Note that distance traveled for each successive bounce is the distance to the floor plus 0.6 of that distance as the ball comes back up.

    Write a program that lets the user enter the initial height of the ball and the number of times the ball is allowed to continue bouncing. Output should be the total distance traveled by the ball. At some point in this process, the distance traveled by the ball becomes negligible. Use the **CONST** section to define a "negligible" distance (for example, 0.00001 inches). Terminate the computing when the distance becomes negligible. When this stage is reached, include the number of bounces as part of the output.

18. Write a program that prints a calendar for one month. Input consists of an integer specifying the first day of the month (1 = Sunday) and an integer specifying how many days are in a month.

■ 19. An amortization table shows the rate at which a loan is paid off. It contains monthly entries showing the interest paid that month, the principal paid, and the remaining balance. Given the amount of money borrowed (the principal), the annual interest rate, and the amount the person wishes to repay each month, print an amortization table. (Be certain that the payment desired is larger than the first month's interest.) Your table should stop when the loan is paid off and should be printed with the following heads.

```
MONTH NUMBER  INTEREST PAID  PRINCIPAL PAID  BALANCE
```

20. Computers work in the binary system, which is based upon powers of 2. Write a program that prints out the first 15 powers of 2, beginning with 2 to the zero power (2^0). Print your output in headed columns.
21. Print a list of the positive integers < 500 that are divisible by either 5 or 7. When the list is complete, print a count of the number of integers found.
22. Write a program that reads in 20 real numbers and then prints the average of the positive numbers and the average of the negative numbers.
■ 23. In 1626, Dutch settlers purchased Manhattan Island from the Indians. According to legend, the purchase price was $24. Suppose the Indians had invested this amount at 3 percent annual interest compounded quarterly. If the money had earned interest from the start of 1626 to the end of last year, how much money would the Indians have in the bank today? (*Hint:* Use nested loops for the compounding.)
24. Write a program to print the sum of the odd integers from 1 to 99.
25. The theory of relativity holds that as an object moves, it gets smaller. The new length of the object can be determined from the formula

$$\text{New length} = \text{Original length} * \sqrt{1 - B^2}$$

where B^2 is the percentage of the speed of light at which the object is moving, entered in decimal form. Given the length of an object, print its new length for speeds ranging from 0 to 99 percent of the speed of light. Print the output in the following columns:

```
Percent of Light Speed  Length
----------------------  ------
```

■ 26. Mr. Christian uses a 90-, 80-, 70-, 60-percent grading scale. Given a list of test scores, print out the number of As, Bs, Cs, Ds, and Fs on the test. Terminate the list of scores with a sentinal value.
27. The mathematician Gottfried Leibniz determined the following formula for estimating the value of π.

$$\frac{\pi}{4} = 1 - \frac{1}{3} + \frac{1}{5} - \frac{1}{7} + \frac{1}{9} - \frac{1}{11} + \ldots$$

Evaluate the first 200 terms of this formula, and print its approximation of π.
28. In a biology experiment, Carey finds that a sample of an organism doubles in population every 12 hours. If she starts with 1000 organisms, in how many hours will she have 1 million?
29. Turbo Pascal does not have a mathematical operator that permits raising a number to a power. We can easily write a program to perform this function, however. Given an integer to represent the base number and a positive integer to represent the power desired, write a program that prints the number raised to that power.
30. Mr. Thomas has negotiated a salary schedule for his new job. He will be paid $0.01 the first day, with the daily rate doubling each day. Write a program that will find his total earnings for 30 days. Print your results in a table set up as follows:

```
Day Number   Daily Salary   Total Earned
    1            .01            .01
    2            .02            .03
    3             .              .
    .             .              .
    .             .              .
    .
   30
```

31. Write a program to print the perimeters and areas of rectangles using all combinations of lengths and widths, running from 1 ft to 10 ft, in increments of 1 ft. Print the output in headed columns.
32. Teachers in most school districts are paid on a salary schedule based upon the number of years of teaching experience. Suppose a beginning teacher in the Babbage School District is paid $19,000 the first year. For each year of experience after this up to 12 years, a 4-percent increase over the preceding year's salary is received. Write a program that prints a salary schedule for teachers in this district. The output should appear as follows:

```
Years Experience       Salary
----------------       ------
        0             $19,000
        1             $19,760
        2             $20,550
        3             $21,372
        .                .
        .                .
        .                .
       12
```

(Actually, most teacher's salary schedules are more complex than this. As an additional problem, you might like to find out how the salary schedule is determined in your school district and write a program to print that schedule.)
33. The Euclidean Algorithm can be used to find the greatest common divisor (GCD) of two positive integers (n_1, n_2). For example, if $n_1 = 72$ and $n_2 = 42$, you can use this algorithm in the following manner.
   a. Divide the larger by the smaller:

      72 = 42 * 1 + 30

   b. Divide the divisor (42) by the remainder (30):

      42 = 30 * 1 + 12

   c. Repeat this process until you get a remainder of zero:

      30 = 12 * 2 + 6
      12 = 6 * 2 + 0

   The last nonzero remainder is the GCD of n_1 and n_2.
   Write a program that lets the user enter two integers and then prints out each step in the process of using the Euclidean Algorithm to find their GCD.
34. Cramer's Rule for solving a system of equations was given in Problem 31, Chapter 4. Add an enhancement to your program by using a loop to guarantee that the coefficients and constants entered by the user are precisely the ones intended.
35. Gaussian Elimination is another method used to solve systems of equations. To illustrate, if the system is

$x - 2y = 1$
$2x + y = 7$

Gaussian Elimination starts with the augmented matrix

$$\left[\begin{array}{cc|c} 1 & -2 & 1 \\ 2 & 1 & 7 \end{array}\right]$$

and produces the identity matrix on the left side

$$\left[\begin{array}{cc|c} 1 & 0 & 3 \\ 0 & 1 & 1 \end{array}\right]$$

At this stage, the solution to the system is seen to be $x = 3$ and $y = 1$.

Write a program in which the user enters coefficients for a system of two equations containing two variables. The program should then solve the system and display the answer. Your program should include the following:

a. A check for bad data
b. A solvable system check
c. A display of partial results as the matrix operations are performed

36. A Pythagorean triple consists of three integers *A*, *B*, and *C* such that $A^2 + B^2 = C^2$. For example, 3, 4, 5 is such a triple because $3^2 + 4^2 = 5^2$. These triples can be generated by positive integers *m* and *n* ($m > n$), where $a = m^2 - n^2$, $b = 2mn$, and $c = m^2 + n^2$. These triples will be primitive (no common factors) if *m* and *n* have no common factors and are not both odd. Write a program that allows the user to enter a value for *m* and then prints out all possible primitive Pythagorean triples such that $m > n$. Use one function to find the greatest common factor of *m* and *n*, another to see if *m* and *n* are both odd, and another to guard against overflow. For the input value of $m = 5$, typical output is

```
m   n    a    b    c    a*a    b*b    c*c
-------------------------------------------
2   1    3    4    5      9     16     25
3   2    5   12   13     25    144    169
4   1   15    8   17    225     64    289
4   3    7   24   25     49    576    625
5   2   21   20   29    441    400    841
5   4    9   40   41     81   1600   1681
```

37. The Focus on Program Design problem in this chapter determines whether or not an integer is prime by checking for divisors less than or equal to the square root of the number. The check starts with 2 and increments trial divisors by 1 each time, as seen by the code

```
Prime := true;
Divisor := 2;
LimitForCheck := sqrt(Candidate);
WHILE (Divisor <= LimitForCheck) AND Prime DO
  IF Candidate MOD Divisor = 0 THEN
    Prime := false
  ELSE
    Divisor := Divisor + 1;
```

Other methods can be used to determine whether or not an integer *N* is prime. For example, you may

a. Check divisors from 2 to $N - 1$, incrementing by 1.
b. Check divisors from 2 to $(N - 1) / 2$, incrementing by 1.
c. Check divisor 2, 3, 5, . . . $(N - 1) / 2$, incrementing by 2.
d. Check divisor 2, 3, 5, . . . sqrt(*N*), incrementing by 2.

Write a program that allows the user to choose between these options in order to compare relative efficiency of different algorithms. Use a function for each option.

38. The prime factorization of a positive integer is the positive integer written as the product of primes. For example, the prime factorization of 72 is

72 = 2 * 3 * 3 * 4

Write a program that allows the user to enter a positive integer and then displays the prime factorization of the integer. A minimal main program could be

```
BEGIN  {  Main program  }
  GetANumber (Num);
  NumberIsPrime := PrimeCheck(Num);
  IF NumberIsPrime THEN
    writeln (Num, ' is prime.')
  ELSE
    PrintFactorization(Num)
END.  {  of main program  }
```

Enhancements to this program could include an error trap for bad data and a loop for repeated trials.

■ Communication in Practice

1. Using a completed program from this chapter, remove all documentation and replace all identifiers with one- or two-letter identifiers. Exchange this version with another student who has prepared a similar version of a different program. Add documentation and change identifiers to meaningful identifiers. Compare your results with the text version of the program. Discuss the similarities and differences with your class.
2. Using the **File** menu, select the file path DEMOS\ and then open the file DIRDEMO.PAS. Identify all repetition statements in this program. Then write documentation for each loop, explaining the purpose of the loop. Discuss your results with another student who has been assigned the same task.
3. As you might expect, instructors of computer science do not agree as to whether a **REPEAT . . . UNTIL** loop or a **WHILE . . . DO** loop is the preferred variable control loop in Turbo Pascal. Interview several computer science instructors at your college or university to determine what preference (if any) they have regarding these two forms of repetition. Prepare a class report based upon your interviews. Include advantages and disadvantages of each form of repetition.
4. Examine the repetition constructs of at least five other programming languages. Prepare a report that compares and contrasts repetition in each of the languages. Be sure to include information such as which languages provide for both fixed and variable repetition and which languages have more than one kind of variable repetition. Which language appears to have the most desirable form of repetition? Include your rationale for this decision in your report.
5. Examine some old computer science texts and talk to some computer science instructors who worked with the early languages to see how repetition was achieved in the "early days." Prepare a brief chronological chart for class display that depicts the various stages in the development of repetition in computer programming.

Text Files and Enumerated Data Types

■ **CHAPTER OUTLINE** ■

Now that you have completed five chapters, you've made a significant step in the process of learning to use a programming language for the purpose of solving problems. We have covered the essential elements of arithmetic, variables, input/output, selection, repetition, and subprograms and are now ready to look at a somewhat different area of Turbo Pascal.

Thus far, you have been unable to work with large amounts of data. In order to write programs that solve problems using large data bases, it is necessary to be able to store, retrieve, and manage the data. In this chapter, we first look at the storage and retrieval of data (text files) and then study a feature of Turbo Pascal (enumerated data types) that facilitates handling the data.

These topics are not closely related, but since both are essential to working with data structures, which are examined in Chapter 7, we present them together. As you study this material, remember that we are "setting the stage" for working with large amounts of data.

■ 6.1 Text Files

Consider the relatively simple problem of using a computer to compute and print water bills for a community of 30,000 customers. If the data needed consist of a customer name, address, and amount of water used, you can imagine that entering all of this information interactively every billing period would involve an enormous amount of time and expense and would result in more errors in the data. Furthermore, it is often desirable to save information between runs of a program for other uses.

To serve these needs, we can store data in some secondary storage device, usually magnetic tapes or disks. Data can be created separately from a program, stored on these devices, and then accessed by programs when necessary. It is also possible to update and save information for other runs of the same program or for running another program using this same data. For now, we will store all data in *text files.* (Other kinds of files are examined in Chapter 10.)

Creating a Text File

Text files can be created by a program or by a text editor in the same manner in which you write a program. For now, we will look at creating text files by using the text editor.

For our first example, open the **File** menu and select the **New** option. This produces a window with the generic name NONAME01.PAS. We can use this window and the editor to create our first text file. Lines of data should be entered just as we wish them to appear. Thus, if we want to have two lines, each containing four integers, we would enter

```
18 26 17 21
```

and press <Enter>. We would then enter a second line, such as

```
19 23 18 22
```

and press <Enter>.

Each line in a text file has an *end-of-line* **(eoln)** *marker,* which has an ASCII representation. For text writing purposes, we use the symbol ▮ to represent this. Thus, the two lines of integer data could be envisioned as

```
18 26 17 21 ▮

19 23 18 22 ▮
```

The end-of-line markers are created by pressing <Enter> after entering a line of data.

Each text file has an *end-of-file* **(eof)** *marker* after the last end-of-line marker. This is placed by the system when you save the file. An end-of-file marker also has an ASCII representation. For text writing purposes, we use the symbol ■ to represent end-of-file. To illustrate, suppose a text file is used to store data for students in a class. If each line consists of an identification number for each student followed by three scores, a typical file can be envisioned as

```
00723 85 93 100 ▮

00131 78 91 85 ▮

00458 82 75 86 ▮ ■
```

Technically, these lines are stored as one continuous stream, with end-of-line markers used to differentiate between lines and an end-of-file marker to signify the end of one file:

```
00723 85 93 100 ▮ 00131 78 91 85 ▮ 00458 82 75 86 ▮ ■
```

However, we frequently use separate lines to illustrate lines in a text file. When characters are read, **eoln** markers are read as blanks. Later in this text, we will see how special functions can be used to detect when end-of-line and end-of-file symbols have been reached when reading data from a data file.

Saving a Text File

After creating a text file by using the text editor, we need to save the file. There are several ways in which this can be done. A recommended method is to select **Save As** from the **File** menu and then enter an appropriate file name for our data file. Although it is not required, it is helpful to include a file name extension of .DAT or .TXT after the file name. Thus, we might choose

DATA1.DAT

for our complete file name. If an extension such as .DAT is not included, the file will be saved as DATA1.PAS by default. The .PAS descriptor should be restricted to files that are to be compiled and subsequently run.

Editing an Existing Text File

If we want to change the data in an existing text file, we first retrieve the file by selecting **Open** (or just <F3>) from the **File** menu and typing the complete file name in the window containing

```
*.PAS
```

Based on our previous example, we would enter DATA1.DAT to create the window

```
DATA1.DAT
```

and then press <Enter>. Turbo then retrieves the indicated text file and makes it available in the active window for editing. When we finish updating the file, we select **Save** (<F2>) from the **File** menu and press <Enter>.

Accessing a Text File from a Program

When a text file is to be used by a program, a file variable must be declared in the variable declaration section. This variable is of type **text.** Thus, the declaration section would include something like

```
VAR
  ClassList : text;
```

The file variable ClassList must be associated with the previously created text file (DATA1.DAT). This is accomplished by using the **assign** procedure as a program statement. The correct form for using **assign** is

> **assign** (<file variable>, '<data file>');

where "file variable" is the variable declared in the declaration section of the program and "data file" is the name of the text file we created using the text editor. Using the identifiers and file names in our illustration, we have

```
assign (ClassList, 'DATA1.DAT');
```

In general, the complete directory path for the stored data file must be specified. Thus, if the data file resides in drive B, the **assign** statement would be

```
assign (ClassList, 'B:DATA1.DAT');
```

If the file has been saved in the default drive it is not necessary to specify a directory.

Files and Program Headings

Turbo Pascal does not require any files to be listed as part of the program heading. However, this is required in standard Pascal. Furthermore, many instructors prefer that users of Turbo Pascal include files in program headings for documentation purposes.

If files are listed, the input file is the keyboard by default and the output file is the monitor by default. Other files are those declared in the variable declaration section. Thus, a program heading could have the form

```
PROGRAM FilePractice (input, output, ClassList);
```

where ClassList is appropriately declared.

In this text, we follow the Turbo Pascal convention of not listing files in the program headings.

Reading from a Text File

Before data can be read from a file, the file must be *opened for reading*. This is done by the statement

```
reset (<file variable>);
```

This statement moves a data pointer to the first position of the first line of the data file to be read. Thus

```
reset (ClassList);
```

positions the pointer as follows:

00723 85 93 100 ▌00131 78 91 85 ▌00458 82 75 86 ▌ ■

↑
pointer

Reading from a text file is very similar to getting input interactively from the keyboard. Standard procedures **read** and **readln** are used with appropriate variables as arguments in either format, as shown.

> **read** (⟨file variable⟩, ⟨input list⟩);
> or
> **readln** (⟨file variable⟩, ⟨input list⟩);

Thus, data from one line of the file of student test scores, ClassList, can be obtained by

```
readln (ClassList, IDNumber, Score1, Score2, Score3);
```

As data items are read using **readln,** values are stored in the designated variables and the pointer is moved to the first position past the end-of-line marker. Thus

```
reset (ClassList);
readln (ClassList, IDNumber, Score1, Score2, Score3);
```

results in

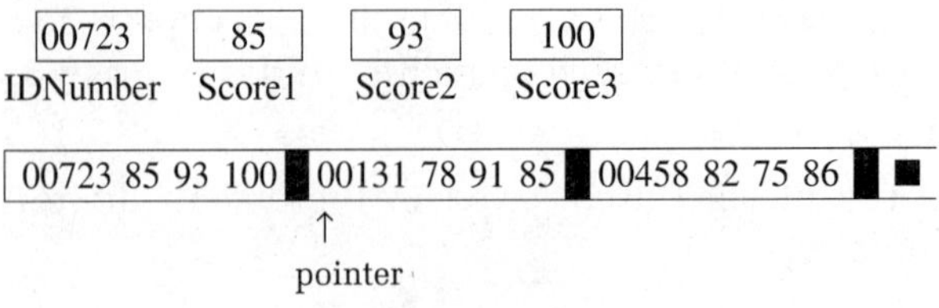

It is not necessary to read all values in a line of data. If only some values are read, a **readln** statement still causes the pointer to move to the first position past the end-of-line marker. Thus

```
reset (ClassList);
readln (ClassList, IDNumber, Score1);
```

results in

00723	85	?	?
IDNumber	Score1	Score2	Score3

00723 85 93 100 ▮	00131 78 91 85 ▮	00458 82 75 86 ▮	■

↑
pointer

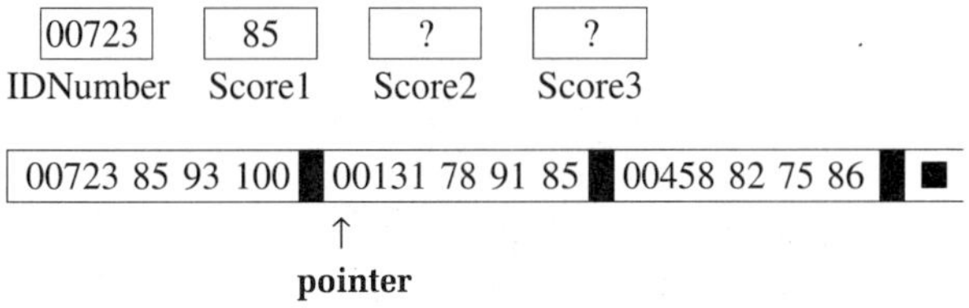

However, when data items are read using **read,** the pointer moves to the first position past the last data item read. Thus, the statement

```
read (ClassList, IDNumber, Score1);
```

results in the following:

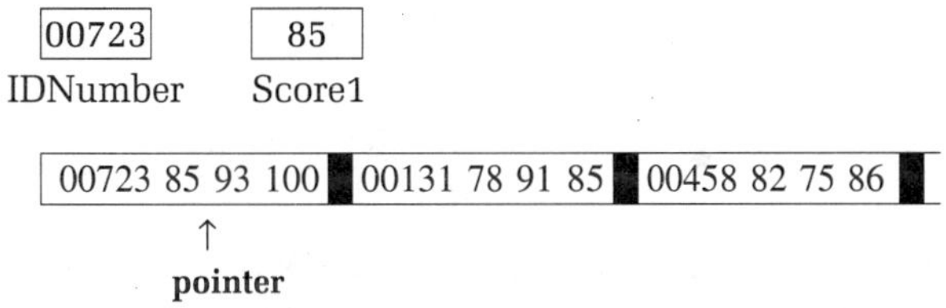

00723	85
IDNumber	Score1

00723 85 93 100 ▮	00131 78 91 85 ▮	00458 82 75 86 ▮

↑
pointer

Variables in the variable list of **read** and **readln** can be listed one at a time or in any combination that does not result in a type conflict. For example

```
readln (ClassList, IDNumber, Score1);
```

can be replaced by

```
read (ClassList, IDNumber);
readln (ClassList, Score1);
```

Turbo Pascal has two Boolean-valued functions that may be used when working with text files: **eoln** (for end-of-line) and **eof** (for end-of-file). If the data pointer is at an end-of-line or end-of-file marker, the Boolean function **eoln** (⟨file variable⟩) is true. Similarly, **eof** (⟨file variable⟩) is true when the data pointer is positioned at the end-of-file marker. This allows both **eoln** (⟨file variable⟩) and **eof** (⟨file variable⟩) to be used as Boolean conditions when designing problem solutions. Thus, part of a solution might be

```
WHILE NOT eof(<file variable>) DO
  (process a line of data)
```

In this loop, data from one line of the text file would typically be read by a **readln** statement. This allows the end-of-file condition to become **true** after the last data line has been read.

Text files can contain any character available in the character set being used. When numeric data are stored, the system converts a number to an appropriate character representation. When this number is retrieved from the file, another conversion takes place to change the character representation to a number.

■ **EXAMPLE 6.1**

Let's now write a short program that uses a text file (ClassList) and the end-of-file (**eof**) condition. Data are stored in the text file Class.DAT. If the problem is to print a listing of student identification numbers, test scores, and test averages, a first-level pseudocode development is

1. Open the file
2. Print a heading
3. **WHILE NOT eof** (⟨file variable⟩) **DO**
   3.1 process a line of data

Step 3.1 can be refined to

   3.1 process a line of data
      3.1.1 get the data
      3.1.2 compute test average
      3.1.3 print the data

A short program to accomplish this task is

```
PROGRAM ClassRecordBook;

{  This program uses data from a text file.  Data for each       }
{  student are on a separate line in the file.  Lines are        }
{  processed until there are no more lines.                      }

USES
  Crt;

VAR
  Score1, Score2, Score3,             {  Test scores              }
  IDNumber : integer;                 {  Student number           }
  TestAverage : real;                 {  Average of three tests   }
  ClassList : text;                   {  Text file                }

{***************************************************************}

FUNCTION Average (Score1, Score2, Score3 : integer) : real;

  {  Given:   Three integers                                     }
  {  Task:    Compute their average                              }
  {  Return:  The average of three integers                      }

  BEGIN
    Average := (Score1 + Score2 + Score3) / 3
  END;  {  of FUNCTION Average  }

{***************************************************************}

PROCEDURE PrintHeading;

  {  Given:   Nothing                                            }
  {  Task:    Print the heading                                  }
  {  Return:  Nothing                                            }

  CONST
    Skip = ' ';
  BEGIN
    ClrScr;
    writeln ('Identification Number', Skip:5, 'Test Scores',
             Skip:5, 'Average');
    writeln ('---------------------', Skip:5, '-----------',
             Skip:5, '-------');
    writeln
  END;  {  of PROCEDURE PrintHeading  }
```

```
{*************************************************************}

BEGIN  {  Main program  }
  assign (ClassList, 'Class.DAT');
  reset (ClassList);
  PrintHeading;
  WHILE NOT eof(ClassList) DO
    BEGIN
      readln (ClassList, IDNumber, Score1, Score2, Score3);
      TestAverage := Average(Score1, Score2, Score3);
      writeln (IdNumber:10, Score1:18, Score2:4, Score3:4,
               TestAverage:12:2)
    END;  {  of WHILE NOT eof DO loop  }
  close (ClassList);
  readln
END.  {  of main program  }
```

When this program is run using the text file Class.DAT with values

00123 85 93 100 ▮ 00131 78 91 85 ▮ 00458 82 75 86 ▮ ■

the output produced is

```
Identification Number     Test Scores   Average
---------------------     -----------   -------

       123                85  93 100     92.67
       131                78  91  85     84.67
       458                82  75  86     81.00
```

A note of caution is in order. Any attempt to read beyond the end of a file results in an error. To illustrate, if

```
read (ClassList, IDNumber, Score1, Score2, Score3);
```

had been used in the previous example instead of

```
readln (ClassList, IDNumber, Score1, Score2, Score3);
```

an error would have occurred because, when **read** is used with the last line of data, the data pointer is positioned as

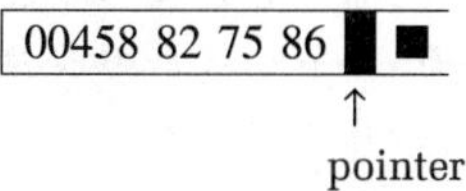

At this point, **eoln** (ClassList) is **true,** but **eof** (ClassList) is still **false** and the loop for processing a line of data would be entered one more time. Using **readln,** however, positions the data pointer as

00458 82 75 86 ▮ ■

↑
pointer

and this causes the end-of-file condition to be **true** when expected.

Writing to a Text File

It is also possible to write to a text file. The file variable must be declared to be of type **text.** Before writing to a file, it must be associated with the file variable by an **assign** statement, such as

`assign` (<file variable> '<data file>');

where "file variable" and "data file" are as previously described. A typical statement would be

```
assign (NewData, 'Data2.DAT');
```

The new file must be *opened for writing* by

```
rewrite (<file variable>);
```

This standard procedure creates an empty file with the specified name. If there were any values previously in the file, they are erased by this statement. Data are then written to the file by using standard procedures **write** and **writeln.** The general form is

> **write** (⟨file variable⟩, ⟨list of values⟩);
> or
> **writeln** (⟨file variable⟩, ⟨list of values⟩);

These both cause the list of values to be written on one line in the file. The difference is that **writeln** causes an end-of-line marker to be placed after the last data item. Using **write** allows the user to continue entering data items on the same line with subsequent **write** or **writeln** statements. If desired,

```
writeln (<file variable>);
```

can be used to place an end-of-line marker at the end of a data line.

Formatting can be used to control spacing of data items in a line of text. For example, since numeric items must be separated, the user might choose to put test scores in a file by

```
writeln (ClassList, Score1:4, Score2:4, Score3:4);
```

If the scores are 85, 72, and 95, the line of data created is

82 72 95 ▮

and each integer is allotted four columns.

Closing Files

When the user has finished reading from or writing to a text file, the file should be closed. This is accomplished by using the procedure **close** in the form

```
close (<file variable>);
```

Although it is not mandatory to close files at these times, there are two reasons why this is a good practice. First, it may be necessary to reopen the file later in the program; in order to do this, the file must have previously been closed. Second, if a file is not closed, it is possible that data intended to be stored on the disk may be lost, because DOS holds data in a buffer before transferring it to the disk. Closing the file causes the buffer to be emptied (data to be transferred to the disk).

A Final Form

Before proceeding with the next example, let's summarize what we have learned about working with text files. Whenever you wish to use an existing text file in a program, you must:

1. Declare a file as type **text** in the variable declaration section.
2. Use **assign** to associate the declared file with the existing text file.

3. Open the file using **reset** or **rewrite.**
4. Close the file (an optional procedure, but a good programming habit to acquire).

Now let's illustrate writing to a file with an example.

■ EXAMPLE 6.2

Let's write a program that allows you to create a text file containing data for students in a class. Each line in the file is to contain a student identification number followed by three test scores. A first-level pseudocode development is

1. Open the file
2. **WHILE** more data **DO**
   2.1 process a line
3. Close the file

Step 2.1 can be refined to

   2.1 process a line
      2.1.1 get data from keyboard
      2.1.2 write data to text file

A complete program for this is

```
PROGRAM CreateFile;

{  This program creates a text file.  Each line of the file      }
{  contains data for one student.  Data are entered inter-       }
{  actively from the keyboard and then written to the file.      }

USES
  Crt;

VAR
  Score1, Score2, Score3,          {  Scores for three tests      }
  IDNumber : integer;              {  Student number              }
  Response : char;                 {  Indicator for continuation  }
  MoreData : boolean;              {  Loop control variable       }
  ClassList : text;                {  Text file                   }

{*************************************************************}

PROCEDURE GetStudentData (VAR IDNumber, Score1, Score2,
                          Score3 : integer);

  {  Given:   Nothing                                          }
  {  Task:    Get IDNumber and three test scores from the      }
  {               keyboard                                     }
  {  Return:  IDNumber, Score1, Score2, Score3                 }

  BEGIN
    write ('Please enter a student ID number.  ');
    readln (IDNumber);
    writeln ('Please enter three test scores.');
    readln (Score1, Score2, Score3)
  END;  {  of PROCEDURE GetStudentData  }

{*************************************************************}
```

```
BEGIN  { Main program }
  ClrScr;
  assign (ClassList, 'NewData.DAT');
  rewrite (ClassList);                          { Open for writing }
  MoreData := true;
  WHILE MoreData DO
    BEGIN
      GetStudentData (IDNumber, Score1, Score2, Score3);
      writeln (ClassList, IDNumber, Score1:4, Score2:4,
               Score3:4);
      { Check for more data }
      writeln;
      writeln ('Any more students?  Y or N');
      readln (Response);
      IF (Response = 'N') OR (Response = 'n') THEN
        MoreData := false
    END;  { of WHILE...DO loop }
  close (ClassList)
END.  { of main program }
```

External and Internal File Names

Names of files declared in the declaration section are referred to as *internal file names.* Names of files that appear in the directory listing are referred to as *external file names.* The **assign** procedure associates an internal file name with an external file name. Thus

```
assign (ClassList, 'Class.DAT');
```

associates the internal file name ClassList with the external file name Class.DAT. All work on a file within the program is done with the internal file name. The external name of a file, which exists in secondary storage, is the name DOS uses to refer to the file. Therefore, DOS rules must be followed when naming external files. A consequence of this is that the directory path may be included in the external name. For example

```
assign (ClassList, 'A:Class.DAT');
```

is a valid statement.

On some occasions, it is desirable to use a file only while the program is running and it is not necessary to save the contents for later use. In such cases, a *temporary* or *scratch file* can be created by declaring a file variable of type **text** in the variable declaration section. Temporary files must also be associated with an external file name by using the **assign** procedure. Temporary files are normally used during file processing when it is desirable to temporarily save the contents of a file that is being altered. The following example illustrates the use of a temporary file.

EXAMPLE 6.3

Let's write a program that allows you to update the text file ClassList by adding one more test score to each line of data. We need two text files in this program: ClassList and TempFile. With these two files, we can create new lines in TempFile by reading a line from ClassList and getting a score from the keyboard. When all lines have been updated, we copy TempFile to ClassList.

A first-level pseudocode solution for this problem is

1. Open the files (**reset** ClassList, **rewrite** TempFile)
2. **WHILE NOT eof** (ClassList) **DO**

   2.1 read one line
   2.2 get new score
   2.3 write one line to TempFile
3. Close the files
4. Open the files (**reset** TempFile, **rewrite** ClassList)
5. Update file
   WHILE NOT eof (TempFile) **DO**
   5.1 read one line from TempFile
   5.2 write one line to ClassList
6. Close the files

A complete program for this problem is

```
PROGRAM UpdateClassList;

{  This program updates an existing text file.  The process      }
{  requires a second file.  Contents of the file are copied to   }
{  a temporary file, and the file is then updated one line at a  }
{  time.                                                         }

USES
  Crt;

VAR
  Score1, Score2,                      {  Scores for four tests  }
  Score3, Score4,
  IDNumber : integer;                  {  Student number         }
  ClassList, TempFile : text;          {  Text files             }

BEGIN  {  Main program  }
  ClrScr;
  assign (ClassList, 'Class.DAT');
  assign (TempFile, 'Temp.DAT');
  reset (ClassList);
  rewrite (TempFile);

  WHILE NOT eof(ClassList) DO
    BEGIN
      readln (ClassList, IDNumber, Score1, Score2, Score3);
      writeln ('Enter a new test score for student ', IDNumber);
      readln (Score4);
      writeln (TempFile, IDNumber, Score1:4, Score2:4,
               Score3:4, Score4:4)
    END;  {  of lines in Classlist  }

  close (ClassList);
  close (TempFile);
  reset (TempFile);
  rewrite (ClassList);  {  Contents of old ClassList are erased  }

  WHILE NOT eof(TempFile) DO
    BEGIN
      readln (TempFile, IDNumber, Score1, Score2, Score3, Score4);
      writeln (ClassList, IDNumber, Score1:4, Score2:4,
               Score3:4, Score4:4)
    END;  {  of copying TempFile to ClassList  }

  close (ClassList);
  close (TempFile)
END.  {  of main program  }
```

■ **EXAMPLE 6.4**

As an illustration of using **eoln,** let's write a program that replaces all blanks in a text file with asterisks. Output is directed to the monitor, and a new text file is created for the purpose of saving the altered form of the original text file. Note that reading a character advances the data pointer only one character position unless **readln** is used.

A first-level pseudocode development is

1. Open the files
2. **WHILE NOT eof** (FileWithBlanks) **DO**
   - 2.1 process one line
   - 2.2 prepare for the next line
3. Close the files

A second-level pseudocode development is

1. Open the files
   - 1.1 open FileWithBlanks
   - 1.2 open FileWithoutBlanks
2. **WHILE NOT eof** (FileWithBlanks) **DO**
   - 2.1 process one line
     - 2.1.1 read a character
     - 2.1.2 **IF** character is a blank **THEN**
       - 2.1.2.1 replace with an asterisk
     - 2.1.3 write character to FileWithoutBlanks
     - 2.1.4 write character to the screen
   - 2.2 prepare for the next line
     - 2.2.1 insert end-of-line in FileWithoutBlanks
     - 2.2.2 end-of-line to screen
     - 2.2.3 advance pointer in FileWithBlanks
3. Close the files

A complete program for this is

```
PROGRAM DeleteBlanks;

{  This program illustrates using eof and eoln with a text    }
{  file.  It replaces blanks with asterisks.                   }

USES
  Crt;

VAR
  FileWithBlanks,             {  Existing text file          }
  FileWithoutBlanks : text;   {  Altered text file           }
  Ch : char;                  {  Used for reading characters  }

BEGIN  {  Program  }
  ClrScr;
  assign (FileWithBlanks, 'Blanks.DAT');
  assign (FileWithoutBlanks, 'NoBlanks.DAT');
  reset (FileWithBlanks);                     {  Open the files  }
  rewrite (FileWithoutBlanks);

  WHILE NOT eof(FileWithBlanks) DO
    BEGIN                                   {  Process one line  }
      WHILE NOT eoln(FileWithBlanks) DO
        BEGIN
          read (FileWithBlanks, Ch);
```

```
          IF Ch = ' ' THEN
            Ch := '*';
          write (FileWithoutBlanks, Ch);
          write (Ch)                  {  Write to the screen  }
        END;  {  of reading one line  }
      writeln (FileWithoutBlanks);    {  Insert end-of-line  }
      writeln;
      readln (FileWithBlanks)         {  Advance the pointer  }
    END;  {  of lines in text file  }

  close (FileWithBlanks);
  close (FileWithoutBlanks);
  readln
END.  {  of program  }
```

On the final time through the loop, readln changes the pointer from

last line	■	■

↑ pointer

to

last line	■	■

↑ pointer

Hence, **eof**(FileWithBlanks) becomes **true**.

When this is run using the text file BLANKS.DAT

```
This is a text file with normal blanks.
After it has been processed by
PROGRAM DeleteBlanks, every blank will
be replaced with an asterisk ''*''.
```

the output to the screen is

```
This*is*a*text*file*with*normal*blanks.
After*it*has*been*processed*by
PROGRAM*DeleteBlanks,*every*blank*will
be*replaced*with*an*asterisk*''*''.
```

The external text file NOBLANKS.DAT also contains the version shown as output.

The material in this section allows us to make a substantial change in our approach to writing programs. We are no longer dependent upon an interactive mode, and we can now proceed assuming that data files exist for a program. This somewhat simplifies program design and also allows us to design programs for large sets of data. Consequently, most programs developed in the remainder of this text use text files for input. If you wish to continue with interactive programs, you should be able to make appropriate modifications.

Exercises 6.1

1. Explain the difference between an external file name and an internal file name. Give appropriate uses for each.
2. Write a test program that allows you to display a line of text from a file to the screen.
3. Explain what is wrong with using

   ```
   writeln (ClassList, Score1, Score2, Score3);
   ```

   if you want to write three scores to the text file ClassList.
4. Write a program that allows you to display a text file line by line.

5. Assume that the text file InFile is as illustrated.

18 ▮ 19M ▮ −14.3 ▮ JO ▮ 142.1F ▮ ■

Also, for each question, assume the pointer is positioned at the beginning of the file and the variable declaration section of a program is

```
VAR
  A, B : integer:
  X, Y : real;
  Ch : char;
  InFile : text;
```

What output is produced from each segment of code?

a.
```
read (InFile, A);
read (Infile, B, Ch);
writeln (A:5, B:5, Ch:5);
```

b.
```
read (Infile, Ch);
write (Ch:10);
readln (InFile, Ch);
writeln (Ch);
read (InFile, Ch);
writeln (Ch:10);
```

c.
```
read (InFile, A, B, Ch, X);
writeln (A, B, Ch, X);
writeln (A:5, B:5, Ch:5, X:10:2);
read (InFile, Ch);
writeln (Ch:5);
```

d.
```
readln (InFile);
read (InFile, Ch, Ch);
readln (InFile, Y);
writeln (Ch:5, Y:10:2);
```

6. Using the same text file and variable declaration section in Exercise 5, indicate the contents of each variable location and the position of the pointer after the segment of code is executed. Assume the pointer is positioned at the beginning for each problem.

a. `read (InFile, Ch, A);`

b. `readln (InFile, Ch, A);`

c. `readln (InFile);`

d.
```
readln (InFile);
readln (InFile);
```

e. `readln (InFile, A, B, Ch, X);`

f. `read (InFile, A, B, Ch, Y);`

g.
```
readln (InFile, A, Ch);
readln (Infile, Ch, Ch, B);
```

h. `read (InFile, A, B, Ch, X, Ch);`

7. Again, use the same text file and variable declaration section in Exercise 5. For each of the following segments of code, indicate if the exercise produces an error and, if so, explain why an error occurs.

a. `read (InFile, X, Y);`

b.
```
readln (InFile, A);
read (InFile, B);
```

c.
```
readln (InFile, Ch);
readln (InFile, Ch);
readln (InFile, Ch);
```

d. `read (InFile, X, A, Ch, B, Ch);`

e.
```
readln (InFile);
read (InFile, Ch, Ch, A, Ch, B);
```

8. Write a complete Turbo Pascal program that reads your (three) initials and five test scores from a text file. Your program should then compute your test average and print out all information in a reasonable form with suitable messages.

9. Write a program that allows you to create a text file that contains your name, address, social security number, and age. Reset the file and have the information printed as output. Save the file in secondary storage for later use.

10. Show what output is produced from the following program. Also indicate the contents of each file after the program is run.

```
PROGRAM Exercise10;
VAR
  Ch : char;
  F1, F2 : text;
BEGIN
  assign (F1, 'F1.DAT');
  assign (F2, 'F2.DAT');
  rewrite (F1);
  rewrite (F2);
  writeln (F1, 'This is a test.');
  writeln (F1, 'This is another line.');
  close (F1);
  reset (F1);
  WHILE NOT eof(F1) DO
    BEGIN
      WHILE NOT eoln(F1) DO
        BEGIN
          read (F1, Ch);
          IF Ch = ' ' THEN
            writeln ('*')
          ELSE
            write (F2, Ch)
        END;
        readln (F1)
    END;
  close (F1);
  close (F2)
END.
```

11. Write a program that deletes all blanks from a text file. Your program should save the revised file for later use.

12. Write a program using a **CASE** statement to scramble a text file by replacing all blanks with an asterisk (*) and interchanging all A's with U's and all E's with I's. Your program should print out the scrambled file and save it for subsequent use.

13. Write a program to update a text file by numbering the lines consecutively as 1, 2, 3, ...

14. Write a program to count the number of words in a text file. Assume each word is followed by a blank or a period.

15. Write a program to find the longest word in a text file. Output should include the word and its length.

16. Write a program to compute the average length of words in a text file.

■ 6.2 TYPE Definitions in Turbo Pascal

Ordinal Data Types

Of the data types we have previously used, all integer types, **char,** and **boolean** are called ordinal data types. A data type is ordinal if values of that type have an immediate predecessor and an immediate successor. The exceptions are that the first listed element has only a successor and the last listed element has only a predecessor. For example, data of type **integer** are ordinal and can be listed as **–maxint,** . . . , –1, 0, 1, 2, . . . , + **maxint.** Boolean values **false** and **true,** and data of type **char** are listed according to the collating sequence shown in Appendix 4. All real data types are not ordinal because a given real has neither an immediate predecessor nor an immediate successor. Permissible values for data of these ordinal data types are summarized as follows:

Data Type	Values
integer	**–maxint** to **maxint**
shortint	–128 . . 127
byte	0 . . 255
word	0 . . 65535
longint	–2147483648 . . 2147483647
char	Character set in a collating sequence
boolean	**true, false**

All data types used thus far are standard data types. We are now ready to see how Turbo Pascal allows us to define other data types called *enumerated data types.*

Simple Enumerated Data Types

The declaration section of a program may contain a **TYPE** definition section that can be used to define an enumerated data type. An *enumerated data type* is one defined by the programmer which allows a discrete number of values for that data type. For example

```
TYPE
  Weekday = (Mon, Tues, Wed, Thur, Fri);
```

After such a definition has been made, the variable declaration section can contain identifiers of the type Weekday. Thus, we could have

```
VAR
  Day : Weekday;
```

Values in an enumerated data type can be any legal identifier. Several comments are now in order concerning the **TYPE** definition.

1. Simple enumerated types are also referred to as *user-defined data types.* (Other user-defined data types include subranges and structured data types, which will be studied later.)
2. This defined type will be an ordinal data type with the first defined constant having ordinal zero. Ordinal values increase by 1 in order from left to right. Every constant except the first has a predecessor, and every constant except the last has a successor. Using the previously defined **TYPE** Weekday, we have

Mon	Tues	Wed	Thur	Fri
↕	↕	↕	↕	↕
0	1	2	3	4

3. Variables can be declared to be of the new type.
4. The values defined in the **TYPE** definition section are constants that can be used in the program. These values must be valid identifiers.
5. No identifier can belong to more than one enumerated data type.

6. Identifiers that are defined values cannot be used as operands in arithmetic expressions.
7. Enumerated data types are for internal use only; you cannot **read** or **write** values of these variables.

Thus, given the previous **TYPE** definition of Weekday and the variable declaration of Day, each of the following would be an appropriate program statement:

1.
```
Day := Tues;
```

2.
```
IF Day = Mon THEN
   .
   .
   .
ELSE
   .
   .
   .
```

3.
```
Day := pred(Day);
```

4.
```
FOR Day := Mon TO Fri DO
  BEGIN
    .
    .
    .
  END;
```

Having seen an example of an enumerated data type and some typical related program statements, let's look at a more formal method of definition. In general, we have

> **TYPE**
> ⟨type identifier⟩ = (⟨constant1⟩, ⟨constant2⟩, . . . , ⟨constant$n$⟩);
> **VAR**
> ⟨identifier⟩ : ⟨type identifier⟩;

The **TYPE** definition section is part of the declaration section of a program. It follows the constant definition section (**CONST**) and precedes the variable declaration section (**VAR**), as shown in Figure 6.1.

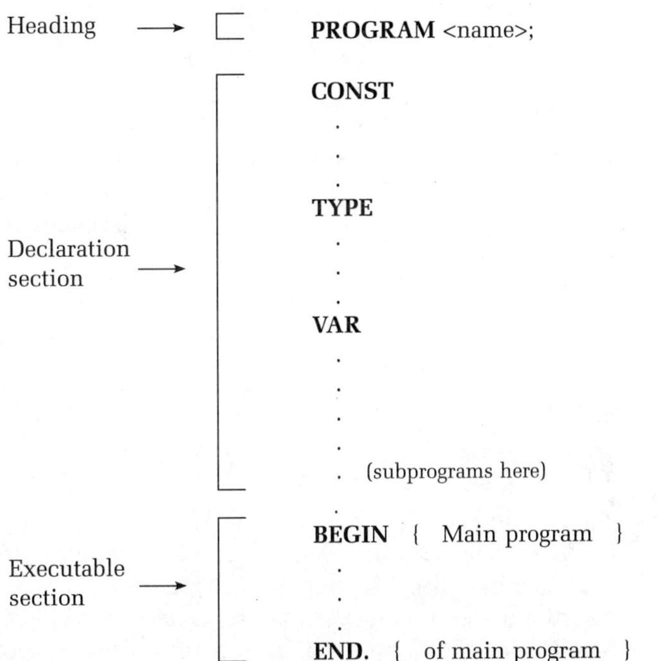

FIGURE 6.1
Placement of **TYPE** definition section

The following short program illustrates the placement and use of enumerated data types.

```
PROGRAM TypePrac;

CONST
  Skip = ' ';

TYPE
  Weekday = (Mon, Tues, Wed, Thur, Fri);

VAR
  Day : Weekday;

BEGIN
  Day := Wed;
  IF Day < Fri THEN
    writeln (Skip:20, 'Not near the weekend.')
  ELSE
    writeln (Skip:20, 'The weekend starts tomorrow.')
END.
```

The output from this program is

```
                    Not near the weekend.
```

Reasons for Using Enumerated Data Types

At first, it may seem like a lot of trouble to define new types for use in a Turbo Pascal program, but there are several reasons for using them. In fact, being able to create enumerated data types is one of the advantages of using Turbo Pascal as a programming language. Why? With enumerated data types, you can express clearly the logical structure of data, enhance the readability of your program, provide program protection against bad data values, and declare parameters in subprograms.

Suppose you are working on a program to count the number of days in the month of a certain year. Enumerated data types allow you to use the following definition and subsequent declaration:

```
TYPE
  AllMonths = (Jan, Feb, March, April, May, June, July,
               Aug, Sept, Oct, Nov, Dec);
VAR
  Month : AllMonths;
```

With this definition, it is easier to understand what the code does. It could contain statements such as

```
FOR Month := Jan TO April DO
    .
    .
    .
```

or

```
IF (Month = Feb) AND (Year MOD 4 = 0) THEN
  NumDays := 29;
```

This second segment of code clearly indicates that you are counting the extra day in February for a leap year. (This is an over simplification of checking for a leap year; see Exercise 7 at the end of this section.)

Enumerated data types may be used in **CASE** statements. For example, movie ticket prices are frequently broken into three categories: youth, adult, and senior citizen. If the definition and declaration

```
TYPE
  Categories = (Youth, Adult, Senior);
VAR
  Patron : Categories;
```

were made, a program statement could be something like

```
CASE Patron OF
  Youth  : Price := YouthPrice;
  Adult  : Price := AdultPrice;
  Senior : Price := Senior Price
END;  {  of CASE Patron  }
```

Once an enumerated data type has been defined at the global level, it is available to all subprograms. Thus, if you have a function for counting the days, a typical function heading might be

```
FUNCTION NumDays (Month : AllMonths;
                  Year : integer) : integer;
```

This aspect of user-defined data types will become more significant when we examine structured data types, including arrays and records.

Recall the limitation imposed on variables that are of an enumerated type: they are for internal use only; you cannot **read** or **write** values of these variables. Thus, in the earlier example using months of the year, we could have the following statement:

```
Month := June;
```

but not

```
writeln (Month);
```

However (as we saw in Section 4.5), use of a **CASE** statement allows translation procedures to be written with relative ease.

A NOTE OF INTEREST

Career Opportunities in Computer Science

The list "Fastest Growing Occupations, 1990–2005", published by the Bureau of Labor Statistics, includes computer programmers and computer system analysts. During this time period, the number of these jobs is expected to increase by 78.9 percent. If this job grouping is broadened to include all computer and data processing professionals, 24,000 workers joined the employment rolls between December 1991 and December 1992. Employment grew 4 percent in this area, compared to 0.5 percent for total nonagricultural employment (*Forecasts: Cahners Economics*). Employment of computer professionals is expected to grow much faster than the average of all occupations through the year 2005 (*Occupational Outlook Handbook*).

In 1992, a total of 751 employers were surveyed to determine which academic disciplines were of greatest interest to employers. Of these, 60 percent mentioned computer science:

The relative rankings of the disciplines has remained very stable since 1980 when they were first compiled. The same three disciplines—computer science, electrical engineering, and mechanical engineering—have been on the top of the list, sought after by about two-thirds of the responding companies. (Peterson, *Job Opportunities*).

Unemployment among computer specialists is traditionally exceptionally low, and almost all who enter the work force find jobs. In 1990, the median annual income was about $38,700 for a system analyst and about $34,000 for a computer programmer (*Occupational Outlook Handbook*).

All able students—particularly women and minorities, who have been traditionally under-represented in the sciences—are encouraged to consider computer science as a career.

We close this section with some typical definitions for enumerated data types that are intended to improve program readability. You are encouraged to incorporate enumerated data types in your subsequent programs. In general, you are limited only by your imagination.

```
TYPE
  SoftDrinks = (Pepsi, Coke, SevenUp, Orange, RootBeer);
  Seasons = (Winter, Spring, Summer, Fall);
  Colors = (Red, Orange, Yellow, Green, Blue, Indigo, Violet);
  ClassStanding = (Freshman, Sophomore, Junior, Senior);
  Fruits = (Apple, Orange, Banana);
  Vegetables = (Corn, Peas, Broccoli, Spinach);
```

Given these type definitions, each of the following would be a reasonable variable declaration:

```
VAR
  Pop, Soda : SoftDrinks;
  Season : Seasons;
  Hue : Colors;
  Class : ClassStanding;
  Appetizer : Fruits;
  SideDish : Vegetables;
```

Exercises 6.2

1. Explain what is meant by ordinal data type.
2. Write a test program to see what happens in each of the following instances.
   a. Try to **write** the value of a variable that is an enumerated data type.
   b. Try to find the predecessor (**pred**) of a defined constant which has zero as its ordinal in an enumerated type.
3. Find all errors in the following definitions.
   a.
   ```
   TYPE
     Names = (John, Joe, Mary, Jane);
     People = (Henry, Sue, Jane, Bill);
   ```
   b.
   ```
   TYPE
     Colors = (Red, Blue, Red, Orange);
   ```
   c.
   ```
   TYPE
     Letters = A, C, E;
   ```
4. Assume the **TYPE** definition
   ```
   TYPE
     Colors = (Red, Orange, Yellow, Blue, Green);
   ```
   has been given. Indicate whether each of the following is **true** or **false**.
   a. `Orange < Blue`
   b. `(Green <> Red) AND (Blue > Green)`
   c. `(Yellow < Orange) OR (Blue >= Red)`
5. Assume the **TYPE** definition and variable declaration
   ```
   TYPE
     AllDays = (Sun, Mon, Tues, Wed, Thur, Fri, Sat);
   VAR
     Day, Weekday, Weekend : AllDays;
   ```
   have been given. Indicate which of the following are valid program statements. For those that are not, give an explanation.

a.
```
Day := Tues;
```
b.
```
Day := Tues + Wed;
```
c.
```
Weekday := Sun;
```
d.
```
IF Day = Sat THEN
  writeln ('Clean the garage.':30);
```
e.
```
IF (Day < Sat) AND (Day > Sun) THEN
  writeln ('It is a workday.':30)
ELSE
  writeln ('It is the weekend.':30);
```
f.
```
FOR Day := Mon TO Fri DO
  writeln (Day);
```
g.
```
read (Day);
IF Day < Sat THEN
  Weekday := Day;
```
h.
```
Wed := Tues + 1;
```

6. Assume the following definitions and declarations have been made in a program.

```
TYPE
  Cloth = (Flannel, Cotton, Rayon, Orlon);
VAR
  Material : Cloth;
  NumberOfYards, Price : real;
```

What would be the output from the following segment of code?

```
Material := Cotton;
NumberOfYards := 3.5;
IF (Material = Rayon) OR (Material = Orlon) THEN
  Price := NumberOfYards * 4.5
ELSE IF Material = Cotton THEN
  Price := NumberOfYards * 2.75
ELSE
  Price := NumberOfYards * 2.5;
writeln (Price:30:2);
```

7. Find the complete definition of a leap year in the Gregorian calendar. Define appropriate data types, and write a segment of code that would indicate whether or not a given year is a leap year.

■ 6.3 Subrange as a Data Type

Defining Subranges

In Section 6.2, we learned how to define new data types by using the **TYPE** definition section. Now we will investigate another way to define new data types.

A *subrange* of an existing ordinal data type may be defined as a data type by

> **TYPE**
> ⟨identifier⟩ = ⟨initial value⟩ . . ⟨final value⟩;

where the initial value and the final value are separated by two periods. For example, we could have a subrange of the integers defined by

```
TYPE
  USYears = 1776..1993;
```

When defining a subrange, the following items should be noted:

1. The original data type must be an ordinal type.
2. Any valid identifier may be used for the name of the type.
3. The initial and final values must be of the original data type.
4. Since the underlying data type is ordinal, it is ordered. In this ordering, the initial value of a defined subrange must occur before the final value.
5. Only values in the indicated subrange (endpoints included) may be assigned to a variable of the type defined by the subrange.
6. The same value may appear in different subranges.

Some of these points are illustrated in the following example.

EXAMPLE 6.5

Consider the subranges Weekdays and Midweek of the enumerated ordinal Days.

```
TYPE
  Days = (Sun, Mon, Tues, Wed, Thur, Fri, Sat);    { Enumerated }
  Weekdays = Mon..Fri;                             { Subrange   }
  Midweek = Tues..Thur;                            { Subrange   }
VAR
  SchoolDay : Weekdays;
  Workday : Midweek;
```

In this case, Days is defined first and we can then define appropriate subranges. With the variable SchoolDay declared as of type Weekdays, you can use any of the values Mon, Tues, Wed, Thur, or Fri with SchoolDay. However, you cannot assign either Sat or Sun to SchoolDay.

Notice that Tues, Wed, and Thur are values that appear in different type definitions. However, since they appear in subranges, this will not produce an error. Furthermore

```
Workday := Tues;
SchoolDay := Workday;
```

are both acceptable statements.

Some other subrange definitions are

```
TYPE
  Grades = 'A'..'E';
  Alphabet = 'A'..'Z';
  ScoreRange = 0..100;
  Months = (Jan, Feb, March, April, May, June,
            July, Aug, Sept, Oct, Nov, Dec);
  Year = Jan..Dec;
  Summer = June..Aug;
```

Months is not a subrange here. Once Months is defined, however, an appropriate subrange, such as Summer, may be defined. With these subranges defined, each of the following declarations would be appropriate:

```
VAR
  FinalGrade : Grades;
  Letter : Alphabet;
  TestScore : ScoreRange;
  SumMonth : Summer;
```

Subrange limits can be ignored. Assignment of a value outside the specified range does not cause a compilation error. However, since the value that will be stored cannot be predicted, subranges should not be used as a form of program protection because program crashes can be caused by inappropriate values.

Compatible and Identical Types

Now that we know how to define subranges of existing ordinal data types, we need to look carefully at the compatibility of variables. Variables are of *compatible type* if they have the same base type. Thus, in

```
TYPE
  AgeRange = 0..110;
VAR
  Age : AgeRange;
  Year : integer;
```

the variables Age and Year are compatible because they both have **integer** as the base type. (AgeRange is a subrange of integers.) If variables are compatible, assignments may be made between them or they may be manipulated in any manner that variables of that base type may be manipulated.

Even when variables are compatible, caution should be exercised when making assignment statements. To illustrate, using Age and Year as previously declared, consider the statements

```
Age := Year;
Year := Age;
```

Since Age is of type AgeRange and AgeRange is a subrange of **integer,** any value in Age is acceptable as a value that can be assigned to Year. Thus

```
Year := Age;
```

is permissible. However, since values for Age are restricted to the defined subrange, it is possible that

```
Age := Year;
```

will produce an error. Since these variables are compatible, there will not be a compilation error, but consider

```
Year := 150;
Age := Year;
```

Since 150 is not in the subrange for Age, a meaningless value may be assigned to Age.

Two variables are said to be of *identical type* if—and only if—they are declared with the same type identifier. It is important to distinguish between compatible and identical types for variables when using subprograms. A value parameter and its argument must be of compatible type; a variable parameter and its argument must be of identical type. A type compatibility error will be generated if these rules are not followed. To illustrate, consider

```
TYPE
  GoodScore = 60..100;
VAR
  Score1, Score2 : GoodScore;
PROCEDURE Compute (HS1 : integer;
                   VAR HS2 : GoodScore);
```

This procedure may be called by

```
Compute (Score1, Score2);
```

Note that HS1 is a value parameter and need only be compatible with Score1, while HS2 is a variable parameter and must be identical in type to Score2.

When used as data types for parameters, **TYPE** definitions must be defined in the main program since they cannot be defined in a subprogram heading. However, **TYPE**s can be defined internally for subprograms.

COMMUNICATION AND STYLE TIPS

The **CONST** and **TYPE** definition sections can be used together to enhance readability and facilitate program design. For example, rather than using the subrange

```
TYPE
  USYears = 1776..1993;
```

you could define an ending constant and then use it as

```
CONST
  CurrentYear = 1993;
TYPE
  USYears = 1776..CurrentYear;
```

Software Engineering Implications

Enumerated types and subranges are features of Turbo Pascal that are consistent with principles of software engineering. As previously stated, communication, readability, and maintenance are essential when developing large systems. The use of enumerated types and subranges is important in all of these areas. To illustrate, suppose a program includes working with a chemical reaction that normally occurs around 180° Fahrenheit. If the definition section includes

```
TYPE
  ReactionRange = 150..210;
```

subsequent modules could use a variable such as

```
VAR
  ReactionTemp : ReactionRange;
```

In Chapter 7, you will see how the use of enumerated or user-defined data types is even more essential to maintaining principles of software engineering. Specifically, defining data structures becomes an important design consideration.

Exercises 6.3

1. Indicate whether the following **TYPE** definitions, subsequent declarations, and uses are valid or invalid. Explain what is wrong with those that are invalid.

a.
```
TYPE
  Reverse = 10..1;
```

b.
```
TYPE
  Bases = (Home, First,
           Second, Third);
  Double = Home..Second;
  Score = Second..Home;
```

c.
```
TYPE
  Colors = (Red, White,
            Blue);
  Stripes = Red..White;
VAR
  Hue : Stripes;
BEGIN
  Hue := Blue;
```

d.
```
TYPE
  Weekdays = Mon..Fri;
  Days = (Sun, Mon, Tues,
          Wed, Thur, Fri, Sat);
```

e.
```
TYPE
  ScoreRange = 0..100;
  HighScores = 70..100;
  Midscores = 50..69;
  LowScores = 20..49;
VAR
  Score1 : Midscores;
  Score2 : HighScores;
BEGIN
  Score1 := 60;
  Score2 := Score1 + 70;
```

2. Write a test program to see what happens when you try to use (assign, read, and so on) a value for a variable that is not in the defined subrange.

3. Explain why each of the following subrange definitions might be used in a program.

a. `Dependents = 0..20;`

b. `HoursWorked = 0..60;`

c. `QuizScores = 0..10;`

d. `TotalPoints = 0..700;`

4. Indicate reasonable subranges for each of the following. Explain your answers.

   a. `TwentiethCentury =`
   b. `Digits =`
   c. `JuneTemp =`
   d. `WinterRange =`
   e. ```
      Colors = (Black, Brown, Red, Pink,
                Yellow, White);
      LightColors =
      ```

5. Assume the declaration section of a program contains

```
TYPE
  ChessPieces = (Pawn, Knight, Bishop, Rook, King, Queen);
  Expendable = Pawn..Rook;
  Valuable = King..Queen;
  LowRange = 0..39;
  Midrange = 40..80;
VAR
  Piece1 : Valuable;
  Piece2 : Expendable;
  Piece3 : ChessPieces;
  Score1 : LowRange;
  Score2 : Midrange;
  Score3 : integer;
```

Indicate which of the following pairs of variables are of compatible type.

   a. `Piece1 and Piece2`
   b. `Piece2 and Piece3`
   c. `Piece3 and Score1`
   d. `Score1 and Score2`
   e. `Score1 and Score3`
   f. `Piece2 and Score3`

6. Assume the declaration section of a program contains the following:

```
TYPE
  PointRange = 400..700;
  FlowerList = (Rose, Iris, Tulip, Begonia);
  Sublist = Rose..Tulip;
VAR
  TotalPts : PointRange;
  Total : integer;
  Flower : Sublist;
  OldFlower : FlowerList;
```

The procedure heading is

```
PROCEDURE TypePrac (A : PointRange;
                    VAR B : integer;
                    Fl : Sublist);
```

Indicate which of the following are valid calls to this procedure.

   a. `TypePrac (TotalPts, Total, Flower);`
   b. `TypePrac (Total, TotalPts, Flower);`
   c. `TypePrac (TotalPts, Total, OldFlower);`
   d. `TypePrac (Total, Total, Flower);`
   e. `TypePrac (Total, Total, OldFlower);`

■ 6.4 Operations on Ordinal Data Types

Functions for Ordinal Data Types

Earlier, we characterized ordinal data types as types in which there is a first and last listed element and each element other than the first and last has an immediate predecessor and an immediate successor. Since the enumerated data types are all ordinal, the functions **ord, pred,** and **succ** may be used on them.
```

Function Call	Value
ord(Sun)	0
ord(Wed)	3
pred(Thur)	Wed
succ(Fri)	Sat
ord(**pred**(Fri))	4

Thus, if we have the definition

```
TYPE
  Days = (Sun, Mon, Tues, Wed, Thur, Fri, Sat);
  Weekdays = Mon..Fri;
```

the function calls have the values shown in the marginal table.

When using functions on enumerated ordinals, the following should be noted:

1. The first-listed identifier has ordinal zero.
2. Successive ordinals are determined by the order in which identifiers are listed.
3. The function call **pred** should not be used on the first identifier; **succ** should not be used on the final identifier.
4. If a subrange data type is defined, the functions return values consistent with the underlying base type; for example, **ord**(Wed) = 3.

Using Ordinal Values of Enumerated Data Types

Now that we are somewhat familiar with ordinal data types and the functions that use them as arguments, let's consider some ways in which they can be incorporated into programs. One typical use is in Boolean expressions. Suppose you are writing a program to compute the payroll for a company that pays time-and-a-half for working on Saturday. Assume the definition and declaration

```
TYPE
  Workdays = (Mon, Tues, Wed, Thur, Fri, Sat);
VAR
  Day : Workdays;
```

have been made. A typical segment of code is

```
Day :=   <some value>;
IF Day = Sat THEN
  ComputeOvertime(<calculation>)
ELSE
  ComputeRegularPay(<calculation>)
```

A second use is with **CASE** statements. As previously explained, one limitation of enumerated data types is that they have no external representation (you cannot **read** or **write** their values). However, this limitation can be circumvented by appropriate use of a **CASE** statement. For example, suppose we have the definition and declaration

```
TYPE
  Colors = (Red, White, Blue);
VAR
  Hue : Colors;
```

If we wish to print the value of Hue, we can do so by

```
CASE Hue OF
  Red   : writeln ('Red':20);
  White : writeln ('White':20);
  Blue  : writeln ('Blue':20)
END;  {  of CASE Hue  }
```

A third use is as a loop index. For example, consider

```
TYPE
  AllDays = (Sun, Mon, Tues, Wed, Thur, Fri, Sat);
VAR
  Day : AllDays;
```

A NOTE OF INTEREST

Computer Ethics: Viruses

Tiny programs that deliberately cause mischief are epidemic among computers and are causing nervousness among those who monitor them.

Written by malicious programmers, the "computer viruses" are sneaked into computer systems by piggybacking them on legitimate programs and messages. There, they may be passed along or instructed to wait until a prearranged moment to burst forth and destroy data.

At NASA headquarters in Washington, several hundred computers had to be resuscitated after being infected. NASA officials have taken extra precautions and reminded their machines' users to follow routine computer hygiene: Don't trust foreign data or strange machines.

Viruses have the eerie ability to perch disguised among legitimate data just as biological viruses hide among genes in human cells, then spring out unexpectedly, multiplying and causing damage. Experts say that even when they try to study viruses in controlled conditions, the programs can get out of control and erase everything in a computer. The viruses can be virtually impossible to stop if their creators are determined enough.

"The only way to protect everybody against them is to do something much worse than the viruses: Stop talking to one another with computers," says William H. Murray, an information-security specialist at Ernst and Whinney financial consultants in Hartford, Connecticut.

Hundreds of programs and files have been destroyed by the viruses, and thousands of hours of repair or prevention time have been logged. Programmers have quickly produced antidote programs with such titles as "Vaccine," "Flu Shot," "Data Physician," and "Syringe."

Experts say known damage is minimal compared with the huge, destructive potential. They express the hope that the attacks will persuade computer users to minimize access to programming and data.

Viruses are the newest of evolving methods of computer mayhem. One type of virus is the "Trojan horse": it looks and acts like a normal program but contains hidden commands that eventually take effect, ordering mischief. The "time bomb" explodes at a set time; the "logic bomb" goes off when the computer arrives at a certain result during normal computation. The "salami attack" executes barely noticeable small acts, such as shaving a penny from thousands of accounts.

A virus typically is written as perhaps only a few hundred characters in a program containing tens of thousands of characters. When the computer reads legitimate instructions, it encounters the virus, which instructs the computer to suspend normal operations for a fraction of a second.

During that time, the virus instructs the computer to check for other copies of itself and, if none are found, to make and hide copies. Instruction to commit damage may be included.

Is Your Machine at Risk?

1. Computer viruses are actually miniature computer programs. Most are written by malicious programmers intent on destroying information in computers for fun.
2. Those who write virus programs often conceal them on floppy disks that are inserted in the computer.
3. A malicious programmer makes the disk available to others, saying it contains a useful program or game. These programs may be lent to others or put onto computerized "bulletin boards," where anyone can copy them for personal use.
4. A computer receiving the programs will "read" the disk and the tiny virus program at the same time. The virus may then order the computer to do a number of things:
   - Tell it to read the virus and follow instructions.
   - Tell it to make a copy of the virus and place it on any disk inserted in the machine today.
   - Tell it to check the computer's clock and, on a certain date, destroy all information that tells where data is stored on any disk: If an operator has no way of retrieving information, it is destroyed.
   - Tell it not to list the virus programs when the computer is asked for an index of programs.
5. In this way, the computer will copy the virus onto many disks—perhaps all or nearly all the disks used in the infected machine. The virus may also be passed over the telephone, when one computer sends or receives data from another.
6. Ultimately hundreds or thousands of people may have infected disks and potential time bombs in their systems.

Each of the following would be an appropriate loop.

1.
```
FOR Day := Mon TO Fri DO
  BEGIN
    .
    .
    .
  END;
```

2.
```
Day := Mon;
WHILE Day < Sat DO
  BEGIN
    Day := succ(Day);
      .
      .
      .
  END;
```

3.
```
Day := Sun;
REPEAT
  Day := succ(Day);
    .
    .
    .
UNTIL Day = Fri;
```

The loop control in a **FOR** loop is based upon the ordinals of the values of the loop index. Thus, the statement

```
FOR Day := Mon TO Fri DO
```

is treated like the statement

```
FOR J := 1 TO 5 DO
```

because **ord**(Mon) is 1 and **ord**(Fri) is 5.

In the **WHILE . . . DO** and **REPEAT . . . UNTIL** loops, the user must be sure to increment (increase the ordinal of) the variable. One method of doing this is to use the function **succ**.

Exercises 6.4

1. Suppose the following **TYPE** definition is given.

```
TYPE
  Trees = (Oak, Ash, Maple, Pine);
  SlackType = (Denim, Cotton, Polyester);
```

Give the value of each of the following expressions. Indicate any expression that is invalid.

a. `pred(Ash)`
b. `succ(Denim)`
c. `ord(Polyester)`
d. `ord(pred(Oak))`
e. `ord(succ(Maple))`
f. `succ(Polyester)`
g. `ord(pred(succ(Oak)))`

2. Write a test program that lists the ordinals of values in a subrange of an enumerated data type.

3. For the ASCII ordering of a character set, **ord**('A') = 65 and **ord**('Z') = 90. Assuming such a sequence, what is the value of each of the following expressions? Indicate any expression that is invalid.

a. `chr(ord('D'))`
b. `ord(chr(10))`
c. `chr(3 * ord('E'))`
d. `ord(chr(10 MOD 3) + chr(20))`
e. `ord(pred('K') + 3)`
f. `succ(chr(ord('Z') - 1))`

4. Write a program that will list the letters of the alphabet and their respective ordinals.
5. Assume the **TYPE** definition and variable declaration

```
TYPE
  AllDays = (Sun, Mon, Tues, Wed, Thur, Fri, Sat);
VAR
  Day : AllDays;
```

are made.

a. What is the output from the following **REPEAT . . . UNTIL** loop?

```
Day := Sun;
REPEAT
  CASE Day OF
    Sat, Sun                   : writeln ('Weekend':20);
    Mon, Tues, Wed, Thur, Fri : writeln ('Weekday':20)
  END;  {  of CASE Day  }
  Day := succ(Day)
UNTIL Day = Sat;
```

b. Rewrite the previous loop as both a **WHILE . . . DO** loop and a **FOR** loop.
c. Find another method to control the loop variable. (For example, replace

```
Day := succ(Day)
```

and make any other necessary changes.)
d. Revise the loop so that all seven days are considered.

6. A standard programming problem is to convert an integer character to its corresponding numeric value (for example, the character '2' to the number 2). Since the digits are listed sequentially in every character set, this could be accomplished by

```
ord('2') - ord('0');
```

a. Write a function to convert a single character digit ('0', '1', . . . , '9') to its corresponding numeric value.
b. Write a function to convert a two-digit number read as consecutive characters to the corresponding numeric value.

7. Suppose you are working with a program that reads an integer representing a month of the year (Jan = 1). Write a function to convert the integer to the appropriate month.

FOCUS ON PROGRAM DESIGN

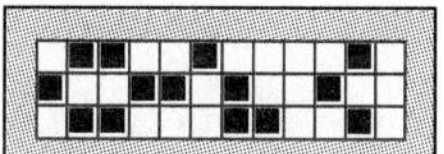

The summary program for this chapter computes the number of days in your birth year from your birthday to the end of the year. Sample input (if you were born on March 16, 1975) would be

```
3 16 75
```

You want the output to be

```
During your birth year, 1975,
you were alive  291 days.
```

Features of this program include enumerated data types and subranges. In particular, note the data type

```
AllMonths = (Jan, Feb, March, April, May, June,
             July, Aug, Sept, Oct, Nov, Dec);
```

A reasonable first-level pseudocode design for this program is

1. Get data
2. Assign month
3. Compute days
4. Print results

A structure chart for this program is given in Figure 6.2.

FIGURE 6.2
Structure chart for **PROGRAM** Birthday

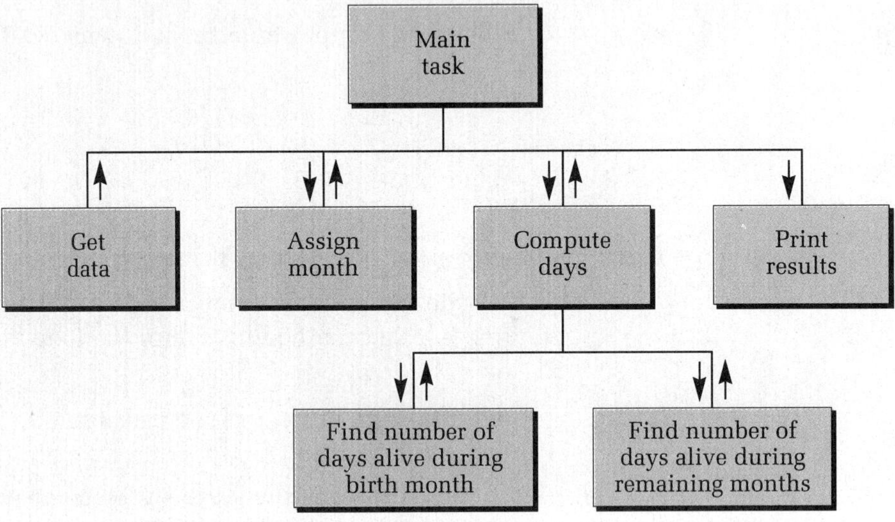

Module specifications for this problem are

1. GetData Module
   Data received: None
   Information returned: Day
   Month
   Year of birth
   Logic: Have the user enter his/her birth date.
2. AssignMonth Module
   Data received: A numeric equivalent of the birth month
   Information returned: The name of the birth month
   Logic: A **CASE** statement assigns the name of the birth month to BirthMonth, which is an enumerated data type.
3. ComputeDays Module
   Data received: Month
   Day
   Year of birth
   Information returned: The number of days alive during the year of birth
   Logic: Compute the number of days alive during the month of birth.
   Compute the number of days in the remaining months.
4. PrintResults Module
   Data received: Number of days alive during the year of birth
   Year of birth
   Information returned: None
   Logic: Use **write(ln)** statements to print the results in a readable form.

GetData merely consists of a **readln** statement; AssignMonth is a procedure using a **CASE** statement (a function could be used here instead), and PrintResults prints the information in a readable form. A function for computing the number of days is further developed as

3. Compute days
   3.1 compute days alive during birth month
   3.2 compute total of days in remaining months

This can be refined to

3. Compute days
   3.1 compute days alive during birth month
      3.1.1 compute for months with 31 days
      3.1.2 compute for months with 30 days
      3.1.3 compute for February
         IF leap year **THEN** use 29 days
         ELSE use 28 days
   3.2 compute total of days in remaining months
      IF NOT December **THEN**
         FOR rest of months **DO**
            add number of days in month

The complete program to solve this problem is

```
PROGRAM Birthday;

{  This program determines how many days you were alive during   }
{  your birth year.  Input is your birth date.  Later, you can   }
{  use this program as the basis for a biorhythm program.        }
{  Note the use of enumerated data types and subranges.          }

USES
  Crt;

TYPE
  AllMonths = (Jan, Feb, March, April, May, June,
               July, Aug, Sept, Oct, Nov, Dec);
  DayRange = 1..31;
  MonthRange = 1..12;
  YearRange = 0..99;

VAR
  BirthMonth : AllMonths;        {  Literal form of birth month    }
  DayNum : DayRange;             {  The day you were born          }
  Month : MonthRange;            {  Birth month                    }
  TotalDays : integer;           {  Days alive in birth year       }
  Year : YearRange;              {  Representation of birth year   }

{************************************************************}

PROCEDURE GetData  (VAR Month : MonthRange;
                    VAR Day : DayRange;
                    VAR Year : YearRange);

  {  Given:   Nothing                                          }
  {  Task:    Enter your birth date in the form 3 16 75        }   1
  {  Return:  Month, day, and year of birth                    }
```

```
  BEGIN
    ClrScr;
    writeln ('Please enter your birth date in the form 3 16 75.');
    writeln ('Press <Enter> when finished.');
    readln (Month, Day, Year)
  END;  {  of PROCEDURE GetData  }

{*****************************************************************}

PROCEDURE AssignMonth (Month : MonthRange;
                       VAR BirthMonth : AllMonths);

  {  Given:   A numerical equivalent of the birth month          }
  {  Task:    Convert to literal BirthMonth                      }
  {  Return:  Literal BirthMonth                                 }

  BEGIN
    CASE Month OF
      1 : BirthMonth := Jan;
      2 : BirthMonth := Feb;
      3 : BirthMonth := March;                                          2
      4 : BirthMonth := April;
      5 : BirthMonth := May;
      6 : BirthMonth := June;
      7 : BirthMonth := July;
      8 : BirthMonth := Aug;
      9 : BirthMonth := Sept;
     10 : BirthMonth := Oct;
     11 : BirthMonth := Nov;
     12 : BirthMonth := Dec
    END  {  of CASE Month  }
  END;  {  of PROCEDURE AssignMonth  }

{*****************************************************************}

FUNCTION ComputeDays (BirthMonth : AllMonths;
                      DayNum : DayRange;
                      Year : YearRange) : integer;

  {  Given:   The month, day, and year of birth                   }
  {  Task:    Compute the days alive during the year of birth     }
  {  Return:  Number of days alive during the year of birth       }

  VAR
    Days : integer;
    Mon : AllMonths;
  BEGIN

    {  Compute days alive in birth month  }
    CASE BirthMonth OF
      Jan, March, May,
           July, Aug, Oct, Dec : Days := 31 - DayNum + 1;              3
      April, June, Sept, Nov   : Days := 30 - DayNum + 1;
      Feb                      : IF Year MOD 4 = 0 THEN
                                   Days := 29 - DayNum + 1
                                 ELSE
                                   Days := 28 - DayNum + 1
    END;  {  of CASE BirthMonth  }

    {  Now compute days in remaining months  }
    IF BirthMonth <> Dec THEN
      FOR Mon := succ(BirthMonth) TO Dec DO
```

```
        CASE Mon OF
          Jan, March, May,
               July, Aug, Oct, Dec : Days := Days + 31;
          April, June, Sept, Nov   : Days := Days + 30;
          Feb                      : IF Year MOD 4 = 0 THEN
                                       Days := Days + 29
                                     ELSE
                                       Days := Days + 28
        END;  {  of CASE Mon  }

    {  Assign total days to function's name  }
    ComputeDays := Days
  END;  {  of FUNCTION ComputeDays  }

{************************************************************}

PROCEDURE PrintResults (TotalDays : integer;
                        Year : YearRange);

  {  Given:   Birth year and total days alive during that year   }
  {  Task:    Print a message indicating the year of birth and   }
  {               number of days alive during that year          }
  {  Return:  Nothing                                            }

  BEGIN
    writeln ('During your birth year,', (Year + 1900):5, ',');
    writeln ('you were alive', TotalDays:5, ' days.');
    writeln
  END;  {  of PROCEDURE PrintResults  }

{************************************************************}

BEGIN  {  Main program  }
  GetData (Month, DayNum, Year);
  AssignMonth (Month, BirthMonth);
  TotalDays := ComputeDays(BirthMonth, DayNum, Year);
  PrintResults (TotalDays, Year);
  readln
END.  {  of main program  }
```

A sample run of this program produces

```
Please enter your birth date in the form 3 16 75.
Press <Enter> when finished.
3 16 75
During your birth year, 1975,
you were alive  291 days.
```

RUNNING AND DEBUGGING HINTS

1. An end-of-line marker is read as a blank. When reading numeric data, this is not a problem. However, when reading data of type **char**, you may forget to advance the pointer to the next line.
2. Text files must be listed in the variable declaration section.
3. Be aware of the possibility of extra blanks at the beginning or end of lines in a text file. Some implementations cause these to be inserted when creating a text file.
4. The end-of-line marker is read as a blank. Thus, when working with character data in a text file, it may appear that extra blanks are in the file.

However, the **eoln** function still returns **true** when the pointer is positioned at an end-of-line marker.

5. Use **assign** to associate an external file name with an appropriately declared internal file name of type **text.**
6. Subranges should be used if the bounds of a variable are known.
7. Enumerated data types should be used to enhance readability.
8. Be careful not to use **pred** on the first element in a list or **succ** on the last element.
9. Make sure variable parameters passed to subprograms are of identical type. For example, using the following definition and declaration

```
TYPE
  Weekdays = (Mon, Tues, Wed, Thur, Fri);
VAR
  Day : Weekdays;
```

if a procedure call is

```
PrintChart (Day);
```

a procedure heading could be

```
PROCEDURE PrintChart (VAR Wkday : Weekdays);
```

10. A value parameter and its argument must be of compatible type.

■ Summary

Key Terms

compatible type
end-of-file (**eof**) marker
end-of-line (**eoln**) marker
enumerated data type
external file name
identical type
internal file name
opened for reading
opened for writing
subrange
temporary (scratch) file
text file
user-defined data type

Keywords

assign **eof** **eoln** **reset** **rewrite** **text** **TYPE**

Key Concepts

- Text files can be used to store data between runs of a program.
- An end-of-line marker (▮) is placed at the end of each line in a text file.
- An end of file marker (■) is placed after the last character in a text file.
- A text file can be declared by

```
VAR
  <file name> : text;
```

- An external file name is the name of a file as it appears in the directory. This is the file name recognized by DOS.
- An internal file name is the name of a file used by a program. If an internal file name is to be associated with an external file name, this association is accomplished by using the **assign** procedure. For example

```
assign (ClassList, 'Class.DAT');
```

associates the internal file name ClassList with the external file name Class.DAT.
- Text files must be opened before they can be written to or read from. Before reading from a file, it can be opened by

reset (⟨file variable⟩);

Before writing to a file, it can be opened by

rewrite (⟨file variable⟩);

- All files should be closed before exiting from a program.
- Reading from a text file can be accomplished by

  read (⟨file variable⟩, ⟨list of variables⟩);
  or
  readln (⟨file variable⟩, ⟨list of variables⟩);

- Writing to a text file can be accomplished by

  write (⟨file variable⟩, ⟨list of values⟩);
  or
  writeln (⟨file variable⟩, ⟨list of values⟩);

- A data type is ordinal if data of that type have a first and last listed element and each element other than the first and last elements has an immediate predecessor and an immediate successor.
- Enumerated data types can be defined by using the **TYPE** definition section. Typical syntax and form are

```
TYPE
  Weekdays = (Mon, Tues, Wed, Thur, Fri);
```

- When a simple enumerated data type has been defined:
  1. The newly defined type will be an ordinal data type.
  2. Variables can be declared to be of the new type.
  3. The identifiers declared in the **TYPE** definition section are constants that can be used in the program.
  4. No identifier can belong to more than one data type.
  5. Identifiers that are defined values cannot be used as operands in expressions.
- You cannot **read** or **write** values of an enumerated data type.
- A subrange of an existing ordinal data type can be defined by

  TYPE
  ⟨identifier⟩ = ⟨initial value⟩ . . ⟨final value⟩;

  For example

```
TYPE
  ScoreRange = 0..100;
  Alphabet = 'A'..'Z';
```

- Type-compatible variables must have the same base type.
- Type-identical variables must have the same type identifier.
- The functions **pred, succ,** and **ord** can be used on enumerated data types and subranges of existing ordinal data types.
- When one of the functions **pred, succ,** or **ord** is used with an argument with a value in a subrange, reference is to the base data type, not to the subrange. Thus, in

```
TYPE
  Letters = 'J'..'O';
```

ord('J') does not have the value 0. Rather, it yields the appropriate ordinal for the collating sequence being used. In the ASCII collating sequence, **ord**('J') yields 74.

■ Programming Problems and Projects

1. Write a program to compute the payroll for a company. Data for each employee is to be on two lines. Line 1 contains an employee number followed by the hourly wage rate. Line 2 contains seven integer entries

indicating the hours worked each day. Wages are to be computed at time-and-a-half for anything over eight hours on a weekday and double time for any weekend work. Deductions should be withheld as follows:

a. state income tax	4.6%	c. social security (FICA)	6.2%
b. federal income tax	21.0%	d. Medicare tax	1.45%

Employee numbers are the subrange 0001 . . 9999. You should define and use a data type for the days of the week.

2. The Caswell Catering and Convention Service (Problem 12, Chapter 3; Problem 14, Chapter 4; and Problem 1, Chapter 5) wants to upgrade its existing computer program. Use the **TYPE** definition section for each of the following, and revise the program you developed previously as appropriate.
   a. The room names are now color-coded as follows:

Room A	RedRoom	Room D	GreenRoom
Room B	BlueRoom	Room E	BrownRoom
Room C	YellowRoom		

   b. Use a subrange for the room rents.
   c. Use defined constants for the low value and high value of the room rents.

■ 3. State University (Problem 15, Chapter 4) wants you to upgrade its computer program by using the **TYPE** definition section for each of the following:
   a. The room types will be Regular or AirConditioned.
   b. Students' numbers will be between 0001 and 9999 (use **CONST** for end values).
   c. Credit hours taken must be between 1 and 25.
   d. The GoodRange for credit hours is 12 to 21.

   The university should be able to use your new version on a data file containing information on several students.

4. Al Derrick (Problem 20, Chapter 4; Problem 10, Chapter 5) wants you to revise his program by using the **TYPE** definition section to enhance readability and ensure protection against bad data. Your new version should run for several wells and include types of wells (Dry, Oil, and Gas), volume for gas (between 10,000 and 100,000), and volume for oil (between 2000 and 50,000).

■ 5. Dr. Lae Z. Programmer is relentless. He wants you to modify your latest version of the grading program (Problems 5, 22, and 23, Chapter 4; Problem 13, Chapter 5) by using the **TYPE** definition section. Your new version should include a range for test scores (from 0 to 100), a range for quiz scores (from 0 to 10), and a range for the final examination (from 0 to 200).

■ 6. Upgrade your most recent version of the Pentagon parking lot program (Problem 26, Chapter 4; Problem 14, Chapter 5) by using the **TYPE** definition section. Time in and time out will be between 0600 and 2200 (6:00 A.M. and 10:00 P.M.). Vehicle type should be denoted by Car, Truck, or Senior.

7. Read a text file containing a paragraph of text. Count the number of words in the paragraph. Assume consecutive words are separated by at least one blank.

8. Write a program that will print the contents of a text file and omit any occurrences of the letter "e" from the output.

9. A text file contains a list of integers in order from lowest to highest. Write a program to read and print the text file with all duplications eliminated.

10. Mr. John Napier, a professor at Lancaster Community College, wants you to develop a program to compute grade point averages. Each line of a text file

contains three initials followed by an unknown number of letter grades. These grades are A, B, C, D, or E. Write a program that reads the file and prints a list of the students' initials and their grade point averages. (Assume an A is 4 points, a B is 3 points, and so on.) Print an asterisk next to any grade point average > 3.75.

11. An amortization table (Problem 19, Chapter 5) shows the rate at which a loan is paid off. It contains monthly entries indicating interest paid, principal paid, and remaining balance. Given the amount of money borrowed (the principal), the annual interest rate, and the amount the person wishes to repay each month, print an amortization table. (The desired payment must be larger than the first month's interest.) Your table should stop when the loan is paid off and should be printed with the following heads:

```
MONTH NUMBER   INTEREST PAID   PRINCIPAL PAID   BALANCE
```

Create an enumerated data type for the month number. Limit this to require that the loan be paid back within 60 months.

12. In 1626, Dutch settlers purchased Manhattan Island from the Indians (Problem 23, Chapter 5). According to legend, the purchase price was $24. Suppose the Indians had invested this amount at 3 percent annual interest compounded quarterly. If the money had earned interest from the start of 1626 to the end of last year, how much money would the Indians have in the bank today? (*Hint:* Use nested loops for the compounding.) Create an enumerated data type for the range of years (1626 to last year) that will be used.

13. Mr. Christian (Problem 26, Chapter 5) uses a 90 percent/80 percent/70 percent/60 percent grading scale on his tests. Given a list of test scores, print the number of As, Bs, Cs, Ds, and Es on the test. Terminate the list of scores with a sentinel value. Use a subrange of the integers for the input grades.

14. Write a program to print the perimeter and area of rectangles using all combinations of lengths and widths running from 1 foot to 10 feet in increments of 1 foot. Print the output in headed columns. Use a subrange to restrict the lengths and widths from 1 to 10.

■ Communication in Practice

1. Select a problem that you have not done from the Programming Problems and Projects section in this chapter. For that problem, write documentation that includes a complete description of the following:
   a. Required input
   b. Required output
   c. Required processing and computation

   Exchange your documentation with another student who has been given the same assignment. Compare your results.
2. Remove all documentation from a program you have written for this chapter. Exchange this version with another student who has done the same thing. Write documentation for the exchanged program. Compare your documentation with that originally written for the program. Discuss the differences and similarities in documentation with the other student.
3. Contact a programmer, graduate student, or upper-division major in computer science and discuss the issue of using enumerated and other user-defined data types. Among other things, find out how often (or even if) that person uses such data types, how important he or she considers such data types to be as part of a programming language, and some specific examples of how he or she uses enumerated data types. Give an oral report of your findings to your class.

4. Enumerated and other user-defined data types are one advantage of Turbo Pascal as a programming language. Examine several other programming languages to see if they include a comparable feature. Prepare a chart that summarizes your findings.
5. Using a team of three or four students, contact businesses and offices that use computers for data storage. Find out exactly how they enter, store, and retrieve data. Discuss how they use their data bases and how large the data bases are. Determine what they like and dislike about data entry and retrieval. Ask if they have suggestions for modifying any aspect of working with their data bases. Prepare a report for class that summarizes your team's findings.

One-Dimensional Arrays

■ CHAPTER OUTLINE ■

This chapter begins a significant new stage of programming. Until now, we have been unable to manipulate and store large amounts of data in a convenient way. For example, if we wanted to work with a long list of numbers or names, we had to declare a separate variable for each number or name. Fortunately, Turbo Pascal (and all other programming languages) provides several structured variables to facilitate solving problems that require working with large amounts of data. Simply put, a structured variable uses one identifier to reserve a large amount of memory. This memory is capable of holding several individual values. Structured variables included in this text are arrays, records, files, and sets.

Arrays, the topic of this chapter, are designed to handle large amounts of data of the same type in an organized manner. They are used whenever there is a need to store data for subsequent use in a program. Using arrays permits us to set aside a group of memory locations that we can then manipulate either as a single entity or as separate components. Some very standard applications for array variables include creating tabular output (tables), alphabetizing a list of names, analyzing a list of test scores, manipulating character data, and keeping an inventory.

■ 7.1 Arrays

Basic Idea and Notation

In many instances, several variables of the same data type are required. At this point, let's work with a list of five integers: 18, 17, 21, 18, and 19. Prior to this chapter, we would have declared five variables (A, B, C, D, and E) and assigned them appropriate values or read them from an input file. This would have produced five values in memory, each accessed by a separate identifier:

18	17	21	18	19
A	B	C	D	E

If the list is very long, however, this is an inefficient way to work with these data. An alternative is to use an array. In Turbo Pascal, we declare a variable as an array variable by using either of the following methods:

1.
```
VAR
  List : ARRAY [1..5] OF integer;
```
2.
```
TYPE
  Numbers = ARRAY [1..5] OF integer;
VAR
  List : Numbers;
```

Given either of these declarations, we now have five integer variables with which to work. They are denoted by

List[1]	List[2]	List[3]	List[4]	List[5]

and each is referred to as a *component,* or *element, of the array.* A good method of visualizing these variables is to assume memory locations are aligned in a column on top of each other and the name of the column is List. If we then assign the five values of our list to these five variables, we have the following in memory:

List

18	List[1]
17	List[2]
21	List[3]
18	List[4]
19	List[5]

The components of an array are referred to by their relative position in the array. This relative position is called the *subscript,* or *index,* of the component. In the array of our five values, the component List[3] has an index of 3 and a value of 21.

For the sake of convenience, you may choose to depict an array by listing only the index beside its appropriate component. Thus, List could be shown as

List

	1
	2
	3
	4
	5

If you choose this method, remember the array elements are referenced by the array name and the index (for example, List[3] for the third component). Whichever method you use, it is important to remember each array component is a variable and can be treated exactly as any other declared variable of that base type in the program.

Declaring an Array

An array type can be defined as a user-defined type, and then an appropriate variable can be declared to be of this type. An earlier declaration was

```
TYPE
  Numbers = ARRAY [1..5] OF integer;
VAR
  List : Numbers;
```

Now let's examine this declaration more closely. Several comments are in order.

1. The data type Numbers is a user-defined data type.
2. **ARRAY** is a reserved word and is used to indicate that an array type is being defined.
3. [1 . . 5] is the syntax that indicates the array consists of five memory locations accessed by specifying each of the numbers 1, 2, 3, 4, and 5. We frequently say the array is "of length 5." The information inside the brackets is the *index type* and is used to refer to components of an array. The index type can be any ordinal data type that specifies a beginning value and an ending value. However, subranges of data type **integer** are the most easily read and frequently used index types.
4. The reserved word **OF** refers to the data type for the components of the array.
5. The key word **integer** indicates the data type for the components. This can, of course, be any valid data type.
6. The identifier List can be any valid identifier. As always, it is good practice to use descriptive names to enhance readability.

The general form for defining an array type is

> **TYPE**
> ⟨name⟩ = **ARRAY** [⟨index type⟩] **OF** ⟨component type⟩;

where "name" is any valid identifier, "index type" is any ordinal data type, except **longint** or any subrange of **longint,** that specifies both an initial value and a final value, and "component type" is any predefined or user-defined data type (except files). The syntax diagram for this is

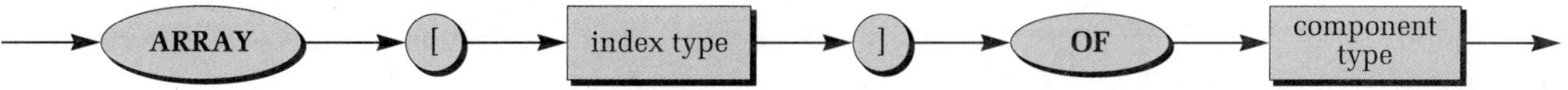

The following example illustrates another declaration of an array variable.

■ EXAMPLE 7.1

Suppose you want to create a list of 10 integer variables for the hours worked by 10 employees as shown in the marginal table. Declare an array that has 10 components of type **integer,** and show how it can be visualized. A descriptive name could be Hours. There are 10 items, so we will use **ARRAY** [1 . . 10] in the definition. Since the data consist of integers, the component type will be **integer**. An appropriate definition and subsequent declaration could be

```
TYPE
  HourList = ARRAY [1..10] OF integer;
VAR
  Hours : HourList;
```

Employee No.	Hours
1	35
2	40
3	20
4	38
5	25
6	40
7	25
8	40
9	20
10	45

At this stage, the components can be visualized as

Hours	
	Hours[1]
	Hours[2]
	Hours[3]
	Hours[4]
	Hours[5]
	Hours[6]
	Hours[7]
	Hours[8]
	Hours[9]
	Hours[10]

After making appropriate assignment statements, Hours can be visualized as

Hours	
35	Hours[1]
40	Hours[2]
20	Hours[3]
38	Hours[4]
25	Hours[5]
40	Hours[6]
25	Hours[7]
40	Hours[8]
20	Hours[9]
45	Hours[10]

Other Indices and Data Types

The previous two arrays use index types that are subranges of the **integer** data type. Although this is a common method of specifying the index to an array, we can use subranges of any ordinal type for this declaration. The following examples illustrate some array definitions with other indices and data types.

■ **EXAMPLE 7.2**

Suppose you want to declare an array to allow you to store the hourly price for a share of IBM stock. A descriptive name could be StockPrice. A price is quoted at each hour from 9:00 A.M. to 3:00 P.M., so **ARRAY** [9 . . 15] should be used in the declaration section. Since the data consist of reals, the data type must be **real**. A possible declaration could be

```
TYPE
  StockPriceList = ARRAY [9..15] OF real;
VAR
  StockPrice : StockPriceList;
```

This will allow you to store the 9:00 A.M. price in StockPrice[9], the 1:00 P.M. price in StockPrice[13], and so on.

■ **EXAMPLE 7.3**

The declaration

```
TYPE
  AlphaList = ARRAY [-2..3] OF char;
VAR
  Alpha : AlphaList;
```

will reserve components, which can be depicted as

Alpha

Alpha[-2]
Alpha[-1]
Alpha[0]
Alpha[1]
Alpha[2]
Alpha[3]

Each component is a character variable.

■ **EXAMPLE 7.4**

The declaration

```
TYPE
  TotalHoursList = ARRAY ['A'..'E'] OF integer;
VAR
  TotalHours : TotalHoursList;
```

will reserve components, which can be depicted as

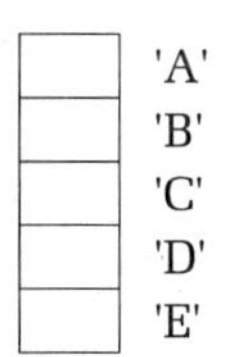

Components of this array are integer variables.

■ **EXAMPLE 7.5**

The declaration

```
TYPE
  FlagValues = ARRAY [1..4] OF boolean;
VAR
  Flag : FlagValues;
```

will produce an array with components that are **boolean** variables.

COMMUNICATION AND STYLE TIPS

Descriptive constants and type identifiers should be utilized when working with arrays. For example, if you are working with an array of test scores for a class of 35 students, you could have

```
CONST
  ClassSize = 35;
TYPE
  TestScores = 0..100;
  ScoreList = ARRAY [1..ClassSize] OF TestScores;
VAR
  Score : ScoreList;
```

It is important to note that in each example, the array components have no assigned values until the program specifically makes some kind of assignment. Declaring an array does not assign values to any of the components.

Two additional array definitions and subsequent declarations follow:

1.
```
TYPE
  Days = (Mon, Tues, Wed, Thur, Fri, Sat, Sun);
  Workdays = ARRAY [Mon..Fri] OF real;
VAR
  HoursWorked : Workdays;
```

2.
```
TYPE
  List50 = ARRAY [1..50] OF real;
  List25 = ARRAY [1..25] OF integer;
VAR
  PhoneCharge : List50;
  Score : List25;
  A, B, C, D : List50;
```

Assignment Statements

Suppose we have declared an array

```
A : ARRAY [1..5] OF integer;
```

and we want to put the values 1, 4, 9, 16, and 25 into the respective components. We can accomplish this with the assignment statements

```
A[1] := 1;
A[2] := 4;
A[3] := 9;
A[4] := 16;
A[5] := 25;
```

If variables B and C of type **integer** are declared in the program, then the following are also appropriate assignment statements:

```
A[3] := B;
C := A[2];
A[2] := A[5];
```

If we want to interchange values of two components (for example, exchange A[2] with A[3]), we could use a third integer variable:

```
B := A[2];
A[2] := A[3];
A[3] := B;
```

This exchange is frequently used in sorting algorithms, so let us examine it more closely. Assume B contains no previously assigned value and A[2] and A[3] contain 4 and 9, respectively, as follows.

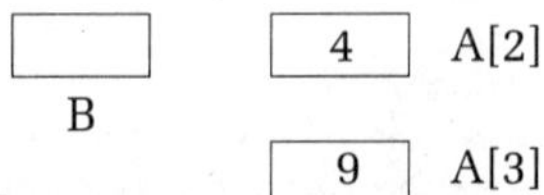

The assignment statement

```
B := A[2];
```

produces

4 4 A[2]
B
9 A[3]

The assignment statement

```
A[2] := A[3];
```

produces

4		9	A[2]
B		9	A[3]

and finally the assignment statement

```
A[3] := B;
```

produces

4		9	A[2]
B		4	A[3]

in which the original values of A[2] and A[3] are interchanged.

The next example illustrates the use of a **TYPE** definition and a subsequent assignment statement.

■ EXAMPLE 7.6

Given the following definitions and declaration

```
TYPE
  Seasons = (Fall, Winter, Spring, Summer);
  TemperatureList = ARRAY [Seasons] OF real;
VAR
  AvTemp : TemperatureList;
```

an assignment statement such as

```
AvTemp[Fall] := 53.2;
```

is appropriate. The array is then

AvTemp

53.2	Fall
	Winter
	Spring
	Summer

Arithmetic

Components of an array can also be used in any appropriate arithmetic operation. For example, suppose A is the array of integers

A

1	A[1]
4	A[2]
9	A[3]
16	A[4]
25	A[5]

and the values of the components of the array are to be added. This can be accomplished by the statement

```
Sum := A[1] + A[2] + A[3] + A[4] + A[5];
```

Each of the following is also a valid use of an array component:

```
B := 3 * A[2];
C := A[4] MOD 3;
D := A[2] * A[5];
```

For the array A given, these assignment statements produce

55	12	1	100
Sum	B	C	D

Some invalid assignment statements and the reasons they are invalid follow:

`A[0] := 7;`	(0 is not a valid subscript.)
`A[2] := 3.5;`	(Component A[2] is not of type **real**.)
`A[2.0] := 3;`	(A subscript of type **real** is not allowed.)

Reading and Writing

Since array components are names for variables, they can be used with **read, readln, write,** and **writeln**. For example, if Score is an array of five integers and we want to input the scores 65, 43, 98, 75, and 83 from a data file, we could use the code

```
readln (Data, Score[1], Score[2], Score[3], Score[4], Score[5]);
```

This would produce the array

Score	
65	Score[1]
43	Score[2]
98	Score[3]
75	Score[4]
83	Score[5]

If we want to print the scores above 80, we could use the code

```
writeln (Score[3]:10, Score[5]:10);
```

to produce

```
        98        83
```

It is important to note that we cannot **read** or **write** values into or from an entire array by a reference to the array name. (An exception will be explained in Section 7.5.) Statements such as

```
read (A);
writeln (A);
```

are invalid if A is an array.

Out-of-range array references should be avoided. For example, if the array A has index values 1 . . 5, a reference to A[6] or A[0] will produce an error. This will become more of a problem when we start processing arrays with loops in the next section.

Exercises 7.1

1. Using descriptive names, define an array type and declare subsequent variables for each of the following.

   a. A list of 35 test scores

   b. The prices of 20 automobiles

A NOTE OF INTEREST

Monolithic Idea: Invention of the Integrated Circuit

One of the most significant breakthroughs in the history of technology occurred in the late 1950s. Prior to 1958, computer circuitry was limited because transistors, diodes, resistors, and capacitors were separate units that had to be wired together and soldered by hand. Although designers could design intricate computer supercircuits using 500,000 transistors, they were almost impossible to build because of the extensive handwork involved. For example, a circuit with 100,000 components could require over 1,000,000 soldered connections. It was virtually impossible to assemble that many components without human error. Thus, the electronics industry was faced with an apparently insurmountable limit.

About this time, Jack St. Clair Kilby developed what has come to be known as the Monolithic Idea. He decided you could put the components of an entire circuit in a monolithic block of silicon. The idea, together with Robert Noyce's work on interconnecting circuits, allowed electronics engineers to overcome the obstacle presented by separate components. Kilby and Noyce's work resulted in the integrated circuit, the most important new product in the history of electronics. For their efforts, both men were awarded the National Medal of Science.

c. The answers to 50 true-or-false questions

d. A list of letter grades for the classes you are taking this semester

2. Write a test program in which you declare an array of three components, read values into each component, sum the components, and print out the sum and value of each component.

3. Find all errors in the following definitions of array types.

a.
```
TYPE
  Time = ARRAY [1..12] OF Hours;
```
b.
```
TYPE
  Scores = ARRAY [1..30] OF integer;
```
c.
```
TYPE
  Alphabet = ARRAY OF char;
```
d.
```
TYPE
  List = ARRAY [1 TO 10] OF real;
```
e.
```
TYPE
  Answers = ARRAY [OF boolean];
```
f.
```
TYPE
  X = ARRAY [1...5] OF real;
```

4. Assume the array List is declared as

```
TYPE
  Scores = ARRAY [1..100] OF integer;
VAR
  List : Scores;
```

and all other variables have been appropriately declared. Label the following as valid or invalid. Include an explanation for any expression that is invalid.

a. `read (List[3]);`

b. `A := List[3] + List[4];`

c. `writeln (List);`

d. `List[10] := 3.2;`

e. `Max := List[50];`

f. `Average := (List[1] + List[8]) / 2;`

g. `write (List[25, 50, 75, 100]);`

h. `write ((List[10] + List[90]):25);`

i.
```
FOR J := 1 TO 100 DO
  read (List);
```

j. `List[36] := List[102];`

k. `Scores[47] := 92;`

l. `List[40] := List[41] / 2;`

5. Change each of the following so that the **TYPE** definition section is used to define the array type.

a.
```
VAR
  LetterList : ARRAY [1..100] OF 'A'..'Z';
```

b.
```
VAR
  CompanyName : ARRAY [1..30] OF char;
```

c.
```
VAR
  ScoreList : ARRAY [30..59] OF real;
```

6. Consider the array declared by

```
TYPE
  ListOfSizes = ARRAY [1..5] OF integer;
VAR
  WaistSize : ListOfSizes;
```

a. Sketch how the array should be envisioned in memory.

b. After assignments

```
WaistSize[1] := 34;
WaistSize[3] := 36;
WaistSize[5] := 32;
WaistSize[2] := 2 * 15;
WaistSize[4] := (WaistSize[1] + WaistSize[3]) DIV 2;
```

have been made, sketch the array and indicate the contents of each component.

7. Let the array Money be declared by

```
TYPE
  List3 = ARRAY [1..3] OF real;
VAR
  Money : List3;
```

Let Temp, X, and Y be real variables, and assume Money has the values

Money	
19.26	Money[1]
10.04	Money[2]
17.32	Money[3]

Assuming Money contains these initial values before each segment is executed, indicate what the array would contain after each of the following sections of code.

a.
```
Temp := 173.21;
X := Temp + Money[2];
Money[1] := X;
```

b.
```
IF Money[2] < Money[1] THEN
  BEGIN
    Temp := Money[2];
    Money[2] := Money[1];
    Money[1] := Temp
  END;
```
c.
```
Money[3] := 20 - Money[3];
```

8. Let the array List be declared by
```
TYPE
  Scores = ARRAY [1..5] OF real;
VAR
  List : Scores;
```
Write a program segment to initialize all components of List to 0.0.

■ 7.2 Using Arrays

Loops for Input and Output

One advantage of arrays is the small amount of code needed when loops are used to manipulate array components. For example, suppose a list of 100 scores stored in a data file is to be used in a program. If an array is declared by

```
TYPE
  List100 = ARRAY [1..100] OF integer;
VAR
  Score : List100;
  J : integer;
  Data : text;
```

the values in file Data can be read into the array using a **FOR** loop as follows:

```
FOR J := 1 TO 100 DO
  read (Data, Score[J]);
```

Remember, a statement such as **read** (Data, Score) is invalid. Data may only be read into individual components of the array.

Loops can be similarly used to produce output of array components. For example, if the array of test scores just given is to be printed in a column,

```
FOR J := 1 TO 100 DO
  writeln (Score[J]);
```

will accomplish this. If the components of Score contain the values

Score

78	Score[1]
93	Score[2]
.	.
.	.
.	.
82	Score[100]

the loop for writing produces

```
78
93
.
.
.
82
```

Note that we cannot cause the array components to be printed by a statement such as **write** (Score) or **writeln** (Score). These are invalid. We must refer to the individual components.

Loops for output are seldom this simple. Usually, we are required to format the output in some manner. For example, suppose the array Score is as declared and we wish to print these scores 10 to a line, each with a field width of 5 spaces. The following segment of code would accomplish this:

```
FOR J := 1 TO 100 DO
  BEGIN
    write (Score[J]:5);
    IF J MOD 10 = 0 THEN
      writeln
  END;
```

Loops for Assigning

Loops can also be used to assign values to array components. At certain times, we might want an array to contain values that are not read from an input file. The following examples show how loops can be used in such instances.

EXAMPLE 7.7

Recall array A in Section 7.1, in which we made the following assignments:

```
A[1] := 1;
A[2] := 4;
A[3] := 9;
A[4] := 16;
A[5] := 25;
```

These assignments could have been made with the loop

```
FOR J := 1 TO 5 DO
  A[J] := J * J;
```

EXAMPLE 7.8

Suppose the components of an array must contain the letters of the alphabet in order from A to Z. Using the ASCII character set, the desired array could be declared by

```
TYPE
  Letters = ARRAY [1..26] OF char;
VAR
  Alphabet : Letters;
```

The array Alphabet could then be assigned the desired characters by the statement

```
FOR J := 1 TO 26 DO
  Alphabet[J] := chr((J - 1) + ord('A'));
```

If

```
J := 1;
```

we have

```
Alphabet[1] := chr(ord('A'));
```

Thus

```
Alphabet[1] := 'A';
```

Similarly, for

```
J := 2;
```

we have

```
Alphabet[2] := chr(1 + ord('A'));
```

Eventually, we obtain

Alphabet

'A'	Alphabet[1]
'B'	Alphabet[2]
'C'	Alphabet[3]
.	.
.	.
.	.
'Z'	Alphabet[26]

Assignment of values from components of one array to corresponding components of another array is a frequently encountered problem. For example, suppose the arrays A and B are declared as

```
TYPE
  List50 = ARRAY [1..50] OF real;
VAR
  A, B : List50;
```

If B has been assigned values and we want to put the contents of B into A, component by component, we could use the loop

```
FOR J := 1 TO 50 DO
  A[J] := B[J];
```

However, for problems of this type, Turbo Pascal allows the entire array to be assigned by

```
A := B;
```

This aggregate assignment actually causes 50 assignments to be made at the component level. The arrays must be of the same data type to do this.

Processing with Loops

Loops are especially suitable for reading, writing, and assigning array components and can be used in conjunction with arrays to process data. For example, suppose the arrays A and B are declared as

```
TYPE
  List100 = ARRAY [1..100] OF real;
VAR
  A, B : List100;
```

If we want to add the values of components of B to the respective values of components of A, we could use the loop

```
FOR J := 1 TO 100 DO
  A[J] := A[J] + B[J];
```

It would appear that since

```
A := B;
```

is valid, this could be accomplished by

```
A := A + B;
```

Not true. Turbo Pascal does not allow the aggregate addition of A + B where A and B are arrays.

The following examples illustrate additional uses of loops for processing data contained in array variables.

EXAMPLE 7.9

Earlier in this section, we read 100 test scores into an array. Assume the scores have been read and you now wish to find the average score and the largest score. Assume variables Sum, Max, and Average have been appropriately declared. The following segment of code will compute the average:

```
Sum := 0;
FOR J := 1 TO 100 DO
  Sum := Sum + Score[J];
Average := Sum / 100;
```

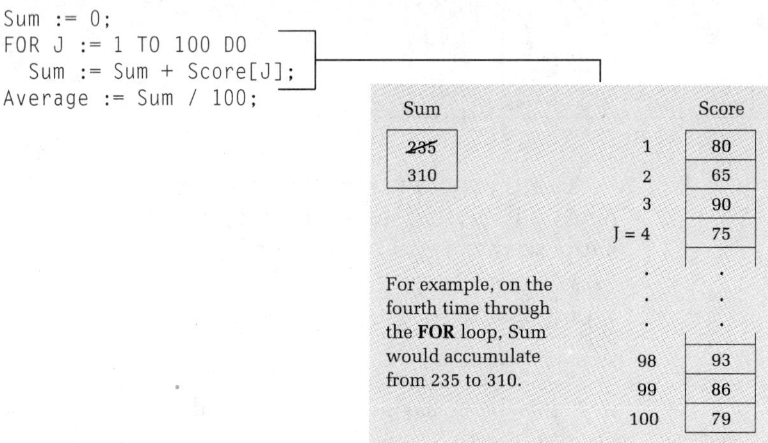

The maximum score can be found by using the following segment of code.

```
Max := Score[1];
FOR J := 2 TO 100 DO
  IF Score[J] > Max THEN
    Max := Score[J];
```

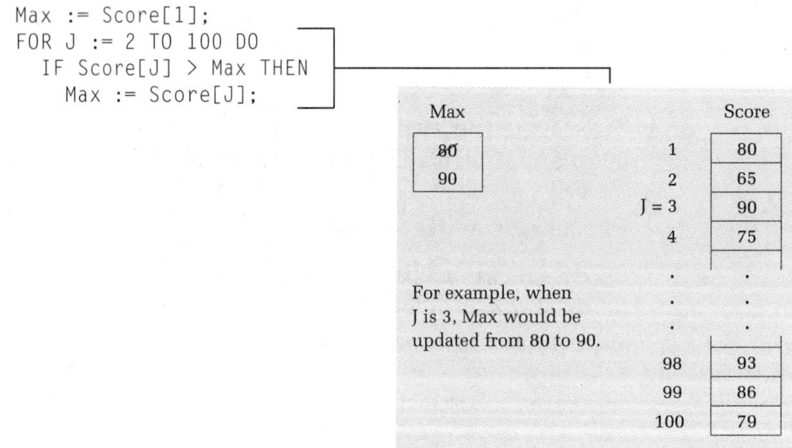

EXAMPLE 7.10

Write a segment of code to find the smallest value of array A and the index of the smallest value. Assume the variables have been declared as

```
TYPE
  Column100 = ARRAY [1..100] OF real;
VAR
  A : Column100;
  Min : real;
  Index : integer;
```

and the values have been read into components of A. The following algorithm will solve the problem.

1. Assign 1 to Index
2. **FOR** J := 2 **TO** 100 **DO**
   IF A[J] < A[Index] **THEN** assign J to Index
3. Assign A[Index] to Min

The segment of code is

```
Index := 1;
FOR J := 2 TO 100 DO
  IF A[J] < A[Index] THEN
    Index := J;
Min := A[Index];
```

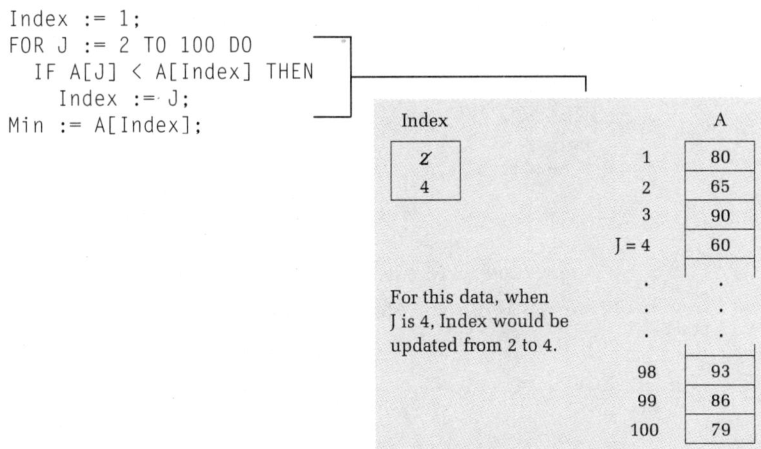

A very standard problem encountered when working with arrays is what to do when we don't know exactly how many components of an array will be needed. In such instances, we must decide some upper limit for the length of the array. A standard procedure is to declare a reasonable limit, keeping two points in mind.

1. The length must be sufficient to store all the data.
2. The amount of storage space must not be excessive; do not set aside excessive amounts of space that will not be used.

To guard against the possibility of not reading all the data into array elements, an **IF . . . THEN** statement, such as

```
IF NOT eof(Data) THEN
  writeln ('There are more data.');
```

could be included in the procedure used to get data from the data file. These points are illustrated in the following example. The array will be partially filled when the number of checks is less than the array length. This information can be retained by including a program statement such as

```
NumberOfChecks := J;
```

after the loop is exited.

■ EXAMPLE 7.11

Suppose an input file contains an unknown number of dollar amounts from personal checks. We want to write a segment of code to read them into an array and output the number of checks. Since the data are in dollars, we use real components and the identifier Check:

```
TYPE
  List = ARRAY [1..?] OF real;
VAR
  Check : List;
```

If we think there are fewer than 50 checks, we can define a constant

```
CONST
  MaxChecks = 50;
```

and then define List by

```
List = ARRAY [1..MaxChecks] OF real;
```

The data can then be accessed using a **WHILE . . . DO** loop:

```
J := 0;
WHILE NOT eof(Data) AND (J < MaxChecks) DO
  BEGIN
    J := J + 1;
    readln (Data, Check[J])
  END;
IF NOT eof(Data) THEN
  writeln ('There are more data.');
NumberOfChecks := J;
```

Now we have the data in the array, we know the number of data items, and we can use NumberOfChecks as a loop limit. Then the loop

```
FOR J := 1 TO NumberOfChecks DO
  BEGIN
    writeln;
    writeln ('Check number':20, J:4, '$':5, Checks[J]:7:2)
  END;
```

will print the checks on every other line.

Range Check Errors

S The Turbo Pascal compiler includes a directive that checks to see if the indices of an array are within the prescribed range. The directive {$R+} enables this option. The default setting is {$R–}. When this option is enabled, any out-of-range errors produce the run-time error message

```
Error 201: Range check error.
```

To illustrate, consider the test program

```
PROGRAM RangeCheck;

{$R+}                          {  Range check option is on  }

VAR
  Component = ARRAY [1..5] OF integer;
  Index : integer;

BEGIN
  FOR Index := 1 TO 6 DO       {    Use out-of-range value  }
    BEGIN
      Component[Index] := Index;
      writeln (Component[Index])
    END
END.
```

When this program is run, the error message

```
Error 201: Range check error.
```

appears at the top of the screen in the edit window and the output window contains

```
1
2
3
4
5
Runtime error 201 at 0B2A:0033
```

If the compiler directive is disabled by changing it to {$R–} and the revised program is run, the output is

```
1
2
3
4
5
6
```

and no error message is displayed.

A good way to take advantage of Turbo Pascal's range-checking feature is to use the compiler directive {$R+} until the program is completely debugged and tested. At that time, the directive may be confidently disabled.

We close this section with a final example that illustrates the use of more elaborate **TYPE** definitions, loops, and arrays.

■ **EXAMPLE 7.12**

```
PROGRAM Economy;

{  This program illustrates the use of TYPE definitions, loops, and      }
{  arrays.  Values are read into an array, and the maximum and average   }
{  are found.  The array contents, maximum, and average are printed.     }

USES
  Crt;

CONST
  StartYear = 1982;
  LastYear = 1991;

TYPE
  RecentYears = StartYear..LastYear;
  EconIndicator = ARRAY [RecentYears] OF real;

VAR
  GrossNatlProd : EconIndicator;    {  Array of gross national product    }
  Max : real;                       {  Maximum value in the array         }
  Sum : real;                       {  Total of values in the array       }
  Average : real;                   {  Average of values in the array     }
  NumYears : integer;               {  Number of years used               }
  Year : RecentYears;               {  Years from StartYear to LastYear   }
  Data : text;                      {  File of GNPs                       }

BEGIN  {  Program  }
  ClrScr;

  {  Get the data  }
  assign (Data, 'GNPData.DAT');
  reset (Data);
  Sum := 0;
  FOR Year := StartYear TO LastYear DO
    BEGIN
      readln (Data, GrossNatlProd[Year]);
      Sum := Sum + GrossNatlProd[Year]
    END;
```

```
  {  Find the maximum  }
  Max := GrossNatlProd[StartYear];                  {  Get initial value  }
  FOR Year := StartYear + 1 TO LastYear DO
    IF GrossNatlProd[Year] > Max THEN             {  Check for larger value  }
      Max := GrossNatlProd[Year];

  {  Find the average  }
  NumYears := LastYear - StartYear + 1;
  Average := Sum / NumYears;

  {  Now display all data  }
  writeln ('Year', 'Gross National Product':30);
  writeln ('(in billions)':29);
  writeln ('----', '----------------------':30);
  writeln;
  FOR Year := StartYear TO LastYear DO
    writeln (Year, GrossNatlProd[Year]:20:1);

  {  Now display the maximum and average  }
  writeln;
  writeln ('The greatest GNP in recent years was',
           Max:8:2, ' billion dollars.');
  writeln ('The average GNP for ', NumYears, ' years was',
           Average:8:2, ' billion dollars.');
  writeln;
  readln;
  close (Data)
END.  {  of program  }
```

The output for this program is

```
Year        Gross National Product
                (in billions)
----        ----------------------

1982              3160.0
1983              3405.7
1984              3772.2
1985              4014.9
1986              4231.6
1987              4524.3
1988              4880.6
1989              5200.8
1990              5463.6
1991              5685.8

The greatest GNP in recent years was 5685.80 billion dollars.
The average GNP for 10 years was 4433.95 billion dollars.
```

Exercises 7.2

1. Assume the following array declarations.

```
TYPE
  NumList = ARRAY [1..5] OF integer;
  AnswerList = ARRAY [1..10] OF boolean;
  NameList = ARRAY [1..20] OF char;
VAR
  List, Score : NumList;
  Answer : AnswerList;
  Name : NameList;
```

COMMUNICATION AND STYLE TIPS

Indices with semantic meaning can be useful when working with arrays. For example, suppose you are writing a program that includes the inventory for shoe styles in a shoe store. If the styles are docksider, high pump, loafer, low pump, plain tie, and wing tip, you would define

```
TYPE
  Style = (Docksider, HighPump, Loafer
           LowPump, PlainTie, WingTip);
  ShoeInventory = ARRAY [Docksider..WingTip] OF integer;
VAR
  Stock : ShoeInventory;
  ShoeType : Style;
```

Typical program statements could be

```
Stock[WingTip] := 25;
Stock[Loafer] := Stock[Loafer] - 3;
FOR ShoeType := Docksider TO WingTip DO
  writeln (Stock[ShoeType]);
```

Indicate the contents of the arrays after each segment of code.

a.
```
FOR J := 1 TO 5 DO
  List[J] := J DIV 3;
```

b.
```
FOR J := 2 TO 6 DO
  BEGIN
    List[J-1] := J+3;
    Score[J-1] := List[J-1] DIV 3
  END;
```

c.
```
FOR J := 1 TO 10 DO
  IF J MOD 2 = 0 THEN
    Answer[J] := true
  ELSE
    Answer[J] := false;
```

d.
```
FOR J := 1 TO 20 DO
  Name[J] := chr(J+64);
```

2. Write a test program to illustrate what happens when you try to use an index that is not in the defined subrange for an array. For example, try to use the loop

```
FOR J := 1 TO 10 DO
  read (Data, A[J]);
```

when A has been declared as

```
TYPE
  NumList = ARRAY [1..5] OF integer;
VAR
  A : NumList;
```

3. Let the array Best be declared by

```
TYPE
  List30 = ARRAY [1..30] OF integer;
VAR
  Best : List30;
```

and assume test scores have been read into Best. What does the following section of code do?

```
Count := 0;
FOR J := 1 TO 30 DO
  IF Best[J] > 90 THEN
    Count := Count + 1;
```

4. Declare an array, and write a segment of code to:

   a. Read 20 integer test scores into the array.

   b. Count the number of scores ≥ 55.

5. Assume the array A is declared as

```
TYPE
  List100 = ARRAY [1..100] OF real;
VAR
  A : List100;
```

Write a segment of code that uses a loop to initialize all components to zero.

6. Let the array List be declared by

```
TYPE
  Numbers = ARRAY [11..17] OF integer;
VAR
  List : Numbers;
```

and assume the components have values of

List

-2	List[11]
3	List[12]
0	List[13]
-8	List[14]
20	List[15]
14	List[16]
-121	List[17]

Show what the array components would be after the following program segment is executed:

```
FOR J := 11 TO 17 DO
  IF List[J] < 0 THEN
    List[J] := 0;
```

7. Assume an array has been declared as

```
TYPE
  List50 = ARRAY [1..50] OF integer;
VAR
  TestScore : List50;
```

Write a segment of code to print a suitable heading (assume this is a list of test scores) and then output a numbered list of the array components.

8. The following segment of code can be used to input the values in Example 7.11:

```
FOR J := 1 TO 50 DO
  IF NOT eof(Data) THEN
    readln (Data, Check[J]);
```

Discuss the differences between this code and the code in the example.

9. Let arrays A, B, and C be declared as

```
TYPE
  FirstList = ARRAY [21..40] OF real;
  SecondList = ARRAY [-4..15] OF real;
VAR
  A, B : FirstList;
  C : Secondlist;
```

Indicate if the following segments of code are valid or invalid. Include an explanation for those that are invalid.

a.
```
FOR J := 21 TO 40 DO
  A[J] := C[J - 25];
```

b. `A := B;`

c. `A := C;`

d.
```
FOR J := 1 TO 10 DO
  B[J + 20] := C[J + 10];
```

e.
```
FOR J := 11 TO 20 DO
  B[J + 20] := A[J + 20];
```

10. Write a program segment to read 100 real numbers from a data file, compute the average, and find both the largest and smallest values.

■ 7.3 Selection Sort and Bubble Sort

A common problem involving arrays is sorting the components of the array in either ascending or descending order. Other sorting algorithms are given in Chapter 11, but here we consider two of the easier methods: the selection sort and the bubble sort.

Selection Sort

Suppose we have an array A of five integers that we wish to sort from smallest to largest. The values currently in A are as depicted on the left; we wish to end up with values as on the right.

A			A	
6	A[1]		1	A[1]
4	A[2]		4	A[2]
8	A[3]		6	A[3]
10	A[4]		8	A[4]
1	A[5]		10	A[5]

The basic steps for a *selection sort* are:

1. Find the smallest number in the array, and exchange it with A[1].
2. Find the smallest number among A[2] through A[5], and exchange it with A[2].
3. Continue this process until the array is sorted.

The first step produces

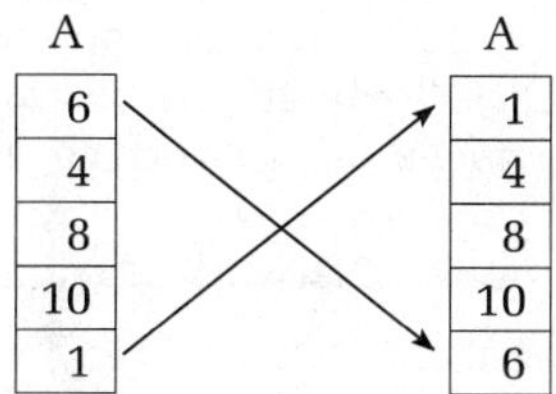

The second, third, and fourth steps produce

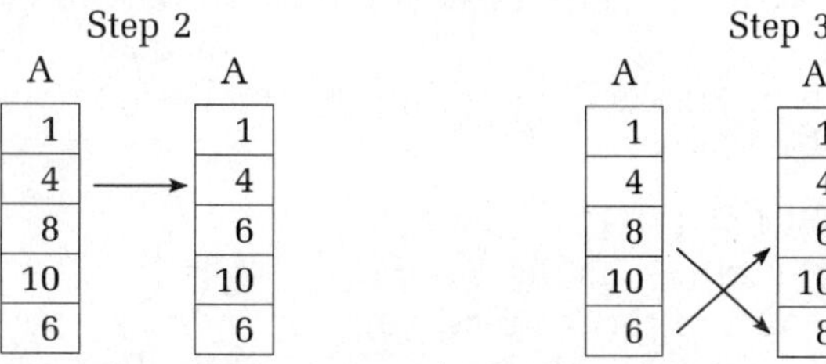

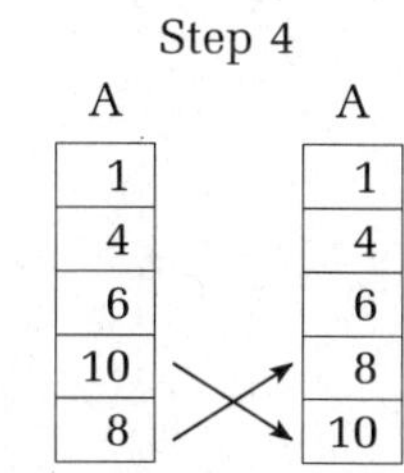

Notice that since the second smallest number is already in place in the second step, we do not need to exchange anything. Before writing the algorithm for this sorting procedure, note the following:

1. If the array is of length n, we need $n - 1$ steps.
2. We must be able to find one of the smallest remaining numbers.
3. We need to exchange appropriate array components.

A NOTE OF INTEREST

Too Few Women in the Computer Science Pipeline

Studies show that women in computer science programs in U.S. universities terminate their training earlier than men do. Historically, women have earned about 35 percent of all B.A. degrees and 27 percent of all M.A. degrees in computer science. ("Spertus, Why Are so Few Women Computer Scientists?"). The latest Taulbee Survey states:

> *The percentage of Ph.D.s in CS [computer science] has stayed where it has been since the early 1970s—between 10 and 14 percent. There are far too few women in our field, and our record of retention of women in the faculty is abysmal. There are only 243 female faculty members (7 percent) in the 163 CS and CE [computer engineering] Ph.D.-granting departments!*

This pattern of decreasing representation is often described as "pipeline shrinkage": as women move along the academic pipeline, their percentage continues to shrink.

The ACM Committee on the Status of Women has made a number of recommendations to promote change ["Becoming a Computer Scientist," *Communications of the ACM* (November 1990)]. These recommendations include

- Ensure equal access to computers for young girls and boys, and develop educational software appealing to both.
- Establish programs (such as science fairs, scouting programs, and conferences in which women speak about their careers in science and engineering) to encourage high school girls to continue with math and science.
- Develop programs to pair undergraduate women with women graduate students or faculty members who serve as role models, providing encouragement and advice.
- Provide women with opportunities for successful professional experiences (such as involvement in research projects), beginning as early as the undergraduate years.
- Establish programs that make women computer scientists visible to undergraduate and graduate students. Women can be invited to campuses to give talks or to serve as visiting faculty members (as for example, in the National Science Foundation's Visiting Professorship for Women).
- Encourage men and women to serve as mentors for young women in the field.
- Maintain lists of qualified women computer scientists to increase the participation of women in influential positions, such as program committees, editorial boards, and policy boards.
- Establish more reentry programs that enable women who have stopped their scientific training prematurely to retrain as computer scientists.
- Increase awareness of and sensitivity to subtle discrimination and its effects.
- Develop and enforce safety procedures on campus. Provide safe access at all hours to public terminal areas, well-lit routes from offices to parking lots, and services to escort those walking on campus after dark.
- Provide affordable, quality childcare.

To provide support for woman computer professionals, several organizations have been established that focus on networking, including Systers, the Association for Women in Computing (AWC), and the International Network of Women in Technology (WITI).

When searching for one of the smallest remaining numbers, it is not necessary to exchange equal values. Thus, strict inequality (<) rather than weak inequality (<=) is used when looking for the smallest remaining value. The algorithm to sort by selection is

1. **FOR** J := 1 **TO** N − 1
   1.1 find the smallest value among A[J], A[J + 1], . . . A[N] and store the index of the smallest value in Index
   1.2 exchange the values of A[J] and A[Index], if necessary

In Section 7.2 (Example 7.10), we wrote the segment of code required to find the smallest value of array A. With suitable changes, we incorporate this into the segment of code for a selection sort:

```
Index := 1;
FOR J := 2 TO ArrayLength DO
```

```
IF A[J] < A[Index] THEN
  Index := J;
```

Let A be an array of length *n*, and assume all variables have been appropriately declared. Then the following will sort A from low to high.

```
FOR J := 1 TO N - 1 DO      {  Find the minimum N - 1 times  }
  BEGIN
    Index := J;
    FOR K := J + 1 TO N DO
      IF A[K] < A[Index] THEN
        Index := K;  {  Find index of smallest number  }
    IF Index <> J THEN
      BEGIN
        Temp := A[Index];
        A[Index] := A[J];
        A[J] := Temp
      END  {  of exchange  }
  END;  {  of FOR J loop  }
```

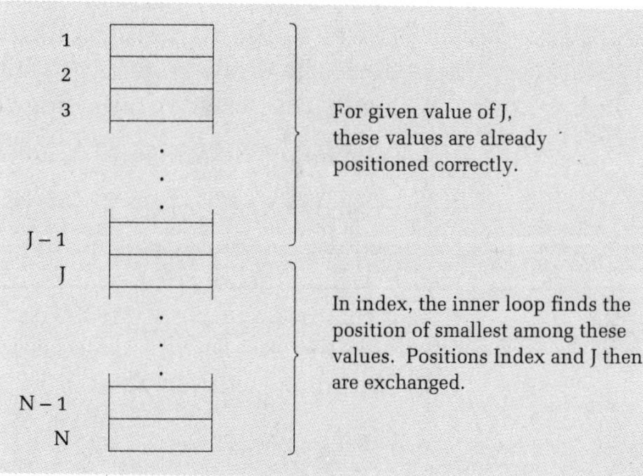
1
2
3
J − 1
J
N − 1
N
For given value of J, these values are already positioned correctly.
In index, the inner loop finds the position of smallest among these values. Positions Index and J then are exchanged.

Now let's trace this sort for the five integers in the array we sorted at the beginning of this section:

A	
6	A[1]
4	A[2]
8	A[3]
10	A[4]
1	A[5]

For J := 1, Index := 1, and this produces

1
Index

K	Index
2	2
3	2
4	2
5	5

For the loop **FOR** K := 2 **TO** 5, we get successive assignments as shown in the margin table.

The statements

```
Temp := A[Index];
A[Index] := A[J];
A[J] := Temp;
```

produce the partially sorted array

A

1	A[1]
4	A[2]
8	A[3]
10	A[4]
6	A[5]

Each successive J value continues to partially sort the array until J := 4. This pass produces a completely sorted array.

■ EXAMPLE 7.13

Our concluding example:

1. Inputs real numbers from a data file.
2. Echo prints the numbers in a column with a width of six spaces, with two places to the right of the decimal (:6:2).
3. Sorts the array from low to high.
4. Prints the sorted array using the same output format.

An expanded pseudocode development for this is

1. Print header—prints a suitable explanation of the program and includes a heading for the unsorted list
2. Get data (echo print)—uses a **WHILE** loop to read the data and print it in the same order in which it is read
3. Sort list—uses the selection sort to sort the array from low to high
4. Output sorted list—uses a **FOR** loop to output the sorted list

```
PROGRAM ArraySample;

{  This program illustrates the use of a sorting algorithm       }
{  with an array of reals.  Output includes data in both an      }
{  unsorted and a sorted list.  The data are formatted and       }
{  numbered to enhance readability.                              }

USES
  Crt;

CONST
  Skip = ' ';
  ListMax = 20;

TYPE
  NumList = ARRAY [1..ListMax] OF real;

VAR
  Index : integer;       {  Stores position of an element            }
  J, K : integer;        {  Indices                                  }
  NumReals : integer;    {  Length of the list                       }
  Temp : real;           {  Temporary storage for array elements     }
  List : NumList;        {  Array of reals                           }
  DataFile : text;       {  File of data                             }

{*****************************************************************}

PROCEDURE PrintHeading;
```

```
  {  Given:    Nothing                                                }
  {  Task:     Print a heading for the output                         }
  {  Return:   Nothing                                                }

  BEGIN
    writeln;
    writeln (Skip:10, 'This sample program does the following:');
    writeln;
    writeln (Skip:12, '<1> Gets reals from a data file.');
    writeln (Skip:12, '<2> Echo prints the data.');
    writeln (Skip:12, '<3> Sorts the data from low to high.');
    writeln (Skip:12, '<4> Prints a sorted list of the data.');
    writeln
  END;  {  of PROCEDURE PrintHeading  }

{************************************************************}

BEGIN {  Main program  }
  ClrScr;

  {  Print the heading  }
  PrintHeading;

  {  Get the data and echo print it  }
  assign (DataFile, 'Ex713.DAT');
  reset (DataFile);
  writeln (Skip:10, 'The original data are as follows:');
  writeln;
  NumReals := 0;
  WHILE NOT eof(DataFile) AND (NumReals < ListMax} DO
    BEGIN
      NumReals := NumReals + 1;
      readln (DataFile, List[NumReals]);
      writeln (Skip:12, '<', NumReals:2, '>', List[NumReals]:6:2)
    END;  {  of WHILE NOT loop  }
  IF NOT eof(DataFile) THEN
    writeln ('There are more data.');

  {  Now sort the list  }
  FOR J := 1 TO NumReals - 1 DO
    BEGIN
      Index := J;
      FOR K := J + 1 TO NumReals DO
        IF List[K] < List[Index] THEN
          Index := K;
      IF Index <> J THEN
        BEGIN
          Temp := List[Index];
          List[Index] := List[J];
          List[J] := Temp
        END  {  of exchange  }
    END;  {  of FOR loop (selection sort)  }

  {  Now print the sorted list  }
  writeln;
  writeln (Skip:10, 'The sorted list is as follows:');
  writeln;
  FOR J := 1 TO NumReals DO
    writeln (Skip:12, '<' J:2 '>', List[J]:6:2);
  close (DataFile)
END.  {  of main program  }
```

The output for this program is

```
This sample program does the following:

  <1> Gets reals from a data file.
  <2> Echo prints the data.
  <3> Sorts the data from low to high.
  <4> Prints a sorted list of the data.

The original data are as follows:

  < 1> 34.56
  < 2> 78.21
  < 3> 23.30
  < 4> 89.90
  < 5> 45.00
  < 6> 56.80
  < 7> 39.01
  < 8> 45.56
  < 9> 34.40
  <10> 45.10
  <11> 98.20
  <12>  5.60
  <13>  8.00
  <14> 45.00
  <15> 99.00
  <16> 56.78
  <17> 56.78
  <18> 45.00

The sorted list is as follows:

  < 1>  5.60
  < 2>  8.00
  < 3> 23.30
  < 4> 34.40
  < 5> 34.56
  < 6> 39.01
  < 7> 45.00
  < 8> 45.00
  < 9> 45.00
  <10> 45.10
  <11> 45.56
  <12> 56.78
  <13> 56.78
  <14> 56.80
  <15> 78.21
  <16> 89.90
  <17> 98.20
  <18> 99.00
```

Echo printing is not necessary in Turbo Pascal when a version that has Watch windows is used. In such cases, echo printing can be simulated by selecting the appropriate variable for inclusion in the Watch window. However, we choose to include the technique of echo printing here to emphasize the process. At some point, you may be using a language or system that does not have Watch Windows.

Bubble Sort

The sorting algorithm commonly referred to as a *bubble sort* rearranges the components of an array until they are in either ascending or descending order. Like the selection sort, an extra array is not used. Basically, a bubble sort starts at the beginning of an array and compares two consecutive elements of the array. If they are in the correct order, the next pair of elements is compared. If they are not in the correct order, they are switched and the next pair is compared. When this has been done for the entire array, the correct element will be in the last position.

Starting at the top (the beginning) each time, successive passes through the array are made until the array is sorted. Two items should be noted here.

1. A flag is needed to indicate whether or not an exchange was made during a given pass through the array. If none was made, the array is sorted.
2. Since each pass filters the largest (or smallest) element to the bottom of the array, the length of what remains to be sorted can be decreased by 1 after each pass.

To illustrate how this algorithm works, assume the array is

A
12
0
3
2
8

The first pass through the array produces

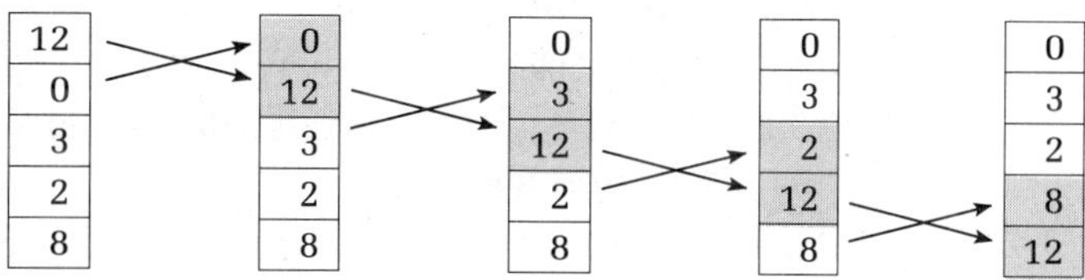

Since an exchange was made, we need to make at least one more pass through the array. However, the length is decreased by one because there is no need to compare the last two elements as the largest element is in its correct position. A second pass produces

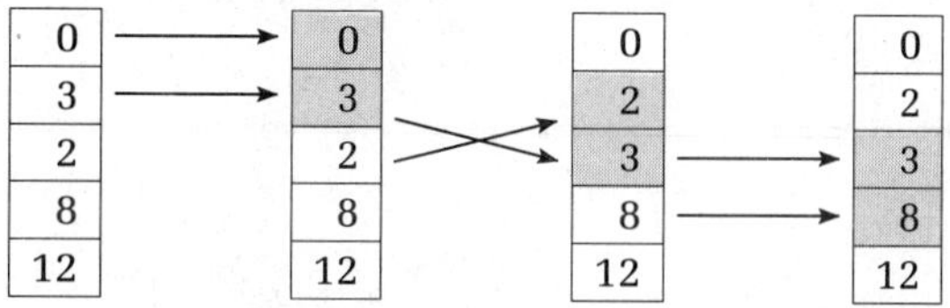

At this stage, the array is sorted, but because an exchange was made, the length is decreased by 1 and another pass is made. Since no exchange is made during this third pass, the sorting process is terminated.

Assuming the variable declaration section includes

```
VAR
  ExchangeMade : boolean;
  J, Length, Last, Temp : integer;
```

the values to be sorted are in the array A, and Length has been assigned a value, an algorithm for a bubble sort could be

```
Last := Length - 1;
REPEAT
  ExchangeMade := false;
  FOR J := 1 TO Last DO
```

```
      IF A[J] > A[J+1] THEN
        BEGIN{  Exchange values  }
          Temp := A[J];
          A[J] := A[J+1];
          A[J+1] := Temp;
          ExchangeMade := true
        END;
    Last := Last - 1 {  Decrement length  }
  UNTIL (NOT ExchangeMade) OR (Last = 0);
```

Exercises 7.3

1. Assume the following array Column is to be sorted from low to high using the selection sort.

   Column

−20
10
0
10
8
30
−2

   a. Sketch the contents of the array after each of the first two passes.
   b. How many exchanges are made during the sort?
2. Write a test program that prints the partially sorted arrays after each pass during a selection sort.
3. Change the code for the selection sort so it sorts an array from high to low.
4. Write a complete program to
   a. Read 10 reals into an array from an input file.
   b. Sort the array from high to low if the first real is positive; sort the array from low to high if it is negative.
   c. Print a numbered column containing the sorted reals using the format :10:2.
5. The array

17
0
3
2
8

   requires five exchanges of elements when sorted using a bubble sort. Since each exchange requires three assignment statements, there are 15 assignments for elements in the array. Sort the same array using the selection sort, and determine the number of assignments made.
6. Modify the selection sort by including a counter that counts the number of assignments of array elements made during a sort.
7. Using the modification in Exercise 6, sort lists of differing lengths that contain randomly generated numbers. On a graph similar to the one shown

here, display the number of assignments made for each sort. Use lists with lengths of multiples of 10.

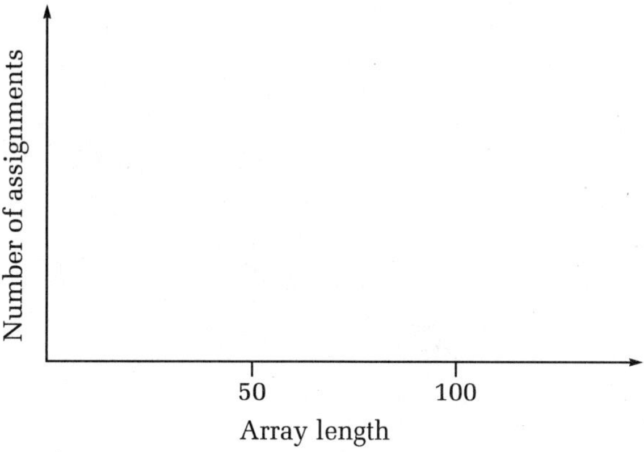

8. Modify the bubble sort to include a counter for the number of assignments made during a sort.
9. Use the modified versions of both sorts to examine their relative efficiency; that is, run them on arrays of varying lengths and plot the results on a graph. What are your conclusions?
10. Modify the bubble sort to sort from high to low rather than low to high.
11. It is common practice to sort parallel arrays (for example, an array of names and a corresponding array of scores on a test). Modify both sorts so you can sort a list of initials and associated test scores.

■ 7.4 Arrays and Subprograms

Basic Idea and Syntax

Procedures and functions should be used with arrays to maintain the structured design philosophy. Before we look at specific examples, let's examine the method and syntax required to pass an array to a procedure. Recall that to pass either a value or a variable parameter to a procedure, we must declare an actual parameter of exactly the same type as the formal parameter in the procedure heading. In addition, if more than one parameter is passed, there must be a one-for-one ordered matching of the actual parameters with the formal parameters in the heading of the procedure. Consider, for example, the following program that reads two integer test scores, computes their average in a procedure called CalcMean, and outputs the results.

■ EXAMPLE 7.14

```
PROGRAM AverageOfTwo;

USES
  Crt;

VAR
  Num1, Num2 : integer;
  Ave : real;

{*********************************************************}
```

```
PROCEDURE CalcMean (Num1, Num2 : integer;
                    VAR Ave : real);

  {  Given:   Two integers                                   }
  {  Task:    Compute their average                          }
  {  Return:  Average of the two integers                    }

  VAR
    Sum : integer;
  BEGIN
    Sum := Num1 + Num2;
    Ave := Sum / 2.0
  END;  {  of PROCEDURE CalcMean  }

{*****************************************************}

BEGIN  {  Main program  }
  ClrScr;
  writeln ('Please enter two integers and press <Enter>.');
  readln (Num1, Num2);
  CalcMean (Num1, Num2, Ave);
  writeln ('The average of ', Num1, ' and ', Num2,
           ' is ', Ave:6:2);
  readln
END.  {  of main program  }
```

The procedure call

```
CalcMean (Num1, Num2, Ave);
```

and the procedure heading

```
PROCEDURE CalcMean (Num1, Num2 : integer;
                    VAR Ave : real);
```

illustrate the desired matching of variables.

Let us now modify the program so it will determine the average of 100 test scores in the array Scores. The procedure call in the program will be

```
CalcMean (Scores, Ave);
```

and the procedure heading will have to match these variables. If Scores also is the variable name to be used in the procedure heading, we have

```
PROCEDURE CalcMean (Scores : ???;
                    VAR Ave : real);
```

Turbo Pascal requires that a **TYPE** definition be given. For example, if we have

```
CONST
  MaxLength = 100;
TYPE
  List = ARRAY [1..MaxLength] OF integer;
VAR
  Scores : List;
```

the procedure heading can be

```
PROCEDURE CalcMean (Scores : List;
                    VAR Ave : real);
```

This is consistent with allowing only identifiers of identical or compatible types to be associated. A common mistake is to attempt to build a data type inside the procedure heading. This will not work. The statement

```
PROCEDURE CalcMean (Scores : ARRAY [1..MaxLength] OF integer;
                    VAR Ave : real);
```

produces an error message because Turbo Pascal compilers check for name equivalence rather than structure equivalence. To illustrate, we could have two arrays

```
Position : ARRAY [1..3] OF real;
Nutrition : ARRAY [1..3] OF real;
```

where Position is used to represent coordinates of a point in space and Nutrition is used to represent the volume, weight, and caloric content of a serving of food. Although Position and Nutrition have the same structure, they have significantly different meanings. Thus, by insisting on name equivalence, the chances of inadvertent or meaningless uses of structured variables are decreased. Also, compiler implementation of name equivalence is easier than compiler implementation of structure equivalence.

We can now write a revised version of the program in Example 7.14 to find the average and include a procedure that requires passing an array variable.

EXAMPLE 7.15

```
PROGRAM Average;

USES
  Crt;

CONST
  MaxLength = 100;

TYPE
  List = ARRAY [1..MaxLength] OF integer;

VAR
  Scores : List;
  Ave : real;
  J, Len : integer;
  ScoreFile : text;

{*******************************************************}

PROCEDURE CalcMean (Scores : List;
                    VAR Ave : real;
                    Len : integer);

  {  Given:   An array of scores and number of scores in  }
  {               the array                               }
  {  Task:    Compute the average of scores in the array  }
  {  Return:  The average score                           }

  VAR
    J, Sum : integer;
  BEGIN
    Sum := 0;
    FOR J := 1 TO Len DO
      Sum := Sum + Scores[J];
    Ave := Sum / Len
  END;  {  of PROCEDURE CalcMean  }

{*******************************************************}

BEGIN  {  Main program  }
  ClrScr;
  assign (ScoreFile, 'Ex715.DAT');
  reset (ScoreFile);
```

```
  Len := 0;
  WHILE NOT eof(ScoreFile) AND (Len < MaxLength) DO
    BEGIN
      Len := Len + 1;
      readln (ScoreFile, Scores[Len])
    END;  {  of WHILE NOT eof  }
  CalcMean (Scores, Ave, Len);
  writeln ('The average of':20);
  writeln;
  FOR J := 1 TO Len DO
    writeln (Scores[J]:12);
  writeln;
  writeln ('is':10, Ave:8:2);
  readln;
  close (ScoreFile)
END.  {  of main program  }
```

7.0 Before we consider more procedures with arrays, we restate a rule: To pass an array to a procedure or function, the array must be declared with an identifier that uses a **TYPE** identifier; the matching variable in the procedure must use the same **TYPE** identifier.

Now that we know how to pass an array, let's rewrite our last example using a completely modular development. In this version, CalcMean is a function instead of a procedure. The first-level pseudocode development is

1. Get the scores (**PROCEDURE** GetData)
2. Compute the average (**FUNCTION** CalcMean)
3. Print a heading (**PROCEDURE** PrintHeader)
4. Print the results (**PROCEDURE** PrintResults)

The procedure to get the scores requires a **VAR** declaration in the procedure heading for the array. If List is defined as a data type, we have

```
PROCEDURE GetData (VAR Scores : List;
                   VAR Length : integer);
  BEGIN
    Length := 0;
    WHILE NOT eof(ScoreFile) AND (Length < MaxLength) DO
      BEGIN
        Length := Length + 1;
        readln (ScoreFile, Scores[Length])
      END
  END;  {  of PROCEDURE GetData  }
```

The average score can be computed by the function CalcMean:

```
FUNCTION CalcMean (Scores : List;
                   Length : integer) : real;
  VAR
    J, Sum : integer;
  BEGIN
    Sum := 0;
    FOR J := 1 TO Length DO
      Sum := Sum + Scores[J];
    CalcMean := Sum / Length
  END;  {  of FUNCTION CalcMean  }
```

A procedure to print a heading is written in a manner similar to the one we have used previously. If we want the output to be

```
Test Scores
---- ------

   99
   98
   97
   96
   95

The average score on this test was 97.00.
```

the procedure for the heading can be

```
PROCEDURE PrintHeader;
  BEGIN
    writeln;
    writeln ('Test Scores');
    writeln ('---- ------');
    writeln
  END;  {  of PROCEDURE PrintHeader  }
```

A procedure to print the results is

```
PROCEDURE PrintResults (Scores : List;
                        Ave : real;
                        Length : integer);
  VAR
    J : integer;
  BEGIN
    FOR J := 1 TO Length DO
      writeln (Scores[J]:5);
    writeln;
    writeln ('The average score on this test was',
             Ave:6:2, '.')
  END;  {  of PROCEDURE PrintResults  }
```

This procedure can be called by

```
PrintResults (Scores, Ave, Length);
```

where Ave is found by

```
Ave := CalcMean(Scores, Length);
```

The following example is a complete program for this development.

EXAMPLE 7.16

```
PROGRAM TestScores;

USES
  Crt;

CONST
  MaxLength = 100;

TYPE
  List = ARRAY [1..MaxLength] OF integer;

VAR
  Scores : List;
  Ave : real;
  Length : integer;
  ScoreFile : text;

{*********************************************************}

PROCEDURE GetData (VAR Scores : List;
                   VAR Length : integer);
```

```
  {  Given:   Nothing                                      }
  {  Task:    Read scores from a data file into an array    }
  {  Return:  Array of scores (with length)                 }

  BEGIN
    IF NOT eof(ScoreFile) THEN
      BEGIN
        Length := 0;
        WHILE NOT eof(ScoreFile) AND (Length < MaxLength) DO
          BEGIN
            Length := Length + 1;
            readln (ScoreFile, Scores[Length])
          END  {  of WHILE NOT eof  }
      END  {  of IF NOT eof  }
    ELSE
      writeln ('ScoreFile is empty')
  END;  {  of PROCEDURE GetData  }

{************************************************************}

FUNCTION CalcMean (Scores : List;
                   Length : integer) : real;

  {  Given:   A list of scores                             }
  {  Task:    Compute the average score                    }
  {  Return:  The average score                            }

  VAR
    J, Sum : integer;
  BEGIN
    Sum := 0;
    FOR J := 1 TO Length DO
      Sum := Sum + Scores[J];
    CalcMean := Sum / Length
  END;  {  of FUNCTION CalcMean  }

{************************************************************}

PROCEDURE PrintHeader;

  {  Given:   Nothing                                      }
  {  Task:    Print a heading for the output               }
  {  Return:  Nothing                                      }

  BEGIN
    writeln;
    writeln ('Test Scores');
    writeln ('---- ------');
    writeln
  END;  {  of PROCEDURE PrintHeader  }

{************************************************************}

PROCEDURE PrintResults (Scores : List;
                        Ave : real;
                        Length : integer);

  {  Given:   Array of scores and average score            }
  {  Task:    Print the scores in a list and print the     }
  {               average score                            }
  {  Return:  Nothing                                      }
```

```
  VAR
    J : integer;
  BEGIN
    FOR J := 1 TO Length DO
      writeln (Scores[J]:5);
    writeln;
    writeln ('The average score on this test was',
             Ave:6:2, '.')
  END;  {  of PROCEDURE PrintResults  }

{*********************************************************}

BEGIN  {  Main program  }
  ClrScr;
  assign (ScoreFile, 'Ex716.DAT');
  reset (ScoreFile);
  GetData (Scores, Length);
  Ave := CalcMean(Scores, Length);
  PrintHeader;
  PrintResults (Scores, Ave, Length);
  readln;
  close (ScoreFile)
END.  {  of main program  }
```

7.0

Sorting arrays is a standard problem for programmers. Now that we can pass arrays to procedures and functions, let's consider a problem in which an unknown number of reals are to be read from an input file and a sorted list (high to low) is to be printed as output. A first-level pseudocode design is

1. Get data (**PROCEDURE** GetData)
2. Sort list (**PROCEDURE** Sort)
3. Print a heading (**PROCEDURE** PrintHeader)
4. Print sorted list (**PROCEDURE** PrintData)

Since the number of data items is unknown, we will have to declare an array that is of sufficient length to store all the data but that does not use an unreasonable amount of memory. The nature of the problem will provide sufficient information for this declaration. For now, assume we know there are at most 50 data items. Then the following declaration is sufficient:

```
CONST
  MaxLength = 50;
TYPE
  NumList = ARRAY [1..MaxLength] OF real;
VAR
  List : NumList;
  Length : integer;
```

The procedure to sort the array uses a version of the selection sort in Section 7.3. Both the array and the number of data items need to be passed to the procedure. An appropriate procedure is

```
PROCEDURE Sort (VAR List : NumList;
                Length : integer);

  VAR
    J, K, Index : integer;
    Temp : real;
```

```
BEGIN
  FOR J := 1 TO Length-1 DO
    BEGIN
      Index := J;
      FOR K := J + 1 TO Length DO
        IF List[K] > List[Index] THEN
          Index := K;
      IF Index <> J THEN
        BEGIN
          Temp := List[Index];
          List[Index] := List[J];
          List[J] := Temp
        END  { of exchange  }
    END  {  of FOR J loop  }
END;  {  of PROCEDURE Sort  }
```

This procedure can be called by the statement

```
Sort (List, Length);
```

After suitable procedures are written for getting the data, printing a heading, and printing the data, the main body of the program could be

```
BEGIN  {  Main program  }
  GetData (List, Length);
  Sort (List, Length);
  PrintHeader;
  PrintData (List, Length)
END.  {  of main program  }
```

Arrays and Variable Parameters

Now let's reconsider the issue of value parameters and variable parameters used with arrays. Because value parameters require separate memory of approximately the same size as that used by actual parameters in the main program, value parameters that are array types can require a great deal of memory. Thus, many programmers use only variable parameters when they work with arrays. This saves memory and speeds execution. Since most of your programs are relatively short and process small data files, this will not be a major problem. However, as data bases become larger and you use more elaborate structures, you may wish to consider using variable parameters even when changes are not made in the variables.

Software Engineering Implications

Passing arrays is a software engineering concern. Passing arrays by reference results in a significant saving of memory. The problem this creates when several modules (teams) use the same array is that inadvertent changes made in an array within a specific module now become changes in the array used by other modules. These side effects do not occur if the array is passed as a value parameter.

How do designers solve this problem? There is no clear solution. If the arrays are fairly small and memory allocation is not a problem, arrays should be passed as value parameters when possible. When conditions require arrays to be passed by reference, it is extremely important to guarantee that no unwanted changes are made. This requirement increases the need for careful and thorough documentation.

Data Abstraction

Now that you are somewhat comfortable with the concept of an array as a data structure, it is time to take a broader look at how data relate to structures used to store and manipulate data. When designing the solution to a problem, it is not important to be initially concerned about the specifics of how data will be manipulated. These implementation details can (and should) be dealt with at a fairly low level in a modular development. The properties of a data structure will, however, be part of the design at a fairly high level.

The separation between the conceptual definition of a data structure and its eventual implementation is called *data abstraction.* This process of deferring details to the lowest possible level parallels the method of designing algorithms; that is, design first and do implementation details last.

Data abstraction is not a well-defined process, but we will attempt to illustrate it here. Suppose you are designing a program that will be required to work with a list of names and an associated list of numbers (student names and test scores). Reasonable tasks would be to

1. Get the data
2. Sort the lists by name or number
3. Print the lists

In your design, you might have procedures such as

```
GetNames (<procedure here>);
GetScores (<procedure here>);
SortByName (<procedure here>);
SortByScore (<procedure here>);
PrintNamesAndScores (<procedure here>);
```

Even though you have not yet worked with the implementation details required to write the procedures, you could use data structure properties in a design. For example, at this point, you probably could design a problem solution using some previously mentioned procedures that work with an array of names and/or an array of associated test scores.

Abstract Data Types

Two abstraction concepts have been previously discussed: procedural abstraction and data abstraction. A third form of abstraction arises from the use of defined types. Specifically, an *abstract data type* (*ADT*) consists of a class of objects, a defined set of properties of these objects, and a set of operations for processing the objects.

Our work thus far has been fairly limited in terms of what can be considered an abstract data type. However, it is possible to think of an array as a list. The class of objects is then lists. Some properties of these lists include identical element type, order, varying lengths, and direct access to individual components. Operations for processing the lists include searching for an element, sorting in ascending or descending order, inserting an element, and deleting an element.

As before, it is not necessary to be overly concerned about specific implementation details at this point. But your growth as a computer scientist will be enhanced if you develop a perspective of abstract data types and use this perspective in the design of problem solutions.

Much of the remainder of this book is devoted to developing properties of data structures and operations for processing these structures. As you progress through the material on higher-dimensional arrays, records, files, and sets, try to analyze each structure with related properties and operations as an abstract data type.

Exercises 7.4

1. Assume the following declarations have been made in a program.

```
TYPE
  Row = ARRAY [1..10] OF integer;
  Column = ARRAY [1..30] OF real;
  Week = (Sun, Mon, Tues, Wed, Thur, Fri, Sat);
VAR
  List1, List2 : Row;
  Aray : Column;
  Day : Week;
  A, B : ARRAY [1..10] OF integer;
```

   Indicate which of the following are valid **PROCEDURE** declarations. Write an appropriate line of code that will call each procedure that is valid. Include an explanation for declarations that are invalid.

   a. `PROCEDURE NewList (X : Row; Y : Column);`

   b. `PROCEDURE NewList (VAR X : Row : VAR Y : Column);`

   c. `PROCEDURE NewList (X : ARRAY [1..10] OF integer);`

   d. `PROCEDURE NewList (VAR X, Y : Row);`

   e. `PROCEDURE NewList (VAR Column : Column);`

   f. `PROCEDURE WorkWeek (Days : ARRAY [Mon..Fri] OF Week);`

   g. `PROCEDURE GetData (X : Week);`

   h. `PROCEDURE Table (VAR X : Row; VAR Y : Row);`

2. Write a test program that illustrates what happens when you define an array structure in a procedure heading. For example

```
PROCEDURE Sort (List : ARRAY [1..20] OF real);
```

3. When possible, use the **TYPE** and **VAR** declaration sections in Exercise 1 to write **PROCEDURE** declarations so each of the following statements in the main program is an appropriate call to a procedure. Explain any inappropriate calls.

   a. `OldList (List1, Aray);`

   b. `ChangeList (List1, Day);`

   c. `Scores (A, B);`

4. Write an appropriate **PROCEDURE** declaration and a line of code to call the procedure for each of the following.

   a. A procedure to **read** 20 test scores into an array and save them for later use.
   b. A procedure to count the number of occurrences of the letter A in an array of 50 characters.
   c. A procedure to take two arrays of 10 integers each and produce a sorted array of 20 integers for later use.
   d. A procedure to **read** integer test scores from a data file, count the number of scores, count the number of scores ≥ 90, and save this information for later use.

5. Assume the following declarations have been made.

```
TYPE
  Column10 = ARRAY [1..10] OF integer;
```

```
VAR
  List1, List2 : Column10;
  K : integer;
```

Indicate the contents of each array after the call to the corresponding procedure.

a.
```
PROCEDURE Sample (VAR List1 : Column10;
                      List2 : Column10);
  VAR
    J : integer;
  BEGIN
    FOR J := 1 TO 10 DO
      BEGIN
        List1[J] := J * J;
        List2[J] := List1[J] MOD 2
      END
  END;  {  of PROCEDURE Sample  }

BEGIN  {  Main program  }
  .
  .
  .
  FOR K := 1 TO 10 DO
    BEGIN
      List1[K] := 0;
      List2[K] := 0
    END;
  Sample (List1, List2);
```

b. Replace the procedure call with

```
Sample (List2, List1);
```

c. Replace the procedure call with the consecutive calls

```
Sample (List1, List2);
Sample (List2, List1);
```

6. Write **PROCEDURE** BubbleSort for the bubble sort in Section 7.3. Show how it would be called from the main program.

7. Write a procedure to examine an array of integers and then return the maximum value, minimum value, and number of negative values to the main program.

8. Suppose you have an array of student names and an array of these students' test scores. How would the array of names be affected if you sorted the test scores from high to low?

9. Write **PROCEDURE** Exchange for the bubble sort that exchanges values of array components. Then rewrite the bubble sort using **PROCEDURE** Exchange.

■ 7.5 Strings and Packed Arrays

S

Recall from our earlier work in Chapters 1 and 2 that Turbo Pascal provides a **string** data type. Standard Pascal does not provide such a data type. However, this data type can be simulated in standard Pascal by using a variation of an array of characters. We now briefly consider the standard Pascal simulation of a **string** data type and some applications of type **string** in Turbo Pascal. If you are not concerned about how standard Pascal differs from Turbo Pascal, you may skip the following section entitled "Basic Idea and Notation of Packed Arrays."

Basic Idea and Notation of Packed Arrays

Arrays, as you recall, are useful for handling large amounts of data. One of the disadvantages of using arrays, however, is that they require large amounts of memory. In particular, arrays of character data use much more memory than is necessary. To illustrate, let's take a closer look at an array declared by

```
VAR
  Examine : ARRAY [1..5] OF char;
```

When this structured variable is declared, the following variables are reserved:

Examine	
	Examine[1]
	Examine[2]
	Examine[3]
	Examine[4]
	Examine[5]

Each component of the array Examine is one *word* in memory, and each word consists of several bytes. Let's consider the array Examine in which each word consists of four bytes. The array can be pictured as

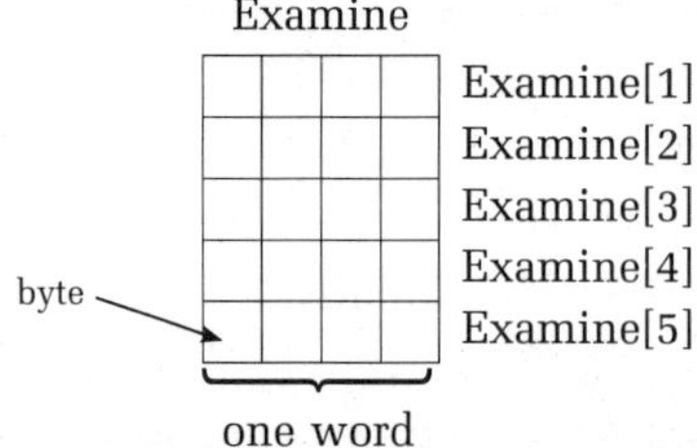

We could assign the word "HELLO" to the array Examine by either

```
Examine[1] := 'H';
Examine[2] := 'E';
Examine[3] := 'L';
Examine[4] := 'L';
Examine[5] := 'O';
```

or

```
Examine := 'HELLO'
```

depending upon which version of Pascal is being used. In either case, after the assignment, the array will look like

Examine				
H				Examine[1]
E				Examine[2]
L				Examine[3]
L				Examine[4]
O				Examine[5]

because a *byte* is the unit of storage necessary for storing a character variable.

As you can see, 20 bytes of storage have been reserved, but only five have been used. Pascal provides a more efficient way of defining arrays that does not use unnecessary amounts of storage space. Instead of declaring a variable as an array, we can declare a variable as a *packed array.* With this declaration, the computer then packs the data in consecutive bytes. In Turbo Pascal, the word **PACKED** has no effect. Instead, packing occurs automatically whenever possible.

Packed arrays can be used with any data type. However, it is not always wise to do so because it takes longer to access individual components of a packed array than it does to access individual components of an array that has not been declared as packed. Storage space is saved, but time may be lost.

Now let's consider the declaration

```
TYPE
  String5 = PACKED ARRAY [1..5] OF char;
VAR
  Examine : String5;
```

and the assignment of the word "HELLO" as before. Using a packed array, we then have the following in memory:

Examine

H	E	L	L	O			

Notice that less than two words (five bytes) are used to store what previously required five words (20 bytes). We can still access the individual components as before. For example

```
writeln (Examine[2]);
```

produces

```
E
```

as a line of output.

Character Strings

Every programming language must be able to handle character data. Names, words, phrases, and sentences are frequently part of some information that must be analyzed. In Turbo Pascal, character strings are formed by declaring a variable to be of type **string** or **string** [*n*]. Thus, a typical declaration is

```
VAR
  Name : string;
```

Now that you have completed some work with arrays, we can analyze **string** variables further. A **string** data type in Turbo Pascal is a packed array. The most general declaration is

```
<identifier> : string [n];
```

where [n] specifies the array length. If no length is given, the default length is 255 characters. Thus, the declaration

```
Name : string;
```

is equivalent to the definition and subsequent declaration

```
TYPE
  String255 = PACKED ARRAY [1..255] OF char;
VAR
  Name : String255;
```

One ramification of viewing strings as arrays of characters is that they can be accessed character by character. The notation is identical to that used for arrays. Thus, if we have the declaration

```
VAR
  Name : string;
```

then Name[1] refers to the first character, Name[2] refers to the second character, and so on. To illustrate this notation, the following example shows how to print a name vertically.

EXAMPLE 7.17

Let's write an interactive program that allows the user to enter a name from the keyboard and then displays the name horizontally and vertically. For this program, we use the default length for our string variable. A complete program for this task is

```
PROGRAM StringPrac;

USES
  Crt;

VAR
  Index : integer;
  Name : string;

BEGIN
  ClrScr;
  writeln ('Please enter your name and press <Enter>.');
  readln (Name);
  writeln (Name);
  writeln;
  FOR Index := 1 TO Length(Name) DO
    writeln (Name[Index]);
  writeln;
  readln
END.
```

A sample run of this program produces

```
Please enter your name and press <Enter>.
Veronica Kyler
Veronica Kyler

V
e
r
o
n
i
c
a

K
y
l
e
r
```

Note that the string function **Length** is used as a loop limit.

Comparing String Variables

S Strings can be compared using the standard relational operators "=, <, >, <>, <=, and >=." For example, if 'Smith' and 'Jones' are strings, then 'Smith' < 'Jones', 'Smith' <> 'Jones', and so on are all valid Boolean expressions. The Boolean value is determined by the collating sequence. Using the collating sequence for the

ASCII character set, the following comparisons yield the indicated values:

Comparison	Boolean Value
'Smith' < 'Jones'	**false**
'Jake' < 'Johnson'	**true**
'ABC' = 'ABA'	**false**
'Smith Doug' < 'Smith Jonathan'	**true**

What happens if we want to evaluate 'William Joe' < 'Williams Bo'? Since a character-by-character comparison is implemented by the computer, no decision is made until the blank following the "m" of William is compared to the "s" in Williams. Using the full ASCII character code, this Boolean expression is **true,** which is how these strings are alphabetized.

We are now ready to write a short program using strings. Suppose we want to get two names from a data file, arrange them alphabetically, and then print the alphabetized list. Assume the names are to appear on two adjacent lines in the data file. A first-level pseudocode development is

1. Get the data (**PROCEDURE** GetData)
2. Arrange the data alphabetically (**PROCEDURE** Alphabetize)
3. Print the data (**PROCEDURE** PrintData)

A procedure to get one line of data is

```
PROCEDURE GetData (VAR Name : string);
  BEGIN
    readln (DataFile, Name)
  END;  {  of PROCEDURE GetData  }
```

After the two names are read from the input file, they can be arranged alphabetically by

```
PROCEDURE Alphabetize (VAR Name1, Name2 : string);
  VAR
    Temp : string;
  BEGIN
    IF Name2 < Name1 THEN
      BEGIN  {  Exchange when necessary  }
        Temp := Name1;
        Name1 := Name2;
        Name2 := Temp
      END  {  of IF...THEN  }
  END;  {  of PROCEDURE Alphabetize  }
```

The procedure for printing the name should include some heading and some formatting of the names. For example, suppose we want to say

```
The alphabetized list is below.
--- ------------ ---- -- -----
```

and then print the list indented 10 spaces after skipping two lines. A procedure to do this is

```
PROCEDURE PrintData (Name1, Name2 : string);
  BEGIN
    writeln;
    writeln (Skip:10, 'The alphabetized list is below.');
    writeln (Skip:10, '--- ------------ ---- -- -----');
    writeln;
    writeln (Skip:20, Name1);
    writeln (Skip:20, Name2)
  END;  {  of PROCEDURE PrintData  }
```

We can now write the complete program.

```
PROGRAM SampleNames;

USES
  Crt;

CONST
  Skip = ' ';

VAR
  Name1, Name2 : string;
  DataFile : text;

{*********************************************************}

PROCEDURE GetData (VAR Name : string);

  {  Given:   Nothing                                          }
  {  Task:    Read a name from the data file                   }
  {  Return:  One name                                         }

  BEGIN
    readln (DataFile, Name)
  END;  {  of PROCEDURE GetData  }

{*********************************************************}

PROCEDURE Alphabetize (VAR Name1, Name2 : string);

  {  Given:   Two names                                        }
  {  Task:    Sort the names alphabetically                    }
  {  Return:  The names in sorted order                        }

  VAR
    Temp : string;
  BEGIN
    IF Name2 < Name1 THEN
      BEGIN                     {  Exchange when necessary  }
        Temp := Name1;
        Name1 := Name2;
        Name2 := Temp
      END  {  of IF...THEN  }
  END;  {  of PROCEDURE Alphabetize  }

{*********************************************************}

PROCEDURE PrintData (Name1, Name2 : string);

  {  Given:   Names in alphabetical order                      }
  {  Task:    Print the names                                  }
  {  Return:  Nothing                                          }

  BEGIN
    writeln;
    writeln (Skip:10, 'The alphabetized list is below.');
    writeln (Skip:10, '--- ------------ ---- -- -----');
    writeln;
    writeln (Skip:20, Name1);
    writeln (Skip:20, Name2)
  END;  {  of PROCEDURE PrintData  }

{*********************************************************}
```

```
BEGIN  {  Main program  }
  ClrScr;
  assign (DataFile, 'Names.DAT');
  reset (DataFile);
  GetData (Name1);
  GetData (Name2);
  Alphabetize (Name1, Name2);
  PrintData (Name1, Name2);
  readln;
  close (DataFile)
END.  {  of main program  }
```

Strings as Parameters

7.0 Using strings as parameters in procedure calls requires some caution. When variable parameters are used, the actual parameter used in the procedure call must be identical to the variable formal parameter used in the procedure. To illustrate, consider the definition and declaration

```
TYPE
  String20 = string [20];
VAR
  LastName : String20;
```

If we have a procedure GetData with the procedure heading

```
PROCEDURE GetData (VAR Surname : String20);
```

a program statement such as

```
GetData (LastName);
```

is acceptable because LastName and Surname are identical in type. However, if the procedure heading is

```
PROCEDURE GetData (VAR Surname : string);
```

the program statement

```
GetData (LastName);
```

results in a type-compatibility error. In this case, the variable formal parameter Surname is compatible with the actual parameter LastName but not identical to it.

When value parameters are used in procedures in place of variable parameters, it is only necessary that the actual and formal parameters be compatible. Thus, a procedure heading

```
PROCEDURE StringPrac (Surname : string);
```

allows the statement

```
StringPrac (LastName);
```

Why are we so concerned about the use of strings as parameters? Since we can always use type **string,** why not just do so and not worry about compatibile versus identical types? Part of the problem is the portability and expandability of the program. Variable parameters that are not identical may be encountered if other procedures are used or libraries are accessed.

Fortunately, Turbo Pascal provides a solution to this problem. The compiler directive {$V–} enables the user to bypass strict type checking for string variables. Thus, an actual parameter and a variable formal parameter need only be compatible. This means the use of string types such as **string** [20] or **string** does not interfere with access to any other string type in a procedure, as long as the compiler directive {$V–} is active.

Exercises 7.5

1. Indicate whether the following string comparisons are **true** or **false**.

   a. `'Mathematics' <> 'CompScience'`

   b. `'Jefferson' < 'Jeffersonian'`

   c. `'Smith Karen' < 'Smithsonian'`

   d. `'#45' <= '$45'`

   e. `'Hoof in mouth' = 'Foot in door'`

   f. `'453012' > '200000'`

2. Write a test program that allows you to examine the Boolean expression

   `'William Joe' < 'Williams Bo'`

3. Suppose Message is declared as

```
TYPE
  String50 = string [50];
VAR
  Message : String50;
```

   and the input file consists of the line

   `To err is human. Computers do not forgive.`

   What output is produced by each of the following segments?

   a.
```
FOR J := 1 TO 50 DO
  IF NOT eoln(Data) THEN
    read (Data, Message[J])
  ELSE
    Message[J] := ' ';
writeln (Message);
```

   b.
```
FOR J := 1 TO 50 DO
  IF NOT eoln(Data) THEN
    read (Data, Message[J])
  ELSE
    Message[J] := ' ';
Count := 0;
FOR J := 1 TO 50 DO
  IF Message[J] = ' ' THEN
    Count := Count + 1;
writeln (Message);
writeln ('There are', Count:3,
         'blanks.':8);
```

   c.
```
FOR J := 1 TO 20 DO
  read (Data, Message[2+J]);
FOR J := 21 TO 40 DO
  Message[J] := ' ';
FOR J := 41 TO 50 DO
  Message[J] := '*';
writeln (Message);
```

   d.
```
FOR J := 1 TO 50 DO
  IF NOT eoln(Data) THEN
    read (Data, Message[J])
  ELSE
    Message[J] := ' ';
writeln (Message);
FOR J := 50 DOWNTO 1 DO
  write (Message[J]);
```

4. Write a short program that prompts the user to enter three names. Output should consist of two lists: one with the names displayed in alphabetical order, and one with the names listed according to length.

5. Assume a string Message of length 100 has been declared and data have been read into it from an input file. Write a segment of the code to count the number of occurrences of the letter "M" in the string Message.

7.6 Searching Algorithms

The need to search an array for a value is a common problem. For example, we may wish to replace a test score for a student, delete a name from a directory or mailing list, or upgrade the pay scale for certain employees. These and other problems require us to be able to examine elements in some list until the desired value is located. When it is found, some action is taken. In this section, we assume all lists are nonempty.

Sequential Search

The first searching algorithm we will examine is the most common method, a *sequential (linear) search.* This process is accomplished by examining the first element in some list and then proceeding to examine the elements in the order in which they appear until a match is found. Variations of this basic process include searching a sorted list for the first occurrence of a value, searching a sorted list for all occurrences of a value, and searching an unsorted list for the first occurrence of a value.

To illustrate a sequential search, suppose we have an array A of integers and we want to find the first occurrence of some particular value (Num). If the desired value is located as we search the array, its position should be printed. If the value is not in the array, an appropriate message should be printed. The code for such a search is

```
Index := 1;
WHILE (Num <> A[Index]) AND (Index < Length) DO
  Index := Index + 1;
```

A reasonable message for output is

```
IF Num = A[Index] THEN
  writeln (Num, ' is in position', Index:5)
ELSE
  writeln (Num, ' is not in the list.')
```

Now let's consider some variations of this problem. Our code works for both a sorted and an unsorted list. However, if we are searching a sorted list, the algorithm can be improved. For example, if the array components are sorted from low to high, we need to continue the search only until the value in an array component exceeds the value of Num. At that point, there is no need to examine the remaining components. The only change required in the loop for searching is to replace

```
Num <> A[Index]
```

with

```
Num > A[Index]
```

Thus, we have

```
Index := 1;
WHILE (Num > A[Index]) AND (Index < Length) DO
  Index := Index + 1;
```

A relatively easy modification of the sequential search is to examine a list for all occurrences of some value. In searching an array, we would generally print the positions and values when a match is found. To illustrate, if A is an array of integers and Num has an integer value, we can search A for the number of occurrences of Num by

```
Count := 0;
FOR Index := 1 TO Length DO
  IF Num = A[Index] THEN
    BEGIN
      Count := Count + 1;
      writeln (Num, ' is in position', Index:5)
    END;
```

This code works for an unsorted list. A modification of the code for working with a sorted list is included as an exercise.

Binary Search

Searching relatively small lists sequentially does not require much computer time. However, when the lists get longer (for example, telephone directories and lists of credit-card customers), sequential searches are inefficient. In a sense, they correspond to looking up a word in the dictionary by starting at the first word and proceeding word-by-word until the desired word is found. Since extra computer time means considerably extra expense for most companies where large amounts of data must be frequently searched, a more efficient way of searching is needed.

If the list to be searched has been sorted, it can be searched for a particular value by a method referred to as a binary search. Essentially, a *binary search* consists of examining the middle value of an array to see which half contains the desired value. The middle value of this half is then examined to see which half of the half contains the value in question. This halving process is continued until the value is located or it is determined that the value is not in the list. (Remember, however, in order to use a binary search, the list must be sorted; the sorting process has its own costs, which should be evaluated, but this subject is outside the scope of this text.)

The code for this process is relatively short. If A is the array to be searched for Num, and First, Mid, and Last are integer variables such that First contains the index of the first possible position to be searched and Last contains the index of the last possible position, the code for a list in ascending order is

```
Found := false;
WHILE NOT Found AND (First <= Last) DO
  BEGIN
    Mid := (First + Last) DIV 2;
    IF Num < A[Mid] THEN
      Last := Mid - 1
```

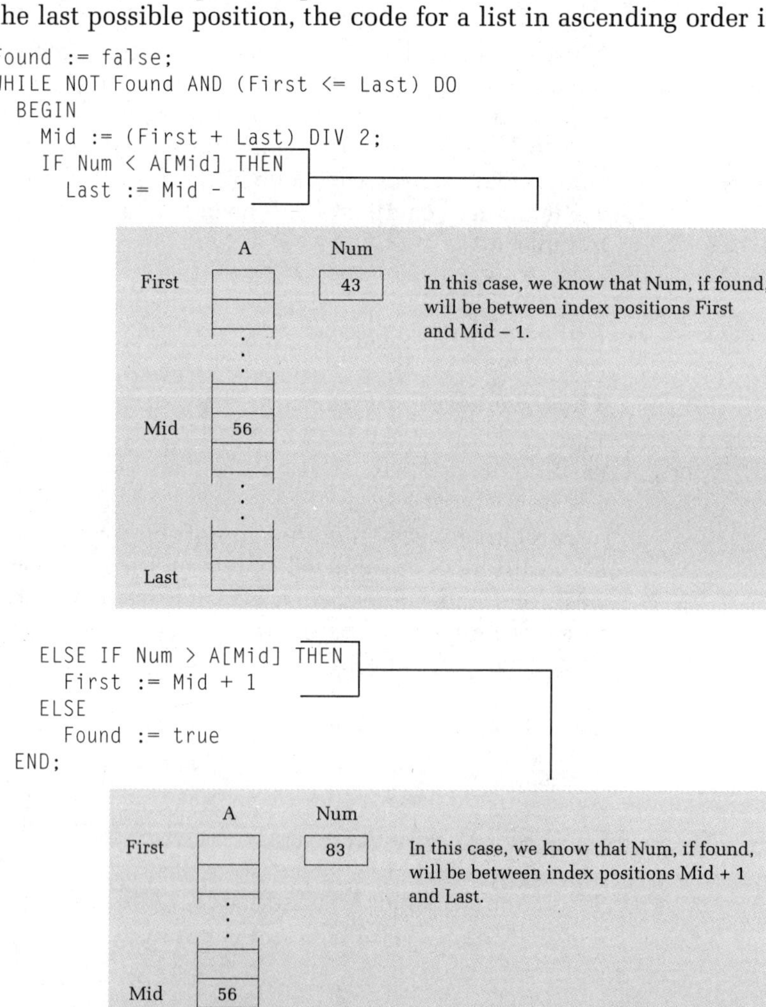
A
Num
First
43
In this case, we know that Num, if found, will be between index positions First and Mid – 1.
Mid
56
Last

```
    ELSE IF Num > A[Mid] THEN
      First := Mid + 1
    ELSE
      Found := true
  END;
```

A
Num
First
83
In this case, we know that Num, if found, will be between index positions Mid + 1 and Last.
Mid
56
Last

When this loop is executed, it is exited when the value is located or it is determined that the value is not in the list. Depending upon what is to be done with the value being looked for, we can modify action at the bottom of the loop or use the values in Found and Mid outside the loop. For example, if we just want to know where the value is, we can change

```
Found := true
```

to

```
BEGIN
  Found := true;
  writeln (Num, ' is in position', Mid:5)
END;
```

Before continuing, let's walk through this search to better understand how it works. Assume A is the array

4	7	19	25	36	37	50	100	101	205	220	271	306	321
A[1]													A[14]

with values as indicated. Furthermore, assume Num contains the value 25. Then First, Last, and Num have the initial values

1	14	25
First	Last	Num

A listing of values by each pass through the loop produces

	First	Last	Mid	A[Mid]	Found
Before loop	1	14	Undefined	Undefined	**false**
After first pass	1	6	7	50	**false**
After second pass	4	6	3	19	**false**
After third pass	4	4	5	36	**false**
After fourth pass	4	4	4	25	**true**

To illustrate what happens when the value being looked for is not in the array, suppose Num contains 210. The listing of values then produces

	First	Last	Mid	A[Mid]	Found
Before loop	1	14	Undefined	Undefined	**false**
After first pass	8	14	7	50	**false**
After second pass	8	10	11	220	**false**
After third pass	10	10	9	101	**false**
After fourth pass	11	10	10	205	**false**

At this stage, First > Last and the loop is exited.

Inserting and Deleting in a Sorted Array

Arrays are typically searched because we want to either insert an element into the array or delete an element from the array. To illustrate, let's consider array A

2	5	8	10	10	12	15	18	21	30
A[1]	A[2]								A[10]

If we remove the element 12 from the array, we end up with

2	5	8	10	10	15	18	21	30
A[1]	A[2]							A[9]

Note 12 has been deleted from the array and then elements listed "after" 12 in the array have been "advanced" one position.

To illustrate what happens when an element is to be inserted into an array, again consider the array A

2	5	8	10	10	12	15	18	21	30
A[1]	A[2]								A[10]

If we want to insert 17 into the sorted array, we first determine it belongs between 15 and 18. We then reassign elements 18, 21, and 30 to produce

2	5	8	10	10	12	15		18	21	30
A[1]	A[2]						↑ 17 goes here			A[11]

The number 17 is then assigned to the appropriate array component to produce the array

2	5	8	10	10	12	15	17	18	21	30
A[1]	A[2]									A[11]

Writing the code for inserting and deleting elements in a sorted array is deferred to the exercises at the end of this section.

Relative Efficiency of Searches

Now let's examine briefly the efficiency of a binary search compared to a sequential search. For purposes of discussion, assume a sequential search on a list of 15 items requires at most 15 microseconds. The nature of a sequential search is such that every time the list length is doubled, the maximum searching time is also doubled; Figure 7.1 illustrates this increase.

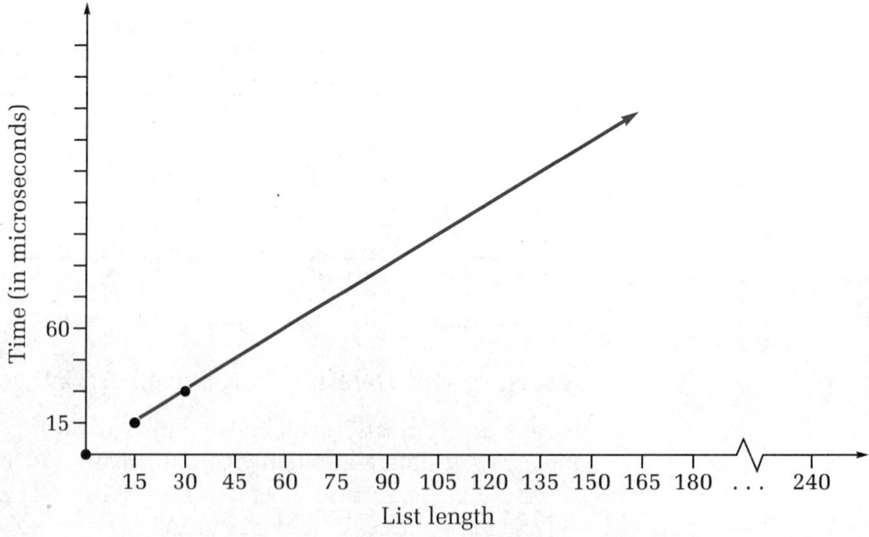

FIGURE 7.1
Sequential search

Next, assume a list of 15 items requires a maximum of 60 microseconds when searched by a binary search. Since this process consists of successively halving the list, at most four passes will be required to locate the value. This means each pass uses 15 microseconds. When the list length is doubled, it requires only one more pass. Thus, a list of 30 items requires 75 microseconds and a list of 60 items requires 90 microseconds. This is shown graphically in Figure 7.2. The comparison of these sequential and binary searches is shown on the graph in Figure 7.3.

FIGURE 7.2
Binary search

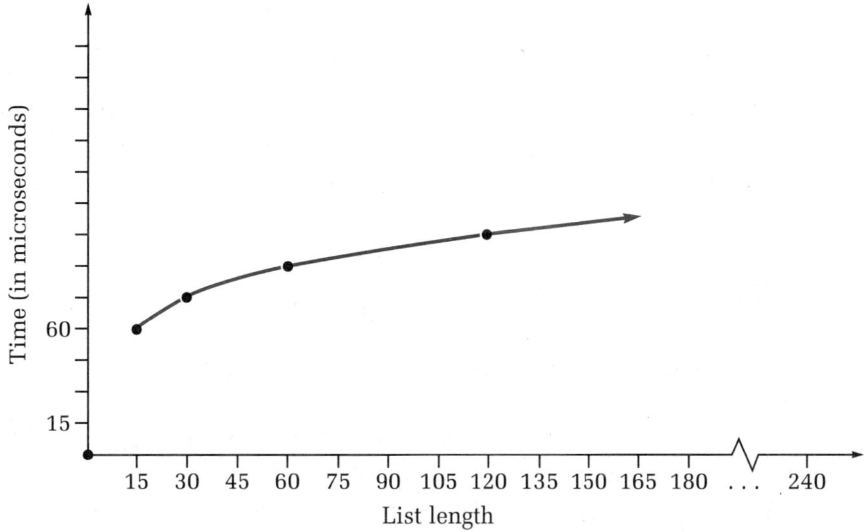

FIGURE 7.3
Sequential search versus binary search

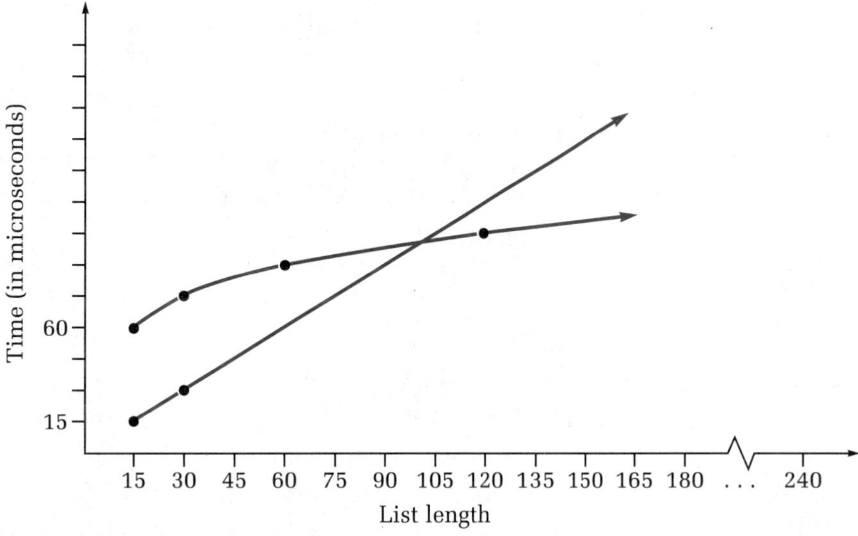

Exercises 7.6

1. Write a sequential search using a **FOR** loop to locate and print all occurrences of the same value.
2. Write a procedure for the sequential search, and show how it can be called from the main program.
3. Modify the sequential search by putting a counter in the loop to count how many passes are made when searching a sorted array for a value. Write and

run a program that uses this version on lists of length 15, 30, 60, 120, and 240. In each case, search for a value that is

a. In the first half b. In the second half c. Not there

and plot your results on a graph.

4. Repeat Exercise 3 for a binary search.
5. Suppose the array A is

18	25	37	92	104
A[1]				A[5]

Trace the values using a binary search to look for

a. 18 b. 92 c. 76

6. Write a procedure to search a sorted list and remove all duplicates.
7. Suppose a sorted list of social security numbers is in secondary storage in a file named StudentNum.
    a. Show how this file can be searched for a certain number using a sequential search.
    b. Show how this file can be searched for a certain number using a binary search.
    c. Show how a binary search can be used to indicate where a new number can be inserted in proper order.
    d. Show how a number can be deleted from the file.
8. Write a procedure to read text from a data file and determine the number of occurrences of each vowel.
9. Using a binary search on an array of length 35, what is the maximum number of passes through the loop that can be made when searching for a value?
10. Using worst-case possibilities of 3 microseconds for a sequential search of a list of 10 items and 25 microseconds for a binary search of the same list, construct a graph illustrating the relative efficiency of these two methods applied to lists of longer lengths.
11. Modify the sequential search you developed in Exercise 1 to list all occurrences of a value so it can be used on a sorted list; that is, have the search stop after the desired value has been passed in the list.
12. Discuss methods that can be used to design programs to guard against searching empty lists.
13. Write a section of code for each of the following.
    a. Insert an element into a sorted array.
    b. Delete an element from a sorted array.
14. The length of a string is the number of positions from the first nonblank character to the last nonblank character. Thus, the packed array

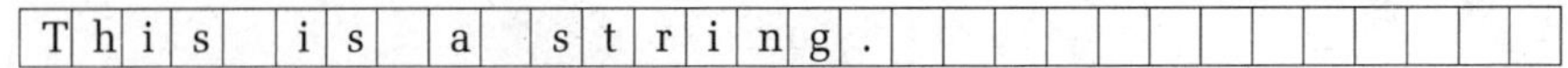

would have length = 17. Write a function that receives a packed array of type [1 . . 30] of **char** and returns the length of the string.

FOCUS ON PROGRAM DESIGN

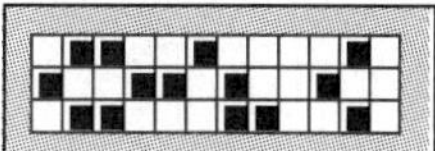

The sample program for this chapter features the use of arrays and subprograms. Since sorting an array is a common practice, it has been included as part of the program. Specifically, suppose the Home Sales Realty Company, Inc., wants to print a list containing the amounts of all sales for a month. Each sale amount is recorded on a separate line of input, and the number of homes sold is < 20. Write a program to do the following:

1. Read the data from the input file.
2. Print the data in the order in which it is read and a suitable header and format.
3. Print a sorted list (high to low) of sales and a suitable heading and format.
4. Print the total number of sales for the month, the total amount of sales, the average sale price, and the company commission (7 percent).

Sample input would be

```
 85000
 76234
115100
 98200
121750
 76700
```

where each line represents the sale price of a home. Typical output would include an unsorted list of sales, a sorted list of sales, and appropriate summary data.

A first-level pseudocode development is

1. Get data (**PROCEDURE** GetData)
2. Print heading (**PROCEDURE** PrintH1)
3. Print unsorted list (**PROCEDURE** PrintList)
4. Sort list (**PROCEDURE** Sort)
5. Print heading (**PROCEDURE** PrintH2)
6. Print sorted list (**PROCEDURE** PrintList)
7. Compute data (**FUNCTION** Total and **PROCEDURE** Compute)
8. Print results (**PROCEDURE** PrintResults)

Notice **PROCEDURE** PrintList is called twice and **PROCEDURE** PrintResults includes output for total number of sales, total amount of sales, average sale price, and company commission. These are printed with suitable headings. A structure chart for the program is given in Figure 7.4.

FIGURE 7.4
Structure chart for Home Sales Realty Company, Inc., program

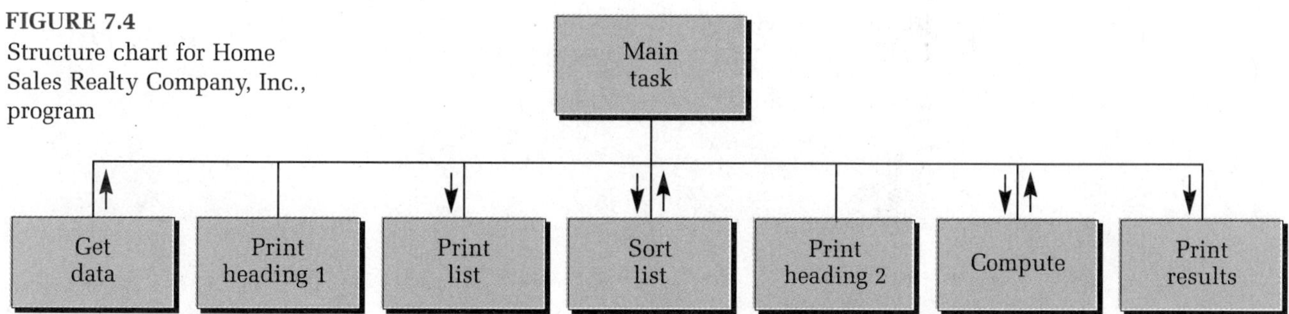

Module specifications for the main modules are

1. GetData Module
   Data received: None
   Information returned: Sales for a month
   Number of sales
   Logic: Use a **WHILE** loop to read entries into an array.
2. PrintHeading1 Module
   Data received: None
   Information returned: None
   Logic: Use **writeln** statements to print a suitable heading for the unsorted list.
3. PrintList Module
   Data received: Array of sales with number of sales
   Information returned: None
   Logic: Use a **FOR** loop with the array length as a loop control variable to print the list of sales for a month.
4. Sort Module
   Data received: Unsorted array of sales
   Number of sales
   Information returned: Sorted array of sales
   Logic: Use a selection sort to sort the array.
5. PrintHeading2 Module
   Data received: None
   Information returned: None
   Logic: Use **writeln** statements to print a suitable heading for the sorted list.
6. Compute Module
   Data received: Array of sales with number of sales
   Information returned: Total sales
   Average sale
   Company commission
   Logic: Use a function to compute the total sales.
   Use a procedure to compute the average sale.
   Compute company commission by using a defined constant, CommissionRate.
7. PrintResults Module
   Data recieved: Number of sales
   Total sales
   Average sale
   Company commission
   Information returned: None
   Logic: Use **writeln** statements to print a summary report.

The main program is

```
BEGIN  { Main program }
  ClrScr;
  assign (SalesList, 'Sales.DAT');
  reset (SalesList);
  GetData (JuneSales, Length);
  PrintHeading1;
  PrintList (JuneSales, Length);
  Sort (JuneSales, Length);
  PrintHeading2;
  PrintList (JuneSales, Length);
  Compute (TotalSales, AverageSale, CompanyCom, JuneSales, Length);
```

```
  PrintResults (TotalSales, AverageSale, CompanyCom, Length);
  readln;
  close (SalesList)
END.  {  of main program  }
```

The complete program for this problem is

```
PROGRAM MonthlyList;

{  This program illustrates the use of arrays with procedures and  }
{  functions.  Note the use of both value and variable parameters. }
{  Also note a procedure is used to sort the array.                }

USES
  Crt;

CONST
  Skip = ' ';
  CommissionRate = 0.07;
  MaxLength = 20;

TYPE
  List = ARRAY [1..MaxLength] OF real;

VAR
  JuneSales : List;                    {  Number of June sales       }
  TotalSales,                          {  Total of June sales        }
  AverageSale,                         {  Amount of average sale     }
  CompanyCom : real;                   {  Commission for the company }
  Length : integer;                    {  Array length of values     }
  SalesList : text;                    {  Data file of sales         }

{*****************************************************************}

PROCEDURE GetData (VAR JuneSales : List;
                   VAR Length : integer);

  {  Given:   Nothing                                              }
  {  Task:    Read selling prices into array JuneSales             }
  {  Return:  Array of JuneSales and array length                  }

  BEGIN                                                                  1
    Length := 0;
    WHILE NOT eof(SalesList) AND (Length < MaxLength) DO
      BEGIN
        Length := Length + 1;
        readln (SalesList, JuneSales[Length])
      END  {  of WHILE NOT eof  }
  END;  {  of PROCEDURE GetData  }

{*****************************************************************}

PROCEDURE PrintHeading1;

  {  Given:   Nothing                                              }
  {  Task:    Print a heading for the unsorted list of sales       }
  {  Return:  Nothing                                              }

  BEGIN                                                                  2
    writeln ('An unsorted list of sales for the');
    writeln ('month of June is as follows:');
    writeln ('---------------------------------');
    writeln
  END;  {  of PROCEDURE PrintHeading1  }
```

```
{*******************************************************************}

PROCEDURE PrintList (JuneSales : List;
                     Length : integer);

  {  Given:   An unsorted array (with length) of sales for June     }
  {  Task:    Print the list                                        }
  {  Return:  Nothing                                               }
                                                                        3
  VAR
    J : integer;
  BEGIN
    FOR J := 1 TO Length DO
      writeln (Skip:4, '<', J:2, '>', '$':2, JuneSales[J]:11:2)
  END;  {  of PROCEDURE PrintList  }

{*******************************************************************}

PROCEDURE Sort (VAR JuneSales : List;
                Length : integer);

  {  Given:   An unsorted array (with length) of sales for June     }
  {  Task:    Use a selection sort to sort the list                 }
  {  Return:  A sorted list of sales for June                       }

  VAR
    J, K, Index : integer;
    Temp : real;
  BEGIN
    FOR J := 1 TO Length - 1 DO
      BEGIN                                                             4
        Index := J;
        FOR K := J + 1 TO Length DO
          IF JuneSales[K] > JuneSales[Index] THEN
            Index := K;
        IF Index <> J THEN
          BEGIN
            Temp := JuneSales[Index];
            JuneSales[Index] := JuneSales[J];
            JuneSales[J] := Temp
          END  {  of exchange  }
      END  {   of FOR J loop   }
  END;  {   of PROCEDURE Sort  }

{*******************************************************************}

PROCEDURE PrintHeading2;

  {  Given:   Nothing                                               }
  {  Task:    Print a heading for the sorted list of sales          }
  {  Return:  Nothing                                               }

  BEGIN
    writeln;                                                            5
    writeln ('Sales for the month of June');
    writeln ('sorted from high to low are:');
    writeln ('-----------------------------');
    writeln
  END;  {  of PROCEDURE PrintHeading2  }

{*******************************************************************}
```

```
FUNCTION Total (JuneSales : List;
                Length : integer) : real;

  {  Given:   An array (with length) of sales for June           }
  {  Task:    Sum the array components                           }
  {  Return:  Total of sales for June                            }

  VAR
    J : integer;
    Sum : real;
  BEGIN
    Sum := 0;
    FOR J := 1 TO Length DO
      Sum := Sum + JuneSales[J];
    Total := Sum
  END;  {  of FUNCTION Total  }

{*******************************************************************}   6

PROCEDURE Compute (VAR TotalSales, AverageSale, CompanyCom : real;
                   VAR JuneSales : List;
                   Length : integer);

  {  Given:   An array (with length) of sales for June           }
  {  Task:    Compute TotalSales, AverageSale, and CompanyCom     }
  {               for the month of June                          }
  {  Return:  TotalSales, AverageSale, and CompanyCom             }

  BEGIN
    TotalSales  := Total(JuneSales, Length);
    AverageSale := TotalSales / Length;
    CompanyCom  := TotalSales * CommissionRate
  END;  {  of PROCEDURE Compute  }

{*******************************************************************}

PROCEDURE PrintResults (TotalSales, AverageSale, CompanyCom : real;
                        Length : integer);

  {  Given:   TotalSales, AverageSale, CompanyCom, and number     }
  {               of sales (Length) for June                     }
  {  Task:    Print summary information for the month           }
  {  Return:  Nothing                                            }

  BEGIN
    writeln;
    writeln ('There were', Length:2, ' sales during June.');   7
    writeln;
    writeln ('The total sales were', '$':2, TotalSales:12:2);
    writeln;
    writeln ('The average sale was', '$':2, AverageSale:12:2);
    writeln;
    writeln ('The company commission was', '$':2, CompanyCom:12:2);
    writeln
  END;  {  of PROCEDURE PrintResults  }

{*******************************************************************}

BEGIN  {  Main program  }
  ClrScr;
  assign (SalesList, 'Sales.DAT');
```

```
  reset (SalesList);
  GetData (JuneSales, Length);
  PrintHeading1;
  PrintList (JuneSales, Length);
  Sort (JuneSales, Length);
  PrintHeading2;
  PrintList (JuneSales, Length);
  Compute (TotalSales, AverageSale, CompanyCom, JuneSales, Length);
  PrintResults (TotalSales, AverageSale, CompanyCom, Length);
  readln;
  close (SalesList)
END.  { of main program }
```

The output for this program is

```
An unsorted list of sales for the
month of June is as follows:
---------------------------------

    < 1> $   85000.00
    < 2> $   76234.00
    < 3> $  115100.00
    < 4> $   98200.00
    < 5> $  121750.00
    < 6> $   76700.00

Sales for the month of June
sorted from high to low are:
----------------------------

    < 1> $  121750.00
    < 2> $  115100.00
    < 3> $   98200.00
    < 4> $   85000.00
    < 5> $   76700.00
    < 6> $   76234.00

There were 6 sales during June.

The total sales were $   572984.00

The average sale was $    95497.33

The company commission was $    40108.88
```

RUNNING AND DEBUGGING HINTS

1. Be careful not to misuse type identifiers. For example, in

```
TYPE
  List = ARRAY [1..100] OF real;
VAR
  Score : List;
```

List is a data type; hence, a reference such as List[5] := 95 is incorrect.

2. Do not attempt to use a subscript that is out of range. For example, given

```
VAR
  List : ARRAY [1..6] OF integer;
```

an inadvertent reference such as

```
FOR J := 1 TO 10 DO
  writeln (List[J]);
```

may produce an error message indicating that the subscript is out of range.

3. Counters are frequently used with loops and arrays. Be sure the final value is the correct value. For example

```
Count := 1;
WHILE NOT eof(<file name>) DO
  BEGIN
    readln (<file name>), (A[Count]);
    Count := Count + 1
  END;
```

used on the data file

18	■	21	■	33	■	■

will have a value of 4 in Count when this loop is exited. This could be corrected by rewriting the segment as

```
Count := 0;
WHILE NOT eof(<file name>) DO
  BEGIN
    Count := Count + 1;
    readln (<file name>), (A[Count])
  END;
```

4. Comparing array components can lead to errors in using subscripts. Two common misuses are shown.
   a. Attempting to compare A[J] to A[J+1]. If this does not stop at array length – 1, then J + 1 will be out of range.
   b. Attempting to compare A[J–1] to A[J]. This presents the same problem at the beginning of an array. Remember, J – 1 cannot have a value less than the initial index value.
5. Make sure the array index is correctly initialized. For example

```
J := 0;
WHILE NOT eof(<file name>) DO
  BEGIN
    J := J + 1;
    readln (<file name>), (A[J])
  END;
```

Note that the first value is then read into A[1].

6. After using a sequential search, make sure you check to see if the value has been found. For example, if Num contains the value 3 and A is the array

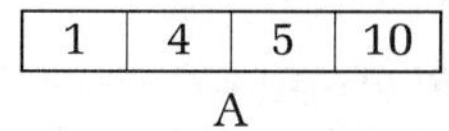

1	4	5	10

A

the search

```
Index := 1;
WHILE (Num <> A[Index]) AND (Index < Length) DO
  Index := Index + 1;
```

yields the values

3	4	10
Num	Index	A[Index]

Depending upon program use, you should check for Num = A[Index] or use a Boolean flag to indicate if a match has been found.

Summary

Key Terms

abstract data type (ADT)
array
binary search
bubble sort
byte
component (element) of an array
data abstraction
index type
packed array
selection sort
sequential (linear) search
subscript (index)
word

Keywords

ARRAY
PACKED

Key Concepts

- An array is a structured variable; a single declaration can reserve several variables.
- It is good practice to define array types in the **TYPE** declaration section and then declare a variable of that type; for example

```
TYPE
  List5 = ARRAY [1..5] OF real;
VAR
  X : List5;
```

- Arrays can be visualized as lists; thus, the previous array could be envisioned as

X	
	1
	2
	3
	4
	5

- Each component of an array is a variable of the declared type and can be used in the same way as any other variable of that type.
- Loops can be used to read data into arrays; for example

```
J := 0;
WHILE NOT eof(<file name>) AND (J < MaxLength) DO
  BEGIN
    J := J + 1;
    readln (<file name>, List[J])
  END;
```

- Loops can be used to print data from arrays; for example, if Score is an array of 20 test scores, they can be printed by

```
FOR J := 1 TO 20 DO
  writeln (Score[J]);
```

- Manipulating components of an array is generally accomplished by using the index as a loop variable; for example, assuming the previous Score, to find the smallest value in the array we can use

```
Small := Score[1];
FOR J := 2 TO 20 DO
  IF Score[J] < Small THEN
    Small := Score[J];
```

- A selection sort is one method of sorting elements in an array from high to low or low to high; for example, if A is an array of length n, a low-to-high sort is

```
FOR J := 1 TO N - 1 DO
  BEGIN
    Index := J;
    FOR K := J + 1 TO N DO
      IF A[K] < A[Index] THEN
        Index := K;
```

```
    IF Index <> J THEN
      BEGIN
        Temp := A[Index];
        A[Index] := A[J];
        A[J] := Temp
      END  { of exchange }
  END;  { of selection sort }
```

- A bubble sort sorts an array by comparing consecutive elements in the array and exchanging them if they are out of order; several passes through the array are made until the list is sorted.
- When arrays are to be passed to subprograms, the type should be defined in the **TYPE** section; thus, we could have

```
TYPE
  List200 = ARRAY [1..200] OF real;

PROCEDURE Practice (X : List200);
```

- If the array being passed is a variable parameter, it should be declared accordingly; for example

```
PROCEDURE GetData (VAR X : List200);
```

- Sorting arrays is conveniently done by using procedures; such procedures facilitate program design.
- Data abstraction is the process of separating a conceptual definition of a data structure from its implementation details.
- An abstract data type (ADT) consists of a class of objects, a defined set of properties for these objects, and a set of operations for processing the objects.
- Character strings can be compared; this facilitates alphabetizing a list of names.
- A sequential search of a list consists of examining the first item in a list and then proceeding through the list in sequence until the desired value is found or the end of the list is reached; code for this search is

```
Index := 1;
WHILE (Num <> A[Index]) AND (Index < Length) DO
  Index := Index + 1;
```

- A binary search of a list consists of deciding which half of the list contains the value in question and then which half of that half contains the value, and so on; code for this search is

```
Found := false;
WHILE NOT Found AND (First <= Last) DO
  BEGIN
    Mid := (First + Last) DIV 2;
    IF Num < A[Mid] THEN
      Last := Mid - 1
    ELSE IF Num > A[Mid] THEN
      First := Mid + 1
    ELSE
      Found := true
  END;
```

■ Programming Problems and Projects

1. Write a program to read an unknown number of integer test scores from an input file (assume at most 150 scores). Print out the original list of scores, the scores sorted from low to high, the scores sorted from high to low, the highest score, the lowest score, and the average score.
2. Write a program to help you balance your checkbook. The input should consist of the beginning balance and then a sequence of transactions, each followed by a transaction code. Deposits should be followed by a D and withdrawals by a W. The output should consist of a list of transactions, a

running balance, an ending balance, the number of withdrawals, and the number of deposits. Include an appropriate message for overdrawn accounts.

3. Write a program to read a line of text as input. Print out the original line of text, the line of text in reverse order, and the number of vowels contained in the line.
4. Write a program that sorts data of type **real** as it is read from the input file. Do this by putting the first data item in the first component of an array and then inserting each subsequent number in the array in order from high to low. Print out the sorted array. Assume there are at most 25 numbers.
5. A palindrome is a word (or number) that is the same forward and backward. Write a program to read several lines of text as input. Inspect each word to see if it is a palindrome. The output should list all palindromes and a count of the number of palindromes in the message.
6. One of the problems faced by designers of word processors is to print text without separating a word at the end of a line. Write a program to read several lines of text as input. Then print the message with each line starting in column 10 and no line exceeding column 70. No word should be separated at the end of a line.
7. Your local state university has to raise funds for an art center. As a first step, they are going to approach 20 previously identified donors and ask for additional donations. Because the donors wish to remain anonymous, only the respective totals of their previous donations are listed in a data file. After they are contacted, the additional donations are listed at the end of the data file in the same order as the first 20 entries. Write a computer program to read the first 20 entries into one array and the second 20 entries into a second array. Compute the previous total donations and the new donations for the art center. Print the following.
   a. The list of previous donations
   b. The list of new donations
   c. An unsorted list of total donations
   d. A sorted list of total donations
   e. Total donations before the fund drive
   f. Total donations for the art center
   g. The maximum donation for the art center
8. Write a program that can be used as a text analyzer. Your program should be capable of reading an input file and keeping track of the frequency of occurrence of each letter of the alphabet. There should also be a count of all characters (including blanks) encountered that are not in the alphabet. Your output should be the data file (printed line-by-line) followed by a histogram reflecting the frequency of occurrence of each letter in the alphabet. For example, the following histogram indicates five occurrences of a, two of b, and three of c:

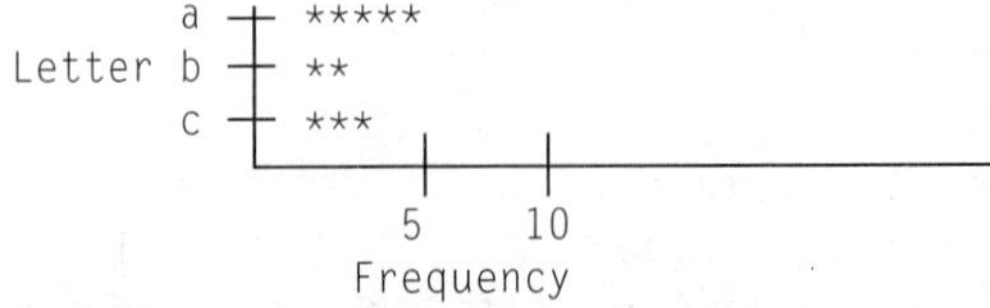

9. The Third Interdenominational Church has on file a list of all of its benefactors (a maximum of 20 names, each up to 30 characters) and an unknown number of amounts that each has donated to the church. You have been asked to write a program that does the following.

a. Print the name of each donor and the amount (in descending order) of any donations given by each.
b. Print the total amounts in ascending order.
c. Print the grand total of all donations.
d. Print the largest single amount donated and the name of the benefactor who made this donation.

10. Read in a list of 50 integers from the data file NumberList. Place the even numbers into an array called Even, the odd numbers into an array called Odd, and the negatives into an array called Negative. Print all three arrays after all numbers have been read.
11. Read in 300 real numbers. Print the average of the numbers followed by all the numbers that are greater than the average.
12. Read in the names of five candidates in a class election and the number of votes received by each. Print the list of candidates, the number of votes each received, and the percentage of the total vote they received sorted into order from the winner to the person with the fewest votes.
13. In many sports events, contestants are rated by judges, with an average score being determined by discarding the highest and lowest scores and averaging the remaining scores. Write a program in which eight scores are entered and the average score for a contestant is computed.
14. Given a list of 20 test scores (integers), print the score that is nearest to the average.
15. The Game of Nim is played with three piles of stones. There are three stones in the first pile, five stones in the second, and eight stones in the third. Two players alternate taking as many stones as they like from any one pile. Play continues until someone is forced to take the last stone. The person taking the last stone loses. Write a program that permits two people to play the game of Nim using an array to keep track of the number of stones in each pile.
16. There is an effective strategy that can virtually guarantee victory in the game of Nim. Devise a strategy and modify the program in Problem 15 so that the computer plays against a person. Your program should be virtually unbeatable if the proper strategy is developed.
17. The median of a set of numbers is the value in the middle of the set if the set is arranged in order. The mode is the number listed most often. Given a list of 21 numbers, print the median and mode of the list.
18. Rewrite Problem 17 to permit the use of any length list of numbers.
19. The standard deviation is a statistic frequently used in education measurement. Write a program that, given a list of test scores, will find and print the standard deviation of the numbers. The standard deviation formula can be found in most statistics books.
20. Revise Problem 19 so that after the standard deviation is printed, you can print a list of test scores that are more than one standard deviation below the average and a list of the scores that are more than one standard deviation above the average.
21. The z-score is defined as the score earned on a test divided by the standard deviation. Given a data file containing an unknown number of test scores (maximum of 100), print a list showing each test score (from highest to lowest) and the corresponding z-score.
22. ■ Salespeople for the Wellsville Wholesale Company earn a commission based on their sales. The commission rates are shown in the following table.

Sales	Commission
$0–1000	3%
1001–5000	4.5%
5001–10000	5.25%
over 10000	6%

In addition, any salesperson who sells above the average of all salespeople receive a $50 bonus, and the top salesperson receives an additional $75 bonus.

Given the names of 20 salespeople and the amounts sold by each, write a program that prints a table showing the salesperson's name, the amount sold, the commission rate, and the total amount earned. The average sales should also be printed.

23. Ms. Alicia Citizen, your school's Student Government advisor, has come to you for help. She wants a program to total votes for the next Student Government election. There are 15 candidates running in the election and five positions to be filled. Each person can vote for up to five candidates. The five highest vote getters will be the winners.

    A data file called VoteList contains a list of candidates (by candidate number) voted for by each student. Any linc of the file may contain up to five numbers; if it contains more than five numbers, it is discarded as a void ballot. Write a program to read the file and print a list of the total votes received by each candidate. Also print the five highest vote-getters in order from highest to lowest vote totals.

24. The data file InstructorList contains a list of the instructors in your school along with the room number to which each is assigned. Write a program that, given the name of the instructor, does a linear search to find and print the room to which the instructor is assigned.

25. Rewrite Problem 24 so that, given a room number, the name of the instructor assigned to that room is found by using a binary search. Assume the file is arranged in order of room numbers.

26. Write a language translation program that permits the entry of a word in English and prints the corresponding word in another language. The dictionary words can be stored in parallel arrays, with the English array being sorted into alphabetical order prior to the first entry of a word. Your program should first sort the dictionary words.

27. Elementary and middle school students are often given the task of converting numbers from one base to another. For example, 19 in base 10 is 103 in base 4 ($1 \times 4^2 + 0 \times 4^1 + 3 \times 4^0$). Conversely, 123 in base 4 is 27 in base 10. Write an interactive program that allows the user to choose from the following:

```
<1>  Convert from base 10 to base A
<2>  Convert from base A to base 10
<3>  Quit
```

    If options 1 or 2 are chosen, the user should then enter the intended base and the number to be converted. A sample run of the program would produce the following output.

```
This program allows you to convert between bases.
Which of the following would you like?

     <1>  Convert from base 10 to base A
     <2>  Convert from base A to base 10
     <3>  Quit
```

```
Enter your choice and press <Enter>.
1

Enter the number in base 10 and press <Enter>.
237

Enter the new base and press <Enter>.
4

The number 237 in base 4 is:  3231

Press <Enter> to continue

This program allows you to convert between bases.
Which of the following would you like?
     <1>  Convert from base 10 to base A
     <2>  Convert from base A to base 10
     <3>  Quit

Enter your choice and press <Enter>.
2

What number would you like to have converted?
2332

Converting to base 10, we get:

     2 *    1 =          2
     3 *    4 =         12
     3 *   16 =         48
     2 *   64 =        128
                     -----
The base 10 value is   190

Press <Enter> to continue

This program allows you to convert between bases.
Which of the following would you like?

     <1>  Convert from base 10 to base A
     <2>  Convert from base A to base 10
     <3>  Quit

Enter your choice and press <Enter>.
3
```

■ Communication in Practice

1. Write a short paper containing the following.
   a. A description of the selection sort
   b. A description of the bubble sort
   c. A discussion of the advantages and disadvantages of each sort
2. Prospective high school teachers are often faced with the challenge of creating classroom demonstrations to illustrate various concepts and processes. Assume you are working with prospective teachers to develop a complete scenario that allows students to "walk through" a demonstration of the bubble sort. For purposes of illustration, you might have randomly selected students stand in front of the class and then use the bubble sort to sort them according to height. Write a complete description of the demonstration, including how it can be incorporated in a classroom setting.
3. One of the principles underlying the concept of data abstraction is that implementation details of data structures should be deferred to the lowest

possible level. To illustrate, consider the high-level design to which we referred in our previous discussion of data abstraction. Our program required you to work with a list of student names and an associated list of test scores. The following first-level design was suggested:

1. GetNames (⟨procedure here⟩);
2. GetScores (⟨procedure here⟩);
3. SortByName (⟨procedure here⟩);
4. PrintNamesAndScores (⟨procedure here⟩);
5. SortByScore (⟨procedure here⟩);

Write complete documentation for each of these modules, including a description of all parameters and data structures required. Present your documentation to the class. Ask if your classmates have questions about the number or type of parameters, the data structures required, and/or the main tasks to be performed by each module.

4. Contact programmers at your university and/or some businesses, and discuss with them the use of lists as a data type. Ask what kinds of programming problems require the use of a list, how the programmers handle data entry (list length), and what operations they perform on the list (search, sort, and so on). Give an oral report of your findings to the class.
5. Select a programming problem from this chapter that you have not yet worked. Construct a structure chart and write all documentary information necessary for the problem you have chosen. Do not write code. When you are finished, have a classmate read your documentation to see if it makes clear precisely what is to be done.

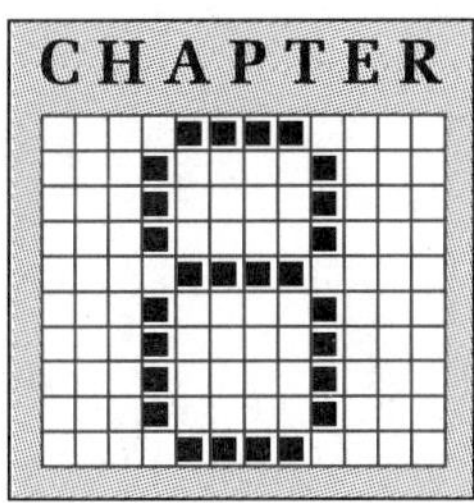

Arrays of More Than One Dimension

■ CHAPTER OUTLINE ■

Chapter 7 illustrated the significance and uses of one-dimensional arrays. There are, however, several kinds of problems that require arrays of more than one dimension. For example, if we want to work with a table that has both rows and columns, a one-dimensional array will not suffice. Such problems can be solved using arrays of more than one dimension.

■ 8.1 Two-Dimensional Arrays

Basic Idea and Notation

One-dimensional arrays are very useful when working with a row or column of numbers. However, suppose we want to work with data that are best represented in tabular form. For example, box scores in baseball are reported with one player name listed for each row and one statistic listed for each column. Another example is an instructor's grade book in which a student name is listed for each row and test and/or quiz scores are listed for each column. In both cases, a multiple reference is needed for a single data item.

Turbo Pascal accomplishes multiple reference by using *two-dimensional arrays*. In these arrays, the row subrange always precedes the column subrange and the two subranges are separated by commas. To illustrate, suppose we want to print the table

1	2	3	4
2	4	6	8
3	6	9	12

where we need to access both the row and column for a single data entry. This table could be produced by either of the following declarations.

1. ```
   VAR
     Table : ARRAY [1..3, 1..4] OF integer;
   ```
2. ```
   TYPE
     Matrix = ARRAY [1..3, 1..4] OF integer;
   VAR
     Table : Matrix;
   ```

The index [1 . . 3, 1 . . 4] of each of these declarations differs from one-dimensional arrays. These declarations reserve memory that can be visualized as three rows, each of which holds four variables. Thus, 12 variable locations have been reserved, as shown.

Table

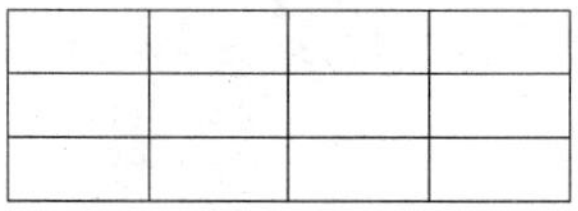

As a second illustration of the use of two-dimensional arrays, suppose we want to print the batting statistics for a softball team of 15 players. If the statistics consist of at bats (AB), hits (H), runs (R), and runs batted in (RBI) for each player, we naturally choose to work with a 15 × 4 table. Hence, a reasonable variable declaration is

```
TYPE
  Table15X4 = ARRAY [1..15, 1..4] OF integer;
VAR
  Stats : Table15X4;
```

The reserved memory area can be visualized as

Stats

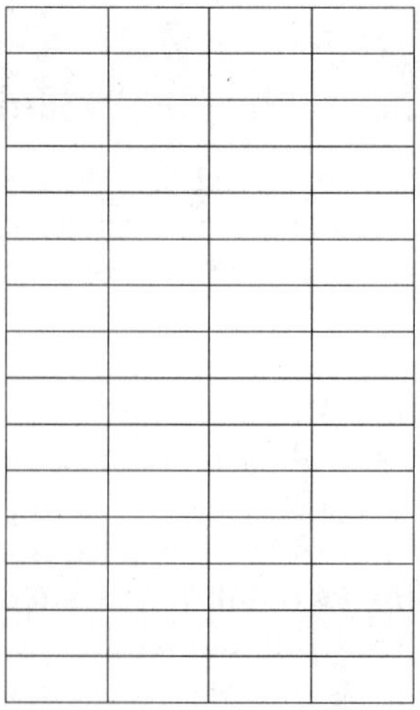

with 60 variable locations reserved.

Before proceeding further, let's examine another method of declaring two-dimensional arrays. Our 3 × 4 table could be thought of as three arrays, each of length four, as follows:

Hence, we have a list of arrays and we could declare the table by

```
TYPE
  Row = ARRAY [1..4] OF integer;
  Matrix = ARRAY [1..3] OF Row;
VAR
  Table : Matrix;
```

The softball statistics could be declared by

```
CONST
  NumberOfStats = 4;
  RosterSize = 15;
TYPE
  PlayerStats = ARRAY [1..NumberOfStats] OF integer;
  TeamTable = ARRAY [1..RosterSize] OF PlayerStats;
VAR
  Stats : TeamTable;
```

Semantic indices could be utilized by

```
TYPE
  Stat = (AtBat, Hits, Runs, RBI);
  StatChart = ARRAY [1..RosterSize, Stat] OF integer;
VAR
  Player : StatChart;
```

In this case, a typical entry would be

```
Player[5, Hits] := 2;
```

In general, a two-dimensional array can be defined by

> **ARRAY** [<row index>, <column index>] **OF** <element type>;
>
> or
>
> **TYPE**
> RowType = **ARRAY** [<column index>] **OF** <element type>;
> Matrix = **ARRAY** [<row index>] **OF** RowType;

Whichever method of declaration is used, the problem now becomes one of accessing individual components of the two-dimensional array. For example, in the table

1	2	3	4
2	4	6	8
3	6	9	12

the 8 is in row 2 and column 4. Note that both the row and column positions of an element must be indicated. Therefore, in order to put an 8 in this position, we use an assignment statement such as

```
Table[2,4] := 8;
```

COMMUNICATION AND STYLE TIPS

When working with charts or tables of a fixed grid size (say 15 × 4), descriptive identifiers could be

```
Chart15X4
```

or

```
Table15X4
```

If the numbers of rows and columns vary for different runs of the program (for example, the number of players on a team could vary from year to year), you could define a type by

```
CONST
  NumRows = 15;
  NumColumns = 4;
TYPE
  RowRange = 1..NumRows;
  ColumnRange = 1..NumColumns;
  Table = ARRAY [RowRange, ColumnRange] OF integer;
VAR
  Stats : Table;
```

This assignment statement could be used with either of the declaration forms mentioned earlier.

Next, let's assign the values just given to the appropriate variables in Table by 12 assignment statements, as follows:

```
Table[1,1] := 1;
Table[1,2] := 2;
Table[1,3] := 3;
Table[1,4] := 4;
Table[2,1] := 2;
Table[2,2] := 4;
Table[2,3] := 6;
Table[2,4] := 8;
Table[3,1] := 3;
Table[3,2] := 6;
Table[3,3] := 9;
Table[3,4] := 12;
```

As you can see, this is extremely tedious. Instead, we can note the relationship between the indices and the assigned values and make the row index Row and the column index Column. The values to be assigned are then Row * Column, and we can use nested loops to perform these assignments, as follows:

```
FOR Row := 1 TO 3 DO
  FOR Column := 1 TO 4 DO
    Table[Row, Column] := Row * Column;
```

Since two-dimensional arrays frequently require working with nested loops, let's examine what this segment of code does more closely. When Row := 1, the loop

```
FOR Column := 1 TO 4 DO
  Table[1, Column] := 1 * Column;
```

is executed. This performs the four assignments

```
Table[1,1] := 1 * 1;
Table[1,2] := 1 * 2;
Table[1,3] := 1 * 3;
Table[1,4] := 1 * 4;
```

and we have the memory area

Table

1	2	3	4

Similar results hold for Row := 2 and Row := 3, and we produce a two-dimensional array that can be visualized as

Table

1	2	3	4
2	4	6	8
3	6	9	12

The following examples will help you learn to work with and understand the notation for two-dimensional arrays.

■ EXAMPLE 8.1

Assume the declaration

```
TYPE
  Table5X4 = ARRAY [1..5, 1..4] OF integer;
VAR
  Table : Table5X4;
```

has been made, and consider the segment of code

```
FOR Row := 1 TO 5 DO
  FOR Column := 1 TO 4 DO
    Table[Row, Column] := Row DIV Column;
```

When Row := 1, the loop

```
FOR Column := 1 TO 4 DO
  Table[1, Column] := 1 DIV Column;
```

is executed, resulting in the assignment statements

```
Table[1,1] := 1 DIV 1;
Table[1,2] := 1 DIV 2;
Table[1,3] := 1 DIV 3;
Table[1,4] := 1 DIV 4;
```

The contents of the memory area after that first pass through the loop are

Table

1	0	0	0

When Row := 2, the assignments are

```
Table[2,1] := 2 DIV 1;
Table[2,2] := 2 DIV 2;
Table[2,3] := 2 DIV 3;
Table[2,4] := 2 DIV 4;
```

Table now has the following values:

Table

1	0	0	0
2	1	0	0

The contents of Table after the entire outside loop has been executed are

Table

1	0	0	0
2	1	0	0
3	1	1	0
4	2	1	1
5	2	1	1

■ EXAMPLE 8.2

Declare a two-dimensional array and write a segment of code to produce the memory area and contents depicted as follows:

2	3	4	5	6	7	8
3	4	5	6	7	8	9
4	5	6	7	8	9	10
5	6	7	8	9	10	11

An appropriate definition is

```
TYPE
  Table4X7 = ARRAY [1..4, 1..7] OF integer;
```

or

```
TYPE
  Table4X7 = ARRAY [1..4] OF
             ARRAY [1..7] OF integer;
VAR
  Table : Table4X7;
```

and a segment of code to produce the desired contents is

```
FOR Row := 1 TO 4 DO
  FOR Column := 1 TO 7 DO
    Table[Row, Column] := Row + Column;
```

Reading and Writing

Most problems using two-dimensional arrays require reading data from an input file into the array and writing values from the array to create some tabular form of output. For example, consider the two-dimensional array for softball statistics

```
TYPE
  Table15X4 = ARRAY [1..15, 1..4] OF integer;
VAR
  Stats : Table15X4;
```

If the data file consists of 15 lines and each line contains statistics for one player as follows,

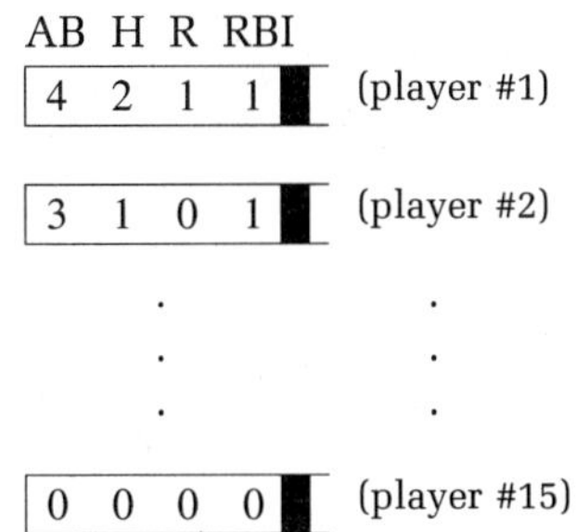

we can get the data from the file by reading it one line at a time for 15 lines. This is done by using nested loops as follows:

```
FOR Row := 1 TO 15 DO
  BEGIN
    FOR Column := 1 TO 4 DO
      read (Stats[Row, Column]);
    readln
  END;
```

When Row := 1, the loop

```
FOR Column := 1 TO 4 DO
  read (Stats[Row, Column]);
```

reads the first line of data. In a similar manner, as Row assumes the values 2 through 15, the lines 2 through 15 are read. After reading the data into an array, some operations and/or updating will be performed and we will output the data in tabular form. For example, suppose we want to print the softball statistics in the 15 × 4 table using only three spaces for each column. We note the following:

1. Three spaces per column can be controlled by formatting the output.
2. One line of output can be generated by a **FOR** loop containing a **write** statement; for example

   ```
   FOR Column := 1 TO 4 DO
     write (Stats[Row, Column]:3);
   ```

3. The output buffer is dumped to the printer after each **write** loop by using **writeln**.
4. We do this for 15 lines by employing another loop:

   ```
   FOR Row := 1 TO 15 DO
     BEGIN
       FOR Column := 1 TO 4 DO
         write (Stats[Row, Column]:3);
       writeln
     END;
   ```

This last segment of code produces the desired output.

In actual practice, we will also be concerned about headings for our tables and controlling where the data occur on the page. For example, suppose we want to identify the columns of softball statistics as AB, H, R, and RBI, underline the headings, and start the output (AB) in column 25. The following segment of code accomplishes our objectives:

```
writeln (Skip:24,'AB H  R RBI');
writeln (Skip:24,'-----------');
writeln;
```

```
FOR Row := 1 TO 15 DO
  BEGIN
    write (Skip:22);  {  Set the left margin  }
    FOR Column := 1 TO 4 DO
      write (Stats[Row, Column]:3);
    writeln  {  Advance to next line  }
  END;
```

The data file used earlier for our ballplayers causes an output of

```
AB H  R RBI
-----------

4  2  1  1
3  1  0  1
   .
   .
   .
0  0  0  0
```

Manipulating Two-Dimensional Array Components

Often we want to work with some but not all of the components of an array. For example, suppose we have a two-dimensional array of test scores for students in a class. If there are 20 students with five scores each, an appropriate two-dimensional array could be declared as

```
TYPE
  Table20X5 = ARRAY [1..20, 1..5] OF integer;
VAR
  Score : Table20X5;
```

After scores have been read into the array Score, we can envision the memory area as follows:

Score

98	86	100	76	95	(student #1)
72	68	65	74	81	(student #2)
85	81	91	84	83	(student #3)
					.
					.
					.
					.
					.
					.
					.
					.
					.
					.
					.
					.
					.
					.
					.
					.
76	81	72	87	80	(student #20)

When printing a table with test scores, it is necessary to compute several items, including total points for each student, percentage grade for each student, and average score for each test. Let's examine what is required for each of these computations. First, to get the total points for each student, we declare a one-dimensional array to store these values, so we can assume the declaration

```
TYPE
  List20 = ARRAY [1..20] OF integer;
VAR
  TotalPoints : List20;
```

Since the first student's test scores are in the first row, we can write

```
TotalPoints[1] := Score[1,1] + Score[1,2] +
                  Score[1,3] + Score[1,4] +
                  Score[1,5];
```

To compute this total for each student, we can use the loop

```
FOR Student := 1 TO 20 DO
  TotalPoints[Student] := Score[Student, 1] +
                          Score[Student, 2] +
                          Score[Student, 3] +
                          Score[Student, 4] +
                          Score[Student, 5];
```

which produces the array of totals

TotalPoints

455	TotalPoints[1]
360	TotalPoints[2]
424	TotalPoints[3]
.	.
.	.
.	.
396	TotalPoints[20]

If the two-dimensional array has several columns, we can use a loop to sum an array of numbers. We can, for instance, write a loop to sum the five test scores for the first student in our table:

```
TotalPoints[1] := 0;
FOR Test := 1 TO 5 DO
  TotalPoints[1] := TotalPoints[1] + Score[1, Test];
```

To do this for each student, we use a second loop:

```
FOR Student := 1 TO 20 DO
  BEGIN
    TotalPoints[Student] := 0;
    FOR Test := 1 TO 5 DO
      TotalPoints[Student] := TotalPoints[Student] +
                              Score[Student, Test]
  END;
```

The second task in our problem is to compute the percentage grade for each student. If we want to save these percentages, we can declare an array as follows:

```
TYPE
  Column20 = ARRAY [1..20] OF real;
VAR
  Percent : Column20;
```

and include a segment of code

```
FOR Student := 1 TO 20 DO
  Percent[Student] := TotalPoints[Student] / 5;
```

The third task is to find the average score for each test. To find these numbers, we need to add all 20 scores for each test and divide the respective total by 20. First, we need to find the sum of each column and declare an array in which to store the averages. The declaration can be

```
TYPE
  List5 = Array [1..5] OF real;
VAR
  TestAv: List5;
```

We now need a loop to find the total of each column. Assuming that an integer variable Sum is declared, we can sum column one by

```
Sum := 0;
FOR Student := 1 TO 20 DO
  Sum := Sum + Score[Student, 1];
```

We can now find the average score by

```
TestAv[1] := Sum / 20;
```

To do this for each column, we can use a second loop:

```
FOR Test := 1 TO 5 DO           {  Test is the column subscript  }
  BEGIN
    Sum := 0;
    FOR Student := 1 TO 20 DO   {  Student is the row subscript  }
      Sum := Sum + Score[Student, Test];
    TestAv[Test] := Sum / 20
  END;
```

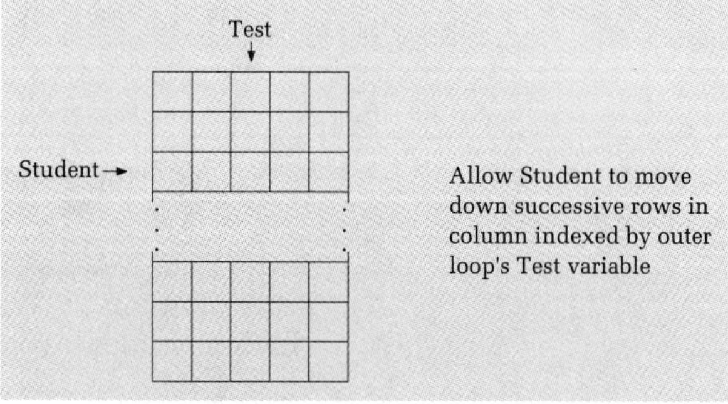
Test
Student
Allow Student to move down successive rows in column indexed by outer loop's Test variable

A concluding example of manipulating elements of two-dimensional arrays follows.

■ EXAMPLE 8.3

Assume we have the declarations

```
CONST
  NumRows = 20;
  NumColumns = 50;
TYPE
  TableSize = ARRAY [1..NumRows,
                     1..NumColumns] OF integer;
  List = ARRAY [1..NumRows] OF integer;
VAR
  Table : TableSize;
  Max : List;
```

and values have been read into the two-dimensional array from an input file. Let's write a segment of code to find the maximum value in each row and then store this value in the array Max. To find the maximum of row one, we can write

```
Max[1] := Table[1,1];
FOR Column := 2 TO NumColumns DO
  IF Table[1, Column] > Max[1] THEN
    Max[1] := Table[1, Column];
```

To do this for each of the rows, we can use a second loop:

```
FOR Row := 1 TO NumRows DO
  BEGIN
    Max[Row] := Table[Row, 1];
    FOR Column := 2 TO NumColumns DO
      IF Table[Row, Column] > Max[Row] THEN
        Max[Row] := Table[Row, Column]
  END;
```

Procedures and Two-Dimensional Arrays

When we start writing programs with two-dimensional arrays, we will use procedures as before to maintain the top-down design philosophy. As with one-dimensional arrays, there are three relatively standard uses of procedures in most problems involving two-dimensional arrays: to get the data, to manipulate the data, and to display the data.

When using procedures with data that require the use of an array as a data structure, the array type must be defined in the **TYPE** section. The actual parameters and formal parameters can then be of the defined array type. As with one-dimensional arrays, we pass two-dimensional arrays by reference to conserve memory allocation.

EXAMPLE 8.4

Western Jeans, Inc., wants to develop a program to keep track of its inventory of jeans. The jeans are coded by waist size and inseam. The waist sizes are the integer values from 24 to 46, and the inseams are the integer values from 26 to 40. Thus, there are 23 waist sizes and 15 inseams for each waist size. The first 23 lines of the data file contain the starting inventory. Each line corresponds to a waist size and contains 15 integers, one for each inseam. The next 23 lines of the data file contain the sales information for a day. Let's write a program to find and print the closing inventory.

A first-level pseudocode development for this program is

1. Get starting inventory
2. Get new sales
3. Update inventory
4. Print heading
5. Print closing inventory

Each of these steps uses a procedure.

Since there are 23 waist sizes and 15 inseams, we can use the following definitions:

```
CONST
  FirstWaist = 24;
  LastWaist = 46;
  FirstInseam = 26;
  LastInseam = 40;
TYPE
  WaistSizes = FirstWaist..LastWaist;
  InseamSizes = FirstInseam..LastInseam;
  Table = ARRAY [WaistSizes, InseamSizes] OF integer;
```

and declare the following variables:

```
VAR
  Inventory : Table;
  Sales : Table;
```

Assuming variables have been declared and constants have been defined as needed, we write the following procedure to get the starting inventory:

```
PROCEDURE GetData (VAR Matrix : Table);
  VAR
    Row, Column : integer;
  BEGIN
    FOR Row := FirstWaist TO LastWaist DO
      BEGIN
        FOR Column := FirstInseam TO LastInseam DO
          read (Data, Matrix[Row, Column]);
        readln (Data)
      END
  END;
```

This procedure can be called from the main program by

```
GetData (Inventory);
```

The next task is to get the sales for a day. Since this merely requires reading the next 23 lines from the data file, we do not need to write a new procedure. We can call GetData again by

```
GetData (Sales);
```

A NOTE OF INTEREST

What the Future Holds in the '90s

Daniel E. Kinnaman, News Editor for *Technology & Learning*, has addressed the issue of technology-literate classrooms in the 1990s. He visited several top research and development programs in search of the most promising projects, products, and ideas related to the future role of technology in the classroom. A partial list of projects, project directors, and summary comments regarding programs follows.

- The Technical Education Research Centers (TERC) and Dr. Robert Tinker are developing programs designed to involve students and teachers from around the world in conducting global ecology research with full-time scientists.
- The Massachusetts Institute of Technology and Dr. Seymour Papert are working on a project involving the development of robotic kits that allow children to build computer intelligence into a robot.
- Harvard's Educational Technology Center (ETC) and Dr. Judah Schwartz are working on software whose purpose is to teach children how to think. One current project is a series called "Visualizing Algebra."
- Institute for Research on Learning (IRL) is working on "Dynagrams," a project that allows students to interact with dynamic diagrams on a computer screen.

In summarizing what these and other educational leaders have to say, Kinneman states,

> *Many of these thinkers hold similar perspectives on the uses of technology in schools—perspectives that strongly influence their development efforts. These common beliefs include the following:*

- All of education, from the physical organization of schools to instructional methods and assessment, needs to be open to review and change.
- Inquiry-centered, process-oriented learning environments in which students are active participants on an academic adventure are heavily favored over the traditional classroom setting.
- There is a decided emphasis, at least presently, on improving math and science education.
- In the 1990s, schools will look to technology more than ever before for educational solutions.
- Although computer power will continue to increase at astounding rates, technology is still just a vehicle. It isn't a destination. It can be a critical ingredient of successful school experience for children, but its usefulness is dependent upon the context in which it is used.

We now need a procedure to update the starting inventory. This updating can be accomplished by sending both two-dimensional arrays to a procedure and then finding the respective differences of components:

```
PROCEDURE Update (VAR Inventory : Table;
                  VAR Sales : Table);
  VAR
    Row, Column : integer;
  BEGIN
    FOR Row := FirstWaist TO LastWaist DO
      FOR Column := FirstInseam TO LastInseam DO
        Inventory[Row, Column] := Inventory[Row, Column] -
                                  Sales[Row, Column]
  END;
```

This is called by the statement

```
Update (Inventory, Sales);
```

The procedure for the heading is the same as before, so we do not need to write it here. Let's assume the arrays have been assigned the necessary values. The output procedure then will be

```
PROCEDURE PrintData (VAR Inventory : Table);
  CONST
    Mark = ' !';
  VAR
    Row, Column : integer;
  BEGIN
    FOR Row := FirstWaist TO LastWaist DO
      BEGIN
        write (Row:6, Mark);
        FOR Column := FirstInseam TO LastInseam DO
          write (Inventory[Row, Column]:4);
        writeln;
        writeln (Mark:6)
      END  {  of printing one row  }
  END;
```

This procedure can be called from the main program by

```
PrintData (Inventory);
```

Once these procedures are written, the main program becomes

```
BEGIN
  assign (Data, 'Sales.DAT');
  reset (Data);
  GetData (Inventory);
  GetData (Sales);
  Update (Inventory, Sales);
  PrintHeading;
  PrintData (Inventory);
  close (Data)
END.  {  of main program  }
```

Exercises 8.1

1. Define a two-dimensional array type for each of the following using both the **ARRAY** [. . , . .] and **ARRAY** [. .] **OF ARRAY** [. .] forms.
   a. A table with real number entries that shows the prices for four different drugs charged by five drug stores.
   b. A table with character entries that shows the grades earned by 20 students in six courses.

c. A table with integer entries that shows the 12 quiz scores earned by 30 students in a class.

2. Write a test program to read integers into a 3 × 5 array and then print out the array components, together with each row sum and each column sum.

3. For each of the following declarations, sketch what is reserved in memory. In each case, state how many variables (memory locations) are available to the programmer.

a.
```
TYPE
  ShippingCostTable = ARRAY [1..10] OF
                      ARRAY [1..4] OF real;
  GradeBookTable = ARRAY [1..35, 1..6] OF integer;
VAR
  ShippingCost : ShippingCostTable;
  GradeBook : GradeBookTable;
```

b.
```
TYPE
  Matrix = ARRAY [1..3, 2..6] OF integer;
VAR
  A : Matrix;
```

c.
```
TYPE
  Weekdays = (Mon, Tues, Wed, Thur, Fri);
  Chores = (Wash, Iron, Clean, Mow, Sweep);
  ScheduleTable = ARRAY [Weekdays, Chores] OF boolean;
VAR
  Schedule : ScheduleTable;
```

d.
```
TYPE
  Questions = 1..50;
  Answers = 1..5;
  Table = ARRAY [Questions, Answers] OF char;
VAR
  AnswerSheet : Table;
```

4. Assume array A has been declared as

```
TYPE
  Table3X5 = ARRAY [1..3, 1..5] OF integer;
VAR
  A : Table3X5;
```

Indicate the array contents produced by each of the following.

a.
```
FOR J := 1 TO 3 DO
  FOR K := 1 TO 5 DO
    A[J,K] := J - K;
```

b.
```
FOR J := 1 TO 3 DO
  FOR K := 1 TO 5 DO
    A[J,K] := J;
```

c.
```
FOR K := 1 TO 5 DO
  FOR J := 1 TO 3 DO
    A[J,K] := J;
```

d.
```
FOR J := 3 DOWNTO 1 DO
  FOR K := 1 TO 5 DO
    A[J,K] := J MOD K;
```

5. Let the two-dimensional array A be declared by

```
TYPE
  Table3X6 = ARRAY [1..3, 1..6] OF integer;
VAR
  A : Table3X6;
```

Write nested loops that cause the following values to be stored in A.

a. A

3	4	5	6	7	8
5	6	7	8	9	10
7	8	9	10	11	12

b. A

0	0	0	0	0	0
0	0	0	0	0	0
0	0	0	0	0	0

c. A

2	2	2	2	2	2
4	4	4	4	4	4
6	6	6	6	6	6

6. Declare a two-dimensional array, and write a segment of code that reads the following input file into the array.

```
13.2 15.1 10.3 8.2 43.6 ■
37.2 25.6 34.1 17.0 15.2 ■
```

7. Suppose an input file contains 50 lines of data and the first 20 spaces of each line are reserved for a customer's name. The rest of the line contains other information. Declare an array of strings to hold the names, and write a segment of code to read the names into the array. A sample line of input is

```
Smith John O        268-14-1801
                    ↑
                    position 21
```

8. Assume the declaration

```
TYPE
  Table4X5 = ARRAY [1..4, 1..5] OF real;
VAR
  Table : Table4X5;
```

has been made and values have been read into Table as follows:

Table

-2.0	3.0	0.0	8.0	10.0
0.0	-4.0	3.0	1.0	2.0
1.0	2.0	3.0	8.0	-6.0
-4.0	1.0	4.0	6.0	82.0

Indicate what the components of Table will be after each of the following segments of code is executed.

a.
```
FOR J := 1 TO 4 DO
  FOR K := 1 TO 5 DO
    IF J MOD K = 0 THEN
      A[J,K] := 0.0
    ELSE
      A[J,K] := -1.0;
```

b.
```
FOR J := 1 TO 4 DO
  IF A[J,1] <> 0.0 THEN
    FOR K := 1 TO 5 DO
      A[J,K] := A[J,K] / A[J,1];
```

c.
```
FOR K := 1 TO 5 DO
  IF A[1,K] = 0.0 THEN
    FOR J := 2 TO 4 DO
      A[J,K] := 0.0;
```

9. Let the two-dimensional array Table be declared as in Exercise 8. Declare additional arrays as needed, and write segments of code for each of the following.

   a. Find and save the minimum of each row.
   b. Find and save the maximum of each column.
   c. Find the total of all the components.

10. Example 8.4 illustrates the use of procedures with two-dimensional arrays. For actual use, Western Jeans would also need a list indicating what to order to maintain the inventory. Write a procedure (assuming all declarations have been made) to print a table indicating which sizes of jeans have a supply of < 4. Do this by putting '*' in the cell if the supply is low or ' ' in the cell if the supply is adequate.

11. Suppose you want to work with a table that has three rows and eight columns of integers.

   a. Declare an appropriate two-dimensional array that can be used with procedures.
   b. Write a procedure to replace all negative numbers with zero.
   c. Show what is needed to call this procedure from the main program.

12. If A and B are matrices of size m × n, their sum A + B is defined by A + B = $[a+b]_{ij}$, where a and b are corresponding components in A and B. Write a program to do the following.

   a. Read values into two matrices of size $m \times n$.
   b. Compute the sum.
   c. Print out the matrices together with the sum.

13. If A and B are matrices of sizes $m \times n$ and $n \times p$, respectively, their product is defined to be the $m \times p$ matrix AB where

$$\text{AB} = [c_{ik}],\ c_{ik} = \sum_{j=1}^{n} a_{ij}b_{jk}$$

   Write a program to do the following.

   a. Read values into two matrices that have a defined product.
   b. Compute their product.
   c. Print out the matrices together with their product.

A NOTE OF INTEREST

Inspections: Debugging in the 1990s

(The following information was provided at the author's request by Franco E. Mau, Development Engineer at Tandem Computers Incorporated, Cupertino, California.)

The process of debugging software has become multifaceted. One form of finding code defects currently used by Tandem Computers Incorporated is the use of "inspections." This inspection process was pioneered by Bill Fagan at IBM in the late 1970s and was introduced at Tandem Computers Incorporated in 1989.

Simply stated, an inspection is a team process of finding defects, particularly in software packages and smaller segments of computer code. An inspection team consists of at least five members: the author (code writer), a moderator, a reader, and two inspectors, one of whom also serves as a recorder. A typical session is about two hours long; many sessions are required to inspect a single software package.

Prior to an inspection session, the reader and both inspectors spend about two hours examining the package or code to be reviewed. At the beginning of the inspection process for a document, initial rules are established concerning what kinds of defects (logical, syntactic, and so on) are being sought. Subsequently, all defects are related to these initial rules.

During a session, authors are available only to make clarifications and otherwise are not involved in the discussion. All members of the inspection team are active participants in the inspection. The moderator sets the pace, makes sure all participants are prepared, inspects code, and generally coordinates the session. The reader provides an oral description of what the code is attempting to accomplish. The recorder records code defects on forms. The code line numbers are listed with respective references to how the lines relate to the defects being sought.

All participants in an inspection are encouraged to stress professionalism. They must be willing to communicate and share their technical expertise. When discussing defects in the code or algorithms, they are expected to make technical comments and to avoid personal references. Inspections focus on the work—not on the author. The style of the code or algorithms are not criticized; the sole purpose of an inspection is to find defects. Consistent with this philosophy, managers are not present at inspections and inspection results may not be used to evaluate employee performance.

Inspections are typically conducted before the code is run. Particular importance is paid to the boundary conditions associated with the software package. This helps to identify defects that may not be apparent because the "program runs." A defect can be something that is incorrect or something that is missing. All defects identified in the inspection become part of a data base. If no defects are found, it is assumed the inspection is not sufficient.

The primary positive result of an inspection is that it does identify defects. In a typical two-hour session, while inspecting 200–300 lines of code, four to six defects may be identified. However, a second, but important, byproduct of inspections is the training of personnel. Authors of code learn more about how to avoid defects in the future; readers and inspectors learn how to improve their own work. Finally, all involved learn from the shared expertise of the inspection team. This is especially helpful when the team consists of members with diverse backgrounds.

In summary, inspections have proved to be very valuable. They result in improved communication, higher morale, in-service training, and better software packages.

■ 8.2 Arrays of String Variables

Basic Idea and Notation

Recall from Section 7.5 our work with strings. A typical declaration for a name 20 characters in length is

```
TYPE
  String20 = string [20];
VAR
  Name : String20;
```

Thus, Name could be envisioned as

Name

It is a natural extension to consider the problem of working with an array of strings. For example, if we need a data structure for 50 names, this can be declared by

```
TYPE
  String20 = string [20];
  NameList = ARRAY [1..50] OF String20;
VAR
  Name : NameList;
```

Name can then be envisioned as

Name

Name[1]
Name[2]
Name[3]
.
.
.
Name[50]

where each component of Name is a string of at most 20 characters.

Alphabetizing a List of Names

One standard problem that programmers face is alphabetizing a list of names. For example, programs that work with class lists, bank statements, magazine subscriptions, names in a telephone book, or credit card customers require alphabetizing. As indicated, Turbo Pascal provides the facility for using an array of strings as a data structure for such lists.

Problems that require the user to alphabetize names contain at least three main tasks: get the data, alphabetize the list, and print the list. Before writing procedures for each of these tasks, let's consider some associated problems. When getting the data, the programmer will usually encounter one of three formats. First, data may be entered with a constant field width for each name. Each name is then typically followed by some additional data item. Thus, if each name uses 20 character positions and position 21 contains the start of numeric data, the data file might be

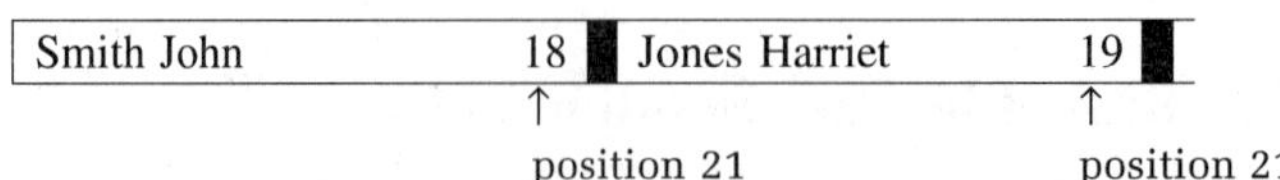

In this case, the name can be read into the appropriate component by a **read** statement. The first name can be accessed by

```
read (Data, Name[1]);
```

and the second name can be accessed by

```
read (Data, Name[2]);
```

A second form for entering data is to use some symbol to indicate the end of a name. When the data are in this form, the user must be able to recognize the symbol. Thus, the data file could be

Smith John*18	Jones Harriet*19

In this case, the first name can be obtained by

```
K := 0;
read (Data, Ch);
WHILE (Ch <> '*') AND (K < 20) DO
  BEGIN
    K := K + 1;
    Name[1,K] := Ch;
    read (Data, Ch)
  END;
```

Thus, Name[1] is

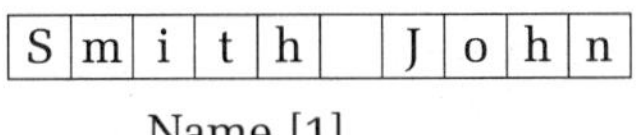

Name [1]

A second name in the data file would be similarly read. The only change is from Name[1, K] to Name[2, K].

A third possibility is that the name is entered on a separate line from other related data items. Thus, the data file could be

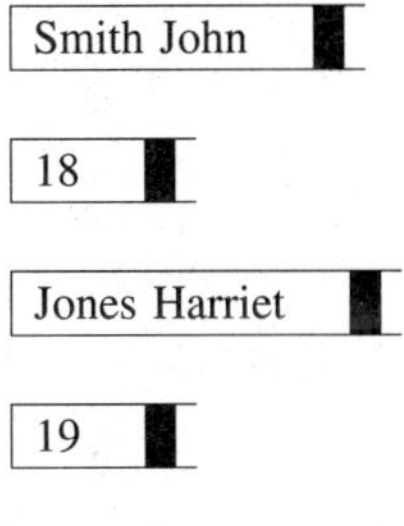

.
.
.

In this case, an end-of-file condition can be used to read the data. Typical code for input would be

```
Index := 1;
WHILE NOT eof(Data) DO
  BEGIN
    readln (Data, Name[Index]);
    readln (Data, Age[Index]);
    Index := Index + 1
  END;
```

The next problem in getting data is determining how many lines are available. If the number of lines is known, a **FOR** loop can be used. More realistically, however, there will be an unknown number of lines and the user will need the **eof** condition in a variable control loop and a counter to determine the number of names. To illustrate, assume there are an unknown number of data lines and each line contains a name. If the declaration section of a program is

```
TYPE
  String20 = string [20];
  NameList = ARRAY [1..50] OF String20;
VAR
  Name: NameList;
  Length : integer;
  Data : text;
```

then a procedure to get the data is

```
PROCEDURE GetData (VAR Name : NameList;
                   VAR Length : integer);
  VAR
    K : integer;
  BEGIN
    reset (Data);
    Length := 0;
    WHILE NOT eof(Data) AND (Length < 50) DO
      BEGIN
        Length := Length + 1;                 {  Increment counter  }
        readln (Data, Name [Length,])         {  Get a name         }
      END;
    IF NOT eof(Data) THEN
      writeln ('There are more data.')
  END;  {  of PROCEDURE GetData  }
```

This procedure is called from the main program by

```
GetData (Name, Length);
```

Now let's consider the problem of alphabetizing a list of names. If we assume the same data structure and let Length represent the number of names, a procedure to sort the list alphabetically (using the selection sort discussed in Section 7.3) is

```
PROCEDURE SelectionSort (VAR Name : NameList;
                              Length : integer);
  VAR
    J, K, Index : integer;
    Temp : String20;
  BEGIN
    FOR J := 1 TO Length - 1 DO
      BEGIN
        Index := J;
        FOR K := J + 1 TO Length DO
          IF Name[K] < Name[Index] THEN
            Index := K;
        IF Index <> J THEN
          BEGIN
            Temp := Name[Index];
            Name[Index] := Name[J];
            Name[J] := Temp
          END  {  of exchange  }
      END  {  of sort  }
  END;  {  of PROCEDURE SelectionSort  }
```

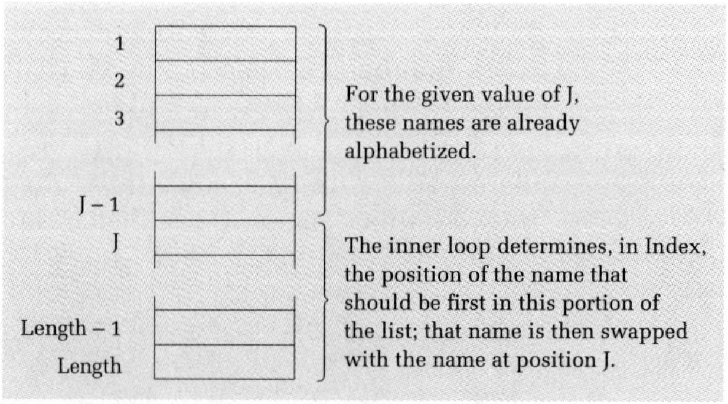

1
2
3
J − 1
J
Length − 1
Length

For the given value of J, these names are already alphabetized.

The inner loop determines, in Index, the position of the name that should be first in this portion of the list; that name is then swapped with the name at position J.

This procedure is called from the main program by

```
SelectionSort (Name, Length);
```

Once the list of names has been sorted, the user often wants to print the sorted list. A procedure to do this is

```
PROCEDURE PrintData (VAR Name : NameList;
                     Length : integer);
  VAR
    J : integer;
  BEGIN
    FOR J := 1 TO Length DO
      writeln (Name[J]:50)
  END;  {  of PROCEDURE PrintData  }
```

This is called from the main program by

```
PrintData (Name, Length);
```

We can now use the procedures in a simple program that gets the names, sorts them, and prints them as follows:

```
BEGIN  {  Main program  }
  assign (Data, 'NameFile.DAT');
  reset (Data);
  GetData (Name, Length);
  SelectionSort (Name, Length);
  PrintData (Name, Length);
  close (Data)
END.  {  of main program  }
```

Exercises 8.2

1. Assume the declarations and definitions

```
TYPE
  String20 = string [20]
  StateList = ARRAY [1..50] OF String20;
VAR
  State : StateList;
```

have been made and an alphabetical listing of the 50 states of the United States of America is contained in the data structure State. Further, assume each state name begins in position one of each component. Indicate the output for each of the following.

a.
```
FOR J := 1 TO 50 DO
  IF State[J,1] = 'O' THEN
    writeln (State[J]:35);
```

b.
```
FOR J := 50 DOWNTO 1 DO
  IF J MOD 5 = 0 THEN
    writeln (State[J]:35);
```

c.
```
FOR J := 1 TO 50 DO
  writeln (State[J,1]:10, State[J,2]);
```

d.
```
CountA := 0;
FOR J := 1 TO 50 DO
  FOR K := 1 TO 20 DO
    IF State[J,K] = 'A' THEN
      CountA := CountA + 1;
writeln (CountA:20);
```

2. Assume you have a sorted list of names in the form "last name, first name." Write a fragment of code to inspect the list of names and print the full name of each Smith on the list.

3. The procedure used in this section to get names from a data file assumed the names in the data file were of fixed length and there were an unknown number of data lines. Modify the procedure for each of the following situations.

   a. Variable length names followed by '*' and a known number of data lines
   b. Variable length names followed by '*' and an unknown number of data lines
   c. Fixed length names (20 characters) and a known number of data lines

d. Names entered in the form first name, space, last name that are to be sorted by last name.

4. If each line of a data file contains a name followed by an age, such as,

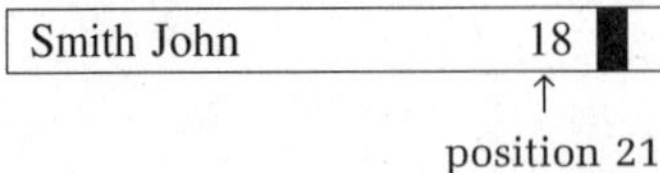

the data will be put into two arrays: one for the names, and one for the ages. Show how the sorting procedure can be modified so the array of ages will keep the same order as the array of names.

5. Write a complete program to read 10 names from an input file (where each line contains one name of 20 characters), sort the names in reverse alphabetical order, and print the sorted list.

■ 8.3 Processing Strings

S

Two string functions, **length** and **concat,** were examined briefly in Section 2.5. Recall **length**(StringName) returns the number of characters currently stored in StringName and **concat**(String1, String2) joins strings String1 and String2 into a single string.

In this section, we consider several more functions and procedures that work with strings. None of these are part of standard Pascal. However, since many applications are concerned with manipulation of character data, it is important to understand how such data is handled.

str and val

Two procedures, **str** and **val**, allow a program to convert between strings and numeric representations: **str** converts a numeric value to its string representation, and **val** converts a string value to a numeric representation.

The correct form and syntax for using **str** are

str (<number>, <string>);

where <number> is any integer-type or real-type expression and <string> is a string-type variable. For example

```
str (216, StringName);
```

causes the integer 216 to be stored in StringName as the string '216'.

The first argument in **str** can be formatted. Formatting causes desired strings to be stored in StringName in the same manner as **writeln** causes formatted output to appear on the screen. To illustrate, Table 8.1 contains several examples of numeric values converted to strings.

TABLE 8.1
Results of using **str**

Procedure Call	Result Stored in StringName
str (8, StringName)	'8'
str (8:3, StringName)	' 8'
str (185.3, StringName)	'1.8530000000E+02'
str (185.3:8:2, StringName)	' 185.30'

In several instances, it is desirable to work with the string representation of a numeric value. In general, specially formatted output of numeric data can be achieved by using calls to **str.** One classic example is when we wish to produce a column of dollar amounts complete with dollar signs, commas, and a decimal point. We include such an example later in this section.

Converting from a string value to a numeric representation is accomplished by using the procedure **val.** The correct form and syntax for using **val** are

val (<string>, <number>, <code>);

where <string> may be any string-type expression and <number> is an integer-type or real-type variable. Appropriately used, the string would contain some integer-type or real-type value stored as a string. The variable represented by <number> is used to store the numeric representation of the string. Thus, the call

```
val ('325', Number, Code);
```

results in the variable Number receiving the integer value 325.

Code is a variable of type **integer.** It receives a value of zero if the character representation in the string is properly formed. Thus, if Number is of type **integer**

```
val ('325', Number, Code);
```

results in Code receiving a value of zero. If Number is of type **real**

```
val ('3.25', Number, Code);
```

also results in Code receiving a value of zero.

If the character representation in the string is not properly formed, Code is assigned the value of the first (reading from left to right) improperly placed character in the string. Thus, if Number is of type **integer,** the call

```
val ('185.3', Number, Code);
```

results in Code receiving a value of 4. Several calls to **val** and resulting assignments to Code are shown in Table 8.2

Table 8.2
Results of using **val**

Procedure Call	Data Type of Number	Value of Code
val ('15', Number, Code)	**integer**	0
val ('15', Number, Code)	**real**	0
val ('1,563', Number, Code)	**integer**	2
val ('1563.5', Number, Code)	**integer**	5
val ('.15', Number, Code)	**real**	1
val ('1.5E+02', Number, Code)	**real**	0

A classic use of **val** in interactive programming is as a guard against invalid input. The following example illustrates this use.

■ **EXAMPLE 8.5**

This example shows how **val** can be used to guarantee that input from the keyboard is an integer. Input is read as a string, and Code must have a value of zero before continuation is allowed.

```
REPEAT
  writeln ('Please enter an integer and press <Enter>.');
  readln (StringName);
  val (StringName, Number, Code)
UNTIL Code = 0;
```

Sample runs of this segment of code produce

```
Please enter an integer and press <Enter>.
1.2
Please enter an integer and press <Enter>.
12,345
Please enter an integer and press <Enter>.
45
```

Incorporating the code of Example 8.5 into a procedure is deferred to the exercises at the end of this section.

copy

Recall strings are really arrays of characters that can be accessed character by character using the index (position) of the desired character. Thus, if we have the assignment

```
StringName := 'This is a string.';
```

then

```
writeln (StringName[4]);
```

produces s because it is the character in position 4 of the string. Turbo Pascal extends this idea of extracting a single character to extracting any substring of a given string. The function **copy** is used for this purpose. The correct form and syntax for **copy** are

copy(<string>, <index>, <count>);

where <string> is a string-type expression, <index> is the position at which copying is to begin, and <count> is the number of positions in the desired substring. For example, using the code

```
FullName := 'Rob Vasquez';
LastName := copy(FullName, 5, 7);
```

the function **copy** results in the substring 'Vasquez' being assigned to LastName.

pos

A second function that works with substrings is **pos.** This function searches a string for a specific substring. The correct form and syntax for **pos** are

pos(<substring>, <string>);

where <substring> and <string> are both string-type expressions. Substring is the expression being searched for in the string. If the desired substring is found, **pos** returns the index of the first character of the expression within the string. Otherwise, **pos** returns zero. To illustrate

```
StringName := 'This is a sentence.';
Substring := 'is';
Location := pos(Substring, StringName);
```

produces a value of 3 in Location. Now let's consider an example that uses **copy** and **pos.**

■ EXAMPLE 8.6

Let's develop a procedure that prints last names only from a list of names where each name in the list is in the form 'LastName, FirstName'. The basic idea is to locate the comma and then print the part of the string that precedes the comma. The comma can be located by

```
Comma := ',';
CommaLocation := pos(Comma, Name);
```

The last name can then be selected by

```
LastName := copy(Name, 1, CommaLocation - 1);
```

If we assume the original list of names is in the text file FullNames, a procedure for printing all last names is

```
PROCEDURE PrintLastNames (Names : NameList);
  CONST
    Comma = ',';
  VAR
    Name, LastName : string;
    CommaLocation : integer;
  BEGIN
    assign (FullNames, 'Names.DAT');
    reset (FullNames);
    WHILE NOT eof(FullNames) DO
      BEGIN
        readln (FullNames, Name);
        CommaLocation := pos(Comma, Name);
        LastName := copy(Name, 1, CommaLocation - 1);
        writeln (LastName)
      END;  {  of WHILE loop }
    close (FullNames)
  END;  {  of PROCEDURE PrintLastNames }
```

---

insert and **delete**

Two fundamental operations for processing strings are the ability to insert something into a string and the ability to delete something from a string. In Turbo Pascal, the procedures **insert** and **delete** provide for these operations. Procedure **insert** inserts a given substring into a string. The correct form and syntax for **insert** are

insert (<substring>, <old string>, <location>);

where <substring> is a string-type expression and <old string> is a string-type variable. Substring is the material to be inserted into the old string; <location> is of type **integer** and is the index of the position in the old string where the new substring will begin. To illustrate

```
Country := 'The United States America';
insert ('of ', Country, 19);
writeln (Country);
```

produces

```
The United States of America
```

Since strings are limited to 255 characters, if **insert** results in a string of more than 255 characters, the string is truncated after the character in position 255.

Procedure **delete** reverses the process of **insert.** It deletes characters from a given string. The correct form and syntax for **delete** are

delete (<old string>, <position>, <count>);

where <old string> is a string-type variable and <position> and <count> are integer-type expressions. Position represents the character index where the deletion is to begin; count represents the number of characters to be deleted. For example

```
Statement := 'I will not wash the car.';
delete (Statement, 8, 4);
writeln (Statement);
```

results in

```
I will wash the car.
```

Our final example in this section considers the problem of printing dollar amounts. Using procedures and functions just developed, we can format the output with the following properties:

1. Decimal points are aligned.
2. Dollar signs are included.
3. Commas are used to express numbers when appropriate.
4. Amounts are rounded to the nearest cent.

Thus, typical amounts would be shown as

```
 $1,625.92
$14,300.00
    $65.50
```

EXAMPLE 8.7

Let's develop a procedure that formats financial amounts as just shown. The procedure receives a real number (such as 1426.538) and prints it as desired, with the decimal point in column 20. The procedure first needs to convert the real number to a string. This can be accomplished by using

```
str (Amount, NumString);
```

Since we want two decimal places and the amounts rounded to the nearest cent, we format Amount to get

```
str (Amount:4:2, NumString);
```

This assures rounding, as well as leading and trailing zeros when necessary.

We now use the length of NumString to insert commas where appropriate. NumString can be thought of as the string – – – – – – – – – – . – –, and the first comma should appear six positions from the right end of the string. Therefore, we define

```
CommaPosition := length(NumString) - 5;
```

where length (NumString) – 5 gives the index of the character in the sixth position from the right end of the string. The comma is then inserted in this sixth position, and the remaining six characters are written to the right of the comma.

A comma can then be inserted at CommaPosition by

```
insert (',', NumString, CommaPosition);
```

CommaPosition is then decremented by 3, and the process is repeated as long as commas are to be inserted. This results in the loop

```
WHILE CommaPosition > 1 DO
  BEGIN
    insert (',', NumString, CommaPosition);
    CommaPosition := CommaPosition - 3
  END;  {  of WHILE loop  }
```

At this stage, all commas and decimals have been inserted into the string. A dollar sign is affixed to the string by concatenation as

```
NumString := '$' + NumString;
```

Since the decimal points are to be aligned in column 20, NumString is printed by

```
writeln (NumString:22);
```

The entire procedure for formatted output of amounts of money is then

```
PROCEDURE MoneyFormat (Amount : real);
  VAR
    NumString : string;
    CommaPosition : integer;
  BEGIN
    str (Amount:4:2, NumString);  {  Rounds and assures correct form  }
    CommaPosition := length(NumString) - 5;
    WHILE CommaPosition > 1 DO
      BEGIN
        insert (',', NumString, CommaPosition);
        CommaPosition := CommaPosition - 3
      END;  {  of WHILE loop  }
    NumString := '$' + NumString; {  Add a dollar sign  }
    writeln (NumString:22)
  END;  {  of PROCEDURE MoneyFormat  }
```

A summary of the string processing procedures and functions is contained in Table 8.3.

TABLE 8.3
String processing procedures and functions

Procedure or Function	Result
length(<string>)	Returns the number of characters in <string>
concat(<string1>, . . . , <string*n*>)	Concatenates specified strings
str (<number>, <string1>)	Causes <number> to be stored as a string in <string1>
val (<string>, <number>, <code>)	Converts <string> to <number> if properly represented; if not, <code> indicates position of improperly entered character
copy(<string>, <index>, <count>)	Returns a substring of <string> that begins at <index> and is <count> characters long
pos(<substring>, <string>)	Returns the starting position of <substring> in <string>
insert (<substring>, <string>, <location>)	Inserts <substring> into <string>, beginning at <location>
delete (<string>, <position>, <count>)	Deletes <count> characters from <string>, beginning with the character in <position>

Exercises 8.3

1. Write a test program to see what happens when **str** is used if a real number is formatted with only a single field width. For example, show what is stored in StringName by the call

   ```
   str (185.3:8, StringName)
   ```

2. Enhance the code of Example 8.5 into a procedure that guarantees input is a positive integer ≤ 100.
3. Write a test program to see what ranges of integers are allowed for Index and Count in
```
copy(StringName, Index, Count);
```
For example, what happens if the ranges are negative or if Count exceeds the remaining string length?
4. Write a program that locates and prints the longest word in a sentence. If there is more than one word of that length, all longest words should be printed. Assume words are separated by a single space.
5. Write a program that finds the average length of all words in a sentence. Assume words are separated by a single space.
6. Modify Example 8.6 by creating a new text file that contains the list of last names printed from the list of full names.
7. Write a test program to show what values are allowed for the integer-type arguments in procedures **insert** and **delete.**
8. Using the procedure developed in Example 8.7, write a program that gets real numbers from a text file and then displays a column of properly formatted dollar amounts.
9. Using the procedure developed in Example 8.7, write an interactive program that allows the user to enter real numbers and then have them displayed as formatted. The process should terminate when a negative number is entered.
10. Assume each line of the text file BirthDates contains a birthdate in the form 'MMM DD YYYY', where 'MMM' is the month in three letters, 'DD' is the date in two positions, and 'YYYY' is the year. Write a procedure that extracts and prints the dates ('DD') contained in the list.
11. Write a program that counts the number of words in a paragraph of text. Assume all words are separated by a single space.

■ 8.4 Parallel Arrays

In many practical situations, more than one type of array is required to handle the data. For example, we may wish to keep a record of names of people and their donations to a charitable organization. We could accomplish this by using an array of names and an equally long array of donations. Programs for such situations can use *parallel arrays*—arrays of the same length with elements in the same relative positions in each array. These arrays have the same index type. However, most uses of parallel arrays have the added condition of different data types for the array components; otherwise, a two-dimensional array would

COMMUNICATION AND STYLE TIPS

Since parallel arrays use the same index type, definitions can have the form
```
CONST
  NumberOfDonors = 30;
TYPE
  String20 = string [20];
  IndexType = 1..NumberOfDonors;
  NameList = ARRAY [IndexType] OF String20;
  AmountList = ARRAY [IndexType] OF integer;
```

suffice. Generally, situations that call for two or more arrays of the same length but of different data types are situations in which parallel arrays can be used. Later, we will see that this situation can also be handled as a single array of records.

Using Parallel Arrays

Let's look at a typical problem that requires working with both a list of names and a list of numbers. Suppose the input file consists of 30 lines, each of which contains a name in the first 20 spaces and an integer starting in space 21 that is the amount of a donation. We are to read all data into appropriate arrays, alphabetize the names, print the alphabetized list with the amount of each donation, and find the total of all donations.

This problem can be solved using parallel arrays for the list of names and the list of donations. Appropriate declarations are

```
CONST
  NumberOfDonors = 30;
TYPE
  String20 = string [20];
  IndexType = 1..NumberOfDonors;
  NameList = ARRAY [IndexType] OF String20;
  AmountList = ARRAY [IndexType] OF integer;
VAR
  Donor : NameList;
  Amount : AmountList;
```

A procedure to read the data from an input file is

```
PROCEDURE GetData (VAR Donor : NameList;
                   VAR Amount : AmountList);
  VAR
    J : integer;
  BEGIN
    FOR J := 1 TO NumberOfDonors DO
      readln (Data, Donor[J], Amount[J])
  END;  {  of PROCEDURE GetData  }
```

This procedure can be called by

```
GetData (Donor, Amount);
```

After this procedure has been called from the main program, the parallel arrays can be envisioned as

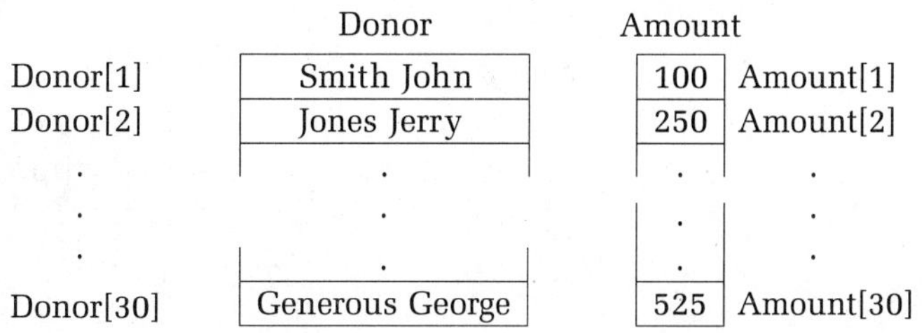

	Donor	Amount	
Donor[1]	Smith John	100	Amount[1]
Donor[2]	Jones Jerry	250	Amount[2]
.	.	.	.
.	.	.	.
.	.	.	.
Donor[30]	Generous George	525	Amount[30]

The next task is to alphabetize the names. However, we must be careful to keep the amount donated with the name of the donor. This can be accomplished by passing both the list of names and the list of donations to the sorting procedure and modifying the code to include exchanging the donation amount whenever the names are exchanged. Since NumberOfDonors is defined in the constant section, a Length argument is not needed. Using the procedure heading

A NOTE OF INTEREST

Computer Ethics: Worms

In *The Shockwave Rider* (1975), John Brunner developed the notion of an omnipotent "tapeworm" program running loose through a network of computers—an idea that seemed rather disturbing but was then well beyond our capabilities. The basic model, however, is a very provocative one: a program or a computation that can move from machine to machine, harnessing resources as needed and replicating itself when necessary.

On November 2, 1988, Cornell computer science graduate student Robert Morris released a worm program into the ARPANET. Over an eight-hour period, it invaded between 2500 and 3000 VAX and Sun computers running the Berkeley UNIX operating system. The worm program disabled virtually all of the computers by replicating rampantly and clogging them with many copies. Many of the computers had to be disconnected from the network until all copies of the worm could be expurgated and until the security loopholes that the worm used to gain entry could be plugged. Most computers were fully operational within two or three days. No files were damaged on any of the computers invaded by the worm.

This incident gained much public attention and produced a widespread outcry in the computing community, perhaps because so many people saw that they had been within a hair's breadth of losing valuable files. After an investigation, Cornell suspended Morris and decried his action as irresponsible. In July 1989, a grand jury brought an indictment against Morris for violation of the Federal Computer Privacy Act of 1986. He was tried and convicted in January 1990.

```
PROCEDURE Sort (VAR Donor : NameList;
                VAR Amount : AmountList);
```

the code for sorting is changed in order to interchange both a name and an amount. Thus

```
Temp := Donor[Index];
Donor[Index] := Donor[J];
Donor[J] := Temp;
```

becomes

```
Temp := Donor[Index];
TempAmount := Amount[Index];
Donor[Index] := Donor[J];
Amount[Index] := Amount[J];
Donor[J] := Temp;
Amount[J] := TempAmount;
```

The procedure for sorting the list of names and rearranging the list of donations accordingly is called by

```
Sort (Donor, Amount);
```

Our next task is to print the alphabetized list together with the donations. If Donor and Amount have been sorted appropriately, we can use the following procedure to produce the desired output:

```
PROCEDURE PrintData (VAR Donor : NameList;
                     VAR Amount : AmountList);
  VAR
    J : integer;
  BEGIN
    FOR J := 1 TO NumberOfDonors DO
      BEGIN
        write (Donor[J]:40);
        writeln ('$':3, Amount[J]:5)
      END
  END;  {  of PROCEDURE PrintData  }
```

This is called by

```
PrintData (Donor, Amount);
```

The last task this program requires is to find the total of all donations. The following function can perform this task:

```
FUNCTION Total (Amount : AmountList) : integer;
  VAR
    Sum, J : integer;
  BEGIN
    Sum := 0;
    FOR J := 1 TO NumberOfDonors DO
      Sum := Sum + Amount[J];
    Total := Sum
  END;  {  of FUNCTION Total  }
```

This function is called by

```
TotalDonations := Total(Amount);
```

where TotalDonations has been declared as an **integer** variable. A complete program for this problem follows.

```
PROGRAM Donations;

{  This program reads data from an input file where each line   }
{  consists of a donor name followed by the amount donated.     }
{  Output consists of an alphabetically sorted list together    }
{  with the amount of each donation.  This is accomplished by   }
{  using parallel arrays.  The total amount donated is also     }
{  listed.                                                      }

USES
  Crt;

CONST
  NumberOfDonors = 30;

TYPE
  String20 = string [20];
  IndexType = 1..NumberOfDonors;
  NameList = ARRAY [IndexType] OF String20;
  AmountList = ARRAY [IndexType] OF integer;

VAR
  Donor : NameList;            {  An array for donor names       }
  Amount : AmountList;         {  An array for amounts donated   }
  TotalDonations : integer;    {  Total amount donated           }
  Data : text;                 {  Names and amounts donated      }

{************************************************************}

PROCEDURE GetData (VAR Donor : NameList;
                   VAR Amount : AmountList);

  {  Given:   Nothing                                         }
  {  Task:    Read names and donations into respective arrays }
  {  Return:  Parallel arrays of names and donations          }

  VAR
    J : integer;
  BEGIN
    FOR J := 1 TO NumberOfDonors DO
      readln (Data, Donor[J], Amount[J])
  END;  {  of PROCEDURE GetData  }
```

```
{*************************************************************}

PROCEDURE SelectionSort (VAR Donor : NameList;
                         VAR Amount : AmountList);

  {  Given:   Unsorted parallel arrays of names and donations  }
  {  Task:    Sort alphabetically                              }
  {  Return:  An alphabetically sorted list of names with      }
  {               respective donations                         }

  VAR
    TempDonor : String20;
    TempAmount : integer;
    J, K, Index : integer;
  BEGIN
    FOR J := 1 TO NumberOfDonors - 1 DO
      BEGIN
        Index := J;
        FOR K := J + 1 TO NumberOfDonors DO
          IF Donor[K] < Donor[Index] THEN
            Index := K;
        IF Index <> J THEN           {  Exchange if necessary  }
          BEGIN
            TempDonor := Donor[Index];
            TempAmount := Amount[Index];
            Donor[Index] := Donor[J];
            Amount[Index] := Amount[J];
            Donor[J] := TempDonor;
            Amount[J] := TempAmount
          END  {  of exchange  }
      END  {  of one pass  }
  END;  {  of PROCEDURE SelectionSort  }

{*************************************************************}

FUNCTION Total (Amount : AmountList) : integer;

  {  Given:   An array of amounts                              }
  {  Task:    Sum the components of the array                  }
  {  Return:  The total of array components                    }

  VAR
    Sum, J : integer;
  BEGIN
    Sum := 0;
    FOR J := 1 TO NumberOfDonors DO
      Sum := Sum + Amount[J];
    Total := Sum
  END;  {  of FUNCTION Total  }

{*************************************************************}

PROCEDURE PrintHeading;

  {  Given:   Nothing                                          }
  {  Task:    Print a heading for the output                   }
  {  Return:  Nothing                                          }

  BEGIN
    writeln ('Donor Name':34, 'Donation':15);
    writeln ('----------':34, '--------':15);
    writeln
  END;  {  of PROCEDURE PrintHeading  }
```

```
{*************************************************************}

PROCEDURE PrintData (VAR Donor : NameList;
                     VAR Amount : AmountList;
                     TotalDonations : integer);

  {  Given:   Parallel arrays of names/donations and total     }
  {                donations                                   }
  {  Task:    Print a list of names and amounts donated; end   }
  {                with the total of all donations             }
  {  Return:  Nothing                                          }

  VAR
    J : integer;
  BEGIN
    FOR J := 1 TO NumberOfDonors DO
      BEGIN
        write (Donor[J]:40);
        writeln ('$':2, Amount[J]:5)
      END;  {  of FOR J loop  }
    writeln ('------':47);
    writeln ('Total':40, '$':2, TotalDonations:5);
    writeln
  END;  {  of PROCEDURE PrintData  }

{*************************************************************}

BEGIN  {  Main program  }
  ClrScr;
  assign (Data, 'DonorDat.DAT');
  reset (Data);
  GetData (Donor, Amount);
  SelectionSort (Donor, Amount);
  TotalDonations := Total(Amount);
  PrintHeading;
  PrintData (Donor, Amount, TotalDonations);
  readln;
  close (Data)
END.  {  of main program  }
```

Output created from an input file of 30 lines is

```
    Donor Name        Donation
    ----------        --------

Alexander Candy      $  300
Anderson Tony        $  375
Banks Marj           $  375
Born Patty           $  100
Brown Ron            $  200
Darnell Linda        $  275
Erickson Thomas      $  100
Fox William          $  300
Francis Denise       $  350
Generous George      $  525
Gillette Mike        $  350
Hancock Kirk         $  500
Higgins Sam          $  300
Janson Kevin         $  200
Johnson Ed           $  350
Johnson Martha       $  400
Jones Jerry          $  250
Kelly Marvin         $  475
Kneff Susan          $  300
```

```
Lasher John          $  175
Lyon Elizabeth       $  425
Moore Robert         $  100
Muller Marjorie      $  250
Smith John           $  100
Trost Frostie        $   50
Trudo Rosemary       $  200
Weber Sharon         $  150
Williams Art         $  350
Williams Jane        $  175
Wilson Mary          $  275
                     ------
               Total $ 8275
```

Exercises 8.4

1. Which of the following are appropriate declarations for parallel arrays? Explain.

   a.
   ```
   TYPE
     String15 = string [15]
     List15 = ARRAY [1..15] OF real;
   VAR
     Names : ARRAY [1..10] OF String15;
     Amounts : List15;
   ```
   b.
   ```
   TYPE
     Chart = ARRAY [1..12, 1..10] OF integer;
     String10 = string [10];
     List = ARRAY [1..12] OF String10;
   VAR
     Table : Chart;
     Names : List;
   ```

2. Write a test program to read names and amounts from a data file. Your program should print out both lists and the total of the amounts. Assume each line of data is similar to

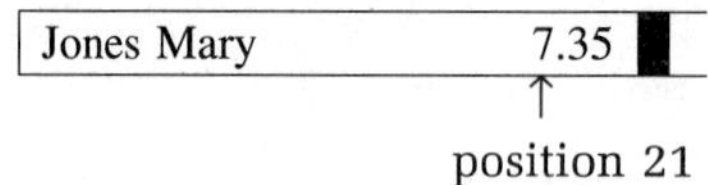

3. Parallel arrays can be used when working with a list of student names and the grades the students receive in a class.
   a. Define array types, and declare subsequent arrays that could be used in such a program.
   b. Write a function that counts the number of occurrences for each letter grade A, B, C, D, and E.

4. Declare appropriate arrays and write a procedure to read data from an input file with an unknown number of lines (but < 100), where each line contains a name (20 spaces), an age (integer), a marital status (character), and an income (real). A typical data line is

Smith John 35M 28502.16

5. Modify the code in Exercise 4 to accommodate data entered in the data file in the following format:

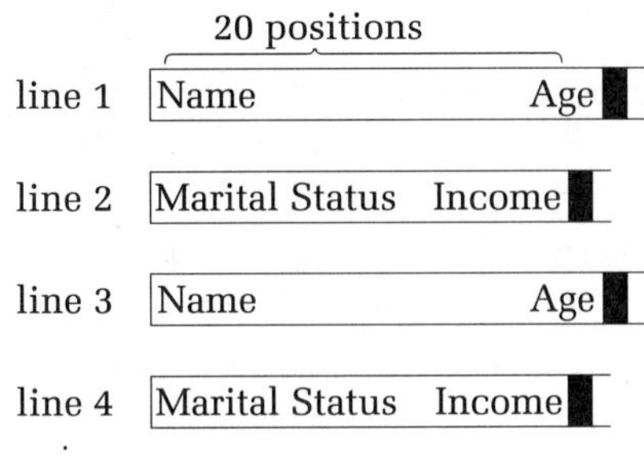

6. Write a procedure to sort the arrays in Exercise 4 according to income.

■ 8.4 Higher-Dimensional Arrays

Thus far, we have worked with arrays of one and two dimensions. Arrays of three, four, or higher dimensions can also be declared and used. Tubro Pascal places no limitation on the number of dimensions of an array.

Declarations of Higher-Dimensional Arrays

Declarations of *higher-dimensional arrays* usually assume one of two basic forms. First, a three-dimensional array type can be defined using the form

```
ARRAY [1 . . 3, 1 . . 4, 1 . . 5] OF <data type>;
```

Each dimension can vary in any of the ways used for arrays of one or two dimensions, and the data type can be any standard or user-defined ordinal data type. Second, a three-dimensional array can be defined as an array of two-dimensional arrays using the form

```
ARRAY [1 . . 3] OF ARRAY [1 . . 4, 1 . . 5] OF <data type>;
```

Each of these declarations will reserve 60 locations in memory. This can be visualized as shown in Figure 8.1.

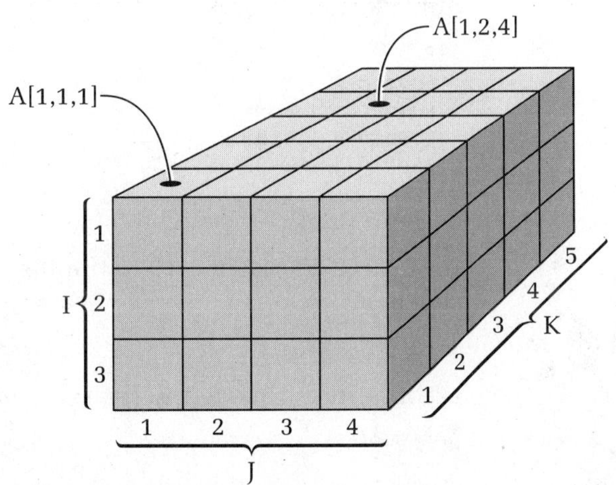

FIGURE 8.1
Three-dimensional array with components A[I, J, K]

An array of dimension n can be defined by

ARRAY [1 . . a_1, 1 . . a_2, . . . , 1 . . a_n] **OF** <data type>;

which would reserve $a_1 * a_2 * \ldots * a_n$ locations in memory. A general definition is

ARRAY [a_1 . . b_1, a_2 . . b_2, . . . , a_n . . b_n] **OF** <data type>;

where $a_i \leq b_i$ for $1 \leq i \leq n$.

Declarations and uses of higher-dimensional arrays are usually facilitated by descriptive names and user-defined data types. For example, suppose we want to declare a three-dimensional array to hold the contents of a book of tables. If there are 50 pages and each page contains a table of 15 rows and 10 columns, a reasonable declaration is

```
TYPE
  Page = 1..50;
  Row = 1..15;
  Column = 1..10;
  Book = ARRAY [Page, Row, Column] OF integer;
VAR
  Item : Book;
```

When this declaration is compared to

```
TYPE
  Book = ARRAY [1..50, 1..15, 1..10] OF integer;
VAR
  Item : Book;
```

we realize both arrays are identical in structure. However, in the first declaration, it is easier to see what the dimensions represent.

Accessing Components

Elements in higher-dimensional arrays are accessed and used in a manner similar to two-dimensional arrays. The difference is that in a three-dimensional array, each element needs three indices for reference. A similar result holds for other dimensions. To illustrate using this notation, recall the declaration

```
TYPE
  Page = 1..50;
  Row = 1..15;
  Column = 1..10;
  Book = ARRAY [Page, Row, Column] OF integer;
VAR
  Item : Book;
```

If we want to assign a 10 to the item on page three, row five, column seven, the statement

```
Item[3,5,7] := 10;
```

accomplishes this. Similarly, this item can be printed by

```
write (Item[3,5,7]);
```

Using this same declaration, we can do the following.

1. Print the fourth row of page 21 with the segment of code

```
FOR K := 1 TO 10 DO
  write (Item[21,4,K]:5);
writeln;
```

2. Print the top row of every page by using

```
FOR I := 1 TO 50 DO
  BEGIN
    FOR K := 1 TO 10 DO
      write (Item[I,1,K]:5);
    writeln
  END;
```

3. Print page 35 by using

```
FOR J := 1 TO 15 DO
  BEGIN
    FOR K := 1 TO 10 DO
      write (Item[35,J,K]:5);
    writeln
  END;
```

4. Print every page that does not have a zero in the first row and the first column by using

```
FOR I := 1 TO 50 DO
  IF Item[I,1,1] <> 0 THEN
    FOR J := 1 TO 15 DO
      BEGIN
        FOR K := 1 TO 10 DO
          write (Item[I,J,K]:5);
        writeln
      END;
```

As another illustration of the use of higher-dimensional arrays, consider the situation in which the manager of a high-rise office complex wants a program that keeps track of the tenants in each office. Suppose there are 20 floors, each having the floor plan shown in Figure 8.2. Each wing contains five rooms.

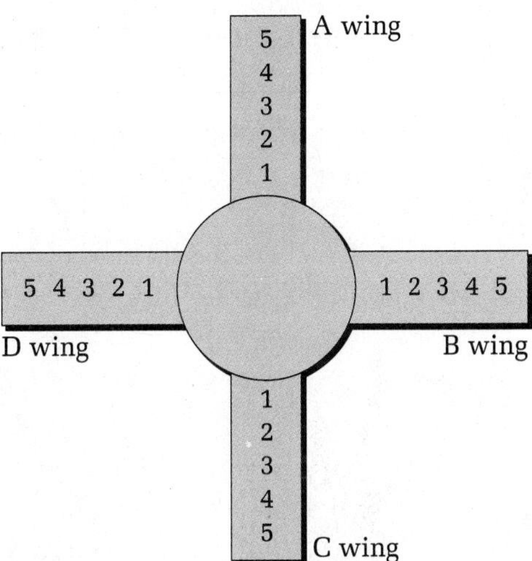

FIGURE 8.2
High-rise floor plan

First let's declare an appropriate array where the tenant's name can be stored. (Assume each name consists of 20 characters.) This can be accomplished by

```
TYPE
  Floors = 1..20;
  Wings = 'A'..'D';
  Offices = 1..5;
  Name = string [20];
  Occupant = ARRAY [Floors, Wings, Offices] OF Name;
VAR
  Tenant : Occupant;
  Floor : Floors;
  Wing : Wings;
  Office : Offices;
```

Now let's write a segment of code to print a list of names of all tenants on the top floor. To get the names of all tenants on the twentieth floor, we need to print the names for each office in each wing. Assuming a field width of 30 columns, the following code completes the desired task:

```
FOR Wing := 'A' TO 'D' DO
  FOR Office := 1 TO 5 DO
    writeln (Tenant[20, Wing, Office]:30);
```

How would we write a segment of code to read the name of a new tenant on the third floor (B wing, room 5) from the data file? Tenant [3,'B',5] is the variable name. Since this is a string, the code for reading is

```
  read (Tenant[3,'B',5]);
```

Assume the string 'Unoccupied' has been entered for each vacant office and we are to write a segment of code to list all vacant offices. This problem requires us to examine every name and print the location of the unoccupied offices. Hence, when we encounter the name 'Unoccupied', we want to print the respective indices. This is accomplished by

```
FOR Floor := 1 TO 20 DO
  FOR Wing := 'A' TO 'D' DO
    FOR Office := 1 TO 5 DO
      IF Tenant[Floor, Wing, Office] = 'Unoccupied' THEN
        writeln (Floor:5, Wing:5, Office:5);
```

As you can see, working with higher-dimensional arrays requires very careful handling of the indices. Nested loops are frequently used to process array elements, and proper formatting of output is critical.

Exercises 8.4

1. How many memory locations are reserved in each of the following declarations?

   a.
   ```
   TYPE
     Block = ARRAY [1..2, 1..3, 1..10] OF char;
   VAR
     A : Block;
   ```
   b.
   ```
   TYPE
     Block = ARRAY [-2..3] OF ARRAY [2..4, 3..6] OF real;
   VAR
     A : Block;
   ```
   c.
   ```
   TYPE
     Color = (Red, Black, White);
     Size = (Small, Large);
     Year = 1950..1960;
     Specifications = ARRAY [Color, Size, Year];
   VAR
     A : Specifications;
   ```

d.
```
TYPE
  String15 = string [15];
  List10 = ARRAY [1..10] OF String15;
  NameTable = ARRAY [1..4] OF List10;
VAR
  A : NameTable;
```

2. Write a test program to read values into an array of size 3 × 4 × 5. Assuming this represents three pages, each of which contains a 4 × 5 table, print out the table for each page together with a page number.
3. Declare a three-dimensional array that a hospital could use to keep track of the types of rooms available: private (P), semiprivate (S), and ward (W). The hospital has four floors, five wings, and 20 rooms in each wing.
4. Consider the declaration

```
TYPE
  Pages = 1..50;
  Rows = 1..15;
  Columns = 1..10;
  Book = ARRAY [Pages, Rows, Columns] OF integer;
VAR
  Page : Pages;
  Row : Rows;
  Column : Columns;
  Item : Book;
```

a. Write a segment of code to do each of the following.
   i. Print the fourth column of page 3.
   ii. Print the top seven rows of page 46.
   iii. Create a new page 30 by adding the corresponding elements of page 31 to page 30.

b. What is a general description of the output produced by the following segments of code?

i.
```
FOR Page := 1 TO 15 DO
  BEGIN
    FOR Column := 1 TO 10 DO
      write (Item[Page, Page, Column]:4);
    writeln
  END;
```

ii.
```
FOR Page := 1 TO 50 DO
  FOR Column := 1 TO 10 DO
    writeln (Item[Page, Column, Column]:(Column+4));
```

Use the following problem statement, definitions, and declarations for Exercises 5–8.

An athletic conference consisting of 10 universities wishes to have a program to keep track of the number of athletic grants-in-aid for each team at each institution. The conference programmer has defined the following structure:

```
CONST
  MaxGrants = 90;

TYPE
  Schools = 'A'..'J';
  Sports = (Baseball, Basketball, CrossCountry,
            FieldHockey, Football, Golf, Gymnastics,
            Swimming, Tennis, Track, Volleyball, Wrestling);
```

```
  Sex = (Male, Female);
  NumberOfGrants = 0..MaxGrants;
  GrantChart = ARRAY [Schools, Sports, Sex] OF NumberOfGrants;

VAR
  NumGrants : integer;
  Grants : GrantChart;
  School : Schools;
  Sport : Sports;
  Gender : Sex;
```

5. How many memory locations are reserved in the array Grants?
6. Explain what tasks are performed by each of the following segments of code.
   a.
```
NumGrants := 0;
FOR School := 'A' TO 'J' DO
  FOR Sport := Baseball TO Wrestling DO
    NumGrants := NumGrants + Grants[School, Sport, Female];
```
   b.
```
Sum := 0;
FOR School := 'A' TO 'J' DO
  FOR Sport := Baseball TO Wrestling DO
    FOR Gender := Male TO Female DO
      IF Grants[School, Sport, Gender] = 0 THEN
        Sum := Sum + 1;
```
7. Write a segment of code for each of the following tasks.
   a. Find the total number of grants for each university.
   b. Find the total number of grants for each sport.
   c. List all schools that have 10 or more grants in field hockey.
8. Explain how a **CASE** statement can be used to help display all sports (indicate male or female) and the number of grants in each sport for school D.

FOCUS ON PROGRAM DESIGN

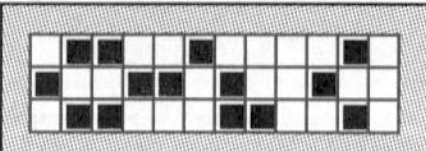

This program simulates the solution to a problem that could be posed by a small airline. Mountain-Air Commuters, Inc., is a small airline commuter service. Each of its planes is a 30-passenger plane with a floor plan as follows:

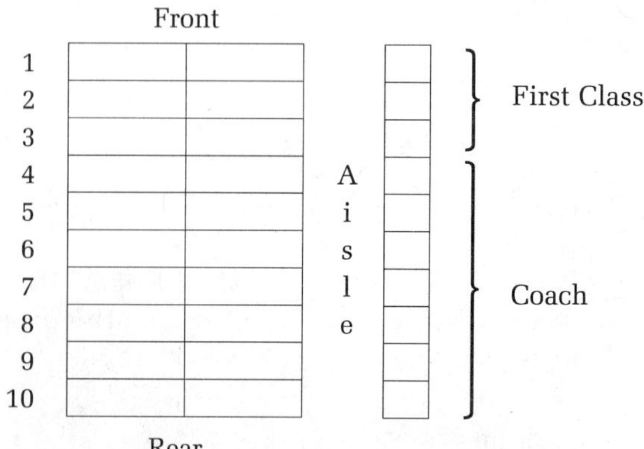

The first three rows are designated as first class because the seats are wider and there is more leg room. (In reality, most commuter planes do not have a first-class section. However, rather than include the large data base needed for larger planes, we simulate the problem using a seating plan with only 10 rows.)

Write a program that assigns seats to passengers on a first-come, first-served basis according to the following rules:

1. First-class and coach requests must be honored; if seats in the requested sections are all full, the customer's name should go on a waiting list for the next flight.
2. Specific seat requests should be honored next; if a requested seat is occupied, the person should be placed in the same row, if possible.
3. If a requested row is filled, the passenger should be seated as far forward as possible.
4. If all seats are filled, the passenger's name should be put on a waiting list for the next flight.

Output should include a seating chart with passenger names appropriately printed and a waiting list for the next flight. Each data line (input) contains the passenger's name, first class (F) or coach (C) designation, and seat request indicating the row and column desired.

A typical line of data would be

```
Smith John              C 5 2
```

where C represents a coach choice, 5 is a request for row five, and 2 represents the preferred seat.

A first-level pseudocode development for this problem is

1. Initialize variables
2. **WHILE NOT eof DO** process a name
3. Print a seating chart
4. **IF** there is a waiting list **THEN** print the list

A complete structure chart for this problem is given in Figure 8.3.

Module specifications for the main modules are

1. Initialize Module
   Data received: None
   Information returned: Value for WaitCount
   Value for EmptyWaitingList
   Value for SeatPlan
   Logic: Assign beginning values to the parameters.
   Use nested loops to initialize the array SeatPlan.
2. ProcessAName Module
   Data received: None
   Information returned: A seating chart
   A Boolean value for extra passengers
   A waiting list for the next flight
   Logic: Get a name, section choice, and seat preference.
   Search to see if a seat can be found.
   If yes, then ticket.
   If no, then save relevant information.
3. PrintSeatingChart Module
   Data received: A two-dimensional array of names of ticketed passengers
   Information returned: None
   Logic: Print the seating plan, indicating row, seat, and section choice for each passenger.

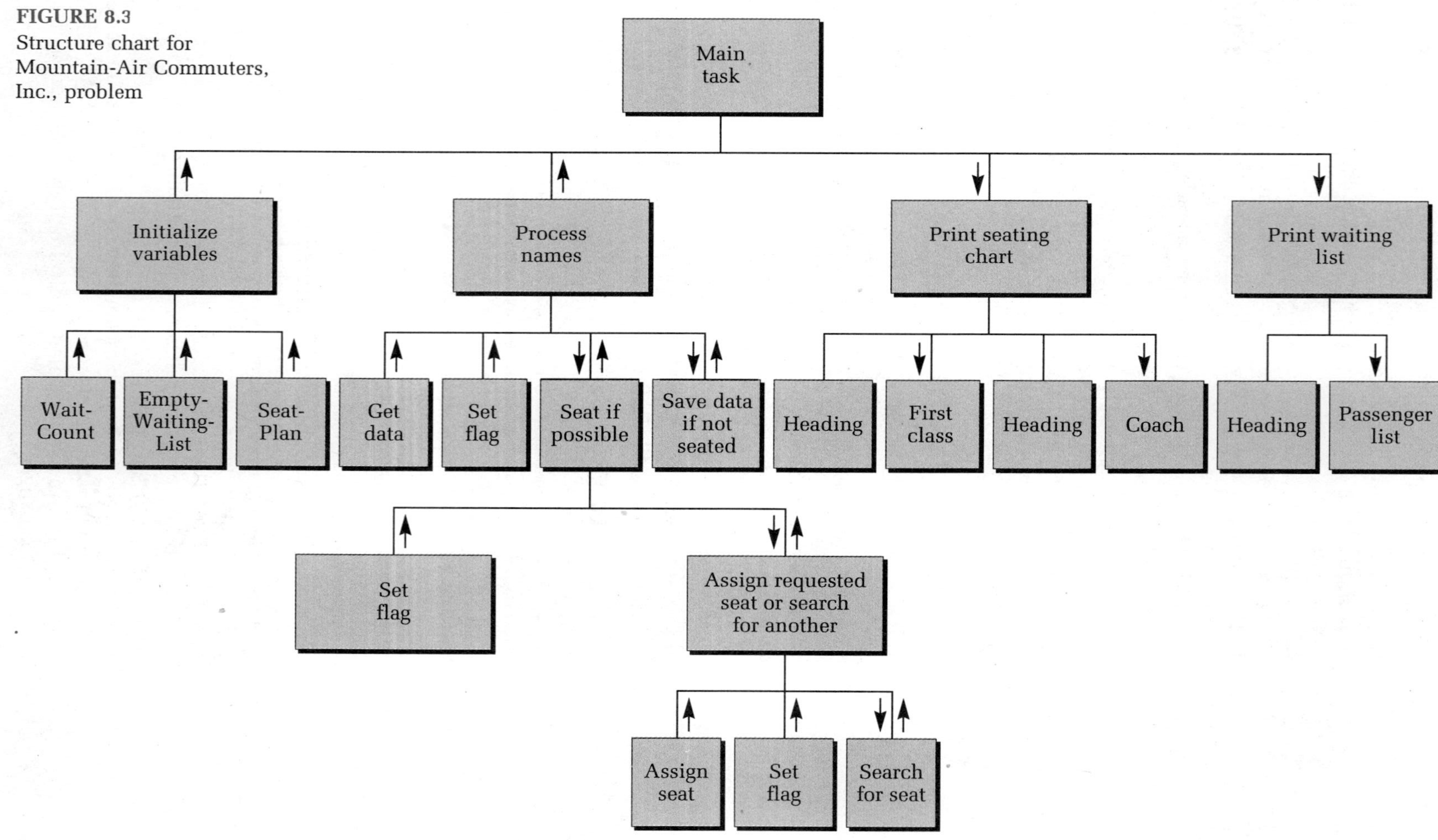

FIGURE 8.3
Structure chart for Mountain-Air Commuters, Inc., problem

4. PrintWaitingList Module
   Data received: Parallel arrays for the passenger's name, section choice, and seat preference
   Information returned: None
   Logic: Use a loop to print an appropriately titled list of passengers for the next flight.

A further development of the pseudocode is

1. Initialize variables
   1.1 initialize WaitCount
   1.2 initialize EmptyWaitingList
   1.3 initialize SeatPlan
2. **WHILE NOT eof DO** process a name
   2.1 get passenger information
   2.2 set Boolean flag Seated for **false**
   2.3 seat if possible
   2.4 **IF NOT** seated **THEN** save relevant information
3. Print a seating chart
   3.1 print a heading
   3.2 print the first-class section
   3.3 print a heading
   3.4 print the coach section
4. **IF** there is a waiting list **THEN** print the list
   4.1 print a heading
   4.2 print passenger list with four columns

Step 2.3 needs some additional refinement. Further development yields

   2.3 seat if possible
      2.3.1 set Seated to **false**
      2.3.2 **IF** requested seat is available **THEN**
         2.3.2.1 assign seat
         2.3.2.2 set Seated to **true**
         ELSE
         2.3.2.3 search for another seat

A complete program for this is

```
PROGRAM AirlineSeating;

{  This program prints a seating plan for an airline.  Passengers     }
{  are assigned seats on a first-come, first-served basis.  Requests  }
{  for first class or coach must be honored.  If all seats are        }
{  filled in a section, the passenger's name and seat preference are  }
{  placed on a waiting list for the next flight.  Features of this    }
{  program include:  defined constants, user-defined data types,      }
{  multidimensional arrays, and subprograms for modular development.  }

USES
  Crt;

CONST
  NumRows = 10;
  NumColumns = 3;
  MaxLength = 50;
  FirstClassBegin = 1;
  FirstClassEnd = 3;
```

```
  CoachBegin = 4;
  CoachEnd = 10;
  EmptyString = '                    ';
  Skip = ' ';

TYPE
  String20 = string [20];
  SeatingPlan = ARRAY [1..NumRows, 1..NumColumns] OF String20;
  NotSeatedList = ARRAY [1..MaxLength] OF String20;
  SectionOptionList = ARRAY [1..MaxLength] OF char;
  SeatChoiceList = ARRAY [1..MaxLength, 1..2] OF integer;

VAR
  Seated : boolean;                     { Indicator for seat found    }
  WaitingList : NotSeatedList;          { Name list for next flight   }
  WaitCount : integer;                  { Counter for waiting list    }
  EmptyWaitingList : boolean;           { Indicator for empty list    }
  Seat : SeatingPlan;                   { 2-dim array of seats        }
  Name : String20;                      { String for names            }
  SectionChoice : char;                 { First class or coach        }
  RowChoice, ColumnChoice : integer;    { Seat preference             }
  SectionOption : SectionOptionList;    { Array of section options    }
  SeatChoice : SeatChoiceList;          { Array of seat choices       }
  Data : text;                          { Names, section/seat choice  }


{**********************************************************************}


PROCEDURE Initialize (VAR Seat : SeatingPlan);

  {  Given:   A two-dimensional array of strings                       }
  {  Task:    Initialize all cells to an empty string                  }
  {  Return:  An initialized two-dimensional array                     }

  VAR
    J, K : integer;                                                        1
  BEGIN
    FOR J := 1 TO NumRows DO
      FOR K := 1 TO NumColumns DO
        Seat[J,K] := EmptyString
  END;  {  of PROCEDURE Initialize  }

{**********************************************************************}


PROCEDURE GetAName (VAR Name : String20;
                    VAR SectionChoice : char;
                    VAR RowChoice, ColumnChoice : integer);

  {  Given:   Nothing                                                  }
  {  Task:    Read a name, section and seat preferences from the       }
  {               input file                                           }
  {  Return:  Passenger name, section and seat preferences             }

  BEGIN
    read (Data, Name);
    readln (Data, SectionChoice, RowChoice, ColumnChoice)
  END;  {  of PROCEDURE GetAName  }

{**********************************************************************}
```

```
PROCEDURE SeatIfPossible (Name : String20;
                          VAR Seat : SeatingPlan;
                          RowChoice, ColumnChoice : integer;
                          SectionChoice : char;
                          VAR Seated : boolean);

  {  Given:   Passenger name, section and seat preferences         }
  {  Task:    If requested seat is available, assign to seat; if   }
  {               seat is not available, use Search to check for an }
  {               alternate seat                                    }
  {  Return:  Seat assignment if one has been made; Boolean flag to }
  {               indicate if seat was found                        }

  PROCEDURE Search (Name : String20;
                    VAR Seat : SeatingPlan;
                    VAR Seated : boolean;
                    FirstRow, LastRow : integer);

    {  Given:   Passenger name, current seating chart, row designa-  }
    {               tors for first-class and coach sections          }
    {  Task:    Search indicated rows to see if an alternate seat is }
    {               available; if yes, assign passenger to it        }
    {  Return:  Updated seating plan and Boolean flag indicating     }
    {               whether or not a seat was found                  }

    VAR
      Row, Column : integer;                                          2
    BEGIN  {  PROCEDURE Search  }
      Seated := false;
      Row := FirstRow;
      REPEAT
        Column := 1;                              {  Start searching rows  }
        REPEAT                                          {  Search one row  }
          IF Seat[Row, Column] = EmptyString THEN
            BEGIN
              Seat[Row, Column] := Name;
              Seated := true
            END
          ELSE
            Column := Column + 1;
        UNTIL Seated OR (Column > NumColumns);
        Row := Row + 1                                 {  Search next row  }
      UNTIL Seated OR (Row > LastRow)
    END;  {  of PROCEDURE Search  }

  BEGIN  {  PROCEDURE SeatIfPossible  }
    Seated := false;
    IF Seat[RowChoice, ColumnChoice] = EmptyString THEN
      BEGIN
        Seat[RowChoice, ColumnChoice] := Name;
        Seated := true
      END
    ELSE
      CASE SectionChoice OF
        'F' : Search (Name, Seat, Seated,
                      FirstClassBegin, FirstClassEnd);
        'C' : Search (Name, Seat, Seated,
                      CoachBegin, CoachEnd)
      END  {  of CASE SectionChoice  }
  END;  {  of PROCEDURE SeatIfPossible  }

{**********************************************************************}
```

```
PROCEDURE PrintSeatingChart (VAR Seat : SeatingPlan);

  {  Given:   The seating chart, a two-dimensional array of names      }
  {  Task:    Print the passenger names in rows and columns accord-    }
  {                   ing to their assigned seats                      }
  {  Return:  Nothing                                                  }

  VAR
    J, K : integer;
  BEGIN
    writeln;
    writeln (Skip:20, 'MOUNTAIN-AIR COMMUTERS');
    writeln (Skip:25, 'Seating Chart');
    writeln;
    writeln ('First-class section');
    writeln ('-------------------');
    writeln;
    FOR J := 1 TO FirstClassEnd DO
      BEGIN                                                               3
        FOR K := 1 TO NumColumns DO
          write (Seat[J,K]:22);
        writeln
      END;  {  of FOR J loop  }
    writeln;
    writeln ('Coach section');
    writeln ('-------------');
    writeln;
    FOR J := CoachBegin TO CoachEnd DO
      BEGIN
        FOR K := 1 TO NumColumns DO
          write (Seat[J,K]:22);
        writeln
      END;  {  of FOR J loop  }
    writeln
  END;  {  of PROCEDURE PrintSeatingChart  }

{*******************************************************************}

PROCEDURE PrintWaitingList (VAR WaitingList : NotSeatedList;
                            VAR SectionOption : SectionOptionList;
                            VAR SeatChoice : SeatChoiceList;
                            WaitCount : integer);

  {  Given:   An array of names of passengers not seated, and the      }
  {                   section and seat preferences for each            }
  {  Task:    Print a waiting list for the next flight                 }
  {  Return:  Nothing                                                  }

  VAR
    J : integer;
  BEGIN                                                                   4
    writeln;
    writeln (Skip:20, 'Waiting list for next flight');
    writeln;
    writeln ('NAME':10, 'SECTION CHOICE':27,
             'ROW NUMBER':25, 'COLUMN NUMBER':15);
    write ('---------------------------------');
    writeln ('---------------------------------');
    writeln;
    FOR J := 1 TO WaitCount DO
      writeln ('<', J:2, '>', WaitingList[J]:22, SectionOption[J]:4,
               SeatChoice[J,1]:18, SeatChoice[J,2]:13)
  END;  {  of PROCEDURE PrintWaitingList  }
```

```
{*******************************************************************}

BEGIN  {  Main program  }
  ClrScr;
  WaitCount := 0;
  EmptyWaitingList := true;
  Initialize (Seat);
  assign (Data, 'Flight.DAT');
  reset (Data);
  WHILE NOT eof(Data) DO
    BEGIN
      GetAName (Name, SectionChoice, RowChoice, ColumnChoice);
      Seated := false;
      SeatIfPossible (Name, Seat, RowChoice, ColumnChoice,
                      SectionChoice, Seated);
      IF NOT Seated THEN        {  Save information for waiting list  }
        BEGIN
          WaitCount := WaitCount + 1;
          WaitingList[WaitCount] := Name;
          SectionOption[WaitCount] := SectionChoice;
          SeatChoice[WaitCount, 1] := RowChoice;
          SeatChoice[WaitCount, 2] := ColumnChoice;
          EmptyWaitingList := false
        END  {  of IF NOT Seated  }
    END;  {  of WHILE NOT eof  }
  PrintSeatingChart (Seat);
  IF NOT EmptyWaitingList THEN
    PrintWaitingList (WaitingList, SectionOption, SeatChoice,
                      WaitCount);
  readln;
  close (Data)
END.  {  of main program  }
```

Using the data file

```
Smith John          F 3 2
Alexander Joe       C 9 3
Allen Darcy         F 3 2
Jones Mary          C 8 1
Humphrey H          C 8 2
Johnson M           F 3 1
Eastman Ken         F 1 1
Winston Sam         C 8 3
Smythe Susan        C 9 1
Hendricks J B       C 9 2
Hanson Cynthia      C 9 3
Zoranson Steve      C 10 1
Radamacher Joe      C 10 3
Borack Bill         C 10 2
Seracki Don         C 9 2
Henry John          F 1 2
Steveson Enghart    F 1 3
Johansen Mary       F 2 1
Smith Martha        F 2 2
Jones Martha        F 2 3
Rinehart Jim        F 3 3
Rinehart Jane       F 3 2
Swenson Cecil       C 4 1
Swenson Carol       C 4 2
Byes Nikoline       C 4 3
Byes Jennifer       C 5 3
Harris John         C 5 2
Harris Judy         C 5 1
```

```
Hartman F G        C 6 1
Hartman D T        C 6 2
Lakes William      C 6 3
Lampton George     C 7 1
Hayes Woodrow      C 7 2
Champion M G       C 7 3
Thomas Lynda       C 8 1
Sisler Susan       C 8 2
Stowers Steve      C 8 3
Banks M J          C 5 3
Banks H W          C 5 2
Brown Susan        C 3 1
Wince Ann          C 8 2
Wince Joanne       C 8 1
```

sample output is

```
                    MOUNTAIN-AIR COMMUTERS
                         Seating Chart

First-class section
-------------------

  Allen Darcy          Eastman Ken          Henry John
  Steveson Enghart     Johansen Mary        Smith Martha
  Johnson M            Smith John           Jones Martha

Coach section
-------------

  Hanson Cynthia       Seracki Don          Swenson Cecil
  Swenson Carol        Byes Nikoline        Byes Jennifer
  Harris John          Harris Judy          Hartman F G
  Hartman D T          Lakes William        Lampton George
  Jones Mary           Humphrey H           Winston Sam
  Smythe Susan         Hendricks J B        Alexander Joe
  Zoranson Steve       Borack Bill          Radamacher Joe

                    Waiting list for next flight

      NAME             SECTION CHOICE     ROW NUMBER  COLUMN NUMBER
----------------------------------------------------------------------
< 1>  Rinehart Jim            F                3             3
< 2>  Rinehart Jane           F                3             2
< 3>  Hayes Woodrow           C                7             2
< 4>  Champion M G            C                7             3
< 5>  Thomas Lynda            C                8             1
< 6>  Sisler Susan            C                8             2
< 7>  Stowers Steve           C                8             3
< 8>  Banks M J               C                5             3
< 9>  Banks H W               C                5             2
<10>  Brown Susan             C                3             1
<11>  Wince Ann               C                8             2
<12>  Wince Joanne            C                8             1
```

RUNNING AND DEBUGGING HINTS

1. Use subrange types with descriptive identifiers to specify index ranges. For example

```
TYPE
  Page = 1..50;
```

```
Row = 1..15;
Column = 1..10;
Book = ARRAY [Page, Row, Column] OF real;
```

2. Develop and maintain a systematic method of processing nested loops. For example, students with mathematical backgrounds will often use I, J, and K as index variables for three-dimensional arrays.
3. Be careful to properly subscript multidimensional array components.
4. When sorting one array in a program that uses parallel arrays, remember to make similar component exchanges in all arrays.
5. Define all data structures in the **TYPE** definition section.

■ Summary

Key Terms

higher-dimensional array   parallel array   two-dimensional array

Key Words

copy	**insert**	**str**
delete	**pos**	**val**

Key Concepts

- Two-dimensional arrays can be declared in several ways; one descriptive method is

```
TYPE
  Chart4X6 = ARRAY [1..4, 1..6] OF real;
VAR
  Table : Chart4X6;
```

- Nested loops are frequently used to **read** and **write** values in two-dimensional arrays; for example, data can be read by

```
FOR Row := 1 TO 4 DO
  FOR Column := 1 TO 6 DO
    read (Table[Row, Column]);
```

- When processing the components of a single row or single column, leave the appropriate row or column index fixed and let the other index vary as a loop index; for example, to sum row three, use

```
Sum := 0;
FOR Column := 1 TO NumOfColumns DO
  Sum := Sum + A[3, Column];
```

  To sum column three, use

```
Sum := 0;
FOR Row := 1 TO NumOfRows DO
  Sum := Sum + A[Row, 3];
```

- An array of strings in Turbo Pascal is a special case of a two-dimensional array; the data structure is an array of strings and can be declared by

```
TYPE
  String20 = string [20];
  NameList = ARRAY [1..50] OF String20;
VAR
  Name : NameList;
```

- Arrays of strings can be alphabetized by using the selection sort.
- Three standard procedures used in programs that work with arrays of strings are (1) get the data, (2) alphabetize the array, and (3) print the alphabetized list.
- Parallel arrays may be used to solve problems that require arrays of the same index type but of different data types.

- A typical problem in which parallel arrays would be used involves working with a list of names and an associated list of numbers (for example, test scores). In Chapter 9, we will see that this can also be done with a single array of records.
- A typical data structure declaration for using names and scores is

```
TYPE
  String20 = string [20];
  NameList = ARRAY [1..30] OF String20;
  ScoreList = ARRAY [1..30] OF integer;
VAR
  Name : NameList;
  Score : ScoreList;
```

- The procedure **str** converts a number to a string.
- The procedure **val** converts a string to a number.
- The function **copy** returns a substring of a string.
- The function **pos** searches for a substring.
- The procedure **insert** inserts a substring into a string.
- The procedure **delete** delets a substring from a string.
- Data structures for solving problems can require arrays of three or more dimensions.
- A typical declaration for an array of three dimensions is

```
TYPE
  Dim1 = 1..10;
  Dim2 = 1..20;
  Dim3 = 1..30;
  Block = ARRAY [Dim1, Dim2, Dim3] OF real;
VAR
  Item : Block;
```

In this array, a typical component is accessed by

```
Item[I,J,K]
```

- Nested loops are frequently used when working with higher-dimensional arrays; for example, all values on the first level of array Item as just declared can be printed by

```
FOR J := 1 TO 20 DO
  BEGIN
    FOR K := 1 TO 30 DO
      BEGIN
        write (Item[1,J,K]:5:2);
        writeln
      END;  {  of 1 line  }
    writeln
  END;  {  of 20 lines  }
```

- When working with subprograms, array variables are usually passed by reference.

■ Programming Problems and Projects

■ 1. The local high school sports boosters are conducting a fund drive to help raise money for the athletic program. As each donation is received, the person's name and donation amount are entered on one line in a data file. Write a program to do the following.

   a. Print an alphabetized list of all donors together with their corresponding donations.

   b. Print a list of donations from high to low together with the donors' names.

   c. Compute and print the average and total of all donations.

■ 2. Because they did not meet their original goal, your local high school sports boosters (Problem 1) are at it again. For their second effort, each donor's name and donation are added on a separate line at the end of the previously sorted list. Write a program to produce the lists, average, and total in Problem 1. No donor's name should appear more than once in a list.

■ 3. Dr. Lae Z. Programmer (Problems 5, 22, and 23, Chapter 4; Problem 13, Chapter 5; and Problem 5, Chapter 6) now expects you to write a program to do all record keeping for the class. For each student, consecutive lines of the data file contain the student's name, 10 quiz scores, six program scores, and three examination scores. Your output should include the following.
   a. An alphabetized list together with
      i. quiz total
      ii. program total
      iii. examination total
      iv. total points
      v. percentage grade
      vi. letter grade
   b. The overall class average
   c. A histogram depicting the grade distribution
4. The All Metro Basketball Conference consists of 10 teams. The conference commissioner has created a data file in which each line contains one school's name, location, and nickname for the school team. You are to write a program to read this data and then produce three lists, each of which contains all information about the school. All lists are to be sorted alphabetically: the first, by school name; the second, by school location; the third, by nickname.
5. Upgrade the program for Mountain-Air Commuters, Inc., in the Focus on Program Design so it can be used for each of five daily flights. Passengers on a waiting list must be processed first. Print a seating chart for each flight.
6. Add yet another upgrade to the Mountain-Air Commuters, Inc., program. Write an interactive version to consider the possibility of seating passengers who wish to sit together in the same row. If no such seating is possible, these passengers should be given a choice of alternate seating (if possible) or of taking a later flight.
7. Salespersons at McHenry Tool Corporation are given a monthly commission check. The commission is computed by multiplying the salesperson's gross monthly sales by the person's commission rate.

   Write a program to compute a salesperson's monthly commission to the nearest cent. The program should prepare a list of all salespersons in descending order based upon monthly commission earned, with the person earning the highest commission on top. Each salesperson's commission should be printed next to his or her name. At the bottom of the list, indicate the total monthly commission (summed across all salespersons) and the average commission per salesperson. McHenry never employs more than 60 salespersons.

   Any names of persons who have invalid data should be printed out separately. Data are invalid if the commission rate is not between 0.01 and 0.50 or if the gross monthly sales figure is negative.
8. In order to reduce their costs, the McHenry Tool Corporation (Problem 7) is switching from monthly to biannual commission checks. The commission is now computed by multiplying a person's commission rate by the sum of his or her gross monthly sales for a six-month period. McHenry has asked you to develop the necessary computer program. The program should differ from Problem 7 in the following ways.
   a. Each name on the output should be followed by the six figures for gross monthly sales. The columns should be labeled "January" through "June." Total six-month gross sales should be given next, followed by the rate of commission and the amount of the six-month commission check rounded to the nearest cent.

b. Commission rates are based upon gross six-month sales as follows.

Sales	Commission Rate (%)
0–$19,999	3.0
$20,000–$39,999	5.0
$40,000–59,999	5.5
$60,000–79,999	6.0
$80,000–89,999	6.5
$90,000 or more	8.0

c. At the bottom of each column, the program should provide the total and the mean for that column. (The column for commission rates does not require a total, only a mean.)

9. The dean of a small undergraduate college (with an enrollment of < 2000) has asked you to write a program to figure grade point averages for an unknown number of students. The output should be an alphabetized roster showing the sex, identification number (social security number), grade point average (rounded to three decimal places), and class status (freshman, sophomore, junior, or senior) for each student.

   The data provide the name, gender (M or F), social security number (ID), and number of semesters completed. Also provided are the number of courses taken and the letter grade and number of credits for each course. The possible letter grades are A (4 points), B (3 points), C (2 points), D (1 point), and E (0 points). Class status is determined by the number of credits as follows:

1–25 credits	freshman
26–55 credits	sophomore
56–85 credits	junior
86 or more credits	senior

10. You have just started to work for the Michigan Association of Automobile Manufacturers and have been asked to analyze sales data gathered on five subcompact cars over the last six months. Your analysis should be in table form and should include the name of each make and model, a model's sales volume for each month, a model's total and average sales volume for six months, a model's total sales revenue for six months, and the total and average sales volumes for each month. In addition, your output should include the total and average sales volumes of all models for the entire six months and the make and model name of the car with the largest total sales revenue and the amount of that revenue.

11. You have been asked to write a program to assist with the inventory and ordering for Tite-Jeans, Inc. The company manufactures three styles: straight, flair, and peg. In each style, waist sizes vary by integer values from 24 to 46 and inseams vary by integer values from 26 to 40. Write a program to do the following.
   a. Read in the starting inventory.
   b. Read in daily sales.
   c. Print the ending inventory for each style.
   d. Print order charts for each style that is low in stock (fewer than three).
   e. Print an emergency order list for each style that is out of stock.

12. You have been asked to write a program that will grade results of a true-false quiz and display the results in tabular form. The quiz consists of 10 questions. The data file for this problem consists of (1) correct responses (answer key) on line one and (2) a four-digit student identification number followed by that student's 10 responses on each successive line. Thus, the data file would be

```
TFFTFTTFTT
0461 TTFTTFTFTT
3218 TFFTTTTFTT
.
.
.
```

Your program should read the key and store it in an array. It should then read the remaining lines, storing the student identification numbers in one array and the number of correct responses in a parallel array. Output should consist of a table with three columns: one for the student identification number, one for the number of correct responses, and one for the quiz grade. Grade assignments are A (10 correct), B (9), C (8–7), D (6–5), E (4–0). Your output should also include the quiz average for the entire class.

13. A few members (total unknown, but no more than 25) at Oakland Mountain Country Club want to computerize their golf scores. Each member plays 20 games: some play 18 holes; some, 9 holes. Each member's name (no more than 20 characters) is written on a data card, followed on a second card by the 20 scores. Each score is immediately followed by E or N, indicating 18 or 9 holes, respectively.

Write a program to read all the names and scores into two parallel two-dimensional arrays. Calculate everyone's 18-hole average. (Double the 9-hole scores before you store them in the array, and treat them as 18-hole scores.) Calculate how much each average is over or under par (Par is 72 and should be declared as a constant.) Output should be each name, average, difference from par, and scores.

14. Write a program to keep statistics for a basketball team consisting of 15 players. Statistics for each player should include shots attempted, shots made, and shooting percentage; free throws attempted, free throws made, and free throw percentage; offensive rebounds and defensive rebounds; assists; turnovers; and total points. Appropriate team totals should be listed as part of the output.

15. A magic square is a square array of positive integers such that the sum of each row, column, and diagonal is the same constant. For example

16	3	2	13
5	10	11	8
9	6	7	12
4	15	14	1

is a magic square with a constant of 34. Write a program to input four lines of four positive integers. The program should then determine whether or not the square is a magic square.

16. Pascal's Triangle can be used to recognize coefficients of a quantity raised to a power. The rules for forming this triangle of integers are such that each row must start and end with a one and each entry in a row is the sum of the two values diagonally above the new entry. Thus, four rows of Pascal's Triangle are

```
      1
    1   1
  1   2   1
1   3   3   1
```

This triangle is a convenient way to determine the coefficients of a quantity of two terms raised to a power (binomial coefficients). For example

$$(a + b)^3 = 1a^3 + 3a^2b + 3ab^2 + 1b^3$$

where the coefficients 1, 3, 3, and 1 come from the fourth row of Pascal's Triangle.

Write a complete program to print out Pascal's Triangle for 10 rows.

17. Your former high school principal wants you to develop a program to maintain a list of the 20 students in the school with the highest scores on the SAT test. Input is from a text file containing the name (20 characters) and the total SAT score (verbal plus mathematical). Write a program that reads all the data and then prints out a list of the 20 highest scores from highest to lowest and the students' names. Assume no two students have the same score.

18. The transpose of a matrix (table) is a new matrix with the row and column positions reversed. Thus, the transpose of matrix A, an $M \times N$ matrix, is an $N \times M$ matrix with each element $A[m,n]$ stored in $B[n,m]$. Given a 3×5 matrix of integers, create a matrix that is its transpose. Print both the original matrix and the new matrix.

■ 19. Mr. Laven, a mathematics instructor at your college, wants you to write a program to help him keep his students' grades. He wants to keep track of up to 30 grades for each of up to 35 students. Your program should read grades and names from a text file and then print the following.
   a. A table showing the names in alphabetical order and the grades received by each student.
   b. An alphabetical list of students with their corresponding total points and average score.
   c. A list of averages from highest to lowest with corresponding students' names.

20. Write a program in which a person can enter data into a 5×7 matrix. Print the original matrix along with the average of each row and column.

21. Matrix M is symmetric if it has the same number of rows as columns and if each element $M[x,y]$ is equal to $M[y,x]$. Write a program to check a matrix entered by the user to see if it is symmetric or not.

22. The following table shows the total sales for salespeople at the Falcon Manufacturing Company.

Salesperson	Week 1	Week 2	Week 3	Week 4
Anna, Michael	30	25	45	18
Henderson, Marge	22	30	32	35
Johnson, Fred	12	17	19	15
Striker, Nancy	32	30	33	31
Ryan, Renee	22	17	28	16

The price of the product being sold is $1,985.95. Write a program that permits the input of the previous data and prints both a replica of the original table and a table showing the dollar value of sales for each individual during each week along with his or her total sales. Also, print the total sales for each week and the total sales for the company.

23. The computer science office wants you to develop a computerized system for finding telephone numbers of students. The program should read a list of up to 20 students and their telephone numbers from a text file. It should permit the entry of a student's name and then print the name and telephone number. (A binary search could be used for this.) If the name is not found, an appropriate message should be printed.
24. Write a program to permit two people to play the game of Battleship. Your program should record the ship positions, hits, misses, and ship sinkings for each player.
25. Rewrite the Battleship program (Problem 24) to have a person play against the computer.
26. Create a text editor that is capable of performing some editing operations on a line of text. A menu should allow the user to choose from the following:

```
<1>  Enter a string
<2>  Delete from the string
<3>  Insert into the string
<4>  Search for a substring
<5>  Replace a substring
<6>  Quit
```

Your program should guarantee valid input for menu options. Each menu option should be developed as a separate procedure.

■ Communication in Practice

1. Select a problem from the Programming Problems and Projects of this chapter that you have not done. Write documentation for that problem that includes a complete description of the following.
   a. Required input
   b. Required output
   c. Required processing and computation
2. Assume you are directing the development of a spelling checker to be used in conjunction with a text editor. Work up a complete set of specifications that can be used by the team who will do the actual development. Your specifications should include a description of the main tasks to be performed by the team, a statement of the expected form of input and output for the finished product, and documentation standards to be included in the development of each component.
3. Arrange a visit with a travel agent or an airline reservations agent, and discuss the information the agent requests from prospective passengers. If possible, have the agent set up a mock booking using the computerized reservations system. Examine the screen displays.

   Prepare a report of your visit for the class. Be sure to discuss how the designers of the reservations system may have used multidimensional arrays.
4. Contact someone who uses a spreadsheet as part of his or her daily work. Have the person show you several routine operations with the spreadsheet. In particular, find out how to adjust the size of the spreadsheet, sum rows, sum columns, and use functions to define entries for specific locations.

   Give an oral report of your findings to your class. Explain how the various spreadsheet operations relate to what you have studied about two-dimensional arrays.

5. Select a problem from the Programming Problems and Projects of this chapter that you have not done. Construct a structure chart and write all documentary information necessary for the problem you have chosen. Do not write code. When you are finished, have a classmate read your documentation to see if precisely what is to be done is clear.
6. Delete all documentation from one of the programs you prepared for this chapter. Exchange your modified version with a student who has prepared a similar version. Write documentation for the exchanged program. Compare your results with your classmate's original version.

Records

CHAPTER OUTLINE

Chapters 7 and 8 dealt extensively with the concept of the structured data type **ARRAY.** When we declare an array, we reserve a predetermined number of memory locations. The variables representing these memory locations are of the same base type and can be accessed by reference to the index of an array element.

All components of an array must be of the same data type—a serious limitation since this is not possible in many situations. For example, a bank may wish to keep a record of the name, address, telephone number, marital status, social security number, annual salary, total assets, and total liabilities of each customer. Fortunately, Turbo Pascal provides another structured data type, **RECORD,** which allows heterogeneous information to be stored, accessed, and manipulated. A record contains fields, which can be of different data types. In this chapter, we will learn how to declare records, how to access the various fields within a record, and how to work with arrays of records.

9.1 Record Definitions

RECORD as a Structured Data Type

A *record* is a collection of *fields* that may be treated as a whole or individually. To illustrate, a record that contains fields for a customer's name, age, and annual income could be visualized as shown in Figure 9.1.

This schematic representation may help you understand why a record is considered a structured data type and may help familiarize you with the idea of using fields in a record.

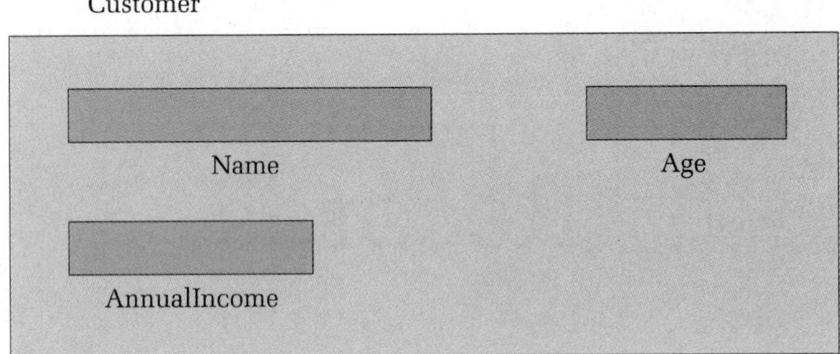

FIGURE 9.1
Fields in a record

RECORD Definition and Declaration

Now let's consider our first example of a formally declared record. Assume we want a record to contain a customer's name, age, and annual income. The following type definition and subsequent declaration can be made:

```
TYPE
  CustomerInfo = RECORD
                   Name : string [30]
                   Age : integer;
                   AnnualIncome : real
                 END;  {  of RECORD CustomerInfo  }
VAR
  Customer : CustomerInfo;
```

Components of a record are called fields, and each field has an associated data type. The general form for defining a record data type using the **TYPE** definition section is

> **TYPE**
> <type identifier> = **RECORD**
> <field identifier 1> : <data type 1>;
> <field identifier 2> : <data type 2>;
> .
> .
> .
> <field identifier *n*> : <data type *n*>
> **END;** { of **RECORD** definition }

The syntax diagram for this is

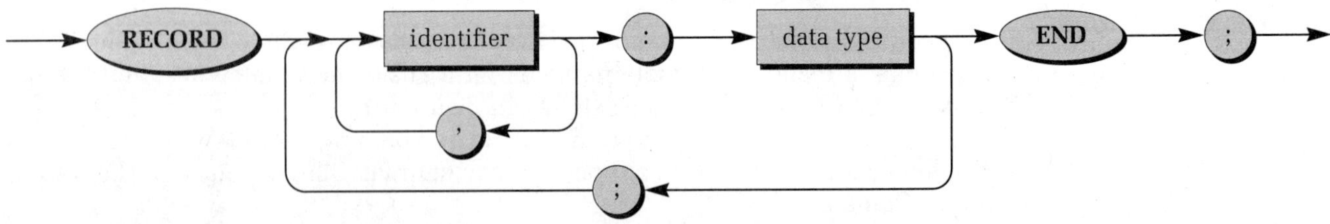

The following comments are in order concerning this form.

1. The type identifier can be any valid identifier. It should be descriptive to enhance program readability.
2. The reserved word **RECORD** must precede the field identifiers.

3. Each field identifier within a record must be unique. However, field identifiers in different records may use the same name. Thus

```
FirstRecord = RECORD
                Name : string [30];
                Age : integer
              END;  {  of RECORD FirstRecord  }
```

and

```
SecondRecord = RECORD
                 Name : string [30];
                 Age : integer;
                 IQ : integer
               END;  {  of RECORD SecondRecord  }
```

can both be defined in the same program.

4. Data types for fields can be user-defined. Thus, our earlier definitions could have been

```
TYPE
  String30 = string [30];
  CustomerInfo = RECORD
                   Name : String30;
                   Age : integer;
                   AnnualIncome : real
                 END;  {  of RECORD CustomerInfo  }
VAR
  Customer : CustomerInfo;
```

5. **END;** is required to signify the end of a **RECORD** definition. This is the second instance (remember **CASE**?) in which **END** is used without a **BEGIN.**
6. Fields of the same base type can be declared together. Thus

```
Info = RECORD
         Name : String30;
         Age, IQ : integer
       END;  {  of RECORD Info  }
```

is appropriate. However, it is good practice to list each field separately to enhance readability and to reinforce the concept of fields in a record. The following example defines another record.

EXAMPLE 9.1

Suppose you want to keep a record for a college student. The record is to contain a field for each of the following: student's name (Smith Jane), social security number (111-22-3333), class status (Fr, So, Jr, or Sr), previous credit hours earned (56), credit hours being taken (17), and grade point average (3.27). We can define a record and declare an appropriate variable as follows:

```
TYPE
  String30 = string [30];
  String11 = string [11];
  Class = (Fr, So, Jr, Sr);
  StudentInfo = RECORD
                  Name : String30;
                  SSN : String11;
                  Status : Class;
                  HoursEarned : 0..999;
                  HoursTaking : 0..30;
                  GPA : real
                END;  {  of RECORD StudentInfo  }
VAR
  Student : StudentInfo;
```

Fields in a Record

Now that we know how to define a record, we need to examine how to access fields in a record. For our discussion, let's consider a record defined by

```
TYPE
  String30 = string [30];
  Employee = RECORD
               Name : String30;
               Age : integer;
               MaritalStatus : char;
               Wage : real
             END;  {  of RECORD Employee  }
VAR
  Programmer : Employee;
```

Programmer can be visualized as shown in Figure 9.2.

FIGURE 9.2
Defined fields in Programmer

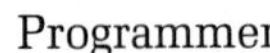

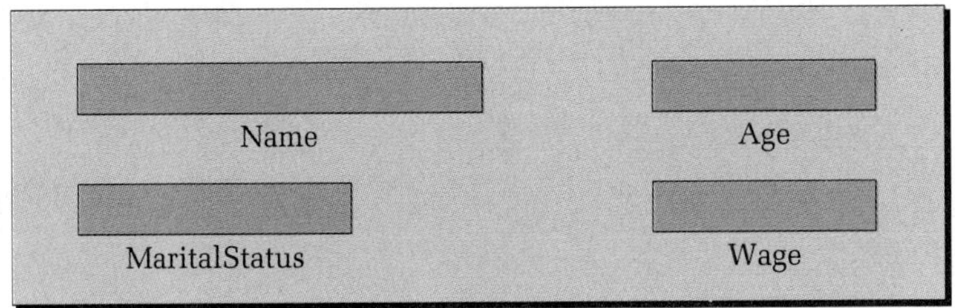

Each field within a record is a variable and can be uniquely identified by

<record name> . <field name>

where a period separates the record name from the field name. Thus, the four field variables are

```
Programmer.Name
Programmer.Age
Programmer.MaritalStatus
Programmer.Wage
```

Each of these variables may be used in any manner consistent with the defined base type. To illustrate, if Programmer.Name and Programmer.Age have been assigned values and we wish to print the names of those employees under 30 years of age, we could have a fragment of code such as

```
IF Programmer.Age < 30 THEN
  writeln (Programmer.Name:40);
```

If we wish to compute gross salary, we might have

```
read (Hours);
Gross := Hours * Programmer.Wage;
```

Other Fields

Thus far, our fields have been defined directly. Sometimes when the structure of a record is being established, the data type of a field needs more development. For example, suppose we wish to declare a record for each student in a class and the record is to contain student name, class name, four test scores, 10 quiz scores, final average, and letter grade. This can be visualized as shown in Figure 9.3. In this case, Test and Quiz are both arrays. Thus, a subsequent development is shown in Figure 9.4.

FIGURE 9.3
Fields in Student

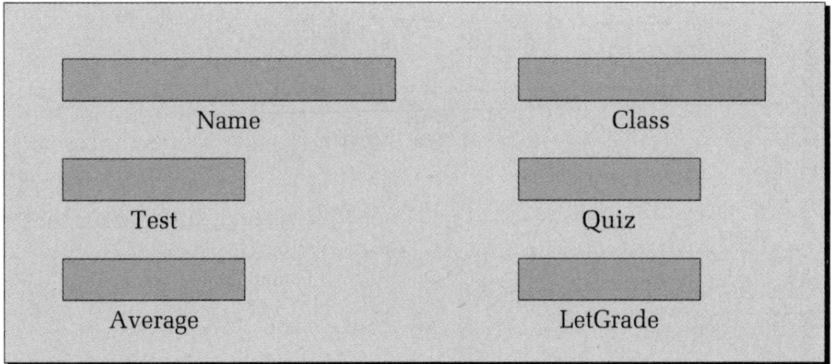

FIGURE 9.4
Arrays as fields in a record

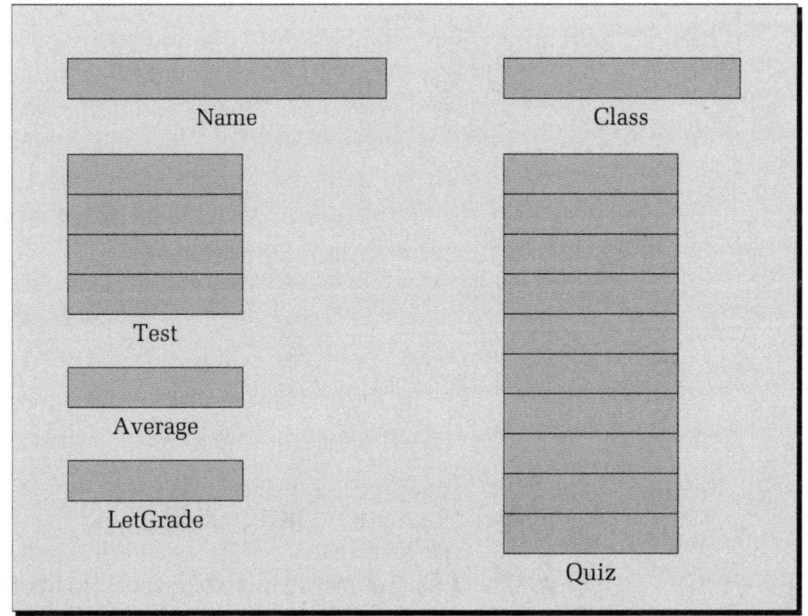

The record in Figure 9.4 can now be formally defined by

```
TYPE
  String30 = string [30];
  String10 = string [10];
  TestScores = ARRAY [1..4] OF integer;
  QuizScores = ARRAY [1..10] OF integer;
  StudentInfo = RECORD
                  Name : String30;
                  Class : String10;
                  Test : TestScores;
                  Quiz : QuizScores;
                  Average : real;
                  LetGrade : char
                END;  {  of RECORD StudentInfo  }
VAR
  Student : StudentInfo;
```

declaration can then use it in prog

If the student associated with this record earns an 89 on the first test and a 9 (out of 10) on the first quiz, this information can be entered by reading the values or by assigning them appropriately. Thus, either of the following will suffice:

COMMUNICATION AND STYLE TIPS

Use descriptive field names, appropriate subranges, and a descriptive variable name when defining records. For example, if you want a record to contain fields for a student's name, age, gender, and class status, you can use

```
TYPE
  String20 = string [20];
  StudentRecord = RECORD
                    Name : String20;
                    Age : 0..99;
                    Gender : (Male, Female);
                    ClassStatus : (Fr, So, Jr, Sr)
                  END;  {  of RECORD StudentRecord  }
VAR
  Student : StudentRecord;
```

The fields are then

```
Student.Name
Student.Age
Student.Gender
Student.ClassStatus
```

and you can use program statements such as

```
IF Student.Gender = Male THEN
```

or

```
IF Student.Age < 21 THEN
```

```
read (Student.Test[1], Student.Quiz[1]);
```

or

```
Student.Test[1] := 89;
Student.Quiz[1] := 9;
```

Exercises 9.1

1. Explain why records are structured data types.
2. Write a test program to
   a. Define a **RECORD** type in which the record contains fields for your name and your age.
   b. Declare a record variable to be of this type.
   c. Read in your name and age from a data file.
   d. Print out your name and age.
3. Discuss the similarities and differences between arrays and records as structured data types.
4. Use the **TYPE** definition section to define each of the three records illustrated in Figure 9.5. In each case, declare a record variable of the defined type.
5. Draw a schematic representation of each of the following record definitions.
   a.
```
TYPE
  String30 = string [30];
  String11 = string [11];
  EmployeeInfo = RECORD
                   Name : String30;
                   SSN : String11;
                   NumOfDep : integer;
                   HourlyWage : real
                 END;
VAR
  Employee : EmployeeInfo;
```

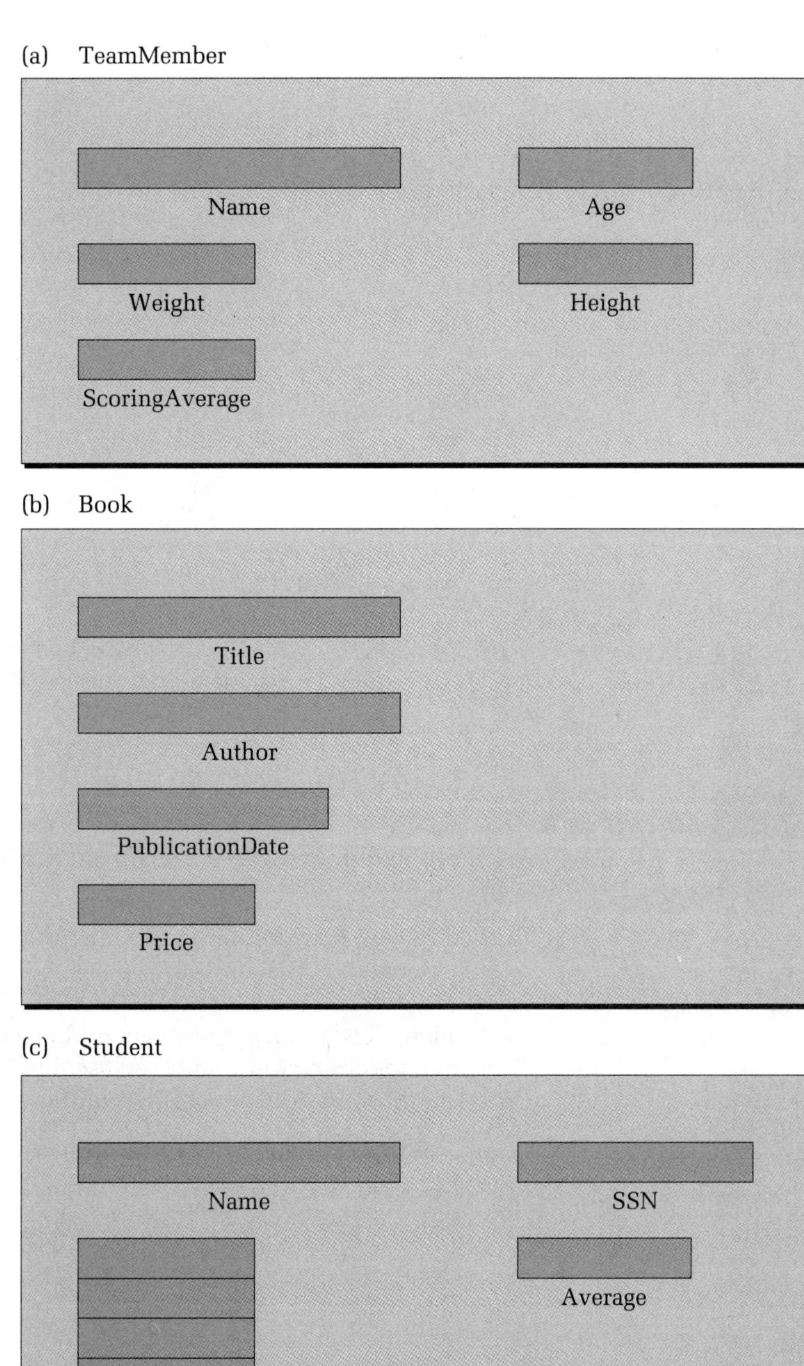

FIGURE 9.5
Records with fields illustrated

b.
```
TYPE
  HouseInfo = RECORD
                Location : string [20]
                Age : integer;
                NumRooms : integer;
                NumBaths : integer;
                BuildingType : (Brick, Frame);
                Taxes : real;
                Price : real
              END;
VAR
  House : HouseInfo;
```

c.
```
TYPE
  String20 = string [20];
  String30 = string [30];
  String8 = string [8];
  PhoneBook = RECORD
                Name : String30;
                Address : ARRAY [1..4] OF String20;
                PhoneNum : String8
              END;
VAR
  PhoneListing : PhoneBook;
```

6. Use the **TYPE** definition section to define an appropriate **RECORD** type for each of the following. In each case, also declare an appropriate record variable.

   a. Families in your former school district: each record should contain the last name, parents' first and last names, address, number of children, and ages of children.

   b. Students in a school system: each record should contain the student's name, identification number, classification (Fr, So, Jr, or Sr), courses being taken (at most six), and grade point average.

7. Find all errors in each of the following definitions or declarations.

a.
```
TYPE
  Info : RECORD
           Name = string [30];
           Age : 0..100
         END;
```

b.
```
TYPE
  Member = RECORD
             Age : integer;
             IQ : integer
           END;
VAR
  Member : Member;
```

c.
```
VAR
  Member = RECORD
             Name : string [30];
             Age : 0..100;
             IQ = 50..200
           END;
```

8. Given the record defined by

```
TYPE
  String30 = string [30];
  Weekdays = (Mon, Tues, Wed, Thur, Fri);
  ListOfScores = ARRAY [1..5] OF integer;
  Info = RECORD
           Name : String30;
           Day : Weekdays;
           Score : ListOfScores;
           Average : real
         END;
VAR
  Contestant : Info;
  Sum : integer;
```

assume values have been assigned as shown in Figure 9.6. Indicate which of the following are valid; explain any invalid statements.

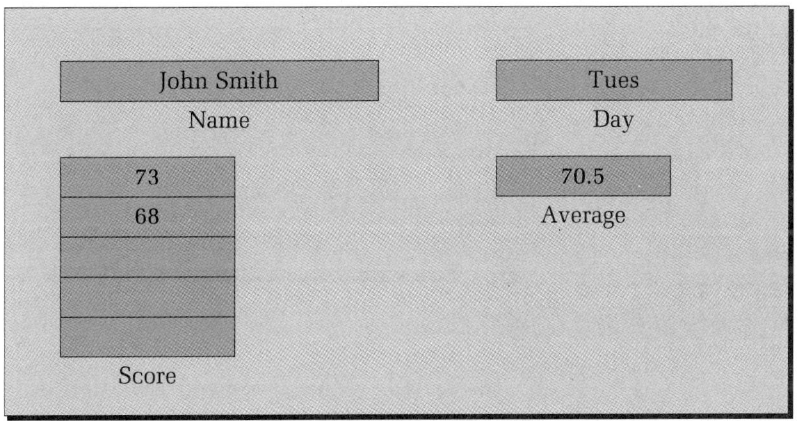

FIGURE 9.6
Values in fields of Contestant

a. `Day := Wed;`

b. `Contestant.Day := Wed;`

c. `Score := 70;`

d. `Score[3] := 70;`

e. `Contestant.Score[3] := 70;`

f. `Contestant[3].Score := 70;`

g.
```
FOR J := 1 TO 5 DO
  Sum := Sum + Contestant.Score[J];
```

h. `Contestant.Score[3] := Score[2];`

i. `Contestant.Score[3] := Contestant.Score[2] + 3;`

j. `Average := (Score[1] + Score[2] + Score[3]) / 3;`

k.
```
IF Contestant.Day < Wed THEN
  Contestant.Average := Contestant.Score[1] +
                        Contestant.Score[2];
```

l. `writeln (Contestant.Name:40, Contestant.Average:10:2);`

■ 9.2 Using Records

The previous section introduced the concept of **RECORD** as a structured data type. At this stage, you should be comfortable with this concept and be able to use the **TYPE** definition section to define such a data type. In this section, we will examine methods of working with records.

WITH . . . DO Using Records

Let's consider a record that contains fields for a student's name, three test scores, and test average. It can be defined by

```
TYPE
  String20 = string [20];
  List3 = ARRAY [1..3] OF integer;
  StudentRecord = RECORD
                    Name : String20;
                    Score : List3;
                    Average : real
                  END;  {  of RECORD StudentRecord  }
VAR
  Student : StudentRecord;
```

and envisioned as shown in Figure 9.7.

FIGURE 9.7
Fields in Student

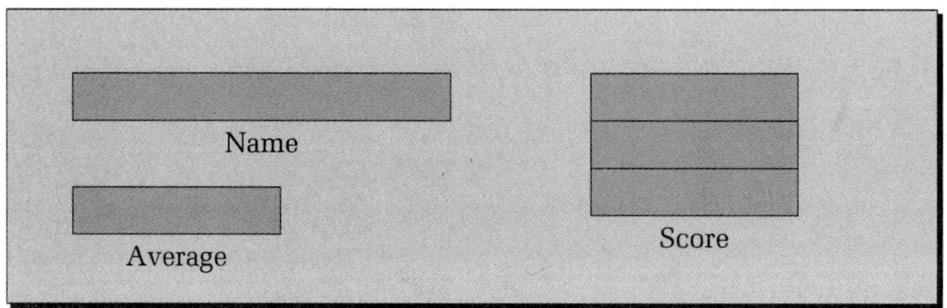

To use this record, we need to assign or read data into appropriate fields. We assume a line of data is

```
Washington Joe      79 83 94
```

This data can be read by the fragment of code

```
read (DataFile, Student.Name);
FOR J := 1 TO 3 DO
  read (DataFile, Student.Score[J]);
readln (DataFile);
```

The average can be computed by

```
Student.Average := (Student.Score[1] +
                    Student.Score[2] +
                    Student.Score[3]) / 3;
```

Notice each field identifier includes the record name. Fortunately, when working with fields of a record, Turbo Pascal provides a more convenient method of referring to these fields: a **WITH . . . DO** statement. Using this option, the previous fragment can be rewritten as

```
WITH Student DO
  BEGIN
    read (DataFile, Name);
    FOR J := 1 TO 3 DO
      read (DataFile, Score[J]);
    readln (DataFile);
    Average := (Score[1] + Score[2] + Score[3]) / 3
  END;  {  of WITH...DO  }
```

Formally, a **WITH . . . DO** statement has the form

> **WITH** <record name> **DO**
> **BEGIN**
> <statement 1>;
> <statement 2>;
> .
> .
> .
> <statement *n*>
> **END;**

where the statements used may refer to the field identifiers but do not include the record name as part of the field identifier. This eliminates use of the period following the record name. Thus, instead of Student.Score[J], we can use Score[J].

As a second illustration, suppose we have a record defined as

```
TYPE
  String20 = string [20];
  PatientInfo = RECORD
                  Name : String20;
                  Age : integer;
                  Height : integer;
                  Weight : integer;
                  Gender : char
                END;  {  of RECORD PatientInfo  }
VAR
  Patient : PatientInfo;
```

Values can be assigned to the various fields specifically by

```
Patient.Name := 'Jones Connie';
Patient.Age := 19;
Patient.Height := 67;
Patient.Weight := 125;
Patient.Gender := 'F';
```

or by

```
WITH Patient DO
  BEGIN
    Name := 'Jones Connie';
    Age := 19;
    Height := 67;
    Weight := 125;
    Gender := 'F'
  END;  {  of WITH...DO  }
```

A single **WITH . . . DO** statement can be used with more than one record. For example, using the previous two record definitions, it is possible to write

```
WITH Student, Patient DO
  BEGIN
    Average := (Score[1] + Score[2] + Score[3]) / 3;
    Age := 19
  END;  {  of WITH...DO  }
```

This is equivalent to the nested use of **WITH . . . DO,** as follows:

```
WITH Student DO
  WITH Patient DO
    BEGIN
      Average := (Score[1] + Score[2] + Score[3]) / 3;
      Age := 19
    END;
```

In this nesting, the record identifier is associated with each field defined in that record. Thus

```
Age := 19
```

can be thought of as

```
Patient.Age := 19
```

Since Average is not a field in Patient, it will not be associated with the record identifier Patient. It will, however, be associated with the record identifier Student.

When using more than one record in a single **WITH . . . DO** statement, each field identifier should have a unique reference to exactly one of the listed records. If a field identifier is used in more than one of the records, the reference intended by the programmer may be ambiguous and a logic error may result. Thus

```
WITH Student, Patient DO
  writeln (Name);
```

could produce a result different than expected because it is not clear whether the reference is to Student.Name or to Patient.Name. In Turbo Pascal, the association is always with the innermost correct field identifier. Since Name is a field in both Student and Patient, Patient.Name would be printed. However, the intent may have been to print Student.Name. In general, you are advised to use separate **WITH . . . DO** statements for records with identical field names.

Copying Records

How can information contained in one record be transferred to another record? This must be done, for example, when we want to sort an array of records. To illustrate how records can be copied, consider the following definitions and declarations:

```
TYPE
  InfoA = RECORD
            Field1 : integer;
            Field2 : real;
            Field3 : char
          END;  { of RECORD InfoA  }
  InfoB = RECORD
            Field1 : integer;
            Field2 : real;
            Field3 : char
          END;  { of RECORD InfoB  }
VAR
  Rec1, Rec2 : InfoA;
  Rec3 : InfoB;
```

The three records declared can be envisioned as shown in Figure 9.8.

Now, suppose data have been assigned to Rec1 by

```
WITH Rec1 DO
  BEGIN
    Field1 := 25;
    Field2 := 89.5;
    Field3 := 'M'
  END;  { of WITH...DO  }
```

These data can be copied to the corresponding fields of Rec2 by

```
Rec2 := Rec1;
```

FIGURE 9.8
Copying records

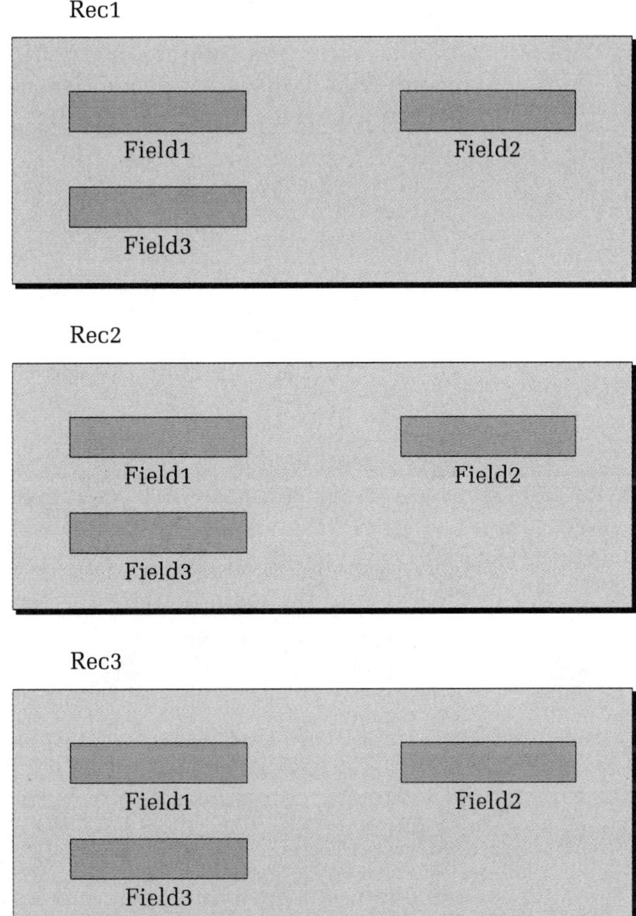

This single assignment statement accomplishes all of the following:

```
Rec2.Field1 := Rec1.Field1;
Rec2.Field2 := Rec1.Field2;
Rec2.Field3 := Rec1.Field3;
```

It is important to note that such an assignment can only be made when the records are of identical type. For example, notice that InfoA and InfoB have the same structure but have been defined as different types. In this case, if we wish to assign the values in the fields of Rec1 to the corresponding fields of Rec3, the statement

```
Rec3 := Rec1;
```

produces a compilation error. Although Rec1 and Rec3 have the same structure, they are not of identical type. In this case, the information can be transferred by

```
WITH Rec3 DO
  BEGIN
    Field1 := Rec1.Field1;
    Field2 := Rec1.Field2;
    Field3 := Rec1.Field3
  END;  {  of WITH...DO  }
```

Reading Data into a Record

Once a record has been defined for a program, one task is to get data into the record. This is usually accomplished by reading from a data file. To illustrate, assume we have a record defined by

```
TYPE
  String20 = string [20];
  PatientInfo = RECORD
                  Name : String20;
                  Age : integer;
                  Height : integer;
                  Weight : integer;
                  Gender : char
                END;  {  of RECORD PatientInfo  }
VAR
  Patient : PatientInfo;
```

and a line of data is

Smith Mary 21 67 125F ▌

One method of getting the data is to use a **WITH . . . DO** statement like the following in the main body of a program as follows:

```
BEGIN  {  Main program  }
  assign (DataFile, 'Patient.DAT');
  reset (DataFile);
  WITH Patient DO
    BEGIN
      read (DataFile, Name);
      readln (DataFile, Age, Height, Weight, Gender)
    END;  {  of WITH...DO  }
```

S However, good program design would have us use a procedure for this task. In order to use a procedure, we must be careful to use the user-defined data type PatientInfo and a variable parameter in the procedure heading. With these two considerations, an appropriate procedure is

```
PROCEDURE GetData (VAR Patient : PatientInfo);
  VAR
    J : integer;
  BEGIN
    WITH Patient DO
      BEGIN
        read (DataFile, Name);
        readln (DataFile, Age, Height, Weight, Gender)
      END  {  of WITH...DO  }
  END;  {  of PROCEDURE GetData  }
```

This is called from the main program by

```
GetData (Patient);
```

As a second example of getting data for a record, suppose we are writing a program to be used to compute grades of students in a class. As part of the program, a record type can be declared as

```
CONST
  NumQuizzes = 10;
  NumTests = 4;
TYPE
  String20 = string [20];
  QuizList = ARRAY [1..NumQuizzes] OF integer;
  TestList = ARRAY [1..NumTests] OF integer;
```

```
  StudentRecord = RECORD
                    Name : String20;
                    Quiz : QuizList;
                    Test : TestList;
                    QuizTotal : integer;
                    TestAverage : real;
                    LetterGrade : 'A'..'E'
                  END;  {  of RECORD StudentRecord  }
VAR
  Student : StudentRecord;
```

If each line of data contains a student's name, 10 quiz scores, and four test scores and looks like

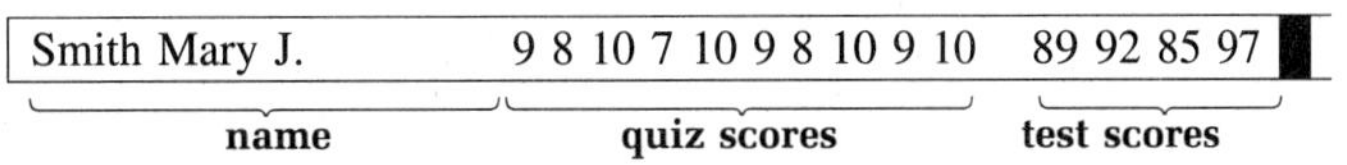

a procedure to get these data is

```
PROCEDURE GetData (VAR Student : StudentRecord);
  VAR
    J : integer;
  BEGIN
    WITH Student DO
      BEGIN
        read (DataFile, Name);
        FOR J := 1 TO NumQuizzes DO
          read (DataFile, Quiz[J]);
        FOR J := 1 TO NumTests DO
          read (DataFile, Test[J])
      END;{  of WITH...DO  }
    readln (DataFile)
  END;  {  of PROCEDURE GetData  }
```

This is called from the main program by

```
GetData (Student);
```

Now let's continue this example by writing a function to compute the test average for a student. Since this average is found by using the four test scores in the record, such a function can be

```
FUNCTION TestAv (Test : TestList) : real;
  VAR
    J : integer;
    Sum : integer;
  BEGIN
    Sum := 0;
```

A NOTE OF INTEREST

Using Key Fields in Records

The need to search records by certain key fields is a basic and very important process. To illustrate, consider how Ted Celentino, a former director of PARS applications for the on-line reservation system of TWA, responded to the question, "How are reservations indexed?" He said:

"By the passenger's name, flight number, and departure date. All three are needed. If a passenger forgets his or her flight number, the agent can try to find a record of it by looking through all flights to the appropriate destination at that particular travel time. It's rare that a passenger doesn't know at least a couple of pieces of information that lead to his or her record."

```
    FOR J := 1 TO NumTests DO
      Sum := Sum + Test[J];
    TestAv := Sum / NumTests
  END;  { of FUNCTION TestAv }
```

Since the array of test scores is the only parameter sent to the function and the average is normally stored in the field TestAverage, this function can be called by

```
Student.TestAverage := TestAv(Student.Test);
```

Printing Data from a Record

After data has been entered in fields of a record and appropriate calculations have been made, we want to print information from the record. Since this is frequently done in a procedure, let's assume the previous record for a student has the values illustrated in Figure 9.9.

FIGURE 9.9
Fields with values

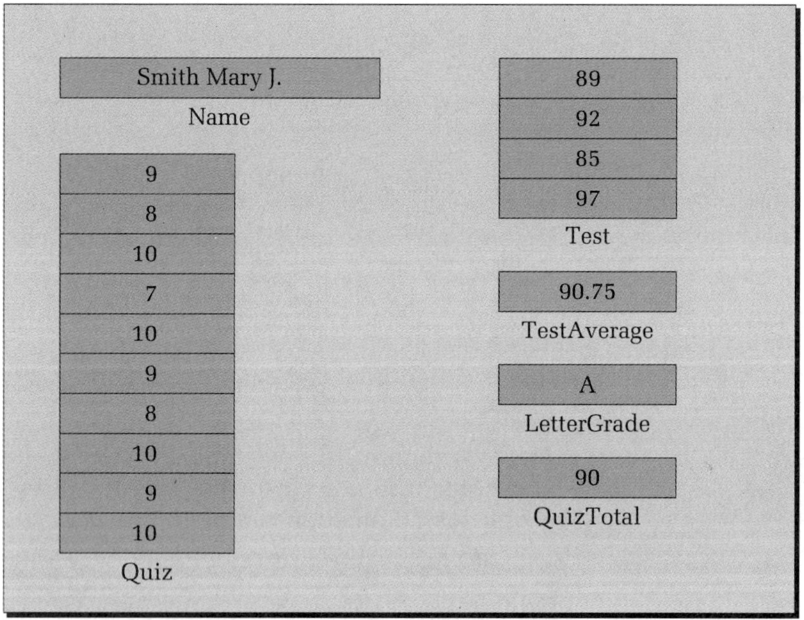

If we want the output for a student to be

```
Name:          Smith Mary J.
Quiz Scores:   9  8 10  7 10  9  8 10  9 10
Quiz Total:    90
Test Scores:   89  92  85  97
Test Average:  90.75
Letter Grade:  A
```

a procedure for producing this is

```
PROCEDURE PrintData (Student : StudentRecord);
  CONST
    Skip = ' ';
  VAR
    J : integer;
BEGIN
    writeln;
    WITH Student DO
```

```
      BEGIN
        writeln ('Name:', Skip:9, Name);
        write ('Quiz Scores:');
        FOR J := 1 TO NumQuizzes DO
          write (Quiz[J]:3);
        writeln;
        writeln ('Quiz Total:', QuizTotal:5);
        write ('Test Scores:');
        FOR J := 1 TO NumTests DO
          write (Test[J]:4);
        writeln;
        writeln ('Test Average:', TestAverage:6:2);
        writeln ('Letter Grade:', LetterGrade:2)
      END  {  of WITH...DO  }
  END;  {  of PROCEDURE PrintData  }
```

This procedure is called from the main program by

```
PrintData (Student);
```

■ EXAMPLE 9.2

As a concluding example, let's consider a short, interactive program that uses records and procedures to perform the arithmetic operation of multiplying two fractions. The program declares a record for each fraction and uses procedures to get the data, multiply the fractions, and print the results.

Before writing this program, let's examine appropriate record definitions and a procedure for computing the product. A definition is

```
TYPE
  RationalNumber = RECORD
                     Numerator : integer;
                     Denominator : integer
                   END;  {  of RECORD RationalNumber  }
VAR
  X, Y, Product : RationalNumber;
```

A procedure for computing the product is

```
PROCEDURE ComputeProduct (X, Y : RationalNumber;
                          VAR Product : RationalNumber);
  BEGIN
    WITH Product DO
      BEGIN
        Numerator := X.Numerator * Y.Numerator;
        Denominator := X.Denominator * Y.Denominator
      END  {  of WITH...DO  }
  END;  {  of PROCEDURE ComputeProduct  }
```

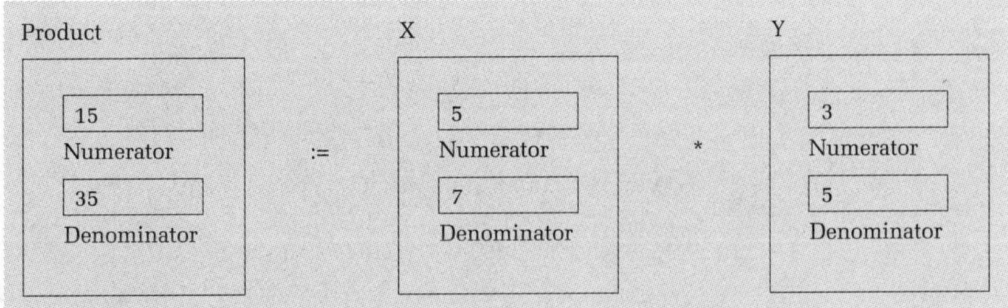

This procedure is called from the main program by

```
ComputeProduct (X, Y, Product);
```

A complete program for this problem follows.

```
PROGRAM Fractions;

{  This program illustrates the use of records with procedures.  }
{  In particular, procedures are used to get the data, perform   }
{  computations, and print the results.  The specific task is    }
{  to compute the product of two rational numbers.               }

USES
  Crt;

TYPE
  RationalNumber = RECORD
                     Numerator : integer;
                     Denominator : integer
                   END;  {  of RECORD RationalNumber  }

VAR
  X, Y, Product : RationalNumber;
  MoreData : boolean;
  Response : char;

{*************************************************************}

PROCEDURE GetData (VAR X, Y : RationalNumber);

  {  Given:   Nothing                                          }
  {  Task:    Have entered from the keyboard the numerator and }
  {               denominator of two fractions                 }
  {  Return:  Two records, each containing a field for the     }
  {               numerator and denominator of a fraction      }

  BEGIN
    WITH X DO
      BEGIN
        write ('Enter the numerator a of a/b.  ');
        readln (Numerator);
        write ('Enter the denominator b of a/b.  ');
        readln (Denominator)
      END;  {  of WITH X DO  }
    WITH Y DO
      BEGIN
        write ('Enter the numerator a of a/b.  ');
        readln (Numerator);
        write ('Enter the denominator b of a/b.  ');
        readln (Denominator)
      END  {  of WITH Y DO  }
  END;  {  of PROCEDURE GetData  }

{*************************************************************}

PROCEDURE ComputeProduct (X, Y : RationalNumber;
                          VAR Product : RationalNumber);

  {  Given:   Records for two fractions                        }
  {  Task:    Compute the product and store result             }
  {  Return:  Product of the fraction                          }

  BEGIN
    WITH Product DO
      BEGIN
        Numerator := X.Numerator * Y.Numerator;
        Denominator := X.Denominator * Y.Denominator
      END  {  of WITH...DO  }
  END;  {  of PROCEDURE ComputeProduct  }
```

```
{*****************************************************************}

PROCEDURE PrintResults (X, Y, Product : RationalNumber);

  {  Given:   Records for each of two given fractions and their  }
  {               product                                         }
  {  Task:    Print an equation stating the problem and answer;  }
  {               standard fraction form should be used as        }
  {               output                                          }
  {  Return:  Nothing                                             }

  BEGIN
    writeln;
    writeln (X.Numerator:13, Y.Numerator:6, Product.Numerator:6);
    writeln ('--- * --- = ---':26);
    writeln (X.Denominator:13, Y.Denominator:6,
             Product.Denominator:6);
    writeln
  END;  {  of PROCEDURE PrintResults  }

{*****************************************************************}

BEGIN  {  Main program  }
  ClrScr;
  MoreData := true;
  WHILE MoreData DO
    BEGIN
      GetData (X, Y);
      ComputeProduct (X, Y, Product);
      PrintResults (X, Y, Product);
      write ('Do you wish to see another problem?  <Y> or <N>  ');
      readln (Response);
      MoreData := (Response = 'Y') OR (Response = 'y');
      writeln
    END  {  of WHILE...DO  }
END.  {  of main program  }
```

A sample run of this program produces

```
Enter the numerator a of a/b.  3
Enter the denominator b of a/b.  4
Enter the numerator a of a/b.  1
Enter the denominator b of a/b.  2

            3     1     3
           --- * --- = ---
            4     2     8

Do you wish to see another problem?  <Y> or <N>  Y

Enter the numerator a of a/b.  3
Enter the denominator b of a/b.  2
Enter the numerator a of a/b.  7
Enter the denominator b of a/b.  10

            3     7    21
           --- * --- = ---
            2    10    20

Do you wish to see another problem?  <Y> or <N>  Y

Enter the numerator a of a/b.  2
Enter the denominator b of a/b.  3
```

```
Enter the numerator a of a/b. 4
Enter the denominator b of a/b. 5

         2     4     8
        --- * --- = ---
         3     5    15

Do you wish to see another problem? <Y> or <N> N
```

Exercises 9.2

1. Assume a program contains the following **TYPE** definition and **VAR** declaration sections:

```
TYPE
  Info1 = RECORD
            Initial : char;
            Age : integer
          END;
  Info2 = RECORD
            Initial : char;
            Age : integer
          END;
VAR
  Cust1, Cust2 : Info1;
  Cust3, Cust4 : Info2;
```

Indicate which of the following statements are valid. Give an explanation for those that are invalid.

a. `Cust1 := Cust2;`

b. `Cust2 := Cust3;`

c. `Cust3 := Cust4;`

d.
```
WITH Cust1 DO
  BEGIN
    Initial := 'W';
    Age := 21
  END;
```

e.
```
WITH Cust1, Cust2 DO
  BEGIN
    Initial := 'W';
    Age := 21
  END;
```

2. Write a test program to see what happens when two different records with the same field name are used in a single **WITH . . . DO** statement. Use the declarations and **TYPE** definitions in Exercise 1. For example

```
WITH Student1, Student2 DO
  Age := 21;
writeln (Student1.Age);
writeln (Student2.Age);
```

3. Assume the **TYPE** and **VAR** sections of a program include

```
TYPE
  String11 = string [11];
  String20 = string [20];
  Info = RECORD
           Name : String20;
           SSN : String11;
           Age : integer;
           HourlyWage : real;
           HoursWorked : real;
           Volunteer : boolean
         END;
VAR
  Employee1, Employee2 : Info;
```

a. Show three different methods of transferring all information from the record for Employee1 to the record for Employee2.
b. Suppose you wished to transfer all information from the record for Employee1 to the record for Employee2 except HoursWorked. Discuss different methods for doing this. Which do you feel is the most efficient?

4. Assume the **TYPE** and **VAR** sections of a program are the same as in Exercise 3. Write a procedure to be used to read information into such a record from a data file. A typical line of data is

```
Smith Jane M.          111-22-3333 25 10.50 41.5Y
```

where Y indicates the worker is a volunteer (**true**) and N indicates the worker is not a volunteer (**false**).

5. Assume a record has been declared by

```
TYPE
  String20 = string [20];
  StudentInfo = RECORD
                  Name : String20;
                  TotalPts : 0..500;
                  LetterGrade : char
                END;
VAR
  Student : StudentInfo;
```

Write a function to compute the student's letter grade based on cutoff levels of 90 percent, 80 percent, 70 percent, and 60 percent. Show how this function is used in a program to assign the appropriate letter grade to the appropriate field of a student's record.

6. Review Example 9.2, in which two fractions are multiplied. In a similar fashion, write procedures for:
   a. Dividing two fractions (watch out for zero)
   b. Adding two fractions
   c. Subtracting two fractions

7. Some instructors throw out the lowest test score for each student when computing the student's test average. Assume a record Student of type StudentRecord has been declared and data have been read into the appropriate fields.
   a. Write a function to compute the test average using the best three scores.
   b. Show how a constant in the **CONST** section can be used to generalize this function to find the best $n - 1$ of n scores.
   c. Rewrite the function using a sort to sort the array of scores from high to low, and then add the first three scores from the array.
   d. Must the entire array be sorted in order to find the three highest scores? Explain.

8. Show how the program Fractions in Example 9.2 can be modified to check for nonzero denominators.

■ 9.3 Data Structures with Records

Nested Records

The first concept to be examined in this section is that of a *nested record,* or a record which is a field in another record. For example, suppose you are working on a program to be used by a biology department and part of your work is to declare a record for a faculty member. This record is to contain fields for the person's name, office number, telephone number, and supply order. Let's assume that the supply order information is to contain the company name, a description of the item ordered, its price, and the quantity ordered. The record for each faculty member, with SupplyOrder as a record within a record, can be visualized as shown in Figure 9.10.

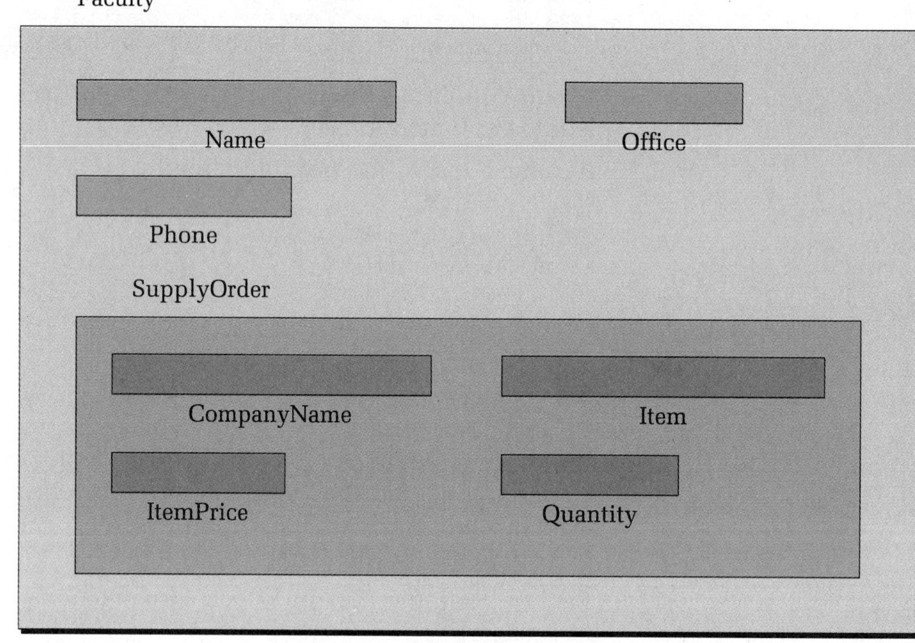

FIGURE 9.10
Illustration of a nested record

Let's look at how such a record can be declared. One possible method is

```
TYPE
  String20 = string [20];
  String12 = string [12];
  OrderInfo = RECORD
                CompanyName : String20;
                Item : String20;
                ItemPrice : real;
                Quantity : integer
              END;  {  of RECORD OrderInfo  }
  FacultyInfo = RECORD
                  Name : String20;
                  Office : integer;
                  Phone : String12;
                  SupplyOrder : OrderInfo
                END;  {  of RECORD FacultyInfo  }
VAR
  Faculty : FacultyInfo;
```

We must now consider how to access fields in the nested record. We do this by continuing our notation for field designators. Thus

```
Faculty.Name
Faculty.Office
Faculty.Phone
```

refer to the first three fields of Faculty, and

```
Faculty.SupplyOrder.CompanyName
Faculty.SupplyOrder.Item
Faculty.SupplyOrder.ItemPrice
Faculty.SupplyOrder.Quantity
```

are used to access fields of the nested record

```
Faculty.SupplyOrder
```

Using WITH . . . DO

As expected, **WITH . . . DO** can be used with nested records. Let's consider the problem of assigning data to the various fields of Faculty as previously declared. Assume we wish to have values assigned as in Figure 9.11.

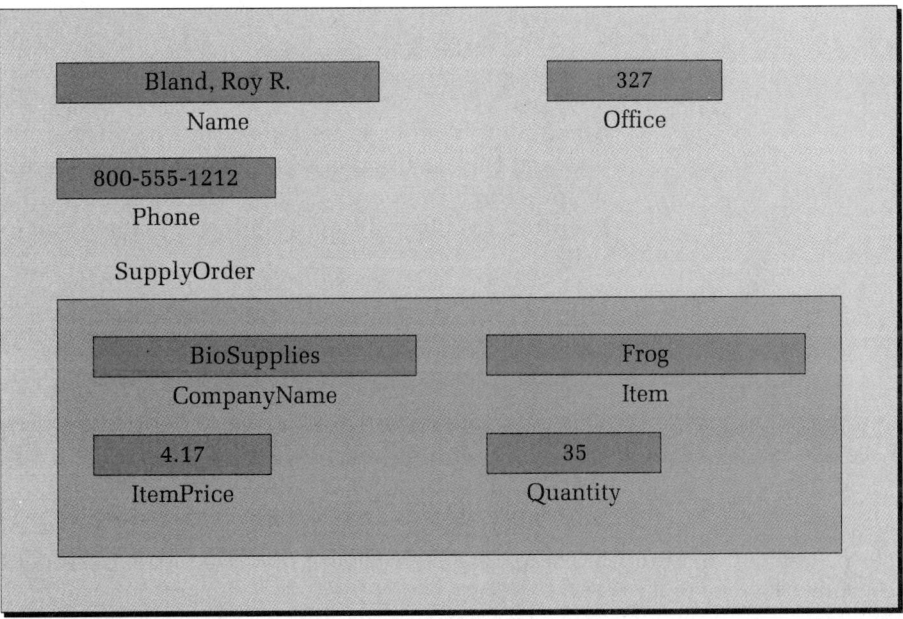

FIGURE 9.11 Values in fields of a nested record

We can then use the following assignment statements:

```
WITH Faculty DO
  BEGIN
    Name := 'Bland Roy R.';
    Office := 327;
    Phone := '800-555-1212';
    SupplyOrder.CompanyName := 'BioSupplies';
    SupplyOrder.Item := 'Frog';
    SupplyOrder.ItemPrice := 4.17;
    SupplyOrder.Quantity := 35
  END;
```

Note that the last four assignment statements all use fields in the record SupplyOrder. Thus, a **WITH . . . DO** statement can be used there in the following manner:

```
WITH Faculty DO
  BEGIN
    Name := 'Bland Roy R.';
    Office := 327;
    Phone := '800-555-1212';
    WITH SupplyOrder DO
```

```
        BEGIN
          CompanyName := 'BioSupplies';
          Item := 'Frog';
          ItemPrice := 4.17;
          Quantity := 35
        END  {  of WITH SupplyOrder DO  }
    END;  {  of WITH Faculty DO  }
```

A third way to accomplish our task is to use **WITH . . . DO** with both the main record name and the nested record name, as follows:

```
WITH Faculty, SupplyOrder DO
  BEGIN
    Name := 'Bland Roy R.';
    Office := 327;
    Phone := '800-555-1212';
    CompanyName := 'BioSupplies';
    Item := 'Frog';
    ItemPrice := 4.17;
    Quantity := 35
  END;  {  WITH...DO  }
```

Since SupplyOrder is nested within Faculty, each reference is distinctly identified and the fragment accomplishes our objective. When using nested records, it is important to identify fields distinctly. To illustrate, suppose Faculty1 and Faculty2 are also of type FacultyInfo. Then each of the following statements is valid:

```
Faculty1.Name := Faculty2.Name;
Faculty1.SupplyOrder.Item := Faculty2.SupplyOrder.Item;
Faculty1.SupplyOrder := Faculty2.SupplyOrder;
```

A NOTE OF INTEREST

History Stuck on Old Computer Tapes

A slice of recent U.S. history has become as unreadable as Egyptian hieroglyphics before the discovery of the Rosetta stone. And more historic, scientific, and business data is in danger of dissolving into a meaningless jumble of letters, numbers, and computer symbols.

Paying millions to preserve the information is part of the price for the country's embrace of more and more powerful computers. Much information from the past 30 years is stranded on computer tape from primitive or discarded systems—it's unintelligible or soon to be so.

Hundreds of thousands of Americans researching family history—the largest use of the National Archives—will find records of their relatives beyond reach. Detection of diseases, environmental threats, or shifts in social class could be delayed because data was lost before researchers even knew which questions to ask.

"The ability to read our nation's historical records is threatened by the complexity of modern computers," said Representative Bob Wise, chairman of a House information subcommittee that wants the government to start buying computers to preserve data for future researchers. A number of records already are lost or out of reach:

- Two hundred reels of 17-year-old Public Health Service computer tapes were destroyed because no one could find out what the names and numbers on them meant.
- The government's Agent Orange Task Force, asked to determine whether Vietnam soldiers were sickened by exposure to the herbicide, was unable to decode Pentagon computer tapes containing the date, site, and size of every U.S. herbicide bombing during the war.
- The most extensive record of Americans who served in World War II exists only on 1600 reels of microfilm of computer punch cards. No staff, money, or machine is available to return the data to a computer so citizens can trace the war history of their relatives.
- Census data from the 1960s and NASA's early scientific observations of the earth and planets exist on thousands of reels of old tape. Some may have decomposed; others may fall apart if run through the balky equipment that survives from that era.

Note that in the third statement, the contents of an entire record are being transferred. This statement is valid because both records are of type OrderInfo.

To illustrate some attempts to use inappropriate designators, let's assume Faculty, Faculty1, and Faculty2 are of type FacultyInfo and consider the following inappropriate references. In the designator

```
Faculty.Item := 'Frog';   (Incorrect)
```

the intermediate descriptor is missing. Thus, something like

```
Faculty.SupplyOrder.Item
```

is needed. In

```
SupplyOrder.Quantity := 35;   (Incorrect)
```

no reference is made to which record is being accessed. A record name must be stated, such as

```
Faculty1.SupplyOrder.Quantity
```

As our final example of working with nested records, let's write a procedure to get data from a data file for a record of type FacultyInfo with the following definitions and declarations:

```
TYPE
  String20 = string [20];
  String12 = string [12];
  OrderInfo = RECORD
                CompanyName : String20;
                Item : String20;
                ItemPrice : real;
                Quantity : integer
              END;  {  of RECORD OrderInfo  }
  FacultyInfo = RECORD
                  Name : String20;
                  Office : 100..399;
                  Phone : String12;
                  SupplyOrder : OrderInfo
                END;  {  of RECORD FacultyInfo  }
VAR
  Faculty : FacultyInfo;
```

If we assume the data for a faculty member are on two lines of the data file as

(line 1)	Bland Roy R.	327 800-555-1212	
(line 2)	BioSupplies	Frog	4.17 35

a procedure to obtain this data is

```
PROCEDURE GetData (VAR Faculty : FacultyInfo);
  VAR
    J : integer;
    Blank : char;
  BEGIN
    WITH Faculty, SupplyOrder DO
      BEGIN
        readln (Data, Name, Office, Phone);

  {  Now read the second line  }
        read (Data, CompanyName, Item);
        readln (Data, ItemPrice, Quantity)
      END  {  of WITH Faculty, SupplyOrder DO  }
  END;  {  of PROCEDURE GetData  }
```

This procedure is called from the main program by

```
GetData (Faculty);
```

Array of Records

Next, we will use structured data types to look at an *array of records.* It is easy to imagine needing to make a list of information about several people, events, or items. Furthermore, it is not unusual for the information about a particular person, event, or item to consist of several different data items. When this situation occurs, a record can be defined for each person, event, or item and an array of these records can be used to achieve the desired result. In such situations, an array of records is frequently used instead of a parallel array.

For example, suppose the local high school sports boosters want you to write a program to enable them to keep track of the names and donations of its members. Assume a maximum of 50 members are making a donation. This problem was solved in Chapter 8 by using parallel arrays; it can now be solved by using an array of records. Each record will have two fields: the donor's name, and the amount donated. The record can be visualized as shown in Figure 9.12.

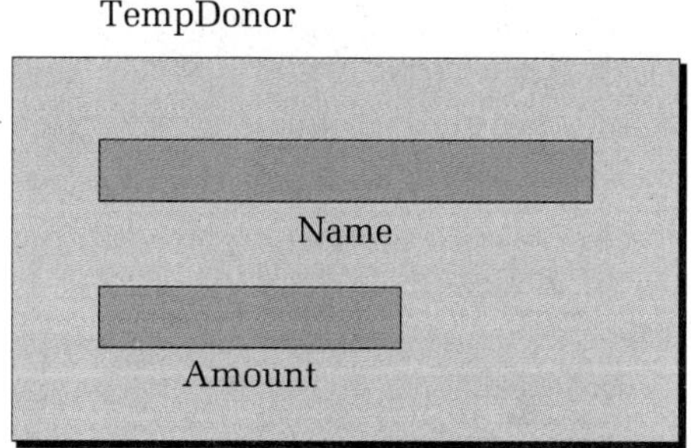

FIGURE 9.12
Fields in TempDonor

We will now declare an array of these records to produce the arrangement shown in Figure 9.13. The definitions and declarations needed are

```
CONST
  ClubSize = 50;
TYPE
  String20 = string [20];
  MemberInfo = RECORD
                 Name : String20;
                 Amount : real
               END;  {  of RECORD MemberInfo  }
  DonorList = ARRAY  [1..ClubSize] OF MemberInfo;
VAR
  Donor : DonorList;
  TempDonor : MemberInfo;
  Count : integer;
```

Before we proceed, the following should be noted:

1. Structures are built in the **TYPE** definition section to facilitate later work with procedures and functions.
2. Each record is now an array element and can be accessed by a reference to the index. Thus, if the third member's name is Tom Jones and he donates $100.00, we can write

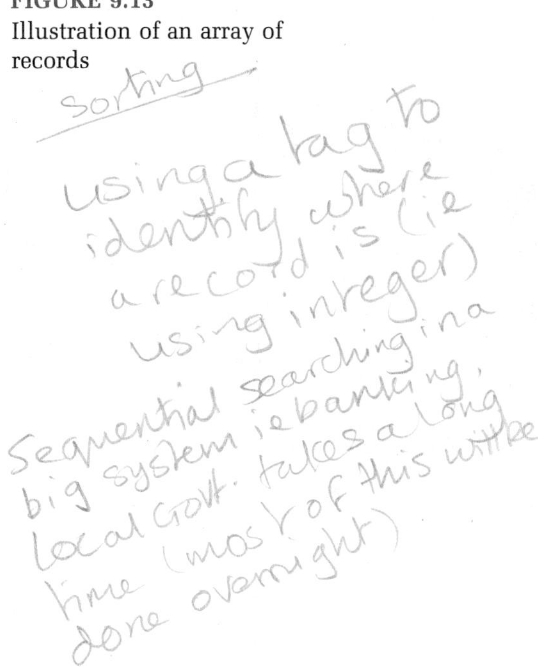

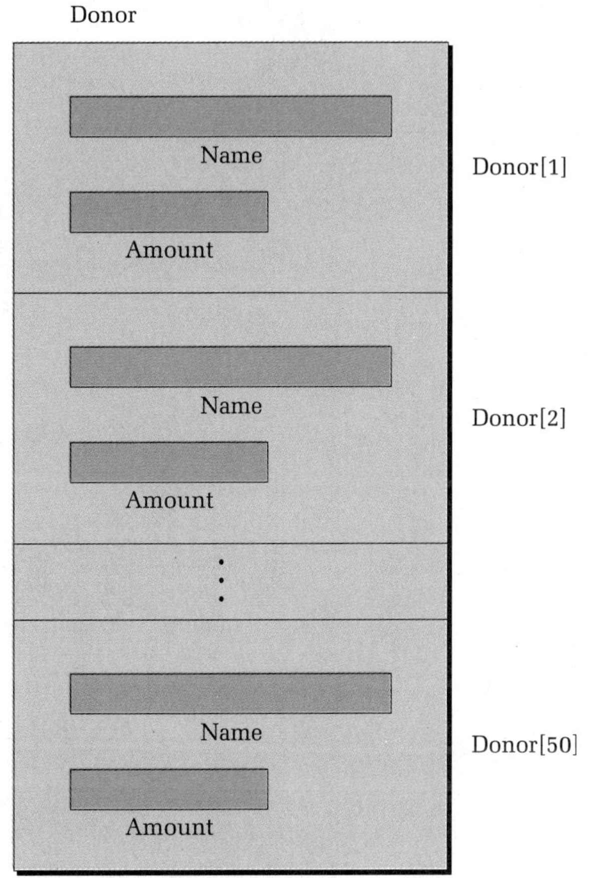

FIGURE 9.13
Illustration of an array of records

```
Donor[3].Name := 'Jones Tom';
Donor[3].Amount := 100.0;
```

Better still, we can use **WITH . . . DO** to get

```
WITH Donor[3] DO
  BEGIN
    Name := 'Jones Tom';
    Amount := 100.0
  END;  {  of WITH...DO  }
```

3. Since all records in an array are of identical type, the contents of two records can be interchanged by

```
TempDonor := Donor[J];
Donor[J] := Donor[K];
Donor[K] := TempDonor;
```

This is needed if records are to be sorted by one of their fields.

4. The distinction in syntax should be noted when using an array of records versus an array as a field within a record. For example, if an array of five scores has been defined as a field in the array of records as shown in Figure 9.14, note the following distinctions:

a. `Student[2].Average` (Average for student 2)
b. `Student[2].Score[4]` (Score on test 4 for student 2)
c. `Student.Score[2]` (Not defined; Student is an array)

FIGURE 9.14
Array of records

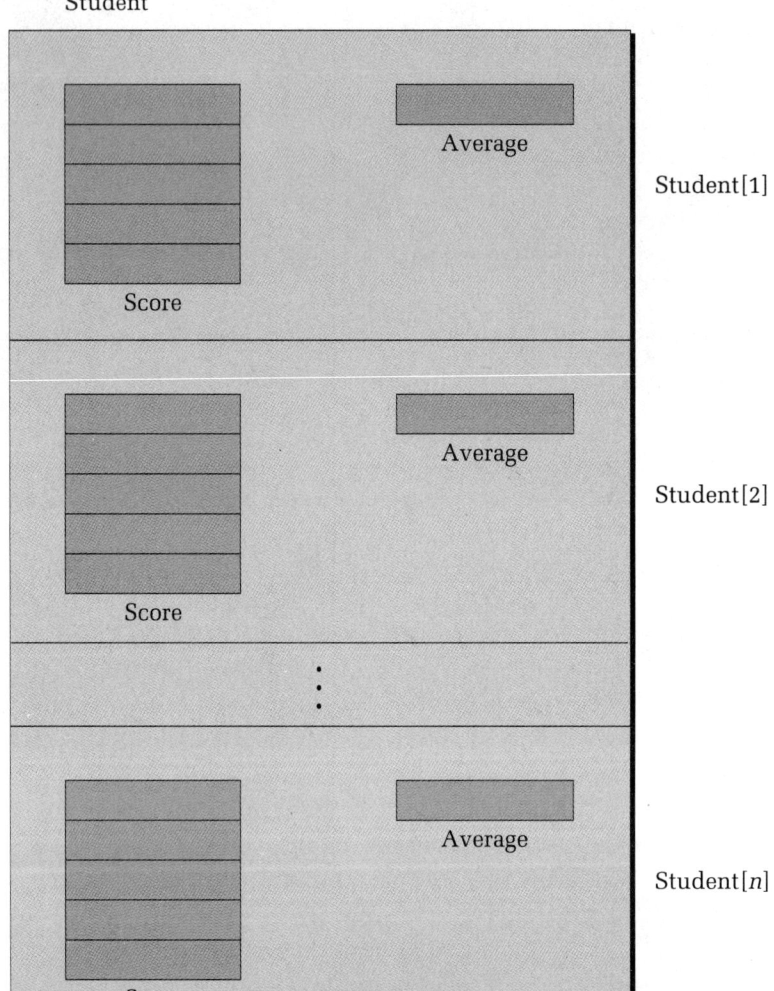

Now let's return to the problem posed by the sports boosters. A first-level pseudocode design is

1. Get the data
2. Sort alphabetically by name
3. Print the sorted list

If we assume each line of the data file is of the form

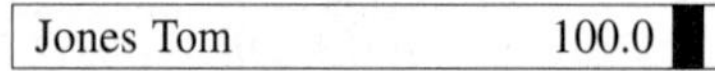

a procedure to get the data is not difficult. We have to remember, however, to count the actual number of donors read. Such a procedure is

```
PROCEDURE GetData (VAR Donor : DonorList;
                   VAR Count : integer);
  VAR
    J : integer;
```

```
BEGIN
  Count := 0;
  WHILE NOT eof(DataFile) AND (Count < ClubSize) DO
    BEGIN
      Count := Count + 1;
      WITH Donor[Count] DO
        readln (DataFile, Name, Amount)
    END  {  of WHILE NOT eof  }
END;  {  of PROCEDURE GetData  }
```

This procedure is called from the main program by

```
GetData (Donor, Count);
```

and Count will contain the actual number of donors after the procedure is called.

The next procedure in this problem requires a sort. A sort that actually exchanges entire records is not very efficient. When working with an array of records, it is more efficient to use an *index sort*, which essentially uses a separate array to reorder the indices in the desired order. However, the formal development of this sorting technique is deferred to a subsequent course. For now, recall the selection sort developed in Chapter 7 as follows:

```
FOR J := 1 TO N - 1 DO            {  Find the minimum N - 1 times  }
  BEGIN
    Index := J;
    FOR K := J + 1 TO N DO
      IF A[K] < A[Index] THEN          {    Find smallest number  }
        Index := K;
    IF Index <> J THEN
      BEGIN
        Temp := A[Index];
        A[Index] := A[J];
        A[J] := Temp
      END  {  of exchange  }
  END;  {  of one pass  }
```

With suitable changes, the array of records can be sorted alphabetically by

```
PROCEDURE Sort (VAR Donor : DonorList;
                Count : integer);
  VAR
    J, K, Index : integer;
    Temp : MemberInfo;
  BEGIN
    FOR J := 1 TO Count - 1 DO
      BEGIN
        Index := J;
        FOR K := J + 1 TO Count DO
          IF Donor[K].Name < Donor[Index].Name THEN
            Index := K;
        IF Index <> J THEN
          BEGIN
            Temp := Donor[Index];
            Donor[Index] := Donor[J];
            Donor[J] := Temp
          END  {  of exchange  }
      END  {  of FOR loop  }
  END;  {  of PROCEDURE Sort  }
```

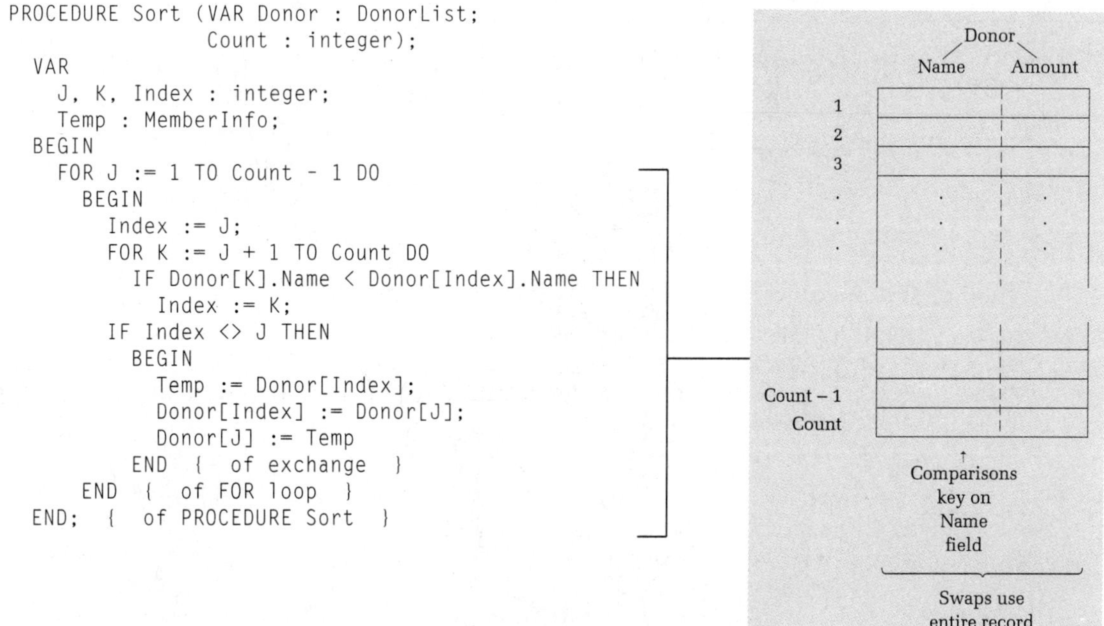

This procedure is called from the main program by

```
Sort (Donor, Count);
```

In this procedure, note that the sort is by only one field in the record—specifically, the donor's name:

```
IF Donor[K].Name < Donor[Index].Name THEN
```

However, when the names are to be exchanged, the contents of the entire record are exchanged by

```
Temp := Donor[Index];
```

We conclude this example by writing a procedure to print the results. If we want the output to be

```
           Local Sports Boosters
               Donation List
-----------------------------------------


   Name                          Amount
   ----                          ------


Anerice Sue                      150.00
Compton John                     125.00
    .                                 .
    .                                 .
    .                                 .
```

a procedure to produce this is

```
PROCEDURE PrintList (VAR Donor : DonorList;
                     Count : integer);
  CONST
    Skip = ' ' ;
  VAR
    J : integer;
  BEGIN
    writeln;
    writeln (Skip:21, 'Local Sports Boosters');
    writeln (Skip:25, 'Donation List');
    writeln (Skip:10, '----------------------------------------');
    writeln;
    writeln (Skip:13, 'Name', Skip:27, 'Amount');
    writeln (Skip:13, '----', Skip:27, '------');
    writeln;

  {  Now print the list  }

    FOR J := 1 TO Count DO
      WITH Donor[J] DO
        writeln (Skip:10, Name, Amount:20:2);
    writeln
  END;  {  of PROCEDURE PrintList  }
```

With these three procedures available, the main program is then

```
BEGIN  {  Main program  }
  assign (DataFile, 'Donor.DAT');
  reset (DataFile);
  GetData (Donor, Count);
  Sort (Donor, Count);
  PrintList (Donor, Count);
  close (DataFile)
END.  {  of main program  }
```

This example is less involved than many of your problems will be, but it does illustrate an array of records, appropriate notation for fields in an array of records, how to sort an array of records by using one field of the records, and the use of procedures with an array of records.

Exercises 9.3

1. Consider the declaration

```
TYPE
  B = RECORD
        C : real;
        D : integer
      END;
  A = RECORD
        E : boolean;
        F : B
      END;
VAR
  G : A;
```

   a. Give a schematic representation of the record G.
   b. Indicate which of the following are valid references.

i.	G.E	**vi.**	A.F.C
ii.	G.C	**vii.**	A.E
iii.	G.F.D	**viii.**	WITH G DO
iv.	F.D	**ix.**	WITH G, F DO
v.	G.A	**x.**	G.F.C

   c. Why would it be incorrect to define record A before record B?

2. Write a test program that illustrates the difference between an array of records and a record with an array component.

3. Give an appropriate definition and declaration for a record that is to contain fields for a person's name, address, social security number, annual income, and family information. Address is a record with fields for street address, city, state abbreviation, and zip code. Family information is a record with fields for marital status (S, M, W, or D) and number of children.

4. Consider the following definitions and subsequent declarations.

```
TYPE
  String20 = string [20];
  Mood = (Quiet, Bright, Surly);
  CurrentHealth = (Poor, Average, Good);
  PatientStatus = RECORD
                    Mental : Mood;
                    Physical : CurrentHealth
                  END;  { of RECORD PatientStatus }
  PatientInfo = RECORD
                  Name : String20;
                  Status : PatientStatus;
                  PastDue : boolean
                END;  { of RECORD PatientInfo }
VAR
  Patient1, Patient2 : PatientInfo;
```

   a. Give a schematic representation for Patient1.
   b. Show how a single letter (Q, B, or S) can be read from a data file, and then have the appropriate value assigned to Patient1.Status.Mental.

c. Write a procedure to read a line of data and assign (if necessary) appropriate values to the various fields. A typical data line is

Smith Sue	BAF

and indicates that Sue Smith's mood is bright, her health is average, and her account is not past due.

5. Declare an array of records to be used for 15 players on a basketball team. The following information is needed for each player: name, age, height, weight, scoring average, and rebounding average.

6. Declare an array of records to be used for students (at most 40) in a classroom. Each record should contain fields for a student's name, social security number, 10 quiz scores, three test scores, overall average, and letter grade.

7. Consider the following declaration of an array of records.

```
CONST
  ClassSize = 35;
TYPE
  String20 = string [20];
  Attendance = (Excellent, Average, Poor);
  TestList = ARRAY [1..4] OF integer;
  StudentInfo = RECORD
                  Name : String20;
                  Atten : Attendance;
                  Test : TestList;
                  Aver : real
                END;
  StudentList = ARRAY [1..ClassSize] OF StudentInfo;
VAR
  Student : StudentList;
```

a. Give a schematic representation for Student.

b. Explain what the following function accomplishes:

```
FUNCTION GuessWhat (Test : TestList) : real;
  VAR
    K, Sum : integer;
  BEGIN
    Sum := 0;
    FOR K := 1 TO 4 DO
      Sum := Sum + Test[K];
    GuessWhat := Sum / 4
  END;
```

c. Write a procedure to print out the information for one student. In this procedure, the entire word describing attendance is to be printed.

8. Reconsider the problem in this section that kept a record of the name and amount donated for each member of the local high school boosters club. Expanding on that problem, write a procedure or function for each of the following.

a. Find the maximum donation, and print out the amount together with the donor's name.

b. Find the sum of all donations.

c. Find the average of all donations.

d. Sort the array according to size of the donation (largest first.)

■ 9.4 Record Variants

You should have noticed by now that when records are defined, each record has certain fixed fields. Since it is sometimes desirable to use a record structure in which the number and type of fields vary, Turbo Pascal allows records to be defined with a *variant part*. For example, a real estate company might want the records for its customers to contain different information depending upon

A NOTE OF INTEREST

Program Documentation—EDS Style

(The following information was provided by Patrick J. Goss, Systems Engineer Supervisor for EDS (Electronic Data Systems). He is employed at the Lansing (MI) Regional Support Center. His primary function is to supervise support of the Sales, Service, and Marketing systems of the Oldsmobile Division of General Motors.)

Program documentation plays a significant part in the training and subsequent work efforts of the systems engineering group at EDS, as it does in any software development group. To illustrate the importance of documentation in software systems developed and maintained by EDS, consider the emphasis at EDS on documentation standards, reasons for stressing documentation, training for and enforcement of coding standards, and specific examples of using documentation.

Documentation Standards

Standards for documentation by systems engineers include:

- The use of "flower boxes" (enclosure by asterisks) to physically separate and identify elements
- Strict naming conventions for variables, data sets, and programs
- Emphasis on structured, modularized code
- Complete documentation of the purpose of each routine within the program
- Complete documentation of the overall function of the total program, with particular emphasis on the business function it serves
- Complete documentation of the subsystem interfaces
- The use of descriptive and standard variable names that are consistent throughout the program, system, and related subsystems
- The consistent use of indentation and alignment to improve program readability

Reasons for Stressing Documentation

EDS has several reasons for placing a heavy emphasis on program documentation. First, well-documented systems are easier to maintain; the work can be streamlined when changes need to be made. Second, the use of personnel is more flexible, so staff members can be moved in and out of assignments with little or no decline in productivity. Third, the learning curve on systems support is reduced, and fourth, stress on production support/abend resolutions (system stop) is also reduced. Finally, on-call responsibilities can be rotated because it is easier to solve problems with well-documented systems.

Training and Enforcement

Systems engineers at EDS receive uniform and intensive training in program development and the use of documentation. Initial training occurs during a 10-week course in Plano, Texas. It is not unusual for program participants to work 12–15 hours per day, seven days a week. Approximately 20 percent of their time is spent on documentation-related issues. The successful completion rate by participants is sometimes less than 50 percent.

After the training session, maintenance of documentation skills and in-service training is provided by "walk throughs" on every system change. These inspections involve a team of at least three peers and a secretary to record comments. During these sessions, developers are told to "check your ego at the door." Graduates from recent Technical Training sessions are often used as peers in order to guarantee adherence to current standards. (The Note of Interest on page 383 elaborates on inspections.)

Some Current Examples

The result of EDS's emphasis on program documentation is perhaps best illustrated by examining some current programs.

A recent capstone project from the Technical Training session is a program that contains 1934 lines, of which 670 (35 percent) are comment lines. When the systems engineers return to their jobs, they put their practice to work. Three programs in use in 1993 consist of length and documentation as follows:

Program Length	*Comment Lines*	*Percent Documentation*
1213	397	33
1236	247	20
3234	854	26

whether the property for sale is a house or a business. For houses, the number of bedrooms and bathrooms and the presence or absence of a fireplace could be indicated; for businesses, the number of offices and amount of possible rental income could be listed.

Defining a Variant Part

In order to define the variant part of a record, we use a form of the **CASE** statement to specify which fields should be included. Then, depending upon the value of the identifier in the **CASE** part of the definition, the desired fields are listed. In the real estate example, we could have

```
TYPE
  PropertyType = (House, Business);
  Listing = RECORD
              CASE Kind : PropertyType OF
                House    : (NumBedrms : integer;
                            NumBaths : integer;
                            Fireplace : boolean);
                Business : (NumOffices : integer;
                            RentalIncome : integer)
            END;  { of RECORD Listing }
VAR
  Property : Listing;
```

Now Property is a record with a variant part. Kind is not a reserved word; it is called the *tag field*. Depending upon the value assigned to Kind, the appropriate fields are available. If the assignment

```
Property.Kind := House;
```

is made, the record can be envisioned as shown in Figure 9.15(a). If the assignment

```
Property.Kind := Business;
```

is made, the record can be envisioned as illustrated in Figure 9.15(b).

FIGURE 9.15
Fields in a variant record

(a) Property

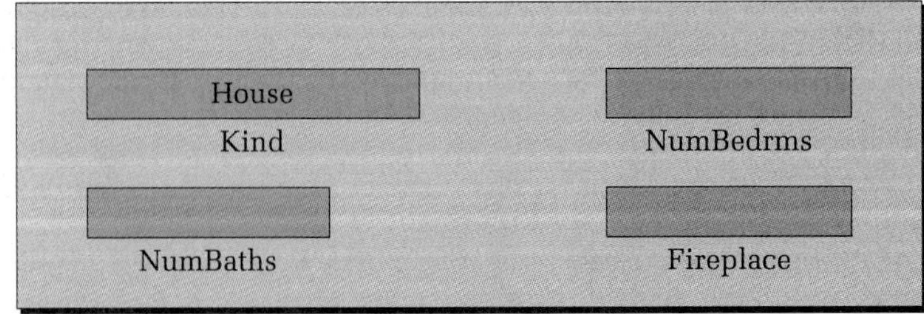

(b) Property

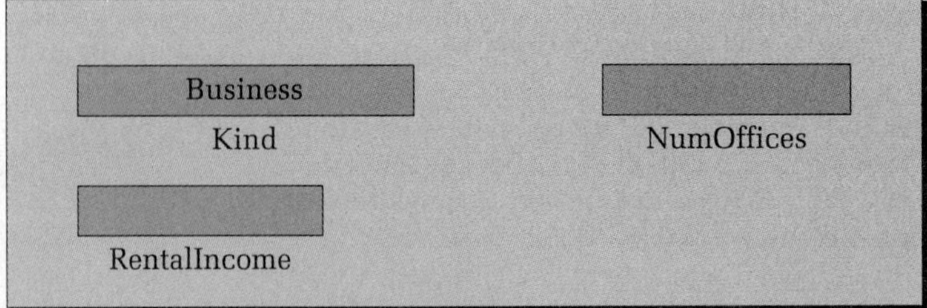

In actual practice, records with variant parts usually have fixed parts also. Suppose the address and price of each property listed for sale is to be included. Since fields for these must be defined for every record, these fields are referred to as the *fixed part*. A complete definition is

```
TYPE
  PropertyType = (House, Business);
  String30 = string [30];
  Listing = RECORD
              Address : String30;                      } fixed
              Price : integer;                         } part
              CASE Kind : PropertyType OF
                House    : (NumBedrms : integer;       ]
                            NumBaths : integer;        ] variant
                            Fireplace : boolean);      ] part
                Business : (NumOffices : integer;      ]
                            RentalIncome : integer)    ]
            END;  {  of RECORD Listing  }
VAR
  Property : Listing;
```

The following points concerning variant parts should now be made.

1. The variant part of a record must be listed after the fixed part.
2. Only one variant part can be defined in a record.
3. The data type for the tag field must be ordinal.
4. Only one **END** statement is used to terminate the definition. It terminates both **CASE** and **RECORD.**

Records with variant parts are defined by the following form:

```
<record name> = RECORD
                  <field 1> : <type>;           ]
                  <field 2> : <type>;           ]
                      .                         ] fixed
                      .                         ] part
                      .                         ]
                  <field n> : <type>;           ]
                  CASE <tag field> : <tag type> OF
                    <value 1> : (<field list>); ]
                    <value 2> : (<field list>); ]
                        .                       ] variant
                        .                       ] part
                        .                       ]
                    <value m> : (<field list>)  ]
                END;
```

It is possible to completely avoid the use of variant parts of a record by listing all possible fields in the fixed part and then using them appropriately. However, this usually means that more storage is required. To illustrate, let's consider how memory is allocated. For each field in the fixed part of the previous example, an area in memory is reserved as

Address   Price

For the variant part of the record, a single area is reserved that will subsequently be utilized by whichever fields are determined by the value of the tag field. In this sense, they overlap as indicated:

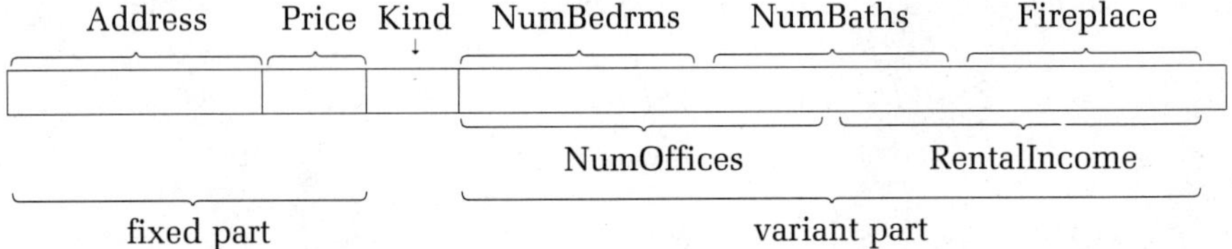

A note of caution is in order when variant records are included as part of programs. Careful programming is needed to properly initialize the variant part or unexpected results may be obtained. For example, using the previous illustration, suppose the initial value of Kind is House, with values for NumBedrms, NumBaths, and Fireplace. If a subsequent value of Kind is Business and no new data are read or assigned, the value of NumOffices may in fact be NumBedrms.

We close this section with an example that illustrates a definition and subsequent use of a record with a variant part.

■ EXAMPLE 9.3

Define a record to be used when working with plane geometric figures. The record should have fixed fields for the type of figure (a single character designator) and area. The variant part should have fields for information needed to compute the area. After the record is defined, write a procedure to get data from a line of the data file. Then write a function that can be used to compute the area of the plane figure.

To complete the definition of the record, assume you are working with at most the geometric figures circle, square, and triangle (C, S, and T, respectively). An appropriate definition is

```
TYPE
  FigureShape = (Circle, Square, Triangle);
  FigureInfo = RECORD
                 Object : char;
                 Area : real;
                 CASE Shape : FigureShape OF
                   Circle   : (Radius : real);
                   Square   : (Side : real);
                   Triangle : (Base, Height : real)
               END;  {  of RECORD FigureInfo  }
VAR
  Figure : FigureInfo;
```

Circle
Radius
Shape
Square
Side
Triangle
Base
Height

Each data line has a single character designating the kind of figure followed by appropriate information needed to compute the area. For example

```
T 6.0 8.0 ■
```

represents a triangle with base 6.0 and height 8.0. A procedure to get a line of data is

```
PROCEDURE GetData (VAR Figure : FigureInfo);
  BEGIN
    WITH Figure DO
      BEGIN
        read (Data, Object);
        CASE Object OF
          'C' : BEGIN
                  Shape := Circle;
                  readln (Data, Radius)
                END;
          'S' : BEGIN
                  Shape := Square;
                  readln (Data, Side)
                END;
          'T' : BEGIN
                  Shape := Triangle;
                  readln (Data, Base, Height)
                END
        END  { of CASE Object  }
      END  { of WITH...DO  }
  END;  { of PROCEDURE GetData  }
```

This is called from the main program by

```
GetData (Figure);
```

Finally, a function to compute the area is

```
FUNCTION ComputeArea (Figure : FigureInfo) : real;
  BEGIN
    WITH Figure DO
      BEGIN
        CASE Shape OF
          Circle   : ComputeArea := Pi * sqr(Radius);
          Square   : ComputeArea := Side * Side;
          Triangle : ComputeArea := 0.5 * Base * Height
        END  { of CASE Shape  }
      END   {of WITH...DO  }
  END;  { of FUNCTION ComputeArea  }
```

This function is called by

```
Figure.Area := ComputeArea(Figure);
```

Exercises 9.4

1. Explain how memory can be saved when records with variant parts are declared.
2. Assume a record is defined by

```
TYPE
  TagType = (One, Two);
  Info = RECORD
           Fixed : integer;
           CASE Tag : TagType OF
             One : (A, B : integer);
```

```
            Two : (X : real;
                   Ch : char)
        END;
```

and the variable declaration section of a program includes

```
VAR
  RecordCheck : Info;
```

What is the output from the following fragment of code?

```
WITH RecordCheck DO
  BEGIN
    Fixed := 1000;
    Tag := One;
    A := 100;
    B := 500;
    writeln (Fixed:15, A:15, B:15);
    Tag := Two;
    X := 10.5;
    Ch := 'Y';
    writeln (Fixed:15, X:15.2, Ch:15);
    writeln (A:15, B:15, X:15:2, Ch:15)
  END;
```

3. Find all errors in the following definitions.

a.
```
TYPE
  Info = RECORD
           A : real;
           CASE Tag : TagType OF
             B : (X, Y : real);
             C : (Z : boolean)
         END;
```

b.
```
TYPE
  TagType = (A, B, C);
  Info = RECORD
           D : integer;
           Flag : boolean;
           CASE Tag : TagType OF
             A : (X, Y : real);
             B : (Z : real)
         END;
```

c.
```
TYPE
  TagType = (A, B, C);
  Info = RECORD
           D : integer;
           Flag : boolean
           CASE Tag OF
             A : (X : real);
             B : (Y : real);
             C : (Z : real)
         END;
```

d.
```
TYPE
  TagType = (A, B, C);
  Info = RECORD
           D : integer;
           CASE Tag1 : TagType OF
             A : (X : real);
             B : (Y : real);
             C : (Z : real)
           END;  {  of CASE  }
           CASE Tag2 : TagType OF
             A : (X1 : real);
             B : (Y1 : real);
             C : (Z1 : real)
         END;  {  of RECORD Info  }
```

4. Redefine the following record without using a variant part.

```
TYPE
  Shapes = (Circle, Square, Triangle);
  FigureInfo = RECORD
                 Object : char;
                 Area : real;
                 CASE Shape : Shapes OF
                   Circle   : (Radius : real);
```

```
                    Square   : (Side : real);
                    Triangle : (Base, Height : real)
                END;
VAR
  Figure : FigureInfo;
```

5. Using the record defined in Exercise 4, indicate the names of the fields available and provide an illustration of these fields after each of the following assignments is made.
   a. `Shape := Circle;`
   b. `Shape := Square;`
   c. `Shape := Triangle;`
6. Redefine the record in Exercise 4 to include rectangles and parallelograms.
7. Define a record with a variant part to be used for working with various publications. For each record, there should be fields for the author, title, and date. If the publication is a book, there should be fields for the publisher and city. If the publication is an article, there should be fields for the journal name and volume number.

FOCUS ON PROGRAM DESIGN

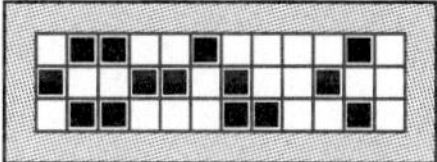

The sample program for this chapter features working with an array of records. The array is first sorted using the field containing a name and then sorted using the field containing a real number.

Let's write a program to help your local high school sports boosters keep records of donors and amounts donated. The data file consists of a name (first 20 positions) and an amount donated (starting in position 21) on each line. For example

Jones Jerry	250 ▮

Your program should get the data from the data file and read it into a record for each donor. Output should consist of two lists:

1. An alphabetical listing together with the amount donated
2. A listing sorted according to the amount donated

A first-level pseudocode development for this problem is

1. Get the data
2. Sort by name
3. Print the first list
4. Sort by amount
5. Print the second list

Module specifications for the main modules are

1. <u>GetData Module</u>
   Data received: None
   Information returned: Array of records containing names, amounts, and array length
   Logic: Use a **WHILE NOT eof** loop with a counter to read the data file.

2. SortByName Module
   Data received: Unsorted array of records containing names and amounts with the list length
   Information returned: An alphabetized list of names with associated amounts
   Logic: Use a selection sort to sort the array of records.
3. PrintList Module
   Data received: Array of records
   Array length
   Information returned: None
   Logic: Call procedure PrintHeading.
   Use a loop to print the names and amounts.
4. SortByAmount Module
   Data received: Array of records sorted alphabetically
   List length
   Information returned: Array of records sorted by size of donation
   Logic: Use a selection sort to sort the list of donations.

A refinement of the pseudocode yields

1. Get the data
   WHILE NOT eof DO
   1.1 get a name
   1.2 get the amount
2. Sort by name (use selection sort)
3. Print the first list
   3.1 print a heading
   3.2 print the names and amounts
4. Sort by amount (use selection sort)
5. Print the second list
   5.1 print a heading
   5.2 print the names and amounts

A complete structure chart is given in Figure 9.16.

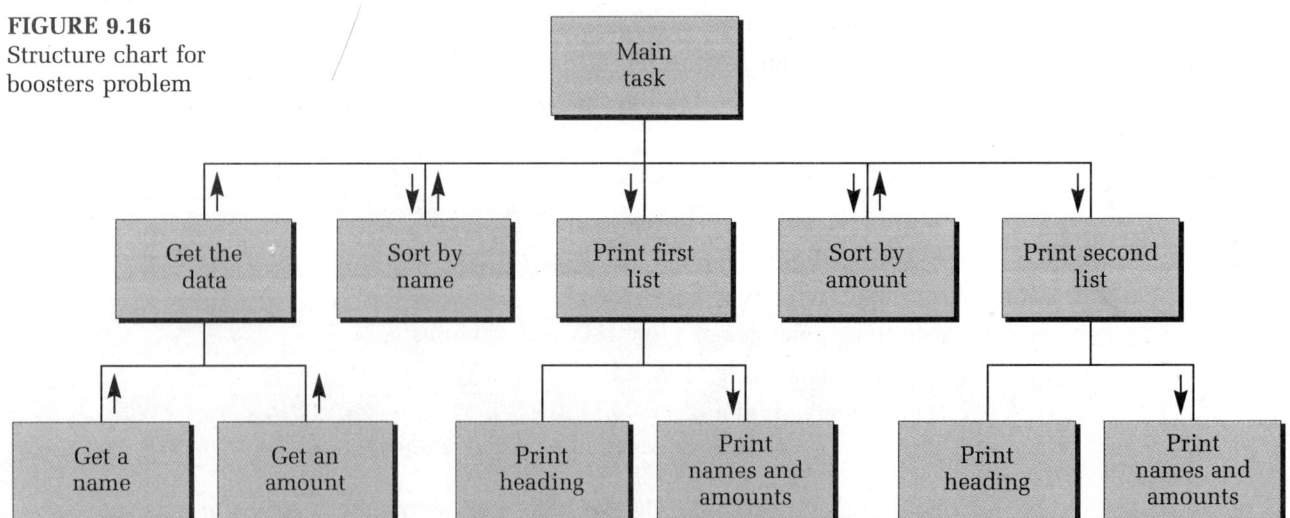

FIGURE 9.16 Structure chart for boosters problem

The main driver for the program is

```
BEGIN  {  Main program  }
  assign (Data, 'Donor.DAT');
  reset (Data);
  GetData (Donor, Count);
  SortByName (Donor, Count);
  PrintList (Donor, Count);
  SortByAmount (Donor, Count);
  PrintList (Donor, Count);
  close (Data)
END.  {  of main program  }
```

A complete program for this problem is

```
PROGRAM Boosters;

{  This program uses an array of records to process information     }
{  for donors to the local high school sports boosters.  Output     }
{  includes two lists:  one sorted by name, and one sorted by       }
{  amount donated.  Information is stored in the text file, Data.   }
{  Lst is used with writeln statements to direct output to the      }
{  printer because of the lengths of the lists.                     }

USES
  Crt,
  Printer;

CONST
  ClubSize = 50;

TYPE
  String20 = string [20];
  MemberInfo = RECORD
                 Name : String20;
                 Amount : real
               END;  {  of RECORD MemberInfo  }
  DonorList = ARRAY [1..ClubSize] OF MemberInfo;

VAR
  Count : integer;          {  Counter for number of donors          }
  Donor : DonorList;        {  Array of records, one for each donor  }
  Data : text;              {  Data file of names and amounts        }

{*****************************************************************}

PROCEDURE GetData (VAR Donor : DonorList;
                   VAR Count : integer);

  {  Given:   Nothing                                               }
  {  Task:    Read donor names and amounts from the text file,      }
  {               Data, into an array of records                    }
  {  Return:  An array of records and number of donors              }
                                                                       1
  VAR
    J : integer;
  BEGIN
    Count := 0;
    WHILE NOT eof(Data) AND (Count < ClubSize) DO
```

```
      BEGIN
        Count := Count + 1;
        WITH Donor[Count] DO
          readln (Data, Name, Amount)
      END;  {  of WHILE NOT eof  }
    IF NOT eof(Data) THEN
      writeln ('Not all data read.')
  END;  {  of PROCEDURE GetData  }

{*************************************************************}

PROCEDURE SortByName (VAR Donor : DonorList;
                      Count : integer);

  {  Given:   An array of records and number of records          }
  {  Task:    Sort alphabetically by the field Donor[J].Name     }
  {  Return:  An alphabetized array of records                   }

  VAR
    J, K, Index : integer;
    Temp : MemberInfo;
  BEGIN
    FOR J := 1 TO Count - 1 DO
      BEGIN                                                          2
        Index := J;
        FOR K := J + 1 TO Count DO
          IF Donor[K].Name < Donor[Index].Name THEN
            Index := K;
        IF Index <> J THEN
          BEGIN
            Temp := Donor[Index];
            Donor[Index] := Donor[J];
            Donor[J] := Temp
          END  {  of exchange  }
      END  {  of FOR J loop  }
  END;  {  of PROCEDURE SortByName  }

{*************************************************************}

PROCEDURE SortByAmount (VAR Donor : DonorList;
                        Count : integer);

  {  Given:   An array of records and number of records          }
  {  Task:    Sort by amount donated, Donor[J].Amount            }
  {  Return:  An array of records sorted by amount donated       }

  VAR
    J, K, Index : integer;
    Temp : MemberInfo;
  BEGIN
    FOR J := 1 TO Count - 1 DO
      BEGIN
        Index := J;
        FOR K := J + 1 TO Count DO                                   4
          IF Donor[K].Amount > Donor[Index].Amount THEN
            Index := K;
        IF Index <> J THEN
          BEGIN
            Temp := Donor[Index];
            Donor[Index] := Donor[J];
            Donor[J] := Temp
          END  {  of exchange  }
```

```
      END  {  of FOR J loop  }
  END;  {  of PROCEDURE SortByAmount  }

{******************************************************************}

PROCEDURE PrintHeading;

  {  Given:   Nothing                                               }
  {  Task:    Print a heading for the output; output directed to    }
  {               the printer                                       }
  {  Return:  Nothing                                               }

  CONST
    Skip = ' ';
  BEGIN
    writeln (lst, Skip:7, 'Local Sports Boosters');
    writeln (lst, Skip:11, 'Donation List');
    writeln (lst, '-----------------------------------');
    writeln (lst);
    writeln (lst, Skip:5, 'Name', Skip:20, 'Amount');
    writeln (lst, Skip:5, '----', Skip:20, '------');
    writeln (lst)
  END;  {  of PROCEDURE PrintHeading  }

{******************************************************************}

PROCEDURE PrintList (VAR Donor : DonorList;                             3
                     Count : integer);

  {  Given:   An array of records and number of records             }
  {  Task:    Print a list containing one column for the name and   }
  {               one column for the amount donated; output         }
  {               directed to the printer                           }
  {  Return:  Nothing                                               }

  CONST
    Skip = ' ';
  VAR
    J : integer;
  BEGIN
    PrintHeading;
    FOR J := 1 TO Count DO
      WITH Donor[J] DO
        writeln (lst, Name, '$':8, Amount:7:2);
    writeln (lst);
    writeln (lst);
    writeln (lst)
  END;  {  of PROCEDURE PrintList  }

{******************************************************************}

BEGIN  {  Main program  }
  ClrScr;
  assign (Data, 'Booster.DAT');
  reset (Data);
  GetData (Donor, Count);
  SortByName (Donor, Count);
  PrintList (Donor, Count);
  SortByAmount (Donor, Count);
  PrintList (Donor, Count);
  readln;
  close (Data)
END.  {  of main program  }
```

The output from this program is

```
         Local Sports Boosters
             Donation List
-----------------------------------

     Name                     Amount
     ----                     ------

Alexander Candy             $ 300.00
Banks Marj                  $ 375.00
Brown Ron                   $ 200.00
Erickson Thomas             $ 100.00
Francis Denise              $ 350.00
Generous George             $ 525.00
Hancock Kirk                $ 500.00
Janson Kevin                $ 200.00
Kneff Susan                 $ 300.00
Lyon Elizabeth              $ 425.00
Muller Marjorie             $ 250.00
Trost Frostie               $  50.00
Weber Sharon                $ 150.00
Williams Art                $ 350.00
Williams Jane               $ 175.00


         Local Sports Boosters
             Donation List
-----------------------------------

     Name                     Amount
     ----                     ------

Generous George             $ 525.00
Hancock Kirk                $ 500.00
Lyon Elizabeth              $ 425.00
Banks Marj                  $ 375.00
Francis Denise              $ 350.00
Williams Art                $ 350.00
Kneff Susan                 $ 300.00
Alexander Candy             $ 300.00
Muller Marjorie             $ 250.00
Brown Ron                   $ 200.00
Janson Kevin                $ 200.00
Williams Jane               $ 175.00
Weber Sharon                $ 150.00
Erickson Thomas             $ 100.00
Trost Frostie               $  50.00
```

■ RUNNING AND DEBUGGING HINTS

1. Be sure to use the full field name when working with fields in a record. You may only leave off the record name when using **WITH . . . DO**.
2. Terminate each record definition with an **END** statement. This is an instance when **END** is used without a **BEGIN**.

3. Although field names in different record types can be the same, you are encouraged to use distinct names. This enhances readability and reduces the chances of making errors.
4. Be careful to note the distinction in syntax when using an array of records versus an array as a field within a record. For example, be able to distinguish between Student[K].Average, Student.Score[J], and Student[K].Score[J].

■ Summary

Key Terms

array of records
field
fixed part
index sort
nested record
record
tag field
variant part

Keywords

RECORD **WITH**

Key Concepts

- A **RECORD** is a structured data type that is a collection of fields; the fields may be treated as a whole or individually.
- Fields in a record can be of different data types.
- Records can be declared or defined by

```
<record name> = RECORD
                  <field identifier 1> : <data type 1>;
                  <field identifier 2> : <data type 2>;
                           .
                           .
                           .
                  <field identifier n> : <data type n>
                END;   {    of RECORD definition    }
```

- Fields can be accessed as variables by
  <record name>.<field identifier>
- Records can be schematically represented as shown in Figure 9.17.

FIGURE 9.17
Fields in a record

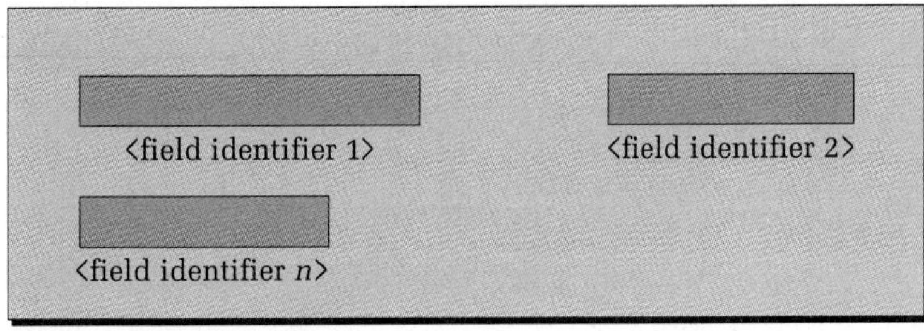

- **WITH** <record name> **DO** can be used in place of a specific reference to the record name with each field of a record; thus, you can have

```
WITH Student DO
  BEGIN
    Name := 'Smith John';
    Average := 93.4;
    Grade := 'A'
  END;
```

instead of

```
Student.Name := 'Smith John';
Student.Average := 93.4;
Student.Grade := 'A';
```

- If two records, A and B, are of identical type, the contents of all fields of one record may be assigned to the corresponding fields of the other by a single assignment statement, such as

```
A := B;
```

- Either entire records or fields within a record can be passed to appropriate subprograms.
- A record can be used as a field in another record.
- A **WITH . . . DO** statement can be used to access fields of nested records.
- Records can be used as components of an array.
- An array of records can be sorted by one of the fields in each record.
- Records with variant parts list all fixed fields (if any) first and then list the variant fields using a **CASE** statement; for example

```
TYPE
  MaritalStatus = (Married, Single, Divorced);
  String20 = string [20];
  Info = RECORD
           Name : String20;
           CASE Status : MaritalStatus OF
             Married  : (SpouseName : String20;
                         NumKids : integer);
             Single   : (Gender : char;
                         Age : integer);
             Divorced : (NumKids : integer;
                         Age : integer;
                         Gender : char;
                         LivesAlone : boolean)
         END;  { of RECORD Info }
VAR
  Customer : Info;
```

- After a value has been assigned to a tag field, the remaining record fields are the ones listed in the **CASE** part of the definition; for example, using the previous definition and assuming

```
Customer.Status := Divorced;
```

the record fields can be envisioned as shown in Figure 9.18.

FIGURE 9.18
Value of a tag field

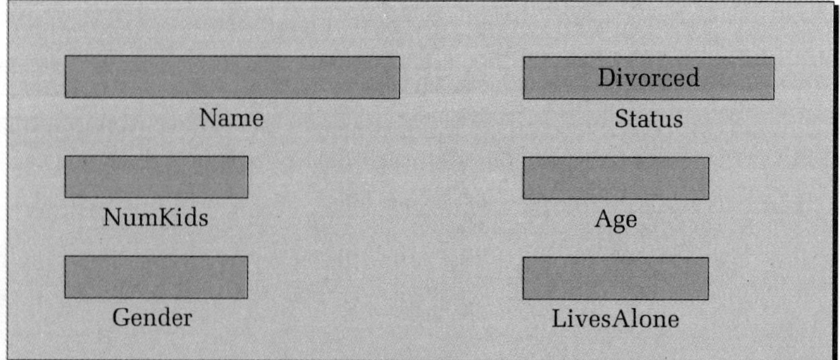

■ Programming Problems and Projects

1. Write a program to be used by the registrar of a university. The program should get information from a data file and the data for each student should include student name, student number, classification (1 = freshman, 2 = sophomore, 3 = junior, 4 = senior, or 7 = special student), hours taking, hours completed, and grade point average. Output should include an alphabetical list of all students, an alphabetical list of students in each class, and a list of all students in order by grade point average.
2. Robert Day, basketball coach at Indiana College, wants you to write a program to help him analyze information about his basketball team. He wants a record for each player to contain the player's name, position played, high school graduated from, height, scoring average, rebounding average, grade point average, and seasons of eligibility remaining.

   The program should read the information for each player from a data file. The output should include an alphabetized list of names together with other pertinent information, a list sorted according to scoring average, an alphabetized list of all players with a grade point average above 3.0, and an alphabetized list of high schools together with an alphabetized list of players who graduated from each school.
3. ■ Final grades in Dr. Lae Z. Programmer's (Problems 5, 22, and 23, Chapter 4; Problem 13, Chapter 5; Problem 5, Chapter 6; and Problem 3, Chapter 8) computer science class are to be computed using the following course requirements:

Requirement		***Possible Points***
1. Quiz scores (10 points each; count the best 10 out of 12)		100
2. Two hourly tests (100 points each)		200
3. Eight programming assignments (25 points each)		200
4. Two test program assignments (50 points each)		100
5. Final examination		100
	Total	700

   Cutoff percentages for grades of A, B, C, and D are 90 percent, 80 percent, 70 percent, and 55 percent, respectively; grade E is less than 55 percent.

   Write a program to keep a record of each student's name, social security number, quiz scores (all 12), hourly test scores, programming assignment scores, test program scores, and final examination score. Your program should read data from a data file, compute total points for each student, calculate the letter grade, and output results. The output should be sorted by total points from high to low and should include all raw data, the 10 best quiz scores, total points, percentage score, and letter grade. Use procedures and functions where appropriate.
4. Write a program to input an unknown number of pairs of fractions with an operation sign (+, −, *, or /) between the fractions. The program should perform the operation on the fractions or indicate that the operation is impossible. Answers should be reduced to lowest terms.

Sample Input	*Sample Output*
3/4 + 5/6	$\frac{3}{4} + \frac{5}{6} = \frac{19}{12}$
4/9 - 1/6	$\frac{4}{9} - \frac{1}{6} = \frac{5}{18}$
4/5 / 0/2	$\frac{4}{5}$ / $\frac{0}{2}$ = Impossible
4/3 + 7/0	$\frac{4}{3} + \frac{7}{0}$ = Impossible
6/5 * 20/3	$\frac{6}{5} * \frac{20}{3} = \frac{8}{1}$

5. Complex numbers are numbers of the form $a + bi$, where a and b are real and i represents $\sqrt{-1}$. Complex number arithmetic is defined by

Sum	$(a+bi)+(c+di) = (a+c)+(b+d)i$
Difference	$(a+bi)-(c+di) = (a-c)+(b-d)i$
Product	$(a+bi)(c+di) = (ac-bd)+(ad+bc)i$
Quotient	$\frac{a + bi}{c + di} = \frac{ac + bd}{c^2 + +d^2} + \frac{bc - ad}{c^2 + d^2} i$

Write a program to be used to perform these calculations on two complex numbers. Each line of data consists of a single character designator (S, D, P, or Q) followed by four reals representing two complex numbers. For example, $(2 + 3i) + (5 - 2i)$ is represented by

```
S2 3 5 -2
```

A record should be used for each complex number. The output should be in the form $a + bi$.

■ 6. The ReadMore Public Library wants you to develop a program to keep track of books checked out. Information for each book should be kept in a record, and the fields should include the author's name, a nonfiction designator (**boolean**), the title, the library catalog number, and the copyright date. Each customer can check out at most 10 books.

Your program should read information from a data file and print two lists alphabetized by author name: one for nonfiction, and the other for fiction. A typical data line is

```
Kidder Tracy        T Soul of a New Machine        81.6044 1982
                    ↑                              ↑
                    position 21                    position 52
```

■ 7. Modify Problem 6 so a daily printout is available that contains a summary of the day's transactions at the ReadMore Public Library. A record for each customer should contain the customer's name and library card number. Be sure to make a provision for books that are returned.

8. Write a program to be used to keep track of bank accounts. Define a record that includes each customer's name, account number, starting balance, transaction record, and ending balance. The transaction record should list all deposits and withdrawals. A special message should be printed whenever there are insufficient funds for a withdrawal. When a name is read from the data file, all previous records should be searched to see if the user is processing a new account. The final output for each customer should look like a typical bank statement.

9. Write a program that uses records to analyze poker hands. Each hand consists of five records (cards). Each record should contain one field for the suit and one field for the value. Rankings for the hands from high to low are

   a. straight flush
   b. four of a kind
   c. full house
   d. flush
   e. straight
   f. three of a kind
   g. two pair
   h. one pair
   i. none of the options given

   Your program should read data for five cards from a data file, evaluate the hand, and print out the hand together with a message indicating its value.

10. Problem 9 can be modified in several ways. One modification is to compare two different hands using only the ranks indicated. A second (more difficult) modification is to also compare hands that have the same ranks; for example, a pair of 8s is better than a pair of 7s. Extend Problem 9 to incorporate some of these modifications.

11. Divers at the Olympics are judged by seven judges. Points for each dive are awarded according to the following procedure:

    a. Each judge assigns a score between 0.0 and 10.0, inclusive.
    b. The high score and low score are eliminated.
    c. The five remaining scores are summed, and this total is multiplied by 0.6. This result is then multiplied by the degree of difficulty of the dive (0.0 to 3.0).

    The first level of competition consists of 24 divers, each making 10 dives. Divers with the 12 highest totals advance to the finals.

    Write a program to keep a record for each diver. Each record should contain information for all 10 dives, the diver's name, and the total score. One round of competition consists of each diver making one dive. A typical line of data consists of the diver's name, degree of difficulty for the dive, and seven judges' scores. Part of your output should include a list of divers who advance to the finals.

12. The University Biology Department has a Conservation Club that works with the state Department of Natural Resources. Its project for the semester is to help capture and tag migratory birds. You have been asked to write a computer program to help the club store information. In general, the program must enable the user to enter information for each tagged bird interactively into an array of records and then store these data in a text file for subsequent use. For each bird tagged, you need a field for the tag number, tagging site, sex, bird type, date, and name of the DNR officer doing the tagging. After all data have been entered, the program should print one list sorted by tag number and one list sorted by bird type.

■ 13. Ada Crown, your computer science instructor, wishes to monitor the maintenance record of her computers and has turned to you for help. She wants to keep track of the type of machine, its serial number (up to 10 characters), the year of purchase, and whether or not the machine is under service contract (a **boolean** variable).

Write a program that permits the entry of records and then prints a list of machines under warranty and a list of those not under warranty. Both lists should be arranged in order of serial number.

14. Most microcomputer owners soon develop a large, often unorganized library of software on several floppy disks. This is your chance to help them. Define a record that contains the disk number of each disk and a list of up to 30 program titles on each disk. Write a program to read a text file containing the information for a disk and then print an alphabetized list of the program titles on that disk.

15. Revise the program you developed in Problem 14 to permit the user to enter the program name desired and have the program print the number of disk(s) containing the program.

16. Write a program to read records that contain the names, addresses, telephone numbers, and classes of some of your friends. Print a list of the names of the students in the file who are in your class.

■ 17. The Falcon Manufacturing Company (Problem 22, Chapter 8) wishes to keep computerized records of its telephone-order customers. The records are to contain the name, street address, city, state, and zip code for each customer and include either T if the customer is a business or F if the customer is an individual. A 30-character description of each business and an individual's credit limit are also to be included in the record.

Write a program to read the information for the customer from a text file and print a list of the information for businesses and a separate list of the information for individuals. There are no more than 50 records in the file.

■ Communication in Practice

1. Write a short paper that explains why the existence of the structured data type **RECORD** eliminates the need for working with parallel arrays. As part of your paper, show specifically how **PROGRAM** Donations in Section 8.3. can be rewritten using records.
2. Suppose you are part of a team that has been asked to develop a spreadsheet. Your specific task is to write all documentation for the sorting feature of the spreadsheet. The documentation is to include complete descriptions of forms of input and output, a logical development of the sorting process, and a description of the user interface messages. Prepare a report that includes this documentation.
3. Visit your local registrar, and discuss how records of students are processed. Discover what data are kept in each record, how the data are entered, and what the fields of each record are. Have the registrar explain what operations are used with a student's record. Specifically, how is information added to or deleted from a record? Discuss the issue of sorting records. What kinds of lists must the registrar produce for those within the system who need information about students?

   Prepare a written report of your visit for the class. Be sure to include a graphic that shows how a student's record can be envisioned.
4. Select an unworked problem from the previously listed programming problems in this chapter. Construct a structure chart and write all documentary information necessary for this problem. Do not write code. When finished,

have a classmate read your documentation to see if precisely what is to be done is clear.

5. Modify one of the programs you developed in this chapter by deleting all documentation. Exchange your modified version with another student who has prepared a similar version. Write documentation for the exchanged program. Compare your results with the other student's original version.
6. Select a problem from the Programming Problems and Projects of this chapter that you have not done. For that problem, write documentation that includes a complete description of the following:
   a. Required input
   b. Required output
   c. Required processing and computation

   Exchange your documentation with another student who has the same assignment. Compare your results.

More about Files

CHAPTER OUTLINE

Chapter 6 introduced the concept of text files that are used to provide data for a program and to store data between runs of a program. All data in a text file are stored as a sequence of characters of type **char.** We are now ready to examine files in more detail, beginning with the definition and use of binary files.

10.1 Binary Files

Files that cannot be defined as text files are *binary files.* Information is stored in binary files by using the internal binary representation of each component. This method differs from data storage in a text file, where components are stored as lines of characters.

The advantage of using binary files is that they can be much more efficiently processed. Because the binary representation of data is already available, conversion between character representation and appropriate binary representation is not needed. A disadvantage of using binary files is that they cannot be created, examined, or modified by using a text editor. Binary files must be created by a program. Furthermore, all operations with binary files must be done within programs. In the following sections, we see how these operations are performed.

Basic Idea and Notation

Information can be saved between runs of a program by using secondary storage devices such as tapes or disks. (Personal computers use floppy or hard disks.) As a beginning programmer, you need not normally be concerned with the actual physical construct of these storage devices, but you do need to know how to work with them. To oversimplify, you need to be able to get data into a program, manipulate these data, and save the data (and results) for later use. For example, if we write a program that computes grades for students in a class, we need to periodically enter data for processing. Turbo Pascal solves this problem with the structured data type **FILE.** A *file* is a data structure that consists of a sequence of components that are all of the same type. A **FILE** data type is defined by

> **TYPE**
> <file identifier> = **FILE OF** <data type>;
> **VAR**
> <file name> : <file identifier>;

Thus, if we wish to work with a file of integers, we define

```
TYPE
  FileOfInt = FILE OF integer;
VAR
  File1 : FileOfInt;
```

In this case, File1 is the desired file. Several comments are now in order.

1. Data entries in a file are called *components of the file.*
2. All components of a file must be of the same data type.
3. The only data type not permitted as a component of a file is another file type. This differs from arrays in that

   ARRAY [ ] **OF ARRAY** [ ] **OF** <data type>;

   is permitted, but

   FILE OF FILE OF <data type>;

   is not permitted.

Each of the following is a valid definition of a file type:

```
TYPE
  Identifier1 = FILE OF real;
  Identifier2 = FILE OF ARRAY [1..20] OF integer;
  Identifier3 = FILE OF boolean;
```

Files of records are frequently used in programs. Thus, to keep a record for each student in a class, we could have the definition

```
TYPE
  String20 = string [20];
  ExamScores = ARRAY [1..4] OF integer;
  QuizScores = ARRAY [1..10] OF integer;
  StudentInfo = RECORD
                  Name : String20;
                  IDNumber : 0..999;
                  Exam : ExamScores;
                  Quiz : QuizScores;
                  Average : real;
                  Grade : char
                END;  {  of RECORD StudentInfo  }
  StudentFile = FILE OF StudentInfo;
VAR
  Student : StudentFile;
```

There is a difference between a text file and a file of characters. Although a text file consists of a sequence of characters, it also has "lines" separated by

A NOTE OF INTEREST

Relational Data Bases

One advance in data management that has gained tremendously in popularity and, in fact, is revolutionizing system development practices, is the increased use of the data base management system, known as DBMS. An especially important development in data base technology is the relational data base.

The relational DBMS is based upon the concept of multiple "flat files" that are "related" via common fields. A flat file is essentially a two-dimensional matrix of columns and rows, where columns represent the fields contained in a record and rows contain different records. A simple example of the flat file concept is a spreadsheet, such as Lotus 1-2-3, although the analogy is somewhat misleading since spreadsheets are most commonly used for purposes other than data base management.

In a relational data base, there are usually several flat files, each of which is used to store information about a different "entity" in the world. The objectives of relational technology are to ensure that each file in the data base contains information about only the entity with which it is associated and to provide linkages between files that represent the relationships between those entities that exist in the real world.

Let's look at a simple example of a relational data base that is used to process customer orders. Such a relational data base would contain at least two files: one for customer data, and one for order data. The customer file would contain information (that is, fields) such as the customer's account number, name, address, and phone number; the order file would contain fields such as product number, product name, order quantity, unit cost, and total order cost. To enable the system to match an order to the customer who placed it, the customer's account number would also be contained in the order file. Thus, when the user needs combined order and customer information (for example, to prepare and mail an invoice), the two files can be temporarily "joined" together based upon common values in each file's respective customer account number fields.

At the mainframe level of computing, the relational DBMS is one of several types of data base management systems; other types are hierarchical and network systems. At the microcomputer level, however, DBMS software is almost exclusively relational. Common packages, such as dBASE III, RBase System V, and SQLBase, are all relational and provide essentially the same basic structures and capabilities, even though they require different syntax to accomplish similar activities.

end-of-line markers. A file of characters, which is of the type **FILE OF char,** does not have line separators.

Comparison to Arrays

Files and one-dimensional arrays have some similarities. Both are structured data types, and the components of both must be of the same type. There are, however, some important differences.

1. Files permit the user to store and retrieve information between runs of a program.
2. Only one component of a file is available at a time.
3. In standard versions of Pascal, files must be sequentially accessed; that is, when working with files, the user starts at the beginning and processes the components in sequence. It is not possible (as with arrays) to access some component directly without first having somehow moved through the previous components. Turbo Pascal does provide for direct access of file components, as will be shown later.
4. Files do not have a defined length. Once a file has been defined, the number of components is limited only by the amount of storage available. However, this is usually so large it can be considered unbounded.
5. Files are stored in secondary storage; arrays are only stored in memory.

Exercises 10.1

1. Discuss the similarities between arrays and files.
2. Discuss the differences between arrays and files.
3. Which of the following are valid declarations of files. Explain those that are invalid. State the component type for those that are valid.

   a.
   ```
   TYPE
     FileOfAges = FILE OF 0..120;
   VAR
     AgeFile : FileOfAges;
   ```
   b.
   ```
   TYPE
     String20 = string [20];
     FileOfNames = ARRAY [1..100] OF String20;
   VAR
     NameFile : FileOfNames;
   ```
   c.
   ```
   TYPE
     FileA = FILE OF real;
     FileB = FILE OF FileA;
   VAR
     RealFile : FileB;
   ```
   d.
   ```
   TYPE
     FileOfInt = FILE [1..100] OF integer;
   VAR
     File1 : FileOfInt;
   ```
   e.
   ```
   TYPE
     IntFile = FILE OF integer;
   VAR
     OldFile, NewFile, TempFile : IntFile;
   ```
4. Define a file type and then declare a file to be used with records of patients for a physician. Information should include the name, address, height, weight, age, gender, and insurance company of each patient.

10.2 Working with Files

Now that we have examined the concepts of files, we need to see how values are transmitted to and from file components. Let's first examine the process of putting data into a file.

Creating a File

Once a file has been declared in a program, entering data to the file is referred to as *writing to the file.* Before writing to a file, the file must be opened. We do this by using the standard procedure **rewrite.** This is referred to as *opening a file.* Thus, if FileA is declared by

```
TYPE
  IntFile = FILE OF integer;
VAR
  FileA : IntFile;
```

then

```
rewrite (FileA);
```

opens FileA to receive values of type **integer.** (Turbo Pascal offers the user a more sophisticated method, but it is beyond the scope of this text.) At this stage, FileA is ready to receive the first component. Any components previously stored in

FileA are no longer available. Successive components may be stored in FileA, and each new component is appended to the previous list of components. When a program has finished writing components to a binary file, the file can be closed by the code

```
close (<file name>);
```

This is referred to as *closing a file.*

Turbo Pascal allows values to be written to a file using the procedure **write.** When this procedure is used, the arguments for **write** are the file variable followed by variables that are of the same type as the file component type. For each variable written, the current file position is advanced to the next component. For example, we can store the values 10, 20, and 30 in FileA by using

```
Num1 := 10;
Num2 := 20;
Num3 := 30;
rewrite (FileA);
write (FileA, Num1, Num2, Num3);
```

FileA can then be envisioned as

The procedure **writeln** can only be used with files of type **text.**

Binary files can be created either interactively or by translating data from an existing text file into a binary file. The following example illustrates how a binary file can be created when data are entered from the keyboard.

■ EXAMPLE 10.1

Let's write an interactive program that allows the user to enter and store integer data in a binary file. The file identifier in the program is IntFile. It is associated with the disk file INTPRAC.DAT by using the **assign** procedure. A complete program follows.

```
PROGRAM FilePrac;

USES
  Crt;

TYPE
  IntegerFile = FILE OF integer;

VAR
  IntFile : IntegerFile;
  Num : integer;
  Response : char;

BEGIN  {  Program  }
  ClrScr;
  assign (IntFile, 'IntPrac.DAT');
  rewrite (IntFile);
  REPEAT
    writeln ('Enter an integer and press <Enter>.');
    readln (Num);
    write (IntFile, Num);  {  Write integer to binary file  }
    write ('Any more?  <Y> or <N>  ');
    readln (Response)
  UNTIL (Response = 'N') OR (Response = 'n');
  close (IntFile)
END.  {  of program  }
```

A sample run of this program produces

```
Enter an integer and press <Enter>.
2
Any more?  <Y> or <N>  Y
Enter an integer and press <Enter>.
4
Any more?  <Y> or <N>  N
```

At this stage, the binary file IntPrac.DAT is stored on the disk. It contains the binary representations of the integers 2 and 4 and can be accessed by subsequent programs.

Accessing Binary Files

The process of entering and retrieving data from binary files is similar to the operations used when working with text files. For the purpose of illustration, the declaration

```
TYPE
  IntFile = FILE OF integer;
VAR
  File1 : IntFile;
```

can be used to produce a file with components illustrated by

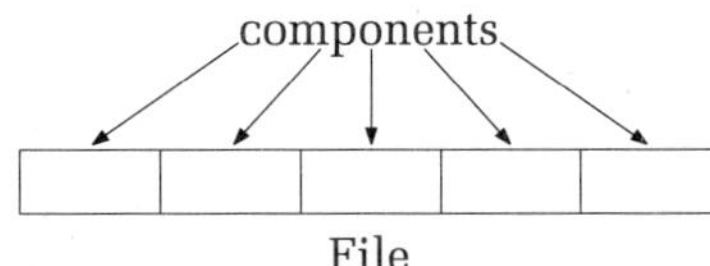

File

A data pointer keeps track of which component is to be written next or which component is to have data copied from it. Thus, File1 can be envisioned as

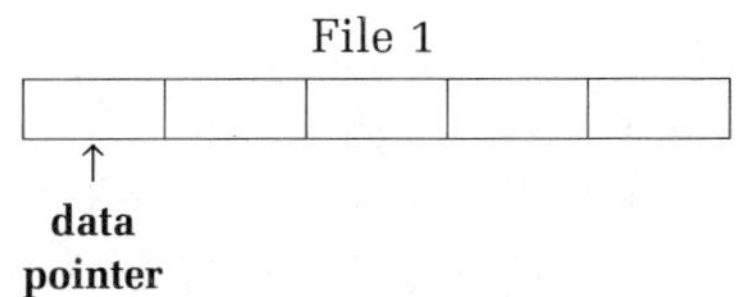

In this instance, the first compoent of File1 can be accessed for data transmission.

The Standard Function **eof**

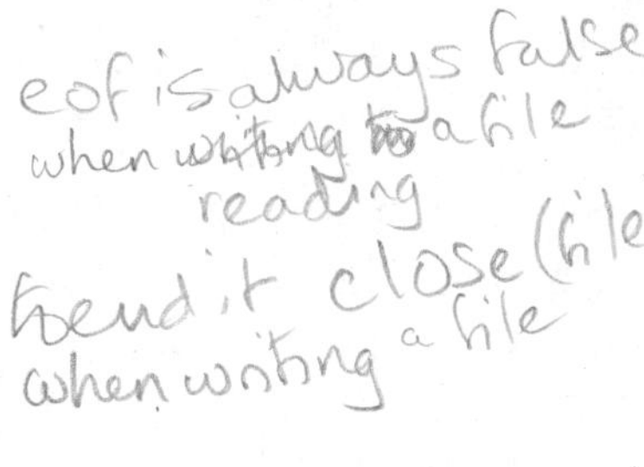

The Boolean function **eof** can be used on binary files in much the same way it is used on text files. When a file is opened for writing, an end-of-file marker is placed at the beginning of the file. When a value is transferred into the file by **write,** the end-of-file marker is advanced to the next component position. The reason for this is relatively obvious. When retrieving data from a file, we need to know when we have reached the end of the file. The function **eof** is used with the file name for an argument. As expected, **eof** (<file name>) is **true** when the pointer is positioned at the end-of-file marker. When writing to a file, **eof** (<file name>) is always **true.**

Retrieving File Data

S The process of retrieving data from a file is referred to as *reading from a file.* To retrieve data from a file, we open the file by using the standard procedure **reset.** Correct syntax is

reset (<file name>);

This has the effect of repositioning the pointer at the beginning of the file.

The standard procedure **read** can be used to transfer data from a file. After the file has been opened for reading, **read** can be used with the file name and variable names as arguments. If the binary FileA contains the values depicted as

the following code can be used to read values from the file:

```
reset (FileA);
read (FileA, N1);
read (FileA, N2);
read (FileA, N3);
```

This would result in the variables N1, N2, and N3 receiving the values in the first three components, respectively, of FileA. Thus, we would have

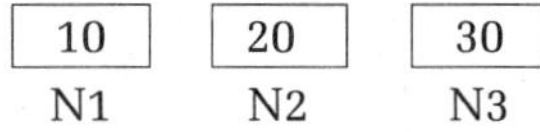

and the data pointer would be positioned as

FileA

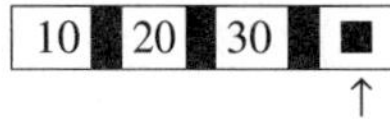

The same result can be achieved by

```
read (FileA, N1, N2, N3);
```

Opening Files

Turbo Pascal permits both reading from and writing to binary files that are opened by using either the **reset** or **rewrite** statement. However, the development of file manipulation using this practice is deferred to Section 10.4. For now, we assume files cannot be open for both reading and writing at the same time (see Section 6.1).

When a file is opened for writing, it remains open to receive values that are appended to the file until the window is repositioned by either the **rewrite** or **reset** statement or until the program is terminated. Thus, we may create a file and then add to it later in the program without reopening it. Similarly before we first read from a file, it must be opened by **reset** (<file name>). Values can then be transferred from the file by using the **read** statement.

Now let's consider a short example in which we do something with each component of a file.

EXAMPLE 10.2

Suppose we have a file of reals and we want to create another file by subtracting 5.0 from each component. Assume the following definitions and declarations:

```
TYPE
  RealFile = FILE OF real;
VAR
  OldFile : RealFile;
  NewFile : RealFile;
  Num : real;
```

We can accomplish our objective by

```
reset (OldFile);      {  Open OldFile  }
rewrite (NewFile);    {  Open NewFile  }
WHILE NOT eof(OldFile) DO
  BEGIN
    read (OldFile, Num):
    Num := Num - 0.5;
    write (NewFile, Num)
  END;
```

Procedures and Files

Much of the work of processing files is accomplished by using procedures. Thus, we should continue to use the **TYPE** definition section to define file types. Files can be used as arguments in a procedure call; however, in the procedure heading, files must be listed as variable parameters. This requirement is implicit in the fact that a file variable cannot be assigned all at once (as a value parameter can be).

EXAMPLE 10.3

Let's write a procedure to accomplish the task outlined in Example 10.2:

```
PROCEDURE Subtract5 (VAR OldFile, NewFile : RealFile);
  BEGIN
    reset (OldFile);
    rewrite (NewFile);
    WHILE NOT eof(OldFile) DO
      BEGIN
        read (OldFile, Num);
        Num := Num - 0.5;
        write (NewFile, Num)
      END  {  of WHILE...DO  }
  END;  {  of PROCEDURE Subtract5  }
```

This procedure is called from the main program by

```
Subtract5 (OldFile, NewFile);
```

Even though no changes are made in OldFile, it is passed as a variable parameter.

Internal and External Files

Recall from Chapter 6 file variables defined in the variable declaration of a program are referred to as internal files. These files are available to the program but are not recognized by a disk operating system (DOS). File identifiers that appear in the directory list and that are recognized by DOS are external files. As is the case with text files, binary files use the **assign** procedure to associate internal file variables with external files. Thus, in the program in Example 10.1

```
VAR
  IntFile : IntegerFile;
```

followed by the program statement

```
assign (IntFile, 'IntPrac.DAT');
```

associates the external file IntPrac.DAT with the internal file IntFile. Any changes made to IntFile are then saved in IntPrac.DAT until IntPrac.DAT is used again by the program or by some other program. The following example creates a binary file of integers from an existing text file.

■ **EXAMPLE 10.4**

This example is a complete program that creates a binary file of integers from an existing text file that has been created using the Turbo Pascal editor. The text file has been saved as IntData.DAT.

```
PROGRAM FilePrac;

USES
  Crt;

VAR
  Num : integer;
  NewFile : FILE OF integer;
  OldFile : text;

BEGIN  {  Program  }
  ClrScr;
  assign (OldFile, 'IntData.DAT');
  assign (NewFile, 'NewData.DAT');
  reset (OldFile);
  rewrite (NewFile);
  writeln ('OldFile', 'Values to NewFile':29);
  writeln ('-------', '-----------------':29);
  WHILE NOT eof(OldFile) DO
    BEGIN
      readln (OldFile, Num);
      write (Num:4);                        {  Output to the screen  }
      Num := Num * 10;
      writeln (Num:24);
      write (NewFile, Num)          {  Output to the binary file  }
    END;  {  of WHILE NOT eof  }
  close (OldFile);
  close (NewFile);
  writeln;

  {  Now display contents of the binary file  }
  writeln ('Values from NewFile');
  writeln ('-------------------');
  reset (NewFile);
  WHILE NOT eof(NewFile) DO
    BEGIN
      read (NewFile, Num);  {  Read value from the binary file  }
      writeln (Num:10)
    END;  {  of WHILE NOT eof  }        {  Output to the screen  }
  readln;
  close (NewFile)
END.  {  of program  }
```

Output from this program is

```
OldFile           Values to NewFile
-------           -----------------
   2                     20
   4                     40
   6                     60
   8                     80
  10                    100

Values from NewFile
-------------------
        20
        40
        60
        80
       100
```

Processing Files

Before looking at a specific problem about processing files, let's consider the general problem of updating an external file. Since we eventually will **rewrite** the external file, we must be careful not to erase the original contents before they have been saved and/or processed in some temporary file. We accomplish this by working with the temporary files until the desired tasks are completed. At this point, we then copy the appropriate temporary file to the external file.

Now let's consider a relatively short example of updating a file of test scores for students in a class. A detailed treatment of processing files is given in Section 10.4.

■ EXAMPLE 10.5

Assume the external file TOTALS.DAT consists of total points for each student in a class. Furthermore, assume the data file TestData contains test scores that are to be added (in the same order) to the previous totals to obtain new totals. A first-level pseudocode solution to this problem is

1. Sum the scores in TotalPts and NewScores
2. Copy new total to TotalPts

Assume the definitions and declarations are

```
TYPE
  IntFile = FILE OF integer;

VAR
  TotalPts : IntFile;
  NewScores : IntFile;
  TempFile : IntFile;
```

A procedure to copy the contents from one file to another is

```
PROCEDURE Copy (VAR OldFile, NewFile : IntFile);
  VAR
    Num : integer;
  BEGIN
    reset (OldFile);
    rewrite (NewFile);
    WHILE NOT eof(OldFile) DO
      BEGIN
        read (OldFile, Num);
        write (NewFile, Num)
      END;  {  of WHILE NOT eof  }
    close (OldFile);
    close (NewFile)
END;  {  of PROCEDURE Copy  }
```

We use the scratch file ScratchFile to contain the sum of previous scores added to the new test scores. A procedure for this is

```
PROCEDURE AddScores (VAR TotalPts, NewScores,
                     ScratchFile : IntFile);
  VAR
    Total, NewScore : integer;
  BEGIN
    reset (TotalPts);
    reset (NewScores);
    rewrite (ScratchFile);
    WHILE NOT eof(TotalPts) DO
      BEGIN
        read (TotalPts, Total);
```

```
        read (NewScores, NewScore);
        Total := Total + NewScore;
        write (ScratchFile, Total)
      END;  { of WHILE NOT eof  }
    close (TotalPts);
    close (NewScores);
    close (ScratchFile)
  END;  { of PROCEDURE AddScores  }
```

This procedure is called from the main program by

```
AddScores (TotalPts, NewScores, TempFile);
```

At this stage, the updated scores are in TempFile and they need to be stored in the file TotalPts before the program is exited. This is done by a call to Copy in the main program. Thus

```
Copy (TempFile, TotalPts);
```

achieves the desired results. The main program is then

```
BEGIN  {  Main program  }
  assign (TotalPts, 'Totals.DAT');
  assign (NewScores, 'TestData.DAT');
  assign (TempFile, 'Scratch.DAT');
  AddScores (TotalPts, NewScores, TempFile);
  copy (TempFile, TotalPts)
END.
```

Example 10.5 obviously overlooks some significant points. For example, how do we know that the scores match up or that each student's new score is added to that student's previous total? We will address these issues later in the chapter. Now let's see how one file can be appended to an existing file.

EXAMPLE 10.6

Assume the files are named OldFile and NewFile and the task is to append NewFile to OldFile. We will use the temporary file TempFile to complete this task. A first-level pseudocode development for this problem is

1. Reset OldFile and NewFile
2. Open TempFile for writing
3. **WHILE NOT eof** (OldFile) **DO**
   3.1 read component from OldFile
   3.2 write component to TempFile
4. **WHILE NOT eof** (NewFile) **DO**
   4.1 read component from NewFile
   4.2 write component to TempFile
5. Copy TempFile to OldFile

The complete code for this example is left as an exercise.

Exercises 10.2

1. Review the difference between internal files and external files.
2. Write test programs that illustrate:
   a. What happens when you try to write to a file that has not been opened for writing.

   b. What happens when you try to get data from a file that has not been reset.
   c. What happens when a procedure uses a file as a value parameter.

3. Declare an appropriate file, and store the positive multiples of 7 that are < 100.

4. After writing and running the program in Example 10.1:
   a. Exit Turbo Pascal and use DOS to examine the directory to see how IntPrac is listed.
   b. Open the file by using the editor (F3) and then typing the file name IntPrac.DAT. Discuss what happens.

5. Consider the file with integer components

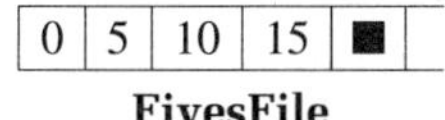

FivesFile

Write a segment of code that would assign the values to variables A, B, C, and D, respectively, by using the **read** statement.

6. Consider the following file with component values as illustrated:

```
TYPE
  RealFile = FILE OF real;
VAR
  Prices : RealFile;
```

15.95	17.99	21.95	19.99	■	

Prices

   a. Declare a new file, and put values in the components that are 15 percent less than the values in the components of Prices.
   b. Update the values in Prices so each value is increased by 10 percent.

7. Discuss the difference between **reset** and **rewrite.**

8. You have been asked to write a program to examine a file of integers and replace every negative number with zero. Assume IntFile has been appropriately declared and contains five integer values. Why will the following segment of code not work?

```
rewrite (IntFile);
FOR J := 1 TO 5 DO
  BEGIN
    read (IntFile, Num);
    IF Num < 0 THEN
      BEGIN
        Num := 0;
        write (IntFile, Num)
      END
  END;
```

9. Consider the files declared by

```
TYPE
  FileOfInt = FILE OF integer;
VAR
  File1, File2 : FileOfInt;
```

Find all errors in each of the following.

a.
```
reset (File1);
FOR J := 1 TO 5 DO
  write (File1, J);
```

b.
```
reset (File2);
WHILE NOT eof(File1) DO
  BEGIN
    read (File1, Num);
    write (File2, Num)
  END;
```

c.
```
rewrite (File1);
FOR J := 1 TO 5 DO
  write (File1, 10 * J);
```

d.
```
reset (File2);
rewrite (File1);
WHILE NOT eof(File2) DO
  BEGIN
    read (File2, Num);
    write (File1, Num)
  END;
```

10. Assume the files OldFile and NewFile are declared as

```
TYPE
  IntFile = FILE OF integer;
VAR
  OldFile, NewFile : IntFile;
```

Furthermore, for each of the following, assume OldFile has the component values

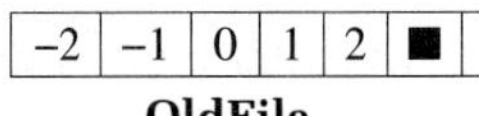

–2	–1	0	1	2	■

OldFile

Indicate the values in components of both OldFile and NewFile after each of the following segments of code.

a.
```
reset (OldFile);
rewrite (NewFile);
WHILE NOT eof(OldFile) DO
  BEGIN
    read (OldFile, Num);
    Num := abs(Num);
    write (NewFile, Num)
  END;
rewrite (OldFile);
reset (NewFile);
WHILE NOT eof(NewFile) DO
  BEGIN
    read (NewFile, Num);
    write (OldFile, Num)
  END;
```

b.
```
reset (OldFile);
rewrite (NewFile);
WHILE NOT eof(OldFile) DO
  BEGIN
    read (OldFile, Num);
    IF Num > 0 THEN
      write (NewFile, Num)
  END;
```

11. Assume OldFile and NewFile are as declared in Exercise 10. Furthermore, assume OldFile contains the values

8	–17	0	–4	21	■

OldFile

Indicate the output from the following segment of code and the values of the components in OldFile and NewFile:

```
reset (OldFile);
rewrite (NewFile);
WHILE NOT eof(OldFile) DO
  BEGIN
    read (OldFile, Num);
    IF Num < 0 THEN
      writeln (Num)
    ELSE
      write (NewFile, Num)
  END;
```

12. Assume you have declared three files (File1, File2, and File3) in a program such that the component type for each file is **real.** Furthermore, assume both File1 and File2 contain unknown numbers of values. Write a segment of code to transfer the corresponding sum of components from File1 and File2 to File3. Since File1 and File2 may have different numbers of components, after one end-of-file is reached, you should add zeros until the next end-of-file is reached. Thus, your segment will produce

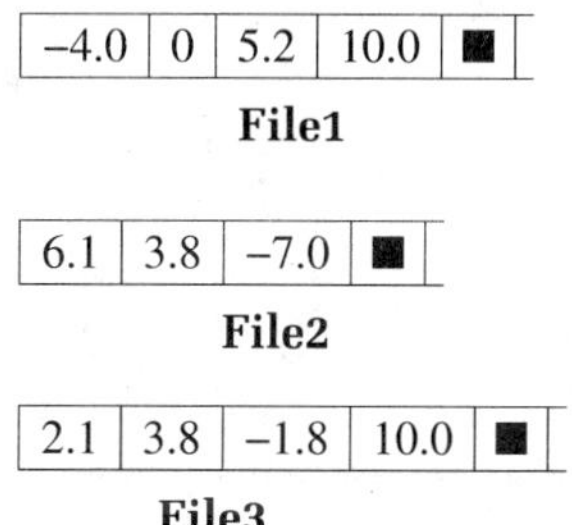

13. Write a complete program that finishes the work started in Example 10.6. Your program should print out the contents of each file used and of the final file.

■ 10.3 Files with Structured Components

In actual practice, components of files are frequently some structured data type. A program might use a file of arrays or a file of records; when such a file is desired, the user declares an internal file, uses the procedure **assign** to associate the internal file variable with an external file, and then creates components from a text file. Once the data have been converted, the user can access an entire array or record rather than individual fields or components. The data are also saved in structured form between runs of a program. When data have been stored in structured components, it is relatively easy to update and work with these files. For example, a doctor may have a file of records of patients and wish to insert or delete records of the patients, examine the individual fields of each record, print an alphabetical list, or print a list of patients with unpaid bills.

Now let's examine a typical declaration. Suppose we are writing a program to use a file of records. Each record contains information about a student in a computer science class: in particular, the student's name, three test scores (in an array), identification number, and test average. A declaration for such a file could be

```
TYPE
  String20 = string [20];
  Scores = ARRAY [1..3] OF 0..100;
  StudentInfo = RECORD
                  Name : String20;
                  Score : Scores;
                  Average : real;
                  IDNumber : 0..999
                END;  {  of RECORD StudentInfo  }
  StudentFile = FILE OF StudentInfo;
VAR
  StudentList : StudentFile;
  StudentRec : StudentInfo;
```

StudentList is a file of records that can be illustrated as shown in Figure 10.1.

FIGURE 10.1
File StudentList

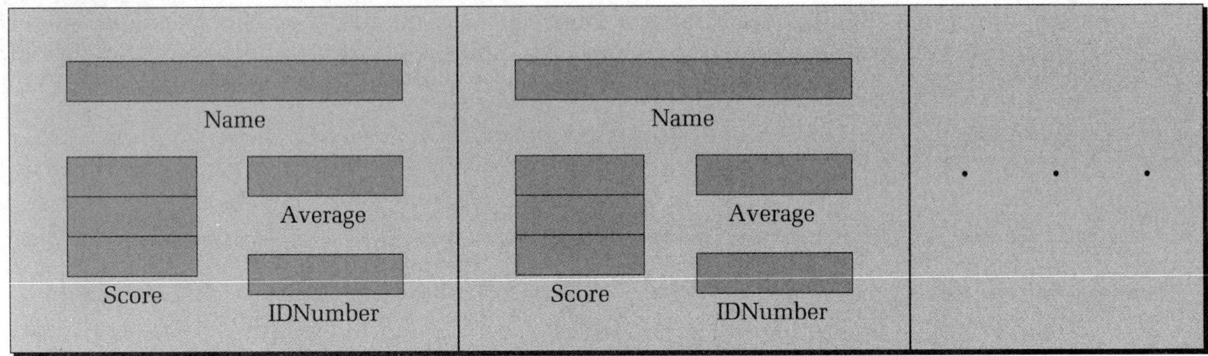

After StudentList is opened for reading by **reset** (StudentList), the statement

```
read (StudentList, StudentRec);
```

causes the contents of a record to be transferred to StudentRec. The field identifiers are

```
StudentRec.Name
StudentRec.IDNumber
StudentRec.Score
StudentRec.Average
```

StudentRec.Score is an array. Components of this array are

```
StudentRec.Score[1]
StudentRec.Score[2]
StudentRec.Score[3]
```

If we wish to compute the average for a student, we can write

```
Sum := 0;
WITH StudentRec DO
  BEGIN
    FOR J := 1 TO 3 DO
      Sum := Sum + Score[J];
    Average := Sum / 3
  END;
```

Creating a File of Records

One of the first problems to be solved when working with files that contain structured variables is to transfer data from some text file to the appropriate file of structured components. Once the new file with structured components is created, it can be saved in secondary storage, since the internal file variable is now associated with an external file. To illustrate the process of creating a file of records, let's continue the example of the file of records for students in a computer science class. Recall the definitions and subsequent declaration

```
TYPE
  String20 = string [20];
  Scores = ARRAY [1..3] OF 0..100;
  StudentInfo = RECORD
                  Name : String20;
                  Score : Scores;
                  Average : real;
                  IDNumber : 0..999
                END;  {  of RECORD StudentInfo  }
```

```
  StudentFile = FILE OF StudentInfo;
VAR
  StudentList : StudentFile;
  StudentRec : StudentInfo;
```

Before we can create the file of records, we need to know how data were entered in the text file. For purposes of this example, assume data for each student are contained on a single line, 20 positions are used for the name, and an identification number is followed by three test scores. Thus, the data file could be

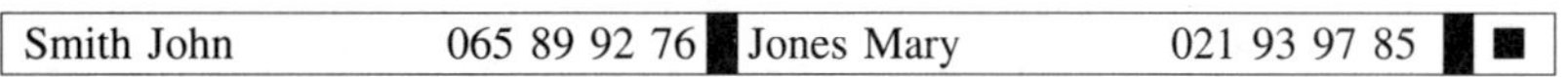

A procedure to create the file of records is

```
PROCEDURE CreateFile (VAR StudentList : StudentFile);
  VAR
    J : integer;
    StudentRec : StudentInfo;
  BEGIN

  {  The file StudentList has already been associated  }
  {  with an external file by assign (StudentList,     }
  {  'Students.DAT') in the main program               }

  rewrite (StudentList);          {   Open for writing  }
  reset (Data);
  WHILE NOT eof(Data) DO      {   Data is the text file  }
    BEGIN                     { Get data for one record  }
      WITH StudentRec DO
        BEGIN
          read (Data, Name, IDNumber);
          readln (Data, Score[1], Score[2], Score[3])
        END;  {  of WITH...DO  }
      write (StudentList, StudentRec)
    END;  {  of WHILE NOT eof  }
  close (StudentList);
  close (Data)
END;  {  of PROCEDURE CreateFile  }
```

This procedure is called from the main program by

```
CreateFile (StudentList);
```

After it is executed, we have the records shown in Figure 10.2.

FIGURE 10.2
File StudentList with values

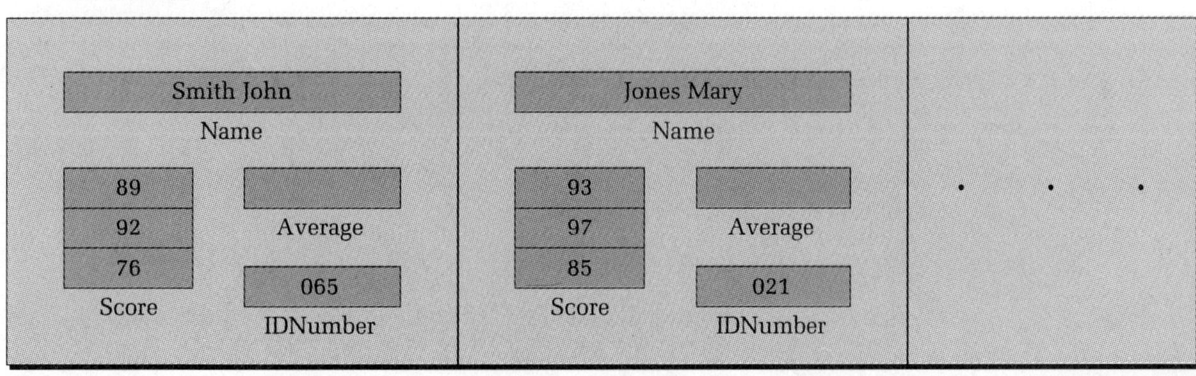

It is also possible to create a file of records where input to the file comes from the keyboard rather than from an existing text file, as shown in Example 10.7.

EXAMPLE 10.7

In Programming Problem 9 at the end of this chapter, it is necessary to work with a file of records that contains flight information for airlines. Specifically, for each flight, we need a record containing the flight number, expected departure and arrival times, origin, and destination of the flight. The following program illustrates how an appropriate file of records can be interactively generated.

```
PROGRAM CreateDataFile;

USES
  Crt;

TYPE
  Flight = RECORD
             FlightNumber : integer;
             ETA : 0..2400;
             ETD : 0..2400;
             Orig, Dest : string [15]
           END;  { of RECORD Flight  }

VAR
  FlightFile : FILE OF Flight;
  FlightRec : Flight;
  MoreData : boolean;
  Continue : char;

BEGIN  {  Program  }
  assign (FlightFile, 'NewFile.DAT');
  rewrite (FlightFile);
  MoreData := true;
  WHILE MoreData DO                           {  Get one flight record  }
    BEGIN
      WITH FlightRec DO
        BEGIN
          ClrScr;
          writeln ('Enter a data line and press <Enter>.');
          writeln;
          write ('Origin        *Destination    *');
          writeln ('ETA':5, 'ETD':5, 'Flight Number':16);
          writeln;
          readln (Orig, Dest, ETA, ETD, FlightNumber)
        END;  {  of WITH...DO  }
      write (FlightFile, FlightRec);  {  Write one record to file  }
      write ('Continue?  <Y> or <N>  ');
      readln (Continue);
      MoreData := (Continue = 'Y') OR (Continue = 'y')
    END;  {  of WHILE...DO  }
  close (FlightFile);

  {  Display contents of the binary file  }

  reset (FlightFile);
  WHILE NOT eof(FlightFile) DO
    BEGIN
      read (FlightFile, FlightRec);
      WITH FlightRec DO
        writeln (Orig:15, Dest:15, ETA:15, ETD:5, FlightNumber:11)
    END;  {  of WHILE NOT eof  }
```

```
  close (FlightFile);
  readln
END. {  of program  }
```

A sample run of this program produces the binary file

```
Detroit        Chicago                        752  756  521
Chicago        Tampa                         1157  857  923
```

File Manipulation

Several problems are typically involved with manipulating files and file components. Generally, a program starts with an existing file, revises it in some fashion, and then saves the revised file. Because files in standard Pascal must be accessed sequentially, this usually necessitates copying the existing external file to a temporary file, revising the temporary file, and copying the revised file to the external file. The existing external file is often referred to as the *master file.* The file containing changes to be made in the master file is called the *transaction file.*

To illustrate a simple update problem, let's reconsider the problem using the file containing records for students in a computer science class. Assume the external file is named Student.DAT and the associated internal file is named StudentList. Now suppose we wish to delete a record from StudentList (master file) because some student moved to Australia. This problem can be solved by searching StudentList sequentially for the record in question. As the name in each record is examined, if the record is to be kept, it is put in a temporary file. The desired record is not transferred, thus accomplishing the update. Finally, StudentList is rewritten by copying the contents of the temporary file to StudentList.

A first-level pseudocode development is

1. Get the name to be deleted
2. Search StudentList for a match and copy each nonmatch to TempFile
3. Copy the remainder of StudentList to TempFile
4. Copy TempFile to StudentList

Using the previous declarations and assuming that the name of the student whose record is to be deleted has been read into MovedAway, step 2 can be solved by

```
reset (StudentList);  {  Open the files  }
rewrite (TempFile);
Found := false;
WHILE NOT eof(StudentList) AND NOT Found DO
  BEGIN
    reset (StudentList);  {  Open the files  }
    rewrite (TempFile);
    Found := false;
    WHILE NOT eof(StudentList) AND NOT Found DO
      BEGIN
        read (StudentList, StudentRec);
        IF StudentRec.Name = MovedAway THEN
          Found := true
        ELSE
          write (TempFile, StudentRec)
      END;  {  of search for a student name  }

{  Now copy the rest of student file  }
```

```
WHILE NOT eof(StudentList) DO
  BEGIN
    read (StudentList, StudentRec);
    write (TempFile, StudentRec)
  END;
close (StudentList);
close (TempFile);
```

We now need to copy TempFile to StudentList so the revised master file is saved as an external file. A procedure for this was developed in Section 10.2; it is called from the main program by

```
Copy (TempFile, StudentList);
```

As a second illustration of file manipulation, let's consider the standard problem of merging two sorted files. For example, suppose the master file is a file of records and each record contains a field for the name of a customer. Further, assume this file has been sorted alphabetically by name. Now suppose an alphabetical listing of new customers is to be merged with the old file to produce a current file containing records for all customers sorted alphabetically by name.

As before, we use a temporary file to hold the full sorted list and then copy the temporary file to the master file. This can be seen as illustrated in Figure 10.3.

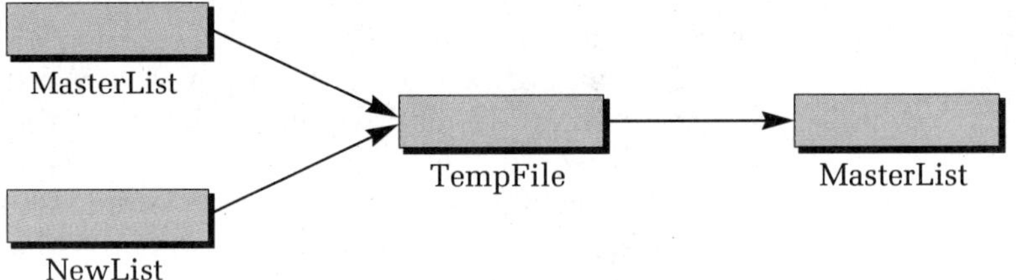

FIGURE 10.3
Merging files

An algorithm for the merge is not too difficult. First all files are opened. Then the initial records from MasterList and NewList are compared. The record containing the name that comes first alphabetically is transferred to TempFile. Then, as shown in the graphic documentation for the following program segment, the next record is obtained from the file containing the record that was transferred. This process continues until the end of one file is reached. At that time, the remainder of the other file is copied into TempFile.

Assuming each record has a field identified by Name, which is of type String30, and FileType has been defined as the type for files being used, a procedure for merging follows.

```
PROCEDURE Merge (VAR Master, NewFile : FileType);
  VAR
    TempFile : FileType;
    MasterRec, NewRec : RecordType;
  BEGIN
    reset (Master);
    reset (NewFile);
    assign (TempFile, 'Scratch.DAT');
    rewrite (TempFile);

  {  Compare top records until an eof of one of the  }
  {  input files is reached.                           }

    read (Master, MasterRec);
    read (NewFile, NewRec);
```

```
WHILE NOT eof(Master) AND NOT eof(NewFile) DO
  IF MasterRec.Name < NewRec.Name THEN
    BEGIN
      write (TempFile, MasterRec);
      read (Master, MasterRec)
    END
  ELSE
    BEGIN
      write (TempFile, NewRec);
      read (TempFile, NewRec)
    END;
```

Current
last
record
Current
record
Current
record
Master
NewFile
TempFile
The smaller of
these two records
must be transferred
to the end of Tempfile.
Then advance within
the file from which
the record was taken.

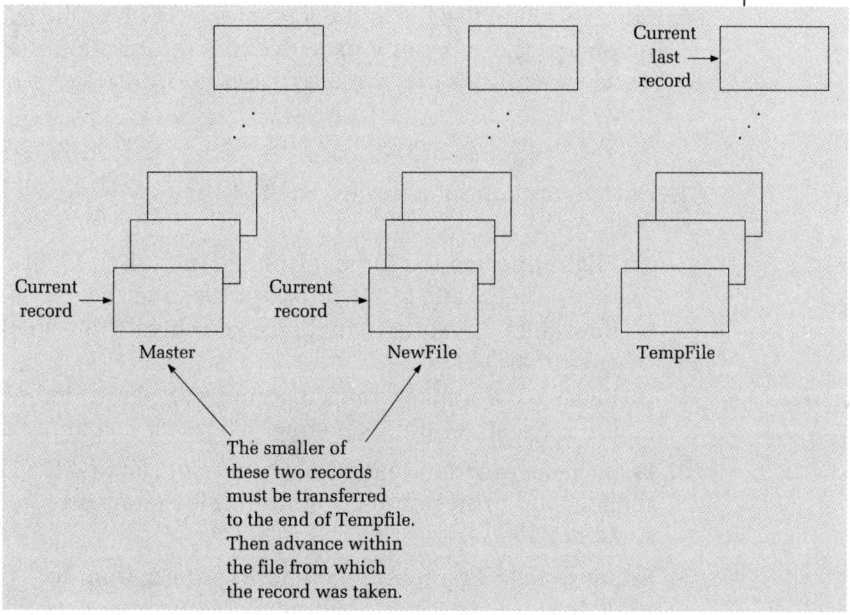

```
{  Now copy the remaining names  }

  WHILE NOT eof(Master) DO
    BEGIN
      write (TempFile, MasterRec);
      read (Master, MasterRec)
    END;
  close (Master);
  WHILE NOT eof(NewFile) DO
    BEGIN
      write (TempFile, NewRec);
      read (NewFile, NewRec)
    END;
  close (TempFile);

{  Now copy back to Master  }

  rewrite (Master);
  reset (TempFile);
  WHILE NOT eof(TempFile) DO
    BEGIN
      read (TempFile, MasterRec);
      write (Master, MasterRec)
    END;
```

```
    close (Master);
    close (TempFile)
  END;  {  of PROCEDURE Merge  }
```

This procedure is called from the main program by

```
Merge (Master, NewFile);
```

A final comment is in order. It is frequently necessary to work with files of records that have been sorted according to a field of the record. Since we might want to work with the records sorted by some other field, we must first be able to sort an unsorted file. In general, this is done by transferring the file components to array components, sorting the array, and transferring the sorted array components back to the file. This means that we must have some idea of how many components are in the file and declare the array length accordingly. The physical setting of a problem usually provides this information. For example, physicians will have some idea of how many patients (100, 200, or 1000) they see.

Exercises 10.3

1. Declare appropriate files for each of the following. Fields for each record are indicated.
   a. Flight information for an airplane, including flight number, airline, arrival time, origin, departure time, and destination
   b. Bookstore inventory, including author, title, stock number, price, and quantity
   c. Records for a magazine subscription agency, including name and address (indicate street number, street name, city, state, and zip code)
2. Write a test program that allows you to declare a file of records, read data into the file, and print information from selected records according to the value in some key field.
3. Suppose data in a text file contains information for students in a class. The information for each student appears on three data lines as illustrated.

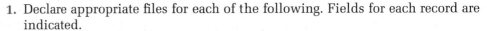

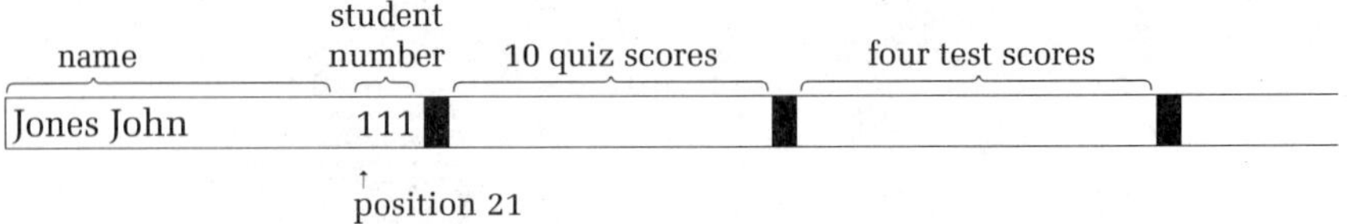

   a. Declare a file of records to be used to store this data.
   b. Write a procedure to create a file of records containing appropriate information from the text file.
   c. Write a procedure to sort the file alphabetically.
4. Illustrate the values of components and fields in StudentList and StudentRec during the first pass through the loop in **PROCEDURE** CreateFile on page 489.
5. Consider the file StudentList declared by

```
TYPE
  String20 = string [20];
  Scores = ARRAY [1..3] OF 0..100;
  StudentInfo = RECORD
                  Name : String20;
                  Score : Scores;
                  Average : real
```

```
                 IDNumber : 0..999
               END;
  StudentFile = FILE OF StudentInfo;
VAR
  StudentList : StudentFile;
  StudentRec : StudentInfo;
```

Write a procedure for each of the following tasks. In each case, show how the procedure is called from the main program. (Assume the file has been alphabetized.)

a. Add one record in alphabetical order.
b. Add one record to the bottom of the file.
c. Update the record of 'Smith Jane' by changing her score on the second test from an 82 to an 89.
d. The scores from the third test have just been entered into a data file. Each line contains an identification number followed by three integer scores. Update StudentList to include these scores. (The first two scores have already been transferred to the appropriate student records.)
e. Assume all test scores have been entered. Update StudentList by computing the test average for each student.
f. Print a list containing each student's name and test average; the list should be sorted by test average from high to low.

■ 10.4 Direct Access Files

S

All text and binary files studied thus far have been *sequential access files.* Such files are processed by starting with the first component and then moving sequentially through all the components of a file. Standard Pascal does not provide any other method of accessing files.

As you might imagine, there is a need for a more efficient way to access files. For example, banks, credit card companies, and hospitals frequently want to be able to access a particular file component immediately. If the data base is quite large, sequential access would be far too slow.

Fortunately, Turbo Pascal provides for *direct access* (also called *random access*) of file components. Conceptually, direct access of files is not difficult. The user specifies the desired component and then modifies it appropriately. However, putting this deceptively easy concept into practice requires some development.

The Turbo Pascal Method

For purposes of this discussion, we will work with the following definitions and declarations:

```
TYPE
  String20 = string [20];
  Scores = ARRAY [1..3] OF 0..100;
  StudentInfo = RECORD
                  Name : String20;
                  Score : Scores;
                  Average : real;
                  IDNumber : 0..999
                END;  { of RECORD StudentInfo  }
  StudentFile = FILE OF StudentInfo;
VAR
  StudentList : StudentFile;
  StudentRec : StudentInfo;
```

Thus, StudentList is a file of records. We further assume there are *n* records in the file.

Turbo Pascal provides the built-in procedure **seek,** which moves the current file position to a specified component. Thus, if we want to modify the fifteenth record in StudentList, we first locate it by using

```
seek (StudentList, 14);
```

We use 14 because file components are numbered beginning with zero. The current file position is then at the fifteenth record, and we can proceed with appropriate modifications. In general, the form of the **seek** procedure is

> **seek** (<file variable>, <position – 1>);

where <file variable> is the identifier representing the file and <position> specifies which file component we want.

Turbo Pascal also provides the functions **FileSize** and **FilePos** for working with direct access files. The function

```
FileSize (<file variable>)
```

returns the current size of a file. thus, if we have 35 records in StudentList (numbered 0–34)

```
FileSize (StudentList)
```

would return a value of 35. The function

```
FilePos (<file variable>)
```

returns the current file position. If the current file position is at the beginning of the file, **FilePos** returns zero. If the current file position is at the end of the file, **FilePos** is equal to **FileSize.**

The **seek** procedure and the function **FileSize** are often used together when working with direct access files. To guarantee that the record for which we are looking is in the file, typical program statements are

```
IF (RecordPos >= 0) AND (RecordPos < FileSize (StudentList)) THEN
  BEGIN
    seek (StudentList, RecordPos);  {  Locate the record  }
       .
       .  (process record here)
       .
```

Hashing

You may have realized by now that a significant problem exists when using direct access files: How do we know which record is in which position? For example, if our file is in order alphabetically, which position is occupied by the record of Susan Smythe? If our file contains records for parts in a manufacturing process and each part has a part number, which position is occupied by the part numbered 12407?

Associating some field of a record with a relative position in a file is referred to as *hashing.* This area of study is beyond the scope of this text. Hashing is an extensive field that is absolutely essential in applications using direct access files. In our examples, we assume a very simple association between a field record and its file position. Specifically, each record has a field that contains its position. In the case of our file of student records, the ID number is used for this purpose. Thus, in a class of 35 students; the ID numbers would range from zero to 34. This means we need a separate list that associates the students' names with their ID numbers.

Reading and Writing

In Turbo Pascal, any binary file is a direct access file. When the **seek** procedure is used to access a component, the user may both **read** and **write** without having to **close** and reopen the file. First, the file must be opened for input by using **reset** before using **seek.** Thus, typical code would be

```
reset (StudentList);
IF (IDNumber >= 0) AND (IDNumber < FileSize(StudentList)) THEN
  BEGIN
    seek (StudentList, IDNumer);   {  Locate the record  }
    read (StudentList, StudentRec);  {  Obtain the record  }
      .
      .  (process record here)
      .
```

After a record has been updated, the new version needs to replace the old version in the file. This is accomplished by using **write.** However, the current file position must be moved to the appropriate component. Since **read** is used to obtain the component in consideration, the file position advances to at least the next component. The pointer can be repositioned by a subsequent call to **seek** before using **write.** This results in code for updating a record in a direct access file as follows:

```
reset (StudentList);  {  Open the file  }
IF (IDNumber > = 0) AND (IDNumber < FileSize(StudentList)) THEN
  BEGIN
    seek (StudentList, IDNumber);
    read (StudentList, StudentRec);
      .
      .  (appropriate change in record)
      .
    seek (StudentList, IDNumber);
    write (StudentList, StudentRec)
  END;
```

Adding Records to a File

Records can be added to an existing direct access file by inserting a record into the file or by appending a record to the end of the file. If a file is to have records inserted, it is appropriate to create a file with empty components; that is, reserve a field containing the record position in RecordPos and then initialize the other fields to zeros or blanks, as appropriate. To insert a record, merely **seek** the appropriate position and assign the desired field values.

To append a record to the end of a file

```
seek (<file variable>, FileSize(<file variable>));
```

places the current file position at the end of the file. A record then can be appended by using

```
write (<file variable>, <record>);
```

Using our defined variables, this would yield

```
seek (StudentList, FileSize(StudentList));
write (StudentList, StudentRec);
```

Deleting Records from a File

Deleting a record from a direct access file is actually a misnomer because the record is not physically removed from the file. Typically, the desired record is located and the fields are reinitialized to zeros and blanks. The value in the field that contains the position is retained.

Exercises 10.4

1. Discuss the difference between the sequential access and the direct access of files.
2. Provide examples of situations in which:
   a. Sequential access of files is more appropriate than direct access.
   b. Direct access of files is more appropriate than sequential access.
3. What is wrong with the following segment of code?

```
BEGIN
  seek (StudentList, 10);
  read (StudentList, StudentRec);
  StudentRec.Score[2] := 89;
  write (StudentList, StudentRec)
END;
```

4. Using the definitions for StudentList and StudentRec given at the beginning of this section, show how a partial credit adjustment can be made on a student's score on the first test. Specifically, suppose that Susan Smythe (position 27) had her test regraded and her score changed from 89 to 93.
5. Write a test program to see what happens in each of the following cases.
   a. **seek** is used on an empty file.
   b. **seek** (<file variable>, Position) is used when Position > FileSize(<file variable>).
6. One method of hashing is to assign each record a number that differs from its position by a constant. For example, a file of 20 records for parts can have fields for part numbers that range from 101 through 120. Discuss how these numbers can be used to locate the relative positions of zero through 19 in a direct access file.
7. Write a program that creates a binary file of records in which each record has the following fields:

```
PartRecord = RECORD
               PartNum : integer;
               PartName : string [15];
               Price : real;
               OnHand : integer
             END;
```

   Your file should contain 30 records with part numbers beginning at 101. Initialize all other fields to zeros or blanks, as appropriate.
8. Write an interactive program that uses the binary file created in Exercise 7. The program should allow the user to enter any part number between 101 and 130 and then examine and/or modify any of the fields in the record.

FOCUS ON PROGRAM DESIGN

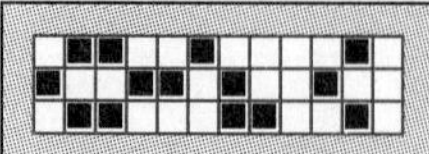

The summary program for this chapter is an elementary version that could be expanded to a comprehensive programming project. Suppose the registrar at your institution wants you to develop a program for updating a file of student records. A master file of student records currently exists; it is sorted alphabetically. Each record contains a field for the student's name, ID number, grade point average, and total hours completed. This file is to be updated by information contained in a transaction file. Each line in the transaction file contains a student number, letter grade for a course taken, and number of credit hours for the course. A typical data line is

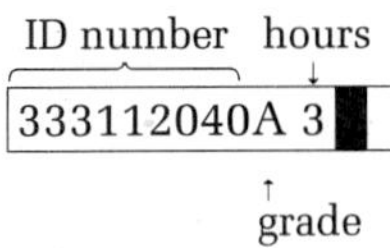

For each data line in the transaction file, your program should search the contents of the master file for a match. If a match is found, appropriate changes should be made in grade point average and total hours completed. If no match is found, the information should be printed in an Exception Report. After all transactions are completed, an alphabetized list should be printed and the master file should be updated.

A first-level pseudocode development for this program is

1. Prepare the files
2. Copy contents of MasterFile to an array
3. Update the records
4. Print the list
5. Update MasterFile

A complete structure diagram for this program is given in Figure 10.4.

FIGURE 10.4
Structure chart for the file update program

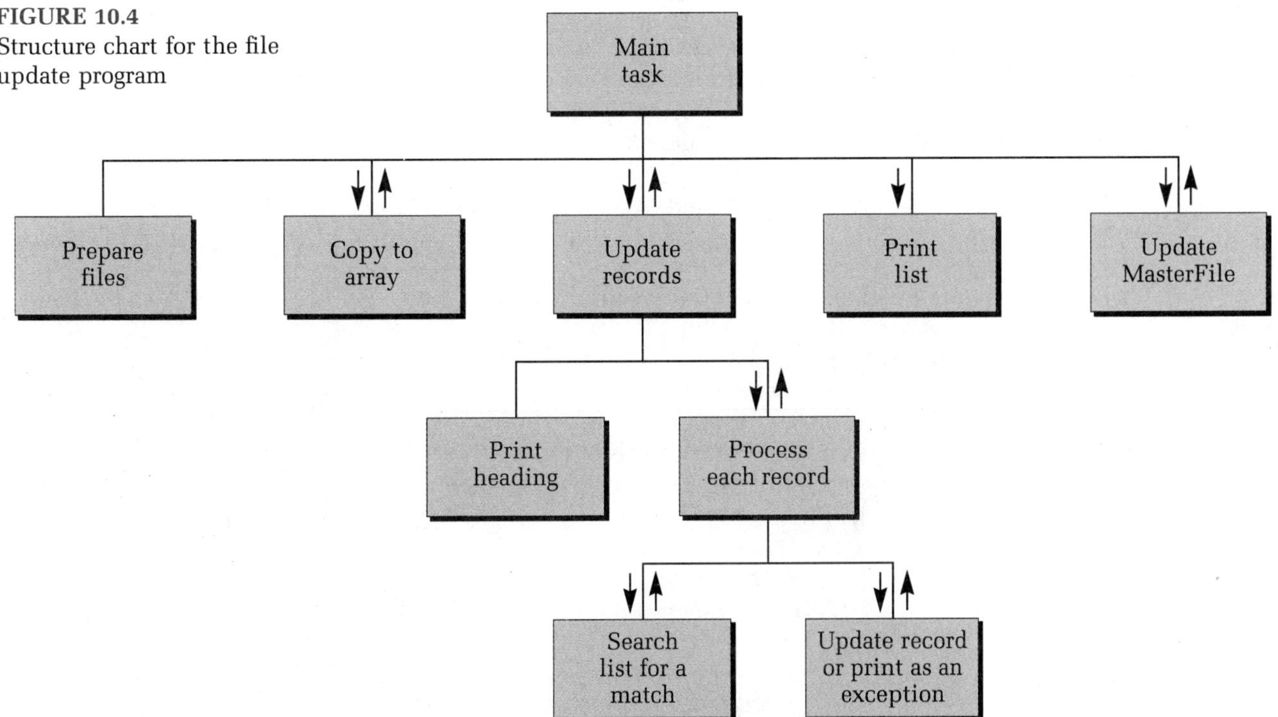

Module specifications for the main modules are

1. PrepareFiles Module
   Data received: None
   Information returned: None
   Logic: Use **reset** to prepare files for reading.

2. LoadArray Module
   Data received: File of records
   Information returned: Array of records
   Number of records
   Logic: Copy contents of each record in MasterFile to a record in Student.
   Count the number of records in the array.

3. UpdateRecords Module
   Data received: An array of records
   Length of the array
   A transaction file
   Information returned: An updated array of records
   Logic: For each data line in TransactionFile, search for a match in the array.
   IF a match is found, **THEN**
   update the record
   ELSE
   print out an Exception Report

4. PrintList Module
   Data received: A sorted array of records
   Length of the array
   Information returned: None
   Logic: Print a heading.
   Print contents of each record.

5. UpdateMasterFile Module
   Data received: An array of records
   Length of the array
   MasterFile of records
   Information returned: An updated MasterFile
   Logic: For each record in Student, copy contents into a record in MasterFile.

Further pseudocode development is

```
1. Prepare the files
   1.1 reset MasterFile
   1.2 reset TransactionFile
2. Copy contents of MasterFile to an array
   2.1 set counter to zero
   2.2 REPEAT
         2.2.1 increment counter
         2.2.2 copy contents of one record
       UNTIL eof (MasterFile)
3. Update the records
   3.1 print Exception Report heading
   3.2 WHILE NOT eof (TransactionFile) DO
         3.2.1 search for a match
         3.2.2 IF NOT Found THEN
                 print as part of Exception Report
               ELSE
                 update the record
4. Print the list
   4.1 print a heading
   4.2 print an alphabetized list
```

5. Update MasterFile
   5.1 **rewrite** MasterFile
   5.2 **FOR** each record in the array **DO**
         copy contents to a record in MasterFile

Step 3.2.1 is a sequential search of the array. If a match is found, the array position is returned; if not, a zero is returned. The portion of step 3.2.2 designed to update the record consists of incrementing the grade point average. A **CASE** statement is used to direct action for grades of 'A', 'B', 'C', 'D', 'E', 'W', and 'I'. This program assumes valid data are contained in TransactionFile. A complete program for this problem follows.

```
PROGRAM FileUpdate;

{  This program updates a file of student records.  Transactions     }
{  are stored in the text file TransactionFile.  Each line consists  }
{  of a student number, grade for a course taken, and credit hours   }
{  for the course.  The file of records is copied to an array of     }
{  records for processing.  This facilitates searching for matches   }
{  of student numbers.  It is assumed the master file is alphabe-    }
{  tized.  If it is not, one could add a procedure to sort the       }
{  array before rewriting the master file.                           }

USES
  Crt,
  Printer;

CONST
  MaxLength = 200;

TYPE
  String9 = string [9];
  String20 = string [20];
  StudentRecord = RECORD
                    Name : String20;
                    IDNumber : String9;
                    GPA : real;
                    Hours : integer
                  END;  { of RECORD StudentRecord }
  StudentList = ARRAY [1..MaxLength] OF StudentRecord;
  RecordsFile = FILE OF StudentRecord;

VAR
  NumberOfRecords : integer;        {  Number of records read          }
  Student : StudentList;            {  Array of student records        }
  MasterFile : RecordsFile;         {  Master file of student records  }
  TransactionFile : text;           {  Transaction file for updating   }

{*******************************************************************}

PROCEDURE PrepareFiles (VAR MasterFile : RecordsFile;
                        VAR TransactionFile : text);

  {  Given:   Nothing                                           }
  {  Task:    Open the files for reading                        }
  {  Return:  MasterFile and TransactionFile ready to be read   }

  BEGIN                                                              1
    assign (MasterFile, 'Records.DAT');
    assign (TransactionFile, 'Updated.DAT');
    reset (MasterFile);
    reset (TransactionFile)
  END;  { of PROCEDURE PrepareFiles }
```

```
{*******************************************************************}

PROCEDURE LoadArray (VAR MasterFile : RecordsFile;
                     VAR Student : StudentList;
                     VAR NumberOfRecords : integer);

  {  Given:   Master file containing data for each student          }
  {  Task:    Create an array of student records from MasterFile    }
  {  Return:  Array of student records and number of records        }

  BEGIN
    NumberOfRecords := 0;                                                  2
    WHILE NOT eof(MasterFile) AND (NumberOfRecords < MaxLength) DO
      BEGIN
        NumberOfRecords := NumberOfRecords + 1;
        read (MasterFile, Student[NumberOfRecords])
      END;  {  of WHILE NOT eof  }
    IF NOT eof(MasterFile) THEN
      writeln ('There are more data.');
    close (MasterFile)
  END;  {  of PROCEDURE LoadArray  }

{*******************************************************************}

FUNCTION NewGPA (Hours, CourseHours : integer;
                 GPA, HonorPoints : real) : real;

  {  Given:   Total hours accumulated, credit hours for the course  }
  {               completed, current GPA, HonorPoints corresponding }
  {               to the letter grade received                      }
  {  Task:    Compute the new grade point average                   }
  {  Return:  New grade point average                               }

  VAR
    OldHours : integer;
  BEGIN
    OldHours := Hours;
    Hours := Hours + CourseHours;
    NewGPA := (OldHours * GPA + CourseHours * HonorPoints) / Hours
  END;  {  of FUNCTION NewGPA  }

{*******************************************************************}

FUNCTION SeqSearch (Student : StudentList;
                    IDNumber : String9;
                    NumberOfRecords : integer) : integer;

  {  Given:   An array of student records, a student ID number, and }
  {               the number of records                             }
  {  Task:    Sequentially search the array to find a match for the }
  {               ID number                                         }
  {  Return:  The index of the record where a match was found;      }
  {               return 0 if no match is found                     }

  VAR
    Found : boolean;
    LCV : integer;
  BEGIN
    SeqSearch := 0;
    Found := false;
    LCV := 0;
```

```
    WHILE (LCV < NumberOfRecords) AND (NOT Found) DO
      BEGIN
        LCV := LCV + 1;
        IF Student[LCV].IDNumber = IDNumber THEN
          BEGIN
            SeqSearch := LCV;
            Found := true
          END  {  of IF...THEN  }
      END  {  of WHILE...DO  }
  END;  {  of FUNCTION SeqSearch  }

{*******************************************************************}

PROCEDURE UpdateRecords (VAR TransactionFile : text;
                         VAR Student : StudentList;
                         NumberOfRecords : integer);

  {  Given:   A transaction file for updating records, an array of    }
  {               student records, and number of student records      }
  {  Task:    Read a line from the transaction file; search array     }
  {               Student for a match of IDNumber; if a match,        }
  {               update hours and GPA; if not, print as part of      }
  {               Exception Report                                    }
  {  Return:  An updated array of student records                    }

  CONST
    Skip = ' ';
  VAR
    J, Index, CourseHours : integer;
    IDNumber : String9;
    Grade : char;
    MatchFound : boolean;                                                  3
  BEGIN

  {  Print heading for the Exception Report  }
    writeln (lst, 'EXCEPTION REPORT':35);
    writeln (lst, 'ID NUMBER':20, 'GRADE':12, 'HOURS':10);
    writeln (lst, Skip:10, '-------------------------------');
    writeln (lst);

  {  Now read the transaction file  }
    WHILE NOT eof(TransactionFile) DO
      BEGIN
        read (TransactionFile, IDNumber);
        readln (TransactionFile, Grade, CourseHours);
        Index := SeqSearch(Student, IDNumber, NumberOfRecords);
        MatchFound := Index <> 0;
        IF MatchFound THEN                  {  Update student record  }
          WITH Student[Index] DO
            CASE Grade OF
              'A' : BEGIN
                      GPA := NewGPA(Hours, CourseHours, GPA, 4.0);
                      Hours := Hours + CourseHours
                    END;
              'B' : BEGIN
                      GPA := NewGPA(Hours, CourseHours, GPA, 3.0);
                      Hours := Hours + CourseHours
                    END;
              'C' : BEGIN
                      GPA := NewGPA(Hours, CourseHours, GPA, 2.0);
                      Hours := Hours + CourseHours
                    END;
```

```
              'D' : BEGIN
                      GPA := NewGPA(Hours, CourseHours, GPA, 1.0);
                      Hours := Hours + CourseHours
                    END;
              'E' : BEGIN
                      GPA := NewGPA(Hours, CourseHours, GPA, 0.0);
                      Hours := Hours + CourseHours
                    END;
              'W', 'I' : {  do nothing  }
            END  {  of CASE Grade  }
        ELSE
          writeln (lst, IDNumber:20, Grade:10, CourseHours:10)
      END;  {  of WHILE NOT eof  }
    close (TransactionFile)
  END;  {  of PROCEDURE TransactionFile  }

{***************************************************************}

PROCEDURE PrintList (VAR Student : StudentList;
                     NumberOfRecords : integer);

  {  Given:   An array of student records and number of records     }
  {  Task:    Print a list of records with appropriate heading      }
  {  Return:  Nothing                                               }

  VAR
    J : integer;
  BEGIN

    {  Print a heading for the revised list  }
    writeln (lst);
    writeln (lst, 'UPDATED REPORT':30);                                  4
    writeln (lst, 'STUDENT FILE LISTING':34);
    writeln (lst);
    writeln (lst, 'NAME':10, 'ID NUMBER':25, 'GPA':8, 'CREDITS':10);
    write (lst, '----------------------------');
    writeln (lst, '-----------------------');
    writeln (lst);

    {  Now print the list  }
    FOR J := 1 TO NumberOfRecords DO
      WITH Student[J] DO
        writeln (lst, Name:20, IDNumber:15, GPA:8:2, Hours:8)
  END;  {  of PROCEDURE PrintList  }

{***************************************************************}

PROCEDURE UpdateMasterFile (VAR MasterFile : RecordsFile;
                            VAR Student : StudentList;
                            NumberOfRecords : integer);

  {  Given:   An array of student records and the array length      }
  {  Task:    Copy the records into MasterFile for storage          }
  {  Return:  A file of student records                             }  5

  VAR
    J : integer;
  BEGIN
    rewrite (MasterFile);
    FOR J := 1 TO NumberOfRecords DO
      write (MasterFile, Student[J])
  END;  {  of PROCEDURE UpdateMasterFile  }
```

```
{*******************************************************************}

BEGIN  {  Main program  }
  ClrScr;
  PrepareFiles (MasterFile, TransactionFile);
  LoadArray (MasterFile, Student, NumberOfRecords);
  UpdateRecords (TransactionFile, Student, NumberOfRecords);
  PrintList (Student, NumberOfRecords);
  UpdateMasterFile (MasterFile, Student, NumberOfRecords);
  readln
END.  {  of main program  }
```

If you use data in MasterFile as

```
Barrett Roda         345678901 3.67 23
Borgnine Ernist      369325263 3.12 14
Cadabra Abra         123450987 3.33 23
Djikstra Edgar       345998765 3.90 33
Garzeloni Randy      444226666 2.20 18
Glutz Agatha         320678230 3.00 22
Holbruck.Hall        321908765 3.50 29
Hunter Michael       234098112 2.50 22
Johnson Rosalyn      345123690 3.25 20
Locklear Heather     369426163 4.00 30
McMann Abagail       333112040 3.97 41
Mildew Morris        234812057 3.67 34
Morse Samuel         334558778 3.00 28
Novak James          348524598 1.50 13
Oherlahe Terry       333662222 2.75 21
Rackham Horace       345878643 4.00 30
Snyder Judith        356913580 2.75 24
Vandersys Ralph      367120987 3.23 22
Vaughn Sarah         238498765 3.00 24
Widget Wendell       444113333 1.25 10
Wilson Phillip       345719642 3.00 25
Witwerth January     367138302 2.10 20
Worden Jack          359241234 3.33 25
Wourthy Constance    342092834 3.50 32
```

and data in TransactionFile as

```
333112040A 3
333112040A 4
333112040A 4
444113333A 3
444113333A 4
444113333A 3
444113333A 2
238498765A 3
238498765A 3
238498766A 4
238498765A 4
369325263A 3
369325263A 3
369325263A 4
369325263C 4
320678230A 5
320678230A 3
320678230A 3
320678230A 4
444226666A 3
444226666A 4
444226666A 3
```

```
444226667A 4
367138302A 3
367138302A 3
367138302A 3
367138302B 3
367120987A 4
367120987A 4
367120987A 3
367120987I 3
367120987A 3
369426163A 4
369426163A 3
345678901A 3
345678901A 4
345678901A 3
345678900A 4
123450987A 3
123450987A 3
123450987A 4
123450987E 3
234098112A 3
234098112A 3
444226666D 3
367138302D 3
123450987C 4
123450987D 3
123450987A 2
333112040D 4
333112040A 3
444113333D 4
444113333A 3
369235263D 4
369235263A 3
320678230D 3
320678230D 4
320678230W 3
334229023D 4
```

output for this program is

```
                   EXCEPTION REPORT
           ID NUMBER        GRADE     HOURS
          --------------------------------

           238498766          A         4
           444226667          A         4
           345678900          A         4
           369235263          D         4
           369235263          A         3
           334229023          D         4

                      UPDATED REPORT
                   STUDENT FILE LISTING

      NAME                  ID NUMBER     GPA   CREDITS
-----------------------------------------------------

BARRETT RODA                345678901    3.77       33
BORGNINE ERNIST             369325263    3.27       28
CADABRA ABRA                123450987    3.01       45
DJIKSTRA EDGAR              345998765    3.90       33
GARZELONI RANDY             444226666    2.66       31
GLUTZ AGATHA                320678230    3.02       44
HOLBRUCK HALL               321908765    3.50       29
```

```
HUNTER MICHAEL           234098112   2.82   28
JOHNSON ROSALYN          345123690   3.25   20
LOCKLEAR HEATHER         369426163   4.00   37
MCMANN ABAGAIL           333112040   3.78   59
MILDEW MORRIS            234812057   3.67   34
MORSE SAMUEL             334558778   3.00   28
NOVAK JAMES              348524598   1.50   13
OHERLAHE TERRY           333662222   2.75   21
RACKHAM HORACE           345878643   4.00   30
SNYDER JUDITH            356913580   2.75   24
VANDERSYS RALPH          367120987   3.53   36
VAUGHN SARAH             238498765   3.29   34
WIDGET WENDELL           444113333   2.64   29
WILSON PHILLIP           345719642   3.00   25
WITWERTH JANUARY         367138302   2.57   35
WORDEN JACK              359241234   3.33   25
WOURTHY CONSTANCE        342092834   3.50   32
```

RUNNING AND DEBUGGING HINTS

1. Be sure all files are properly opened for reading and writing. Remember, you must **reset** before reading from a file and **rewrite** before writing to a file.
2. Don't try to read past the end-of-file marker. This is a common error that occurs when trying to **read** without a sufficient check for **eof.**
3. Be careful to use file names correctly in **read, readln, write, writeln,** and **eof** statement.
4. Use the **assign** procedure to associate internal files with external files.
5. Be sure all files listed in a procedure heading are variable parameters.
6. Protect against working with empty files or empty lines of a text file.
7. Create "empty" files for direct access processing.

Summary

Key Terms

binary file
closing a file
component of a file
direct (random) access file
hashing
master file
opening a file
reading from a file
sequential access file
transaction file
writing to a file

Keywords

FILE **FileSize** **FilePos** **seek**

Key Concepts

- A file is a sequence of components that are all of the same data type; a typical declaration is

```
TYPE
  RealFile = FILE OF real;
VAR
  FileA : RealFile;
```

- In standard implementations of Pascal, files must be accessed sequentially.
- Turbo Pascal provides for direct access of file components by

```
seek (<file variable>), <position - 1>)
```

- It is possible to **read** components from and **write** components to a binary file.
- Binary files must be created through a program.
- Before transferring values to a file (writing to a file), the file must be opened for writing by **rewrite** (<file name>). Values can then be transferred to the file using **write** (<file name>, <value>); for example

```
rewrite (NewFile);
write (NewFile, Num);
```

- Before transferring values from a file (reading from a file), the file must be opened for reading by **reset** (<file name>). Values can then be transferred from the file by using **read** (<file name>, <variable name>); for example

```
reset (NewFile);
read (NewFile, Num);
```

- An end-of-file marker is automatically placed at the end of the file as **eof** (<file name>) when a file is created.
- When a file is declared as a parameter in a procedure heading, it must be listed as a variable parameter; for example

```
PROCEDURE Update (VAR OldFile, NewFile : <file type>);
```

- Components of a file can be arrays; the declaration

```
VAR
  F : FILE OF ARRAY [1..10] OF real;
```

can be depicted as shown in Figure 10.5, where each component is an array.

FIGURE 10.5
File of arrays

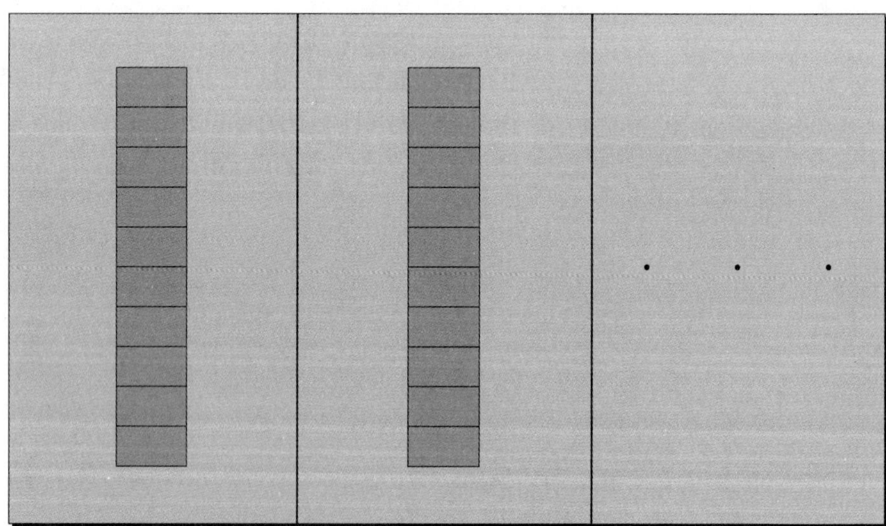

- File components can also be records and can be declared by

```
TYPE
  RecType = RECORD
              Name : string [20];
              Age : 0..120;
              Gender : char
            END;  { of RECORD RecType }
VAR
  F : FILE OF RecType;
```

and depicted as shown in Figure 10.6. In this case, each component is a record.

FIGURE 10.6
File of records

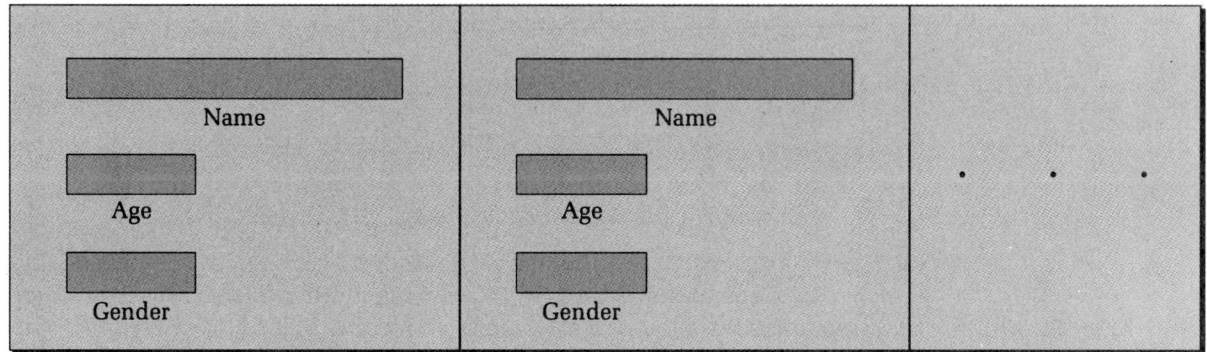

- Files with structured components frequently have to be processed and/or updated; for a file of records, you might insert or delete a record, sort the file by a field, merge two files, update each record, or produce a printed list according to some field.
- When updating or otherwise processing a file, changes are normally made in a transaction (temporary) file and then copied back into the master (permanent) file.
- Since input data are generally in a text file, you need to create a file of structured components from the text file; you can then use **read** and **write** to transfer entire structures at one time.

Programming Problems and Projects

1. *The Pentagon* is a mathematics magazine published by Kappa Mu Epsilon, a mathematics honorary society. Write a program to be used by the business manager for the purpose of generating mailing labels. The subscribers' information should be read into a file of records. Each record should contain one subscriber's name; address, including street and street number, apartment number (if any), city, two-letter abbreviation for the state, and zip code; and expiration information, including month and year.

   Your program should create an alphabetically sorted master file, print an alphabetical list for the office, print a mailing list sorted by zip code for bulk mailing, and denote all last issues by a special symbol.
2. The relentless Dr. Lae Z. Programmer (Problems 5, 22, and 23, Chapter 4; Problem 13, Chapter 5; Problem 5, Chapter 6; Problem 3, Chapter 8; Problem 3, Chapter 9) now wants you to create a file of records for students in his computer science course. You should provide fields for the student's name, 10 quiz scores, six program scores, and three examination scores. Your program should do the following.
   a. Read in the names from a text file.
   b. Include procedures for updating quiz, program, and examination scores.
   c. Be able to update the file by adding or deleting a record.
   d. Print an alphabetized list of the data base at any given time.
3. Write a program to do part of the work of a word processor. Your program should read a text file and print it in paragraph form. The left margin should be in column 10; the right margin, in column 72. In the input file, periods will designate the end of sentences and the symbol (*) will denote a new paragraph. No word should be split between lines. Your program should save the edited file in a file of type **text.**

4. Slow-pitch softball is rapidly becoming a popular summer pastime. Assume your local community is to have a new women's league this year consisting of eight teams, with 15 players on each team. This league gets the field one night per week for four games. They will play a double round-robin, so each team will play every other team twice, resulting in 14 games. Write a program to do the following.
   a. Create a file of records (one record for each team) in which the team name is included.
   b. Print a schedule.
   c. List the teams alphabetically by team name.
   d. Print a list of players for each team.

5. The registrar at State University (Problem 15, Chapter 4; Problem 3, Chapter 6) wants you to write an interactive program to assist with record keeping. Your program should create a file of records. The record for each student should contain the student's name, identification number, credit hours completed, number of credit hours in which currently enrolled, and grade point average. Your program should also contain a procedure for each of the following updates.
   a. List semester-end data of hours completed and grade point average for the semester.
   b. Insert a record.
   c. Delete a record.
   d. Print a list sorted alphabetically.
   e. Print a list sorted by grade point average.

6. The local high school sports boosters (Problems 1 and 2, Chapter 8) need more help. They want you to write a program to create a file of records in which each record contains the parents' names, the children's first names (at most 10 children), and the names of the sports in which the children have participated.

   A typical record is shown in Figure 10.7. Your program should create a file from a text file and save it for later use, print an alphabetical list of parents' names, and print a list of the names of parents of football players.

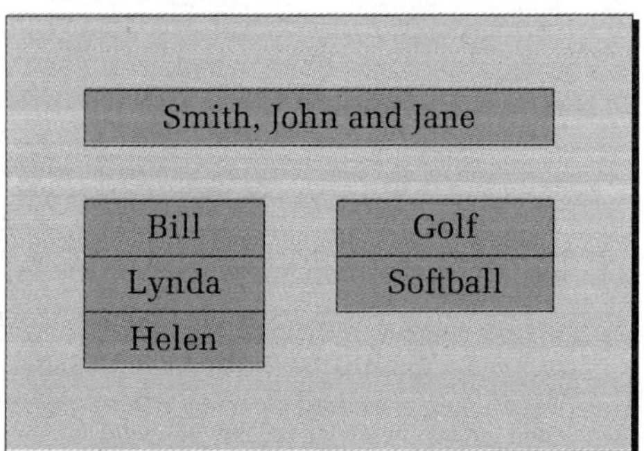

FIGURE 10.7
Typical values for fields in a record

7. A popular use of text files is to help teachers create a bank of test items from which to generate quizzes using some form of random selection. Write a program to allow you to create files of type **text** that contain questions for each of three chapters. Then, generate two quizzes of three questions for each of the three chapters.

8. Public service departments must always be on the lookout for people who try to abuse the system by accepting assistance from similar agencies in different geographic areas. Write a program that compares names from one county with those from another county and prints all of the names on both lists.
9. Write a program to be used by flight agents at an airport (see Exercise 1a, Section 10.3). Your program should use a file of records; the record for each flight should contain flight number, airline, arrival time, origin, departure time, and destination. Your program should list incoming flights sorted by time, list departing flights sorted by time, add flights, and delete flights.
10. Congratulations! You have just been asked to write a program that will assign dates for the Valentine's Day dance. Each student record should contain the student's name, age, gender (M or F), and the names of three date preferences (ranked). Your program should do the following.
    a. Create a master file from the input file.
    b. Create and save alphabetically sorted files of males and females.
    c. Print a list of couples for the dance. The genders must be opposite, and the age difference may be no more than three years. Dating preferences should be in the following form.

	CAN'T MISS!	
First request	Matches	First request
	GOOD BET!	
First request	Matches	Second request
Second request	Matches	First request
	GOOD LUCK!	
	Any other matches	
	OUT OF LUCK!	
	You are not on any list	

It's obvious (isn't it?) that a person can have at most one date for the dance.

11. A data file consists of an unknown number of real numbers. Write a program to read the file and print the highest value, lowest value, and average of the numbers in the file.
12. ■ The Falcon Manufacturing Company (Problem 22, Chapter 8; Problem 17, Chapter 9) wants you to write an inventory file program. The file should contain a 30-character part name, an integer part number, the quantity on hand, and the price of an item. The program should permit the entry of new items into and the deletion of existing items from the file. The items to be changed will be entered from the keyboard.
13. ■ Write a program for the Falcon Manufacturing Company (Problem 12) to allow a secretary to enter an item number, a quantity, and whether an item is to be added to or deleted from the stock. The program should prepare a new data file with the updated information. If the user requests to remove more items than are on hand, an appropriate warning message should be issued.
14. ■ Write a program to read the inventory file of the Falcon Manufacturing Company (Problems 12 and 13) and then print a listing of the inventory. The program should print an asterisk (*) next to any quantity that is < 50.
15. ■ Revise the program that you wrote in answer to Problem 22 in Chapter 8 to permit the sales figures of the Falcon Manufacturing Company to be read from a file. Also revise the program so the information on the total dollar amount of sales for each product by each salesperson is written to a file for later use.

■ 16. Write a program to read the total dollar sales file from Problem 15 for last month and the corresponding file for this month and print out a table showing the total sales by each salesperson for each product during the two-month period.

17. A data file contains an alphabetized list of the secondary students in your former high school; another data file contains an alphabetized list of the elementary students. Write a program to merge these two files and print an alphabetized list of all students in your former school.

18. The Andover Telephone Company (its motto is, "We send your messages of Andover") wants you to develop a computerized directory information system. The data file should contain the customer names and telephone numbers. Your program should permit the following.
    a. The entry of new customers' names and telephone numbers
    b. The deletion of existing customers' names and telephone numbers
    c. The printing of all customers' names and telephone numbers
    d. The entry from the keyboard of a customer's name with the program printing the telephone number (if found)

    Whenever customers' names and numbers are to be added or deleted, the file should be updated accordingly. You may assume there are no more than 50 customers.

19. Revise the program written to keep the grades of Mr. Laven's students (Problem 19, Chapter 8) to read the grades entered previously from a file and, when the program is complete, print the updated list of grades.

20. Recognizing your talents as a programmer, the principal of the local high school wants you to write a program to work with a data file containing the names of the students who are absent at the start of the school day. These names are kept as strings. The program should permit the principal to enter the name of a student later in the day to check to see if the student was absent at the start of the day.

21. Revise Problem 13 from Chapter 9 to permit Mrs. Crown's computer maintenance records to be kept in a file. Your program should allow the data on a machine to be changed and new machines to be added.

■ Communication in Practice

1. Select a program from the Programming and Problem Solving section of this chapter that you have not yet worked. Construct a structure chart and write all documentary information for this program. Include variable definitions, subprogram definitions, required input, and required output. When you are finished, have a classmate read your documentation to see if precisely what is to be done is clear.
2. Remove all documentation from a program you have written for this chapter. Exchange this modified version with another student who has done the same thing. Write documentation for the exchanged program. Compare your documentation with that originally written for the program. Discuss the differences and similarities with the other students in the class.
3. Contact a programmer at your university or some company or corporation to discuss data structures. Find out how much (if any) he or she uses arrays, records, and files. If the programmer does use arrays, records, or files, what kinds of programming problems require their use? Find out what kinds of operations are used with these data structures. What limitations do these structures exhibit when applied to the problems that need to be solved? Write a complete report summarizing your discussion.

4. Problems involving data management are routinely addressed in nonprogramming courses taught in schools of business. These courses may be taught in departments such as Management Information Systems (MIS) or Business Information Systems (BIS). Contact an instructor of such a course, and discuss the issue of using data structures to manage information. How are data structures presented to the classes? What are some typical real-world problems?

   Give an oral report of your discussion to your class. Compare and contrast the instructor's presentations with those provided in your own class. Use charts with transparencies as part of your presentation.
5. Select an unworked problem from the programming problems for this chapter. Construct a structure chart and write all documentary information necessary for this problem. Do not write code. When finished, have a classmate read your documentation to see if precisely what is to be done is clear.

Recursion and Sorting

CHAPTER OUTLINE

The previous chapters have presented techniques for working with structured variables. In particular, we have seen how to sort lists in either ascending or descending order, search lists for some specific value, and merge lists that may or may not be sorted. In this chapter, we will examine additional techniques for working with structured variables. First, however, we will look at recursion—a powerful process available in Turbo Pascal. In subsequent chapters, we will use recursion to implement more sophisticated algorithms. These algorithms should make you aware of the problems associated with recursion and sorting.

Unfortunately, this chapter cannot answer all of the questions associated with recursion and sorting. This text and most beginning courses defer more extensive treatment and examination of other methods and their relative efficiency to later programming courses. A list of suggestions for further reading is included at the end of this chapter.

11.1 Recursion

In our previous work with subprograms, we have seen instances in which one subprogram calls another. In Chapter 5 on repetition, we saw how to use the **FOR**, **WHILE**, and **REPEAT** statements in Turbo Pascal to control iterative processes. Now let's consider how we can use a subprogram that calls itself to control an iterative process.

Recursive Processes

Many problems can be solved by having a subtask call itself as part of the solution. This process is called *recursion;* subprograms that call themselves are *recursive subprograms.* Recursion is frequently used in mathematics. Consider, for example, the definition of $n!$ (n factorial) for a nonnegative integer n, which is defined by

$0! = 1$
$1! = 1$
for $n > 1$, $n! = n * (n - 1)!$

Thus,

$$
\begin{aligned}
6! &= 6 * 5! \\
&= 6 * 5 * 4! \\
&= 6 * 5 * 4 * 3! \\
&= 6 * 5 * 4 * 3 * 2! \\
&= 6 * 5 * 4 * 3 * 2 * 1
\end{aligned}
$$

Another well-known mathematical example is the Fibonacci sequence, in which the first term is 1, the second term is 1, and each successive term is defined to be the sum of the previous two terms. More precisely, the Fibonacci sequence

$a_1, a_2, a_3, \ldots, a_n$

is defined by

$a_1 = 1$
$a_2 = 1$
$a_n = a_{n-1} + a_{n-2}, \quad \text{for } n > 2$

This generates the sequence

1, 1, 2, 3, 5, 8, 13, 21, . . .

In both examples, note that the general term is defined by using the previous term or terms.

What applications does recursion have for computing? In many instances, a procedure or function can be written to accomplish a recursive task. If the language allows a subprogram to call itself (Turbo Pascal does; FORTRAN does not), it is sometimes easier to solve a problem by applying this process.

■ EXAMPLE 11.1

As an example of a recursive function, consider the sigma function, denoted by $\sum_{i=1}^{n} i$, which is used to compute the sum of integers from 1 to n:

```
FUNCTION Sigma (N : integer) : integer:
  BEGIN
    IF N <= 1 THEN
      Sigma := N
    ELSE
      Sigma := N + Sigma(N - 1)
  END;  { of FUNCTION Sigma}
```

To illustrate how this recursive function works, suppose it is called from the main program by a statement such as

```
Sum := Sigma(5);
```

In the **ELSE** portion of the function, we first have

```
Sigma := 5 + Sigma(4)
```

At this stage, note that Sigma(4) must be computed. This call produces

```
Sigma := 4 + Sigma(3)
```

If we envision these recursive calls as occurring on levels, we have

```
1. Sigma := 5 + Sigma(4)
   2. Sigma := 4 + Sigma(3)
      3. Sigma := 3 + Sigma(2)
         4. Sigma := 2 + Sigma(1)
            5. Sigma := 1
```

The end of the recursion has been reached. Now the steps are reversed for assigning values. Thus, we have

```
            5. Sigma := 1
         4. Sigma := 2 + 1  (= 3)
      3. Sigma := 3 + 3  (= 6)
   2. Sigma := 4 + 6  (= 10)
1. Sigma := 5 + 10  (= 15)
```

Thus, Sigma is assigned the value 15.

Before we analyze what happens in memory when recursive subprograms are used, two comments about recursion are in order.

1. The recursive process must have a well-defined termination. This termination is referred to as a *stopping state.* In Example 11.1, the stopping state is

```
IF N <= 1 THEN
  Sigma := N
```

2. The recursive process must have well-defined steps that lead to the stopping state. These steps are usually called *recursive steps.* In Example 11.1, these steps are

```
Sigma := N + Sigma(N - 1)
```

Note that in the recursive call, the parameter is simplified toward the stopping state.

FIGURE 11.1
Stack for **FUNCTION** Sigma

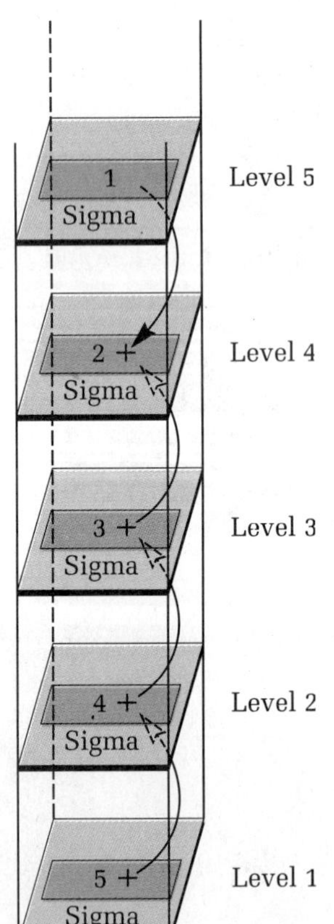

What Really Happens?

What really happens when a subprogram calls itself? First, we need to examine the idea of a *stack.* Imagine a stack as a pile of cafeteria trays: the last one put on the stack is the first one taken off the stack. This is what occurs in memory when a recursive subprogram is used. Each call to the subprogram can be thought of as adding a tray to the stack. In the previous function, the first call creates a level of recursion that contains the partially complete assignment statement

```
Sigma := 5 + Sigma(4)
```

This corresponds to the first tray in the stack. In reality, this is an area in memory waiting to receive a value for 5 + Sigma(4). At this level, operation is temporarily suspended until a value is returned for Sigma(4). However, the call Sigma(4) produces

```
Sigma := 4 + Sigma(3)
```

This corresponds to the second tray on the stack. As before, operation is temporarily suspended until Sigma(3) is computed. This process is repeated until finally the last call, Sigma(1), returns a value.

At this stage, the stack may be envisioned as illustrated in Figure 11.1. Since different areas of memory are used for each successive call to Sigma, each variable Sigma represents a different memory location.

The levels of recursion that have been temporarily suspended can now be completed in reverse order. Thus, since the assignment

```
Sigma(1) := 1
```

has been made

```
Sigma(2) := 2 + Sigma(1)
```

becomes

```
Sigma(2) := 2 + 1
```

This then permits

```
Sigma(3) := 3 + Sigma(2)
```

to become

```
Sigma(3) := 3 + 3
```

Continuing until the first level of recursion has been reached, we obtain

```
Sigma := 5 + 10
```

This "unstacking" is illustrated in Figure 11.2.

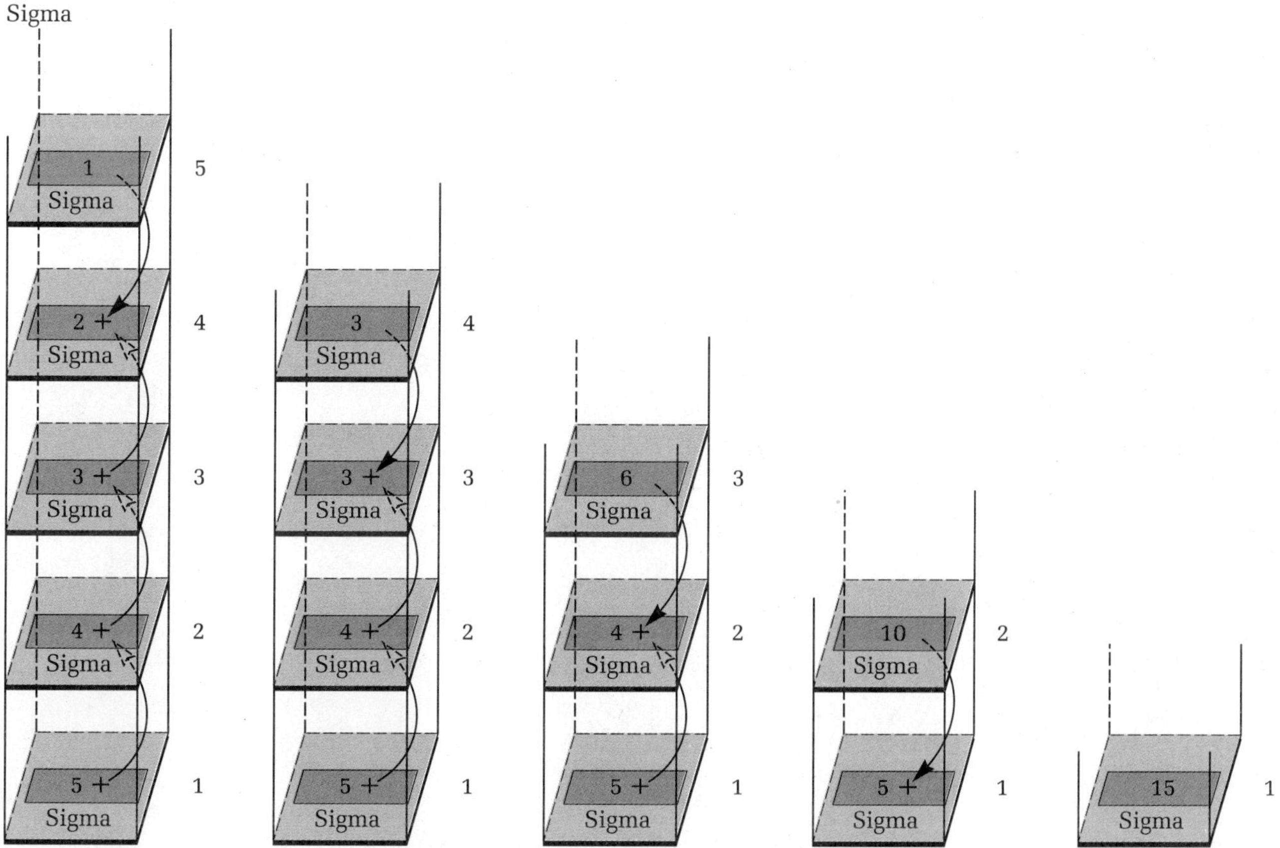

FIGURE 11.2
"Unstacking" **FUNCTION** Sigma

Note that the recursive function illustrated in Example 11.1 uses a value parameter. In general, any formal parameter that relates to the size of the problem must be a value parameter. If the formal parameter (N, for example) were variable, it would not be possible to use the expression N – 1 as an actual parameter in a recursive call.

■ EXAMPLE 11.2

Now let's consider a second example of recursion in which a procedure is used recursively to print a line of text in reverse order. Assume the line of text has only one period and it is at the end of the line. The stopping state occurs when the character read is a period. Using the data line

This is a short sentence. ■

a complete program follows.

```
PROGRAM LineInReverse;

{  This program uses a procedure recursively to print a     }
{  line of text in reverse.                                 }

USES
  Crt;

VAR
  Data : text;

{*********************************************************}

PROCEDURE StackItUp;

  {  Given:   Nothing                                       }
  {  Task:    Read one character;  print if a period;       }
  {                if not, call this same procedure         }
  {  Return:  Nothing                                       }

  VAR
    OneChar : char;
  BEGIN
    read (Data, OneChar);
    IF OneChar <> '.' THEN
      StackItUp;
    write (OneChar)
  END;  {  of PROCEDURE StackItUp  }

{*********************************************************}

BEGIN  {  Main program  }
  ClrScr;
  assign (Data, 'RecurDat.DAT');
  reset (Data);
  StackItUp;
  writeln;
  readln;
  close (Data)
END.  {  of main program  }
```

Output from this program is

```
.ecnetnes trohs a si sihT
```

In this program, as each character is read, it is placed on a stack until the period is encountered. At that time, the period is printed. Then, as each level in the stack is passed through in reverse order, the character on that level is printed. The stack created while this program is running is illustrated in Figure 11.3.

FIGURE 11.3
Stack created by **PROCEDURE** StackItUp

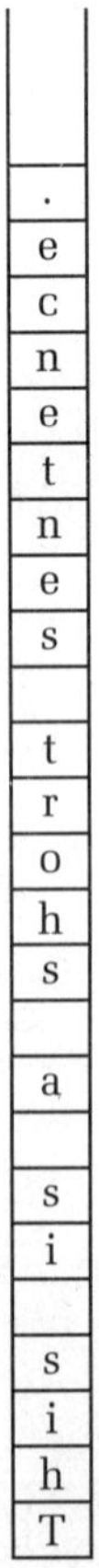

.
e
c
n
e
t
n
e
s
t
r
o
h
s
a
s
i
s
i
h
T

EXAMPLE 11.3

Now let's consider another example of a recursive function. Recall the factorial of a nonnegative integer n is defined to be

$$1 * 2 * 3 * \cdots * (n-1) * n$$

and is denoted by $n!$. Thus

$$4! = 1 * 2 * 3 * 4$$

For the sake of completing this definition, $1! = 1$ and $0! = 1$. A recursive function to compute $n!$ is

```
FUNCTION Factorial (N : integer) : integer;
  BEGIN
    IF N = 0 THEN
      Factorial := 1
    ELSE
      Factorial := N * Factorial(N - 1)
  END;  {  of FUNCTION Factorial  }
```

If this function is called from the main program by a statement such as

```
Product := Factorial(4);
```

we envision the levels of recursion as

```
1.   Factorial := 4 * Factorial(3)
  2.   Factorial := 3 * Factorial(2)
    3.   Factorial := 2 * Factorial(1)
      4.   Factorial := 1 * Factorial(0)
        5.   Factorial(0) := 1
```

Successive values would then be assigned in reverse order to produce

```
        5.   Factorial(0) := 1
      4.   Factorial := 1 * 1
    3.   Factorial := 2 * 1
  2.   Factorial := 3 * 2
1.   Factorial := 4 * 6
```

Why Use Recursion?

You may have noticed that the previous recursive functions Sigma and Factorial could have been written using other iterative control structures. For example, we could write

```
FUNCTION NonRecursiveSigma (N : integer) : integer;
  VAR
    J, Sum : integer;
  BEGIN
    Sum := 0;
    For J := 1 TO N DO
      Sum := Sum + J;
    NonRecursiveSigma := Sum
  END;  {  of FUNCTION NonRecursiveSigma  }
```

It is not coincidental that the recursive function Sigma can be rewritten using the function NonRecursiveSigma. In principle, any recursive subprogram can be rewritten in a nonrecursive manner. Furthermore, recursion generally requires more memory than equivalent nonrecursive iteration and is usually difficult for beginning programmers to comprehend. Why then do we use recursion? There are several reasons. First, a recursive thought process may be the best way to think about solving the problem. If so, it naturally leads to using recursion in a program. A classical example of this is the Towers of Hanoi problem, which involves a sequence of moving disks on pegs. This problem is fully developed as our next example.

Second, some recursive solutions can be very short compared to other iterative solutions. Some nonrecursive solutions may require an explicit stack and unusual coding. In some instances, use of a recursive algorithm can be very simple, and some programmers consider recursive solutions elegant because of this simplicity. The Towers of Hanoi problem in Example 11.4 provides an example of such elegance.

Third and finally, subsequent work in Turbo Pascal can be aided by recursion. For example, one of the fastest sorting algorithms available, the quick sort, uses recursion (see Section 11.2). Also, recursion is a valuable tool when working with dynamic data structures (Chapter 15).

Having now seen several reasons why recursion should be used, let's consider when recursion should not be used. If a solution to a problem is easier to obtain by using nonrecursive methods, it is usually preferable to use them. A nonrecursive solution may require less execution time and use memory more efficiently. Referring to the previous examples, the recursive function Factorial should probably be written by using iteration, but reversing a line of text would typically be done by using recursion because a nonrecursive solution is difficult to write.

In summary, recursion is a powerful and necessary programming technique. You should become familiar with using recursive subprograms, learn to recognize when a recursive algorithm is appropriate, and be able to implement a recursive subprogram.

EXAMPLE 11.4

A classic problem called the Towers of Hanoi problem involves three pegs and disks, as depicted in Figure 11.4. The object is to move the disks from peg A to peg C. The rules are that only one disk may be moved at a time and a larger disk can never be placed on a smaller disk. (Legend has it that this problem—but with 64 disks—was given to monks in an ancient monastery. The world was to come to an end when all 64 disks were in order on peg C.)

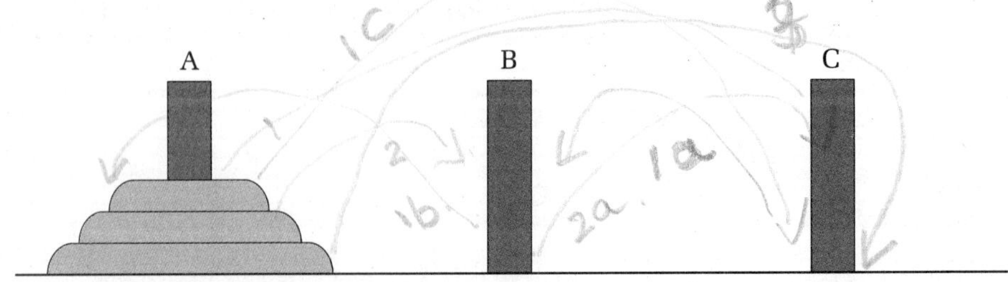

FIGURE 11.4
Towers of Hanoi problem

To see how this problem can be solved, let's start with a one-disk problem. In this case, merely move the disk from peg A to peg C. The two-disk problem is almost as easy. Move disk 1 to peg B, then move disk 2 to peg C, and use the solution to the one-disk problem to move disk 1 to peg C. (Note the reference to the previous solution.)

Things get a little more interesting with a three-disk problem. First, use the two-disk solution to get the top two disks in order on peg B. Then move disk 3 to peg C. Finally, use the two-disk solution to move the two disks from peg B to peg C. Again, note the reference to the previous solution. By now you should begin to see the pattern for solving the problem. However, before generalizing, let's look at the four-disk problem. As expected, the solution is to:

1. Use the three-disk solution to move disks 1, 2, and 3 to peg B.
2. Move disk 4 to peg C.
3. Use the three-disk solution to move the three disks from peg B to peg C.

This process can be generalized as a solution to the problem for n disks:

1. Use the $(n - 1)$ disk solution to move $(n - 1)$ disks to peg B.
2. Move disk n to peg C.
3. Use the $(n - 1)$ disk solution to move $(n - 1)$ disks from peg B to peg C.

This general solution is recursive in nature because each particular solution depends upon a solution for the previous number of disks. This process continues until there is only one disk to move. This corresponds to the stopping state when a recursive program is written to solve the problem. A complete interactive program that prints out each step in the solution to this problem follows.

```
PROGRAM TowersOfHanoi;

{  This program uses recursion to solve the classic Towers of   }
{  Hanoi problem.                                               }

USES
  Crt;

VAR
  NumDisks : integer;

{***********************************************************}

PROCEDURE ListTheMoves (NumDisks : integer;
                        StartPeg, LastPeg, SparePeg : char);

  {  Given:   The number of disks to move, the initial peg      }
  {               StartPeg, the working peg SparePeg, and the   }
  {               destination peg LastPeg                       }
  {  Task:    Move NumDisks from StartPeg to LastPeg using      }
  {               SparePeg (involves recursive calls)           }
  {  Return:  Nothing                                           }

  BEGIN
    IF NumDisks = 1 THEN
      writeln ('Move a disk from ', StartPeg, ' to ', LastPeg)
    ELSE
      BEGIN
        ListTheMoves (NumDisks - 1, StartPeg, SparePeg, LastPeg);
        writeln ('Move a disk from ', StartPeg, ' to ', LastPeg);
        ListTheMoves (NumDisks - 1, SparePeg, LastPeg, StartPeg)
      END  {  of ELSE option  }
  END;  {  of PROCEDURE ListTheMoves  }

{***********************************************************}
```

```
BEGIN  { Main program }
  ClrScr;
  write ('How many disks in this game?  ');
  readln (NumDisks);
  writeln;
  writeln ('Start with ', NumDisks, ' disks on Peg A');
  writeln;
  writeln ('Then proceed as follows:');
  writeln;
  ListTheMoves (NumDisks, 'A', 'C', 'B');
  readln
END.  { of main program }
```

Sample runs for three-disk and four-disk problems produce the following:

```
How many disks in this game?  3

Start with 3 disks on Peg A

Then proceed as follows:

Move a disk from A to C
Move a disk from A to B
Move a disk from C to B
Move a disk from A to C
Move a disk from B to A
Move a disk from B to C
Move a disk from A to C

How many disks in this game?  4

Start with 4 disks on Peg A

Then proceed as follows:

Move a disk from A to B
Move a disk from A to C
Move a disk from B to C
Move a disk from A to B
Move a disk from C to A
Move a disk from C to B
Move a disk from A to B
Move a disk from A to C
Move a disk from B to C
Move a disk from B to A
Move a disk from C to A
Move a disk from B to C
Move a disk from A to B
Move a disk from A to C
Move a disk from B to C
```

Exercises 11.1

1. Explain what is wrong with the following recursive function:

```
FUNCTION Recur (X : real) : real;
  BEGIN
    Recur := Recur(X / 2)
  END;
```

2. Write a recursive function that reverses the digits of a positive integer. If the integer used as input is 1234, output should be 4321.

3. Consider the following recursive function:

```
FUNCTION A (X : real;
            N : integer) : real;
  BEGIN
    IF N = 0 THEN
      A := 1.0
    ELSE
      A := X * A(X, N - 1)
  END;  { of FUNCTION A }
```

   a. What is the value of Y for each of the following?

      i. `Y := A(3.0, 2);`
      ii. `Y := A(2.0, 3);`
      iii. `Y := A(4.0, 4);`
      iv. `Y := A(1.0, 6);`

   b. Explain what standard computation is performed by **FUNCTION** A.
   c. Rewrite **FUNCTION** A by using iteration rather than recursion.

4. Recall the Fibonacci sequence

   1, 1, 2, 3, 5, 8, 13, 21, . . .

   where for $n > 2$, the nth term is the sum of the previous two terms. Write a recursive function to compute the nth term in the Fibonacci sequence.

5. Write a function that uses iteration to compute $n!$.

■ 11.2 Sorting Algorithms

Several algorithms can be used to sort elements in arrays and files. We have worked with the selection sort since Chapter 7, where we also discussed the bubble sort. Two other commonly used sorting methods are the insertion sort and the quick sort. All of these sorts work relatively well when sorting small lists of elements.

However, when large data bases need to be sorted, a direct application of an elementary sorting process usually requires a great deal of computer time. Thus, some other sorting method is needed—one that might involve using a different algorithm or dividing the lists into smaller parts, sorting these parts, and then merging the lists back together. In more advanced courses, you will examine the relative efficiency of sorts and methods for handling large data bases. For now, let's consider these two sorting methods.

Insertion Sort

The purpose of a sort is to produce an array of elements sorted in either ascending or descending order. These elements are normally read from an input file into an array. Now let's see how an insertion sort arranges numbers in ascending order in an unsorted array.

The main principles of an *insertion sort* are:

1. Put the first K elements of an array in order.
2. Move the K + 1 element into Temp.
3. Move the sorted elements (1 to K) down, one at a time, until the value in Temp can be placed in order in the previously sorted portion of the array.

To illustrate how this works, consider the array of integers

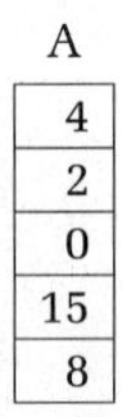

The first step is to put the value from A[2] into Temp by using

```
Temp := A[2];
```

This produces

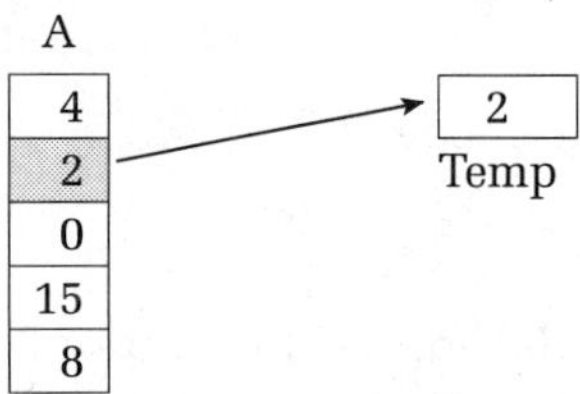

where the shaded cell can be thought of as waiting to receive a value. The value in Temp is then compared to values in the array before A[2]. Since A[1] > A[2], the value in A[1] is "moved down" to produce

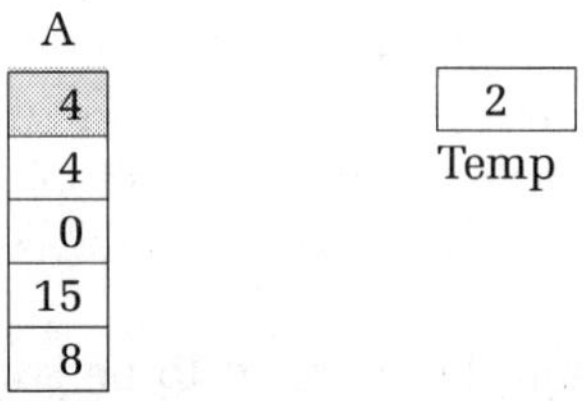

Since we are at the top of the array, the value in Temp is placed in A[1] to yield

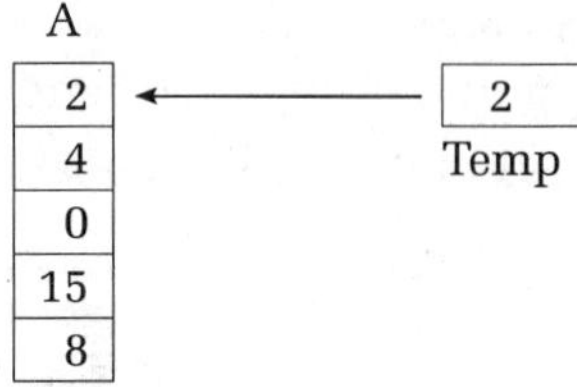

During the next pass, the value of A[3] is put into Temp and we have

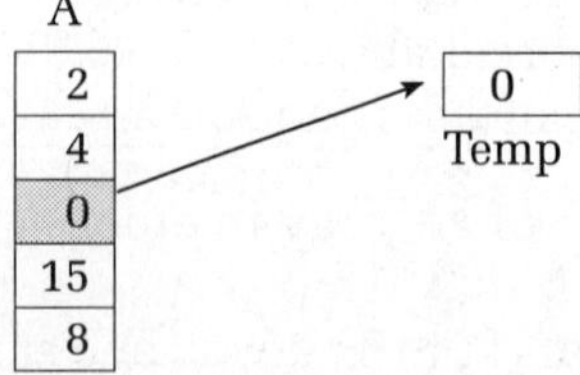

This value is compared to those above it. As long as Temp is less than an array element, the array element is shifted down. This process produces

A	
2	Temp: 0
2	
4	
15	
8	

At this stage, the value in Temp is inserted into the array to produce the partially sorted array

A
0
2
4
15
8

At the start of the next pass, Temp receives the value in A[4] to yield

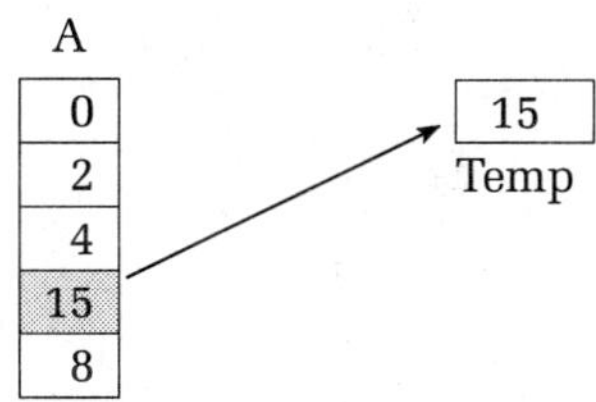

When the value in Temp is compared to A[3], the process terminates because Temp > A[3]. Thus, using the partially sorted array improves the efficiency of the sort. On the last pass, Temp receives the value from A[5] and we have

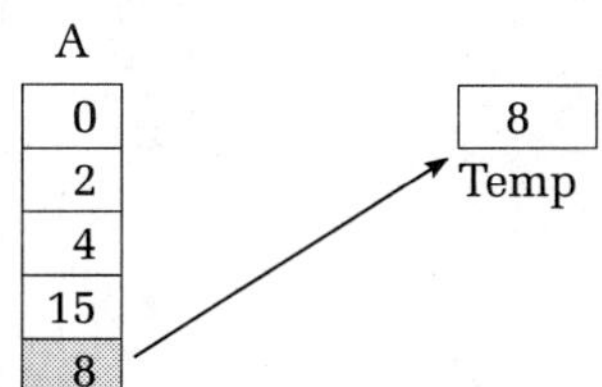

Since Temp < A[4], we next get

A	
0	Temp: 8
2	
4	
15	
15	

At this stage, Temp > A[3], so we insert the value of Temp into A[4] to produce the sorted array

A
0
2
4
8
15

In summary, the idea of an insertion sort is to do the following.

1. Remove an element from position (K + 1) in the array.
2. Slide the previously sorted elements down the array until a position is found for the new element.
3. Insert the element in its proper position.
4. Continue until the array is sorted.

A procedure for the insertion sort follows.

```
PROCEDURE InsertionSort (VAR List : SortArray;
                             ListLength : integer);

  {  Given:   An array List with entries in locations 1         }
  {               through ListLength                            }
  {  Task:    Apply insertion sort logic to List                }
  {  Return:  The array List with entries sorted in             }
  {               ascending order.                              }

  VAR
    Index, K : integer;
    Temp : ElementType;
    Done : boolean;
  BEGIN
    FOR Index := 2 TO ListLength DO
      BEGIN
        Temp := List[Index];
        K := Index;
        Done := false;
        WHILE (K >= 2) AND (NOT Done) DO
          IF Temp < List[K-1] THEN
            BEGIN                        {  Move elements down  }
              List[K] := List[K-1];
              K := K - 1
            END
          ELSE
            Done := true;         {  Found position for insertion  }
        List[K] := Temp                   {  Insert into array  }
      END  {  of FOR loop  }
  END;  {  of PROCEDURE InsertionSort  }
```

This procedure is called from the main program by

```
InsertionSort (UnsortedList, Length);
```

As expected, records can be sorted by examining some key field and then assigning the entire record accordingly. Thus, if an array type is

```
TYPE
  .
  .
  .
  StudentInfo = RECORD
                  Name : String20;
                  Score : integer
                END;
  List = ARRAY [1..ListLength] OF StudentInfo;
```

and the array is to be sorted according to student scores, the field comparison in **PROCEDURE** InsertionSort could be

```
IF Temp.Score < Student[K-1].Score
```

A NOTE OF INTEREST

Gene Mapping: Computer Scientists Examine Problems of Genome Project

Deciphering the human genome is much like trying to read the instructions on a computer disk filled with programs written in the zeros and ones of electronic code—without knowing the programming language.

That was the message from molecular biologists to computer scientists at a meeting sponsored by the National Research Council. The biologists hope to involve the computer scientists in the U.S. Human Genome Project, a 15-year, $3-billion effort to identify and locate the information contained in human chromosomes.

Computer scientists, with their experience in managing information and using arcane programming languages to store data and convey instructions, could be particularly valuable in helping to read and organize the three billion "letters" that make up the human genetic code, the biologists said.

"The entire program for making *me* is about 10 to the 10 bits" (about 10 trillion pieces of information), said Gerald J. Sussman, a professor of electrical engineering and computer science at the Massachusetts Institute of Technology. "It is no bigger than the U.S. Tax Code or the design documents for the U.S. space shuttle." Figuring out what that program is, he said, is a computer-science problem.

Biologists said they need computer scientists to

- Design easy-to-use data bases that can handle the millions of pieces of information that need to be correlated to fully understand genetics—and life.
- Design computer networks that will allow biologists to share information conveniently.
- Create procedures that will allow biologists to analyze information pulled from laboratory experiments.
- Write programs that will let biologists simulate the formation and development of proteins.

Quick Sort

One of the fastest sorting techniques available is the *quick sort.* It uses recursion and is based upon the idea of separating a list of numbers into two parts. One part contains numbers smaller than some number in the list; the other part contains numbers larger than the number. Thus, if an unsorted array originally contains

14	3	2	11	5	8	0	2	9	4	20
A[1]	A[2]				A[6]					A[11]

we select the element in the middle position, A[6], and then pivot on the value in A[6], which is 8 in our illustration. Our process then puts all values smaller than 8 on the left side and all values larger than 8 on the right side. This first subdividing produces

						Pivot ↓				
4	3	2	2	5	0	8	11	9	14	20
A[1]										A[11]

Now, each sublist is subdivided in the same manner until all sublists are in order. The array is then sorted. This is a recursive process.

Before writing a procedure for this sort, let's examine how it works. First, why do we choose the value in the middle position? Ideally, we would like to pivot on the median of the list. However, it is not efficient to find this value first, so we choose the value in the middle as a compromise. The index of this value is found by (First + Last) **DIV** 2, where First and Last are the indices of the initial and final array elements. We then identify a LeftArrow and a RightArrow on the far left and far right respectively. This can be envisioned as

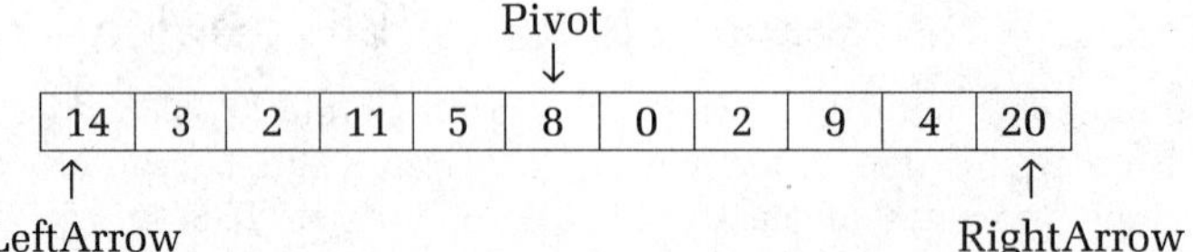

where LeftArrow and RightArrow represent the respective indices of the array components. Starting on the right, RightArrow is moved left until a value less than or equal to the pivot is encountered. Similarly, LeftArrow is moved right until a value greater than or equal to the pivot is encountered. This produces

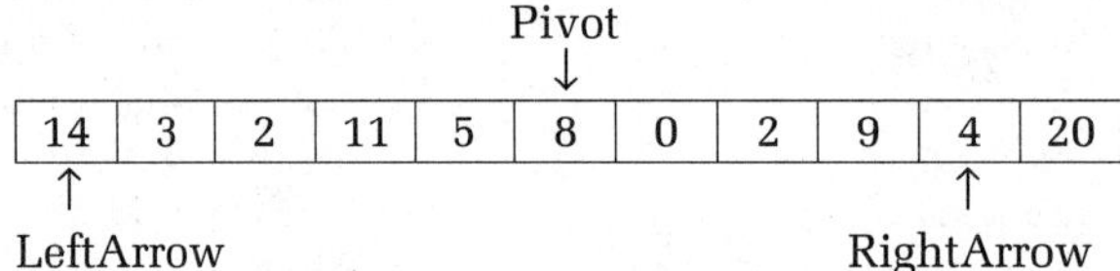

Since LeftArrow is already at a value greater than (or equal to) the pivot, it is not moved. The contents of the two array components are now switched to produce

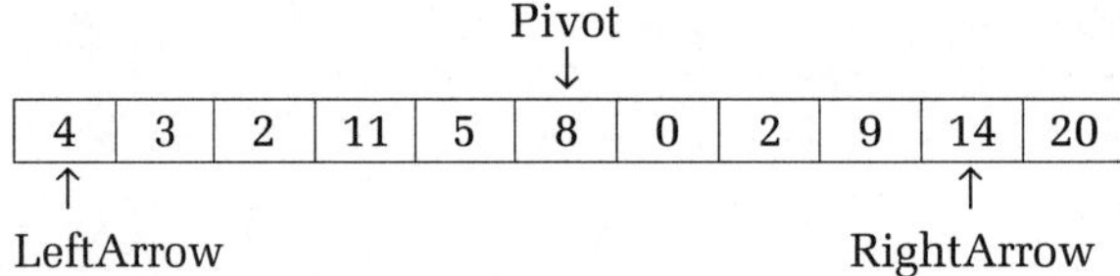

We continue by moving RightArrow left to produce

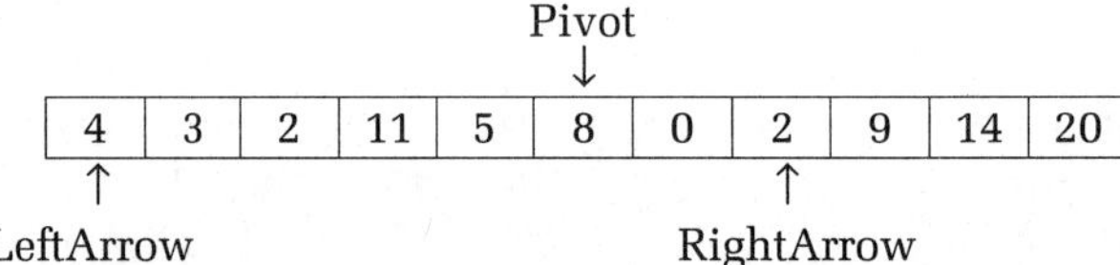

and by moving LeftArrow right to obtain

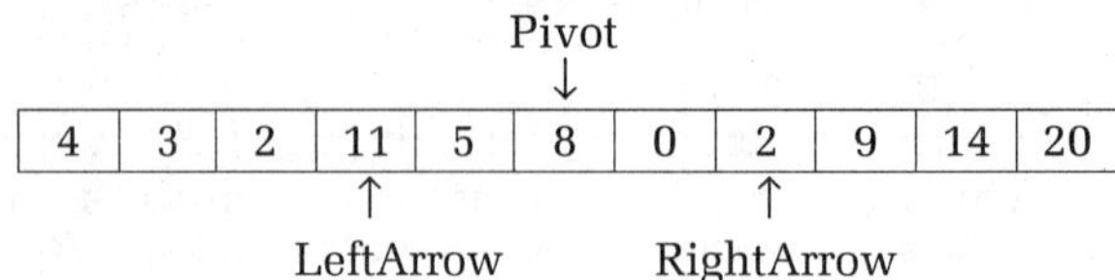

These values are exchanged to produce

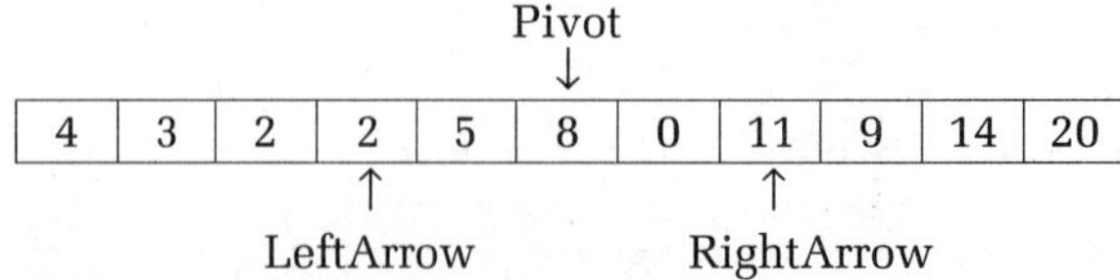

This process stops when LeftArrow > RightArrow is **true**. Since this is still **false** at this point, the next RightArrow move to the left produces

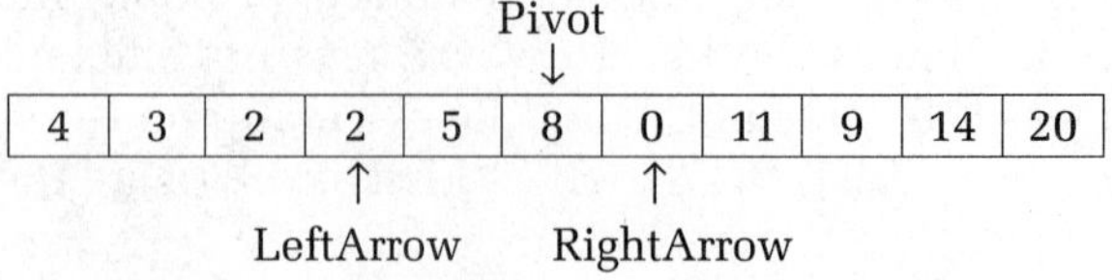

and the next LeftArrow move to the right yields

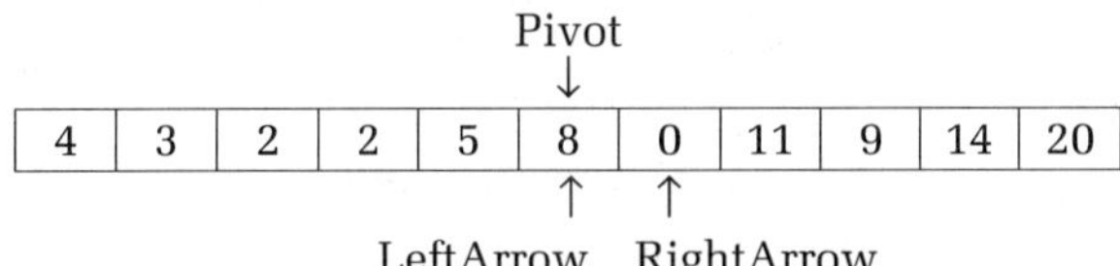

Since LeftArrow < Pivot is **false,** LeftArrow stops moving and an exchange is made to produce

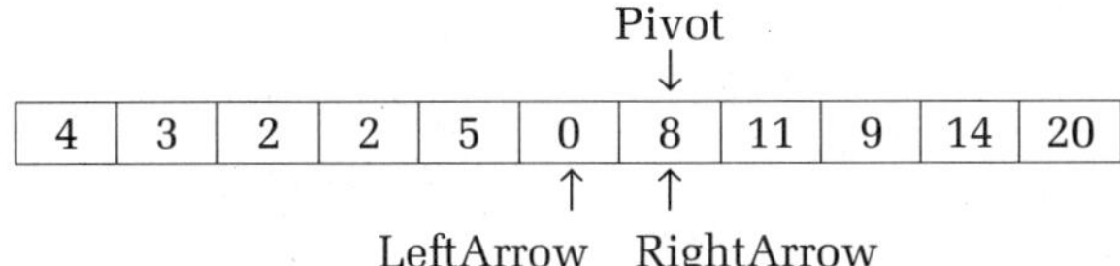

Notice that the pivot, 8, has been exchanged and now occupies a new position. This is acceptable because Pivot is the value of the component, not the index. As before, RightArrow is moved left and Left Arrow is moved right to produce

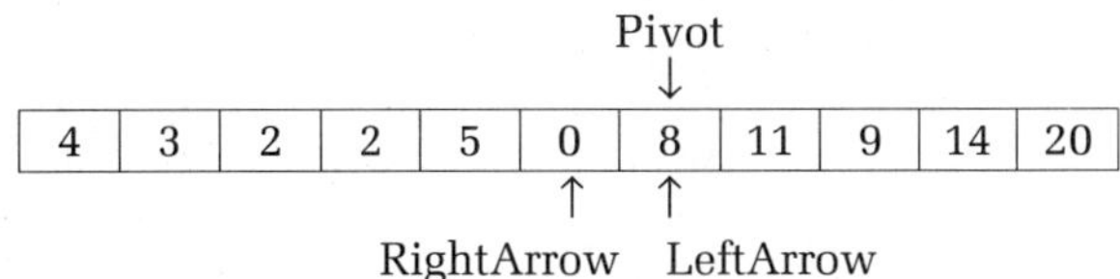

Since RightArrow < LeftArrow is **true,** the first subdividing is complete. At this stage, numbers smaller than Pivot are on the left side and numbers larger than Pivot are on the right side. This produces two sublists that can be envisioned as

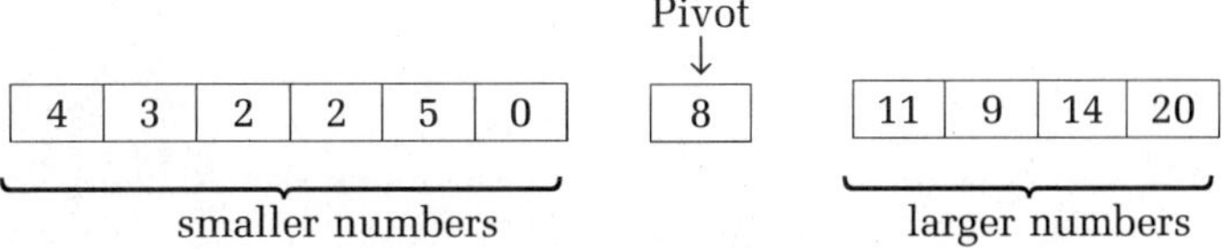

Each sublist can now be sorted by the same procedure. This requires a recursive call to the sorting procedure. In each case, the array is passed as a variable parameter together with the right and left indices for the appropriate sublist. A procedure for this sort follows.

```
PROCEDURE QuickSort (VAR Num : List;
                     Left, Right : integer);
  VAR
    Pivot, Temp, LeftArrow, RightArrow : integer;
  BEGIN
    LeftArrow := Left;
    RightArrow := Right;
    Pivot := Num[(Left + Right) DIV 2];
    REPEAT
      WHILE Num[RightArrow] > Pivot DO
        RightArrow := RightArrow - 1;
      WHILE Num[LeftArrow] < Pivot DO
        LeftArrow := LeftArrow + 1;
      IF LeftArrow <= RightArrow THEN
        BEGIN
          Temp := Num[LeftArrow];
          Num[LeftArrow] := Num[RightArrow];
          Num[RightArrow] := Temp;
```

```
          LeftArrow := LeftArrow + 1;
          RightArrow := RightArrow - 1
        END  {  of switching elements and then moving arrows  }
    UNTIL RightArrow < LeftArrow;
    IF Left < RightArrow THEN
      QuickSort (Num, Left, RightArrow);
    IF LeftArrow < Right THEN
      QuickSort (Num, LeftArrow, Right)
  END;  {  of PROCEDURE QuickSort  }
```

The design for a complete interactive program to illustrate the use of quick sort is

1. Fill the array
2. Sort the numbers
3. Print the list

The complete program follows.

```
PROGRAM UseQuickSort;

{ This program illustrates the quick sort as a sorting           }
{ algorithm. The array elements are successively subdivided      }
{ into ''smaller'' and ''larger'' elements in parts of the array. }
{ Recursive calls are made to PROCEDURE QuickSort.               }

USES
 Crt;

CONST
 MaxLength = 30;

TYPE
 List = ARRAY [1..MaxLength] OF integer;

VAR
 Num : List;
 First, Last, Length : integer;

{****************************************************************}

PROCEDURE FillArray (VAR Num : List;
                     VAR Length : integer);

  {  Given:   Nothing                                          }
  {  Task:    Read numbers entered from the keyboard into the  }
  {               array Num                                    }
  {  Return:  An array of numbers, Num, and number of elements }
  {               in the array                                 }

VAR
  Index : integer;
BEGIN
   Index := 0;
   REPEAT
     Index := Index + 1;
     write ('Enter an integer, -999 to quit. ');
     readln (Num[Index])
   UNTIL Num[Index] = -999;
  Length := Index - 1
END;  { of PROCEDURE FillArray }

{****************************************************************}
```

```
PROCEDURE QuickSort (VAR Num : List;
                     Left, Right : integer);

  {  Given:  An unsorted array of integers and array length      }
  {  Task:   Sort the array                                      }
  {  Return: A sorted array of integers                          }

VAR
  Pivot, Temp, LeftArrow, RightArrow : integer;
BEGIN
  LeftArrow := Left;
  RightArrow := Right;
  Pivot := Num[(Left + Right) DIV 2];
  REPEAT
     WHILE Num[RightArrow] > Pivot DO
     RightArrow := RightArrow - 1;
  WHILE Num[LeftArrow] < Pivot DO
    LeftArrow := LeftArrow + 1;
  IF LeftArrow <= RightArrow THEN
    BEGIN
      Temp := Num[LeftArrow];
      Num[LeftArrow] := Num[RightArrow];
      Num[RightArrow] := Temp;
      LeftArrow := LeftArrow + 1;
      RightArrow := RightArrow - 1
    END  {  of IF...THEN  }
  UNTIL RightArrow < LeftArrow;
  IF Left < RightArrow THEN
    QuickSort (Num, Left, RightArrow);
  IF LeftArrow < Right THEN
    QuickSort (Num, LeftArrow, Right)
END; {of PROCEDURE QuickSort }

{*****************************************************************}

PROCEDURE PrintList (VAR Num : List;
                     Length : integer);

  {  Given:   A sorted array of numbers and array length        }
  {  Task:    Print the numbers                                 }
  {  Return:  Nothing                                           }

VAR
  Index : integer;
BEGIN
  writeln;
  writeln ('The sorted list is:');
  writeln;
  FOR Index := 1 TO Length DO
    writeln (Num[Index]);
  readln
END;  {  of PROCEDURE PrintList }

{*****************************************************************}

BEGIN  {  Main program  }
  ClrScr;
  FillArray (Num, Length);
  QuickSort (Num, 1, Length);
  PrintList (Num, Length)
END.  {  of main program  }
```

A sample run of this program using the previous data produces

```
Enter an integer, -999 to quit. 14
Enter an integer, -999 to quit. 3
Enter an integer, -999 to quit. 2
Enter an integer, -999 to quit. 11
Enter an integer, -999 to quit. 5
Enter an integer, -999 to quit. 8
Enter an integer, -999 to quit. 0
Enter an integer, -999 to quit. 2
Enter an integer, -999 to quit. 9
Enter an integer, -999 to quit. 4
Enter an integer, -999 to quit. 20
Enter an integer, -999 to quit. -999

The sorted list is:

0
2
2
3
4
5
8
9
11
14
20
```

Exercises 11.2

1. Modify the insertion sort so it sorts numbers from an input file rather than from an array. Explain why **PROCEDURE** InsertionSort inserts the first element of the unsorted list into the first position of the sorted list.
2. Using the bubble sort discussed in Chapter 7, the array

17
0
3
2
8

   requires five exchanges of elements. Since each exchange requires three assignment statements, there are 15 assignments for elements in the array. Sort the same array using the insertion sort, and determine the number of assignments made.
3. Modify the insertion sort by including a counter that counts the number of assignments of array elements made during a sort.
4. Using the modification in Exercise 3, sort lists of differing lengths that contain randomly generated numbers. Display the number of assignments made for each sort on a graph similar to the one shown in Figure 11.5. (Use lists with lengths of multiples of 10.)
5. Modify both the bubble sort and the selection sort discussed in Chapter 7 to include counters for the number of assignments made during a sort.
6. Use the modified version of all sorts to examine their relative efficiency; that is, run them on arrays of varying lengths and plot the results on a graph. What are your conclusions?

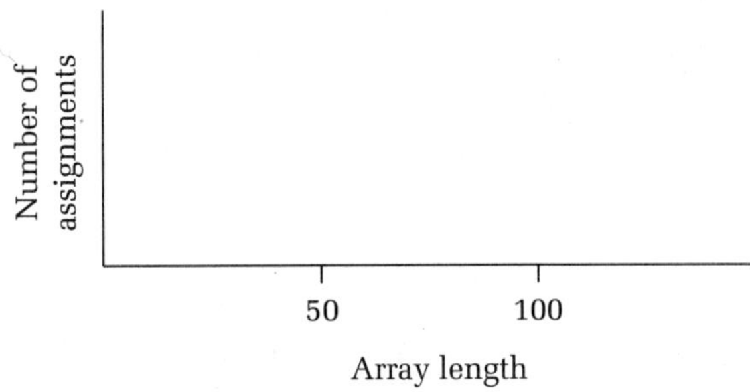

FIGURE 11.5
Array length

7. Write a short program to read numbers into an array, sort the array, print the sorted numbers, and save the sorted list for later use by some other program.
8. Modify all sorts to sort from high to low rather than from low to high.
9. Sorting parallel arrays is a common practice. An example of parallel arrays is an array of names and a corresponding array of scores on a test. Modify the insertion sort and the quick sort so you can sort a list of names and test scores.
10. Explain how an array of records with the key field Name can be sorted using the quick sort.
11. Suppose you are using a program that contains an array of records in which each record is defined by

```
TYPE
  .
  .
  .
  CustomerInfo = RECORD
                   Name : String20;
                   AmountDue : real
                 END;
```

    a. Use the quick sort to sort and then print the records alphabetically.
    b. Resort the array by the field AmountDue. Print a list ordered by AmountDue in which anyone with an amount due of more than $100 will be designated with a triple asterisk (***).
12. Modify **PROCEDURE** QuickSort in this section to use the first element (not the middle element) in an array as the pivot.

RUNNING AND DEBUGGING HINTS

1. Make sure recursive subporgrams reach a stopping state.
2. Make sure recursive subprograms have well-defined recursive steps.
3. Use value parameters for any formal parameters that relate to the size of the problem in a recursive subprogram.
4. Sorting large files or long arrays can be very time consuming. Depending upon the number of elements to be processed, use some form of "divide and conquer"; that is, divide the list, sort the elements, and then merge them. Very large data bases may require several subdivisions and subsequent merges.
5. When sorting records using a key field, be careful to compare only the key field and then exchange the entire record accordingly.

■ Summary

Key Terms

insertion sort
quick sort
recursion
recursive step
recursive subprogram
stack
stopping state

Key Concepts

- Recursion is a process whereby a subprogram calls itself.
- A recursive subprogram must have a well-defined stopping state.
- Recursive solutions are usually elegant and short, but they generally require more memory than iterative solutions.
- An insertion sort creates a sorted array from an unsorted array by inserting elements one at a time in their respective order.
- A quick sort is one of the fastest sorting techniques available. It uses recursion and is based upon the idea of separating a list into two parts.

■ Suggestions for Further Reading

Recursion and sorting are the subjects of numerous articles and books. This chapter provided some samples of each process. For variations and improvements on the information included here as well as on other techniques, the interested reader is referred to the following books, which many consider to be classics in the field.

Baase, Sara. "Sorting." Chapter 2 in *Computer Algorithms: Introduction to Design and Analysis.* Reading, MA: Addison-Wesley Publishing Co., 1978.

Gear, William. *Applications and Algorithms in Engineering and Science.* Chicago: Science Research Associates, 1978.

Horowitz, Ellis, and Sartaz, Sahmi. "Divide and Conquer." Chapter 3 in *Fundamentals of Computer Algorithms.* Potomac, MD.: Computer Science Press, 1978.

Knuth, Donald. *The Art of Computer Programming.* Vol. 3, *Sorting and Searching.* Reading, MA: Addison-Wesley Publishing Co., 1975.

■ Programming Problems and Projects

■ **1.** Write a program to update a mailing list. Assume you have a sorted master file of records and each record contains a customer's name, address, and expiration code. Your program should input a file of new customers, sort the file, and merge the file with the master file to produce a new master.

■ **2.** Assume the ReadMore Public Library (Problems 6 and 7, Chapter 9) stores information about books on their shelves in a file of records named OldFile. Information about a new shipment of books is contained in the data file. Both files are sorted alphabetically by book title. Write a program to be used to update OldFile. For each book in the input file, your program should search the existing file to see if the additional book is a duplicate. If it is, change a field in the record to indicate that an additional copy has been obtained. If it is not a duplicate, insert the record in sequence in the file.

3. The Bakerville Manufacturing Company has to lay off all employees who started working after a certain date. Write a program to do the following.
   a. Input a termination date.
   b. Search an alphabetical file of employee records to determine who will get a layoff notice.
   c. Create a file of employee records for those who are being laid off.
   d. Update the master file to contain only records of current employees.
   e. Produce two lists of those being laid off: one ordered alphabetically and one ordered by hiring date.

4. The Bakerville Manufacturing Company (Problem 3) has achieved new prosperity and can rehire 10 employees who were recently laid off. Write a program to do the following.
   a. Search the file of previously terminated employees to find the ten with the most seniority.
   b. Delete those 10 records from the file of employees who were laid off.
   c. Insert the 10 records alphabetically into the file of current employees.
   d. Print four lists.
      i. An alphabetical list of current employees
      ii. A seniority list of current employees
      iii. An alphabetical list of employees who were laid off
      iv. A seniority list of employees who were laid off
5. The Shepherd Lions Club sponsors an annual cross-country race for area schools. Write a program to do the following.
   a. Create an array of records for the runners; each record should contain the runner's name, school, identification number, and time (in a seven-character string, such as 15:17:3).
   b. Print an alphabetical listing of all runners.
   c. Print a list of schools entered in the race.
   d. Print a list of runners in the race; order the list by school name.
   e. Print the final finish order by sorting the records according to the order of finish and printing a numbered list according to the order of finish.
6. The greatest common divisor of two positive integers a and b, GCD(a,b), is the largest positive integer that divides both a and b. Thus, GCD(102, 30) = 6, which can be found by using the division algorithm as follows:

   ```
   102 = 30 * 3 + 12
   30  = 12 * 2 + 6
   12  = 6 *  2 + 0
   ```

   Note that

   $$\begin{aligned} GCD(102, 30) &= GCD(30, 12) \\ &= GCD(12, 6) \\ &= 6 \end{aligned}$$

   In each case, the remainder is used for the next step. The process terminates when a remainder of zero is obtained. Write a recursive function that returns the GCD of two positive integers.
7. A palindrome is a number or word that is the same when read either forward or backward. As examples, 12321 and mom are palindromes. Write a recursive function that can be used to determine whether or not an integer is a palindrome. Use this function in a complete program that reads a list of integers and then displays the list with an asterisk following each palindrome.
8. Recall the Fibonacci sequence discussed at the beginning of this chapter. Write a recursive function that returns the nth Fibonacci number. Input for a call to the function will be a positive integer.
9. Probability courses often contain problems that require students to compute the number of ways r items can be chosen from a set of n objects. It is shown that there are

   $$C(n,r) = \frac{n!}{r!(n-r)!}$$

such choices. This is sometimes referred to as "n choose r." To illustrate, if you wish to select three items from a total of five possible objects, there are

$$C(5,3) = \frac{5!}{3!(5-3)!} = \frac{5*4*3*2*1}{(3*2*1)\,(2*1)} = 10$$

such possibilities.

In mathematics, the number $C(n,r)$ is a binomial coefficient because for appropriate values of n and r, it produces coefficients in the expansion of $(x + y)^n$. Thus

$$(x + y)^4 = C(4,0)x^4 + C(4,1)x^3y + C(4,2)xy^2 + C(4,3)xy^3 + C(4,4)y^4$$

a. Write a function that returns the value $C(n,r)$. Arguments for a function call will be integers n,r such that $n > r > 0$. (*Hint:* Simplify the expression

$$\frac{n!}{r!(n-r)!}$$

before computing.)

b. Write an interactive program that receives as input the power to which a binomial is to be raised. Output should be the expanded binomial.

■ Communication in Practice

1. Select a programming problem that you have not worked from the Programming Problems and Projects section of this chapter. Construct a structure chart and write all documentary information for this program. Include variable definition, subprogram definition, required input, and required output. When you are finished, have a classmate read your documentation to see if it is clear precisely what is to be done.
2. Remove all documentation from a program you have written for this chapter. Exchange this modified version with another student who has done the same thing. Write documentation for the exchanged program. Compare your documentation with the original program. Discuss the differences and similarities with the other students in your class.
3. Form a team of three or four students, and identify some local business that has not yet computerized its customer records. The team should talk to the owner or manager to determine how the customer records are used and then design an information processing system for the business. The system should include complete design specifications. Particular attention should be paid to searching and sorting.
   The team should then give an oral presentation to the class and use appropriate charts and diagrams to illustrate their design.
4. Write a short paper that describes how the quick sort works. Prepare a model that can be used to demonstrate this sorting technique to your class.

Sets

CHAPTER OUTLINE

Thus far we have investigated structured data types, arrays, records, and files. These data types are structured because when each one is declared, a certain structure is reserved to subsequently hold values. In an array, a predetermined number of elements that are all of the same type can be held. A record contains a predetermined number of fields that can hold elements of different types. A file is somewhat like an array but the length is not predetermined.

Another structured data type available in Turbo Pascal is a set. The goal of this chapter is to enable you to use sets when writing programs to solve problems. One fairly common use of sets is as a guard against inadvertent keystrokes when users are working with interactive programs. But before you can use sets in a program, you must understand certain fundamentals. In particular, you must be able to properly define sets and use set operations.

12.1 Declarations and Terms

Basic Idea and Notation

A *set* in Turbo Pascal is a structured data type consisting of a collection of distinct elements from an indicated base type (which must be an ordinal data type). Sets in Turbo Pascal are defined and used in a manner consistent with the use of sets in mathematics. A set type is defined by

```
TYPE
    <type name> = SET OF <base type>;
```

A set variable is then declared by

```
VAR
    <variable name> : <type name>;
```

In a program working with characters of the alphabet, we might have

```
TYPE
  Alphabet = SET OF 'A'..'Z';
VAR
  Vowels, Consonants : Alphabet;
```

In a similar fashion, if our program analyzes digits and arithmetic symbols, we might have

```
TYPE
  Units = SET OF 0..9;
  Symbols = SET OF '*'..'/';  {  Arithmetic symbols  }
VAR
  Digits : Units;
  ArithSym : Symbols;
```

In these examples, Alphabet, Units, and Symbols are set types. Vowels, Consonants, Digits, and ArithSym are set variables.

A set can contain elements; these elements must be of the defined base type, which must be an ordinal data type. Thus, none of the real data types can be used as a base type. The maximum set size in Turbo Pascal is 256 elements. The base type must not have more than 256 possible values. The ordinal values of the upper and lower bounds of the base type must be within the range of zero to 255. For these reasons, the base type of a set cannot be **shortint, integer, longint,** or **word.**

Assignments to Sets

Once a set variable has been declared, it is undefined until an assignment of values is made. The syntax for making such an assignment is

<set name> := [<values>];

For example, we can have

```
Vowels := ['A', 'E', 'I', 'O', 'U'];
Consonants := ['B'..'D', 'F'..'H', 'J'..'N',
               'P'..'T','V'..'Z'];
Digits := [0..9];
ArithSym := ['+', '-', '*', '/'];
```

Notice the assigned values must be included in brackets and must be of the defined base type. Appropriate values depend upon the character set being used. Also, subranges of the base type can be used; thus

```
Consonants := ['B'..'D'];
```

is the same as

```
Consonants := ['B', 'C', 'D'];
```

It is also possible to have set constants. Just as 4, 'H', and −56.20 are constants, [2, 4, 6] is a constant. In the previous example, this could be caused by

```
Digits := [2,4,6];
```

As mentioned, sets are structured data types because, in a sense, they can be thought of as containing a list of elements. However, in listing the elements, notice each element can be listed only once and order makes no difference; thus, [2, 4, 6] is the same as [4, 2, 6].

A NOTE OF INTEREST

Fractal Geometry and Benoit Mandelbrot

Fractal geometry as a serious mathematical endeavor began [in about 1975] with the pioneering work of Benoit B. Mandelbrot, a Fellow of the Thomas J. Watson Research Center, IBM Corporation. Fractal geometry is a theory of geometric forms so complex they defy analysis and classification by traditional Euclidean means. Yet fractal shapes occur universally in the natural world. Mandelbrot has recognized them not only in coastlines, landscapes, lungs, and turbulent water flow but also in the chaotic fluctuation of prices on the Chicago commodity exchange.

Source: From *For All Practical Purposes: Introduction to Contemporary Mathematics.* By Consortium for Mathematics and Its Applications. Copyright © 1991 by COMAP, Inc. Reprinted by permission of W. H. Freeman and Company.

Although Mandelbrot's first comprehensive publication of fractal theory took place in 1975, mathematicians were aware of some of the basic elements during the period from 1875 to 1925. However, because mathematicians at that time thought such knowledge of "fractal dimension" deserved little attention, their discoveries were left as unrelated odds and ends. Also, the creation of fractal illustrations—a laborious and nearly impossible task at the turn of the twentieth century—can now be done quickly and precisely using computer graphics. (Even personal computers can now be used to generate fractal patterns with relative ease.)

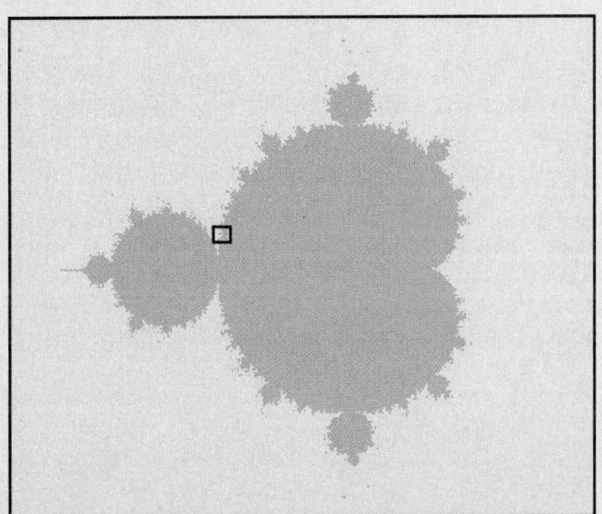

The figure to the left shows an enlargement of the area of the Mandelbrot set defined in the rectangle in the figure above.

Other Terminology

Once a value of the base type has been assigned to a set, it is an *element of the set.* Thus, if we have

```
Digits := [2,4,6];
```

2, 4, and 6 are elements of Digits. Testing membership in a set is discussed in the next section.

As in mathematics, any set that contains all possible values of the base type is called the *universal set.* In

```
Digits := [0..9];
```

Digits is a universal set. It is also possible to consider a set constant as a universal set. Thus, ['A' . . 'Z'] is a universal set if the **TYPE** definition section contains

```
<type name> = SET OF 'A'..'Z';
```

If A and B have been declared as sets of the same type and all of the elements of set A are also contained in set B, A is a *subset* of B. If we have

```
VAR
  A, B : Units;
```

and the assignments

```
A := [1,2,3,4,5];
B := [0..6];
```

have been made, A is a subset of B. However, notice B is not a subset of A because B contains two elements (0 and 6) that are not contained in A.

The *empty set,* or *null set,* is a set that contains no elements. It is denoted by [ ].

These definitions permit set theory results of mathematics to hold in Turbo Pascal. Some of these results follow.

1. The empty set is a subset of every set.
2. If A is a subset of B and B is a subset of C, then A is a subset of C.
3. Every set (of the base type) is a subset of the universal set.

Exercises 12.1

1. Find all errors in the following definitions and declarations. Explain your answers.

   a.
   ```
   TYPE
     Numbers = SET OF real;
   ```
   b.
   ```
   TYPE
     Numbers = SET OF integer;
   ```
   c.
   ```
   TYPE
     Alphabet : SET OF 'A'..'Z';
   ```
   d.
   ```
   TYPE
     Alphabet = SET OF ['A'..'Z'];
   ```
   e.
   ```
   TYPE
     Conditions = (Sunny, Mild, Rainy, Windy);
     Weather = SET OF Conditions;
   VAR
     TodaysWeather : Weather;
   ```

2. Write a test program to do the following.
   a. Discover if **char** is a permissible base type for a set.
   b. Determine the limitation on the size of the base type for a set.

3. Suppose set A is declared by

   ```
   TYPE
     Letters = SET OF 'A'..'Z';
   VAR
     A : Letters;
   ```

   a. Show how set A can be made to contain the letters in your name.
   b. Assign the letters in the word PASCAL to set A.
   c. Assuming the assignment

   ```
   A := ['T', 'O', 'Y'];
   ```

   has been made, list all elements and subsets of set A.

4. Let the sets A, B, and U be declared by

```
TYPE
  Alphabet = SET OF 'A'..'Z';
VAR
  A, B, U : Alphabet;
```

and the assignments

```
A := ['B', 'F', 'J'..'T'];
B := ['O'..'S'];
U := ['A'..'Z'];
```

be made. Indicate whether each of the following is **true** or **false**.

a. [ ] is a subset of B.
b. B is an element of A.
c. B is a subset of A.
d. 'B' is an element of A.
e. 'B' is a subset of A.
f. A is a subset of U.
g. 'O' is an element of A.

5. Assume A, B, and U are declared as in Exercise 4. Find and explain all errors in the following assignment statements.

a. `A := 'J'..'O';`
b. `U := [];`
c. `B := [A..Z];`
d. `A := ['E', 'I', 'E', 'I', 'O'];`
e. `[] := ['D'];`
f. `B := ['A'..'T', 'S'];`

6. Let set A be declared by

```
TYPE
  NumRange = 0..100;
VAR
  A : SET OF NumRange;
  M, N : integer;
```

Indicate if the following assignment statements are valid or invalid. For those that are valid, list the elements of set A. For those that are invalid, explain why.

a. `A := [19];`

b.
```
M := 80;
N := 40;
A := [M + N, M MOD N, M DIV N];
```

c. `A := 19;`

d.
```
M := 10;
N := 2;
A := [M, M * N, M / N];
```

7. Define a set type and declare a set variable to be used for each of the following.
   a. Set values consist of colors of the rainbow.
   b. Set values consist of class in school (Freshman, Sophomore, Junior, or Senior).
   c. Set values consist of fruits.
   d. Set values consist of grades for a class.

8. Explain why **SET** is not an enumerated type.

■ 12.2 Set Operations and Relational Operators

Set Operations

Turbo Pascal provides for the set operations union, intersection, and difference where, in each case, two sets are combined to produce a single set. If A and B are sets of the same type, these operations are defined as follows:

- The *union* of A and B is A + B, where A + B contains any element that is in A or that is in B.
- The *intersection* of A and B is A * B, where A * B contains the elements that are in both A and B.

- The *difference* of A and B is A – B, where A – B contains the elements that are in A but that are not in B.

To illustrate, suppose A and B are sets that contain integer values and the assignment statements

```
A := [1..5];
B := [3..9];
```

are made. The values produced by set operations are shown in the marginal table.

Set Operation	Values
A + B	[1..9]
A * B	[3,4,5]
A - B	[1,2]
B - A	[6..9]

Multiple operations can be performed with sets. When such an expression is encountered, the same operator priority exists as for evaluating the comparable arithmetic expression. Thus, if A and B contain the values previously indicated

```
A + B - A * B
```

produces

```
[1..5] + [3..9]   -   [1..5] * [3..9]
                              ↓
[1..5] + [3..9]   -        [3,4,5]
        ↓
    [1..9]        -        [3,4,5]
                  ↓
             [1,2,6..9]
```

Relational Operators

Relational operators can also be used with sets in Turbo Pascal. These operators correspond to the normal set operators equal, not equal, subset, and superset. In each case, a Boolean value is produced. If A and B are sets, these operators are defined as shown in Table 12.1. Boolean values associated with some set expressions follow.

Set Expression	Boolean Value
[1,2,3] <= [0..10]	**true**
[0..10] <= [1,2,3]	**false**
[0..10] = [0..5, 6..10]	**true**
[] = ([1,2] - [0..10])	**true**
[1..5] <> [1..3, 4, 5]	**false**
[] <= [1,2,3]	**true**

TABLE 12.1
Set operations

Operator	Relational Expression	Definition
= (equal)	A = B	A is equal to B; that is, every element in A is contained in B and every element in B is contained in A.
< > (not equal)	A < > B	A does not equal B; that is, either A or B contains an element that is not contained in the other set.
<= (subset)	A <= B	A is a subset of B; that is, every element of A is also contained in B.
>= (superset)	A >= B	A is a superset of B (B is a subset of A); that is, every element of B is also contained in A.

Set Membership

Membership in a set is indicated in Turbo Pascal by the reserved word **IN**. The general form is

<element> **IN** <set>

This returns a value of **true** if the element is in the set and a value of **false** if it is not. To illustrate, suppose A and B are sets and the assignments

```
A := [0..20];
B := [5..10];
```

are made. The values of expressions using **IN** follow.

Expression	Boolean Value
`10 IN A`	**true**
`5 IN (A - B)`	**false**
`20 IN B`	**false**
`7 IN (A * B)`	**true**
`80 DIV 20 IN A * B`	?

Notice the last expression cannot be evaluated until priorities are assigned to the operators. Fortunately, these priorities are identical to those for arithmetic expressions; **IN** is on the same level as relational operators, as shown in Table 12.2.

TABLE 12.2
Operator priorities including set operations

Priority Level	Operators
1	( )
2	**NOT**
3	*, /, **MOD, DIV, AND**
4	+, –, **OR, XOR**
5	<, >, <=, >=, =, < >, **IN**

Operations at each level are performed in order from left to right as they appear in an expression. Thus, the expression

```
80 DIV 20 IN A * B
```

produces

```
80 DIV 20 IN A * B
    ↓
    4     IN A * B
               ↓
    4     IN [5..10]
          ↓
        false
```

Exercises 12.2

1. When using sets in Turbo Pascal, is >= the logical complement of <=? Give an example to illustrate your answer.
2. Let A and B be sets defined such that A := [0 . . 10] and B := [2,4,6,8,10] are valid. Write a test program to show each of the following.
   a. A + B = A   **b.** A * B = B   **c.** A – B = [0, 1, 3, 5, 7, 9]

3. For each of the following sets A and B, find A + B, A * B, A – B, and B – A.
   a. A := [–3 . . 2, 8, 10], B := [0 . . 4, 7 . . 10]
   b. A := [0, 1, 5 . . 10, 20], B := [2, 4, 6, 7 . . 11]
   c. A := [ ], B := [1 . . 15]
   d. A := [0 . . 5, 10, 14 . . 20], B := [3, 10, 15]
4. Given the following sets
   A := [0, 2, 4, 6, 8, 10];
   B := [1, 3, 5, 7, 9];
   C := [0 . . 5];
   indicate the values in each of the following sets.
   a. A * B – C
   b. A * (B – C)
   c. A * (B + C)
   d. A * B + A * C
   e. A – B * C
   f. A – (B – (A – B))
   g. A * (B * C)
   h. (A * B) * C
5. Using sets A, B, and C with values assigned as in Exercise 4, indicate whether each of the following is **true** or **false**.
   a. A * B = [ ]
   b. C <= A + B
   c. [5] <= B
   d. A + B < > C
   e. A – B >= [ ]
   f. (A + B = C) **OR** ([ ] <= B – C)
6. In mathematics, when x is an element of set A, this is denoted by $x \in A$. If x is not in A, we write $x \notin A$. Let B be a set declared by

```
VAR
  B : SET OF 0..10;
```

   Examine the following for validity, and decide how Turbo Pascal handles the "not an element of" concept.
   a. `4 NOT IN B`
   b. `4 NOT (IN B)`
   c. `NOT 4 IN B`
   d. `NOT (4 IN B)`
   e. `4 IN NOT B`
   f. `4 IN (NOT B)`
7. Write a short program to count the number of uppercase vowels in a text file. Your program should include the set type

```
TYPE
  AlphaUppercase = SET OF 'A'..'Z';
```

   and the set variable VowelsUppercase declared by

```
VAR
  VowelsUppercase : AlphaUppercase;
```

■ 12.3 Using Sets

Uses for Sets

Now that we know how to declare sets, assign values to sets, and operate with sets, we need to examine some uses of sets in programs. First, however, we need to note an important limitation of sets: as with other structured variables, sets cannot be read or written directly. However, the two processes—generating a set and printing the elements of a set—are not difficult to code. To illustrate generating a set, suppose we wish to create a set and have it contain all the characters in the alphabet in a line of text. (For this example we assume the text file does not contain lowercase letters.) We can declare this set with

```
TYPE
  AlphaSymbols = 'A'..'Z';
  Symbols = SET OF AlphaSymbols;
VAR
  Alphabet : Symbols;
  SentenceChar : Symbols;
  Ch : char;
```

Code to generate the set SentenceChar is

```
Alphabet := ['A'..'Z'];
SentenceChar := [];
WHILE NOT eoln(Data) DO
  BEGIN
    read (Data, Ch);
    IF Ch IN Alphabet THEN
      SentenceChar := SentenceChar + [Ch]
  END;
```

In many examples, we assume the text file does not contain lowercase letters. As you will see in the Focus on Program Design section at the end of this chapter, a slight modification can be made to accommodate both uppercase and lowercase letters. For example, we can use both uppercase and lowercase letters by changing the set definitions to

```
TYPE
  Symbols = SET OF char;
VAR
  UppercaseAlphabet : Symbols;
  LowercaseAlphabet : Symbols;
  Alphabet: Symbols;
```

Alphabet can then be formed in the program by

```
UppercaseAlphabet := ['A'..'Z'];
LowercaseAlphabet := ['a'..'z'];
Alphabet := UppercaseAlphabet + LowercaseAlphabet;
```

or

```
Alphabet := ['A'..'Z', 'a'..'z']
```

The general procedure of placing values into a set is to initialize the set by assigning the empty set and then use set union to add elements to the set.

COMMUNICATION AND STYLE TIPS

Sets with appropriate names are particularly useful for checking data. For example, a typical problem when working with dynamic variables (discussed in Chapter 15) is to examine an arithmetic expression for correct form. Thus, 3 + 4 is a valid expression but 3 + * 4 is not. As part of a program that analyzes such expressions, you might choose to define the following sets.

```
TYPE
  ValidDigits = SET OF '0'..'9';
  Symbols = SET OF char;
VAR
  Digits : ValidDigits;
  ValidOperator : Symbols;
  LeftSymbol, RightSymbol : Symbols;
```

These sets can now be assigned values such as

```
Digits := ['0'..'9'];
ValidOperator := ['+', '*', '-', '/'];
LeftSymbol := ['(', '[', '{'];
RightSymbol := [')', ']', '}'];
```

The process of printing values of elements in a set is equally short. Assuming we know the data type of the elements in the set, a loop can be used where the loop control variable ranges over values of this data type. Whenever a value is in the set, it is printed. To illustrate, assume the set SentenceChar contains some alphabetical characters and we wish to print these characters. Since we know the data type of the elements in SentenceChar is characters in 'A' . . 'Z', we can print the contained values by

```
FOR Ch := 'A' TO 'Z' DO
  IF Ch IN SentenceChar THEN
    write (Ch:2);
writeln;
```

This fragment of code produces the output

```
A B C D E H I K L M N O P S T U V Y
```

when the set SentenceChar is formed from the line of text

```
THIS LINE (OBVIOUSLY MADE UP!) DOESN'T MAKE MUCH SENSE.
```

Now that you are familiar with how to generate elements in a set and subsequently print contents of a set, let's examine some uses for sets in programs. Specifically, let's look at using sets to replace complex Boolean expressions, to protect a program against bad data, and to aid in interactive programming.

Suppose we are writing a program to analyze responses to questions on a standard machine-scored form. If we want a certain action to take place for every response of A, B, or C, instead of

```
IF (Response = 'A') OR (Response = 'B') OR (Response = 'C') THEN
```

we can use

```
IF Response IN ['A', 'B', 'C'] THEN
        .
        .
        .
```

To demonstrate protecting a program against bad data, suppose we are writing a program to use a relatively large data file. Furthermore, suppose the data are entered by operators in such a fashion that the first entry on the first line for each customer is a single-digit code followed by appropriate data for the customer. To make sure the code is properly entered, we can define a set ValidSym and assign it all appropriate symbols. Our program design could be

```
read (Data, Sym);
IF Sym IN ValidSym THEN
  BEGIN
      .
      .  (action here)
      .
  END
ELSE
  (error message here)
```

Specifically, a program for printing mailing labels might require a 3, 4, or 5 to indicate the number of lines for the name and address that follow. If we are writing a program that also partially edits the data file, we can have

```
read (Data, NumLines);
IF NumLines IN [3,4,5] THEN
  BEGIN
      .
      .  (process number of lines)
      .
```

```
  END
ELSE
  (error message here)
```

A third use of sets is as an aid in writing interactive programs. Frequently a user will be asked to respond by pressing a certain key or keys. For example, the following message may be given:

```
Do you wish to continue?
<Y> or <N> and press <Enter>.
```

In such cases, two problems can occur. First, the user may use uppercase or lowercase letters for a correct response. Second, the user may inadvertently strike the wrong key. To make this part of the program correct and guard against bad data, we can have a set declared and initialized as

```
GoodResponse := ['Y', 'y', 'N', 'n'];
```

and then use a **REPEAT . . . UNTIL** loop as follows:

```
REPEAT
  writeln ('Do you wish to continue?');
  writeln ('<Y> or <N> and press <Enter>.');
  readln (Response)
UNTIL Response IN GoodResponse;
```

We can then use a **boolean** variable Continue by first assigning it a value **false** and then follow the **REPEAT . . . UNTIL** loop with

```
Continue := Response IN ['Y', 'y'];
```

Sets with Functions

Sets can be used with subprograms. In general, set types can be used as parameters in much the same way that arrays, records, and files are used. However, when working with functions, sets cannot be returned as values of a function because functions cannot return structured types.

To illustrate using sets with functions, let's consider two examples.

EXAMPLE 12.1

Let's write a function to determine the cardinality (size or number of elements) in a set. Assuming appropriate **TYPE** definitions, such a function can be

```
FUNCTION Cardinality (S : <set type>) : integer;
  VAR
    Ct : integer;
    X : <base type for set>;
  BEGIN
    Ct := 0;
    FOR X := <initial value> TO <final value> DO
      IF X IN S THEN
        Ct := Ct + 1;
    Cardinality := Ct
  END;
```

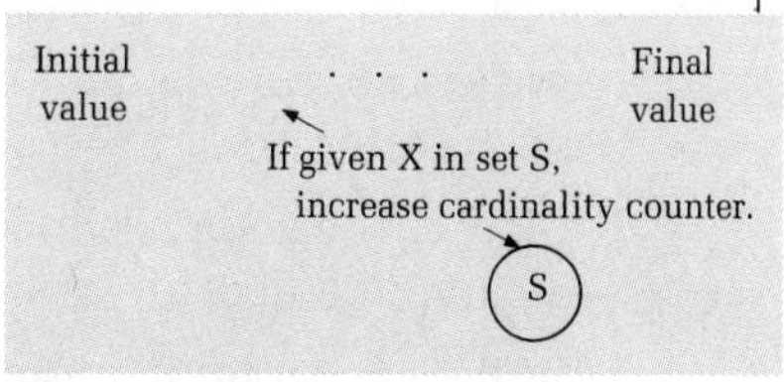

Initial value . . . Final value
If given X in set S, increase cardinality counter.
S

This is called from the main program by

```
SetSize := Cardinality(<set name>);
```

EXAMPLE 12.2

In our second example, let's consider a function to find the maximum (largest ordinal) element of a set. This function is typically applied to a set that contains elements in some subrange of the integers, but you can easily modify the function by considering the ordinals of set elements.

```
FUNCTION MaxElement (S : <set type>) : <base type>;
  VAR
    Temp : <base type>;
    X : <base type>;
  BEGIN
    IF S = [] THEN
      BEGIN
        writeln ('You are working with an empty set!':40);
        MaxElement := <initial value>
      END
    ELSE
      BEGIN
        Temp := <initial value>;
        FOR X := <initial value> TO <final value> DO
          IF (X IN S) AND (X > Temp) THEN
            Temp := X;
          MaxElement := Temp
      END  {  of ELSE option  }
  END;  {  of FUNCTION MaxElement  }
```

Initial value
. . .
Final value
Any new value of X which is also in S causes Temp to be adjusted.
S

This is called from the main program by

```
Largest := MaxElement(<set name>);
```

Sets with Procedures

Recall sets cannot be returned as values of a function. However, when a program requires a set to be returned from a subprogram, the set can be used as a variable parameter with a procedure. In this manner, sets can either be generated or modified with subprograms. The Focus on Program Design section at the end of this chapter illustrates such a use.

Exercises 12.3

1. Modify the function MaxElement used in Example 12.2 to find the character in a line of text that is latest in the alphabet. Use this function with the Focus on Program Design code presented at the end of this chapter.
2. Write a test program to create a set containing all the consonants from a line of text. Your program should also print all elements in the set.
3. Write a short program to reproduce a text file in which every vowel is replaced by an asterisk.
4. Modify the code used to find all the alphabet characters in a line of text so that a complete text file rather than just one line can be analyzed.
5. Write a program to simulate the arithmetic operations indicated in a text file. Arithmetic expressions should always be of the form digit-symbol-digit (9 +

8), where all digits and symbols are given as data of type **char**. Your program should protect against bad operation symbols, bad digits (actually, nondigits), and division by zero.

6. Write a function that returns the length of a string passed to the function as a packed array. Punctuation marks and internal blanks should add to the string length. Blanks at the beginning or end should not add to the length of the string.
7. Write a Boolean function to analyze an integer between −9999 and 9999 that returns the value **true** if the integer contains only odd digits (1731) and **false** otherwise.

FOCUS ON PROGRAM DESIGN

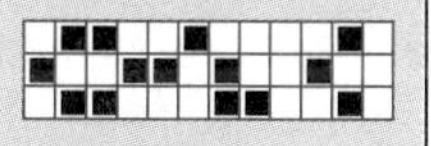

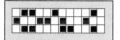

The sample program for this chapter illustrates a set used as a variable parameter in a procedure. The specific problem is to write a program to determine the alphabetical characters used in a line of text. Output from the program is an echo print of the text line, a list of letters in the text, and the number of distinct letters used in the line.

A first-level pseudocode development for this problem is

1. Get the characters
2. Print distinct characters
3. Determine the cardinality of the set
4. Print a closing message

A structure chart for this program is given in Figure 12.1.

FIGURE 12.1
Structure chart for
PROGRAM SymbolCheck

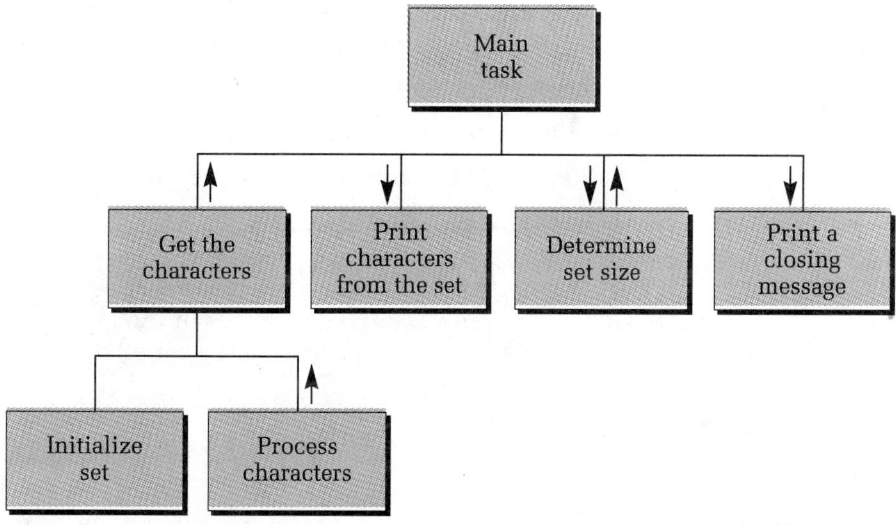

Module specifications for the main modules are

1. GetLetters Module
   Data received: None
   Information returned: A set of letters from a sentence
   Logic: Initialize the set.
   Add (union) distinct letters from a line of text.

2. PrintSet Module
   Data received: A set of letters
   Information returned: None
   Logic: Use a **FOR** loop to scan the alphabet and print the distinct letters contained in the set.

3. Cardinality Module
   Data received: A set of letters
   Information returned: The cardinality of the set
   Logic: Use a function to count the number of distinct elements in a set.

4. PrintMessage Module
   Data received: The cardinality of the set
   Information returned: None
   Logic: Print a message indicating the set size.

A refinement of the pseudocode produces

1. Get the characters
   1.1 initialize set
   1.2 **WHILE NOT eoln DO**
       1.2.1 process a character
2. Print distinct characters
   2.1 **FOR** Ch := 'A' **TO** 'z' **DO**
         IF Ch is in the set **THEN**
           print Ch
3. Determine the cardinality of the set
   3.1 initialize counter to zero
   3.2 **FOR** Ch := 'A' **TO** 'z' **DO**
         IF Ch is in the set **THEN**
           increment counter
   3.3 assign count to function name
4. Print a closing message

Step 1.2.1 can be refined to

    1.2.1 process a character
          1.2.1.1 read a character
          1.2.1.2 write a character (echo print)
          1.2.1.3 **IF** character is in the alphabet **THEN**
                    add it to the set of characters

The main program is

```
BEGIN  { Main program }
  ClrScr;
  assign (Data, 'DataFP12.DAT');
  reset (Data);
  GetLetters (SentenceChar);
  PrintSet (SentenceChar);
  SetSize := Cardinality(SentenceChar);
  PrintMessage (SetSize);
  close (Data);
  readln
END.  { of main program }
```

A complete program follows.

```
PROGRAM SymbolCheck;

{  This program illustrates working with sets.  It reads a line   }
{  of text and determines the number of distinct letters in       }
{  that line.  Output includes the distinct letters and the set   }
{  cardinality.  Information for this program is stored in the   }
{  text file Data.                                                }

USES
  Crt;

CONST
  Skip = ' ';

TYPE
  AlphaSymbols = SET OF char;

VAR
  SentenceChar : AlphaSymbols;       {  Set of possible letters   }
  SetSize : integer;                 {  Cardinality of the set    }
  Data : text;                       {  Data file                 }

{*************************************************************}

PROCEDURE GetLetters (VAR SentenceChar : AlphaSymbols);

  {  Given:   Nothing                                            }
  {  Task:    Read characters from the text file Data; echo      }
  {               print them; store the alphabetical characters  }
  {               in a set                                       }
  {  Return:  The set of letters contained in the line of text   }

  VAR
    Ch : char;
    Alphabet : AlphaSymbols;
  BEGIN
    SentenceChar := [];
    Alphabet := ['A'..'Z'] + ['a'..'z'];                                   1
    writeln (Skip:10, 'The line of text is below:');
    writeln; write (Skip:10);
    WHILE NOT eoln(Data) DO
      BEGIN
        read (Data, Ch);
        write (Ch);                                {  Echo print  }
        IF Ch IN Alphabet THEN
          SentenceChar := SentenceChar + [Ch]
      END;  {  of WHILE NOT eoln  }               {  of one line  }
    writeln
  END;  {  of PROCEDURE GetLetters  }

{*************************************************************}

PROCEDURE PrintSet (SentenceChar : AlphaSymbols);

  {  Given:   A set of characters                                }
  {  Task:    Print all characters in the set                    }
  {  Return:  Nothing                                            }

  VAR
    Ch : char;
  BEGIN                                                                    2
    writeln;
    writeln (Skip:10, 'The letters in this line are:');
    writeln; write (Skip:10);
```

```
    FOR Ch := 'A' TO 'z' DO
      IF Ch IN SentenceChar THEN
        write (Ch:2);
    writeln
  END;  {  of PROCEDURE PrintSet  }

{*************************************************************}

FUNCTION Cardinality (SentenceChar : AlphaSymbols) : integer;

  {  Given:   A set of characters                             }
  {  Task:    Determine the number of characters in the set   }
  {  Return:  The set size (cardinality)                      }

  VAR
    Ct : integer;
    X : char;                                                     3
  BEGIN
    Ct := 0;
    FOR X := 'A' TO 'z' DO
      IF X IN SentenceChar THEN
        Ct := Ct + 1;
    Cardinality := Ct
  END;  {  of FUNCTION Cardinality  }

{*************************************************************}

PROCEDURE PrintMessage (SetSize : integer);

  {  Given:   The cardinality of the set                      }
  {  Task:    Print a closing message                         }
  {  Return:  Nothing                                         }   4

  BEGIN
    writeln; write (Skip:10);
    writeln ('There are', SetSize:5, ' letters in this sentence.')
  END;  {  of PROCEDURE PrintMessage  }

{*************************************************************}

BEGIN  {  Main Program  }
  ClrScr;
  assign (Data, 'DataFP12.DAT');
  reset (Data);
  GetLetters (SentenceChar);
  PrintSet (SentenceChar);
  SetSize := Cardinality(SentenceChar);
  PrintMessage (SetSize);
  close (Data);
  readln
END.  {  of main program  }
```

When this program is run on the line of text

```
The numbers -2, 5, 20 and symbols '?', ':' should be ignored.
```

the output is

```
          The line of text is below:

          The numbers -2, 5, 20 and symbols '?', ':' should be ignored.
```

```
The letters in this line are:

 T a b d e g h i l m n o r s u y

There are   16 letters in this sentence.
```

RUNNING AND DEBUGGING HINTS

1. When defining a set type, do not use brackets in the definition. Thus, the following definition is incorrect:

```
TYPE
  Alphabet = SET OF ['A'..'Z'];
```

   The correct form is

```
TYPE
  Alphabet = SET OF 'A'..'Z';
```

2. Remember to initialize a set before using it in a program. Declaring a set does not give it a value. If your declaration is

```
VAR
  Vowels : Alphabet;
```

   the program should contain

```
Vowels := ['A', 'E', 'I', 'O', 'U'];
```

3. Attempting to add an element to a set rather than a set to a set is a common error. If you wish to add 'D' to the set ['A', 'B', 'C'], you should write

```
['A', 'B', 'C'] + ['D']
```

   rather than

```
['A', 'B', 'C'] + 'D'
```

   This is a particular problem when the value of a variable is to be added to a set:

```
['A', 'B', 'C'] + Ch;
```

   should be

```
['A', 'B', 'C'] + [Ch];
```

4. Avoid confusing arrays and array notation with sets and set notation.
5. Remember certain operators (+, –, and *) have different meanings when used with sets.

Summary

Key Terms

difference	intersection	union
element of a set	set	universal set
empty (null) set	subset	

Keywords

IN **SET**

Key Concepts

- In Turbo Pascal, a **SET** is a structured data type that consists of distinct elements from an indicated base type; sets can be declared by

```
TYPE
  Alphabet = SET OF char;
VAR
  Vowels : Alphabet;
  GoodResponse : Alphabet;
```

In this definition and declaration, Alphabet is a **SET** type and Vowels and GoodResponse are set variables.

- Values must be assigned to a set; as for example,

```
Vowels := ['A', 'E', 'I', 'O', 'U'];
GoodResponse := ['Y', 'y', 'N', 'n'];
```

- When listing elements in a set, order makes no difference and each element may be listed only once.
- Standard set operations in Turbo Pascal are defined to be consistent with set operations of mathematics; to illustrate, if

```
A := [1,2,3,4];
```

and

```
B := [3,4,5];
```

the union, intersection, and difference of these sets are as follows:

Term	Expression	Value
Union	`A + B`	`[1..5]`
Intersection	`A * B`	`[3,4]`
Difference	`A - B`	`[1,2]`
	`B - A`	`[5]`

- Set membership is denoted by using the reserved word **IN**. Such an expression returns a Boolean value, as shown for

```
A := [1,2,3,4];
```

Expression	Value
`2 IN A`	**true**
`6 IN A`	**false**

- The relational operators (<=, >=, < >, and =) can be used with sets to form Boolean expressions and return values consistent with expected subset and set equality relationships. This is illustrated for

```
A := [1,2,3];
B := [0..5];
C := [2,4];
```

Expression	Value
`A <= B`	**true**
`B <= C`	**false**
`B >= C`	**true**
`A = B`	**false**
`B <> C`	**true**

- Priority levels for set operations are consistent with those used for arithmetic expressions; they are

Priority Level	Operation
1	( )
2	**NOT**
3	*, /, **MOD, DIV, AND**
4	+, –, **OR, XOR**
5	<, >, <=, >=, <>, =, **IN**

- Sets cannot be used with **read** or **write**; however, a set can be generated by initializing the set, assigning the empty set, and using set union to add elements to the set. For example, a set of characters in a text line can be generated by

```
S := [];
WHILE NOT eoln(Data) DO
  BEGIN
    read (Data, Ch);
    S := S + [Ch]
  END;
```

  This set can be printed by using

```
FOR Ch := <initial value> TO <final value> DO
  IF Ch IN S THEN
    write (Ch:2);
```

- Three uses for sets in programs are to replace complex Boolean expressions, to protect a program (or segment) from bad data, and to aid in interactive programming.
- Sets can be used as parameters with subprograms.
- Sets cannot be returned as values of a function.
- Sets can be generated or modified through subprograms by using variable parameters with procedures.

■ Programming Problems and Projects

Each of the following programming problems can be solved with a program using sets. Hints are provided to indicate some of the uses; you may, of course, find others.

Symptom	Code
Headache	1
Fever	2
Sore throat	3
Cough	4
Sneeze	5
Stomach pain	6
Heart pain	7
Muscle pain	8
Nausea	9
Back pain	10
Exhaustion	11
Jaundice	12
High blood pressure	13

1. Write a program to be used to simulate a medical diagnosis. Assume the symptoms are coded as indicated in the marginal table.

   Further, assume each of the following diseases is characterized by the symptoms indicated in the following table.

Disease	Symptoms
Cold	1, 2, 3, 4, 5
Flu	1, 2, 6, 8, 9
Migraine	1, 9
Mononucleosis	2, 3, 11, 12
Ulcer	6, 9
Arteriosclerosis	7, 10, 11, 13
Appendicitis	2, 6

   Your program should accept as input a person's name and symptoms (coded) and provide a preliminary diagnosis. Sets can be used for the following.
   a. Bad data check
   b. Symptoms = 1 . . 13;
      Disease = **SET OF** Symptoms;
   c. Cold, Flu, Migraine, Mononucleosis, Ulcer, Arteriosclerosis, Appendicitis : Disease;
2. Write a program to serve as a simple text analyzer. Input is any text file. Output should be three histograms: one each for vowel frequency, consonant frequency, and other symbol frequency. Your program should use a set for vowels, a set for consonants, and a set for other symbols.

3. Typists often complain that the standard QWERTY keyboard

Q W E R T Y U I O P
A S D F G H J K L ;
Z X C V B N M , . /
space bar

is not efficient. As you can see, many frequently used letters (E, T, N, R, and I) are not on the middle row. A new keyboard, the Maltron keyboard, has been proposed. Its design is

Q P Y C B V M U Z L
A N I S F E D T H O R ; : .
J G W K X
space bar

Write a program to analyze a text file to see how many jumps are required on each keyboard. For purposes of this program, a jump is any valid symbol not on the middle row. Output should include the number of valid symbols read and the number of jumps on each keyboard.

4. Write a program to serve as a simple compiler for a Turbo Pascal program. Your compiler should work on a program that uses only single-letter identifiers. Your compiler should create a set of identifiers and make sure identifiers are not declared twice, all identifiers on the left of an assignment are declared, and no type mismatch errors occur. For purposes of your compiler program, assume the following:
   a. Variables are declared between **VAR** and **BEGIN**; for example

```
VAR
  X, Y : real;
  A, B, C : integer;
  M : char;
BEGIN
```

   b. Each program line is a complete Turbo Pascal statement.
   c. The only assignments are of the form X := Y.

   Output should include the program line number and an appropriate error message for each error. Run your compiler with several short Turbo Pascal programs as text files. Compare your error list with the one given in Appendix 5.

5. A number in exponential notation preceded by a plus or minus sign may have the form

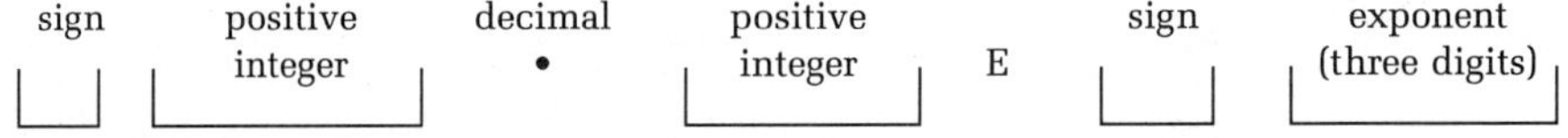

For example, −45.302E+002 is the number −4530.2. If the number is in standard form, it will have exactly one digit on the left side of the decimal (−4.5302E+003).

Write a program to read numbers in exponential form from a text file, one number per line. Your program should check to see if each number is in proper form. For numbers that are in proper form, print out the number as given and the number in standard form.

6. Write a program to analyze a text file for words of differing lengths. Your program should keep a list of all words of length 1, 2, . . . , 10. It should also count the number of words with lengths exceeding 10.

A word ends when one alphabetical character is followed by a character not in the alphabet or when an end-of-line marker is reached. All words start with letters (7UP is not a word). Your output should be an alphabetized list for each word length. It should also include the number of words with lengths exceeding 10 characters. An apostrophe does not add to the length of a word.

7. The Falcon Manufacturing Company (Problem 22, Chapter 8; Problem 17, Chapter 9; Problems 12–16, Chapter 10) wants you to develop a computerized system that determines if customers are approved for credit. A customer number should be entered from the keyboard, and the program should print the credit limit for the customer if credit has been approved and "No credit" if it has not. Each line of a text file contains a customer number and credit limit. Valid customer numbers range from 100 to 999; credit limits are $100, $300, $500, $1000, and unlimited credit.
8. Write a program in which you read a text file and print out the number of times a character in the file matches a character in your name.
9. The Court Survey Corporation wishes to conduct a poll by sending questionnaires to men and women between 25 and 30 years of age who live in your state or any state adjacent to it. A text file containing names, street addresses, cities, states, zip codes, and ages is to be read. The program should print the names and addresses of those persons who match the criteria.
10. Write a program to test your ESP and that of a friend. Each of you should secretly enter 10 integers between 1 and 100. The program should check each list and print the values in both lists and the number of values in both lists.
11. Modify the Wellsville Wholesale Company commission problem (Problem 22, Chapter 7) to define the sales ranges as sets. Use these sets to verify input and determine the proper commission rate.
12. The Ohio Programmers' Association offices are in a large building with five wings lettered A through E. The office numbers in the wings are given in the marginal table. Write a program that enables the receptionist, Miss Lovelace, to enter an office number from the keyboard and then have the computer print the wing in which the office is located.

Wing	Rooms
A	100–150; 281–300
B	151–190; 205–220
C	10 – 50; 191–204
D	1 – 9; 51–99
E	221–280; 301–319

■ Communication in Practice

1. Select a program from the Programming Problems and Projects section of this chapter that you have not yet worked. Construct a structure chart and write all documentary information for this program. Include variable definition, subprogram definition, required input, and required output. When you are finished, have a classmate read your documentation to see if it is clear precisely what is to be done.
2. Remove all documentation from a program you have written for this chapter. Exchange this modified version with another student who has done the same thing. Write documentation for the exchanged program. Compare your documentation with that originally written for the program. Discuss the differences and similarities with the other students in your class.
3. Not all programming languages include sets as a data structure. Examine several other languages to determine what data structures they include. Prepare a chart that compares and contrasts the data structures of Turbo Pascal (arrays, records, files, and sets) with the data structures of other languages. Give an oral presentation of your results to the class.

Graphics

■ CHAPTER OUTLINE ■

S

In this chapter, we will discover how Turbo Pascal allows us to create graphics displays on the screen. All prior output to the screen has been text: letters, numbers, and a few special symbols. Now we will see how geometric designs, charts, and other graphic displays are produced.

A note of caution is in order. This chapter is written for users of Turbo Pascal who have common display systems. If you are not using Turbo Pascal or if your display system is not consistent with what is presented in this chapter, you will need to refer to some other source to see how your system handles graphics.

■ 13.1 Fundamentals of Graphics

In this section, we examine the fundamental aspects necessary to produce graphics displays beginning with how the screen is configured. Next we consider color options, getting into and out of the graphics mode, and various forms of initialization for graphics. Then, we learn how to enter and exit the graphics mode, after which we investigate the elementary properties of plotting points and drawing lines.

The Screen

The standard display screen for personal computers contains 25 lines, each capable of holding 80 text characters. This can be envisioned as shown in Figure 13.1.

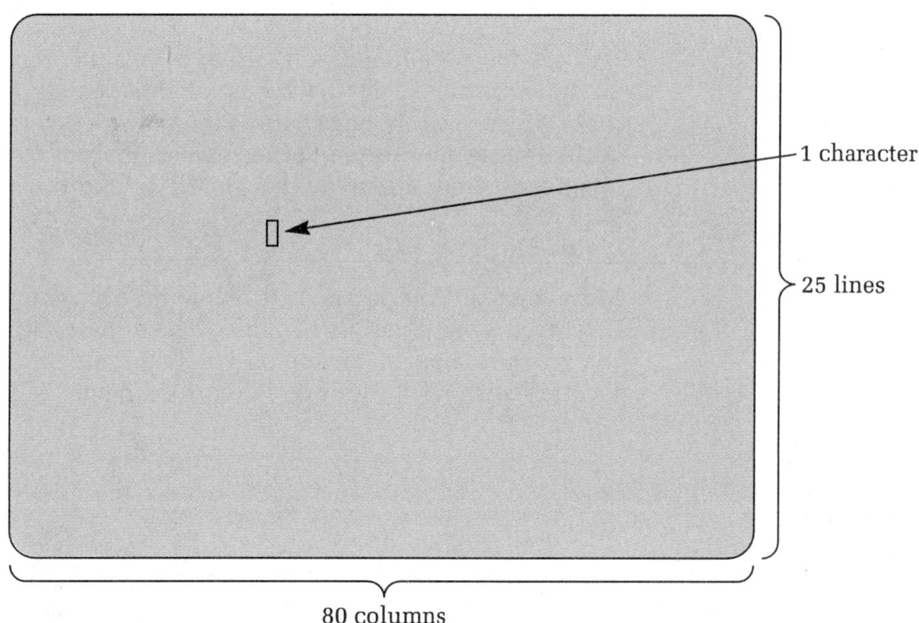

FIGURE 13.1
Standard display screen for text characters

Because there are 80 characters in each of 25 lines, you may think there are $80 \times 25 = 2000$ positions on the screen. Actually, there are many more than 2000 positions on a display screen because the screen actually consists of *pixels,* which is short for *picture elements.* A pixel is the smallest picture element on the display. When we work in a graphics mode, we work with these pixels instead of the character positions as when we use text characters.

Many graphics screens are 320 pixels across and 200 pixels down, as shown in Figure 13.2.

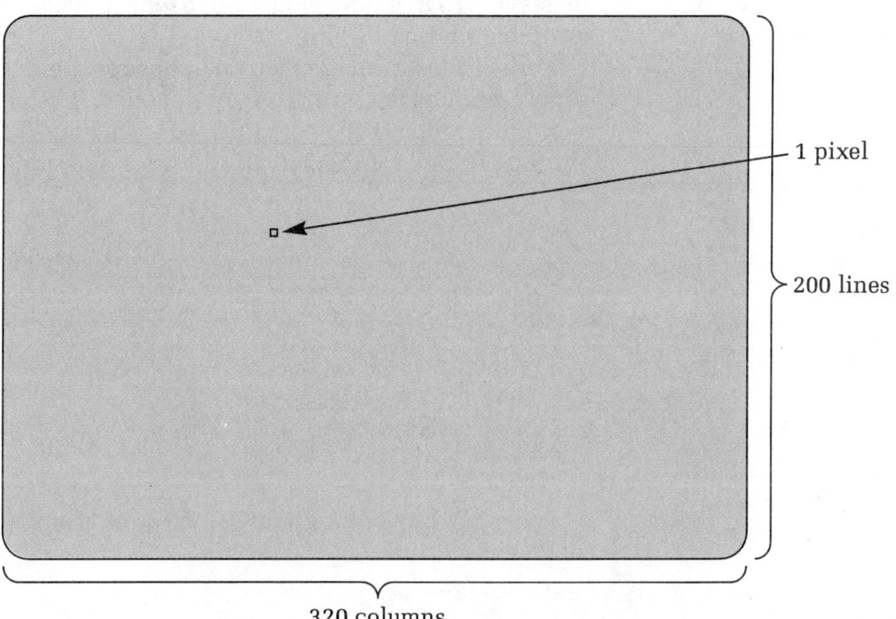

FIGURE 13.2
Pixels on a screen

Such a screen contains 64,000 (320 × 200) pixels. Graphics displays using screens that are 320 × 200 pixels are said to be in a *medium resolution mode.* If you have an option available that lets you use more pixels, you will be in *high resolution mode.* (Systems that have 640 × 200 or 640 × 360 pixels are examples.) Although both of these options (and others) are available on some systems, the work in this chapter assumes a display that is 320 × 200 pixels.

Color Options

Most personal computers have color graphics adapters that permit graphics to be displayed using a variety of colors. The number of colors available depends upon the graphics mode available on your computer. A list of several graphics modes, together with resolutions and colors available, is given in Table 13.1.

TABLE 13.1
Graphics modes, resolution, and colors available

Mode			Number of Colors Available
Name	Code	Resolution	
CGAC0	0	320 × 200	4
CGAC1	1	320 × 200	4
CGAC2	2	320 × 200	4
CGAC3	3	320 × 200	4
VGALo	0	640 × 200	16
VGAMed	1	640 × 350	16
VGAHi	2	640 × 480	16
EGALo	0	640 × 200	16
EGAHi	1	640 × 350	16
HercMonoHi	0	720 × 348	monochrome

The examples in this chapter have been developed on the assumption you are using a color monitor and working in one of the CGA modes. If you are working in some other mode, you will be in a high resolution mode with 16 colors available instead of four.

Turbo Pascal provides four palettes for the CGA modes. Each palette contains a background color and three other colors. The palettes are selected by specifying a graphics mode at the beginning of a program. The colors available in each mode are represented by integers 0, 1, 2, or 3 and are listed in Table 13.2

TABLE 13.2
Colors available in each mode

CGA	COLOR NUMBER			
Mode	0	1	2	3
0	Background	LightGreen	LightRed	Yellow
1	Background	LightCyan	LightMagenta	White
2	Background	Green	Red	Brown
3	Background	Cyan	Magenta	LightGray

When we first enter graphics, we select the mode we want by using a program statement such as

```
GraphMode := CGAC1;
```

or the equivalent

```
GraphMode := 1;
```

We then have available the colors LightCyan, LightMagenta, White, and a background color of our choice. It is possible to change the mode later in the program.

After the mode is selected, any of the 16 colors can be specified as a background color by using the predefined procedure **SetBkColor.** The background colors are listed in Table 13.3.

TABLE 13.3
Background colors

Background colors			
Number	**Color**	**Number**	**Color**
0	Black	8	DarkGray
1	Blue	9	LightBlue
2	Green	10	LightGreen
3	Cyan	11	LightCyan
4	Red	12	LightRed
5	Magenta	13	LightMagenta
6	Brown	14	Yellow
7	LightGray	15	White

SetBkColor requires a single argument, which can be any integer from zero to 15, inclusive. Turbo Pascal also permits the use of predefined constants that describe the colors provided by each integer. Thus, if we wish the background color to be Green, we can use either

```
SetBkColor(2);
```

or

```
SetBkColor(Green);
```

During the running of a graphics program, we can control the colors we use by changing the mode and/or changing the color in each mode. Mode changes are accomplished by the predefined procedure

SetGraphMode (<argument>);

where the argument is an integer that specifies the mode. For the CGA medium resolution mode, the argument will be one of the integers 0, 1, 2, or 3, as shown in Table 13.2.

We can then specify a foreground color by using the predefined procedure

SetColor (<argument>)

where the argument is an integer or a predefined constant. For the CGA medium resolution mode, the argument will be 0, 1, 2, or 3. An argument of 0 will make the current drawing color the same as the background color (in effect, erasing it!). Arguments of 1, 2, or 3 will specify the respective colors listed in Table 13.2. Thus, if we are in CGA mode 1

```
SetColor(2);
```

will cause the current drawing color to be LightMagenta. Table 13.4 contains a summary list of the procedures to use in establishing the modes and colors when working with graphics.

TABLE 13.4
Procedures for selecting colors

Procedure	Purpose
`SetBkColor (<selection>)`	Establishes a background color
`SetGraphMode (<selection>)`	Sets and/or changes modes for different color palettes
`SetColor (<selection>)`	Specifies a foreground color

Getting into Graphics Mode

Before we can do anything in graphics, we must get into the graphics mode. We will be using the units **Graph** and **Crt,** so our programs will begin with

```
PROGRAM GraphDemo;
USES
  Crt, Graph;
```

Before using any graphics in the main program, we must use the predefined procedure

InitGraph (<driver>, <mode>, <file path>);

where <driver> and <mode> are variable parameters of type **integer.** The parameter <driver> specifies which graph driver is to be used. Turbo Pascal internally associates each driver with a unique integer value. However, it is not necessary to know these values. Predefined constants CGA, VGA, EGA, and others can represent values of the parameter. Our examples will all use the CGA driver. Since this is a variable parameter, we use the variable GraphDriver to produce

```
GraphDriver := CGA;
InitGraph (GraphDriver, <mode>, <file path>);
```

The second parameter <mode> is also a variable parameter. Turbo Pascal supports any of the modes listed in conjunction with the names given in Table 13.1. Thus, if we want the mode CGAC1, we can use either

```
GraphMode := CGAC1;
```

or

```
GraphMode := 1;
```

where GraphMode is declared as a variable of type **integer.** Both the driver and the mode selection should be made before the call to **InitGraph.** Typically, a graphics program begins

```
PROGRAM GraphPrac;

USES
  Crt, Graph;

VAR
  GraphDriver, GraphMode : integer;

BEGIN
  GraphDriver := CGA;
  GraphMode := 1;
  InitGraph (GraphDriver, GraphMode, <file path>);
      .
      .
      .
```

The third parameter <file path> is the path required to locate the directory containing the BGI driver files (*.BGI). If Turbo Pascal has been installed so that the user is already in that directory, the file path can just be the null string ' '. If Turbo Pascal is not in the same directory as the BGI driver, the file path must be specified. For example, the file path could be

```
'C:\TP\BGI'
```

In this case, the **InitGraph** procedure would be

```
InitGraph (GraphDriver, GraphMode, 'C:\TP\BGI');
```

Default Values

It is possible to enter the graphics mode with less fanfare. Turbo Pascal provides a method that automatically examines the hardware being used and determines which driver is needed. This mechanism uses the name **detect** as follows:

```
GraphDriver := detect;
```

One advantage of using **detect** is the user does not need to know which driver your hardware supports or what the code for the driver is. A second advantage of using **detect** to specify the driver is it also delivers the value of the mode when the **InitGraph** procedure is processed. A program using **detect** begins

```
GraphDriver := detect;
InitGraph (GraphDriver, GraphMode, '');
```

provided we are in the directory containing the driver specified in the first argument. If we do not want the default mode or if we want to change the mode at some point in the program, we merely assign a different mode by using

```
GraphMode := <value>;
```

For a more complete explanation of how the mode is specified when using **detect,** see the Turbo Pascal Library Reference Manual.

The examples in this chapter do not use default values provided by **detect.** We assume a CGA driver and always specify a mode of 0, 1, 2, or 3. We also specify a file path for the BGI driver files. Therefore, our typical program begins

```
GraphDriver := CGA;
GraphMode := 1;
InitGraph (GraphDriver, GraphMode, 'C:\TP\BGI');
```

Getting Out of Graphics Mode

After we finish with graphics, we need to exit the graphics mode. This is accomplished by a call to the procedure **CloseGraph,** which requires no arguments and appears as a single line of code:

```
CloseGraph;
```

Calling this procedure has the effect of restoring the original screen mode before graphics was initialized. It also frees the memory allocated for graphics.

When it is necessary to move back and forth between graphics and text several times within a program, the procedure **RestoreCrtMode,** rather than **CloseGraph,** should be used. **RestoreCrtMode** returns the user to text mode but retains the current graphics settings. These settings can be reinstated by using the predefined procedure

```
SetGraphMode (GraphMode);
```

rather than going through **InitGraph** again. The procedure **SetGraphMode** can also be used to change the mode in a program by

A NOTE OF INTEREST

Artist of Interface

Millions of people encounter the graphic art of Susan Kare every day, and many more will experience her unusual work in the months ahead. Her carefully crafted images have won a place among the cultural symbols of our age, yet few people have any idea who she is or where her work can be seen.

Only a handful of industry insiders know that Kare is the artist responsible for the graphic appearance of some of the country's best-known computer software. Based in San Francisco, she designed most of the distinctive icons, typefaces and other graphic elements that gave the original Macintosh computer its characteristic—and widely emulated—appearance. Many consider her to be the mother of the famous Macintosh trash can.

Since then, Kare has parlayed her initial work for Apple Computer, Inc., into a full-time business, designing graphic user interfaces, or GUIs, for computer companies and software developers. The user interface is the software that allows an operator to control a personal computer and direct its functions. A decade ago, most interfaces forced the user to type cryptic commands in a blank space on the display.

With the introduction of the Macintosh in 1984, Apple pushed the world toward the graphic interface, which provides greater ease of use. A graphic interface allows an operator to control the computer by manipulating symbols displayed on its monitor, usually with a mouse or trackball.

The growing demand for graphic user interfaces has forced Kare to turn down work. She has rejected potential clients in part because she refuses to hire people to share the work load. "I do every job myself because I think of it as an art," she said. She works almost entirely on a computer, shunning traditional artist's tools for their electronic successors. "Anything that's bound for the screen, I do on the screen," she said. If there is a secret to her work, it is simplicity, restraint, and common sense.

```
GraphMode := 2;
SetGraphMode (GraphMode);
```

Modes can be changed as often as desired. When graphics is left for the final time, **CloseGraph** should be used.

Guarding against Initialization Errors

A call to **InitGraph** may not properly complete the initialization process. The predefined function **GraphResult** tests for proper initialization. If everything is correct, **GraphResult** is zero. Otherwise, **GraphResult** returns an integer from −1 to −14, inclusive. These numbers indicate different errors, which are listed in the Turbo Pascal Library Reference Manual.

GraphResult can be used in a fairly direct manner to guard against initialization errors. Since **GraphResult** must be zero to proceed in the graphics mode, an **IF . . . THEN . . . ELSE** statement of the form

```
IF GraphResult = 0 THEN
        .
        .  (program action here)
        .
ELSE
        .
        .  (error message here)
        .
```

can be used. Here, the error message could be

```
writeln ('Could not enter the graphics mode.');
```

It is possible to develop a more elaborate initialization process to be used with each graphics program. It is also possible to develop a procedure to find a specific error that prevents entry into the graphics mode. Let's look at the development of such a procedure.

GraphResult is reset to zero after it is called, so we store the value it returns in the variable ErrorResult. We also declare the variable InitError of type **boolean** and assign it a value by using

```
InitError := (ErrorResult <> 0);
```

The predefined functions **GraphErrorMsg** and **Halt** are used during the termination process when initialization is not successful. **GraphErrorMsg** returns a specific error message; **Halt** causes a return to the operating system. Using these functions, the initialization procedure contains the code

```
ErrorResult := GraphResult;
InitError := (ErrorResult <> 0);
IF InitError THEN
  BEGIN
    writeln ('There is a graphics error.');
    writeln (GraphErrorMsg(ErrorResult));
    writeln ('Program aborted.');
    Halt
  END;
```

A complete initialization procedure is

```
PROCEDURE InitializeGraphics;

  { Given:   Nothing                                       }
  { Task:    Initialize graphics; provide error message    }
  { Return:  Nothing                                       }

VAR
  GraphDriver, GraphMode,
  ErrorResult : integer;
  InitError : boolean;
BEGIN
  GraphDriver := CGA;
  GraphMode := 1;
  InitGraph (GraphDriver, GraphMode, 'C:\TP\BGI');
  ErrorResult := (GraphResult);
  InitError := (ErrorResult <> 0);
  IF InitError THEN
    BEGIN
      writeln ('There is a graphics error.');
      writeln (GraphErrorMsg(ErrorResult));
      writeln ('Program aborted.');
      Halt
    END
END;  { of PROCEDURE InitializeGraphics  }
```

This procedure is called from the main program by

```
InitializeGraphics;
```

If an error message is printed, it can be seen by opening the output window.

A Final Form

By now, you are probably becoming a little impatient with the process of getting into and out of graphics mode. That is only natural. However, once you master the entry and exit problems of graphics, you will be able to move on to creating graphic designs. We summarize the information presented thus far with two typical outlines for a graphics program.

Without using an initialization procedure, we have

```
PROGRAM Graphics;

USES
  Crt, Graph;

VAR
  GraphDriver,
  GraphMode : integer;

BEGIN
  GraphDriver := CGA;
  GraphMode := 1;
  InitGraph (GraphDriver, GraphMode, 'CT\TP\BGI');
  IF GraphResult = 0 THEN
           .
           .  (main part of graphics program here)
           .
  ELSE
           .
           .  (error message here)
           .
  CloseGraph
END.
```

If we use the initialization procedure developed earlier, we have

```
PROGRAM Graphics;

USES
  Crt, Graph;

PROCEDURE InitializeGraphics;
   .
   .  (code for procedure here)
   .

BEGIN  {  Main program  }
  InitializeGraphics;
           .
           .  (main part of program here)
           .
  CloseGraph
END.  {  of program  }
```

We use this form for our graphics programs in this chapter. Generally, we will only refer to the procedure InitializeGraphics and not rewrite the procedure for each program.

Plotting Points

The most basic operation in graphics is plotting a point. For the sake of referencing coordinates, screens have the point with coordinates (0,0) in the upper-left corner. The *x*-axis, or first coordinate, is numbered left to right, and the maximum coordinate value produces a point on the right side of the screen. Thus, if we are in medium resolution with 320 × 200 pixels, the upper-right corner has coordinates (319,0). Note the pixel positions range from 0 to 319.

The vertical coordinates range from 0 to 199, with the numbers increasing as we move down the screen. Thus, (0,50) is above (0,100) on the screen. Coordinates of corners and a typical point are shown in Figure 13.3.

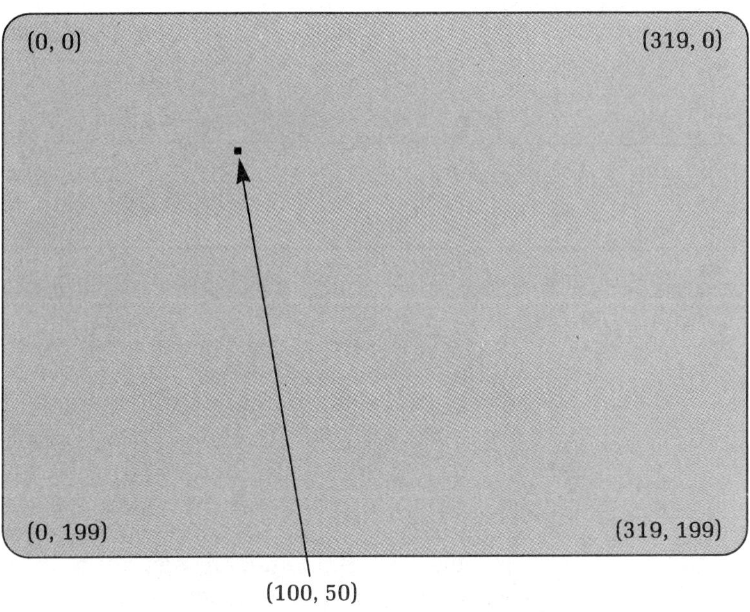

FIGURE 13.3
Screen coordinates in medium resolution with 320 × 200 pixels

The predefined functions **GetMaxX** and **GetMaxY** return the maximum values of X and Y, respectively. These functions are used for centering, determining boundaries, and many other purposes when creating graphic designs.

Points are placed on the screen by the predefined procedure **PutPixel.** The general from of this procedure is

PutPixel (<X Value>, <Y value>, <color>);

Thus, the line of code

```
PutPixel (100, 50, 3);
```

selects the pixel in position (100,50) and colors it with color number 3 of whatever color mode is in effect when the procedure is called. Use of the functions **GetMaxX** and **GetMaxY** to determine screen boundaries is shown in the following example.

■ **EXAMPLE 13.1**

Let's write a short program that plots a point in the middle of your graphics screen.

```
PROGRAM CenterPlot;

USES
  Crt, Graph;

VAR
  MidX, MidY : integer;

PROCEDURE InitializeGraphics;
   .
   .  (code for procedure here)
   .
```

```
BEGIN
  InitializeGraphics;
  SetBkColor (Green);
  MidX := GetMaxX DIV 2;
  MidY := GetMaxY DIV 2;
  PutPixel (MidX, MidY, 1);
  readln;
  CloseGraph
END.  { of program }
```

When you run this program, you will need to look very closely to see the pixel in the middle of the screen. Also notice a **readln** statement is used to hold the screen before returning you to text mode. You must press <Enter> to continue. Later, we will learn to make messages appear with graphics on the screen.

Drawing Lines

The second fundamental operation in graphics is drawing a line. This is accomplished by the predefined procedure **Line.** A typical call to this procedure is

```
Line (0, 0, 100, 100);
```

which causes a line to be drawn from the endpoint (0,0) to the endpoint (100,100). In general, procedure **Line** requires four integer arguments of the form

Line (X1, Y1, X2, Y2);

where (X1,Y1) are coordinates of one endpoint and (X2,Y2) are coordinates of the other endpoint.

In graphics mode, an invisible *current pointer* keeps track of the current pixel position. This is analogous to the cursor visible on the screen in text mode. The current pointer can be moved in two different ways. If we know the specific location to which we want the current pointer to move, we can write

```
MoveTo (X,Y);
```

where (X,Y) is the desired location. We may also move the current pointer relative to its location. Thus, if we want to move it 10 positions to the right and 15 positions down, we write

```
MoveRel (10,15);
```

In general, the predefined procedures for moving the current pointer are

MoveTo (X,Y);

and

MoveRel (DeltaX, DeltaY);

where X, Y, DeltaX, and DeltaY are integer variables. The variables X and Y range from 0 to **GetMaxX** and **GetMaxY**, respectively. Ranges for the arguments of **MoveRel** are

–GetMaxX < DeltaX < **GetMaxX**
–GetMaxY < DeltaY < **GetMaxY**

A negative argument for DeltaX moves the current pointer to the left from its current position; a positive argument moves it to the right. A negative argument for DeltaY moves the current pointer up from its current position; a positive argument moves it down. Moving the current pointer off the screen using **MoveRel** does not cause an error, but this possibility can be averted by using appropriate boundary values.

A second procedure for drawing lines is the predefined procedure **LineTo.** The general form of this procedure is

> **LineTo** (X,Y);

where X and Y are integer variables. This causes a line to be drawn from the current pointer to the point with coordinates (X,Y). The uses of these procedures are shown in the following example.

■ **EXAMPLE 13.2**

Let's see how a line with the endpoints (0,30) and (100,30) can be drawn using both the **Line** and **LineTo** procedures. Using the **Line** procedure, this can be accomplished with

```
Line (0, 30, 100, 30);
```

Using the **LineTo** procedure, we first position the current pointer at one end of the desired line using **MoveTo** and then finish the task using **LineTo** as follows:

```
MoveTo (0,30);
LineTo (100,30);
```

The **Line** procedure does not cause the current pointer to be moved. However, **LineTo** does cause the current pointer to be positioned at the point given by the coordinates that are arguments of the **LineTo** procedure. Thus, the previous call to

```
LineTo (100,30)
```

will leave the current pointer at (100,30).

A third predefined procedure can be used to draw a line segment. **LineRel** causes a line to be drawn from the current pointer to an endpoint with coordinates that are determined in relation to the current pointer. Thus, if we want a line to go from the current pointer to a point 20 pixels to the right and 30 pixels down, we write

```
LineRel (20,30);
```

LineRel moves the current pointer to the position indicated by its arguments. The general form for **LineRel** is

> **LineRel** (X,Y);

The advantage of this procedure is that we do not need to know the coordinates of the new endpoint. We only need to know where they are relative to the current pointer. **MoveRel** and **LineRel** are useful for drawing a shape with a starting point that can be changed, so the same shape can be drawn in different locations on the screen.

Variations of a Line

All lines drawn thus far have been drawn in a default mode. Turbo Pascal allows the user to specify three characteristics of a line—style, pattern, and thickness—which are specified by using the predefined procedure **SetLineStyle** of the form

SetLineStyle (<style>, <pattern>, <thickness>);

The line styles available for this procedure are illustrated in Table 13.5.

TABLE 13.5
Line styles

Style	Value	Result
SolidLn	0	________________________________
DottedLn	1	....
CenterLn	2	— — — — — — — — — — — — — — — —
DashedLn	3	------------------------------
UserBitLn	4	(result varies)

All arguments of **SetLineStyle** are variables of type **word.** If the variable declaration section includes

```
VAR
  Style : word;
```

we can use either

```
Style := DottedLn;
```

or

```
Style := 1;
```

to draw a dotted line.

The style **UserBitLn** allows the user to specify a particular 16-bit pattern. This option will not be developed here. The interested reader is directed to the Turbo Pascal Library Reference Manual.

A zero value is always used for the pattern argument. Nonzero values must be hexadecimal values, which specify the bit pattern when the first argument <style> is **UserBitLn.**

The third argument <thickness> can have a value of either 1 or 3. A value of 1 causes a line to be drawn that is one pixel wide. A value of 3 causes a line to be drawn that is three pixels wide. The predefined constants **NormWidth** and **ThickWidth** may also be used. The next example illustrates several methods of using **SetLineStyle.**

EXAMPLE 13.3

Let's illustrate different ways to specify drawing a dotted line with extra thickness (three pixels). If we assume the variable declaration section includes

```
VAR
  Style, Pattern, Thickness : word;
```

then each of the following sections of code is appropriate:

1.
```
Style := DottedLn;
Pattern := 0;
Thickness := ThickWidth;
SetLineStyle (Style, Pattern, Thickness);
```

2.
```
Style := DottedLn;
Pattern := 0;
Thickness := 3;
SetLineStyle (Style, Pattern, Thickness);
```

3.
```
Style := 1;
Pattern := 0;
Thickness := 3;
SetLineStyle (Style, Pattern, Thickness);
```

4.
```
SetLineStyle (DottedLn, 0, ThickWidth);
```

5.
```
SetLineStyle (1, 0, 3);
```

As you can see, several variations for using **SetLineStyle** are available. In general, code is more readable when identifiers are used as shown in method (1). The line style you define remains in effect until you define a different setting or until you leave the graphics mode by using **CloseGraph.**

Clearing the Screen

Eventually, we will want to clear the screen while in graphics mode. This is accomplished by a call to the procedure **ClearDevice,** which uses no arguments and appears as a single line of code:

```
ClearDevice;
```

We conclude this section with a short graphics program that draws a border around the screen and then draws two diagonals in the rectangle that borders the screen. A variety of line styles and colors are used. Note a **readln** statement is used to stop the program. When the program is run, <Enter> is pressed to continue. Later, we will examine different ways of stopping and slowing down the graphics display.

A first-level pseudocode development for this program is

1. Initialize graphics
2. Set colors
3. Determine screen size
4. Draw the diagonals
5. Draw the border

A second-level development is

1. Initialize graphics
2. Set colors
   2.1 set background color
   2.2 set current color
3. Determine screen size
   3.1 get maximum width (X)
   3.2 get maximum height (Y)
4. Draw the diagonals
   4.1 draw first diagonal
   4.2 position pointer
   4.3 draw second diagonal
5. Draw the border
   5.1 set style
   5.2 draw side borders
   5.3 change line style
   5.4 draw top and bottom borders

A complete program for this problem follows.

```
PROGRAM LineExample;

{  This program uses the Line and LineTo procedures to draw    }
{  diagonals on the screen and then draw a border around the   }
{  screen. Different line styles and widths are used.          }

USES
  Crt, Graph;

VAR
  MaxX, MaxY : integer;

{*************************************************************}

PROCEDURE InitializeGraphics;

  {  Given:   Nothing                                           }
  {  Task:    Initialize graphics. Provide error message        }
  {                for unsuccessful initialization.             }
  {  Return:  Nothing                                           }

  VAR
    GraphDriver, GraphMode,
    ErrorResult : integer;
    InitError : boolean;
  BEGIN
    GraphDriver := CGA;
    GraphMode := 1;
    InitGraph (GraphDriver, GraphMode, 'C:\TP\BGI');
    ErrorResult := GraphResult;
    InitError := (ErrorResult <> 0);
    IF InitError THEN
      BEGIN
        writeln ('There is a graphics error.');
        writeln (GraphErrorMsg(ErrorResult));
        writeln ('Program aborted.');
        Halt
      END
  END;  {  of PROCEDURE InitializeGraphics  }

{*************************************************************}

PROCEDURE GetScreenSize (VAR MaxX, MaxY : integer);

  {  Given:   Nothing                                           }
  {  Task:    Get screen limits for X and Y.                    }
  {  Return:  Maximum values for X and Y                        }

  BEGIN
    MaxX := GetMaxX;
    MaxY := GetMaxY
  END;  {  of PROCEDURE GetScreenSize  }

{*************************************************************}

PROCEDURE DrawDiagonals (MaxX, MaxY : integer);
```

```
  {  Given:    Screen limits for X and Y                         }
  {  Task:     Draw both diagonals                               }
  {  Return:   Nothing                                           }

  BEGIN
    Line (0, 0, MaxX, MaxY);            {  Draw one diagonal  }
    readln;                               {  Hold the screen  }
    MoveTo (0, MaxY);
    LineTo (MaxX, 0);             {  Draw the other diagonal  }
    readln                                {  Hold the screen  }
  END;  {  of PROCEDURE DrawDiagonals  }

{************************************************************}

PROCEDURE DrawBorder (MaxX, MaxY : integer);

  {  Given:    Screen limits for X and Y                         }
  {  Task:     Draw the screen border                            }
  {  Return:   Nothing                                           }

  VAR
    Style, Thickness : word;
  BEGIN

    {  Draw the right-side border  }
    Style := DottedLn;                    {  Change the style  }
    Thickness := NormWidth;
    SetLineStyle (Style, 0, Thickness);
    LineTo (MaxX, MaxY);             {  Draw the right border  }
    readln;                               {  Hold the screen  }

    {  Draw the left-side border  }
    MoveTo (0,0);                      {  Position the cursor  }
    LineTo (0, MaxY);                   {  Draw the left border  }
    readln;

    {  Draw the bottom border  }
    SetColor (2);  {  Switch from LightCyan to LightMagenta  }
    Thickness := ThickWidth;            {  Now use thick width  }
    Style := CenterLn;               {  Change the style again  }
    SetLineStyle (Style, 0, Thickness);
    LineTo (MaxX, MaxY);             {  Draw the bottom border  }
    readln;

    {  Draw the top border  }
    Style := DashedLn;                     {  Try a new style  }
    SetLineStyle (Style, 0, Thickness);
    Line (0, 0, MaxX, 0);               {  Draw the top border  }
    readln
  END;  {  of PROCEDURE DrawBorder  }

{************************************************************}

BEGIN  {  Main program  }
  InitializeGraphics;
  SetBkColor (Green);
  SetColor (1);
  GetScreenSize (MaxX, MaxY);
  DrawDiagonals (MaxX, MaxY);
  DrawBorder (MaxX, MaxY);
  CloseGraph
END.  {  of main program  }
```

Output from this program (without color) is

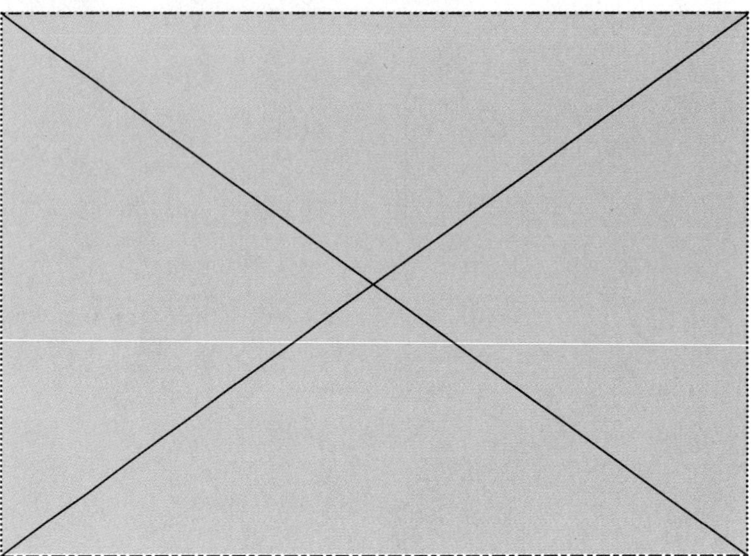

Exercises 13.1

1. Explain why **InitGraph** (CGA, GraphMode) and **InitGraph** (GraphDriver, 2) are not valid calls to the procedure **InitGraph.**
2. Discuss the advantages and disadvantages of using background constants Black, Blue, and so forth, rather than their ordinals (0, 1, . . .), as arguments for **SetBkColor.**
3. Write a "graphics shell" that can be used as the basis for all of your graphics programs. This shell should include the following:
   a.
   ```
   USES
     Crt, Graph;
   ```
   b. An initialization procedure that contains:
      i. The definition and initialization of GraphDriver and GraphMode
      ii. An **InitGraph** statement
      iii. An **IF . . . THEN** statement for displaying an appropriate initialization error message
   c. A **CloseGraph** statement

   Save this shell, and make modifications to it when you want to write a graphics program.
4. Write a test program to determine what values are returned by **GetMaxX** and **GetMaxY** for the screen you are using.
5. Use the functions **GetMaxX** and **GetMaxY** to locate the center of your screen. After finding the pixel that represents this center, do the following.
   a. Put a nine-pixel square in the center of the screen.
   b. Draw horizontal and vertical lines through this square.

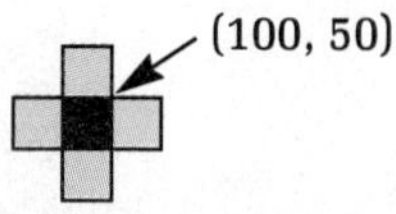

6. A single pixel is hard to see. Solve this problem by writing a procedure to plot a point that is actually five pixels with the indicated pixel in the middle. Thus, if you wish to see the point (100,50), your procedure will actually display the five pixels shown in the margin.

7. Write a test program that shows the default colors available when you enter the graphics mode using

```
GraphDriver := detect;
InitGraph (GraphDriver, GraphMode, 'C\TP\BGI');
```

8. Use nested loops in a short program to display two thick lines of each color available on your screen.

9. Write a program that does the following.
   a. Use a loop and **LineRel** to fill your screen with horizontal lines that are 10 pixels apart.
   b. Use a loop and **Line** to fill your screen with vertical lines that are 10 pixels apart.

10. Use **MoveTo** and **LineRel** to draw a 10 pixel × 10 pixel square with the upper-left vertex at (100,100).

11. Write a program that displays 10 pixel × 10 pixel squares on a diagonal from the upper-left corner of the screen to the bottom of the screen (probably at (199,199).

12. Modify your program in Exercise 11 by changing the color of the squares on the diagonal.

13. Discuss the differences among the procedures **Line**, **LineTo**, and **LineRel**.

14. Use **GetMaxX** and **GetMaxY** in a program that allows you to normalize the screen in the following manner.
   (1) The normalized origin is in the lower-left corner of the screen.
   (2) The screen range of the first coordinate of a point is from 0 to 1, moving left to right.
   (3) The screen range of the second coordinate of a point is from 0 to 1, moving up the screen.

   The normalized corners of your screen are then

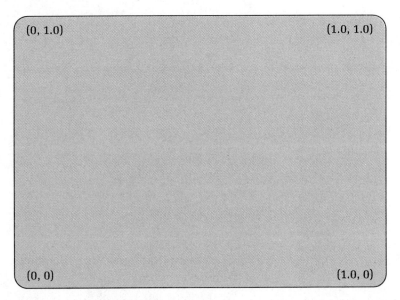

and the screen center is (0.5,0.5). (*Hint:* If you use LargestX := **GetMaxX** and LargestY := **GetMaxY**, the normalized center is (round(0.5 * LargestX), round(0.5 * LargestY)).

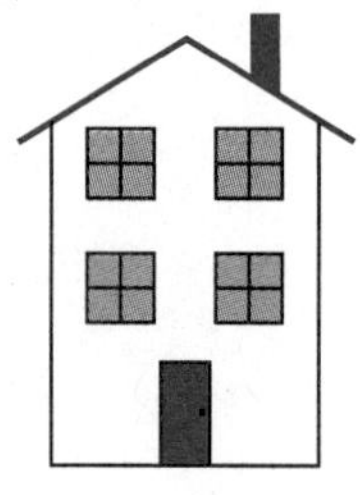

15. Modify Exercise 9 so different line styles and widths are used to make the grid. Include examples of different styles and widths used in the same grid.
16. Use procedures to create a "house," as shown in the margin. Vary the colors for the roof, chimney, windows, and door.
17. Write a procedure that creates a design by using only the relative movements **LineRel** and **MoveRel**. Use this procedure in a program to show how the design can be moved around the screen by specifying different starting positions.

■ 13.2 Graphics Figures

Several procedures in Turbo Pascal allow the user to construct geometric figures. In this section, we will see how to use a single procedure to display a rectangle, circle, arc, or ellipse.

Rectangles

A rectangle is determined by four vertices and can be displayed by using a sequence of **Line**, **LineRel**, or **LineTo** procedures. Thus, a rectangle with an upper-left vertex of (10,10) and dimensions of 100 × 50 can be shown by

```
ClearDevice;
MoveTo (10,10);
LineTo (110,10);
LineTo (110,60);
LineTo (10,60);
LineTo (10,10);
```

When this segment of code is executed from graphics mode, the display shown in Figure 13.4 results.

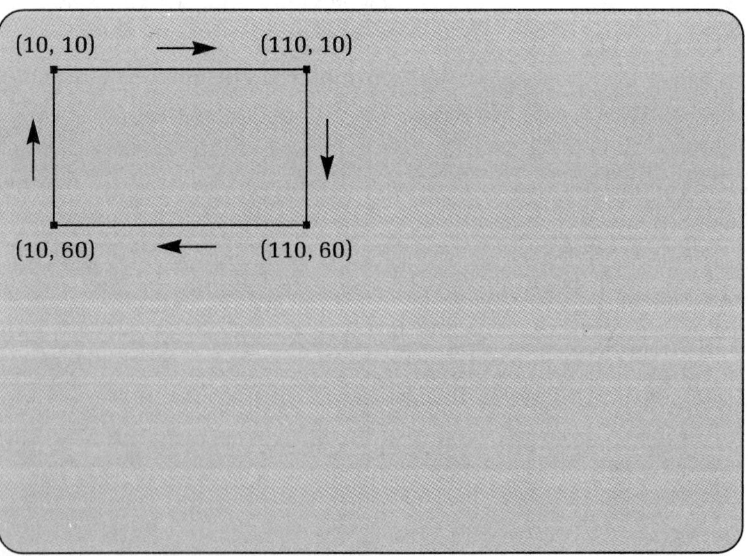

FIGURE 13.4
A rectangle 100 × 50

Fortunately, the procedure **Rectangle** performs the same task. Using this procedure.

```
Rectangle (10, 10, 110, 60);
```

causes the same figure to be displayed. The general form of procedure **Rectangle** is

Rectangle (X1, Y1, X2, Y2);

where (X1,Y1) is the upper-left vertex and (X2,Y2) is the lower-right vertex. Variables X1, Y1, X2, and Y2 are of type **integer** with the respective ranges

0 < X1 < X2 < **GetMaxX**
0 < Y1 < Y2 < **GetMaxY**

Aspect Ratio

Looking at your 100 × 50 rectangle, you probably notice the length (100) is less than twice the width (50). To see even more clearly that displays may be different from what you expect, draw a square of side length 150 by using

```
Rectangle (0, 0, 150, 150);
```

When this line of code is executed, the display shown in Figure 13.5 results.

FIGURE 13.5
A square of side length 150

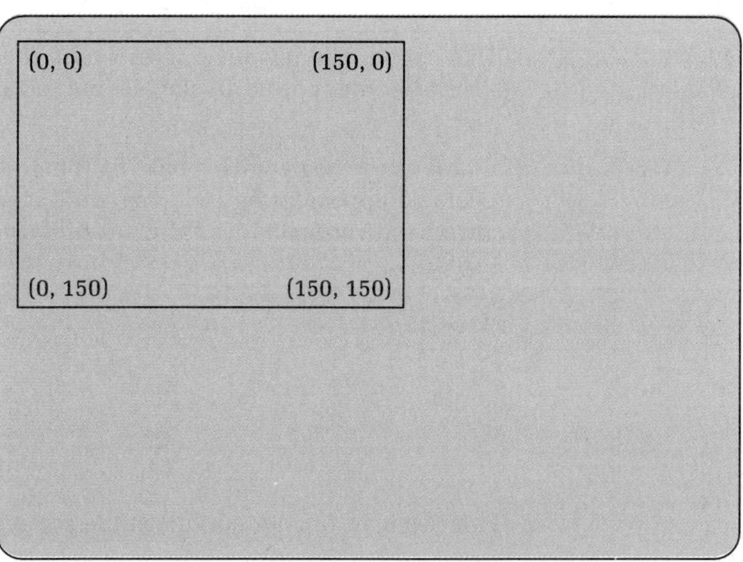

FIGURE 13.6
Shape of a pixel

(a) length > width

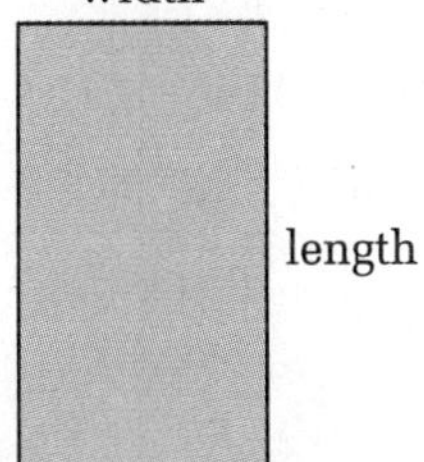

(b) length < width

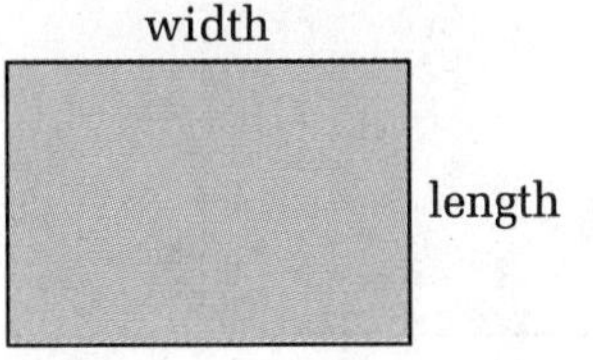

The distortion from the expected results arises from the fact that pixels are not square. They are rectangles with lengths and widths that differ according to what computer you are using. Thus, a pixel can be envisioned as shown in Figure 13.6.

We can correct for this distortion by using the procedure **GetAspectRatio**. The general form of this procedure is

GetAspectRatio (Xasp, Yasp);

where Xasp and Yasp are variables of type **word.** The ratio of these variables can then be used to correct the distortion, so squares look square and rectangles are proportional. The segment of code

```
GetAspectRatio (Xasp, Yasp);
AspRatio := Xasp / Yasp;
```

produces a value of approximately 6/5 (or 5/6), which can then be used to adjust one pair of sides of a rectangle to eliminate distortion. To illustrate, consider the segment of code

```
GetAspectRatio (Xasp, Yasp);
AspRatio := (Xasp / Yasp);
X1 := 10;
Y1 := 10;
DeltaX := 100;
DeltaY := round(100 * AspRatio);  {  AspRatio is a real  }
X2 := X1 + DeltaX;
Y2 := Y1 + DeltaY;
Rectangle (X1, Y1, X2, Y2);
```

When this code is run, a square of horizontal side length 100 is produced by starting at coordinates (10,10) and going clockwise through (110,10), (110,Y2), (10,Y2), and (10,10). The square now looks like a square. [You may have to use AspRatio := Yasp/Xasp if your pixels appear as shown in Figure 13.6(b)].

An examination of the previous code reveals the vertical (Y) coordinates have been adjusted so the change in Y looks the same as the change in X. The horizontal (X) values are absolute, and the vertical (Y) values are relative, as determined by the aspect ratio. This is illustrated in the following example.

EXAMPLE 13.4

Let's construct a rectangle with a base that appears to be twice its height. Recall our earlier attempt to display such a rectangle used the line of code

```
Rectangle (10, 10, 110, 60);
```

to draw a rectangle with a base of 100 and a height of 50. We can now make this rectangle appear to be twice as wide as it is high by using the aspect ratio to correct the vertical sides for distortion as follows:

```
GetAspectRatio (Xasp, Yasp);
AspRatio := (Xasp / Yasp);
X1 := 10;
Y1 := 10;
DeltaX := 100;
DeltaY := round(50 * AspRatio);  {  Correct distortion  }
X2 := X1 + DeltaX;
Y2 := Y1 + DeltaY;
Rectangle (X1, Y1, X2, Y2);
```

This segment of code produces the screen display shown in Figure 13.7.

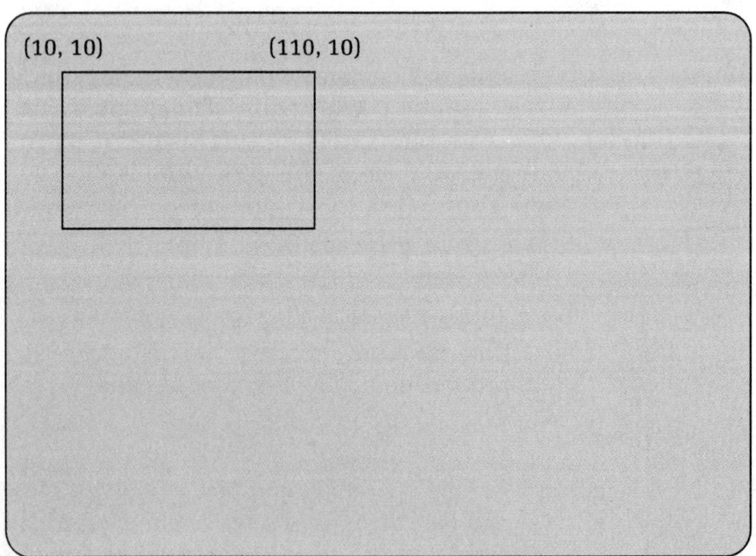

FIGURE 13.7
Rectangle using aspect ratio

Using delay

Some method is required to hold the graphics display on the screen long enough to enable the user to see what is being displayed. Thus far, we have been using the **readln** statement for this purpose. Since no message appears on the screen, we assume the user knows to press <Enter> to continue.

Another method for holding the screen display is the procedure **delay.** This is a procedure in the **Crt** unit, not in the **Graph** unit. The form of the **delay** procedure is

delay (LengthOfPause);

where LengthOfPause is a variable of type **word.** The value of LenghOfPause is the approximate number of milliseconds the computer pauses before executing the subsequent line of code. Thus, if we want a display to appear for approximately one second, we use the code

```
LengthOfPause := 1000;
delay (LengthOfPause);
```

The **delay** feature allows the user to create animation. For example, we can make a square appear to move across the screen by the following process:

1. Select a color palette
2. Select a background color
3. Select a current color
4. Create a moving square by following these steps
   4.1 set coordinates
   4.2 display a square
   4.3 pause
   4.4 erase the square
   4.5 repeat this process until the motion is to be terminated

The program in the next example creates animation.

■ EXAMPLE 13.5

This example uses the **delay** procedure to provide our first look at animation. Note that a constant is used to define LengthOfPause. Given this definition, we can easily change the rate at which the object moves. The following program moves a square of side length 20 across the top of the screen.

```
PROGRAM Animation;

{  This program demonstrates simple animation.  A square        }
{  appears to move horizontally by a sequence of drawing the    }
{  square, erasing the square, and then redrawing the square    }
{  to the right of the previous position.                       }

USES
  Crt, Graph;

CONST
  LengthOfPause = 100;
  SideLength = 10;

VAR
  X1, Y1, X2, Y2 : word;
  AspRatio : real;
  DeltaX, DeltaY : integer;
```

```
{*****************************************************************}

PROCEDURE InitializeGraphics;

  {  Given:   Nothing                                             }
  {  Task:    Initialize graphics. Provide error message for      }
  {                unsuccessful initialization.                   }
  {  Return:  Nothing                                             }

  VAR
    GraphDriver, GraphMode,
    ErrorResult : integer;
    InitError : boolean;
  BEGIN
    GraphDriver := CGA;
    GraphMode := 1;
    InitGraph (GraphDriver, GraphMode, 'C:\TP\BGI');
    ErrorResult := GraphResult;
    InitError := (ErrorResult <> 0);
    IF InitError THEN
      BEGIN
        writeln ('There is a graphics error.');
        writeln (GraphErrorMsg(ErrorResult));
        writeln ('Program aborted.');
        Halt
      END
  END;  {  of PROCEDURE InitializeGraphics  }

{*****************************************************************}

PROCEDURE SetAspectRatio (VAR AspRatio : real);

  {  Given:   Nothing                                             }
  {  Task:    Set the aspect ratio                                }
  {  Return:  The aspect ratio                                    }

  VAR
    Xasp, Yasp : word;
  BEGIN
    GetAspectRatio (Xasp, Yasp);
    AspRatio := Yasp / Xasp
  END;  {  of PROCEDURE SetAspectRatio  }

{*****************************************************************}

BEGIN  {  Main program  }
  InitializeGraphics;
  SetBkColor (0);
  SetAspectRatio (AspRatio);

  {  Initialize the first square  }
  X1 := 0;
  Y1 := 0;
  DeltaX := SideLength;
  DeltaY := round(SideLength * AspRatio);
  X2 := X1 + DeltaX;
  Y2 := Y1 + DeltaY;

  {  Display and erase squares across the screen  }
  REPEAT
    SetColor (1);
    Rectangle (X1, Y1, X2, Y2);
```

```
      delay (LengthOfPause);
      SetColor (0);                       { Erase the square }
      Rectangle (X1, Y1, X2, Y2);
      X1 := X1 + DeltaX;
      X2 := X2 + DeltaX
    UNTIL X2 > GetMaxY;
    readln;
    CloseGraph
END. { of main program }
```

Circles

The procedure **Circle** in Turbo Pascal allows the user to display a circle. The correct form of this procedure is

Circle (Xcoor, Ycoor, Radius);

where Xcoor and Ycoor are variables of type **integer** and represent the coordinates of the center of the circle. Radius is of type **word**, and its value is the number of pixels contained in the radius of the circle. To illustrate, a circle at the center of the screen with a radius of 50 can be displayed by using

```
Xcoor := GetMaxX DIV 2;
Ycoor := GetMaxY DIV 2;
Radius := 50;
Circle (Xcoor, Ycoor, Radius);
```

This segment of code produces the circle shown in Figure 13.8.

The circle is drawn in the current color, and the interior of the circle is in the background color. Later, we will see how to vary the color of the interior of a circle.

Note the circle displayed when **Circle** is called looks like a circle. No distortion is caused by the difference in the width and height of a pixel because the aspect ratio is automatically applied when **Circle** is called. The following example illustrates multiple use of the **Circle** procedure.

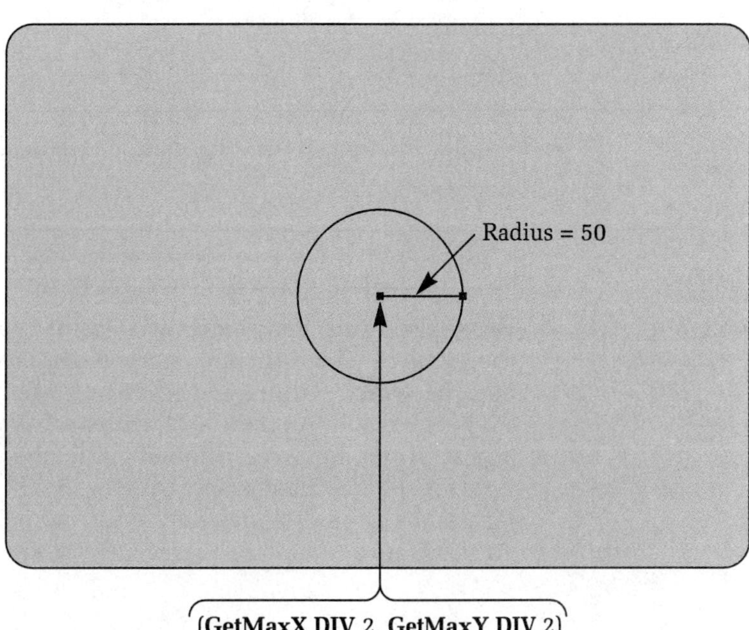

FIGURE 13.8
A circle with a radius of 50

■ EXAMPLE 13.6

In this example, we use the **Circle** procedure to display concentric circles, all of which are centered at the middle of the screen. We increase the radius by 20 pixels each time. The segment of code that accomplishes this task is

```
Xcoor := GetMaxX DIV 2;
Ycoor := GetMaxY DIV 2;
Radius := 20;
REPEAT
  Circle (Xcoor, Ycoor, Radius);
  delay (100);
  Radius := Radius + 20
UNTIL Radius > GetMaxY DIV 2;
```

After running this segment of code, the screen display is

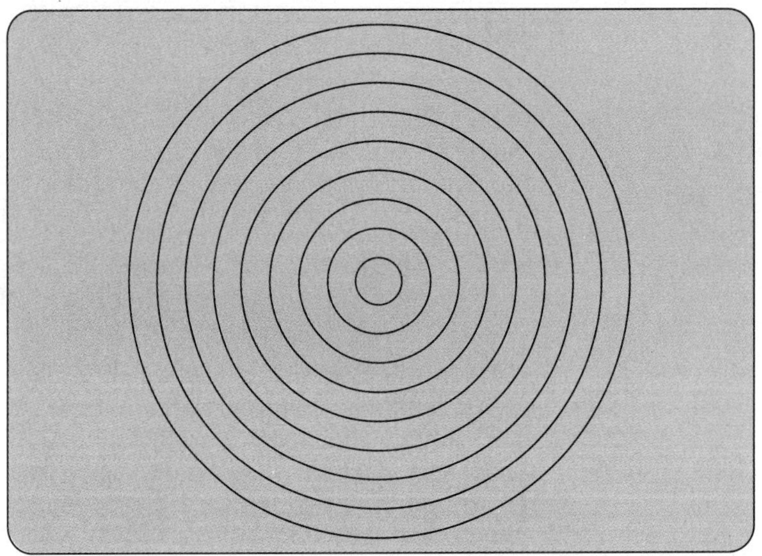

Arcs

The fundamental portion of any curve in two dimensions is an arc. Turbo Pascal provides the procedure **Arc**, which allows the user to draw arcs. The form of the **Arc** procedure is

Arc (Xcoor, Ycoor, AngleStart, AngleFinish, Radius);

Here, Xcoor and Ycoor are variables of type **integer** and represent the center of the circle of which the arc is a portion. AngleStart, AngleFinish, and Radius are of type **word.** Radius is the radius of the circle of which arc is a portion. AngleStart and AngleFinish represent, respectively, the initial and terminal angles of the arc. An AngleStart of 0° means the arc begins horizontally to the right of the specified center (in the 3 o'clock position). An AngleFinish of 90° means the arc ends above the center and is formed in a counterclockwise manner. To illustrate

```
Arc (100, 100, 0, 90, 50);
```

produces the arc shown in Figure 13.9.

FIGURE 13.9
Arc (100, 100, 0, 90, 50)

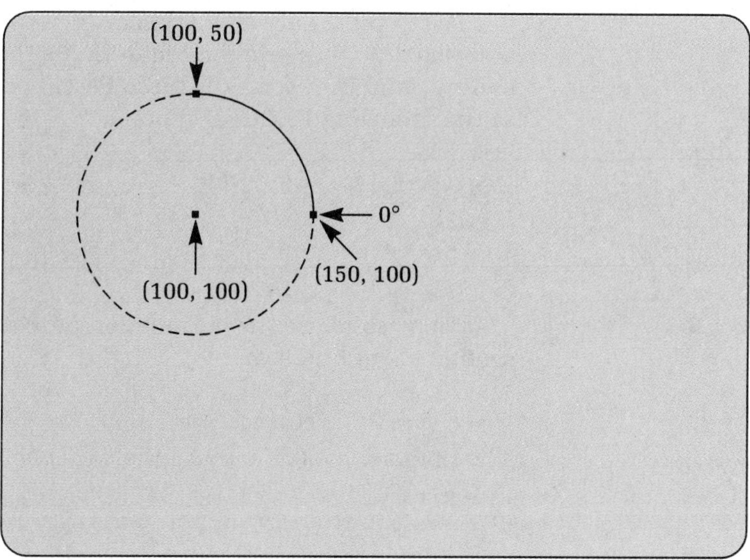

As with circles, the arc is drawn in the current color. Also note arcs do not need to be adjusted for distortion because the aspect ratio is automatically applied when **Arc** is called.

Elaborate curves can be displayed by joining the ends of arcs of differing radii. It may also be necessary to join the ends of an arc with a line segment. For these

A NOTE OF INTEREST

Impact of Computers on Art

Dana J. Lamb recently discussed the impact of computers on the arts in an article appearing in *Academic Computing.* Among other things, she reported part of a conversation held with Alice Jones, a freelance graphic designer, a member of a summer arts program studying developments in full-color graphics on personal computers. When Jones was asked about the use of computers in her professional pursuits, she indicated her study led her to believe the time required to produce a typical paste-up could be reduced by as much as 75 percent, depending upon the proficiency of the graphic artist. She pointed out that the traditional means of producing art required the teamwork of a graphic artist, typesetter, copy camera operator, photographer, and/or illustrator. The logistics of even the simplest paste-up of a few black and white photographs often required days in transit as copy was typeset at one location and photos and illustrations were created and then reduced or enlarged at two other locations—all traveling from each place of business to another while the graphic designer sits waiting. Jones observed that this dispersion of design components has been suddenly unified and put into the hands of the designer.

Later in the article, Lamb addressed the issue of how artists perceive the computer. According to Lamb, the opinions of those in the art world can be divided into three major groups:

1. Those who deny the computer has any legitimate place in the creation of art
2. Those who believe the computer should be included in the realm of traditional and/or nontraditional tools in the creation of art
3. Those who believe the computer, together with its fundamental structure, is an art medium unto itself

Lamb concludes her article with the following paragraph:

It is easy to forget that we are witnessing the infancy of this medium in relationship to the arts because of its phenomenal growth in eight years. Artists have been using computers since the 1950s but up to the last decade were viewed as oddities with few arenas to exhibit or share their work. Those days are over, and as the image of these machines becomes less a philosophical issue and simply another tool in the creative process, we can move on to develop the "clear path" between the visual concept and final product espoused.

purposes, procedure **GetArcCoords** returns the coordinates of three points associated with an arc: the center (X,Y), the starting point (Xstart,Ystart), and the ending point (Xend,Yend). Turbo Pascal provides the predefined **ArcCoordsType** as the following **RECORD** type:

```
TYPE
  ArcCoordsType = RECORD
                    X, Y : integer;
                    Xstart, Ystart : integer;
                    Xend, Yend : integer
                  END;
```

If we wish to use the information provided by **GetArcCoords**, your declaration section should include

```
VAR
  ArcCoords : ArcCoordsType;
```

The program could then use the variable ArcCoords in a manner such as

```
GetArcCoords (ArcCoords);
WITH ArcCoords DO
  BEGIN
    .
    .        (Use coordinates here)
    .
  END;
```

For example, we can join the endpoints of an arc by using

```
GetArcCoords (ArcCoords);
WITH ArcCoords DO
  Line (Xend, Yend, Xstart, Ystart);
```

The following segment of code displays an arc that is one-quarter of a circle and then joins the endpoints after a slight delay:

```
SetColor (2);
SetBkColor (Green);
Arc (100, 100, 0, 90, 50);
delay (1000);
GetArcCoords (ArcCoords);
WITH ArcCoords DO
  Line (Xend, Yend, Xstart, Ystart);
```

This code produces the screen display shown in Figure 13.10.

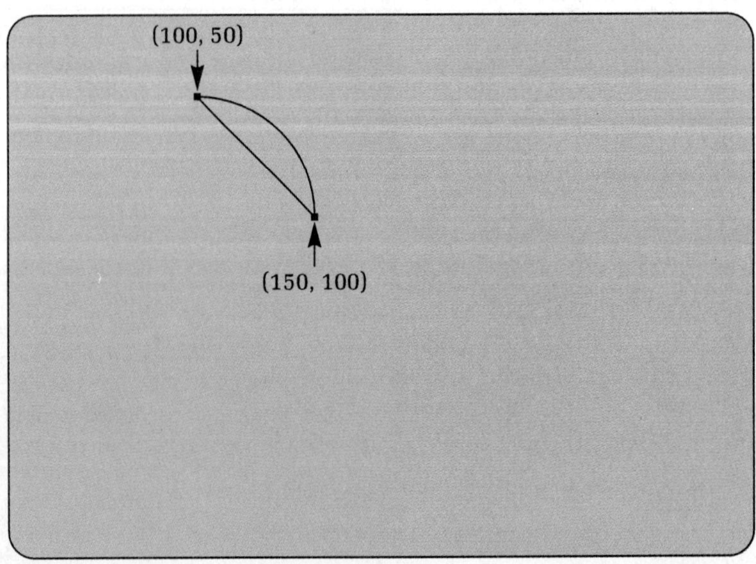

FIGURE 13.10
Arc with chord drawn

Ellipses

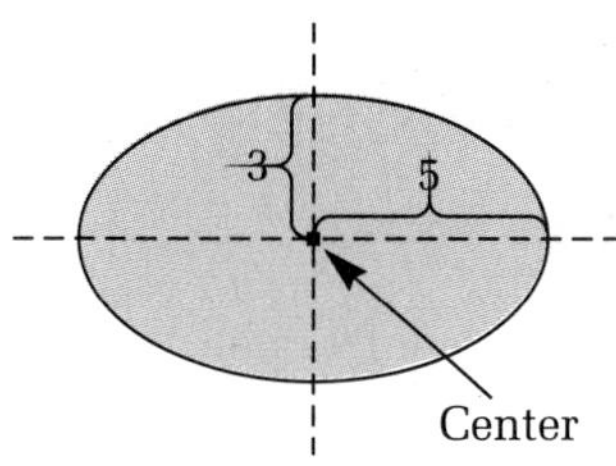

FIGURE 13.11
An ellipse with a major axis of 10 and a minor axis of 6

The final geometric shape we consider is that of an ellipse. An ellipse differs from a circle in that it has a major axis and a minor axis, not just a radius. An example of an ellipse is shown in Figure 13.11.

The **Ellipse** procedure in Turbo Pascal is used to display an ellipse. The form of this procedure is

> **Ellipse** (Xcoor, Ycoor, AngleStart, AngleFinish, Xrad, Yrad);

Here, Xcoor and Ycoor are variables of type **integer** and represent the center of the ellipse; that is, they are coordinates of the point of intersection of the major and minor axes.

AngleStart and AngleFinish are variables of type **word** and represent the same functions they do for the **Arc** procedure. Thus, the portion of the ellipse that is displayed begins at AngleStart with a value of 0°, which is horizontally to the right of (Xcoor, Ycoor). The ellipse (or portion of it) is sketched in a counterclockwise manner until an angle of AngleFinish is reached. A complete ellipse is displayed anytime AngleFinish – AngleStart = 360°. Typically, the user begins at 0° and finishes at 360°.

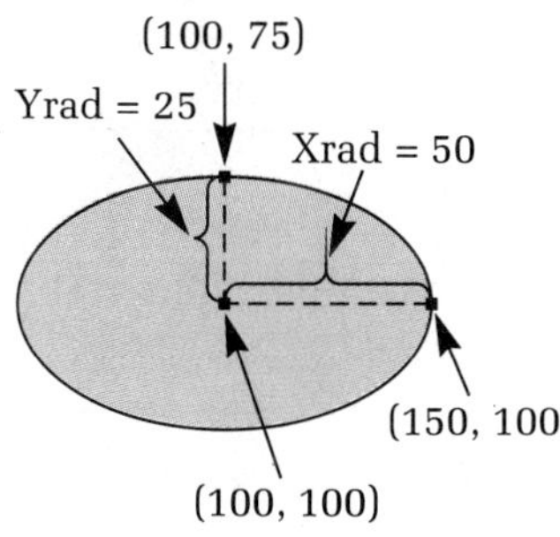

FIGURE 13.12
The ellipse displayed by **Ellipse** (100, 100, 0, 360, 50, 25)

Xrad and Yrad represent the horizontal axis and vertical axis, respectively. Xrad is the distance in pixels from the center of the ellipse to the point on the ellipse that is a horizontal distance Xrad pixels to the right of (Xcoor,Ycoor). This point is (Xcoor + Xrad,Ycoor). Yrad works in a similar manner in the vertical direction. To illustrate, the ellipse generated by

```
Ellipse (100, 100, 0, 360, 50, 25);
```

is shown in Figure 13.12.

The ellipse is displayed in the current color. The interior of the ellipse is drawn in the background color.

Using parts of ellipses allows us to work with arcs that are not parts of circles, which provides greater flexibility in creating designs. As with arcs, information about an ellipse or a portion of an ellipse can be retrieved by using the procedure **GetArcCoords**, which returns the center (X,Y), starting point (Xstart,Ystart), and ending point (Xend,Yend) of the portion of the ellipse last drawn. To illustrate, the following segment of code draws the top half of an ellipse and then draws a line connecting the endpoints:

```
Ellipse (100, 100, 0, 180, 50, 25);
GetArcCoords (ArcCoords);
WITH ArcCoords DO
  Line (Xend, Yend, Xstart, Ystart);
```

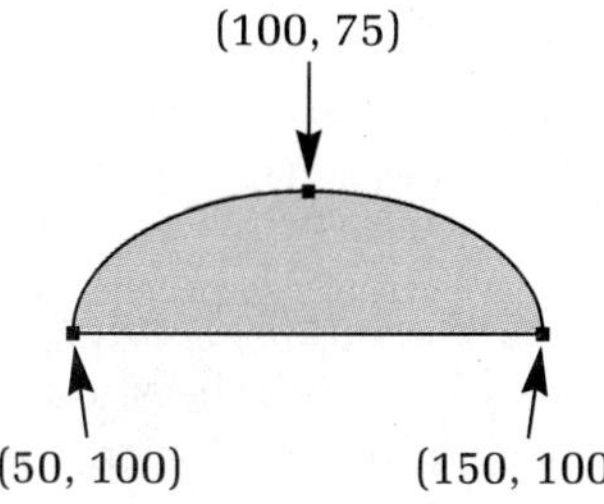

FIGURE 13.13
Display using **GetArcCoords**

The display created by this code is shown in Figure 13.13.

The procedures discussed in this section are summarized in Table 13.6.

Exercises 13.2

1. Recall how the procedure **LineTo** is used to display a rectangle with dimensions of 100 × 50 and an upper-left vertex at (10,10).
   a. Show how this rectangle can be produced using the **Line** procedure.
   b. Show how this rectangle can be produced using the **LineRel** procedure.
2. Write a test program to display the values of the arguments used in the procedure **GetAspectRatio** as well as the aspect ratio found when the quotient of these arguments is computed.

TABLE 13.6
Procedures for geometric designs

Form and Parameters	Result of Call
`Rectangle (X1, Y1, X2, Y2);`	Displays a rectangle with upper-left vertex (X1,Y1) and lower-right-vertex (X2,Y2).
`GetAspectRatio (Xasp, Yasp);`	Returns values that can be used to correct for distortion due to nonsquare pixels.
`delay (LengthOfPause);`	Causes a display to remain on the screen for LengthOfPause milliseconds.
`Circle (Xcoor, Ycoor, Radius);`	Displays a circle with a center given by (Xcoor, Ycoor) and a radius of Radius.
`Arc (Xcoor, Ycoor, AngleStart, AngleFinish, Radius);`	Displays an arc as a portion of a circle with a center given by (Xcoor,Ycoor) and a radius of Radius. The arc begins at AngleStart and terminates at AngleFinish, moving counterclockwise. An AngleStart of 0° is horizontally to the right of (Xcoor,Ycoor) in the 3 o'clock position.
`GetArcCoords (ArcCoords);`	ArcCoords is of the predefined **RECORD** type **ArcCoordsType**. The procedure **GetArcCoords** returns the center (X,Y), starting point (Xstart,Ystart), and ending point (Xend,Yend) of an arc.
`Ellipse (Xcoor, Ycoor, AngleStart, AngleFinish, Xrad, Yrad);`	Displays all or a portion of an ellipse with a center given by (Xcoor,Ycoor). The ellipse begins at AngleStart and moves counterclockwise to AngleFinish. Xrad is the horizontal distance from the center of the ellipse to the point on the ellipse that is Xrad pixels to the right of (Xcoor,Ycoor); Yrad is the same in the vertical direction.

3. Explain how a conversion can be made that allows you to think of the argument for **delay** in terms of seconds rather than milliseconds. Thus, the form of the **delay** procedure would become

```
delay (NumSeconds);
```

4. Recall a square moved across the top of the screen in Example 13.5.
   a. Write a program that causes a square to move down the diagonal from the upper-left vertex to the lower-right vertex.
   b. Discuss why the animation does not appear to be "smooth." Make changes in the program to provide better animation.
5. Expand on Exercise 4 by moving a square across the top of the screen and then moving a circle across the bottom of the screen.
6. Use squares and circles to create a border for your screen. You can accomplish this by varying Exercises 4 and 5 so you do not erase the previous display.
7. Use a loop and the erase technique of drawing in the background color to produce a dotted circle. Arcs on the circumference of the circle should alternate by an equal number of degrees from the background color to the current color. Use the **Arc** procedure.
8. Use the procedures discussed in this section to create a medium-sized face, complete with eyes, ears, nose, and mouth.
9. Write a program that causes the face you created in Exercise 8 to move across the screen.
10. Modify Exercise 8 so that a smile changes to a frown and one eye blinks.
11. Write a test program that demonstrates how the **Circle** procedure corrects for distortion. Your program should display a circle with a given radius and then

plot two points on the circle. One point should be at angle 0°, the other, at angle 90°. Something like

```
Circle (100, 100, 50);
PutPixel (150, 100, 1);
PutPixel (100, 50, 1);
```

should suffice. Discuss the results of your test program.

12. Use the procedures discussed in this section to display the outline of an automobile.

■ 13.3 Filling Patterns

There are many ways to change the color and design of the interior of closed regions. In this section, we will look at some of the methods available.

Selecting a Pattern and a Color

The basic method for filling a region is a two-step process:

1. Select the pattern and the color of the interior.
2. Fill the region.

Turbo Pascal provides procedures to accomplish both of these tasks. The **SetFillStyle** procedure allows us to select a particular style and color for our filling pattern. The form of this procedure is

SetFillStyle (<pattern>, <color>);

where <pattern> is a variable (or predefined constant) of type **word** that can have any value listed in Table 13.7 and <color> is a variable of type **word** that specifies the color to be used to fill the region.

The values 0 through 12 can be used for arguments of **SetFillStyle** if desired. However, the constant identifiers **EmptyFill** . . . **UserFill** are recommended because they are more descriptive.

The fill pattern **UserFill** requires special mention. You may use this to define your own filling pattern. It requires a call to **SetFillPattern** in which you define your own bit pattern. For further information, see the Turbo Pascal Library Reference Manual.

Filling Regions

Once a pattern and color have been selected, an enclosed region may be filled by using one of several available procedures. The first procedure we examine is **FloodFill.** The form of this procedure is

FloodFill (<Xcoor>, <Ycoor>, <bordercolor>);

Here, Xcoor and Ycoor are variables of type **integer** and may be the coordinates of any point in the interior of the region to be filled. <bordercolor> is a variable of type **word** and represents the color of the border of the enclosed region.

When **FloodFill** is called, it fills the interior of the enclosed region with the current fill pattern and color established by **SetFillStyle.** The method used is to color pixels outward from the designated pixel until the border is reached. Thus, the coloring appears to spread from the selected pixel to the borders.

TABLE 13.7
Patterns for procedure **SetFillStyle**

Value	Predefined Constant	Pattern
0	**EmptyFill**	Background color
1	**SolidFill**	Solid fill with color
2	**LineFill**	————————
3	**LtSlashFill**	(light)
4	**SlashFill**	(thick)
5	**BkSlashFill**	(thick)
6	**LtBkSlashFill**	(light)
7	**HatchFill**	
8	**XHatchFill**	
9	**InterleaveFill**	
10	**WideDotFill**	
11	**CloseDotFill**	
12	**UserFill**	**SetFillPattern** defines pattern

To see how **FloodFill** works, let's consider the rectangle defined by

```
Rectangle (0, 0, 100, 50);
```

If the border color is Red and we wish to fill this rectangle with a light backslash, we select **LtBkSlashFill** and a desired color with **SetFillStyle** before calling **FloodFill.** Thus, the segment of code

```
Rectangle (0, 0, 100, 50);
SetFillStyle (LtBkSlashFill, Green);
FloodFill (1, 1, Red);
```

causes the defined rectangle to be filled with the **LtBkSlashFill** pattern against the background color Green, as shown in Figure 13.14.

If you run a short program containing these three lines of code, it appears the rectangle is being filled with the pattern and color when it is originally drawn. To get a better look at how **FloodFill** works, use **delay** before **FloodFill** and increase the dimensions of your rectangle. For example

```
Rectangle (0, 0, 200, 150);
delay (2000);
SetFillStyle (LtBkSlashFill, Green);
FloodFill (100, 75, Red);
```

allows you to better see how the rectangle gets filled.

It is important to remember that the point represented by (Xcoor,Ycoor) in

```
FloodFill (Xcoor, Ycoor, BorderColor);
```

FIGURE 13.14
A pattern-filled rectangle

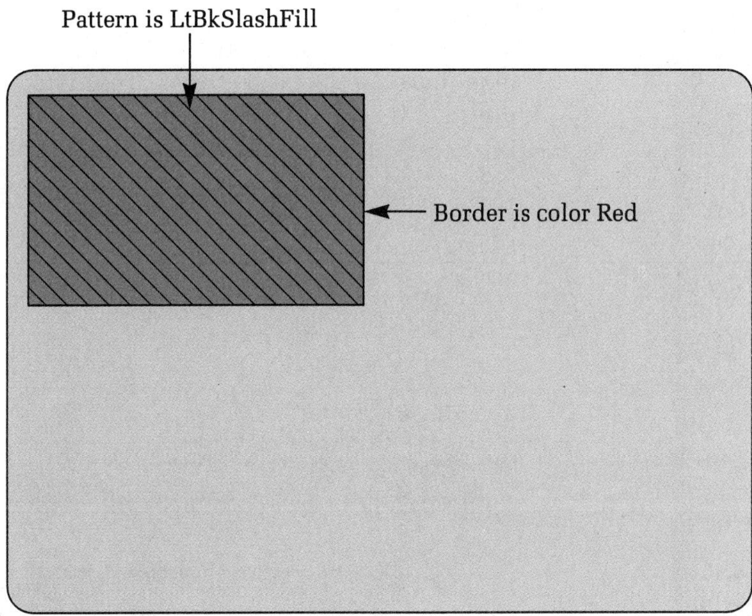

must be located in the interior of the region to be filled. If it is located outside an enclosed region, the entire exterior will be filled. If it is located on the border of the region, nothing will happen.

Another filling procedure available is **FillEllipse.** The form of this procedure is

FillEllipse (<Xcoor>, <Ycoor>, <Xrad>, <Yrad>);

Here, Xcoor and Ycoor are variables of type **integer** and represent the center of the ellipse. Xrad and Yrad are variables of type **word** and represent the horizontal and vertical radii, respectively.

When **FillEllipse** is called, it causes the ellipse specified by (Xcoor, Ycoor, Xrad, Yrad) to be drawn and filled in with the current filling pattern. Note there are no arguments for either a beginning angle or an ending angle because **FillEllipse** can be used only with a complete ellipse. Hence, the default arguments are always from 0° to 360°.

A third, more general procedure for filling regions is also available. The procedure **FillPoly,** which allows the user to specify a polygonal region to be filled, is not developed here, however; refer to the Turbo Pascal Library Reference Manual for further information.

The following example illustrates the use of filling patterns with circles.

EXAMPLE 13.7

This example creates a pattern of concentric circles in which each ring is filled with a different pattern. In Example 13.6 in Section 13.2, concentric circles are generated by the code

```
Xcoor := GetMaxX DIV 2;
Ycoor := GetMaxY DIV 2;
Radius := 20;
REPEAT
  Circle (Xcoor, Ycoor, Radius);
  delay (100);
  Radius := Radius + 20
UNTIL Radius > GetMaxY DIV 2;
```

We now modify this code by changing the filling pattern after each circle is drawn and then filling the ring with the new pattern. Note that an appropriate pixel must be selected in each ring. The new segment of code is

```
SetBkColor (White);
SetColor (Blue);
Xcoor := GetMaxX DIV 2;
Ycoor := GetMaxY DIV 2;
Radius := 20;
Pattern := EmptyFill;
REPEAT
  Circle (Xcoor, Ycoor, Radius);
  SetFillStyle (Pattern, LightRed);
  FloodFill ((Xcoor + Radius - 5), Ycoor, Blue);
  delay (100);
  Radius := Radius + 20;
  Pattern := succ(Pattern)
UNTIL Radius > GetMaxY DIV 2;
```

This segment of code produces the display shown in Figure 13.15.

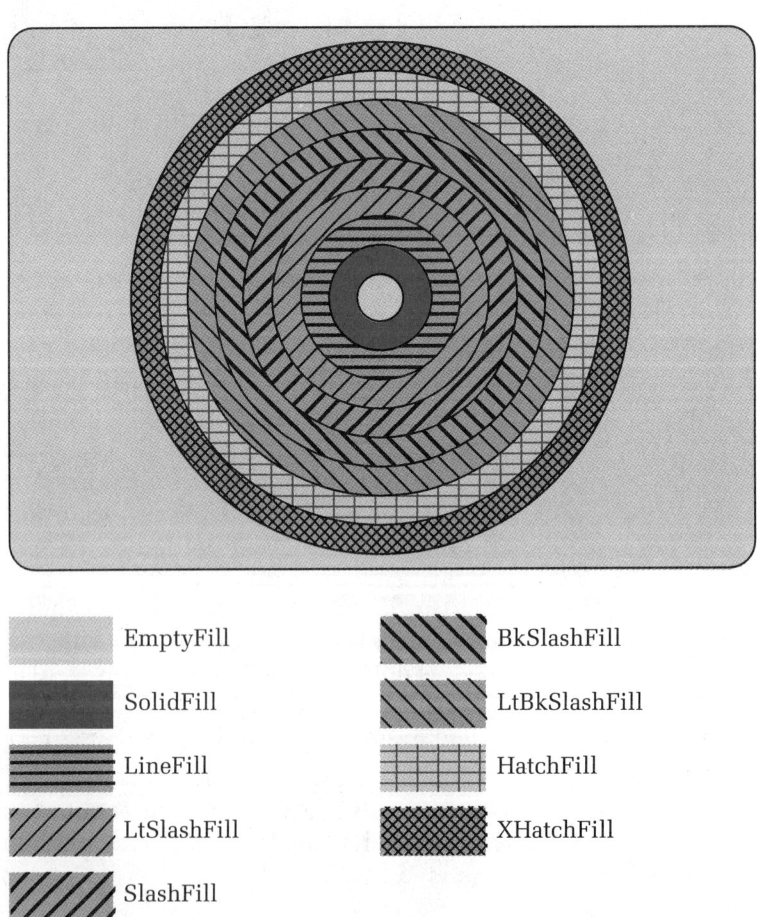

FIGURE 13.15
Concentric circles with various patterns

Exercises 13.3

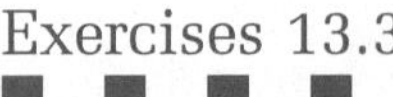

1. Write test programs to investigate what happens when procedure **FloodFill** is used with arguments that do not satisfy the conditions specified when **FloodFill** was defined. In particular, what happens when each of the following occurs?

a. A color is used that is not the border color of the defined region.
b. The point (Xcoor,Ycoor) is outside the defined region.
c. The point (Xcoor,Ycoor) is on the border of the defined region.

2. Write a test program to see what happens when **FloodFill** is used when the region containing (Xcoor,Ycoor) is not an enclosed region. (Put a gap in the side of a rectangle.)
3. Write a program that displays rectangles across the screen with different filling patterns.
4. Discuss how you could reverse the background color and the current drawing color of a graphics program.
5. Write a program that adds animation to Exercise 3; that is, have the rectangles move as they change patterns across the screen.
6. Modify Exercise 5 by having ellipses with different patterns move down a diagonal, starting in the upper-left corner.
7. Concentric circles containing different filling patterns are displayed in Example 13.7. The point in each region to be filled has the coordinates (Xcoor + Radius – 5,Ycoor).
   a. Discuss other ways you could vary the X coordinate.
   b. Would the same system work with the Y coordinate? Why or why not?
8. Create an outline of a house, and use different filling patterns for the door, windows, chimney, and siding.

■ 13.4 Bar Graphs and Charts

There are several convenient ways to display bars, bar graphs, and charts. In this section, we will examine the available procedures and how they can be used to create graphic displays.

Bars

The underlying requirement for constructing bar graphs is the ability to construct a single bar. This ability is provided by using the procedure **Bar.** The correct form of this procedure is

Bar (<UpLeftX>, <UpLeftY>, <LowRightX>, <LowRightY>);

where all variables are of type **integer.** As expected, (UpleftX, UpleftY) represents the corrdinates of the upper-left vertex of the bar and (LowRightX,LowRightY) represents the coordinates of the lower-right vertex. We frequently use notation consistent with how rectangles are defined. Thus

```
Bar (X1, Y1, X2, Y2);
```

is the bar displayed in Figure 13.16.

More specifically, Figure 13.17 contains a bar with an upper-left vertex of (10,10) and a lower-right vertex of (40,80).

The **Bar** procedure closely resembles the **Rectangle** procedure. The difference is that it automatically fills the interior with the border color. Thus

```
Bar (10, 10, 40, 80);
```

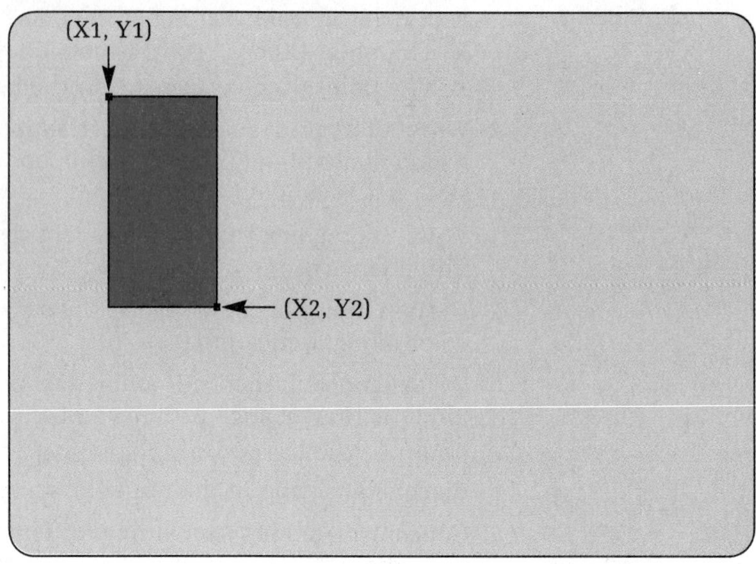

FIGURE 13.16
The bar defined by
Bar (X1, Y1, X2, Y2)

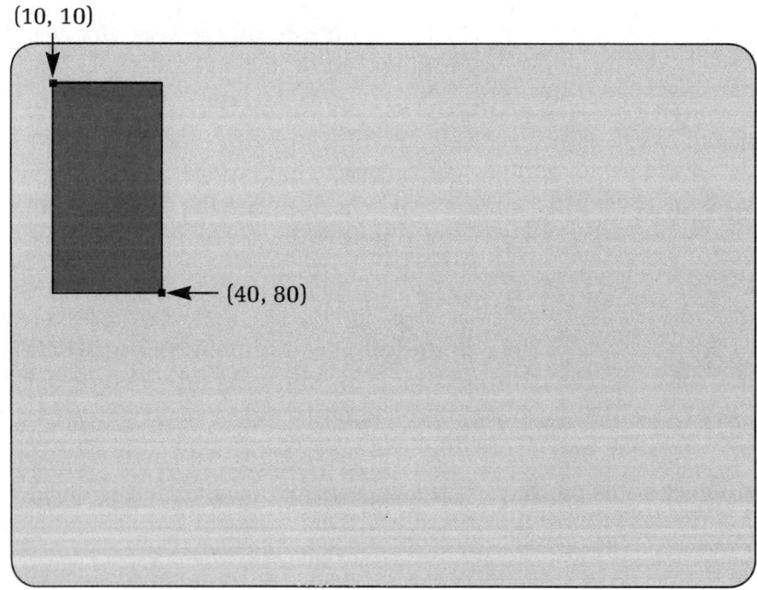

FIGURE 13.17
The bar defined by
Bar (10, 10, 40, 80)

has the same effect as

```
Rectangle (10, 10, 40, 80);
FloodFill (11, 11, 3);
```

assuming color 3 is the border color for the rectangle.

It is possible to vary the color and pattern used to fill the interior of a bar by using the procedure **SetFillStyle.** Thus, if we want to fill a bar with the **SlashFill** pattern using color 2, we use the code

```
SetFillStyle (SlashFill, 2);
Bar (10, 10, 40, 80);
```

Bar Graphs

Bars can be used to create bar graphs. Suppose we want to display the grade distribution for some class. For sample data, let's assume the grades for 30 students are grouped as follows: A, 5; B, 7; C, 10; D, 6; E, 2.

Before we can create a bar graph to display these data, several issues must be considered. First, what are the relative heights of the bars? Given this particular range of numbers (2–10), an easy choice is to let each integer be represented by 10 pixels. Thus, the bar representing C's will be 100 pixels high and the one representing E's will be 20 pixels high.

Second, where do we want the bottom line of our graph to be located? If we want the graph to be centered vertically, we must determine how much of the vertical part of the screen is not being used by the bars. Since the tallest bar is 100 pixels, this leaves **GetMaxY** – 100 pixels not in use. We want one-half of these pixels to be above the graph and one-half to be below, so we define BottomEdge to be

```
BottomEdge := 100 + round((GetMaxY - 100) / 2);
```

which can be simplified to 50 + round(**GetMaxY**/2). This is illustrated in Figure 13.18.

FIGURE 13.18
Centering a bar of 100 pixels

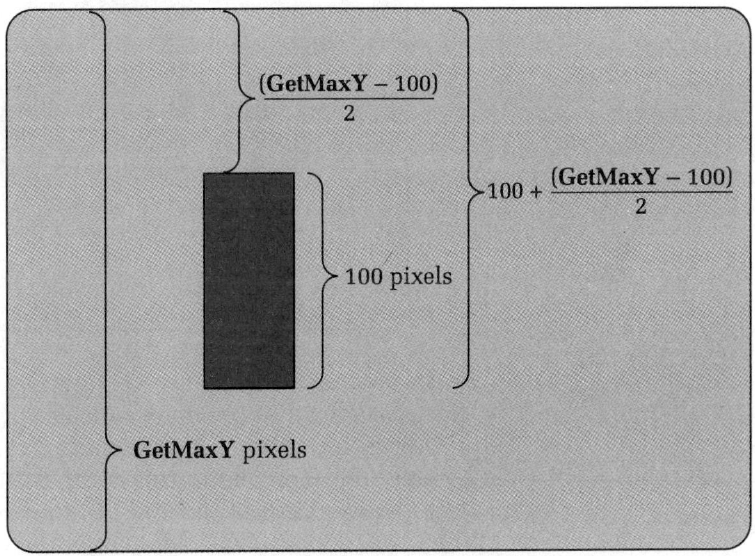

With the bottom edge of the graph now defined, the Y coordinates of the bar representing the number of Cs will be Y1 = BottomEdge – 100 and Y2 = BottomEdge.

Third, how wide should our bars be? The width of the bars is a matter of choice. Our example uses a width of 10 pixels.

Fourth, how far apart should our bars be? Again, this is a matter of choice. Our example separates the bars by 10 pixels.

Finally, where should the bars start? We could center the chart horizontally in a similar manner to the way we centered them vertically. However, we choose to leave a left margin of 30 pixels.

Now that these decisions have been made, our first bar graph is created by the code

```
BottomEdge := 50 + round(GetMaxY / 2);
LeftEdge := 30;
Bar (LeftEdge, BottomEdge - 50,
     LeftEdge + 10, BottomEdge);      {  Bar for A's  }
Bar (LeftEdge + 20, BottomEdge - 70,
     LeftEdge + 30, BottomEdge);      {  Bar for B's  }
Bar (LeftEdge + 40, BottomEdge - 100,
     LeftEdge + 50, BottomEdge);      {  Bar for C's  }
Bar (LeftEdge + 60, BottomEdge - 60,
     LeftEdge + 70, BottomEdge);      {  Bar for D's  }
Bar (LeftFdge + 80, BottomEdge - 20,
     LeftEdge + 90, BottomEdge);      {  Bar for E's  }
```

When this segment of code is run, the display shown in Figure 13.19 results.

FIGURE 13.19
A bar graph

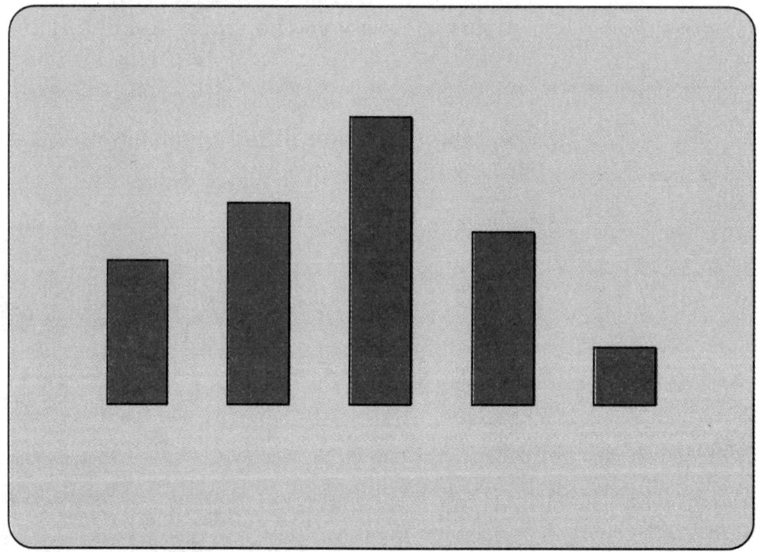

You may notice the previous code is not very elegant. Since the intent was to help you see how the **Bar** procedure can be used to produce a bar graph, we deliberately left the code in this form. Several suggestions for modifications are made in the exercises at the end of this section.

When we constructed the bar graph in this example, we simplified an important consideration. We allowed our tallest bar to be 10 times the number of C's because the range of values was 2–10. In general, such easy choices are not usually available. A better method is to define the tallest bar to be a percentage (integer) of the vertical portion of the screen we want to use. We call this value MaxBarHeight. Then each remaining bar height can be determined relative to the tallest bar. For example, if the values range from 100 to 1300 and one of the values is 685, the bar height for that bar will be 685/1300 * MaxBarHeight. You will be required to use this technique in an exercise at the end of this section.

Three-Dimensional Bars

A three-dimensional bar can also be used to construct bar graphs. Such a bar adds both depth and a top (optional) to a two-dimensional bar. The procedure for a three-dimensional bar is **Bar3D.** The correct form of this procedure is

Bar3D (X1, Y1, X2, Y2, <depth>, <top>);

Here, X1, Y1, X2, and Y2 are the same as the variables used in the **Bar** procedure. Depth is of type **word** and represents the depth desired for perspective; no standard exists for this, but the depth of most three-dimensional bars is 25–35 percent of the bar width. Top is a variable of type **boolean:** a value of **true** means a top is included; a value of **false** means a top is not included. We would exclude the top of a bar if we wanted to "stack" another bar on top of it. To illustrate, consider the three-dimensional bars displayed by

```
Bar3D (20, 20, 50, 70, 10, true);
Bar3D (100, 20, 130, 70, 10, false);
```

which are illustrated in Figure 13.20.

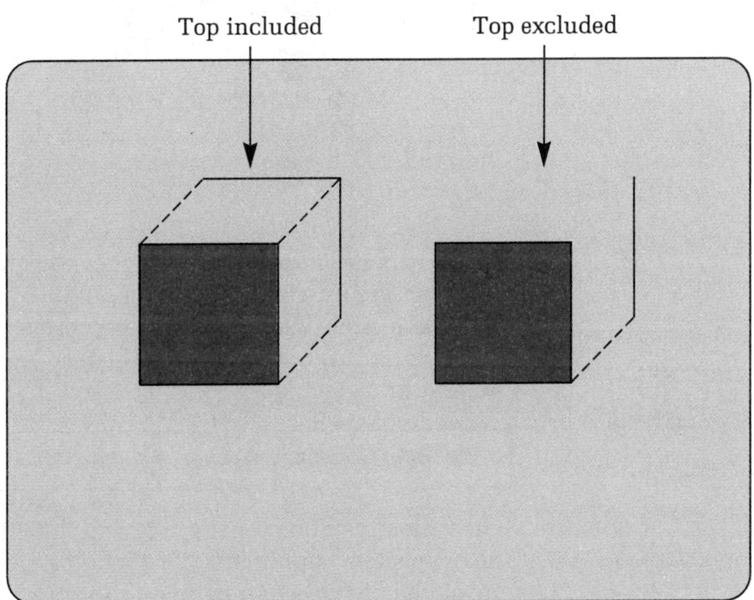

FIGURE 13.20
Two three-dimensional bars

Default settings are used to fill in the "faces" of three-dimensional bars with the border color. We can change the filling pattern and color by using **SetFillStyle** before a call to **Bar3D.** The three-dimensional outline of the bar is drawn in the current line style, and color is determined by **SetLineStyle** and **SetColor.**

To illustrate the difference between a two-dimensional and a three-dimensional bar graph, let's reconsider the earlier example in which we displayed the results of a distribution of grades in a class in two dimensions, as shown in Figure 13.19. Changing the **Bar** procedure

```
Bar (LeftEdge, BottomEdge - 50,
     LeftEdge + 10, BottomEdge);
```

to

```
Bar3D (LeftEdge, BottomEdge - 50,
       LeftEdge + 10, BottomEdge, 3, true);
```

yields a depth of 30 percent of the bar width (10 pixels) and puts a top on each bar. After similar changes are made in the remaining bars, the segment of code produces the display shown in Figure 13.21.

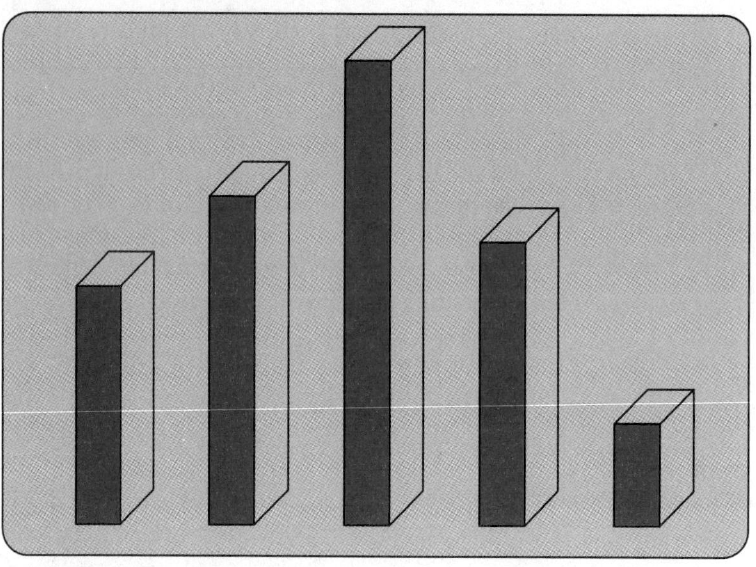

FIGURE 13.21
A three-dimensional bar graph

Sectors

Just as bars are needed to construct bar graphs, sectors of a circle are needed to construct pie charts. We create a sector by joining the endpoints of an arc to the center of a circle. However, this process requires that we identify the coordinates of the endpoints of the arc. Fortunately, the procedure **PieSlice** provides an easier method for drawing a sector. The correct form of this procedure is

PieSlice (<Xcoor>, <Ycoor>, <anglestart>, <anglefinish>, <radius>);

where the five arguments are of the same types and serve the same purposes as the respective arguments for **Arc.** The difference is that **PieSlice** causes the endpoints of the arc to be joined to the center of the circle of which the arc is a portion. To illustrate, let's consider

```
Arc (100, 100, 0, 45, 50);
```

and

```
PieSlice (100, 100, 0, 45, 50);
```

The results of these procedures are displayed in Figure 13.22(a) and (b), respectively.

Note the sector is filled with the border color by default. In general, the interior can be controlled by using **SetFillStyle** to specify a pattern and a color. To illustrate

```
SetColor (1);
SetBkColor (4);
SetFillStyle (SlashFill, 2);
PieSlice (100, 100, 0, 90, 50);
```

produces the sector shown in Figure 13.23 on page 598.

If we are in CGA mode 3, the background color is red(4), the current drawing color is cyan(1), and the **SlashFill** pattern is drawn with magenta(2).

There is also a procedure **Sector,** which can be used to display a portion of an ellipse. The correct form of this procedure is

FIGURE 13.22

(a) **Arc** (100, 100, 0, 45, 50)

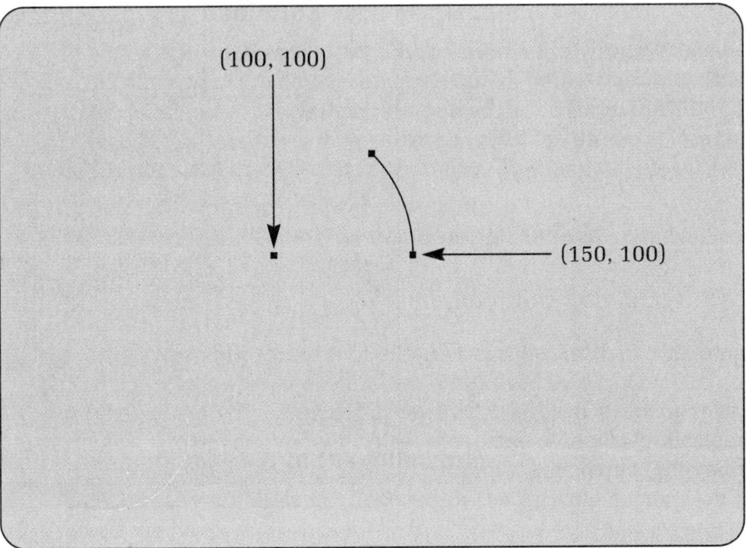

(b) **PieSlice** (100, 100, 0, 45, 50)

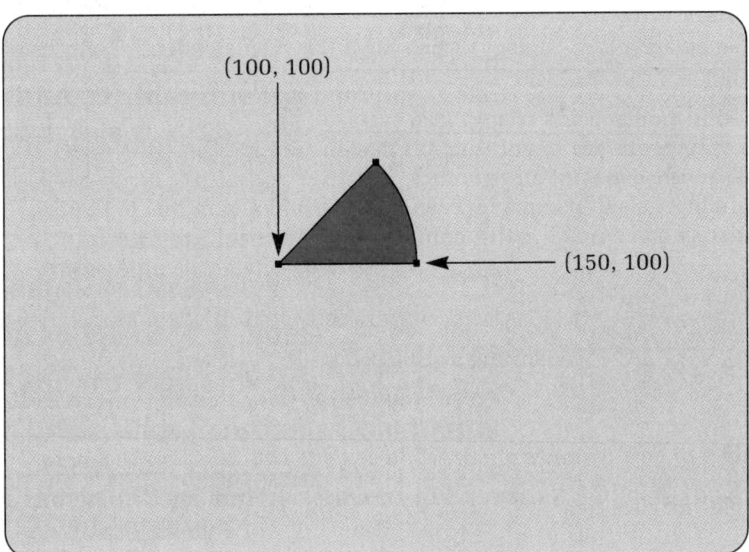

Sector (<Xcoor>, <Ycoor>, <anglestart>, <anglefinish>, <Xrad>, <Yrad>);

The types and purposes of the arguments of **Sector** are identical to those in procedure **Ellipse**. The procedure **Sector** draws the indicated portion of the ellipse and then fills the interior in the same manner that **PieSlice** fills the interior of a sector.

Pie Charts

A pie chart is an alternative method for displaying data graphically. The size of the central angle of a sector of a circle corresponds to the height of a particular bar in a bar graph. Procedure **PieSlice** can be used to produce a pie chart.

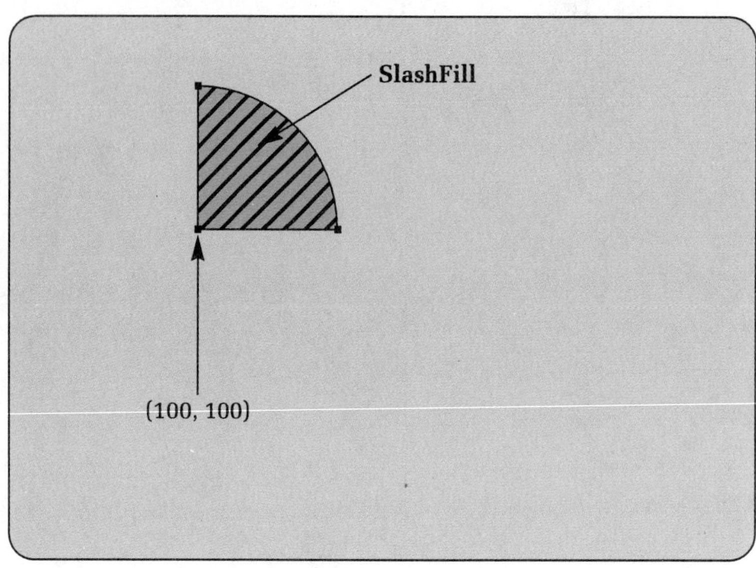

FIGURE 13.23
Filling and coloring a sector

To illustrate how a pie chart is formed, let's reconsider the data we used to produce the bar graph in Figure 13.19. The grade distribution for a class of 30 students is A, 5; B, 7; C, 10; D, 6; E, 2. Since the total number of grades is 30, each grade is represented by 360/30, or (12) degrees. Thus, the central angle for the sector representing the number of A's is 5 × 12° = 60°. In general, we can determine the degree representation for each data item by the quotient 360/number of items. If we define

```
ItemAngleSize := 360 / TotalItems;
```

the central angle for each item is

```
ItemAngleSize * <number of items>
```

Using our grade distribution example, we have

```
ItemAngleSize := 360 / 30;
```

Central angles for data items A–E are indicated in Table 13.8.

TABLE 13.8
Central angles for data items

Data Item	Number of Items	ItemAngle Size × Number of Items (slice size)
A	5	$\frac{360}{30} \times 5 = 60$
B	7	$\frac{360}{30} \times 7 = 84$
C	10	$\frac{360}{30} \times 10 = 120$
D	6	$\frac{360}{30} \times 6 = 72$
E	2	$\frac{360}{30} \times 2 = 24$

When we write code to produce a pie chart, the sector representing A's will have a central angle of 60°, the sector representing B's will have a central angle of 84°, and so on.

Next, we must determine how to start and end each sector. If we assume an angle start of 0°, the sector for A's will be generated by

```
AngleStart := 0;
AngleFinish := 60;
```

Several methods can be used to keep track of successive starting and finishing angles. In our example, we use the code

```
AngleStart := AngleFinish;  {  from previous slice  }
AngleFinish := AngleStart + SliceSize;
```

It is also customary to vary the filling pattern for each slice in a pie chart. This can be controlled by using **SetFillStyle** before each call to **PieSlice.** We use the technique of

```
Pattern := succ(pattern);
```

after suitable initialization of Pattern.

Based on the concepts developed in this section, the following program causes a pie chart to be displayed that represents the data used to produce the bar graph shown in Figure 13.19.

```
PROGRAM PieChart;

{  This program uses the procedure PieSlice to produce      }
{  a pie chart.  Note how sectors are determined and        }
{  filled in PROCEDURE GraphSector.                         }

USES
  Crt, Graph;

CONST
  NumDataItems = 30;
  Radius = 50;
  Xcoor = 100;
  Ycoor = 100;

VAR
  AngleStart, AngleFinish : word;
  Pattern : word;
  SliceSize : word;
  ItemAngleSize : real;
  NumItems : integer;

{*********************************************************}

PROCEDURE InitializeGraphics;

  {  Given:   Nothing                                        }
  {  Task:    Initialize graphics; provide error message     }
  {  Return:  Nothing                                        }

  VAR
    GraphDriver, GraphMode,
    ErrorResult : integer;
    InitError : boolean;
  BEGIN
    GraphDriver := CGA;
    GraphMode := 1;
    InitGraph (GraphDriver, GraphMode, 'C:\TP\BGI');
    ErrorResult := GraphResult;
    InitError := (ErrorResult <> 0);
    IF InitError THEN
```

```
      BEGIN
        writeln ('There is a graphics error.');
        writeln (GraphErrorMsg(ErrorResult));
        writeln ('Program aborted.');
        Halt
      END
  END;  {  of PROCEDURE InitializeGraphics  }

{*******************************************************}

PROCEDURE GraphSector (NumItems : integer;
                       ItemAngleSize : real;
                       AngleStart : word;
                       VAR AngleFinish : word;
                       VAR Pattern : word);

  {  Given:   Number of items for the sector, angle size   }
  {               per item, angle start position, fill     }
  {               pattern for the last sector              }
  {  Task:    Create one sector of a pie chart             }
  {  Return:  Angle finish position and pattern used       }
  {               for the sector                           }

  VAR
    SliceSize : word;
  BEGIN
    SliceSize := round(NumItems * ItemAngleSize);
    AngleStart := AngleFinish;
    AngleFinish := AngleStart + SliceSize;
    SetFillStyle (Pattern, 2);
    PieSlice (Xcoor, Ycoor, AngleStart, AngleFinish, Radius);
    Pattern := succ(Pattern)
  END;  {  of PROCEDURE GraphSector  }

{*******************************************************}

BEGIN  {  Main program  }
  InitializeGraphics;

  {  Initialize  }
  SetBkColor (Green);
  AngleFinish := 0;
  Pattern := LineFill;
  ItemAngleSize := 360 / NumDataItems;

  {  Draw the pie sectors  }
  NumItems := 5;
  GraphSector (NumItems, ItemAngleSize, AngleStart,
               AngleFinish, Pattern);
  NumItems := 7;
  GraphSector (NumItems, ItemAngleSize, AngleStart,
               AngleFinish, Pattern);
  NumItems := 10;
  GraphSector (NumItems, ItemAngleSize, AngleStart,
               AngleFinish, Pattern);
  NumItems := 6;
  GraphSector (NumItems, ItemAngleSize, AngleStart,
               AngleFinish, Pattern);
  NumItems := 2;
  GraphSector (NumItems, ItemAngleSize, AngleStart,
               AngleFinish, Pattern);
  readln;
  CloseGraph
END.  {  of main program  }
```

When this program is run, the screen display shown in Figure 13.24 results.

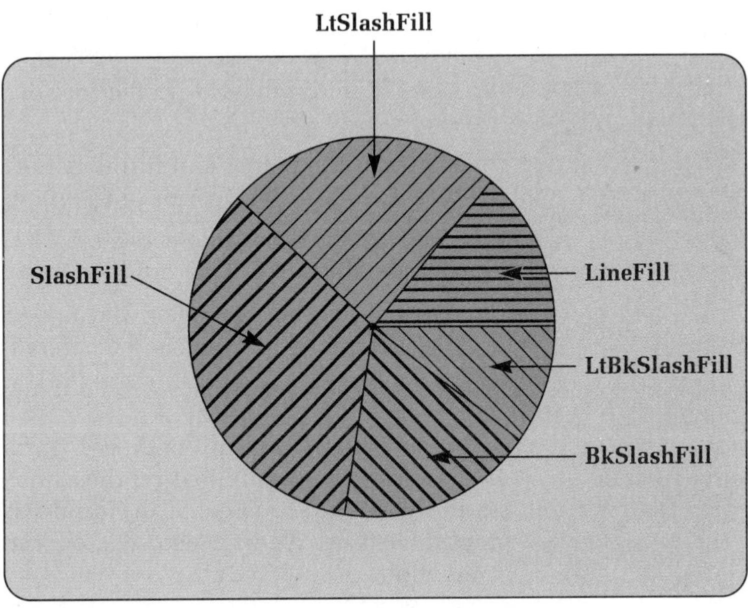

FIGURE 13.24
A pie chart

Exercises 13.4

1. Write a procedure to display vertical bars of width 10 and height 50 that are filled with different filling patterns. Have the base separated by a horizontal distance of five pixels.
2. Reconsider the bar graph example in this section. Modify the segment of code on page 594 in each of the following ways.
   a. Define and use a height for each bar, such as AHeight := 50.
   b. Define and use a bar width.
   c. Define and use a distance between bars.
   d. Revise the code to use a **FOR** loop to display the bars. A general form is

```
FOR Number := 1 TO 5 DO
  BEGIN
    .
    .    (set coordinates here)
    .
    Bar (X1, Y1, X2, Y2)
  END;
```

3. Reconsider the bar graph referred to in Exercise 2. Experiment with LeftEdge, bar width, and distance between bars to find the most appealing display.
4. Review the discussion in this section (page 594) about using relative bar heights, where the tallest bar is defined to be of height **MaxBarHeight.** Use this technique to draw a bar graph of the values 120, 135, 180, 240, 290, and 345.
5. Three-dimensional bars without tops are used when stacking bars. Write a short program to display five three-dimensional bars in a stack. Vary the patterns on the faces of the bars.
6. Find the average monthly rate of precipitation for the region in which your college or university is located. Display the results for one year in a two-dimensional bar graph.
7. Change your program so your display in Exercise 6 uses three-dimensional bars.

8. Write an interactive program that allows the user to experiment with different depths when displaying a three-dimensional bar. The user should be able to enter any depth between 0 and 100 percent of the bar width. Use **delay** to create a significant pause to allow the user to view each display.
9. Make a color wheel by using **PieSlice** and changing the color of the sector every 45°.
10. How can the colors and filling patterns be used to produce the outline of a sector? (Make the interior of the sector the same as the screen background.)
11. Use both **PieSlice** and **Sector** to fill a semicircle with a radius of 50. Compare the two displays. What are your conclusions?
12. Reconsider the pie chart developed in this section. Revise **PROGRAM** PieChart so the grades can be entered interactively.

■ 13.5 Text in Graphics Mode

As is true of most graphics packages, Turbo Pascal permits the combined display of graphics features and text on the same screen. In this section, we will look at several procedures available in Turbo Pascal for printing characters while in a graphics setting. We will also see how the characters can vary in font, size, and orientation.

Graphics Characters

A standard-size character displayed while in the graphics mode occupies an 8 × 8 pixel square. Thus, when working with a 200 × 320 pixel screen, there are 25 lines of 40 characters each.

Displaying Characters with OutText

There are two basic procedures for displaying characters in a graphics mode: **OutText** and **OutTextXY.** The correct form of procedure **OutText** is

OutText (<message>);

where <message> is a **string** or a variable of type **string.** If <message> is an actual string rather than a variable, it must be enclosed in quotes. Thus, we can print HI THERE by using either

```
OutText ('HI THERE');
```

or

```
Message := 'HI THERE';
OutText (Message);
```

When **OutText** is used to display characters, it starts printing at the current pointer position, which is the upper-left corner of the 8 × 8 pixel square used to display the first character of the string. To illustrate, assume we have just entered the graphics mode and the default setting of the current pointer is at (0,0). The segment of code

```
OutText ('HI THERE');
MoveTo (4,9);
OutText ('HI THERE');
```

then produces the display shown in Figure 13.25.

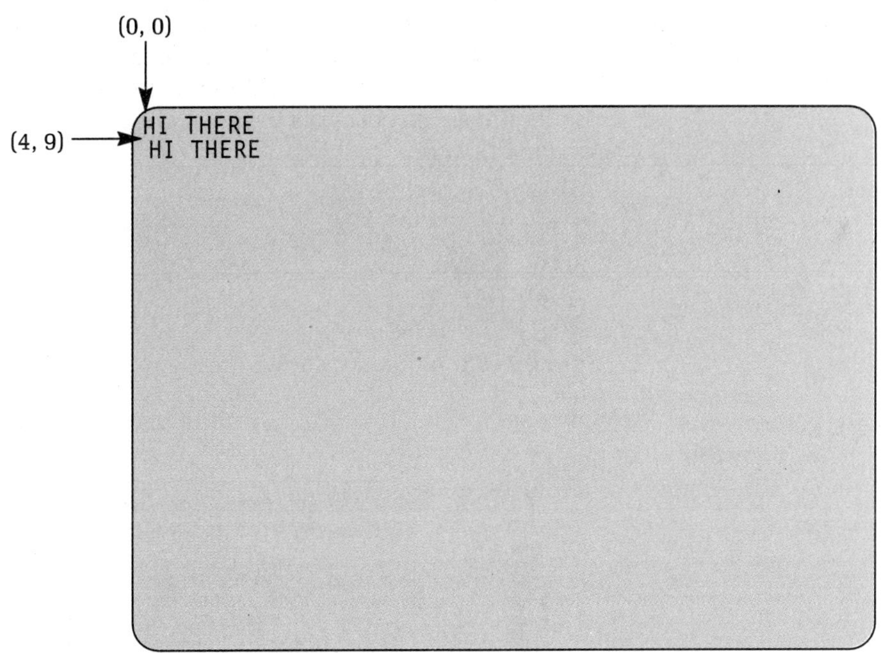

FIGURE 13.25
Display using **OutText**

Use of **OutText** causes the current pointer to move. Its position becomes the upper-left corner of the next available 8 × 8 pixel square after the last character in the string has been printed. Thus, if the current pointer is at (0,0) and we print

```
OutText ('HI THERE');
```

the current pointer is then positioned as shown in Figure 13.26.

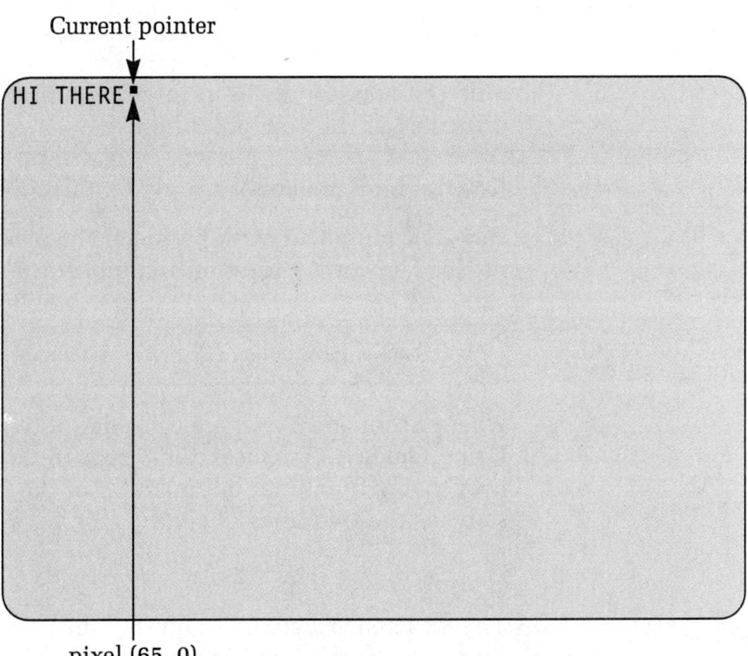

FIGURE 13.26
Position of the current pointer after printing the first string

Text characters in graphics are not confined to the 25 lines of 40 characters on a 200 × 320 pixel screen. We can position a string to begin at any pixel on the screen by using **MoveTo.** After a call to **MoveTo,** the next character is displayed so its upper-left corner is in the position designated by **MoveTo.** To illustrate, the segment of code

```
Message := 'HI THERE';
OutText (Message);
MoveTo (65,4);
OutText (Message);
MoveTo (69,12);
OutText (Message);
```

produces the display shown in Figure 13.27.

FIGURE 13.27
Display using **MoveTo**

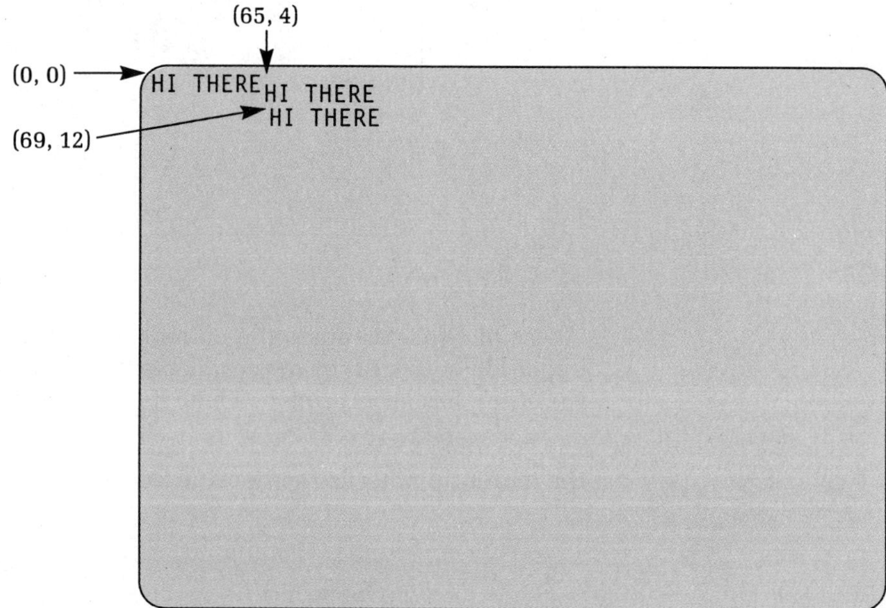

If the message to be printed using **OutText** is too long for the screen, it is truncated at the viewpoint border.

Displaying Characters with OutTextXY

The procedure **OutTextXY** can also be used to print messages while in a graphics mode. The correct form of this procedure is

OutTextXY (<Xcoor>, <Ycoor>, <message>);

where Xcoor and Ycoor are variables of type **integer** and message is of type **string.** Using **OutTextXY** causes the string to be printed with pixel position (Xcoor,Y-coor) being the upper-left position of the first character. Thus, the display is the same as the two lines of code

```
MoveTo (Xcoor,Ycoor);
OutText (Message);
```

The difference between **OutText** and **OutTextXY** is that **OutTextXY** does not cause the current pointer to be moved. This means we can print a message anywhere we choose and the current pointer will remain where it was before **OutTextXY** was used. The next example illustrates how this feature can enhance your graphics work.

EXAMPLE 13.8

This example uses **OutTextXY** to display a "continuation message" at the bottom of the graphics screen. Until now, we have been using a **readln** statement or the procedure **delay** to hold the graphics screen and no message to press <Enter> to continue has been given. We can make our programs more user-friendly by writing a procedure that displays a message directing the user appropriately. A typical procedure follows.

```
PROCEDURE ContinuationMessage;
  VAR
    Xcoor, Ycoor : integer;
  BEGIN
    Message := 'Press <Enter> to continue.';
    Xcoor := (GetMaxX - 8 * Length(Message)) DIV 2;
    Ycoor := GetMaxY - 8;
    OutTextXY (Xcoor, Ycoor, Message);
    readln
  END;  {  of PROCEDURE ContinuationMessage  }
```

Note we have centered this message on the last line available for printing. If we use this procedure in conjunction with a modification of the earlier code used to display HI THERE on the screen, we have

```
Message := 'HI THERE';
OutText (Message);
ContinuationMessage;
OutTextXY (65, 4, Message);
ContinuationMessage;
OutTextXY (69, 12, Message)
ContinuationMessage;
```

When this code is run, the displays shown in Figures 13.28(a), (b), and (c) result.

FIGURE 13.28
Display using a continuation message

(a)

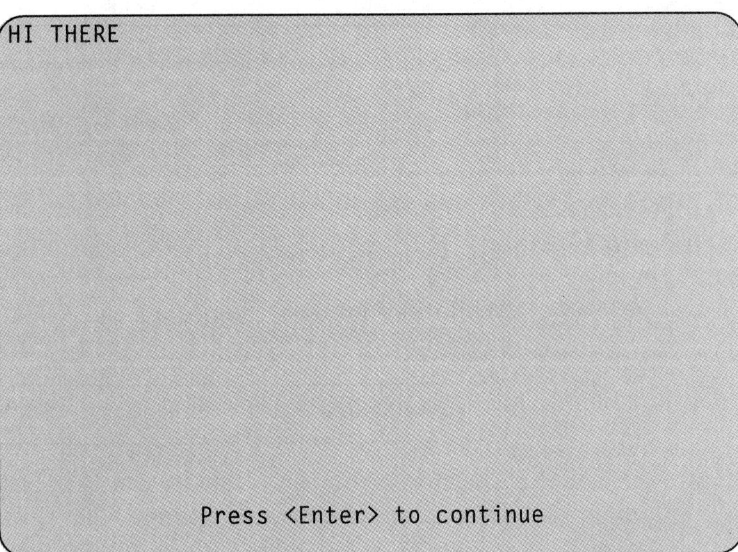

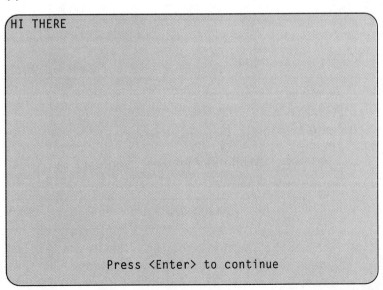

FIGURE 13.28
(continued)

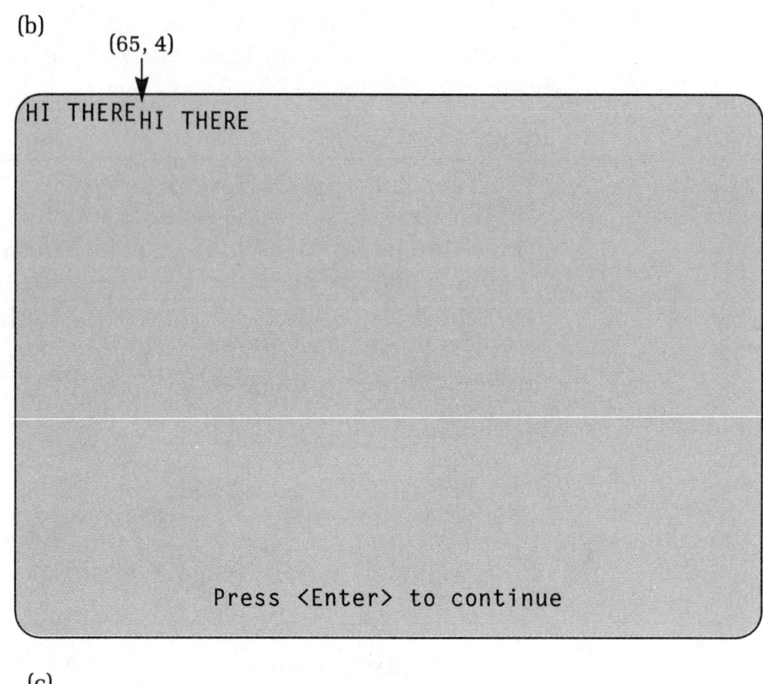

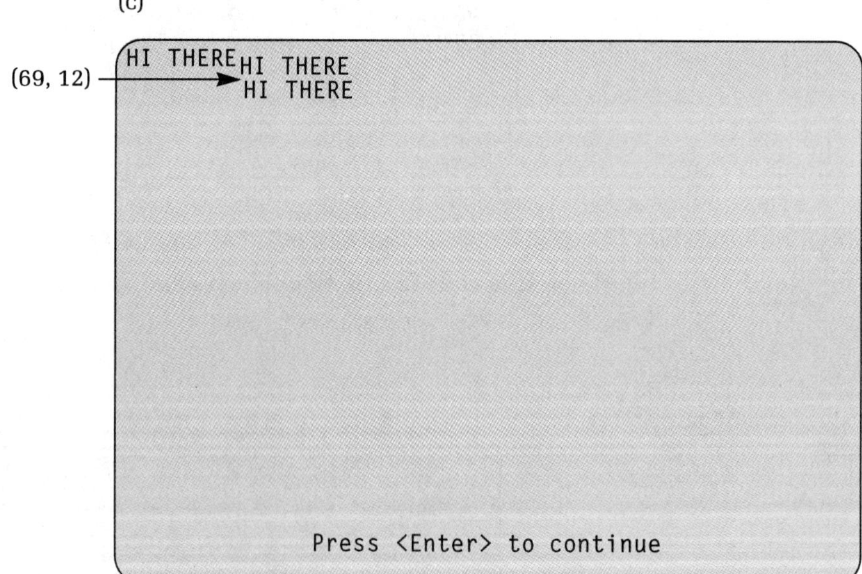

Changing the Characters

While in a graphics mode, we can vary the characters used with a call to the procedure **SetTextStyle.** The correct form of this procedure is

SetTextStyle (<font>, <direction>, <size>);

The first argument, <font>, is a variable of type **word** that allows the user to select from five available fonts. These predefined constants and how they look when displayed are shown in Table 13.9.

TABLE 13.9
Fonts

Font Name	Font Value	Font Style
DefaultFont	0	Default Font
TriplexFont	1	Triplex Font
SmallFont	2	Small Font
SansSeriFont	3	Sans Serif Font
GothicFont	4	Gothic Font

The constant DefaultFont has value zero. This font is referred to as a *bit-mapped font,* and characters appear in an 8 × 8 pixel square. The other fonts are *stroked fonts,* so called because of the manner in which the characters are constructed. These fonts do not appear in 8 × 8 pixel squares.

After a font is selected using **SetTextStyle,** all text displayed will be in that font until a different font is selected. Either the value (0, 1, 2, 3, or 4) of the font or the predefined constant identifier may be used. As usual, we recommend using identifiers to improve the readability of the code.

TABLE 13.10
Orientation

Orientation Name	Orientation Value
HorizDir	0
VertDir	1

The second argument in **SetTextStyle,** <direction>, is a variable of type **word** that allows the user to select either vertical or horizontal display for the text. The two predefined constants and their values are listed in Table 13.10.

The default setting is HorizDir. If we select VertDir, the text will begin to be printed at the indicated position and then move up (rather than down) the screen.

The third argument in **SetTextStyle**, <size>, is a variable of type **word.** It allows the user to set the size of each character, with allowable values ranging from 1 to 10. Character sizes are magnified by multiples of the 8 × 8 pixel square. Thus, if we select a value of 2, each character is displayed in a 16 × 16 pixel square. A value of 3 yields 24 × 24 pixel squares, and so on, until a value of 10 produces an 80 × 80 pixel square. This information is summarized in Table 13.11.

TABLE 13.11
Character size

Size Value	Size of Character Display (in pixels)
1	8 × 8
2	16 × 16
3	24 × 24
4	32 × 32
5	40 × 40
6	48 × 48
7	56 × 56
8	64 × 64
9	72 × 72
10	80 × 80

The following example illustrates some displays that are available **SetText-Style** is used in a graphics mode.

A NOTE OF INTEREST

Artificial Intelligence

Artificial intelligence (AI) research seeks to understand the principles of human intelligence and to apply those principles to the creation of smarter computer programs. The original goal of AI research was to create programs with humanlike intelligence and capabilities, yet after many years of research, little progress has been made toward this goal.

In recent years, however, AI researchers have pursued much more modest goals with much greater success. Programs based on AI techniques are playing increasingly important roles in such down-to-earth areas as medicine, education, recreation, business, and industry. Such programs come nowhere near to achieving human levels of intelligence, but they often have capabilities that are not easily achieved with non-AI programs.

The main principles of AI can be summarized as follows:

Search: The computer solves a problem by searching through all logically possible solutions.

Rules: Knowledge about what actions to take in particular circumstances is stored as rules; each rule has the form

IF <situation> **THEN** <action or conclusion>

Reasoning: Programs can use reasoning to draw conclusions from the facts and rules available to the program.

Planning: The control program plans the actions that must be taken to accomplish a particular goal, and then modifies the plan if unexpected obstacles are encountered; this is most widely used in robot control.

Pattern recognition: This is important for rule-based systems. The IF part of a rule specifies a particular pattern of facts; the rule is to be applied when that pattern is recognized in the facts known to the program.

Knowledge bases: Locations where the facts and rules that govern the operation of an AI program are stored.

EXAMPLE 13.9

Let's write a segment of code to compare the five fonts available using **SetTextStyle.** Our segment uses the default values for orientation and size. The code is

```
Ycoor := 0;
FOR Font := DefaultFont TO GothicFont DO
  BEGIN
    SetTextStyle (Font, HorizDir, 1);
    OutTextXY (30, Ycoor, 'Can you read this?');
    Ycoor := Ycoor + 20
  END;
```

When this segment of code is run, the display shown in Figure 13.29 results.

FIGURE 13.29
Comparing fonts

Default Font
Triplex Font
Small Font
Sans Serif Font
Gothic Font

Several other text-related procedures are available, including **SetTextJustify, GetTextSettings, TextHeight,** and **TextWidth.** Detailed analyses of these procedures are beyond the scope of this text. The interested reader is referred to the Turbo Pascal Library Reference Manual.

The primary use of text in graphics is to generate more informative screen displays than those produced using graphics procedures without text. Graphs and charts require axes and labels. Headings can be produced for displayed text. Explanatory paragraphs can be put in rectangles using a combination of **Rectangle** and **OutTextXY.** These and many other capabilities should become a standard part of your program development when you are using graphics. The Focus on Program Design for this chapter illustrates a combined use of graphics and text.

Exercises 13.5

1. Write a test program to see what happens in each of the following situations.
   a. **OutText** is used with a message that is too long for the viewing screen.
   b. You try to print a character at the bottom of the screen when you do not have a complete 8 × 8 pixel square available.
2. Reconsider Example 13.8. In centering the message, why was the variable Xcoor defined as **(GetMaxX** – 8 * Length(Message)) **DIV** 2 rather than as **(GetMaxX** – Length(Message)) **DIV** 2?
3. Modify the program on page 594 that displays a bar graph of grades by pausing with a continuation message before each successive bar is displayed.
4. Modify **PROGRAM** PieChart on pages 599–600 by adding a legend that explains the filling pattern used in each sector. Your output should be

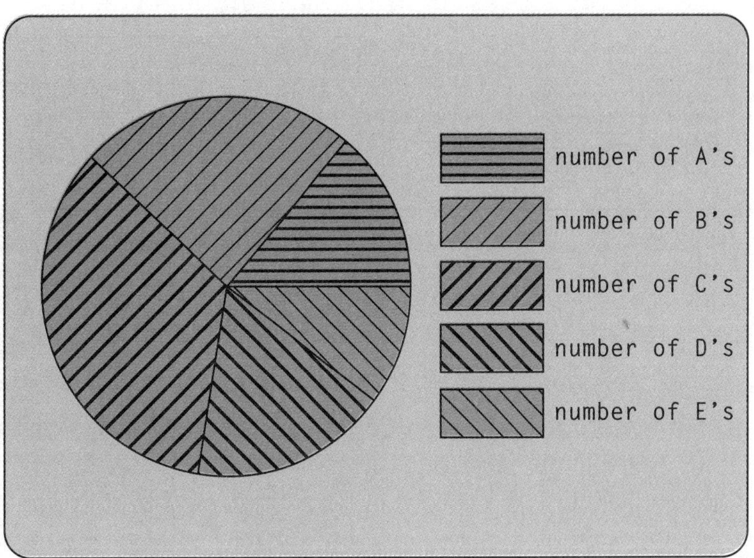

5. Use the procedures **Rectangle** and **OutTextXY** to display a message in a box. Do this for both vertical and horizontal messages.
6. Reconsider the code in Example 13.9. Develop and run similar code segments that allow you to compare text direction and text size.

7. Combine Example 13.9 and Exercise 6 to produce a program that allows the user to compare text fonts, direction, and size with a continuation message at the bottom of each screen display.

FOCUS ON PROGRAM DESIGN

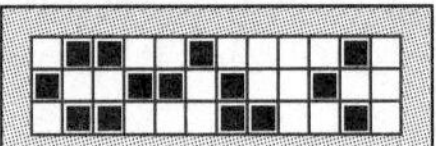

The summary program combines several of the concepts and program segments we have discussed thus far. In particular, this is an interactive program that allows the user to enter the grade distribution for a class and then elect to see these grades displayed in either a bar graph or a pie chart. A menu allows the user to choose the appropriate program action. This menu is

```
This program will graphically display the
distribution of grades for a class.  Please
choose one of the following and press <Enter>.

    <1> Enter grades

    <2> View bar graph

    <3> View pie chart

    <4> Quit
```

Both the bar graph and the pie chart combine graphics and text as part of the screen display. The bar graph display shows the letter grade below the appropriate bar. A title and continuation message appear as part of each display. A typical screen is

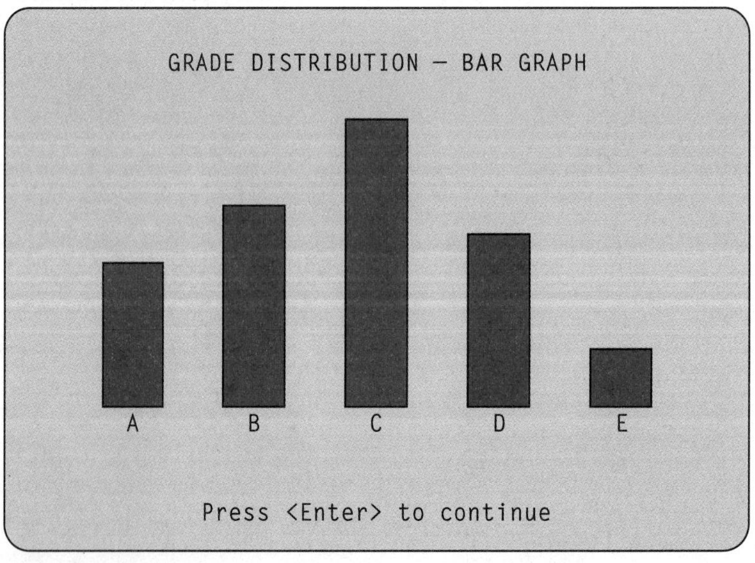

The pie chart display includes a legend that explains the various filling patterns in the sectors. A typical screen is

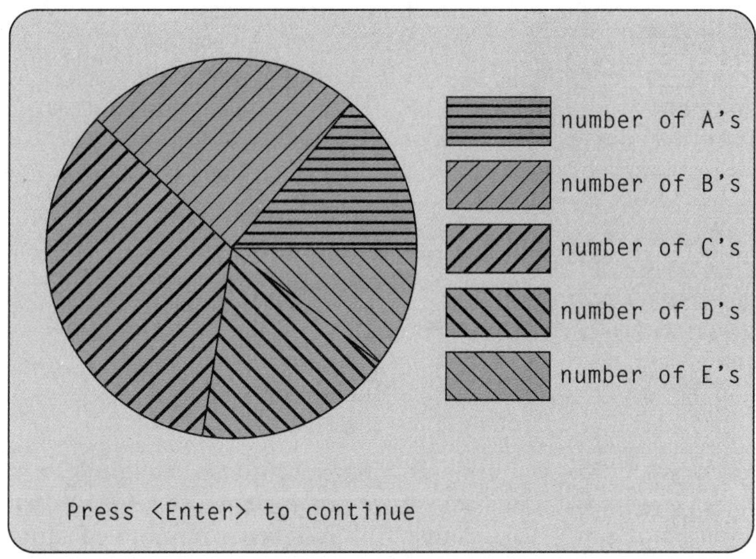

A first-level pseudocode development for this problem is

```
REPEAT
  1. Display a menu
  CASE MenuChoice OF
     2. Enter grades
     3. Display a bar graph
     4. Display a pie chart
     5. Exit the program
UNTIL program is exited
```

A second-level pseudocode development is

```
REPEAT
   1. Display a menu
      1.1 clear the screen
      1.2 print directions
      1.3 print selections
      1.4 get user choice
   CASE MenuChoice OF
      2. Enter grades
         2.1 clear the screen
         2.2 input grades
      3. Display a bar graph
         3.1 initialize graphics
         3.2 set boundaries and spacings for bars
         3.3 print a heading
         3.4 display the bars
         3.5 print a continuation message
         3.6 close graphics
      4. Display a pie chart
         4.1 initialize graphics
         4.2 initialize angles and patterns
```

        4.3 print a heading
        4.4 display the sectors
        4.5 display the legends
        4.6 print a continuation message
        4.7 close graphics
    5. Exit the program
UNTIL program is exited

In this second-level pseudocode stage, the following steps need additional development:

2.2 input grades
3.4 display the bars
4.4 display the sectors
4.5 display the legends

As part of entering grades, the program should have the user input how many of each grade were given, accumulate the total number of grades given, and determine the maximum number of any one grade. Thus, step 2.2 is further developed as

2.2 input grades
    2.2.1 get number for a grade

FIGURE 13.30 (a–d) Structure chart for **PROGRAM** GradeGraphs

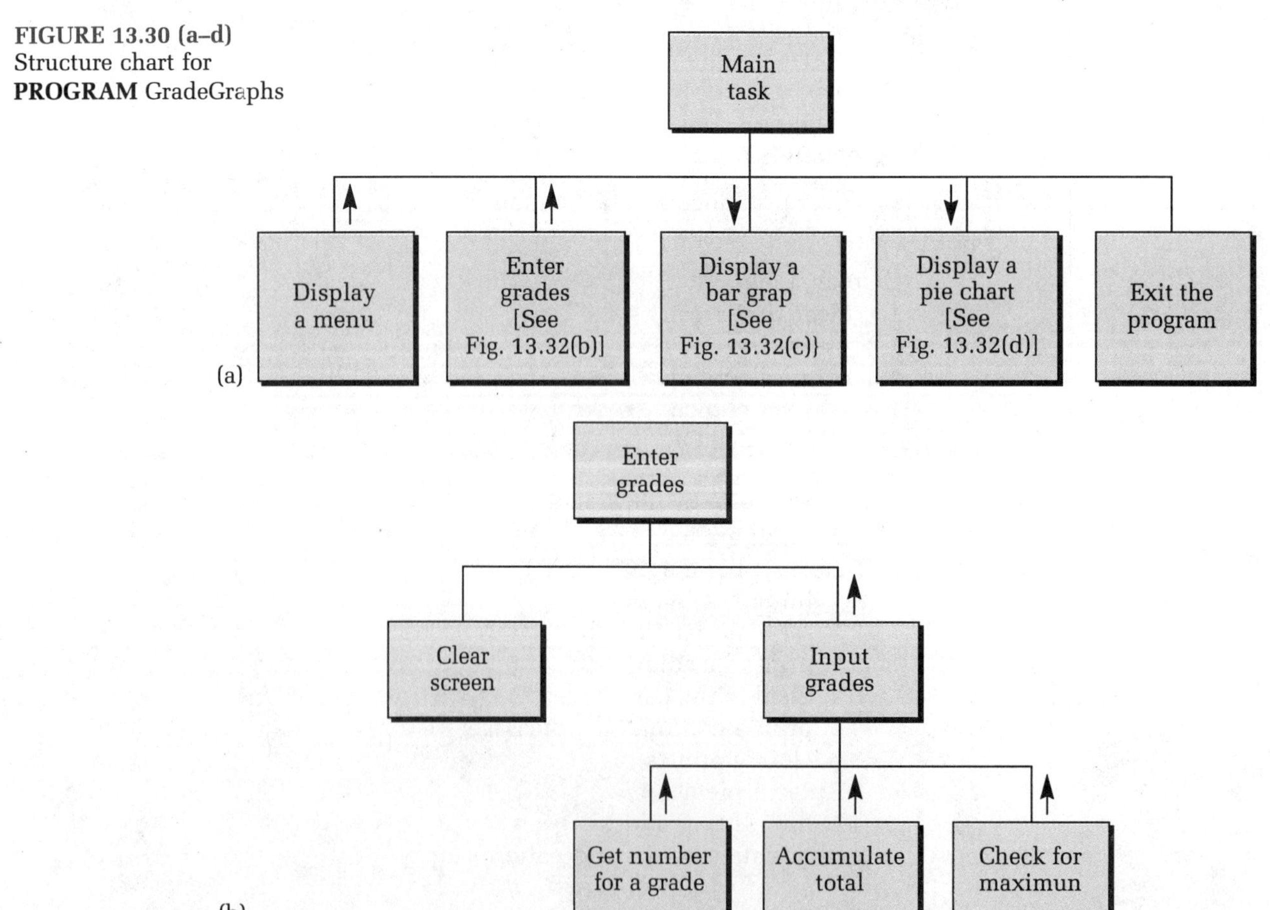

2.2.2 accumulate total
2.2.3 check for maximum

Further development of steps 3.4, 4.4, and 4.5 is not included here because these subjects were discussed in detail earlier in this chapter. What was not shown earlier was the combining of text with graphics. You should look closely at how this capability is incorporated into the program. You should also pay particular attention to how the bar heights are scaled relative to the tallest bar.

A structure chart for **PROGRAM** GradeGraphs is shown in Figure 13.30. The module specifications for the main modules are

1. Menu Module
   Data received: None
   Information returned: Menu choice
   Logic: Display choices and request the user to enter choice from the keyboard.
2. EnterGrades Module
   Data received: None
   Information returned: Number for each grade (A, B, C, D, E)
   Total number of grades
   Maximum for any one grade
   Logic: Have the user enter the number for each grade.
   Accumulate a total.
   Find the maximum for any one grade.

FIGURE 13.30
Structure chart for **PROGRAM** GradeGraphs

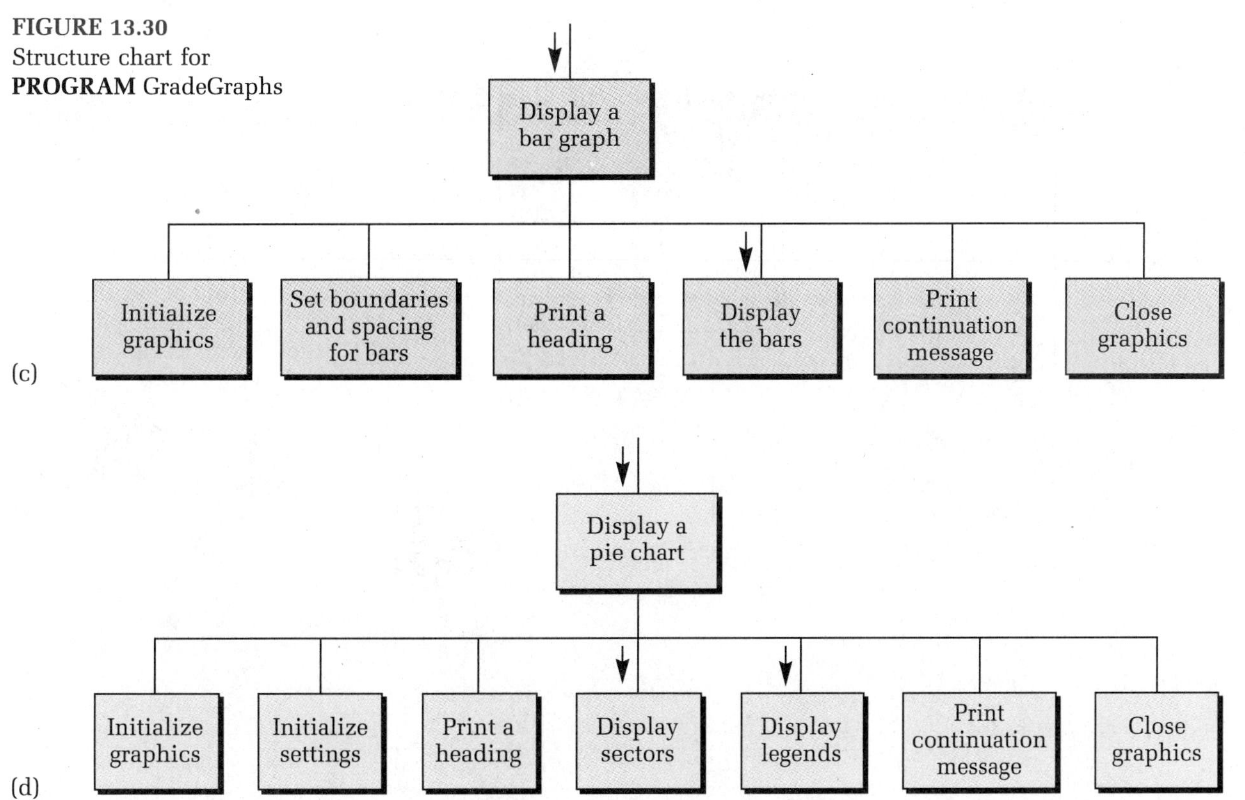

3. MakeBarGraph Module
   Data received: Number for each grade
   Total number of grades
   Maximum for any one grade
   Information returned: None
   Logic: Display a bar for each grade, using the maximum for scaling purposes. Include a heading, continuation message, and description of each bar.
4. MakePieChart Module
   Data received: Total number of grades
   Number for each grade
   Information returned: None
   Logic: Display a sector for each grade. Include a heading, continuation message, and legend for the sector patterns.
5. Exit Program Module
   This option in the **CASE** statement consists of the null statement that permits an exit from the program.

The main program for this problem is

```
BEGIN  {  Main program  }
  InitializeGraphics;
  RestoreCrtMode;
  REPEAT
    Menu (Choice);
    CASE Choice OF
      1 : EnterGrades (NumGrades, MaxGrades, Total);
      2 : MakeBarGraph (NumGrades, MaxGrades, Total);
      3 : MakePieChart (NumGrades, Total);
      4 :   {  null statement - exit option  }
    END  {  of CASE Choice statement  }
  UNTIL Choice = 4
END.  {  of main program  }
```

A complete program for this problem follows.

```
PROGRAM GradeGraphs;

{  This program is a culmination of most of what has been   }
{  presented in this graphics supplement.  It features bar  }
{  graphs, pie charts, text in graphics, and user inter-    }
{  action.  The user is instructed to enter grades and      }
{  choose a display of a bar graph or a pie chart for       }
{  viewing the distribution of grades.                      }

USES
  Crt, Graph;

CONST
  Indent = ' ';

TYPE
  GradeList = ARRAY['A'..'E'] OF integer;

VAR
  MaxGrades,
  Total, Choice : integer;
  NumGrades : GradeList;

{************************************************************}
```

```
PROCEDURE Menu (VAR Choice : integer);

  {  Given:   Nothing                                     }
  {  Task:    Have the user enter an option for further   }
  {                action                                  }
  {  Return:  Option for further action                    }

  BEGIN
    ClrScr;
    writeln ('This program will graphically display the');
    writeln ('distribution of grades for a class.  Please');
    writeln ('choose one of the following and press <Enter>.');
    writeln;
    writeln (Indent:4, '<1> Enter grades');
    writeln;
    writeln (Indent:4, '<2> View bar graph');
    writeln;
    writeln (Indent:4, '<3> View pie chart');
    writeln;
    writeln (Indent:4, '<4> Quit');
    readln (Choice)
  END;   {  of PROCEDURE Menu  }

{*********************************************************}

PROCEDURE InitializeGraphics;

  {  Given:   Nothing                                      }
  {  Task:    Initialize graphics. Provide error message   }
  {                for unsuccessful initialization.        }
  {  Return:  Nothing                                      }

  VAR
    GraphDriver, GraphMode,
    ErrorResult : integer;
    InitError : boolean;
  BEGIN
    GraphDriver := CGA;
    GraphMode := 1;
    InitGraph (GraphDriver, GraphMode, 'C:\TP\BGI');
    ErrorResult := GraphResult;
    InitError := (ErrorResult <> 0);
    IF InitError THEN
      BEGIN
        writeln ('There is a graphics error.');
        writeln (GraphErrorMsg(ErrorResult));
        writeln ('Program aborted.');
        readln;
        Halt
      END
  END;  {  of PROCEDURE InitializeGraphics  }

{*********************************************************}

PROCEDURE Continuation;

  BEGIN
    SetColor (2);
    OutTextXY (10, GetMaxY - 10, 'Press <Enter> to continue');
    readln
  END;  {  of PROCEDURE Continuation  }
```

```
{**********************************************************}

PROCEDURE EnterGrades (VAR NumGrades : GradeList;
                       VAR MaxGrades, Total : integer);

  {  Given:   Nothing                                          }
  {  Task:    Have the user enter the grade distribution       }
  {                for a class                                 }
  {  Return:  The grade distribution for a class,              }
  {                the total number of grades, and             }
  {                the maximum for any one grade               }

  VAR
    Grade : char;
  BEGIN
    ClrScr;

    {  Initialize variables  }
    MaxGrades := 0;
    Total := 0;

    {  Get input interactively  }
    FOR Grade := 'A' TO 'E' DO
      BEGIN
        write ('How many ',Grade,'''s?  ');
        readln (NumGrades[Grade]);
        Total := Total + NumGrades[Grade];
        IF NumGrades[Grade] > MaxGrades THEN
          MaxGrades := NumGrades[Grade]  { Find the maximum }
      END  {  of FOR loop  }
  END;  {  of PROCEDURE EnterGrades  }

{**********************************************************}

PROCEDURE MakeBarGraph (NumGrades : GradeList;
                        MaxGrades, Total : integer);

  {  Given:   The grade distribution for a class and           }
  {                the total number of students in the         }
  {                class                                       }
  {  Task:    Make and display a bar graph of the grades       }
  {  Return:  Nothing                                          }

  CONST
    LeftEdge = 50;
    BarWidth = 10;
    BarSeparation = 15;
  VAR
    BottomEdge,
    MaxHeight,
    BarScale,
    X1, X2, Y1, Y2 : integer;
    Grade : char;

  {========================================================}

  PROCEDURE DisplayBar (VAR X1,X2 : integer;
                        BottomEdge, BarScale : integer;
                        Num : integer);

    {  Given:   Ending position of the last bar (X2),          }
    {                distance between bars, bottom edge,       }
    {                scale for height and number of grades     }
```

```
    {  Task:    Display one bar                              }
    {  Return:  The new edges (X1,X2)                        }

    BEGIN
      X1 := X2 + BarSeparation;
      Y1 := BottomEdge - NumGrades[Grade] * BarScale;
      X2 := X1 + BarWidth;
      Bar (X1, Y1, X2, Y2)
    END;  {  of PROCEDURE DisplayBar  }

  {==========================================================}

  BEGIN  {  PROCEDURE MakeBarGraph  }
    SetGraphMode (1);
    SetBkColor (Green);

    {  Set the boundaries and spacings for the bars  }
    BottomEdge := GetMaxY - 50;
    X2 := LeftEdge - BarSeparation;
    Y2 := BottomEdge;
    MaxHeight := GetMaxY - 100; { Leave margins of 50 pixels }
    BarScale := round(MaxHeight/MaxGrades); {  Scale height }

    {  Print a heading  }
    OutTextXY (0,10, 'GRADE DISTRIBUTION - BAR GRAPH');

    {  Display the bars  }
    FOR Grade := 'A' TO 'E' DO
      BEGIN
        DisplayBar (X1, X2, BottomEdge,
                    BarScale, NumGrades[Grade]);
        OutTextXY (X1, Y2 + 10, Grade)
      END;  {  of display for one bar  }
    Continuation;
    RestoreCrtMode
  END;  {  of PROCEDURE MakeBarGraph  }

{**********************************************************}

PROCEDURE MakePieChart (NumGrades : GradeList;
                        Total : integer);

  {  Given:   The grade distribution for a class and       }
  {                the total number of students in the     }
  {                class                                   }
  {  Task:    Make and display a pie chart of the grades   }
  {  Return:  Nothing                                      }

  CONST
    Radius = 50;
    Xcoor = 100;
    Ycoor = 100;
    Ystart = 45;
  VAR
    AngleStart, AngleFinish, SliceSize : integer;
    Pattern : word;
    ItemAngleSize : real;
    Grade : char;
    Y1 : integer;

  {==========================================================}
```

```
PROCEDURE GraphSector (NumItems : integer;
                       ItemAngleSize : real;
                       AngleStart : integer;
                       VAR AngleFinish : integer;
                       VAR Pattern : word);

  {  Given:   Number of items for the sector, angle size  }
  {                per item, angle start position, fill   }
  {                pattern for the last sector            }
  {  Task:    Create one sector of a pie chart            }
  {  Return:  Angle finish position and pattern used      }
  {                for the sector                         }

  VAR
    SliceSize : word;
  BEGIN
    SliceSize := round(NumItems * ItemAngleSize);
    AngleStart := AngleFinish;
    AngleFinish := AngleStart + SliceSize;
    IF AngleFinish > 360 THEN
      AngleFinish := 360;
    Pattern := succ(Pattern);
    SetFillStyle (Pattern, 2);
    PieSlice (Xcoor, Ycoor, Anglestart, AngleFinish, Radius)
  END;  {  of PROCEDURE GraphSector  }

{===========================================================}

PROCEDURE DisplayLegend (VAR Y1 : integer;
                         VAR Pattern : word;
                         Grade : char);

  {  Given:    Initial Y, pattern for fill and Grade      }
  {  Task:     Draw a bar, pattern fill, show legend      }
  {  Return:   Ending Y and pattern used                  }

  CONST
    X1 = 175;
    X2 = 200;
    DeltaY = 15;
    BetweenBars = 10;
  VAR
    X, Y2 : integer;
  BEGIN
    Y2 := Y1 + DeltaY;
    Pattern := succ(Pattern);
    SetFillStyle (Pattern, 2);
    Bar (X1, Y1, X2, Y2);
    X := X2 + 10;
    OutTextXY (X, Y1, Grade);
    Y1 := Y2 + BetweenBars
  END;  {  of PROCEDURE DisplayLegend  }

{===========================================================}

BEGIN  {  PROCEDURE MakePieChart  }

  {  Perform initialization  }
  SetGraphMode (1);
  SetBkColor (Blue);
```

```
    AngleFinish := 0;
    Pattern := SolidFill;
    ItemAngleSize := 360 / Total;

    {  Print a heading  }
    OutTextXY (0, 10, 'GRADE DISTRIBUTION - PIE CHART');

    {  Display sectors of the pie chart  }
    FOR Grade := 'A' TO 'E' DO
      GraphSector (NumGrades[Grade], ItemAngleSize,
                   AngleStart, AngleFinish, Pattern);

    {  Display legend for the sectors  }
    Y1 := Ystart;
    Pattern := SolidFill;
    FOR Grade := 'A' TO 'E' DO
      DisplayLegend (Y1, Pattern, Grade);
    Continuation;
    RestoreCrtMode
  END;  {  of PROCEDURE MakePieChart  }

{***********************************************************}

BEGIN  {  Main program  }
  InitializeGraphics;
  RestoreCrtMode;
  REPEAT
    Menu (Choice);
    CASE Choice OF
      1 : EnterGrades  (NumGrades, MaxGrades, Total);
      2 : MakeBarGraph (NumGrades, MaxGrades, Total);
      3 : MakePieChart (NumGrades, Total);
      4 :   {  null statement - exit option  }
    END  {  of CASE statement  }
  UNTIL Choice = 4
END.  {  of main program  }
```

A sample run of this program produces the following output.

```
This program will graphically display the
distribution of grades for a class.  Please
choose one of the following and press <Enter>.

       <1> Enter grades

       <2> View bar graph

       <3> View pie chart

       <4> Quit
1
```

Screen 1

```
How many A's?  4
How many B's?  7
How many C's?  10
How many D's?  5
How many E's?  3
```

Screen 2

```
This program will graphically display the
distribution of grades for a class.  Please
choose one of the following and press <Enter>.


      <1> Enter grades


      <2> View bar graph


      <3> View pie chart


      <4> Quit
2
```

Screen 3

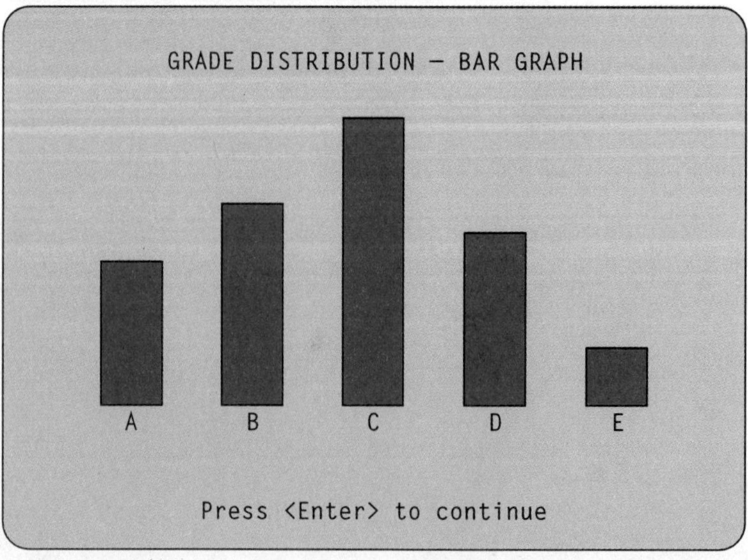

Screen 4

```
This program will graphically display the
distribution of grades for a class.  Please
choose one of the following and press <Enter>.

      <1> Enter grades

      <2> View bar graph

      <3> View pie chart

      <4> Quit
3
```

Screen 5

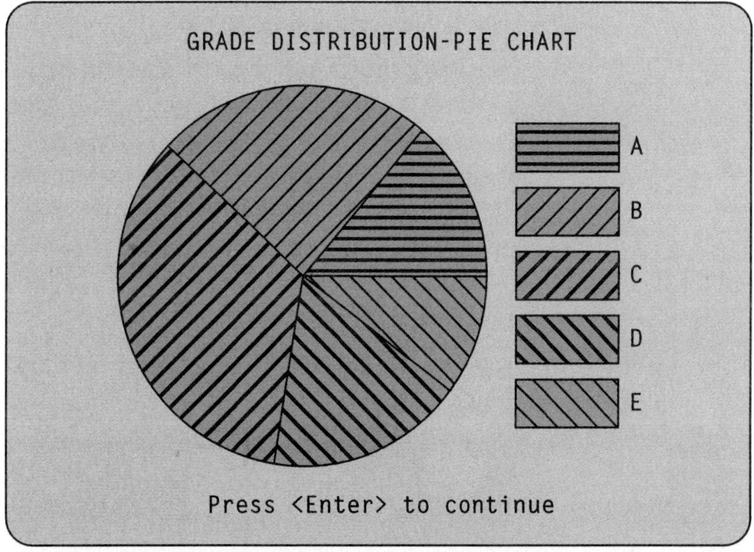

Screen 6

```
This program will graphically display the
distribution of grades for a class.  Please
choose one of the following and press <Enter>.

      <1> Enter grades

      <2> View bar graph

      <3> View pie chart

      <4> Quit
4
```

Screen 7

RUNNING AND DEBUGGING HINTS

1. Include both **Crt** and **Graph** in the **USES** section of your program when you plan to use graphics. A typical statement is

```
USES
  Crt, Graph;
```

2. If Turbo Pascal is in the same directory as the BGI driver file (*.BGI), you can use

```
GraphDriver := detect;
InitGraph (GraphDriver, GraphMode, '');
```

to initialize graphics.

3. If Turbo Pascal is not in the same directory as the BGI driver file (*.BGI), you must specify a file path in the **InitGraphics** procedure. The path could be C:\TP\BGI.
4. Use **SetBkColor** and **SetColor** to control screen colors for backgrounds and for the current drawing color.
5. Use **SetGraphMode** to change the available colors.
6. Use **RestoreCrtMode** (not **CloseGraph**) if you are going back and forth between graphics and text.
7. Use **GetAspectRatio** (Xasp,Yasp) to determine the relative width and height of a pixel. Then define an aspect ratio as AspectRatio := Xasp/Yasp. Use this ratio to produce proper perspectives for shapes.
8. Use **readln** to hold displays on the screen for an indefinite amount of time.
9. Use **delay** to hold displays on the screen for a predetermined amount of time.
10. Achieve animation by using **delay** and erasing the figure by drawing it in the background color.
11. Use a sequence of calls to **bar** to produce a bar graph.
12. Determine bar heights for bar graphs as a function of the tallest bar.
13. Determine a bottom edge for bar graphs by using **GetMaxY.**
14. Use a sequence of calls to **PieSlice** to produce a pie chart.
15. Vary the patterns in a pie chart by using **succ**(Pattern) and **SetFillStyle** before calling **PieSlice.**
16. Display a legend for a pie chart to explain what the sectors represent.
17. Develop a continuation message by writing a procedure that uses **OutTextXY** to print a message at the bottom of a graphics display.
18. When making a pie chart, always make the last ending angle 360°.

Summary

Key Terms

bit-mapped font
current pointer
high resolution mode
medium resolution mode
picture element
pixel
stroked font

Keywords

Arc
ArcCoordsType
Bar
GetMaxY
GetTextSettings
GothicFont
Rectangle
RestoreCrtMode
SansSeriFont

Bar3D	**GraphErrorMsg**	**SetBkColor**
BkSlashFill	**GraphResult**	**SetColor**
CenterLn	**Halt**	**SetFillStyle**
Circle	**HatchFill**	**SetGraphMode**
ClearDevice	**HorizDir**	**SetLineStyle**
CloseDotFill	**InterleaveFill**	**SetTextJustify**
CloseGraph	**InitGraph**	**SetTextStyle**
DashedLn	**Line**	**SlashFill**
DefaultFont	**LineFill**	**SmallFont**
delay	**LineRel**	**SolidFill**
Detect	**LineTo**	**SolidLn**
DottedLn	**LtBkSlashFill**	**TextHeight**
Ellipse	**LtSlashFill**	**TextWidth**
EmptyFill	**MoveRel**	**ThickWidth**
FillEllipse	**MoveTo**	**TriplexFont**
FillPoly	**NormWidth**	**UserBitLn**
FloodFill	**OutText**	**UserFill**
GetArcCoords	**OutTextXY**	**VertDir**
GetAspectRatio	**PieSlice**	**WideDotFill**
GetMaxX	**PutPixel**	**XHatchFill**
Graph	**Sector**	

Key Concepts

- The predefined functions **GetMaxX** and **GetMaxY,** respectively, can be used to determine the number of pixels horizontally and vertically.
- Individual pixels can be plotted using **PutPixel** (X, Y, <color>).
- Lines can be drawn using **Line** (X1, Y1, X2, Y2) or **LineTo** (X,Y).
- The current pointer can be moved using **MoveTo** (X,Y).
- Four standardized styles of lines are available for **SetLineStyle.**
- Rectangles can be drawn using **Rectangle** (X1, Y1, X2, Y2).
- Circles can be drawn using **Circle** (Xcoor, Ycoor, Radius).
- **delay** (LengthOfPause) can be used to hold a screen image a predetermined amount of time.
- Arcs can be drawn using **Arc** (Xcoor, Ycoor, AngleStart, AngleFinish, Radius).
- Ellipses can be drawn using **Ellipse** (Xcoor,Ycoor, AngleStart, AngleFinish, Xrad, Yrad).
- Several filling patterns are available; these patterns are set by a call to **SetFillStyle** (Pattern, Color).
- **FloodFill** (Xcoor, Ycoor, BorderColor) can be used to fill a closed region.
- **FillEllipse** (Xcoor, Ycoor, Xrad, Yrad) can be used to fill an ellipse.
- A bar can be drawn by using **Bar** (X1, Y1, X2, Y2).
- Sectors of a circle can be drawn by using **PieSlice** (Xcoor, Ycoor, AngleStart, AngleFinish, Radius).
- Either **OutText** or **OutTextXY** can be used to display text while in the graphics mode.
- Five predetermined fonts are available for text characters while in the graphics mode.
- The text font, direction, and size can be determined by a call to **SetTextStyle.**

■ Programming Problems and Projects

1. Write a program that produces a kaleidoscope that fills your screen with varying patterns of different colors.
2. Write a program that produces a bouncing ball and moves it across the screen. Use **delay** to achieve animation and to erase previous images. Use **Circle** in a procedure to display a single image.
3. Earlier in this chapter, you were asked to design a display of an automobile. Put this design in a procedure (if you haven't already done so), and then use the technique of animation to move the automobile around the screen.

4. Several modifications can be made in the Focus on Program Design program in this chapter. Write a complete program that includes the following enhancements.
   a. Enter the bar graph.
   b. Center and place the headings in a rectangle, such as

```
GRADE DISTRIBUTION - BAR GRAPH
```

   c. Put a vertical scale on the graph to indicate the bar heights.
   d. Indicate the percent represented by each sector in the pie chart.
5. Write a program that displays closing prices on the New York Stock Exchange for several weeks. Your graph should have a horizontal axis and a vertical axis. Let the daily closing prices be plotted as nine pixel squares and connected by lines to the center of each square. Let the range for each day be shown by a vertical line. Typical output would be similar to the following graph.

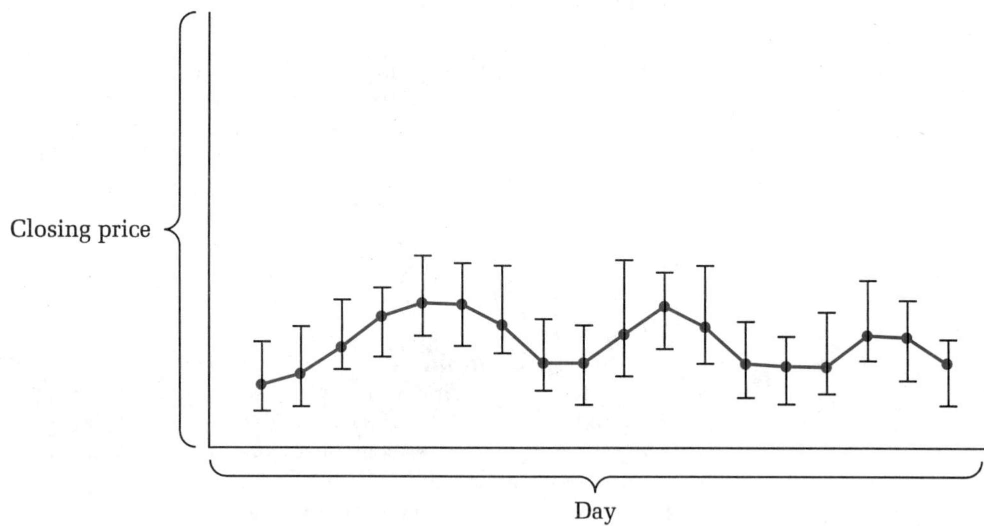

6. Examine the graphics features available in several spreadsheets. In particular, note how they can be used to display bar graphs, three-dimensional bar graphs, and pie charts. After running several sample graphs, compare your results with the results you obtain when you run the Focus on Program Design program at the end of this chapter. Based on your findings, prepare a report for the class indicating what design specifications you believe the software engineers used to create the graphics part of the spreadsheets.
7. Develop a procedure that allows text display to be printed vertically "down" the screen, rather than "up" the screen as is the case when **SetTextStyle** has a second argument (direction) of 1. Use your procedure in a program that allows the user to select from the following menu of orientations:

   0—horizontal
   1—vertical (up)
   2—vertical (down)

8. Prepare an interactive program that allows the user to experiment with the background colors and the current drawing colors available. The user should be allowed to make the following choices:

   (1) Figure of a circle or square (3) Background color
   (2) Value of a radius or side length (4) Current drawing color

9. Modify the program you created in Problem 8 to allow the user additional choices of filling patterns and colors.
10. Develop a system for normalizing the screen coordinates in a graphics mode. In your normalized system, (0,0) is in the lower-left corner and (1,1) is in the upper-right corner. The *x*-axis extends from 0 to 1, left to right; the *y*-axis extends from 0 to 1, bottom to top. The center of this screen is (0.5,0.5). Thus, your normalized screen would look like this:

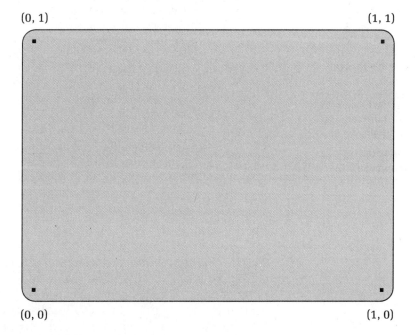

    Give a report of your system to the students in your class. Show them how they can plot points and draw lines, rectangles, and other graphics figures using the normalized system.
11. Contact your local weather service bureau and determine the average precipitation in your region for each month of the year. Write a program that displays the distribution in a bar graph. Be sure to include suitable headings and messages as part of your output.

■ Communication in Practice

Select and run BGIDEMO.PAS. Obtain a hard copy of this program. Run the program again, and trace out the code as you progress through the various screens. Discuss the documentation provided with the program. Make a list of the suggestions you have for modifying the documentation, and present these suggestions to the class.

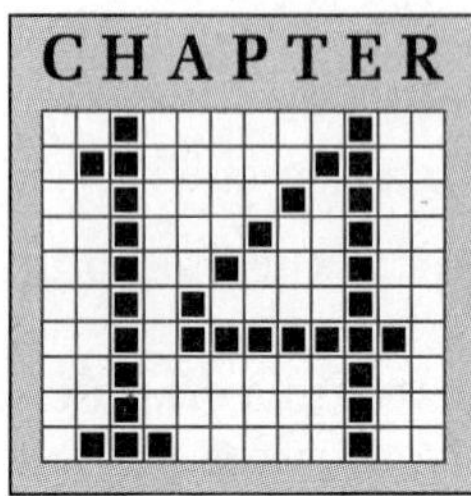

Object-Oriented Programming (OOP)

CHAPTER OUTLINE

S

Object-oriented programming (OOP) is an extension of a programming language. In this sense, we must be aware of syntax, data structures, and programming language constructs before we can write and use objects in object-oriented programming; thus, OOP is discussed at the end of a programming text. On the other hand, object-oriented programming requires us to think about program development in such a different way that it arguably could be studied as a self-contained entity instead of an entity embedded in a programming language.

Object-oriented programming is causing a revolution in software engineering. It provides a new way for software engineers to develop, design, update, and maintain software systems. Although it is relatively new, OOP is a rapidly growing approach to creating software systems.

One feature of OOP is the creation of a large library of object definitions that can be reused both in the maintenance of existing softwear and in the creation of new software. The ability to manipulate existing objects to accomplish program tasks greatly simplifies the writing of new programs. Using objects from your library will enable you to solve new problems faster and to have greater confidence in the correctness of your solutions.

The concepts, processes, terminology, syntax, development, and uses of objects in object-oriented programming will be slowly introduced in this chapter. Although it is not the purpose of this chapter to make you an expert in object-oriented programming, you should be comfortable with the basic concepts and uses of objects in object-oriented programming by the time you complete this chapter. Just relax, be patient, and enjoy this introductory look at a new design methodology.

■ 14.1 What Is an Object?

We previously worked with structures containing data fields when we worked with arrays, records, and files. As we examined these structures, we developed operations for manipulating the data fields, such as sorting, finding the largest value, inserting, deleting, and so forth. The goal of object-oriented programming is to combine the data fields and subsequent operations into a unified package in such a manner that the user can manipulate the object without being concerned about implementation details.

Encapsulation

An *object* in object-oriented programming is a structure that contains:

1. Fields for data
2. A list of operations, called *methods,* that can be performed on the data fields

The data fields and all methods (procedures and functions) necessary to access these fields are contained in the same structure. The process of including the operations that can be performed on the data fields as part of the structure is referred to as *encapsulation.* To illustrate, the definition of our first object type, which can be used to represent a point in a plane, is

```
TYPE
  Point = OBJECT
            X : real;}
            Y : real;}                                          data fields

            PROCEDURE Init;                                  }
            PROCEDURE SetCoordinates (Xcoor, Ycoor : real);  }
            FUNCTION GetX : real;                            }  methods
            FUNCTION GetY : real;                            }
            PROCEDURE Print;                                 }
          END;  {  of OBJECT Point   }
```

With this definition, an object of this type can be declared in the variable declaration part of the program as

```
VAR
  Dot : Point;
```

Dot is referred to as an *instance of the object* type Point.

The object type Point allows us to consider that a point in the plane is determined by two coordinates. Furthermore, it allows us to think about some of the operations we may wish to perform on a point in a plane. Specifically, we can initialize the coordinates to (0, 0), set values in the coordinates, retrieve the X or Y coordinates, and print the coordinates.

Using Methods

Before we proceed, let's look more closely at the methods listed in the object type Point. Why do we need procedures for initialization, setting coordinates, and printing values or functions for retrieving the values of the coordinates? We need these methods because a program should never operate directly on the data fields of an object. A method should be written for every operation, and the methods should be then used to work with the object. This process permits the details of

A NOTE OF INTEREST

IBM and Apple = Pinstrips and T-Shirts

After signing the Treaty of Amiens in 1802, Napolean said, "What a beautiful fix we are in now; peace has been declared." In July 1991, representatives of IBM and Apple announced an alliance that similarly shocked many industry analysts. IBM has long been positioned in the mainstream of the computer industry, gaining its reputation more from selling the reliability of its corporate image than from technological innovation. Apple, on the other hand, has based its claim to fame on bold new technologies developed by computer enthusiasts with a distinct bent toward "hacking." For instance, the window-based environment of the first Apple Macintosh in 1983 established a new and exciting mode of human-computer interaction. When IBM and Microsoft later "copied" the "look and feel" of the Mac environment to an IBM-compatible operating system, Apple promptly took them to court. The effects of this case on the software industry are still being debated.

Small wonder that eyebrows have been raised by the agreement between these two corporate antagonists. What are the underlying reasons for the move? According to joint press releases, the companies will cooperate on four fronts:

1. IBM will take steps to better integrate the Mac into IBM-based computer networks.
2. Apple will build future machines using IBM's RISC architecture chip technology.
3. The companies will work together to develop data standards for multimedia.
4. There will be a joint endeavor to produce a new, object-oriented operating system that will eventually be marketed for both IBM and Apple computers.

The last of these ventures is the one that seems to be generating the most excitement on an industry-wide basis. The two companies had been working individually on object-oriented operating systems. Apple had been calling their exploratory system Pink; IBM had called its system Metaphor. It now appears that the Pink and Metaphor research groups will combine their efforts, with the long-range goal that users and third-party software developers will only have to deal with one common interface for a variety of different machines from the two companies. By taking advantage of the abstraction emphasized by the object-oriented approach, the details of the particular machine will be completely hidden.

It all sounds good in theory, but can researchers from two such historically different companies really define a common set of goals? If they can, will it destroy their own individual initiatives? Only time will tell.

implementation to be hidden from the user. Thus, the user's only concern is that the message sent to the object is clear. If it is clear, the task will be accomplished.

Form and Syntax

The general form for defining an object type is

```
TYPE
  <identifier> = OBJECT
                 <field 1> : <data type 1>;  ┐
                     .           .           │
                     .           .           │ data fields
                     .           .           │
                 <field n> : <data type n>;  ┘
                 <method 1>;                 ┐
                     .                       │
                     .                       │ methods
                     .                       │
                 <method m>;                 ┘
                 END;
```

This form resembles the data type for a record. Note the following characteristics of this definition:

1. The first part contains the data fields to be assigned to the object type.
2. The second part contains methods to be used to perform operations on the data fields; these methods are procedures and functions.
3. The listing of these methods is a form of forward declaration; that is, they are listed as part of the object structure, but the actual code for them is written later as part of the subprogram definition section.
4. Variables of this defined type may be declared in the **VAR** declaration section. This is called *instantiation.*
5. A semicolon is required after the last method and before the **END** of the definition.

Objects can be used in a program wherever records can be used, with one exception. Objects cannot be used as components of files.

Use in a Program

Now let's write a short, complete program that defines an object type, develops written code for each method, declares an instance of an object, and then uses the object. In the following program, we declare an object type Point (as before), give the point some coordinates, and then print the coordinates of the point.

```
PROGRAM ObjectPoint;

USES
  Crt;

TYPE
  Point = OBJECT
            X : real;
            Y : real;

            PROCEDURE Init;
            PROCEDURE SetCoordinates (Xcoor, Ycoor : real);
            FUNCTION GetX : real;
            FUNCTION GetY : real;
            PROCEDURE Print;
          END;  {  of OBJECT Point  }

VAR
  P, Q : Point;
  NewX, NewY : real;

{*********************************************************}

{  Now write procedures and functions for the methods.  }

{--------------------------------------------------------}

PROCEDURE Point.Init;
  BEGIN
    X := 0.0;
    Y := 0.0
  END;  {  of PROCEDURE Point.Init  }

{--------------------------------------------------------}
```

```
PROCEDURE Point.SetCoordinates (Xcoor, Ycoor : real);
  BEGIN
    X := Xcoor;
    Y := Ycoor
  END;  {  of PROCEDURE Point.SetCoordinates  }

{-----------------------------------------------------------}

FUNCTION Point.GetX : real;
  BEGIN
    GetX := X
  END;  {  of FUNCTION Point.GetX  }

{-----------------------------------------------------------}

FUNCTION Point.GetY : real;
  BEGIN
    GetY := Y
  END;  {  of FUNCTION Point.GetY  }

{-----------------------------------------------------------}

PROCEDURE Point.Print;
  VAR
    Xcoor, Ycoor : real;
  BEGIN
    Xcoor := GetX;
    Ycoor := GetY;
    writeln ('The coordinates are X = ', Xcoor:6:2,
             '  Y = ', Ycoor:6:2)
  END;  {  of PROCEDURE Point.Print  }

{***********************************************************}

{  All methods have been written.  }
{  Now begin the main program.     }

BEGIN  {  Main program  }
  ClrScr;
  P.Init;
  Q.Init;
  P.SetCoordinates (3,5);
  P.Print;
  NewX := 2 * P.GetX;
  NewY := 2 * P.GetY;
  Q.SetCoordinates (NewX, NewY);
  Q.Print;
  readln  {  Hold the display  }
END.  {  of main program  }
```

A sample run of this program produces

```
The coordinates are X =   3.00  Y =   5.00
The coordinates are X =   6.00  Y =  10.00
```

Scope

With this program in mind, let's consider some aspects of using objects in object-oriented programming. Let dot (the object) be an instance of the object type Point. It may be envisioned as

Dot

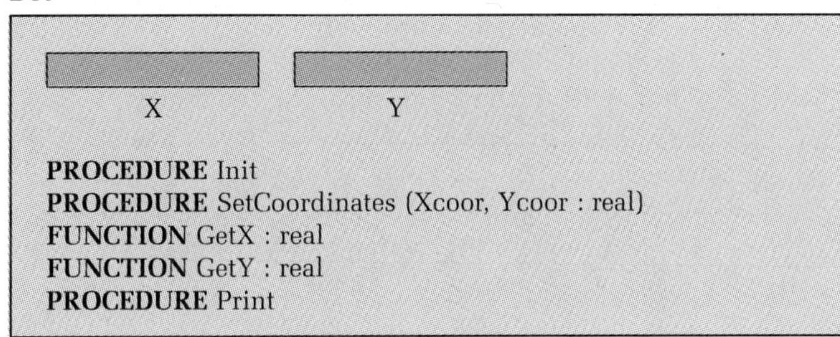

The data fields of an object are available to that object's methods. Since **PROCEDURE** Init is defined in the object type Point, it has the same scope as X and Y. In general, the method bodies and the object data fields share the same scope. Thus, in the procedure

```
PROCEDURE Point.Init;
  BEGIN
    X := 0.0;
    Y := 0.0
  END;
```

since X and Y are fields in the object type, references to them in **PROCEDURE** Point.Init are unique.

Initially, we define all object types in the outermost scope of a program. Later, we will see how Turbo Pascal permits these definitions to be local.

Because the fields and methods of an object share the same scope, no field identifiers may be identical to a formal parameter. If we had written

```
TYPE
  Point = OBJECT
            X : real;
            Y : real;
              .
              .
              .
            PROCEDURE SetCoordinates (X, Y : real);
```

it would have caused the compilation error

```
Error 4 : Duplicate identifier
```

When methods for an object type are listed in the definition, they are treated as **FORWARD** declarations. When they are actually written later, they must contain a unique reference to the object type in which they are defined. This method of reference requires the object type identifier to be followed by a period. Thus, if the object type is

```
TYPE
  Point = OBJECT
            X : real;
            Y : real;

            PROCEDURE Init;
              .
              .
              .
```

when **PROCEDURE** Init is written, the procedure heading is

```
PROCEDURE Point.Init;
```

This uniquely identifies **PROCEDURE** Init with the object type Point.

A consequence of uniquely identifying **PROCEDURE** Point.Init with the object type Point is that the data fields of Point (X and Y) are available to the procedure. Thus, within the procedure, the references

```
X := 0.0;
Y := 0.0;
```

uniquely identify data fields of the variables. In our program, Dot.Init causes fields X and Y to be initialized as follows:

Dot

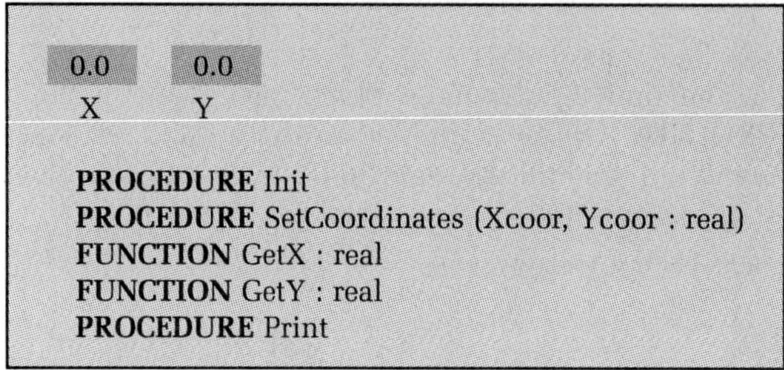

Object References

References to the methods of an object require periods in the same manner as do references to the fields of a record. Thus, to initialize Dot, we write

```
Dot.Init;
```

It is also possible to use the **WITH . . . DO** statement (see Chapter 9) when referring to the methods of an object. Using this construct, the main program can be written

```
BEGIN
  ClrScr;
  WITH Dot DO
    BEGIN
      Init;
      SetCoordinates (3, 5);
      Print;
      NewX := 2 * GetX;
      NewY := 2 * GetY;
      SetCoordinates (NewX, NewY);
      Print
    END; {  of WITH...DO  }
  readln  {  Hold the screen   }
END.
```

In this introductory look at object-oriented programming, we will usually make explicit references to the fields of an object instead of utilizing the **WITH . . . DO** statement.

The Self Parameter

Let's reconsider **PROCEDURE** Point.SetCoordinates from **PROGRAM** Object-Point. Code for this procedure is

```
PROCEDURE Point.SetCoordinates (Xcoor, Ycoor : real);
  BEGIN
    X := Xcoor;
    Y := Ycoor
  END;
```

In this procedure, the identifiers X and Y are used with no explicit reference to the object type Point. The code

```
BEGIN
  X := Xcoor;
  Y := Ycoor
END;
```

works the same as if it had been written

```
WITH Point DO
  BEGIN
    X := Xcoor;
    Y := Ycoor
  END;
```

or, equivalently

```
BEGIN
  Point.X := Xcoor;
  Point.Y := Ycoor
END;
```

Why is no explicit reference to Point needed? Turbo Pascal provides an invisible parameter, called the *self parameter*, that links an object and its methods in scope. Thus, the procedure can be thought of as

```
PROCEDURE Point.SetCoordinates (Xcoor, Ycoor : real);
  BEGIN
    Self.X := Xcoor;
    Self.Y := Ycoor
  END;
```

where **Self** links the data fields X and Y to the object type Point.

The good news is we do not normally need to be concerned about how **Self** works or about using **Self** in methods. Explicit use of **Self** is permissible but should be avoided unless absolutely necessary. This necessity can occur if there is an identifier conflict within a method (same identifier; different scope). Rather than using the **Self** parameter, identifiers within methods should be chosen judiciously to avoid identifier conflicts in the first place. For further elaboration, see the Turbo Pascal User's Guide.

The Init Procedure

One feature of object-oriented programming is that objects should be initialized before they are used. In general, it is good practice to initialize fields before they are used. Later, we will consider a modification of the object type definition that requires initialization before use.

It is possible to use formal parameters with an initialization method such as

```
PROCEDURE Init (Xcoor, Ycoor);
```

and then to use Init, rather than the method

```
PROCEDURE SetCoordinates (Xcoor, Ycoor);
```

when we wish to assign values as coordinates of a point. If we had done this, the main program in **PROGRAM** ObjectPoint would have been

```
BEGIN
  Dot.Init (0,0);
  Dot.Init (3,5);
      .
      .
      .
```

or just

```
BEGIN
  Dot.Init (3,5);
        .
        .
        .
```

Although this works, it is not good practice. True initialization is a separate task, and a method should be written for it. Since only a small amount of extra code is required, it is better to think of initialization as a separate process from assigning values to data fields.

Using Objects

By now, you certainly should be wondering why we go to so much trouble to define and use a record with two fields. The answer underlies one of the basic premises of object-oriented programming. Earlier, we stated that a program should never operate directly with the data fields of an object; rather, access should be via some method. This concept has come to be known as *sending a message* to the object. Think of the boss (main program) sending messages asking a secretary (methods) to Initialize, SetCoordinates, and so on. (Actually, we only care that the secretary makes sure the job gets done; responsibility for actual task completion may be subsequently delegated to others.)

Sending messages to manipulate objects is a significant process. It causes the programmer to think of code and data together during design. If the programmer is thorough, enough methods can be provided so a user of the object never has to access a field directly. To further illustrate this point, suppose we are designing a program that is to read data for successive coordinates of a point. Although we can read them directly into their respective fields by using

```
readln (Dot.X, Dot.Y);
```

we should use declared variables to read the values and then use a method such as SetCoordinates to assign the values to their respective fields, which would result in something like

```
readln (NewX, NewY);
Dot.SetCoordinates (NewX, NewY);
```

This discussion leads to another basic premise of OOP. To put a value into the field of an object, we, call a method belonging to the object that assigns a value to that field. To get a value from the field of an object, we call a method belonging to the object that returns the value of the desired field.

We conclude this section with another illustration of an object: we define an object type for a person's name. Included as part of the definition are methods for initialization, putting a name into the field, and retrieving a name from the field. Although it may not yet be clear why we define an object type for this purpose, you will soon see how the definition can be used as a basis for creating other objects, which is the topic of the next section. For now, we define the type as previously indicated and then use it in a short program. The object type is

```
TYPE
  NameString = OBJECT
                 Name : string;                              } data field

                 PROCEDURE Init;                             ]
                 PROCEDURE SetName (NameStr : string);       } methods
                 FUNCTION GetName : string;                  
                 PROCEDURE Print;                            ]
               END;  { of OBJECT NameString }
```

In the following program, we declare an instance of NameString as

```
VAR
  FullName : NameString;
```

FullName can now be envisioned as

FullName

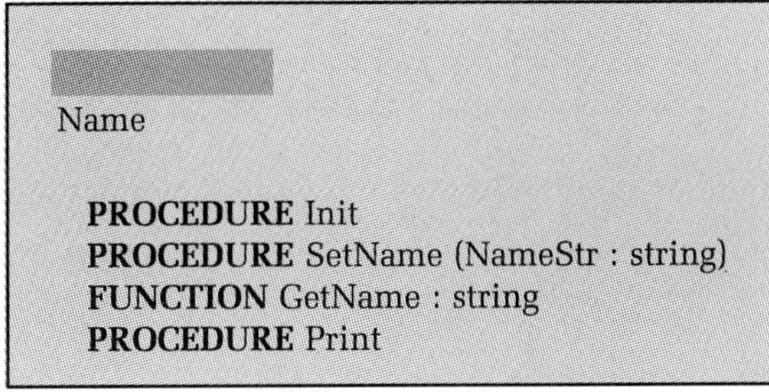

Next, we write code for the four methods defined in the object type. These methods allow the user to initialize the data field, put a value into it, retrieve a value from it, and print the contents. Code for these methods is

```
PROCEDURE NameString.Init;
  BEGIN
    Name := ' '
  END;  {  of PROCEDURE NameString.Init  }

{-----------------------------------------------------------}

PROCEDURE NameString.SetName (NameStr : string);
  BEGIN
    Name := NameStr
  END;  {  of PROCEDURE NameString.SetName  }

{-----------------------------------------------------------}

FUNCTION NameString.GetName : string;
  BEGIN
    GetName := Name
  END;  {  of FUNCTION NameString.GetName  }

{-----------------------------------------------------------}

PROCEDURE NameString.Print;
  BEGIN
    write (Name)
  END;  {  of PROCEDURE NameString.Print  }
```

A complete program that uses the object type NameString follows.

```
PROGRAM NameStrPrac;

USES
  Crt;

TYPE
  NameString = OBJECT
                 Name : string;

                 PROCEDURE Init;
                 PROCEDURE SetName (NameStr : string);
                 FUNCTION GetName : string;
                 PROCEDURE Print;
               END;  {  of OBJECT NameString  }
```

```
VAR
  FullName : NameString;
  MyName : string;

{*************************************************************}

{  Write all methods for the object type NameString.  }

{-------------------------------------------------------------}

PROCEDURE NameString.Init;
  BEGIN
    Name := ' '
  END;  {  of PROCEDURE NameString.Init  }

{-------------------------------------------------------------}

PROCEDURE NameString.SetName (NameStr : string);
  BEGIN
    Name := NameStr
  END;  {  of PROCEDURE NameString.SetName  }

{-------------------------------------------------------------}

FUNCTION NameString.GetName : string;
  BEGIN
    GetName := Name
  END;  {  of FUNCTION NameString.GetName  }

{-------------------------------------------------------------}

PROCEDURE NameString.Print;
  BEGIN
    write (Name)
  END;  {  of PROCEDURE NameString.Print  }

{*************************************************************}

{  All methods have been written.  }
{  Now begin the main program.  }

BEGIN  {  Main program  }
  ClrScr;
  FullName.Init;
  writeln ('Enter your full name and press <Enter>');
  readln (MyName);                       {  Get the user's name  }
  FullName.SetName (MyName);         {  Use an object's methods  }
  MyName := FullName.GetName;  {   Retrieve data using a method  }
  writeln;
  writeln ('The name stored in the data field Name is ', MyName);
  writeln;
  writeln ('This can be printed using a method.  You get ');
  writeln;
  FullName.Print;
  readln
END.  {  of main program  }
```

The output from a sample run of this program is

```
Enter your full name and press <Enter>
Kathy Stowers
```

```
The name stored in the data field Name is Kathy Stowers

This can be printed using a method.  You get

Kathy Stowers
```

We seem to be going to a lot of effort to perform fairly simple tasks. However, this is a necessary basis for subsequent work with objects. In particular, notice in **PROGRAM** NameStrPrac that we never dealt directly with the data fields in the object FullName. Rather, we sent messages such as

```
FullName.Init;
FullName.SetName (MyName);
MyName := FullName.GetName;
FullName.Print;
```

Exercises 14.1

1. State the similarities between an object type and a record type.
2. State the differences between an object type and a record type.
3. Explain what encapsulation means.
4. Explain why a compilation error is caused by the following object type definition:

```
TYPE
  Player = OBJECT
             Weight : real;
             Height : real;
             PROCEDURE Init;
             PROCEDURE SetWeight (Weight : real);
           END;
```

5. Consider the object type defined as

```
TYPE
  Rectangle = OBJECT
                Length : real;                          } data fields
                Width : real;

                PROCEDURE Init;                          ]
                PROCEDURE SetRectangle (L, W : real);    } methods
                FUNCTION GetLength : real;               ]
                FUNCTION GetWidth : real;
              END;
```

Indicate which of the following are valid and which are invalid. Explain what is wrong with each procedure or function that is invalid.

a.
```
PROCEDURE Init;
  BEGIN
    Length := 0;
    Width := 0
  END;
```

b.
```
PROCEDURE Rectangle.SetRectangle (Len, Wid : real);
  BEGIN
    Len := Length;
    Wid := Width
  END;
```

c.
```
FUNCTION Rectangle.GetLength : real;
  BEGIN
    Rectangle.GetLength := Length
  END;
```

d.
```
FUNCTION Rectangle.GetWidth : real;
  BEGIN
    GetWidth := Length
  END;
```

e.
```
FUNCTION Rectangle.GetWidth : real;
  BEGIN
    Width := GetWidth
  END;
```

6. Consider the data fields of the object type definition

```
TYPE
  Point = RECORD
            X : real;
            Y : real
          END;
  Line = OBJECT
           P1 : point;
           P2 : point;
           MidPt : point;
           Length : real;
              .
              .  (methods)
              .
```

Write a method for each of the following tasks.

a. Initialize the object.
b. Assign values to endpoints P1 and P2.
c. Retrieve values from endpoints P1 and P2.
d. Find the midpoint of the line segment.
e. Find the length of the line segment.

7. Consider the object type defined in Exercise 5.

a. Extend the definition to include a method for finding the area of the rectangle.
b. Write the method to implement this task.

8. Again, consider the object type defined in Exercise 5.

a. Declare an instance of a variable of type Rectangle.
b. Use the method SetRectangle to put values of 5 and 8 into the data fields Length and Width, respectively.
c. If the variable declaration includes

```
VAR
  Rect : Rectangle;
```

what would happen if the main program included the line of code

```
Rect.Length := 5;
```

9. Discuss the difference between directly accessing the data fields of an object and using methods to access the data fields of an object.

10. Define an object type that can be used for a fraction. Fields should allow for both a numerator and a denominator. Methods should allow the user to perform the following tasks.

a. Initialize the fraction. (Don't divide by zero!)
b. Put values into the fraction.
c. Retrieve values from the fraction.
d. Print the fraction.
e. Print the decimal equivalent of the fraction.

11. Write a complete program that uses the object type defined in Exercise 10. Your program should allow the user to enter the numerator and the denominator from the keyboard, check for division by zero, put values into the fraction, retrieve values from the fraction, print the fraction, and print the decimal equivalent of the fraction.
12. Define an object type for a complex number. Include methods that allow the user to initialize, set values, add two complex numbers, and display a complex number in the form $a + bi$.
13. Write a complete program using the object type developed in Exercise 12. Your program should allow the user to initialize objects, read two complex numbers from the keyboard, put values in appropriate fields in instances of the object type, use a method to find the sum of the two complex numbers, and display the results.

■ 14.2 Inheritance

We are now ready to consider the most significant new concept associated with object-oriented programming, *inheritance.* According to the process of inheritance, a new object type may be defined by using an existing object type. In this case, the new type inherits the data fields and methods of the previously defined type. To illustrate, reconsider the object type Point from Selection 14.1:

```
TYPE
  Point = OBJECT
            X : real;
            Y : real;

            PROCEDURE Init;
            PROCEDURE SetCoordinates (Xcoor, Ycoor : real);
            FUNCTION GetX : real;
            FUNCTION GetY : real;
            PROCEDURE Print;
          END;  {  of OBJECT Point  }
```

Now suppose we want to define the object type Circle with data fields for a center and a radius. Since a center can be thought of as a point, the object type definition is

```
Circle = OBJECT (Point)
           Radius : real;

           PROCEDURE Init;
           PROCEDURE SetValues (Xcoor, Ycoor, Rad : real);
           PROCEDURE GetCenter (VAR Xcoor, Ycoor : real);
           FUNCTION GetRadius : real;
           FUNCTION ComputeArea : real;
           PROCEDURE Print;
         END;  {  of OBJECT Circle  }
```

In this definition, the new object type Circle inherits all the fields and methods from Point. This is accomplished by listing Point in parentheses after the reserved word **OBJECT** in the definition as

```
Circle = OBJECT (Point)
```

This means a variable object of type Circle can be envisioned as shown in Figure 14.1.

Although the graphic description of an inherited object type in Figure 14.1 is valid, a somewhat better way to illustrate the hierarchy of the relationship is shown in Figure 14.2.

FIGURE 14.1
Object type Circle

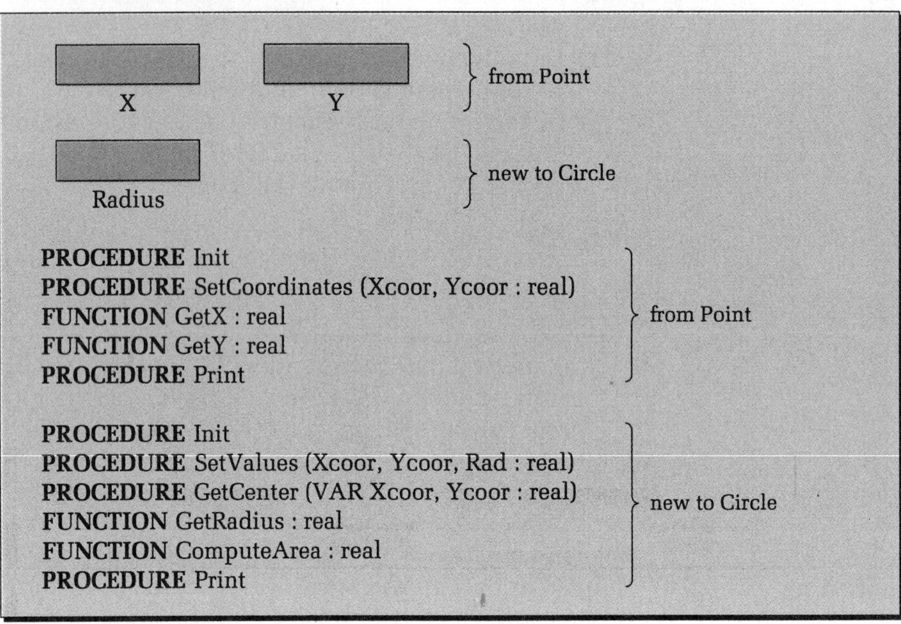

FIGURE 14.2
Object type Circle inherits object type Point

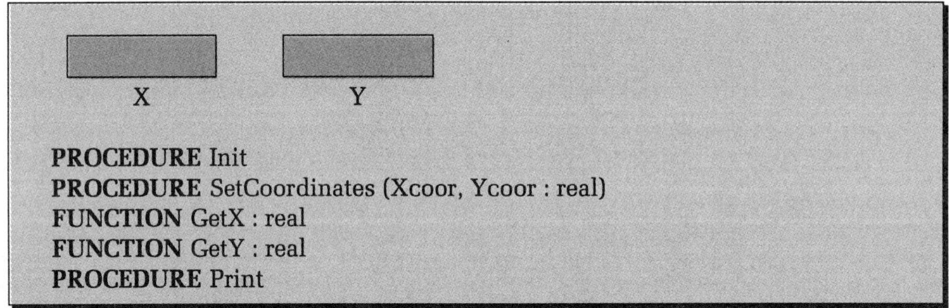

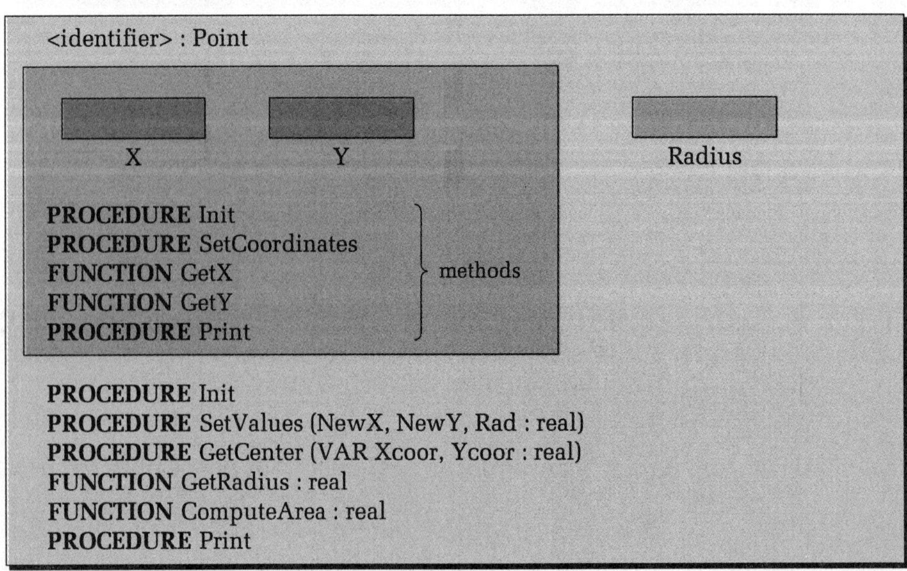

We will use this method to illustrate hierarchies throughout the remainder of this section.

In the definition of object type Circle, it is not necessary to define a new data field for Center. The inherited fields X and Y from Point serve as the center of the circle.

Terminology

The newly defined type (Circle) is a *descendant* of the previously defined type (Point). Thus, Point is an *ancestor* of Circle. This ancestor-descendant relationship resembles the hierarchical classifications frequently used in other areas. Consider, for example, the following classifications.

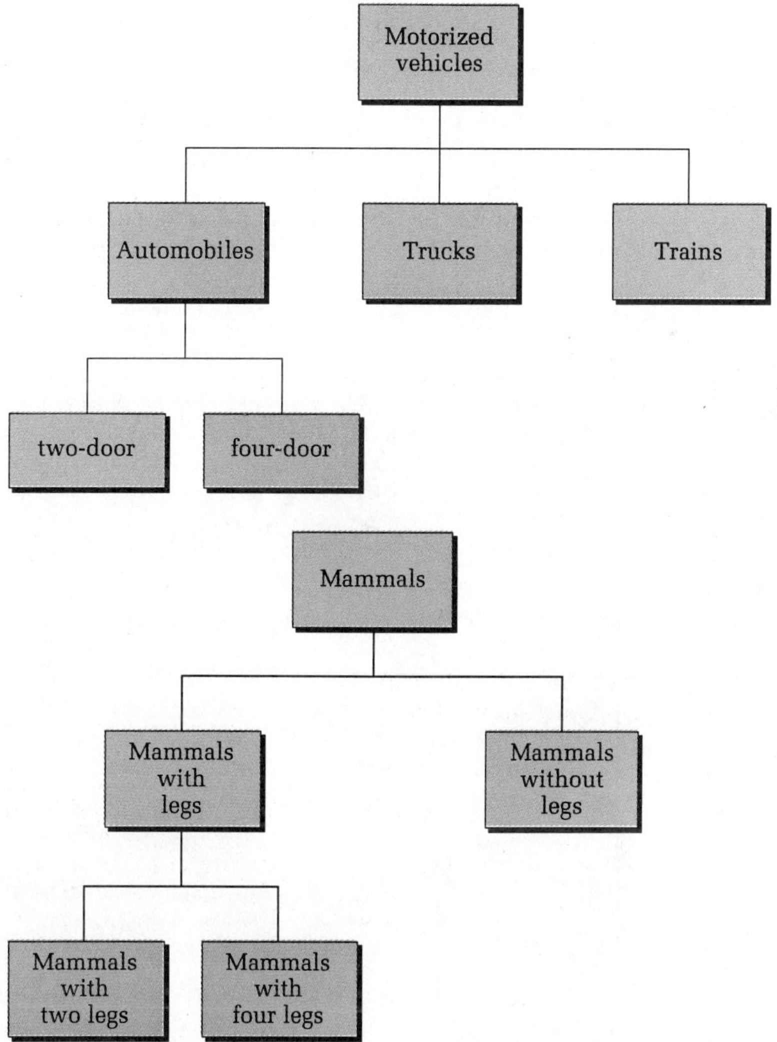

These hierarchies suggest the use of more specific terminology. An object type may be thought of as a base *class.* Descendants then belong to a *subclass* of the ancestor.

Data Fields and Methods

As previously mentioned, the data fields of the ancestor are available to the methods of the descendant. Using the object type Circle, we can declare a variable of type Circle as

```
VAR
  Figure : Circle;
```

Circles are uniquely determined by their center and radius. By our definition, we can think of Figure as having a radius that is defined in Circle and a center that is an object of type Point.

When we enter values for the center and radius, the main program contains the statement

```
Figure.SetValues (Xcoor, Ycoor, Rad);
```

The procedure SetValues is then

```
PROCEDURE Circle.SetValues (Xcoor, Ycoor, Rad : real);
  BEGIN
    Point.SetCoordinates (Xcoor, Ycoor);
    Radius := Rad
  END;
```

Notice the method SetValues in Circle can use the existing method SetCoordinates in Point. This allows full use of the methods already written for Point.

COMMUNICATION AND STYLE TIPS

The intended portability and reusability of objects makes it essential to carefully and completely document all methods in an object type. It should be clear what the method receives, what task the method accomplishes, and what the method returns. To illustrate, consider the method SetCoordinates from the object type Point:

```
PROCEDURE Point.SetCoordinates (Xcoor, Ycoor : real);
  BEGIN
    X := Xcoor;
    Y := Ycoor
  END;
```

To add documentation to this procedure, we will deviate from the Given/Task/Return form we have been using for procedures and functions. Instead, we will use a Precondition/Task/Postcondition form, which more accurately reflects how the methods of an object should be used. Thus, we get

```
PROCEDURE Point.SetCoordinates (Xcoor, Ycoor : real);

{  Precondition:   Coordinates of a point already exist  }
{                  by initialization or previous use of  }
{                  SetCoordinates.                       }
{  Task:           Assign new values to coordinates of   }
{                  a point.                              }
{  Postcondition:  Coordinates of the point contain new  }
{                  values.                               }

  BEGIN
    X : Xcoor;
    Y : Ycoor
  END;  {  of PROCEDURE Point.SetCoordinates  }
```

Override

Next let's consider **PROCEDURE** Init from the object type Circle, which is written

```
PROCEDURE Circle.Init;
  BEGIN
    Point.Init;
    Radius := 0.0
  END;
```

7.0 Two things should be noted here. First, Circle.Init simply uses Point.Init to initialize the coordinates of the center. This makes use of the inherited property of Point.Init. Second, the method name Init in Circle is the same as the method name Init in Point. In this case, Circle.Init is said to be an *override* of Point.Init.

In general, the user may override the methods of an object by using the same identifier in the methods of a descendant. The method being overriden is usually called by the new method (in the descendant). This is good style and good practice. The method being overriden (in the ancestor) may have some subtle properties that were carefully thought out when that method was written. By calling that method from the new method, the user does not have to worry about these subtleties.

Now let's write all the methods for the object type Circle. Recall from Figure 14.2 that Circle is defined as

```
Circle = OBJECT (Point)
           Radius : real;

           PROCEDURE Init;  {  override  }
           PROCEDURE SetValues (Xcoor, Ycoor; Rad : real);
           PROCEDURE GetCenter (VAR Xcoor, Ycoor : real);
           FUNCTION GetRadius : real;
           FUNCTION ComputeArea : real;
           PROCEDURE Print;  {  override  }
         END;  {  of OBJECT Circle  }
```

The methods for this object type follow.

```
PROCEDURE Circle.Init;
  BEGIN
    Point.Init;
    Radius := 0.0
  END;

{--------------------------------------------------------}

PROCEDURE Circle.SetValues (Xcoor, Ycoor, Rad : real);
  BEGIN
    Point.SetCoordinates (Xcoor, Ycoor);
    Radius := Rad
  END;

{--------------------------------------------------------}

PROCEDURE Circle.GetCenter (VAR Xcoor, Ycoor : real);
  BEGIN
    Xcoor := X;
    Ycoor := Y
  END;

{--------------------------------------------------------}
```

```
FUNCTION Circle.GetRadius : real;
  BEGIN
    GetRadius := Radius
  END;

{--------------------------------------------------------}

FUNCTION Circle.ComputeArea : real;
  BEGIN
    ComputeArea := Pi * sqr(Radius)
  END;

{--------------------------------------------------------}

PROCEDURE Circle.Print;
  VAR
    CircleRad : real;
    CircleArea : real;
  BEGIN
    writeln;
    writeln ('The center is: ');
    Point.Print;
    CircleRad := GetRadius;
    writeln  ('The radius is  ', CircleRad:6:2);
    CircleArea := ComputeArea;
    writeln  ('The area is  '  , CircleArea:6:2)
  END;
```

Notice both methods Circle.Init and Circle.Print are overrides of methods from an ancestor.

We will now see how object inheritance is used in a short program. This program performs the following tasks.

1. Enters values from the keyboard.
2. Stores the values in appropriate data fields.
3. Prints the values from the data fields.
4. Changes the values in the data fields.
5. Prints the changed values from the data fields.

Be aware that this is a contrived problem. Remember our current purpose is to become familiar with the concept of inheritance and the use of objects in object-oriented programming. The complete program follows.

```
PROGRAM InheritanceDemo;

USES
  Crt;

TYPE
  Point = OBJECT
            X : real;
            Y : real;

            PROCEDURE Init;
            PROCEDURE SetCoordinates (Xcoor, Ycoor : real);
            FUNCTION GetX : real;
            FUNCTION GetY : real;
            PROCEDURE Print;
          END;  {  of OBJECT Point  }
```

```
  Circle = OBJECT (Point)
             Radius : real;

             PROCEDURE Init;              {  Override  }
             PROCEDURE SetValues (Xcoor, Ycoor, Rad : real);
             PROCEDURE GetCenter (VAR Xcoor, Ycoor : real);
             FUNCTION GetRadius : real;
             FUNCTION ComputeArea : real;
             PROCEDURE Print;             {  Override  }
           END;  {  of OBJECT Circle  }

VAR
  Figure : Circle;
  Xvalue, Yvalue : real;
  Rad : real;

{*********************************************************}

{  Write all methods for OBJECT Point.  }

{---------------------------------------------------------}

PROCEDURE Point.Init;
  BEGIN
    X := 0.0;
    Y := 0.0
  END;  {  of PROCEDURE Point.Init  }

{---------------------------------------------------------}

PROCEDURE Point.SetCoordinates (Xcoor, Ycoor : real);
  BEGIN
    X := Xcoor;
    Y := Ycoor
  END;  {  of PROCEDURE Point.SetCoordinates  }

{---------------------------------------------------------}

FUNCTION Point.GetX : real;
  BEGIN
    GetX := X
  END;  {  of FUNCTION Point.GetX  }

{---------------------------------------------------------}

FUNCTION Point.GetY : real;
  BEGIN
    GetY := Y
  END;  {  of FUNCTION Point.GetY  }

{---------------------------------------------------------}

PROCEDURE Point.Print;
  VAR
    Xcoor, Ycoor : real;
  BEGIN
    Xcoor := GetX;
    Ycoor := GetY;
    writeln ('The coordinates are X =  ', Xcoor:4:2,
             '  Y =  ', Ycoor:4:2)
  END;  {  of PROCEDURE Point.Print  }
```

```
{*********************************************************}

{  Write all methods of OBJECT Circle  }

{--------------------------------------------------------}

PROCEDURE Circle.Init;       {  Override  }
  BEGIN
    Point.Init;
    Radius := 0.0
  END;  {  of PROCEDURE Circle.Init  }

{--------------------------------------------------------}

PROCEDURE Circle.SetValues (Xcoor, Ycoor, Rad : real);
  BEGIN
    Point.SetCoordinates (Xcoor, Ycoor);
    Radius := Rad
  END;  {  of PROCEDURE Circle.SetValues  }

{--------------------------------------------------------}

PROCEDURE Circle.GetCenter (VAR Xcoor, Ycoor : real);
  BEGIN
    Xcoor := X;
    Ycoor := Y
  END;  {  of PROCEDURE Circle.GetCenter  }

{--------------------------------------------------------}

FUNCTION Circle.GetRadius : real;
  BEGIN
    GetRadius := Radius
  END;  {  of FUNCTION Circle.GetRadius  }

{--------------------------------------------------------}

FUNCTION Circle.ComputeArea : real;
  BEGIN
    ComputeArea := Pi * sqr(Radius)
  END;  {  of FUNCTION Circle.ComputeArea  }

{--------------------------------------------------------}

PROCEDURE Circle.Print;         {  Override  }
  VAR
    CircleRad : real;
    CircleArea : real;
  BEGIN
    writeln;
    writeln ('The center is:');
    Point.Print;
    CircleRad := GetRadius;
    writeln ('The radius is  ', CircleRad:6:2);
    CircleArea := ComputeArea;
    writeln ('The area is  ', CircleArea:6:2)
  END;  {  of PROCEDURE Circle.Print  }

{****************************************************************}

{  All methods have been written.  }
{  Now begin the main program.  }
```

```
BEGIN  {  Main program  }
  ClrScr;
  Figure.Init;

  {  Get values from the keyboard  }
  writeln ('Please enter coordinates for the center of a circle.');
  write ('X coordinate = ');
  readln (Xvalue);
  write ('Y coordinate = ');
  readln (Yvalue);
  write ('The radius is ');
  readln (Rad);

  {  Use Circle's methods  }
  Figure.SetValues (Xvalue, Yvalue, Rad);
  Figure.Print;

  {  Move the center, and change the radius  }
  Xvalue := Xvalue + 3;
  Yvalue := Yvalue + 1;
  Rad := 2 * Rad;

  {  Use Circle's methods again  }
  Figure.SetValues (Xvalue, Yvalue, Rad);
  Figure.Print;
  readln
END.  {  of main program  }
```

Output from this program is

```
Please enter coordinates for the center of a circle.
X coordinate = 1
Y coordinate = 1
The radius is 2

The center is:
The coordinates are X =  1.00  Y =  1.00
The radius is    2.00
The area is   12.57

The center is:
The coordinates are X =  4.00  Y =  2.00
The radius is    4.00
The area is   50.27
```

This sample program contains two procedures, Init and Print, that override the ancestor's procedures. Also note how **PROCEDURE** Circle.SetValues uses the ancestor method Point.SetCoordinates. This use ensures that the descendant object includes the ancestor's functionality. This use also guarantees that changes made to the ancestor's method automatically affect the descendants.

As we have seen, the methods of an object type may be overridden in a descendant by using the same method identifier and a different body. It is also possible to override methods that contain parameter lists. However, the parameter list in the new method must contain at least as many appropriate parameters as are contained in the ancestor's method being overridden.

Data fields cannot be overridden. Once we define a data field in an object type, no descendant type can contain a data field with the same identifier.

Multiple Descendants

A single object type may have several descendants. Our next example uses the object type Name to illustrate this. However, an object type may have only one ancestor. (Some other OOP languages allow multiple or nonlinear inheritance.) The inheritance property may extend for several levels. The analogy of subclasses to generations within a family is appropriate here. Of course, the inheritance of subsequent object types is more predictable than the inheritance of a physical characteristic such as red hair. The example in Section 14.3 illustrates multiple levels of inheritance.

Object Type Compatibility

If Figure1 and Figure2 are both instances of the object type Circle, the assignment statement

```
Figure1 := Figure2;
```

is valid. This assignment copies contents of the data fields of Figure2 into the data fields of Figure1 in the same manner that contents of fields of records are copied in an assignment statement that assigns one record to another. In general, if Obj1 and Obj2 are of the same object type, the assignment statement

```
Obj1 := Obj2;
```

is valid.

Some assignments of inherited objects are also possible. The general rule is a descendant object can be assigned to an ancestor. When this happens, fields in the ancestor receive values from appropriate fields in the descendant. Thus, if Parent is an instance of ParentType and Child is an instance of the descendant ChildType

```
Parent := Child;
```

is valid. Assignments in the other direction are not valid.

Object type compatibility also extends to formal parameters declared as object types. To illustrate, suppose we have object types

```
TYPE
  ParentType = OBJECT
       .
       .
       .
  ChildType = OBJECT (ParentType)
       .
       .
       .
```

If a procedure heading is

```
PROCEDURE CompatPrac (Parent : ParentType);
```

we can invoke this procedure by using either

```
CompatPrac (Parent);
```

or

```
CompatPrac (Child);
```

where Parent and Child are instances of ParentType and ChildType, respectively.

Exercises 14.2

1. In this section, a hierarchy starting with mammals is used to illustrate the concept of inheritance. Describe at least three other hierarchies that illustrate the same concept.

2. Write a separate test program to illustrate what happens in each of the following cases.
   a. An ancestor and its descendant have a method with the same identifier.
   b. An ancestor and its descendant have a data field with the same identifier.
   c. A method in a descendant accesses a data field of its ancestor.
3. Consider the object type defined as

```
TYPE
  Rectangle = OBJECT
                Length : real;
                Width : real;

                PROCEDURE Init;
                PROCEDURE SetValues (Len, Wid : real);
                FUNCTION GetLength : real;
                FUNCTION GetWidth : real;
                FUNCTION GetArea : real;
              END;
```

   Define a descendant object type Box. Box should have a data field for Height and methods that perform the following tasks.
   a. Assign values to all data fields.
   b. Retrieve values from data fields.
   c. Compute the volume of a box.
4. Reconsider the object types in Exercise 3.
   a. Write code for all of the methods in Rectangle.
   b. Write code for all of the methods in Box.
5. Reconsider the object type Rectangle in Exercise 3. Suppose a descendant type Box includes the following as part of its definition:

```
Box = OBJECT (Rectangle);
        Height : real;
          .
          .
          .
        FUNCTION ComputeVolume : real;
```

   Also suppose the method ComputeVolume has been developed as

```
FUNCTION ComputeVolume : real;
  BEGIN
    ComputeVolume := Length * Width * Height
  END;
```

   a. Will this method work when used with an instance of Box?
   b. Should this method be used in this way? Why or why not?
6. Consider the descendant type

```
Circle = OBJECT (Point)
```

   in this section. This object type contains the method

```
PROCEDURE Circle.Print;
```

   This method contains the lines of code

```
writeln ('The center is: ');
Point.Print;
```

   What happens if Point.Print is replaced with

```
Print;
```

7. Consider the object type NameString in Section 14.1.
   a. Define a descendant type Student that has an additional field for GPA.
   b. Write methods for the descendant type Student.
   c. Define a descendant type Pet that has an additional field for the type of pet (bird, cat, dog, fish, other).
8. Explain how a descendant's method can override a method in the ancestor. Discuss when this action is appropriate.
9. Consider the object type definitions

```
TYPE
  NameString = OBJECT
                 Name : string;

                 PROCEDURE Init;
                 PROCEDURE SetName (NameStr : string);
                 PROCEDURE PrintName;
               END;

  PersonData = OBJECT (NameString)
                 Age : integer;
                 Gender : char;
               END;
```

   Suppose the variable declaration section contains the following instances of NameString and PersonData:

```
VAR
  MyName, YourName : NameString;
  MySelf, YourSelf : PersonData;
```

   Assuming suitable initialization, which of the following are valid and which are invalid? Explain what is wrong with each assignment statement that is invalid.

   a. `MyName := YourName;`
   b. `MyName := MySelf;`
   c. `YourName := MySelf;`
   d. `MySelf := MyName;`
   e. `MySelf := YourName;`
   f. `YourSelf := MySelf;`
10. Create a hierarchy of object types that contains four levels. Include the complete development of all method headings.

14.3 Using Objects

Before we consider another example, let's take a second look at the philosophy of and the rationale for using objects in object-oriented programming.

Why Use Objects?

If the uses of objects were limited to the kinds of examples presented thus far, their design and purpose would be subject to question. However, the use of objects is far more sophisticated than has yet been demonstrated.

Objects for software development can be developed independently and then made available to a wider audience. This projected availability allows the software engineer to concentrate on the form and manipulation of data and to spend time on designing the main program instead of worrying about the details of coding.

Using objects is a way to implement abstract data types. Someone else can develop the object (ADT) to be used in a program. For example, when we direct output to the screen while writing a program in Turbo Pascal, we include the statement

```
USES
  Crt;
```

as part of the program. We can think of Crt as an object. Similarly, suppose we are designing a program that is to work with a list of items. If an appropriate object is written that includes an array (or similar structure) and methods for working with the array, such as GetData, AccessComponent, Sort, Print, and so on, the statement

```
USES
  List;
```

may be all that is required to utilize properties of the list in a program. As part of our design, we can use the properties of the object by sending the appropriate messages from the main program in the form of such statements as

```
ClassList.GetData (<parameters>);
ClassList.Sort (<parameters>);
ClassList.Print (<parameters>);
```

We only have to worry about the form and manipulation of data, not about the details of writing code for getting, sorting, and printing the data.

Software designed using objects therefore possesses more structure and modularity than software designed without using objects. This process also leads to more abstraction. Code written using objects is more structured and easier to extend and to maintain.

Reusability is another issue to consider when designing objects. For example, given the object type List previously mentioned, whenever the program design requires the use of a List type, we can use the same object, which was originally designed for some other program. Actually, the object type List (or several versions of List) will probably be designed independently of any one program. This object type can then be encoded, placed on a disk, and accessed as a Unit (see Section 14.4) whenever it is needed.

One advantage of object-oriented design is that a large library of reusable objects can be accumulated. Writing new programs then becomes a matter of using selected objects from this library. This improves both the speed and correctness of new programs.

Constructing Objects

With a little practice, constructing objects can become an enjoyable task. Initially, some of the work may seem a bit tedious. However, as you become familiar with the conceptual use of an object and with the process of inheritance, you will see the need for care in the development of objects. The selection of meaningful identifiers is important. Complete documentation is essential because the objects will be read by other users. Remember that, once prepared, objects are available to a large audience.

Polymorphism

The three key ingredients to object-oriented programming are encapsulation, inheritance, and polymorphism. We have already discussed encapsulation and inheritance. *Polymorphism* refers to giving an action one name that is shared up

A NOTE OF INTEREST

When Will Object Technology Meet Its Potential?

Rebecca Wirfs-Brock, Director of Object Technology Services at Digitalk, addressed the issue of the potential of object technology in a guest editorial in a recent publication of the Journal of Object-Oriented Programming. *A summary of her comments follows.*

When will it be so easy to use objects that other competing technologies won't even be considered? Can we have a future in which objects nicely coexist with more traditional software? These questions are on the minds of industry watchers, application developers, and object technology suppliers alike. Sure, people really are starting to use objects. It isn't as controversial to start an object-oriented project as it used to be. Objects have come out of the research labs and are being used on management information systems (MIS) and engineering projects. For some, the rich development and prototyping environment alone is sufficient for them to switch. For others, touted benefits come with too high a risk factor and retraining cost. These people are waiting until enormous gains are well established and guaranteed.

I'm delighted that people are delivering software written in Smalltalk, C++, Eiffel, and CLOS. Proponents of object technology say it is easy to use. But developing applications with objects isn't a routine procedure just yet. It needs to get simpler.

Reusing software and constructing applications from standard components is a great idea. However, there are some fundamental hurdles that need to be cleared before we can efficiently build software this way.

Object-oriented application construction has many different dimensions that don't directly map to the ways engineers develop hardware. To achieve that next higher level of software productivity, we need to address the following needs.

- We need components that are easy to mix and match (for example, classes and subsystems of cooperating classes) supplied by different vendors written in different languages with application-specific components.
- We must be able to use components in a variety of different contexts. Vendors need to supply us with components that work across different platforms.
- We need well-documented, standardized component libraries, subsystems, and architectural frameworks for building applications. We need to be able to construct simple applications largely by assembling them from components found in preexisting catalogs.
- For more complex applications, we need to construct applications out of subsystems, frameworks, and components organized and described in ways that are understandable without resorting to reading code. We need to be able to easily grasp accepted patterns for connecting these components.
- Finally, we need to enhance our ability to develop applications by refining existing components. Programming by refinement is an extremely powerful metaphor. It shouldn't be dropped when we adopt the mentality of construction from preexisting components. Refinement is what enables developers to add application-specific functionality while reusing most of an existing design.

and down an object hierarchy. Each object in the hierarchy then implements the action in a manner appropriate to itself. More simply, polymorphism permits a process that is common to many objects to have a different implementation for each type of object. "Polymorphism" is Greek for "many shapes."

As a first example of polymorphism, consider how Turbo Pascal uses the "+" operator. When used with integers, it means integer addition. When used with strings, it represents concatenation. When used with sets, it is interpreted as set union. These three instances are conceptually similar as a binary operation. However, the implementation differs in each system.

As a second example, consider the previous hierarchy of a Point type and let Circle be a descendant type of Point. In a graphics setting, it would be appropriate to think of displaying each data type on the screen. As additional Figure types are defined for squares, rectangles, triangles, and so on, it would be natural to design a method for each type that would also allow it to be displayed on the screen. Thus, each figure should have the property that it can be "displayed." The single word, Display is used to display many shapes. However, the method by which each shape is shown varies according to the specific figure.

These two examples illustrate the nature of polymorphism. It is the property that allows us to use a single method call to manipulate an object, whether it is an ancestor object type or one of its descendants.

Having discussed the concept of polymorphism, now let's consider its implementation. Dynamic type binding is the final ingredient required for methods to be polymorphic. The issue of binding methods in Turbo Pascal is discussed in Section 14.4. The study of dynamic objects is beyond the scope of this text. In a subsequent course, you will see how polymorphism becomes an essential property in object-oriented design.

A Final Example

We conclude this section with an example that includes both different subclasses of a single object type and a subclass of a subclass to demonstrate the use of different levels of inheritance. We use the object type NameStr (see Section 14.1) as the base class. A subclass of NameStr is Person and subclasses of Person are Student and Professor. This hierarchy is shown in Figure 14.3.

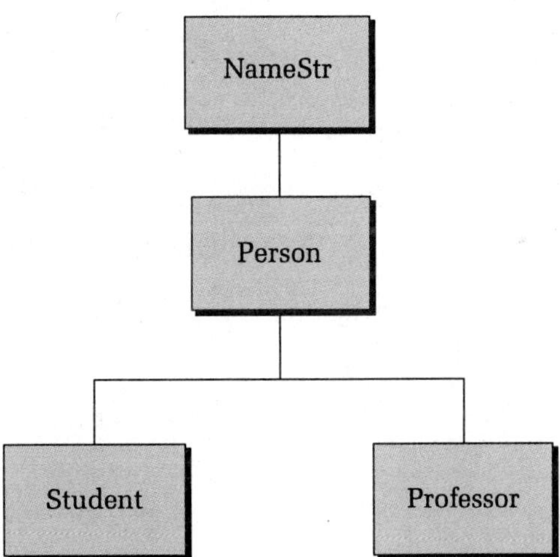

FIGURE 14.3
Inheritance hierarchy with multiple subclasses

In this program, we define five object types, write code for all of their methods, and then use the methods as needed. The program does the following:

1. Puts information for a Professor into appropriate data fields
2. Creates an array of students
3. Sorts the array alphabetically
4. Displays the information about the Professor and his or her students

This example is slightly more elaborate than the others thus far. We define the object type List, which has an array of objects as one field. Since implementation details are hidden from the user, notice this array could subsequently be modified to a linked list (Section 15.2) . A pseudocode development follows:

1. Initialize
   1.1 initialize Professor
   1.2 initialize Student List
2. Get data
   2.1 read Professor data from keyboard
   2.2 read Student List from keyboard
3. Sort Student List

4. Compute class GPA
5. Print data
   5.1 print data about Professor
   5.2 print data about each Student

Prior to writing the program, let's consider the object type definitions to be used. The base type is

```
TYPE
  NameStr = OBJECT
              Name : string;

              PROCEDURE Init;
              PROCEDURE SetName (TheName : string);
              PROCEDURE Print;
            END;  {  of OBJECT NameStr  }
```

The object type NameStr is illustrated in Figure 14.4.

FIGURE 14.4
Object type NameStr

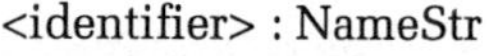

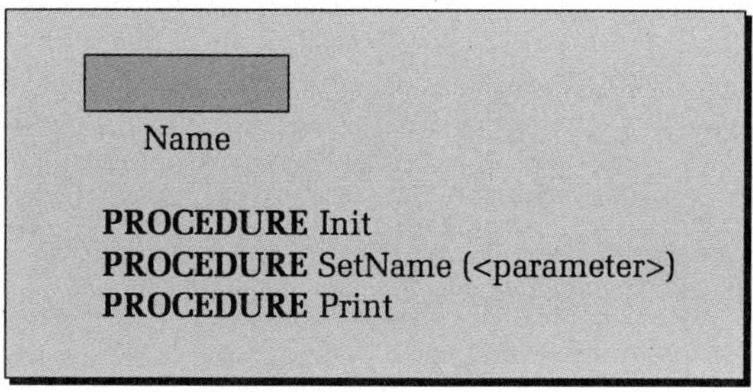

A descendant type of NameStr is

```
PersonType = OBJECT (NameStr)
               Age : integer;
               Gender : char;

               PROCEDURE Init;  {  Override  }
               PROCEDURE GetData;
               PROCEDURE Print;  {  Override  }
             END;  {  of OBJECT PersonType  }
```

This descendant type is illustrated in Figure 14.5.

FIGURE 14.5
Object type PersonType

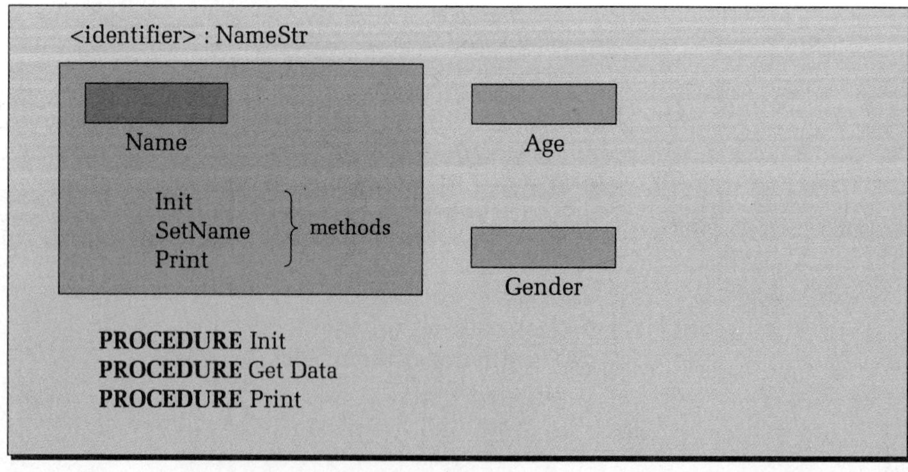

We now define a descendant type of PersonType as

```
StudentType = OBJECT (PersonType)
                ID : string;
                GPA : real;

                PROCEDURE Init;  {  Override  }
                PROCEDURE GetData;  {  Override  }
                FUNCTION GetID : string;
                FUNCTION GetGPA : real;
                PROCEDURE Print;  {  Override  }
              END;  {  of OBJECT StudentType  }
```

This descendant type is illustrated in Figure 14.6.

Next, we define a second descendant type of PersonType as

FIGURE 14.6
Object type StudentType

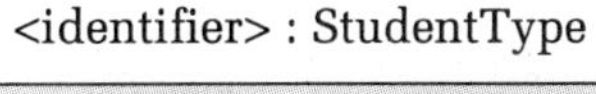

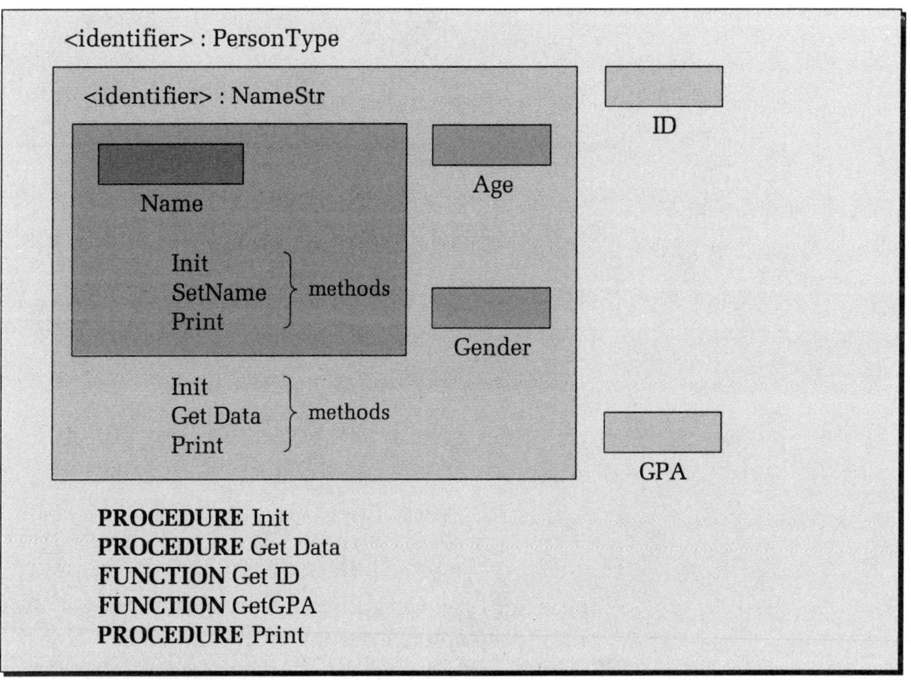


```
ProfessorType = OBJECT (PersonType)
                  Dept : string;
                  Rank : string;
                  Office : string;
                  PhoneNum : string;

                  PROCEDURE Init;  {  Override  }
                  PROCEDURE GetData;  {  Override  }
                  PROCEDURE Print;  {  Override  }
                END;  {  of OBJECT ProfessorType  }
```

This descendant type is illustrated in Figure 14.7. The hierarchy of these object types is illustrated in Figure 14.8.

The program requires us to work with a list of students. Since we have defined the object type StudentType, we use an array of StudentType as our data structure. Furthermore, we define an object type ClassList, which contains this

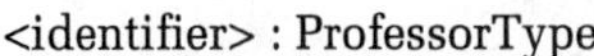

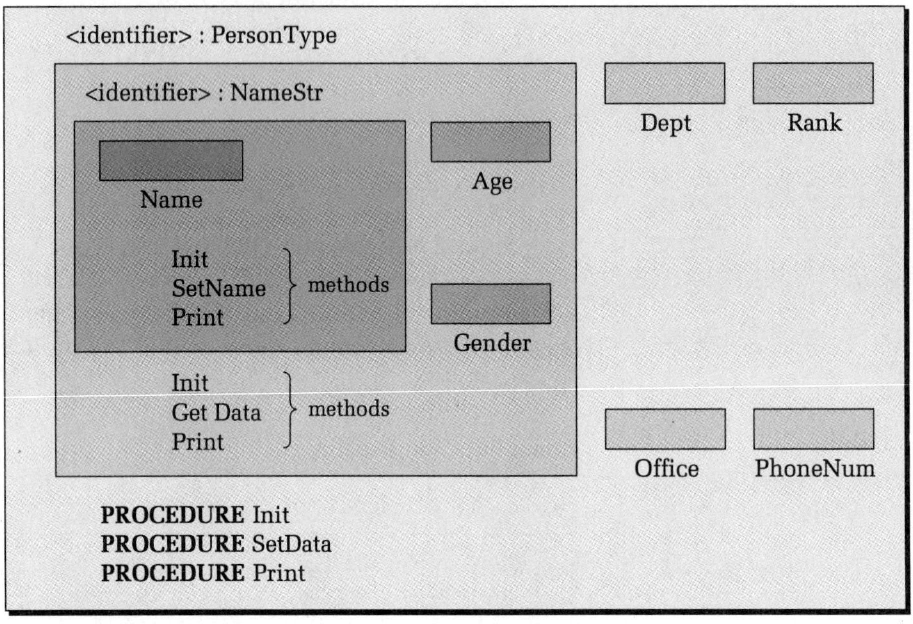

FIGURE 14.7
Object type ProfessorType

data structure as well as the methods required for utilizing the structure. The definition is

```
ListOfStudents = ARRAY [1..ClassSize] OF StudentType;
ClassList = OBJECT
              ListSize : integer;
              Student : ListOfStudents;

              PROCEDURE Init;  {  Override  }
              PROCEDURE GetListData;
              PROCEDURE Sort;
              FUNCTION ComputeGPA : real;
              PROCEDURE Print;  {  Override  }
            END;  {  of OBJECT ClassList  }
```

The object type ClassList can be envisioned as shown in Figure 14.9.

The complete program utilizing these object types follows. Notice only **PROCEDURE** PersonType.GetData has appropriate documentation. You are asked to provide documentation for the methods as part of the exercises at the end of this section.

```
PROGRAM ListPrac;

USES
  Crt;

CONST
  ClassSize = 30;

TYPE

  {============================================================}

  {  Define the OBJECTS  }

  {============================================================}
```

FIGURE 14.8
Hierarchy of object types

NameStr

Name

Init
SetName
Print

PersonType

NameStr

Age
Gender

Init
GetData
Print

StudentType

PersonType

ID
GPA

Init
GetData
GetID
GetGPA
Print

ProfessorType

PersonType

Dept
Rank
Office
PhoneNum

Init
GetData
Print

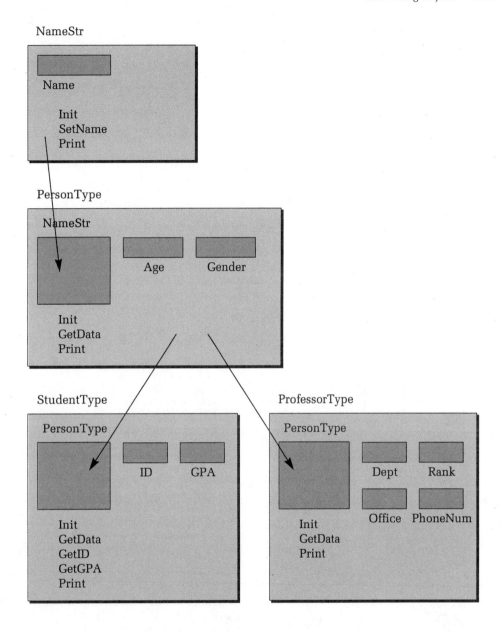

FIGURE 14.9
Object type ClassList

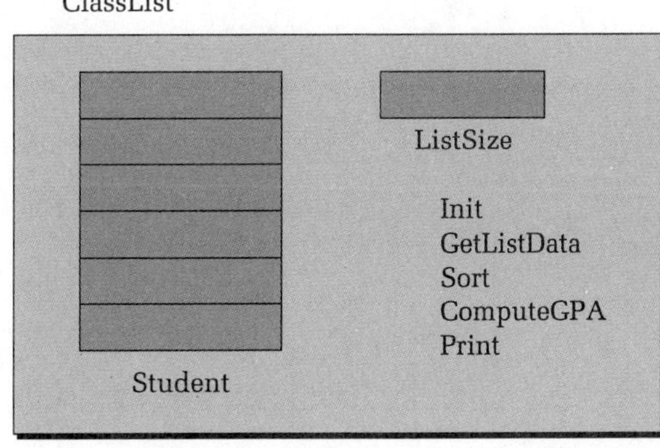

```
NameStr = OBJECT
            Name : string;

            PROCEDURE Init;
            PROCEDURE SetName (TheName : string);
            PROCEDURE Print;
          END; {  of OBJECT NameStr  }

{============================================================}

PersonType = OBJECT (NameStr)
               Age : integer;
               Gender : char;

               PROCEDURE Init;         {  Override  }
               PROCEDURE GetData;
               PROCEDURE Print;        {  Override  }
             END; {  of OBJECT PersonType  }

{============================================================}

StudentType = OBJECT (PersonType)
                ID : string;
                GPA : real;

                PROCEDURE Init;        {  Override  }
                PROCEDURE GetData;     {  Override  }
                FUNCTION GetID : string;
                FUNCTION GetGPA : real;
                PROCEDURE Print;       {  Override  }
              END; {  of OBJECT StudentType  }

{============================================================}

ProfessorType = OBJECT (PersonType)
                  Dept : string;
                  Rank : string;
                  Office : string;
                  PhoneNum : string;

                  PROCEDURE Init;      {  Override  }
                  PROCEDURE GetData;   {  Override  }
                  PROCEDURE Print;     {  Override  }
                END; {  of OBJECT ProfessorType  }

{============================================================}

ListOfStudents = ARRAY [1..ClassSize] OF StudentType;
ClassList = OBJECT
              ListSize : integer;
              Student: ListOfStudents;

              PROCEDURE Init;          {  Override  }
              PROCEDURE GetListData;
              PROCEDURE Sort;
              FUNCTION ComputeGPA : real;
              PROCEDURE Print;         {  Override  }
            END; {  of OBJECT ClassList  }

{  All OBJECTS have been defined  }

{============================================================}
```

```
VAR
  Prof : ProfessorType;
  StuList : ClassList;
  ClassGradeAv : real;

{*************************************************************}

{  Write methods for the OBJECTS  }

{=============================================================}

{  Methods for NameStr  }

PROCEDURE NameStr.Init;
  BEGIN
    Name := ' '
  END;

PROCEDURE NameStr.SetName (TheName : string);
  BEGIN
    Name := TheName
  END;

PROCEDURE NameStr.Print;
  BEGIN
    writeln (Name)
  END;

{=============================================================}

{  Methods for PersonType  }

PROCEDURE PersonType.Init;       {  Override  }
  BEGIN
    NameStr.Init;
    Age := 0;
    Gender := ' '
  END;

PROCEDURE PersonType.GetData;

  {  Precondition:   The object has fields for Name, Age,      }
  {                  and Gender, which have been initialized   }
  {                  but currently contain no useful values.   }
  {  Task:           Read data from the keyboard for the       }
  {                  fields Name, Age, and Gender.             }
  {  Postcondition:  Fields Name, Age, and Gender now have     }
  {                  new values.                               }

  BEGIN
    write ('Name:  (last name first)      ');
    readln (Name);
    write ('Age:                          ');
    readln (Age);
    write ('Gender:  <M or F>             ');
    readln (Gender)
  END;

PROCEDURE PersonType.Print;      {  Override  }
  BEGIN
    write ('Name:                ');
    NameStr.Print;
```

```
    writeln ('Age:                    ', Age);
    writeln ('Gender:                 ', Gender)
  END;

{==============================================================}

{  Methods for StudentType  }

PROCEDURE StudentType.Init;
  BEGIN
    PersonType.Init;
    ID := ' ';
    GPA := 0.0
  END;

PROCEDURE StudentType.GetData;
  BEGIN
    PersonType.GetData;
    write ('ID:                       ');
    readln (ID);
    write ('Current GPA:              ');
    readln (GPA)
  END;

FUNCTION StudentType.GetID : string;
  BEGIN
    GetID := ID
  END;

FUNCTION StudentType.GetGPA : real;
  BEGIN
    GetGPA := GPA
  END;

PROCEDURE StudentType.Print;            {  Override  }
  BEGIN
    PersonType.Print;
    writeln ('ID:                     ', ID);
    writeln ('GPA:                    ', GPA:4:2)
  END;

{==============================================================}

{  Methods for ProfessorType  }

PROCEDURE ProfessorType.Init;
  BEGIN
    PersonType.Init;
    Dept := ' ';
    Rank := ' ';
    Office := ' ';
    PhoneNum := ' '
  END;

PROCEDURE ProfessorType.GetData;
  BEGIN
    ClrScr;
    writeln ('Enter data for the class Professor.');
    writeln;
    writeln ('For each of the following questions, please enter');
    writeln ('the requested information and press <Enter>');
    writeln;
```

```
    PersonType.GetData;
    write ('Department?                ');
    readln (Dept);
    write ('Rank?                      ');
    readln (Rank);
    write ('Office number?             ');
    readln (Office);
    write ('Phone number?              ');
    readln (PhoneNum);
    writeln;
    write ('Thank you for your patience.  Press <Enter> to');
    writeln (' continue.');
    readln
  END;

PROCEDURE ProfessorType.Print;
  BEGIN
    ClrScr;
    writeln;
    writeln ('PROFESSOR DATA');
    writeln ('--------------');
    writeln;
    PersonType.Print;
    writeln ('Department:            ', Dept);
    writeln ('Rank:                  ', Rank);
    writeln ('Office number:         ', Office);
    writeln ('Phone number:          ', PhoneNum);
    writeln
  END;

{=================================================================}

{  Methods for ClassList  }

PROCEDURE ClassList.Init;
  VAR
    Index : integer;
  BEGIN
    ListSize := 0;
    FOR Index := 1 TO ClassSize DO
      Student[Index].Init
  END;

PROCEDURE ClassList.GetListData;
  VAR
    Response : char;
    NoMoreStudents : boolean;
  BEGIN
    ClrScr;
    writeln ('Please enter data for students in the class.');
    writeln ('Press <Enter> after each entry.');
    writeln;
    writeln;
    ListSize := 0;
    REPEAT
      ListSize := ListSize + 1;
      Student[ListSize].GetData;
      writeln;
      write ('Any more students?  <Y or N>  ');
      readln (Response);
      NoMoreStudents := (Response = 'N') OR (Response = 'n')
    UNTIL NoMoreStudents
  END;
```

```
PROCEDURE ClassList.Sort;
  VAR
    J, K, Index : integer;
    Temp : StudentType;
  BEGIN
    FOR J := 1 TO ListSize - 1 DO
      BEGIN
        Index := J;
        FOR K := J + 1 TO ListSize DO
          IF Student[K].Name < Student[Index].Name THEN
            Index := K;
        IF Index <> J THEN
          BEGIN
            Temp := Student[Index];
            Student[Index] := Student[J];
            Student[J] := Temp
          END  {  of IF...THEN  }
      END  {  of FOR J loop  }
  END;  {  of the sort  }

FUNCTION ClassList.ComputeGPA : real;
  VAR
    Index : integer;
    GPASum : real;
  BEGIN
    GPASum := 0.0;
    FOR Index := 1 TO ListSize DO
      GPASum := GPASum + Student[Index].GPA;
    IF ListSize <> 0 THEN
      ComputeGPA := GPASum / ListSize
    ELSE
      BEGIN
        writeln ('Error:  ListSize is Zero');
        ComputeGPA := 0.0
      END  {  of ELSE option  }
  END;

PROCEDURE ClassList.Print;
  VAR
    Index : integer;
  BEGIN
    ClrScr;
    writeln;
    writeln ('Data for students in the class are as follows:');
    FOR Index := 1 TO ListSize DO
      BEGIN
        writeln;
        Student[Index].Print
      END;
    writeln
  END;

{==================================================================}

{  Methods for all OBJECTS have been written  }
{  Now begin the main program  }

BEGIN  {  Main program  }
  Prof.Init;
  StuList.Init;
```

```
  Prof.GetData;
  StuList.GetListData;
  StuList.Sort;
  Prof.Print;
  readln;
  StuList.Print;
  ClassGradeAv := StuList.ComputeGPA;
  writeln;
  writeln ('The class GPA is ', ClassGradeAv:6:3);
  readln
END.  {  of main program  }
```

A sample run of this program produces the following display.

```
Enter data for the class Professor.

For each of the following questions, please enter
the requested information and press <Enter>

Name:  (last name first)      Winsor Robert
Age:                          52
Gender: <M or F>              M
Department?                   Computer Science
Rank?                         Professor
Office number?                PE 221
Phone Number?                 (111) 231 3311

Thank you for your patience.   Press <Enter> to continue.


Please enter data for students in the class.
Press <Enter> after each entry.


Name:  (last name first)     Curtiss Patrice
Age:                         19
Gender:  <M or F>            F
ID:                          111 22 1212
Current GPA:                 3.45

Any more students? <Y or N>   Y
Name:  (last name first)     Cripps Tom
Age:                         21
Gender:  <M or F>             M
ID:                          111 12 2222
Current GPA:                 3.67

Any more students? <Y or N>   Y
Name:  (last name first)      Adams Karen
Age:                         31
Gender:  <M or F>             F
ID:                          666 55 1234
Current GPA:                 3.80

Any more students? <Y or N>   N
```

```
PROFESSOR DATA
--------------

Name:                  Winsor Robert
Age:                   52
Gender:                M
Department:            Computer Science
Rank:                  Professor
Office number:         PE 221
Phone number:          (111) 231 3311


Data for students in the class are as follows:

Name:                 Adams Karen
Age:                  31
Gender:               F
ID:                   666 55 1234
GPA:                  3.80

Name:                 Cripps Tom
Age:                  21
Gender:               M
ID:                   111 12 2222
GPA:                  3.67

Name:                 Curtiss Patrice
Age:                  19
Gender:               F
ID:                   111 22 1212
GPA:                  3.45


The class GPA is   3.640
```

Exercises 14.3

1. Consider **PROGRAM** ListPrac in this section. Extend the hierarchy of object types to include a subclass for buildings. (Assume a building has a name.) Also create subclasses of students so there is an object type for full-time students and an object type for part-time students.
2. Consider Exercise 1. Suppose you wish to define object types for students who commute and for students who live on campus. Where would they fit in your hierarchy?
3. Discuss how the concept of polymorphism can be applied to automobiles.
4. Returning to **PROGRAM** ListPrac, redefine the object ProfessorType so records are used for the data fields Dept, Rank, Office, and PhoneNum.
5. Consider the object type ClassList in **PROGRAM** ListPrac. The **PROCEDURE** GetListData uses the object to get data from the keyboard. Modify the program so data is entered into variable fields and a method is then used to send the data to the object type. (In other words, data entry is not a method in the object.)
6. Modify **PROGRAM** ListPrac so input is from a text file stored on a disk.
7. Write documentation for all the methods in **PROGRAM** ListPrac.

■ 14.4 Implementation of Objects

In the first three sections of this chapter, we have discussed the philosophy, syntax, examples, and implementation of objects in object-oriented programming. We now consider some features of object-oriented programming that are developed and implemented in Borland's Turbo Pascal.

Static Methods

In the examples in this chapter thus far, all methods written in objects are *static methods.* All connections, allocations, and references between methods and data fields in a hierarchy are resolved at compilation time.

The process of using static methods works well for these short examples. However, as the inheritance hierarchies get more involved and more overrides are used in methods, it is possible to encounter situations in which the early determination of references is not sufficient. In particular, some override methods do not produce the desired result.

A complete explanation of how use of static methods can cause programming problems is beyond the scope of this introductory chapter on object-oriented programming. It is sufficient for you to know that such problems can occur.

Virtual Methods

Turbo Pascal avoids the problems associated with the compile-time resolution of method calls through the use of *virtual methods.* When a method is indicated as **VIRTUAL**, the resolution of connections, allocations, and references is not determined until run time. Now let's consider the following example of an object type, which contains virtual methods:

```
TYPE
  Point = OBJECT
            X : real;
            Y : real;

            CONSTRUCTOR Init;
            DESTRUCTOR Done; VIRTUAL;
            PROCEDURE SetCoordinates  (Xcoor,Ycoor : real); VIRTUAL;
            FUNCTION GetX : real : VIRTUAL;
            FUNCTION GetY : real : VIRTUAL;
            PROCEDURE Print; VIRTUAL;
          END;
```

Notice we have used the previously defined object type Point and changed the methods from static to virtual. This is accomplished by including the reserved word **VIRTUAL** after the method when the object type is defined. This is the only syntax change necessary. The methods are still written the same way.

Using Constructors

It is important to note that **PROCEDURE** Init has been replaced by **CONSTRUCTOR** Init in the preceding object type. Objects containing virtual methods must be initialized at run time by using methods listed as *constructors.* The constructor must be called before any virtual method is called. Failure to do this can cause the system to "lock up."

Each instance of an object must be initialized by a separate constructor call. In particular, notice it is not sufficient to initialize one instance of an object and then assign it to another instance. This also may cause the system to lock up.

What do constructors do? It is possible to use constructors without knowing what they do. However, understanding their function may help you to remember to always call them before you call a virtual method. According to the Turbo Pascal User's Guide.

> *"Every object type has something called a* virtual method table (VMT) *in the data segment. The VMT contains the object type's size and, for each of its virtual methods, a pointer to the code implementing that method. What the constructor does is establish a link between the instance calling the constructor and the object type's VMT.*

Turbo Pascal does provide a way to guard against system lock up by failure to use a **CONSTRUCTOR** call appropriately. If the compiler directive {$R+} is activated, all virtual method calls are checked for the initialization status of the instance making the call. If the constructor has not been called before the virtual method call, a range check run-time error occurs. This is certainly preferable to a system lock up. After the program is up and running, the {$R+} compiler directive can be removed.

Using Destructors

The method **DESTRUCTOR** Done has been added to the preceding object type. This method can be used when the user has finished working with an object. Calling a *destructor* allows reserved memory to be released. Failure to use a **DESTRUCTOR** call is normally not a problem. All of the memory is simply not released until the program finishes.

Descendant Methods

One final note should be made before looking at a complete program using virtual methods. In establishing an object-type hierarchy, care must be taken when defining methods in descendants. If an ancestor method is **VIRTUAL,** all methods of the same name in any descendant must be **VIRTUAL.**

Now let's look at a complete program using virtual methods.

EXAMPLE 14.1

The program in this example is a revision of the InheritanceDemo program in Section 14.2.

```
PROGRAM InheritanceDemo;

{  This version of InheritanceDemo has been changed to illustrate    }
{  the use of VIRTUAL methods.  Note the use of CONSTRUCTOR and      }
{  DESTRUCTOR.                                                       }

{$R+}  {  This is a compiler directive  }

USES
  Crt;

TYPE
  Point = OBJECT
            X : real;
            Y : real;

            CONSTRUCTOR Init;
            DESTRUCTOR Done; VIRTUAL;
```

```
              PROCEDURE SetCoordinates (Xcoor, Ycoor : real); VIRTUAL;
              FUNCTION GetX : real; VIRTUAL;
              FUNCTION GetY : real; VIRTUAL;
              PROCEDURE Print; VIRTUAL;
            END;  {  of OBJECT Point  }

  Circle = OBJECT (Point)
               Radius : real;

               CONSTRUCTOR Init;              {  Override  }
               DESTRUCTOR Done; VIRTUAL;
               PROCEDURE SetValues (Xcoor, Ycoor, Rad : real); VIRTUAL;
               PROCEDURE GetCenter (VAR Xcoor, Ycoor : real); VIRTUAL;
               FUNCTION GetRadius : real; VIRTUAL;
               FUNCTION ComputeArea : real; VIRTUAL;
               PROCEDURE Print; VIRTUAL;      {  Override  }
             END;  {  of OBJECT Circle  }

VAR
  Figure : Circle;
  Xvalue, Yvalue : real;
  Rad : real;

{******************************************************************}

{  Write all methods for OBJECT Point.  }

{------------------------------------------------------------------}

CONSTRUCTOR Point.Init;
  {  Must be called before any virtual method  }
  BEGIN
    X := 0.0;
    Y := 0.0
  END;  {  of CONSTRUCTOR Point.Init  }

{------------------------------------------------------------------}

PROCEDURE Point.SetCoordinates (Xcoor, Ycoor : real);
  BEGIN
    X := Xcoor;
    Y := Ycoor
  END;  {  of PROCEDURE Point.SetCoordinates  }

{------------------------------------------------------------------}

FUNCTION Point.GetX : real;
  BEGIN
    GetX := X
  END;  {  of FUNCTION Point.GetX  }

{------------------------------------------------------------------}

FUNCTION Point.GetY : real;
  BEGIN
    GetY := Y
  END;  {  of FUNCTION Point.GetY  }

{------------------------------------------------------------------}
```

```
PROCEDURE Point.Print;
  VAR
    Xcoor, Ycoor : real;
  BEGIN
    Xcoor := GetX;
    Ycoor := GetY;
    writeln ('The coordinates are X =  ', Xcoor:4:2,
             '  Y =  ', Ycoor:4:2)
  END;  {  of PROCEDURE Point.Print  }

{-------------------------------------------------------------------}

DESTRUCTOR Point.Done;
  {  Terminates the instance and releases memory  }
  {  To be called when finished with the instance  }
  BEGIN
  END;  {  of DESTRUCTOR Point.Done  }

{*******************************************************************}

{  Write all methods of OBJECT Circle  }

{-------------------------------------------------------------------}

CONSTRUCTOR Circle.Init;        {  Override  }
  {  Must be called before any virtual method  }
  BEGIN
    Point.Init;
    Radius := 0.0
  END;  {  of CONSTRUCTOR Circle.Init  }

{-------------------------------------------------------------------}

PROCEDURE Circle.SetValues (Xcoor, Ycoor, Rad : real);
  BEGIN
    Point.SetCoordinates (Xcoor, Ycoor);
    Radius := Rad
  END;  {  of PROCEDURE Circle.SetValues  }

{-------------------------------------------------------------------}

PROCEDURE Circle.GetCenter (VAR Xcoor, Ycoor : real);
  BEGIN
    Xcoor := X;
    Ycoor := Y
  END;  {  of PROCEDURE Circle.GetCenter  }

{-------------------------------------------------------------------}

FUNCTION Circle.GetRadius : real;
  BEGIN
    GetRadius := Radius
  END;  {  of FUNCTION Circle.GetRadius  }

{-------------------------------------------------------------------}

FUNCTION Circle.ComputeArea : real;
  BEGIN
    ComputeArea := Pi * sqr(Radius)
  END;  {  of FUNCTION Circle.ComputeArea  }

{-------------------------------------------------------------------}
```

```
PROCEDURE Circle.Print;          {  Override  }
  VAR
    CircleRad : real;
    CircleArea : real;
  BEGIN
    writeln;
    writeln ('The center is:');
    Point.Print;
    CircleRad := GetRadius;
    writeln ('The radius is  ', CircleRad:6:2);
    CircleArea := ComputeArea;
    writeln ('The area is  ', CircleArea:6:2)
  END;  {  of PROCEDURE Circle.Print  }

{-------------------------------------------------------------------}

DESTRUCTOR Circle.Done;
  {  Terminates the instance and releases memory  }
  {  To be called when finished with the instance  }
  BEGIN
  END;

{*******************************************************************}

{  All methods have been written.  }
{  Now begin the main program.  }

BEGIN  {  Main program  }
  ClrScr;
  Figure.Init;  {  This is a CONSTRUCTOR call  }

  {  Get values from the keyboard  }
  writeln ('Please enter coordinates for the center of a circle.');
  write ('X coordinate = ');
  readln (Xvalue);
  write ('Y coordinate = ');
  readln (Yvalue);
  write ('The radius is ');
  readln (Rad);

  {  Use Circle's methods  }
  Figure.SetValues (Xvalue, Yvalue, Rad);
  Figure.Print;

  {  Move the center, and change the radius  }
  Xvalue := Xvalue + 3;
  Yvalue := Yvalue + 1;
  Rad := 2 * Rad;

  {  Use Circle's methods again  }
  Figure.SetValues (Xvalue, Yvalue, Rad);
  Figure.Print;
  readln;
  Figure.Done  {  This is a DESTRUCTOR call  }
END.  {  of main program  }
```

Output from a sample run of this program is

```
Please enter coordinates for the center of a circle.
X coordinate = 3
Y coordinate = 2
The radius is 1
```

```
The center is:
The coordinates are X =  3.00  Y =  2.00
The radius is    1.00
The area is    3.14

The center is:
The coordinates are X =  6.00  Y =  3.00
The radius is    2.00
The area is   12.57
```

Early Binding versus Late Binding

There is yet another way to think of the difference between virtual methods and static methods. Using a static method can be thought of as making a decision now; using a virtual method can be thought of as delaying the decision as long as possible. Since the connections to static methods are made when the program is compiled, this process is referred to as *early binding.* On the other hand, the connections to virtual methods are made as late as possible, so this process is referred to as *late binding.*

Virtual Methods and Polymorphism

One significant feature of late binding by using virtual methods is how it enhances the concept and use of polymorphism in program designs. When late binding is used, any descendant type of the parameter type can be passed in the parameter. Thus, the user does not need to know which object type the parameter is receiving. This means the exact type of the parameter can be unknown during program compilation. In this sense, the actual parameter is a polymorphic object.

This significant new concept is radically different from standard Pascal. Initially, you may not be able to think of examples that utilize this property. However, if you expand your work in object-oriented programming, it will become a regular part of your thought process as you design software systems.

We will not pursue this aspect of object-oriented programming in Turbo Pascal in this introductory chapter. However, you should be aware of the use of late binding and polymorphic objects if you continue your work in this area.

Object Types as Units

Recall from earlier discussion that encapsulation is enhanced through the use of objects in a program. Turbo Pascal provides an even better vehicle to accommodate this process. Units are designed specifically to allow users to access their features without dealing with how they are implemented. For example, if we want to use the printer and the screen for output, we include the statement

```
USES
  Crt, Printer;
```

as part of our program. Crt and Printer are units. We know and use their features but are unaware of how they are implemented.

Now let's see how object types can be written as units. The form and syntax required for creating a unit follow.

```
UNIT <identifier>;

INTERFACE
USES <unit1, unit2, . . . unitn>; { optional }
   <constants>   ┐
   <data types>  │
   <variables>   ├ (public declaration;
   <procedures>  │  visible to other units or programs)
   <functions>   ┘

IMPLEMENTATION
USES <unit1, unit2, . . . unitn>; {  optional  }
        .
        .            (implementation of procedures and functions)
        .
BEGIN
        .
        .            (initialization section; optional)
        .
END. { of the unit }
```

The Interface Section

The *interface section* or public part of a unit contains definitions of constants, data types, variables, procedures, and functions. This section begins with the reserved word **INTERFACE** and ends when the reserved word **IMPLEMENTATION** is encountered. When it is applied to an object type definition, this structure allows all constants, data types, object types, and methods to be listed in the interface section. To illustrate, the object type Point written as a unit PointUn has the following interface section:

```
INTERFACE

TYPE
  Point = OBJECT
            X : real;
            Y : real;

            CONSTRUCTOR Init;
            DESTRUCTOR Done; VIRTUAL;
            PROCEDURE SetCoordinates (Xcoor, Ycoor : real); VIRTUAL;
            FUNCTION GetX : real; VIRTUAL;
            FUNCTION GetY : real; VIRTUAL;
            PROCEDURE Print; VIRTUAL;
          END;  {  of OBJECT Point  }
```

Every item in this interface section is now available to programs that use this unit.

The Implementation Section

All implementation details are contained in the *implementation section* of a unit. This section begins with the reserved word **IMPLEMENTATION** and ends with **END** followed by a period. Everything defined in the interface section is available to the implementation section. If we continue the example using the object type Point, the implementation portion of the unit is

```
IMPLEMENTATION

CONSTRUCTOR Point.Init;
  {  Must be called before any virtual method. }
  BEGIN
    X := 0.0;
    Y := 0.0
  END;    {  of CONSTRUCTOR Point.Init  }

PROCEDURE Point.SetCoordinates (Xcoor, Ycoor : real);
  BEGIN
    X := Xcoor;
    Y := Ycoor
  END;  {  of PROCEDURE Point.SetCoordinates  }

FUNCTION Point.GetX : real;
  BEGIN
    GetX := X
  END;  {  of FUNCTION Point.GetX  }

FUNCTION Point.GetY : real;
  BEGIN
    GetY := Y
  END;  {  of FUNCTION Point.GetY  }

PROCEDURE Point.Print;
  VAR
    Xcoor, Ycoor : real;
  BEGIN
    Xcoor := GetX;
    Ycoor := GetY;
    writeln ('The coordinates are X =  ', Xcoor:4:2,
             '  Y =  ', Ycoor:4:2)
  END;  {  of PROCEDURE Point.Print  }

DESTRUCTOR Point.Done;
  {  Terminates the instance and releases memory.  }
  {  To be called when finished with the instance. }
  BEGIN
  END;  {  of DESTRUCTOR Point.Done  }

END. {  of UNIT PointUn  }
```

We now have a unit available to other units and programs. Thus, when we write a unit for the object type Circle, we can access the unit just written by

```
USES
  PointUn;
```

The unit for the object type Circle then becomes the following.

```
UNIT CircleUn;
INTERFACE

USES
  PointUn;  {  A call to a UNIT  }
```

```
TYPE
  Circle = OBJECT (Point)
             Radius : real;

             CONSTRUCTOR Init;          {  Override  }
             DESTRUCTOR Done; VIRTUAL;
             PROCEDURE SetValues (Xcoor, Ycoor, Rad : real); VIRTUAL;
             FUNCTION GetRadius : real; VIRTUAL;
             FUNCTION ComputeArea : real; VIRTUAL;
             PROCEDURE Print; VIRTUAL;  {  Override  }
           END;  {  of OBJECT  Circle  }

IMPLEMENTATION

{*******************************************************************}

{ Write all methods for object type Circle  }

{-------------------------------------------------------------------}

CONSTRUCTOR Circle.Init;  {  Override  }
  {  Must be called before any virtual method  }
  BEGIN
    Point.Init;
    Radius := 0.0
  END;  {  of CONSTRUCTOR Circle.Init  }

{-------------------------------------------------------------------}

PROCEDURE Circle.SetValues (Xcoor, Ycoor, Rad : real);
  BEGIN
    Point.SetCoordinates (Xcoor, Ycoor);
    Radius := Rad
  END;  {  of PROCEDURE Circle.SetValues  }

{-------------------------------------------------------------------}

FUNCTION Circle.GetRadius : real;
  BEGIN
    GetRadius := Radius
  END;  {  of FUNCTION Circle.GetRadius  }

{-------------------------------------------------------------------}

FUNCTION Circle.ComputeArea : real;
  BEGIN
    ComputeArea := Pi * sqr(Radius)
  END;  {  of FUNCTION Circle.ComputeArea  }

{-------------------------------------------------------------------}

PROCEDURE Circle.Print;  {  Override  }
  VAR
    CircleRad : real;
    CircleArea : real;
  BEGIN
    writeln;
    writeln ('The center is:');
    Point.Print;
    CircleRad := GetRadius;
    writeln ('The radius is  ', CircleRad:6:2);
    CircleArea := ComputeArea;
```

```
    writeln ('The area is  ', CircleArea:6:2);
    writeln
  END;  {  of PROCEDURE Circle.Print  }


{-------------------------------------------------------------------}

DESTRUCTOR Circle.Done;
  {  Terminates the instance and releases memory.  }
  {  To be called when finished with the instance. }
  BEGIN
  END;  {  of DESTRUCTOR Circle.Done  }

{*******************************************************************}

END.  {  of UNIT CircleUn  }
```

We can now rewrite the program InheritanceDemo to take advantage of the existence of these units for the object types Point and Circle. Notice with these units available, we can go directly to the main program.

```
PROGRAM UnitPrac;

{$R+}  {  Check for Init with VIRTUAL methods  }

USES
  Crt,
  CircleUn;  {  CircleUn contains USES PointUn  }

VAR
  Figure : Circle;
  Xvalue, Yvalue : real;
  Rad : real;

BEGIN  {  Program  }
  ClrScr;
  Figure.Init;

  {  Get values from the keyboard  }
  writeln ('Please enter coordinates for the center of a circle.');
  write ('X coordinate = ');
  readln (Xvalue);
  write ('Y coordinate = ');
  readln (Yvalue);
  write ('Now enter the radius:  ');
  readln (Rad);

  {  Use Circle's methods  }
  Figure.SetValues (Xvalue, Yvalue, Rad);
  Figure.Print;

  {  Move the center and change the radius  }
  Xvalue := Xvalue + 3;
  Yvalue := Yvalue + 1;
  Rad := 2 * Rad;

  {  Use Circle's methods again  }
  Figure.SetValues (Xvalue, Yvalue, Rad);
  Figure.Print;
  readln;
  Figure.Done
END.  {  of main program  }
```

Private Declarations

At times, we may not want to make the data fields and/or methods in an object or unit available to the user of that object or unit. To achieve this, Turbo Pascal allows private fields and methods to be specified within object-type definitions. These private fields and methods are defined immediately following the regular fields and methods and must be preceded by the reserved word **PRIVATE.** We do not illustrate this feature here. The interested reader is directed to the Turbo Pascal User's Guide.

7.0

Initialization Section

An optional initialization section can be included in a unit. If written, it is part of the **IMPLEMENTATION** section. After writing code for the implementation of all procedures and functions, we use the reserved word **BEGIN** to signal the start of the initialization section. We may then proceed to initialize any data structures or variables that the unit uses or makes available to the program using the unit. The initialization section may also be used to open files for later use in the program. When a program is run, the unit's initialization section is called before the main body of the program is run.

Exercises 14.4

1. Discuss the difference between static and virtual methods.
2. What is the purpose of **CONSTRUCTOR** Init?
3. What happens if an instance of an object containing a virtual method is used before it is initialized?
4. What is the purpose of **DESTRUCTOR** Done?
5. What changes in an object-type definition using static methods are required if you want to use virtual methods?
6. Why would you want to use virtual methods rather than static methods in an object-type definition?
7. Recall the hierarchy in Section 14.3 that used the object types NameStr, PersonType, StudentType, and ProfessorType. Rewrite each object-type definition so all methods are virtual rather than static.
8. Explain what is wrong with the following definitions:

```
PROGRAM Exercise8;

  Object1 = OBJECT
              X : real;
              CONSTRUCTOR Init;
              PROCEDURE GetData; VIRTUAL;
                       .
                       .
                       .
            END;

  Object2 = OBJECT (Object1)
              N : integer;
              CONSTRUCTOR Init;
              PROCEDURE GetData;
                       .
                       .
                       .
            END;
```

9. Discuss how the concept of late binding using virtual methods enhances the concept of polymorphism in object-oriented programming.
10. What is the interface section of a unit?
11. What is the implementation section of a unit?
12. Reconsider **PROGRAM** ListPrac in Section 14.3.
    a. Write a separate unit for each of the object types NameStr, PersonType, StudentType, ProfessorType, and ClassList.
    b. Rewrite the program using the units you wrote in (a).

RUNNING AND DEBUGGING HINTS

1. When defining an object, place a semicolon as a separator between the last method and **END**. For example

```
TYPE
  Point = OBJECT
             .
             .              } data fields
             .

             .
             .              } methods
             .
          PROCEDURE Print;
        END;
```

2. Always initialize the data fields of an object by using **PROCEDURE** Init.
3. You cannot use objects as components of a file.
4. Never make a field identifier identical to a formal parameter. For example

```
TYPE
  Point = OBJECT
            X : real;
            Y : real;
               .
               .
               .
            PROCEDURE SetCoordinates (X,Y : real);
          END;
```

causes a compilation error.

5. Do not use an object-type identifier when referring to an instance of the object. Thus, if you have

```
TYPE
  Circle = OBJECT (Point)
     .
     .
     .
VAR
  Figure : Circle;
```

a reference in the program to Circle.Init produces an error. The reference should be Figure.Init.

6. When overriding an ancestor's method, you must make a unique reference to that method. Thus, in

```
PROCEDURE Circle.Init;
  BEGIN
    Point.Init;
    Radius := 0.0
  END;
```

note that Point.Init refers to the initialization method for object type Point.

7. Never override a data field. Once you define a data field in an object type, no descendant type can contain a data field with the same identifier.
8. You can assign a descendant object to an ancestor, but the converse is not true. Thus, if Child is a descendant of Parent, then

```
Parent := Child
```

is valid, but

```
Child := Parent
```

is not valid.

9. Use **CONSTRUCTOR** Init rather than **PROCEDURE** Init when defining an object type with virtual methods.
10. Call the constructor before you call any virtual method.
11. Initialize each individual instance of an object by a separate constructor call.
12. If an ancestor method is **VIRTUAL**, you must make all methods of the same name in any descendant **VIRTUAL**.

■ Summary

Key Terms

ancestor
class
constructor
descendant
destructor
early binding
encapsulation process
implementation section
inheritance
instance of an object
instantiation
interface section
late binding
method
object
object-oriented programming (OOP)
override
polymorphism
self parameter
sending a message
static method
subclass
virtual method
virtual method table (VMT)

Keywords

CONSTRUCTOR
DESTRUCTOR
IMPLEMENTATION
INTERFACE
OBJECT
PRIVATE
Self
VIRTUAL

Key Concepts

- An object contains fields for data, and methods for operating on the data.
- A typical definition of an object type is

```
TYPE
  Point = OBJECT
            X : real;                 }
            Y : real;                 } data fields

            PROCEDURE Init;            }
            PROCEDURE SetCoordinates;  }
            FUNCTION GetX;             } methods
            FUNCTION GetY;             }
            PROCEDURE Print;           }
          END;
```

- Encapsulation is the process of including the operations that can be performed on the data fields as part of the program structure.
- An instance of the object type is an object declared in the variable declaration section as

```
VAR
  Dot : Point;
```

- A program should never operate directly with the data fields of an object. A method should be written for every operation; the methods should then be used to work with data fields of the object.
- The data fields of an object are available to the methods of that object.
- The method's bodies and the object's data fields share the same scope.
- Methods for an object type must contain a unique reference to that object type. A typical heading is

```
PROCEDURE Point.Init;
```

- References to an object's methods require a period. A typical reference is

```
Dot.Init
```

- **WITH . . . DO** can be used in a manner similar to that used with fields of a record.
- To put a value into an object's field, call a method belonging to the object that assigns a value to that field.
- To get a value from an object's field, call a method belonging to the object that returns the value of the desired field.
- A new object type can be defined using an existing object type. The new type inherits the data fields and methods of the previous type.
- A descendant can use an ancestor's methods. For example, in

```
PROCEDURE Circle.SetValues (Xcoor, Ycoor, Rad : real);
  BEGIN
    Point.SetCoordinates (Xcoor, Ycoor);
    Radius = Rad
  END;
```

  the method SetValues in Circle uses the existing method SetCoordinates in Point.
- A descendant's methods can override an ancestor's methods by using the same identifier in a descendant's method.
- Polymorphism permits a process that is common to many objects to have a different implementation for each type of object.
- Using static methods, all connections, allocations, and references between methods and data fields in a hierarchy are resolved at compilation time. This is referred to as early binding.
- Using virtual methods, the resolution of connections, allocations, and references is not determined until run time. This is referred to as late binding.
- Virtual methods are defined by including the word **VIRTUAL** after the method is listed in an object type. For example, in

```
TYPE
  Point = OBJECT
            X : real;
            Y : real;

            CONSTRUCTOR Init;
            DESTRUCTOR Done; VIRTUAL;
            PROCEDURE SetCoordinates (Xcoor, Ycoor : real); VIRTUAL;
            FUNCTION GetX : real; VIRTUAL;
            FUNCTION GetY : real; VIRTUAL;
            PROCEDURE Print; VIRTUAL;
          END;
```

  the methods Done, SetCoordinates, GetX, GetY, and Print are virtual methods.
- Object types lend themselves to be developed as units.

- Units contain an interface section and an implementation section and may contain an initialization section.

■ Programming Problems and Projects

1. Design a software package that allows the user to work with fractions in horizontal form. Use an object type for a fraction. Menu options should allow you to do the following.
   a. Get two fractions.
   b. Get the desired operation (+, –, *, /).
   c. Write the answer in nonreduced form.
   d. Write the answer in reduced form.
   e. Quit.
2. Design a software package that works with a hierarchy of geometric shapes. The ancestor type should be for Figure with fields of Shape, Area, and Perimeter. Descendants should be Circle, Rectangle, Square, and RightTriangle. Your system should allow the user to enter the choice of Figure together with minimal pertinent data. Output should include a display of the characteristics of Figure, including Shape, Area, and Perimeter.
3. Develop a unit for working with a list of names. Each name is a string of at most 25 characters. The unit should allow the user to perform the following operations on the list.
   a. Get data (from a disk file).
   b. Add names to the list.
   c. Delete names from the list.
   d. Sort the list.
   e. Search the list for a name, returning the position of the name if a match is found.
   f. Display a name from the list (after search is **true**).
   g. Display the list.
   h. Display the length of the list.

   Use the unit in a program. Include enough sample runs to verify each list operation.
4. Write an object type that calculates and displays the mean, median, and mode of a set of at most 100 numbers. Data for the object is stored in an unsorted array. Encapsulate the object as a unit. Use the unit in a program that allows the user to enter a set of test scores from the keyboard.
5. Consider the Focus on Program Design problem in Chapter 5 (page 000), where a program is written that lists all primes less than or equal to a given positive integer. Write an object that can be used as a "prime number checker." Input to the object is a positive integer. The object should indicate whether or not the positive integer is prime. Encapsulate the object as a unit, and write a program that uses the unit. Input and output for the program should be similar to that for the program in Chapter 5.
6. Refer to the Focus on Program Design problem in Chapter 10 (page 000). Rewrite that program using object types for Name, StudentRecord, and StudentList.

■ Communication in Practice

Using the **File** menu, select the file path DEMOS\ and then open the file BREAKOUT.PAS. Compile and run this program, and obtain a hard copy of the program listing. List all suggestions you have for changing the documentation used in this program. Examine the methods used in this program, and create documentation for each. Compare your results with those of other students who have been given the same assignment.

Dynamic Variables and Data Structures

CHAPTER OUTLINE

Material in the previous chapters has focused almost exclusively on *static variables,* which have the following characteristics:

1. Their size (array length, for example) is fixed at compilation time.
2. A certain amount of memory is reserved for each variable, and this memory is retained for the declared variables as long as the program or subprogram in which the variable is defined is active.
3. They are declared in a variable declaration section.
4. The structure or existence of a variable cannot be changed during a run of the program. (Two exceptions are the length of a file and records with variant parts).

A disadvantage of using only static variables and data structures is that the number of variables needed in a program must be predetermined. Thus, if we are working with an array and we anticipate the need for 1000 locations, we would define

```
<name> = ARRAY [1..1000] OF <base type>;
```

This creates two problems. We may overestimate the length of the array and use only part of it, thereby wasting memory. Or we may underestimate the necessary array length and be unable to process all the data until the program is modified.

Fortunately, Turbo Pascal solves these problems with the use of *dynamic variables.* Some of their characteristics follow.

1. Dynamic variable types are defined in the **TYPE** section.
2. Memory for dynamic variables is created as needed and returned when not needed during the execution of a program. Therefore, unneeded memory is not wasted and the programmer is limited only by the available memory.
3. A new (and significant) technique must be developed to form a list of dynamic variables; these lists are referred to as *dynamic structures.*

4. In some instances, working with dynamic structures can be a slower process than working with static structures; in particular, direct access of an array element has no analogue.
5. A significantly different method of accessing values stored in dynamic variables must be developed because memory locations are not predetermined.

A complete development of dynamic variables and data structures is left to other courses in computer science. However, when you have finished this chapter, you should have a reasonable understanding of dynamic variables and data structures, and be able to use them in a program. Here, we will carefully develop one type of dynamic data structure (the linked list) and then introduce three others—the stack, queue, and binary tree.

You may find this material somewhat difficult. If so, do not get discouraged. Two reasons for the increased level of difficulty are that some of the work is not intuitive and that the level of abstraction is different from that of previous material. Therefore, as you work through this chapter, you are encouraged to draw several diagrams and write several short programs to help you understand concepts. You also may need to reread the chapter or particular sections to grasp the mechanics of working with dynamic variables.

■ 15.1 Pointer Variables

Computer Memory

Computer memory can be envisioned as a sequence of memory locations, as shown in Figure 15.1(a). A memory location is an area where a value can be stored. When a variable is declared in the variable declaration section of a program, a memory location is reserved during execution of that program block. This memory location can be accessed by a reference to the variable name, and only data of the declared type can be stored there. Thus, if the declaration section is

```
VAR
  Sum : integer;
```

we can envision it as shown in Figure 15.1(b). If the assignment

```
Sum := 56;
```

is made, we have the arrangement shown in Figure 15.1(c).

Each memory location has an *address*. This is an integer value that the computer must use as a reference to the memory location. When static variables such as Sum are used, the address of a memory location is used indirectly by the

FIGURE 15.1(a)
Computer Memory

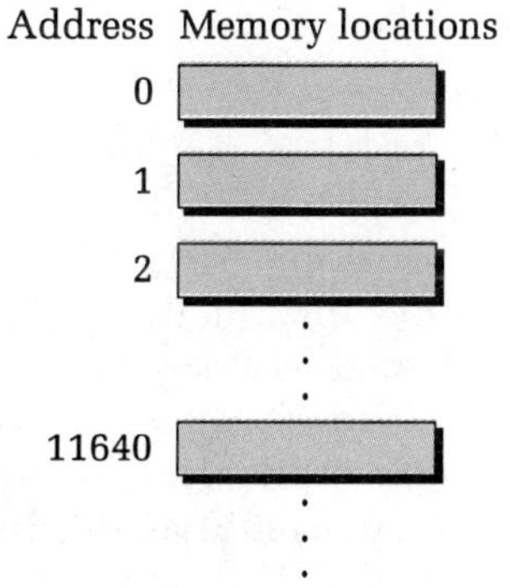

Address	Memory locations
0	
1	
2	
.	
.	
.	
11640	
.	
.	
.	

FIGURE 15.1(b)
Variable location in memory

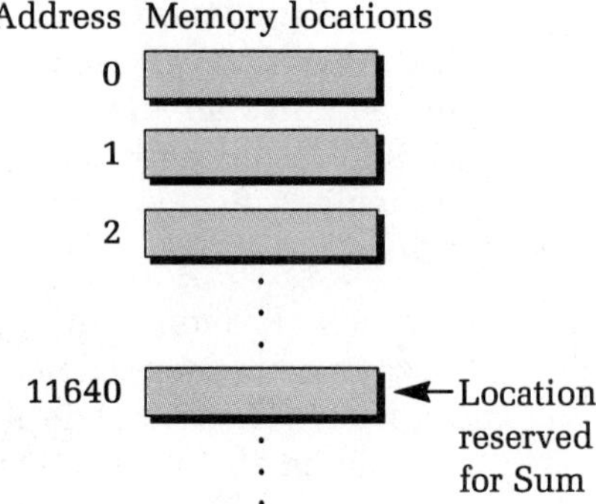

FIGURE 15.1(c)
Value in variable Sum

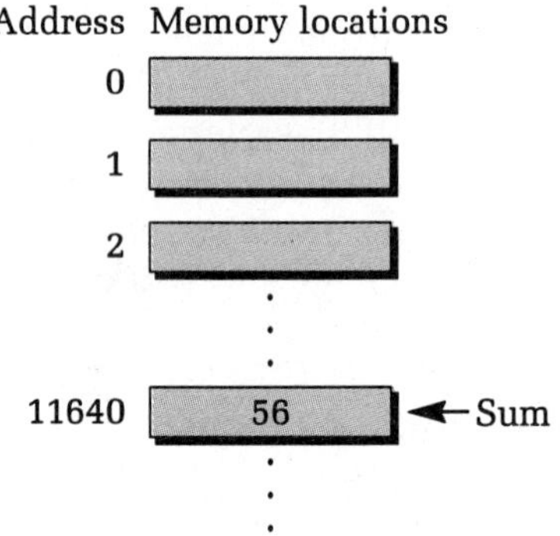

FIGURE 15.1(d)
Relationship between pointer and memory location

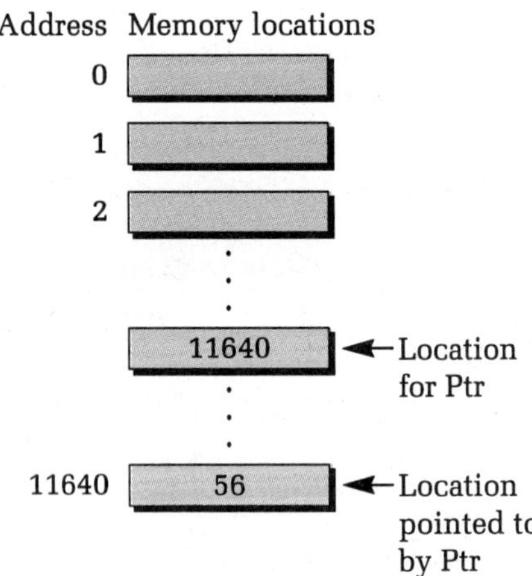

underlying machine instruction. However, when dynamic variables are used, the address is used directly as a reference or pointer to the memory location.

The *value* that is the address of a memory location must be stored somewhere in memory. In Turbo Pascal, the value is stored in a *pointer variable* (frequently denoted by Ptr), which is a variable of a predefined type that is used to contain the address of a memory location. To illustrate, assume Ptr is declared as a pointer variable. If 56 is stored in a memory location with the address 11640, we can envision it as shown in Figure 15.1(d).

Working with Pointer and Dynamic Variables

S Pointer variables are declared by using a caret (^) in front of the type name. Thus

```
TYPE
  Ages = 0..120;
  PointerToAges = ^Ages;
VAR
  Ptr : PointerToAges;
```

declares Ptr as a pointer variable. Ptr cannot be assigned values of type Ages; Ptr can only contain addresses of locations with values of type Ages.

Once this declaration has been made, a dynamic variable can be created. A dynamic variable, designated as Ptr^, is a variable accessed by a pointer variable; a dynamic variable is not declared in the declaration section of a program. Using the standard procedure **new** with a pointer variable

```
new (Ptr);  {  This initializes a value for Ptr  }
```

creates the dynamic variable Ptr^. This can be illustrated by

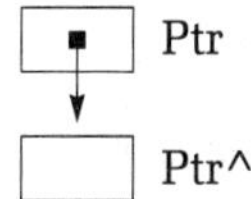

The pointer variable followed by a caret is always the identifier for a dynamic variable. We usually read Ptr^ as the object (variable) pointed to by Ptr.

To illustrate the relationship between pointer variables and dynamic variables, assume we have the previous declaration and the code

```
new (Ptr);
Ptr^ := 56;
```

This stage can be envisioned as

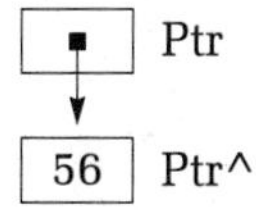

where Ptr contains the address of Ptr^.

Dynamic variables can be destroyed by using the standard procedure **dispose.** Thus, if we no longer need the value of a dynamic variable Ptr^,

```
dispose (Ptr);
```

causes the pointer variable Ptr to no longer contain the address for Ptr^. In this sense, Ptr^ does not exist because nothing is pointing to it. This location has been returned to the computer for subsequent use.

Since pointer variables contain only addresses of memory locations, they have limited use in a program. Pointer variables of the same type can be used only for assignments and comparisons for equality. They cannot be used with **read, write,** or any arithmetic operation. To illustrate, assume we have the definition and declaration

```
TYPE
  Ages = 0..120;
VAR
  Ptr1, Ptr2 : ^Ages;
```

COMMUNICATION AND STYLE TIPS

Ptr or some identifier containing Ptr (for example, DataPtr) is frequently used when declaring pointer variables. This reinforces the difference between working with a pointer variable (Ptr) and working with a dynamic variable (Ptr^).

Then

```
new (Ptr1);
new (Ptr2);
```

create the dynamic variables Ptr1^ and Ptr2^, respectively. If the assignments

```
Ptr1^ := 50;
Ptr2^ := 21;
```

are made, we can envision this as

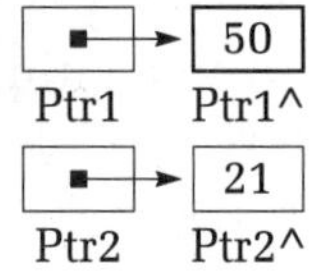

Then Ptr1 = Ptr2 is **false** and Ptr1 < > Ptr2 is **true.** If the assignment

```
Ptr1 := Ptr2;
```

is made, we can envision

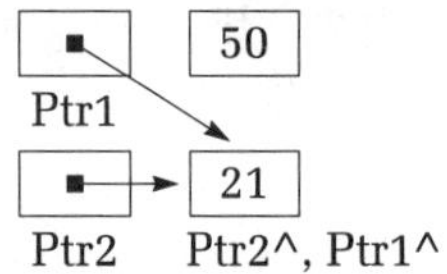

Then Ptr1 = Ptr2 is **true** and Ptr1 < > Ptr2 is **false.**

Notice that in this last illustration, 50 no longer has anything pointing to it. Thus, there is now no way to access this value. Since we did not use **dispose,** the location has not been returned for subsequent reuse. Be careful to use **dispose** when necessary, or you could eventually run out of memory.

Dynamic variables can be used in any context used by static variables of the same type. To illustrate, assume the previous declarations for Ptr1 and Ptr2. If appropriate values (50 and 21) are in a data file, the segment

```
new (Ptr1);
new (Ptr2);
readln (Data, Ptr1^, Ptr2^);
writeln ('The average of', Ptr1^:5, ' and', Ptr2^:5,
         ' is', (Ptr1^ + Ptr2^) / 2:6:2);
```

produces

```
The average of   50 and   21 is 35.50
```

Defining and Declaring Pointer Variables

The previous definition and declarations of pointer types and pointer variables are relatively uncomplicated. However, in actual practice, pointer types and variables are a bit more complex. In the next section, for example, we will work with a dynamic variable as a record type where one of the fields in the record type is a pointer of the same type. Thus, we can have

```
TYPE
  String20 = string [20];
  DataPtr = ^StudentInfo;
  StudentInfo = RECORD
                  Name : String20;
                  Next : DataPtr
                END;  {  of RECORD StudentInfo  }
VAR
  Student : DataPtr;
```

Notice DataPtr makes a reference to StudentInfo before StudentInfo is defined. StudentInfo then contains a field of type DataPtr. This instance is an exception to the rule in Turbo Pascal that an identifier cannot be used before it is defined. Specifically, the following exception is permitted: pointer type definitions can precede definitions of their reference types. The reverse is not true; a structure cannot contain a field or component of a pointer type that has not yet been defined. We frequently want each record to point to another record. Using a record definition with one field for a pointer permits this.

Another note about working with pointers should be mentioned here. The reserved word **NIL,** which has the value of the null pointer that does not point to anything, can be assigned to a pointer variable. Thus, we can have

```
new (Student);
Student^.Next := NIL;
```

This allows pointer variables to be used in Boolean expressions and is needed in later work. For example, if we are forming a list of dynamic variables and each dynamic variable contains a pointer variable for pointing to the next dynamic variable, we can use **NIL** to know when we are at the end of a list. This idea and the concept of pointer type definitions are fully developed in the next section.

Exercises 15.1

1. Discuss the difference between static variables and dynamic variables.
2. Write a test program to declare a single pointer variable with an associated dynamic variable that can have values in the subrange 0 . . 50 and then do the following.
   a. Create a dynamic variable, assign the value 25, and print the value.
   b. Create another dynamic variable, assign the value 40, and print the value.

   At this stage of your program, where is the value 25 stored?
3. Illustrate the relationship between pointer variables and dynamic variables produced by

```
TYPE
  Ptr = (Red, Yellow, Blue, Green);
VAR
  Ptr1, Ptr2 : ^Ptr;
BEGIN
  new (Ptr1);
  new (Ptr2);
  Ptr1^ := Blue;
  Ptr2^ := Red
END.
```

4. Assume the **TYPE** and **VAR** sections given in Exercise 3. Find all errors in the following.
   a. `new (Ptr1^);`
   b. `new (Ptr2);`
      `Ptr2 := Yellow;`

c.
```
new (Ptr1);
new (Ptr2);
Ptr1^ := Red;
Ptr2^ := Ptr1^;
```

d.
```
new (Ptr1);
new (Ptr2);
Ptr1^ := Red;
Ptr1^ := Ptr2^;
```

e.
```
new (Ptr1);
new (Ptr2);
Ptr1^ := Red;
Ptr2^ := Ptr1;
```

5. Assume pointer variables are declared in the variable declaration section as

```
VAR
  RealPtr1, RealPtr2 : ^real;
  IntPtr1, IntPtr2 : ^integer;
  BoolPtr1, BoolPtr2 : ^boolean;
```

Indicate if the following are valid or invalid references. Give an explanation for each invalid reference.

a. `IntPtr1 := IntPtr1 + 1;`

b. `writeln (RealPtr2:30:2);`

c. `writeln (BoolPtr1^:15, IntPtr1^:15, RealPtr1^:15:2);`

d.
```
IF IntPtr1 < IntPtr2 THEN
  writeln ('All done');
```

e.
```
IF BoolPtr NOT NIL THEN
  new (BoolPtr2);
```

f.
```
IF RealPtr1 <> RealPtr2 THEN
  writeln (RealPtr1^:15:2, RealPtr2^:15:2);
```

g.
```
IF BoolPtr2 THEN
  new (BoolPtr1);
```

h.
```
IF BoolPtr2^ THEN
  new (BoolPtr1);
```

6. Assume the declarations given in Exercise 5. What is the output from the following fragment of code?

```
new (IntPtr1);
new (IntPtr2);
new (RealPtr1);
new (BoolPtr1);
IntPtr1^ := 95;
IntPtr2^ := 55;
RealPtr1^ := (IntPtr1^ + IntPtr2^) / 2;
BoolPtr1^ := true;
WHILE BoolPtr1^ DO
  BEGIN
    writeln (RealPtr1^:20:2);
    RealPtr1^ := RealPtr1^ - 5;
    IF RealPtr1^ < 0 THEN
      BoolPtr1^ := false
  END;
```

■ 15.2 Linked Lists

A *linked list* can be implemented as a dynamic data structure and can be thought of as a list of data items with each item linked to the next one by means of a pointer. Such a list can be envisioned as

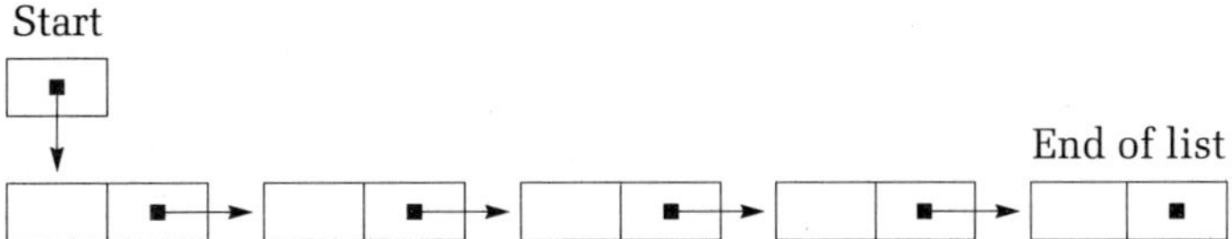

Items in a linked list are called *components* or *nodes.* These lists are similar to arrays; data of the same type can be stored in each node. As shown in the previous illustration, each node of a linked list can store certain data as well as point to the next node. Consequently, a record is used for each node, and one field of the record is reserved for the pointer. If names of students are to be stored in a linked list, we can use the record definition from Section 15.1 as follows:

```
TYPE
  String20 = string [20];
  DataPtr = ^StudentInfo;
  StudentInfo = RECORD
                  Name : String20;
                  Next : DataPtr
                END;  { of RECORD StudentInfo  }
```

Thus, we can envision a list of names as

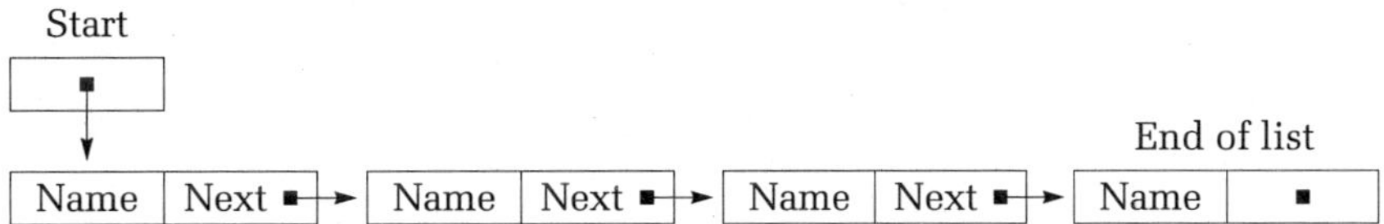

COMMUNICATION AND STYLE TIPS

When working with linked lists, the identifier Next is frequently used as the name of the field in the record that is the pointer variable. This is to remind you that you are pointing to the next record. It makes code such as

```
P := P^.Next;
```

more meaningful.

Creating a Linked List

To create a linked list, we need to be able to identify the first node, the relationship (pointer) between successive nodes, and the last node. Pointers are used to point to both the first and last node. An auxiliary pointer is also used to point to the newest node. The pointer to the first node (Start) is not changed unless a new node is added to the beginning of the list. The other pointers change as the linked list grows. Once a linked list is created, the last node is usually designated by assigning **NIL** to the pointer. To illustrate, let's see how a linked list that holds five names can be formed. Using the **TYPE** definition section

```
TYPE
  String20 = string [20];
  DataPtr = ^StudentInfo;
  StudentInfo = RECORD
                  Name : String20;
                  Next : DataPtr
                END;  { of RECORD StudentInfo  }
```

and the variable declaration section

```
VAR
  Start, Last, Ptr : DataPtr;
```

we can generate the desired list with the following segment of code:

```
BEGIN
  new (Start);
  Ptr := Start;  {  Pointer moves to first node  }
  FOR J := 1 TO 4 DO
    BEGIN
      new (Last);
      Ptr^.Next := Last;
      Ptr := Last
    END;
  Ptr^.Next := NIL;
```

When this code is executed

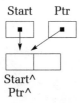

```
new (Start);
```

causes

Start

Start^

and

```
Ptr := Start;
```

produces

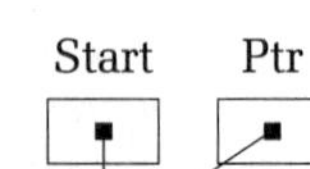

Now that we have started our list, the first pass through the **FOR** loop produces the results shown in Table 15.1.

Similarly, the second pass through the **FOR** loop causes the list to grow as shown in Table 15.2.

Each pass through the body of the **FOR** loop adds one element to the linked list and causes both Ptr and Last to point to the last node of the list. After the loop has been executed four times, we have the following list:

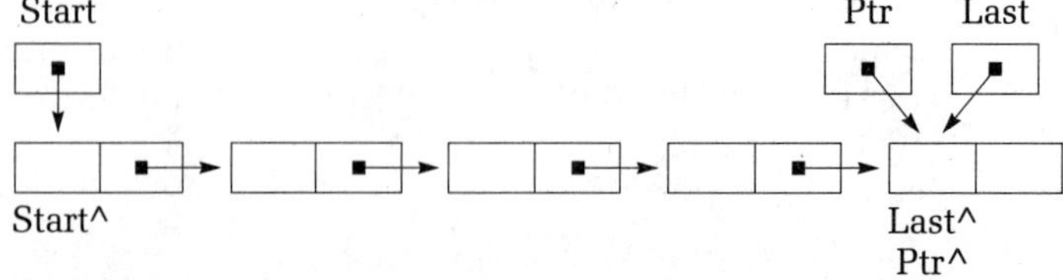

At this stage, the loop is exited and

```
Ptr^.Next := NIL;
```

produces

TABLE 15.1
Adding a second node to a linked list

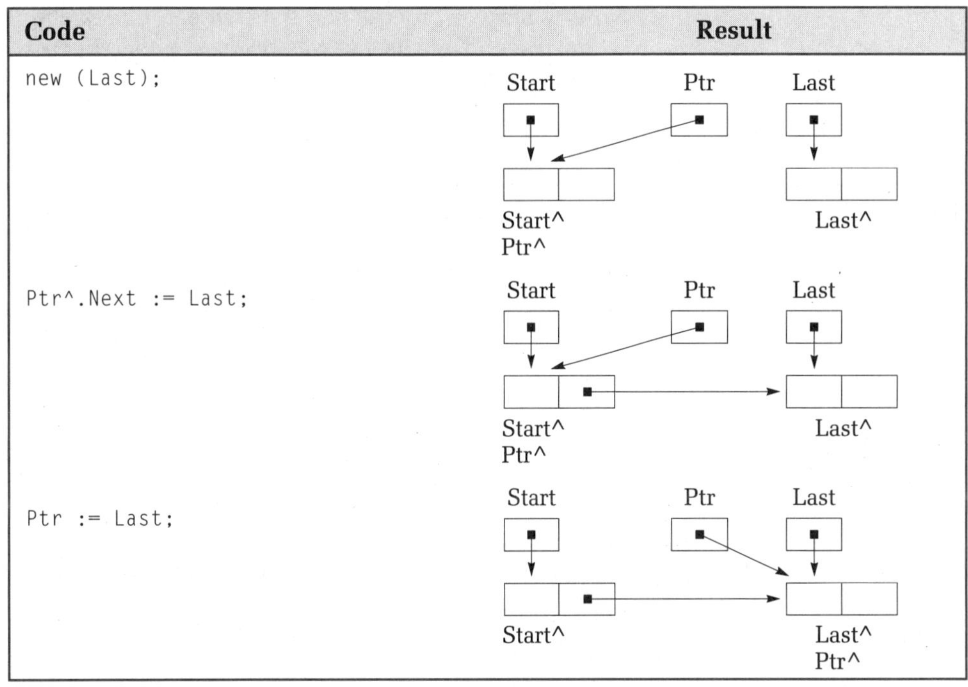

Code	Result
`new (Last);`	Start, Ptr, Last; Start^ Ptr^; Last^
`Ptr^.Next := Last;`	Start, Ptr, Last; Start^ Ptr^; Last^
`Ptr := Last;`	Start, Ptr, Last; Start^; Last^ Ptr^

TABLE 15.2
Adding a third node to a linked list

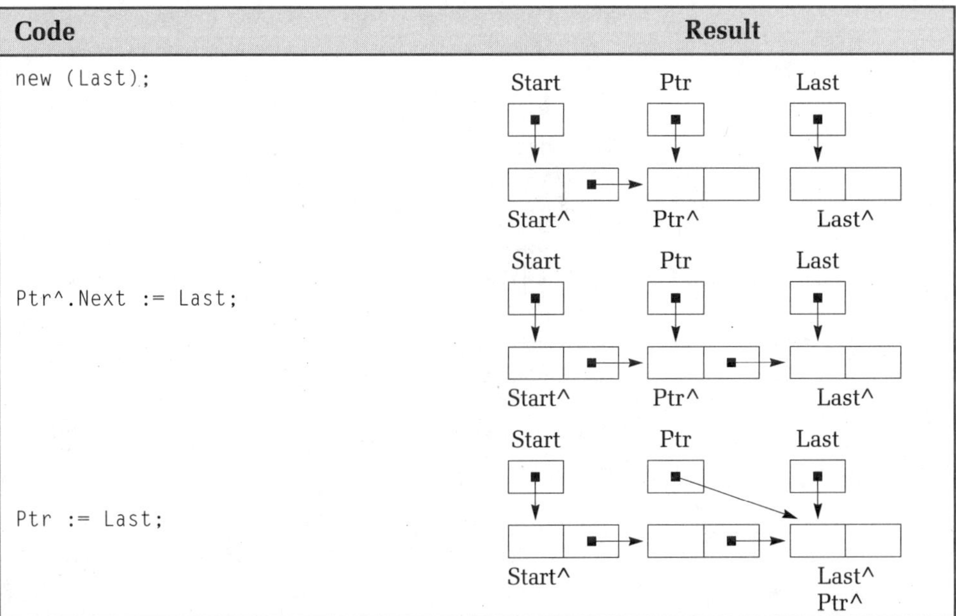

Code	Result
`new (Last);`	Start, Ptr, Last; Start^; Ptr^; Last^
`Ptr^.Next := Last;`	Start, Ptr, Last; Start^; Ptr^; Last^
`Ptr := Last;`	Start, Ptr, Last; Start^; Last^ Ptr^

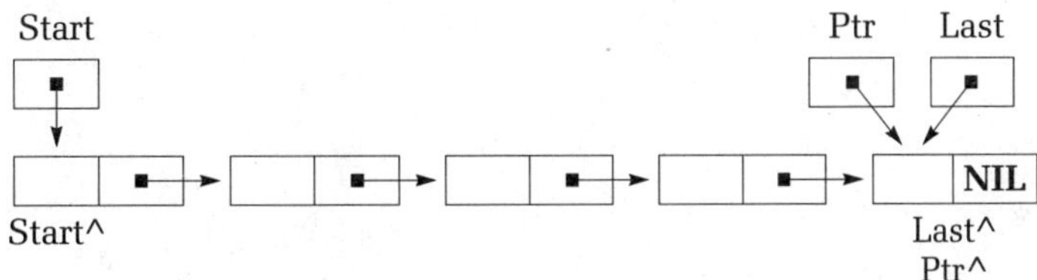

Now when we process the list, we can check the field name Next to determine when the end of the list has been reached. In this sense, the use of **NIL** here is similar to the use of **eof** with files.

EXAMPLE 15.1

Now let's create a linked list that can be used to simulate a deck of playing cards. We need 52 nodes, each of which is a record with a field for the suit (club, diamond, heart, or spade), a field for the number (1 to 13), and a field for the pointer. Such a record can be defined as

```
TYPE
  Pointer = ^Card;
  Suits = (Club, Diamond, Heart, Spade);
  Card = RECORD
           Suit : Suits;
           Num : 1..13;
           Next : Pointer
         END;  {  of RECORD Card  }
```

As before, we need three pointer variables; they can be declared as

```
VAR
  Start, Last, Ptr : Pointer;
```

If an ace is represented by the number 1, we can start our list with

```
BEGIN
  new (Start);
  Start^.Suit := Club;
  Start^.Num := 1;
  Ptr := Start;
  Last := Start;
```

This beginning can be envisioned as

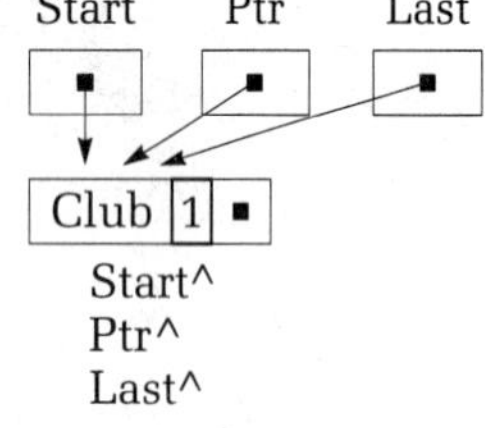

We can then generate the rest of the deck with

```
FOR J := 2 TO 52 DO
  BEGIN
    new (Last);
    IF Ptr^.Num = 13 THEN  {  Start a new suit  }
      BEGIN
        Last^.Suit := succ(Ptr^.Suit);
        Last^.Num := 1
      END
    ELSE  {  Same suit, next number  }
      BEGIN
        Last^.Suit := Ptr^.Suit;
        Last^.Num := Ptr^.Num + 1
      END;
    Ptr^.Next := Last;
    Ptr := Last
  END;
Ptr^.Next := NIL;
```

The first time through this loop produces

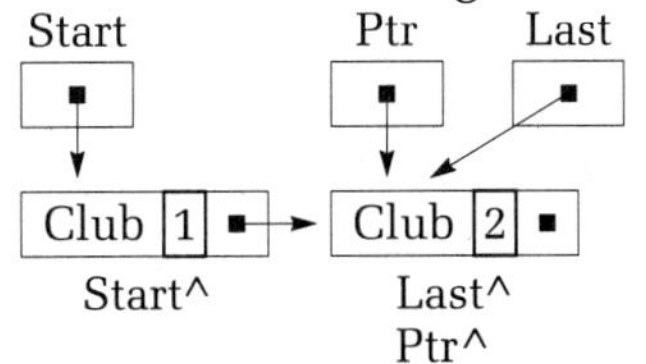

This loop is processed all 51 times and then exited, so when

```
Ptr^.Next := NIL;
```

is executed, we have the list shown in Figure 15.2.

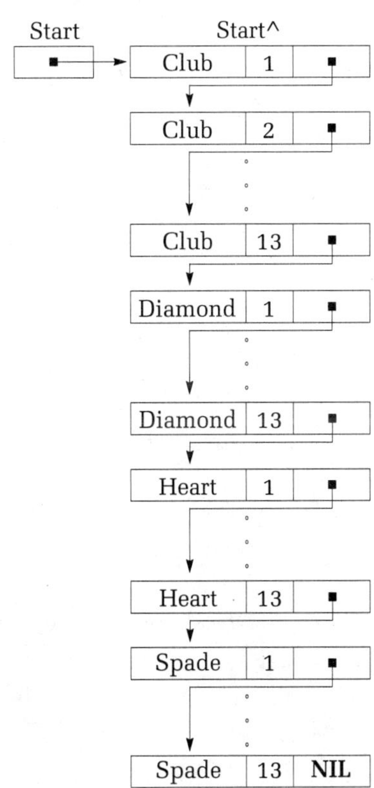

FIGURE 15.2
A linked list simulating a deck of cards

Printing from a Linked List

Thus far, we have seen how to create a dynamic structure and assign data to components of such a structure. We conclude this section with a look at how to print data from a linked list.

The general idea is to start with the first component in the list, print the desired information, and then move sequentially through the list until the last component (**NIL**) is reached. Two aspects of this algorithm need to be examined. First, the loop control depends upon examining the current record for the value of **NIL** in the pointer field. If P is used to denote this field, we have

```
WHILE P <> NIL DO
  BEGIN
    .
    .
    .
  END;
```

Second, the loop increment is to assign the value of the Next field of the current record to the pointer (P) that is used as a loop control variable. To illustrate, assume the previous definitions and declarations are used to form a list of student names. If we declare the variable P by

```
VAR
  P : DataPtr;
```

we can then print the names with

```
BEGIN  { Print names in list }
  P := Start;
  WHILE P <> NIL DO
    BEGIN
      writeln (P^.Name);
      P := P^.Next
    END
END;  { of printing names }
```

In general, printing from a linked list is done with a procedure. In this case, only the external pointer (Start, in our examples) needs to be used as a parameter. To illustrate, a procedure to print the previous list of names is

```
PROCEDURE PrintNames (Start : DataPtr);
  VAR
    P : DataPtr;
  BEGIN
    P := Start;
    WHILE P <> NIL DO
      BEGIN
        writeln (P^.Name);
        P := P^.Next
      END
  END;  { of PROCEDURE PrintNames }
```

This is called from the main program by

```
PrintNames (Start);
```

Exercises 15.2

1. Discuss the differences and similarities between arrays and linked lists.
2. Write a test program to transfer an unknown number of integers from a data file into a linked list and then print the integers from the linked list.
3. Write a procedure to be used with the test program you wrote in Exercise 2 to print the integers.
4. Explain why it is preferable to use a linked list when you are getting an unknown number of data items from a data file.
5. Suppose you are going to create a linked list of records, each of which contains the following information about a student: name, four test scores, 10 quiz scores, average, and letter grade.
   a. Define a record to be used for this purpose.
   b. What pointer type(s) and pointer variable(s) are needed?
   c. Assume the data for each student appears on one line in the data file in the following form:

Smith Mary	97 98 85 90 9 8 7 10 6 9 10 8 9 7

   i. Show how to get the data for the first student into the first component of a linked list.
   ii. Show how to get the data for the second student into the second component.

6. Why are three pointers (Start, Last, Ptr) used when creating a linked list?

7. Consider the following definitions and declarations.

```
TYPE
  P = ^Node;
  Node = RECORD
           Num : integer;
           Next : P
         END;
VAR
  A, B, C : P;
```

a. Show how the schematic

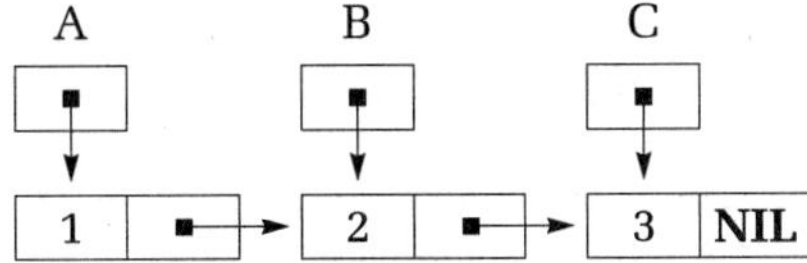

would be changed by each of the following:

i. `A := A^.Next;`

ii. `B := A;`

iii. `C := A^`

iv. `B^.Num := C^.Num;.Next;`

v. `A^.Num := B^.Next^.Num;`

vi. `C^.Next := A;`

b. Write one statement to change

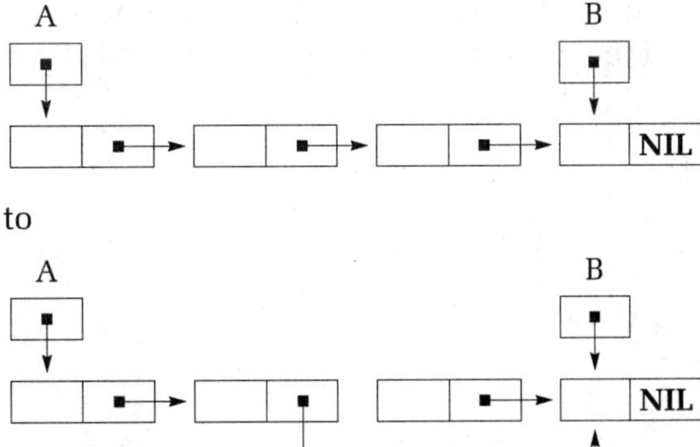

8. Assume the definitions and declarations in Exercise 7. Indicate the output for each of the following.

a.
```
new (A);
new (B);
A^.Num := 10;
B^.Num := 20;
B := A;
A^.Num := 5;
writeln (A^.Num, B^.Num);
```

b.
```
new (C);
C^.Num := 100;
new (B);
B^.Num := C^.Num MOD 8;
new (A);
A^.Num := B^.Num + C^.Num;
writeln (A^.Num, B^.Num, C^.Num);
```

c.
```
new (A);
new (B);
A^.Num := 10;
A^.Next := B;
A^.Next^.Num := 100;
writeln (A^.Num, B^.Num);
```

9. Write a function Sum to sum the integers in a linked list of integers. Show how the function is called from the main program.

■ 15.3 Working with Linked Lists

In this section, we will examine some of the basic operations required when working with linked lists. Working with a list of integers, we will learn how to create a sorted list by inserting elements. We will then update a linked list by searching it for a certain value and deleting that element from the list.

The following **TYPE** definition is used in most of this section:

```
TYPE
  DataPtr = ^Node;
  Node = RECORD
           Num : integer;
           Next : DataPtr
         END;
```

Since most of the operations examined here will be used later in this section, procedures are written for them.

COMMUNICATION AND STYLE TIPS

When working with linked lists of records, Node is frequently used as the record identifier. This facilitates the readability of program comments. Thus, comments such as "Get new node," "Insert a node," and "Delete a node" are meaningful.

Inserting an Element

The dynamic nature of a linked list implies that we are able to insert an element into a list. The three cases considered are inserting an element at the beginning, in the middle, and at the end of a list.

The procedure for inserting an element at the beginning of a list is commonly called *Push.* Before we write code for this procedure, let's examine what should be done with the nodes and pointers. If the list is illustrated by

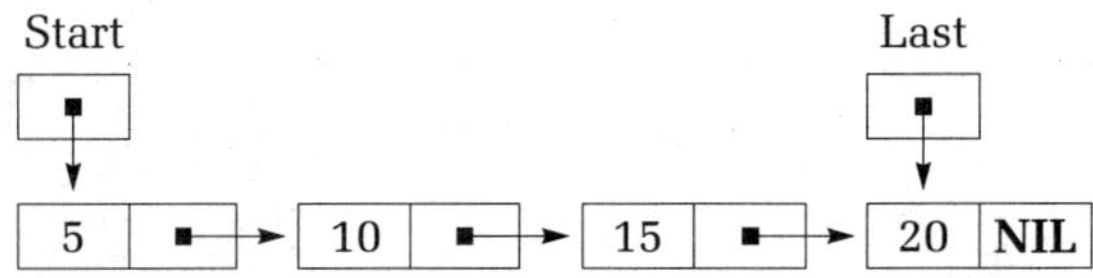

and we wish to insert

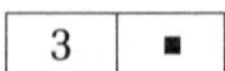

at the beginning of it, we need to get a new node with

```
new (P);
```

assign the appropriate value to Num, using

```
P^.Num := 3;
```

and reassign the pointers to produce the desired result. After the first two steps, we have the list

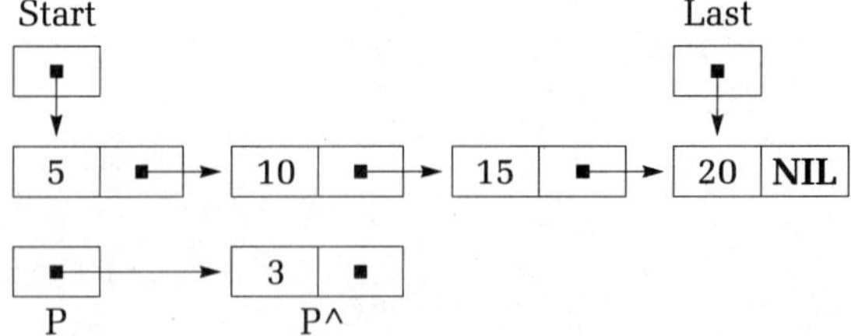

At this point,

```
P^.Next := Start;
```

yields the list

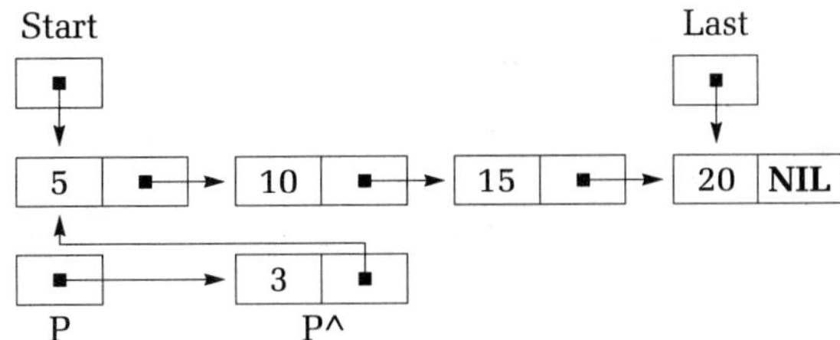

Then

```
Start := P;
```

yields the following list, in which **PROCEDURE** Push is now complete.

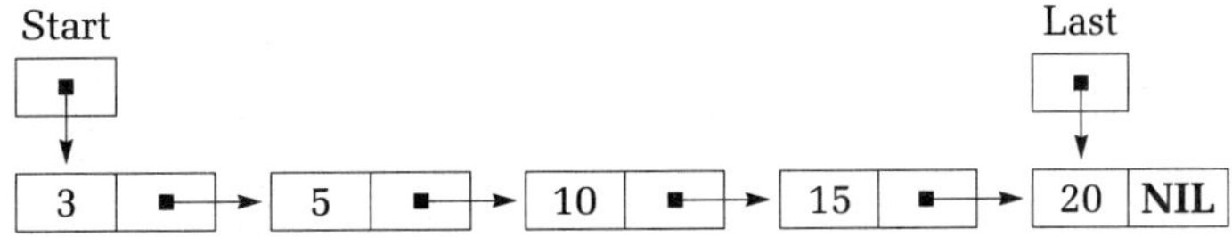

A procedure for this can be written as

```
PROCEDURE Push (VAR Start : DataPtr;
                NewNum : integer);
  VAR
    P : DataPtr;
  BEGIN
    new (P);              {  Get another node  }
    P^.Num := NewNum;     {  Assign the data value  }
    P^.Next := Start;     {  Point to the first node  }
    Start := P;           {  Point to the new first node  }
    IF Start^.Next = NIL THEN
      Last := Start       {  For a list with only one node  }
  END;
```

This procedure is called from the main program by

```
Push (Start, 3);
```

A note of caution is in order. This procedure is written assuming there is an existing list with **NIL** assigned to the pointer in the final node. If this procedure is implemented as the first step in creating a new list, the assignment

```
Start := NIL;
```

must have been made previously.

The basic process of inserting a node somewhere in a linked list other than at its beginning or end is to get a new node, find where it belongs, and put it in the list. In order to do this, we must start at the beginning of a list and search it sequentially until we find where the new node belongs. When we next change pointers to include the new node, we must know between which pair of elements in the linked list the new node is to be inserted. Thus, if

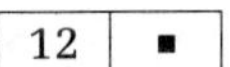

is to be inserted in an ordered linked list such as

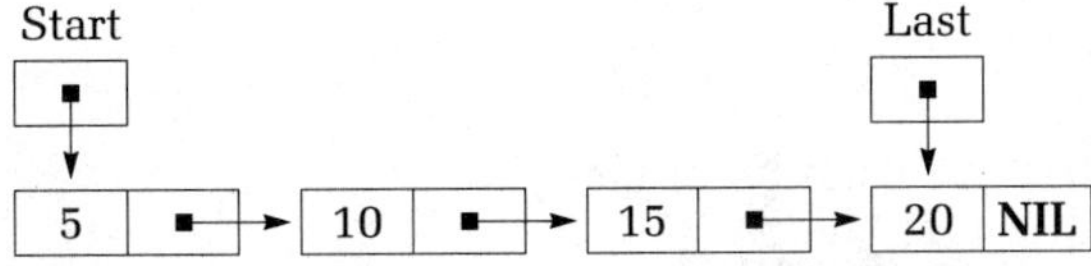

we need to know the link

is in the list. Once this pair of nodes is identified, the pointers will be changed to produce

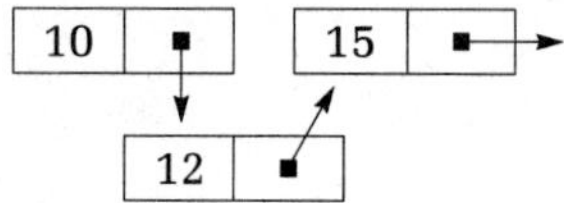

so the new list with the new node inserted is

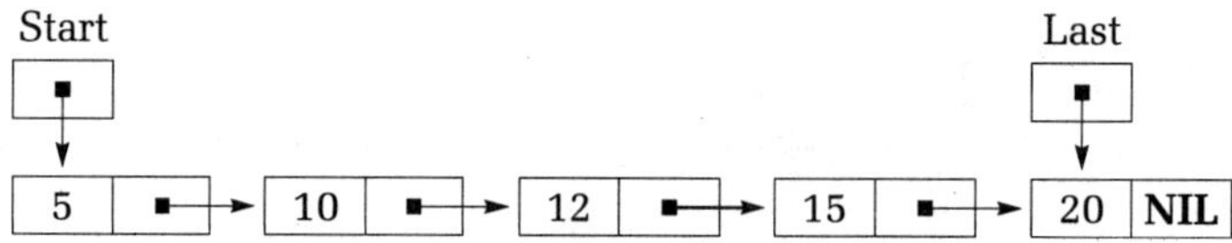

Now let's see how this can be done. We can get a new node with

```
new (P);
P^.Num := NewNum;  {  Where NewNum has the value 12  }
```

To find where it belongs, we need two pointer variables to keep track of successive pairs of elements as we traverse the list. Assume Before and Ptr have been appropriately declared. Then

```
Ptr := Start;
WHILE (Ptr <> NIL) AND (Ptr^.Num < NewNum) DO
  BEGIN
    Before := Ptr;
    Ptr := Ptr^.Next
  END;
```

will search the list for the desired pair. (We assume the node to be inserted is not at the beginning of the list.) Using the previous numbers, when this loop is completed, we have the arrangement

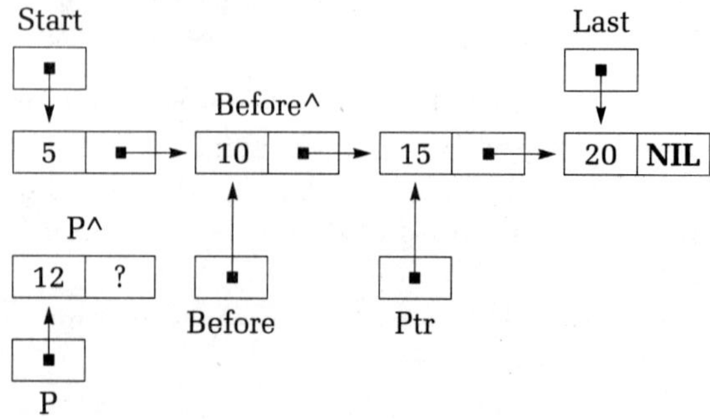

We can put the new node in the list by reassigning the pointers using

```
P^.Next := Ptr;
Before^.Next := P;
```

The list can then be envisioned as

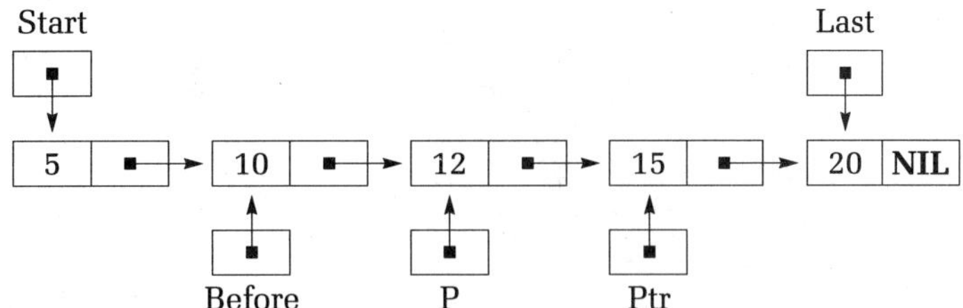

When this code is written together, we have

```
PROCEDURE InsertMiddle (Start : DataPtr;
                        NewNum : integer);
  VAR
    P, Ptr, Before : DataPtr;
  BEGIN

  {  Get a new node  }
    New (P);
    P^.Num := NewNum;

  {  Find where it belongs  }
    Ptr := Start;
    WHILE (Ptr <> NIL) AND (Ptr^.Num < NewNum) DO
      BEGIN
        Before := Ptr;
        Ptr := Ptr^.Next
      END;

  {  Insert the new node  }
    P^.Next := Ptr;
    Before^.Next := P
  END;  {  of PROCEDURE InsertMiddle  }
```

This procedure is called from the main program by

```
InsertMiddle (Start, 12);
```

The next problem to consider is how to insert a node at the end of a list. In the previous code, when Ptr is **NIL,** a reference to Ptr^ causes an error so it cannot be used for inserting an element at the end of a list. This problem can be solved by using the Boolean variable Looking, initializing it to **true,** and changing the loop control to

```
WHILE (Ptr <> NIL) AND Looking DO
```

The body of the loop then becomes the **IF . . . THEN . . . ELSE** statement

```
IF Ptr^.Num > NewNum THEN
  Looking := false
ELSE
  BEGIN
    Before := Ptr;
    Ptr := Ptr^.Next
  END;
```

The loop is followed by the statement

```
P^.Next := Ptr;
```

Thus, we have

```
new (P);
P^.Num := NewNum;
Ptr := Start;
Looking := true;
```

```
WHILE (Ptr <> NIL) AND Looking DO
  IF Ptr^.Num > NewNum THEN
    Looking := false
  ELSE
    BEGIN
      Before := Ptr;
      Ptr := Ptr^.Next
    END;
P^.Next := Ptr;
Before^.Next := P;
Last := P;
```

To see how this segment of code permits insertion at the end of a list, suppose NewNum is 30 and the list is

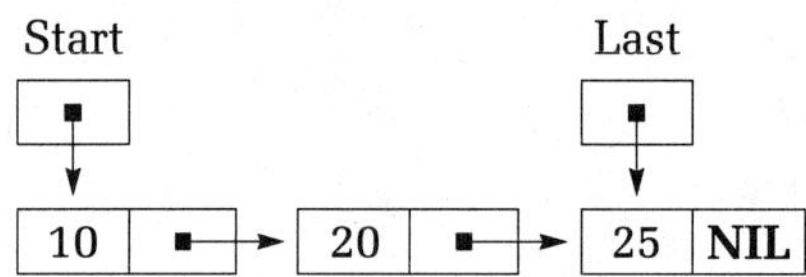

The initialization produces the list shown in Figure 15.3(a). Since Ptr < > **NIL** and Looking is **true,** the loop is entered. Ptr^.Num > NewNum (10 > 30) is **false,** so the **ELSE** option is exercised to produce the list shown in Figure 15.3(b). At this stage, Ptr < > **NIL** and Looking is still **true,** so the loop is entered again. Ptr^.Num > NewNum (20 > 30) is **false,** so the **ELSE** option produces the list illustrated in Figure 15.3(c). Since Ptr is not yet **NIL,** Ptr < > **NIL,** and Looking is **true,** the loop is entered. Ptr^.Num > NewNum is **false,** so the **ELSE**

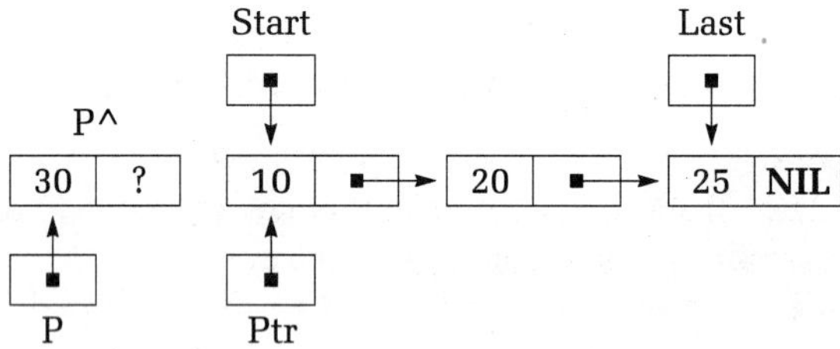

FIGURE 15.3(a) Getting a new node for a linked list

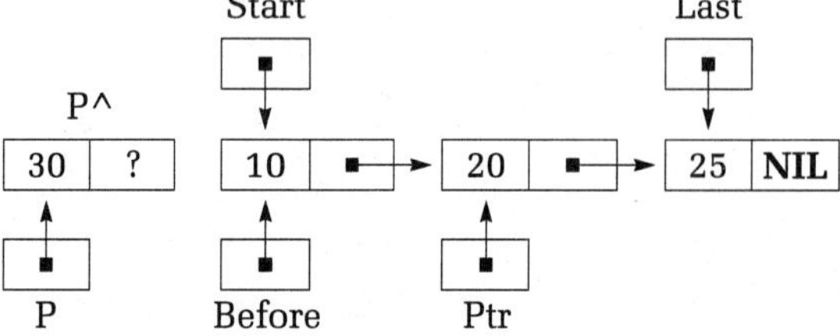

FIGURE 15.3(b) Positioning Before and Ptr

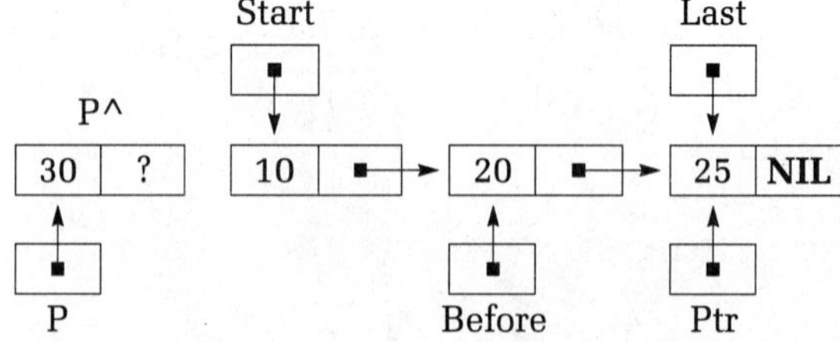

FIGURE 15.3(c) Moving Before and Ptr

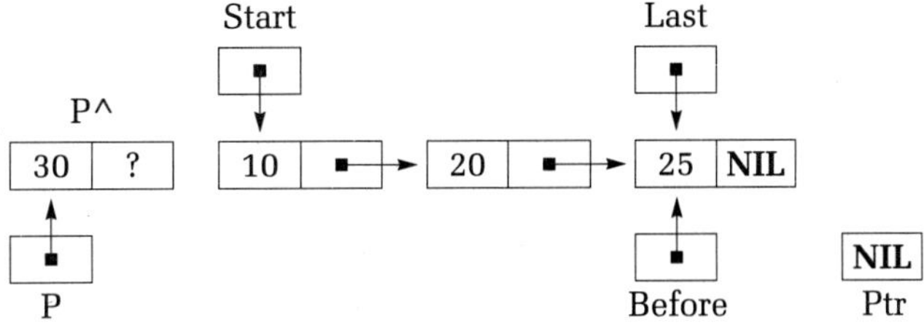

FIGURE 15.3(d)
Before and Ptr ready for insertion

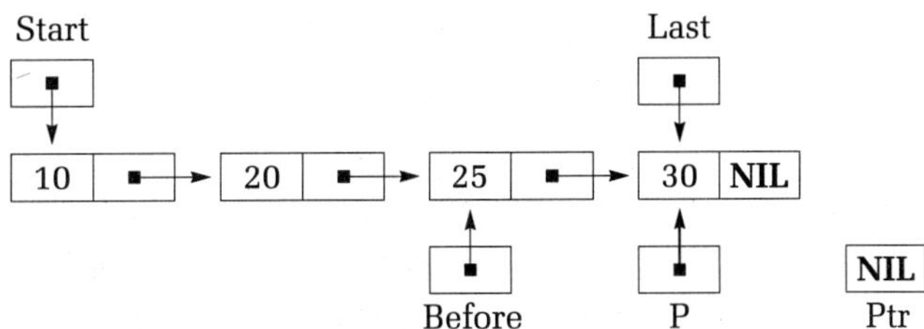

FIGURE 15.3(e)
Insertion at end of linked list complete

option produces the list shown in Figure 15.3(d). Now the condition Ptr < > **NIL** is **false,** so control is transferred to

```
P^.Next := Ptr;
```

When this line of code and the two lines following it are executed, we get the arrangement shown in Figure 15.3(e).

One final comment is in order. A slight modification of this procedure accommodates an insertion at the beginning of a list. You may choose to reserve Push for this purpose. However, a single procedure that will insert anywhere in a linked list follows.

```
PROCEDURE Insert (VAR Start, Last : DataPtr;
                  NewNum : integer);
  VAR
    P, Ptr, Before : DataPtr;
    Looking : boolean;
  BEGIN

  {  Initialize  }
    new (P);
    P^.Num := NewNum;
    Before := NIL;
    Ptr := Start;
    Looking := true;

  {  Check for empty list  }
    IF Start = NIL THEN
      BEGIN
        P^.Next := Start;
        Start := P
      END
    ELSE
      BEGIN  {  Now start the loop  }
        WHILE (Ptr <> NIL) and Looking DO
          IF Ptr^.Num > NewNum THEN
            Looking := false
          ELSE
            BEGIN
              Before := Ptr;
              Ptr := Ptr^.Next
            END;
```

```
        {  Now move the pointers  }
        IF Looking THEN
          Finish := Ptr;
        P^.Next := Ptr;

        {  Check for insert at beginning  }
        IF Before = NIL THEN
          Start := P
        ELSE
          Before^.Next := P
      END
  END;  {  of PROCEDURE Insert  }
```

■ EXAMPLE 15.2

To illustrate how **PROCEDURE** Insert can be used to create a linked list of integers sorted from high to low, let's develop a short program to read integers from a data file, create a linked list sorted from high to low, and print the contents of components in the linked list. A first-level pseudocode development of this is

1. Create the list
2. Print the list

Step 1 can be refined to

1. Create the list
   1.1 create the first node
   1.2 **WHILE NOT eof DO**
       insert in the list

A program which uses procedures for inserting an element and printing the list follows.

```
PROGRAM LinkListPrac;

{  This program is an illustration of using linked lists.  It   }
{  creates a sorted linked list from an unsorted data file and  }
{  then prints the contents of the list.  Procedures are used   }
{  to (1) insert into the list, and (2) print the list.         }

USES
  Crt;

TYPE
  DataPtr = ^Node;
  Node = RECORD
           Num : integer;
           Next : DataPtr
         END;  {  of RECORD Node  }

VAR
  Number : integer;     {  Number to be inserted               }
  Start,                {  Pointer for the beginning of the list }
  Finish : DataPtr;     {  Pointer for the end of the list     }
  Data : text;          {  Data file                           }

{*************************************************************}

PROCEDURE Insert (VAR Start, Finish : DataPtr;
                  Number : integer);
```

```
  {  Given:   A linked list and number to be inserted in order  }
  {  Task:    Insert the number in numerical order in the       }
  {           linked list                                       }
  {  Return:  Nothing                                           }

  VAR
    P, Ptr, Before : DataPtr;
    Looking : boolean;
  BEGIN

    {  Initialize  }
    new (P);
    P^.Num := Number;
    Before := NIL;
    Ptr := Start;
    Looking := true;

    {  Now start the loop  }
    WHILE (Ptr <> NIL) AND Looking DO
      IF Ptr^.Num > Number THEN
        Looking := false
      ELSE
        BEGIN
          Before := Ptr;
          Ptr := Ptr^.Next
        END;  {  of ELSE option  }

    {  Now move the pointers  }
    IF Looking THEN
      Finish := Ptr;
    P^.Next := Ptr;

    {  Check for insert at beginning  }
    IF Before = NIL THEN
      Start := P
    ELSE
      Before^.Next := P
  END;  {  of PROCEDURE Insert  }

{****************************************************************}

PROCEDURE PrintList (Start : DataPtr);

  {  Given:   A pointer to the start of a linked list           }
  {  Task:    Print numbers from nodes of the linked list       }
  {  Return:  Nothing                                           }

  VAR
    P : DataPtr;
  BEGIN
    P := Start;
    WHILE P <> NIL DO
      BEGIN
        writeln (P^.Num);
        P := P^.Next
      END  {  of WHILE loop  }
  END;  {  of PROCEDURE PrintList  }

{****************************************************************}
```

```
BEGIN  {  Main program  }
  assign (Data, 'Data132.DAT');
  reset (Data);
  ClrScr;

  {  Start the list  }
  new (Start);
  readln (Data, Number);
  Start^.Num := Number;
  Start^.Next := NIL;
  new (Finish);
  Finish := Start;        {  List has only one node  }

  {  Now create the remainder of the list  }
  WHILE NOT eof(Data) DO
    BEGIN
      readln (Data, Number);
      Insert (Start, Finish, Number)
    END;  {  of WHILE NOT eof  }
  PrintList (Start);
  readln;
  close (Data)
END.  {  of main program  }
```

When this program is run on the data file

the output is

```
-10
0
2
42
45
52
78
86
91
99
100
```

Deleting a Node

A second standard operation when working with linked lists is deleting a node. First, let's consider the problem of deleting the first node in a list. This process is commonly called *Pop*. Before we write code for this procedure, however, let's examine what should be done with the pointers.

Deleting the first node essentially requires a reversal of the steps used when inserting a node at the beginning of a list. If the list is

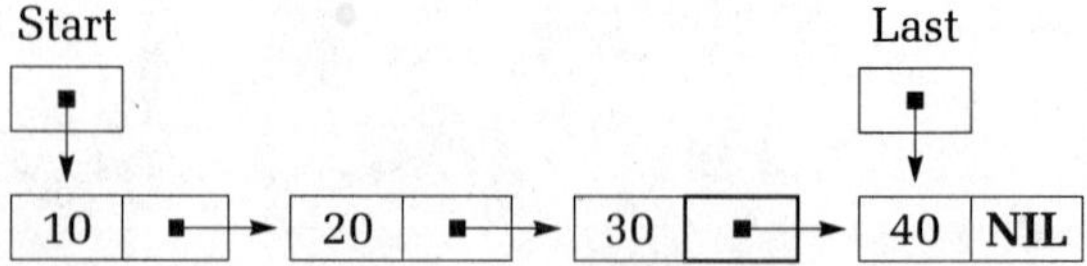

and we wish to produce the list

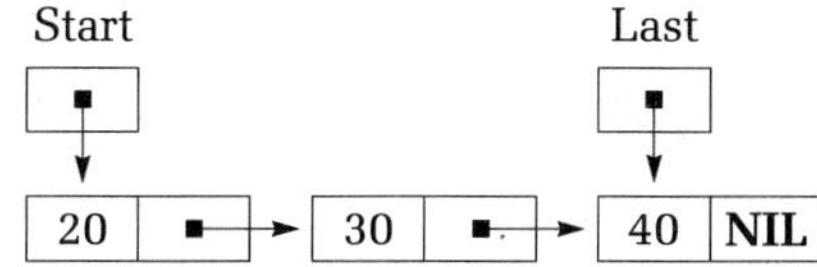

we may think

```
Start := Start^.Next;
```

can accomplish this. Not true. The use of this method poses two problems. First, we may (and probably will) want the values of some data fields returned to the main program. Thus, the values of the appropriate fields must be assigned to variable parameters. A second problem is the first node has not been returned to the computer for subsequent reuse. Since an advantage of using dynamic variables is unused storage is not wasted, the procedure **dispose** should be used with this node.

We can now write a procedure to delete the first node. Assuming the data value is to be returned to the main program, the procedure is

```
PROCEDURE Pop (VAR Start : DataPtr;
               VAR Number : integer);
  VAR
    P : DataPtr;
  BEGIN
    P := Start;                      { Use a temporary pointer  }
    Number := P^.Num;           { Return value to main program }
    Start := Start^.Next;            { Move start to next node  }
    dispose (P)                      { Return P^ for later use  }
  END;  { of PROCEDURE Pop  }
```

The next kind of deletion we examine is when the list is searched for a certain key value and the node containing this value is removed from the linked list. For example, if the list contains records for customers of a company, we might want to update the list when a former customer moves away. To illustrate the process, suppose the list is

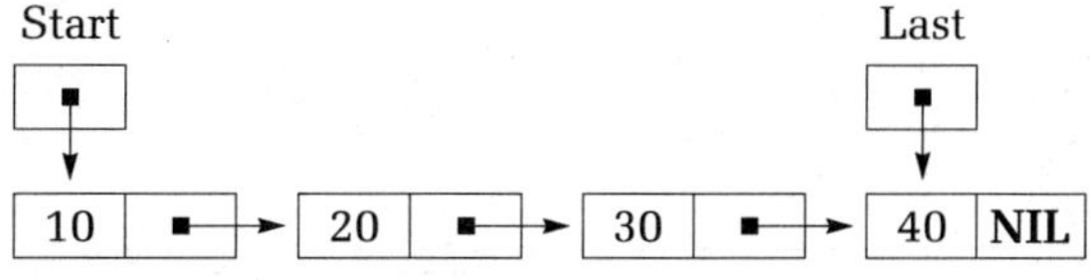

and we wish to delete

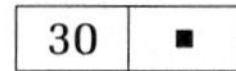

The new list is

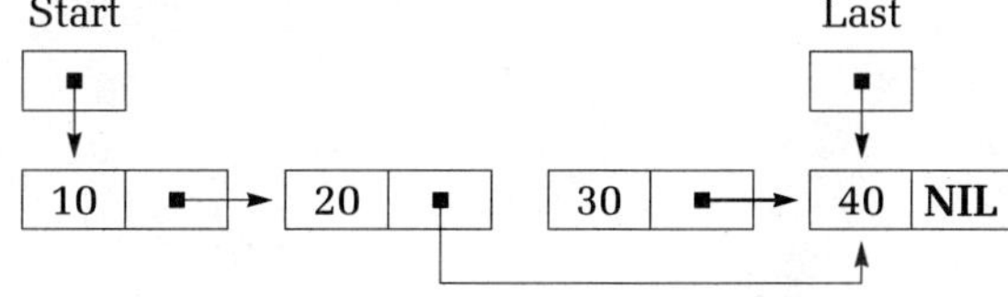

and the procedure **dispose** can be used to return the deleted node, producing

This method uses two temporary pointers. One pointer searches the list for the specified data value; once it is located, the second pointer points to it so we can use **dispose** to return it for subsequent use. If Before and P are the temporary pointers, the code is

```
BEGIN
  Before := Start;
  WHILE Before^.Next^.Num <> NewNum DO
    Before := Before^.Next;
  P := Before^.Next;
  Before^.Next := P^.Next;
  dispose (P)
END;
```

Now let's see how this segment of code deletes

from the previous list. First

```
Before := Start;
```

yields the list

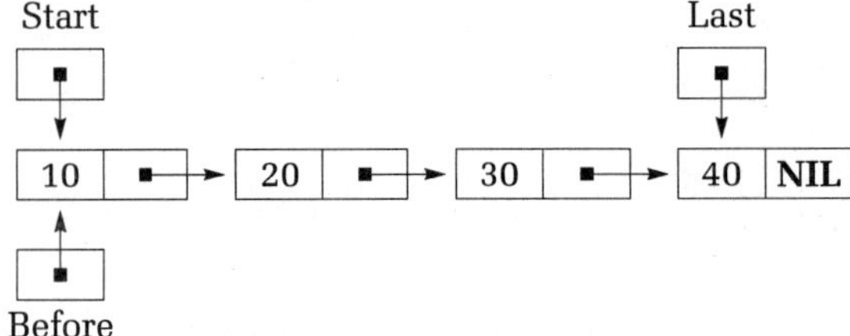

At this stage, NewNum is 30 and Before^.Next^.Num is 20. Since these values are not equal, the pointer Before is moved by

```
Before := Before^.Next;
```

Thus, we have the list

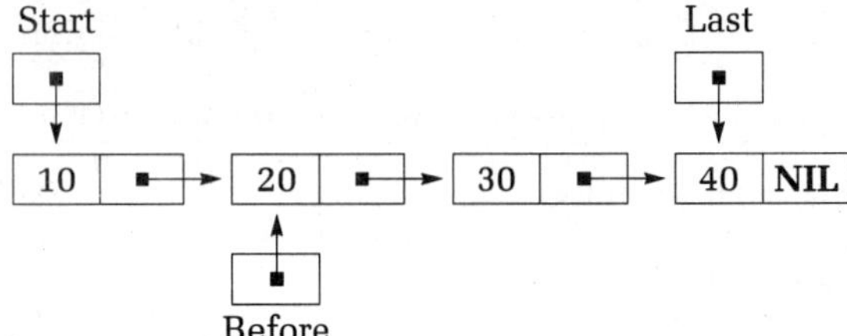

Now Before^.Next^.Num = NewNum (30), so the **WHILE** loop is exited and

```
P := Before^.Next;
```

produces the list

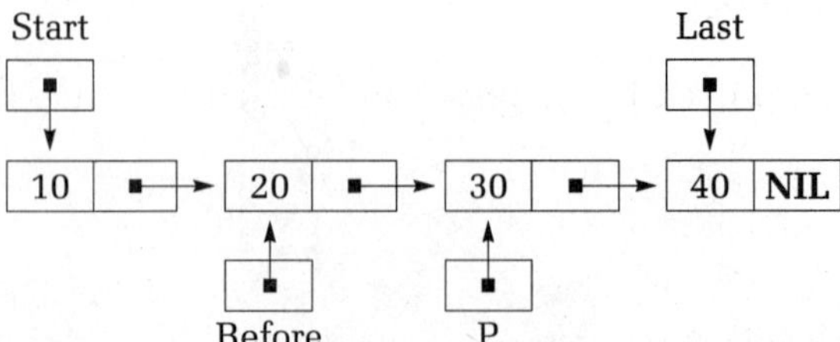

Now

```
Before^.Next := P^.Next;
```

yields the list

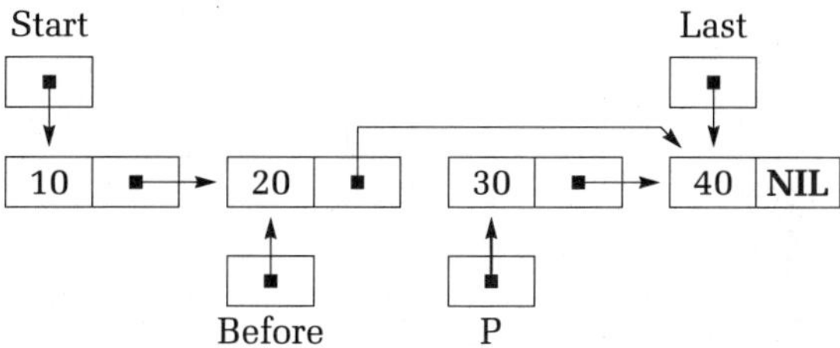

Finally **dispose** (P) returns the node, resulting in the list

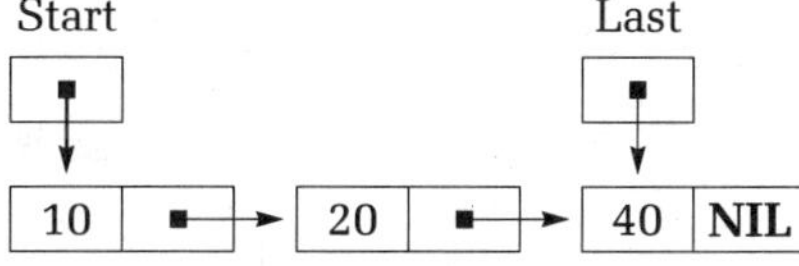

This process can be combined with deleting the first node to produce the following procedure:

```
PROCEDURE Delete (VAR Start : DataPtr;
                  Number : integer);
  VAR
    Before, P : DataPtr;
  BEGIN
    IF Number = Start^.Num THEN
      Pop (Start, Number)
    ELSE
      BEGIN
        Before := Start;
        WHILE Before^.Next^.Num <> Number DO
          Before := Before^.Next;
        P := Before^.Next;
        IF P^.Next = NIL THEN  {  Reset Last  }
          BEGIN
            Last := Before;
            Last^.Next := NIL
          END
        ELSE
          Before^.Next := P^.Next;
        dispose (P)
      END
  END;  {  of PROCEDURE Delete  }
```

This procedure can now be used to delete any node from a linked list. However, it will produce an error if no match is found. A modification to protect against this possibility is left as an exercise.

Exercises 15.3

1. Illustrate how **PROCEDURE** Insert works when inserting a node in the middle of a linked list.
2. Write a test program to see what happens when Ptr is **NIL** and a reference is made to Ptr^.
3. Revise **PROCEDURE** Insert so it calls **PROCEDURE** Push if a node is to be inserted at the beginning of a list.

A NOTE OF INTEREST

Using Pointers

Caution must be exercised when using pointers. Unless they are carefully described, they can easily to make a program hard to follow. Speaking to this point, Nazim H. Madhavji states: "It is often necessary to traverse deeply into the structure in order to access the required data, as can be seen in the following example, using pointers P1 and P2:

```
P1 := P2^.IDType^.ElementType^.Fields ...
```

Such 'spaghetti-like' directions get more cumbersome as SomeType gets more complex. Often, access paths of this kind are diagrammatically represented with no absolute certainty of their correctness." Madhavji continues, saying: "By raising the level of description of dynamic data structures, the visibility of these structures in programmed text can be increased."

4. Modify **PROCEDURE** Delete to protect against the possibility of not finding a match when the list is searched.
5. Modify **PROCEDURE** Pop so no data value is returned when Pop is called.
6. Write a complete program that allows the user to do the following.
   a. Create a linked list of records where each record contains a person's name and an amount of money donated to a local fund-raising group; the list should be sorted alphabetically.
   b. Use the linked list to print the donor names and amounts.
   c. Read a name that is to be deleted and then delete the appropriate record from the list.
   d. Print the revised list.
7. Modify **PROCEDURE** Delete to delete the *n*th node rather than a node with a particular data value.
8. Write a procedure to copy the integers in a linked list of integers into a file of integers.
9. Write a complete program that uses a linked list to sort a file of integers. Your program should create a sorted list, print the list, and save the sorted list for later use.
10. Write a procedure to delete duplicate records. Assume the list of records is ordered.

■ 15.4 Other Dynamic Data Structures

In this final section, we briefly examine three additional dynamic data structures: stacks, queues, and binary trees. All of these data structures have significant computer-oriented applications.

We used stacks in our earlier work with recursion in Chapter 11. Recall each recursive call adds something to a stack until a stopping state is reached. Stacks are also used when evaluating arithmetic expressions that contain parentheses; partial computations are put "on hold" until needed later in the process.

Queues are used when data do not arrive in an orderly manner. A typical setting is the allocation of priorities to computer users in a time-sharing system. Another example of a queue is a single waiting line for multiple service windows, as might be found at an airport or a bank.

Binary trees are used in programs in which a series of yes/no questions relate to the data. Examples include sorting, computer games, and data that can be stored in the form of a matrix.

Here, the concepts behind stacks, queues, and binary trees and their elementary uses are emphasized. This section should serve as an introduction to these dynamic data structures. A suggested reading list is included for students who desire more detailed development of these concepts.

Stacks

A stack can be implemented as a dynamic data structure in which access can be made from only one end. Think of a stack as paper in a copying machine or trays in a cafeteria line. In both cases, the last one in will be the first one out; that is, items are put in, one at a time, at the top and removed, one at a time, from the top. This *last-in, first-out order* is referred to as *LIFO;* stacks are therefore often termed LIFO structures.

A stack can be envisioned as

E
D
C
B
A

In this illustration, item E is considered the top element in the stack.

The two basic operations needed to work with a stack are the insertion of an element to create a new stack top (Push) and the removal of an element from the top of the stack (Pop). If a stack is represented by a linked list, Push and Pop are merely "insert at the beginning" and "delete from the beginning", respectively, as developed in Section 15.3.

To illustrate the use of a stack in a program, let's consider a program that checks an arithmetic expression to make sure parentheses are correctly matched (nested). Our program considers

```
(3 + 4 * (5 MOD 3))
```

to make sure the number of left parentheses matches the number of right parentheses. A first-level pseudocode for this problem is

1. Read a character
2. **IF** it is a "(" **THEN**
   Push it onto the stack
3. **IF** it is a ")" **THEN**
   Pop the previous "("
4. Check for an empty stack

The growing and shrinking of the stack is illustrated in Table 15.3.

Two points need to be made concerning this program. First, since the stack is represented by a linked list, the illustration could be

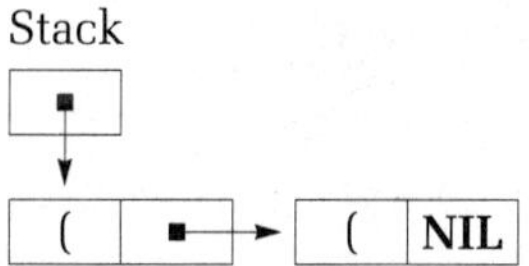

Second, before Pop is used on a stack, a check must be made to make sure the stack is not already empty. Thus, **PROCEDURE** Pop is replaced by **PROCEDURE** PopAndCheck, in which a suitable error message will appear if the user tries to pop an empty stack.

TABLE 15.3
Using a stack

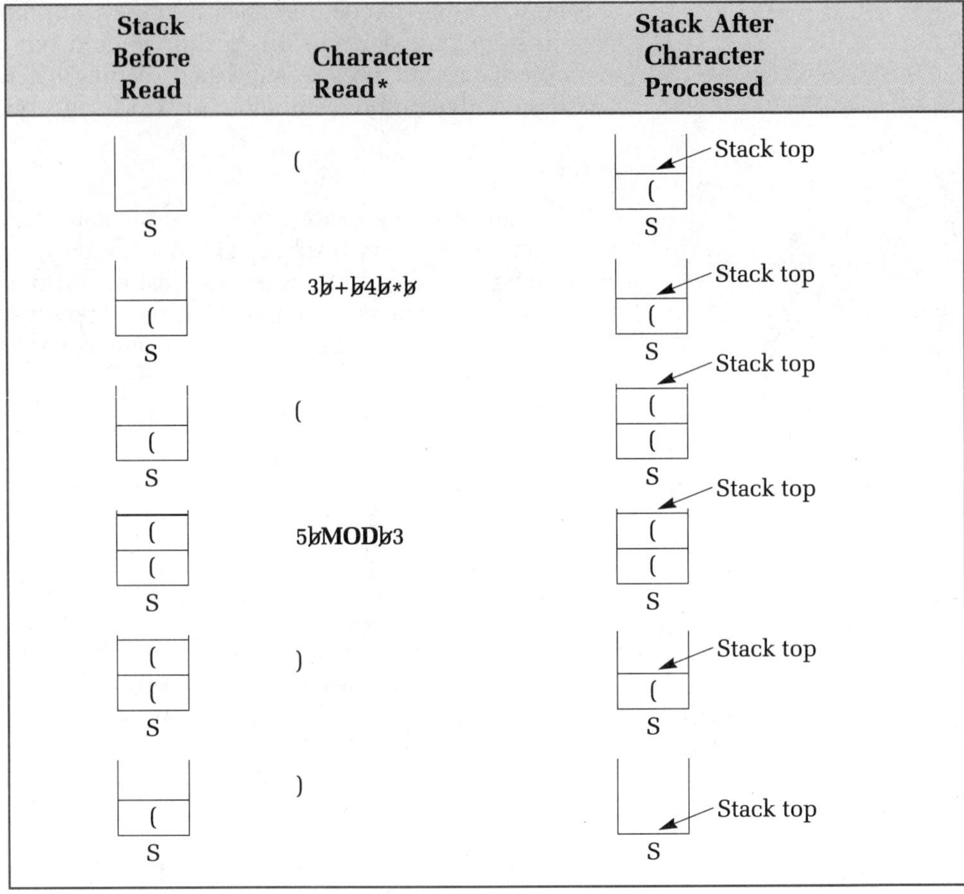

*b̸ represents a blank space.

Now let's prepare code for the previous problem. The following definitions are used:

```
TYPE
  DataPtr = ^Node;
  Node = RECORD
           Sym : char;
           Next : DataPtr
         END;
VAR
  Stack : DataPtr;
```

The **PROCEDURE** Push is

```
PROCEDURE Push (VAR Stack : DataPtr;
                Symbol : char);
  VAR
    P : DataPtr;
  BEGIN
    new (P);
    P^.Sym := Symbol;
    P^.Next := Stack;
    Stack := P
  END;  { of PROCEDURE Push  }
```

The **PROCEDURE** PopAndCheck is

```
PROCEDURE PopAndCheck (VAR Stack : DataPtr);
  VAR
    P : DataPtr;
  BEGIN
    IF Stack = NIL THEN  {  Check for empty stack  }
      writeln ('The parentheses are not correct.')
    ELSE
      BEGIN  {  Pop the stack  }
        P := Stack;
        Stack := Stack^.Next;
        dispose (P)
      END
  END;  {  of PROCEDURE PopAndCheck  }
```

With these two procedures, the main body of a program that examines an expression for correct use of parentheses follows.

```
BEGIN  {  Main program  }
  Stack := NIL;
  assign (Data, 'EXPRCHK.DAT');
  reset (Data);
  WHILE NOT eoln(Data) DO
    BEGIN
      read (Data, Symbol);
      IF Symbol = '(' THEN
        Push (Stack, Symbol);
      IF Symbol = ')' THEN
        PopAndCheck (Stack)
    END;

{  Now check for an empty stack  }
  IF Stack <> NIL THEN
    writeln ('The parentheses are not correct.');
  close (Data)
END.  {  of main program  }
```

Several modifications of this short program are available and are suggested in the exercises at the end of this section.

Queues

A *queue* can be implemented as a dynamic data structure in which access can be made from both ends. Elements are entered from one end (the rear) and removed from the other end (the front). This *first-in, first-out order* is referred to as *FIFO;* queues are termed FIFO structures. A queue is like a waiting line. Think of people standing in line to purchase tickets: each new customer enters at the rear of the line and exits from the front. A queue implemented as a linked list can be illustrated as

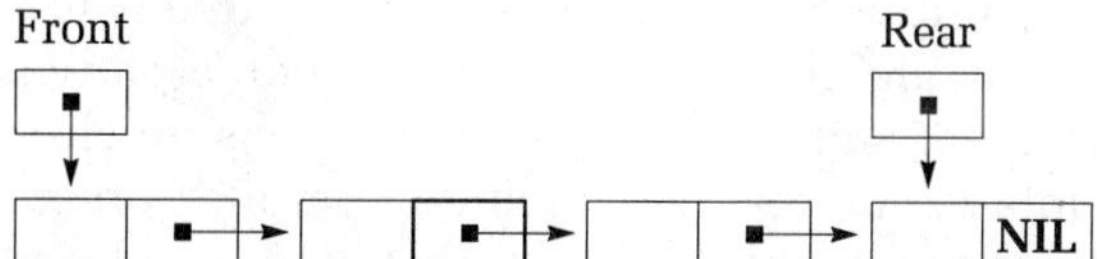

The two basic operations needed to work with queues are the removal of an element from the front of the list and the insertion of an element at the rear of the list. If we use the definitions

```
TYPE
  DataPtr = ^Node;
  Node = RECORD
           Num : integer;
           Next : DataPtr
         END;
```

we can use variables declared by

```
VAR
  Front, Rear : DataPtr;
```

when working with such a structure.

Removing an element from the front of a queue is similar to the use of **PROCEDURE** PopAndCheck with a stack. The only difference is that after an element has been removed, if the queue is empty, Rear must be assigned the value **NIL.** A procedure for removing an element from the front of a queue follows. It is assumed that the value of the element removed is to be returned to the main program via a variable parameter.

```
PROCEDURE Remove (VAR Front, Rear : DataPtr;
                  VAR Number : integer);
  VAR
    P : DataPtr;
  BEGIN
    IF Front = NIL THEN  {  Check for empty queue  }
      writeln ('The queue is empty.')
    ELSE
      BEGIN  {  Pop the queue  }
        P := Front;
        Front := Front^.Next;
        Number := P^.Num;
        dispose (P)
      END;
    IF Front = NIL THEN  {  Set pointers for empty queue  }
      Rear := NIL
  END;  {  of PROCEDURE Remove  }
```

This procedure is called from the main program by

```
Remove (Front, Rear, Number);
```

A procedure to insert an element at the rear of a queue (assuming there is at least one element in the queue) is similar to the procedure given in Section 15.3 for inserting an element at the end of a linked list. You are asked to write the code as an exercise.

Trees

A *tree* can be implemented as a dynamic data structure consisting of a special node called a *root* that points to zero or more other nodes, each of which points to zero or more other nodes, and so on. In general, a tree can be visualized as illustrated in Figure 15.4. The root of a tree is its first, or top, node. *Children* are nodes that are pointed to by an element, a *parent* is the node that is pointing to its children, and a *leaf* is a node that has no children.

Applications for trees include compiler programs, artificial intelligence, and game-playing programs. In general, trees can be applied in programs that call for information to be stored so it can be retrieved rapidly. As illustrated in Figure 15.4, pointers are especially appropriate for implementing a tree as a dynamic data structure. An external pointer is used to point to the root and each parent uses pointers to point to its children. A more detailed tree is illustrated in Figure 15.5.

Binary Trees. From this point on, we will restrict our discussion of trees to binary trees. A *binary tree* is a tree such that each node can point to at most two children. A binary tree is illustrated in Figure 15.6.

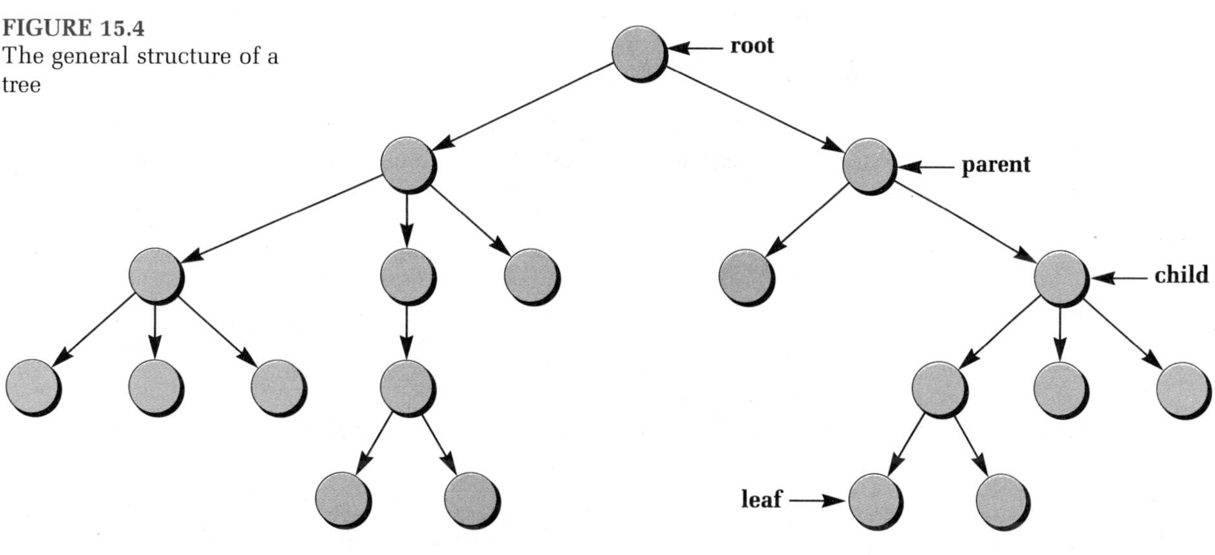

FIGURE 15.4
The general structure of a tree

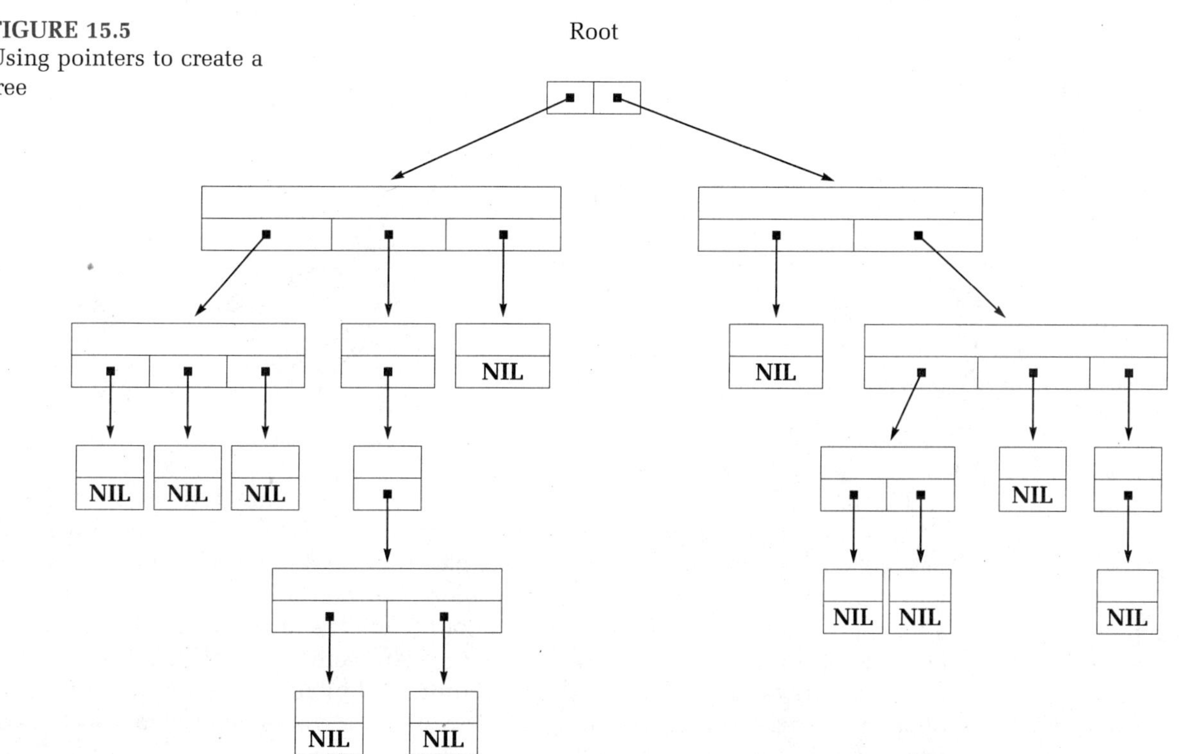

FIGURE 15.5
Using pointers to create a tree

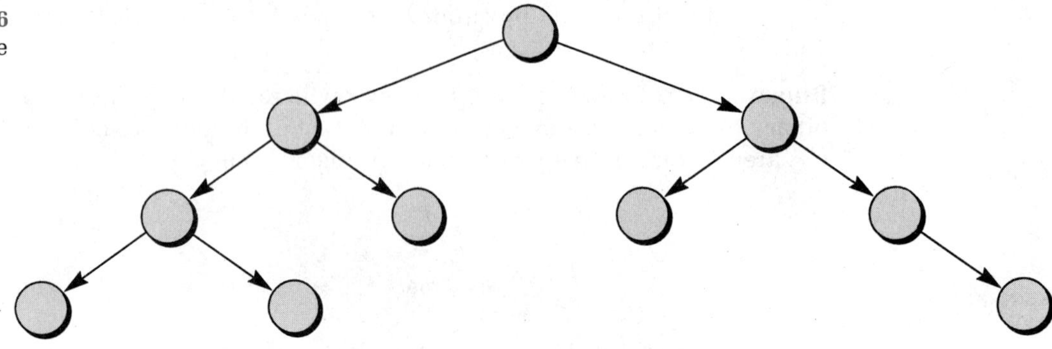
FIGURE 15.6
A binary tree

If a binary tree is used to store integer values, a reasonable definition for the pointer type is

```
TYPE
  Pointer = ^TreeNode;
  TreeNode = RECORD
               Info : integer;
               RightChild : Pointer;
               LeftChild : Pointer
             END;
```

A particularly important kind of binary tree is a *binary search tree,* which is a binary tree formed according to the following rules:

1. The information in the key field of any node is greater than the information in the key field of any node of its left child and any children of the left child.
2. The information in the key field of any node is less than the information in the key field of any node of its right child and any children of the right child.

Figure 15.7 illustrates a binary search tree.

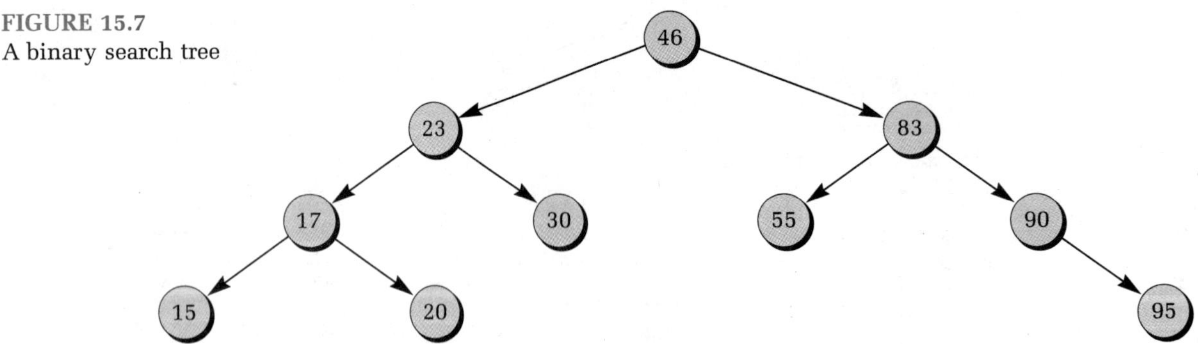

FIGURE 15.7
A binary search tree

The reference to "search" is made because such trees are particularly efficient when we must search for a value. To illustrate, suppose we wish to see whether or not 30 is in the tree. At each node, we check to see if the desired value has been found. If it has not, we determine on which side to continue looking until either a match is found or the value **NIL** is encountered. If a match is not found, we are at the appropriate node for adding the new value (creating a child). As we search for 30, we traverse the tree via the path indicated by heavier arrows. Notice after only two comparisons (<46, >23), the desired value has been located, as illustrated in Figure 15.8.

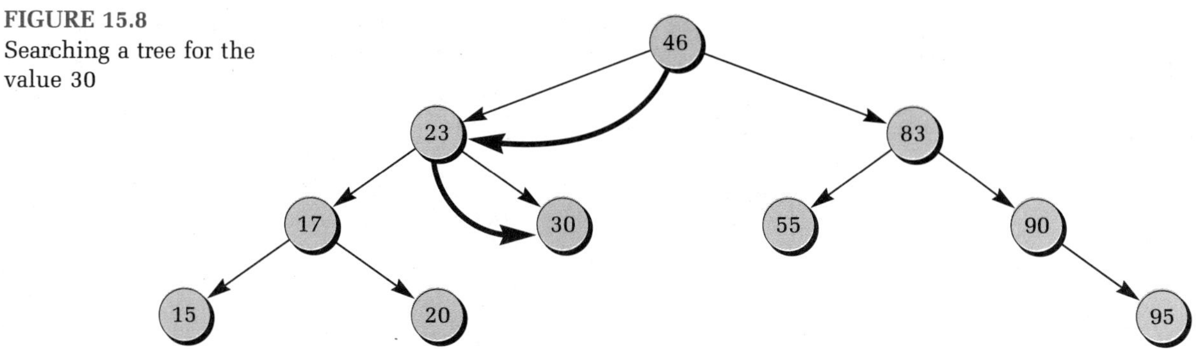

FIGURE 15.8
Searching a tree for the value 30

Now suppose we search the tree for the value 65. The path (again indicated by heavier arrows) is shown in Figure 15.9. At this stage, the right child is **NIL** and the value has not been located. It is now relatively easy to add the new value to the tree.

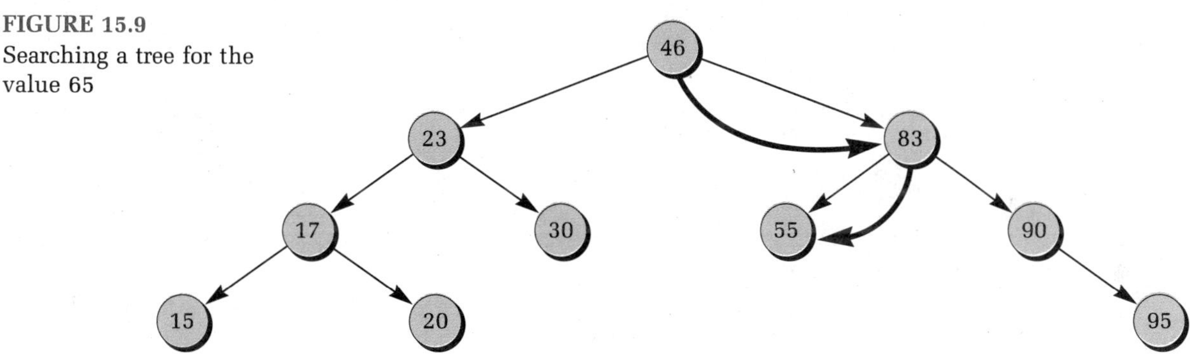

FIGURE 15.9
Searching a tree for the value 65

Binary search trees can be used to store any data that can be ordered. For example, the registrar of a university might want to quickly access the record of a particular student. If the records are stored alphabetically by student name in a binary search tree, quick retrieval is possible.

Implementing Binary Trees. We conclude this chapter with a relatively basic implementation of binary search trees: a program to create a binary search tree from integers in a data file. We print the integers in order, using a variation of the general procedure for searching a tree. The operations of inserting and deleting nodes are left as exercises.

Before we develop algorithms and write code for these implementations, we need to discuss the recursive nature of trees. (You may wish to reread Section 11.1 at this time.) When we move from one node to a right or left child, we are (in a sense) at the root of a subtree. Thus, the process of traversing a tree is

1. **IF** LeftChild < > **NIL THEN**
   traverse left branch
2. Take desired action
3. **IF** RightChild < > **NIL THEN**
   traverse right branch

Steps 1 and 3 are recursive; each return to them saves values associated with the current stage together with any pending action. If the desired action is to print the values of nodes in a binary search tree, step 2 is

2. Print the value

and when this procedure is called, the result is to print an ordered list of values contained in the tree. If we use the previous definitions

```
TYPE
  Pointer = ^TreeNode;
  TreeNode = RECORD
               Info : integer;
               RightChild : Pointer;
               LeftChild : Pointer
             END;
```

a procedure for printing is

```
PROCEDURE PrintTree (T : Pointer);
  BEGIN
    IF T = NIL THEN
      {  Do nothing  }
    ELSE
      BEGIN
        PrintTree (T^.LeftChild);
        writeln (T^.Info);
        PrintTree (T^.RightChild)
      END
  END;  {  of PROCEDURE PrintTree  }
```

This procedure is called from the main program by

```
PrintTree (Root);
```

Notice how the recursive nature of this procedure provides a simple, efficient way to inspect the nodes of a binary search tree.

The process of creating a binary search tree is only slightly longer than the process of printing one. A first-level pseudocode is

1. Initialize root to **NIL**
2. **WHILE NOT eof DO**
   2.1 get a number
   2.2 add a node

A recursive procedure can be used to add a node. An algorithm for this is

2.2 add a node
   2.2.1 if the current node is **NIL,** store the value and stop
   2.2.2 if the new value is less than the current value, point to the left child and add the node to the left subtree
   2.2.3 if the new value is greater than the current value, point to the right child and add the node to the right subtree

Notice the recursive procedure to add a node adds only nodes containing distinct values. A slight modification (left as an exercise) allows duplicate values to be included. A procedure for adding a node to a binary search tree is

```
PROCEDURE AddNode (VAR Node : Pointer;
                   Number : integer);
  BEGIN
    IF Node = NIL THEN  {  Add a new node  }
```

```
      BEGIN
        new (Node);
        Node^.Info := Number;
        Node^.LeftChild := NIL;
        Node^.RightChild := NIL
      END
    ELSE IF Number < Node^.Info THEN
      AddNode (Node^.LeftChild, Number)
    ELSE
      AddNode (Node^.RightChild, Number)
  END;  {  of PROCEDURE AddNode  }
```

A complete program to read unordered integers from a data file, create a binary search tree, and then print an ordered list follows.

```
PROGRAM TreePrac;

{  This program illustrates working with a binary tree.  Note   }
{  the recursion used in AddNode and PrintTree.  Input is an    }
{  unordered list of integers.  Output is a sorted list of      }
{  integers that is printed from a binary search tree.          }

USES
  Crt;

TYPE
  Pointer = ^TreeNode;
  TreeNode = RECORD
               Info : integer;
               RightChild : Pointer;
               LeftChild : Pointer
             END;  {  of RECORD  }

VAR
  Root : Pointer;          {  Pointer to indicate the tree root  }
  Number : integer;        {  Integer read from the data file    }
  Data : text;             {  Data file                          }

{****************************************************************}

PROCEDURE AddNode (VAR Node : Pointer;
                   Number : integer);

  {  Given:   The root of a binary tree and a number            }
  {  Task:    Insert the number in the binary tree              }
  {  Return:  Nothing                                           }

  BEGIN
    IF Node = NIL THEN                      {  Add a new node  }
      BEGIN
        new (Node);
        Node^.Info := Number;
        Node^.LeftChild := NIL;
        Node^.RightChild := NIL
      END
    ELSE IF Number < Node^.Info THEN     {  Move down left side  }
      AddNode (Node^.LeftChild, Number)
    ELSE
      AddNode (Node^.RightChild, Number)
  END;  {  of PROCEDURE AddNode  }

{****************************************************************}
```

```
PROCEDURE PrintTree (Node : Pointer);

  {  Given:    The root of a binary tree                              }
  {  Task:     Print numbers in order from nodes of the binary        }
  {                tree                                               }
  {  Return:   Nothing                                                }

  BEGIN
    IF Node = NIL THEN
      {  Do nothing  }
    ELSE
      BEGIN
        PrintTree (Node^.LeftChild);
        writeln (Node^.Info);
        PrintTree (Node^.RightChild)
      END  {  of ELSE option  }
  END;  {  of PROCEDURE PrintTree  }

{***************************************************************}

BEGIN  {  Main program  }
  assign (Data, 'TreeData.DAT');
  reset (Data);
  ClrScr;
  new (Root);
  Root := NIL;
  WHILE NOT eof(Data) DO
    BEGIN
      readln (Data, Number);
      AddNode (Root, Number)
    END;  {  of WHILE NOT eof  }
  PrintTree (Root);
  readln;
  close (Data)
END.  {  of main program  }
```

When this is run on the data file

16	■	8	■	-5	■	20	■	30	■	101	■	0	■	10	■	18	■	■

the output is

```
-5
0
8
10
16
18
20
30
101
```

Exercises 15.4

1. Using the program for checking parentheses at the beginning of this section, illustrate how the stack grows and shrinks when the following expression is examined:

   ```
   (5 / (3 - 2 * (4 + 3) - (8 DIV 2)))
   ```

2. Write a test program to check an arithmetic expression for correct nesting of parentheses.

3. Modify the program in Exercise 2 so several expressions may be examined; then give more descriptive error messages. Finally, include a **SET** for the parentheses symbols "(" and ")".
4. Write a program that utilizes a stack to print a line of text in reverse order.
5. Stacks and queues can also be implemented using arrays rather than linked lists. With this in mind, do the following.
   a. Give appropriate definitions and declarations for using arrays for these data structures.
   b. Rewrite all procedures using array notation.
6. Write a procedure for inserting an element at the rear of a queue. Illustrate changes made in the linked list when such a procedure is executed.
7. Write a program that uses a stack to check an arithmetic expression for correct use of parentheses "( )," brackets "[ ]," and braces "{ }."
8. Indicate which of the following are binary search trees. Explain what is wrong with the ones that are not.

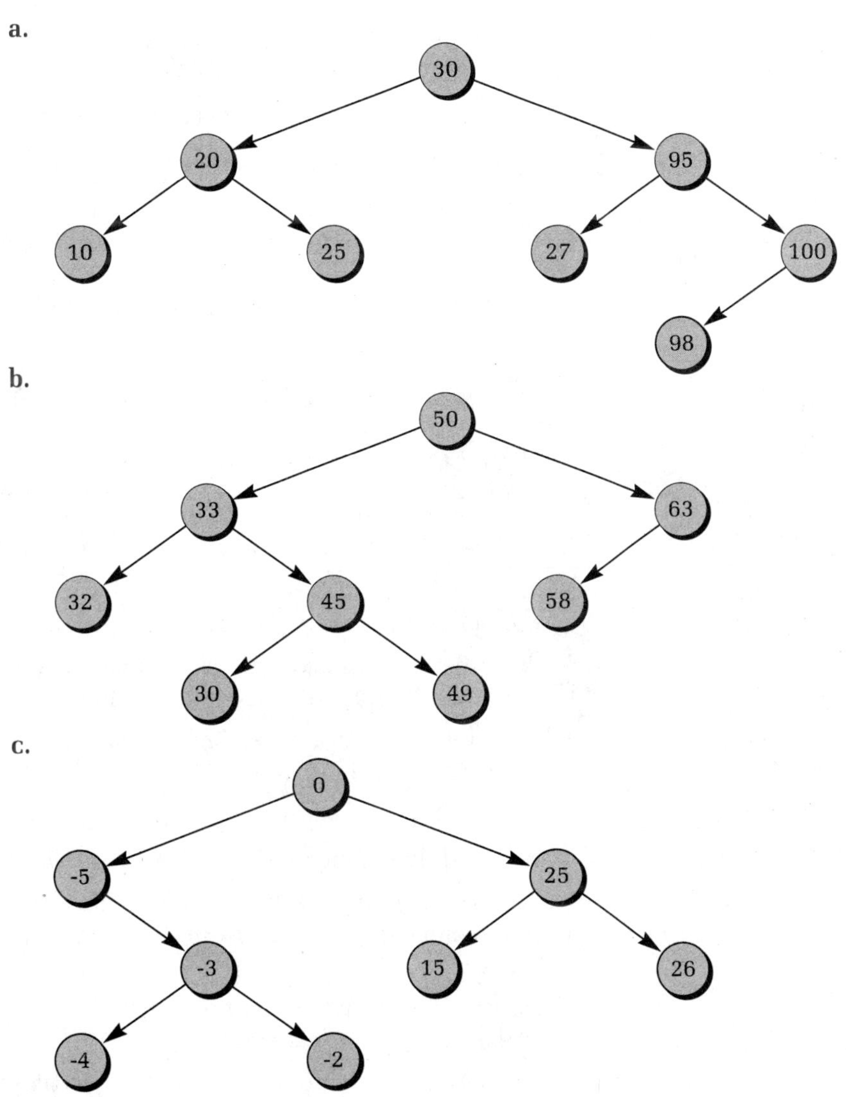

d.

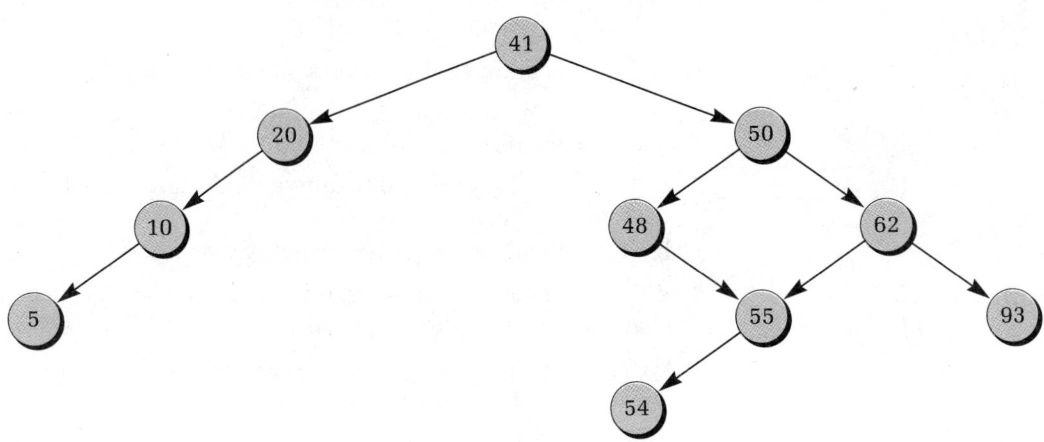

9. Modify **PROCEDURE** AddNode to include the possibility of having nodes of equal value.
10. Write a procedure that allows the user to insert a node in a binary search tree.
11. Write a function to search a binary search tree for a given value. The function should return **true** if the value is found and **false** if it is not found.
12. Write a procedure that allows the user to delete a node from a binary search tree.
13. Illustrate what binary search tree is created when **PROGRAM** TreePrac is run using the data file

RUNNING AND DEBUGGING HINTS

1. Be careful to distinguish between a pointer and its associated dynamic variable. Thus, if Ptr is a pointer, the variable is Ptr^.
2. When a dynamic variable is no longer needed in a program, use **dispose** so the memory location can be reallocated.
3. After using **dispose** with a pointer, its referenced variable is no longer available. If you use **dispose** (Ptr), then Ptr^ does not exist.
4. Be careful not to access the referenced variable of a pointer that is **NIL.** Thus, if the assignment

   ```
   Ptr := NIL;
   ```

   is made, a reference to Ptr^.Info results in an error.
5. When using pointers with subprograms, be careful to pass the pointer—not the referenced variable—to the subprogram.
6. When creating dynamic data structures, be careful to initialize properly by assigning **NIL** where appropriate and keep track of pointers as your structures grow and shrink.
7. Operations with pointers require that they be of the same type. Thus, exercise caution when comparing or assigning them.

8. Values may be lost when pointers are inadvertently or prematurely reassigned. To avoid this, use as many auxiliary pointers as you wish. This is better than trying to use one pointer for two purposes.

Summary

Key Terms

address (of a memory location)
binary search tree
binary tree
children
component (of a linked list)
dynamic structure
dynamic variable
first-in, first-out order (FIFO)
last-in, first-out order (LIFO)
leaf
linked list
node
parent
pointer variable
Pop
Push
queue
root
static variable
tree
value (of a memory location)

Keywords

dispose **new** **NIL**

Key Concepts

- Values are stored in memory locations; each memory location has an address.
- A pointer variable contains the address of a memory location; pointer variables are declared by

```
TYPE
  AgeRange = 0..99;
VAR
  Ptr : ^AgeRange;
```

  where the caret (^) is used before the predefined data type.
- A dynamic variable is a variable that is referenced through a pointer variable. Dynamic variables can be used in the same context as any other variable of the same type, and they are not declared in the variable declaration section. In the declaration

```
TYPE
  AgeRange = 0..99;
VAR
  Ptr : ^AgeRange;
```

  the dynamic variable is Ptr^ and is available after **new** (Ptr) is executed.
- Dynamic variables are created by

```
new (Ptr);
```

  and destroyed (memory area made available for subsequent reuse) by

```
dispose (Ptr);
```

- Assuming the definition

```
TYPE
  AgeRange = 0..99;
VAR
  Ptr : ^AgeRange;
```

  the relationship between a pointer and its associated dynamic variable is illustrated by the code

```
new (Ptr);
Ptr^ := 21;
```

  which can be envisioned as

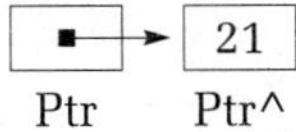

- The only legal operations on pointer variables are assignments and comparisons for equality.
- **NIL** can be assigned to a pointer variable; this is used in a Boolean expression to detect the end of a list.
- Dynamic data structures differ from static data structures in that they are modified during the execution of the program.
- A linked list is a dynamic data structure formed by having each component contain a pointer that points to the next component; generally, each component is a record with one field reserved for the pointer.
- A node is a component of a linked list.
- When creating a linked list, extra pointers are needed to keep track of the first, last, and newest component.
- When creating a linked list, the final component should have **NIL** assigned to its pointer field.
- Printing from a linked list is accomplished by starting with the first component in the list and proceeding sequentially through the list until the last component is reached; a typical procedure for printing from a linked list is

```
PROCEDURE Print (First : DataPtr);
  VAR
    P : DataPtr;
  BEGIN
    P := First;
    WHILE P <> NIL DO
      BEGIN
        writeln (P^.<field name>);
        P := P^.Next
      END
  END;  {  of PROCEDURE Print  }
```

- The insertion of a node in a linked list should encompass three cases: insertion at the beginning, in the middle, and at the end of a list.
- Inserting an element at the beginning of a linked list is a frequently used procedure and is referred to as Push; one version of this procedure is

```
PROCEDURE Push (VAR Start : DataPtr;
                NewNum : integer);
  VAR
    P : DataPtr;
  BEGIN
    new (P);
    P^.New := NewNum;
    P^.Next := Start;
    Start := P
  END;  {  of PROCEDURE Push  }
```

- Searching an ordered linked list to see where a new node should be inserted is accomplished by

```
Ptr := Start;
WHILE Ptr^.Num < NewNum DO
  BEGIN
    Before := Ptr;
    Ptr := Ptr^.Next
  END;
```

- When deleting a node from a linked list, delete the first node or search for a particular node and then delete it.
- Deleting the first node is referred to as Pop; one version is

```
PROCEDURE Pop (VAR Start : DataPtr;
               VAR NewNum : integer);
  VAR
    P : DataPtr;
```

```
BEGIN
  P := Start;
  NewNum := P^.Num;
  Start := Start^.Next;
  dispose (P)
END;  {  of PROCEDURE Pop  }
```

- When a node is deleted from a linked list, it should be returned for subsequent use; this is done by using the standard procedure **dispose.**
- A stack is a dynamic data structure where access can be made from only one end; stacks are referred to as LIFO (last-in, first-out) structures.
- A queue is a dynamic data structure where access can be made from both ends; queues are referred to as FIFO (first-in, first-out) structures.
- A tree is a dynamic data structure consisting of a special node (called a root) that points to zero or more other nodes, each of which points to zero or more other nodes, and so on. Trees are represented symbolically as

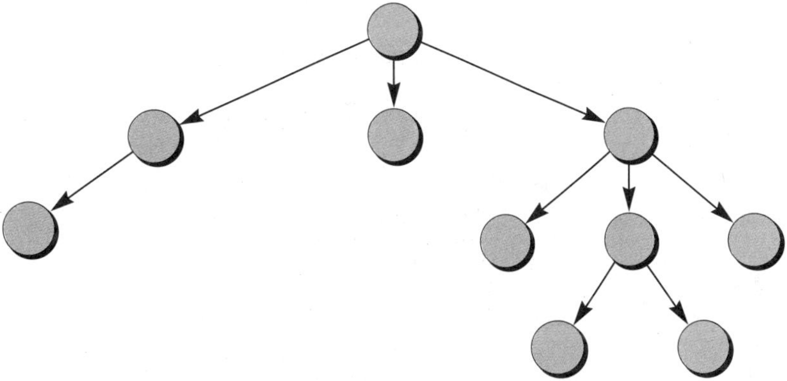

- A root is the first or top node of a tree.
- Trees are particularly useful in programs that use data that can be ordered and that need to be retrieved quickly.
- Binary trees are trees where each node points to at most two other nodes; parent, right child, and left child are terms frequently used when working with binary trees. An illustration of a binary tree is

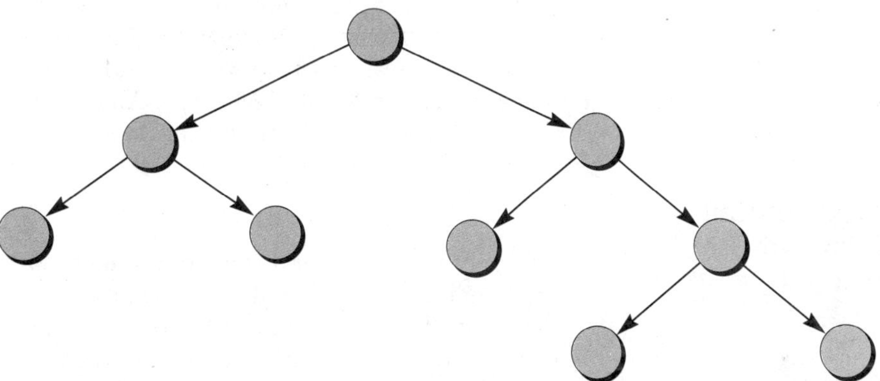

- Binary search trees are binary trees in which the information in any node is greater than the information in any node of its left child and any children of the left child and the information in any node is less than the information in any node of its right child and any children of the right child. An illustration of a typical binary search tree is

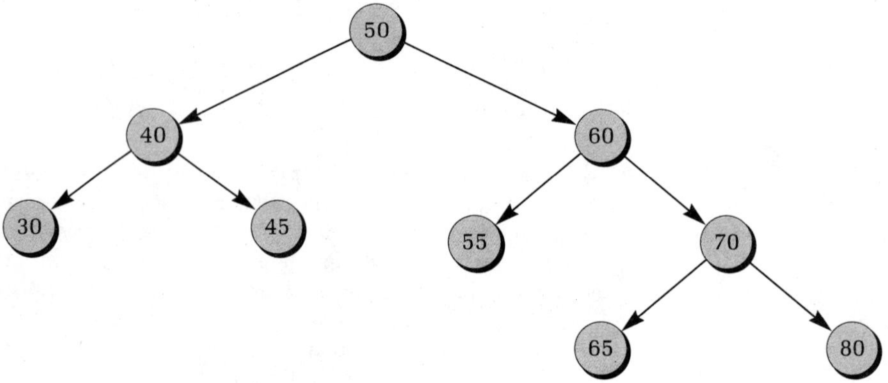

- Recursive procedures can be used when working with trees; to illustrate, the values in the nodes of a binary search tree can be printed (sequentially) with the following procedure:

```
PROCEDURE PrintTree (T : Pointer);
  BEGIN
    IF T = NIL THEN
      {  Do nothing  }
    ELSE
      BEGIN
        PrintTree (T^.LeftChild);
        writeln (T^.Info);
        PrintTree (T^.RightChild)
      END
  END  {  of PROCEDURE PrintTree  }
```

■ Suggestions for Further Reading

Nance, Douglas W., and Thomas L. Naps. *Introduction to Computer Science: Programming, Problem Solving, and Data Structures, 2nd ed.* St. Paul, MN: West Publishing Company, 1992.

Naps, Thomas L., and Bhagat Singh. *Program Design with Pascal: Principles, Algorithms, and Data Structures.* St. Paul, MN: West Publishing Company, 1988.

Naps, Thomas L., and Douglas W. Nance. *Introduction to Computer Science: Programming, Problem Solving, and Data Structures, 2nd alternate ed.* St. Paul, MN: West Publishing Company, 1992.

Naps, Thomas L., and George Pothering. *Introduction to Data Structures and Algorithm Analysis with Pascal.* St. Paul, MN.: West Publishing Company, 1992.

Tenenbaum, Aaron M., and Moshe J. Augenstein. *Data Structures Using Pascal.* Englewood Cliffs, NJ: Prentice-Hall, 1981.

■ Programming Problems and Projects

1. Creating an index for a textbook can be accomplished by a Turbo Pascal program that uses dynamic data structures and works with a text file. Assume that input for a program is a list of words to be included in an index. Write a program that scans the text and produces a list of page numbers indicating where each word is used in the text.
2. One of the problems faced by businesses is how to best manage their lines of customers. One method is to have a separate line for each cashier or station. Another is to have one feeder line where all customers wait and the customer at the front of the line goes to the first open station. Write a program to help a manager decide which method to use by simulating both options. Your program should allow for customers arriving at various intervals. The manager wants to

know the average wait in each system, the average line length in each system (because of its psychological effect on customers), and the longest wait required.

3. Write a program to keep track of computer transactions on a mainframe computer. The computer can process only one job at a time. Each line of input contains a user's identification number, a starting time, and a sequence of integers representing the duration of each job. Assume all jobs are run on a first-come, first-serve basis. Output should include a list of identification numbers, starting and finishing times for each job, and the average waiting time for a transaction.
4. Several previous programming problems have involved keeping records and computing grades for students in some class. If linked lists are used for the students' records, such a program can be used for a class of 20 students or a class of 200 students. Write a recordkeeping program that utilizes linked lists. Input is from an unsorted data file. Each student's information consists of the student's name, 10 quiz scores, six program scores, and three examination scores. Output should include the following
   a. A list, alphabetized by student name, incorporating each student's quiz, program, and examination totals; total points; percentage grade; and letter grade
   b. Overall class average
   c. A histogram depicting class averages
5. Modify the program you developed for the ReadMore Public Library (Problems 6 and 7, Chapter 9, and Problem 2, Chapter 11) to incorporate a dynamic data structure. Use a linked list to solve the same problem.
6. Mailing lists are frequently kept in a data file sorted alphabetically by customer name. However, when they are used to generate mailing labels for a bulk mailing, they must be sorted by zip code. Write a program to input an alphabetically sorted file and produce a list of labels sorted by zip code. The data for each customer are:
   a. Name
   b. Address, including street (plus number), city, two-letter abbreviation for state, and zip code
   c. Expiration information, including the month and year

   Use a binary tree to sort by zip code. Your labels should include some special symbol for all expiring subscriptions (see Problem 1, Chapter 11).

■ Communication in Practice

1. Select a program from the Programming Problem and Projects section of this chapter that you have not yet worked. Construct a structure chart, and write all documentary information for this program. Include variable definition, subprogram definition, required input, and required output. When you are finished, have a classmate read your documentation to see if it is clear in terms of precisely what is to be done.
2. Remove all documentation from a program you have written for this chapter. Exchange this modified version with another student who has done the same thing. Write documentation for the exchanged program. Compare your documentation with that originally written for the program. Discuss the differences and similarities with the other students in your class.
3. Linked lists, stacks, and queues can be presented by using either dynamic variables or static variables (arrays). Talk with a computer science instructor who prefers the dynamic variable approach and with one who prefers the static variable approach. List the advantages and disadvantages of each method. Give an oral report to your class summarizing your conversations with the instructors. Create a chart to use as part of your presentation.

Appendixes

Appendix 1 Reserved Words

The following words have predefined meanings in Turbo Pascal and cannot be changed. Each of these reserved words (except **GOTO** and **LABEL**) has been developed in the text. The **GOTO** and **LABEL** statements are discussed in Appendix 10.

AND	**END**	**MOD**	**SET**
ARRAY	**FILE**	**NIL**	**THEN**
BEGIN	**FOR**	**NOT**	**TO**
CASE	**FORWARD**	**OBJECT**	**TYPE**
CONST	**FUNCTION**	**OF**	**UNTIL**
CONSTRUCTOR	**GOTO**	**OR**	**VAR**
DESTRUCTOR	**IF**	**PRIVATE**	**VIRTUAL**
DIV	**IMPLEMENTATION**	**PROCEDURE**	**WHILE**
DO	**IN**	**PROGRAM**	**WITH**
DOWNTO	**INTERFACE**	**RECORD**	**XOR**
ELSE	**LABEL**	**REPEAT**	

Appendix 2
Standard Identifiers

The standard identifiers for constants, types, files, functions, and procedures are given in this appendix. All have predefined meanings that can (but probably should not) be changed in a program. Summary descriptions are given for the functions and procedures.

Constants	*Types*	*Files*
false	**boolean**	**input**
maxint	**byte**	**output**
true	**char**	**lst**
	comp	
	double	
	extended	
	integer	
	longint	
	real	
	shortint	
	single	
	string	
	text	
	word	

Functions

Function	Parameter Type	Result Type	Value Returned
abs(x)	**integer**	**integer**	Absolute value of x
	real	**real**	
arctan(x)	**integer**	**real**	Arctangent of x *(radians)*
	real		
chr(a)	**integer**	**char**	Character with ordinal a
concat	**string(s)**	**string**	Single string
copy	**string** and two **integers**	**string**	Substring of a string
cos(x)	**integer**	**real**	Cosine of x (radians)
	real		
eof(F)	**file**	**boolean**	End-of-file test for F
eoln(F)	**file**	**boolean**	End-of-line test for F
exp(x)	**integer**	**real**	e^x
	real	**real**	
GetMaxX	none	**integer**	Maximum X coordinate of a pixel
GetMaxY	none	**integer**	Maximum Y coordinate of a pixel
length	**string**	**integer**	Length of the string
ln(x)	**integer** (positive)	**real**	Natural logarithm of x
	real (positive)		
odd(a)	**integer**	**boolean**	Tests for a (an odd integer)
ord(x)	nonreal scalar	**integer**	Ordinal number of x
pred(x)	nonreal scalar	same as x	Predecessor of x
pos	two **strings**	**byte**	Position of substring
round(x)	**real**	**integer**	Rounds off x
sin(x)	**integer**	**real**	Sine of x
	real		
sqr(x)	**integer**	**integer**	Square of x
	real	**real**	
sqrt(x)	**integer**	**real**	Square root of x
	real		
succ(x)	nonreal scalar	same as x	Successor of x
trunc(x)	**real**	**integer**	Truncated value of x

Procedures

Procedure Call	Purpose of Procedure
Arc (X, Y, StAngle, FinAngle, Radius)	Draws a circular arc from StAngle to FinAngle using (X,Y) as the center
assign (Data, 'Ex13-4.DAT')	Assigns the name of an external file to a file variable
Bar (X1, Y1, X2, Y2)	Draws a bar using the current fill style and color
Bar3D (X1, Y1, X2, Y2, Depth, Top)	Draws a three-dimensional bar using the current fill style and color
Circle (X, Y, Radius)	Draws a circle with center (X,Y) and specified radius
CloseGraph	Shuts down the graphics system
delay (MilliSec)	Delays a specified number of milliseconds
delete (<string>, N1, N2)	Deletes a substring
dispose (Ptr)	Returns variable referenced by Ptr to available space list
Ellipse (X, Y, StAngle, FinAngle, Radius)	Draws an elliptical arc from StAngle to FinAngle using (X,Y) as the center
FilePos (F)	Returns the current file position
FileSize (F)	Returns the current size of a file
FillEllipse (X, Y, XRad, YRad)	Draws a filled ellipse
FloodFill (X, Y, Border)	Fills a bounded region with the current fill pattern
GetAspectRatio (Xasp, Yasp)	Returns the effective resolution of the graphics screen from which the aspect ratio (Xasp : Yasp) can be computed
InitGraph (Driver, Mode, Path)	Initializes the graphics system and puts the hardware into graphics mode
insert (<source>, <string>, N)	Inserts a string
Line (X1, Y1, X2, Y2)	Draws a line from (X1, Y1) to (X2, Y2)
LineRel (DeltaX, DeltaY)	Draws a line to a point that is a relative distance from the current pointer
LineTo (X,Y)	Draws a line from the current pointer to (X,Y)
MoveTo (X,Y)	Moves the current pointer to (X,Y)
new (Ptr)	Creates a variable of the type referenced by Ptr^ and stores a pointer to the new variable in Ptr
OutText (<string>)	Sends a string to the output device at the current pointer
OutTextXY (X, Y, <string>)	Sends a string to the output device at the specified position
page (F)	Starts printing the next line of text F at the top of a new page
PieSlice (X, Y, StAngle, FinAngle, Radius)	Draws and fills a pie slice
PutPixel (X, Y, Color)	Plots a point in the specified color
read (F, <variable list>)	Reads values from file F into indicated variables; if F is not specified, **input** is assumed
readln (F, <variable list>)	Executes the same as **read** and then advances the file pointer to the first position following the next end-of-line marker
Rectangle (X1, Y1, X2, Y2)	Draws a rectangle using the current line style and color

Procedures (continued)

Procedure Call	Purpose of Procedure
reset (F)	Resets the pointer in file F to the beginning for the purpose of reading from F
RestoreCrtMode	Restores the screen mode to its original state before graphics was initialized
rewrite (F)	Resets the pointer in file F to the beginning for the purpose of writing to F
Seek (F, Num)	Moves the current position of a file to a specified component
SetAspectRatio (Xasp, Yasp)	Changes the default aspect-ratio correction factor
SetBkColor (ColorNum)	Sets the current background color using the palette
SetColor (Color)	Sets the current drawing color using the palette
SetFillPattern (Pattern, Color)	Selects a user-defined fill pattern
SetFillStyle (Pattern, Color)	Sets the fill pattern and color
SetGraphMode (Mode)	Sets the system to graphics mode and clears the screen
SetTextStyle (Font, Direction, Size)	Sets the current text font, style, and character size
str (N, <string>)	Converts a numeric value to its string representation
val (<string>, V, Code)	Converts a string value to its numeric representation
write (F, <parameter list>)	Writes values specified by parameter list to text file F; if F is not specified, **output** is assumed
writeln (F, <parameter list>)	Executes the same as **write** and then places an end-of-line marker in F

Appendix 3 Syntax Diagrams

Syntax diagrams in this appendix are listed and numbered in the following order:

1. Program

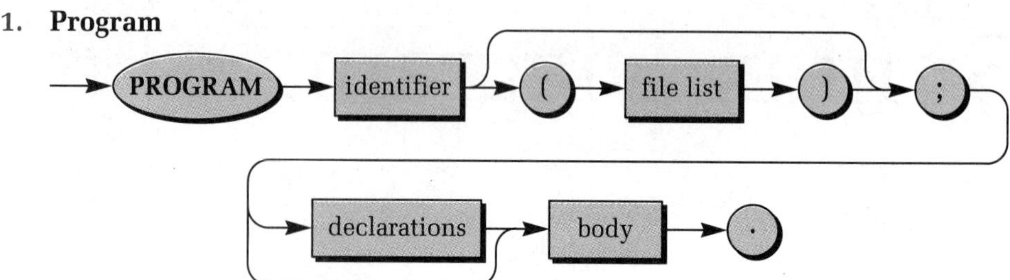

2. Identifier

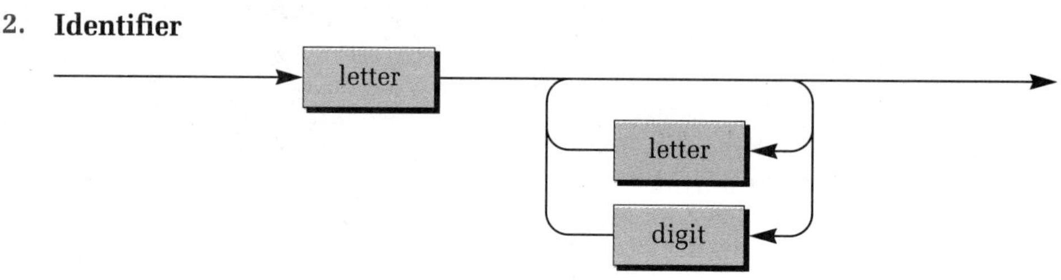

3. File List

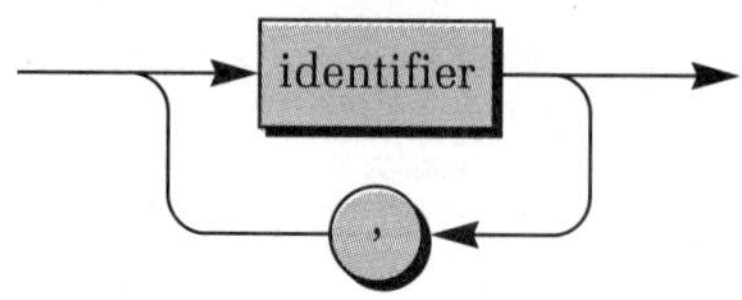

4. Declarations and Definitions

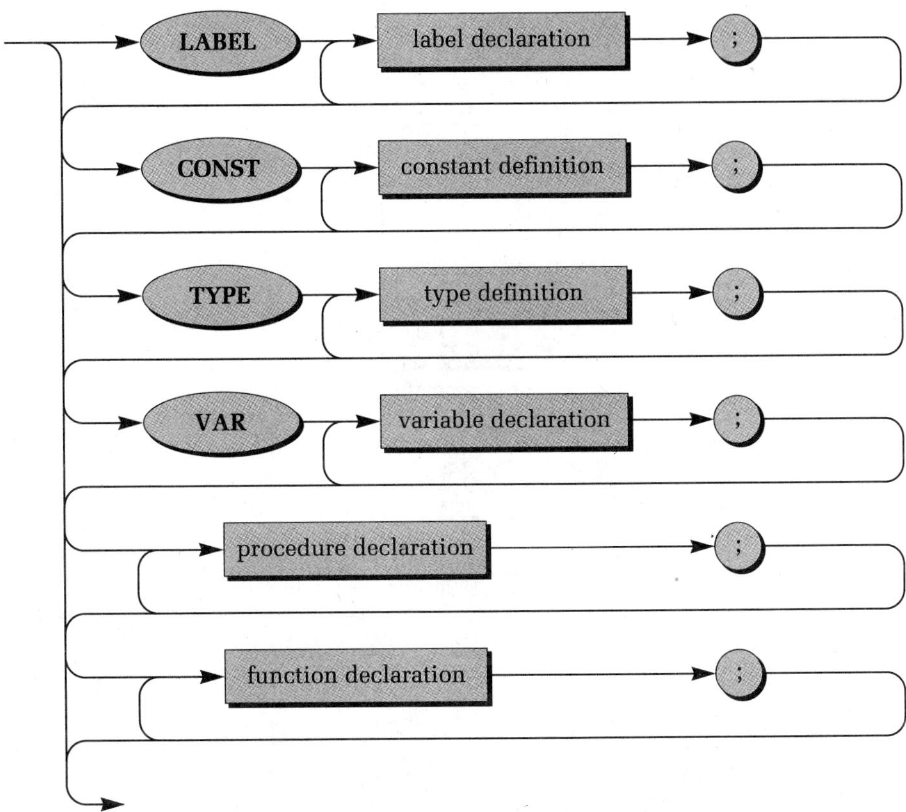

5. Label Declaration

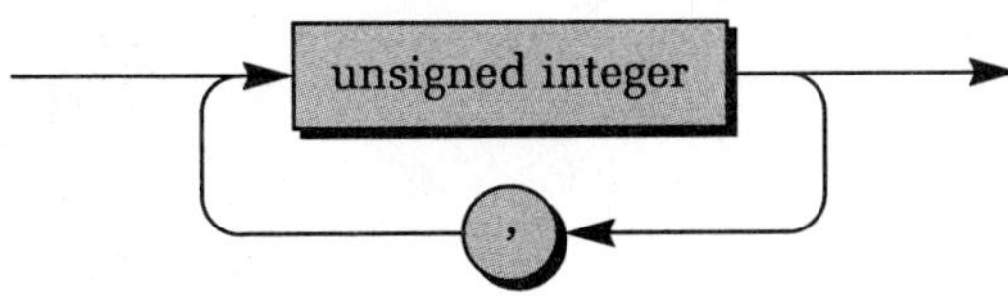

6. Constant Definition

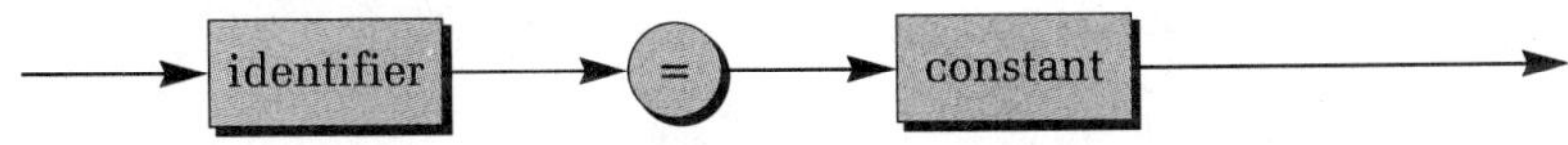

7. Type Definition

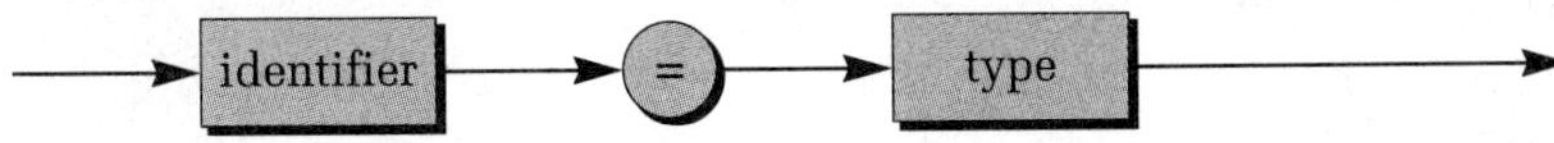

8. **Type**

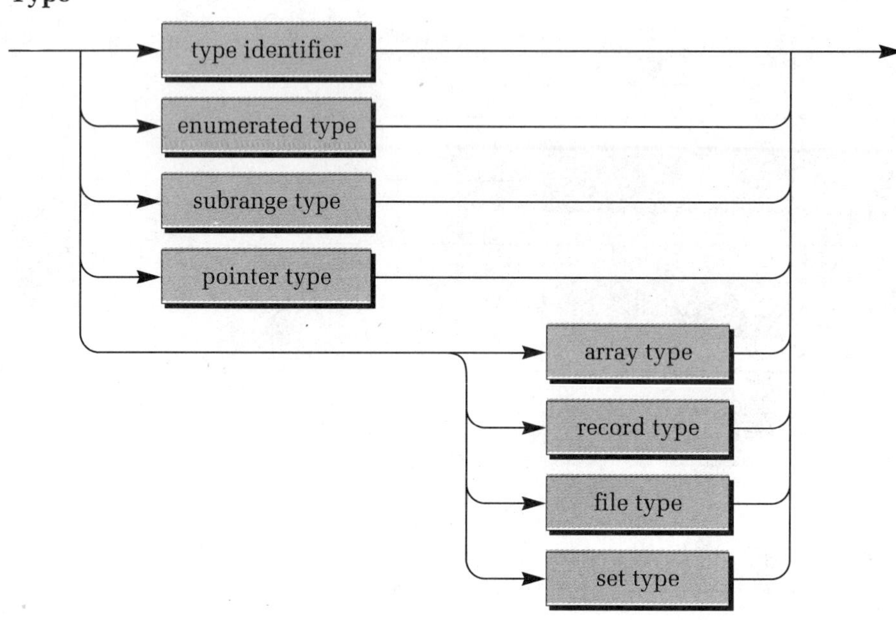

9. **Enumerated Type**

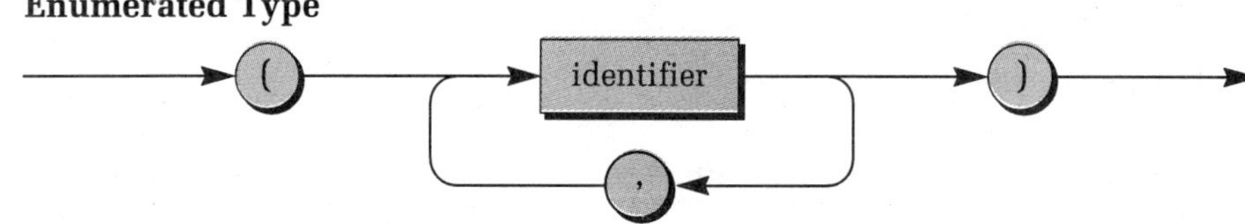

10. **Subrange Type**

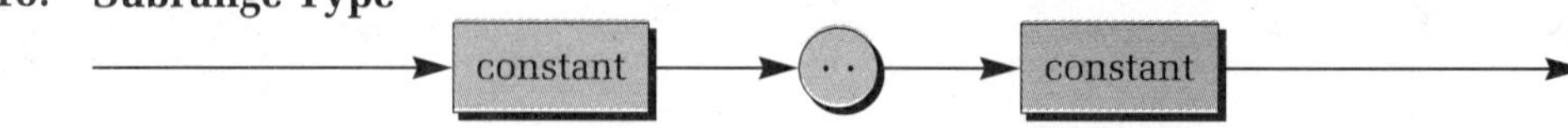

11. **Pointer Type**

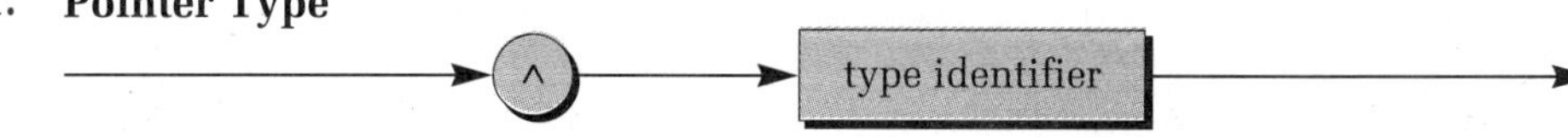

12. **Array Type**

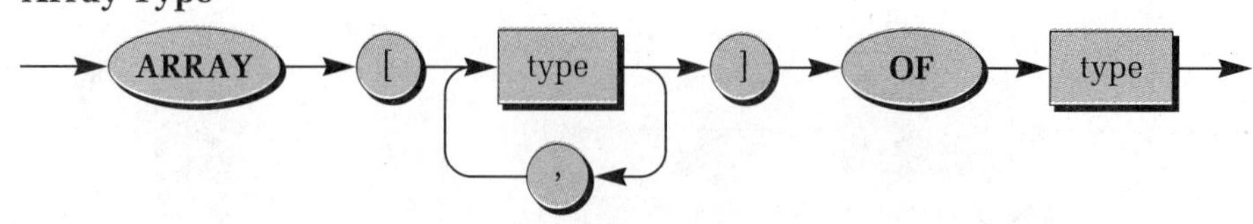

13. Record Type

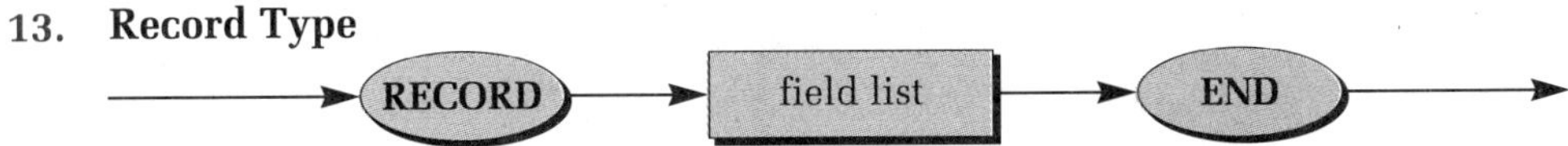

14. Field List

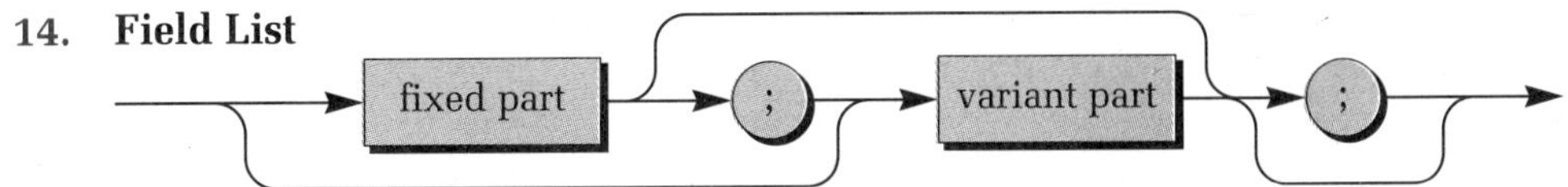

15. Fixed Part

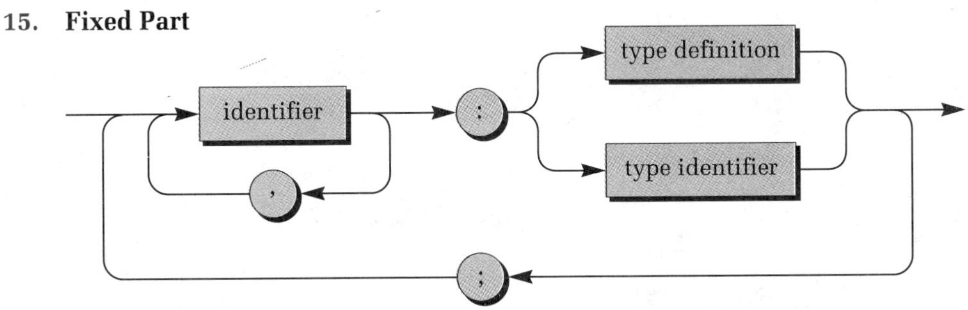

16. Variant Part

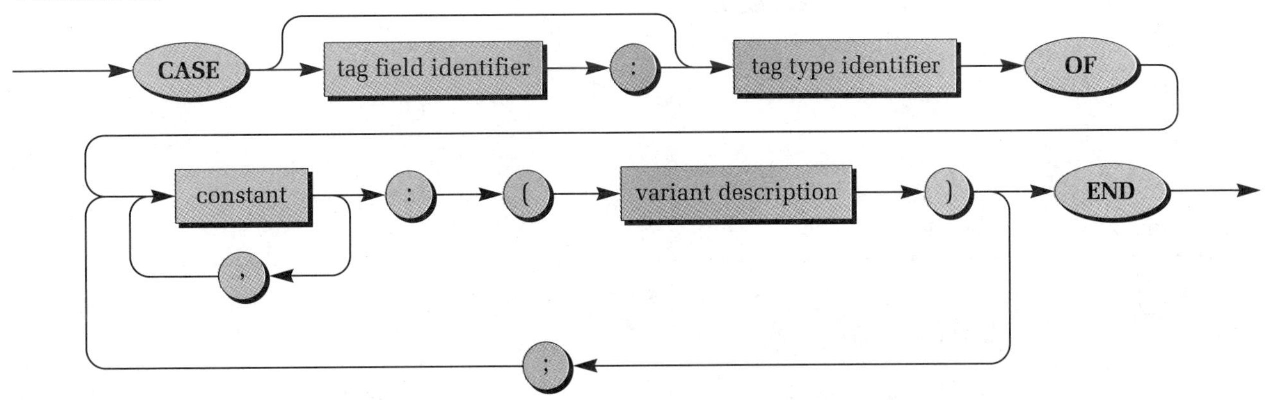

17. Variant Description

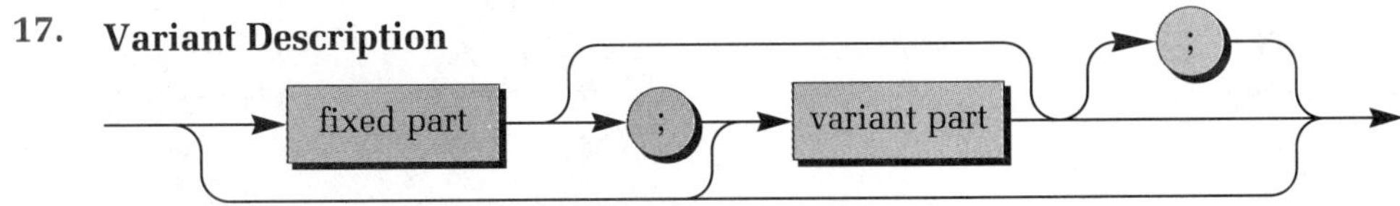

18. File Type

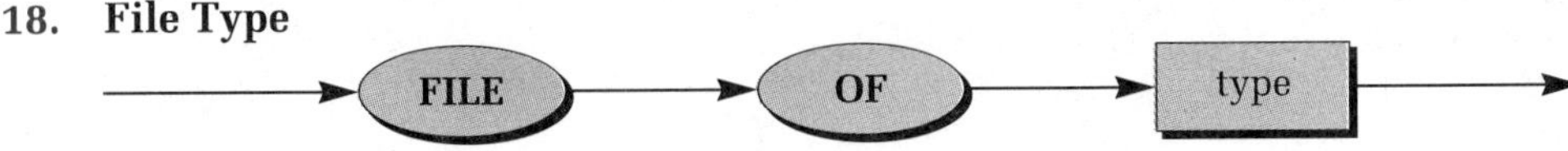

19. Set Type

20. Variable Declaration

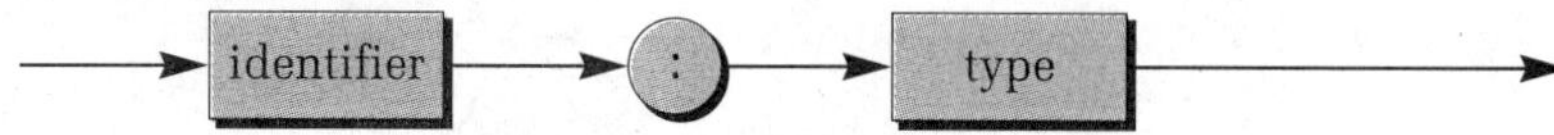

21. Procedure and Function Declarations

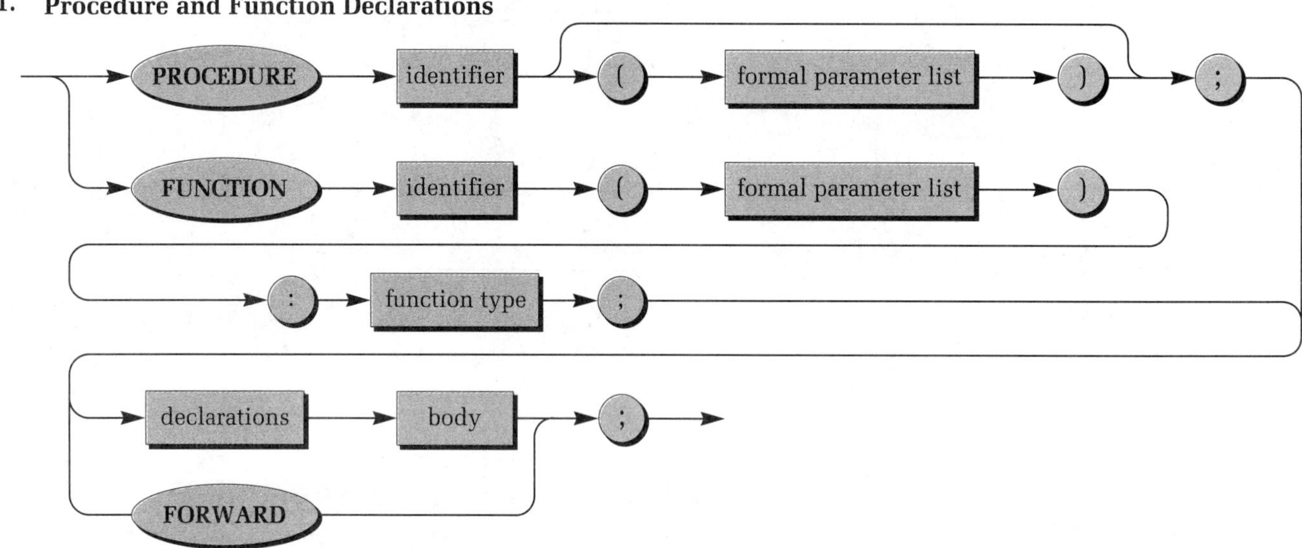

22. Formal Parameter List

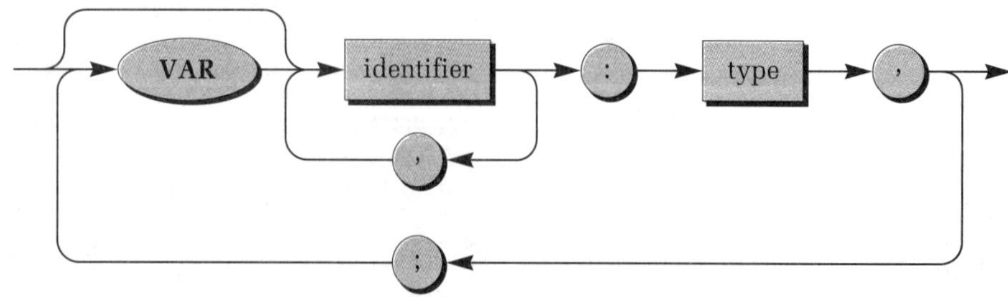

23. Body

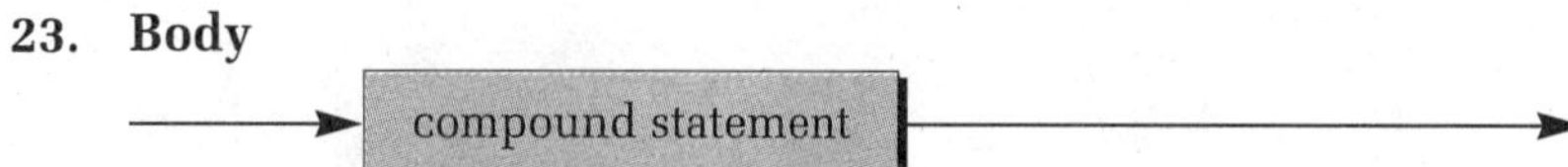

24. Compound Statement

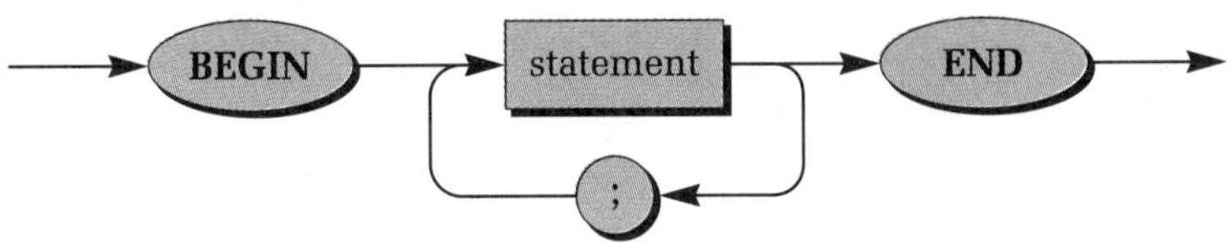

25. Statement

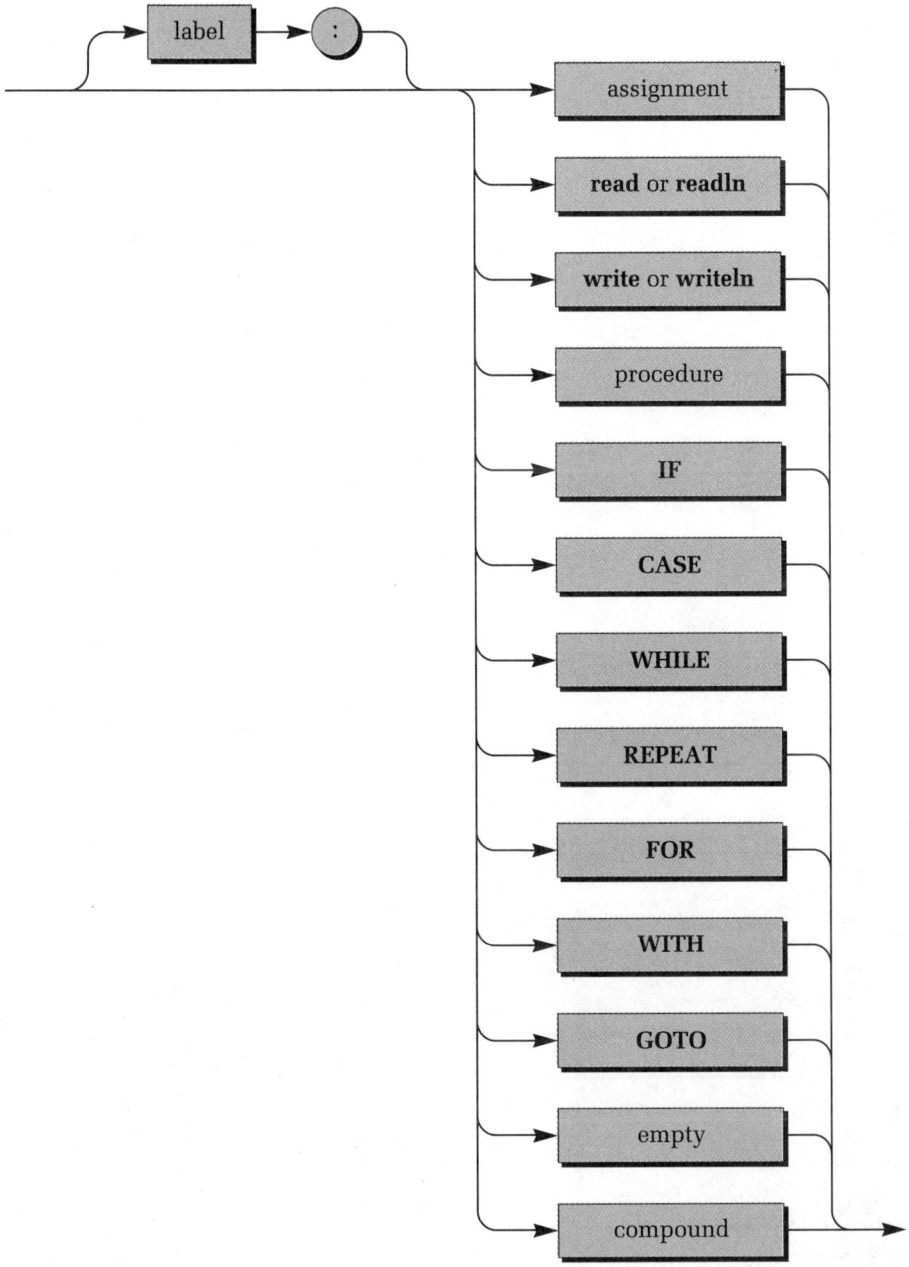

label
:
assignment
read or **readln**
write or **writeln**
procedure
IF
CASE
WHILE
REPEAT
FOR
WITH
GOTO
empty
compound

26. Assignment Statement

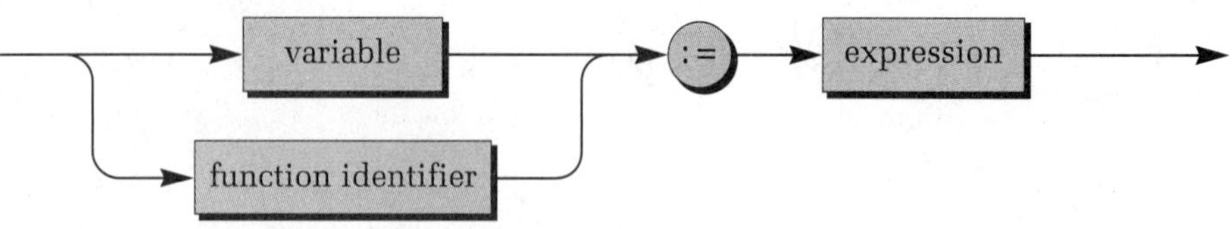

27. Expression

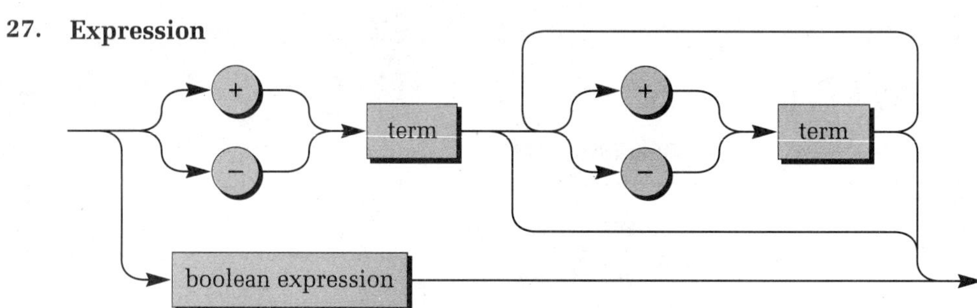

28. Term

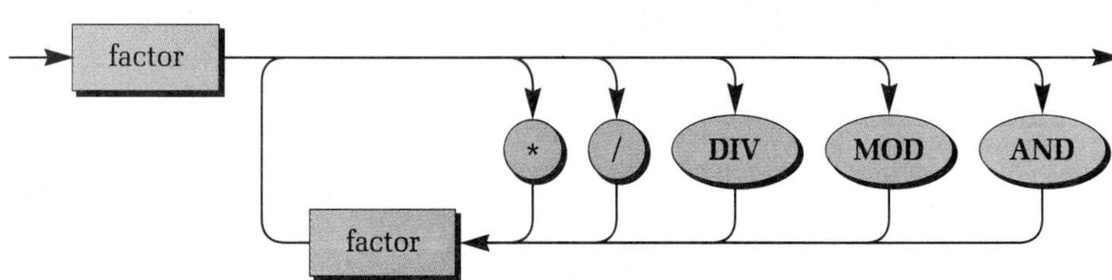

29. Factor

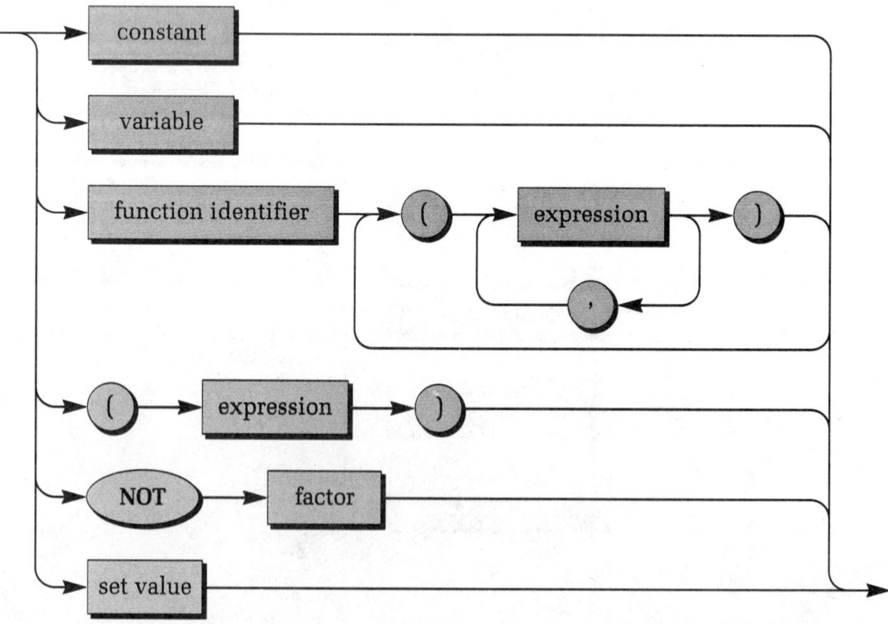

30. Variable

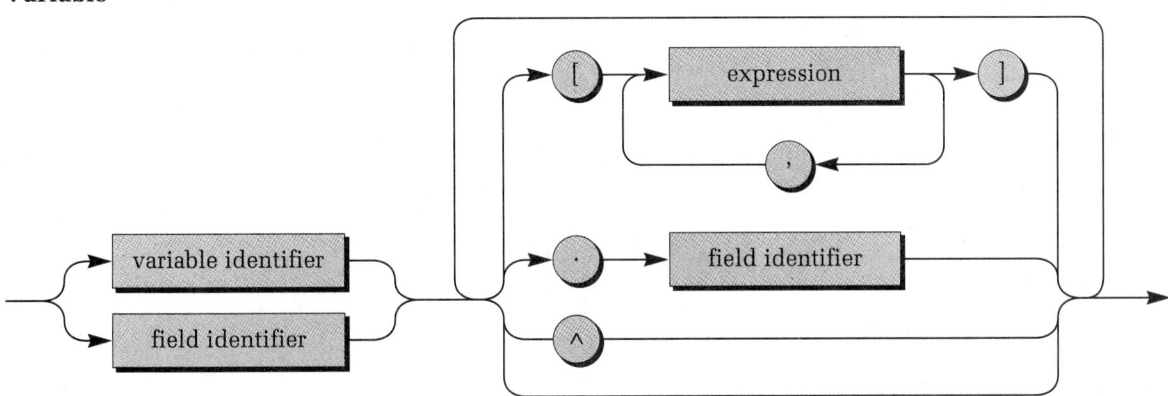

31. Set Value

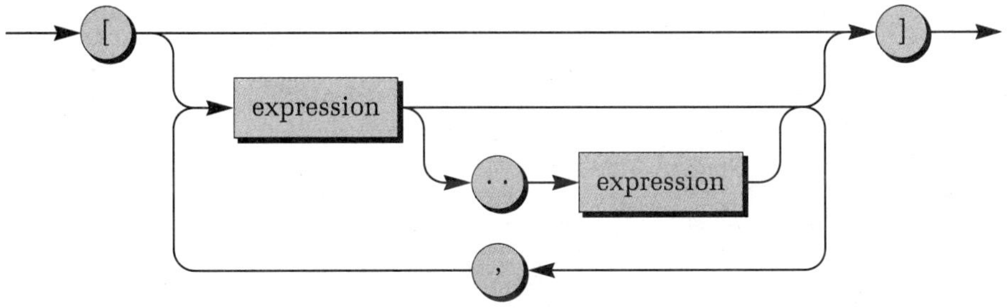

32. Boolean Expression

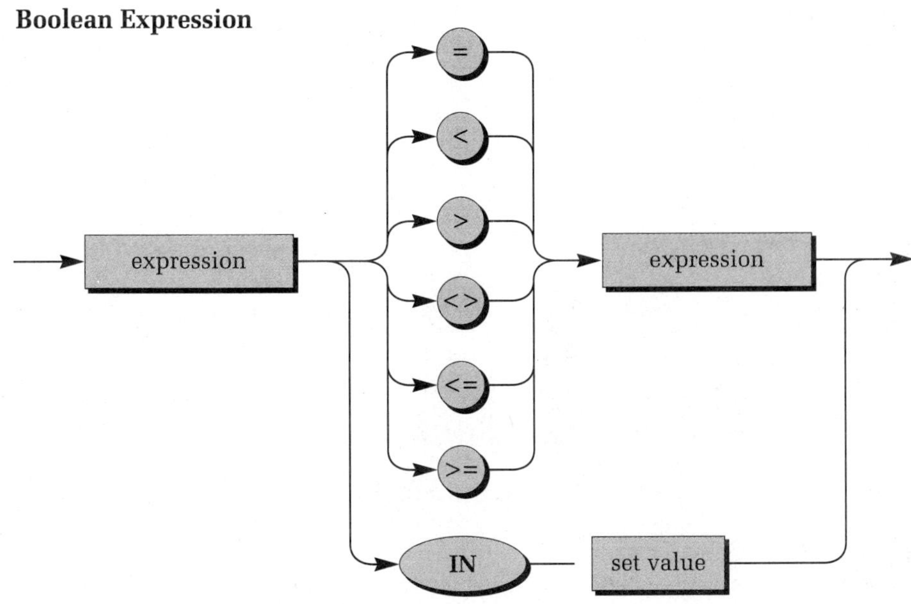

33. read or readln Statement

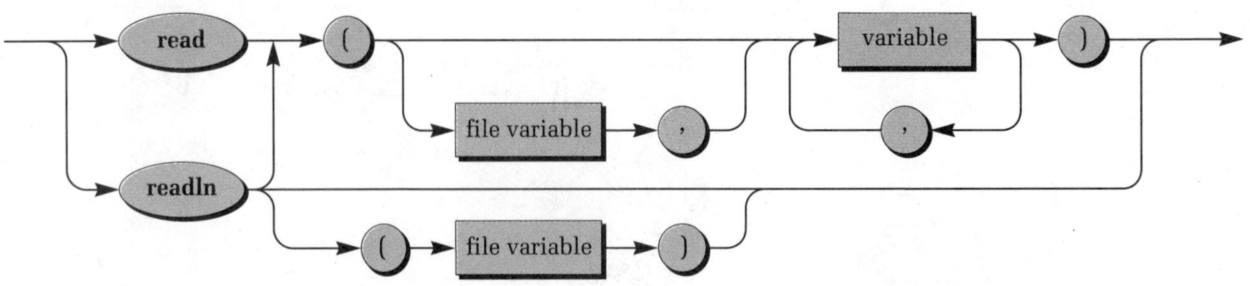

34. write or writeln Statement

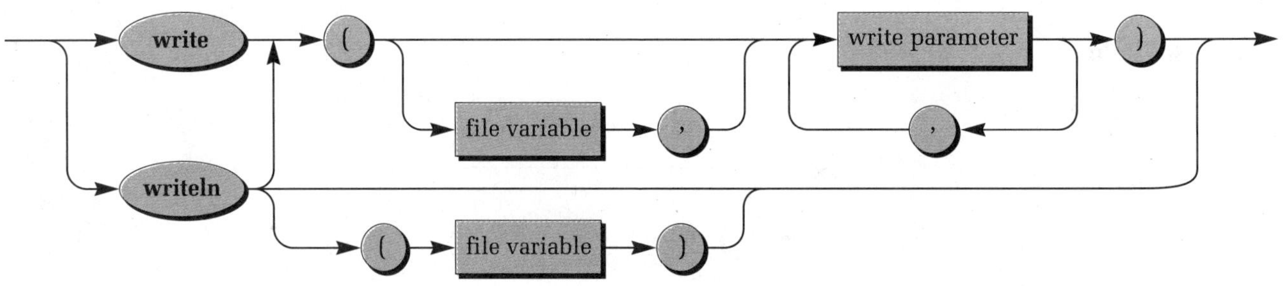

35. Procedure Statement

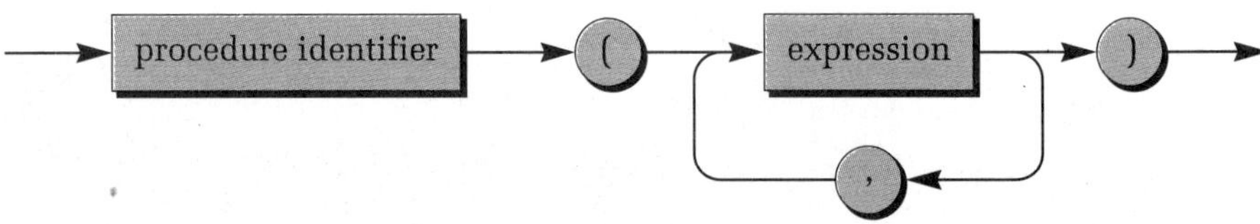

36. IF Statement

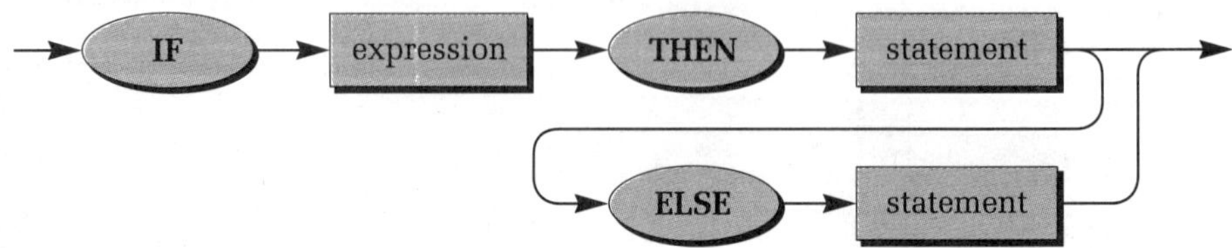

37. **CASE Statement**

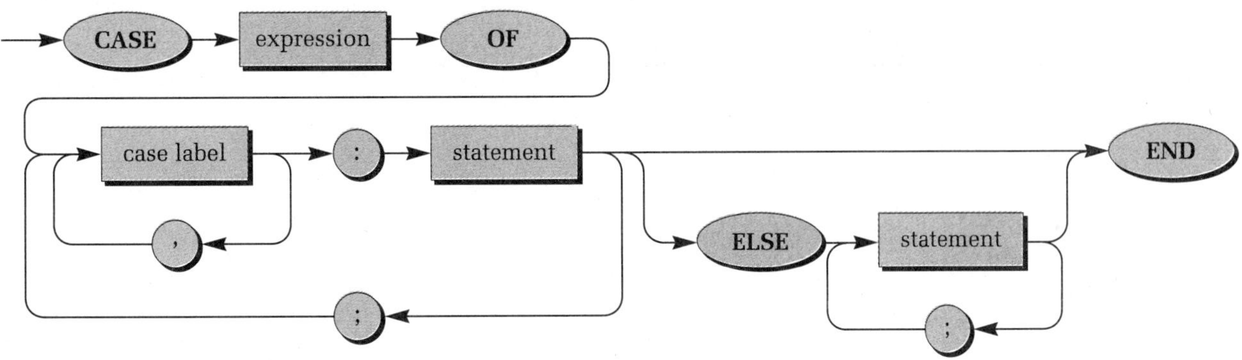

38. **Case Label**

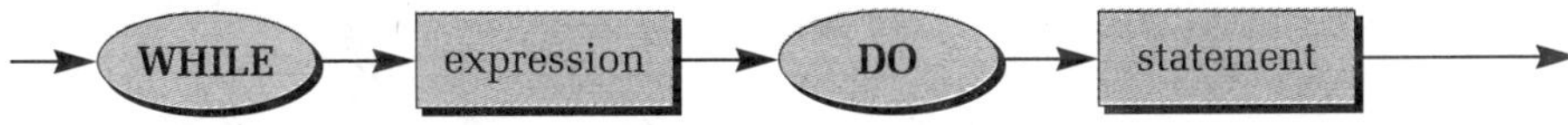

39. **WHILE Statement**

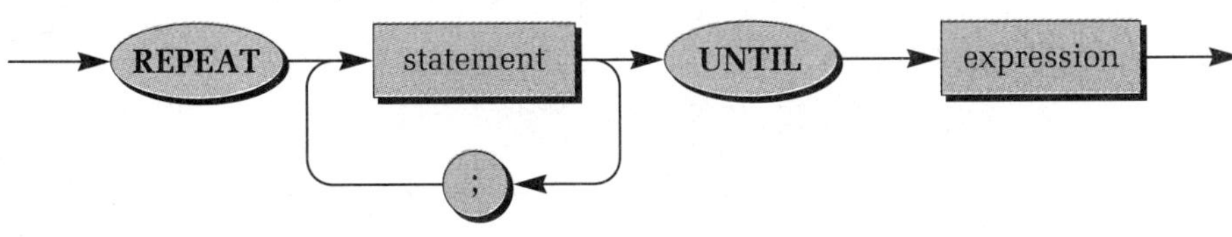

40. **REPEAT Statement**

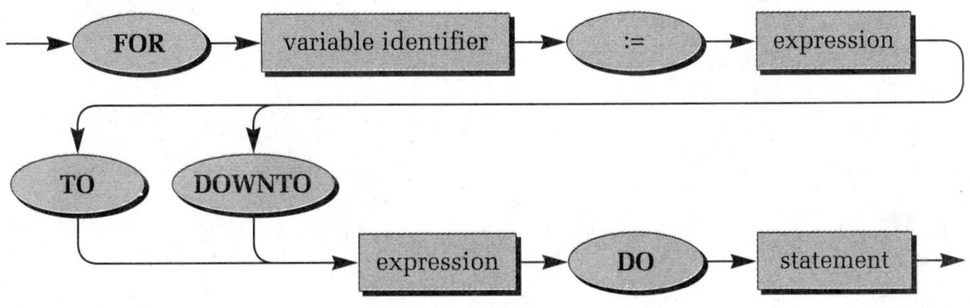

41. **FOR Statement**

42. WITH Statement

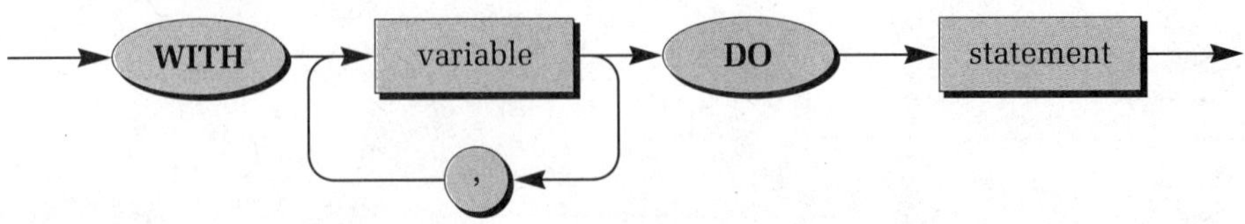

43. GOTO Statement

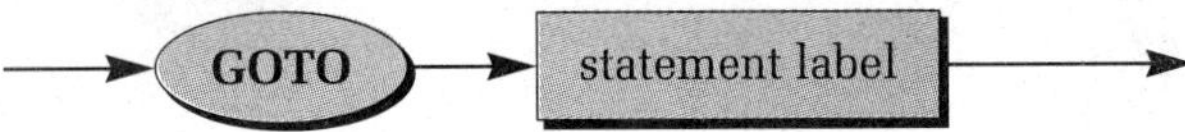

44. Empty Statement

Appendix 4
ASCII Character Set

This table shows the American Standard Code for Information Interchange (ASCII) ordering for a character set. Notice only printable characters are shown. Ordinals without character representations either do not have standard representation or are associated with unprintable control characters. The blank is denoted by "b̸".

The American Standard Code for Information Interchange (ASCII)

Left Digit(s)	Right Digit 0	1	2	3	4	5	6	7	8	9
3			b̸	!	"	#	$	%	&	'
4	(	)	*	+	,	−	.	/	0	1
5	2	3	4	5	6	7	8	9	:	;
6	<	=	>	?	@	A	B	C	D	E
7	F	G	H	I	J	K	L	M	N	O
8	P	Q	R	S	T	U	V	W	X	Y
9	Z	[	\	]	^	—	`	a	b	c
10	d	e	f	g	h	i	j	k	l	m
11	n	o	p	q	r	s	t	u	v	w
12	x	y	z	{	|	}	~			

*Codes less than 32 or greater than 126 are nonprintable.

Appendix 5 Error Messages

Compiler Error Messages

This list contains error messages that may be displayed during the compilation stage. Whenever possible, additional diagnostic information is displayed. Further descriptions of these messages are contained in the Turbo Pascal Programmer's Guide.

```
 1  OUT OF MEMORY.
 2  IDENTIFIER EXPECTED.
 3  UNKNOWN IDENTIFIER.
 4  DUPLICATE IDENTIFIER.
 5  SYNTAX ERROR.
 6  ERROR IN REAL CONSTANT.
 7  ERROR IN INTEGER CONSTANT.
 8  STRING CONSTANT EXCEEDS LINE.
 9  TOO MANY NESTED FILES.
10  UNEXPECTED END OF FILE.
11  LINE TOO LONG.
12  TYPE IDENTIFIER EXPECTED.
13  TOO MANY OPEN FILES.
14  INVALID FILE NAME.
15  FILE NOT FOUND.
16  DISK FULL.
17  INVALID COMPILER DIRECTIVE.
18  TOO MANY FILES.
19  UNDEFINED TYPE IN POINTER DEFINITION.
20  VARIABLE IDENTIFIER EXPECTED.
21  ERROR IN TYPE.
22  STRUCTURE TOO LARGE.
23  SET BASE TYPE OUT OF RANGE.
24  FILE COMPONENTS MAY NOT BE FILES OR OBJECTS.
25  INVALID STRING LENGTH.
26  TYPE MISMATCH.
27  INVALID SUBRANGE BASE TYPE.
28  LOWER BOUND GREATER THAN UPPER BOUND.
29  ORDINAL TYPE EXPECTED.
30  INTEGER CONSTANT EXPECTED.
31  CONSTANT EXPECTED.
32  INTEGER OR REAL CONSTANT EXPECTED.
33  POINTER TYPE IDENTIFIER EXPECTED.
34  INVALID FUNCTION RESULT TYPE.
```

35 LABEL IDENTIFIER EXPECTED.
36 BEGIN EXPECTED.
37 END EXPECTED.
38 INTEGER EXPRESSION EXPECTED.
39 ORDINAL EXPRESSION EXPECTED.
40 BOOLEAN EXPRESSION EXPECTED.
41 OPERAND TYPES DO NOT MATCH OPERATOR.
42 ERROR IN EXPRESSION.
43 ILLEGAL ASSIGNMENT.
44 FIELD IDENTIFIER EXPECTED.
45 OBJECT FILE TOO LARGE.
46 UNDEFINED EXTERNAL.
47 INVALID OBJECT FILE RECORD.
48 CODE SEGMENT TOO LARGE.
49 DATA SEGMENT TOO LARGE.
50 DO EXPECTED.
51 INVALID PUBLIC DEFINITION.
52 INVALID EXTRN DEFINITION.
53 TOO MANY EXTRN DEFINITIONS.
54 OF EXPECTED.
55 INTERFACE EXPECTED.
56 INVALID RELOCATABLE REFERENCE.
57 THEN EXPECTED.
58 TO OR DOWNTO EXPECTED.
59 UNDEFINED FORWARD.
60 TOO MANY PROCEDURES.
61 INVALID TYPECAST.
62 DIVISION BY ZERO.
63 INVALID FILE TYPE.
64 CANNOT READ OR WRITE VARIABLES OF THIS TYPE.
65 POINTER VARIABLE EXPECTED.
66 STRING VARIABLE EXPECTED.
67 STRING EXPRESSION EXPECTED.
68 CIRCULAR UNIT REFERENCE.
69 UNIT NAME MISMATCH.
70 UNIT VERSION MISMATCH.
71 DUPLICATE UNIT NAME.
72 UNIT FILE FORMAT ERROR.
73 IMPLEMENTATION EXPECTED.
74 CONSTANT AND CASE TYPES DO NOT MATCH.
75 RECORD VARIABLE EXPECTED.
76 CONSTANT OUT OF RANGE.
77 FILE VARIABLE EXPECTED.
78 POINTER EXPRESSION EXPECTED.
79 INTEGER OR REAL EXPRESSION EXPECTED.
80 LABEL NOT WITHIN CURRENT BLOCK.
81 LABEL ALREADY DEFINED.
82 UNDEFINED LABEL IN PRECEDING STATEMENT PART.
83 INVALID @ ARGUMENT.
84 UNIT EXPECTED.
85 ‘‘;’’ EXPECTED.
86 ‘‘:’’ EXPECTED.
87 ‘‘,’’ EXPECTED.
88 ‘‘(’’ EXPECTED.
89 ‘‘)’’ EXPECTED.
90 ‘‘=’’ EXPECTED.
91 ‘‘:=’’ EXPECTED.
92 ‘‘[’’ or ‘‘(.’’ EXPECTED.
93 ‘‘]’’ or ‘‘).’’ EXPECTED.
94 ‘‘.’’ EXPECTED.
95 ‘‘..’’ EXPECTED.
96 TOO MANY VARIABLES.
97 INVALID FOR CONTROL VARIABLE.

98 INTEGER VARIABLE EXPECTED.
99 FILE AND PROCEDURE TYPES ARE NOT ALLOWED HERE.
100 STRING LENGTH MISMATCH.
101 INVALID ORDERING OF FIELDS.
102 STRING CONSTANT EXPECTED.
103 INTEGER OR REAL VARIABLE EXPECTED.
104 ORDINAL VARIABLE EXPECTED.
105 INLINE ERROR.
106 CHARACTER EXPRESSION EXPECTED.
107 TOO MANY RELOCATION ITEMS.
112 CASE CONSTANT OUT OF RANGE.
113 ERROR IN STATEMENT.
114 CANNOT CALL AN INTERRUPT PROCEDURE.
116 MUST BE IN 8087 MODE TO COMPILE THIS.
117 TARGET ADDRESS NOT FOUND.
118 INCLUDE FILES ARE NOT ALLOWED HERE.
120 NIL EXPECTED.
121 INVALID QUALIFIER.
122 INVALID VARIABLE REFERENCE.
123 TOO MANY SYMBOLS.
124 STATEMENT PART TOO LARGE.
126 FILES MUST BE VAR PARAMETERS.
127 TOO MANY CONDITIONAL SYMBOLS.
128 MISPLACED CONDITIONAL DIRECTIVE.
129 ENDIF DIRECTIVE MISSING.
130 ERROR IN INITIAL CONDITIONAL DEFINES.
131 HEADER DOES NOT MATCH PREVIOUS DEFINITION.
132 CRITICAL DISK ERROR.
133 CANNOT EVALUATE THIS EXPRESSION.
134 EXPRESSION INCORRECTLY TERMINATED.
135 INVALID FORMAT SPECIFIER.
136 INVALID INDIRECT REFERENCE.
137 STRUCTURED VARIABLES ARE NOT ALLOWED HERE.
138 CANNOT EVALUATE WITHOUT SYSTEM UNIT.
139 CANNOT ACCESS THIS SYMBOL.
140 INVALID FLOATING-POINT OPERATION.
141 CANNOT COMPILE OVERLAYS TO MEMORY.
142 PROCEDURAL OR FUNCTION VARIABLE EXPECTED.
143 INVALID PROCEDURE OR FUNCTION REFERENCE.
144 CANNOT OVERLAY THIS UNIT.
147 OBJECT TYPE EXPECTED.
148 LOCAL OBJECT TYPES ARE NOT ALLOWED.
149 VIRTUAL EXPECTED.
150 METHOD IDENTIFIER EXPECTED.
151 VIRTUAL CONSTRUCTORS ARE NOT ALLOWED.
152 CONSTRUCTOR IDENTIFIER EXPECTED.
153 DESTRUCTOR IDENTIFIER EXPECTED.
154 FAIL ONLY ALLOWED WITHIN CONSTRUCTOR.
155 INVALID COMBINATION OF OPCODE AND OPERANDS.
156 MEMORY REFERENCE EXPECTED.
157 CANNOT ADD OR SUBTRACT RELOCATABLE SYMBOLS.
158 INVALID REGISTER COMBINATION.
159 286/287 INSTRUCTIONS ARE NOT ENABLED.
160 INVALID SYMBOL REFERENCE.
161 CODE GENERATION ERROR.
162 ASM EXPECTED.

Run-Time Error Messages

Run-time errors cause the program to display an error message and terminate. They are divided into four categories: DOS errors (1–99), I/O errors (100–149), Critical errors (150–199), and Fatal errors (200–255). Several examples of each are listed here. More complete descriptions can be found in the Turbo Pascal Programmer's Guide.

DOS Error Messages

```
  1  INVALID FUNCTION NUMBER.
  2  FILE NOT FOUND.
  3  PATH NOT FOUND.
  4  TOO MANY OPEN FILES.
  5  FILE ACCESS DENIED.
  6  INVALID FILE HANDLE.
 12  INVALID FILE ACCESS CODE.
 15  INVALID DRIVE NUMBER.
 16  CANNOT REMOVE CURRENT DIRECTORY.
 17  CANNOT RENAME ACROSS DRIVES.
```

I-O Error Messages

These errors cause termination if the particular statement was compiled in the {$I+} state. In the {$I–} state, the program continues to execute and the error is reported by the **IOResult** function.

```
100  DISK READ ERROR.
101  DISK WRITE ERROR.
102  FILE NOT ASSIGNED.
103  FILE NOT OPEN.
104  FILE NOT OPEN FOR INPUT.
105  FILE NOT OPEN FOR OUTPUT.
106  INVALID NUMERIC FORMAT.
```

Critical Error Messages

```
150  DISK IS WRITE-PROTECTED.
151  UNKNOWN UNIT.
152  DRIVE NOT READY.
153  UNKNOWN COMMAND.
154  CRC ERROR IN DATA.
155  BAD DRIVE REQUEST STRUCTURE LENGTH.
156  DISK SEEK ERROR.
157  UNKNOWN MEDIA TYPE.
158  SECTOR NOT FOUND.
159  PRINTER OUT OF PAPER.
160  DEVICE WRITE FAULT.
161  DEVICE READ FAULT.
162  HARDWARE FAILURE.
```

Fatal Error Messages

These errors always immediately terminate the program.

```
200  DIVISION BY ZERO.
201  RANGE CHECK ERROR.
202  STACK OVERFLOW ERROR.
203  HEAP OVERFLOW ERROR.
204  INVALID POINTER OPERATION.
205  FLOATING-POINT OVERFLOW.
206  FLOATING-POINT UNDERFLOW.
207  INVALID FLOATING-POINT OPERATION.
208  OVERLAY MANAGER NOT INSTALLED.
209  OVERLAY FILE READ ERROR.
210  OBJECT NOT INITIALIZED.
211  CALL TO ABSTRACT METHOD.
212  STREAM REGISTRATION ERROR.
213  COLLECTION INDEX OUT OF RANGE.
214  COLLECTION OVERFLOW ERROR.
```

Appendix 6
Compiler Directives

A *compiler directive* is a feature that controls Turbo Pascal's compiler. Compiler directives appear as special comments having the specific syntax

```
{$<directive>}
```

or

```
{$<directive>, <directive>, ...}
```

Some directives are *switch directives,* which act as a toggle to either enable or disable a particular feature. The enabling sign is "+," and the disabling sign is "–". Thus

```
{$B+}
```

enables the complete Boolean evaluation feature, while

```
{$B-}
```

causes short-circuit Boolean evaluation to be performed. Each switch directive has a default setting.

Other directives are *parameter directives* of the form

```
{$<parameter>}
```

For example

```
{$I<file name>}
```

causes the compiler to include the named file in the compilation.

The following table contains a list of the most frequently used compiler directives. The Turbo Pascal Programmer's Guide contains a more complete listing and descriptions of compiler directives.

Compiler directives

Compiler Directive	**Default Setting**	**Effect on Compiler**
{$B<+,–>}	{$B–}	Enables/disables complete Boolean evaluation
{$D<+,–>}	{$D+}	Enables/disables generation of debugging information
{$E<+,–>}	{$E+}	Enables/disables the program to access a floating-point, run-time library, which emulates the 8087 numeric coprocessor
{$I<+,–>}	{$I+}	Enables/disables the automatic code generation that checks the result of a call to an I/O procedure; when disabled, I/O error results should be checked using the **IOResult** function
{$I<file name>}		Instructs the compiler to include the file name in the compilation at the point at which the directive appears
{$L<+,–>}	{$L+}	Enables/disables the generation of debugging information for local variables; {$L+} has no effect if the program (or unit) is compiled using {$D–}
{$N<+,–>}	{$N–}	Enables/disables different models of floating-point code generation; {$N+} causes the compiler to generate code to perform real-type calculations using the 8087 numeric coprocessor, which allows use of the extended **real** data types **single, double, extended,** and **comp**
{$R<+,–>}	{$R–}	Enables/disables the generation of range-checking code; {$R+} enables the generation of code for subscript range checking, so this option should be active when debugging a program that includes subscripts
{$S<+,–>}	{$S+}	Enables/disables the generation of stack overflow checking code; when active, stack overflow causes a run-time error; when passive, stack overflow is likely to cause a system crash
{$V<+,–>}	{$V+}	Enables/disables type checking on strings passed as variable parameters; when active, strict type checking requires formal and actual parameters to be of identical type; when passive, any **string** type is allowed as an actual parameter

Appendix 7 Turbo Pascal 7.0 Notes

Using Turbo Pascal 7.0 instead of 6.0 should have little, if any, effect on the programming done in your first course. The differences between 6.0 and 7.0 are generally of importance only to professional programmers. Three interactive development environments are offered in Turbo 7.0, as opposed to only one in Turbo 6.0. These three are:

- The real mode IDE
- The protected mode IDE
- The Microsoft Windows IDE

The real mode IDE corresponds to the only IDE available in Turbo 6.0. Our assumption throughout this text and appendix is that you are working in the real mode IDE. The protected mode and Microsoft Windows IDEs are designed for controlling extremely large software projects consisting of many source files. You should consult the *Turbo Pascal User's Guide* if you are interested in using these environments and the advanced features that are available in them.

7.0

The remainder of this appendix consists of specific page references in bold type, followed by appropriate comments and examples concerning Turbo 7.0. Turbo 7.0 logos (shown at the left) are used throughout the text to indicate a reference to this appendix.

Turbo 7.0 Notes

page 27: Depending on which variant of Turbo 7.0 is used by your institution, it may be installed in a directory called BP (for Borland Pascal) instead of TP. Check with your instructor if it is necessary to be in this directory before running Turbo.

page 27: The Turbo Pascal 7.0 main menu appears in a slightly different form from that of Turbo 6.0. The 7.0 main menu appears in Figure A. Note that the triple-bar menu item (≡) from Turbo 6.0 no longer appears in Turbo 7.0. The main function of this item in Turbo 6.0 was to clear your desktop of all windows. This can be done by choosing the "Close All" option from the Windows menu item in Turbo 7.0. Note also that the Turbo 7.0 main menu offers a Tools item that did not appear in the Turbo 6.0 main menu. The main purpose of this item is to run a utility file search program called **Grep.** Consult the *Turbo 7.0 User's Guide* if you want to learn about **Grep.**

Figure A
The Turbo 7.0 main menu

page 37: Clearing your desktop can be done by choosing the "Close All" option from the Windows menu item in Turbo 7.0. The triple-bar (≡) option, used for this purpose in Turbo 6.0, is not available in Turbo 7.0.

page 87: Some additional standard functions and procedures available in Turbo 7.0 are **high, continue, break, and exit.** Use of these will be discussed later in this appendix.

pages 105 and 112: Turbo 7.0 introduces a class of parameters called *constant parameters* in addition to **VAR** and value parameters. The keyword **CONST** preceding a group of parameters indicates that these parameters are value parameters that cannot be locally altered within the procedure or function to which the parameter list belongs. This is in contrast to normal value parameters that can be altered locally without having such alteration affect the value of the actual parameter upon exit from the procedure or function. The following clarifies this difference.

```
PROCEDURE ShowDifference  (X : integer; {  Normal value parameter   }
                           VAR Y : integer; {  VAR parameter        }
                           CONST Z : integer); {  CONST parameter   }

BEGIN
   .
   .
   .
   X := ... {  Assignment to X is allowed although the actual parameter
               associated with X will not be changed.  }
   Y := ... {  Assignment to Y is allowed, and the actual parameter
               associated with Y will be changed.  }
   Z := ... {  Assignment to Z is detected and generates a syntax error.   }
   .
   .
   .
END;
```

page 134: In Turbo 7.0, the library procedure **exit** can be used to control the execution of a procedure or a function. It causes an immediate termination and return from the currently executing procedure or function. For example, the following procedure will return control immediately to the calling program unit upon finding an employee whose hours worked equal zero.

```
PROCEDURE ComputePay (VAR TotalPay);
  BEGIN
    readln (Data, Hours, Payrate);
    IF Hours = 0 THEN
      exit;
    {  Rest of procedure skipped upon finding Hours = 0.  }
    .
    .
    .
  END;
```

Check with your instructor before using the **exit** procedure since many programmers would criticize it as being unstructured in its logical control.

pages 213, 222, 229: In Turbo 7.0, the library procedure **continue** can be used to control loop iteration. It causes the innermost enclosing **FOR**, **WHILE**, or **REPEAT** statement to immediately proceed with the next iteration. For example, the following loop will skip processing all employees whose hours worked equal zero.

```
WHILE NOT eof(Data) DO
  BEGIN
    readln(Data, Hours, Payrate);
    IF Hours = 0 THEN
      continue;
    .
    .
    .
  END;
```

Check with your instructor before using the **continue** procedure since many programmers would criticize it as being unstructured in its logical control.

pages 213, 222, 229: In Turbo 7.0, the library procedure break can be used to control loop iteration. It causes the innermost enclosing **FOR**, **WHILE**, or **REPEAT** statement to be exited immediately. For example, the following loop will terminate upon finding an employee whose hours worked equal zero.

```
WHILE NOT eof(Data) DO
  BEGIN
    readln (Data, Hours, Payrate);
    IF Hours = 0 THEN
      break;
    .
    .
    .
  END;
```

Check with your instructor before using the **break** procedure since many programmers would criticize it as being unstructured in its logical control.

pages 332 and 335: In Turbo 7.0, open array parameters allow arrays of varying sizes to be passed to the same procedure or function. For example, an open array parameter List for integer arrays would be declared as follows in a procedure's formal parameter list:

```
FUNCTION Sum (List : ARRAY OF integer) : integer;
```

Within **FUNCTION** Sum, the parameter is regarded as an array indexed from 0 to N-1, where N is the physical size of the actual parameter that is associated with List. Note that the actual parameter need not be indexed starting from zero; the only requirement imposed upon it is that its base data type be **integer**. Hence, we could write the body of **FUNCTION** Sum to return the sum of the values in any array of integers.

```
FUNCTION Sum (List : ARRAY OF integer) : integer;
  VAR
    Total, K : integer;
  BEGIN
    Total := 0;
```

```
    FOR K := 0 TO high(List) DO
      Total := Total + List[K];
    Sum := Total
  END;
```

Here the library function **high** is used to return the index of the last element in the open array parameter. **FUNCTION** Sum could now be used to determine the total of values in arrays of two different types.

```
VAR
  A1 : ARRAY [1..100] of integer;
  A2 : ARRAY [-5..5] of integer;
BEGIN
  .
  .
  .
  writeln (Sum(A1), Sum(A2));
  .
  .
  .
END.
```

Open array parameters can also appear as **VAR** parameters. For instance, the following SelectionSort procedure could be used to sort any array of reals.

```
PROCEDURE SelectionSort (N : integer;
                         VAR List : ARRAY OF real);
  VAR
    K, J, MinPosition : integer;
    Temp : real;
  BEGIN
    FOR K := 0 TO N - 2 DO  {  Put smallest in position K  }
      BEGIN
        MinPosition := K;  {  Initially assume Kth is smallest  }
        FOR J := K + 1 TO N - 1 DO  {  Test previous smallest  }
          IF List[J] < List[MinPosition] THEN
            MinPosition := J;  {  Index, not array element, assigned here  }
        Temp := List[K];  {  Now swap smallest outside the inner loop  }
        List[K] := List[MinPosition];
        List[MinPosition] := Temp
      END
  END;  {  of PROCEDURE SelectionSort  }
```

page 345: For Turbo strings, open string parameters achieve the same goal that open array parameters achieve for arrays. That is, they allows us to pass an actual parameter of any string type into a procedure. Within the procedure, the maximum length of the formal parameter will be the same as that of the actual parameter. For instance, consider the following procedure that is designed to assign the longest possible string of A's to the parameter S.

```
PROCEDURE AssignA (VAR S : OpenString);
  VAR I : integer;
  BEGIN
    S[0] := chr(high(S));     {  Assign string length  }
    FOR I := 1 TO high(S) DO  {  Assign characters in string  }
      S[I] := 'A'
  END;
```

Here the keyword OpenString establishes S as an open string parameter. Within the procedure, the library **high** function is used to determine the declared maximum size of the actual parameter that is associated with S. Hence, if the strings S1 and S2 were declared by

```
VAR
  S1 : string[10];
  S2 : string[20];
```

then calls of the form

```
AssignA (S1);
AssignA (S2);
```

would assign 10 A's to S1 and 20 A's to S2 respectively.

pages 643: In Turbo 7.0, the keyword **INHERITED** can be used to denote the ancestor of the enclosing method's object type. To illustrate, suppose that the object type Circle is derived from the object type Point.

```
TYPE
  Circle = OBJECT (Point);
```

Then, within **CONSTRUCTOR** Init for Circle we could refer to **CONSTRUCTOR** Init for Point by using **INHERITED** instead of explicitly referring to Point.

```
PROCEDURE Circle.Init;
  BEGIN
    INHERITED Init;  {  Use INHERITED instead of Point.Init  }
    Radius := 0.0
  END;
```

pages 625: In addition to the reserved word **PRIVATE**, Turbo 7.0 also offers the reserved word **PUBLIC**. Used along with **PRIVATE**, **PUBLIC** allows you to intersperse those components of an object's declaration in any order that you wish to make available to users of the object. With only **PRIVATE** available in Turbo 6.0, you are forced to place all available components first (before the **PRIVATE** declaration) in an object's definition. For more detail, consult the *Turbo Pascal Language Guide.*

Appendix 8 Standard Pascal Notes

S

This text has been prepared using Turbo Pascal. Although Turbo Pascal has most of the features of standard Pascal, there are a few differences. This appendix contains descriptions of many of these differences. Specific page references to the text appear in bold type followed by appropriate comments. Standard logos (shown at left) are used throughout the text to indicate a reference to this appendix.

page 25: All of Section 1.4 is Turbo Pascal specific. Due to implementation differences in Pascal, no attempt is made here to explain the various ways of getting into a Pascal programming environment. It is assumed your instructor will provide this information.

page 38: **Crt** and **ClrScr** are not available in standard Pasal.

page 39: **XOR** is not standard.

page 40: **byte, comp, double, extended, longint, lst, shortint, single, string,** and **word** are not standard.

page 49: **shortint, longint, byte,** and **word** are not available in standard Pascal.

page 50: **single, double, extended,** and **comp** are not available in standard Pascal.

page 52: Standard Pascal simulates strings by using packed arrays. These are examined in Chapter 7.

page 53: **lst** is not required in standard Pascal.

page 55: Most versions of standard Pascal also default to the minimum field width required to print what is specified.

page 65: Overflow is handled a variety of ways in different systems. Some systems give a message, such as ARITHMETIC OVERFLOW; other systems merely assign a meaningless value and continue with the program.

page 67: A variable usually holds a meaningless value until an assignment is made.

page 76: File names are typically included as part of the program heading. When data are obtained for a program, the standard file **input** must be listed. When output is produced, the standard file **output** must be listed. Thus, a typical program heading is

```
PROGRAM <program name> (input, output);
```

When other files are used, the file list must contain them.

page 81: **string** is not a data type in standard Pascal.

page 91: Since **string** is not a data type in standard Pascal, the **string** related functions described in the subsection on **string** functions do not exist in standard Pascal.

page 152: Some implementations do not support the output of Boolean variables.

page 155: The logical operator **XOR** does not exist in standard Pascal.

page 186: **ELSE** is not available as part of a **CASE** statement in standard Pascal. Several implementations use **OTHERWISE** in the same manner that Turbo Pascal uses **ELSE** as part of a **CASE** statement.

page 214: The index of a **FOR** loop may not retain the last value assigned in the loop. The index variable may be assigned a meaningless value once the loop has been completed.

page 264: The creation and use of text files is very system-dependent. If you are not using Turbo Pascal, your instructor will probably need to provide examples and explanations that suit your particular environment.

page 265: **assign** is not available in standard Pascal.

page 266: In standard Pascal, the file variable must also be included as part of the file list in the program heading. Thus, a heading might be

```
PROGRAM FilePrac (input, output, ClassData);
```

page 316: Range-checking errors are not part of most standard Pascal compilers.

page 339: Many programmers and instructors believe a significant weakness of standard Pascal is the absence of a **string** data type. Although strings can be simulated using packed arrays, the work is tedious and must be delayed until after arrays have been studied.

page 342: Strings must be of the same length to be compared in standard Pascal.

page 383: Since standard Pascal simulates strings by using packed arrays of **char**, an array of strings is a two-dimensional array.

page 388: See the standard Pascal note for page 91.

page 432: In standard Pascal, strings are read by reading one character at a time into a packed array. Thus

```
read (DataFile, Student.Name);
```

would be replaced by

```
FOR J := 1 TO 20 DO
  read (DataFile, Student.Name[J]);
```

This procedure could easily be the main part of a procedure for reading strings. For example

```
PROCEDURE StringRead (VAR Data : text;
                      VAR StringChar : string20);
VAR
  J : integer;
BEGIN
  FOR J := 1 TO 20 DO
    read (Data, StringChar[J])
END;
```

This procedure could then be called from the main program by

```
StringRead (DataFile, Student.Name);
```

page 436: See the standard Pascal note for page (432).

page 475: Accessing files in standard Pascal is quite different from working in Turbo Pascal. A brief introduction to file definition and access in standard Pascal follows.

First, we examine the concepts of a *file window* and a *buffer variable.* A file can be visualized as a sequence of components as follows:

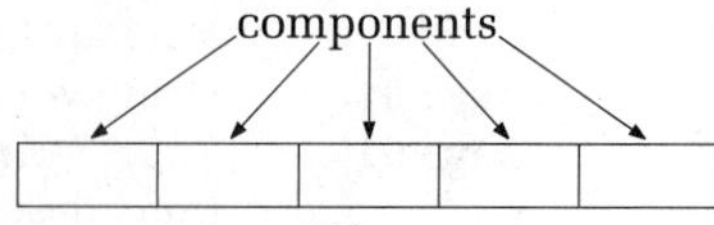

File 1

Only one of these components can be "seen" at a time. An imaginary window is associated with a file, and values can be transferred to (or from) a component of the file only through this window. Thus, the window must be properly positioned before the user attempts to transmit data to or from a component.

This imaginary window, which is called a file window, has no name in Pascal. However, a related concept, called buffer variable, is the actual vehicle through which values are passed to or from the file component. When a file is declared in a program, a buffer variable is automatically declared and available to the programmer. To illustrate, given the following declaration of File A

```
TYPE
  FileInfo = FILE OF integer;
VAR
  FileA : FileInfo;
```

the buffer variable (FileA^ or FileA↑) can be used in the program. The buffer variable is always the file name followed by a caret (^) or an up arrow (↑). Historically, the phrase "up arrow" has been used to refer to buffer variables. However, we will use the caret symbol to designate buffer variables because it is available on computer keyboards (above the 6).

The buffer variable is not declared in the variable declaration section. In general, we have

Declaration	**Buffer Variable**
VAR <file name> : **FILE OF** <data type>;	<file name>^

The buffer variable is of the same data type as one component of the file. It allows the user to access data at the position of the file marker or pointer used when illustrating text files. Although its intended use is for passing values to and from a file, it can be used very much like a regularly declared variable of that type. Specifically, from FileA, FileA^ is a variable of type **integer** and statements such as

```
FileA^ := 21;
Age := FileA^
GetData (FileA^);   (where GetData is a procedure)
```

are appropriate.

page 496: See note for page 495.

page 478: Standard Pascal allows the use of constants when writing to a file. Thus

```
write (FileA, 10);
```

could be used.

page 478: Most versions of Pascal allow values to be written to a file by assigning the desired value to the buffer variable and using the standard procedure **put** with the buffer variable as an argument. We can, for example, store the value 10 in FileA with

```
rewrite (FileA);
FileA^ := 10;
put (FileA);
```

The **put** procedure transfers the value of the buffer variable to the component in the window and then advances the window to the next component.

page 479: In standard Pascal, when a file is open for reading, the value of the file component in the window is automatically assigned to the buffer variable. The window can be advanced to the next file component by a call to the standard procedure

```
get (<file name>);
```

Using the values for FileA as

10	20	30	■

FileA

values can be transferred to the main program by

```
reset (FileA);
N1 := FileA^;
get (FileA);
N2 := FileA^;
get (FileA);
N3 := FileA^;
```

This example of retrieving data is a bit contrived, since we know there are exactly three components before the end-of-file marker. A more realistic retrieval would use the **eof** function; for example

```
reset (FileA);
WHILE NOT eof(FileA) DO
  BEGIN
    .
    .  (process FileA^)
    .
  get (FileA)
END;
```

page 480: Standard Pascal does not permit a file to be open for writing and reading at the same time.

page 483: A comparable procedure in standard Pascal is

```
PROCEDURE Copy (VAR OldFile, NewFile : IntFile);
  BEGIN
    reset (OldFile);
    rewrite (NewFile);
    WHILE NOT eof(OldFile) DO
      BEGIN
        NewFile^ := OldFile^;
        put (NewFile);
        get (OldFile)
      END  {  of WHILE...DO  }
  END;  {  of PROCEDURE Copy  }
```

page 487: In standard Pascal, the variable declaration section would be

```
VAR
  Student : StudentFile;
```

It is not necessary to declare a record variable because Student^ contains the desired structure. Typical field identifiers are

```
Student^.Name
Student^.IDNumber
Student^.Score
Student^.Average
```

page 495: Direct access files are not available in standard Pascal.

page 538: Most implementations of Pascal limit the maximum size of the base type of a set. This limit is such that a base type of **integer** is not allowed. Often the limit is at least 128, so base type **char** and subranges of **integer** within (0..127) can usually be used.

page 558: Graphics are not part of standard Pascal.

page 626: Standard Pascal does not support object-oriented programming (OOP). However, many implementers of Pascal compilers, aware of the increasing trend to use OOP, are beginning to offer object-oriented extensions to their versions of Pascal.

page 683: Pointer variables may be declared by using a caret(^) or an up arrow (↑).

Appendix 9 DOS Utilities Programs/Commands

Several DOS utilities programs are available. Some of the more useful ones are listed here for your convenience. Complete descriptions of these commands and of other available DOS utilities are contained in your DOS Operating Manual. For our purposes, we will separate commands into three categories: general-purpose commands, commands associated with directories, and commands associated with file manipulation.

General-purpose commands

Command	Resulting Action
DATE	Displays the current date
DATE <mmddyy>	Changes to new date
TIME	Displays the current time
TIME <hhmm>	Changes to new time
<Ctrl><Break>	Aborts program execution
<Shift><Prt Sc>	Prints the current screen
<Ctrl><Prt Sc>	Off/on toggle for continuous screen printing
<Ctrl>	Start/stop feature during a continuous screen display

Directory commands

Command	Resulting Action
`DIR`	Displays the current directory of the active drive
`DIR <drive:>`	Displays the directory of the specified drive
`DIR/W`	Displays the directory of the active drive, using a wide format
`DIR *.<extension>`	Displays all files in the current directory with the designated extension; for example, `DIR *.PAS` displays all files with a PAS extension
`CD <directory name>`	Changes to designated directory
`CD..`	Changes to parent of the current directory (back up one level)
`CD\`	Resets to root directory
`MD <directory name>`	Creates (makes) a subdirectory in the current directory
`RD <directory name>`	Deletes (removes) the specified directory; the directory must be empty to be deleted
`FORMAT <drive:>`	Formats the disk in the specified drive; for example, `FORMAT A:` formats the disk in drive A

File commands

Command	Resulting Action
`TYPE <file name>`	Displays the specified file on the screen
`MORE <file name>`	Displays the specified file one screen at a time
`PRINT <file name>`	Prints the designated file
`COPY <source file> <target file>`	Copies a file as specified
`RENAME <old file> <new file>`	Renames a file as specified
`ERASE <file name>`	Erases the specified file

Appendix 10
Turbo Pascal Debugger

Versions 5.0 and higher of Turbo Pascal provide powerful debugging programs to assist you in debugging the programs you write. In this appendix, we discuss several debugging features that may be helpful as you develop increasingly complex programs.

General Notes

For your reference, we list four frequently used keys together with descriptions of their functions:

1. Press <Esc> to close a dialog box.
2. Press <F6> to toggle between or cycle among active windows; for example, Watches—Editor.
3. Press <F7> to step through a program one line at a time. (This is the **Trace into** option on the **Run** menu.)
4. Press <Ctrl><F2> (program reset) to reinitialize the debugging system.

A Sample Program

The following sample program is used as a frame of reference in this appendix. This interactive program accumulates the sum of five integers and then displays the total and average of the numbers entered.

```
Program DebugPrac;

USES
  Crt;

VAR
  Index : integer;
  Sum, Num : integer;
  Average : real;

BEGIN
  ClrScr;
  Sum := 0;
  FOR Index := 1 TO 5 DO
```

```
    BEGIN
      writeln ('Enter an integer and press <Enter>');
      readln (Num);
      Sum := Sum + Num
    END;  {  of FOR loop  }
  Average := Sum / 5;
  writeln ('The total is  ', Sum:10);
  writeln ('The average is ', Average:10:2)
END.
```

Using Trace Into (F7)

The first debugging feature we examine is **Trace into** (<F7>). This option is contained on the **Run** menu, but we use the <F7> key both to access and to process the option. This debugging feature allows us to step through the program one line at a time.

The first time we press the <F7> key, the program in the current work space (edit window) is compiled. If the compilation is successful, an active bar is placed over the BEGIN statement at the start of the processing section, as illustrated in Figure A.1.

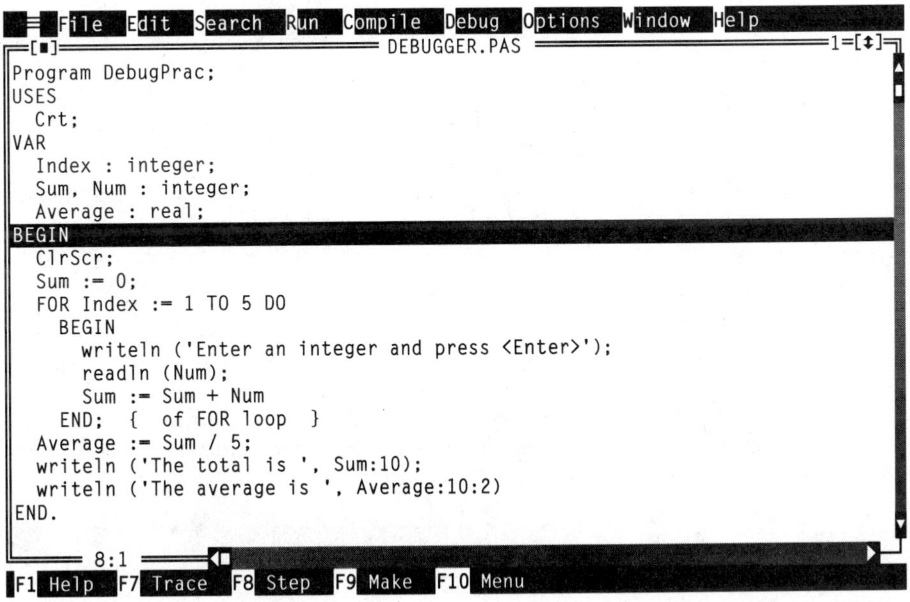

Figure A.1
First use of <F7>

```
 ≡ File  Edit  Search  Run  Compile  Debug  Options  Window  Help
[■]═══════════════════ DEBUGGER.PAS ═══════════════════1=[↕]
Program DebugPrac;
USES
  Crt;
VAR
  Index : integer;
  Sum, Num : integer;
  Average : real;
BEGIN
  ClrScr;
  Sum := 0;
  FOR Index := 1 TO 5 DO
    BEGIN
      writeln ('Enter an integer and press <Enter>');
      readln (Num);
      Sum := Sum + Num
    END;  {  of FOR loop  }
  Average := Sum / 5;
  writeln ('The total is ', Sum:10);
  writeln ('The average is ', Average:10:2)
END.
═══ 8:1 ═══
 F1 Help  F7 Trace  F8 Step  F9 Make  F10 Menu
```

Each time we press <F7>, the line covered by the active bar is executed and the next executable line is highlighted by the active bar. Any **BEGIN** statements other than those at the beginning of a processing section are skipped. If a subprogram is called, the highlight bar goes to the called subprogram in the same order dictated by program execution.

Using our previous sample program, we press <F7> once to compile the program and position the highlight bar at the **BEGIN** statement for the main program. We then press <F7> four more times to highlight the line

```
writeln ('Enter an integer and press <Enter>');
```

as shown in Figure A.2.

We continue pressing <F7> to execute the program one line at a time. Notice how control of the program cycles through the **FOR** loop. Remember we may exit the step-through process by pressing <Ctrl><F2> to reset the debugging system.

Figure A.2
Using <F7> to step through a program

```
 ≡ File  Edit  Search  Run  Compile  Debug  Options  Window  Help
[■]═══════════════════════ DEBUGGER.PAS ═══════════════════════1=[↕]
Program DebugPrac;
USES
  Crt;
VAR
  Index : integer;
  Sum, Num : integer;
  Average : real;
BEGIN
  ClrScr;
  Sum := 0;
  FOR Index := 1 TO 5 DO
    BEGIN
      writeln ('Enter an integer and press <Enter>');
      readln (Num);
      Sum := Sum + Num
    END;  {  of FOR loop  }
  Average := Sum / 5;
  writeln ('The total is ', Sum:10);
  writeln ('The average is ', Average:10:2)
END.
═══13:1 ════
F1 Help  F7 Trace  F8 Step  F9 Make  F10 Menu
```

Using Step Over (<F8>)

A second step-through debugging feature is **Step over** (<F8>) from the **Run** menu. **Step over** (<F8>) works just like **Trace into** (<F7>) except that when control is passed to a subprogram, the active bar goes to the next line of code rather than to the designated subprogram.

Viewing the Output

Several methods can be used to view program output. First, we can press <Alt><F5> at any time to view the User screen. Use of this method provides a full-screen output. We can return to the edit window by pressing either <F5> or <F6>.

A second method is to select **Output** from the **Window** menu, which provides a split screen. The Output window occupies the lower portion of the screen, as shown in Figure A.3.

Figure A.3
Viewing the Output window

```
 ≡ File  Edit  Search  Run  Compile  Debug  Options  Window  Help
─────────────────────── DEBUGGER.PAS ───────────────────────1───
Program DebugPrac;
USES
  Crt;
VAR
  Index : integer;
  Sum, Num : integer;
  Average : real;
BEGIN
  ClrScr;
  Sum := 0;
  FOR Index := 1 TO 5 DO
    BEGIN
      writeln ('Enter an integer and press <Enter>');
      readln (Num);
      Sum := Sum + Num
[■]═══════════════════════ Output ═══════════════════════2=[↑]

F1 Help  ↑↓→← Scroll  F10 Menu
```

We can use <F6> to toggle between the split screen and the edit window. Notice the use of <F6> changes the active window.

The third (and probably the best) method of viewing output while debugging is by using a Watch window, as discussed in the next section.

Using Watch Windows

Watch windows allow us to specify variables and then observe their values as we step through a program using <F7> (or <F8>). A Watch window is activated first by selecting the **Debug** menu and then by using the up/down arrow keys to select the **Watches** menu option. We press <Enter> to get a submenu, as shown in Figure A.4.

Figure A.4
The **Watches** submenu

```
 ≡ File  Edit  Search  Run  Compile  Debug  Options  Window  Help
[■]═══════════════════════ DEB                                 1=[↕]
Program DebugPrac;                Evaluate/modify...  Ctrl-F4
USES                              Watches                   ►
  Crt;                                                      8
VAR                                Add watch...   Ctrl-F7
  Index : integer;                 Delete watch
  Sum, Num : integer;              Edit watch...
  Average : real;                  Remove all watches
BEGIN
  ClrScr;
  Sum := 0;
  FOR Index := 1 TO 5 DO
    BEGIN
      writeln ('Enter an integer and press <Enter>');
      readln (Num);
      Sum := Sum + Num
    END;  {  of FOR loop  }
  Average := Sum / 5;
  writeln ('The total is ', Sum:10);
  writeln ('The average is ', Average:10:2)
END.

═══ 13:1 ═══
F1 Help │ Insert a watch expression into the Watch window
```

We use the up/down arrow keys (or <Ctrl> <F7>) to select the **Add Watch** option of the submenu. We press <Enter> to get an Add Watch dialog box, as shown in Figure A.5.

Figure A.5
Add Watch dialog box

```
 ≡ File  Edit  Search  Run  Compile  Debug  Options  Window  Help
[■]══════════════════════ DEBUGGER.PAS ══════════════════════1=[↕]
Program DebugPrac;
USES
  Crt;
VAR
  Index : integer;
  Sum, Num : integer;
  Average ╔[■]═══════════════ Add Watch ═══════════════╗
BEGIN     ║                                            ║
  ClrScr; ║ Watch expression                           ║
  Sum := 0║ FOR                                   |↓|  ║
  FOR Inde║                                            ║
    BEGIN ║                  OK      Cancel     Help   ║
      writ║                                            ║
      read║                                            ║
      Sum ╚════════════════════════════════════════════╝
    END;  {  of FOR loop  }
  Average := Sum / 5;
  writeln ('The total is ', Sum:10);
  writeln ('The average is ', Average:10:2)
END.

═══ 11:3 ═══
F1 Help │ Enter expression to add as watch
```

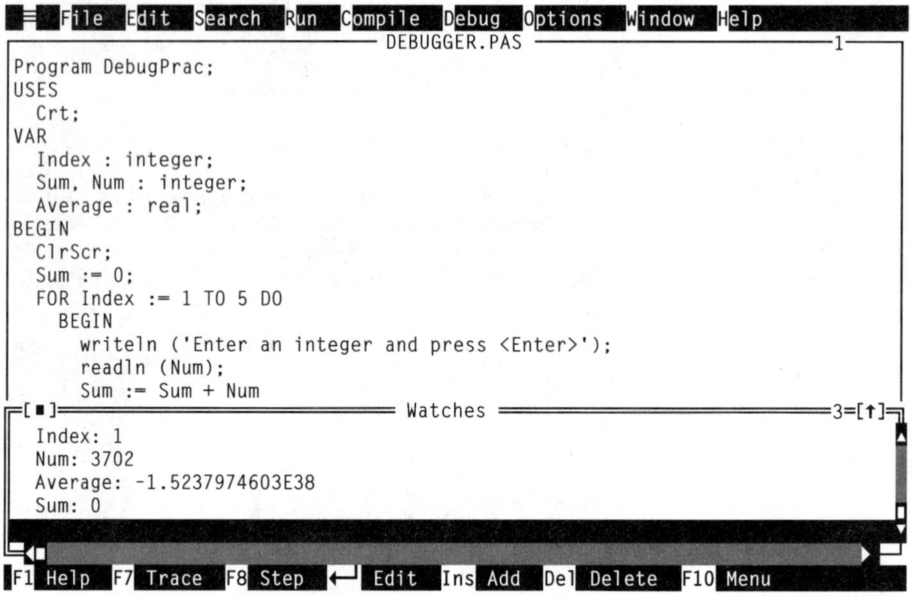

Figure A.6(a)
A Watch window with four variables at initialization

```
 ≡ File Edit Search Run Compile Debug Options Window Help
──────────────────────── DEBUGGER.PAS ─────────────────────────1─
Program DebugPrac;
USES
  Crt;
VAR
  Index : integer;
  Sum, Num : integer;
  Average : real;
BEGIN
  ClrScr;
  Sum := 0;
  FOR Index := 1 TO 5 DO
    BEGIN
      writeln ('Enter an integer and press <Enter>');
      readln (Num);
      Sum := Sum + Num
═[■]══════════════════════ Watches ══════════════════════3=[↑]═
  Index: 1
  Num: 3702
  Average: -1.5237974603E38
  Sum: 0

F1 Help  F7 Trace  F8 Step  ↵ Edit  Ins Add  Del Delete  F10 Menu
```

We then type the desired variable in the line designated for Watch expression and press <Enter> to obtain a split screen. The lower portion of the screen contains by the Watch window, which shows the designated variable with its current value displayed. We canthen use <F7> (or <F8>) to step through the program and watch the values of the designated variable change.

We may also select a variable for the Watch window by placing the cursor below the first letter of the desired variable at any place where the variable appears in the edit window and then pressing <Ctrl> <F7>. This places the desired variable in the Add Watch window. We then press <Enter> to add the specified variable to the Watch window.

Adding More Watches. It is possible for several variables to appear simultaneously in the Watch window. We can add a variable to the Watch window by pressing <Ctrl><F7> or by selecting **Add Watch** from the **Watches** submenu. As before, we type in the desired variable or select it by using the cursor method from the program. In either case, this process will yield another variable in the Watch window. We can repeat this process as often as we wish. Figure A.6(a) illustrates a Watch window in which four variables are specified before program execution begins. Figure A.6(b) illustrates a Watch window with the same four variables after the loop has been executed three times.

Deleting Watches. It is possible to delete any or all variables from the Watch window. If we want to delete a single variable, we use the up/down arrow keys to highlight that variable in the Watch window. Then we select **Delete watch** from the **Watches** submenu and press <Enter>, and the desired variable is deleted from the Watch window.

We may also remove all variables from the Watch window. If we select **Remove all watches** from the **Watches** submenu and press <Enter>, an empty Watch window results.

Breakpoints

Occasionally, we may wish to run parts of a program at regular speed and then slow down to step through other parts of the program. For example, we may know a loop works correctly but may want to check the program carefully after the loop is completed. We can do this by setting *breakpoints* in the program.

Setting Breakpoints. A breakpoint can be set in a program in one of two ways. In either case, the cursor first must be positioned in the edit window on the line which is to be used

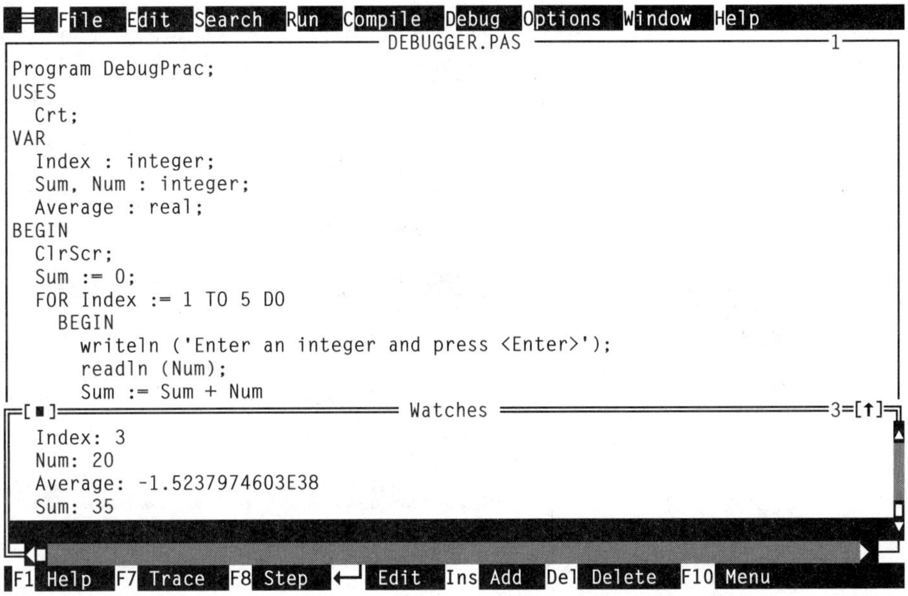

Figure A.6(b)
A Watch window with four variables during program execution

```
 ≡ File Edit Search Run Compile Debug Options Window Help
┌──────────────────────── DEBUGGER.PAS ─────────────────────1──┐
Program DebugPrac;
USES
  Crt;
VAR
  Index : integer;
  Sum, Num : integer;
  Average : real;
BEGIN
  ClrScr;
  Sum := 0;
  FOR Index := 1 TO 5 DO
    BEGIN
      writeln ('Enter an integer and press <Enter>');
      readln (Num);
      Sum := Sum + Num
=[■]==================== Watches ==========================3=[↑]=
  Index: 3
  Num: 20
  Average: -1.5237974603E38
  Sum: 35

F1 Help  F7 Trace  F8 Step  ←┘ Edit  Ins Add  Del Delete  F10 Menu
```

as a breakpoint. We then press <Ctrl> <F8> or select **Toggle breakpoint** from the **Debug** menu. Either action causes the designated line to be highlighted and to serve as a breakpoint when the program is executed at regular speed.

To illustrate, in our sample program, the first line after the **FOR** loop is set as a breakpoint, as shown in Figure A.7.

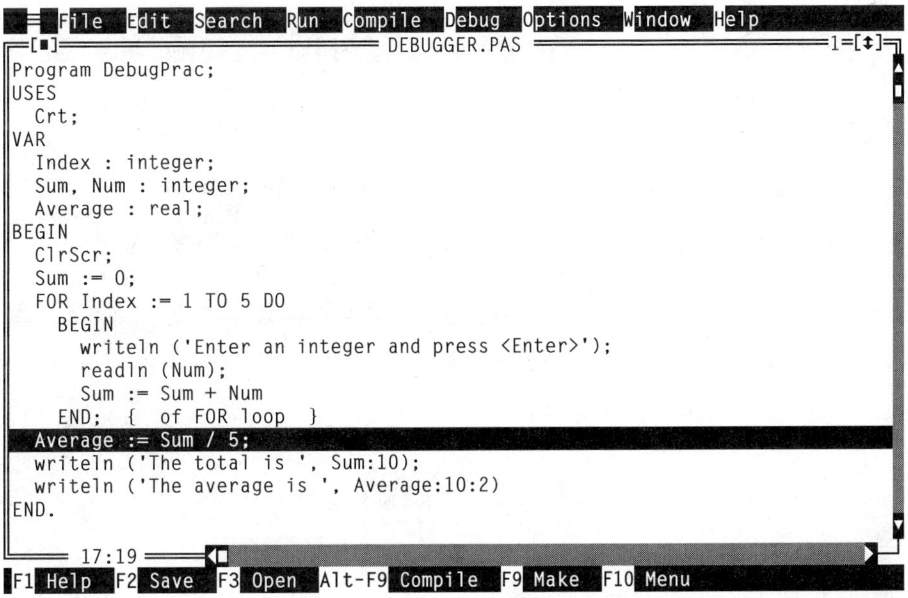

Figure A.7
Setting a breakpoint

```
 ≡ File Edit Search Run Compile Debug Options Window Help
=[■]===================== DEBUGGER.PAS ===================1=[↕]=
Program DebugPrac;
USES
  Crt;
VAR
  Index : integer;
  Sum, Num : integer;
  Average : real;
BEGIN
  ClrScr;
  Sum := 0;
  FOR Index := 1 TO 5 DO
    BEGIN
      writeln ('Enter an integer and press <Enter>');
      readln (Num);
      Sum := Sum + Num
    END;  {  of FOR loop  }
  Average := Sum / 5;
  writeln ('The total is ', Sum:10);
  writeln ('The average is ', Average:10:2)
END.

==== 17:19 ====
F1 Help  F2 Save  F3 Open  Alt-F9 Compile  F9 Make  F10 Menu
```

When this program is run at normal speed (<Ctrl> <F9>), execution terminates with the last line preceding the designated breakpoint line. We can then use <F7> or <F8> to step through lines as before. At any point, of course, we can use <Ctrl> <F9> to resume execution at normal speed.

Removing Breakpoints. Breakpoints may be removed by repeating the process used to set a breakpoint because the breakpoint switch is actually a toggle. Thus, if the cursor is moved to a line designated as a breakpoint and <Ctrl> <F8> is pressed, the line is no longer a breakpoint.

Multiple Breakpoints. Multiple breakpoints can be established by repeating the process for setting a single breakpoint. As many as 21 breakpoints can be designated in a program. Each line serving as a breakpoint is highlighted. Whenever one of these lines is deselected, the highlight bar is removed from that line.

Working with Breakpoints. It is possible to work with breakpoints in a more sophisticated manner than has been shown thus far by using the **Breakpoints . . .** option from the **Debug** menu. For purposes of illustration, two breakpoints were set in the sample program and then the **Breakpoints . . .** option was selected to produce the display shown in Figure A.8.

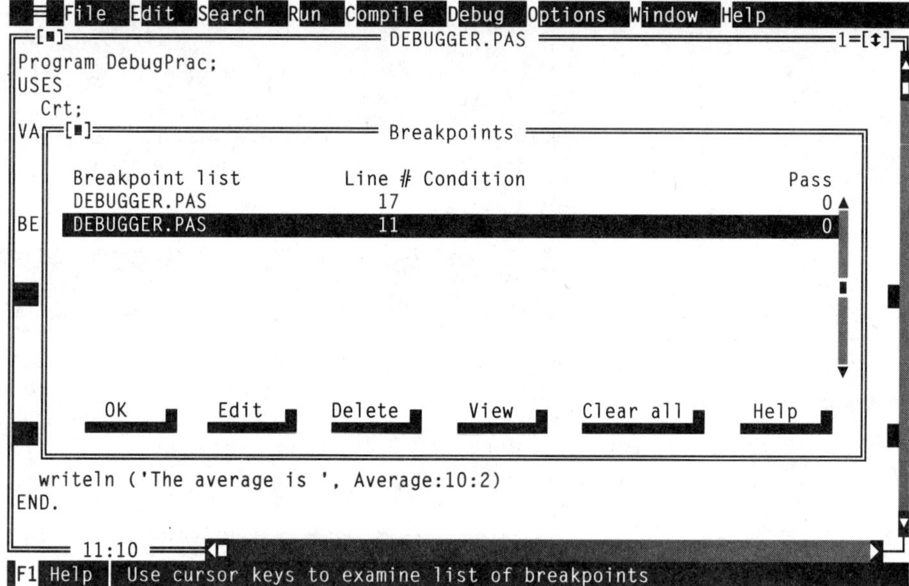

Figure A.8
A dialog box using **Breakpoints . . .** from the **Debug** menu

Looking at the bottom of the dialog box, notice it is possible to accept, edit, delete, view, or clear all breakpoints. To edit or delete a breakpoint, we first highlight the breakpoint by using the up/down arrow keys. We then use the mouse (or tab key) to specify the desired option. Once the option is selected, we press <Enter> to achieve the desired result.

Of the options listed at the bottom of the **Breakpoints . . .** dialog box, the **Edit** option requires some elaboration. If we select this option, we obtain another dialog box similar to the one shown in Figure A.9.

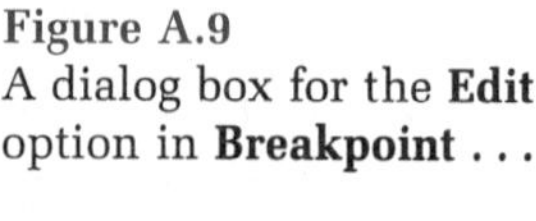
Figure A.9
A dialog box for the **Edit** option in **Breakpoint . . .**

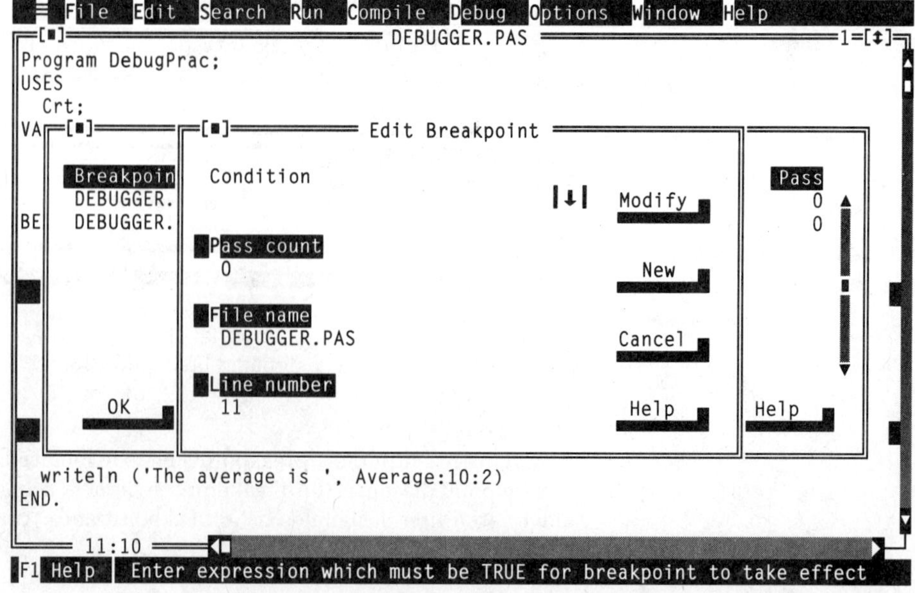

We can use this dialog box to add new breakpoints. We use the mouse (or tab key) to move to the Line number field. We then enter the new line number and use the mouse (or tab key) to select New. This causes the specified line to become a new breakpoint.

The Condition field contains any Boolean conditions that were set for the specified line. We can change these conditions using any valid Boolean condition. Execution then terminates only when the prescribed Boolean condition is **true.**

The Pass count field is used to specify how many times the designated breakpoint line should be skipped before program execution is terminated. This is sometimes helpful when debugging loops.

After all changes are made, we select Modify and press <Enter> to record the changes.

Leaving the Debugging Environment

When we have finished debugging our program, we press <Ctrl> <F2> to reset it. This releases all memory that was set aside during the debugging session.

Appendix 11 GOTO Statement

In your work with computers, you may have heard of a **GOTO** statement. This statement allows a programmer to transfer control within a program. The **GOTO** statement has the effect of an immediate, unconditional transfer to an indicated designation. You should not use **GOTO** statements in a Turbo Pascal program, but for the sake of completeness, you should be aware of their existence and how they work.

Early programming languages needed a branching statement; therefore, both FORTRAN and BASIC were designed using a **GOTO** statement for branching. Subsequent languages, particularly Pascal, included more sophisticated branching and looping statements. These statements led to an emphasis on structured programming, which is easier to design and read. If you are a beginning programmer and have not used the **GOTO** statement in another language, you should continue to develop your skills without including this statement. If you have already written programs in a language that uses **GOTO** statements, you should still attempt to write all Turbo Pascal programs without **GOTO** statements.

One instance in which **GOTO** statements might be appropriate is in making a quick exit from some part of the program. For example, if we are getting data from somewhere within a program and we wish to check for valid data, our design could include a program segment such as

```
read data
IF (<bad data>) THEN
  BEGIN
    <write error message>;
    GOTO <end of program>
  END
ELSE
  <process data>
```

Keeping the previous admonitions about the use of **GOTO** statements in mind, we now briefly examine the form, syntax, and flow of control for these statements.

GOTO statements require the use of numerically labeled statements. Thus, our program could contain

```
LABEL
  <label 1>,
  <label 2>;
      .
      .
      .
```

```
GOTO 100;
      .
      .
      .
100 : <program statement>;
      .
      .
      .
```

All labels must be declared in a label declaration section that precedes the constant definition section in a program. Each label can be used only for a single program statement. The form for the label declaration section is

```
LABEL
  ⟨label 1⟩,
  ⟨label 2⟩,
      .
      .
      .
  ⟨label n⟩;
```

The correct form for a **GOTO** statement is

```
GOTO ⟨numeric label⟩;
```

where numeric label is an integer from 1 to 9999, inclusive. Declared labels are then used with appropriate statements in a program. The proper syntax for labeling a statement is

```
⟨label⟩ : ⟨program statement⟩;
```

Consider the fragment of code

```
BEGIN
  read (Num);
  IF Num < 0 THEN
    GOTO 100
  ELSE
    Sum := Sum + Num;
        .
        .
        .
  100 : writeln ('Data include a negative number.':40)
END.
```

In this instance, when a negative number is encountered as a data item, an appropriate message is printed and the program is terminated.

GOTO statements permit the immediate transfer out of any control structure. As stated, we recommend you avoid the use of this statement whenever possible. If you must use it, use it only to make an immediate exit from some point in the program; never use it to construct a loop in Turbo Pascal.

Glossary

abstract data type (ADT) A form of abstraction that arises from the use of defined types. An ADT consists of a class of objects, a defined set of properties of those objects, and a set of operations for processing the objects.

accumulator A variable used for the purpose of summing successive values of some other variable.

actual parameter A variable or expression contained in a procedure or function call and passed to that procedure or function. *See also* **formal parameter.**

address (of a memory location) an integer value that the computer can use to reference a location. *See also* **value.**

algorithm A finite sequence of effective statements that, when applied to the problem, will solve it.

ancestor An object type that is used by a subsequently defined object type. See also **descendant.**

application software Programs designed for a specific use.

argument A value or expression passed in a function or procedure call.

arithmetic/logic unit (ALU) The part of the central processing unit (CPU) that performs arithmetic operations and evaluates expressions.

array A structured variable designed to handle data of the same type.

array index The relative position of the components of an array.

array of records An array with the component type **record.**

ASCII collating sequence The American Standard Code for Information Interchange ordering for a character set.

assembly language A computer language that allows words and symbols to be used in an unsophisticated manner to accomplish simple tasks. Also referred to as *low-level language.*

assertion Special comments used with selection and repetition that state what is expected to happen and when certain conditions will hold.

assignment statement A method of putting values into memory locations.

batch input Input for a program being run in batch mode. Also referred to as *stream input.*

batch processing A technique of executing the program and data from a file that has been created. User interaction with the computer is not required during execution. Also referred to as *stream input.*

BEGIN. . .END block The segment of code between **BEGIN** and **END** that is treated as a single statement when a compound statement is executed within a program.

binary digit A digit, either 0 or 1, in the binary number system. Program instructions are stored in memory using a sequence of binary digits. Binary digits are called *bits.*

binary file Nontext files where information is stored using binary representation for each component.

binary search The process of examining a middle value of a sorted array to see which half of the array contains the value in question and halving that half until the value is located.

binary search tree A binary tree such that the information in the key field of any node (1) is greater than the information in the key field of any node of its left child and any of its children and (2) is less than the information in the key field of any node of its right child and any of its children.

binary tree A tree such that each node can point to at most two children.

bit *See* **binary digit.**

bit-mapped font The default font for text display. Each character appears in an 8 × 8 pixel square. See also **stroked font.**

block A program in Turbo Pascal can be thought of as a heading and a block. The block contains an optional declaration part and a compound statement. The block structure for a subprogram is a subblock. *See also* **subblock.**

Boolean expression An expression that has a value of either true or false. *See also* **compound Boolean expression** and **simple Boolean expression.**

bottom-up testing Independent testing of modules.

bubble sort A sorting method that rearranges elements of an array until they are in either ascending or descending order. Consecutive elements are compared to move (bubble) the elements to the top or bottom, accordingly, during each pass. *See also* **index sort, insertion sort, quick sort,** and **selection sort.**

built-in function *See* **standard function.**

bus A group of wires imprinted on a circuit board to facilitate communication between components of a computer.

byte A sequence of bits used to encode a character in memory. *See also* **word.**

call Any reference to a subprogram by an executable statement. Also referred to as *invoke.*

central processing unit (CPU) A major hardware component that consists of the arithmetic/logic unit (ALU) and the control unit.

character set The list of characters available for data and program statements. *See also* **collating sequence.**

children Nodes pointed to by an element in a tree.

class An object type that has descendants. See also **subclass.**

closing a file The use of the procedure **close** when finished with a file.

code (writing) The process of writing executable statements that are part of a program to solve a problem.

cohesive subprogram A subprogram designed to accomplish a single task.

collating sequence The particular order sequence for a character set used by a machine. *See also* **ASCII collating sequence.**

comment A nonexecutable statement used to make a program more readable.

compatible type Variables that have the same base type. A value parameter and its argument must be of compatible type. *See also* **identical type.**

compilation error An error detected when the program is being compiled. A complete list of compilation error messages is set forth in Appendix 5. *See also* **design error, logic error, run-time error,** and **syntax error.**

compiler A computer program that automatically converts instructions in a high-level language to machine language.

compiler directive A special comment which controls the compiler.

component of a file One element of the file data type.

component of a linked list *See* **node.**

component of an array One element of the array data type.

compound Boolean expression The complete expression when logical connectives and negation are used to generate Boolean values. *See also* **Boolean expression** and **simple Boolean expression.**

compound statement The use of the reserved words **BEGIN** and **END** to make several simple statements into a single compound statement.

concatenation The process of joining strings one after another.

conditional statement *See* **selection statement.**

constant The contents of a memory location that cannot be changed in the body of the program.

constant definition section The section in which program constants are defined for subsequent use.

constructor A method for initializing objects that contain virtual methods.

control structure A structure that controls the flow of execution of program statements.

control unit The part of the central processing unit (CPU) that controls the operation of the rest of the computer.

counter A variable used to count the number of times some process is completed.

current pointer An invisible indicator of the current pixel position when in graphics mode.

data The particular characters that are used to represent information in a form suitable for storage, processing, and communication.

data abstraction The separation between the conceptual definition of a data structure and its eventual implementation.

data type A formal description of the set of values that a variable can have. Also referred to as *type.*

data validation The process of examining data prior to its use in a program.

debugging The process of eliminating errors or "bugs" from a program.

declaration section The section used to declare (name) all symbolic constants, data types, variables, and subprograms that are necessary to the program.

decrement To decrease the value of a variable.

descendant An object type that uses a previously defined object type. See also **ancestor.**

design error An error such that a program runs but produces unexpected results. Also referred to as a *logic error. See also* **compilation error, run-time error,** and **syntax error.**

destructor An object method for releasing reserved memory.

difference The difference of set A and set B is A – B, where A – B contains the elements that are in A but are not in B. *See also* **intersection, subset,** and **union.**

direct access files Files whose components can be accessed specifically rather than by sequential access. *See also* **sequential access files.**

dynamic structure A data structure that may expand or contract during execution of a program.

dynamic variable Frequently designed as Ptr^ or Ptr↑, a dynamic variable is a variable accessed by a pointer variable.

early binding The process of making connections to static methods at compile time. See also **late binding.**

echo checking A debugging technique in which values of variables and input data are displayed during program execution.

edit window The main portion of the screen used when entering or editing a program.

effective statement A clear, unambiguous instruction that can be carried out.

element of an array *See* **component of an array.**

element of a set A value that has been assigned to a set.

empty set A set containing no elements. Also called a *null set.*

empty statement A semicolon used to indicate that no action is to be taken. Also referred to as a *null statement.*

empty string A string containing no characters.

encapsulation The process of hiding the implementation details of a subprogram.

end-of-file marker (eof) A special marker inserted by the machine to indicate the end of the data file. In this text, **eof** is represented by a black square (■).

end-of-line marker (eoln) A special marker inserted by the machine to indicate the end of a line in the data. In this text, **eoln** is represented by a black column (▮).

entrance controlled loop *See* **pretest loop.**

enumerated data type A data type that is defined in the **TYPE** definition section by the programmer. Also referred to as *user-defined data type.*

error *See* **compilation error, design error, logic error, run-time error,** and **syntax error.**

executable section Contains the statements that cause the computer to do something. Starts with the reserved word **BEGIN** and concludes with the reserved word **END.**

executable statement The basic unit of grammar in Turbo Pascal, consisting of valid identifiers, standard identifiers, reserved words, numbers, and/or characters together with appropriate punctuation.

execute To perform a program step-by-step.

exit controlled loop *See* **posttest loop.**

exponential form *See* **floating point.**

extended IF statement Nested selection in which additional **IF . . . THEN . . . ELSE** statements are used in the **ELSE** option. *See also* **nested IF statement.**

external file A file used to store data in secondary storage between runs of a program. *See also* **internal file.**

field A component of a record.

field width The phrase used to describe the number of columns used for various output. *See also* **formatting.**

FIFO structure First-in, first-out structure. *See* **queue.**

file A data structure that consists of a sequence of components that are all of the same type.

fixed part The part of a record structure in which the number and type of data fields are fixed for all records of a particular type. *See also* **variant part.**

fixed-point The method of writing decimal numbers in which the decimal is placed where it belongs in the number. *See also* **floating point.**

fixed repetition loop A loop used when it is known in advance the number of times a segment of code needs to be repeated. **FOR . . . TO . . . DO** is a fixed repetition loop. Also referred to as an *iterated loop.*

floating-point A method for writing numbers in scientific notation to accommodate numbers that may have very large or very small values. Exactly one nonzero digit must appear on the left of the decimal. *See also* **fixed point.**

FOR loop A fixed repetition loop that causes a fragment of code to be executed a predetermined number of times. **FOR . . . TO . . . DO** and **FOR . . . DOWNTO . . . DO** are **FOR** loops.

formal parameter A variable that is declared and used in a procedure or function declaration but is replaced by an actual parameter when the procedure or function is called.

formatting Designating the desired field width when printing integers, reals, Boolean values, and character strings. *See also* **field width.**

forward reference A method of listing a subprogram heading without writing the subprogram. This allows a subprogram to be referenced by other subprograms before it appears as a complete subprogram in the list of subprograms.

function *See* **standard function** and **user-defined function.**

global identifier An identifier that can be used by the main program and all subprograms in a program. Also referred to as a *global variable.*

global variable *See* **global identifier.**

hardware The actual computing machine and its support devices.

hashing The process of associating a field of a record with the record's relative position in a file. *See also* **direct access files.**

higher-dimensional array An array of more than two dimensions.

high-level language Any programming language that uses words and symbols to make it relatively easy to read and write a program. *See also* **assembly language** and **machine language.**

high resolution Graphics displays that use more pixels than are available in medium resolution.

hot keys Function keys that are used instead of key-stroke sequences to accomplish tasks. Also called *quick keys.*

identical type Variables that are declared with the same type identifier. A variable parameter and its argument must be of identical type. *See also* **compatible type.**

identifiers Words that must be created according to a well-defined set of rules but that can have any meaning subject to these rules. *See also* **standard identifiers.**

implementation section The private part of a unit. It contains implementation details. *see also* **unit.**

index *See* **array index** or **loop index.**

index sort A sorting method that sorts an array by ordering the indices of the components rather than by exchanging the components.

index type The data type used to specify the range for the index of an array. The index type can be any ordinal data type that specifies an initial and a final value.
infinite loop A loop in which the controlling condition is not changed in a manner that allows the loop to terminate.
inheritance The property of a new object type that has access to the data fields and methods of a previously defined object type. *See also* **inherits.**
inherits The process of making the data fields and methods of a previously defined object type available to a newly defined type. *See also* **inheritance.**
input Data obtained by a program during its execution. *See also* **batch input** and **interactive input. See also nonlocal identifier.**
input assertion A precondition for a loop.
input device A device that provides information to the computer. Typical devices are keyboards, disk drives, card readers, and tape drives. *See also* **I/O device** and **output device.**
input statements Procedures **read** and **readln** which are used to obtain input.
insertion sort A sorting method that sorts an array of elements in either ascending or descending order, starting with an empty array and inserting elements one at a time in their proper order. *See also* **bubble sort, index sort, quick sort,** and **selection sort.**
instance A declared identifier of an object type. *See also* **instantiation.**
instantiation Declaring a variable of a defined object type. *See also* **instance.**
integer arithmetic operations Operations allowed on data of type **integer**, which include addition, subtraction, multiplication, **MOD,** and **DIV** to produce integer answers.
interactive input A method of getting data into the program from the keyboard. User interaction is required during execution.
interactive program A program that requires the user to enter data from a keyboard.
interface A formal statement of how communication occurs between subprograms, the main driver, and other subprograms.
interface section The public part of a unit. It contains public declarations available to users of a unit. *See also* **unit.**
internal file A file that is used only for processing and is not saved in secondary storage. Also referred to as a *temporary* or *scratch file. See also* **external file.**
intersection The intersection of set A and set B is A * B, where A * B contains the elements that are in both A and B. *See also* **difference, subset,** and **union.**
invariant expression An assertion that is true before the loop and after each iteration of the loop.
invoke *See* **call.**
I/O device Any device that allows information to be transmitted to or from a computer. *See also* **input device** and **output device.**
iterated loop *See* **fixed repetition loop.**
iteration *See* **loops.**
keywords Either reserved words or predefined identifiers.
late binding The process of making connections to virtual methods at run time. *See also* **early binding.**
leaf In a tree, a node that has no children.
length of an array The number of components of an array.
LIFO Last-in, first-out structure. *See* **stack.**
linear search *See* **sequential search.**
linked list A list of data items in which each item is linked to the next one by means of a pointer.
local identifier An identifier that is restricted to use within a subblock of a program. Also referred to as a *local variable. See also* **nonlocal identifier.**
local variable *See* **local identifier.**
logical operator Either logical connective **(AND, OR)** or negation **(NOT).**
logic error *See* **design error.**
loop index Variable used for control values in a **FOR** loop.
loop invariant An assertion that expresses a relationship between variables that remains constant throughout all iterations of the loop.
loops Program statements that cause a process to be repeated. *See also* **FOR loop, REPEAT . . . UNTIL loop,** and **WHILE . . . DO loop.**
loop variant An assertion that changes in terms of truth between the first and final execution of the loop.
loop verification The process of guaranteeing that a loop performs its intended task.
low-level language *See* **assembly language.**
machine language The language used directly by the computer in all its calculations and processing.
main block The part of a program that consists of both the declaration and executable sections.
main driver The main program when subprograms are used to accomplish specific tasks. *See* **executable section.**
mainframe Large computers typically used by major companies and universities. *See also* **microcomputer** and **minicomputer.**
main (primary) memory Memory contained in the computer. *See also* **memory** and **secondary memory device.**
main unit The central processing unit (CPU) and the main (primary) memory of a computer, hooked to an input device and an output device.
master file An existing external file.
maxint The largest integer constant available to a particular system.
medium resolution Graphics displays using screens that are 320 × 200 pixels.
memory The ordered sequence of storage cells that can be accessed by address. The instructions and variables of a program are temporarily held here while the program is executed. *See also* **main memory** and **secondary memory device.**
memory location A storage cell that can be accessed by address. *See also* **memory.**

menu bar The shaded bar at the top of the screen.

merge The process of combining lists; typically refers to files or arrays.

method An operation, listed in an object, that can be performed on a data field.

microcomputer A personal computer with relatively limited memory, generally used by one person at a time. *See also* **mainframe** and **minicomputer.**

minicomputer A small version of a mainframe computer that can be used by several people at once. *See also* **mainframe** and **microcomputer.**

mixed mode An expression containing data of both **integer** and **real** types; the value will be given as a real, not as an integer.

modular development The process of developing an algorithm using modules. *See also* **module.**

modularity The property possessed by a program that is written using modules.

module An independent unit that is part of a larger development; usually a procedure or function. *See also* **modular development.**

module specifications A description of data received, information returned, and logic used in the module.

negation The use of the logical operator **NOT** to negate the Boolean value of an expression.

nested IF statement A selection statement used within another selection statement. *See also* **extended IF statement.**

nested loop A loop that appears as one of the statements in the body of another loop.

nested record A record that appears as a field in another record.

nested selection Any combination of selection statements within another selection statement. *See also* **selection statement.**

nested subprograms A function or procedure within another function or procedure.

node One data item in a linked list.

nonlocal identifier An identifier used in a block in which the identifier was not declared. *See also* **local identifier.**

null set *See* **empty set.**

null statement *See* **empty statement.**

object In object-oriented programming, a structure that contains fields for data together with a list of operations that can be performed on the data fields.

object code *See* **object program.**

object-oriented programming An extension of a programming language. Objects are defined and utilized for software development. *See also* **object.**

object program The machine code version of the source program. Also referred to as *object code.*

opened for reading Positions a pointer at the beginning of a file for the purpose of reading from the file.

opened for writing Positions a pointer at the beginning of a file for the purpose of writing to the file.

opening a file Positions a pointer at the beginning of a file. *See also* **opened for reading,** and **opened for writing.**

operating system A large program that allows the user to communicate with the hardware.

ordinal data type A data type ordered in some association with the integers; each integer is the ordinal of its associated character.

output Information that is produced by a program.

output assertion A postcondition for a loop.

output device A device that allows the user to see the results of a program; typically a monitor or printer. *See also* **input device** and **I/O device.**

overflow In arithmetic operations, if a value is too large for the computer's memory location, a meaningless value may be assigned to avoid an error message. *See also* **underflow.**

override The process of using the same identifier for a method in a descendant object type.

packed array An array in which data is placed in consecutive bytes.

parallel arrays Arrays of the same length but with different component data types.

parameter *See* **argument.**

parameter directive A compiler directive which causes the compiler to include the named file in the compilation. *See also* **compiler directive.**

parameter list A list of parameters. An actual parameter list is contained in the procedure or function call. A formal parameter list is contained in the procedure or function heading.

parent In a tree, the node that is pointing to its children.

passed by reference When variable parameters are used in subprograms.

peripheral memory *See* **secondary memory device** and **memory.**

picture element *See* **pixel.**

pixel The smallest picture element on a screen display.

pointer variable Frequently designated as Ptr, a pointer variable contains the address of a memory location. *See also* **address** and **dynamic variable.**

polymorphism Giving an action one name that is shared up and down an object hierarchy. Each object in the heirarchy may implement the action in a manner appropriate to itself.

pop A procedure to delete a node from a linked list.

postcondition An assertion written after a segment of code.

posttest loop A loop in which the control condition is tested after the loop is executed. **REPEAT . . . UNTIL** is a posttest loop. Also referred to as an *exit controlled loop.*

precondition An assertion written before a particular statement.

pretest condition A condition that controls whether or not the body of the loop is executed before going through the loop.

pretest loop A loop in which the control condition is tested before the loop is executed. **WHILE . . . DO** is a pretest loop. Also referred to as an *entrance controlled loop.*

primary memory *See* **main memory** and **memory.**

procedural abstraction The process of considering only what a procedure is to do rather than the details of the procedure.

procedure A subprogram designed to perform a specific task as part of a larger program. Procedures are not limited to returning a single value to the main program.

program A set of instructions that tells the machine (the hardware) what to do.

program heading The first statement of any Turbo Pascal program; it must contain the reserved word **PROGRAM.**

programming language Formal language that computer scientists use to give instructions to the computer.

program proof An analysis of a program that attempts to verify the correctness of program results.

program protection A method of using selection statements to guard against unexpected results.

program walk through The process of carefully following, using pencil and paper, the steps the computer uses to solve the problem given in a program. Also referred to as a *trace.*

prompt A marker on the terminal screen that requests input data.

protection *See* **program protection.**

pseudocode A stylized, half-English, half-code language written in English but that suggests Pascal code.

push A procedure for adding a node to the beginning of a linked list.

queue A dynamic data structure in which elements are entered from one end and removed from the other end. Also referred to as a *FIFO structure.*

quick keys *See* **hot keys.**

quick sort A relatively fast sorting technique that uses recursion. *See also* **bubble sort, index sort, insertion sort,** and **selection sort.**

random access files *See* **direct access files.**

reading from a file Retrieving data from a file.

real arithmetic operations Operations allowed on data of type **real,** including addition, subtraction, multiplication, and division.

record A data structure that is a collection of fields that may be treated as a whole or that allows the user to work with individual fields.

recursion The process of a subprogram calling itself. A clearly defined stopping state must exist. Any recursive subprogram can be rewritten using iteration.

recursive step A well-defined step that leads to the stopping state in the recursive process.

recursive subprogram *See* **recursion.**

relational operator An operator used to compare data items of the same type.

REPEAT . . . UNTIL loop A posttest loop that examines a Boolean expression after causing a fragment to be executed. *See also* **FOR loop, loops,** and **WHILE . . . DO loop.**

repetition *See* **loops.**

reserved words Words that have predefined meanings that cannot be changed. Reserved words are highlighted in the text in capital boldface print; a list of reserved words in Turbo Pascal appears in Appendix 1.

return type The data type for a function name.

robust The state in which a program is completely protected against all possible crashes from bad data and unexpected values.

root The first or top node in a tree.

run-time error An error that is detected after compilation is complete when an error message results instead of the correct output. *See also* **compilation error, design error, logic error,** and **syntax error.**

scope of identifier The largest block in which the identifier is available.

scratch file *See* **internal file.**

secondary memory device An auxiliary device for memory; usually a disk or magnetic tape. Also referred to as *peripheral memory. See also* **main memory** and **memory.**

selection sort A sorting algorithm that sorts the components of an array in either ascending or descending order. This process puts the smallest or largest element in the top position and repeats the process on the remaining array components. *See also* **bubble sort, index sort, insertion sort,** and **quick sort.**

selection statement A control statement that selects some particular logical path based upon the value of an expression. Also referred to as a *conditional statement.*

self-documenting code Code that is written using descriptive identifiers.

self parameter An invisible parameter that links an object and its methods in scope.

sending a message In object-oriented programming, the process of using methods of the object to access data fields.

sentinel value A special value that indicates the end of a set of data or of a process.

sequential access files Files whose components are accessed by starting with the first component and then moving sequentially through the file. *See also* **direct access files.**

sequential algorithm *See* **straight-line algorithm.**

sequential search The process of searching a list by examining the first component and then examining successive components in the order in which they occur. Also referred to as *linear search.*

set A structured data type that consists of a collection of distinct elements from an indicated base type, which must be ordinal.

side effect An unintentional change in a variable that results from some action taken in a program.

simple Boolean expression An expression in which two numbers or variable values are compared using a single relational operator. *See also* **Boolean expression** and **compound Boolean expression.**

software Programs that make the machine (the hardware) do something, such as word processing, data-base management, or games.

software engineering The process of developing and maintaining large software systems.

software system life cycle The development, maintenance, and demise of a software system. Phases include analysis, design, coding, testing/verification, maintenance, and obsolescence.

sort merge The process of repeatedly subdividing a long list, sorting shorter lists, and then merging them to obtain a single sorted list.

source program A program written by a programmer. *See also* **system software.**

stack A dynamic data structure which can be accessed from only one end. Also referred to as a *LIFO structure.*

standard function A built-in function available in most versions of Pascal.

standard identifiers Predefined words whose meanings can be changed if needed. Standard identifiers are highlighted in the text in lowercase boldface print; a list of standard identifiers in Turbo Pascal appears in Appendix 2.

standard simple types The predefined data types **boolean, char, integer,** and **real.**

static method The method by which all connections, allocations, and references are resolved at compilation time. *See also* **virtual method.**

static variable A variable of a size (for example, array length) that is fixed at compilation time. A certain memory area is reserved for each variable, and this location is retained for the declared variable as long as the program or subprogram in which the variable is defined is active.

stepwise refinement The process of repeatedly subdividing tasks into subtasks until each subtask is easily accomplished. *See also* **structured programming** and **top-down design.**

stopping state The well-defined termination of a recursive process.

straight-line algorithm An algorithm that consists of a sequence of simple tasks. Also referred to as *sequential algorithm.*

stream input *See* **batch input.**

string An abbreviated name for a string constant.

string constant One or more characters used as a constant in a program.

string data type A data type that permits a sequence of characters. The **string** data type is not available in standard Pascal but can be simulated using a packed array of characters.

stroked font Any of the four nondefault fonts. Characters do not appear in 8 × 8 pixel squares.

structure chart A graphic method of indicating the relationship between modules when designing the solution to a problem.

structured programming Programming that parallels a solution to a problem achieved by top-down design. *See also* **stepwise refinement** and **top-down design.**

stub program A no-frills, simple, and often incomplete version of a final program.

subblock A block structure for a subprogram. *See also* **block.**

subclass The collection of the immediate descendants of an object type. *See also* **class.**

subprogram A program within a program. Procedures and functions are subprograms.

subrange The defined subset of values of an existing ordinal data type.

subscript *See* **array index** or **loop index.**

subset Set A is a subset of set B if all the elements in A are also in B. *See also* **difference, intersection,** and **union.**

switch directive A compiler directive which acts as a toggle. *See also* **compiler directive.**

syntax The formal rules governing construction of valid statements.

syntax diagramming A method used to formally describe the legal syntax of language structures; syntax diagrams are given in Appendix 3.

syntax error An error in the spelling, punctuation, or placement of certain key symbols in a program. *See also* **compilation error, design error, logic error,** and **run-time error.**

system software The programs that allow users to write and execute other programs, including operating systems such as DOS.

tag field A field used in defining variant records. Values of the tag field determine the variant record structure.

temporary file *See* **internal file.**

test program A short program written to provide an answer to a specific question.

text file A file of characters that is divided into lines.

top-down design A design methodology for solving a problem whereby the problem is first stated and the main task is then subdivided into major subtasks. Each subtask is then subdivided into smaller subtasks. This process is repeated until each remaining subtask can be easily solved. *See also* **stepwise refinement** and **structured programming.**

trace *See* **program walk through.**

transaction file A file containing changes to be made in a master file.

tree A dynamic data structure consisting of a special node (a root) that points to zero or more other nodes, each of which points to zero or more other nodes, and so on.

two-dimensional array An array in which each element is accessed by a reference to a pair of indices.

two-way merge The process of merging two sorted lists.

type *See* **data type.**

underflow If an arithmetic value is too small to be represented by a computer, the value is automatically replaced by zero. *See also* **overflow.**

union The union of set A and set B is A + B, where A + B contains any element that is in A or that is in B. *See also* **difference, intersection,** and **subset.**

universal set Any set that contains all possible values of the base type.

user-defined data type *See* **enumerated data type.**

user-defined function A subprogram (function) written by the programmer to perform a specific task. Functions return one value when called.

user-friendly program An interactive program with clear, easy-to-follow messages for the user.

value (of a memory location) refers to the value of the contents of a memory location. *See also* **address.**

value parameter A formal parameter that is local to a subprogram. The value of this parameter is not returned to the calling program.

variable A memory location, referenced by an identifier, with a value that can be changed during a program.

variable condition loop A repetition statement in which the loop control condition changes within the body of the loop.

variable declaration section The section of the declaration section in which program variables are declared for subsequent use.

variable dictionary A listing of the meanings of variables used in a program.

variable parameter A formal parameter that is not local to a subprogram. The value of this parameter is returned to the calling program.

variant part The part of a record structure in which the number and type of data fields can vary. *See also* **fixed part.**

virtual method A method where the resolution of connections, allocations, and references is not determined until run time. See also **static method.**

virtual method table A table containing an object type's size and pointers to the code implementing virtual methods.

WHILE . . . DO loop A pretest loop that examines a Boolean expression before causing a fragment to be executed.

word A unit of memory consisting of one or more bytes. Words can be addressed.

writing to a file The process of entering data to a file.

Answers to Selected Exercises

This section contains answers to selected exercises from the exercise sets at the end of each section in the text. In general, answers to odd-numbered exercises are given.

CHAPTER 1

Section 1.3

1. **a.** and **c.** are effective statements.

   b. is not effective because you cannot determine when to perform the action.

   d. is not effective because there is no smallest positive fraction.

   e. is not effective because you cannot determine in advance which stocks will increase in value.

3. **a.** 1. Select a topic
   2. Research the topic
   3. Outline the paper
   4. Refine the outline
   5. Write the rough draft
   6. Read and revise the rough draft
   7. Write the final paper

   c. 1. Get a list of colleges
   2. Examine criteria (programs, distance, money, and so on)
   3. Screen to a manageable number
   4. Obtain further information
   5. Make a decision

5. **a.** First-level development:

   1. Get information for first employee
   2. Perform computations for first employee
   3. Print results for first employee
   4.
   5. } repeat for second employee
   6.

   Second-level development:

   1. Get information for first employee
      1.1 get hourly wage
      1.2 get number of hours worked per week
   2. Perform computations for first employee
      2.1 compute gross pay
      2.2 compute deductions
      2.3 compute net pay
   3. Print results for first employee
      3.1 print input data
      3.2 print gross pay
      3.3 print deductions
      3.4 print net pay
   4.
   5. } repeat for second employee
   6.

   Third-level development:

   1. Get information for first employee
      1.1 get hourly wage
      1.2 get number of hours worked per week
   2. Perform computations for first employee
      2.1 compute gross pay
      2.2 compute deductions
         2.2.1 federal withholding
         2.2.2 state withholding
         2.2.3 social security
         2.2.4 union dues
         2.2.5 compute total deductions
      2.3 compute net pay
         2.3.1 subtract total deductions from gross pay
   3. Print results for first employee
      3.1 print input data
         3.1.1 print hourly wage
         3.1.2 print number of hours worked per week
      3.2 print gross pay
      3.3 print deductions
         3.3.1 print federal withholding
         3.3.2 print state withholding
         3.3.3 print social security
         3.3.4 print union dues
         3.3.5 print total deductions
      3.4 print net pay
   4.
   5. } repeat for second employee
   6.

7. There are several ways to solve this problem, one of which follows:
    1. Get the numbers as input
    2. Put them in order (Small, Large)
    3. Check for a divisor
        3.1 **IF** Small is a divisor of Large **THEN**
            3.1.1 GCD is Small
            ELSE
            3.1.2 decrease Small until a common divisor is found
    4. Print the results
            3.1.2 can be further refined as
            3.1.2 decrease Small until a common divisor is found
                3.1.2.2 **REPEAT**
                    IF GCDCandidate is a common divisor **THEN**
                        GCD is GCDCandidate
                    ELSE
                        decrease GCDCandidate by 1
                    UNTIL a common divisor is found

Section 1.4

1. As part of your response, consider both the user who works in an environment without a mouse and the user who works in an environment with a mouse. If possible, talk with one of each.

5. You will need to do the following.
    a. Enter Turbo as before.
    b. Select the **File** menu and the Open option (<F3>).
    c. Select the desired file from the "Open a File" window, and press <Enter>.
    d. Edit the file.
    e. Select "Save As . . . " from the **File** menu.
    f. Type in the desired name, and press <Enter>.

Section 1.5

3. a., b., e., and g are valid. However, a semicolon must be used between the heading in a. and the next line of code.
    c. does not begin with the reserved word **PROGRAM.**
    d. is missing an identifier for the program name.
    f. and h. use improper identifiers for the program name.

5. A typical constant definition statement is

```
CONST
  Name = 'Julie Adams';
  Age = 18;
  BirthDate = 'November 10, 1973';
  Birthplace = 'Carson City, MI';
```

Section 1.6

1. a., d., e., and g. are valid.
    b. has a decimal.
    c. has a comma.
    f. is probably larger than **maxint.**
    h. is a real.

3. a. 1.73E2 d. 1.4768E1
    b. 7.43927E11 e. –5.2E0
    c. –2.3E–8

5. a. and d. are integers. b., c., and g. are **reals.** e. and f. are string constants.

7. a.
```
writeln ('Score':14);
writeln ('-----':14);
writeln (86:13);
writeln (82:13);
writeln (79:13);
```

CHAPTER 2

Section 2.1

1. a. 11 e. 126 h. 140
    b. –41 f. 63 i. –2
    c. 3 g. 48 j. 7
    d. 24

3. a. and b. are valid; type **integer.** c., e., f., g., h., and i. are valid; type **real.** d. and j. are invalid.

5. Output will vary according to local implementation.

7. Since the maximum value of a real is 10E38, try to assign a greater value than this to a **real** variable.

Section 2.2

1. a., b., e., f., and h. are valid assignment statements.
    c. is invalid. A real cannot be assigned to an integer variable.
    d. is invalid. An operand cannot be on the left of an assignment statement.
    g. is invalid. IQ/3 is a real.

3.
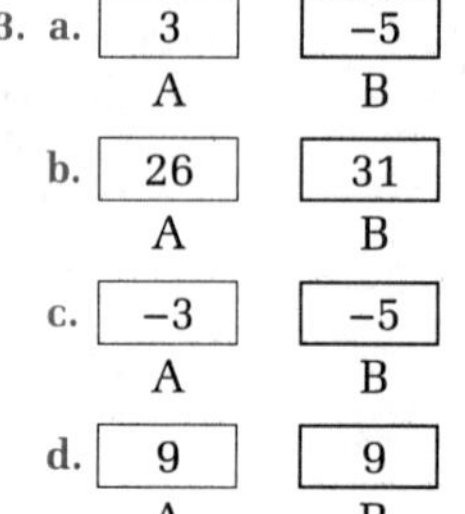

5.
```
Gender      M
Age         23
Height      73 inches
Weight      186.5 lbs
```

7. column 11

```
**********************************
*                                *
*     Name      Age     Gender   *
*     ----      ---     -----    *

*     Jones      21        M     *
*                                *
**********************************
```

9. column 10

```
         ↓
         This  reviews string formatting.
When a letterAis used,
         Oops! I forgot to format.
         When a letter A is used,
         it is a string of length one.
```

Section 2.3

5. a.

83	95	' '	100.0
Num1	Num2	Ch	Num3

b. Error 106: Invalid, numeric format.

c.

83	−72	' '	93.5
Num1	Num2	Ch	Num3

d.

83	−72	' '	93.5
Num1	Num2	Ch	Num3

e. Error 106: Invalid, numeric format.

f. Error 106: Invalid, numeric format.

g.

91	92	' '	93.0
Num1	Num2	Ch	Num3

h.

−76	−81	'−'	−16.5
Num1	Num2	Ch	Num3

Section 2.4

3.

```
   CPS 150                   TEST #2
----------------------------------------

   Total points                100
   My score                     93
   Class average              82.3
```

Section 2.5

1. a. 15.2   c. 0   e. **−4.5**

   b. 14   d. 36   f. −11.98

3. a. `sqrt(A * A + B * B)`

   b. `(-B + sqrt(B * B - 4 * A * C)) / (2 * A)`
   and
   `(-B - sqrt(B * B - 4 * A * C)) / (2 * A)`

5. `(round(10 * X)) / 10.0`

7. a. `-4.30  4.30   -4   -4`

   b.
   ```
   4
   65
   ```

   c. `   L    K    M`

9. a.
   ```
   Uppercase := chr(ord(Lowercase)
                - ord('a') + ord('A'));
   ```

   b.
   ```
   IntValue := ord(Digit) - ord('0');
   (Also see val in Section 8.3.)
   ```

CHAPTER 3

Section 3.2

3. a. A and B are variable parameters. X is a value parameter.

   b. A and X are variable parameters. B and Ch are value parameters.

   c. X, Y, and Z are variable parameters. A, B, and Ch are value parameters.

5. a. `Prob5 (Num1, Num2, Letter);`

   b. `PrintHeader;`

   c. `FindMax (Num1, Num2, Max);`

   d. `Switch (Num1, Num2);`

7. b.
```
PROCEDURE MaxAndAver (X, Y, Z : real;
                      VAR Max, Aver : real);
  BEGIN
    Max := X;
    IF Y > Max THEN
      Max := Y;
    IF Z > Max THEN
      Max := Z;
    Aver := (X + Y + Z) / 3.0
  END;
```

Section 3.3

7. Identifiers for this program are represented schematically by the figure at right.

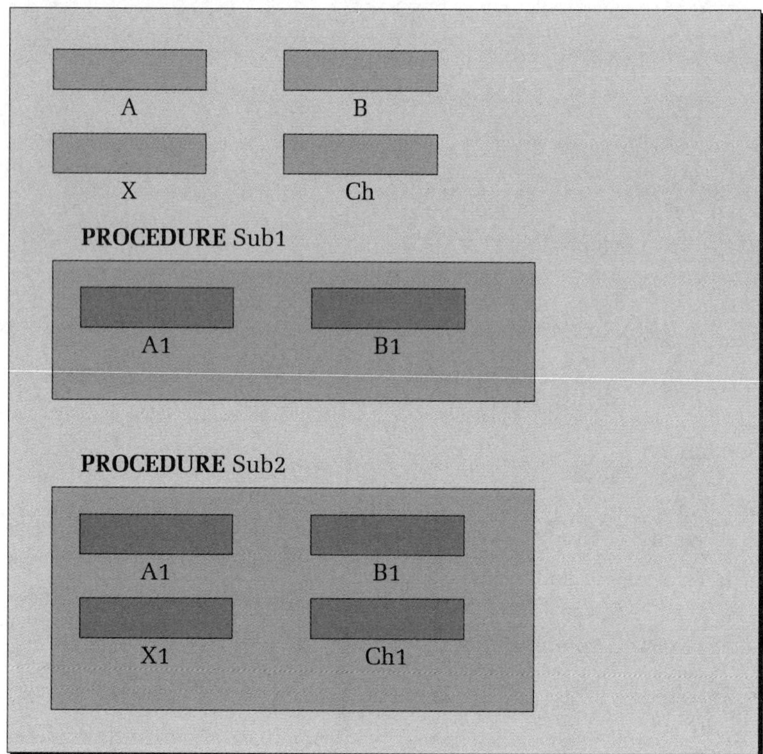

9.
```
10
20
10
30
30
```

11. a. Average cannot be used as a procedure name since it has already been declared as an identifier with scope that includes that procedure.

    b. No errors; the variables declared in the procedure heading are local to it.

    c. No errors.

13. The main program is trying to access an identifier that is not available. The line

    ```
    writeln (X1:20:2);
    ```

    in the main program is inappropriate because the scope of X1 is **PROCEDURE** Sub1.

Section 3.4

3. c. and d. are valid.

   a. is invalid. The data type for what will be returned to the calling program must be listed:

   ```
   FUNCTION RoundTenth (X : real) : real;
   ```

   b. is invalid. Data types must be listed for X and Y.

   e. is invalid. The comma following **char** should be a semicolon.

CHAPTER 4

Section 4.1

1.
```
TRUE TRUE  FALSE
              FALSE
```

3. Only c. and f. are valid.

5. a., b., d., and g. are **true.** c., e., and f. (which compare as reals) are **false.**

7. a., b., and c. are **true.** d. and e. are **false.**

Section 4.2

1. a. 10 5

   b. No output

   c. 5 0

   d. 10 5

   e. 15 4
      15 4

   f. 10 5

3. a. should be

```
IF A = 10 THEN ...
```

   b. `3 < X < 10`

   cannot be evaluated. It should be changed to

```
(3 < X) AND (X < 10)
```

   c. This expression needs a **BEGIN . . . END** statement to be consistent with indentation requirements. It should be changed to

```
IF A > 0 THEN
  BEGIN
    Count := Count + 1;
    Sum := Sum + A
  END;
```

   d. `IF Ch = 'A' OR 'B' THEN`

   should be

```
IF (Ch = 'A') OR (Ch = 'B') THEN
```

5. Yes

9.
```
BEGIN
  readln (Num1, Num2, Num3);
  Total := Total + Num1 + Num2 + Num3;
  writeln (Num1:5, Num2:5, Num3:5);
  writeln;
  writeln (Total)
END;
```

11.
```
read (Ch1, Ch2, Ch3);
IF (Ch1 <= Ch2) AND (Ch2 <= Ch3) THEN
  writeln (Ch1, Ch2, Ch3);
```

This can also be written

```
read (Ch1, Ch2, Ch3);
IF Ch1 <= Ch2 THEN
  IF Ch2 <= Ch3 THEN
    writeln (Ch1, Ch2, Ch3);
```

Section 4.3

1. a. -14 14   c. 10 5
                   5 0

   b. 50 25
      1 75

3. a. Since the intent appears to be a statement that counts characters other than periods, a **BEGIN . . . END** block should be included in the **IF . . . THEN** option, so

```
IF Ch <> '.' THEN
  BEGIN
    CharCount := CharCount + 1;
    writeln (Ch)
  END
ELSE
  PeriodCount := PeriodCount + 1;
```

   b. The semicolon between **END** and **ELSE** should be omitted.

   c. Technically, this fragment will run. However, since it appears that OldAge := OldAge + Age is to be included in the **ELSE** option, the programmer probably meant

```
ELSE
  BEGIN
    OldCount := OldCount + 1;
    OldAge := OldAge + Age
  END;
```

Section 4.4

1.

	X	Y
a.	38.15	763.0
b.	-21.0	21.0
c.	600.0	1200.0
d.	3000.0	9000.0

3. a.
```
IF Ch = 'M' THEN
  IF Sum > 1000 THEN
    X := X + 1
  ELSE
    X := X + 2
ELSE IF Ch = 'F' THEN
  IF Sum > 1000 THEN
    X := X + 3
  ELSE
    X := X + 4;
```

   b.
```
readln (Num);
  IF Num > 0 THEN
    IF Num <= 10000 THEN
      BEGIN
        Count := Count + 1;
        Sum := Sum + Num
      END
    ELSE
      writeln ('Value out of range':27)
  ELSE
    writeln ('Value out of range':27);
```

   c.
```
IF A > 0 THEN
  IF B > 0 THEN
    writeln ('Both positive':22)
  ELSE
    writeln ('Some negative':22)
ELSE
  writeln ('Some negative':22);
```

   d.
```
IF C <= 0 THEN
  IF A > 0 THEN
    IF B > 0 THEN
      writeln ('Option one':19)
    ELSE
      writeln ('Option two':19)
  ELSE
    writeln ('Option two':19)
ELSE
  writeln ('Option one':19);
```

5.
```
IF Average < 90 THEN
  IF Average < 80 THEN
    IF Average < 70 THEN
      IF Average < 55 THEN
        Grade := 'E'
      ELSE Grade := 'D'
    ELSE Grade := 'C'
  ELSE Grade := 'B'
ELSE Grade := 'A';
```

This can be written using sequential **IF . . . THEN** statements. For example

```
IF (Average <= 100) AND (Average >= 90) THEN
  Grade := 'A';
IF (Average < 90) AND (Average >= 80) THEN
  Grade := 'B';
     .
     .
     .
```

The disadvantage of this method is that each Boolean expression of each statement will always be evaluated. This is relatively inefficient.

7.

8	13	104
A	B	C

Section 4.5

3. In Turbo Pascal, the **ELSE** option is used:

```
CASE Age DIV 10 OF
     .
     .
     .
ELSE
  writeln ('Value of Age is ', Age)
END;  {  of CASE Age  }
```

Standard Pascal uses an **IF . . . THEN . . . ELSE** statement, such as

```
IF (Age >= 1) AND (Age <= 10) THEN
  CASE Age DIV 10 OF
     .
     .
     .
  END  {  of CASE Age  }
ELSE
  writeln ('Value of Age is ', Age);
```

5. a. 5 3. 125

b. You have purchased Super Unleaded gasoline

c. 3 -3

d. 5 10 -5

7. Assume there is a variable ClassType. The design of the fragment to compute fees is then

```
read (ClassType);
CASE ClassType OF
  'U' :
  'G' :
  'F' :   (list options here)
  'S' :
END;  {  of CASE ClassType  }
```

CHAPTER 5

Section 5.2

1. a.
```
*
 *
  *
   *
    *
     *
```

b.
```
 1 :      9
 2 :      8
 3 :      7
 4 :      6
 5 :      5
 6 :      4
 7 :      3
 8 :      2
 9 :      1
10 :      0
```

c.
```
**   2
**   3
**   4
**   5
**   6
**   7
**   8
**   9
**  10
**  11
**  12
**  13
**  14
**  15
**  16
**  17
**  18
**  19
**  20
```

d.
```
 1
 2
 3
 4
 5
 6
 7
 8
 9
10
11
12
13
14
15
16
17
18
19
20
21
```

3. a.
```
FOR J := 1 TO 4 DO
  writeln ('*':2);
```

b.
```
FOR J := 1 TO 8 DO
  writeln ('***':J + 3);
```

c.
```
writeln ('*':6);
FOR J := 1 TO 3 DO
  writeln ('*':6 - J, '*':2 * J);
writeln (' **** ****');
FOR J := 1 TO 2 DO
  writeln ('* *':7);
writeln ('***':7);
```

d. This "look ahead" problem can be solved by using a loop within a loop. This idea is developed in Section 5.6.

```
FOR J := 5 DOWNTO 1 DO
  BEGIN
    write (' ':(6 - J));  {  Indent a line  }
    FOR K := 1 TO (2 * J - 1) DO  {  Print
                                     a line  }
      write ('*');
    writeln
  END;
```

5. a.
```
FOR J := 1 TO 5 DO
  write (J:3);
FOR J := 5 DOWNTO 1 DO
  write (6 - J:3);
```

b.
```
FOR J := 1 TO 5 DO
  writeln ('*':J);
FOR J := 5 DOWNTO 1 DO
  writeln ('*':(6 - J));
```

7.
```
FOR J := 2 TO 10 DO
  writeln (12 - J:12 - J);
```

9. The key loop in this program will be something like

```
FOR J := -10 TO 10 DO
  BEGIN
    Num := 5 * J;
    writeln (Num:10, Num * Num:10,
                 Num * Num * Num:10)
  END;  {  of printing the chart  }
```

Section 5.3

3. a.
```
 1
 2
 3
 4
 5
 6
 7
 8
 9
10
```

b.
```
1     0
2     1
3     2
4     1
5     2
```

c.
```
54        50
```

d.
```
The partial sum is    1
The partial sum is    3
The partial sum is    6
The partial sum is   10
The partial sum is   15
The count is    5
```

e.
```
    96.00       2.00
```

5. a.
```
WHILE Num > 0 DO
  BEGIN
    writeln (Num:10:2);
    Num := Num - 0.5
  END;
```

Section 5.4

1. A pretest loop tests the Boolean expression before executing the loop. A posttest loop tests the Boolean expression after the loop has been executed.

3. a.
```
1    9
2    8
3    7
4    6
5    5
6    4
```

b.
```
  2
  4
  8
 16
 32
 64
128
```

c.
```
 1
 2
 3
 4
 5
 6
 7
 8
 9
10
```

d.
```
1   0
2   1
3   2
4   1
5   2
```

5. a.
```
IF Num > 0 THEN
  REPEAT
    writeln (Num:10:2);
    Num := Num - 0.5
  UNTIL Num <= 0;
```

Section 5.6

1. a.
```
FOR K := 1 TO 5 DO
  BEGIN
    write (' ':K);
    FOR J := K TO 5 DO
      write ('*');
    writeln
  END;
```

c.
```
FOR K := 1 TO 7 DO
  IF K < 5 THEN
    BEGIN
      FOR J := 1 TO 3 DO
        write ('*');
      writeln
    END;
  ELSE
    BEGIN
      FOR J := 1 TO 5 DO
        write ('*');
      writeln
    END;
```

3.
```
4   5   6   7
4   5   6   7
4   5   6   7
4   5   6   7

5   6   7
5   6   7
5   6   7

6   7
6   7
```

Section 5.7

1. a. This is an infinite loop.

b. There is no error. However, the index K should be assigned a value before being used as something other than a loop index.

CHAPTER 6

Section 6.1

3. The variables should be formatted so the integers will be separated by blanks.

You should check your answers to Exercises 5–7 on your computer due to possible differences in reading text files.

11.
```
PROGRAM DeleteBlanks;
VAR
  NoBlank,Data : text;
  Ch : char;
BEGIN
  assign (Data, 'Ex6-1-11.DAT');
  assign (NoBlank, 'FWOBLANK.DAT');
  reset (Data);
  rewrite (NoBlank);  {  Open for writing  }
  WHILE NOT eof(Data) DO
```

```
      BEGIN
        WHILE NOT eoln(Data) DO
          BEGIN
            read (Data, Ch);
            IF Ch <> ' ' THEN
              write (NoBlank, Ch)
          END;  { of WHILE NOT eoln  }
        readln(Data);
        writeln (NoBlank)
      END  { of WHILE NOT eof  }
    Close (Data);
    Close (NoBlank)
  END.  {  of main program  }
```

Section 6.2

3. a. Jane is listed in both type Names and type People.

   b. Red is listed twice in type Colors.

   c. Parentheses are needed around the values:

```
TYPE
  Letters = (A, C, E);
```

5. a., d., and e. are valid.

   b. is invalid; Tues + Wed is not defined.

   c. is valid (but a poor choice).

   f. is invalid; you cannot **write** user-defined values.

   g. is invalid; you cannot **read** user-defined ordinals.

   h. is invalid; the operation Tues + 1 is not defined.

Section 6.3

1. a. The definition is invalid; 10 . . 1 is not a subrange of an existing ordinal data type.

   b. Bases and Double are valid. Score is invalid because Second . . Home is not a subrange.

   c. All definitions and declarations are valid. However, Hue := Blue is an invalid use because Blue is not in the subrange defined for Stripes.

   d. The definitions are invalid because the type Days must be defined before the subrange Weekdays.

   e. All definitions and declarations are valid, but Score2 := Score1 + 70 causes a meaningless value to be stored in Score2.

3. a. Dependents usually refers to the number of single-family dependents for tax purposes; 20 is a reasonable maximum.

   b. Assuming hours worked in one week, 0 . . 60 is a reasonable subrange.

   c. This subrange is for a maximum score of 10. It would vary for other maximum scores.

   d. This subrange is used for total points with a maximum of 700. It might be used in some grading programs.

5. a. and b. are compatible. The base type is ChessPieces.

   c. and f. are incompatible.

   d. and e. are compatible. The base type is **integer.**

Section 6.4

1. a. Oak

   b. Cotton

   c. 2

   d. −1, but this expression should be avoided.

   e. 3

   f. 3, but this expression should be avoided.

   g. 0

3. a. 'D'

   b. 10

   c. '0'

   d. Invalid; addition of characters is not defined.

   e. Invalid; **pred**('K') is a character; thus, the operation '+' is not defined.

   f. 'Z'

5. a.

```
Weekend
Weekday
Weekday
Weekday
Weekday
Weekday
```

   b. For a **WHILE** . . . DO loop, you could use the Boolean expression **WHILE** Day < Sat **DO**:

```
          Day := Sun;
WHILE Day < Sat DO
  BEGIN
    .
    .     (body of loop here)
    .
  END;
```

   A **FOR** loop could be controlled by the Boolean expression

```
FOR Day := Sun TO Fri DO
  BEGIN
    .
    .     (body of loop here)
    .
  END;
```

   c. This can be accomplished by using ordinal values. For example, if OrdValue is declared, the loop can be

```
OrdValue := 0;
  REPEAT
    CASE OrdValue OF
      0             :}
      1, 2, 3, 4, 5 :}  (action here)
    END;  {  of CASE OrdValue  }
    OrdValue := OrdValue + 1
  UNTIL OrdValue = 6;
```

   d. The last value (Sat) is not being considered. This can be altered by using a **FOR** loop and including Sat or by using a variable control loop and adding a **writeln** statement, such as

```
writeln ('Weekend':20);
```

   outside the loop.

7. Assume variables MonthNum and Month are appropriately declared. A function can then be

```
FUNCTION Month (MonthNum : integer) : MonthName;
  BEGIN
    CASE MonthNum OF
      1  : Month := Jan;
      2  : Month := Feb;
              .
              .
              .
      12 : Month := Dec
    END   {  of CASE MonthNum  }
  END;  {  of FUNCTION Month  }
```

CHAPTER 7

Section 7.1

1. a.
```
TYPE
  ScoreList = ARRAY [1..35] OF integer;
VAR
  Score : ScoreList;
```

b.
```
TYPE
  PriceList = ARRAY [1..20] OF real;
VAR
  CarCost : PriceList;
```

c.
```
CONST
  NumQuestions = 50;
TYPE
  AnswerList = ARRAY [1..NumQuestions] OF char;
VAR
  Answer : AnswerList;
```

Note: It is possible to use an array of element type **boolean** here.

d.
```
TYPE
  GradeList = ARRAY [1..6] OF char;
VAR
  Grade : GradeList;
```

3. a. There is no error if Hours has been defined as a constant.

b. No error

c. No index range has been given for the array.

d. The index range should be [1 . . 10] rather than [1 **TO** 10].

e. The index range is not appropriate; something like **ARRAY** [⟨index range⟩] **OF boolean** should be used.

f. [1 . . . 5] should be [1 . . 5].

5. a.
```
TYPE
  LetterList = ARRAY [1..100] OF 'A'..'Z';
VAR
  Letter : LetterList;
```

b.
```
TYPE
  Name = ARRAY [1..30] OF char;
VAR
  CompanyName : Name;
```

c.
```
TYPE
  ScoreList = ARRAY [30..59] OF real;
VAR
  Score : ScoreList;
```

7. a. Money

183.25	Money[1]
10.04	Money[2]
17.32	Money[3]

b. Money

10.04	Money[1]
19.26	Money[2]
17.32	Money[3]

c. Money

19.26	Money[1]
10.04	Money[2]
2.68	Money[3]

Section 7.2

1. a. List

0	List[1]
0	List[2]
1	List[3]
1	List[4]
1	List[5]

b. List

5	List[1]
6	List[2]
7	List[3]
8	List[4]
9	List[5]

Score

1	Score[1]
2	Score[2]
2	Score[3]
2	Score[4]
3	Score[5]

c. Answer

false	Answer[1]
true	Answer[2]
false	Answer[3]
true	Answer[4]
false	Answer[5]
true	Answer[6]
false	Answer[7]
true	Answer[8]
false	Answer[9]
true	Answer[10]

d. Name

A	Name[1]
B	Name[2]
.	.
.	.
.	.
T	Name [20]

3. The section counts the number of scores > 90.

5.
```
FOR J := 1 TO 100 DO
  A[J] := 0.0;
```

7.
```
writeln ('Test Number', 'Score':10);
writeln ('-----------', '-----':10);
writeln;
FOR J := 1 TO 50 DO
  writeln ('<':4, J:2, '>', TestScore[J]:11);
```

9. a. Valid; the range for each array is not exceeded.

   b. Valid; the entire arrays are set equal, component by component.

   c. Invalid; the arrays are not of the same type.

   d. Invalid; the range of C is exceeded.

   e. Valid.

Section 7.3

1. a. After one pass: After two passes:

After one pass
−20
10
0
10
8
30
−2

After two passes
−20
−2
0
10
8
30
10

   b. Three exchanges are made.

3. A high to low sort is achieved by changing

```
IF A[K] < A[Index] THEN
```

to

```
IF A[K] > A[Index] THEN
```

Section 7.4

1. a. is valid; it can be called by

```
NewList (List1, Aray);
```

   b. is invalid; a semicolon is needed after Row.

   c. is invalid; array declaration cannot be included in the heading.

   d. is valid; it can be called by

```
NewList (List1, List2);
```

   e. is invalid; Column cannot be used as a variable name.

   f. is invalid; array declaration cannot be included in the heading.

   g. is valid; it can be called by

```
GetData (Day);
```

   h. is valid; it can be called by

```
Table          (List1,          List2);
```

3. a.
```
PROCEDURE OldList (X : Row;
                   Y : Column);
```

   b.
```
PROCEDURE ChangeList (X : Row;
                      D : Week);
```

   c. This call is inappropriate because the data type for A and B has not been defined in the **TYPE** section.

5. a.

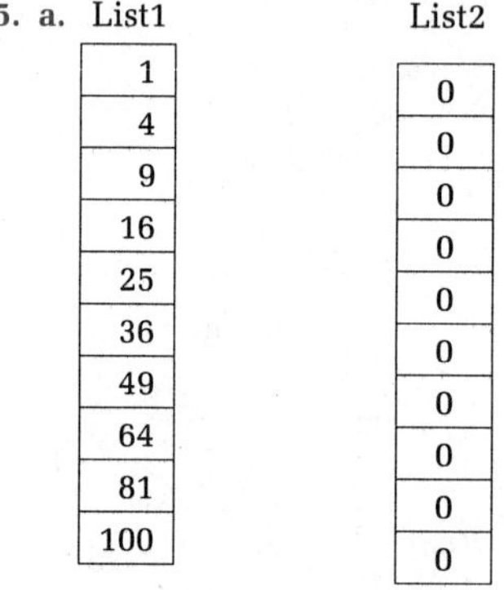

List1
1
4
9
16
25
36
49
64
81
100
List2
0
0
0
0
0
0
0
0
0
0

Section 7.5

1. a., b., c., d., and f are **true.**

   e. is **false.**

3. a.
```
To err is human. Computers do
```

   b.
```
To err is human. Computers do not forgive.
                          (10 blanks)
                              ↓
```

   c.
```
To err is human. Com                ************
                   ↑                      ↑
             position 20         (12 asterisks)
```

   d.
```
To err is human. Computers do not forgive.
.evigrof ton od sretupmoC .namuh si rre oT
```

5.
```
MCount := 0;
FOR J := 1 TO length(Message) DO
  IF Message[J] = 'M' THEN
    MCount := MCount + 1;
```

Section 7.6

1.
```
FOR J := 1 TO Length DO
  IF Num = A[J] THEN
    writeln (Num, ' is in position', J:5);
```

3. The value of Index in the loop can be used as a counter.

5. a. `Num = 18`

	First	Last	Mid	A[Mid]	Found
Before loop	1	5	Undefined	Undefined	**false**
After first pass	1	2	3	37	**false**
After second pass	1	2	1	18	**true**

c. `Num = 76`

	First	Last	Mid	A[Mid]	Found
Before loop	1	5	Undefined	Undefined	**false**
After first pass	4	5	3	37	**false**
After second pass	4	3	4	92	

Since First > Last, the loop will be exited and an appropriate message should be printed.

7. Algorithmic developments for this problem follow.

   a. 1. Copy file components into an array
      2. Get number to look for
      3. Search sequentially for a match

   c. 1. Copy file components into an array
      2. Get new number
      3. Use a binary search until Last < First
      4. Assign First to Position
      5. Move array components ahead one from Position to the end of the list:

```
FOR J := Length DOWNTO Position DO
  A[J + 1] := A[J];
```

      6. Assign new number to

```
A[Position];
```

9. There will be a maximum of five passes.

CHAPTER 8

Section 8.1

1. a.
```
DrugPrice = ARRAY [1 ..4, 1..5] OF real;
DrugPrice = ARRAY [1..4] OF ARRAY [1..5] OF
real;
```

   b.
```
Grade = ARRAY [1..20, 1..6] OF char;
Grade = ARRAY [1..20] OF ARRAY [1..6] OF char;
```

   c.
```
QuizScore = ARRAY [1..30, 1..12] OF integer;
QuizScore = ARRAY [1..30] OF ARRAY [1..12] OF
integer;
```

3. a. ShippingCost

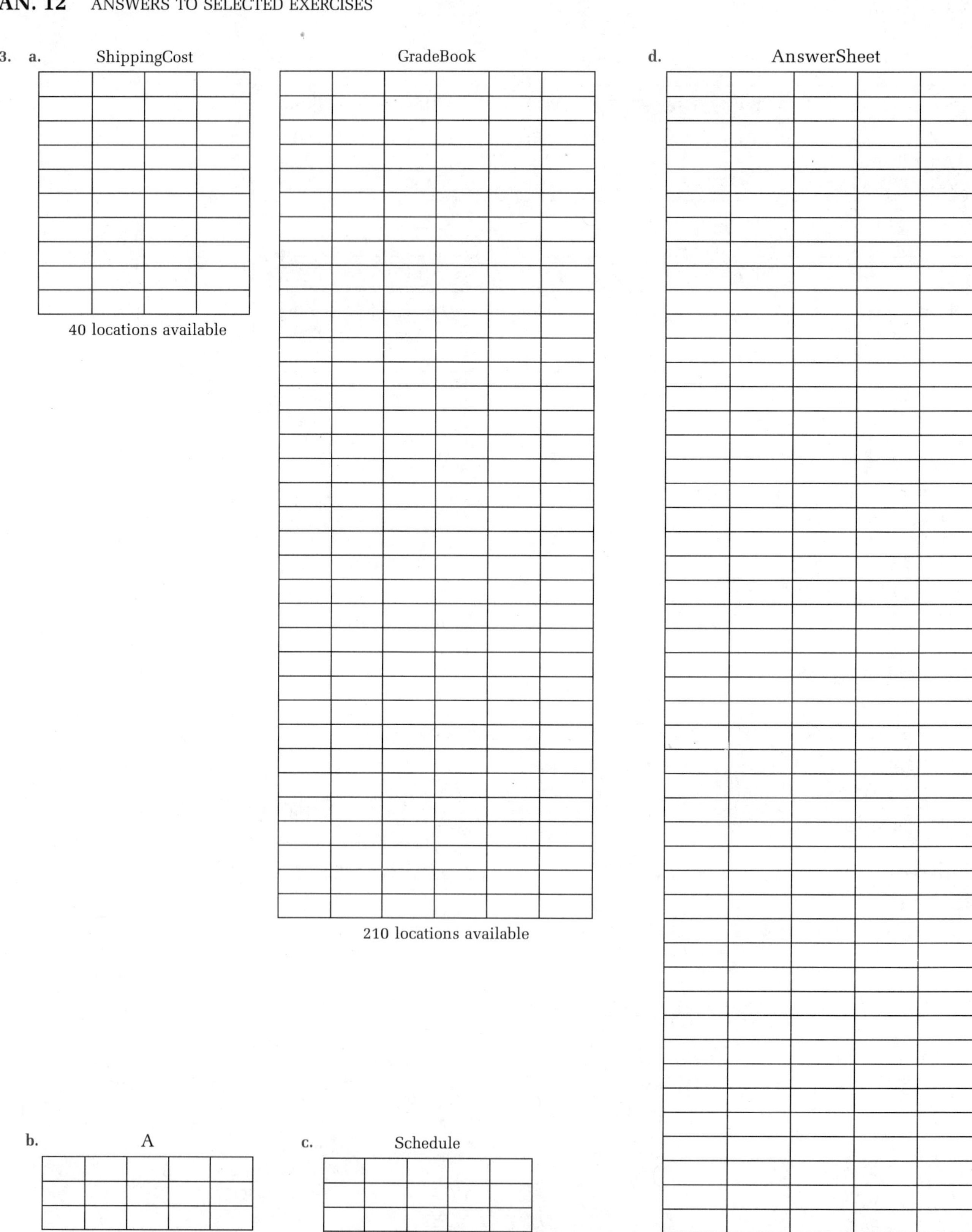

40 locations available

GradeBook

210 locations available

d. AnswerSheet

250 locations available

b. A

15 locations available

c. Schedule

25 locations available

5. a.
```
FOR J := 1 TO 3 DO
  FOR K := 1 TO 6 DO
    A[J,K] := 2 * J + K;
```
b.
```
FOR J := 1 TO 3 DO
  FOR K := 1 TO 6 DO
    A[J,K] := 0;
```
c.
```
FOR J := 1 TO 3 DO
  FOR K := 1 TO 6 DO
    A[J,K] := 2 * J;
```

7.
```
TYPE
  String20 = string [20];
  NameList = ARRAY [1..50] OF String20;
VAR
  Name: NameList;

FOR J := 1 TO 50 DO
  readln (Data, Name[J]);
```

9. a.
```
FOR J := 1 TO 4 DO
  BEGIN
    MinRow[J] := Table[J,1];
    FOR K := 2 TO 5 DO
      IF Table[J,K] < MinRow[J] THEN
        MinRow[J] := Table [J,K]
  END;
```
c.
```
Total := 0;
FOR J := 1 TO 4 DO
  FOR K := 1 TO 5 DO
    Total := Total + Table[J,K];
```

11. a.
```
TYPE
  Table = ARRAY [1..3, 1..8] OF integer;
```
b.
```
PROCEDURE Replace (VAR A : Table);
  VAR
    J, K : integer;
  BEGIN
    FOR J := 1 TO 3 DO
      FOR K := 1 TO 8 DO
        IF A[J,K] < 0 THEN
          A[J,K] := 0
  END;  { of PROCEDURE Replace }
```
c. **PROCEDURE** Replace in **b.** can be called by

```
Replace (Table3X5);
```

13. a. Reading values into matrices A and B depends upon how data are arranged in the data file.

b.
```
FOR H := 1 TO M DO
  FOR J := 1 TO P DO
    BEGIN
      Sum := 0;
      FOR K := 1 TO N DO
        Sum := Sum + A[H,K] * B[K,J];
      C[H,J] := Sum
    END;
```

Section 8.2

1. a. This prints an alphabetical listing of the states that begin with the letter O.

b. This prints every fifth state in reverse alphabetical order.

c. This lists the first two letters of each state.

d. This counts all occurrences of the letter A in the names of the states.

3. Assume the number of data lines is in NumLines.

a.
```
FOR J := 1 TO NumLines DO
  BEGIN
    read (Data, Name[J,1]);
    K := 2;
    WHILE Name[J,K] <> '*' DO
      BEGIN
        read (Data, Name[J,K]);
        K := K + 1
      END;
    readln (Data)
  END;
```
c.
```
FOR J := 1 TO NumLines DO
  readln (Data, Name[J])
  END;
```

Section 8.3

1. The code
```
str (185.3:8, StringName);
writeln (StringName);
```
produces the output
```
1.9E+02
```

5. After suitable initialization and a priming read, a loop to process the data line is
```
WHILE Ch <> '.' DO
  BEGIN
    read (Data, Ch);
    WHILE (Ch <> ' ') AND (Ch <> '.') DO
      BEGIN
        WordLength := WordLength + 1;
        read (Data, Ch)
      END;
    SumOfLengths := SumOfLengths + WordLength;
    WordLength := 0;
    WordCount := WordCount + 1
  END;
```

Section 8.4

1. a. These declarations are not appropriate because Names is an array of 10 elements while Amounts is an array of 15 elements.

b. These declarations are appropriate because both Table and Names can be thought of as an array of length 12.

3. b. Assume an array type is defined as

```
TYPE
  GradeCount = ARRAY ['A'..'E'] OF integer;
```

If Count is a variable of type GradeCount, the frequency of each grade can be determined by

```
FOR Ch := 'A' TO 'E' DO  {  Initialize  }
  Count[Ch] := 0;
FOR J := 1 TO ListLength DO
  CASE Grade[J] OF
```

```
        'A' : Count['A'] := Count['A'] + 1;
        'B' : Count['B'] := Count['B'] + 1;
        'C' : Count['C'] := Count['C'] + 1;
        'D' : Count['D'] := Count['D'] + 1;
        'E' : Count['E'] := Count['E'] + 1
      END;  {  of CASE Grade[J]  }
```

Section 8.5

1. a. 2 * 3 * 10 = 60

   b. 6 * 3 * 4 = 72

   c. 3 * 2 * 11 = 66

3.
```
TYPE
  Floor = 1..4;
  Wing = 1..5;
  Room = 1..20;
  FloorPlan = ARRAY [Floor,
                     Wing, Room] OF char;
VAR
  RoomType : FloorPlan;
```

5. There are 10 schools, 12 sports, and 2 genders. Thus, 10 * 12 * 2 (240) memory locations are reserved.

7. a.
```
{  Initialize to zero.  }
FOR School := 'A' TO 'J' DO
  NumGrants[School] := 0;
FOR School := 'A' TO 'J' DO  {  Consider each school.  }
  FOR Sport := Baseball TO Wrestling DO  {  Consider each sport.  }
    FOR Gender := Male TO Female DO  {  Consider each gender.  }
      NumGrants[School] := NumGrants[School] +
                           Grants[School, Sport, Gender];
```

CHAPTER 9

Section 9.1

5. a. Employee

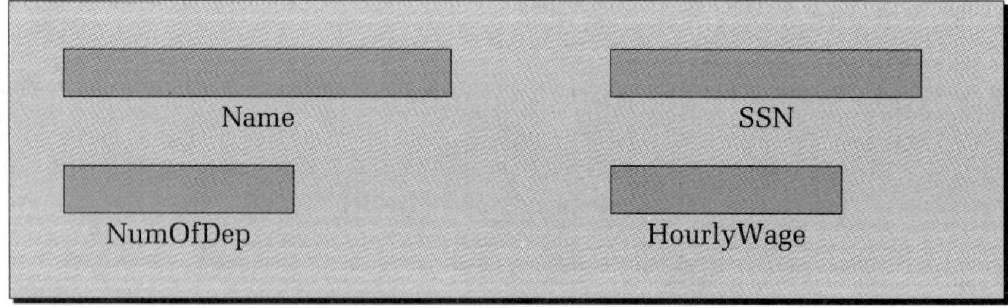

b. House

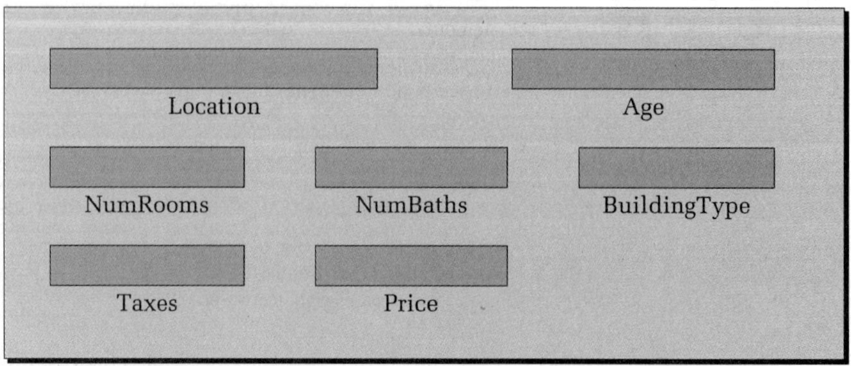

c. PhoneListing

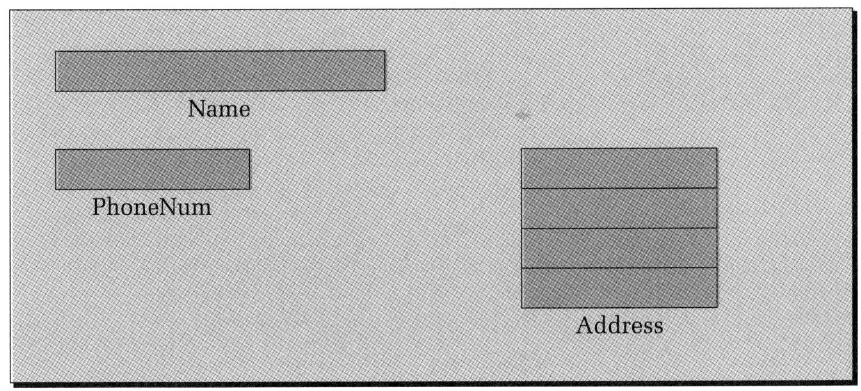

7. **a.**

```
Info : RECORD
```

should be

```
Info = RECORD
```

b. Member is used as both a variable and a data type.

c.

```
IQ = 50..200
```

should be

```
IQ : 50..200
```

Section 9.2

1. **a., c.,** and **d.** are valid.

   b. is invalid; Cust2 and Cust3 are not of identical type.

   e. is valid but demonstrates a poor practice. For better readability, you should always determine precisely which fields are being used.

3. **a.** The three different methods you could use are

   (1)
```
Employee2 := Employee1;
```

   (2)
```
WITH Employee2 DO
  BEGIN
    Name := Employee1.Name;
    SSN := Employee1.SSN;
    Age := Employee1.Age;
    HourlyWage := Employee1.HourlyWage;
    Volunteer := Employee1.Volunteer
  END;  { of WITH...DO }
```

   (3)
```
WITH Employee1 DO
  BEGIN
    Employee2.Name := Name;
    Employee2.SSN := SSN;
    Employee2.Age := Age;
    Employee2.HourlyWage := HourlyWage;
    Employee2.Volunteer := Volunteer
  END;  { of WITH...DO }
```

   b. Did you consider doing the following?

```
WITH Employee2 DO
  BEGIN
    Temp := HoursWorked;
    Employee2 := Employee1;
    HoursWorked := Temp
  END;
```

5.
```
FUNCTION Grade (Pts : integer) : char;
  VAR
    Percent : real;
  BEGIN
    Percent := Pts / 5;  {  Compute percent.  }
    IF Percent < 60 THEN
      Grade := 'E'
    ELSE IF Percent < 70 THEN
      Grade := 'D'
    ELSE IF Percent < 80 THEN
      Grade := 'C'
    ELSE IF Percent < 90 THEN
      Grade := 'B'
    ELSE
      Grade := 'A'
  END;
```

This function can be called by

```
With Student DO
  LetterGrade := Grade(TotalPts);
```

Section 9.3

1. **a.** See the following figure.

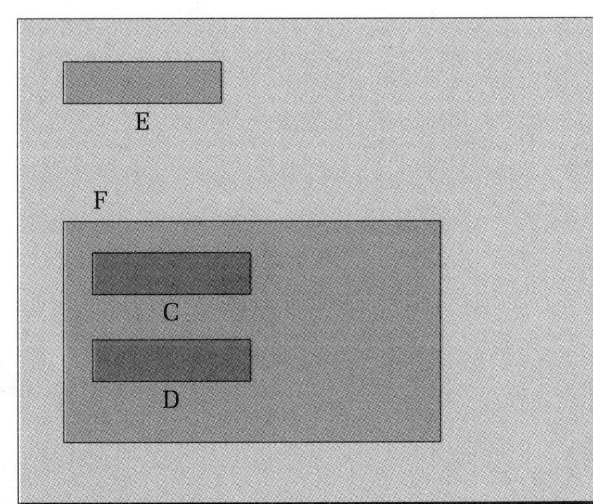

b. **i., iii., iv., viii., ix.,** and **x.** are valid references.

ii., v., vi., and **vii.** are invalid references.

3.
```
TYPE
  String20 = string [20];
  Status = ('S', 'M', 'W', 'D');
  NumKids = 0..15;
  FamilyRec = RECORD
                MaritalStatus : Status;
                Children : NumKids
              END;  { of FamilyRec }
  AddressRec = RECORD
                 Street : String20;
                 City : String20;
                 State : string [2];
                 ZipCode : integer
               END;  { of AddressRec }
  CustomerInfo  = RECORD
                    Name : String20;
                    Address : AddressRec;
                    SSN : string [11];
                    AnnualIncome : real;
                    FamilyInfo : FamilyRec
                  END;  { of CustomerInfo }
VAR
  Customer : CustomerInfo;
```

5.
```
CONST
  SquadSize = 15;
TYPE
  String20 = string [20];
  AgeRange = 15..25;
  HeightRange = 70..100;
  WeightRange = 100..300;
  PlayerInfo = RECORD
                 Name : String20;
                 Age : AgeRange;
                 Height : HeightRange;
                 Weight : WeightRange;
                 ScoringAv : real;
                 ReboundAv : real
               END;  { of PlayerInfo }
  PlayerList = ARRAY [1..SquadSize] OF Player-
Info;
VAR
  Player : PlayerList;
```

7. a. Student

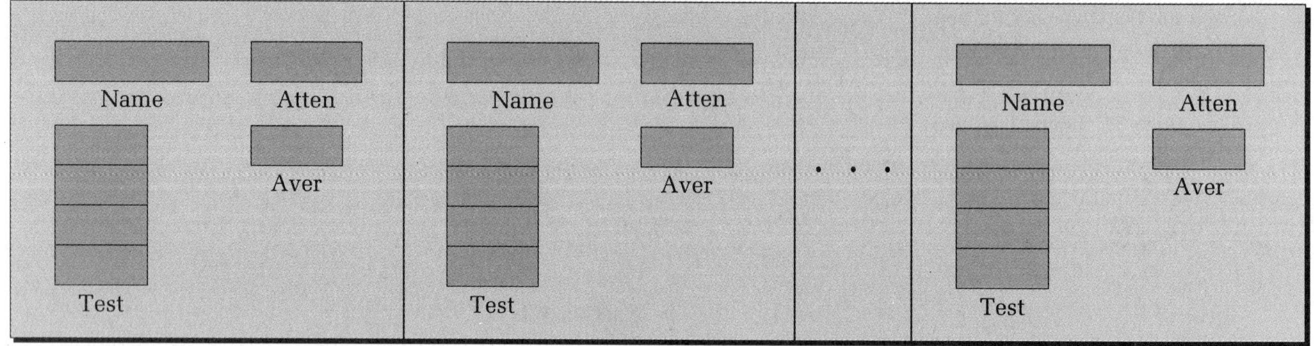

b. This function computes the test average for one student. It can be called by

```
WITH Student[K] DO
  Aver := GuessWhat(Test);
```

c. Format and headings will vary according to personal preference. However, your procedure should include

```
WITH St DO  { Printout for St }
  BEGIN
    .
    .
    .
    write ('Your attendance was ');
    CASE Atten OF
      Excellent : writeln ('excellent.');
      Average   : writeln ('average.');
      Poor      : writeln ('poor.')
    END;  { of CASE }
    .
    .
    .
  END;  { of WITH...DO }
```

Section 9.4

3. a. The type TagType for the tag field Tag has not been defined.

   b. No value is listed for C in the tag field.

   c. There is a syntax error. A semicolon is needed between **boolean** and **CASE.** A type has not been given for the tag field. It should be

   ```
   CASE Tag : TagType OF
   ```

   d. Only one variant part can be defined in a record

5. a. Figure

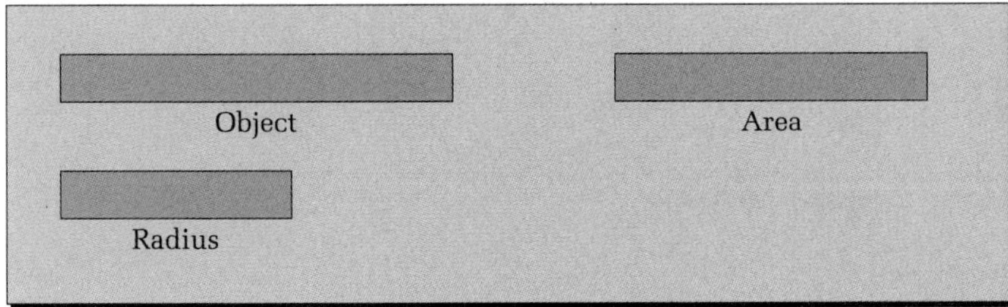

   b. Figure

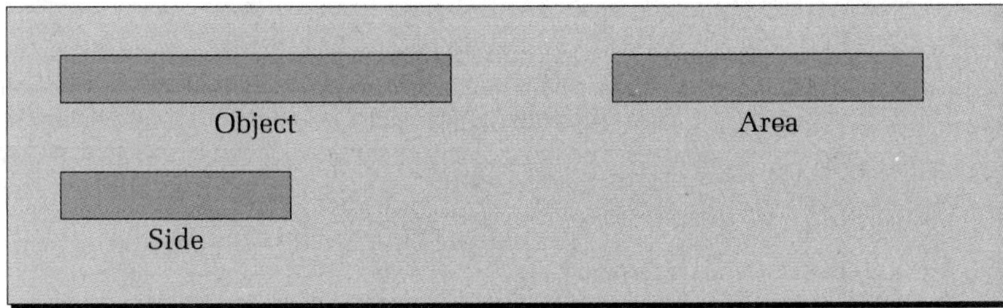

   c. Figure

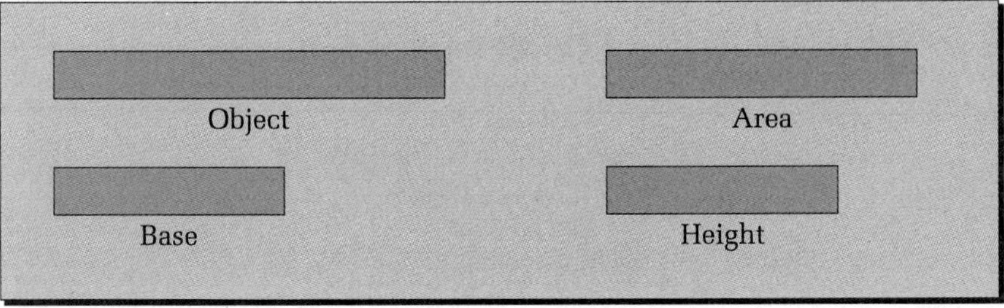

7.
```
PubType = (Book, Article);
DataRange = 1600..2000;
PublicationInfo = RECORD
                    Author : String30;
                    Title : String30;
                    Date : DataRange;
                    CASE Pub : PubType OF
                      Book   : (Publisher : String30;
                                 City : String30);
                      Article : (JournalName : String30;
                                 VolumeNumber : integer)
                  END;
```

CHAPTER 10

Section 10.1

3. a. is valid; the component type is an integer in the subrange 0 . . 120

   b. is invalid; no file type has been defined.

   c. is invalid; the component type for a file cannot be another file.

   d. is invalid; the expression **FILE**[1 . . 100] has no meaning.

   e. is valid; the component type is **integer.**

4.
```
TYPE
  String20 = string [20];
  AddressType = ARRAY [1..3] OF String20;
  GenderType = (M, F);
  PatientInfo = RECORD
                  Name : String20;
                  Address : AddressType;
                  Height : 0..200;
                  Weight : 0..300;
                  Age : 0..120;
                  Gender : GenderType;
                  InsuranceCo : String20
                END;  { of PatientInfo  }
  PatientFile = FILE OF PatientInfo;
VAR
  Patient : PatientFile;
```

Section 10.2

3.
```
TYPE
  FileType = FILE OF integer;
VAR
  SevenMult : FileType;
  Num, Sevens : integer;
```

A fragment of code for this problem is

```
rewrite (SevenMult);  {  Open the file.  }
Num := 1;
Sevens := 7;
WHILE Sevens < 100 DO
  BEGIN
    write (SevenMult, Sevens);
    Num := Num + 1;
    Sevens := 7 * Num
  END;  {  of WHILE...DO  }
```

5. Either of the following work.

```
reset (FivesFile);
read (FivesFile, A, B, C, D);
```

or

```
reset (FivesFile);
read (FivesFile, A);
read (FivesFile, B);
read (FivesFile, C);
read (FivesFile, D);
```

7. The **reset** procedure opens a file so values may be read from the file. Contents of the file are not altered by this command.
   The **rewrite** procedure opens a file so values may be written to the file. When **rewrite**(⟨file name⟩) is executed, any previous contents are lost.

9. a. The **reset** procedure opens the file for reading from the file. It appears

```
reset(File1);
```

should have been

```
rewrite(File1);
```

   b. The files are mixed up. It appears that the intent is to copy the contents of File1 into File2.

   c. No errors.

   d. No errors; this is a correct version of a problem similar to the one posed in **b.**

11. The output is

```
-17
-4
```

The files contain these.

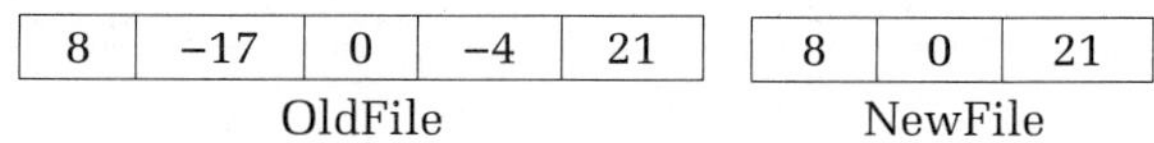

8	−17	0	−4	21

OldFile

8	0	21

NewFile

Section 10.3

1. b.
```
TYPE
  String20 = string [20];
  BookInfo = RECORD
               Author : String20;
               Title : String20;
               StockNumber : integer;
               Price : real;
               Quantity : 0..500
             END;  {  of RECORD BookInfo  }
  BookFile = FILE OF BookInfo;
VAR
  Book : BookFile;
```

3. a.
```
TYPE
  String20 = string [20];
  QuizList = ARRAY [1..10] OF 0..10;
  TestList = ARRAY [1..4] OF 0..100;
  StudentRec = RECORD
                 Name : String20;
                 Number : integer;
                 Quiz : QuizList;
                 Test : TestList
               END;  {  of RECORD StudentRec  }
  StudentFile = FILE OF StudentRec;
VAR
  Student : StudentFile;
```

b.
```
PROCEDURE GetData (VAR St : StudentFile;
                   VAR Data : text);
  VAR
    J : integer;
    OneRec : StudentRec;
  BEGIN
    rewrite (St);  {  Open the files.  }
    reset (Data);
    WHILE NOT eof(Data) DO
      BEGIN
        WITH OneRec DO
          BEGIN
            read (Data, Name, Number); {  Get Name, ID.     }
            FOR J := 1 TO 10 DO
              read (Data, Quiz[J]);    {  Get quiz scores. }
            FOR J := 1 TO 4 DO
              read (Data, Test[J]     { Get test scores.  }
          END;  {  of data for OneRec  }
        readln;  {  Advance the pointer.  }
        write (St, OneRec)  {  Put record in binary file.  }
      END  {  of WHILE NOT eof (Data)  }
  END;  {  of PROCEDURE  GetData  }
```

c. The basic design for this task is to.
   1. Transfer records to an array
   2. Sort the array
   3. Transfer records from the array back to the file

   Assuming suitable definitions and declarations have been made, a procedure to accomplish this follows.

```
PROCEDURE SortFile (VAR St : StudentFile);
  VAR
    Temp : StudentRec;
    J, K, Length, Index : integer;
    TempList : ARRAY [1..MaxSize] OF StudentRec;
  BEGIN
    reset (St);
    J := 0;
    WHILE NOT eof(St) DO  {  Copy to array.  }
      BEGIN
        J := J + 1;
        read (St, TempList[J])
      END;
    Length := J;
    close (St);

  {  Now sort the array.  }

    FOR J := 1 TO Length - 1 DO
      BEGIN
        Index := J;
        FOR K := J + 1 TO Length DO
          IF TempList[K].Name < TempList[Index].Name THEN
            Index := K;
        IF Index <> J THEN
          BEGIN
            Temp := TempList[Index];
            TempList[Index] := TempList[J];
            TempList[J] := Temp
          END  {  of exchange  }
      END;  {  of one pass  }

  {  Now copy back to the file.  }

      rewrite (St);
      FOR J := 1 TO Length DO
        write (St, TempList[J]);
    close (St)
  END;  {  of PROCEDURE SortFile  }
```

Section 10.4

3. It appears the intent is to modify an existing record. Thus, after the change is made, you should use **seek** to reposition the pointer before using **write.** A correct version is

```
BEGIN
  seek (StudentList, 10);
  read (StudentList, StudentRec);
  StudentRec.Score[2] := 89;
  seek (StudentList, 10);
  write (StudentList, StudentRec)
END;
```

7. Use a variation of **PROGRAM** CreateDataFile in Section 10.3. For this problem, replace the data type Flight with the data type PartRecord. Replace the **WHILE** MoreData **DO** loop with **FOR** Index := 1 **TO** 30 **DO.** Within the **FOR** loop, use the assignment statement
`PartRec.PartNum := Index + 100;`
Since the default values are zeros or blanks, it is not necessary to assign explicit values to the other fields. If you choose to do so, however, use a **WITH . . . DO** statement, as is done in **PROGRAM** CreateDataFile.

CHAPTER 11

Section 11.1

1. There is no stopping state.

3. a. **i.** Y = 9.0
   ii. Y = 8.0
   iii. Y = 256.0
   iv. Y = 1.0

5.

```
FUNCTION IterFactorial (N : integer) : integer;
  VAR
    PartialProduct,
    NextFactor : integer;
  BEGIN
    PartialProduct := 1;
    FOR NextFactor := 2 TO N DO
      PartialProduct := PartialProduct
                        * NextFactor;
    IterFactorial := PartialProduct
  END;  {  of FUNCTION IterFactorial  }
```

Section 11.2

1.
```
PROCEDURE InsertionSort (VAR B : List);
  VAR
    Num, Index, N : integer;
    Found : boolean;
  BEGIN
    NewLength := 0;
    WHILE NOT eof(Data) DO
      BEGIN
        Index := 1;
        Found := false;
        readln (Data, Num);
        WHILE NOT Found AND
          (Index <= NewLength) DO
          IF Num < B[Index] THEN
            Found := true
          ELSE
            Index := Index + 1;
        FOR N := NewLength DOWNTO Index DO
          B[N + 1] := B[N];
        B[Index] := Num;
        NewLength := NewLength + 1
      END  {  of WHILE NOT eof  }
  END;  {  of PROCEDURE InsertionSort  }
```

3. After initializing Count, change

```
BEGIN
  List[K] := List[K-1];
  K := K - 1
END
```

to

```
BEGIN
  List[K] := List[K-1];
  K := K - 1;
  Count := Count + 1
END;
```

9. The insertion sort modification is

```
FOR Index := 2 TO ListLength DO
  BEGIN
    TempA := List1[Index];
    TempB := List2[Index];
    K := Index;
    Done := false;
    WHILE (K >= 2) AND (NOT Done) DO
      IF TempA < List1[K - 1] THEN
        BEGIN
          List1[K] := List1[K - 1];
          List2[K] := List2[K - 1]
        END
      ELSE
        Done := true;
    List1[K] := TempA;
    List2[K] := TempB
  END;  {  of FOR loop  }
```

CHAPTER 12

Section 12.1

1. a. **real** is not an ordinal data type.

   b. **integer** will exceed the maximum size for a set.

   c. : should be =.

   d. Brackets should not be used.

   e. No errors

3. a. `A := ['J', 'I', 'M'];`

   b. `A := ['P', 'A', 'S', 'C', 'L'];`

   c. The elements are 'T', 'O', and 'Y'. The eight subsets are [ ], ['T'], ['O'], ['Y'], ['T', 'O'], ['T', 'Y'], ['O','Y'], and ['T', 'O', 'Y'].

5. a. Brackets are needed:

   `A := ['J'..'O'];`

   b. No errors

   c. Single quotation marks are needed:

   `B := ['A'..'Z'];`

   d. 'E' and 'I' are listed more than once.

   e. [ ] is not a set variable.

   f. Since 'S' is in the subrange 'A' . . 'T', it is listed more than once.

7. a.
```
TYPE
  Hues = (Red, Orange, Yellow, Green, Blue,
          Indigo, Violet);
  RainbowSet = SET OF Hues;
VAR
  Rainbow : RainbowSet;
```

   c.
```
TYPE
  SomeFruits = (Apple, Orange, Banana, Grape,
                Pear, Peach, Strawberry);
  FruitSet = SET OF SomeFruits;
VAR
  Fruit : FruitSet;
```

Section 12.2

1. No; when A = B, both A >= B and A <= B are **true**.

3. a. A + B = [−3 . . 4, 7 . . 10]
   A ∗ B = [0, 1, 2, 8, 10]
   A − B = [−3, −2, −1]
   B − A = [3, 4, 7, 9]

   c. A + B = B
   A ∗ B = A
   A − B = A
   B − A = B

5. All of these are **true.**

7. Code for this is

```
VowelsUppercase := ['A', 'E', 'I', 'O', 'U'];
VowelCount := 0;
WHILE NOT eof(Data) DO
  BEGIN
    read(Data, Ch);
    IF Ch IN VowelsUppercase THEN
      VowelCount := VowelCount + 1
  END;
```

Section 12.3

3. Modify **PROGRAM** DeleteBlanks in Example 6.4 in Section 6.1, by changing

```
IF Ch = ' ' THEN
  Ch := '*';
```

to

```
IF Ch IN Vowels THEN
  write '*'
ELSE
  write (Ch);
```

7.
```
FUNCTION AllOddDigits (Num : integer) : boolean;
  TYPE
    Digits = SET of 0..9;
  VAR
    EvenDigits : Digits;
    NumDigits, J, Digit : integer;
  BEGIN
    EvenDigits := [0, 2, 4, 6, 8];
    IF Num DIV 1000 = 0 THEN  {  Num < 1000  }
      IF Num DIV 100 = 0 THEN  {  Num < 100  }
        IF Num DIV 10 = 0 THEN  {  Num < 10  }
          NumDigits := 1
        ELSE NumDigits := 2
      ELSE NumDigits := 3
    ELSE NumDigits := 4;
    AllOddDigits := true;
    FOR J := 1 TO NumDigits DO
      BEGIN
        Digit := abs(Num MOD 10);
        IF Digit IN EvenDigits THEN
          AllOddDigits := false;
        Num := Num DIV 10
      END  {  of FOR loop  }
  END;  {  of FUNCTION AllOddDigits  }
```

CHAPTER 13

Section 13.1

1. The driver and the mode are both variable parameters. Thus, constants CGA and 2 cannot be used.

3. Combining **PROCEDURE** InitializeGraphics with **PROGRAM** Graphics in this section produces

```
PROGRAM Graphics;
USES
  Crt, Graph;
VAR
  .
  .
  .
PROCEDURE InitializeGraphics;
  VAR
    GraphDriver, GraphMode,
    ErrorResult : integer;
    InitError : boolean;
  BEGIN
    GraphDriver := detect;
    GraphMode := 1;
    InitGraph (GraphDriver, GraphMode, ' ');
    ErrorResult := GraphResult;
    InitError := (ErrorResult < > 0);
    IF InitError THEN
      BEGIN
        writeln ('There is a graphics error.');
        writeln (GraphErrorMsg(ErrorResult));
        writeln ('Program aborted.');
        Halt;
      END
  END;  {  of PROCEDURE InitializeGraphics  }

BEGIN  {  Main program  }
  InitializeGraphics;
        .
        .  (main part of program here)
        .
   CloseGraph
END.  {  of  PROGRAM  Graphics  }
```

5. a. Find the coordinates of the center by using

```
Xvalue := GetMaxX DIV 2;
Yvalue := GetMaxY DIV 2;
```

One way to create a nine-pixel square with center (Xvalue, Yvalue) is to use

```
FOR Y := Yvalue - 1 TO Yvalue + 1 DO
  Line (Xvalue - 1, Y, Xvalue + 1, Y);
```

9. a. Consider the fragment of code

```
FOR Y := 0 TO GetMaxY DIV 10 DO
  BEGIN
    MoveTo (0,10 * Y);  {  Start at the
                           left edge.  }
    LineRel (GetMaxX,0) {  Draw the
                           horizontal line.  }
  END;
```

11. One method of accomplishing this is to use

```
NumSquares := GetMaxY DIV 10;
MoveTo (0,0);
FOR J := 1 TO NumSquares DO
  BEGIN
    MoveRel (10,10);  {  Start at the lower
                         right corner.  }
    LineRel (0,-10);
    LineRel (-10,0);
    LineRel (0,10);
    LineRel (10,0)
  END;
```

Section 13.2

1. a. The following code produces the same rectangle.

```
ClearDevice;
Line (10, 10, 110, 10);
Line (110, 10, 110, 60);
Line (110, 60, 10, 60);
Line (10, 60, 10, 10);
```

3. The default unit for delay is approximately one millisecond. Thus, the pause length in seconds should be multiplied by 1000 before making a call to **Delay.**

7. Consider the code

```
SetBkColor (Green);
SetColor (Blue);
Circle (100, 100, 50);  {  Draw the circle.  }
SetColor (Green);
FOR Theta := 0 TO 180 DO  {  Erase alternate
                             degree arcs.  }
  arc (100, 100, 2 * Theta, 2 * Theta + 1, 50);
```

Section 13.3

1. **a.** Try something like

```
SetColor (2);
Rectangle (10, 10, 100, 100);
FloodFill (15, 15, 3);
```

3. One method of accomplishing the task is to use the code

```
Pattern := LkBkSlashFill;
FOR J := 1 TO 5 DO  {  Draw five rectangles.  }
  BEGIN
    X1 := 50 * J;
    X2 := X1 + 40;
    Y1 := 20;
    Y2 := 100;
    Rectangle (X1, Y1, X2, Y2);    {  Draw the rectangle.  }
    Pattern := succ(Pattern);      {  Change the pattern.  }
    SetFillStyle (Pattern, 2);
    FloodFill (X1 + 1, Y1 + 1, 3)  {  Fill the rectangle.  }
  END;
```

5. Use a combination of **Delay** and **ClearDevice** for animation.

Section 13.4

1.

```
PROCEDURE DrawPatternBars (NumBars : integer);
  VAR
    Pattern : word;
    X1, X2, Y1, Y2, J : integer;
  BEGIN
    Pattern := 0;  {  Select lowest ordinal.   }
    X1 := 20;      {  Initialize coordinates   }
    Y1 := 20;      {  for the first bar.       }
    X2 := X1 + 10;
    Y2 := 70;
    FOR J := 1 TO NumBars DO
      BEGIN
        SetFillStyle (Pattern, 2);
        Bar (X1, Y1, X2, Y2);
        Pattern := succ(Pattern);  {  Change the pattern.  }
        X1 := X1 + 15;
        X2 := X1 + 10
      END  {  of FOR loop  }
  END;  {  of PROCEDURE DrawPatternBars  }
```

5. One way to accomplish the task is with the following code.

```
{  Initialize for the first bar.  }

Pattern := 0;
SetFillStyle (Pattern, 2);
X1 := 100;
DeltaX := 40;
X2 := X1 + DeltaX;
Y1 := GetMaxY - 30;                    {  Start at the screen bottom.  }
Y2 := Y1 + 30;
Depth := DeltaX DIV 4;                 {  Use 25% depth.               }
Bar3D (X1, Y1, X2, Y2, Depth, false);  {  Draw the first bar.          }

{  Draw the remaining bars.  }

FOR index := 2 TO 5 DO            {  Draw successive bars.     }
  BEGIN
    Delay (500);                  {  Slow down the display.    }
    Y2 := Y1;                     {  Coordinates for new bar   }
    Y1 := Y1 - 30;
    Pattern := succ(Pattern)      {  Change the pattern.       }
    SetFillStyle (Pattern, 2);
    Bar3D (X1, Y1, X2, Y2, Depth, false)
  END;  {  of FOR loop for drawing bars  }
```

9. Alternating colors in sectors of 45° can be generated by the code

```
{  Initialize the settings.  }

SetGraphMode (1);
X := 100;  {  Coordinates for center.  }
Y := 100;
Rad := 50;
AngleSize := 45;

FOR Quadrant := 1 TO 4 DO
  BEGIN

    {  Color one sector.  }

    SetColor (1);  {  Select a color.  }
    AngleStart := 90 * Quadrant - 2 * AngleSize;
    AngleFinish := AngleStart + AngleSize;
    PieSlice (X, Y, AngleStart, AngleFinish, Rad);
    Delay (200);

    {  Color the next sector in Quadrant.  }

    SetColor (2);  {  Change the color.  }
    AngleStart := AngleFinish;
    AngleFinish := 90 * Quadrant;
    PieSlice (X, Y, AngleStart, AngleFinish, Rad);
    Delay (500)
  END;
```

Section 13.5

1. b. Try something like
   MoveTo (GetMaxY – 4);
   OutText ('What happens?');

3. Use **PROCEDURE** ContinuationMessage in this section, and call it from **PROCEDURE** GraphSector:

```
PROCEDURE GraphSector (<parameter list>);
  VAR
    .
    .
    .
  BEGIN
    .
    .
    .
    PieSlice (<arguments>);
    ContinuationMessage
  END;
```

5. To illustrate a horizontal message, modify **PROCEDURE** ContinuationMessage to be

```
PROCEDURE ContinuationMessage;
  VAR
    .
    .
    .
  BEGIN
    Message := ('Press <Enter> to continue.');

    {  Set coordinates for message.  }

    Xcoor := (GetMaxX - 8 * Length(Message)) DIV 2;
    Ycoor := GetMaxY - 10;

    {  Set coordinates for rectangle.  }

    X1 := Xcoor - 2;
    Y1 := Ycoor - 2;
    X2 := X1 + 8 * Length(Message) + 2;
    Y2 := Y1 + 10;
    Rectangle (X1, Y1, X2, Y2);  {  Draw the rectangle.  }
    OutText XY (Xcoor, Ycoor, Message)  {  Print the message.  }
  END;
```

The same principle is used when displaying vertical messages. In this case, however, use

```
SetTextStyle (<font>, 1, <size>);
```

to produce the vertical display.

CHAPTER 14

Section 14.1

5. a. The procedure heading should be
   `PROCEDURE Rectangle.Init;`

   b. The references to fields should be
   ```
   Length := Len;
   Width := Wid
   ```

   c. The function body should be
   `GetLength := Length`
   rather than
   `Rectangle.GetLength := Length`

   d. This one works; however, it doesn't accomplish the desired task. If you want the width, the function body should be
   `GetWidth := Width`

   e. The function body should be
   `GetWidth := Width`

7. a. Add the method
   `FUNCTION ComputeArea;`

   b.
   ```
   FUNCTION Rectangle.ComputeArea : real;
     BEGIN
       ComputeArea := Length * Width
     END;
   ```

Section 14.2

3.
```
Box = OBJECT (Rectangle)
        Height : real;

        PROCEDURE Init;
        PROCEDURE SetDimensions (Len, Wid, Hght : real);
        PROCEDURE GetDimensions (Len, Wid, Hght : real);
        FUNCTION ComputeVolume : real;
      END;
```

5. a. Yes

b. No; since the ancestor type Rectangle has a method for computing area, use that method to find the area of the base and then multiply that number by the height. For example

```
AreaOfBase := Rectangle.GetArea;
ComputeVolume := AreaOfBase * Height
```

7. a.
```
Student = OBJECT (NameString)
            GPA : real;

            PROCEDURE Init;
            PROCEDURE SetValue (GradePtAv : real);
            PROCEDURE GetValue (GradePtAv : real);
            PROCEDURE Print;
          END;
```
This assumes the computation of GPA will not be a method.

c.
```
TYPE
  PetType = (Bird, Cat, Dog, Fish, Other);

Pet = OBJECT (NameString)
        KindOfPet : PetType;

        PROCEDURE Init;
        PROCEDURE SetType (WhatKind : PetType);
        PROCEDURE GetType (WhatKind : PetType);
        PROCEDURE PrintType;
      END;
```

9. a. Valid; same object type

b. Valid; a descendant can be assigned to an ancestor.

c. Valid; a descendant can be assigned to an ancestor.

d. Invalid; an ancestor cannot be assigned to a descendant.

e. Invalid; an ancestor cannot be assigned to a descendant.

f. Valid; same object type

Section 14.3

1. A subclass of part-time students could be
```
PartTimeType = OBJECT (StudentType)
                 NumHour : integer;
                 ExternalJob : boolean;
                PROCEDURE Init;
                PROCEDURE GetData;
                FUNCTION GetNumHours : integer;
                FUNCTION GetExternalJob : boolean;
                PROCEDURE Print;
              END;
```

5. Due to the GetData overrides, all ancestor methods that assume interactive input would have to be modified to read data from a file.

Section 14.4

3. You will not get a compilation error. However, during execution, the error message

```
Error 210: Object not initialized.
```

will appear when an attempt is made to use an instance of the uninitialized object.

5. The inialization procedure is replaced by **CONSTRUCTOR** Init. The keyword **VIRTUAL** is listed after each virtual method. **DESTRUCTOR** Done is listed as a virtual method and should be used to release memory once a program is no longer using an object.

11. The implementation section of a unit contains all implementation details. Everything defined in the interface section is available to the implementation section.

CHAPTER 15

Section 15.1

3.

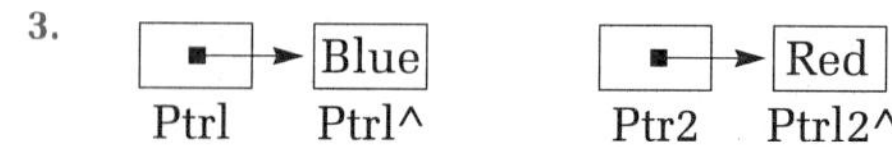

5. c., f., and h. are valid.

a. is invalid; IntPtr1 + 1 is not allowed.

b. is invalid; pointers cannot be used with **writeln.**

d. is invalid; < is not a valid comparison for pointers.

e. is invalid;

```
BoolPtr NOT NIL
```

should be

```
BoolPtr2 < > NIL
```

g. is invalid; BoolPtr2 is not a Boolean expression.

Section 15.2

3. Assume the file name is Num. A procedure is then

```
PROCEDURE PrintNumbers (First : DataPtr);
  VAR
    P : DataPtr;
  BEGIN
    P := First;
    WHILE P <> NIL DO
      BEGIN
        writeln (P^.Num);
        P := P^.Next
      END
  END;  {  of PROCEDURE PrintNumbers  }
```

This procedure is called by

```
PrintNumbers (Start);
```

5. a.
```
TYPE
  String20 = string [20];
  TestList = ARRAY [1..4] OF 0..100;
  QuizList = ARRAY [1..10] OF 0..10;
  DataPtr = ^StudentInfo;
  StudentInfo = RECORD
                  Name : String20;
                  Test : TestList;
                  Quiz : QuizList;
                  Average : real;
                  Grade : char;
                  Next : DataPtr
                END;  { of RECORD StudentInfo }
VAR
  Student : DataPtr;
```

b. The pointer variable is Student. The pointer type is DataPtr.

c. i. Assume Start, Ptr, and Last have been declared to be of type DataPtr. Data for the first student can then be obtained by using

```
reset (Data);
new (Start);
Ptr := Start;
Last := Start;
WITH Start^ DO
   BEGIN
     read (Data, Name);
     FOR J := 1 TO 4 DO
       read (Data, Test[J]);
     FOR J := 1 TO 10 DO
       read (Data, Quiz[J]);
     Next := NIL
   END;
readln;
```

ii. Data for the second student can be obtained by

```
new (Last);
Ptr^.Next := Last;
Ptr := Last;
WITH Last^ DO
  BEGIN
    read (Data, Name);
    FOR J := 1 TO 4 DO
      read (Data, Test[J]);
    FOR J := 1 TO 10 DO
      read (Data, Quiz[J])
  END;
readln;
Ptr^.Next := NIL;
```

7. a. Working from the original

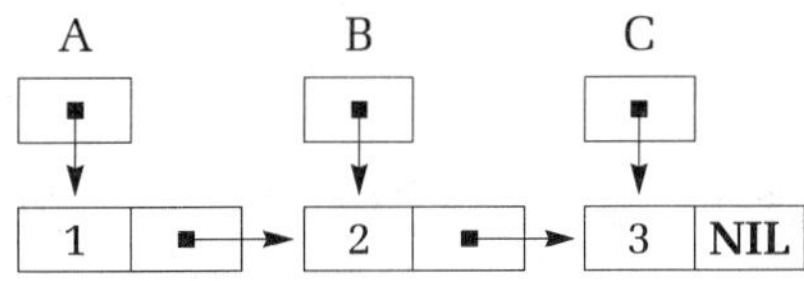

each time, we get

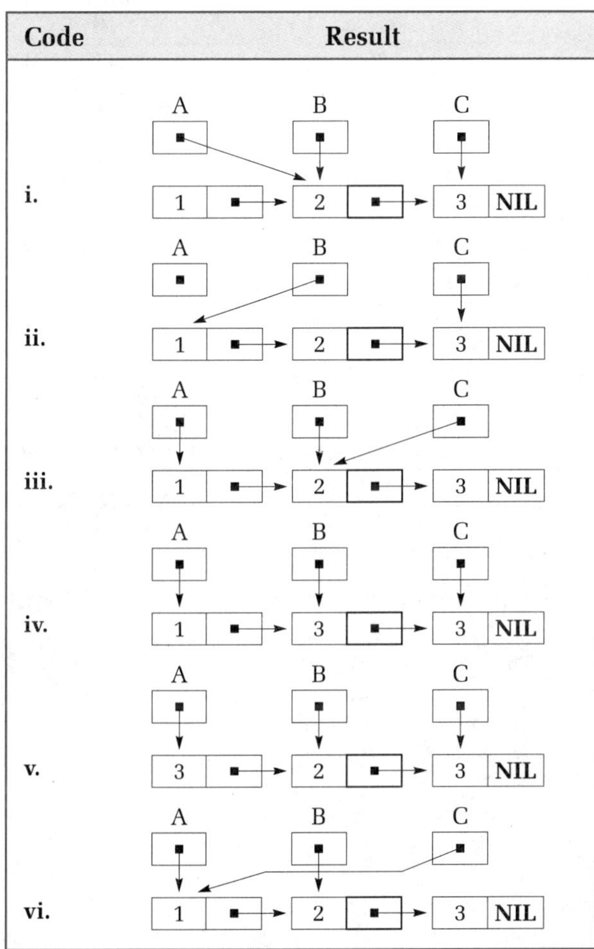

b. `A^.Next^.Next := B;`

9. Assume the linked list has been declared and values have already been read into the field Num for each component of the list. Furthermore, assume Start is the pointer to the first node. A function for summing is then

```
FUNCTION Sum (First : DataPtr) : integer;
  VAR
    Total : integer;
    P : DataPtr;
  BEGIN
    Total := 0;
    P := First;
    WHILE P <> NIL DO
      BEGIN
        Total := Total + P^.Num;
        P := P^.Next
      END;
    Sum := Total
  END;  {  of FUNCTION Sum  }
```

Section 15.3

1. Assume the original list can be envisioned as

and you wish to insert 25 into the list. The initialization produces

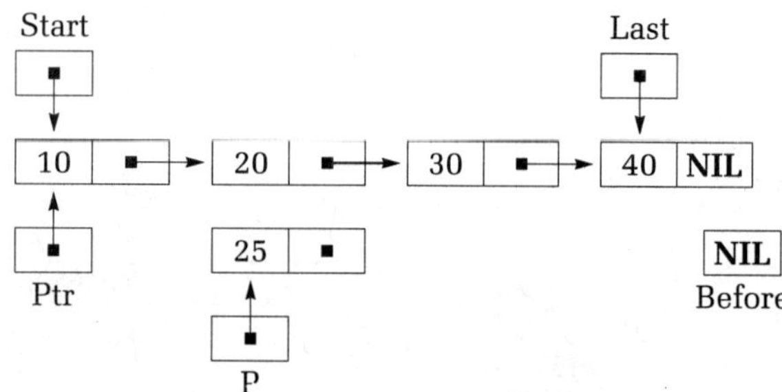

Since the loop is not empty, the **WHILE . . . DO** loop will be executed until we have

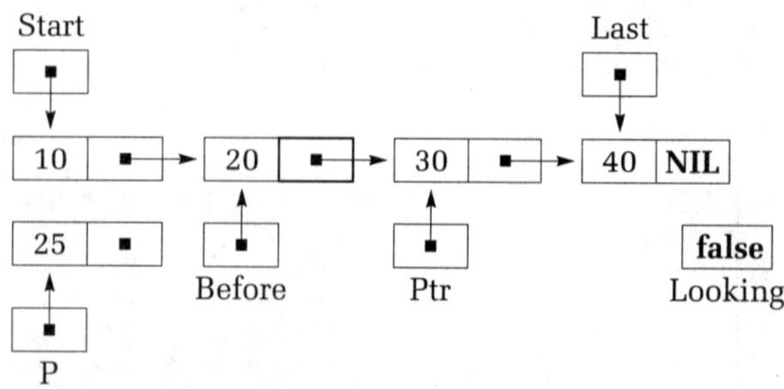

The pointers are then moved to obtain

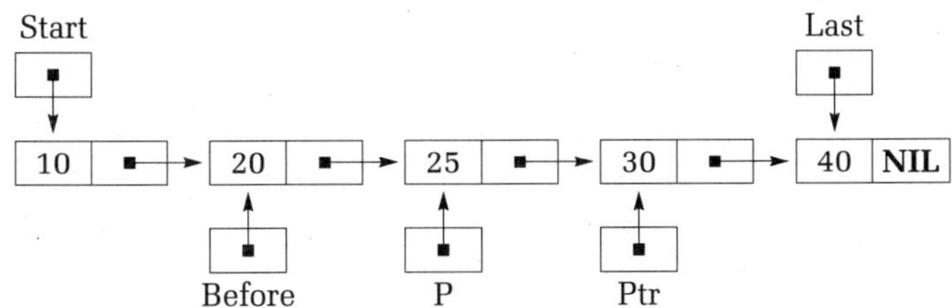

The new code is

```
IF Before = NIL THEN
  Push (Start, NewNum)      {  call to Push  }
ELSE
  Before^.Next := P;
```

5. The heading becomes

```
PROCEDURE Pop (VAR Start : DataPtr);
```

and the line

```
NewNum := P^.Num
```

should be deleted.

7.
```
PROCEDURE Delete (VAR Start : DataPtr;
                  Position : integer);
  VAR
    Before, P : DataPtr;
  BEGIN
    IF Position = 1 THEN
      Pop (Start, Start^.Num)
    ELSE
      BEGIN
        Before := Start;
        FOR J := 1 TO (Position - 2) DO
          Before := Before^.Next;
        P := Before^.Next;
        Before^.Next := P^.Next;
        dispose (P)
      END  {  of ELSE option  }
  END;  {  of modified PROCEDURE Delete  }
```

Section 15.4

1. Illustrating only the parentheses, you get

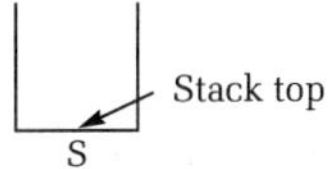

Character Read	New Stack
"("	(
"("	((
"("	(((
")"	((
"("	(((
")"	((
")"	(
")"	

5. a.
```
CONST
  MaxStack = <value>;
TYPE
  Stack = RECORD
            Item : ARRAY [1..MaxStack]
                   OF <data type>;
            Top : 0..MaxStack
          END;
VAR
  S : Stack;
```

b. Push becomes

```
PROCEDURE Push (VAR S : Stack;
                X : integer);
  BEGIN
    IF S.Top = MaxStack THEN
      writeln ('Stack overflow')
    ELSE
      BEGIN
        S.Top := S.Top + 1;
        S.Item[S.Top] := X
      END
  END;  {  of PROCEDURE Push  }
```

PopAndCheck becomes

```
PROCEDURE PopAndCheck (VAR S : Stack;
                       VAR X : integer;
                       VAR Underflow :
                       boolean);
  BEGIN
    IF Empty(S) THEN  {  Check for empty
                         stack.  }
      Underflow := true
    ELSE
      BEGIN
        Underflow := false;
        X := S.Item[S.Top];
        S.Top := S.Top - 1
      END  {  of ELSE option  }
  END;  {  of PROCEDURE PopAndCheck  }
```

9. Change the **ELSE** option to

```
ELSE IF Num = Node^.Info THEN
  writeln (Num, ' is a duplicate value.')
ELSE IF Num < Node^.Info THEN
  AddNode (Node^.LeftChild, Num)
ELSE
  AddNode (Node^.RightChild, Num)
```

11.
```
FUNCTION Search (Node : Pointer;
                 NewNum : integer) : boolean;
  VAR
    Found : boolean;
    Current : Pointer;
  BEGIN
    Current := Node;
    Found := false;
    WHILE (Current <> NIL) AND NOT Found DO
      IF Current^.Num = NewNum THEN
        Found := true
      ELSE IF Current^.Num < NewNum THEN
        Current := Current^.RightChild
      ELSE
        Current := Current^.LeftChild;
    Search := Found
  END;  {  of FUNCTION Search  }
```

13.

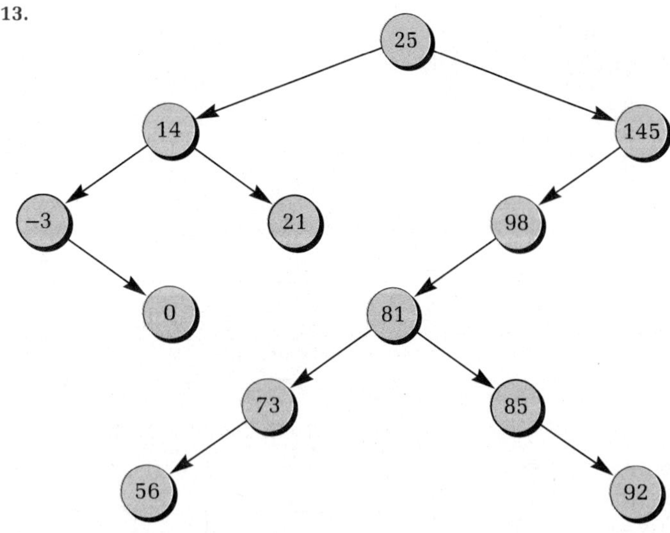

Index

Credits

PHOTOS

Figures 1.4, 1.5a, 1.5b, 1.5c, and 1.6b: Courtesy of IBM Corporation
Figures 1.5d and 1.6a: Courtesy of Apple Computer, Inc.
Figure 1.8: Robert Barclay.

NOTES OF INTEREST

Page 5: Ethics and Computer Science
Page 12: Data Loss on Floppy Disks
Reprinted with permission from *Information Systems in Business: An Introduction,* p. 230, by James O. Hicks, Jr. Copyright © 1990 by West Publishing Company. All rights reserved. Permission for figure is credited to Verbatim Corporation, 1200 W WT Harris Blvd., Charlotte, NC 28213.
Page 15: Why Learn Pascal?
Reprinted with permission from "Pascal," by T. Woteki and A. Freiden, published in the September 1983 issue of *Popular Computing* magazine. © McGraw-Hill, Inc., New York. All rights reserved.
Page 19: Software Verification
From Ivars Peterson, "Finding Fault: The Formidable Task of Eradicating Software Bugs," SCIENCE NEWS, February 16, 1991, Vol. 139. Reprinted with permission from SCIENCE NEWS, the weekly newsmagazine of science. Copyright © 1991 by Science Services, Inc. Photo courtesy of Ontario Hydro.
Page 47: Blaise Pascal
Adapted from William Dunham, *Journey Through Genius: The Great Theorems of Mathematics,* John Wiley & Sons, 1990. Photos: Courtesy of IBM Corporation.
Page 68: Herman Hollerith
Reprinted by permission for *Introduction to Computers with BASIC,* pp. 27–28, by Fred G. Harold. Copyright © 1984 by West Publishing Company. All rights reserved. Photos courtesy of IBM Corporation.
Page 81: Communication Skills Needed
From P. Jackowitz, R. Plishka, J. Sidbury, J. Hartman, and C. White, ACM Press *SIGCSE Bulletin* 22, No. 1 (February 1990). Copyright 1991, Association for Computing Machinery, Inc. Reprinted by permission of Association for Computing Machinery, Inc.
Page 85: Defined Constants and Space Shuttle Computing, *Communications of the ACM* 27, No. 9 (September 1984): 880. Copyright 1984, Association for Computing Machinery, Inc. Reprinted by permission of Association for Computing Machinery, Inc.
Pages 91 and 99: Debugging or Sleuthing?
From J. Bentley, *Communications of the ACM* 28, No. 2 (February 1985): 139. Copyright 1985, Association for Computing Machinery, Inc. Reprinted by permission of Association for Computing Machinery, Inc.
Page 102: Structured Programming
Page 114: Computer Ethics: Hacking and Other Intrusions
Reprinted by permission from *Computers Under Attack: Intruders, Worms, and Viruses,* pp. 150–155, edited by Peter J. Denning, Article 7, "The West German Hacker Incident and Other Intrusions," by Mel Mandell. Copyright 1990, Association for Computing Machinery, Inc.
Page 135: Niklaus Wirth.
Adapted from Niklaus Wirth, Programming Language Design to Computer Construction, 1984 Turing Award Lecture, *Communications of the ACM,* 28, No. 2 (February 1985).
Page 156: George Boole
Adapted from William Dunham, *Journey Through Genius: The Great Theorems of Mathematics,* John Wiley & Sons, 1990. Photo: The Bettmann Archive.
Page 170: New Legal Research Uses English, Not Boolean
Page 190: A Software Glitch
From Ivars Peterson, "Finding Fault: The Formidable Task of Eradicating Software Bugs," SCIENCE NEWS, February 16, 1991, Vol. 139. Reprinted with permission from SCIENCE NEWS, the weekly newsmagazine of science. Copyright 1991 by Science Services, Inc.
Page 219: Charles Babbage
Reprinted by permission from *Introduction to Computers with BASIC,* pp. 24–26, by Fred G. Harold. Copyright © 1984 by West Publishing Company. All rights reserved. Photos courtesy of IBM Corporation.
Page 226: Ada Augusta Byron
Reprinted by permission from *Introduction to Computers with BASIC,* pp. 26–27, by Fred G. Harold. Copyright © 1984 by West Publishing Company. All rights reserved. Photo: The Bettmann Archive.
Page 281: Career Opportunities in Computer Science
From Carol Wilson, Western Kentucky University, Bowling Green, Kentucky, 1991.
Page 289: Computer Ethics: Viruses
From Philip J. Hilts, Science Lab, in *The Washington Post National Weekly Edition,* May 23–29, 1988. Reprinted by permission of The Washington Post.
Page 309: Monolithic Idea: Invention of the Integrated Circuit
Adapted from T. R. Reid, "The Chip," *Science,* February 1985, pp. 32–41.
Page 322: Too Few Women in the Computer Science Pipeline?
From Carol Wilson, Western Kentucky University, Bowling Green, Kentucky, 1991.
Page 378: What the Future Holds in the '90s
From Daniel E. Kinnaman, "The Next Decade: What the Future Holds," *Technology & Learning* 11, No. 1 (September 1990). Reprinted by permission of *Technology & Learning* © 1990, Peter Li, Inc.

Page 383: Inspections: Debugging in the 1990s
Page 396: Computer Ethics: Worms
Reprinted by permission from *Computers Under Attack: Intruders, Worms, and Viruses,* pp. 191 and 265, edited by Peter J. Denning, Article 9, "Computer Security in the Business World," by Maurice V. Wilkes; and Article 16, "The 'Worm' Programs—Early Experience with a Distributed Computation," by John F. Shoch and Jon A. Hupp. Copyright 1990, Association for Computing Machinery, Inc.
Page 437: Using Key Fields in Records
From David Gifford and Alfred Spector: "The TWA Reservations System: An Interview with Carol Flood and Ted Celentio," *Communications of the ACM* 17, No. 7 (July 1984): 650–657, Copyright 1984, Association for Computing Machinery, Inc. Reprinted by permission of Association for Computing Machinery, Inc.
Page 446: History Stuck on Old Computer Tapes
From the *Minneapolis Star/Tribune,* "30 Years of History Stuck on Old Computer Tapes," January 2, 1991. Reprinted by permission of the Associated Press.
Page 455: Program Documentation—EDS Style
Page 476: Relational Data Bases
Page 527: Gene Mapping: Computer Scientists Examine Problems of Genome Project
From *The Chronicle of Higher Education,* May 9, 1990. Reprinted by permission of The Chronicle of Higher Education.
Page 539: Fractal Geometry and Benoit Mandlebrot. Figure from *Integrated Computer Graphics,* p. 128, by Bruce Mielke. Copyright © 1991 by West Publishing Company.
Page 564: Artist of Interface
From Ron Wolf, "Artist a Go-Between for Users, Computers," *The Chicago Tribune,* June 10, 1990. Reprinted by permission from Knight-Ridder Tribune News.
Page 583: Impact of Computers on Art
From Dana J. Lamb, "The Impact of the Computer on the Arts," *Academic Computing,* April, 1989, pp. 22–24. Reprinted by permission from Academic Computing.
Page 608: Artificial Intelligence
Reprinted by permission from *The Mind Tool,* Fifth Ed., pp. 394–398, by Neill Graham. Copyright © 1989 by West Publishing Company. All rights reserved.
Page 628: IBM and Apple-Pinstripes and T-Shirts
Page 652: When Will Object Technology Meet Its Potential?
Reprinted by permission of Sigs Publications, Inc. Copyright © 1992.
Page 706: Using Pointers
From Nazim H. Madhavji, "Visibility Aspects of Programmed Dynamic Data Structures," *Communications of the ACM* 27, No. 8 (August 1984): 766. Copyright 1984, Association for Computing Machinery, Inc. Reprinted by permission of Association for Computing Machinery, Inc.